The Principle of *Numerus Clausus* in European Property Law

The Principle of *Numerus Clausus* in European Property Law

intersentia

METRO

Ius Commune Europaeum

Bram Akkermans
PhD-thesis

The Principle of *Numerus Clausus* in European Property Law

ISBN-13: 978-90-5095-824-0
D/2008/7849/65
NUR 822

www.intersentia.com

PREFACE

It is a great joy to finish a project after having worked on it for a period of four years. The work in this book is the result of research on my Ph.D. thesis at the Faculty of Law of Maastricht University, undertaken in the period from February 2004 until December 2007.

During my research I have had the honour and pleasure to discuss my work with various property law and comparative law experts across the world. Some of them deserve a special word of thanks.

First and foremost I owe gratitude to my supervisor Prof. dr. Sjef van Erp. Few in the world are patient enough to sit and listen to a beginning researcher and always make time to think and reflect with him. Many thanks for opening his incredible network for me. In the past years I have very much enjoyed working together, a cooperation I hope to continue for many more years.

Second, the members of the Ius Commune Casebook Team on Property law must be mentioned. William Swadling of Brasenose College, Oxford University, for hosting me, both in the early as well as in the more advanced stages of my research. Vincent Sagaert for his enthusiastic support and relentless – and very successful – attempts to focus my attention on French and Belgian law. Monika Hinteregger, for keeping my focus on the German tradition and her kind and expertise criticism on my work. Caroline Lebon for sharing my experiences as junior researcher. Michael Milo for always taking an interest in my progress, and Alexandra Braun for showing me new insights in the law of trusts.

Third, during my research I was hosted by Reinhard Zimmermann, director of the Max Planck Institute in Hamburg, who kindly offered me the opportunity to present my work in his workshop in Hamburg, where I first survived critical German views on the law of property. Reiner Schulze, dean of the law faculty and director of CEP in Münster hosted me several times. Also with him I could discuss my research and he kindly allowed me to present my research to his researchers and guests. Christoph Schmid, director of ZERP in Bremen, allowed me to stay at his institute, present my research, and, perhaps most importantly, introduced me to the world of European private international law. Finally, Marius de Waal was kind enough to allow a former student time, space, and host a visit for him in Stellenbosch.

The members of the reading committee of my thesis deserve as special mentioning for their willingness to read through the lengthy manuscript. Special thanks must go to René de Groot, Vincent Sagaert, Reiner Schulze, William Swadling and Marius de Waal, for their willingness to sit on my reading committee. I am honoured by their willingness to read through the whole manuscript.

There are two more groups that deserve mentioning. Of my direct colleagues in Maastricht, I owe special thanks to Lars van Vliet for his relentless support and difficult questions, always sharpening the mind or attempting to crack our brains on the doctrine of the law of property. To Tanja van der Meer for her support and always inspiring views on the law of property, both from a modern, as well as from a historical perspective. It is through her that I really learned to enjoy teaching.

And last, but most certainly not least, my (international) friends and colleagues at the faculty without whom I would never have finished at all. It is through their friendship and support that I kept motivated to continue and finish.

A wise colleague once stated that without a personal live there is no professional life possible. To her thanks for her friendship, but in particular thanks for showing me this insight. To my family, my parents, but to Irene in particular, thanks for your patience and stamina to stick with me. It is to her that this book is dedicated.

Finally, on the contents of this book, the research was closed on 31 December 2007. I have only been able to make small changes and additions after that.

Brussels, July 2008.

TABLE OF CONTENTS

PREFACE v

CHAPTER 1: INTRODUCTION 1

1. Introduction 1
1.1. Personal Rights and Property Rights 2
1.2. Property Law 4
1.2.1. Principles of Property Law 5
1.2.2. *Numerus Clausus* of Property Rights 6
1.3. European Private Law 7

2. Legal Systems 9
2.1. Civil Law: French, German and Dutch Law 10
2.2. Common Law: English Law 11
2.3. South African Law as a Comparative Factor 12

3. Methodology 12

4. Terminology 13

5. Searching for a *Numerus Clausus* 15

CHAPTER 2: THE DEVELOPMENT OF PROPERTY RIGHTS 19

1. Introduction 19

2. (Pre-) Classical Roman Law 21
2.1. Introduction 21
2.2. General Principles of (Pre-) Classical Roman Law 22
2.3. Ownership 24
2.4. Other Property Rights 29
2.5. A *Numerus Clausus* in (Pre-) Classical Roman Law? 43
2.6. Summary 45

3. Codified Roman Law – The *Corpus Iuris Civilis* 45
3.1. Introduction 45

3.2. General Principles of the *Corpus Iuris Civilis* ... 47
3.3. Ownership ... 47
3.4. Other Property Rights ... 50
3.5. A *Numerus Clausus* in the *Corpus Iuris Civilis?* ... 55
3.6. Summary ... 56

4. The *Ius Commune* ... 56
4.1. Introduction ... 56
4.1.1. Sources of Law: Problems with the *Ius Proprium* ... 58
4.2. General Principles of the *Ius Commune* ... 60
4.3. Ownership ... 61
4.4. Other Property Rights ... 64
4.5. Summary ... 66

5. Natural Law and the French Revolution ... 67
5.1. Introduction ... 67
5.2. General Principles ... 69
5.3. Ownership ... 70
5.3.1. Natural Law School ... 70
5.3.2. The French Revolution ... 72
5.4. Other Property Rights ... 74
5.4.1. Natural Law School ... 74
5.4.2. The French Revolution ... 76
5.5. A *Numerus Clausus* after the French Revolution? ... 77
5.6. Summary ... 78

6. Conclusion ... 78
6.1. General Summary ... 78
6.2. Conclusion ... 80

CHAPTER 3: FRENCH LAW ... 83

1. Introduction ... 83

2. The Right of Ownership ... 89
2.1. Ownership ... 91
2.2. Co-Ownership including Apartments ... 99
2.3. Security Ownership ... 105

3. Other Property Rights ... 116
3.1. Real Servitudes ... 118
3.2. Personal Servitudes ... 125
3.3. *Superficies* ... 130
3.4. *Emphyteusis* ... 133
3.5. Pledge ... 136
3.6. Hypothec ... 142
3.7. Priority Rights ... 146

4. Borderline Cases in French Property Law ... 148
4.1. Right of Retention ... 148

4.2. Real Obligations 151
4.3. *Concession Immobilière* 154
4.4. Real Suretyship 156
4.5. *Fiducie* 158
4.6. Lease 159

5. A *Numerus Clausus* in French Property Law? 161

CHAPTER 4: GERMAN LAW 169

1. Introduction 169

2. The Right of Ownership 175
2.1. Normal Ownership 176
2.2. Co-Ownership 180
2.3. Ownership of an Apartment 181
2.4. *Treuhand* Ownership 184
2.5. Security Ownership 186

3. Other Property Rights 191
3.1. Real Servitudes 199
3.2. Personal Servitudes: Usufruct and Limited Personal Servitudes 205
3.3. *Superficies* 211
3.4. Expectation Rights: Pre-Emptive Right and Acquisition Right 214
3.5. Real Burden (*Reallast*) 221
3.6. Pledge 224
3.7. Hypothec 228
3.8. *Grundschuld* 232

4. Borderline Cases in German Property Law 235
4.1. Old Property Rights 235
4.2. Pre-Emptive Registration (*Vormerkung*) 236
4.3. Entitlement to Possession through the Law of Obligations 239
4.4. Lease of Immovable Objects 240
4.5. *Treuhand* Bank Account 243

5. A *Numerus Clausus* in German Property Law? 244

CHAPTER 5: DUTCH LAW 253

1. Introduction 253

2. The Right of Ownership 256
2.1. Normal Ownership 258
2.2. Co-Ownership 262
2.3. Security Ownership 263

3. Other Property Rights 270
3.1. Real Servitudes 272
3.2. Usufruct 275
3.3. *Emphyteusis* 280

3.4. *Superficies* ... 283
3.5. Right of Apartment ... 286
3.6. Pledge ... 289
3.7. Hypothec ... 293

4. Borderline Cases in Dutch Property Law ... 298
4.1. Priority Rights ... 298
4.2. Old Property Rights ... 299
4.3. Lease of Immovable Objects ... 300
4.4. Registration of a Consumer Contract of a Sale of a House ... 302
4.5. After-Effects of Property Rights ... 304
4.6. Privative Mandate ... 306
4.7. Obligations as Part of Property Rights ... 308
4.8. 'Qualitative Duties' and Chain Clauses ... 311
4.9. EC and International Influences ... 315

5. A *Numerus Clausus* in Dutch Property Law? ... 320

CHAPTER 6: ENGLISH LAW ... 331

1. Introduction ... 331
1.1. Terminology ... 332
1.2. Common Law and Equity ... 334
1.3. Personal Property Law and Land Law ... 337
1.4. Commercial Law ... 338
1.5. Trust Law ... 338

2. Property Rights in Respect of Land ... 343
2.1. Fee Simple ... 346
2.2. Lease of Land ... 351
2.3. Easement ... 359
2.4. Profit à Prendre ... 361
2.5. Restrictive Covenant ... 363
2.6. Rentcharges over Land ... 365
2.7. Estate Contracts ... 366
2.8. Options to Purchase ... 367
2.9. Mortgage of Land and Equity of Redemption ... 367
2.10. Charges of Land ... 371

3. Property Rights in Respect of Personalty ... 373
3.1. Title / Ownership ... 373
3.2. Leases / Bailment? ... 376
3.3. Mortgage of Chattels and Equity of Redemption ... 379
3.4. Charges, Fixed and Floating ... 380
3.5. Pledge ... 384
3.6. Liens ... 385

4. A *Numerus Clausus* in English Property Law? ... 387

CHAPTER 7: COMPARATIVE OVERVIEW 397

1. Introduction 397
1.1. Property Law in Development 398
1.2. The Increasing Role of Contract Law 400
1.3. Considering *Numerus Clausus* 402
1.3.1. Requirements of *Numerus Clausus* 402
1.3.2. *Numerus Clausus* as a Principle or as a Rule? 403
1.3.3. Historical Origins of *Numerus Clausus* 403
1.3.4. *Numerus Clausus* as a Principle of 'Constitutional' Property Law, or as a Framework Principle 407

2. The Content of Property Law Systems in Europe 408
2.1. Of Primary Property Rights and Lesser Property Rights 410
2.2. Of Ways to Create a Lesser Property Right 413
2.3. Primary Property Rights 417
2.4. Lesser Rights to Use 420
2.4.1. Lesser Rights to Use for a Limited Period of Time 421
2.4.2. Lesser Rights to Use for an Unlimited Period of Time 423
2.4.3. Lesser Rights to Use of an Apartment 427
2.4.4. Evaluation 428
2.5. Lesser Rights as Security 428
2.5.1. Security Rights in Respect of Movables and Chattels 429
2.5.2. Security Rights in Respect of Immovables and Land 430
2.5.3. Evaluation 432
2.6. Lesser Rights Used to Acquire a Certain Legal Position (Anticipatory Rights) 433

3. *Numerus Clausus* in Property Law Systems in Europe? 436
3.1. Justifications for a *Numerus Clausus* from within the Legal System 437
3.2. Law and Economics on *Numerus Clausus* 440
3.2.1. Fragmentation: Not too Many Rights; on Commons and Anti-Commons 442
3.2.2. *Numerus Clausus* as Optimal Standardisation of Property Rights 445
3.2.3. *Numerus Clausus* as Verification of Property Rights 448
3.2.4. Critical Analysis of the Approach to *Numerus Clausus* in Law and Economics 450
3.3. *Numerus Clausus* in Comparative Analysis 453
3.4. Struycken: Why we Need a *Numerus Clausus* 458
3.5. Füller: Restructuring Property Law but Maintaining a Closed System 464
3.6. Van Erp: a Less Rigid *Numerus Clausus* 467
3.7. Smits and Sagaert: Property Law as a System of Obligations 469
3.8. A Legal System without a *Numerus Clausus*: South African Law 473

4. Conclusion: *Numerus Clausus* in Property Law Systems in Europe 482

CHAPTER 8: *NUMERUS CLAUSUS* IN A EUROPEAN PROPERTY LAW? ... 489

1. Introduction ... 489
1.1. European Property Law ... 489
1.2. Private International Law ... 490
1.3. European Union Law ... 494

2. The European Union and the Need for a European Property Law ... 496
2.1. EC Private Law ... 497
2.1.1. Legal Framework: Primary Community Law ... 497
2.1.2. Legal Framework: Secondary Community Law ... 500
2.1.3. European Commission Initiatives for Future Legislation ... 503
2.2. The ECJ as a Motor for the Development of European Private Law ... 509
2.2.1. Free Movement of Goods ... 510
2.2.1.1. Obstacles to Trade ... 510
2.2.1.2. Grounds for Justification ... 513
2.2.1.3. Proportionality ... 513
2.2.1.4. Moving Towards a Market Access Test? ... 514
2.2.1.5. Conclusion ... 516
2.2.2. Freedom of Establishment and its Effect on Substantive Private Law ... 517
2.3. Voluntary Harmonisation ... 521
2.4. The Effects of European Law on the Law of Property ... 522
2.4.1. Article 295 EC Treaty and European Property Law ... 523
2.4.2. The Effects of Internal Market Law on Property Law ... 525
2.4.2.1. Obstacles to Trade ... 525
2.4.2.2. Grounds for Justification ... 529
2.4.2.3. Proportionality ... 530
2.4.2.4. Example: Krantz ... 532
2.4.2.5. Evaluation ... 534
2.4.2.6. Other Freedoms ... 536
2.4.2.7. Conclusion ... 537

3. The Making of European Property Law ... 538
3.1. The Influence of European Law on National Property Law Systems ... 540
3.2. The Status of European Property Law ... 542
3.3. Two Fundamental Questions for a Coherent European Property Law ... 547
3.3.1. Separation between the Law of Obligations and the Law of Property? ... 547
3.3.2. *Numerus Clausus*: the Available Menu of Property Rights? ... 548
3.4. A Possible Model for a European Property Law: *Numerus Clausus* as a Constitutive Element of European Property Law ... 550
3.4.1. Towards a European Property Law as a Flexible System of Property Rights ... 552
3.4.2. A Limited Open System of Property Relations ... 553
3.4.3. Formulating the Access Test ... 555
3.4.4. Advantages of an Access Test and a Limited Open System of Property Rights ... 558
3.4.5. Possible Objections to an Access Test and to a Limited Open System of Property Rights ... 561

4. Conclusions 563

SUMMARY 565

SAMENVATTING 571

BIBLIOGRAPHY 579

INDEX 651

CURRICULUM VITAE 657

Chapter 1

INTRODUCTION

1. Introduction

Compared with other areas of private law, the law of property in the countries on which this study focuses is usually considered a static area of law.[1] Where in other fields, for example, in contract law and in company law, many changes have been made over time, property law has remained static, upholding principles and methods of doctrinal reasoning that have been used for ages, some even directly derived from Roman law.[2] The reason for this is that property law is not only concerned with legal relations between persons, but also with legal relations that have an effect against third parties, in some cases even an effect against the whole world. Technically speaking, following from legal relations in respect to land - the most valuable object of property law known in pre-industrial societies, in particular in Roman law - a sophisticated system of property rules developed. Rather than having to add new rules to the system, property law was structured so that, when new developments in society arose, these could be included in the existing system.[3]

When objects other than land became valuable, property law concerning these objects also developed. Many existing property rules could be adapted, maintaining the original structure and coherence. The law of property reached maturity much earlier than other legal areas, and for a long time was regarded to be the most important area of private law. Particularly in relation to the law of contract, property law took a more important position for many centuries. The influences of this historical development can still be seen today. The fact that the French Civil Code deals with contract law in a book titled 'Different ways to acquire ownership' is possibly the best example.[4] However, with the rise of contract law in the nineteenth century and this field of private law taking an equally important position next to the law of property, the influences of one area on the other have created a dynamic

1 Van Erp 2006a, p. 1043-1044.
2 So also Füller 2006, p. 2.
3 See, e.g., Terrat 1904, p. 335.
4 In French, *Des différentes manières dont on acquiert la propriété*.

system of interaction.[5] For example, in the German Civil Code, contract law and property law are given equal status and the interaction between contract and property has led to the recognition of new property rights. Nevertheless, under the influence of German scholarship in particular, contract law and property law have been held strictly separate, not only in respect of the effects of the legal relations these areas of law govern, but also in the study of contract and property law.[6] Property law is above all a field of system and doctrine, which will only upon careful examination show its underlying principles and concepts.

1.1. *Personal Rights and Property Rights*

The difference between the law of obligations and the law of property is best viewed in terms of the legal relations that are dealt with by these respective fields of law. The law of obligations, in particular its subspecies contract law, concerns itself with personal rights. Contractual rights concern legal relations entered into by two or more parties that only bind those parties who have agreed to the terms of the legal relation.[7] This basic principle of contract law is known as privity of contract. When a third party interferes with a personal right, the holder of that personal right must resort to the law of obligations to act against such interference.[8] Typically, the law of obligations will provide a remedy in tort law.

Opposed to these personal rights are those legal relations governed by the law of property. These legal relations are not only made between two or more persons, but also affect third parties in respect of an object.[9] It is the link to an object combined with this third-party effect that is characteristic of property rights. As a basic principle of property law, these legal relations, typically known as property rights, have effect against third parties by their nature.[10]

When the object is transferred, property rights in respect of that object will transfer as well.[11] Also when the object falls into the hands of a third party, the property rights will remain resting on the object, enabling the right-holder to act against this third party. In property law theory this third-party effect is commonly known as the right to follow or *droit de suite.* Furthermore, when a property right is created in respect to an object, the holder of that property right as a creditor will be in a privileged position, compared with other creditors of the same debtor. This effect is known in property law theory as the right of preference or *droit de préférence.* In other words, entitlement to a property right allows its holder to act not

5 On the equal position of contract law and the law of property, see Motive III 1888, p. 1-3.

6 Exceptions include, *inter alia*, Rank-Berenschot 1992, Reid 1997b, Rutgers 1999, Von Bar & Drobnig 2002, and Van Erp 2004b, Füller 2006.

7 Moreover, in the other area of the law of obligations, the law of tort, only personal relations arise. However, in respect to these relations, no party agreement is required.

8 See Van Laarhoven 2005, p. 48 *et seq.*

9 Reid 1997b, p. 226-227.

10 I.e. not because the parties have expressed their desire to have third party effect, but through the existence of the property right.

11 However, physical control over the object can be retained by making use of the concept of possession.

only against the person with whom he created the property right, but also against third parties interfering with his rights. In contrast with acting upon interference of a personal right, the holder of a property right may use property law to act against an interfering third party.[12]

In order for parties to grant third-party effect to their legal relation they must submit their relation to the law of property and for this a price must be paid. Parties can elect the third-party effect, but only if they comply with the rules set out by property law. In property law, therefore, party autonomy is limited in exchange for third-party effect. When parties choose to settle for a personal right, property law cannot impose these limits on party autonomy and in principle the parties are free to decide on what they want.[13] In contract law, there is party autonomy, only the parties to the contract, and not third parties, are bound by the terms of that contract.[14]

The other area of the law of obligations, the law of tort, also deals with personal rights. In contrast with contract law, legal relations in the law of tort come into existence upon the occurrence of a factual situation, usually where one party damages another party or the interests of another party. The relation that comes into existence is a personal relation in respect to the person causing the damage and will entitle the victim to compensation.[15]

The difference between personal rights and property rights is therefore directly related to the separation between the law of obligations and the law of property. The law of contract and the law of property are therefore different from each other, especially in respect of the content of the rights that they govern. Under the influence of German legal thinking and because of the fundamentally varying effects of personal and property rights, most legal systems uphold a separation between these two areas of law.[16]

Nevertheless there is also a close relationship between contract law and property law, especially when considered from the perspective of property law. In order for a property right to come into existence, parties must enter into an agreement that first of all will constitute personal rights. When the requirements of property law have been fulfilled, the personal right will become a property right and will be governed by property law. Another example is the transfer of a property right from one party to another. In order for a transfer to succeed an agreement between two parties is needed. Depending on the system of property law the agree-

12 English law forms an exception to this where also in property law the remedies in the law of obligations must be used to protect a property right. Typically in case of movable objects this is the tort of conversion. See Swadling 2000a, p. 218-219, Bridge 2002, p. 47 *et seq.*

13 Reid 1997b, p. 228.

14 Also in contract law, parties can be bound more than just by the limits of the law. In case of specific contracts such as lease of an immovable or a labour contract, contract law imposes formalities and certain content upon these legal relations as well. See, *inter alia,* Atiyah 1979, Trebilcock 1993, Hofer 2001, Farnsworth 2006, p. 918-919.

15 Van Dam 2006, p. 3 *et seq.*

16 Füller 2006, p. 10-13. However, in English law the law of torts is used to protect property rights, creating a strong link between the two areas of law. However, also in English law the law of tort creates only personal relations. See Chapter 6 English Law.

ment as such will transfer the property right or property law will impose additional criteria that must be fulfilled before the property right transfers.[17]

Furthermore, in most legal systems the separation between the law of obligations and the law of property also results in legal relations that do not clearly fall into either of these areas of law. An example of such a right is the right of lease. In many legal systems, especially civil law systems, the right of lease is a personal right binding only the lessor and lessee. However, as a means of protection for lessees, these systems have adopted a rule, albeit mostly with regard to land and buildings, of 'sale does not break a lease'.[18] Under this provision, a lessee who is confronted with an owner who transfers his property right to another person will continue to be a lessee, but now with a new lessor. The right of the lease therefore has limited third-party effect because it binds the new owner to the terms of the lease agreement between the lessee and the principal lessor.[19]

In every legal system where lease is a personal right, the relation between the law of obligations, to which lease belongs in those systems, and the law of property, where the right of lease may seem to belong, is being discussed.[20] However, by making use of doctrinal arguments, such as the separation between the law of obligations and the law of property, the contractual nature of lease is upheld and the limited third-party effect of a lease is considered an exception.[21]

Many legal systems are therefore confronted with a tension between the law of obligations and the law of property. Depending on the legal system, the law of property will be, to a greater or lesser degree, influenced by the law of obligations, in particular by contract law. The discussion on the influence of contract law, in particular if the acceptance of a quasi-property right is the result, will return in each legal system that is discussed in this study.[22]

1.2. *Property Law*

The law of property, or the law of things as it is sometimes called, deals with legal relations between persons in respect of objects (or things).[23] These legal relations, or better, property rights, exist with regard to tangible objects - corporeal movable objects or corporeal immovable objects -, and intangible objects, or incorporeal objects such as claims.

17 See, on different systems of transfer, in this chapter; 4. Terminology, see also Van Vliet 2000.

18 Art. 1749 CC, Para. 566 BGB, Art. 7:226 BW.

19 See Westrik 2001.

20 Even in English law where a lease is a property right, the right originates as a personal right. See Chapter 6; 2.2. Leases of Land.

21 On the place of lease in French, German and Dutch law, see Chapter 3; 4.6. Lease, Chapter 4; 4.4. Lease of Immovable Objects, and Chapter 5; 4.3. Lease of Immovable Objects.

22 See Chapter 3; 4. Borderline Cases in French Property Law, Chapter 4; 4. Borderline Cases in German Property Law, and Chapter 5; 4. Borderline Cases in Dutch Property Law. In respect to English law, because of the different nature of the English legal system, the discussion on the borderline between personal rights and property rights is included in the discussion of property rights. See in particular Chapter 6; 4. A *Numerus Clausus* in English Property Law.

23 See, e.g., Van der Merwe & De Waal 1993, Swadling 2007, p. 220.

The law of property provides rules on property rights in respect of these objects, including their creation, exercise, execution, termination and other forms of destruction. Because of the third-party effect of the rights the law of property deals with, these rules cannot usually - different from other areas of private law - be simply deviated from by party agreement between the parties, in contrast with other areas of private law.

1.2.1. Principles of Property Law

Although property law can be studied from its technical rules, and these rules can be compared between one country and another, this will not provide a complete overview of the law of property. Although many property law systems use the same technical rules for the same purposes, the application of these rules to a certain problem may differ from system to system. Property law as a doctrinally coherent system is governed by a set of principles, according to which any type of property can be expressed. When the comparison is taken to this general level of principles, it becomes possible to place these technical rules into a context, allowing a better and more complete comparative overview.[24]

The basic principles of property law are the principle of *numerus clausus* and the principle of transparency, which can be further divided into the principle of specificity and the principle of publicity.[25] The principle of specificity determines to what extent the object on which a property right is created must be specified. In many legal systems the rules on specificity are under pressure by developments in the field of security rights in respect of claims, where creditors are demanding property security rights in respect of future claims. Future claims are objects of property law that cannot be identified yet, as they do not exist. Many systems face difficulties accepting property rights in respect of these non-existing claims.

The other element of the principle of transparency is the principle of publicity. In property law, because of the effect of property rights in respect of third parties, information is vital.[26] Therefore, many legal systems demand registration of a property right in a register that is publicly accessible so that third parties may find out about the existence of a property rights' existence. In respect of highly valuable objects, such as land and valuable movable objects such as aircraft, trains and ships, registration is almost always required.[27]

Although the principle of transparency is very important to property law, the principle of *numerus clausus* is the principle that decides on the applicability of the law of property, and therefore also on the applicability of the transparency principle. This study therefore concentrates on the principle of *numerus clausus* as the gateway to property law.

24 In the same sense see Van Erp 2006a, p. 1050, Van Erp 2006b, p. 13 *et seq.*, Michaels 2006a, p. 364 *et seq.*

25 Van Erp 2006b, p. 14-16. On principles, fundamental principles and model rules see DCFR Interim Outline 2008, Nos. 10-11, p. 8-9.

26 Van Erp 2006b, p. 15.

27 Van Erp 2006b, p. 14-15.

1.2.2. *Numerus Clausus* of Property Rights

The principle of *numerus clausus* of property rights, or *numerus clausus* for short, refers to the idea that a system of property law imposes limitations on private parties that want to create property rights.[28] After its literal meaning, in many legal systems the term *numerus clausus* in property law refers to a closed list of property rights.

Given its importance to society as a whole, many legal systems provide rules on property law through legislation.[29] In countries as France, Germany and the Netherlands, a separate part in the Civil Code deals with the law of property. When these systems adhere to the principle of *numerus clausus* this means that in principle only those property rights that are allowed by the Civil Codes especially are recognised as property rights.[30] As a result parties can only create property rights that fulfil the criteria set by this legislation, leaving a limited freedom or no freedom at all to shape the content of their property relations.

The origin of the idea of *numerus clausus* can be found in the debates held after the French Revolution. In France, where the feudal system of landholding had been abolished, the legal system returned to a Roman-law inspired law of property in which, in contrast to the period before the Revolution, there was a separation between the law of obligations and the law of property.[31] In order to express the new property law system, the new French legislature wanted to provide an overview in the Civil Code of those property rights that from now on would be recognised.[32]

However, the real discussion on the closed system of property rights as a principle of property law and therefore a part of property law theory originates in nineteenth-century German legal thinking.[33] The German *Bürgerliches Gesetzbuch* (BGB) adopted Von Savigny's theory on *Vermögensrecht*, within which property law and the law of obligations form separate and distinctive parts of the law.[34] In the law of property as a separate area of law, because of its foundations taken from Roman law, the most extensive property right was a unitary and absolute right of ownership. All other property rights were considered rights lesser than the right of ownership but still with third-party effect.

Because of this effect, and to protect the newly created unitary and absolute right of ownership, the Civil Code limited the number, but also the content, of property rights. In doctrinal terms this idea of limitation of property rights or *Typen-gebundenheit* can be expressed with two different terms that have become commonly

28 The term 'private parties' refers also to public legal entities acting as a party in private law.

29 See Smits 2002, p. 249-252, Van Erp 2006b, p. 5-7.

30 Although in some legal systems property rights are also created through special legislation. See, e.g., Chapter 3; 3.4. *Emphyteusis*, and Chapter 4; 3.3. *Superficies*.

31 Pothier 1772, p. 1 *et seq.*, Laurent 1878, p. 92-93, Terré & Simler 1998, p. 67, Gordley 1994, p. 459 *et seq.*

32 See the statement made by Treilhard in *Recueil complet des travaux préparatoires du code civil* 11, p. 33.

33 Wiegand 1987, p. 630 *et seq.*

34 Von Savigny 1981, Paras. 52-57, Wiegand 1987, p. 631, Füller 2006, p. 8 *et seq.*

accepted in explaining the principle of *numerus clausus*; the limitation on the number of rights has become known as *Typenzwang* and the limitation on the content of the rights as *Typenfixierung*.[35]

Strongly connected to the separation between the law of obligations and the law of property, and the resulting distinction between property rights and personal rights, the principle of *numerus clausus* provides a filter to decide whether the law of property applies to a certain legal relation. Depending on the legal system there are different ways of describing the *numerus clausus*. When the principle of *numerus clausus* has found expression in the form of legislation, in particular as a part of the Civil Code, from which parties may not deviate, we could speak of a *rule* of *numerus clausus*. However, there are also legal systems in which the principle has not found expression as a formal rule. In some legal systems, for example, there is no Civil Code, and another source of law has a more important position than general legislation. In these legal systems the principle of *numerus clausus* also finds expression, usually through a decision of a court of law.[36]

Finally, there are also legal systems in the world that explicitly adhere to an open system of property rights, known as *numerus apertus*. These systems do not have a rule of *numerus clausus*, but nevertheless impose limitations on parties when it comes to the creation of new, as yet unknown, property rights.[37]

1.3. *European Private Law*

Comparing property law systems based on one of the principles of property law is more and more relevant from the perspective of the development of a European private law. For many years already the European Union has been active in the field of private law, the law of contract in particular. Since 2001 the European Commission has been working on a more coherent contract law in the form of a research project that might result in a complete revision of the existing contract law *acquis*, including general aspects of contract law.[38]

As part of the preparation for this research project, the Commission published a study on property law and tort law and how they relate to contract law. The objective of this study was to investigate how far harmonisation of contract law would have effects on the law of property.[39] As a result the researchers concluded that a harmonised contract law would certainly affect areas of property law. These

35 The term *Tipizität* is also used instead of *Typengebundenheid*, see Giuffrè 1992, Rainer 1995, p. 415 *et seq.*, Wiegand 1987, p. 633, Rey 1991, p. 71-75.

36 See, e.g., the English case *National Provincial Bank Ltd v Ainsworth* [1965] AC 1175, HL at 1247-1248 *per* Lord Wilberforce.

37 In other words, these systems might not have a rule of *numerus clausus*, but still adhere to the principle by imposing limitations on private parties in the creation of new property rights. Such systems include South African law and Spanish law. South African law will return in the discussion in Chapter 7; 3.8. A Legal System Without a *Numerus Clausus*: South African Law.

38 Action plan 2001, COM(2001) 98, Smits 2006. See Chapter 8; 2.1.3. European Commission Initiatives for Future Legislation.

39 See Von Bar & Drobnig 2002.

areas of property law include the rules on transfer of property rights, property security rights in respect of movable objects and rules on trusts.

Furthermore, the European Union has also taken several initiatives in the field of property law itself. These initiatives include Directives on stolen cultural objects, combatting late payments, and on financial collateral arrangements, as well as the Regulation on Insolvency proceedings.[40] Possible future initiatives of the Commission include the creation of a European property security right in respect of land, the right of Euro-mortgage.[41] Until now there has not been a general measure of European law harmonising the law of property. The fragmented approach of present European legislation leads to fundamental issues of national property law which sometimes cannot be completely resolved.[42]

With the work of the European Commission on the creation of a European private law, the work on comparative property law becomes more important, especially in order to see the effects of European integration on the national property law systems. In respect of the fundamental principles of property law, not much comparative research has been conducted.[43] There is, for instance, no general agreement on the possibility of finding a common core in property law, nor is there agreement on the question of harmonisation of property law.[44] Furthermore, the relation between national property law and European law as well as property law as part of the law in the European Internal Market has often been neglected.[45] Only in respect of property security rights in respect of movable objects has research shown that national property law systems are subject to the law of the Internal Market.[46]

In the study and development of a European private law, the law of property has not always been given the attention it deserves. Fundamental questions of property law have been left aside, sometimes due to a preconception of incompatibility. The current developments in European contract law and their possible effect on private law in the European Union enable property lawyers to look into fundamental questions of property law.[47] The principle of *numerus clausus* as the gatekeeper of property law is one of these fundamental principles that deserve

[40] Directive 93/7/EEC of the Council on of 15 March 1993 on the return of cultural objects unlawfully removed from the territory of a Member State, Directive 2000/35 of the European Parliament and of the Council of 29 June 2000 on combating late payment in commercial transactions, Directive 2002/47/EC of the European Parliament and the Council of 6 June 2002 on financial collateral arrangements, and Council Regulation 1346/2000 of 29 May on insolvency proceedings. On these European Union initiatives see Chapter 8; 2.1.3. European Commission Initiatives for Future Legislation.

[41] See Green Paper Mortgage Credit in the EU COM(2005) 237 final, p. 13-14.

[42] See, *inter alia,* Van Erp 2004c, p. 533 *et seq.*, Van Erp 2005, p. 252 *et seq.*, Van Erp 2006b.

[43] An exception is the work of Van Erp, see Van Erp 2006b, p. 12-14, Van Erp 2008.

[44] See, on the general conception of property law, Gordley 2006a, p. 49-50. On harmonisation, see Kieninger 2004, p. 647 *et seq.*, Rank 2006, p. 201 *et seq.*

[45] However, see Smits 2002, p. 245 *et seq.*, Van Erp 2006b.

[46] See Kieninger 1996a, Kieninger 1996b, Rutgers 1999, Roth 1999.

[47] When fundamental questions of contract law are considered, fundamental questions of property law might be included as well. On the discussion of fundamental elements of contract law, see Schuze 2005, p. 25-27.

much more attention, even more in the light of the development of European private law.

2. Legal Systems

There are various different property law systems in the European Union. Each of the Member States has a separate and distinct property law system and some even use more than one system.[48] Dealing with all property law systems of the EU is therefore almost impossible.[49] In a study on one of the fundamental principles of property law a choice must be made between legal systems.

In the debate on European private law the distinction between civil law and common law systems remains one of the central issues. In particular through the work of Legrand, who argues that no common ground can be found between civil law and common law because of a fundamental difference in the approaches taken by these legal traditions, the differences between civil law and common law might seem larger than ever.[50]

However, work on comparative property law has already shown that common ground in the law of property can be found.[51] When it comes to fundamental principles such as the principle of *numerus clausus*, not much attention has been given to the search for such a common core.[52] A study on the principle of *numerus clausus* should therefore at least include a legal system from the civil law and common law tradition.

Furthermore, even within traditions many differences exist; there is not one common law or civil law system. As a guidance to choose from the many legal systems in the world, in the light of the debate on European private law, a focus on European legal systems seems justified. Within these European legal systems two systems, French and German law, have been very influential. The Civil Codes drafted in these countries have influenced Civil Codes throughout the mainland of Europe, including, for instance, the law of the Netherlands which has been influenced by both. When it comes to common law systems, English law, as the mother of all common law systems, has been immensely influential.

48 English law uses the law of real property or land law and the law on personal property or personal property law. See Chapter 6; 1.1. Terminology.

49 There is only one study on property law in the Member States of the European Union. See Von Bar (ed.) *Sachenrecht in Europa, Schriften zum Internationalen Privatrecht und zur Rechtsvergleichung*, (Osnabrück, 2000), volumes 1-4.

50 Legrand 1996a, p. 779 *et seq.*, Legrand 1996b, p. 52 *et seq.*, Legrand 1997, p. 44 *et seq.*, Legrand 1999, p. 1053 *et seq.* On the role of Legrand in comparative law and other criticism see Michaels 2006a, p. 340-341, Dannemann 2006, p. 389.

51 See, *inter alia*, Van Vliet 2000, p. 201 *et seq.*, Kieninger 2004, p. 647 *et seq.*, Gordley 2006a, p. 49-50.

52 However, see Reid 1997b, Van Erp 2003b, Struycken 2007.

2.1. *Civil Law: French, German and Dutch Law*

In respect of the division between civil law and common law systems, civil law systems are in the vast majority in the European Union.[53] Although these civil law systems differ from each other, they share a common basis in the influence of Roman law.[54] Western European legal systems, such as French and German law, have had an enormous influence on other European legal systems, including those in Eastern Europe. In particular, as a result of the codes of private law in France and in Germany, and the Roman law basis of these codes, many other legal systems have adopted aspects of Roman law.[55]

The Civil Codes of France and Germany were introduced 100 years apart. During the period between the introduction of the French *Code civil* (CC) and the German *Bürgerliches Gesetzbuch* (BGB) new insights on the law of property were developed. In particular under pressure from the German scholar Von Savigny, the German BGB adheres to a much stricter separation between the law of obligations and the law of property than does the French Civil Code.[56]

The development of property law from the French to the German Civil Code shows the development of what has been named the classical system of property law, a system of property law strictly separated from the law of obligations in which legal certainty is the most important value.[57] Under the heading of legal certainty, property relations can only exist when it is clear on which object the property relation is created and third parties can know about its existence. In the case of immovables this requires registration, in the case of movables it requires possession by the right-holder. Although other areas of law continued to develop, the classical model of property law as it was formed in French and German law has remained the same throughout most of the twentieth century. Only recently were changes made in both German and French law.[58]

The classical model of property law also prevailed in countries influenced by the French and German legal systems. Dutch law, from 1838 onwards, used a French-inspired Civil Code and therefore also the French system of property law. Changes inspired by German law were made in 1992, when a large part of the new Dutch *Burgerlijk Wetboek* (BW) came into effect, including the relevant parts on property law. In the new Dutch Civil Code a stronger influence of German law can be seen in a stricter separation between the law of obligations and the law of property as well as a limitation of the law of property, in particular the right of ownership, to corporeal objects.[59]

53 Hondius 1998, p. 9, but also other distinctions have been made. See *inter alia* Zweigert & Kötz 1998, p. 63 *et seq*.

54 On the common basis in Roman law see Chapter 2, Zwalve 2003, p. 23 *et seq*

55 Zwalve 2003, p. 36-42, 43-47,Zweigert & Kötz 1998, p. 85 *et seq*., 143 *et seq*.

56 See Von Savigny 1981.

57 On the classical system of property law see Van Erp 2008, forthcoming.

58 See Chapter 3; 1. Introduction, and Chapter 4; 3.4. Expectation Rights.

59 See Chapter 5; 1. Introduction.

The classical model used in German law, therefore also influenced the classical model of Dutch law, which now combines the historical influence of French law and modern concepts of Dutch law with the new influence of German law. From the perspective of civil law systems, Dutch law therefore offers a middle ground between French and German law, but at the same time offers a complication because of various, often very traditional, choices that were made in the new Civil Code of 1992.

The civil law part of this book will deal with French, German and Dutch law. Only occasionally influences from other civil law jurisdictions will be mentioned. The focus on these three countries enables a comparison of the fundamental concepts of property law, the principle of *numerus clausus* in particular, as well as the content of the closed list of property rights and its deviations.

2.2. *Common Law: English Law*

The common law tradition is in a minority in the European Union. In fact, only England, Wales, Northern Ireland, and Ireland are common law systems at the moment.[60] However, English law also has influence in other parts of the European Union in countries such as Malta, Cyprus and Scotland. These systems are mixed traditions, combining civil law and common law, but remain heavily influenced by English law.

In this study the term common law is used to describe the legal system that has developed in England since 1066.[61] Common law, and its parallel system of equity, underwent its own development, only occasionally under the influence of a certain aspect of the continental Roman law.[62] The result of this development is that, compared with civil law, common law uses different solutions to similar problems. These different solutions include other concepts of property law, but also different legal techniques. From a civil law point of view, the development of land law and personal property law and the separate development of common law and equity until the end of the nineteenth century create a fragmented system of property law.

One of the clearest distinguishing factors between common law and civil law countries in respect of property law is the feudal system of land holding. Where, in civil law systems, the feudal system was abolished as a result of the French Revolution, it remained in force in England.[63] Civil law systems, with the drafting of the various Civil Codes, returned to Roman-law based concepts such as a unitary and absolute right of ownership. In English law feudal concepts such as fees and estates remain, although without an actual feudal system today.

60 Other examples are the Channel Islands of Jersey and Guernsey. See Van Erp 2006a, p. 1058-1059.

61 Zweigert & Kötz 1998, p. 182 *et seq.*, Pierre 1997, p. 243 *et seq.*, Van Caenegem 1988a, p. 3-14.

62 Zweigert & Kötz 1998, p. 181, Stein 1992, p. 1591. See also Gauthier 1996, Reimann 1993, Zimmermann 2002a. See further Chapter 6; 1.1. Terminology.

63 See Van Erp 2008, forthcoming.

A discussion of English law will therefore show the problems comparative property lawyers face in resolving fundamental distinctions, based on the contrast between Roman law and feudal principles.

2.3. *South African Law as a Comparative Factor*

In the debate on comparative property law and the sometimes sharp distinctions between common law and civil law, a third legal tradition may offer useful insights.[64] The law of South Africa, which is confronted with civil law and common law every day, offers such a third tradition. South Africa is a mixed legal system that combines Roman-Dutch civil law with English common law, exactly the legal traditions followed by the countries mentioned above. Being a mixed legal system means that South African law recognises concepts specific to English law, such as trusts, but refuses to recognise equity.[65] Fitting trusts into a property law system without equity requires some fundamental decisions to resolve conflicts, mainly in relation to the ownership of the trust objects and the rights of beneficiaries.[66] In cases like that of trusts, South African law must find solutions for conflicts between common law and civil law concepts on a frequent basis. Possibly these solutions offered by South African law can offer insights and be used as a basis for a European private law.[67]

However, South African law is not a European legal system and, although the solutions it provides are highly relevant in the debate on European private law, South African law will only be dealt with as a comparative factor. When the differences between civil law and common law have become clear, South African law can play its role in helping to find a middle ground.[68] The content of the South African system of property rights, however, will be left aside.

3. Methodology

The distinction between personal rights and property rights, in civil law systems, can be traced back to Roman law. However, this distinction is also recognised by the common law. In common law the distinction also has historical origins, but they are different from those in the civil law.[69] Furthermore, the abolition of the feudal system in the civil law systems as a result of the French Revolution and its continued existence in England shows the different historical origins of these systems of property law.[70]

Property law systems develop on their own, not necessarily logically, sometimes as a reaction to an event or a certain unwanted situation. Without knowing

64 See Michaels 2006a, p. 367-369.

65 On the law of trusts in South African law see De Waal 2000, p. 439 *et seq.*

66 See Honoré et al. 2003.

67 Smits 1999.

68 See Chapter 7; 3.8. A Legal System Without *Numerus Clausus*: South African Law.

69 See Tyler & Palmer 1973, p. 6-7, Simpson 1986, p. 25 *et seq.*, Holdsworth 1927, p. 11 *et seq.*

70 Critically on the results of the French Revolution see Gordley 1994, p. 459 *et seq.*

the historical origins of a legal system it is difficult to explain why ownership in France is such an absolute right, why German law has two types of rights of hypothec on immovable objects, why Dutch law continues to struggle with trusts and transfers of ownership for security purposes, and why in English law a lease is not really realty, but nevertheless a property right. A discussion and comparison of modern property law systems without taking into account the historical development of legal systems is therefore almost impossible in respect of property law.[71]

As this study will show, it is striking that, although there are many differences, there are, even with a different historical basis, also many similarities and similar approaches between these systems. In the light of the debate on European private law looking for a common ground between French, German, Dutch and English law, while taking into account the diversity between legal systems could provide helpful results.[72] This common basis could contribute to the discussion on the development of a European property law.

In order to find these common grounds, a different look at property law will be needed.[73] Property law concepts that are functionally equivalent, in other words, concepts that respond, although they are different concepts, to the same problem, shall be grouped as much as possible.[74] In doing so respect can be maintained for the differences between the concepts in different legal systems, but at the same time bringing them under the same heading.[75] As an example, there is no need to distinguish servitudes on land in civil law systems from easements in English law. The result is an analysis of the system of property rights in French, German, Dutch and English law, expressed in terms that are as neutral as possible. Based on this comparative system, proposals can be made to move towards a European property law. The method used to come to such proposals must consequently be historical-comparative.

4. Terminology

In the course of the discussion on the property law systems of France, Germany, the Netherlands and England, various terms of property law will be used. Some of these are so general that they should be explained here rather than in the respective chapters on the particular legal systems.

This study will speak of 'legal relations' whenever possible.[76] The term 'legal relation' is used to mean any relation between two or more persons with an effect in law. When two parties agree on something, their legal relation will usually be a contract and the rights these parties will receive from this legal relation will be personal rights. Consequently, if parties agree on something in respect to an object and this legal relation falls within the system of property law, when formalities

71 Van Erp 2003a, p. 394 *et seq.*
72 Dannemann 2006, p. 391-394.
73 On the functional method and looking functionally at legal systems see Michaels 2006a.
74 Michaels 2006a, p. 356-359.
75 Michaels 2006a, p. 364-365.
76 See Ginossar 1960, Zenati 1981, Sagaert 2005b.

have been fulfilled, the legal relation will be a property relation and the rights arising from it will be property rights. The term legal relation is therefore intended to be a term preceding the phase and the question which right, whether personal or proprietary, arises. Furthermore, the term 'legal relation' emphasises the connection between the law of obligations and the law of property and makes it possible to approach *numerus clausus* as the principle that decides which legal relation is granted access to property law and therefore will have third-party effect.

Another term that is used throughout the following chapters is the term 'possession'. Depending on the legal system in which the term is used, possession refers to a factual situation in which a person has factual power over an object for himself or on behalf of another, or to a legal situation in which the person with the strongest right of possession holds the best title in an object.

In civil law systems there are two approaches to possession. French and Dutch law reserve the term possession for the person having factual power over an object for himself. When a person has factual power over an object, but not for himself, French and Dutch law use the term 'detention' .[77]

German law uses the concept of possession for both of these factual situations. When a person has factual power over an object for himself, German law speaks of *Eigenbesitz*. When a person has factual power over an object for another, German law speaks of *Fremdbesitz*.[78]

The difference in approaches towards possession is relevant in respect of the actions a possessor may take to protect his possession. These possessory actions are, in French and Dutch law, only open to a possessor and not to a detentor, but in German law also to a *Fremdbesitzer*. The result is a complicated discussion in Germany on the proprietary status of certain legal relations that in French and Dutch law only award detention.[79]

The terms 'possession' and 'detention' should not be confused with the term 'holding'. Holding a property right refers to the entitlement to that property right, not to the factual power over the object on which the property right is created. The term 'right-holder' therefore refers to that person entitled to a property right.

Another term that is used throughout the study is 'the system of transfer' or 'transfer system'. French, German, Dutch and English law all use different requirements for the transfer of a property right in respect of an object to another person. Mostly these requirements are also used for the creation of property rights.

In terms of transfer systems there are two major distinctions. A consensual system allows immediate property effects, the transfer of a property right, from a contract concluded between a buyer and a seller. A tradition system requires, besides a valid contract underlying the transfer, an additional act in the law of property for the transfer to take effect.

A second distinction is between abstract and causal transfer systems. A causal system requires a valid contract to transfer a property right in respect of an object,

77 Malaurie & Aynès 2005, p. 101, Asser, Mijnsen, De Haan & Van Dam 2006, No. 123, p. 107-108.

78 Wieling 2001, p. 43.

79 See Chapter 4; 4.3. Entitlement to Possession Through the Law of Obligations.

not only at the moment of transfer, but also after that. When the contract underlying the transfer is for some reason void or avoided, because of the causal system, the transfer will be void as well. In an abstract system of transfer, a valid agreement is needed to effect the transfer, but once the transfer has taken place, invalidity of the agreement in contract law will, in most circumstances, have no effect on the transfer of the property right anymore.[80]

A final terminological distinction that is made is that of land registration systems. In terms of land registration systems, there are two models. A negative model, as used by French and Dutch law, is one in which a public register is kept of all transactions in respect of immovable objects by registering the deeds underlying these transactions. However, the registrar merely registers the deeds and does not check their contents, apart from some procedural requirements. A positive model, as used in German and in English law, is a system in which a public register is kept of all transactions concluded in respect to immovable objects, in which data taken from deeds is registered after the validity of this data has been checked. These systems, in one way or another, guarantee the correct content of the register.[81] The distinction between these two models of registration systems is needed because of the work of the European Commission on mortgage credit markets in Europe. In order to promote cross-border transactions in immovable property, systems for registration of security rights are becoming more and more integrated. Moreover, a property security right in respect of immovable objects, the existence of which can be proven from a document provided by a positive register, might possibly be introduced in the future.[82]

5. Searching for a *Numerus Clausus*

This study will examine one of the principles of property law, the principle of *numerus clausus*, and the expressions of this principle in the legal systems of France, Germany, the Netherlands and England. In the discussion on these legal systems, not only the existence of the *numerus clausus* but also its content will be central.

These property law systems are under increasing pressure from the law of contract in which party autonomy is used to achieve similar results as can be achieved in property law, or even to achieve results that cannot be achieved in property law, but still bind third parties. As a result several legal systems have been confronted with new property rights or adapted versions of already existing property rights, which they have accepted and included in the law of property.[83]

Furthermore, because of the increased integration of national legal systems in the Internal Market of the European Union, these four legal systems are also subject to influence from each other. Due to the increasing economic and political, as well

80 On these distinctions see Van Vliet 2000, Cámara-Lapuente 2005, p. 808-809.

81 On these distinctions see Cámara-Lapuente 2005, p. 809 *et seq.*

82 On the Euro-mortgage see Chapter 8; 2.3. European Commission Initiatives for Future Legislation.

83 See e.g. Rey 1991, p. 54 *et seq.*, Fesevur 1992, p. 13-15, Kerridge 2000, p. 533 *et seq.*, Wiegand 1987, p. 640-641, Van Erp 2003b, Reid 1997b, p. 229, De Waal 2000, p. 439 *et seq.*

as legal, links between these legal systems, they are increasingly confronted with choices made in other jurisdictions. One example is the recognition of property rights created in another legal system and the legal economic and legal political choices connected to these rights and their recognition.[84]

Finally, also because of further market integration, the European Union has taken and is taking several legislative initiatives in which it introduces new property rights. These new rights include the security interest and the transfer of title under the Financial Collateral Arrangement Directive, as well as a legislative instrument introducing a Euro-mortgage which might be proposed in the near future.[85]

The classical model of property law is therefore under more pressure than ever. In order to understand this pressure and to propose a method to deal with it, this book is divided into three parts. First, the civil law will be looked at. Because of the civil law systems' shared heritage in Roman law, Chapter 2 examines the development of property rights, starting from Roman law, in the civil law. Moreover, as the theory of *numerus clausus* is most developed in civil law systems, this Chapter on the development of property rights will also explore the origins of the *numerus clausus* principle. After that, Chapter 3 will deal with French law, Chapter 4 with German law and Chapter 5 with Dutch law.

Each of these chapters will examine which property rights the legal system recognises and for which purpose these property rights are used. Furthermore, each chapter will devote attention to the distinction between the law of obligations and the law of property and those legal relations that do not fall into either of these areas of private law.

The second section, Chapter 6, will deal with English law. This section will also examine the law of property, but will follow the distinction between land law and personal property law. Chapter 6 will discuss whether the *numerus clausus* principle can also be found in English law and what its place is in that legal system.

The third section comprises a comparative analysis of French, German, Dutch and English law in Chapter 7. In this analysis the content of the property law system of these countries will be compared as well as the place of the *numerus clausus*. An overview is provided of the system of property rights in these legal systems, and the theory of *numerus clausus* is revisited to see what are the arguments for its existence and whether these arguments can still be maintained.

The final chapter, Chapter 8, will discuss the influence on the national systems of property law that result from the impact of private international law and European law, more specifically the law of the European Union. This Chapter will raise the question whether national property law really is only national property law today, when seen from the perspective of European integration. The findings of this thesis lead to a negative answer. Property law systems now function together in a system of European property law. When a European property law is formed, the

84 On this, see Chapter 8.

85 Directive 2002/47/EC of the European Parliament and the Council of 6 June 2002 on financial collateral arrangements, Green Paper Mortgage Credit in the EU COM(2005) 237 final, p. 13-14. See Chapter 8; 2.3. European Commission Initiatives for Future Legislation.

principle of *numerus clausus* will need to take centre stage. At the end of Chapter 8, therefore, a proposal is made for a European property law in which *numerus clausus* is a constitutive element.

Chapter 2

THE DEVELOPMENT OF PROPERTY RIGHTS

1. Introduction

The legal systems of France, Germany and the Netherlands share a common basis in Roman law. Not only historical Roman law, the law from the formative period of Roman law until the codifications of Justinian, but also the Roman law that was rediscovered and received into the legal systems of the territories that are now these nation states.[1] In the period between the original, historical Roman law and the rediscovered and adapted form of Roman law, society had continued to develop and had started to use different legal concepts taken from customary law. Applying Roman law when it was rediscovered was sometimes difficult, as it had to be adapted to the new situations in society. The feudal system of landholding had come into existence between the fall of the Roman Empire and the rediscovery of Roman law. In this system both the feudal lord and tenant held a strong property right in the same land at the same time. It was not very simple to reincorporate principles such as the Roman unitary concept of ownership, *dominium*.[2]

This study searches for the existence of the principle of *numerus clausus* in French, German, Dutch and English law. As was mentioned in Chapter 1, a distinction can be made between a principle of *numerus clausus* and a rule of *numerus clausus*. As mentioned in Chapter 1, and as will be further elaborated in Chapter 4 on German law, the doctrinal theory on the rule of *numerus clausus* finds its origin in the German debate on the separation between the law of obligations and the law of property.[3] Moreover, there is also a strong influence from the French Civil Code. During the drafting process of the French Civil Code some of the drafters expressed their opinion that there was a closed list of property rights in French law and that parties were not free any longer to create new property rights.[4] The origins of the idea that there are limitations on parties in the creation of property rights, or the

1 I.e., when the *Ius Commune* applied. On the term *Ius Commune* see Nève 1995, p. 3 *et seq.*

2 More will be stated about this below in 4.3. Ownership.

3 See Chapter 1; 1.2.2. *Numerus Clausus* of Property Rights, and Chapter 4; 1. Introduction.

4 See Chapter 3; 5. A *Numerus Clausus* in French Property Law.

principle of *numerus clausus*, might therefore be older than the drafting of the German Civil Code.

Projecting the rule of *numerus clausus* to a period before these Civil Codes would not answer the question of the doctrinal origins of this rule of property law, but would require that period to be explained in terms of later legal theory. However, the idea of limiting the available property rights, especially the ideas contained in the *principle* of *numerus clausus*, was not new for German lawyers in the nineteenth century.[5] Private parties have been limited in the possibility to create new property rights from Roman times onwards. Although the reasons for these limitations in Roman law might have been different from the modern day reasons for *numerus clausus*, these reasons should be placed in the time period in which they were used and, in that perspective, remain of value.[6]

Central to this Chapter is therefore not the possible existence of a rule of *numerus clausus* of property rights. Instead the Chapter will focus on the question of how property rights developed and whether, in the legal system in which they functioned, limitations were imposed on the number and content of these rights. When discussing these limitations, the Chapter will search for *numerus clausus* as a principle of property law.[7]

The development of property rights, including the content of property rights, forms a common basis for the civil law systems discussed in the next three Chapters. This Chapter will provide an overview of the common historical basis as well as lay foundations for the discussion on the nature of the modern civil law systems of France, Germany and the Netherlands.[8] This Chapter will also show that this common basis not only concerns the limitation of the number of property rights, but that these civil law systems to a very large extent have also incorporated the same property rights, subjected to the same criteria as developed in historical Roman law. In the discussion below on property rights in the modern civil law systems of France, Germany and the Netherlands, explicit reference will be made back to this Chapter to underline the historical basis.

Because the term Roman law is imprecise regarding the exact period it concerns, and Roman law differed in content depending on the period under consideration, a distinction is made between historical and learned Roman law. The term learned Roman law is used to describe the received Roman law at the time of

5 On the distinction between the rule and the principle of *numerus clausus* see Chapter 1; 1.2.2. *Numerus Clausus* of Property Rights, and Chapter 7; 1.3.2. *Numerus Clausus* as a Principle or as a Rule?

6 However, see Lokin 2003, p. 273. On Lokin's view on the origins of the *numerus clausus* see Chapter 7; 1.3.3. Historical Origins of *Numerus Clausus*. See also in this Chapter; 2.5. A *Numerus Clausus* in (Pre-) Classical Roman Law?

7 *Numerus clausus* as a principle of property law limits party autonomy regarding the creation of property rights, both existing and new rights. Searching for a principle of *numerus clausus* does not include the search for an absolutely closed list of property rights, which is only one of the ways in which the principle of *numerus clausus* can be expressed. See Van Erp 2006b, p. 12 *et seq.*, Van Erp 2008, forthcoming.

8 See Chapter 7; 1.1. Property Law in Development.

the *Ius Commune*.[9] The term historical Roman law is used as a general term for the law that applied at the time the Roman Republic, Principate and Empire actually existed. In historical Roman law a further distinction is made between the period before codification, especially pre-classical and classical Roman law, and the period after codification when the *Corpus Iuris Civilis* was adopted under the authority of Emperor Justinian.[10] The (pre-) classical period, as it will be referred to, concerns the formative period of Roman law from the Late Republic (250 BC) until the end of the second century AD. It should be emphasised that it is not the intention of this study to provide an extensive overview of Roman law. The objective of this Chapter is merely to see which property rights existed at what time and in which system. Was this (1) a system of unlimited freedom for parties to create property rights? or (2) a system in which parties were limited to create new rights? Because of the casuistic nature of Roman law, which was mainly developed by learned writers describing factual cases and by deriving general rules from these cases, a summary will be provided at the end of each section. After the discussion of Roman law, this Chapter will deal with the *Ius Commune*, which was the time in which Roman law was rediscovered and applied to feudal property law and when the law of the Roman Catholic Church, canon law, became more influential, forming the basis of many theoretical property law problems that still exist today. Finally, this Chapter will deal with the development away from the Roman-law inspired *Ius Commune* through the works of the Humanists and the natural law school, as well as the abolition of the feudal system, at least in France, as a result of the French Revolution.[11] It was the abolition of the feudal system that would eventually lead to the adoption of the French Civil Code, reinstating parts of the (pre-)classical Roman concept of 'unitary' ownership as well as (pre-)classical Roman property rights other than ownership.[12]

2. (Pre-) Classical Roman Law

2.1. *Introduction*

A general discussion of the development of property law in the period in Roman law before Justinian's codifications remains somewhat difficult as this period comprises at least three generally recognised sub-periods; pre-classical law, classical law and post-classical or vulgar law. This Chapter combines pre-classical and classical Roman law and seeks to discover what types of property rights were developed in this period and how these rights functioned. From this perspective, the (pre-) classical Roman law, where the Roman legal system was at its most untainted and

9 See below; 4. The *Ius Commune*.

10 This code is the *Corpus Iuris Civilis*, made under the authority of Emperor Justinian. See below; 3. Codified Roman Law – The *Corpus Iuris Civilis*.

11 The different legal systems and the way in which historical legal systems are incorporated are dealt with in the respective Chapters.

12 At the time of the French Revolution there was already work on drafts for a Civil Code in Austria and Prussia.

extensive form, is the most interesting.[13] After the period of classical Roman law the concepts that were developed in a clear way and that had become distinct from other concepts, became, mostly due to economic circumstances, unclear and blurred. It was only in the codification made under the authority of Emperor Justinian that classical Roman law principles were restored.[14]

Furthermore, a distinction can be made between the pre-codification period and the codification period which can be explained from the point of view of the *numerus clausus*. The codification that was ordered by Emperor Justinian is usually regarded as the first codification of law in history.[15] As the intention of Justinian was to codify the law and give this codification exclusive force of law, the property rights contained in this codification may be regarded as the only property rights that could be created.[16] In respect to limitations on private parties concerning the creation of property rights, and given the nature of Justinian's codification, it could be held that a rule of *numerus clausus* was established.[17] However up to the time of codification the law was un-codified and it was a matter for practice and the writers of authority to include and recognise new property rights.[18]

After discussing some general principles, this Chapter will first discuss the concept of ownership, after which attention will be paid to various property rights other than ownership. Finally, when the contents of the property rights - ownership and property rights other than ownership - have been examined, the system of property rights will be examined.

2.2. *General Principles of (Pre-) Classical Roman Law*

Before examining the concept of ownership and the various other property rights it is important to deal with some general principles first. Roman law was based on actions more than on rights.[19] The Romans did not occupy themselves with the question of who had a certain right, but rather with who had a certain *actio* or action to protect a certain legal position. The *actio* was a type of remedy that could be invoked before a judge, legal officer or magistrate. Besides actions there were also interdicts, the difference being one of origin. Because of this system of actions it was unnecessary to provide a general definition of the right of ownership, the question in Roman law would not have been who had ownership but who had an *actio* protecting ownership.

13 Nicholas 1962, p. 34, Kaser & Knütel 2003, p. 4-5.

14 See below; 3. Codified Roman Law - The *Corpus Iuris Civilis*.

15 Lokin & Zwalve 1992, p. 61-64. It should be noted that there had been previous law collections.

16 Zwalve 2003, p. 103, see below; 3.2. General Principles of the *Corpus Iuris Civilis*.

17 See below; 3.5. A *Numerus Clausus* in the *Corpus Iuris Civilis*?

18 See, *inter alia,* Mayer-Maly 1999, p. 97, Johnston 1999, p 69, Watson 1968, p 176-180, Giuffrè 1992, p. 203 *et seq*. However, it should be noted that the existence of a *numerus clausus* in pre-codification times is debatable. It is clear that these writers attempted to categorise new situations into existing property rights.

19 On this see, *inter alia,* Van den Bergh 1988, p. 33-34.

The modern distinction between personal rights and property rights, that is usually held to have been adhered to by Roman law as well, therefore was addressed by the question of against which person or persons a certain *actio* could be initiated. A property relation would be recognised if the *actio* worked against everyone, whereas a personal relation would be characterised by an *actio* only available between the parties. In this respect the term proprietary action or *actio in rem* can be used.

In Roman law it is important to classify the objects of property law.[20] The concept of *res* is of importance. In ancient Roman law, when society was primarily based on agriculture, a distinction was made between those objects required for, especially, agriculture, the *res mancipi*, and those not relevant to such purposes, the *res nec mancipi*.[21] This distinction was important, especially in relation to the ways in which ownership of these objects could be transferred. *Res mancipi* could be transferred by *mancipatio*, which was a formal way to transfer ownership, whereas *res nec mancipi* were transferred by *traditio*, which was a more informal way to transfer ownership.[22] The reason for this distinction becomes clear when the *res mancipi* are examined. The contents of what can be *res mancipi* are listed by Gaius in his *Institutes* and comprise slaves, beasts of burden (oxen, horses, mules and donkeys), Italic land, houses on Italic land and rustic praedial servitudes.[23] These objects were the most important elements in Roman life at that time and therefore these important elements could only be transferred with the utmost formality.

The procedure of *mancipatio* was one of these formal procedures. *Mancipatio*, which is described by Gaius, exists in a ritual enacted before five witnesses, where the *res mancipi* is exchanged for some symbolic amount or quantity of value in bronze.[24] The procedure of *in iure cessio* was also used, where both parties would come before the *praetor* and the claimant would state that an object was his, whereas the defendant would remain silent and the praetor would then adjudicate the *res mancipi* to the claimant by *addictio*.[25] The *traditio* was the least formal procedure and was used to transfer *res nec mancipi*. On delivery, if based on a valid cause, the object

20 See, *inter alia*, Watson 1968, Sohm 1931, Schulz 1992, Nicholas 1962, Borkowski 1997.

21 On this distinction and its possible origin see Van den Bergh 1988, p. 9, Borkowski 1997, p. 156, Kaser & Wubbe 1971, p. 94-95, Giuffrè 1992, p. 121, Nicholas 1962, p. 106, Kaser & Knütel 2003, p. 120, and G. Inst. 2.14a.

22 Moreover, these objects could also be transferred by *in iure cessio*. Kaser & Wubbe 1971, p. 94, 118-120, Borkowski 1997, p. 155-156.

23 G. Inst. 2.14a. The part regarding the beast of burden has been much debated. The list provided by Gaius as examples seems to have been the full list. When, for example, elephants became beast of burden, they were not regarded as *res mancipi*. Borkowski 1997, p. 156, Watson 1968, p. 17-20.

24 Although it should be noted that the symbolic value could be replaced by the actual purchase price, thus transforming the *mancipatio* into a sale transaction. Watson 1968, p. 16 20, Borkowski 1997, p. 200-202, Nicholas 1962, p. 116, Thomas 1976, p. 152-155.

25 Watson 1968, p. 20-21, Borkowski 1997, p. 202, Nicholas 1962, p. 116, Mayer-Maly 1999, p. 74, Thomas 1976, p. 155-157. More will be stated on this mode of transfer in the part on servitudes.

would pass to a new owner.[26] The method of transfer of ownership by *traditio* was considered the most standard form to transfer ownership and would eventually remain as the principal method of transfer.

Finally, the distinction between Roman citizens and Roman objects of property, and people from the rest of the world and other objects of property should be explained. In Roman law, Roman citizens were the only persons who could acquire Roman objects under what is known as a *Quiritian* title. This title, or the right to the *actio* protecting ownership, was the paramount entitlement to an object. People who were not Roman citizens were not capable of this ownership and were forced to make do with a lesser form. Land outside Italy was not covered by the Roman civil law and therefore, under the law that applied to these areas of land, the *Ius Gentium*, all land outside of Italy was owned by the State. It could therefore not be owned by *Quiritian* title or any other title.

The Roman distinction between *Quiritian* ownership and lesser forms of ownership was the result of a distinction between *ius civile*, which applied to Roman citizens only, and *ius gentium*, which applied to the whole territory of the Republic, Principate and Empire respectively. This distinction followed from the general system of Roman law where the *ius civile* was restricted to Roman citizens.

2.3. *Ownership*

Although Roman law did not provide a precise definition of the concept of ownership, it was already regarded as the paramount entitlement to an object, and this does not mean that Roman ownership cannot be defined.[27] In fact, throughout later history attempts have been made to do so.[28] Especially in (pre-) classical Roman law, it was difficult to describe the owner of an object.[29] In terms of a definition, with Roman law looking at actions rather than at rights, the person with ownership was a Roman person who had an object acquired through a Roman legal process to whom the action of vindication belonged.[30]

Originally, Roman society had been organised around families with the *pater familias* or head of the family as the one owned everything. In these ancient times, the ownership of the *pater familias* was protected by the procedure of *legis actio sacramento in rem*. This was a formal procedure, which is considered to date from the time of the law of XII Tables, one of the oldest Roman written laws. In this legal procedure each of the parties would claim that a certain object was his.[31] It was for

26 Or, on *iusta causa*. Nicholas 1962, p. 117, Watson 1968, p. 61-62, Pool 1995, p. 46 *et seq.*, Mayer-Maly 1999, p. 74, Thomas 1976, p. 179-183.

27 Thomas 1976, p. 133, Mayer-Maly 1999, p. 60-61, Van der Merwe 1996, p. 364, Carey Miller 1998, p. 145-148, Nicholas 1962, p. 153, Watson 1968, p. 92, Zwalve 2003, p. 109.

28 For an overview see Schrage 1996.

29 Carey Miller 1998, p. 45-46.

30 Regardless under which procedure this vindication was granted, as will be shown in this section. Thomas 1976, p. 133, Kaser & Wubbe 1971, p. 108-109.

31 Or the words *meum esse aio*. G. Inst. 4.16., the XII Tables date from 450 B.C., Thomas 1976, p. 33. Kaser & Wubbe 1971, p. 130, Kaser 1964, p. 7-8, Sohm 1931, p. 311.

the judge in the procedure to decide which of the parties had the best right and who was therefore considered owner. [32] This specific procedure has given rise to a theory by Kaser that in ancient times the Romans used a concept of relative ownership, since both were able to claim ownership to the object in the procedure.[33] However, several other authors claim that the use of the word 'mine', a party claiming a certain object was his, makes it possible to speak of an absolute concept of ownership and contradicts this assumption.[34] Although Kaser's theory is interesting and would enable a better comparison with modern English law, where an 'owner' is looked at as that person having the best right to an object, the majority of authors reject his views.[35]

The *legis actio sacramento in rem* disappeared in the later law and so did the position of the *pater familias*.[36] In pre-classical law the procedure *per sponsionem* replaced the ancient *legis actio* procedure, although it was still strongly based on it.[37] This procedure was used to decide whether the plaintiff was owner or not by the formula *petitoria* or *rei vindicatio*, or *vindicatio* for short. This formula already existed at the time of the *legis actio* procedure but, in pre-classical law, it became the remaining procedure for vindication.[38] The *formula petitoria* went as follows:

> Let Titius be judge. If it appears that the object which is the subject of the action is Aulus Agerius's by the law of the Quirites, and if that object shall not be restored to Aulus Agerius in response to the judge's decision, for as much as that object shall be worth, for so much in money let the judge condemn Numerius Negidius to Aulus Agerius. If it does not appear, let him absolve.[39]

32 Not only the concept of *meum esse* (mine) has been debated but also the question whether a judge in this procedure had to appoint one person as the owner where it could have been possible that neither really was. See, *inter alia*, Mayer-Maly 1999, p. 62, Ankum & Pool 1989 and Kaser 1964.

33 The approach is very similar to the concept of relativity of title in English law. Kaser 1964, p. 5 *et seq.* and Kaser & Wubbe 1971, p. 108-110, Mayer-Maly 1999, p. 62-63. On English law see Chapter 6; 3.1. Title / Ownership.

34 These words are *meum esse*. Kaser 1964, *contra* Watson 1968, p. 91-96 and Mayer-Maly 1999, p. 62.

35 Kaser & Wubbe 1971, p. 108, Watson 1968, p. 92. An interesting parallel could be drawn to English law that also uses the concept of the better right to an object. In civil law systems it is agued that this approach is contrary to the absolute and unitary concept of ownership since it would allow multiple degrees of possible ownership. That this makes sense is only proved by the Roman-based concept of *duplex dominium*, which will be dealt with below in 4.3. Ownership.

36 Kaser & Wubbe 1971, p. 109, Kaser 1964, p. 10.

37 Kaser 1964, p. 10, Mayer-Maly 1999, p. 63.

38 Although the application of the action was still restricted to specific cases, usually connected with possession. Watson 1968, p. 96-98, Mayer-Maly 1999, p. 63-64, Feenstra 1990, p. 40-42.

39 G. Inst. 4.91-93: 'Titius iudex esto. Si paret hominem Stichum quo de agitur ex iure Quiritum Auli Agerri esse neque is home arbitrio iudicis restituetur, quanda ea res erit, tantam pecunium iudex Numerium Negidium Auolo Agerio condemnato. Si non paret absolvito'. English version cited by Birks 1985, p. 5, note 19. Translation by O. Lenel, *Edictum Perpetuum* 3 ed (1927) 185-186. Latin text and German translation cited by Mayer-Maly 1999, p. 63.

The development of the actions protecting ownership gradually led to a better differentiation of terminology and, from the beginning of (pre-) classical Roman law, the concepts of *dominium* and *proprietas* were used to describe the position of ownership. This does not mean, however, that these concepts became defined; they still denoted that person who had the best right.[40] In other words, *dominium* became the term used for the ultimate entitlement to an object above which there was no other.[41] In this respect it could be stated that in Roman law the concept of ownership was therefore absolute.[42]

The *vindicatio* allowed the owner to assert his ownership in case of interference, but he could also initiate a specific *actio* claiming that his ownership had not been burdened. The owner would have to do so in case someone argued he had a property right other than ownership on the property of that owner. This *actio*, the *actio negatoria*, allowed the *dominus*, or the owner, to claim that he could freely enjoy his right and if necessary claim that any disturbance to his property should be removed.[43]

In addition to *dominium* there were other forms of ownership recognised in (pre-) classical Roman law. First, as stated above, the Romans distinguished between Romans and non-Romans. This distinction was especially important in the law of property since only Romans were able to have *dominium*. In this respect, the concept of *dominium* was the most extensive right held by a Roman person.[44]

Peregrini, foreigners, could not own *ex iure Quiritium*.[45] However the Romans did recognise a form of ownership of Italic land and objects in Italy for foreigners, usually named peregrine ownership.[46] A peregrine owner would not have *dominium ex iure Quiritium*, but was awarded an *actio* comparable to the *vindicatio* in order to protect his position. Moreover, since land outside Italy was not covered by the *ius civile*, which was the law applying to Romans in Italy, it was not possible for any person to acquire *dominium* of so such land. The explanation for this distinction is one of Roman State organisation. Provincial land was governed and therefore 'owned' by the *populus* and, in later imperial times, by the Emperor, under the *ius gentium*.[47] This form of State ownership prevented *peregrini* or *Quirites* from having *dominium*. Nevertheless, Roman law did offer a solution. Similar to peregrine ownership, Romans were granted actions similar to those protecting the ownership of land in Italy to protect their position in respect of land outside Italy.

In short, for a Roman person to acquire *dominium* over an object the acquisition of *dominium* must be have been recognised by the *ius civile*, and in case of any other

40 Kaser & Wubbe 1971, p. 109.

41 Thomas 1976, p. 134.

42 Birks 1985, p. 1 *et seq.*, Honoré 1961, p. 107, Van den Bergh 1988, *contra* Kaser 1964, p. 5 *et seq.*

43 Feenstra 1990, p. 90-91, Kaser & Knütel 2003, p. 171.

44 Also known as ownership under *Quiritary* title or *dominium ex iure Quiritium*, Spruit 2003, p. 168, Thomas 1976, p. 135. On the concept *commercium* see Mayer-Maly 2003, p. 1 *et seq.*

45 Thomas 1976, p. 135, Kaser & Wubbe 1971, p. 110-111.

46 Not much is known about peregrine ownership, but there is clear evidence of its existence. See Borkowski 1997, p. 156, Thomas 1976, p. 135, Van der Walt & Kleyn 1989, p. 228.

47 Thomas 1976, p. 135-135. The distinction gradually lost its meaning through law reforms and was eventually abolished by Justinian.

form of ownership by the *ius gentium*.[48] For a peregrine owner the requirement was that he acquired ownership through a method recognised by the *ius gentium*.

Ownership could be acquired by one of the three procedures described above; the *mancipatio, in iure cessio,* or *traditio,* depending on the nature of the object. Additionally, the right of ownership could be acquired through *usucapio,* which required uninterrupted possession of an object for a certain number of years.[49] As well as uninterrupted possession the requirements included good faith, *bona fides,* of the possessor.[50] This method of prescriptive acquisition was already recognised in early Roman law, it is usually held to originate in the XII Tables, and formed one of the most important elements in the development of another additional form of ownership in (pre-) classical Roman law.

Until the *usucapio* was completed, the holder of the object was merely a possessor and therefore only protected by the interdicts available to possession.[51] These interdicts, although very useful, worked only against immediate dispossessors and not against the original owner using a *vindicatio*.[52] This was especially a problem when a *res mancipi* was transferred using the wrong method. The deliveree would become a possessor, and not owner, and would only acquire *dominium* once the period of prescription had expired. Until that time, the deliveror, who usually was the owner, could vindicate the object. In the late Republic, when the distinction between the various objects became less important, the *praetor,* the main legal magistrate, intervened to prevent these unwanted situations from occurring by offering the possessor protection through the creation of a separate *actio* to vindicate possession.[53]

The *actio* the praetor granted was named the *actio Publiciana*. It offered an *actio* to possessors in *usucapio* that very much resembled the *vindicatio*. In this action a *iudex,* which was a Roman judge, was to assume that the possessor had already possessed the object for the relevant period and therefore was like a fictitious owner.[54] In this way the possessor acquired such a strong position that only the real *dominus* could defeat him in court. In effect, therefore, an additional type of ownership was created, known as praetorian ownership.

48 Important is that the object itself must also be capable of being subject of private ownership. In Roman law some objects could be reserved either for the State or for the gods. Borkowski 1997, p. 157.

49 The periods of uninterrupted possession that were required differed from movable to immovable and were changed, usually made longer, as Roman law developed. Borkowski 1997, p. 203, Kaser & Wubbe 1971, p. 124, Van der Walt & Kleyn 1989, p. 229, Nicholas 1962, p. 122.

50 The full set of requirements for usucaption were *res habilis, titulus, fides, possessio* and *tempus,* Feenstra 1990, p. 70-78, Kaser & Knütel 2003, p. 156, Watson 1968, p. 21-23. Servitudes could, at one time, also be capable of usucaption.

51 The word interdict is deliberately chosen, since the possibilities for a possessor in court were not named actions. See, *inter alia,* Borkowski 1997, p. 159, Thomas 1976, p. 143.

52 Nicholas 1962, p. 125.

53 Nicholas 1962, p. 125, Borkowski 1997, p. 158-159,Thomas 1976, p. 136-137, Mayer-Maly 1999, p. 64-65, Van der Walt & Kleyn 1989, p. 228-232, Ankum & Pool 1989, p. 5, Birks 1985, p. 29, Sohm 1931, p. 284-285.

54 Thomas 1976, 149, Kaser & Wubbe 1971, p. 135-136.

However, there were situations where the Publician possessor wanted to be protected from the original owner as well, especially in case of a transfer of ownership through the wrong method. In the case of sale of a *res mancipi,* where the object was delivered by *traditio,* in other words, by the wrong procedure, the praetor went even further and created another type of ownership called bonitary ownership.[55] Bonitary ownership was seen as a species of the general praetorian ownership created by the *actio Publiciana.* The ownership that was created offered the bonitary owner, who was the actual possessor of the object, actions that enabled him to assert his right over anybody else, including against the original owner.[56] These actions comprised a possibility for the bonitary owner to plead his case against the original owner and prove that he had acquired the property by sale.[57]

Roman law therefore recognised, apart from Quiritian and peregrine ownership, also a praetorian ownership.[58] However, the existence of these separate forms of ownership does not mean that ownership was considered very lightly. Ownership was considered the ultimate legal entitlement; the form seemed only to depend on the circumstances.[59]

The right of ownership could be shared between two or more persons, co-ownership has been possible since (pre-) classical Roman law.[60] In a co-ownership regime, each person would have an indivisible share in the whole object over which other property rights could be created.[61] When the object as a whole was to be alienated, all owners would have to act together, or at least all other owners had to give one of the owners permission to act.[62] In order to prevent one owner from acting on behalf of the property in co-ownership, each of the owners could, in limited cases, initiate an *actio* to stop this one owner or order a separation of the ownership.[63] A fragmentation of ownership in which each co-owner held a separate

55 Although it seems commonly accepted that a sale of a *res mancipi* by *traditio* is the first instance in which bonitary ownership was recognised. Ankum and Pool argue otherwise. Ankum & Pool 1989, p. 38.

56 Borkowski 1997, p. 159, Kaser & Wubbe 1971, p. 135.

57 Or, the *exceptio rei vindicatae et traditae.* Thomas 1976, p. 136, it is proven that the Romans saw this position as more than just a protected possessor. Ankum & Pool 1989, p. 38. The concept of bonitary ownership has been compared to the German *Anwartschaftsrechte* that are recognised in case of a sale and transfer under reservation of ownership clause. See Chapter 4; 3.4. Expectation Rights.

58 The distinction between praetorian and bonitary ownership is not made by every author. See, *inter alia,* Van der Walt & Kleyn 1989, p. 228-332, Borkowski 1997, p. 158-160.

59 Thomas 1976, p. 134, Kaser & Knütel 2003, p. 137 *et seq.*

60 *Comunio pro indiviso,* Kaser & Knütel 2003, p. 145, Mayer-Maly 1999, p. 65, Kaser 1975, p. 272.

61 The German word *Bruchteil* seems more appropriate. On the terminology on indivisible shares see Lawson and Rudden 2002, p. 92-93. D. 17.2.83, Kaser & Knütel 2003, p. 147, Kaser 1975, p. 272.

62 Kaser & Knütel 2003, p. 147, Lawson and Rudden 2002, p. 92-93, Kaser & Wubbe 1971, p. 116.

63 The *actio communi dividundo* and the *actio familiae erciscundae.* Kaser & Wubbe 1971, p. 116, Kaser & Knütel 2003, p. 147.

and fragmented right of ownership was not held to be possible. In this respect Roman ownership, regardless of the type, was also unitary.[64]

2.4. *Other Property Rights*

In Roman law, ownership was not the only property right that was recognised. In addition, rights over another person's object could be created. However, it was not possible to create property rights over one's own objects on behalf of oneself. Although originally some property rights - in particular, the rustic praedial servitudes that were mentioned above and will be further dealt with below - were considered *res mancipi*, which has led to some theories on these rights being a part of the right of ownership, it is commonly accepted that besides the types of *dominium* dealt with above, several property rights other than ownership existed.[65]

The Romans themselves, however, did not consider this question since they did not concern themselves with rights but rather with actions. Once more, Roman law would have looked at which actions protected which situations. Taking this into account and in order to understand Roman law in the best possible way, Roman law scholarship also uses the term 'right' to describe what, in later times have been called *iura in re aliena*.[66]

(Pre-) classical Roman law used a functional categorisation for these rights in which they distinguished praedial servitudes, personal servitudes and security rights.[67] The praedial servitudes were, according to their function, divided into rustic praedial servitudes, *iura praediorum rusticorum*, and urban praedial servitudes, *iura praediorum urbanorum*.[68]

The rights of servitude originate from the practice where two people held adjoining lands and one person needed rights over the other person's land in order to perform a certain function. These functions could, for instance, include a right of passage for persons, water or cattle. Based on factual situations, the (pre-) classical jurists derived several general criteria for servitudes. The first of these, the criterion of *vicinitas* of two pieces of land, followed from an analysis of the fact that servitudes, for example, the right to walk over a neighbour's land or construct a sewer, could only exist when two pieces of land were neighbouring or very close to each other.[69]

64 This is different in English law. See Chapter 6; 1.2. Common Law and Equity. However there are similarities to the French rules governing co-ownership. See Chapter 3; 2.2. Co-Ownership including Apartments.

65 Giuffrè 1992, p. 121, Kaser 1964, p. 7, *contra* Watson 1968, p. 92-96.

66 Although also the term *iura in re* is used. See, *inter alia*, Thomas 1976, p. 195, Zwalve 2003, p. 106, Carey Miller 1998, p. 151, Van der Walt & Kleyn 1989, p. 214, Nicholas 1962, p. 141.

67 It should be noted that the term personal servitudes most likely dates from after the classical Roman era. However, for means of systematisation and some likeness of treatment the term personal servitude is also used when describing classical law. Thomas 1976, p. 202, Bund 1956, p. 163 *et seq.*

68 G. Inst. 2.14, Gordon & Robinson 1988, p. 127-131, Kaser & Wubbe 1971, p. 137, Nicholas 1962, p. 143, Carey Miller 1998, p. 96.

69 Feenstra 1990, p. 87.

Secondly, a servitude could not exist on one's own object. Since a servitude was, like other property rights other than ownership, considered a burden on the ownership of the land over which it ran, the concurrence of the ownership of such land and the burden of the servitude would result in the burden ceasing to exist. Following this reasoning, the maxim *nulli res sua servit* applied to all servitudes.[70] This maxim also includes the impossibility that a right to a servitude would come into the same hands as the right of ownership over which the right of servitude extended. Upon acquisition of the servitude by such an owner, the servitude would mix with the right of ownership and cease to exist.[71]

Thirdly, from (pre-) classical times the rule existed that servitudes could not be possessed. This was relevant for the question of accessibility of possessory interdicts. Except for the servitudes that were considered *res mancipi*, as is set out below, servitudes were incorporeal objects and therefore not capable of possession.[72] However, it should be noted that this rule no longer applied in Justinian's time and that already before the codification the enjoyment of a servitude became protected by actions comparable to the possessory interdicts.[73]

Fourthly, (pre-) classical jurists derived a rule that servitudes must be beneficial in a material sense. The piece of land to which the servitude belonged should benefit from the existence of the servitude, or, as phrased in the Roman maxim, that it was of *utilitas fundi*.[74] An important addition to this rule came with the requirement that the abovementioned benefits should be permanent or should have a permanent reason to exist, known as a *perpetua causa*.[75]

In relation to the absolute notion of ownership, the Romans used the rule that a servitude must be exercised reasonably.[76] This rule suggests that the Romans realised that servitudes imposed burdens on the ownership of those over whose land the right of servitude ran.

Finally, and perhaps most importantly, the requirement *servitus in faciendo consistere nequit* resulted in the impossibility for a servitude to contain an active or, in terms of modern law, positive duty.[77] This requirement formed a strong limitation on the creation of servitudes. Under this rule, an owner of a piece of land over which a right of servitude was created would have to tolerate the servitude but could not be forced to do something. The only duty of this owner was to make sure the holder of the servitude was able to exercise his right. However, there were exceptions to this rule. One exception to this maxim was the servitude of *oneris*

70 D. 7.6.5, D. 8.2.26, Thomas 1976, p. 196, Borkowski 1997, p. 170, Feenstra 1990, p. 88.

71 G. Inst. 2.30, Gordon & Robinson 1988, p. 134-135, D. 8.6.1, Borkowski 1997, p. 170.

72 This was prohibited by the *lex Scribonia*, but this was later again allowed. Borkowski 1997, p. 170, Mayer-Maly 1999, p. 100, Kaser 1971, p. 444-445.

73 Allowing the possession of servitudes also opened the way to the acquisition by *usucapio*. Borkowski 1997, p. 170, Kaser & Wubbe 1971, p. 100.

74 D. 8.1.8, D. 8.1.15pr., Feenstra 1990, p. 87, Thomas 1976, p. 196.

75 D. 8.2.28, Feenstra 1990, p. 87.

76 D. 8.1.9, Borkowski 1997, p. 171. On the absolute nature of Roman ownership see Kaser 1964, Feenstra 1979, Feenstra 1976, Birks 1985.

77 D. 8.1.15.1, Feenstra 1990, p. 88, Borkowski 1997, p. 171, Kaser 1971, p. 443, Giuffrè 1992, p. 41-42.

ferrendi or the right of support, where the owner of a certain building was obliged to support a neighbouring building.[78] In particular this last rule showed that (pre-) classical Roman lawyers were aware of the effects a property right had on the right of ownership.[79] The absolute content of the right of ownership, or the fact that it was the most extensive entitlement to an object, included the full enjoyment of ownership. However, the existence of other property rights burdened this freedom and therefore Roman law was very careful to introduce new property relations.[80]

As mentioned above, with respect to praedial servitudes a distinction was made between rustic and urban servitudes. The development of these servitudes shows that the development of Roman property law was through adaptation of the law because of practical needs. The existence of a principle of *numerus clausus* of property rights in (pre-) classical Roman property law is therefore hard to illustrate.[81] However, several attempts to prove the existence of the principle have been made. In particular, Guarino and Bund succeed, by making use of texts from the Digests, proving the existence of a closed system of property rights.[82] It should be noted that the development of this closed system meant that every now and then new property rights were recognised by the jurists, but that parties themselves were limited by the set of actions that was available to them. On the other side, because of the possibility of extending the list of actions, some authors have held that a *numerus clausus* did not exist.[83] Before dealing with this controversy, an overview of the recognised property rights should be given.

The distinction made in (pre-) classical Roman law between rustic and urban praedial servitudes was one of functionality, referring to agricultural or city-related needs.[84] However, the distinction is not as clear as it might seem and seems to have been developed by practice.[85] The term praedial is used to show that the rights created are attached to the land and are there by virtue of ownership of the land.[86] The distinction is especially important to distinguish these types of servitudes from personal servitudes, which will be dealt with below.

78 D. 8.5.6.2, D. 8.2.33. The owner of the building that needed support could demand security for in case of damage arising from non-support of his building, the *cautio damni infecti*. See, Feenstra 1990, p. 88, Borkowski 1997, p. 171, Watson 1968, p. 198-201.

79 Schulz 1956, p. 153 *et seq.*

80 Or, once more, proprietary actions protecting a specific legal relation. On the relevance of the difference between rights and actions see above; 1. Introduction.

81 The proof of existence of a *numerus clausus* of property rights becomes easy when the nature of the codifications is considered. Justinian intended to codify the law, anything not contained in the codifications therefore lost force of law. See, *inter alia*, Lokin & Zwalve 1992, P. 63-64, note 51. On the *numerus clausus* of property rights in Roman law see below; 2.5. A *Numerus Clausus* in (Pre-) Classical Roman Law?

82 Guarino 2001, p. 497, Bund 1956, p. 159.

83 Kaser & Knütel 2003, p. 176, Giuffrè 1992, p. 203 *et seq.*, Rainer 1995, p. 415 *et seq.*

84 Kaser & Knütel 2003, p. 175.

85 The result of this is that not all text are in line with each other. Some servitudes are considered urban by some where they are considered rustic by others. See, *inter alia*, Thomas 1976, p. 196, Bund 1956, p. 158-159.

86 Also the term *iura praediorum* is sometimes used. Kaser 1971, p. 440. D. 8.4.1.1, Borkowski 1997, p. 171, Bund 1956, p. 160.

Amongst the rustic servitudes were the four classic servitudes; passage of persons, known as *iter,* driving of cattle, known as *actus,* way for vehicles, known as *via,* and of watershed or waterway, known as *aquae ductus.* These were considered *res mancipi* and could therefore only be transferred by *mancipatio.*[87] All other servitudes were incorporeal *res nec mancipi* and could therefore be transferred by the slightly less formal *in iure cessio.*[88]

It is clear that these property rights are the oldest recognised rights, already present in ancient Roman law. In (pre-) classical times, the category of rustic servitudes had been extended with the rights to draw water, *aquae haustus,* the right to channel excess water, *aquam immittere,* the right to water cattle on the land of a neighbour, *pecoris ad aquam appellendi,* the right to let cattle graze on the neighbour's land, *pascendi,* the right to burn lime, *calcis coquendae,* and the right to dig for clay, known as *harenae fodiendae.*[89] In other words, when a practice arose of using land in a certain way and with that the needs for a proprietary action to protect the rights granted on the land of another, new servitudes would be recognised.

When Roman society departed from the traditional agricultural model towards a more urban model with more people living together in a small area, the category of urban praedial servitudes developed beside the rustic praedial servitudes. Servitudes in this category include; the rights to construct a sewer, *cloaca,* to see the sky or light through the neighbour's land, *lumen,* the right to see the sky, *prospectus,* the right to have a wall overhang onto a neighbour's land, *proiciendi* and *protegendive,* to let water drip onto a neighbour's land, *stillicidium,* to let water flow onto a neighbour's land, *flumen,* to have a higher building tolerated, *altius tollendi,* and the right of support by another building, *oneris ferendi.*[90]

The last servitude, *oneris ferendi,* as was already mentioned, takes an exceptional position amongst the servitudes. The burden this servitude imposes is positive in that it allows for the support of a building, especially buildings constructed in such a way that a building could only remain standing if the supporting building is maintained.[91] The exceptional position of this servitude was that it violated the general rule of servitudes that a servitude may not impose an active or

87 See D. 8.3.30, D. Cicero *pro Caecina* 26.74, D. 8.3.8, D. 43.20.8 respectively. As taken from Watson 1968, p. 176, G. Inst. 2.17, Kaser & Knütel 2003, p. 175.

88 G. Inst. 2.14a, although *mancipatio* would also have been possible. Kaser & Knütel 2003, Thomas 1976, p. 200., p. 175-176. Although some doubts exist whether the other rustic servitudes were also considered as *res mancipi,* see, *inter alia,* Mayer-Maly 1991, p. 74.

89 D. 8.3.30; 18.1.40.1, D. 8.3.29; 39.3.2.10, D. 43.20.1.18, D. 8.3.4, D. 8.3.6.1; 8.3.5.1 and D. 8.3.1.1; 8.3.5.1. See Watson 1968, p. 176 *et seq.,* 195, Mayer-Maly 1991, p. 74, Bund 1956, p. 183, Kaser 1971, p. 442, Jörs, Kunkel & Wenger 1987, p. 183-184, Giuffrè 1992, p. 184. It goes beyond the scope of this thesis to provide a full overview of all rights of servitude that existed in classical Roman law. It is important to see that with the increased needs in society the legal system responded with the recognition of new types of servitudes.

90 D 8.3.5.1, D. 8.2.16; D. 8.2.16; 8.2.7, D 8.5.17pr; 8.2.2, D. 39.3.1.17, D. 39.3.1.17, D. 8.2.2, D. 8.5.6.2; 8.2.33, respectively. See Kaser & Wubbe 1971, p. 137, Watson 1968, p. 176, 194 *et seq.,* Mayer-Maly 1991, p. 74, Thomas 1976, p. 197-198, Honsell 1997, p. 67-69, Borkowski 1997, p. 172, Mayer-Maly 1999, p. 97-98.

91 As mentioned above, the holder of the servitude could demand security from the holder of the servient land for possible future damage under the *cautio damni infecti.*

positive duty.[92] The right to support another building does impose a positive duty but seems nevertheless to have been accepted as a valid servitude.[93]

A second type of servitude existed in the form of personal servitudes. These servitudes were not attached to a piece of land, but rather to the person holding the right.[94] A person therefore held these servitudes not in his capacity as owner of a piece of land. The category of personal servitudes comprised several property relations. First, there was the right to use a certain object and to take the fruits it produces, known as *ususfructus*.[95] This right of usufruct, as it is named in modern law, was a strictly personal right, meaning that it was held by a person not in his capacity as the owner of land, but connected to that person holding it, the usufructuary. The right would therefore exist until the person holding it died.[96] Initially only land could be subject of a usufruct, but afterwards usufructs over movable objects also became accepted. At the end of the (pre-) classical Roman era a usufruct could be created over all of a person's assets.[97]

One of the strict requirements for a usufruct was that the object over which the right existed must remain unimpaired. This requirement restricted the usufructuary's right to alter the object under usufruct; this meant that if the object was changed the *ususfructus* would cease to exist.[98] However, the fruits that came from the object over which the usufruct existed could be used or even sold by the usufructuary.[99] The result of this was that the usufructuary was not an owner or even a

92 D. 8.1.15.1. There are some authors who also include other urban praedial servitudes amongst the positive duties, but they seem, in this respect, to hold a minority position. See, *inter alia*, Thomas 1976, p. 197-198, Mayer-Maly 1999, p. 98, Borkowski 1997, p. 171, Honsell 1997, p. 68, Mayer-Maly 1991, p. 74, Kaser & Wubbe 1971, p. 138, Giuffrè 1992, p. 41-42.

93 See also D. 8.5.6.2; 8.5.6.3 where it is attempted to connect the duty to the object (*res*) rather than to the person holding it. See also Thomas 1976, p. 198, note 26. More will be stated about this exception below in 2.5. A *Numerus Clausus* in (Pre-) Classical Roman Law?

94 D. 8.1.1. There is a discussion whether personal servitudes were already recognised in (pre-) classical Roman law. The general opinion seems to be that they were. It is clear that the right of *ususfructus* existed, but whether the rights was already categorised as a personal servitude remains subject for debate. See, *inter alia*, Bund 1956, Watson 1968, p. 203 *et seq.*, *contra* Mayer-Maly 1999, p. 98-99.

95 Although the origin of the right itself has been much debated. A definition is provided in D. 7.1.1., see, *inter alia*, Mayer-Maly 1999, p. 98-99, Kaser 1971, p. 447 *et seq.* Also an elaborate discussion can be held on the exact meaning of a fruit in classical Roman law, but that is beyond the scope of this study. On this see Graziadei 2002a, p. 122 *et seq.*

96 A person could return the usufruct during his lifetime but could never transfer the right itself. Kaser & Wubbe 1971, p. 140-141, Watson 1968, p. 207, Bund 1956, p. 167-168, Giuffrè 1992, p. 153.

97 Kaser & Wubbe 1971, p. 141, Kaser 1971, p. 449-450, *contra* Watson 1968, p. 207 210, 211, Mayer-Maly 1991, p. 74-75.

98 Watson 1968, p. 207, Borkowski 1997, p. 174-175, Mayer-Maly 1991, p. 74-76, Kaser 1971, p. 450-451.

99 Kaser 1971, p. 450-451.

possessor, instead the holder of a usufruct was considered to have the enjoyment of the property.[100]

Granting enjoyment to another person would deprive the owner of most of his powers connected to his ownership. Usufruct was therefore already very early considered as a property relation that would, once created, leave almost nothing of the ownership of the *dominus*.[101]

The requirement to keep and maintain the objects under usufruct could lead to problems, especially when a usufruct was extended over someone's full set of assets. If an object could not be kept or was used up through normal use of the object, the right of usufruct could not exist. To solve this the concept of *quasi-ususfructus* was created. The quasi-usufruct was not really a property right other than ownership, but rather a transfer of ownership. In a quasi-usufruct the usufructuary would become owner of the objects instead of mere right-holder, but was required to give security for the objects he acquired.[102] The security would ensure the original owner of the value of the objects when the quasi-usufruct came to an end.

Closely connected to *ususfructus* was the right of use, known as *usus*, which included the mere right to use a certain object. A person holding the right of *usus* would only be entitled to the use, but not to the fruits of, a certain object. In (pre-) classical Roman law this right included the later rights of *habitatio*, *usus* of a house or lodging and of *operae servorum vel animalium*, right to the services of a slave or animal.[103] The rules on the *usus* were identical to those of the usufruct.[104]

As stated above there were general rules applicable to servitudes and these rules applied to all servitudes, including personal servitudes, but with some exceptions.[105] One exception should be mentioned in respect of the rule against possession of servitudes. The possession of a personal servitude was possible, which created the possibility to receive a personal servitude through *usucapio*.[106] Furthermore, it was also possible to acquire a personal servitude through a legacy, which was not possible for praedial servitudes.[107] However, in late classical Roman law it also became possible to acquire praedial servitudes through *usucapio*.[108]

100 In other words he was the *detentor*, Kaser 1971, p. 451. It was the enjoyment of the right of usufruct that could be shared. D. 7.1.13.3, D. 33.2.31.,Borkowski 1997, p. 174-176, Kaser 1971, p. 450.

101 This situation has been described as *nuda proprietas*. Kaser 1971, p. 448, Borkowski 1997p. 177-178, Mayer-Maly 1991, p. 75.

102 D. 7.5.2.1 J. Inst. 2.4.2, security would be given by the *cautio usufructuaria*. Kaser 1971, p. 543-544, Kaser & Knütel 2003, p. 183, Guarino 2001, p. 735-737.

103 D. 7.8, D. 7.7., although some discussion is held on whether these rights were recognised as such already in classical Roman law. The leading opinion seems to be that they were included in the right of *usus*. Watson 1968, p. 220-221, Bund 1956, p. 167, Thomas 1976, p. 207-208, Kaser 1971, p. 454.

104 D. 7.8.1.1., although it is held that a right of *usus* could not be shared Bund 1956, p. 167-168, Kaser 1971, p. 454.

105 Exceptions include the servitude *oneris ferendi* that constitutes a positive duty Borkowski 1997, p. 170.

106 Mayer-Maly 1999, p. 100-101.

107 Kaser 1971, p. 454, Mayer-Maly 1999, p. 100, Borkowski 1997, p. 179.

108 Borkowski 1997, p. 179.

Since all servitudes were considered incorporeal rights, these could not be created by *traditio*.[109] Except for the original four rustic praedial servitudes that were considered *res mancipi*, all other servitudes would be created through *in iure cessio*. The *res mancipi* servitudes required a *mancipatio* or *in iure cessio* for their creation.[110] In order to create servitudes on provincial land, in alignment with the right of ownership of such land, separate rules existed: a servitude on provincial land could be created by *pactiones et stipulationes*.[111]

The rights of servitude received protection under the *ius civile* through actions comparable to the protection of the right of ownership. As *dominium* became protected by the action of *vindicatio*, servitudes were granted protection through a special type of *vindicatio*, the *vindicatio servitutis* or the *actio confessoria*.[112] The *ususfructus* had its own action to protect the holder of the right, known as the *vindicatio ususfructus*.[113] Furthermore the praetor offered specific protection when necessary, especially in cases where the enjoyment of a servitude was restricted.[114]

The approach towards servitudes, including their creation and protection, is therefore very similar to the approach taken towards ownership. It is therefore understandable that it has been argued that servitudes were considered a part of ownership granted to someone else instead of separate rights. However, although the development of property rights might have originally led to this conclusion, it can no longer be maintained in (pre-) classical Roman law.[115]

In addition to the servitudes, there were also two other rights that entitled one to the usage of another's objects. These rights were not property rights, but personal rights. Because of their development they are classified as property rights. As described in the beginning of this Chapter, Roman law distinguished between land in Italy, which was capable of being subject of ownership under the *ius civile*, and land outside Italy, where only a right comparable to ownership could be held but not *dominium* itself. Originally, on land outside Italy, a right of *ager vectigalis* could be recognised.[116] This right would entitle a person to hold land for a limited period of time or forever in exchange for a payment of a ground rent or *vectigal*.[117] The central authority of the pertinent province awarded this right.[118] The person having

109 Thomas 1976, p. 200, Borkowski 1997, p. 178-179, Kaser 1971, p. 443-444.

110 Kaser 1971, p. 433-444, Mayer-Maly 1999, p. 100.

111 G. Inst. 2.3.1 Feenstra 1990, p. 88, Kaser & Wubbe 1971, p. 139.

112 It should be noted that the term *actio confessoria* dates from the time of Justinian. In classical Roman law the term *vindicatio servitutis* was used, Thomas 1976, p. 198. D. 7.6.5.6; 8.5.2pr., Kaser 1971, p. 446-447, Mayer-Maly 1999, p. 101.

113 Mayer-Maly 1999, p. 101.

114 But this was not under the *ius civile* but under the law of praetor, the *ius honorarium*. These actions allowed by the praetor where possessory interdicts that also came to the unlawful possessor. The owner himself could always assert an action against the existence of a servitude: the *actio negatoria*. Kaser 1971, p. 447.

115 Watson 1968, p. 176, Kaser 1971, p. 440, Jörs, Kunkel & Wenger 1987, p. 182-183.

116 Mayer-Maly 1999, p. 102, Kaser & Knütel 2003, p. 184, Thomas 1976, p. 135, Kaser 1971, p. 455-456, Borkowski 1997, p. 182-183. Cf. J. Inst. 3.24.3.

117 Mayer-Maly 1991, p. 78, Mayer-Maly 1999, p. 102, Kaser & Knütel 2003, p. 187-185, Kaser 1971, p. 455, Borkowski 1997, p. 182-183.

118 Kaser 1971, p. 455.

the right of *ager vectigalis* would be protected by possessory interdict and possibly, in late classical law, also an action comparable to the *vindicatio* would have been available.[119]

The right of *ager vectigalis* was based on the relation of *locatio conductio* or the temporary contract of hire.[120] Its origins are therefore in the law of obligations as a personal right. However, through the protection of the right with possessory interdicts as well as an action comparable to the *vindicatio*, the right entered the law of property. The *ius in agro vectigali* gave a right to land that in principle could be acquired, apart from establishment, by prescription donation and sale.[121]

Besides the *ager vectigalis*, (pre-) classical Roman law recognised the right, for payment of a fee, to have a building on empty municipal land.[122] This right, that is very comparable to the *ager vectigalis*, allowed the holder to erect a building on, initially, land outside of Italy.[123] In late (pre-) classical Roman law it was possible to create this right in respect of private property as well, either empty or already with a building on it.[124] Like the right of *ager vectigalis*, the relationship of the holder of the right and the actual owner was similar to the relation in a *locatio conductio*, although not the same.[125] The right was usually concluded for an indefinite time, but it was possible to agree on a limited time as well.[126] This right, which is known as the right of *superficies*, is also very similar to the right of *habitatio*.[127] It remains doubtful whether this right was already a property right in (pre-) classical Roman law, but it certainly gave its holder the right to have a building on the land of another.

119 Named the *actio in rem vectigalis* by some. See D. 6.3.1.1, Kaser 1971, p. 455, Mayer-Maly 1991, p. 78, Guarino 2001, p. 744-746.

120 Kaser 1971, p. 455, Guarino 2001, p. 745, Borkowski 1997, 281 *et seq*. Because of the interrelation with the contract of hire it has been doubted whether, in classical Roman law, the *ager vectigalis*, which forms the basis for the later right of *emphyteusis*, was a property right. On this see, *inter alia*, Mayer-Maly 1999, p. 102, Guarino 2001, p. 746-747, Kaser & Knütel 2003, p. 184 and the literature mentioned there.

121 Guarino 2001, p. 745-746, Kaser 1971, p. 455, Vogt 1950, p. 73.

122 Where the right was on land outside of Italy the payment would be *vectigalis*, however payment for a right in respect of municipal land was called *solarium*. Rainer 1989, p. 329, 331. Kaser 1971, p. 456, Kaser & Knütel 2003, p. 185, Mayer-Maly 1999, p. 103, Mayer-Maly 1991, p. 79, Borkowski 1997, p. 183.

123 Vogt 1950, p. 64 *et seq*., Guarino 2001, p. 740 *et seq*.

124 The controversy about the possibility of such a right in respect of private land and therefore under the *ius civile* is great. On the possibility see, *inter alia*, Kaser & Knütel 2003, p. 185, Kaser 1971, p. 456, Mayer-Maly 1999, p. 103, Mayer-Maly 1991, p. 79, Guarino 2001, p. 740, Kaden 1951, p. 607 *et seq*., Rainer 1989, p. 329, *contra* Vogt 1950, p. 64 *et seq*.

125 Although it is generally held that this right originated from the relation of a *locatio conductio*, Giuffrè 1992, p. 175-176, Guarino 2001, p. 741, Kaser & Wubbe 1971, p. 145-146.

126 Kaser 1971, p. 456.

127 Both give right to the use of a building, the difference is in the content of the rights. Where the *habitatio* gives the usage of a building for a limited period only, the right of *superficies* gives the right of usage for an unlimited period.

This right was remarkable because Roman law used the principle of *superficies solo cedit* or that whatever is attached to the land is part of it.[128] The result of this rule is that all buildings on the land are considered to be part of the land and therefore to be part of the ownership of the land.[129] Since (pre-) classical Roman law used a unitary concept of ownership, it was impossible for the owner of a house and the owner of a piece of land to have ownership over the same object at the same time. Although the right of superficies did not provide its holder with a right of ownership of a building, it did entitle him to have a building on the land of another. The right of *superficies* came under protection of the praetor by the introduction of the *interdictum de superficiebus*.[130] This interdict that was structured along the lines of the possessory interdict allowed the holder of the right of *superficies* to protect his right against persons who interfered with his right.[131] With this interdict the position of *superficies* worked against everyone who interfered with it and therefore acquired property characteristics. The right of *superficies* could originally be acquired through heritage, however, like the right of *ager vectigalis*, acquisition through sale and donation was recognised later.[132]

Apart from the right to use another's objects or the obligation to tolerate the use by another person of your own objects, there were also rights that were not intended to provide use but to secure the performance of a certain debt.[133] In Roman law it was very common for one person to provide personal security for another.[134] This form of personal security meant that the creditors of a person, in case this person could not pay his debt, could attempt to get the money from the man who gave the personal security. These forms of personal security were contractual agreements with no other effect than between the parties and will therefore not be dealt with.[135] However, there were also agreements that had effects against everyone and therefore should be placed in the area of property law.

Roman law adhered to the rule of *paritas creditorum*, or the rule that all creditors are equal. However, most creditors did not want to run the risk of losing their invested money because of having to share their claim with other creditors. Instead, when the debtor could not pay, creditors wanted to have access to their object

128 Cf. J. Inst. 2.1.29, D. 41.1.7.10, see, *inter alia*, Van Vliet 2002a, p. 67, Rainer 1989, p. 328-329, Guarino 2001, p. 741, Thomas 1976, p. 210.

129 In property law this rule is also known as the principle of accession.

130 The origin of this interdict in (pre-) classical Roman law has been debated, on this see, *inter alia*, Vogt 1950, p. 86 *et seq.*, Kaser 1971, p. 456, Kaser & Knütel 2003, p. 185, Guarino 2001, p. 742-743, Rainer 1989, p. 344.

131 The possessory interdict referred to is the interdict of *uti possidetis*. Kaser & Knütel 2003, p. 185, Kaser 1971, p. 456, Guarino 2001, p. 742, Giuffrè 1992, p. 178-179.

132 Although, some controversy about this remains. See Vogt 1950, p. 73 and Kaser & Knütel 2003, p. 185.

133 On this difference see, *inter alia*, Bund 1956, p. 156, Kaser & Wubbe 1971, p. 146, Nicholas 1962, p. 149. That is not to say that right to use cannot be used for security purposes. What is intended is that the rights which will be discussed are specifically intended to provide security, regardless of what is the content of the given security.

134 Kaser & Knütel 2003, p. 186, Mayer-Maly 1999, p. 84-85, Nicholas 1962, p. 149-150.

135 These rights are therefore in the law of obligations. See Thomas 1976, p. 334 *et seq.* for a good overview of personal security rights in Roman law.

before the other creditors were dealt with. In order to break with the principle of *paritas creditorum*, (pre-) classical Roman law used several security devices.

Originally, if a person needed a large amount of money he would, upon agreement, transfer his *dominium* of a certain object to another in exchange for, usually, money. Depending on the type of object over which the person wanted to transfer ownership, the procedure was the *mancipatio* or the *in iure cessio*.[136] In the agreement that led to the transfer of ownership, the parties would agree that once the debt was paid to the creditor, the creditor would return the ownership of the object. Transferring ownership of the object deprived the original owner of his property right. The agreement was therefore based on mutual trust and was called *fiducia*. Two forms of *fiducia* existed, one where a friend would not so much be creditor but manager, the *fiducia cum amico contracta*, and one where the transfer of ownership was strictly for security purposes, the *fiducia cum creditore contracta*.[137] The latter form was more widely used, and this last type of *fiducia* became the main form of security in early Roman law. It had some undesired consequences, however. To start with, the ownership of the object would be transferred to the creditor, leaving the debtor at most as a *detentor* of the object.[138] For the enjoyment of the object this did not pose a serious problem since the *fiducia* would be created by *mancipatio* or *in iure cessio* that did not, in contrast with the *traditio*, require the transfer of possession of the object. The debtor, albeit as a holder, remained able to use and enjoy the property.

However, without the right of ownership the debtor could not act against interference with the object. It was for the creditor, who was now the owner of the object, to initiate a *vindicatio* or a possessory interdict in order to protect the object serving as security.[139] In terms of ownership, all the powers were now with the creditor, who could do with the object whatever he wanted. In order to protect the debtor, Roman law held that the ownership of the creditor was subject to the condition that it had to be returned to the debtor once the debt had been paid. Furthermore, the creditor was also under the obligation to make sure the object was protected and he was explicitly prohibited to transfer the ownership to someone else.[140]

The condition under which the creditor must return the object to the debtor was formed through a personal relation following from the agreement between

136 *Res mancipi* could only be transferred by *mancipatio, res nec mancipi* would be transferred by *in iure cessio*. Of course, the creditor would not become owner if the debtor was not an owner himself. Nicholas 1962, p. 151, Feenstra 1990, p. 102.

137 G. Inst. 2.60, Feenstra 1990, p. 100-101, Kaser 1971, p. 462, Mayer-Maly 1999, p. 86, Zwalve 2003, p. 485-486, Mayer-Maly 1991, p. 62. The *fiducia cum amico contracta* lead to the development of *commodatum*. On this development see, *inter alia*, Thomas 1976, p. 274 *et seq.*, Noordraven 1999, p. 1 *et seq.*

138 *Detentor* or holder was the only position left after the original owner had transferred his ownership. On the concept of detention see Chapter 1; 4. Terminology.

139 Thomas 1976, p. 330-331, Kaser & Knütel 2003, p. 187-188, Mayer-Maly 1999, p. 85-86.

140 This included the transfer of ownership by sale. This obligation took as long as the debtor kept repaying the debt, if the debtor would not pay the agreement (*pactum fiduciae*) could provide for the power to sell the object. Kaser & Knütel 2003, p. 188.

these two parties. This personal relation only gave the debtor a personal action known as *actio fiduciae* against the creditor. Success of the *actio* for the debtor brought infamy with it for the creditor.[141] The *actio fiduciae* also allowed the debtor to claim the return of the ownership after the debt had been paid. However, in no event could the creditor be forced to return the property by *mancipatio* or *in iure cessio*, instead the debtor would have a claim for compensation, because of the Roman law principle of *condemnatio pecunia*.[142] In the event that the creditor had transferred the ownership to a third person, the creditor could be forced to pay compensation as well.[143]

Creating a security right through a transfer of ownership had disadvantages for the debtor. These disadvantages included the risk of losing the object transferred as security and only receiving compensation in return, even when the object given as security was higher in value than the value of the outstanding debt. In many situations the ownership of a more valuable property was transferred, regardless of the amount of money that was lent. The transfer of ownership for security purposes provided effective protection for the creditor. The reason to create the security interest, for a certain creditor to gain a preferred position in relation to the other creditors, was therefore achieved. As a result of the transfer of ownership, the debtor could no longer create a second security on the same object.[144]

In early (pre-) classical Roman law the *fiducia* was the only type of security that was recognised to have property law consequences. Initially the creditor was subject to strict requirements that had to be imposed through the security agreement or *pactum fiduciae*. This agreement specifically included the powers of the creditor in case of non-payment. However, over time, as the use of the security agreement was standardised, the right to sell the object became presumed to have been included in the transaction.[145] The debtor would then be entitled to the surplus of the sale, if any, for which he could also initiate the *actio fiduciae*.[146]

Although early (pre-) classical Roman law may originally have required it, the creation of a *fiducia* did not require a transfer of factual power. This development strengthened the position of the debtor somewhat because he would continue to have power over the object himself and the creditor would have to take action to gain factual control over the object.[147] In the system of (pre-) classical Roman law, the possession of the debtor offered an advantage to the debtor as he could receive the right of ownership back by *usucapio* after the debt had been paid. To strengthen the position of the debtor in the absence of a voluntary return by the creditor, a

141 A situation that had serious consequences under *ius civile* as well, for instance the prohibition to exercise a public function. Kaser & Knütel 2003, p. 188, 101.

142 Feenstra 1990, p. 102.

143 I.e., the *actio fiduciae* could only been initiated after the debt had been paid. Feenstra 1990, p. 102.

144 This last element formed a guarantee that he had a strong position for the creditor, and would not be rivalled by another security owner.

145 Feenstra 1990, p. 103, Kaser & Knütel 2003, p. 194-195.

146 The surplus was called the *superfluum*. Feenstra 1990, p. 103, Kaser 1971, p. 461-462.

147 Feenstra 1990, p. 104-105.

usucapio ex fiducia was possible after a period of one year.[148] However, although this improved the position of the debtor, the inconvenience of not being able to create a second security on the same object remained.

From the middle of the first century BC, next to *fiducia* another, more informal, form of security developed as well. Instead of transferring ownership to a creditor to give security for the payment of a loan, a separate property right was created on behalf of the creditor, while the debtor remained the owner of the object. Initially, factual power would be transferred to the creditor, but later the right could also be established without such a transfer.[149] The creditor would receive a right of *pignus* or pledge that came under praetorian protection.[150] However, the agreement, and therefore the right of pledge, could not come into existence without the claim of the creditor towards the debtor.[151] By analogy of the *actio fiduciae*, the debtor was awarded a personal action called the *actio pigneraticia* (*in personam*) with which the debtor could claim compensation when the object was not returned properly.[152]

As in the case of a *fiducia*, the pledge would be created by agreement. Up to the period of (pre-) classical Roman law, the position of the debtor in a *pignus* was similar to the position of the debtor in a *fiducia*, with the difference being that pledge would more be used for property of a lesser value.[153] The main difference between the two was that for the creation of a pledge no specific formalities were required, a simple agreement would suffice.[154]

The availability of only a personal *actio* restricted the creditor considerably, in particular when a third party interfered with the object under pledge. Therefore, in (pre-) classical Roman law, the *pignus* agreement became protected by proprietary actions, enabling the creditor to react against third parties if needed. In case a *pignus* had been created with the transfer of possession, the creditor became entitled to use the possessory interdicts to protect his right.[155] Nevertheless, there were many situations where the creditor did not have factual power. As stated above, a pledge without the transfer of possession could also be created. For instance, there could be

148 This special form of usucaption required the completion of a time period of one year, regardless whether the object was immovable or movable and regardless of *bona fides*. G. Inst. 2.59, Feenstra 1990, p. 105, Mayer-Maly 1991, p. 62, Mayer-Maly 1999, p. 86.

149 Feenstra 1990, p. 108.

150 The term *pignus* (general) is not at all clear. First, it includes both the object of, and the relationship between, the debtor and the creditor. Secondly, it is also used to describe the type of security right under which both the right of *hypotheca* and the right of *pignus* (specific) are. For a good overview see Kaser 1971, p. 458-459 and Feenstra 1990, p. 106-107.

151 This principle of accessority made that the right of *pignus* and the claim could not exist apart from each other. If the claim would cease to exist, so would the right and *vice versa*. Kaser & Knütel 2003, p. 190, Mayer-Maly 1991, p. 63, Honsell 1997, p. 72, Kaser 1971, p. 465.

152 Feenstra 1990, p. 109.

153 The procedures of *mancipatio* or *in iure cessio* would not be used. Feenstra 1990, p. 105, 109, Kaser & Knütel 2003, p. 189.

154 Unlike the procedures of *mancipatio* or *in iure cessio* that were required with a *fiducia*.

155 Feenstra 1990, p. 113-114. The possibility to use possessory interdicts in situation where it is not clear that the possessor also holds a property right, has led to discussion in modern law on the nature of possession. See Chapter 4; 4.3. Entitlement to Possession Through the Law of Obligations.

a situation where the factual power of the main object of the pledge had been transferred, and for security of the payment the debtor would pledge objects he brought onto the land to work on the land.[156] These objects could not be given into possession to the creditor, as the debtor needed them to earn money for the repayment of the debt. (Pre-) classical Roman law allowed this but entitled the creditor, when the debtor would not pay, to use the *interdictum Salvianum*, an interdict that would award the creditor possession of the objects.[157] However the interdict would only work against the debtor and not apply to a third party taking possession of the objects.[158]

Besides the *interdictum Salvianum* the creditor could also use the *actio Serviana*. With this action the creditor could act against a third party who had taken possession of the objects.[159] The creditor could try and claim the objects back into his possession comparable to a *vindicatio* of an owner.[160] If a creditor was able to prove that there was a right of pledge created on the property and that he was entitled to payment of the debt and the debt had not yet been paid, he would be able to recover the object over which the right of pledge had been created, even if the object had been passed to third parties.[161]

The *actio Serviana*, the interdict *Salvianum* and the possessory interdicts were available to a creditor in a situation where a right of pledge had been validly created. Initially, Roman law did not concern itself with differences between movable and immovable property.[162] *Pignus* was such an informal and flexible right to create and it therefore won in popularity over the strict and formal *fiducia*.[163] Soon, a pledge could also be created on land and other types of immovable property.

Confusingly, the *pignus* relationship existed both in situations where possession had been transferred as well as when it had not been. In order to avoid confusion, different terminology was occasionally used. Already in (pre-) classical Roman law, the term *hypotheca* was used to describe the relationship where possession was not transferred and the term *pignus* was reserved for a pledge that

156 The *ivecta, illata et importa*. Feenstra 1990, p. 114, Kaser & Knütel 2003, p. 189, Thomas 1976, p. 333.

157 Feenstra 1990, p. 114-115, Nicholas 1962, p. 152, Kaser & Knütel 2003, p. 195.

158 Nicholas 1962, p. 152.

159 Who, for instance, had bought the objects from the debtor. Feenstra 1990, p. 115.

160 J. Inst. 4.6.7. The action has also been referred to as *actio pigneraticia in rem* or *vindicatio pignoris*. See, *inter alia*, Feenstra 1990, p. 116, Kaser & Knütel 2003, p. 196.

161 It should be emphasised that, like the *vindicatio*, the *actio Serviana* could not force another person to hand over the object itself, but could force that person to pay compensation in the form of the *litis aestimatio*. The result would usually have been the return of the object to avoid the payment of such compensation. Against the *vindicatio* of the owner the pledgee, who had taken possession of the object, would have an *exceptio rei pignori datae*. On this topic see, *inter alia*, Feenstra 1990, p. 117 and Wacke 1998, p. 190. Kaser & Knütel 2003, p. 196, Kaser 1971, p. 472-473.

162 Far more important was the distinction between *res mancipi* and *res nec mancipi*.

163 Feenstra 1990, p. 105, Thomas 1976, p. 333.

did include a transfer of possession.[164] In case of a *hypotheca* the *actio Serviana* would be called *actio hypothecaria*, but would be the same in content.[165]

The content of a *pignus* or *hypotheca* is determined by agreement in which a creditor promises to hold a right in respect of the object other than ownership, which the creditor, if necessary, can enforce against everyone. In this agreement specific arrangements could be made about the repayment of the debt. When a certain object would produce fruits and the creditor would have factual power over the object, an agreement could be made that the fruits would be used to repay the interest, if a payment of interest was agreed on, or the debt itself.[166] Instead of using the fruits to pay the interest or to repay the loan, it could also be agreed that the creditor would be entitled to the fruits for the duration of the agreement.[167]

Furthermore, the agreement would cover what would happen if the debtor would not pay the debt. One agreement, known as *lex commissoria,* was the agreement that the creditor was entitled to keep the object under pledge in case of non-performance by the debtor. However, the *lex commissoria* was generally considered unfair and creditors would abuse their powers as pledgee to acquire the objects. It has been argued that in ancient Roman law the object would fall into the set of assets and debts of the creditor under such an arrangement. Later, but still before the (pre-) classical Roman law period, the parties would agree on the power to sell the object if the debtor would not pay.[168] In (pre-) classical Roman law the power to sell was, although the creditor was not the owner, presumed to be included in the agreement of *pignus,* and thus ended the use of the *lex commissoria.*[169] Comparable to the power to sell in a *fiducia* relation, the debtor would be entitled to what was left of the proceeds of sale after the debt had been repaid, also known as the *superfluum.*[170]

Finally, a pledge could also be created on incorporeal objects. In order to decide which incorporeal object could be subject to a pledge, (pre-) classical Roman law would consider whether the object was capable of being sold. If the answer was

164 At least, this seems to be the leading opinion. The terminology was also used the other way around. Also the Romans differed in opinion about the distinction. Marcian D. 20.1.5.1 writes that the only difference between *pignus* and *hypotheca* is the sound of the words, whereas Ulpinian D. 13.7.9.2 writes that *pignus* is a situation where possession is transferred and *hypotheca* is the term used when this is not the case. Feenstra 1990, p. 106-107, Kaser 1971, p. 462-463, Kaser & Knütel 2003, p. 188-189, Thomas 1976, p. 332, Nicholas 1962, p. 152.

165 The term *pignus* also remained in use to describe both *hypotheca* and *pignus* in the narrow sense as a possessory pledge.

166 In the latter case, the debt would eventually cease to exist and therefore so would the right of *pignus*. The end of the claim is also referred to as amortisation. Feenstra 1990, p. 112.

167 This is the *antichresis,* a term received from Greek but also used in Roman law. Feenstra 1990, p. 112.

168 Feenstra 1990, p. 110, Kaser & Knütel 2003, p. 194, *contra* Wacke 1998, p. 168 *et seq.*

169 The *lex commissoria* became prohibited under Constantine. C. 8.34.3, Thomas 1976, p. 331. Only with Imperial permission could the creditor be entitled to include the object in his set of assets. On the power to sell see D. 20.5.7.1, Feenstra 1990, p. 111, Kaser & Knütel 2003, p. 194-195, Kaser 1971, p. 470-471, *contra* Wacke 1998, p. 176.

170 Feenstra 1990, p. 111, Kaser & Knütel 2003, p. 195, Mayer-Maly 1999, p. 91.

positive a pledge could be created.[171] This would not only include claims, but later also praedial servitudes, but only urban servitudes, as well as personal servitudes, *superficies* and, at an even later stage, after the (pre-) classical period, also *emphyteusis* and *pignus*.[172] Now that a pledge could be created on such a wide variety of objects, parties soon tried to create a general pledge covering all of another's assets.[173]

2.5. *A Numerus Clausus in (Pre-) Classical Roman Law?*

Taking the above into consideration together with the already mentioned *caveat* that the doctrine behind the rule of *numerus clausus* is of a later date than Roman law itself, it is difficult to discuss the existence of *numerus clausus* in Roman law. However, by limiting the principle of *numerus clausus* to the general idea that a legal system imposes restrictions on private parties in the creation of property relations, useful insights can be derived from (pre-) classical Roman law.

Because of the formal system of law, a person who wanted to achieve something in law was always required to fulfil certain requirements. Whether this was to create a contract or to establish a property right, the law would prescribe formalities. In this respect Roman law itself formed a closed system in which parties were not free to create their own legal relationships, whether protected with a personal or a proprietary claim.[174] However, because (pre-) classical Roman property law continued to develop itself and kept granting new actions and interdicts, right until the end of the (pre-) classical Roman era, it cannot be stated with certainty that this development had actually been completed. Nevertheless, in respect of *numerus clausus* it is clear that it was not for private persons to create new relations with third-party effect, it was for the magistrates to recognise a relation by protecting it with a new or existing property action or interdict that could be initiated against third parties.

The question whether the list of Roman property relations was closed or not is less relevant in the discussion on the existence of the principle of *numerus clausus*. Also in modern law it is possible for lawmakers to include new property rights within an existing closed system. What seems to be clear is that the concept of property relations used by the (pre-) classical Romans was very wide. As a result parties were relatively free to create their own relations as long as they remained within the boundaries set by the jurists. The servitudes form an excellent example. As long as the relationship fulfilled the criteria of *vicinitas, nulli res sua servit, utilitas fundi, perpetua causa* and *servitus in faciendo consistere non potest*, parties could

171 D. 20.1.10, Kaser 1971, p. 465.

172 D. 20.1.9.1, D. 20.1.11.3 (rustic servitudes), D. 20.1.11.2 (usufruct). It has been argued that servitudes could only be pledge in times of Justinian, on this see Mayer-Maly 1985, p. 173 *et seq*. In general Kaser 1971, p. 465, Mayer-Maly 1999, p. 87, Thomas 1976, p. 332.

173 Feenstra 1990, p. 121-122.

174 For a good overview of the Roman law of obligations in English see Nicholas 1962, Borkowski 1997 or Thomas 1976. Also see Kaser 1971, Kaser & Knütel 2003 and Mayer-Maly 1991 for an overview in German, and Guarino 2001 for an overview in Italian.

attempt to create new relations that would be protected under recognition by the praetor with the *vindicatio servitutis*.[175]

An additional argument supporting the limitation on private parties in the creation of new property relations can be found in the concept of *dominium*. The absolute concept of ownership as the most extensive entitlement a person could have in respect of an object could only work if the legal system exercised caution with the recognition of new actions and interdicts affecting the free use of this ownership.[176] As a result legal historians refer to the relations protected with a proprietary action different from *vindicatio* that were used to protect and enforce a right in respect of one's own object as property rights other than ownership on another person's object. These property rights in respect of another's object are known in Latin as *iura in re aliena*.

It is with the actions that protect these rights that, in my opinion, the *numerus clausus* of property rights is concerned, even though, in this respect, it is better to use the term *numerus clausus* of property actions. The difference between actions and rights is not so fundamental as it seems, as the availability of actions certainly had an effect on the content of the relations protected by those actions as well. In order to stay within the scope of availability of a certain action, in late (pre-) classical Roman law, property relations became standardised.[177] A counter argument could be that, if actions and rights can be interchanged in this way, then in terms of *numerus clausus* the search should not be for new relations, but for new actions. Regarding this line of reasoning, it is clear that it was not possible in (pre-) classical Roman law to create new actions, as the power to do so was with the jurists and the praetor, not with private parties themselves.

However, the similarity between actions and rights does not go that far and does not need to be taken that far. It is not for parties, and has never been, to decide on the actions available to them. The available actions have always been a part of the public side of the system of law, where not parties but the State makes choices on the available remedies. The actions in Roman law, like modern day remedies, protected relations, even though the focus of the whole legal system was on actions. An action in Roman law therefore gave access to a legal relation.[178] In this respect Roman law adhered to a *Typengebundenheid*, meaning that new relation would have to fall under the existing scope of protection of the recognised actions, otherwise it could be excluded.[179]

175 See Lenel 1927, p. 191-194.

176 Schulz 1956, p. 143-144.

177 This could be described as a standardisation of property rights in the sense of a reflection of the principle of *numerus clausus*. This view finds support in Guarino 2001, p. 497, Giuffrè 1992, p. 199, 203, Van der Merwe & De Waal 1993, p. 38, Sohm 1931, p. 322-323, Schulz 1956, p. 155, Birks 1985, p. 4, Jörs, Kunkel & Wenger 1987, p. 183, Kaser 1971, p. 440, Kaser 1975, p. 248, Rainer 1995, p. 415 *et seq.*, but *contra* Kaser & Knütel 2003, p. 176 and Watson 1968, p. 176-179.

178 In modern law this is the other way around: it is the legal relation that grants access to an action.

179 Giuffrè 1992, p. 203, Rainer 1995, p. 415 *et seq.*, Zwalve 2003, p. 103.

The system of law and the fact that law was created by the jurists and not by a modern-type legislator might lead to the conclusion that, by standardising the available actions related to the content of the property relations and the standardising effect this had on the content of these property relations, the principle of *numerus clausus* was effectively adhered to.[180]

2.6. *Summary*

(Pre-) classical Roman law recognised several forms of ownership. Because of the distinction between *res mancipi* and *res nec mancipi* and the distinction between the *Quirites* and the *Peregrini*, Roman citizens were the only persons who could have *dominium ex iure Quiritium* and bonitary ownership. However, peregrine ownership could be combined with some form of praetorian ownership. Important to note is that praetorian ownership offered protection against all but the *dominus ex iure Quiritium*, or bare owner, whereas bonitary ownership, as a species of praetorian ownership, was even able to defeat the bare owner.[181]

Besides the forms of ownership, (pre-) classical Roman law also recognised relations to property other than ownership. These relations that were protected by specific actions not only created rights and duties between the persons establishing them, but also had effect against third parties. It is for this reason that these relations are dealt with in property law. Because of the strict system of available actions that (pre-) classical Roman law used, the number and type of relations with regard to which proprietary actions were available were fixed. The principle of *numerus clausus* was therefore already adhered to in (pre-) classical Roman law.

3. Codified Roman Law - The *Corpus Iuris Civilis*

3.1. *Introduction*

The abstract level of legal science was visible in the many writings by the jurists of (pre-) classical Roman law, even through the case-by-case approach. However, in the period that followed (pre-) classical Roman law, the system and the coherent set of rules developed by these jurists were mostly lost due to the pressure of economic development. The clear distinction between concepts that had been made became blurred and practical solutions often prevailed over general theory.[182]

180 However, in terms of a rule of *numerus clausus* and the doctrinal foundations of the modern day concept of property law, it cannot be held a *numerus clausus* existed. In respect of the standardisation of rights a parallel to modern law can be made, especially to the landmark contributions of Rudden on the *numerus clausus* of property rights from an economic point of view, Rudden 1987 and Rudden 1994, and the contributions of several American authors about the standardisation of property rights in common law jurisdictions, Merrill & Smith 2000 and Hansmann & Kraakman 2002. See Chapter 7; 3. *Numerus Clausus* in Property Law Systems in Europe.

181 See, *inter alia*, Guarino 2001, p. 690 *et seq.*

182 See Nicholas 1962, p. 12-13, 36-38, Kaser 1975, p. 238, Kaser & Knütel 2003, p. 6-7.

This development, known as the vulgarisation of Roman law, became even stronger when in AD 395 Emperor Constantine left the Roman Empire to be divided amongst his two sons. From this moment, the Roman Empire was divided into an Eastern and a Western Empire, each of which underwent a separate development.[183] Although officially each legislative decision was also valid for the other part of the empire, the Eastern Roman Empire eventually prevailed as the most powerful.[184]

Whereas in the Western Roman Empire the vulgarisation of the law continued, in the Eastern Roman Empire vulgarisation came to a halt with the renewed study of (pre-) classical Roman law. In this period lawyers were once again educated in the writings of the (pre-) classical Roman jurists. Although the (pre-) classical Roman law was studied again, lawyers had considerable difficulties with the vast amount of material. Furthermore, it was not always possible to find authentic texts from the (pre-) classical period.[185] Attempts had already been made to compile an authoritative collection of existing writing, but it was not until Emperor Theodosius that an attempt was made at an official compilation with the authority of law.[186]

It was in this renewed school of thought that Justinian, adopted son of Emperor Justin, received his education.[187] Justinian, when he became emperor, would change the law completely by making a codification of law that would incorporate the (pre-) classical concepts. It would be the work that was conducted under the authority of Emperor Justinian that would change Roman law forever and was to continue to form a source of inspiration for lawmakers until today.

Justinian's work started with a collection of imperial constitutions intended to be complete and exclusive, thereby replacing any previous constitutions.[188] Soon Justinian ordered his advisor Tribonian and a commission of skilled jurists to create an authoritive collection of legal literature also. In this collection, known as the *Digests* of Justinian, the work of the (pre-) classical jurists was revisited. If there were contradictions or when daily practice had changed, Tribonian and his commission would correct the text.[189] These two works, together with the *Institutes*, which was a textbook to train new jurists, would form the collection named the *Corpus Iuris Civilis*.[190] For the first time in history, through the work of Justinian,

183 For an overview see, *inter alia*, Nicholas 1962, p. 12 *et seq.*, Lokin & Zwalve 1992, p. 56 *et seq.* and Kaser & Knütel 2003, p. 8 *et seq.*

184 Since both emperors together held the *imperium*, the ownership of and power over the whole territory, was also known as the *consortium imperii*. Lokin & Zwalve 1992, p. 57-58, Nicholas 1962, p. 13-14.

185 Nicholas 1962, p. 37.

186 Earlier attempts include the *Codex Gregorianus* and the *Codex Hermogenianus*. The final result was the *Codex Theodosianus*. Nicholas 1962, p. 38, Lokin & Zwalve 1992, p. 61-63.

187 Nicholas 1962, p. 37-39, Lokin & Zwalve 1992, p. 58-59.

188 The *Codex Justinianus* Lokin & Zwalve 1992, p. 63, Nicholas 1962, p. 39.

189 These are called interpolations. Nicholas 1962, p. 40-41, Lokin & Zwalve 1992, p. 65-72.

190 The *Corpus Iuris Civilis* has been influential in many legal systems, its influence will be dealt with in each specific Chapter. The received form of the *Corpus Iuris Civilis* would also include the *Novellae Constitutiones*, an additional set of Imperial constitutions, not all by Justinian himself.

there was a workable collection of law that could survive in the late days of the Roman Empire

3.2. *General Principles of the Corpus Iuris Civilis*

Although Justinian was educated in a legal school that studied (pre-) classical Roman law, not every aspect of this legal system was incorporated in his *Corpus Iuris Civilis*. The vulgar period had caused most of the sharp (pre-) classical distinctions between legal concepts to disappear and some of the newly arisen situations and concepts were considered very useful and were therefore included.

In (pre-) classical Roman law, the distinction between *res mancipi* and *res nec mancipi* was one of the cornerstones of the system. This was especially the case since ownership of *res mancipi* could not be transferred by *traditio*, but with the praetorian protection for the person receiving a *res mancipi* by *traditio*, the distinction had become unnecessary.[191] Justinian therefore consistently had the term *mancipatio* replaced with *traditio*, in effect abolishing the distinction between *res mancipi* and *res nec mancipi*.[192]

Before Justinian, non-Italic land had become subject to taxation, thereby removing the distinction between Italic and non-Italic land of the (pre-) classical Roman law. Justinian therefore also officially abolished this distinction.[193] As a result it was no longer necessary to recognise the multiple types of 'ownership' of (pre-) classical Roman law, most types of object could now be fully owned by all people living on Roman territory.[194]

The system of actions remained, the question of who was owner or who had a certain servitude would still be answered in terms of who had the relevant action or interdict at his disposal. Many of the actions that were used in the *Corpus Iuris Civilis* were taken from the (pre-) classical Roman law, although some of them were extended or altered to fit new demands.

3.3. *Ownership*

Vulgar law is best characterised by its lack of distinction between ownership and possession. (Pre-) classical Roman law made a sharp distinction between these two concepts, protecting ownership with an *actio* and possession with interdicts. Instead, vulgar law used the terms *proprietas*, *dominium* and *possidere* as synonyms.[195]

191 Kaser & Knütel 2003, p. 120-121, Nicholas 1962, p. 106, Feenstra 1990, p. 54.

192 C. 7.31.1.5, Van Vliet 2000, p. 171, Kaser & Knütel 2003, p. 121, Nicholas 1962, p. 106, Feenstra 1990, p. 55. This mechanical substitution of terminology has led to many problems in respect to *inter alia* the transfer system.

193 Thereby treating non-Italic land as if it was Italic Land, J. Inst. 2.1.40, Kaser 1975, p. 240, Feenstra 1990, 77.

194 Exceptions were, *inter alia*, the *res publica*, publicly held objects, and the *res divini iuris*, objects held for religious purposes usually by the church, Kaser & Knütel 2003, p. 119-120, Kaser 1975, p. 242.

195 Kaser 1975, p. 261, Kaser & Knütel 2003, p. 140.

Furthermore, the distinction between ownership and the rights derived from ownership was, to a considerable extent, also lost.[196] Justinian returned to the (pre-) classical concepts and the sharp distinction between ownership, possession and the property rights other than ownership, the *iura in re aliena*.

With the return to the (pre-) classical concepts and the departure from some of the (pre-) classical distinctions, there was only one unitary and absolute *dominium* that almost everybody could have on almost everything.[197] The *vindicatio* protected *dominium*, and was available against all potential claimants.[198] However, the content of the right of ownership remained undefined, to be filled in on case-to-case base.[199] As in (pre-) classical Roman law the open concept of ownership was more a matter of entitlement. In order for a person to have access to a *vindicatio* that person had to provide evidence of his entitlement to the object.[200] A *vindicatio* could not be initiated against a person who was entitled to hold a certain object under him because of an agreement of sale or lease. Only if the actual owner could prove his entitlement would he be able to vindicate the object.

In (pre-) classical Roman law the applicability of this action had been limited, only resulting in financial compensation, but not in an enforcement of the actual return of the object. Moreover, the procedure of *vindicatio* had been connected to possession of the other party, which further limited its application. Justinian extended and improved the scope of the *vindicatio* to include most cases.[201] The most important change was the effect of the action; instead of compensation, the result of a successful action would be the return of the object to the original owner.[202]

With these changes, Justinian strengthened the (pre-) classical concept of ownership and simplified the method of transfer. Delivery by *traditio*, replacing the old methods of *mancipatio* and *in iure cessio*, had become the principal form of transferring property rights.[203] For a *traditio* to work the parties needed to have the legal capacity to act, the object had to be capable of being subject of ownership and the transferor had to be owner himself.[204] Furthermore, as in (pre-) classical law, there needed to be a valid title or *iusta causa*, an intention of the parties to transfer ownership, and the transfer of possession.[205] The intention to transfer could be

196 Or the *iura in re aliena*. Kaser 1975, p. 262.

197 Only those persons and object excluded from private ownership remained outside. C. 7.25.1, Kaser & Knütel 2003, p. 140.

198 J. Inst. 4.6.15, Carey Miller 1998, p. 45.

199 Nicholas 1962, p. 153-154, Carey Miller 1998, p. 47-48.

200 Carey Miller 1998, p. 46.

201 Justinian removed the link with possession and therefore enabled a wider application of the *vindicatio*. After these modifications, the *vindicatio* could also be initiated against a *detentor*. Feenstra 1990, p. 41-42, Kaser 1975, p. 293-294.

202 Although this method of vindication dates from the post-classical era, Justinian included it in his *Corpus Iuris*. J. Inst. 4.6.17, Feenstra 1990, p. 42-43.

203 Carey Miller 1998, p. 51, Feenstra 1990, p. 55-57.

204 Carey Miller 1998, p. 52-53, G. Inst. 2.10. G, Inst. 2.11, G. Inst. 2.19, G. Inst. 2.20.

205 The meaning of the concept of *iusta causa* has been very controversial and has been equated with the intention to transfer. For a good overview of the discussion see Pool 1995, p. 46 *et seq*., Van Vliet 2000, p. 169 *et seq*. and Gordon 1989, p. 123 *et seq*. Feenstra 1990, p. 57-60, Nicholas 1962, p. 112-115, Kaser 1975, p. 259-261, Kaser & Knütel 2003, p. 153.

enough to transfer ownership, which resulted in the constructive forms of delivery that are still known in modern law.[206]

Ownership could still be acquired through prescription, although some alterations to the rules on prescription were made.[207] In (pre-) classical law the periods for usucaption in Italy had been one year for movable objects and two years for immovable objects. Justinian made *usucapio* only available for movable objects, with a lapsing period of three years.[208] For immovable objects Justinian used the concept that had before been restricted to prescription of land outside of Italy, the *longi temporis praescriptio* or long-term possession.[209] With the same requirements as in case of *usucapio*, ownership of immovable objects could be acquired after ten years or twenty years depending on whether the actual owner was domiciled in the same or in another province.[210] Furthermore, Justinian introduced a new form of prescription. *Usucapio* and long-term possession required a *iusta causa*. When a person possessing land was not in good faith, the *iusta causa* would be missing and no ownership could be acquired. This third form of prescription entitled a person to acquire *dominium* over a certain object without *iusta causa* after thirty years of possession through very long-term possession or *longissimi temporis praescriptio*.[211]

The rules on prescription remained very relevant because Justinian allowed the *actio Publiciana* to remain in his *Corpus Iuris Civilis*. A person who would in time acquire ownership through *usucapio* or long-term possession and who was in good faith would therefore remain protected by the Publician action against third parties during the period of prescription.[212] Praetorian ownership therefore remained as a result of maintaining the Publician action.

Finally, the concept of co-ownership also survived. In vulgar law co-ownership had been regarded as a functional fragmentation of ownership, but as Justinian had restored the (pre-) classical unitary and absolute concept of ownership, so only the (pre-) classical co-ownership in indivisible shares remained in the *Corpus Iuris Civilis*.[213] To protect the co-owners Justinian enlarged the application of the *actio communi dividundo* with which the co-owners could prevent one of the co-owners who attempted to interfere with the object of co-ownership or, if such a person had

206 J. Inst. 2.1.44, Carey Miller 1998, p. 53. The forms of delivery fall outside the scope of this study. For a good overview see Van Vliet 2000, p. 52 *et seq.*

207 J. Inst. 2.6.pr., Carey Miller 1998, p. 55 *et seq.*, Kaser 1975, p. 296, Feenstra 1990, p. 78, Guarino 2001, p. 695-696.

208 J. Inst. 2.6.pr. Feenstra 1990, p. 78, Carey Miller 1998, p. 55 *et seq.*

209 J. Inst. 2.6.pr. Although originally a form of limitation, by the time of Justinian it had become a form of acquisitive prescription. Nicholas 1962, p. 128, Feenstra 1990, p. 78, Carey Miller 1998, p. 55 *et seq.*, Guarino 2001, p. 690.

210 J. Inst. 2.6.pr. Carey Miller 1998, p. 56, Gordon 1989, p. 123-135.

211 Although the term *longissimi temporis praescriptio* dates from the commentators, it is commonly used to describe the Justinian use of the very long term possession as well. C. 7.39.8.1, Kaser & Knütel 2003, p. 158, Feenstra 1990, p. 78, Nicholas 1962, p. 128-129, Kaser & Wubbe 1971, p. 125, Guarino 2001, p. 699.

212 Kaser & Wubbe 1971, p. 135, Feenstra 1990, p. 44-46, Nicholas 1962, p. 126-128.

213 D. 8.2.27.1, Kaser 1975, p. 272, Kaser & Knütel 2003, p. 145-148.

already done so, restore the object to its original situation.[214] By assuming that each owner held the full right of ownership but with the value of an indivisible share in the property, the unitary concept of ownership remained.[215]

3.4. *Other Property Rights*

In vulgar law the distinction between *dominium* and the *iura in re aliena* had disappeared and some *iura in re aliena* were considered types of ownership. Justinian restored the (pre-) classical Roman demarcation between these concepts and dealt with *iura in re aliena* separately.[216] These rights became the rights in respect of another's object categorised according to the (pre-) classical distinction in right to use and security rights.[217]

Although the rustic praedial servitudes had lost some of their earlier importance, the division between rustic and urban praedial servitudes remained in the *Corpus Iuris Civilis*.[218] Also personal servitudes were now officially included in the category of servitudes.[219] Justinian re-introduced the rules from (pre-) classical Roman law, which applied to all servitudes.[220] These rules formed the framework within which servitudes could be created. First, the dominant and servient land should be in the *vicinitas* of each other.[221] Secondly, it was not possible to have a servitude on your own property, as was established by the rule of *nulli res sua servit*.[222] Thirdly, the servitude must be beneficial for the object and not to the person holding the object. In other words, the servitude should have *utilitas fundi*.[223] Fourthly, the servitude should be beneficial to the dominant land continuously, or should have a *perpetua causa*.[224] Finally, the servitude could not constitute a positive duty. This rule of *servitus in faciendo consistere nequit*, which had some exceptions, formed the largest restriction on the content of the rights of servitude.[225]

214 Apart from this action, a co-owner could also use the *actio familiae erciscundae* (inheritance) and the *actio finium regundorum* (land) to stop the co-ownership and divide the object among the co-owners. Kaser & Knütel 2003, p. 148, Kaser & Wubbe 1971, p. 116-117, Mayer-Maly 1999, p. 66, Borkowski 1997, p. 293.

215 See, *inter alia*, Guarino 2001, p. 524.

216 Kaser 1975, p. 248, 298 *et seq*. Although the vulgar law period will mostly be left aside, some aspects of it will be dealt with together with the specific property rights.

217 Although the *res mancipi – res nec mancipi* distinction was no longer made.

218 Bund 1956, p. 216.

219 Also the action protecting the servitudes became one and the same, the *actio confessoria*. Kaser 1975, p. 305, Bund 1956, p. 218-219.

220 See above; 2.4. Other Property Rights, Feenstra 1990, p. 86-87.

221 D. 8.3.5.1, D. 8.3.7.1, Feenstra 1990, p. 87, Kaser & Wubbe 1971, p. 138.

222 D. 8.2.26, D. 8.6.1, Kaser & Wubbe 1971, p. 138, Feenstra 1990, p. 88, Mayer-Maly 1999, p. 96, Borkowski 1997, p. 170.

223 D. 8.1.8pr., Feenstra 1990, p. 87, Kaser & Wubbe 1971, p. 138, Borkowski 1997, p. 170, see note 74.

224 D. 8.2.28, Kaser & Wubbe 1971, p. 138, Feenstra 1990, p. 87.

225 D. 8.1.15.1, Feenstra 1990, p. 88, Borkowski 1997, p. 171, Giuffrè 1992, p. 41-42, Mayer-Maly 1999, p. 95-96.

Originally, the first four rustic praedial servitudes could only be acquired by a *mancipatio* and therefore had been *res mancipi*. Other servitudes could be established by *in iure cessio*. However, since both methods of transfer had disappeared from the *Corpus Iuris Civilis*, another method of creation was necessary. Analogous application of the tradition was problematic due to the requirement of delivery. Already in (pre-) classical Roman law it had been possible to create a servitude by *pactiones et stipulationes*, or, in other words, by a free agreement, pact or formal stipulation.[226] As a general rule Justinian allowed all servitudes to be created by pact and stipulation.[227] Moreover, it had not been possible to possess a servitude.[228] Justinian included all servitudes in his renewed rules on prescription so that servitudes could also be acquired through long-term prescription.[229]

A servitude would be created if the legal relation complied with the abovementioned criteria. In order to protect the servitude the (pre-) classical action of *vindicatio servitutis* was available which became known as the *actio confessoria* in Justinian's law.[230] With this action a claimant could establish that the servitude did in fact exist, as well as attempt to restore the situation as if he would have been able to enjoy the servitude. The *actio confessoria* was a property action and could therefore be initiated against third parties.[231] The owner of the servient land, in his turn, could initiate the *actio negatoria*, an action that, like the *actio confessoria*, resembled the *vindicatio*. With this action the owner could establish that there was no servitude as well as restore the situation to where he would have been able to enjoy his right of ownership. The *actio negatoria* could only be initiated against those who claimed to have a servitude.[232]

Through the collection of (pre-) classical Roman writings in the *Digest*, which formed the major part of the *Corpus Iuris Civilis*, all property rights existing from (pre-) classical Roman law were reinstated. In respect to servitudes, praedial servitudes remained in force and continued to be divided into rustic and urban praedial servitudes. In respect to personal servitudes, the law of Justinian made a larger contribution to the development of property rights, by clearly stating which rights were to belong to this category. In (pre-) classical Roman law the relation between the right of usufruct and the right of ownership had been much debated.[233]

226 Although contractual in nature, these came under praetorian protection. Borkowski 1997, p. 179, Feenstra 1990, p. 88-89, Kaser & Wubbe 1971, p. 138-139, Mayer-Maly 1999, p. 100-101.

227 It has even been suggested that in Justinian law the formal stipulation was even no longer required, however the official text uses pacts and stipulations, J. Inst. 2.3.4, Feenstra 1990, p. 88-89, Mayer-Maly 1999, p. 101, Kaser 1975, p. 304.

228 Borkowski 1997, p. 170.

229 Since these servitudes belonged to the land on which they were established. C. 7.33.12.4, Feenstra 1990, p. 89, Kaser & Wubbe 1971, p. 139, Mayer-Maly 1999, p. 100-101.

230 D. 8.5.2pr., D. 7.6.5.6, Feenstra 1990, p. 90, Kaser 1975, p. 305, Mayer-Maly 1999, p. 101.

231 Feenstra 1990, p. 90.

232 There is a difference with the medieval Romanists who also allowed the initiation of the *actio negatoria* against those who disturbed the holder in the enjoyment of the object. Feenstra 1990, p. 91.

233 Schulz 1956, p. 386, Thomas 1976, p. 205, Kaser 1975, p. 303, Bund 1956, p. 218, Borkowski 1997, p. 174-175.

Justinian established that personal servitudes, although derived from *dominium*, were a separate class of property rights and included the rights of *ususfructus, usus, habitatio* and *operae servorum vel animalium*.[234]

The right of usufruct, and the other personal servitudes, continued to take a special place in the system of servitudes. Although now clearly property relations, the rights remained property rights in respect to persons and not in respect to persons in their capacity as owners. Personal servitudes would therefore terminate on a specific moment or, certainly, because of the connection to a person as holder of the right, on the death of the usufructuary.[235] Moreover, the usufruct could only be vested in perishable objects or objects that were not consumed through use. Like in (pre-) classical Roman law, a quasi-usufruct could be established in which the usufructuary would actually become owner of the objects and would give security for their value.[236] In effect, this made it possible to have a right of usufruct on all types of property. The *vindicatio ususfructus*, the action that has protected the holder of a usufruct in (pre-) classical Roman law, became, with the changes made by Justinian, included in the wide *actio confessoria* and disappeared as a separate *actio*.[237] Of course, an owner could also use the *actio negatoria* to claim the non-existence of a personal servitude.[238]

In the system of the *Corpus Iuris Civilis*, other rights granting the use of another person's objects were also included. In (pre-) classical law there had been a development to allow a private person, in exchange for payment, to hold land outside Italy through a right of *ager vectigalis*.[239] Already in (pre-) classical Roman law a debate arose on the nature of this right, in particular whether it was a sale or a letting or hiring, on which no real final answer was provided.[240] Although many of these situations dealt with State-owned land and therefore public rights, many of the persons who held public land on behalf of the State sub-let it to private persons, creating a private relationship. At first only these specific relations, but in time all relations whereby land was used in exchange for payment, became known as *emphyteusis*.[241]

The development of the *emphyteusis* in vulgar law is highly relevant. The *ius ager vectigalis* became, especially in the West, considered as a part of the right of ownership. This inclusion, which is in line with the functional division of ownership in vulgar Roman law, resulted in the conclusion that both the actual owner and the person having the right of *ager vectigalis* enjoyed ownership, including the possibility to initiate a *vindicatio*.[242] In essence this right was still a contract and the contract

234 J. Inst. 2.4.1, Thomas 1976, p. 202-208, Kaser & Knütel 2003, p. 175, Mayer-Maly 1999, p. 98-100, Carey Miller 1998, p. 66-67.

235 J. Inst. 2.4.3, Carey Miller 1998, p. 66-67.

236 J. Inst. 2.4.2, D. 7.5.2.1, D. 7.5.3, Carey Miller 1998, p. 66, Feenstra 1990, p. 92-93.

237 J. Inst. 4.6.2, Feenstra 1990, p. 95, Mayer-Maly 1999, p. 101, Kaser & Knütel 2003, p. 178, 182.

238 Any damage to the object by the usufructuary could also be recovered under the *lex Aquilia*. D. 7.1.13.2, Johnston 1989, p. 155.

239 See above; 2.4. Other Property Rights.

240 Thomas 1976, p. 209, Kaser 1975, p. 310-311.

241 Kaser 1975, p. 308-310, Kaser & Knütel 2003, p. 184-185, Thomas 1976, p. 209.

242 Kaser & Knütel 2003, p. 184, Kaser 1975, p. 308-309. Thomas 1976, p. 209, Mayer-Maly 1999, p. 102.

itself was known as *contractus emphyteuticarius*, until Emperor Zeno settled the debate on the nature of the right and stated in a *constitutio* that *emphyteusis* was a right *sui generis*.[243] Justinian had *emphyteusis* included in his *Corpus Iuris* and allowed it to be created by contract or by legacy. In Justinian's system the right of *emphyteusis* came under protection of an *actio in rem* comparable to the *vindicatio*.[244] However, instead of awarding the holder of the right a right of ownership, this right remained with the original owner who would not be able to interfere with the object. As long as the ground rent was paid, the holder would have a *ius in re aliena*.[245]

Finally, the right of *superficies* was also recognised as a separate property right.[246] In vulgar law the right of *superficies*, like *emphyteusis*, had been part of the functional concept of ownership. Justinian also changed this and restored the (pre-) classical law distinction. The person having the *superficies* was protected by the interdict *de superficiebus* but *superficies* itself was now recognised as a separate *ius in re* with a corresponding *actio*.[247] This action, like the action connected to the right of *emphyteusis*, resembled the *vindicatio* and could be used as long as the payment for the right, known as *solarium*, was paid.[248] *Superficies* was specifically intended to provide a right to the person having a building on the land of another. By operation of the rule of *superficies solo cedit*, the owner of the land became owner of the buildings erected on it. The creation of a *superficies* would break with this rule in that it would give the *superficarius* not a right of ownership but a property right in the house that could itself serve as an object for the establishment of other property rights.[249]

Like in (pre-) classical law, the *Corpus Iuris Civilis* included, next to property relations granting rights to use, property relations to provide security, usually for a loan. In (pre-) classical law these rights had been the *fiducia cum creditore*, the *pignus* and the *hypotheca*.[250] The fiduciary transfer had, as was stated above, become obsolete due to the development of the other security rights. Now, under the reforms of Justinian, the fiduciary transfer of ownership disappeared completely.[251] Therefore *pignus* and *hypotheca* remained the only available property security rights. Where in (pre-) classical Roman law these rights had been the same, Justinian made

243 Emperor Zeno (474-491 AD). C. 4.66.1, J. Inst. 3.2.3, Kaser & Knütel 2003, p. 185, Thomas 1976, p. 209.

244 The precursor of the right of *emphyteusis* might also have had this action available, but this remains uncertain. See D. 6.3, Thomas 1976, p. 210.

245 Thomas 1976, p. 209.

246 Thomas 1976, p. 210, Kaser 1975, p. 306-308.

247 D. 6.1.74-76, D. 43.18.1. Although *superficies* should only include the building itself, the developments in vulgar law lead to the right itself also being named *superficies*. Kaser 1975, p. 306-307, Thomas 1976, p. 210.

248 Kaser & Knütel 2003, p. 185.

249 D. 43.18.1.9, Carey Miller 1998, p. 74-75.

250 See above; 2.4. Other Property Rights.

251 As all the formal modes of conveyance had been replaced by *traditio*, it was not until the discovery of the works of Gaius in the 19th century that information on the *fiducia cum creditore contracta* was rediscovered. On this see, *inter alia*, Feenstra 1990, p. 105-106.

a distinction.[252] *Hypotheca* was used for non-possessory security and *pignus* was used in cases where possession had been transferred.[253]

Already in very late (pre-) classical Roman law there had been some developments, which caused the *pignus* and *hypotheca* of Justinian to be slightly different from those of (pre-) classical Roman law. Through interference of the legislature some legal hypothecs had come into existence. These hypothecs were property relations not created through agreement between the parties but by operation of law. Examples of situations in which a legal hypothec arose were the case where a guardian bought something for his ward with the ward's money, and the general hypothec of the taxation authority on someone's assets. In both cases a hypothec would come into existence by operation of law either for the ward on the specific property or for the taxation authority on everything a certain person owned.[254]

The legal hypothec of the tax authority especially posed the legal system with a serious problem. A general hypothec covers all assets, including rights and debts. The inclusion of rights and debts into the right of hypothec was achieved because hypothecs were now non-possessory security relations. As a result the *actio Serviana*, the action that protected the relationship, would also be applicable to these specific types of object.[255] However it was of no use if the creditor became entitled to a debt himself. Instead an *actio utilis in personam* was created with which the creditor could act against the debtor of his former debtor.[256]

The rules on the creation of the rights of pledge and hypothec stayed the same. In order to create such a right, an agreement, an object capable of being subject of pledge or hypothec and ownership of that object was required.[257] In cases where a pledge or hypothec came into existence by operation of law, an agreement was not necessary.

When a debtor could not pay his debt the creditor would have the authority to sell the object over which the security right was created. The agreement that the creditor would be entitled to keep the object for himself in case of non-performance by the debtor, known as the *lex commissoria,* had been prohibited since Emperor Constantine and remained prohibited by Justinian.[258] If no buyer could be found the creditor could, with imperial permission, receive the ownership of the object.[259] Any surplus to the sale or the value of the object would have to be paid to the debtor.[260]

252 J. Inst. 4.6.7, but *contra* D. 13.7.9.2, Thomas 1976, p. 332.
253 Kaser 1975, p. 314.
254 Schulz 1992, p. 410, Thomas 1976, p. 333.
255 D. 13.7.18, D. 20.1.20, C. 8.16.4, Feenstra 1990, p. 121.
256 Feenstra 1990, p. 121.
257 Kaser 1975, p. 315.
258 Feenstra 1990, p. 119, Kaser 1975, p. 319-320.
259 Kaser 1975, p. 320.
260 Kaser 1975, p. 321.

3.5. *A Numerus Clausus in the Corpus Iuris Civilis?*

Zwalve argues that because of the nature of Justinian's codification, Justinian intended to codify the law and give it exclusive force, a closed system of property rights existed.[261] The result of this exclusivity was that all other existing sources of law became invalid with the introduction of the separate parts of the *Corpus Iuris Civilis*. In other words, only those relations that were recognised by the *Corpus Iuris Civilis* as property relations were granted a proprietary action. In this respect the principle of *numerus clausus* took, as in (pre-) classical Roman law, the form of a *numerus clausus* of property actions.[262]

A closed system of actions did not automatically prevent parties from entering into new types of property relations. As in (pre-) classical Roman law a proprietary action could be awarded when a legal relation could be brought under the criteria provided by law. This was especially true for servitudes. As long as the requirements for servitudes were fulfilled the relation would be protected with the *actio confessoria*.[263]

At the foundation of the system of the *Corpus Iuris Civilis* remained, as in (pre-) classical Roman law, the distinction between personal and proprietary actions. Only proprietary actions could be initiated against third parties. In the law of Justinian the difference between personal and property relations was made by legislation and from this point of view not only the principle but also the rule of *numerus clausus* applied, albeit with respect to property actions and not property rights.

The difference between actions and rights is relevant. The principle of restricting the number of property relations in respect of the burden they imposed on the unitary and absolute concept of ownership, therefore ensuring legal certainty for third parties, was already present in (pre-) classical Roman law. Like in modern law, the principle of *numerus clausus* itself was not written down in legislation, but nevertheless applied in practice. However due to the codification in the *Corpus Iuris Civilis* this principle found expression as a rule of *numerus clausus* of property actions, where there had only been a principle of *numerus clausus* of property actions in (pre-) classical Roman law. Whether this means there was also a rule of *numerus clausus* in respect of property relations remains, as in (pre-) classical Roman law, difficult to determine.[264] In any case, standardisation of property actions by legislation must have had effect on the contents of the legal relations entered into, to make them fit within these actions.[265]

261 Zwalve 2003, p. 103. Lokin & Zwalve 1992, p. 2, 80 *et seq.*, Varga 1991, p. 35 *et seq.* On codification ideas in general see Hart 1970, p. 158 *et seq.*

262 See above; 2.5. A *Numerus Clausus* in (Pre-) Classical Roman Law?

263 See above; 3.4. Other Property Rights.

264 See above; 2.5. A *Numerus Clausus* in (Pre-) Classical Roman Law?

265 The same *Typizität* or *Typengebundenheid* as in classical Roman law. See above; 2.5. A *Numerus Clausus* in (Pre-) Classical Roman Law?

3.6. *Summary*

Justinian restored and incorporated the clear distinctions of (pre-) classical Roman law in his *Corpus Iuris Civilis*. These include the distinction between ownership and possession, but also between ownership and rights lesser than ownership. These *iura in re aliena*, as they have been named later, are property rights because they were protected with at least one proprietary action. Because of the exclusive codification that was made under Emperor Justinian, the only available property actions were those mentioned in the code. Property relations that meet the criteria for one of these actions were recognised as property rights because of the third-party effect the actions provided to the holders of these rights. Nevertheless, there was a limited freedom for parties to shape their legal relations.

The principle of *numerus clausus* did apply, not only to ensure that the unitary and absolute concept of ownership was not burdened too much, but also in the fact that no other property actions could be created. In this sense even a rule of *numerus clausus* of property actions existed.

4. The *Ius Commune*

4.1. *Introduction*

The downfall of the Western Roman Empire came with the Germanic conquest at the end of the fifth century.[266] In the Roman Empire as it had evolved, the whole population had become subject to Roman law. However, under Germanic law principles, persons were governed by their law of birth.[267] Depending on the origin of a person a different law would apply, therefore, Roman law would only apply to the Roman citizens and their descendants. To the Germanic tribes, specific Germanic laws, which were mainly customary laws, would apply.

The end of the Western Roman Empire led to the disappearance of the State institutions and the end of the Roman tradition of the study of law.[268] Emperor Justinian had introduced his *Corpus Iuris Civilis* in the Eastern Roman Empire, which had halted the vulgarisation of law in the East, but the vulgarisation of law in the West continued and eventually led to the decline of Roman law in general. The central administration vanished and society returned to agriculture.[269]

Apart from the remains of vulgar Roman law and Germanic customary law there were two other relevant sources of law. In the year 800 Charlemagne had himself crowned Emperor in Rome by the Pope, uniting different kingdoms under his reign. With the papal blessing he announced that he, as Emperor, had the power to make legislation in his empire.[270] The law of the Church, which was strongly

266 Zwalve 2003, p. 24, Lange 1997, p. 1.

267 Van Caenegem 1988b, p. 17, 19 Stein 1999, p. 39.

268 Van Caenegem 1988b, p. 17.

269 Stein 1999, p. 38.

270 Later this Empire would grow into the Holy Roman Empire. Stein 1999, p. 41-43.

based on Roman law, became a source of law in the Carolingian Empire. The law of the Roman Catholic Church, which is also known as canon law, primarily dealt with the organisation and dealings of the Church, but there were certain principles that also heavily influenced and changed the Roman private law.[271]

The other source of law was the customary law that came with the system of landholding. The decline of the Roman Empire and the lack of a central government led to a situation of anarchy in which the common man was not sure of his possessions or his life.[272] In exchange for protection of a neighbouring lord, the common person would take an oath of fidelity, which obliged him to go to war in the service of this lord. These relations between common men and lords are known as feudal relations, and these became the principal method for landholding.[273]

The Frankish kings would, in exchange for services in combat, grant parts of their land to warriors. These warriors in their turn would grant part of their land to persons who were faithful to them.[274] Persons who had received land in exchange for a payment of services or money became known as vassals.[275] In this form the feudal system and its principles spread through Europe and became an additional, but very important, source of law.

However, it was not until the end of the eleventh century that Roman law was properly reintroduced. In Italy, technically, Roman law had never lost the force of law. Under the personality principle of Germanic law, Roman law remained applicable to the former Roman citizens and even served as a subsidiary source of law when Germanic customary law could not provide an answer. When more and more people moved to other territories, the population became mixed. At one moment there could be more than twenty different laws applicable in the same square kilometre. Disputes became hard to settle. Therefore, the personality principle slowly made way for the territoriality principle, under which law would apply to a certain region regardless of the origin of the citizens.[276]

At the end of the eleventh century the *Corpus Iuris Civilis* was rediscovered and studied again. The level of legal culture rose with the establishment of law schools and a university in Bologna. The rediscovery and synthesis of Roman law took most of the twelfth century and would lead to a system of learned Roman law.[277] However, Germanic customary law remained the principal source of law, supplemented by feudal law, canon law and, now, the rediscovered Roman law. The renewed study of Roman law therefore required a method to adapt the Roman law to current times.

This adaptation came with the school of the Glossators who, in Bologna, would add a comment, or gloss, to the text of the *Corpus Iuris Civilis* to explain its

271 For example the rule that agreements should be kept. More will be stated about the influence of Canon law below in 4.4. Other Property Rights. Zwalve 2003, p. 62.

272 Zwalve 2003, p. 66.

273 Zwalve 2003, p. 66-67, Van den Bergh 1988, p. 17 *et seq.*, Van Caenegem 1988b, p. 20.

274 Zwalve 2003, p. 67.

275 For a detailed overview see Lévy & Castaldo 2002, p. 380 *et seq.* and Coing 1985, p. 352 *et seq.*

276 Stein 1999, p. 39, Lévy & Castaldo 2002, p. 369.

277 Stein 1999, p. 43 *et seq.*, Wieacker 1995, p. 28 *et seq.*

meaning. The Glossators succeeded in rediscovering most of the *Corpus Iuris Civilis* and to reintroduce it as a subsidiary source of law. The end of the school of Glossators came with the creation of a standard collection of Glosses by Accursius, the *Glossa Ordinaria*.[278] In the next centuries this collection of glosses more than the text of the *Corpus Iuris Civilis* itself, would become the primary source of Roman-based law.[279]

The successors of the Glossators went further and attempted to apply the rediscovered Roman law in their society. These Post-Glossators or Commentators attempted, with the use of specific methods of interpretation, to apply Roman law to their current time.[280] In this sense the Post-Glossators differed from the thirteenth-century Glossators who had sought to explain the texts. The new learned law could also be applied to the study of non-Roman law such as Germanic customary law and feudal law. These non-Roman laws, which were particular to each region, were also known as *ius proprium*.[281] The *ius proprium* became a specific part of the study of the Post-Glossators.[282]

The third school that studied Roman law was the school of the Humanists. Inspired by the renaissance of antiquity the Humanists rejected the approach of the Commentators and corrected many historically incorrect interpretations from both the Glossators and the Commentators.[283] The result of this approach was that study of Roman law lost contact with practice and became more and more an academic discipline.[284] The Humanists, based in France, called their method *mos gallicus* to oppose themselves to the Commentators, whose method had become known as *mos italicus*.[285] The Humanist school of thought remained in force until the seventeenth century when it was replaced by the study of natural law.[286]

4.1.1. Sources of Law: Problems with the *Ius Proprium*

The four sources of law remained in force throughout the whole period, but the differences in the nature of these laws require some explanations:

First, Roman law as it was received throughout Europe spread through its study at the universities, first in Italy, but later also in the rest of Europe. The result was that received Roman law and the addition made to it by the study of learned scholars, became a common law of the continent of Europe.

278 Zwalve 2003, p. 34-36, Stein 1999, p. 46-49, Van Caenegem 1988b, p. 47 *et seq.*, Lange 1997, p. 335 *et seq.*
279 Stein 1999, p. 49.
280 Stein 1999, p. 67-74.
281 Van Caenegem 1988b, p. 53, Zwalve 2003, 29 *et seq.*
282 As far as property law is concerned, the works of Bartolus de Saxoferrato and Baldus de Ubaldis are the most valued works. Van Caenegem 1988b, p. 54, Stein 1999, p. 71 *et seq.*, Zwalve 2003, p. 36.
283 Van Caenegem 1988b, p. 55 *et seq.*, Koschaker 1995, p. 105 *et seq.*, Lange 1997, p. 120 *et seq.*
284 Koschaker 1995, p. 112-113, Van Caenegem 1988b, p. 56-57.
285 Koschaker 1995, p. 108-109.
286 Natural Law will be dealt with below in 5. Natural Law and the French Revolution.

Second, the same can be held for the law of the Roman Catholic Church. Together with the rise of the study of Roman law came the study of canon law, which also led to several compilations and subsequent glosses and commentaries on the compilations.[287] In order to write these glosses and commentaries the canon law scholars used the terminology of the learned Roman law. Furthermore, the Church explicitly lived under Roman law, by which it meant the original *Corpus Iuris Civilis*, as applicable to ecclesiastical matters.[288] The Church was an influential institution, which had spread throughout Europe, and through its influence not only learned Roman law, but also learned canon law became a true European law.

Third, in the second half of the twelfth century, feudal customary rules were collected in what came to be known as the *Libri Feudorum*.[289] The collection of customary law became accepted as a good collection of customary law throughout Europe and was even included in the medieval version of the *Corpus Iuris Civilis*.[290] However, the *Libri Feudorum* never became as authoritative as Roman law and canon law.

These three sources of law applied throughout continental Europe and therefore together became known as the *Ius Commune*, the common law of Europe. However, the *ius proprium*, which was the customary law that differed from place to place, should not be disregarded. This law was known as the *ius proprium* in order to contrast it with the *Ius Commune*.[291] As a result of the primary nature of the *ius proprium* there was no real common law of Europe. In legal practice, the application of the *ius proprium* resulted in a merely subsidiary application of the *Ius Commune*.[292]

Although it did not have exclusive force of law, clever scholarship in the twelfth century made for a strict interpretation of customary law so that the *Ius Commune* had room to apply and develop, not only in scholarship, but also in practice.[293] Furthermore, the lawyers who used and interpreted the *ius proprium* had received legal training based on the *Ius Commune*. Most applications and interpretations were therefore consistent with Roman law principles.[294]

Because of this dual system, the structure of this Section 4.1.1 is different from that of the Sections on Roman law in this Chapter. The local customary law, in so far as it is relevant for modern law in the selected legal systems, will be dealt with in the Chapters dealing with modern law respectively. This Chapter will deal with the learned law or *Ius Commune*. Because this law was common to the continent of Europe and because so many modern legal systems have been inspired by principles and rules following from the sources of the *Ius Commune*, it is worth looking at the *Ius Commune* property law. Due to the hierarchy of sources and the

287 Van Caenegem 1988b, p. 65.

288 Van Caenegem 1988b, p. 65.

289 Stein 1999, p. 61, Zwalve 2003, p. 66, Van Caenegem 1988b, p. 20.

290 Stein 1999, p. 61-62.

291 Zwalve 2003, p. 29 *et seq.*

292 *Libri Feudorum* 2,1 as quoted by Zwalve in Zwalve 2003, p. 29.

293 More will be stated in the next section. The scholar who came with the rules of interpretation was Bartolus de Saxoferrato. Zwalve 2003, p. 68 *et seq.*

294 Zwalve 2003, p. 29 *et seq.*

possible existence of property rights in local customary law that would take preference over Roman law principles as part of the *Ius Commune*, this part will not examine the possible existence of a principle of *numerus clausus* and its application.

4.2. *General Principles of the Ius Commune*

The renewal of the interest in Roman law, especially in Justinian's *Corpus Iuris Civilis*, led to several schools of thought. The Glossators attempted to explain the *Corpus Iuris*, which sometimes confronted them with serious problems, mostly due to changes in society.[295] In order to explain the text the Glossators wrote a gloss at the side of the text that would explain the problem and, if possible, cross-reference to another section. Although Justinian's intention had been to avoid any contradictions in his text, many were left. These contradictions forced the Glossators to come up with solutions.[296] One of these solutions was the use of a technique named *distinctio*. With this technique, it was be possible to provide several meanings for the same word.[297]

The study of Roman law also influenced the study of the other sources of law. The concepts of Roman law were applied to feudal law with the result that in this area customary law became described in Roman law terminology. The Roman system of actions was now applied to the feudal relation, which led to serious problems concerning the classification of the position of the vassal and the question of which action would be available.

Furthermore, the academic study of Roman law, as opposed to its application in practice, led to a critical view of the subject matter. Academics posed the question of whether there was perhaps a *causa* that was at the foundation of a certain *actio* awarded by Roman law.[298] In other words, these academics searched for a reason why a certain action would be available. This search for a *causa* eventually led to the rise of the concept of 'right' that is used in civil law today. However, even though the Glossators already paid attention to the idea of a *causa* behind an action, this change in approach occurred gradually.[299]

Finally an important distinction was made between corporeal and incorporeal objects. Although this distinction was not new, it had been used by Gaius as well, it

295 See below; 4.3. Ownership.

296 This is the reason for the interpolations in the texts, e.g. the replacement of *mancipatio* and in *iure cessio* with the *tradition*, Van Caenegem 1988b, p. 49.

297 Van Caenegem 1988b, p. 49.

298 Feenstra 1979, p. 10.

299 There has been a large debate on the origin of the concept of subjective right, started by Villey, see, *inter alia*, Coing 1962, p. 38 *et seq.*, Schrage 1977, p. 1 *et seq.*, Feenstra 1979, p. 1 *et seq.*, Schrage 1996, p. 55-56 for an overview of this debate. For an extensive overview from a procedural point of view see Kriechbaum 1996, p. 144 *et seq.* This subject will be dealt with below in 4.4. Other Property Rights.

gained importance in relation to the concept of ownership.[300] In the renewed study of Roman law, ownership had become restricted to corporeal objects.[301]

4.3. *Ownership*

The study of Roman law allowed the Glossators to understand the concept of *dominium* in the context of Roman law. Already at the end of the twelfth century, the concept of *dominium* was used to interpret the *Libri Feudorum*.[302] Interpreting feudal law in Roman terminology allowed the Glossators to use the *Libri Feudorum*, besides the *Corpus Iuris*, in teaching.[303] This new method posed for them a problem concerning the relationship between the lord and the vassal in feudal law. In order to solve this, the Glossators looked at the debate on the status of the person having an *emphyteusis* in Roman law.[304] In the Eastern Roman Empire, *emphyteusis* had been a right *sui generis*.[305] However, in the Western Roman Empire *emphyteusis* was considered a right of ownership.[306] Furthermore, there are texts in the *Corpus Iuris* that suggest and underline the relation with *dominium*, especially in granting the holder of an *emphyteusis* an *actio in rem utilis*.[307]

With these concepts of ownership and *emphyteusis* in mind, the Glossators derived the principle that the vassal would have *dominium utile* whereas the feudal lord would have *dominium directum*.[308] Corresponding to these types of ownership there would be a *vindicatio directa* or *vindicatio utile*.[309] This view, which was criticised already at that time, resulted in the generally accepted opinion that the holder of an *emphyteusis*, the holder of a *superficies* and the long-term lessor also held *dominium utile*.[310] Furthermore the term was used for the person who would become owner through *usucapio*.[311]

300 G. Inst. 2, 12, Kaser & Knütel 2003, p. 119.

301 At least, ownership in the narrow sense of the word, see below; 4.3. Ownership.

302 Feenstra 1976, p. 265, Feenstra 1974, p. 215 *et seq.*

303 Feenstra argues that the Glossator who first included the *Libri feudorum* in teaching was Pillius Feenstra 1974, p. 221, Feenstra 1976, p. 265. However, the discussion is wider, see Van der Walt & Kleyn 1989, p. 235-243 for a good overview.

304 See above; 2.4. Other Property Rights and 3.4. Other Property Rights.

305 See above; 3.4. Other Property Rights.

306 Van der Walt & Kleyn 1989, p. 234-235, Zwalve 2003, p. 112-113.

307 C. 11.62.2; C. 11.62.4; C. 11.70.4; C. 11.68.2pr.; C. 11.62.12.1, as quoted by Van der Walt & Kleyn 1989, p. 234-235. See also Feenstra 1976, p. 265-266.

308 See Gloss *Libertates* on C. 11.62.11.1, Spruit & Feenstra 1987, p. 273-274. Feenstra 1976, p. 266, Van der Walt & Kleyn 1989, p. 235-236, Zwalve 2003, p. 112-113, Lévy & Castaldo 2002, p. 386-387, 398 Stein 1999, p. 63, Lange 1997, p. 90.

309 Kriechbaum 1996, p. 232.

310 Van der Walt 1986, p. 308, Van der Walt & Kleyn 1989, p. 236, 241, Zwalve 2003, p. 113, Feenstra 1976, p. 267, Van den Bergh 1988, p. 45, Lévy & Castaldo 2002, p. 386-387, see Kriechbaum 1996, p. 232 *et seq.* for a detailed overview.

311 Such a person would have had the *actio Publiciana* at his disposal in Roman law and would have held praetorian or bonitary ownership. Coing 1962, p. 41. See above; 2.3. Ownership.

A problem would arise if a vassal had *dominium utile* in respect to his lord, but sub-infeudated his property to another vassal.[312] The *Glossa Ordinaria* and most Glossators answered that only the latter vassal would have *dominium utile* leaving the original vassal with nothing.[313] This shows that, although a division of the concept of ownership was held possible, the ownership itself could not be divided. Furthermore there were two different conceptions of ownership. *Dominium* in a wide sense included ownership on all corporeal and incorporeal objects. *Dominium* in a narrow sense of the word was a species of the wider concept and was restricted to corporeal objects. It was in the narrow category that the distinction between dominium *directum* and *utile* was made.[314]

Although this *duplex dominium* was recognised, there still was no definition of ownership.[315] The successors of the Glossators continued and extended the work and succeeded in deriving a definition of ownership.[316] The work of the Post-Glossators was academic in nature and they paid more attention to law outside Roman law as well.[317] They wrote commentaries on the *Corpus Iuris* in which they built on the works of the Glossators.[318] The Post-Glossators also used the two different conceptions of ownership of the Glossators.

In one of the famous commentaries of Bartolus de Saxoferrato, a definition of *dominium* is provided.[319] Bartolus considered ownership as:

> The right in a corporeal object to have...perfectly at one's disposal, unless it is forbidden by law.[320]

In another commentary Bartolus also included incorporeal objects into his definition of *dominium*.[321] However, this definition did not mean that Bartolus only recognised one type of ownership. Instead, he recognised three types; *dominium directum, dominium utile* and *quasi-dominium*.[322] The recognition of these three types should be read together with his definition of ownership as a right perfectly at one's dis-

312 I.e., if a vassal would, in his turn, give land in feudal tenure to others, who are known as sub-vassals.

313 This opinion was not held by all scholars, from the period of the Post-Glossators it became accepted that both vassal and sub-vassal would have *dominium utile*. Feenstra 1976, p. 266-267.

314 Coing 1953, p. 349-350, Coing 1985, p. 291.

315 Although at the time of the Glossators some authors under the influences of canon scholarship attempted to define ownership. Kriechbaum 1996, p. 375 *et seq.*, Schrage 1977, p. 38 *et seq.*

316 Van Caenegem 1988b, p. 52.

317 Van Caenegem 1988b, p. 53.

318 Zwalve 2003, p. 36.

319 Commentary on D. 41.2.17, Schrage 1996, p. 43.

320 ... *ius in re corporali perfecte disponendi nisi lege prohibeatur*, quote and translation from Schrage 1996, p. 43.

321 Commentary on D. 41.2.17, Schrage 1996, p. 44, Van den Bergh 1988, p. 44 *et seq.*

322 Van der Walt & Kleyn 1989, p. 242-243.

posal.[323] Bartolus considered his definition of ownership to be applicable to all three types of ownership.[324]

Like the Glossators, Bartolus reserved the *dominium directum* for the feudal lord. He awarded *dominium utile* to the vassal, the holder of the right of *emphyteusis*, the holder of the right of *superficies* and the long-term possessor.[325] The third type of ownership was reserved for people who were on their way to becoming owner through prescription. This type of ownership was based on the Roman *actio Publiciana* which protected a possessor who, in the future, would acquire ownership through *usucapio*.[326] Although this third type was not as widely accepted as the other two, Bartolus' definition of ownership has become very influential in later writings about the right of ownership.[327]

The end of the feudal system of landholding came with the decline of the school of the Post-Glossators. This is not to say that feudalism no longer existed, but more that because of developments in society the place of feudal relations became less explicit. The new school of legal thought became the Humanist school of Roman law. The Humanists were inspired by the *renaissance* of antiquity and they returned to the (pre-) classical Roman concepts. In doing so they rejected the work and approaches of the Glossators and Post-Glossators as vulgar or non-Roman.[328]

This new approach included the general rejection of the division between *dominium directum* and *dominium utile*.[329] Instead most Humanists preferred the distinction between *dominium plenum* and *dominium minus plenum*.[330] The true *dominium* in the Roman sense of the word remained with the person having the *dominium plenum*, staying closer to what the Humanists considered to be the true Roman ownership. The person who had this *dominium plenum* would have the object perfectly at his disposal.[331] *Dominium minus plenum* consisted of other property rights other than ownership.[332]

However, in certain cases, as for example in respect of a right of *emphyteusis*, the question remained who was the actual owner. The Glossators and Post-Glossators had awarded the true *dominium* to the person with the ultimate entitlement, which they named *dominium directum*. However, in some cases, the

323 Which refers to the words *perfecte disponendi*, see Feenstra 1976, p. 255.
324 Van der Walt & Kleyn 1989, p. 242.
325 Other instances where *dominium utile* was awarded also existed. See Coing 1953, p. 361, Van der Walt & Kleyn 1989, p. 242 and the sources quoted there.
326 See above; 2.3. Ownership, Feenstra 1989, p. 113.
327 Which included the writings of his student Baldus, Feenstra 1978, p. 112, Feenstra 1989, p. 113, Schrage 1996, p. 44, Van der Walt & Kleyn 1989, p. 243.
328 Van Caenegem 1988b, p. 55.
329 Van der Walt & Kleyn 1989, p. 243 *et seq.*
330 Or *dominium (ex iure Quiritium)* and *in bonis esse*, see Van der Walt & Kleyn 1989, p. 244, Feenstra 1978, p. 221-222.
331 However, the meaning of *perfecte disponendi* might have been slightly different from the Post-Glossators. Feenstra 1978, p. 223, Van der Walt & Kleyn 1989, p. 244-245.
332 This distinction is made by Molina, Van der Walt & Kleyn 1989, p. 244, Feenstra 1978, p. 222-223.

Humanists awarded the true ownership to, in terms of the Glossators and Post-Glossators, the person with the *dominium utile*.[333]

4.4. *Other Property Rights*

Modern law usually makes a clear distinction between ownership on the one hand and property rights other than ownership on the other. It should be recalled that Roman law did not made such a clear distinction.[334] Subsequently, each of the schools of renewed Roman study included some of the Roman property rights and new feudal property rights into their various concepts of *dominium*. The discussion and the question whether property rights are distinct from the right of ownership or whether perhaps ownership is a property right came with the search for a *causa* behind an *actio in rem*.

The Glossators were the first to deal with these questions. The concepts of ownership the Glossators used were not very clear and only a general distinction was made between *dominium directum* and *dominium utile*. However, no definition of *dominium* was provided.[335] Schrage and Nörr argue that in the discussion in canon law a subjective notion of a 'right' of ownership was created.[336] Schrage argues that, because of the debate on ownership of the Franciscan friars, this notion had to be dealt with. Franciscan friars, under the oath they had taken, were not allowed to have any ownership. Consequently, a debate arose on who would have the ownership instead.[337] Schrage shows that the writers Bonaventura, Bonagratia and Bartolus answered the problem by looking at the rights the friars would have to give up and which rights the friars would continue to have.[338] Only after these questions were answered was the possible action considered.[339]

Hostiensis, in his *Summa Aurea*, used a concept of *ius* that can be understood as a 'subjective' right.[340] Furthermore Nörr argues that with the technique of *distinctio* the *Glossa Ordinaria* uses the same notion of right.[341] He emphasises that the result of the findings of Hostiensis is not that there was no other concept of right than the 'subjective' right. To the contrary, the Glossators and Canonists still used many concepts of rights.[342] However, the foundations for a later distinction had been laid.

Even though the Glossators were the first to deal with the question of the *causa* behind the *actio in rem* and though they came close to the use of the concept *ius in re* as a property right, most of them considered *dominium*, and not any other right, to be at the basis of the *actio in rem*. Also, the wide definition of *dominium* allowed

333 Van der Walt & Kleyn 1989, p. 244.
334 De Waal 1992, p. 568, Feenstra 1976, p. 260-261, Feenstra 1979, p. 6.
335 Feenstra 1979, p. 10.
336 Schrage 1977, p. 39 *et seq.*, Schrage 1996, p. 55-58, Nörr 1992, p. 193 *et seq.*
337 Save for the ownership of one *tunica*, Schrage 1996, p. 56.
338 Schrage 1977, p. 45-54 (Bonaventura), p. 57-61 (Bonagratia), p. 66-69 (Bartolus).
339 Schrage 1977, p. 69.
340 Nörr 1992, p. 193, 200-202, Lange 1997, p. 102 *et seq.*
341 Nörr 1992, p. 202-204.
342 Nörr 1992, p. 203.

incorporeal objects to be part of the right of ownership. The Roman *iura in re aliena* had been considered as incorporeal objects from the reception of Roman law and could therefore be included in the definition of ownership.[343] However, the search for and description of the *ius in re* by the Glossators would allow the Post-Glossators to develop a category of rights that they would oppose to *ius personale*.[344]

The Post-Glossator Baldus was the first to provide a list of *iura in re* or, as he named them, *iura realia*. Besides the three types of ownership Bartolus described, Baldus mentions; the right of succession, *ius hereditatis*, the rights of servitude, *iura servitutum realium et personalium*, and the right of pledge, *hypotheca* or *pignus*.[345] This set of *iura realia* became generally accepted among the Post-Glossators.[346]

It was not until the fifteenth and sixteenth centuries that scholars made a distinction between property rights and personal rights along the same lines as the modern legal distinction.[347] Feenstra emphasises the importance of the work of Apel, who proposed to make this distinction the foundation of the whole private law system.[348] Donellus made the distinction between *dominium* and *iura in re aliena*, rights other than ownership.[349] In the Humanist school of thought, with its rejection of a split ownership, Donellus concluded that the holder of an *emphyteusis* could not have ownership. Apart from the right of *emphyteusis*, Donellus considered as *iura in rebus alienis* the right of *superficies*, the *ius bonae fidei possessoris*, and *ius pignoris*. Feenstra also argues that Donellus considered those rights as *imminutio* of the rights of the owner.[350] However, others also concerned themselves with the subject, although not as much as Apel and Donellus did.

A well-known exception is Heinrich Hahn, who derived five property rights from five corresponding actions in Roman law.[351] The rights he derived were; *dominium*, *pignus*, *servitus*, *possessio* and *hereditas*. Feenstra has shown that this enumeration, which is known as Hahn's Pentarchy, was not the first of its kind but a selection of the various rights that were recognised at that time.[352] Even though Hahn might not have been the first author to make an enumeration of property

343 Coing 1985, p. 291.
344 Feenstra 1989, p. 112, Feenstra 1979, p. 15 *et seq.*
345 Feenstra 1979, p. 14, Feenstra 1989, p. 113.
346 Although Baldus did not distinguish ownership from other property rights, other Post-Glossators did, though none came as far as the modern day distinction. Feenstra 1989, p. 113.
347 Feenstra 1989, p. 114, Feenstra 1979, p. 16-17.
348 Although the distinction between personal rights and property rights was not new; it had been used before in Canon law, Coing 1985, p. 341, Feenstra 1979, p. 17 *et seq.*, Feenstra 1989, p. 114 *et seq.*, Feenstra 1982, p. 107.
349 Feenstra 1979, p. 26, Feenstra 1989, p. 115.
350 Feenstra 1989, p. 115.
351 The dissertation is called *De jure rerum et juris in re speciebus*, Hahn's enumeration of five property rights, also known as Hahn's Pentarchy, gained special importance in the Netherlands because of an article by Meijers in 1907, Meijers 1907, p. 271 *et seq.*, Feenstra 1982, p. 110.
352 Feenstra 1982, p. 107 *et seq.*, especially 113 *et seq.*

rights, his work is a representation of the general works of his time.[353] It was Hahn's Pentarchy that would influence several European Civil Codes.[354]

In other words, the renewed study of Roman law led to the search for rights behind the actions that were taken from Roman law. The result of this was not only a concept of a right as opposed to an action, but also a further division in personal rights and property rights. Although the development of property rights is visible through the centuries in which the *Ius Commune* applied, the content of most of the property rights remained Roman in nature.[355] Even more, those rights that were not of Roman origin were fitted into the Roman law system when needed.

Fitting non-Roman rights into the Roman system of property relations was not only needed for the relation of the vassal and the lord, which became a type of ownership next to the right of *emphyteusis*, but also with other customary rights.[356] These rights were considered incorporeal objects and were interpreted along the lines of servitudes in Roman law. The result of this approach was that some of the strict rules on servitudes were relaxed in order to fit these rights into the system.[357] The advantage of the inclusion of these non-Roman rights in the Roman system was that the methods of creation and protection were the same as for the Roman servitudes. As a result, these rights were all protected with the *actio confessoria*.[358]

The classification of the various Roman property rights differed as well. Partly under the influence of the other sources of law in the *Ius Commune*, especially the influence of feudal law on the rights of *emphyteusis* and *superficies* that were now seen as parts of the right of ownership, a fragmented system resulted. The right of ownership was recognised but not in its Roman unitary and absolute form. Only from the fifteenth century on, through the works of Apel and Donellus, were property rights seen as different from personal rights and the right of ownership was considered distinct from the other property rights.[359]

4.5. *Summary*

The renewed study of Roman law led to the development of modern concepts of ownership and property rights other than ownership, or *iura in re aliena*. The concept of *dominium* as it was defined by Bartolus, although he might not necessarily have been the first, gained influence and resulted in a breach with the Roman

[353] Feenstra also mentions Donellus, Giphanius, Spiegel, Calvinus and Mynsinger, who in their turn based their work on Apel, Feenstra 1982, p. 114-115.

[354] The Austrian *ABGB*, but also the Dutch *BW*. It was especially Meijers who argued that Hahn's division was the basis for Article 584 of the Old Dutch Civil Code, Meijers 1907, p. 271 *et seq*. On the influence of Hahn's Pentarchy see Feenstra 1982, p. 118.

[355] The work on this is not only of the Humanists, but certainly also of the Glossators and Post-Glossators.

[356] Coing 1985, p. 310-311, 342.

[357] On the rules applying to servitudes see above; 2.4. Other Property Rights. Coing 1985, p. 311 *et seq*.

[358] Coing 1985, p. 347.

[359] However, Feenstra emphasises that the work of Donellus was not generally accepted in his time, Feenstra 1989, p. 117.

unitary concept of ownership.[360] *Dominium* could be understood in a wider sense, including incorporeal objects, but also in a narrow sense, only including corporeal objects. Under the influence of feudal law especially, a division into *dominium directum, utile* and *quasi dominium* was made. Only after the Post-Glossators started to use the concept of *iura realia,* could a distinction of property rights with the right of ownership be made. In the works of Apel in the fifteenth century a clear contrast with personal rights was provided. Donellus then made clear that there was to be a distinction between ownership and rights other than ownership. This opened the way for an investigation into what property rights could be included in the list of rights other than ownership. Of the many authors that searched for the available property rights, Hahn gained the most fame with his Pentarchy of property rights.

5. Natural Law and the French Revolution

5.1. *Introduction*

Now that a new system of private law had been developed, based on the study of Roman law, other schools of thought could develop. Under the influence of the work of Grotius, a new school of thought developed that did not base its reasoning on the *Corpus Iuris Civilis* but on reason, *ratio,* instead. This school of thought, known as the natural law school, had formed part of the study of canon law until the seventeenth century.[361] Natural law focused on reason as opposed to the Roman texts to find authority for law, and it became very influential, especially in the Netherlands where it formed the basis for the Roman-Dutch law.[362]

In 1625 the Dutchman Hugo de Groot, or Grotius, published a book that firmly founded the natural law school of thought.[363] He argued that although Roman law was very useful, the fundamental legal values came from reason and not from the Roman law texts. The justification for the use of Roman law principles was therefore that they formed an excellent example of written reason.[364] These ideas gradually spread through Europe and caused a controversy with the practitioners of the *Ius Commune.*[365] Since the Glossators, the authority of the Roman law had not been questioned and practitioners of the *Ius Commune* saw these fundamental values in

360 Kriechbaum suggests that Ockham might have been the first, although is definition was less technical than Bartolus' definition. Kriechbaum 1996, p. 375 *et seq.*, Villey has also suggested this in his works, on the latter see Schrage 1977, Coing 1953, p. 348 *et seq.*

361 Zwalve 2003, p. 79, 64.

362 On Roman-Dutch law, that still applies in South Africa today see Chapter 7; 3.8. A Legal System Without a *Numerus Clausus*: South African Law.

363 The book is *De iure belli ac pacis*. Grotius is considered by many to be the founder of the modern Natural Law School, see, *inter alia*, Zwalve 2003, p. 79 and Zimmermann 1992, p. 26 *et seq.*

364 Koschaker 1995, p. 242.

365 Zwalve 2003, p. 80.

the text of the *Corpus Iuris* itself.[366] Natural law, although not strong enough to abolish Roman law, questioned its validity.[367]

In practice, *Ius Commune* was applied with all its practical deviations from Roman law, but natural law thinking took over in the work of learned writers. Although natural law scholars had returned to some of the Roman concepts, the feudal system and canon law were still very influential. However, feudal relations were not the same as they had been at the time of the Glossators and Post-Glossators. From the end of the fifteenth century feudal relations became economic in nature. Lords were interested in receiving a yearly sum of money from their vassals instead of services.[368] Furthermore, not all land was held in feudal tenure anymore. These free lands, also known as allodial lands, conflicted with the rule *nulle terre sans seigneur*, or no land without a feudal lord, that had applied in the ages before.[369] Most lands remained under feudal relations, especially because the absolutists kings adhered to the old rules for granting entitlements to land.[370] Although payment of money instead of services was an improvement on the system as it had been before, the feudal relations remained.

Now that natural law had become a learned law, it gained authority in legal theory, and it caused a departure from Roman law principles for the first time in history. At the same time, however, the feudal organisation continued to exist in practice, leaving vassals under feudal tenure having to respect the many feudal privileges of their lords.[371] These feudal privileges and feudal rights could lead to heavy burdens for the vassals. The oppression of vassals by the feudal lords combined with these burdening feudal rights led to discontent that would eventually start a revolution, which in many ways formed the climax of the development towards a unitary concept of ownership and the application of the natural law school's ideas in practice.[372]

The revolution originated in France where the lower class, known as the Third Estate, objected to the way in which they were treated. The Third Estate feared a conspiracy by the aristocrats, that is, the feudal lords, and the king against them.[373] In Paris increased oppression against the Third Estate by both the aristocrats and the king led to the fall of the *Bastille* on 14 July 1789.[374] In the rest of France, peasants, usually vassals, refused to render taxes and other feudal payments, stormed castles and burned the documents on which their feudal obligations rested.[375] The *bourgeoisie* of Paris elected a National Assembly which the king was forced to

366 Koschaker 1995, p. 243.

367 Wieacker 1995, p. 227 *et seq.*

368 However, also old feudal duties remained in existence, Lévy & Castaldo 2002, p. 408.

369 Instead the rule became *nul seigneur sans titre*, Lévy & Castaldo 2002, p. 409.

370 Lévy & Castaldo 2002, p. 409.

371 E.g., hunting rights, Ketelaar 1978, p. 16.

372 In the past the importance of the French Revolution itself has been overestimated. See, *inter alia*, Van den Bergh 1988, p. 51 *et seq.*, Palmer 1959, p. 482, Gordley 1994, p. 459 *et seq.*

373 Palmer focuses on the idea of a feeling of aristocratic conspiracy amongst the Third Estate as a method to understand the whole French Revolution. Palmer 1959, p. 483 *et seq.*

374 Palmer 1959, p. 483.

375 Palmer 1959, p. 483-484.

recognise. This National Assembly took over control of the city of Paris and issued decrees to save what could be saved in the chaos that had resulted from the beginning of the Revolution. On the night of the 4th of August 1789, the National Assembly abolished the feudal system.[376] However, according to the Decree, some feudal rights remained that could only be abolished in exchange for compensation. It was not until 1792 that the remaining privileges and the right to compensation were abolished.[377]

From a legal point of view, the French Revolution marked the turning point from the fragmented system which applied at the time of the *Ius Commune* towards a unitary system of law and of ownership in particular.[378] In this unitary system the sources of law, but also the concepts of law, would become clearer. The right of ownership would become unitary once more.

5.2. *General Principles*

This Chapter has shown that since the (pre-) classical Roman jurists there have been several schools of thought, each of which had their influence on the development of property rights.[379] To the schools that developed during the time the *Ius Commune* applied, this final section adds the natural law school.[380] As mentioned above, the formal study of law became that of the natural law school of thought. This caused a separation between the reality of society and legal theory. With the increased unrest in society, in particular amongst the Third Estate, it was eventually the combination of this unrest with the various schools of thought that led to the French Revolution.

After the French Revolution various schools of thought remained and new schools were even created. However, the period up to the French Revolution was highly relevant in the formation of modern law.[381] It was as a result of this Revolution that the system of property law in Europe was thoroughly reformed. This reform meant the end of the feudal system and introduced a system that would form the basis of most modern codes of civil law.[382] The basis for this reform was found in the writings of the Humanists, scholars who focused on universal human qualities to determine right and wrong, and from that perspective derived rules of law, and who succeeded in questioning the Roman law basis of the law and the

376 The official decree dates a week later: Decree of 11 August 1789 Abolishing the Feudal System.

377 This was done on the 10th August 1792. More will be stated about the abolition of the feudal system below in 5.3. Ownership. Palmer 1970, p. 41-42, Lévy & Castaldo 2002, p. 431.

378 This general unitary nature especially refers to the application of provisions of property law to immovable and movable objects alike. Until the French Revolution, the feudal system had governed immovable objects, whereas movable objects were not included.

379 See above; 2. (Pre-) Classical Roman Law, Codified Roman Law - The *Corpus Iuris Civilis*, and The *Ius Commune*.

380 The other schools are those of the Glossators and Post-Glossators. See above; 4. The *Ius Commune*.

381 See below; 5.3. Ownership.

382 See, *inter alia*, Lokin & Zwalve 1992, p. 156 *et seq.*, Stein 1999, p. 104 *et seq.*

status of Roman law in general.[383] From the work of the Humanists, under the influence of the works of Grotius, the natural law school followed. The discussions of the natural law scholars, although diverse in nature, opened the way for new ideas and the influence of different concepts. The system of Roman law, as it had been received in the *Ius Commune*, had not allowed external influences, for instance, concepts of freedom and unburdened rights, to have effect on the basic concepts of the system.[384]

The desire for a codified civil law is one of the other results of the French Revolution. In the various grievances that the French population brought to Paris at the beginning of the Revolution, many asked for a clear codification of the law. For the common person it had become increasingly difficult to understand what law applied to him or her. Many cases were complicated by the fact that customary law, Roman law and feudal law could all apply.[385] The changes in the property law system, including the right of ownership and the available property rights, that were made as a result of these grievances created legal certainty and formed the basis on which the Civil Codes could be built.

5.3. *Ownership*

5.3.1. Natural Law School

The right of ownership, although still Roman in origin, had been subject to alterations because of the influences of feudal law, canon law, and customary law. The legal scholars of the *Ius Commune* had altered the right of ownership in such a way that the absolute and unitary concept of *dominium* in Roman law no longer existed. Furthermore, because of the influences of the feudal system as the principal form of landholding, it was possible that a vassal would have *dominium utile* in relation to his lord, who had *dominium directum*, and, at the same time, *dominium directum* in relation to his own vassals in case of sub-infeudation.[386]

The natural law school rejected this approach to ownership, but retained some of its *duplex* nature.[387] Nevertheless, the natural law school established a unitary concept of ownership that was distinct from the other property rights.[388] The ideas of the natural law school were not new; natural law existed from the beginning of ancient law.[389] The Catholic Church had continued to use natural law. However, because of the general application of Roman law as a secondary source of law in the

383 Lévy & Castaldo 2002, p. 443, Zwalve 2003, p. 81. On the Humanist school see above; 4.1. Introduction.

384 Instead, it could be held that the system of Roman law had its influences on external factors, such as feudal law. On these influences see Lévy & Castaldo 2002, p. 443, Zwalve 2003, p. 115-116.

385 Lokin & Zwalve 1992, p. 156 *et seq*.

386 Although originally the Glossators opposed to this idea, see above; 4.3. Ownership.

387 Van den Bergh 1988, p. 37.

388 Van den Bergh 1988, p. 37.

389 Wieacker 1995, p. 205.

Ius Commune, there had been no place for natural law.[390] In canon law, natural law theories on ownership had been current since the fifteenth century.[391] In respect to the ownership of the Franciscan Friars, who were not allowed to have any personal belongings, a unitary concept of ownership was developed.[392] These theories on ownership also influenced the Spanish theologians and jurists of the sixteenth century.[393] In all circumstances, natural law remained connected to the law of the Church.

It is in this context that Grotius wrote his works, 'On the Law of War and Peace' and 'An Introduction to Dutch Law'.[394] Grotius distinguished between *ius in rem,* which he named *beheering,* and *ius in personam sive creditum,* which he named *inschuld.*[395] The *ius in rem* he divided into *ius possessionis,* which he named *bezitsrecht,* and *ius dominii vel quasi,* which he named *eigendom.* The last concept denotes ownership, which Grotius further divides into complete ownership and incomplete ownership.[396] Complete ownership means a man is entitled 'to do with an object and to his advantage, anything he pleases which is not forbidden by the law'.[397] 'Incomplete ownership is when there is something missing from this full capacity'.[398] With this distinction Grotius mentions the terms *dominium plenum* and *dominium minus plenum* that were also used by Donellus.[399]

Grotius' concept of full ownership is complete because it awards the absolute power over an object. This natural law approach, focusing on the powers of the owner rather than on the exact contents of the right of ownership, dates back to Aristotle and was commonly used by the canonical, natural law scholars in the time of the Glossators and Post-Glossators.[400] This conception of the right of ownership found its way into the works of the natural law scholars of the sixteenth and seventeenth centuries, including Grotius and Pufendorf.[401]

Incomplete ownership, formulated by Grotius in a negative sense, describes other property rights such as servitudes, usufruct and *emphyteusis,* all of which he

390 Wieacker 1995, p. 206-207.
391 The theories of, *inter alia,* Ockham and Luther, see Wieacker 1995, p. 208-209.
392 The discussion on the Franciscan Friars has also been relevant in relation to the notion of a subjective right and the distinction between ownership and property rights other than ownership. See Van den Bergh 1988, p. 37 *et seq.*
393 Which included, *inter alia,* Molina, Van den Bergh 1988, p. 37-38, Feenstra 1976, p. 270.
394 *De iure belli ac pacis* and *Inleidinge tot de Hollandsche Rechtsgeleerdheid,* Feenstra 1976, p. 270-271.
395 Or *ius reale* and *ius personale.* Feenstra 1976, p. 271, Feenstra 1978, p. 230.
396 Feenstra 1978, p. 231, Feenstra 1989, p. 121. Full or complete ownership is where someone can do with an object as he wishes, within the limits of the law.
397 'Volle is den eigendom waer door iemand met de zake alles mag doen nae sijn geliefte ende t'sijnen bate dat by de wetten onverboden is', De Groot 1926, Book II.3.10, p. 34, Feenstra 1989, p. 119, Feenstra 1978, p. 231.
398 'Gebrecklicke waer aen iet, om zulcs alles to moghen doen, ontbreect', De Groot 1926, Book II.3.11, p. 34, Feenstra 1989, p. 119, Feenstra 1978, p. 231.
399 Feenstra 1978, p. 231.
400 Zwalve 2003, p. 115-116.
401 This approach to the right of ownership would become very influential in the modern codifications, see, *inter alia,* article 544 CC. Zwalve 2003, p. 115-116.

calls *gerechtigheid* or, as it has later been translated, *iura in re aliena*.[402] Grotius explains what he means by incomplete ownership when he describes the situation in which a person has a servitude. In such a case Grotius states that both the owner of the dominant land and the owner of the right of servitude have incomplete ownership. However, the person having the 'greater part' of the ownership is the actual owner; the other has a *gerechtigheid* and is therefore not the owner.[403]

On who would have the greater part of the right of ownership Grotius states in his *Inleidinge*:

> However, to determine which is the greater, which is the lesser share, regard is often paid more to the value than to present profit. Thus, in the case of land held upon hereditary lease the name of owner is given to the person who receives the rent, and who has the right of reversion by virtue of his upper-ownership, and not to the tenant who nevertheless derives the greatest profit from the land.[404]

It seems that Grotius moved towards a unitary and absolute concept of ownership, which he distinguished from rights other than ownership. These rights other than ownership are derived from the right of ownership itself. In this respect Grotius refers to these as incomplete ownership. However, he is not as consistent as it seems at first sight. Feenstra, in his many writings about the work of Grotius, has put forward that in one of the editions Grotius mentioned the term *dominium utile* as a note in the margin when he dealt with a specific form of incomplete ownership.[405]

5.3.2. The French Revolution

In practice the distinction between the different ownership of the lord and the vassal remained. Only in the case of allodial lands was there only one type of ownership at the same time.[406] Furthermore, at the same time many feudal rights and privileges existed that were attached to the feudal relation. In the theory that remained from the scholars of the *Ius Commune*, the *dominium utile* or *dominium minus plenum*, which belonged to the vassal, included the feudal relation and *emphyteusis*.[407] These rights and privileges could be connected to the land on which

402 More will be stated about *gerechtigheden* in the next section. The translation to *iura in re aliena* is not his own. Feenstra 1989, p. 120-121.

403 Feenstra 1989, p. 119, Feenstra 1978, p. 232-233.

404 'Doch om the vinden het meerder ende minder deel zietmen dickmael meer op de waerde als op de baet. Ende daerom noemt men eighenaar van erfpacht-land dien die den erfpacht beurt, ende die 't recht heeft van verval van wegen sijn opper-eigendom: ende niet den erfpachter die nochtans de meeste baet heeft van 't land', De Groot 1926, book II.33.1, Feenstra 1989, p. 120 notes 61 and 62.

405 Although Grotius seems to have deliberately wanted to avoid the structure of the *duplex dominium*. Feenstra 1978, p. 233, Feenstra 1979, p. 26, Feenstra 1989, p. 121.

406 Although the existence of the monarchy complicated the situation. In some theories, the King was also considered as owner of the land, on the basis of which he attempted to raise taxes. Lévy & Castaldo 2002, p. 409 *et seq.*

407 Ketelaar 1978, p. 16 *et seq.*

the vassal was living and which he had inherited, or they could be personal because of the vassal's relation to the lord.

Vassals, especially peasants, had long protested against these feudal rights, including taxes they had to pay, and wanted their land to be free from these burdens.[408] These grievances were recorded in the *cahiers de doléances* and taken to the meeting of the Estates General in Paris. There the peasants, belonging to the Third Estate, were not allowed to sit with the other social classes.[409] After weeks of negotiations the Third Estate, with some followers from the other classes, left the Estates General and established the National Assembly, which they said was the true representative organ of all French people.[410] The National Assembly negotiated with the king and eventually rejected his proposals, which led to the storming of the Bastille in Paris on 14 July 1789. This event created a revolt in the whole of France and the Revolution became a popular movement where previously it had only been an affair for influential lawyers and writers.[411]

As noted above, on 4 August 1789, followed by the Decree of 11 August 1789, the National Assembly 'abolished' the feudal system.[412] The National Assembly declared in the first article of the Decree:

> The National Assembly hereby completely abolishes the feudal system. It decrees that, among the existing rights and dues, both feudal and *censuel*, all those originating in or representing real or personal serfdom shall be abolished without indemnification. All other dues are declared redeemable, the terms and mode of redemption to be fixed by the National Assembly. Those of the said dues which are not extinguished by this decree shall continue to be collected until indemnification shall take place.[413]

The distinction between feudal rights that were abolished without compensation and those that remained until compensation had been paid had been created by the Decree but was left to be 'fixed by the National Assembly'. The rights which were abolished included serfdom, exclusive hunting rights, most tithes, manorial court rights and pecuniary privileges.[414] In order to create a system of compensation for the remaining rights, a special committee, the *Comité de féodalité,* was established.[415]

408 Palmer 1959, p. 482.
409 Palmer 1959, p. 480.
410 Palmer 1959, p. 480-481.
411 Palmer 1959, p. 482.
412 'L'Assemblée Nationale détruit entièrement le régime féodal', Ketelaar 1978, p. 16, Palmer 1970, p. 42, Lokin & Zwalve 1992, p. 158, Chabas 1994, No. 1299, p. 12.
413 'L'Assemblée Nationale détruit entièrement le régime féodal et décrète que tous les droits et devoirs, tant féodaux que censuels, ceux que tiennent à la mainmorte réelle ou personnelle et à la servitude personnelle et ceux qui les représentent, sont abolis sans indemnité; tous les autres sont déclarés rachetables et les prix et le mode de rachat seront fixés par l'Assemblée Nationale. Ceux desdits droits qui ne sont pas supprimés continueront néanmoins à être perçus jusqu'au remboursement'. Decree of 11 August 1789 Abolishing the Feudal System, Article I. English translation from H. Robinson, ed., *Readings in European History,* vol. 2 (Boston, 1906), p. 404-409, French text from Ketelaar 1978, p. 16.
414 Decree of 11 August 1789 Abolishing the Feudal System, Arts. III, IV, V, IX and XI, Lévy & Castaldo 2002, p. 433.
415 Ketelaar 1978, p. 16.

The *Comité* dealt with the distinction between abolished rights and redeemable rights and distinguished, based on origin, between personal rights and property rights.[416] The personal rights were considered to have their basis in the feudal structure and fell in the category *la féodalité dominante*. Property rights were considered rights that had been created by agreement between the lord and the vassal and were therefore *féodalité contractante*.[417]

The category of *féodalité dominante* was abolished without compensation. The category of *féodalité contractante* was redeemable. However, when it could be established that the right originated in feudal oppression, it could be abolished without compensation. A Decree of 3 May 1790 organised the 'sale' of these rights. The result was very unsatisfactory since the prices were high and the proof demanded was often impossible to provide.[418] On 25 August 1792 the burden of proof was shifted from the formal vassals to the lords. The maxim of *nulle terre sans seigneur* was abolished and all land was considered allodial unless proven otherwise.[419]

In a final Decree of 17 July 1793 the National Assembly abolished all remaining feudal rights without a right of compensation. Only normal, non-feudal, property relations were to remain.[420] With these three Decrees the National Assembly had eventually effectively abolished the feudal system. All land was now officially considered free and without feudal burdens. The situation before the Revolution now became referred to as the *ancien régime*.

Compared with the situation before the *ancien régime* the true ownership was now with the vassal who before had always used and benefited from the land under feudal obligations. However, until the late seventeenth century the majority of opinions still considered *dominium directum* to be the actual ownership.[421] The result of the French Revolution was that now *dominium utile* remained as the only form of ownership.[422] When a non-feudal right had been established on that ownership, it could not be ownership and must consequently be another property right.

5.4. *Other Property Rights*

5.4.1. Natural Law School

Although Grotius was not the first to distinguish property rights other than ownership from the right of ownership itself, he has been very influential. In the theory of Grotius these rights were incomplete ownership, specifically *gerechtigheden*. These *gerechtigheden* included the property rights which had been recognised throughout

416 *Droits personnels* and *droits réels*, Ketelaar 1978, p. 18, Lévy & Castaldo 2002, p. 432.

417 Ketelaar 1978, p. 18, Lévy & Castaldo 2002, p. 432 *et seq.*

418 Sometimes the price was up to 50 times the annual rent. Lévy & Castaldo 2002, p. 433-434.

419 Lévy & Castaldo 2002, p. 434, Ketelaar 1978, p. 18.

420 Lévy & Castaldo 2002, p. 434, Ketelaar 1978, p. 19.

421 Compare Grotius who awarded the *dominus directum* actual ownership where the holder of an *emphyteusis*, which he referred to as holder of the *dominium utile*, would have a *gerechtigheid*.

422 See, *inter alia*, Chabas 1994, No. 1299, p. 12.

the *Ius Commune*. Grotius invented a general term for property rights other than servitudes. This term, *tocht*, includes usufruct, *emphyteusis* and feudal tenure.[423] In fact, the term *tocht* was further divided into *lijftocht*, meaning usufruct, and *erftocht*, including *emphyteusis* and feudal tenure.[424]

Although Grotius was clearly a natural lawyer, he followed the contents of the Roman rights. He distinguishes urban praedial servitudes, which he named *huisdienstbaerheden*, and rustic praedial servitudes, which he named *velddienstbaerheden*, and gives examples for each of them, although he does not state that he uses a limited list of examples.[425] However, from these examples general requirements for servitudes can be deducted, as was done with the servitudes in Roman law.[426] In case of *tocht*, Grotius also follows the Roman law *Ius Commune* categorisation and systematisation.[427]

In the final part of the property law section of his *Inleidinge*, Grotius deals with privileged rights and pledge, which he named *onderzettinge*.[428] He recognised that these rights can come into existence either by agreement or by operation of law, recognising the legal hypothecs from Roman law. Furthermore, he also recognised the possessory and non-possessory pledge, though not using the distinction between the terms pledge and hypothec.[429] However, in between the parts on *tocht* mentioned already and the part on *onderzettinge*, Grotius deals with other property rights included in his definition of *tocht*.[430] These include tithes and use, which he translates as *ius decimarum* and *usus*. Furthermore he also deals with the right to tax and the right of *superficies*, which he translates as *census* and *Ius superficiarum*.[431] The works of Grotius show that natural law leaned very much on Roman law as far as substance was concerned. The system as such, although not new in content, is clearly formulated, making it different from the attempts made before.[432] By

423 De Groot 1926, Book II.38.5, '*Tocht* is een gerechtheid om de vruchten van eens anders zaeck te trecken zonder des zaecks vermindering' *Tocht* is a right to take the fruits of another's object without impairing the object itself. Feenstra 1989, p. 121 note 71 (Translation by Feenstra).

424 Personal *tocht* and hereditary *tocht* (own translation), Feenstra 1978, p. 234.

425 De Groot 1926, Book II.34, p. 93 'Wy sullen tot naerder verklaringhe de gebruickelickste huisdienstbaerheden vermanen ...' (In order to explain we shall mention the most common servitudes).

426 The rules on the creation and loss of servitudes also explain some general requirements. De Groot 1926, Book II.36-37, p. 96-97.

427 De Groot 1926, Book II.38 *et seq*, p. 97 *et seq*.

428 De Groot 1926, Book II.48, p. 116-119.

429 De Groot 1926, Book II.48.26, p. 118-119.

430 De Groot 1926, Book II.44-47, p. 111-116.

431 De Groot 1926, Book II.46, p. 114.

432 Feenstra has emphasised that the system was not as clear as it seems at first sight. When dealing with the contracts of *pignus* and *emphyteusis* Grotius refers back to the property law aspects of these contracts as incomplete ownership, the term he earlier substituted with *gerechtigheid* Feenstra 1989, p. 122, note 77, in this article Feenstra corrects his earlier statements about the system of Grotius. The text Feenstra refers to is De Groot 1926, Book III.8.2, p. 140.

following the earlier distinction by Donellus between *dominium* and *iura in re aliena* the fundamental distinction eventually found its way into modern law.[433]

5.4.2. The French Revolution

In feudal relations the distinction between *dominium directum* and *dominium utile* remained, although some changes in the feudal system improved the position of the vassal. The French Revolution abolished the feudal system and, later, the feudal rights and privileges that were once connected to the abolished feudal relations. However, the abolition of feudal rights did not take effect against property relations which were not feudal in origin. Each of the Decrees abolishing feudal rights was strictly limited to feudal rights only.[434]

Other property rights, such as tithes and ground rent, had feudal characteristics and posed a problem to the legislature. These rights provided a substantial income to either the clergy or the owners of large properties, both represented in the legislative assembly.[435] However, based on the same principle that had abandoned feudal rights, each property right that had a feudal character would be abolished, either with or without compensation.[436] In principle all property rights with a feudal character would be abolished without compensation, only those rights which served a purpose for society, such as the ecclesiastical tithes, would continue to exist, but could, in exchange for a certain payment, be abolished.[437]

Many of these rights from the *ancien régime* remained in existence until the twentieth century and courts have been confronted with them long after the French Revolution.[438] These rights were considered property rights *sui generis* without any feudal origin. What remained were the Roman property rights to use and for security.[439] Natural law influences remained and property rights were distinguished from the right of ownership. The system as it had been created by the French Revolution with a unitary and absolute concept of ownership and property rights other than ownership would form the basis for many civil law systems.[440]

433 Grotius' system had a larger impact on private law than did Donellus' because of the influence his writings have had in the 18th and 19th century. Feenstra 1989, p. 122.

434 Lévy & Castaldo 2002, p. 431 *et seq*.

435 Lévy & Castaldo 2002, p. 434-137.

436 Lévy & Castaldo 2002, p. 435.

437 This on the condition that State and Church were separated and that, in fact, these rights were private rights and no longer public rights. Lévy & Castaldo 2002, p. 435.

438 Lévy & Castaldo 2002, p. 436-437. See e.g. *Req*. 13 February 1834, D.P. 1834.I.218, S.1834.I.205. On this case see Chapter 3; 3. Other Property Rights, and in that same chapter; 5 A *Numerus Clausus* in French Property Law.

439 On this distinction see above; 2.4. Other Property Rights.

440 The German system is based on the same fundamental distinction, but differs in its conception of property rights as part of the right of ownership. In German law property rights exist besides the right of ownership and burden it, but do not form part of the right of ownership itself. See Chapter 4; 3. Other Property Rights and Chapter 7; 2.2. Of Ways to Create a Lesser Property Right.

5.5. *A Numerus Clausus after the French Revolution?*

The achievements of the French Revolution in the area of property law are very important. However, at the same time the French Revolution should also be seen as a result of discussions in the preceding centuries.[441] Not only did the Revolution lead to the abolition of the *duplex dominium*, it also created a system of property rights. The *Comité de féodalité* dealt with all feudal property rights and most other property rights as well, since it had to decide which rights were feudal and which were not. Furthermore, the legislative assembly had to deal with other property rights with feudal characteristics which had to be abolished. The natural law works of Grotius and Pufendorf, but also other natural law scholars as Pothier and Domat, were used to create a new legal system. These developments ended in the draft of the *Code Napoléon*, which would eventually form the *Code Civil*.[442]

As far as the Roman property rights were concerned, Roman law requirements applied to them as much as possible.[443] Therefore, the same reasoning with respect to a *numerus clausus* in Roman law applied to Roman-law inspired property rights after the Revolution.[444] However, there were other property rights, which originated in the French customary law and those remaining non-feudal rights as well. Even more, after the Revolution, law in Europe no longer formed a *Ius Commune*. Instead, each country created its own law, usually with its own Civil Code.[445] The question of a *numerus clausus* of property rights therefore became a question that could only be answered from country to country.

Various new schools of legal thought, usually nationally orientated, now dealt exclusively with national legal problems and no longer founded their reasoning solely on Roman law or the *Ius Commune*. However, each of these schools attempted, with a codification, to prevent a return to the *ancien régime*, when nobody had known exactly what rights existed or on which objects they could not exist. The codifications of law also firmly re-established the difference between personal rights and property rights and only those rights the Civil Codes mentioned as property rights could be property rights.[446]

441 On the influences of Natural law on the theories developed in the French Revolution see Van den Bergh 1988, p. 51 *et seq.*

442 On this development see Chapter 3; 1. Introduction.

443 E.g. a servitude not being a positive obligation and the requirement of two lands in each other's vicinity.

444 On the relevance of Roman law for the principle of *numerus clausus* see above; 2.5. A *Numerus Clausus* in (Pre-) Classical Roman Law?

445 On the development of the codifications in the 18th and 19th Centuries see Lokin & Zwalve 2001, p. 161 *et seq.*, 213 *et seq.*, Zweigert & Kötz 1998, p. 98 *et seq.*, 143 *et seq.*

446 Or property rights mentioned in another codification of law besides the general private law codification. On this *rule* of *numerus clausus* see Chapter 7; 1.3.2. *Numerus Clausus* as a Principle or a Rule?

5.6. *Summary*

The common development of property rights in civil law systems ends with the French Revolution, after which property law became a national affair. Natural law was the final school from the period common to civil law systems to have a major effect on modern legal systems. It clarified the distinction between personal rights and property rights and, within the latter category, the distinction between ownership and rights other than ownership. However, many historical property rights and property-like rights that existed in the *ancien régime* complicated this system. The French Revolution abolished, together with the abolition of the feudal system, some of these rights, but many remained in existence. In order to replace the old structure of landholding, the concept of ownership as a unitary and absolute concept was established, based on the natural law theory of Grotius and Pufendorf.[447] Property rights other than ownership were established as rights taken from the right of ownership itself, burdening it for the duration that they are held by someone else.

6. Conclusion

6.1. *General Summary*

Chapter 1 mentioned the distinction between personal rights and property rights as the basis for the private law systems in both common law and civil law.[448] This second Chapter shows that, in respect to civil law systems, this distinction is a result of the historical development of property rights.[449] The Roman law system did not use a concept of 'right', instead it adhered to a concept of action. These actions protected specific relations between people and were either personal or property actions.

Based on this system of actions, the Roman jurists created criteria to establish which action would apply to which situation. In (pre-) classical Roman law, the action protecting the rights of ownership was the *rei vindicatio*. Although initially this action did not, in fact, vindicate the object, it had the same effect because of the obligation of payment of compensation it imposed on an unlawful acquirer.[450]

447 Van der Bergh remarks that many authors have argued that the concept of ownership the French Revolution created was actually a restoration of the Roman concept of ownership. He states that this is incorrect and this Chapter underlines this thesis: The concept of ownership after the French Revolution was influenced by many discussions during the *Ius Commune* period. There are, of course, still many influences from Roman law in the modern day concept of ownership. Van den Bergh 1988, p. 47-56.

448 See Chapter 1; 1.1. Personal Rights and Property Rights.

449 On the common law origin of this distinction in real and personal actions see Chapter 6; 1.3. Personal Property Law and Land Law.

450 In the same sense in modern English law the tort of conversion allows for damages to be paid in case a third party interferes with the possession of a chattel. See Bridge 2002, p. 52-56.

Based on the action protecting ownership there were actions protecting other property relations; servitude, usufruct, *emphyteusis, superficies*, pledge and hypothec.

The property relations and the system of actions in which they originated were received at the time of the Glossators and Post-Glossators into a system that would be known as the *Ius Commune*. Between the application of Roman law and the beginning of the *Ius Commune*, the system of landholding had become a feudal system with a different set of laws that soon also belonged to the *Ius Commune*. Furthermore, other sources of law which had not existed in the Roman law period were very influential. The legal scholars who received the Roman law into their law adapted some general concepts, including the right of ownership. However, they generally applied Roman law concepts to all other sources of law, including customary law.

The distinction between *dominium directum* and *dominium utile*, and all the property relations that were included in this distinction, remained accepted until the Humanist and natural law school movement. The natural law scholars questioned the Roman origins of the *Ius Commune* distinction since, in Roman law, there had been only one owner, although there had been several types of ownership available depending on the object of ownership. Furthermore, the natural law school, like the Glossators and Post-Glossators, searched for 'rights' instead of actions, but also attempted to create a system of these rights, which they thought was at the foundation of the system of actions.

Before the natural law scholars, the search for a right behind a Roman action had already started. The Glossators, the first scholars of Roman law, had searched for a right behind an action. The Post-Glossators who followed them did the same. The late Post-Glossators or Commentators and the natural law scholars continued the search and formed theories on which property rights were built. However, the distinction between personal rights and property rights is an invention of the Humanist and natural law schools, although it might not have found many followers at that time.

The work of the natural law school has had its implications in the study of law. Roman law, as the exclusive authority of law, was challenged and the system of private law was subsequently revised and refined. The system of Grotius in particular would be very influential. He proposed a distinction between personal rights and property rights at the basis of the system of private law. Furthermore, Grotius proposed an almost unitary concept of ownership, in any case distinct from property rights derived from ownership. However, it would not be until the French Revolution that the actual distinction between *dominium directum* and *utile* was abolished. Where, in the works of Grotius, the *dominium directum* remained to prevail, after the French Revolution the only ownership was the former *dominium utile* of the vassal.[451] In other legal systems the distinction between *dominium*

[451] Some Humanists also put this emphasis on the *dominium utile*, see above; 4.3. Ownership.

directum and *dominium utile* remained in force, but would be abolished in the next century as well.[452]

A property relation has effect against everyone and therefore infringes on the relations of others. It is because of this effect that property relations have been given much attention since the time of (pre-) classical Roman law. The most eminent property relation is ownership. In Roman law ownership was the paramount entitlement to an object. Although multiple types of ownership were recognised, mainly depending on the object of ownership, there could be only one owner of each type at a time.[453] Furthermore, the position of ownership was considered as such that the impairment of it should be minimised in order to provide full enjoyment of property. In other words, there was a unitary-like and absolute concept of ownership.

The alterations made by the Glossators and their successors to the Roman-law inspired right of ownership abandoned its unitary and absolute nature. Instead, a *duplex dominium* was created under which several people could have ownership of the same object at the same time. Ownership therefore became fragmented and relative. The feudal system provides a good illustration of *duplex dominium*.[454] The feudal lord would have *dominium directum* whereas the vassal would have *dominium utile*. The ownership of the vassal could also be *directum* in respect of the relation to a sub-vassal in case of sub-infeudation. It was eventually as a result of the French Revolution that the feudal system was abolished and that a return was made to a unitary and absolute ownership.

6.2. *Conclusion*

The right of ownership remained important throughout the development of property law. Property rights other than the right of ownership were limited in number and content in order to protect the right of ownership. In Roman law this resulted in a limitation of situations in which a proprietary action would apply. By stating criteria for each property action Roman law limited the effect of property relations on the right of ownership and, at the same time, created clarity as to which property relations existed.[455]

I have argued that, with this limitation of the system of actions, a principle of *numerus clausus* of property actions existed which had immediate effect on the content of property relations. Especially when the *Corpus Iuris Civilis* was adopted, the available actions became exclusively those mentioned in a codification of law. Accepting a closed system of property actions explains how, once the Glossators started searching for rights behind the proprietary actions, a closed system of rights resulted. However, that is not to say that in times of the application of the *Ius*

452 E.g., in Germany where a series of very influential articles by Thibaut focused on the un-Roman nature of the *duplex dominium*. Thibaut 1817a, p. 23 *et seq.*, Thibaut 1817b, p. 67 *et seq.*

453 See above; 2.6. Summary.

454 However, the *duplex dominium* also existed in other situations, such as with the rights of *emphyteusis* and *ususfructus*.

455 Although not all people had access to legal documents describing these property actions.

Commune there was a closed list of property rights. Apart from Roman law, the *Ius Commune* comprised feudal law and canon law, all of which applied as secondary sources of law next to the *ius proprium*, the local customary law.

Coing has argued that the system of requirements from Roman law was consistently applied to customary and feudal property rights as well.[456] This opens the possibility for the existence of a *numerus clausus* of property rights in the *Ius Commune* as a whole, but because of the diverse nature of customary law and the various methods in which that customary law allowed for the creation of property rights, such a conclusion cannot be made for the full set of possibly available property rights.

The natural law scholars dealt with the right of ownership and rights other than ownership. In this respect Grotius followed the Humanists Apel and Donellus in their distinction between personal rights and property rights and between ownership and rights other than ownership. Although many ideas and influences in natural law were new, many natural law scholars accepted concepts from Roman law as a basis for their ideas. However, in the legal theory of the natural law scholars, Roman, feudal, canon and customary law and consequently property rights following from these sources remained in existence.

The French Revolution and the consequent abolition of the feudal system clarified the distinction between property rights and personal rights and opened the way for the major Civil Codes of the eighteenth and nineteenth centuries. The abolition of feudal rights and the renewed discussion on which property rights remained and which requirements applied to these property rights once more took the specific nature of property rights into account. The conception of unitary and absolute ownership and the freedom to enjoy such a right of ownership eventually resulted in a limitation of the available property rights that would limit this freedom.

The development of property rights other than the right of ownership shows a parallel with the development of the right of ownership itself. In times when the concept of ownership was unitary and absolute, the legal system restricted the existing property rights in order to limit the effects these rights had on the right of ownership. In times when the concept of ownership was fragmented and relative, many other property rights came into existence and the classification of these rights as a part of the right of ownership was very common. When, because of the French Revolution, a unitary and absolute concept of ownership was re-established, once again the property rights were considered different from the paramount right of ownership and parties were limited in the property relations they could create.

This historical relation between the right of ownership and other property rights is still relevant today.[457] The system that resulted from the development of property rights forms the foundations on which each national civil law system built its property law. Because of the third-party effect as well as the potential limitation

456 Coing 1962, p. 311 *et seq*.

457 See Chapter 7; 1.3. Considering *Numerus Clausus*.

on the right of ownership, the number and content of property rights remain limited, in the same way as property rights have been limited throughout history.

Chapter 3

FRENCH LAW

1. Introduction

Since the introduction of the French Civil Code in 1804, the French legal system has been one of the most influential legal systems in Europe.[1] This was not only because it was one of the first civil codes and because of the expansion of the territory of France under Napoléon Bonaparte, but also because of its contents.[2] Before the French Civil Code was drafted, the system of private law in France was fragmented and different laws applied in different areas. Even when, after the French Revolution, Revolutionary legislators passed law after law abolishing the situation as it had been in the period before the Revolution, the *ancien régime*, the legal system remained fragmented.

In times when the original Roman law applied, most of France had been part of Roman territory. During and after the fall of the Western Roman Empire, Germanic tribes conquered large parts of France.[3] Emperor Justinian attempted to unify the old Roman Empire but was unable to reconquer the territories further from Rome, with the result that the *Corpus Iuris Civilis* did not apply even in the regions of France that had been within the Roman Empire. In the south of France, an earlier codification, the *Codex Theodosianus*, applied.[4] However, the influence of the *Corpus Iuris* was substantial. Even the introduction of Germanic codifications, for example, the *Breviarum Alaricianum*, did not resist the eventual renascence of the study and partial applicability of Roman law.

At the time of the *Ius Commune*, under influence from the Italian school of the Glossators, the *Corpus Iuris Civilis* became the subject of study in the south of

1 Most literature referred to in this chapter will be French literature. However, if an English source was available I have tried to mention it where possible.

2 Zweigert & Kötz 1998, p. 74. The influence of the Civil Code has recently been subject to examination on the occasion of the 200th anniversary of the French Civil Code in 2004. See Chirac 2004.

3 Zweigert & Kötz 1998, p. 75.

4 Zwalve 2003, p. 37.

France.[5] The *Corpus Iuris Civilis* gained force and would soon replace the Germanic codes as a source of law, not because it had been forced on the territory, as had been the case in Italy, but because it became a custom of French lawyers to invoke the *Corpus Iuris Civilis*.[6] In this respect, Roman law was customary law in the south of France. In the north of France, Roman law was mostly absent. There, local Germanic customary law applied.[7] Nevertheless, the study of Roman law also gradually filtered through to the north, but, unlike the south, it never wholly replaced the Germanic customary laws.[8]

In short, French law was mainly composed of customary law. In the south the customary law included the written *Corpus Iuris Civilis*, whereas the northern customs consisted mainly of unwritten Germanic law.[9] Because of this difference, the south became known as the region with the written laws, the *pays de droit écrit*, and the north as the region with the unwritten customary law, the *pays de droit coutumier*.[10] The nature of customary law was therefore different across France. However, at the same time Roman law remained, as it had before, a unifying factor, as Roman law would be invoked where customary law, whether it was written or unwritten, could not or did not provide an answer.[11]

In the tenth and eleventh centuries, the north of France had broken apart in many different territories, each with their own customary laws. The result was that a judge in a court could no longer automatically know the exact content of the customary law, leading to a situation of legal uncertainty.[12] In 1454, in an attempt to solve this uncertainty, King Charles VII ordered the recording of the customary laws in order to achieve an overview of the different laws of his territory. In other countries the renewed application of Roman law pushed customary law into the background, but in France, although the drafting of the written customary laws took longer than expected, the body of texts that eventually resulted would resist the reception of Roman law.[13]

5 Zwalve 2003, p. 37. On these developments in general see Chapter 2.
6 Zweigert & Kötz 1998, p. 75, Zwalve 2003, p. 37, 150.
7 Zweigert & Kötz 1998, p. 75.
8 Zweigert & Kötz 1998, p. 75, Zwalve 2003, p. 38.
9 Zwalve 2003, p. 38, Zweigert & Kötz 1998, p. 88.
10 Zwalve 2003, p. 38, Zweigert & Kötz 1998, p. 75. The distinction is not only one of textbooks: Portalis, one of the members of the Drafting committee of the Code Civil (C.civ) uses the terminology to explain the situation in the South regarding property rights in respect of rivers and other waters. See *Loi relative à la Propriété, présentée le 26 nivose au Corps législatif, par les conseillers d'état* Portalis, Berlier *et* Pelet (de la Lozère), *chargés d'en soutenir la discussion*, in: Recueil des lois composant le code civil, Livre Deuxième. Des Biens et des différent Modifications de la Propriété, 1804, p, 61. See also Demolombe 1870, p. 418.
11 This method is different from the Bartolistic method where customary law was to be interpreted as narrow as possible in order to make way for the application of Roman law, see Chapter 2; 4.4. Other Property Rights. Zweigert & Kötz 1998, p. 76.
12 In order to solve this a procedure known as *enquête par tube* could be followed in which the judge would ask a number of local inhabitants to explain the substance of the customary rule. See Zweigert & Kötz 1998, p. 76.
13 Zweigert & Kötz 1998, p. 76-77.

One of the most famous collections of customary law was the collection of Paris, known as the *Coutume de Paris*, which was published in 1510.[14] Of all the collections of written customary law, the *Coutume de Paris* would become the most influential and would soon be applied everywhere in cases where the local customary law would not provide an answer.[15] The *Coutume de Paris* therefore acquired subsidiary force of law and provided a basis for a common law of France. Because the *Coutume de Paris* was French customary law it would be applied before the rediscovered Roman law.[16] It is in this way that the reception of Roman law in France was different from other countries.[17] However, questions concerning contract law and property law would usually be left to Roman law under the *Coutume*.[18]

French law prior to the French Revolution therefore offered a mixed picture of written law in the south, which comprised Roman law from before the *Corpus Iuris Civilis*, written law in the north, which comprised Germanic customary law and the *Coutume de Paris*, and rediscovered Roman law as a secondary or tertiary source of law. In contrast with other countries, especially Germany, where Roman law would become the unifying force, the subsidiary force of the *Coutume de Paris* would form the basis for the idea of a common French private law.[19]

The French Revolution was the turning point in the unification of the law of France. When, as a result of the Revolution, the feudal system was abolished, many other laws and regulations were also closely examined and, if necessary, abolished.[20] Following the new ideas on freedom of the individual and equality for all, the new French legislature was very effective in abolishing almost anything in respect to property rights that had to do with the *ancien régime*.[21] With respect to property law, anything that could be linked to the feudal system was fiercely opposed and abolished. For example, under the feudal system, only the lawful heir of a feudal fee had been able to receive land by inheritance, and other family members would be left without any part of the inheritance.[22] As a reaction against this rule, the power to donate objects, whether on death by last will, or *inter vivos* by contractual donation in direct line, was abolished. As a result, by operation of the standard rules, each family member became heir and each heir would acquire his or her share of the objects of a deceased instead of only the one having the feudal fee.[23] These, sometimes very radical, changes of law would result in system that became known as intermediary law or *droit intermédiaire*.

14 The version was revised and extended in 1580, Zweigert & Kötz 1998, p. 77, Zwalve 2003, p. 41, 150.
15 Zweigert & Kötz 1998, p. 77-78.
16 Zweigert & Kötz 1998, p. 78.
17 On German law see Chapter 4; 1. Introduction.
18 Zwalve 2003, p. 41-42.
19 On German law see Chapter 4; 1. Introduction.
20 *See Decree of 11 August 1789 Abolishing the Feudal System, in general on the creation of the French Civil Code see Halpérin 1992, p 19 et seq.*
21 Zweigert & Kötz 1998, p. 80-81, Zwalve 2003, p. 84.
22 I.e., these other family members were not recognised as legal heirs.
23 Zweigert & Kötz 1998, p. 81.

During the period of the intermediary law, the work on a code of law for the entire population of France continued. In 1793 Cambacérès presented a first draft for a Civil Code for France that was immediately rejected. A second proposal was made in 1794 but was rejected as well. Cambacérès produced a final draft in 1796 that was still under consideration when Napoléon Bonaparte came to power in 1799.[24] Napoléon did not stop the legislative process, and established a commission of only four persons that would submit a draft for a French Civil Code. In this commission there were two representatives from the *pays de droit coutumier*, Tronchet and Bigot de Préameneu, and two representatives from the *pays de droit écrit*, Maleville and the very influential chairman, Portalis.[25]

Despite the philosophical ideas on individuality, freedom, equality, and enlightenment that were strongly advocated during the Revolution, the property law part of the new Civil Code is very traditional.[26] The commission based its ideas on property law on the work of Pothier from the eighteenth century. Pothier, who was an expert in both Roman law and French customary law, developed his ideas on ownership and property law mainly based on the Roman system.[27] This system of property law included the fundamental distinction between property rights and personal rights, which Pothier called *iura in rem* and *iura ad rem*.[28] The first concerned the right to an object, whereas the latter concerned the right to a performance by another person.[29]

It is this system of two different concepts of rights that would also be at the foundation of the French Civil Code. However, although the law of obligations and the law of property are considered separate areas of French private law, a very strict separation between the law of property and the law of obligations was not imposed, as would later be used in the German Civil Code.[30] Although the French code is based on these two Roman-law inspired types of rights, the influence of Germanic customary law, which mixed the two types of rights, can be seen in the fact that personal rights and therefore the law of obligations facilitate property law and do not form a distinct area of law. In other words, in terms of facilitation of property law, a personal relation is seen as a right to acquire or create a property right. Another term used for personal rights in French law is therefore *droit de créance*.[31]

In the French Civil Code party autonomy would, contrary to the law of property, become the starting point of the law of obligations, in particular the law of contract.[32] The law of property and the law of obligations deal with different types of rights, and these areas of law are dealt with in two different books to express the new system of private law and to prevent a return to the feudal system, in which

24 Gordley 1994, p. 486-487, Zweigert & Kötz 1998, p. 82.
25 Gordley 1994, p. 487, Zweigert & Kötz 1998, p. 82. On Portalis see Derine 1955, p. 53 *et seq.*
26 See Gordley 1994, p. 459 *et seq.*, Bürge 1991, p. 85 *et seq.*
27 Zweigert & Kötz 1998, p. 79.
28 Or in French the *droit réel and the droit personnel.* Pothier 1772, p. 1 *et seq.*, Laurent 1878, p. 92-93.
29 Laurent 1878, p. 92, Malaurie & Aynès 2005, p. 87, Rank-Berenschot 1992, p. 36-40.
30 See also Chapter 4; 1. Introduction.
31 Laurent 1878, p. 93, Zwalve 2003, p. 150, Malaurie & Aynès 2005, p. 88-89.
32 Art. 1134 C.civ, see Hervieu 1981, p. 31-32, Bürge 1991, p. 3, 64.

the law of contract and property had been mixed.[33] The law of property and the law of obligations are therefore separated to some extent in French law, but the system is mixed in comparison with the later German Civil Code.[34]

In French law, therefore, there remains a strong link between these two areas of law. Perhaps the best example of this is provided by the system of transfer of property rights. After the entry into force of the Civil Code, French law adhered to a consensual system of transfer.[35] The result is that, leaving some exceptions aside, a property right in respect of an object is transferred by the conclusion of a contract. At the outset of the system no other requirements than the conclusion of a contract are necessary for an effective transfer.[36]

After some severe complications, the work of the commission resulted in the *Code civil des Français* (C.civ) composed of three books.[37] After an initial preliminary book or *Livre préliminaire,* the first book deals, with the law of persons. The second book deals with the law of property. The third book, which is titled 'Of ways to acquire ownership' or *Des différentes manières dont on acquiert la propriété,* deals with the law of obligations, but also certain aspects of property law, such as prescription.[38]

The spirit of the Revolution can be seen throughout the French Civil Code.[39] In the law of obligations, although created to serve the law of property, the starting point became the freedom of contract in which only limitations by law are allowed insofar as they are absolutely necessary. Article 6 of the Civil Code (C.civ) provides in this respect:[40]

33 See Hervieu 1981, p. 22, Sagaert 2005b, p. 987-989.
34 On the German Civil Code see Chapter 4; 1. Introduction.
35 Art. 1138 C.civ. On consensual transfer systems see Van Vliet 2000, p. 73 *et seq.*, Zweigert & Kötz 1998, p. 92.
36 In case of a transfer of a property right in respect of an immovable object, registration requirements must be fulfilled. Zwalve 2003, p. 151. In later codifications, especially German law, the separation between the law of contract and the law of property is expressed through the adoption of an abstract tradition system of transfer in which a contract is nothing more than the initiating act of a transfer, but without immediate effect in property law. See Van Vliet 2000, p. 31 *et seq.*
37 The *Code civil* was introduced by 36 separate laws on 31 March 1804. On the complications during the draft see Gordley 1994, p. 488-489, Zweigert & Kötz 1998, p. 82-84, Hervieu 1981, p. 27 *et seq.*
38 Moreover, there are also aspects of family law still in the Third Book of the French Civil Code. The French word *propriété* has two meanings. First, the term could be used for objects of property rights, as is done in the title of the third book of the French Civil code. Second the term also denotes the right of ownership. In this study the French term *propriété* will be used to describe the right of ownership. See, *inter alia*, Zweigert & Kötz 1998, p. 91, Terré & Simler 1998, p. 63 *et seq.* Furthermore, after the reforms of property law in March 2006 the Code civil now also includes a fourth book dealing with security rights.
39 Terré & Simler 1998, p. 67, for a more critical view see Gordley 1994, p. 459 *et seq.*
40 Zweigert & Kötz 1998, p. 94. Henceforth, all references to the French Civil Code will take the abbreviations 'C.civ'.

> Laws and statutes that are of public order or morality may not be deviated from by agreement between private parties.[41]

Different from the law of contract, in the law of property the starting point is not party autonomy, but limitations on parties in the creation of property rights. Concepts of property law are therefore defined by the Civil Code and only leave room for party autonomy where the legislator specifically intended this. In respect to property rights French law recognises a unitary concept of ownership as well as several property rights other than ownership.[42] On the right of ownership, Article 543 C.civ states:

> On an object one may have a right of ownership, a mere right of enjoyment or only a right of servitude.[43]

Since its introduction in 1804, the Civil Code has been subject to many additions and alterations by both legislation and case law. Moreover, in certain areas of law, case law has completely taken over from the statutory provisions.[44] In respect to property law there had not been many legislative amendments until 23 March 2006, when the French government reformed the law on securities, both personal and proprietary rights.[45] A commission of several influential French property lawyers, headed by Professor Grimaldi, prepared this reform. Moreover, in 2006 and 2007 the French legislature also reformed aspects of property law in a reform of the law of succession, which mostly concerned the provisions on co-ownership, and the law of trusts, known in French as *fiducie*, which directly affect the right of ownership.

Generally, before the security law reform, French property security law was fragmented over different sources. Parts of it were in the Civil Code, parts in the commercial code, and parts were even developed through case law. The reform was intended to end this fragmentation and provide a clear statutory framework of security rights.[46] Furthermore, the part in the Civil Code dealing with security rights had never been reformed since its introduction in 1804.[47] However, the working method of the French government is very interesting for a civil law system. Instead of following a full legislative procedure, the French government took the preparatory work by the Grimaldi group and published an adapted version of the proposals as an *Ordonnance*, taking effect immediately.[48] The *Ordonnance* changed the

41 Art. 6 C.civ, 'On ne peut déroger, par des conventions particulières, aux lois que intéressent l'ordre public et les bonnes mœurs'.

42 See Crocq 1995, p. 192, Bertrel 1994, p. 751-754, Patault 1989, p. 15, 85-86.

43 Art. 543 C.civ will be dealt with elaborately below in 3. Other Property Rights. Art. 543 C.civ, 'On peut avoir sur les biens, ou in droit de propriété, ou un simple droit de jouissance, ou seulement des services foncier à prétendre'.

44 E.g. the law of delict or tort, Arts. 1382-1386 C.civ. See Zweigert & Kötz 1998, p. 90.

45 Ordonnance No. 2006-346 du 23 Mars 2006 relative aux sûretés, JORF 24 March 2006.

46 Legeais 2006a, p. 320-321.

47 Legeais 2006a, p. 321.

48 Ordonnance No. 2006-346 du 23 Mars 2006 relative aux sûretés, JORF 24 March 2006. For the Grimaldi report, Grimaldi et al. 2003.

last part of the Civil Code completely and both re-introduced old property security rights and introduced new ones.

In addition to the security law reform, on 23 June 2006 the French government promulgated a law amending the law of succession, which entered into force on 1 January 2007.[49] Although this law does not directly deal with property law, the provisions on co-ownership were changed to suit the new law of succession. Finally, on 21 February 2007 a law was promulgated introducing a trust-like device, *fiducie*, into French law.[50] Originally, the *fiducie* had been part of the proposals of the Grimaldi commission working on reforms of security rights, but the *Ordonnance* had not adopted this specific proposal.[51] Instead, after a parliamentary initiative, the law introducing the *fiducie* was finally adopted.[52] Although the *fiducie* is a contract, it has various consequences in property law as it limits the powers of the owner over his object.[53] The adoption of the *fiducie* in French law is remarkable because French law had before mostly resisted all trust-like relations.

This chapter will deal first with the right of ownership and the developments to which this right has been subject from the introduction of the Civil Code. Revolutionary ideas, but especially also the influence of customary law, will become apparent. Secondly, this chapter will deal with property rights other than the right of ownership, known as limited property rights. As this Chapter will show, Article 543 C.civ is not as exhaustive as it seems. Furthermore, the development of French private law has also resulted in the recognition of legal relations that are not recognised as property rights as such, but which closely resemble property relations nonetheless. These relations will be examined as well.[54] Finally, the system of property rights in French law will be examined to see whether French law adheres to a rule of *numerus clausus* of property rights.[55]

2. The Right of Ownership

The concept of ownership in French law finds its basis in one of the most fundamental debates of the eighteenth century. The French Revolution, which caused the abolition of the fragmented ownership from the *ancien régime*, gave rise to a new or at least renewed theory on a unitary approach to ownership.[56] Until this renewed conception of ownership was introduced there were effectively two regimes dealing with ownership. One regime, feudal in nature, dealt with ownership of immovable

49 Loi No. 2006-728 du 23 juin 2006, JORF 24 June 2006.
50 Loi No. 2007-211 du 19 février 2007, JORF 21 February 2007.
51 Grimaldi et al. 2003. On the reason for this see Crocq 2007, p. 1-2. See also below; 2.3. Security Ownership.
52 Senateur M. Philippe Marini, Text No. 178 (2004-2005) deposited at the Senate on 8 February 2005. See <http://www.senat.fr/dossierleg/ppl04-178.html>.
53 See in general Legeais 2006a, p. 510-511.
54 One example of such a legal relation is the right of lease. On these special types of legal relations see below; 4. Borderline Cases in French Property Law. On the right of lease specifically see below; 4.6. Lease.
55 See below; 5. A *Numerus Clausus* in French Property Law?
56 See, *inter alia*, Libchaber 2004, p. 305, Crocq 1995, p. 64 *et seq*.

objects, the other regime, non-feudal in nature, dealt with ownership of movable objects.[57] The changes made after the French Revolution resulted in an approach to ownership that applies to both immovable and movable objects.

The Civil Code does not define the object that can be subject of a property right, but it does make a general distinction. A thing, known in French as a *chose,* can be the object of a property right. In legal French, the object of property rights is known as a *bien,* which can be either immovable or movable.[58] The distinction between *chose* and *bien* is complicated and has in the last few decades become the subject of serious criticism.[59] As Libchaber describes, a *chose* is a thing in real life, a *bien* is a thing in law.[60] It is a person's *biens,* the description of objects in law, that form the content of that person's patrimony, the set of objects and debts of a person, *patrimoine* in French, best described as the set of assets and debts a person has.[61]

The concept of *bien* is divided into immovables, in French known as *immeubles,* and movables, *meubles.* Furthermore, the distinction is complicated by the inclusion of rights.[62] In French legal scholarship a property right in respect of an immovable is considered an immovable object by itself.[63] Moreover, a personal right that entitles to an immovable property rights is also an immovable object itself. Consequently, a property right in respect of a movable is a movable object itself.[64] Finally, personal rights can be also characterised as a *bien,* in as far as they entitle the holder of the right to performance by another person.[65] This includes the recognition of what is known as incorporeal movables.[66] Furthermore, French law recognises groups of objects, which as a group can be the subject of a property right. Such a group can be known as a *fonds de commerce,* or the set of assets of a company. A *fonds de commerce*

57 On the feudal system of land holding see Chapter 2; 4.1. Introduction. Terré & Simler 1998, p, 65, Malaurie & Aynès 2005, p. 109-110, Patault 1983, p. 217-218.

58 Terré & Simler 1998, p. 12 *et seq.*, Carbonnier 2000, p. 84-86.

59 See Carbonnier 2000, p. 80, but especially Libchaber 2004, p. 323 *et seq.*

60 Libchaber states: '... *autant les choses sont du côté du monde réel, autant les biens sont du côté du droit*', Libchaber 2004, p. 324.

61 On the concept of patrimony in French property law see Carbonnier 2000, p. 3 *et seq.* The translation of *patrimoine* into patrimony is not uncontroversial. In English property law, the term patrimony is almost unknown. In the rest of this chapter, and this book, the term patrimony is used to include the set of objects (assets) and debts of a person. English lawyers sometimes also use the term 'estate' for this. However, estate also refers to the proprietary entitlement to land - e.g., an estate in fee simple - and should therefore be avoided to prevent confusion.

62 Arts. 516, 517 and 527 C.civ, Malaurie & Aynès 2005, p. 26 *et seq.* For a short overview of the various immovable and movable objects in French law see Terré & Simler 1998, p. 18 *et seq.*

63 Art. 526 C.civ, Terré & Simler 1998, p. 13.

64 Art. 529 C.civ, Terré & Simler 1998, p. 13.

65 This is a *droit de créance,* Art. 529 C.civ, Terré & Simler 1998, p. 12-13, 36-37.

66 The term incorporeal movable seems a contradiction, but is, because of the wide and technical legal meaning of the concept of *bien,* possible. The prime example is the *fonds de commerce,* which is a set of assets of a company, but also intellectual property rights. Consequently, but exceptionally, an incorporeal immovable is can also exist. See Malaurie & Aynès 2005, p. 29, 33-35.

can comprise immovable and movable but also incorporeal objects and is particularly used as the subject of a property security right.[67]

Because certain parts of French property law only apply to immovables, as some parts only apply to movables, the categorisation of objects remains important. These different parts include rules on transfer and the creation of limited property rights.[68] However, as was stated above, the right of ownership applies to both immovable and movable objects, corporeal and incorporeal. The main reason for making a distinction between immovables and movables is historical. When the Civil Code was drafted, land was the principal type of object, because it represented the most important form of wealth. Therefore, the Civil Code is to a large extent centred around rules on immovable objects. However, in the development of society in the two centuries since the introduction of the Civil Code, movable objects have become just as much, and even more, important. Furthermore, developments in the past decades have also shown an increasing number of incorporeal objects becoming of great value.[69]

French law adheres to a unitary concept of ownership. However, for the purposes of discussion, a distinction can be made between normal ownership, co-ownership, which in French law includes the entitlement to apartments, and security ownership. It should be emphasised that, in theory, because the concept of ownership is unitary, the right remains the same, regardless of its application. However, due to the substantial differences between the law applying to a normal owner, the owner of an apartment, and the owner of a security, these concepts are dealt with in separate paragraphs. The question of whether ownership remains one unitary right that can be applied to all situations, including apartment ownership and security ownership, will be returned to at the end of this chapter.[70]

2.1. *Ownership*

The right of ownership in French law is mainly a private law concept, but is also dealt with as a fundamental right. Approaching the right of ownership as a fundamental right, especially as a constitutional concept, ensures that everyone is capable of owning objects. As a result of the French Revolution the right of ownership therefore became seen as a fundamental right, especially a non-feudal right, suitable for everyone to have.[71] This right did not only find its basis in the Civil Code, but, in a

67 See below; 3.5. Pledge.

68 On limited property rights see below; 3. Other Property Rights, see Chabas 1994, No. 1292, p. 8.

69 In general on this development see Libchaber 2004, p. 297 *et seq.*, in particular p. 329-350, see also Malaurie & Aynès 2005, p. 35-39, 105, Terré & Simler 1998, p. 18-19, 27-29, Chabas 1994, Nos. 1301 *et seq.*, p. 12 *et seq.* The draftsmen of the Civil Code worked with the maxim *res mobilis, res vilis,* which is often referred to in French legal literature.

70 See, *inter alia,* Crocq 1995, p. 192-196. See below; 5. A *Numerus Clausus* in French Property Law?

71 Terré & Simler 1998, p. 65, Malaurie & Aynès 2005, p. 109 *et seq.*, Libchaber 2004, p. 352, Jourdain, Marty & Raynaud 1995, p. 37, Chabas 1994, p. 87, Baudry-Lacantinerie & Chauveau 1905, p. 13, Portalis 1844, p. 209 *et seq.*

constitutional form, also in the 1789 Declaration of Rights of Man and the Citizen, or *Déclaration des droits de l'homme et du citoyen*, which states in Article 2:

> The aim of all political association is the preservation of the natural and imprescriptible rights of man. These rights are liberty, ownership, security, and resistance to oppression.[72]

The declaration further specifies the right of ownership in Article 17:

> Since the right of ownership is an inviolable and sacred right, no one shall be deprived thereof except when necessary for public purposes, that have been determined according to law, shall clearly demand it, but only on condition that the owner shall have been equitably indemnified.[73]

The focus on expropriation, which is the taking of ownership by the state, has led to debate in France on the constitutional nature of the right of ownership. It has been argued that the right of ownership is not just a right dealt with by private law, but is by its nature so important that it deserves constitutional protection. In 1982 the *Conseil Constitutionnel* confirmed this view, based on Articles 2 and 17 of the Declaration of Rights of Man and the Citizen, and upheld the constitutional status of the right of ownership as a fundamental right in French law.[74]

Although the constitutional concept of ownership is very important, the vast majority of the rules on ownership are dealt with in the Civil Code. First and foremost the right of ownership is a private law right and only in relation to the protection of that right against state interference is the constitutional concept relevant. The Civil Code defines the right of ownership in French law in Article 544 C.civ:

> Ownership is the right to enjoy and dispose of an object in the most absolute manner, provided that one does not use it in a manner prohibited by law or regulation.[75]

Of all the property rights a person can have in an object, the right of ownership is considered to be the most complete. This completeness of the right is not only emphasised by the words the 'most absolute manner' in Article 544 C.civ, but also forms the starting point from which French legal scholarship considers the right of

72 Déclaration des droits de l'homme et du citoyen, 26 August 1789. Article 2: 'Le but de toute association politique est la conservation des droits naturels et imprescriptibles de l'homme. Ces droits sont la liberté, la propriété, la sûreté et la résistance à l'oppression'.

73 Art. 17: 'La propriété étant un droit inviolable et sacré, nul ne peut en être privé, si ce n'est lorsque la nécessité publique, légalement constatée, l'exige évidemment, et sous la condition d'une juste et préalable indemnité', see, *inter alia*, Crocq 1995, p. 70.

74 Or *caractère fondamental*, Cons. Const. 16 January 1982 JCP 82.II.19788. See Malaurie & Aynès 2005, p. 112-114, Jourdain, Marty & Raynaud 1995, p. 36.

75 Art. 544 C.civ, 'La propriété est le droit de jouir et disposer des choses de la manière la plus absolue, pourvu qu'on n'en fasse pas un usage prohibé par les lois ou par les règlements'. Translation slightly adapted from Zweigert & Kötz 1998, p. 86.

ownership.[76] The right of ownership as defined by the Civil Code reflects aspects of the definition of Bartolus who stated ownership was 'the right in a corporeal thing to have ... perfectly at one's disposal, unless it is forbidden by law'.[77] The drafters of the definition of ownership in Article 544 C.civ aimed to emphasise the unitary concept of ownership. Especially at the time of drafting the code, a unitary right of ownership made it clear that the new Civil Code rejected fragmented ownership. Furthermore, a unitary right of ownership in the new Civil Code also gave the message that France rejected the feudal system that had been abolished during the Revolution.[78]

At a later stage, in particular at the end of the nineteenth century, the part of the definition of ownership referring to the exercise powers 'in the most absolute manner', came to be interpreted as if ownership was an almost unlimited property right, especially in respect to the powers of the owner.[79] Demolombe, for instance, argued that the powers of the owner were so absolute that an owner could not be restricted in any other way than by law. According to him, these absolute powers included the power to do with the object under ownership whatever the owner desired, including the destruction of the object itself, subject to the limits imposed by law.[80] This 'liberal' approach to property law, the right of ownership in particular, as it was advocated at the end of the nineteenth and at the beginning of the twentieth century played an important role in the creation of the modern doctrinal conception of the right of ownership in French property law.[81]

Modern French legal scholarship recognises three elements of the right of ownership; the right to use, *usus*, the right to enjoy, particularly the fruits, *fruc tus*, and the right of disposal, *abusus*. This division, which is derived from the Glossators, continues to be used to explain the content of the right of ownership and to define property rights other than ownership.[82] Furthermore, it is also these three elements that should be read in the definition of Article 544. The right of ownership is the right to use, to enjoy, and the right to dispose of the object under ownership

76 Terré & Simler 1998, p. 40 (*le droit le plus complet*), Chabas 1994, No. 1294, p. 9 (*Le droit réel le plus parfait*), Atias 2005, p. 53 (*La propriété, par définition, c'est tout*), Jourdain, Marty & Raynaud 1995, p. 32 (*L'expression juridique suprême*).

77 See Chapter 2; 4.3. Ownership, Schrage 1996, p. 43, Carbonnier 2000, p. 128, 133-134, Terré & Simler 1998, p. 64, 93. For a critical review of the true Roman origins of the definition of Art. 544 C.civ see Derine 1955, p. 32 *et seq.*, and a review of Article 625 of the Old Dutch Civil Code see Van den Bergh 1988, p. 39-50.

78 It is in this way that the words 'in the most absolute manner' or *de la manière la plus absolue* should be read. See Huc 1893, p. 96-97, Jourdain, Marty & Raynaud 1995, p. 46, Patault 1983, p. 220-221. On the absolute nature of the right of ownership in French law see, *inter, alia* Terré & Simler 1998, p. 65, Malaurie & Aynès 2005, p. 109 *et seq.*

79 Zachariae, Massé & Vergé 1855, p. 55 *et seq.*, Aubry, Rau, Falcimaigne & Gault 1897, p. 255-256, Baudry-Lacantinerie & Chauveau 1905, p. 152, Demolombe 1870, p. 462 *et seq.*. On these authors see also Bürge 1991, p. 29, 42-43, 55, Crocq 1995, p. 68 *et seq.*

80 Demolombe 1870, p. 464-466, see critically Derine 1955, p. 153-155. See also Pothier 1772, p. 103.

81 See, *inter alia*, Patault 1983, p. 221-237.

82 See below; 3. Other Property Rights. Vareilles-Sommières 1905, 448 *et seq.*, Jourdain, Marty & Raynaud 1995, p. 46.

as well as the right of ownership itself.[83] The right to dispose includes the possibility for the owner to separate parts of his ownership, corresponding to these three elements, to another person in the form of a property right other than ownership, for example, a right of usufruct that includes the right to use and to take the fruits of an object.[84]

Moreover, French legal scholarship approaches the right of ownership, apart from its constitutional status as a fundamental right, by distinguishing three major characteristics. First, the right of ownership is *absolute*, which should first and foremost be seen as a rejection of the feudal system with its fragmented and therefore relative, non-absolute, concept of ownership.[85] Another explanation of the absolute nature of the right of ownership can be found in the intention of the drafters to distinguish the right of ownership from the other property rights they recognised.[86] In the system of the French Civil Code the method to create property rights other than ownership makes use of the right of ownership as a source from which these rights are derived. Because these rights are more restricted in content than the right of ownership, the right of ownership is absolute in the sense of it being the most extensive property right available.[87]

Next to the rejection of fragmented ownership and the distinction of the right of ownership from the other property rights, the absoluteness of the right can also be seen in the unlimited powers of the owner, unlimited at least in principle.[88] However, the last part of Article 544 C.civ allows for the limitation of the powers of the owner. This includes limitations that the drafters of the Civil Code, although influenced by the natural law doctrine of unlimited powers of the owner, had foreseen, but also limitations that have been imposed, particularly by case law, in the course of the nineteenth and twentieth centuries.[89] At the beginning of the nineteenth century, partly under the influence of natural law theories, the 'liberal' view of law was that the individual was considered highly important. In respect of the right of ownership this resulted in a rejection of restrictions on individual ownership. These were seen as an infringement of this basic principle of individual freedom.[90] However, in the second half of the nineteenth century the French legislature, but also the courts, started to impose general restrictions on the powers of the owner. In order to

83 Demolombe 1870, No. 543, p. 462, Jourdain, Marty & Raynaud 1995, p. 47, Terré & Simler 1998, p. 93-98, Malaurie & Aynès 2005, p. 119-121, Carbonnier 2000, p. 128-131, Chabas 1994, p. 84-85.

84 Art. 543 C.civ, see below; 3. Other Property Rights.

85 Terré & Simler 1998, p. 107, Carbonnier 2000, p. 129, critically see Derine 1955, p. 42-43.

86 Derine 1955, p. 42-43.

87 See below; 3. Other Property Rights.

88 Terré & Simler 1998, p. 108, Crocq 1995, p. 77.

89 Terré & Simler 1998, p. 108-109, Chabas 1994, p. 87 *et seq*. Chabas uses the term sovereignty of the owner in this respect. However, the importance of the second part of Article 544 C.civ should not be underestimated. Also in 1804 the drafters of the Civil Code knew and foresaw many exceptions to the sovereignty of the owner. Pothier 1772, p. 14, Portalis 1844, p. 219, see Portalis in Recueil complet des travaux préparatoires du code civil 11, p. 116-117. For an overview see Derine 1955, p. 15-18, 40-43, 90 *et seq*., Patault 1989, p. 273-275.

90 Chabas 1994, p. 88, critically see Derine 1955, p. 14, 67 *et seq*.

achieve this the courts used the doctrine of abuse of rights, known in French as *abus de droit*.[91] The abuse of rights jurisprudence is particularly relevant in the area of the law between neighbours. Damage caused by an act of the owner through use, enjoyment or disposal, with the intention to disadvantage another without any benefit for the object of the owner would now constitute an abuse of the right of ownership and would lead to the obligation to remove or stop the disturbance to the third party and pay damages.[92] Finally, the owner himself can also impose limitations on his powers. An owner is entitled to limit his powers through the creation of a property right, taking part of his right of ownership and transferring this to another person in the form of a property right other than ownership, or by the conclusion of a contract, agreeing not to exercise a certain power for a certain time.[93]

The second characteristic of the right of ownership is that it is an *exclusive* right. Exclusivity indicates that only the owner is entitled to use, enjoy or dispose of his ownership and that the right has an effect *erga omnes*, because the owner can exclude anyone from his right to use, enjoy or dispose of his object.[94] In two situations the powers of the owner are less exclusive. First, when certain powers have been temporarily transferred to another by way of a property right other than ownership.[95] Secondly, when the right of ownership has been transferred under condition or the owner transfers ownership under condition that the owner will not have the full set of exclusive powers.[96]

The third characteristic is that the right of ownership is a *perpetual* right.[97] The right of ownership is intended to last as long as the object on which it is created exists.[98] Because the right of ownership is unitary and absolute, a temporary type of ownership would be in violation of these principles.[99] Furthermore, the right of ownership will remain in existence even when the owner does not use his right. This does not only follow from Article 2 of the Declaration of Rights of Man and the Citizen mentioned above, but also from case law of the *Cour de cassation*.

91 *Req.* 3 August 1915, D.P. 1917. 1. 79, *Cass.* 20 January 1964, D. 1964. 518, but also *Cass.* 30 October 1972, *Bull. civ.* III, No. 576, Chabas 1994, p. 89, Terré & Simler 1998, p. 108-109, Zweigert & Kötz 1998, p. 95, Crocq 1995, p. 77. It should be emphasised that the doctrine of abuse of rights was not new, but merely became applied more after 1855. On this development see Derine 1955, p. 178 *et seq.*

92 The abuse of the right of ownership is a specific category of abuse of right, see *Req.* 3 August 1915, D.P. 1917. 1. 79, Carbonnier 2000, 272-273.

93 Crocq 1995, p. 77-78, on the creation of property rights see below; 3. Other Property Rights and 4.2. Real Obligations.

94 Chabas 1994, p. 81, Malaurie & Aynès 2005, p. 131, Terré & Simler 1998, p. 109.

95 A *démembrement du droit de propriété*, see Malaurie & Aynès 2005, p. 131, Chabas 1994, p. 32. In the same sense see Van Erp 2006b, p. 16-17.

96 See Terré & Simler 1998, p. 110-112.

97 Chabas 1994, p. 103, Malaurie & Aynès 2005, p. 133 *et seq.*, Terré & Simler 1998, p. 114, Jourdain, Marty & Raynaud 1995, p. 59 *et seq.*

98 Chabas 1994, p. 103-104.

99 Malaurie & Aynès 2005, p. 133-134, see also Chabas 1994, p. 106 *et seq.*

In French law, the Civil Code stipulates that all actions, including the action of vindication that protects the right of ownership cease to exist after thirty years.[100] However, in 1905 the *Cour de cassation* held that the claim protecting the right of ownership could not cease to exist, because this would violate the principle of perpetuity of the right of ownership.[101] As a result the rules on prescription remain valid, but no longer apply to the action of vindication of ownership.

These three basic characteristics of the right of ownership form the foundation of the system of property law. Parties are able to deviate from these general characteristics only to a very limited extent. Two of these possibilities to deviate, clauses of non-transferability and clauses of conditional transfer, affect the content of the right of ownership in such a way that they need to be described briefly here.

First, through the use of a non-transferability clause the powers of an owner can be limited. Such a clause can be made in a contract of transfer as well as in a last will.[102] These clauses impose limitations in respect of the power of disposal of the owner and can include a prohibition to transfer in general, as well as a prohibition to transfer partially, or to create other property rights. The validity of such a clause has been problematic. For a long time it was held that a non-transferability clause would violate the general principle of French property law stipulated in Article 537 C.civ:

> Private individuals have the freedom to dispose of objects that belong to them, subject to the modifications established by legislation ...[103]

It is precisely because of this, that the Civil Code of 1804 did not provide rules on non-transferability clauses.[104] Also the courts, still having in mind the *ancien régime*, where non-transferability had been one of the main elements of the feudal system, were very reluctant to allow the use of these clauses. Many courts therefore refused to accept the validity of a non-transferability clause, particularly because these clauses were usually made perpetual.[105]

Based on decisions of the French courts, parties searched for possibilities to include valid non-transferability clauses in their contracts and wills. In 1858 the *Cour de cassation* recognised the validity of a non-transferability clause when the

100 Art. 2262 C.civ states 'Toutes les actions, tant réelles que personnelles, sont prescrites par trente ans, sans que celui qui allègue cette prescription soit obligé d'en rapporter un titre ou qu'on puisse lui opposer l'exception déduite de la mauvaise foi', Malaurie & Aynès 2005, p. 133.

101 *Req.* 12 July 1905, D.P. 1907. 1. 141, Malaurie & Aynès 2005, p. 133-134, Chabas 1994, p. 105, 364 *et seq.*, critically see Carbonnier 2000, p. 143-144.

102 Carbonnier 2000, p. 161-163, Terré & Simler 1998, p. 99. Inalienability can result from the law or from judgements, this section deals with the question whether inalienability can also result from agreement.

103 Art. 537 C.civ states 'Les particuliers ont la libre disposition des biens qui leur appartiennent, sous les modifications établies par les lois ...', see also Terré & Simler 1998, p. 98-99, Malaurie & Aynès 2005, p. 14.

104 Terré & Simler 1998, p. 100.

105 See, *inter alia*, *Civ.*, 6 June 1853, D. 1. 191, on perpetuity issues see *Req.* 20 May 1879, D.P. 79. 1. 431, on the former case see Huc 1893, p. 107, on the latter see Terré & Simler 1998, p. 101.

effect of the clause was limited in time, in other words it was not made perpetually, and the clause was inserted in the interest of the persons who made it.[106] This interest can be both on the side of the transferor as well as the transferee, and even the interest of a third party might justify the validity of a clause.[107] From that moment on, non-transferability clauses were accepted in French law, but not until 1971 did the legislature include provisions in the Civil Code affirming this case law.[108]

The starting point remains that a non-transferability clause is invalid because it violates the characteristics of the right of ownership and the principle of free circulation of objects in France, but it can be allowed if the clause is made for a limited period and pursues a legitimate and serious aim. Article 900-1 C.civ, which was introduced by the 1971 legislation, therefore states:

> Non-transferability clauses concerning an object donated or bequeathed are valid only where they are temporary and justified by a serious and legitimate aim. Even in that case, a donee or legatee may be judicially authorised to dispose of the object if the aim which justified the clause has disappeared or if it happens that a more important interest so requires.[109]

The effect of a valid non-transferability clause is that the owner is limited in his power of disposal. This can include the prohibition to transfer the right of ownership, but also in the prohibition to create a property right in respect of the object, particularly a property security right.[110] However, the effect of a transfer of ownership of an object on which a non-transferability claim was validly created is debated.[111]

It is clear that the effect of a valid non-transferability clause in operation should be that a transfer that contravenes the clause is considered void. Furthermore, French legal scholarship agrees that only that person in whose interest the clause was made should be able to invoke the voidance.[112] The debate centres on the question of how this voidance is achieved. Carbonnier works around the central

106 *Civ.*, 20 April 1858, D.P. 58. 1. 154, S. 58. 1. 589.

107 Terré & Simler 1998, p. 102. *Civ.*, 18 March 1903, D.P. 1905. 1. 126, S. 1905. 1. 513.

108 Loi No. 71-526 du 3 juillet 1971 which inserted Art. 900-1 C.civ.

109 Art. 900-1 C.civ states 'Les clauses d'inaliénabilité affectant un bien donné ou légué ne sont valables que si elles sont temporaires et justifiées par un intérêt sérieux et légitime. Même dans ce cas, le donataire ou le légataire peut être judiciairement autorisé à disposer du bien si l'intérêt qui avait justifié la clause a disparu ou s'il advient qu'un intérêt plus important l'exige', see Terré & Simler 1998, p. 100 *et seq.*, Carbonnier 2000, p. 148 *et seq.*, Jourdain, Marty & Raynaud 1995, p. 75 *et seq.* Furthermore, the *Cour de cassation* has held that a stipulation made for life is temporary, see *Civ.*, 8 January 1975, JCP 1976, II, 18240.

110 Terré & Simler 1998, p. 103. However, a property security right coming into operation by force of law and not by agreement between parties will be able to exist since such a security right comes into existence and exists regardless of the power to dispose of the owner. See Carbonnier 2000, p. 162-163.

111 See Carbonnier 2000, p. 151-153, Terré & Simler 1998, p. 103-105, Jourdain, Marty & Raynaud 1995, p. 75-77, Crocq 1995, p. 200-201.

112 Terré & Simler 1998, p. 104-105, Jourdain, Marty & Raynaud 1995, p. 75-76.

question by stating that case law declares the transfer void.[113] Terré and Simler discuss two possibilities; either the clause leads to legal incapacity of the owner, but this cannot be achieved by contract, or the ownership is transferred without the power of disposal, the *abusus*, by analogy of the creation of limited property rights.[114] Jourdain states that the non-transferability clause limits the power of disposal of the owner.[115] This latter approach is also followed by Crocq and also Terré and Simler end up with this solution and could therefore be considered as the leading opinion.[116]

Secondly, the right of ownership can also be transferred under condition.[117] Such a condition can be twofold. First, the transfer can be a transfer made under a resolutive condition. Such a transfer is only effective until the condition occurs, after which the ownership returns to the original owner.[118] Secondly, the transfer can also be a transfer under condition of suspension. This type only takes effect as a transfer of ownership once the condition has occurred.[119]

In French law a transfer under condition always results in a situation whereby one party becomes an owner under resolutive condition and the other party an owner under condition of suspension.[120] Therefore, the transfer of ownership under condition creates, at least until the moment the condition is fulfilled, a temporary fragmentation of the right of ownership.[121] However, the right of ownership in French law is unitary and absolute and cannot, in principle, be fragmented.[122] The result is that the owner under resolutive condition has the right of ownership with all its characteristics; *usus*, *fructus* and *abusus*.[123] However, the owner under condition of suspension also has a right of ownership, but this ownership, until the condition is fulfilled, lacks the characteristics of *usus* and *fructus*. The owner under condition of suspension, as well as the owner under resolutive condition, will have the power to sell and transfer the ownership, *abusus*, to another person.[124] The ownership under condition of suspension exists, but cannot be used until the condition is fulfilled.[125] However, the transfer has already taken effect, and the fulfilment of the condition will not cause another transfer to occur. Instead, the conditional

113 Carbonnier 2000, p. 152.

114 Terré & Simler 1998, p. 103-104. Against the *démembrement* see Crocq 1995, p. 172. On the creation of property rights see below; 3. Other Property Rights.

115 Jourdain, Marty & Raynaud 1995, p. 75-76.

116 Crocq 1995, p. 166, Terré & Simler 1998, p. 104.

117 Arts. 1168 *et seq*. C.civ.

118 Arts. 1181 and 1182 C.civ.

119 Arts. 1183 and 1184 C.civ, Carbonnier 2000, p. 148-149, Terré & Simler 1998, p. 110-111.

120 Terré & Simler 1998, p. 111, Crocq 1995, p. 194.

121 Or when it becomes clear the condition can no longer be fulfilled, e.g. the cancellation of an event. Terré & Simler 1998, p. 112.

122 After all, a fragmentation of ownership as it existed in the *ancien régime* was rejected with the definition of Article 544 C.civ.

123 An owner under resolutive condition can only dispose of the object within the same limits, i.e., under the same resolutive condition, as the one to which he is subject himself. Terré & Simler 1998, p. 112.

124 Art. 1180 C.civ.

125 Art. 1181 C.civ, Malaurie & Aynès 2005, p. 195-197.

right of one of the parties will grow into the full right of ownership by fulfilment of the condition.[126]

When the condition is fulfilled, the owner under condition of suspension will become owner with retroactive effect. The owner under condition of suspension is considered to have been the owner from the moment of transfer. The owner under resolutive condition loses his ownership with retroactive effect at the same moment and is considered never to have had ownership. The situation of fragmented ownership therefore ends and, because of the retroactive effect, is presumed never to have taken place.[127] A similar situation occurs when it becomes clear that the condition cannot be fulfilled. In that case the owner under resolutive condition becomes the definitive owner and the owner under condition of suspension will be considered never to have held a right of ownership.[128] Again, the legal system assumes that fragmented ownership has never existed.[129]

2.2. *Co-Ownership including Apartments*

The concept of co-ownership or *indivision* in French law is subject to so many additional rules compared with the normal concept of ownership that it deserves to be dealt with in a separate section.[130] The term *indivision* covers a situation where there is more than one person exercising a property right in respect of the same object and to the idea that these rights cannot be completely separated. The concept of *indivision* is very wide and applies also to all objects of property rights; immovable, movable, but also personal and property rights.[131] For the purposes of clarity, insofar as *indivision* concerns the right of ownership, the term co-ownership will be used here.

The difficulty with co-ownership is that a co-owner is also considered to be an owner in the sense of the right of ownership under Article 544 C.civ. The right of a co-owner is absolute and meant to last forever, perpetual, but is, because of the reason for its existence, less exclusive than the normal right of ownership. Because the right of ownership cannot be fragmented, a co-owner will not own a specific part but rather will have a share in a community.[132] The shares together, the community as a whole, will comprise the full ownership in the normal sense of Article 544 C.civ. The shares will entitle their holder to a share in this right of ownership. In a double abstraction, the rights to the share itself are owned in turn. In other words, a co-owner is a person owning a share in a right of ownership on an object or set of

126 This is the *effet déclaratif* or declarative effect.

127 Art. 1179 C.civ, see Malaurie & Aynès 2005, p. 196, Terré & Simler 1998, p. 112-113, Carbonnier 2000, p. 149-150.

128 Malaurie & Aynès 2005, p. 196.

129 Terré & Simler 1998, p. 112-113.

130 It has been argued that the concept of co-ownership is so much different from the concept of ownership that it deserves to be dealt with as a separate property right, see Atias 2005, p. 116-117 and carefully Bayard-Jammes 2003, p. 345-347.

131 Atias 2005, p. 117. The terms *indivision* and *copropriété* are used in a different sense depending on the author using them. See, *inter alia*, Carbonnier 2000, p. 145, Chabas 1994, p. 35.

132 Chabas 1994, p. 35, Carbonnier 2000, p. 144-145.

objects. Consequently, now that ownership of a share in the community of objects can be held, the share of the co-owner can be the subject of a transfer or creation of another property right in the same way as any object under ownership.[133]

Co-ownership therefore brings a tension to the unitary and exclusive nature of the right of ownership, especially in the light of the fragmented ownership in the *ancien régime*. Originally, the Civil Code did not deal with co-ownership except in very exceptional cases.[134] In Article 815 of the Civil Code of 1804 the legislator stated:

> No one may be compelled to remain in a situation of co-ownership; and a separation may always be induced, taking prohibitions and conventions into account. It is possible to delay the separation for a limited period: such an agreement is not binding for longer than five years, but it can be renewed.[135]

Co-ownership was considered a deviation from the normal right of ownership and therefore limited in its application. Furthermore, through the provision in Article 883 C.civ, the division would have retroactive effect, resulting in a situation where the co-ownership never existed.[136] In this respect the same technique is applied as in case of a transfer of ownership under condition, where also a temporary fragmentation of ownership results, but is nevertheless allowed, because it is only temporary.[137]

Besides the co-ownership arising from Article 815 C.civ, which provides rules for a general situation of co-ownership, the Civil Code also recognised a form of co-ownership in Article 1873 C.civ, which was a specific type of co-ownership that came into operation by agreement between parties.[138]

However, under pressure from practice, the courts and, especially, the legislature interfered.[139] Through the statutory reforms the rules on co-ownership were amended and completed with a set of more elaborate rules. After these reforms, which took place in 1976, there were two substantial regimes of co-ownership, the co-ownership governed by law in Articles 815 and following, and the co-ownership arising from agreement in Article 1873 and following.[140] Furthermore, in 2006, when the law of succession was thoroughly reformed, the Articles on co-ownership were

133 Terré & Simler 1998, p. 402.

134 Chabas 1994, p. 36, Malaurie & Aynès 2005, p. 202, Terré & Simler 1998, p. 392.

135 Art. 815 Old C.civ as quoted by Chabas 1994, p. 36. See also Terré & Simler 1998, p. 395. 'Nul ne peut être contraint à demeurer dans l'indivision; et le partage peut toujours être provoqué, nonobstant prohibitions et conventions contraires. On peut cependant convenir de suspendre le partage pendant un temps limité: cette convention ne peut être obligatoire au-delà de cinq ans; mais elle peut être renouvelée'.

136 Chabas 1994, p. 36, Terré & Simler 1998, p. 413-414.

137 On conditional transfers of ownership see above; 2.1. Ownership.

138 See Atias 2005, p. 119, Terré & Simler 1998, p. 424.

139 Loi No. 76-1286 du 31 décembre 1976, later corrected by a law in 1978, Loi No. 78-627 du 10 juin 1978. See Terré & Simler 1998, p. 395-396, Chabas 1994, p. 37, Malaurie & Aynès 2005, p. 202-203.

140 Or the *régime legale* (Arts. 815 *et seq.* C.civ) and the *convention d'indivision* (Arts. 1873 *et seq.* C.civ), Chabas 1994, p. 37, Atias 2005, p. 118-119.

also dealt with.[141] In substance the 2006 reforms, which entered into force on 1 January 2007, simplified the rules of co-ownership but did not change their content to any great extent.[142]

Article 815 C.civ and following provide a general set of rules for situations of co-ownership. The reformed Article 815 C.civ states:[143]

> No one may be compelled to remain in a situation of co-ownership; and a separation may always be induced, unless it was order to remain by judgement or agreement.[144]

The new set of rules that were introduced in 1976 provide a regime in which, although co-ownership is still seen as an exception to the normal type of ownership, either by law or through agreement, a situation of co-ownership can be created.[145] Furthermore these new regulations included rules on the preservation, administration and transfer of the object under co-ownership.[146] As a general rule the co-owners each have the right to use and enjoy, *usus* and *fructus*, the object under co-ownership, but because of the nature of their relation must share the object between them.[147] The co-owners are also bound to each other in respect of the transfer of certain objects from the community. Each co-owner who wishes to sell and transfer his rights in an object under co-ownership must give notice of the details of the transaction to the other co-owners.[148] The other co-owners have a right of pre-emption, or *droit de préemption*, which allows them to decide within a month to buy the object themselves instead of allowing the co-owner to sell and transfer. When the other co-owners use their right of pre-emption, the co-owner will have to co-operate in this transaction.[149] If no notification is made, the co-owners will continue to have an action to nullify the transaction for a period of five years.[150] When no right of pre-emption has been exercised or when only one of the co-owners exercises his right of pre-emption, the object or money received from the transaction will become part of the community of co-owners through substitution.[151]

A situation of co-ownership will normally arise when two or more persons enter into an agreement and the Civil Code specifically accommodates such agreements.[152] A co-ownership agreement must be made in writing before it will have

141 Loi No. 2006-728 du 23 juin 2006.
142 See Delmas Saint-Hilaire 2007, p. 40-48, Blanchard 2006, p. 28.
143 Before the reform Art. 815 CC contained an extra sentence dealing with the temporary nature of a co-ownership regime and the role of party agreement in this.
144 Art. 815 C.civ, 'Nul ne peut être contraint à demeurer dans l'indivision et le partage peut être toujours provoqué, à moins qu'il n'y ait été sursis par jugement ou convention'.
145 Art. 815-1 C.civ, Terré & Simler 1998, p. 397-398.
146 Arts. 815-2 and 815-3 C.civ, Chabas 1994, p. 40-41, Malaurie & Aynès 2005, p. 210-213.
147 Art. 815-9 C.civ, Chabas 1994, p. 42, Malaurie & Aynès 2005, p. 205, 209, Terré & Simler 1998, p. 415-416.
148 Art. 815-14 C.civ.
149 Art. 815-14 C.civ, Terré & Simler 1998, p. 403.
150 Art. 815-16 C.civ, Terré & Simler 1998, p. 403.
151 Terré & Simler 1998, p. 402-403, Malaurie & Aynès 2005, p. 203-204.
152 Arts. 815-1 and 1873-2 C.civ, see Chabas 1994, p. 44, Malaurie & Aynès 2005, p. 201.

any effect in property law.[153] Even though the agreement results in the creation of several co-ownership rights, the agreement itself remains subjected to the law of obligations. In the system of the Civil Code, the general provisions of co-ownership apply, but under Article 815-1 C.civ parties may decide otherwise in their agreement.[154] The best example of this is provided by Article 1873-2 C.civ, which allows the co-owners to remain in co-ownership even when one of the co-owners would like to leave the community of co-owners, which would normally bring the co-ownership regime to an end.[155]

Although Article 815 C.civ no longer provides a maximum duration, Article 1873-3 C.civ provides that an agreement of co-ownership is either made for a limited duration, which cannot be longer than five years, after which it must be renewed, or is made for an unlimited duration.[156] However in the latter situation a separation of the objects may be requested at any time.[157]

Furthermore the parties may appoint one or several administrators, *gérants*, who, on their behalf, will take care of the objects under co-ownership.[158] In the agreement, the co-owners may award the administrator certain powers. These powers are constructed through the technique of a mandate and create rights and obligations on the side of the administrator. Rights include general conservation and administration of the object under co-ownership, duties include the duty to inform the other co-owners.[159] However, for important decisions, for example, the sale and transfer of one of the objects under co-ownership, unanimity of the co-owners remains required.[160]

Apart from an agreement, a situation of co-ownership can also arise by operation of law.[161] The Civil Code mentions several situations of co-ownership, known as forced co-ownership or, in French, *indivision forcée*.[162] In respect of forced co-ownership the Civil Code especially deals with the situation of a wall that is co-owned by two neighbours because the wall is placed exactly on the border between them.[163] Other situations can also give rise to a situation of forced co-ownership.[164] Because a situation of forced co-ownership arises from a factual situation, usually

153 It is a *contrat solennel*, Paris 22 March 1989, D. 1989. I.R. 123. See Chabas 1994, p. 45.

154 Terré & Simler 1998, p. 423-425, Carbonnier 2000, p. 147, Chabas 1994, p. 44.

155 See Terré & Simler 1998, p. 424-425.

156 Art. 1873-3 C.civ, Terré & Simler 1998, p. 426.

157 This rule distinguishes the *convention d'indivision* from a situation of forced co-ownership that lasts forever.

158 Art. 1873-5 C.civ, Terré & Simler 1998, p. 427, Chabas 1994, p. 45.

159 Terré & Simler 1998, p. 429-430.

160 Art. 1873-8 C.civ, Chabas 1994, p. 45.

161 When the division is temporary, it is possible that the co-ownership regime will fall under Art. 815 C.civ as a type of coincidental co-ownership. An example is a co-ownership of object between the heirs in the law of succession. When the co-ownership regime is not temporary a forced co-ownership arises that escapes application of Art. 815 C.civ.

162 Malaurie & Aynès 2005, p. 201, Carbonnier 2000, p. 145.

163 Arts. 653-670 C.civ. Particularly in case of a wall co-ownership is presumed, see Art. 653 C.civ, Chabas 1994, p. 47.

164 This includes trees and other buildings between neighbours, but also a co-ownership of apartments. Chabas 1994, p. 47-48, Terré & Simler 1998, p. 436.

with two pieces of land, forced co-ownership is, contrary to normal types of co-ownership, intended to last for a long time, sometimes even forever.

Most situations of forced co-ownership actually concern the law of neighbours and solve problems between them. However, one specific type of forced co-ownership, the co-ownership of apartments, results in such a special situation that it must be dealt with separately.[165] Co-ownership of apartments combines a forced co-ownership of common parts of a building with an exclusive ownership of private parts of a building.[166]

The Civil Code of 1804 did not contain any rules on co-ownership of apartments and could therefore not form the basis for the co-ownership of apartments as it exists today. Only one Article, 664 C.civ, dealt with the division of costs for construction and reparation in situations of forced co-ownership, which was also used in those very exceptional circumstances where a co-ownership of apartments was needed.[167] However, at the beginning of the twentieth century, the courts were confronted with an increasing demand for rules on co-ownership of apartments, which had not existed at the time of drafting of the Civil Code.[168] Due to this demand, in 1938 the legislature interfered, abolishing Article 664 C.civ and introducing a twofold regime.[169] First, the legislation created a possibility to establish a construction association.[170] The construction association, as a legal person, could have a piece of land in ownership and could construct a building on it, to which the shareholders in the association would be entitled.[171] The construction association legislation was reformed in 1971 to suit the practical application for which the construction association had come to be used.[172] These uses included the construction association established by a commercial developer, could then sell the apartments in a co-ownership regime created after construction.[173] Secondly, whereas the co-ownership of apartments had been a normal type of co-ownership, the 1938 legislation introduced a double-ownership regime in which a right of co-ownership of the common parts of the building was combined with a normal right of ownership for the private part of the building.[174] Furthermore, the creation of a co-owner-

165 See in general Terré & Simler 1998, p. 435 *et seq.*, Malaurie & Aynès 2005, p. 219 *et seq.*, Atias 2005, p. 253 *et seq.*

166 See *Cass.* 21 November 1955, J.C.P. 1955. II. 9004, Terré & Simler 1998, p. 435-436.

167 This was Art. 664 C.civ. These exceptional circumstances existed in the cities of Grenoble and Rennes, see Terré & Simler 1998, p. 437, Chabas 1994, p. 53.

168 Terré & Simler 1998, p. 436-437. This was due to the lack of houses after the destructions of the First World War.

169 Loi du 28 juin 1938, Terré & Simler 1998, p. 437, Terré & Simler 1998, Malaurie & Aynès 2005, p. 219-220, Chabas 1994, p. 53.

170 Or *société de construction.*

171 Terré & Simler 1998, p. 437-438, Malaurie & Aynès 2005, p. 220.

172 Loi No. 71-579 du 16 juillet 1971, Terré & Simler 1998, p. 440.

173 In this way the construction-association was not used for what it was intended in 1938, but merely as a vehicle to achieve a simplified building process after which a division could be made. See Terré & Simler 1998, p. 440.

174 Terré & Simler 1998, p. 438.

ship of apartments would have to be combined with a general agreement creating an association of co-owners that could represent the co-owners.[175]

Even though it improved the legal situation in which co-ownership of apartments could be created, the 1938 legislation left room for much improvement. One of the most important problems with the 1938 regime was that unanimity was required to reach a decision between co-owners. In 1965 the legislature therefore interfered again and updated the co-ownership of apartments regime, replacing the 1938 rules on co-ownership.[176] The new regime left much more party autonomy to the co-owners to create an association of co-owners and transfer powers to that association.[177] Finally, after some fine-tuning in the 1980s and 1990s, the law of co-ownership of apartments became widely used.[178]

After all these reforms, the co-ownership of apartments has become structured in a complex way. It combines a right of co-ownership on common parts of a building with a right of normal ownership on private parts of a building, together with membership of an association as well as with an agreement between the parties known as a regulation.[179] In fact, a building is separated into common parts and private parts and these parts are allocated to the various co-owners. These common parts will be in a situation of forced co-ownership to which each of the parties will have a share proportional to their contribution.[180] Depending on the regulation made by the co-owners the parts that are not used exclusively are considered common.[181]

The co-owners are obliged to make regulations defining their relations.[182] The regulations constitute a special type of multi-party agreement that will not only have effect between the parties but will also have effect against those who contract with the co-owners, for instance, lessees and holders of security rights.[183] Because of this limited third-party effect of the regulations, the parties must remain within the legal framework provided for them. Notwithstanding the other agreements the co-owners make, the regulations have to deal with which parts are common and which are private and how they will use the object under co-ownership, the administration of the object and the way in which they will deal with maintenance and reparation of the common parts.[184]

175 Terré & Simler 1998, p. 438, Chabas 1994, p. 54-55.

176 Loi No. 65-557 du 10 juillet 1965, modified by Loi No. 66-1006 du 28 décembre 1966, Terré & Simler 1998, p. 439, Malaurie & Aynès 2005, p. 220-222, Chabas 1994, p. 56.

177 Terré & Simler 1998, p. 439, Chabas 1994, p. 54-55, 63.

178 Loi No. 85-1470 du 31 décembre 1985, Décret No. 86-768 du 9 juin 1986 and Loi No. 94-624 du 21 juillet 1994, Terré & Simler 1998, p. 439, Chabas 1994, p. 55.

179 Art. 10 Loi du 10 juillet 1965, Chabas 1994, p. 63, Malaurie & Aynès 2005, p. 221-222.

180 Art. 1 Loi du 10 juillet 1965, the shares are not defined and can be dealt with by the regulation. In a forced co-ownership shares are known as *millièmes or tantièmes*, Malaurie & Aynès 2005, p. 222, 224, Chabas 1994, p. 57.

181 *Civ.*, 25 March 1966, Bull. Civ. I. 195, Malaurie & Aynès 2005, p. 222-223, Chabas 1994, p. 61.

182 Art. 10 Loi du 10 juillet 1965, Malaurie & Aynès 2005, p. 232-233.

183 Art. 13 Loi du 10 juillet 1965, Malaurie & Aynès 2005, p. 232-233.

184 Art. 8 Loi du 10 juillet 1965, Malaurie & Aynès 2005, p. 233.

Furthermore, the co-owners, by nature of their community, form an association or *syndicat*.[185] This association is used to administer the common parts of the object under co-ownership. Within this association the co-owners must meet at least once a year to decide, by a majority or unanimously depending on the decision they are making, on the administration and management of the common parts.[186] With regard to the management the co-owners appoint a manager, or *syndic,* who, with a mandate from the co-owners, manages the day-to-day business of the association in general.[187] This manager can be one of the co-owners, but can also be a third party paid by the association. Finally, in very complicated co-ownership regimes, a certain part of the co-owners may also form a council or *conseil syndicat* which will support the manager in the day-to-day affairs and function as an intermediary between the manager and the general association of co-owners.[188]

With its complex composition the right of co-ownership of apartments is a unique combination of rights.[189] Its exact legal nature has been the subject of debate in the past and varied from a dualistic approach, combining normal ownership with co-ownership, to a unitary approach.[190] The unitary approach that considers the entitlement to apartments as a special type of co-ownership may be considered the leading opinion.[191] In this view, the exclusive part of the right of co-ownership of apartments should be seen as an exclusive right to use the air of a certain space between the walls, ceiling and floor, which are, in their turn, co-owned.[192]

2.3. *Security Ownership*

The right of ownership is not only used as the paramount entitlement to use and enjoy an object, the *usus* and *fructus,* but can also be used as security for a certain performance by a debtor. In this respect the owner makes use of his power of disposal of the right, the element of *abusus,* to limit the powers of the creditor.[193] The use of the right of ownership for security purposes can be twofold. First the right of ownership can be retained and only transferred upon the performance by the debtor, usually the payment of a sum of money. Secondly, the right of ownership can be transferred to serve as security for the performance by the debtor, usually also payment of a sum of money, and will only be retransferred upon such repayment.

185 Art. 14 Loi du 10 juillet 1965, Malaurie & Aynès 2005, p. 234-235, Chabas 1994, p. 63.

186 Arts. 24-26 Loi du 10 juillet 1965, Malaurie & Aynès 2005, p. 237-238.

187 Malaurie & Aynès 2005, p. 238-240, Chabas 1994, p. 65.

188 Art. 21 Loi du 10 juillet 1965, Malaurie & Aynès 2005, p. 239-240.

189 I.e., a combination of the right of ownership and a right of co-ownership. The right to an apartment constitutes a *bien immeuble,* see Malaurie & Aynès 2005, p. 231-232.

190 For an overview see Chabas 1994, p. 59-61, Malaurie & Aynès 2005, p. 231-232, Terré & Simler 1998, p. 451-454.

191 Chabas 1994, p. 59, Malaurie & Aynès 2005, p. 243-244, Terré & Simler 1998, p. 453, Crocq 1995, p. 80-81.

192 Malaurie & Aynès 2005, p. 231-232, Terré & Simler 1998, p. 521-523. For a similar characterisation of the right of apartment in Dutch law see Van Velten 1989.

193 On the various elements of the right of ownership in French law see above; 2.1. Ownership.

The use of the right of ownership as a security right in French law is complex.[194] The drafters of the Civil Code opted for a unitary concept of ownership and did not foresee this method of using the right of ownership. Part of this structural problem is caused by the general distinction made between principal and accessory property rights.[195] The right of ownership is perceived as a principal property right, whereas security rights are considered accessory rights. The structure of property law in the Civil Code therefore did not include any provisions on security rights and only deals with principal property rights.[196] Nevertheless, over time, the *Cour de cassation* has recognised some security elements in the right of ownership as well. Furthermore, in the 2006 reform of the Civil Code, some of this case law was specifically affirmed by the legislature and included in the Civil Code.[197] Furthermore, in 2007, the introduction of the *fiducie* that can also be used for purposes of security added another security element to the right of ownership.[198]

The reservation of the right of ownership until the payment of a sum of money, usually a purchase price, is known as a *clause de réserve de propriété* or reservation of ownership clause.[199] Until March 2006, the Civil Code did not explicitly mention the possibility of a reservation of ownership.[200] The French Commercial Code recognised the validity and effectiveness of a reservation of ownership in cases of bankruptcy in Articles 121 and 122 of a statute of 25 January 1985.[201] However, long before that statutory recognition, French practice had already developed and recognised the use of the reservation clause.[202] In French law, ownership of a movable object as well as of an immovable object is transferred by the mere conclusion of a contract.[203] This transfer system is known as a consensual transfer system and should be distinguished from the transfer systems in Germany and the Netherlands which follow a *traditio* model, where besides a contract an act in property law is also required to transfer ownership of an object. In French law, the

194 Piedelièvre 2004, p. 187-191, Witz 1981, p. 41 *et seq.*, 141-143, Legeais 1996, p. 326-330.

195 See, *inter alia*, Terré & Simler 1998, p. 40-41, Crocq 1995, p. 59, 87, Simler & Delebecque 2004, p. 308-309. On the distinction see below; 3. Other Property Rights.

196 I.e., Art. 543 C.civ only mentions the rights of ownership, usufruct and servitude. Other property security rights are dealt with by the Civil Code, but not in the second book dealing specifically with property law.

197 Ordonnance No. 2006-346 du 23 mars 2006 relative aux sûretés, JORF 24 mars 2006. Particularly Art. 13 of the Ordonnance, which establishes the accessory character of a reservation of ownership clause.

198 However, see Crocq who has a very critical view on the introduction of the *fiducie* in French law Crocq 2007, p. 1 *et seq.*

199 Legeais 1996, p. 331 *et seq.*, Simler & Delebecque 2004, p. 583 *et seq.*, Campana 2001a, p. 3, Crocq 2006, p. 23-25.

200 This was changed by Article 13 of the Ordonnance of 23 mars 2006, which inserted Arts. 2367-2372 into the Civil Code.

201 Which have now become Art L. 621-122 and L. 621-124 of the French Commercial Code.

202 See *Cass. Req.* 17 July 1895, D.P. 1896, 57, *Cass. Req.* 26 October 1938, D.H. 1939, 84. Huc 1893, p. 107, Crocq 1995, p. 39-40.

203 For the transfer of immovable objects additional requirements must be fulfilled in order for the transfer to take effect against third parties. In general on the transfer system in French property law see Van Vliet 2000, p. 73 *et seq.*

conclusion of a contract of sale makes the ownership pass from the seller to the buyer. However, the inclusion of a reservation of ownership clause can suspend this property effect until the purchase price has been paid, both in case of movables and immovables.[204]

Although the reservation of ownership clause was recognised from the nineteenth century onwards, its effect has been the subject of much debate.[205] The *Cour de cassation* has moved in its jurisprudence from the refusal of effect against third parties, in 1895, to the recognition of such effect in 1938. In 1980 the legislature interfered and firmly established the effect of the reservation clause against third parties, including other creditors of the debtor, in a situation of bankruptcy of the debtor.[206] From the 1980s onwards, the use of the reservation clause has only increased, making it one of the most suitable security devices for a seller.[207]

Another interesting debate dealt with the exact legal nature of the reservation clause.[208] Because of the nature of the French system of transfer of ownership, this aspect of the debate is almost purely on contract law. One of the questions in this debate is whether the reservation clause is part of the contract of sale. When this would be the case, the majority considered that the contract would not exist until the fulfilment of the condition.[209] This point of view is therefore generally rejected.[210] Another option can be found in the separation of the contract of sale and the inclusion of the reservation clause. The reservation clause would then delay the obligation to pay the purchase price and, with that, also delay the effect of the contract and the transfer of the right of ownership.[211] Or, in other words, the property effects of the reservation clause are separated from the contractual effects of the contract of sale.[212]

Finally, another question can be raised on the accessory nature of the reservation clause. This question is highly relevant because in French law all security rights, at least until 2006, were considered accessory rights, which are rights depending on the existence of a claim for performance by a debtor, and not principal property rights.[213] Does the right of ownership, the principal property right *per*

204 Although a reservation clause in case of a sale of immovables is relatively rare. Loi No. 67-3 du 3 janvier 1967, Piedelièvre 2004, p. 191, Crocq 1995, p. 41.

205 On the debate see Crocq 1995, p. 38-40. See *Cass. Req.* 17 July 1895, D.P. 1896, *Cass. Req.* 26 October 1938, D.H. 1939, 84.

206 Loi No. 80-335 du 12 mai 1980, Crocq 1995, p. 39, Legeais 1996, p. 332, Piedelièvre 2004, p. 193, Campana 2001a, p. 3-4. Furthermore, the legislator reformed the requirements for a reservation clause in 1985 by Loi 85-98 du 25 janvier 1985 and in 1994 by Loi 94-475 du 10 juin 1994, see Campana 2001a, p. 4 *et seq.*

207 Legeais 1996, p. 332, Simler & Delebecque 2004, p. 585, Dupichot 2007, p. 5 *et seq.*

208 Simler & Delebecque 2004, p. 584 *et seq.*, Crocq 1995, p. 109 *et seq.*

209 Simler & Delebecque 2004, p. 585, Crocq 1995, p. 109-110.

210 See *Cass. Com.* 1 October 1985, D. 1986, 246.

211 Simler & Delebecque 2004, p. 585, Crocq 1995, p. 115, Campana 2001a, p. 5. It should be emphasised that the contract itself is therefore not under a resolutive condition but the clause itself.

212 In the same sense see Crocq 1995, p. 116.

213 On the distinction between principal and accessory property rights see below; 3. Other Property Rights.

se, that is retained in a reservation of ownership clause become an accessory right? When such a clause is made, the right of ownership of the seller becomes dependent on the payment of the purchase price by the buyer. After the buyer has paid the purchase price in full, the seller automatically loses his right of ownership and the buyer acquires the right of ownership.[214] Not surprisingly, in 1988 the *Cour de cassation* decided on the accessory character of the reservation clause.[215] However, the debate continued and was finally answered by the legislature in the 2006 security rights reform.[216] After the reform Article 2367 C.civ states:

> The ownership of an object can be reserved for security purposes by a reservation of ownership clause which suspends the effect of a contract until the complete performance of the obligation of the other party.
> The right of ownership which is reserved is accessory to the claim for which it serves as security.[217]

Furthermore, the 2006 reform also used the occasion to extend the applicability of the reservation of ownership clauses. Some modifications had already been made in 1985 and in 1994 to extend the scope of the reservation clause. However, the 2006 reform included these extensions in the Civil Code. By way of Article 2370 and 2372 C.civ the reservation of ownership also includes a possibility for real subrogation.[218] This inclusion creates an extended reservation of ownership, under which the reservation clause also envisages a situation in which the object to which the reservation clause applies is incorporated into another object, as well as to the price that is received if the object is sold or to the insurance remuneration in case the object is destroyed.[219] Particularly when the object under reservation of ownership is incorporated into another object and that object can still be separated, the right of

214 See Crocq 1995, p. 59-60.

215 *Cass. Com.* 15 mars 1988, Bull. Civ. IV, 106, D. 1988, 330. See Campana 2001a, p. 6, Piedelièvre 2004, p. 191.

216 See Crocq 2006, p. 23-25. Crocq even considers that the right of security ownership is an element of the claim which performance is secured, because, according to him, only the fulfilment of that claim can lead to fulfilment of the security arrangement.

217 Article 2367 C.civ 'La propriété d'un bien peut être retenue en garantie par l'effet d'une clause de réserve de propriété que suspend l'effet translatif d'un contrat jusqu'au complet paiement de l'obligation que en constitue la contrepartie. La propriété ainsi réservée est l'accessoire de la créance dont elle garantit le paiement'.

218 Before the reform, this possibility also existed, but was not included in the Civil Code. See the report accompanying the *Ordonnance* of 23 March 2006. Rapport au Président de la République relatif à l'ordonnance No. 2006-346 du 23 mars 2006 relative aux sûretés, JORF 24 mars 2006, Para. 1.2.2.4. Crocq 2006, p. 23-25.

219 Art. 2370 C.civ 'L'incorporation d'un meuble faisant l'objet d'une réserve de propriété à un autre bien ne fait pas obstacle aux droits du créancier lorsque ces biens peuvent être séparés sans subir de dommage' and Art. 2372 C.civ 'Le droit de propriété se reporte sur la créance du débiteur à l'égard du sous-acquéreur ou sur l'indemnité d'assurance subrogée au bien'. The incorporated object had already been recognised in the 1994 legislation and the extension to the purchase price had been introduced in 1985, see Campana 2001a, p. 10, Dupichot 2007, p. 5 *et seq.*

ownership over that object is not lost.[220] Because of the accessory nature of the reservation of ownership, the right of ownership of the object will continue to exist until the condition that was agreed upon is fulfilled.[221]

Secondly, the *credit-bail* or financial lease agreement is a contract by which a financial institution, on the instruction of a person or a company, buys or creates an object, movable or immovable, and leases the object to that person or company.[222] In French law, like in other civil law systems, the right of lease is a personal right only.[223] Although the financial institution becomes the owner of the object it acquired or constructed, through the contract most of the prerogatives of the right of ownership are 'transferred' to the lessee.[224] Furthermore, the contract will contain a promise of sale at the end of the lease.[225] The lessee will therefore have, if specifically agreed upon, the option to buy the object and the end of the lease, but may also decide to continue the lease or renounce it without buying and acquiring the object.[226]

The lease agreement uses the right of ownership for security purposes, but, like the reservation of ownership clause, this security application is not the sole purpose for the existence of the transaction.[227] The reservation of ownership clause is part of a sale and the lease agreement is primarily intended for financing purposes. However, the right of ownership is used to encourage the debtor to pay.

Other devices exist which are solely based on the provision of security. French legal scholarship therefore distinguishes between these first two types of security applications of the right of ownership, the reservation of ownership and financial lease agreements, and those which are only intended on the provision of security. These latter transactions are known as devices for security purposes.[228]

The primary example of this second category is the transfer of ownership for security purposes. Until 2006, this technique, known in Roman law as the *fiducia cum creditore*, was unknown to French law as a general security device.[229] The primary reason for the refusal to accept or recognise such a security rule was found

220 Critically on this subject see Crocq 2006, p. 23-24.

221 Normally this will be the payment of the purchase price. Furthermore, the right of ownership will also cease to exist when the object to which it applies can no longer be separated from another object into which it is incorporated.

222 Also a *fonds de commerce* can be subject of a *credit-bail*, Loi No. 86-12 du 6 janvier 1986. See Witz 1981, p. 143, Legeais 1996, p. 334, Piedelièvre 2004, p. 193.

223 However, also in civil law systems leases have some property characteristics. On French law see below; 4.6. Lease.

224 This 'transfer' is not a transfer within the meaning of a transfer of ownership or a transfer of parts of the right of ownership so that a limited property rights comes into existence. Legeais 1996, p. 334.

225 Crocq 1995, p. 43.

226 Piedelièvre 2004, p. 193.

227 See, *inter alia*, Legeais 1996, p. 334-335, Crocq 1995, p. 43-47 and 33-34.

228 Or transferts de propriété réalises à seule fin de garantie, see Legeais 1996, p. 335, or les propriétés-garanties fiduciaires, see Crocq 1995, p. 23.

229 See Witz 1981, p. 41 *et seq.*, Simler & Delebecque 2004, p. 537-538. On the Roman law concept of *fiducia cum creditore* see Chapter 2; 2.4. Other Property Rights.

in the protection of third parties due to the lack of publicity of such a transfer.[230] Particularly the prohibition of the *lex commissoria*, as it was known in Roman law, known in French law as the *pacte commissoire*, was used as the primary reason to refuse a transfer of ownership for security purposes.[231] Under the *lex commissoria* a creditor could be allowed to keep the object serving as security for him in case of non-payment of the debt. This practice was already prohibited in Roman law and its prohibition was considered one of the defining elements of French law.[232]

Nevertheless, French law knows specific situations in which a transfer for security purposes is allowed. First, in 1967, the legislature introduced the possibility for banks or financial institutions to conclude a contract with another bank or financial institution, creating a debt for the first bank or financial institution while at the same time securing that debt with a transfer of the claim the bank or financial institution had outstanding.[233] The agreement would specifically entitle the creditor to execute the claims and receive the money in case of non-payment. In case the claims needed to be re-transferred to the debtor, the claims could be transferred in total by drafting a list.[234] In this method of providing security, the right of ownership of claims was used to secure the payment of the debt created by the contract between banks and financial institutions.[235]

From the very beginning of these transactions the nature of the right of ownership, especially whether the right of ownership was security ownership or normal ownership, was debated.[236] However, it was not until 1981 that the legislature specifically introduced the transfer of claims for security purposes, including the effect of such a transfer against third parties.[237] This transaction became known as *cession Dailly*, after the name of the law, and enables a debtor, acting in his professional capacity, to transfer multiple claims with one single list, or to subject multiple claims to a right of pledge with one single list.[238] The transfer that takes place with

230 On the recognition issues see specifically Witz 1981, p. 203-204. Witz deals with two cases on the recognition of respectively a Dutch and a German ownership for security purposes; both which were fiercely rejected: *Cass. Req.* 24 mai 1933, D.H. 1933, 378, *Cass.* 8 juillet 1969, J.C.P. 1970, II, 16182. Simler & Delebecque 2004, p. 537-538, Witz 1981, p. 204-206.

231 See, *inter alia*, *Cass.* 8 juillet 1969, J.C.P. 1970, II, 16182, Legeais 1996, p. 336. On the *lex commissoria* and its prohibition in Roman law see Chapter 2; 2.4. Other Property Rights. The prohibition of the *lex commissoria* in the Civil Code, Article 2078 C.civ, was abolished by Article 11 of Ordonnance No. 2006-346 du 23 mars 2006.

232 However, as from 2006 a *pacte commissoire* has become allowed, see Simler 2006, p. 597-600, Legeais 2006a, p. 357-358.

233 Ordonnance No. 67-838 du 28 septembre 1967, specifically Art. 4 (the Ordonnance was later almost fully repealed by Loi No. 81-1 du 2 janvier 1981 (Loi Dailly)), Witz 1981, p. 170-173, Crocq 1995, p. 27.

234 Or a transfer *sur bordereau*. Article 14, Ordonnance du 28 septembre 1967, Witz 1981, p. 172-173, Campana 2001b, p. 43.

235 The Ordonnance itself did not specifically deal with the re-transfer. Witz 1981, p. 173.

236 See Witz 1981, p. 172.

237 Now Art. L313-27 Code Monétaire et Financier, Campana 2001b, p. 43, Legeais 2006a, p. 503.

238 Consumers are excluded from the scope of the transaction. The pledge concerns a *nantissement*. Loi No. 81-1 du 2 janvier 1981 *facilitant le crédit aux entreprises* (Loi Dailly), Art. L313-23 →

the use of the *cession Dailly* can be made for security purposes in which case it must be accompanied by the creation of a debt.[239] The transfer can take place between a company, or a person acting in his professional capacity, not as a consumer, and a bank or financial institution.[240] The claims transferred are therefore claims a company or a person in his professional capacity has outstanding in the course of his business.[241] Any rights that are accessory to these claims will transfer with the claim, including reservation of ownership clauses and rights of hypothec.[242]

The moment the contract of transfer is concluded the transfer takes effect, not only between the debtor and creditor, but also against third parties, without any other formalities.[243] A *cession Dailly* is therefore not registered and could be seen as an undisclosed transaction.[244] The result of this lack of registration is that the debtors of the claims that have been transferred for security purposes are unaware of the transfer. The payment of the claim they have outstanding will therefore be made to the creditor of the claim, the debtor of the *cession Dailly*. In order to solve the problem arising from this, that of the creditor receiving the payment of the claims that he no longer owns because the ownership of the claim is transferred for security purposes, any such payment the debtor of the *cession Dailly* will receive as a mandatory for the creditor. After notification of the transaction to the debtor of the transferred claims, payment can only be made to the creditor of the *cession Dailly*.[245]

Furthermore, other transfers for security purposes exist, but usually only in case of professional transactions.[246] These security transfers include the *opérations de pension* and repurchase agreements. The *opération de pension* allows a bank or financial institution to transfer claims or equities to another bank or institution in order to obtain an advance of funds.[247] The transaction is created by contract and includes an agreement on the purchase price as well as the re-purchase price at the end of the transaction. The difference between the two purchase prices is the profit for the

Code Monétaire et Financier, Legeais 1996, p. 336, Crocq 1995, p. 27, Campana 2001b, p. 45, Legeais 2006a, p. 377.

239 A transfer for security purposes is known as a *transfert* (or *cession*) *à titre garantie*, see Campana 2001b, p. 43, Simler & Delebecque 2004, p. 541. See Art. L313-24 Code Monétaire et Financier.

240 Crocq 1995, p. 30-31, Campana 2001b, p. 44, Simler & Delebecque 2004, p. 539-541.

241 Or *créances professionelles*, see Campana 2001b, p. 45, Simler & Delebecque 2004, p. 541-542.

242 Art. L313-27 Code Monétaire et Financier. Although multiple rights in respect of the same claim can also lead to problems, see Simler & Delebecque 2004, p. 545. The specific inclusion of the right of hypothec enables securitisation devices. On securitisation in general and mortgage backed security (MBS) in particular see Nasarre-Aznar 2004, p. 8 *et seq.*

243 Art. L313-27 Code Monétaire et Financier, Simler & Delebecque 2004, p. 542.

244 Or *occulte*, see Legeais 1996, p. 336-337.

245 Art. L313-28 Code Monétaire et Financier, Simler & Delebecque 2004, p. 542, Campana 2001b, p. 46.

246 Additionally the implementation of Directive 2002/47/EC of 6 June 2002 on Financial Collateral arrangements by the Ordonnance No. 2005-171 du 24 février 2005 now Art. L.431-4 *et seq. Code monétaire et financier* created a transfer of money and shares between banks and large financial institutions for security purposes. See Legeais 2006a, p. 505-507.

247 Legeais 1996, p. 337, Crocq 1995, p. 31-32, Simler & Delebecque 2004, p. 538-539, Witz 1981, p. 173 *et seq.*

receiving bank or financial institution.[248] The legal nature of the *opération de pension* is debatable. Originally it was perceived as an alteration on the right of pledge, but it is more and more recognised as a transfer of ownership for security purposes.[249]

Furthermore, in Article 1659 C.civ the possibility to create a *vente à réméré* or a re-purchase agreement is mentioned. The re-purchase agreement is a contract of sale and at the same time an agreement on an option of re-sale at the end of a certain period.[250] The re-purchase agreement as such is not a security device but can be used for security purposes when the purchase price is a debt.[251] In re-purchase agreements the general risk is that the object will devaluate during the time the contract runs. The re-purchase agreement is not restricted to professional claims and can therefore, in theory, also be used by consumers. Perhaps for this reason the *Cour de cassation* has been very careful about recognising the validity of the use of Article 1659 C.civ for security purposes. The *Cour de cassation* has held that the security re-purchase agreement is an attempt to avoid the mandatory rules on pledge, particularly an attempt to avoid the prohibition of the *pacte commissoire*, which was prohibited until 2006.[252] The *Cour de cassation* has therefore, under the regime of the law before the reform, re-qualified the security re-purchase agreement as a right of pledge securing a debt.[253]

Until 2007, the use of the right of ownership for security purposes was mainly restricted to retaining the right until a certain performance took place. Only in exceptional and specifically defined situations could ownership be transferred for security purposes as well. Nevertheless, for many years several influential academics have been pleading for the introduction of a general security device allowing a transfer of ownership for security purposes known as *fiducie*.[254] Although the Grimaldi report, which is at the foundation of the 2006 reforms, proposed the introduction of the *fiducie*, the final 2006 reforms did not include the *fiducie*.[255] The reason for this was that at the same time the French government was working, on the initiative of Senator Marini, on the general introduction of a transfer of ownership for special purposes, including for security purposes, and it was considered a

248 Crocq 1995, p. 31-32.

249 See Crocq 1995, p. 31, Witz 1981, p. 175.

250 Art. 1659 C.civ states 'la faculté de rachat ou de réméré est un pacte par lequel le vendeur se réserve de reprendre la chose cendue, moyennant la restitution du prix principal et le remboursement dont il est parlé à l'article 1673', see Piedelièvre 2004, p. 189, Legeais 1996, p. 335.

251 Piedelièvre 2004, p. 189, Legeais 1996, p. 335.

252 Legeais 1996, p. 336, Piedelièvre 2004, p. 189, Crocq 1995, p. 18.

253 *Cass.* 13 janvier 1965, J.C.P., II, 14469.

254 Most importantly *Avant-projet de Loi instituant la Fiducie* which was proposed in 1989, 1994 and most recently again in 2005 by Senator Marini, see Text No. 178 (2004-2005) de M. Philippe Marini, déposé au Sénat le 8 février 2005. See, *inter alia*, Crocq 1995, p. 36-38, Witz 1981, Crocq 2007, p. 1-2, Kuhn 2007, p. 32.

255 Grimaldi et al. 2005, p. 14. The French *fiducie* is often compared to the English trust, on trusts see Chapter 6; 1.5. Trust Law. Crocq 1995, p. 36-38, Witz 1981. See also below; 5. A *Numerus Clausus* in French Property Law? Particularly the abolishing of the prohibition on the *lex commissoria*, one of the primary reasons the *Cour de cassation* refuses to accept foreign security trust relations, should be considered. On the refusal of the *Cour de cassation* see *Cass.* 8 juillet 1969, J.C.P. 1970, II, 16182.

better improvement of French law for the *fiducie* to be introduced as a general concept and not for security purposes only.[256] Subsequently, on 19 February 2007, the French legislature adopted an Act that introduced the *fiducie*, as a general concept, into French law.[257]

The *fiducie*, a trust-like device, is dealt with in Article 2011 C.civ:

> The *fiducie* is the act by which one or more persons transfer objects, rights or securities, or a set of objects, rights or securities, present or future, to one or more fiduciaries, who will keep the objects separate from their own patrimony, for the benefit of one or more beneficiaries.[258]

The definition of *fiducie* in Article 2011 C.civ is very promising and seems to suggest that a general trust-like device has been created in French law. However, the Ministry of Finance interfered, afraid the *fiducie* as it was generally formulated by Article 2011 C.civ would be used to abuse tax law and the law of succession.[259] Therefore, contrary to the initial proposals, at the last moment the French legislature limited the scope of application of the *fiducie* to legal persons, banks and financial institutions.[260] Only legal persons may be transferee, and only those institutions mentioned in Article L.511-1 of the *Code monétaire et financier* as financial institutions can be a fiduciary. This Article in the *Code monétaire et financier* states that financial institutions are those legal persons that professionally conduct banking operations.[261] In the opinion of the French government, after the 2006 reforms natural persons would already have a sufficient choice in property security rights to obtain the finance they needed. The law on *fiducie* could therefore be limited to financial institutions that require a lower degree of protection.[262]

The *fiducie* revives the Roman *fiducia cum creditore*, a transfer of ownership for security purposes, and the Roman *fiducia cum amico*, a transfer of ownership for management purposes, whereby a contract, the *pactum fiduciae*, limited the owner in his rights over the object that was transferred.[263] Like the Roman law version, the *fiducie* in modern French law comprises a transfer of objects under a contract that limits the owner in his powers over the object.[264] French law allows parties to use

256 Crocq 2007, p. 1-2.

257 Loi No. 2007-211 du 19 février 2007, JORF 21 February 2007.

258 Art. 2011 C.civ, 'La fiducie est l'opération par laquelle un ou plusieurs constituants transfèrent des biens, des droits ou des sûretés, ou un ensemble de biens, de droits ou de sûretés, présents ou futurs, à un ou plusieurs fiduciaires qui, les tenant séparés de leur patrimoine propre, agissent dans un but déterminé au profit d'un ou plusieurs bénéficiaires'.

259 Crocq 2007, p. 2.

260 Arts. 2014 and 2015 C.civ, De Roux 2007, p. 23-24.

261 Art. L511-1 *Code monétaire et financier* states 'les établissement de crédit sont des personnes morales que effectuent à titre de profession habituelle des opérations de banque au sens de l'article L.311-1…'. Kuhn 2007, p. 38-39.

262 De Roux 2007, p. 23-24, Crocq 2007, p. 2.

263 Kuhn 2007, p. 32. On *fiducia cum creditore* see Chapter 2; 2.4. Other Property Rights.

264 Art. 2012 C.civ, De Roux 2007, p. 13, 34, Kuhn 2007, p. 43.

the *fiducie* for both security and management purposes, subject to the same rules.[265] However, how this right of ownership is limited is subject to debate.

When the right of ownership is transferred for security purposes, security ownership arises. This is a right of ownership that is different from a standard right of ownership, as the right of ownership must be returned to the debtor at the end of the security arrangement and the owner is limited in his powers over the object under ownership through the security contract. Senator Marini, who made the original proposal for the *fiducie*, stated that this right of ownership was a form of modified ownership.[266] Senator De Richemont, who was reporter for the proposal in the Senate, qualified the right of ownership as *propriété dégradée* or degraded ownership.[267] In stating this Senator De Richemont wanted to make clear that a *fiducie* does not create a *démembrement* of the right of ownership, but merely contractually limits the owner in his power over his own object.[268]

This limitation on the right of ownership is twofold. First, the contract of *fiducie* limits the purpose for which the owner may use the object. As the general definition of Article 2011 C.civ provides, the instrument creating the *fiducie* must state the purpose for which it is used. A transfer of ownership for security purposes will result in limitations on the right to use, to enjoy and to dispose. Furthermore, the contract will also impose a duty of care on the owner to preserve the object.[269] Secondly, the ownership of the fiduciary will be limited in time. Article 2018(2) C.civ limits the maximum duration of a *fiducie* to thirty-three years.[270] Therefore, the transferee will have a right to the 'remainder', which enables him to reclaim the right of ownership at the end of the *fiducie*.[271]

The security transfer is made for the benefit of a beneficiary, which will usually be the transferee himself, but could also be another person. The new statute on *fiducie* imposes no limitations on who can be a beneficiary.[272] Because the *fiducie* is a contractual relation between a transferee, known as a *constituant,* and a fiduciary for the benefit of a beneficiary, there could be a situation where there are three parties to the contract. As stated before, in case of a transfer for security purposes, the *fiducie* relation usually only concerns two parties. However, when a beneficiary is a third party, he will have to agree to the terms of the contract. By analogy to the provisions on a contract for the benefit of a third party, consent of the beneficiary is

265 However, the use of a *fiducie* in the law of succession, is in principle excluded. See Dupichot 2007, p. 5 *et seq.*

266 Or *propriété modelée*, see *Exposé des motifs de la proposition de loi n 178, session 2004-2005, p. 5.*

267 De Richemont 2006, p. 11.

268 De Richemont 2006, p. 11. In agreement with this conclusion see Crocq 1995, p. 204-206. Of a different opinion see Grimaldi 1991a, p. 913-917.

269 See De Richemont 2006, p. 12.

270 Originally a term of 99 years had been proposed, connected to the duration of legal persons. However, the French government considered 33 years to be sufficiently to provide continuity to the institution. See De Roux 2007, p. 31, Dupichot 2007, p. 5 *et seq.*

271 See Art. 2029 C.civ. In English law the remainder is the right of the holder of a fee simple who has granted a lease to the return of the possession of the object at the end of the lease. See Chapter 6; 1.1. Terminology.

272 Art. 2016 C.civ, De Roux 2007, p. 40-41.

not needed for the validity of the contract, but will enable revocation of the contract.[273] Failure to consent will give the transferee the right to revoke the transfer, but will not make the *fiducie* invalid.[274] Consequently, once the contract has been agreed to by the beneficiary, the terms are set and can no longer be modified, nor revoked.[275]

If the *fiducie* does not result in a *démembrement* of the right of ownership, neither the transferee nor the beneficiary will hold a limited property right.[276] A beneficiary will therefore only have a personal claim on the fiduciary. In order to protect the beneficiary, the fiduciary is under a duty to keep the *fiducie* objects separated from his own patrimony.[277] This separation is achieved in French law through the creation of a new type of patrimony, the *patrimoine d'affectation*. As a result the fiduciary will hold two patrimonies, one for himself and one for the *fiducie*.[278] Consequently, the private creditors of the fiduciary will not be able to claim from the *patrimoine d'affectation,* not even in case of insolvency of the fiduciary.[279]

In order for a *fiducie* to be created the contract must mention the objects, rights or securities that are transferred.[280] When these are future objects, rights, or securities they must be identifiable.[281] Furthermore, the contract must mention the duration of the transfer, not exceeding thirty-three years, a description of the transferee, fiduciary and beneficiary, or provisions that enable identification of a beneficiary and the purpose for which the *fiducie* is created, including the rights and duties of the fiduciary.[282] These requirements are strict and when any of these are missing, the contract will be void.[283] Finally, in order for the contract to remain valid, when these requirements are fulfilled, the *fiducie* must be registered within one month in a new special register.[284]

The *fiducie* therefore introduces a transfer of ownership for security purposes on all objects, but which can only be created by legal persons, banks, and other financial institutions. It results in a transfer of ownership whereby security ownership is created. Although security ownership remains a standard right of ownership doctrinally, because of the limitations imposed by the contract of *fiducie* it can hardly be treated as such.

273 Art. 1121 C.civ, *Cass. Civ.* 1er, 19 December 2000, Bull. Civ. I, No. 333, p. 215, De Roux 2007, p. 54.
274 Art. 2028 C.civ.
275 Art. 2028 C.civ.
276 However, see Grimaldi who has argued that the right of ownership of a *fiduciaire* is not a normal right of ownership, see Grimaldi 1991a, p. 914-917 and Grimaldi 1991b, p. 975-981. *Contra* see Crocq 1995, p. 189-206.
277 Art. 2011 C.civ.
278 De Roux 2007, p. 10.
279 Art. 2024 C.civ, Kuhn 2007, p. 40-41.
280 Dupichot 2007, p. 5 *et seq.*
281 Art. 2018(1) C.civ.
282 Arts. 2018(2), 2018(3), 2018(4), 2018(5) and 2018(6) C.civ.
283 Art. 2018 C.civ.
284 Arts. 2019 and 2020 C.civ. Kuhn 2007, p. 35.

The same reasoning applies to the other type of *fiducie*, the *fiducie gestion*, or transfer of ownership for management purposes.[285] Here not a security but a management contract will limit the ownership of the fiduciary. The choice made by the legislature to introduce general articles on the *fiducie* instead of including it as a part of the security law reforms, results in general rules on *fiducie*, regardless of whether it is a transfer for security or management purposes.

In any case, the introduction of the *fiducie* provides a general framework for transfers for specific purposes. Other types of security transfers that existed before the introduction of these general rules, such as the *cession Dailly*, the *opérations de pension* and the *vente à réméré*, will therefore also fall under these general provisions in the Civil Code as much as possible. They are *fiducies innommées*, in the words of Deputy M. Xavier le Roux, member of the *Assemblée National*.[286]

3. Other Property Rights

In addition to the right of ownership, French law recognises a set of property rights other than ownership. These property rights, known as limited property rights, are derived from the right of ownership through a method known in French law as *démembrement*.[287] Under this method the powers attributed to the right of ownership can be divided into specific parts that can be transferred to another person in the form of a limited property right.[288] This fragmentation of the right of ownership does not lead to multiple concepts of ownership but to the creation of a limited property right. In other words, the limited property right comprises a fragment of the right of ownership.[289]

It is important to recognise the division between the right of ownership on the one hand and the limited property rights on the other hand. The choice the drafters of the Civil Code made for the absolute, unitary and exclusive right of ownership results in the recognition of only one type of ownership as the most extensive property right.[290] Consequently, any other property relation must be different from a right of ownership and must be less in content. In the French system, therefore, the right of ownership serves as a model for the other property rights, named limited property rights.[291]

One of the most debated questions in French law is whether or not the list of recognised limited property rights is closed. The debate centres on the interpretation of Article 543 C.civ, which only recognises the right of ownership, the right of

285 On this type of *fiducie* see below; 4.5. *Fiducie*.
286 De Roux 2007, p. 8.
287 The term *démembrement* does not translate well into English. The term is best defined as fragmentation or subtraction. See Terré & Simler 1998, p. 587-590, Libchaber 2004, p. 356 *et seq*.
288 Libchaber uses the term *découper* which best translates as cut, as in cutting a piece from a pie, Libchaber 2004, p. 357.
289 See Terré & Simler 1998, p. 587.
290 Libchaber 2004, p. 352.
291 Or *droit réels*.

usufruct and the right of servitude as possible property rights.[292] In this debate two principal arguments are brought forward. First, the Civil Code of 1804, although abolishing feudal property rights that had existed before the French Revolution, still had party autonomy at its starting point.[293] The limitation of this free will in terms of private law party autonomy that would be implied in the decision of the French legislature to limit the number and content of property rights is difficult for some to accept.[294]

Secondly, the *Cour de cassation* has, over time, recognised some additional property rights that are not mentioned by Article 543 C.civ. This includes the famous case of *Caquelard v Lemoine* in which the *Cour de cassation* recognised a situation of co-ownership whereby one person was entitled to the use of trees and one to the use of bushes on the same land, fragmenting the right of ownership in a way not recognised by the system of the Civil Code.[295] In this case the *Cour de cassation* stated in respect to the French system of property rights:

> Considering that in law Articles 544, 546 and 552 C.civ. are declarative of the common law in respect to the effects of ownership, but are not prohibitive.; – That neither the articles, nor any other Statute, excludes the different modifications and forms the normal right of ownership may take.[296]

French legal scholarship recognises two categories of property rights: principal and accessory rights.[297] The principal property rights include the right of ownership and its *démembrements* that grant rights of use to third persons. These rights are property rights in respect of an object that are created through the method of *démembrement,* and that are dealt with by book 2 of the Civil Code.[298] Accessory property rights come into existence to secure a claim and are accessory to an agreement creating a debt.[299] These rights are not dealt with in book 2 but are situated in, the newly introduced, book 4 dealing with security rights. Contrary to the principal property rights these rights are not specifically created with regard to an object itself, but have as their object the value of the asset.[300] The latter is also used to justify why the

292 For a discussion on Art. 543 C.civ see below; 5. A *Numerus Clausus* in French Property Law?

293 Or *pouvoir de la volonté,* see Terré & Simler 1998, p. 42, Malaurie & Aynès 2005, p. 90-91, Libchaber 2004, p. 355-357.

294 See Terré & Simler 1998, p. 42-43.

295 *Req.* 13 February 1834, D.P. 1834.I.218, S.1834.I.205, see, *inter alia,* Atias 2005, p. 47-50, Malaurie & Aynès 2005, p. 89-90, Hervieu 1981, p. 57-59.

296 '...; – Attendu en droit que les art. 544, 546 et 552 Cod. Civ., sont déclaratifs du droit commun relativement à la nature et aux effets de la propriété, mais ne sont pas prohibitifs; – Que ni ces articles, ni aucune autre loi, n'excluent les diverses modifications et décompositions dont le droit ordinaire de propriété est susceptible', *Req.* 13 February 1834, D.P. 1834.I.218, S.1834.I.205. For more on this case and the *numerus clausus* in French property law below in 5. A *Numerus Clausus* in French Property Law?

297 Malaurie & Aynès 2005, p. 88-89, Terré & Simler 1998, p. 40-41.

298 This includes the already mentioned Art. 543 C.civ.

299 I.e., accessory to a *créance,* see Malaurie & Aynès 2005, p. 89.

300 Malaurie & Aynès 2005, p. 89.

property security rights, also named accessory property rights, are not mentioned in Article 543 C.civ.[301]

Whether or not the list of property rights is closed, remains open for debate.[302] The leading opinion seems to suggest that the list is closed, but its proponents are forced to recognise that some extensions have been made over time.[303] These extensions include both legislative as well as judiciary interference. This section will deal with the principal property rights apart from the right of ownership and then also discuss the accessory property rights.

3.1. *Real Servitudes*

One of the most important limited property rights in French law is the right of servitude.[304] The right of servitude especially shows the Roman foundations of the system of French property law.[305] The concept of servitude is dealt with in Article 637 C.civ, which states:

> A right of servitude is a charge on an immovable object for the use and utility of an immovable object of another owner.[306]

Originally, the French Civil Code did not speak of a right of servitude but of a *service foncier*, or land service.[307] This different terminology was used to avoid the use of the term servitude, which was associated with the feudal system.[308] However, at the same time the drafters of the Civil Code also recognised the Roman-law, non-feudal, nature of the rights of servitudes and indeed the title dealing with servitudes mentions both terms.[309]

A right of servitude in French law can come into existence in three ways. First and foremost, a right of servitude can be created by agreement between parties. Secondly, a right of servitude can come into existence through operation of law.[310] Operation of law can include special provisions in the Civil Code or other legislation, but can also include certain factual circumstances described in the Civil

301 Atias 2005, p. 54-55, Legeais 2006a, p. 422. The French property law handbooks each have different parts for the principal property rights characterised under the law of things, or *droit des biens* and the law of securities, or *droit des sûretés*.

302 See below; 5. A *Numerus Clausus* in French Property Law?

303 Malaurie & Aynès 2005, p. 91, Chabas 1994, No. 1287, p. 4-6. See below; 5. A *Numerus Clausus* in French Property Law?

304 Traditionally the French handbooks, as well as the Civil Code itself, deal with personal servitudes before they deal with real servitudes. However, for the purposes of general structure in this study, real servitudes will be dealt with before personal servitudes.

305 See Malaurie & Aynès 2005, p. 326.

306 Art. 637 C.civ, 'Une servitude est une charge imposée sur un héritage pour l'usage et l'utilité d'un héritage appartenant à un autre propriétaire'.

307 See the description used in Art. 543 C.civ.

308 Chabas 1994, p. 425.

309 Title IV of Book 2 of the *Code civil* is named 'Of servitudes or land services', in French *Des servitudes ou des services fonciers*.

310 See Chabas 1994, p. 150 *et seq.*, Terré & Simler 1998, p. 656-657.

Code.[311] Finally, a right of servitude can come into existence through the decision of a court.[312] Article 637 C.civ provides a general definition of a right of servitude, after which the Civil Code deals with special provisions for each type of servitude.

The definition used by Article 637 C.civ presupposes that several criteria are fulfilled. First, there must be a dominant and a servient piece of land, the servient land being that which is encumbered with the right of servitude.[313] The existence of the right of servitude implies a limitation on the right of ownership of the owner of the servient land, in other words, a duty to tolerate something from the owner of the dominant land or a prohibition to use the servient land of which he is the owner in a certain way. It is most important that the right of servitude is created between two pieces of land or between the owners or right-holders of two pieces of land. The parties creating and using the right of servitude cannot be bound in their personal capacity, but only in their capacity as an owner or right-holder to either the dominant or servient land.[314] Furthermore, the duty on the servient owner cannot be positive in nature. This very fundamental principle, known in Roman law as *servitus in faciendo consistere nequit*, is a restriction to prevent an owner from being bound in his personal capacity.[315] Under French legal scholarship it is the ownership of the land that is burdened with the right of servitude and not the owner himself. If a servitude contained a positive duty, the owner himself and not the servient land would be forced to do something.[316]

Secondly, the right of servitude must be created for the benefit of the dominant land itself.[317] Not the owner personally, but the owner in his capacity as an owner must benefit from the existence of the right of servitude.[318] It is therefore usually held that the right of servitude must have an objective, at least indirect, relation to the use of the dominant land. If more than one owner is involved, and there is a situation of co-ownership, then each of the co-owners must benefit from the existence of the servitude.[319] The requirement of benefit therefore restricts the possible servitudes that could be created, for instance, excluding rights to hunt or pick fruits, which cannot be a created as a right of servitude.[320] However, a right of servitude with a non-competition clause has been allowed as a valid right of servitude benefiting the owner of the dominant land.[321] Like the restriction to

311 Some examples will be provided below in this Section.

312 Art. 639 C.civ. Although the article does not mention the fourth possibility, a servitude arising from a court decision was introduced by the Decree of 4 December 1958 and are now in the *Code de l'urbanisme*, Art. L451-1 s., see Terré & Simler 1998, p. 657, 661-662, Atias 2005, p. 325.

313 Terré & Simler 1998, p. 648-649, Malaurie & Aynès 2005, p. 329-330.

314 Art. 686 C.civ, Terré & Simler 1998, p. 649, Malaurie & Aynès 2005, p. 330-331.

315 On the Roman maxim see Chapter 2; 2.4. Other Property Rights.

316 However, accessory to a negative duty, a positive duty can be recognised.

317 Malaurie & Aynès 2005, p. 331.

318 Terré & Simler 1998, p. 649-650, Atias 2005, p. 331, Malaurie & Aynès 2005, p. 331-332.

319 Terré & Simler 1998, p. 653.

320 See Art. 686 C.civ, Terré & Simler 1998, p. 650.

321 *Cass.* 15 July 187, Bull. Civ. IV, No. 184, D. 1988, II, 360, see Sagaert 2004b, p. 53-54. See Malaurie & Aynès 2005, p. 334-335. However, French law does not, contrary to German law, recognise the application of rights of servitude with a non competition clause for security →

negative duties, with the situation of the *ancien régime* in mind, the requirement that the dominant land must benefit also limits rights of servitude to the land and not to persons themselves. For example, a right to hunt does not benefit the land but the owner of the land personally, and therefore cannot be a right of servitude.

Thirdly, the owner of the dominant land must be a different owner from the owner of the servient land. Following the Roman maxim *nulli res sua servit*, the combination of the burden over the ownership of the land and the ownership itself leads to the destruction of the right of servitude.[322] However, this rule is applied in a strict sense and does not apply when, for instance, one of the owners only becomes co-owner of the other piece of land.[323] The requirement of two different owners forms part of the minimum requirements for a right of servitude and cannot be deviated from except in circumstances prescribed by law or by agreement that only takes effect after one of the pieces of land is sold and transferred to another owner.[324]

Finally, the right of servitude is linked to the ownership of the dominant land. French legal scholarship confusingly brings this under the heading of accessority, which is also used to explain how a property security right is connected to the claim for performance it seeks to secure. These security rights are known as accessory property rights. As long as the ownership of the dominant land exists, the right of servitude will remain in existence. A right of servitude in French law therefore has a perpetual nature.[325] The parties can decide on a shorter duration of the servitude by agreement, but in the absence of such agreement the servitude will remain in existence. In this respect the right of servitude is accessory to the right of ownership, but remains a principal property right.[326]

The Civil Code provides a very broad definition of a right of servitude. In general, it is for the parties to decide on the content of the property right, as long as they stay within the limits of the law. Depending on the agreement between the parties, the right of servitude will have a specific name such as a servitude of way, of water, of view and of restriction.[327] As a specific exception to the rules above, French law recognises one type of servitude as imposing a positive burden in the form of a right of support.[328] Any other positive burden will not take the form of a property right, but will remain a mere personal right.[329]

purposes, known in German as *Sicherungsdienstbarkeiten*. On the German security servitudes see Chapter 4; 3.1. Real Servitude.

322 Art. 705 C.civ, Terré & Simler 1998, p. 650-651.

323 Terré & Simler 1998, p. 651.

324 See Art. 693 C.civ, that creates a *servitude de destination du père de famille*. Terré & Simler 1998, p. 651.

325 Terré & Simler 1998, p. 652, Malaurie & Aynès 2005, p. 338-339.

326 Terré & Simler 1998, p. 652-653, Malaurie & Aynès 2005, p. 338-339. On principal and accessory property rights see above; 3. Other Property Rights.

327 Malaurie & Aynès 2005, p. 339-340.

328 Terré & Simler 1998, p. 649, Chabas 1994, p. 429, Jourdain, Marty & Raynaud 1995, p. 8-9, Atias 2005, p. 332.

329 See Sagaert 2004b, p. 56-59.

It is the content of the agreement between the parties that becomes the content of the right of servitude.[330] Article 686 C.civ states in this respect:

> Owners may create on their land or in favour of their land such servitudes as seem fit to them, provided however that the duties the servitude creates are not imposed on a person, nor in favour of a person, but solely on a piece of land and on behalf of a piece of land, and provided that these duties are not contrary to public policy'.
> The use and the extent of the servitude is established by the title that creates it; without a title, by the rules following this article.[331]

The general prohibition of imposing a positive duty is considered to be implied in the requirement not to impose a duty on a person but on a piece of land. It is only a person who can perform a positive duty and not a piece of land itself.[332] The *Cour de cassation* has been strict in maintaining this restriction. For example, a prohibition not to build on a piece of land in order to impose a duty to build was rejected as a valid right of servitude.[333] The reason for this restriction should be seen in historical perspective as a general rejection of the personal duties a person would have had to perform under the feudal system.[334] The restriction of servitudes to negative burdens should therefore be seen as the primary restriction of the freedom for the parties creating a right of servitude.

However, a positive duty that is connected to a negative duty, which itself is the subject of a right of servitude, can be allowed.[335] The distinction between these positive duties that are connected, *accessoire*, to the right of servitude and those who are not is a complicated distinction.[336] The exceptions that have been allowed include a duty of maintenance of a road in the case of a right of servitude of way, but also a duty to mine coal for the exercise of an industrial servitude for a glassworks company.[337] Furthermore, a duty to repair in case of non-performance by the owner of the servient land can also become a connected obligation.[338] In these cases, the otherwise personal obligation does not become part of the right of

330 Malaurie & Aynès 2005, p. 345-346.

331 Art. 686 C.civ 'Il est permis aux propriétaires d'établir sur leurs propriétés, ou en faveur de leurs propriétés, telles servitudes que bon leur semble, pourvu néanmoins que les services établis ne soient imposés ni à la personne, ni en faveur de la personne, mais seulement à un fonds et pour un fonds, et pourvu que ces services n'aient d'ailleurs rien de contraire à l'ordre public. L'usage et l'étendue des servitudes ainsi établies se règlent par le titre qui les constitue; à défaut de titre, par les règles ci-après'.

332 Terré & Simler 1998, p. 649, Malaurie & Aynès 2005, p. 332-333.

333 *Cass. Civ.* 3e, 6 May 1980, Bull. Civ. III, No. 90. It could, however, constitute a valid personal right. Malaurie & Aynès 2005, p. 346.

334 It is because of this requirement that a right to hunt or a right to fish cannot be subject of a right of servitude, i.e. these rights do not benefit the land but benefit the persons living on the land. See Malaurie & Aynès 2005, p. 330, 333-334, Sagaert 2004b, p. 53.

335 Another term would be an accessory relation between the negative and the positive duty.

336 On the debate see Sagaert 2004b, p. 56-59, Sagaert 2004a, No. 16.

337 *Req.* 22 February 1814, DP 1881, I, 111 and *Cass. Civ.* 9 January 1901, DP 1901, I, 451, S. 1901, I, 169.

338 See Arts. 701 and 697 C.civ, Aberkane 1957, p. 2, 6, Sagaert 2004b, p. 56-57.

servitude but will transfer with the right and will have effect against third parties.[339] They are known as qualitative or real obligations.[340]

Although the starting point of Article 686 C.civ remains party autonomy, the *Cour de cassation* has also imposed limitations. Besides the requirement that the right must concern two different pieces of land between which there must be an objective relation, the requirement of *ordre public*, or public policy, restricts the parties' freedom. In the case of servitudes created by the parties themselves, the *Cour de cassation* has used a wide concept of public policy. In the view of the court, the concept of public policy includes the provisions following Article 686 C.civ that restrict the content of servitudes as well as other provisions in and outside of the Civil Code.[341] Finally, the *Cour de cassation* has also restricted the content of a servitude that takes away all the powers to use and enjoy of the owner.[342] However, a right of servitudes that takes away only a part of the powers of an owner is a normal servitude and thus allowed.[343]

A right of servitude takes effect between the parties creating it from the moment of agreement. However, for the enforceability against third parties, particularly against those who acquire the servient piece of land, or the land on which the burden runs, registration is required.[344] Registration is therefore not a requirement for the right of servitude to come into existence, but merely for the opposability against third parties.

An interesting application of the general rules on servitudes is the right of servitude created by the *pater familias*.[345] When two pieces of land are in the same hand, the owner of these two pieces may create a factual situation, in French known as the *destination du père de famille* or purpose of the *pater familias*, resembling the exercise of a right of servitude, for instance, of a waterway or a view.[346] The factual situation must be visible to the outside world in order to have effect after one of the pieces of land is transferred to another owner. When these requirements have been fulfilled and the ownership of one of the pieces of land is transferred to another person, the effect is the immediate creation of a right of servitude on behalf of the new owner. Prior to the separation of the two pieces of land, a right of servitude

339 Malaurie & Aynès 2005, p. 332.

340 See below; 4.2. Real Obligations.

341 Examples are the law of neighbours and environmental law, see Malaurie & Aynès 2005, p. 346.

342 Or: a right of servitude may not exclude an owner, see *Cass. Civ.* 3e, 24 May 2000, Bull. Civ. III, No. 113, D. 2001.151, with a note by R. Libchaber. Malaurie & Aynès 2005, p. 338, 346.

343 Malaurie & Aynès 2005, p. 346 and Libchaber in his note under *Cass. Civ.* 3e, 24 May 2000, D. 2001, 151, p. 153.

344 The acquirer of the dominant land, i.e. the ownership of land to which the right the servitude grants is connected, will usually benefit from the right of servitude also without registration. *Cass.* 27 October 1993, Bull. Civ. IIIème, No. 132, p. 86, *contra* see Carbonnier 2000, p. 265-266. Although, if the acquirer did know of the existence of the right of servitude, he is also bound by it, see *Cass. Civ.* 17 July 1918, DP, 1918.I.71, see Malaurie & Aynès 2005, p. 339.

345 See Malaurie & Aynès 2005, p. 350 *et seq.*

346 Art. 692 C.civ, Malaurie & Aynès 2005, p. 350.

cannot exist. The requirement of two separate pieces of land with different owners resists a right of servitude coming into being.[347]

Besides the servitudes created by the parties themselves, a right of servitude in French law can also come into existence by operation of law.[348] These rights are, to a large extent, considered property rights and therefore have effect against third parties. However, because they are rights arising by operation of law, registration is not required for third party effect.[349] French legal scholarship divides these servitudes into two categories; natural and legal servitudes.[350]

Natural servitudes are those servitudes that come into existence by force of law when a specific factual situation between two pieces of land arises. These servitudes primarily deal with a situation in which one owner must allow water from another piece of land to run over his land.[351] Such a factual situation can occur when one of the pieces of land is located higher than the other piece of land. Naturally the water from the higher piece of land will flow over the lower piece. The owner of the lower piece of land must therefore tolerate the flow of water and may not block it.[352] A factual situation between two pieces of land may also give rise to a right of an owner to oblige another owner to set the boundaries between their respective pieces of land.[353] Furthermore, each owner is also entitled to enclose his land with a fence or wall, which must be tolerated by the other owner.[354] Although these latter two situations are dealt with under the heading of servitudes, they technically do not give rise to the creation of a right of servitude. It is only the factual situation that is similar, the two pieces of land neighbouring each other, but not the rights arising from it.[355]

The second category contains the legal servitudes. These rights of servitude come into existence by operation of law and can, in their turn, be divided into two. Article 649 C.civ states:

> Rights of servitude created by law are for the public or communal purposes, or for private purposes'[356]

The legal servitudes for private purposes deal to a large extent with the law of co-ownership, particularly common walls and ditches.[357] These provisions do not

347 Malaurie & Aynès 2005, p. 352-353.

348 Or just by one party. A right of servitude can also be created through a last will or testament. See Malaurie & Aynès 2005, p. 345-346.

349 Malaurie & Aynès 2005, p. 339.

350 See Terré & Simler 1998, p. 192.

351 Art. 640 C.civ, *Cass.* Civ. Ier 1 June 1965, Bull. Civ. 1965, I, No. 362, Terré & Simler 1998, p. 656.

352 Art. 640 C.civ, Terré & Simler 1998, p. 215-218.

353 Known as *bornage*, see Art. 646 C.civ, Terré & Simler 1998, p. 195-199, Malaurie & Aynès 2005, p. 287-288.

354 Known as *clôture,* see Art. 647 C.civ, Terré & Simler 1998, p. 199- 203, Malaurie & Aynès 2005, p. 288-289.

355 See Terré & Simler 1998, p. 201.

356 Art. 649 C.civ, 'Les servitudes établies par la loi ont pour objet l'utilité publique ou communale, ou l'utilité des particuliers'.

create a right of servitude, there is no dominant or servient piece of land and their place in the Civil Code is therefore criticised.[358] However, four other situations are recognised which do create a right of servitude by force of law.[359] French legal scholarship deals with these situations in the law of neighbours and not the law of servitudes.[360] They include a duty to keep a distance from the border of the land in order to prevent nuisance to a neighbour, a duty to refrain from having drain water flow onto the land of a neighbour, a right of view over a neighbours land, and the right to a way out from an enclosed piece of land.[361] The last servitude is of particular interest. When a piece of land is enclosed by other pieces of land so that no public space, usually a road, can be reached without going over one of the enclosing pieces of land, a legal servitude comes into existence enabling the enclosed owner to have a way to the public space, subject to payment of compensation.[362] Furthermore, even if there is a way to the public space but this way is not suitable for its regular agricultural, industrial or commercial purpose, a legal servitude may come into existence.[363] Furthermore, the legal servitude does not only apply for a right of way for human traffic, but can also come into existence for pipes or waterways.[364]

Although the legal servitude runs on the land of the neighbour and therefore, as a limited property right, burdens the full ownership of that neighbour, the legal servitude may only be exercised in relation to its purpose. The way of exercise of the servitude, in particular the exact place where it has to be exercised, may either be agreed on by the parties themselves or, in case of dispute, by a court decision.[365] Furthermore, continuous use of a legal servitudes can also set the content, for example, through the uninterrupted use of a certain path for thirty years, the exact location where the legal servitude runs can be determined.[366] However, the way to the public space must be found in a way that causes the least amount of damage to the servient land.[367]

Finally, the second type of legal servitudes, those for public purposes, should be mentioned. These servitudes are used for those pieces of land that serve a public benefit, such as roads or public transmission lines, including electricity or telecom-

357 Which includes a wall placed under a natural servitude, Art. 647 C.civ, Terré & Simler 1998, p. 202-203, 650.

358 Terré & Simler 1998, p. 650, Malaurie & Aynès 2005, p. 343-344.

359 This includes section I of chapter II of title IV on servitudes of the Civil Code. Terré & Simler 1998, p. 203-208.

360 Terré & Simler 1998, p. 192-194.

361 Respectively Arts. 674, 675, 681 and 682 C.civ. On the right of view: this right restricts a neighbour putting up a wall. See Terré & Simler 1998, p. 206-207.

362 Art. 682 C.civ.

363 Originally the text of Art. 682 C.civ only used the agricultural purpose. However, by Loi du 20 août 1881 the industrial purpose and by Loi du 30 décembre 1967 the commercial purpose were added. See Terré & Simler 1998, p. 209.

364 *Cass.* 22 November 1937, D. 1938, 62, note M. Voirin. Such lines may also run above the land, see *Cass.* 24 February 1930 DP 1932.1.9. note Besson.

365 Terré & Simler 1998, p. 211.

366 Art. 685 C.civ, Terré & Simler 1998, p. 211.

367 Art. 683 C.civ, Terré & Simler 1998, p. 212.

munication.[368] Apart from two provisions in the Civil Code, these servitudes are dealt with by public law regulations.[369] Although these rights are dealt with under the heading of servitudes, they are considered different from any of the other rights of servitude.[370] There is no dominant land, but a public legal person who serves in this function and, one of the most fundamental principles of the law of servitudes, the prohibition of imposing a positive duty, does not apply for legal servitudes for a public purpose.[371] Nevertheless, these servitudes burden the ownership of the owner over whose land the servitude runs, and therefore should be mentioned.

3.2. *Personal Servitudes*

From the perspective of some legal systems the term personal servitude is a contradiction in terms. After the abolition of the feudal system, the general idea developed that persons were no longer bound by property rights other than in their capacity as right-holder of an object on which a property right was created. Because of this the rule against positive duties in case of real servitudes is strongly applied. The term personal servitude was taken from Roman law without a reference to the feudal system and refers to a property right that is held by a person not in his capacity as right-holder to an object.[372]

The category of personal servitudes contains the right of usufruct and, derived from the right of usufruct, rights of use and habitation.[373] Different from a right of real servitude, which is created on a piece of land on behalf of an owner of that land, personal servitudes are created on an object on behalf of a person in his personal capacity, in other words, not in the capacity of holder of a property right in respect of that object. However, and herein lies the difficulty, personal servitudes are property rights and therefore have effect against third parties.[374] The result of this personal nature is a connection between the property right and the person who holds the property right. Therefore in general the maximum duration a personal servitude exists is the life of the person on whose behalf the right is created.[375]

The right of usufruct is the most important right amongst the personal servitudes. It is created either by operation of law, resulting in a legal usufruct, or by a private act, usually a gift or a testament.[376] Legal usufructs include specific situations in the law of succession, which are very common, but also a right of

368 Terré & Simler 1998, p. 234-235, 237, Malaurie & Aynès 2005, p. 363.
369 Arts. 649 and 650 C.civ, Terré & Simler 1998, p. 234-235, Malaurie & Aynès 2005, p. 364.
370 Terré & Simler 1998, p. 238.
371 Terré & Simler 1998, p. 238-239.
372 On the Roman law category of personal servitudes see Chapter 2; 2.4. Other Property Rights.
373 Recueil des lois composant le code civil, Livre Deuxième. Des Biens et des différent Modifications de la Propriété, 1804, p. 117 et seq.
374 Malaurie & Aynès 2005, p. 254-256, Atias 2005, p. 143.
375 See Malaurie & Aynès 2005, p. 252-253, Terré & Simler 1998, p. 591.
376 Furthermore, a right of usufruct can also be created through acquisitive prescription. Malaurie & Aynès 2005, p. 595, 261, Atias 2005, p. 145.

parents over objects owned by their minor children.[377] Moreover, there is the right of usufruct created by a private party. The right of usufruct is explicitly dealt with by the Civil Code, which states in Article 578 C.civ:

> The right of usufruct is the right to use and enjoy an object of another in the same way as an owner himself, but on the condition that the substance of the object is preserved.[378]

A right of usufruct, which finds its basis in Roman law, is a *démembrement* of the right of ownership and comprises the right to use and enjoy, the *usus* and *fructus*, of the owner.[379] Traditionally, the right of usufruct has always been considered not to comprise the right of disposal, the *abusus*, which consequently remains with the owner.[380] In modern French scholarship, however, the view is also defended that the holder of a right of usufruct may dispose of the objects under usufruct in so far as this is in line with the purpose for which the objects are to be used.[381]

In any case, the right of ownership that remains after a right of usufruct is created is deprived of most of its elements. French legal scholarship therefore describes the ownership that remains after a right of usufruct has been created as bare ownership or *nue-propriété*.[382] Consequently, the right of ownership is not complete until the right of usufruct ceases to exist.[383] It is of great importance that the right of usufruct is temporary. Should the right of usufruct be perpetual, it would revive the situation of fragmented ownership from the *ancien régime*.[384] In general, a right of usufruct is created for the duration of a person's life, in case of a legal person, for a maximum of thirty years.[385] Nevertheless, a specific agreement on the duration of a usufruct can be made, but the death of the usufructuary will end the usufruct in any case.[386]

Although the existence of a right of usufruct is connected to a person, the right can be transferred to another person, except if otherwise agreed upon.[387] However, the existence of the right will remain connected to the person to whom it was

377 See Arts. 767 and 1094 C.civ on the law of succession, as well as Art. 382 C.civ on the legal usufruct of parents. Terré & Simler 1998, p. 596.

378 Article 578 C.civ, 'L'usufruit est le droit de jouir des choses dont un autre a la propriété, comme le propriétaire lui-même, mais à la charge d'en conserver la substance'.

379 Malaurie & Aynès 2005, p. 250, 256, Vareilles-Sommières 1905, p. 449. Different see Carbonnier 2000, No. 104, p. 180-181.

380 Terré & Simler 1998, p. 607-608, Malaurie & Aynès 2005, p. 256.

381 Dockès 1995, p. 479 *et seq*. In respect to the same development in Belgian law see Verbeke 1999, p. 530 *et seq*.

382 Or *nue-propriété*, Terré & Simler 1998, p. 591.

383 See Art. 617 C.civ, Malaurie & Aynès 2005, p. 253.

384 Malaurie & Aynès 2005, p. 253.

385 Art. 619 C.civ, Malaurie & Aynès 2005, p. 254.

386 *Ch. Réunies*, 16 June 1933, DH., 1933.393, see Malaurie & Aynès 2005, p. 254, Terré & Simler 1998, p. 630-631.

387 Art. 595 C.civ, A transfer of a right of usufruct occurs very often in legal practice. Terré & Simler 1998, p. 616-617.

granted first.[388] In this way the original usufructuary and the bare owner remain connected, including the liability of the original usufructuary in certain situations.[389]

The right of usufruct can be created on all objects, whether movable, immovable, corporeal or incorporeal, as well as on certain sets of objects as an estate or a *fonds de commerce*.[390] The Civil Code requires two obligations from the future holder of a right of usufruct. First, an inventory of the objects that will be under the right of usufruct has to be made.[391] Usually this inventory will be part of the document creating the right of usufruct, for instance, of a testament or of an agreement. Secondly, the holder of a usufruct is forced to appoint a surety for payments the usufructuary would have to make pursuant to the compliance with his obligations.[392] When the right of usufruct is created on an immovable object, it will have to be registered in order to have effect against third parties who acquire the immovable object.[393] One of the most important requirements is duty for the usufructuary to preserve the object under usufruct. This requirement restricts the usufructuary in his freedom to dispose of the object under usufruct. At the end of the right of usufruct, the object must be returned to the bare owner, who will then become full owner of it.

Until the right of usufruct ceases to exist, French legal scholarship considers the bare ownership and the usufruct as two distinct property rights that can be transferred independent of each other.[394] However, at the same time both rights are linked to each other through the existence of the right of usufruct. After all, the bare owner may expect to become full owner again at the end of the usufruct, which includes the return of the object under usufruct.

The holder of a usufruct is under the obligation to take care of the objects under usufruct as a good *pater familias*, which includes the aforementioned obligation to maintain the objects. Furthermore this obligation contains the duty to preserve the purpose for which the objects are used.[395] The standard of the *pater familias* imposes several obligations on the usufructuary, which include the prevention of deterioration of the objects, unless they are destroyed without his fault, and the duty to protect the object under usufruct from interference from third parties, including a duty to notify the owner when such interference concerns the right of ownership itself.[396] Furthermore, the usufructuary takes over the obligations of the owner in respect of the use and enjoyment of the object. This includes the payment

388 *Cass. Civ.* 3eme 26 January 1972, D. 1975, p. 22, JCP 1972, éd. G, II, 17104.

389 Terré & Simler 1998, p. 617.

390 Terré & Simler 1998, p. 597-598, 600, Malaurie & Aynès 2005, p. 258-259.

391 Art. 600 C.civ, Malaurie & Aynès 2005, p. 262, Atias 2005, p. 157.

392 Art. 601 C.civ, *Cass. Civ.* 5 February 1897, DP 1897, 1, 601, Malaurie & Aynès 2005, p. 262, Atias 2005, p. 157.

393 Terré & Simler 1998, p. 597-598, 645.

394 Terré & Simler 1998, p. 593-594, Malaurie & Aynès 2005, p. 255, Atias 2005, p. 147.

395 Art. 601 C.civ, Terré & Simler 1998, p. 618, Malaurie & Aynès 2005, p. 266-268, Atias 2005, p. 150-153.

396 Arts. 614 and 605 C.civ, Terré & Simler 1998, p. 620, Malaurie & Aynès 2005, p. 268-269, Atias 2005, p. 154-155.

of taxes, loans and maintenance, but also the costs of a common wall or serious repairs.[397] However, extraordinary costs are for the account of the owner.[398]

The holder of a right of usufruct who fulfils his obligations is entitled to use and enjoy the object under usufruct as well as to take the fruits from that object. Fruits are those objects that are periodically produced from the object under usufruct.[399] In this respect French legal scholarship distinguishes between fruits and products, the former to which the usufructuary is entitled, the latter are for the bare owner. The distinction between fruits and products is made by the criterion of objects periodically produced. If an object periodically produces the same kind of objects, these are known as fruits.[400] An object that is not produced periodically is not a fruit but a product. This distinction is subject to alteration by the agreement between parties. An object produced by an object under usufruct might be seen as product, for instance, branches from trees in a forest, but when periodically cut in the course of a business exercised with the right of usufruct, they become fruits, regardless of whether they are cut by the bare owner or the holder of the right of usufruct.[401]

In respect of fruits French legal scholarship distinguishes three types: natural, industrial and civil.[402] Natural fruits are those objects produced by nature, such as fruits from a tree. Industrial fruits are those objects that are produced with the help of man, such as a garden or a vineyard.[403] Civil fruits are those periodic proceeds from an object that are paid by third parties, such as the payment for a lease of the object under usufruct. Finally, as the object under usufruct can be movable, immovable, corporeal and incorporeal, the fruits the object produces differ depending on the nature of the object.[404]

The duty to preserve the object under usufruct limits the right to those objects that do not perish by their nature.[405] The creation of a right of usufruct on those objects would result in a situation where the usufructuary would be unable to take care of the objects and return them to the owner at the end of the usufruct. After all, the *abusus*, the power of disposal, which includes the power to consume the object, has traditionally not been considered to be part of a right of usufruct, but is considered to be left with the bare owner.[406] However, modern French legal scholarship accepts the possibility for a holder of a right of usufruct to transfer objects.[407] This view focuses on the purpose for which the objects are given in usufruct. When, by making use of the objects, for instance, by trading them, the purpose of the

397 Art. 608 C.civ, Terré & Simler 1998, p. 621.

398 Art. 609 C.civ, Terré & Simler 1998, p. 621, Malaurie & Aynès 2005, p. 268.

399 Terré & Simler 1998, p. 95, Malaurie & Aynès 2005, p. 49-51.

400 Terré & Simler 1998, p. 95-96, 608-610, Malaurie & Aynès 2005, p. 49-50.

401 Terré & Simler 1998, p. 96.

402 Terré & Simler 1998, p. 95, 610, Malaurie & Aynès 2005, 49, 263.

403 Terré & Simler 1998, p. 95, 610.

404 See Terré & Simler 1998, p. 610-613.

405 In French known as *consomptibles*, see Terré & Simler 1998, p. 598, Malaurie & Aynès 2005, p. 258-259.

406 Terré & Simler 1998, p. 598.

407 Dockès 1995, p. 479 *et seq.*

usufruct can be fulfilled, the power of the holder of the usufruct to transfer objects is accepted.[408]

However, on objects that perish by their nature, a right of usufruct cannot be created. On these objects, French law, following the Roman law example, recognises a quasi-usufruct.[409] Like in Roman law, a quasi-usufruct in French law is actually a transfer of ownership with the duty to return, at the end of the quasi-usufruct, similar objects to the original owner.[410] In this respect Article 587 C.civ states:

> When a right of usufruct is created on objects which cannot be used without being consumed, such as money, grain, liquors, the usufructuary has a right to use them, but with the obligation, at the end of the usufruct, to return either objects of the same quantity and quality or their value estimated at the date or return.[411]

The possibility to create a quasi-usufruct enables parties to include perishable objects into their construction. It can therefore be used as a right combined, accessory, to a normal right of usufruct.[412] In such a legal construction, those objects that are not perishable fall under the normal right of usufruct, and the perishable objects fall under the quasi-usufruct.

A slightly different but comparable situation can arise when a right of usufruct is created on a *fonds de commerce*. The holder of the right of usufruct will have the power to use and enjoy the objects that are not perishable, but will be owner of those which are perishable.[413] Because of the general nature of a *fonds de commerce*, the right created in it is a normal right of usufruct, preventing the usufructuary from disposing of the *fonds de commerce* itself.[414] Any new object entering the *fonds de commerce* will be subject to the right of usufruct, as the right is created on the *fonds* itself, and not on the specific objects. The new object will then substitute the object that has left the *fonds*.[415]

Apart from the right of usufruct, the category of personal servitudes also includes the rights of use and habitation. These rights very closely resemble the right of usufruct, but are less in content.[416] They are created and also cease to exist in the same way as the right of usufruct, but are not as often used.[417] Furthermore, these rights are created on behalf of a person *intuitu personae*, or not in his capacity as a right-holder to a property right.

408 It is not entirely clear whether all French property law authors have taken over this view. See, e.g., Terré & Simler 1998, p. 598.
409 See Chapter 2; 2.4. Other Property Rights.
410 Zentati 2001, p. 605 *et seq.*
411 Art. 587 C.civ, 'Si l'usufruit comprend des choses dont on ne peut faire usage sans les consommer, comme l'argent, les grains, les liqueurs, l'usufruitier a le droit de s'en servir, mais à la charge de rendre, à la fin de l'usufruit, soit des choses de même quantité et qualité soit leur valeur estimée à la date de la restitution'.
412 Terré & Simler 1998, p. 599-601.
413 Terré & Simler 1998, p. 600-601, Carbonnier 2000, p. 181-182.
414 *Cass. Civ.* 13 December 1842, S. 1843, 1, p. 22, see Terré & Simler 1998, p. 601.
415 Known in French law as *subrogation réelle*, see, Terré & Simler 1998, p. 600-601.
416 Terré & Simler 1998, p. 641, Malaurie & Aynès 2005, p. 275.
417 Art. 625 C.civ, Terré & Simler 1998, p. 641-642.

The right of use does not include a right to take the fruits the object produces, except for those fruits that the right-holder and his family need.[418] The right of habitation is a specific right for a person to live in a house, to use a house, or to use a part of a house with their family.[419] The articles of the Civil Code on the right of usufruct apply to the rights of use and habitation in as much the same way as possible.[420] However, differences exist. The rights of use and habitation are strictly personal and cannot be transferred or leased to another person.[421] Because these rights cannot be transferred they can also not be made subject of a security property right, such as a right of hypothec.[422] Finally, the *Cour de cassation* has, pursuant to the impossibility of transferring or burdening these rights, declared these rights incapable of seizure.[423]

3.3. *Superficies*

Like its Roman law equivalent, the right of *superficies* is a right to have ownership of an immovable object on someone else's land.[424] The ownership of an immovable object on someone else's land, without the ownership of that land, is difficult. French law adheres to the principle of *superficies solo cedit*, which results in a situation where the person who owns the land owns any immovable object on that land.[425] In this respect Article 552 C.civ states:

> Ownership of land includes ownership of that what is below or above it.
> An owner may place any plantations or constructions on his land which he deems fit, save for exceptions in the title on servitudes.
> He may make any such excavations or constructions under the ground as he deems fit, and take from these excavations all products which they provide, save the limitations resulting from statutes and regulations on mines, and police statutes and regulations.[426]

It is the right of *superficies* that allows a deviation from this rule, separating the ownership of the land from the ownership of the constructions or plants above or

418 Art. 630 C.civ, Malaurie & Aynès 2005, p. 275-276.
419 Art. 633 C.civ, Terré & Simler 1998, p. 643, Malaurie & Aynès 2005, p. 277.
420 See Arts. 625, 626, and 627 C.civ, Terré & Simler 1998, p. 644.
421 Arts. 631 and 634 C.civ, *Cass. Civ.* 3ème 3 January 1978, Bull. Civ. III, No. 3, p. 3, Terré & Simler 1998, p. 645, Malaurie & Aynès 2005, p. 276.
422 On the right of hypothec see below; 3.6. Hypothec, Terré & Simler 1998, p. 646.
423 *Cass. Civ.* 5 August 1878, DP 1879, 1, p. 75, see Terré & Simler 1998, p. 646.
424 See, *inter alia*, Beudant 1938, p. 60, Sagaert 2006, p. 37.
425 See Chapter 2; 2.4. Other Property Rights. Malaurie & Aynès 2005, p. 279, Terré & Simler 1998, p. 714.
426 Art. 552 C.civ, 'La propriété du sol emporte la propriété du dessus et du dessous. Le propriétaire peut faire au-dessus toutes les plantations et constructions qu'il juge à propos, sauf les exceptions établies au titre "Des servitudes ou services fonciers". Il peut faire au-dessous toutes les constructions et fouilles qu'il jugera à propos, et tirer de ces fouilles tous les produits qu'elles peuvent fournir, sauf les modifications résultant des lois et règlements relatifs aux mines, et des lois et règlements de police'.

below it.[427] Under the *ancien régime*, the right of *superficies* was used to allow multiple owners of the same object each with a different type of ownership.[428] Patault has shown that under the influence of customary laws especially the *Cour de cassation* continued to apply pre-Revolutionary multiple rights of ownership, or *propriétés simultanées*.[429] In particular in a situation where an object is situated on a piece of land, the ownership of the land would also comprise the ownership of that object.[430] With the use of the concept of co-ownership the *Cour de cassation* managed to continue to apply these customary principles.[431] The court generally held that the owner of such an object would be co-owner, as well as the owner of the land, who would also be characterised as a co-owner. Patault shows that only from 1858 onwards the *Cour de cassation* abandoned its doctrine of co-ownership and recognised a separate property right enabling the right-holder to have a separate and distinct right of ownership from the owner of the land.[432] This change in approach of the *Cour de cassation* enabled the use of a singular and unitary concept of ownership, which either rests on the object on the land or on the land itself. It is from this perspective that Article 553 C.civ should be read[433]:

> Any construction, plantations or works on or within a piece of land are presumed to be made by the owner, at his expense and in his ownership, if the contrary is not proven; Without prejudice to the ownership which a third party has acquired or could acquire by prescription, whether of a basement under the building of another, or of any part of the building.[434]

The right of *superficies* separates the ownership of an object, known as *superficiaire*, from the ownership of a piece of land on which it is constructed, known as *tréfonds*.[435] A right created, usually by agreement, forms the proof that the ownership of the construction, plantation or work is in different hands than the ownership of the land.[436] In the absence of such an agreement the owner of the land will become owner of the constructions placed on his land by a third party through application of Article 552 C.civ.[437] Therefore, the right of *superficies* can, although

427 Malaurie & Aynès 2005, p. 279, Chabas 1994, p. 16, Larroumet 2004, p. 439.

428 See Pataault 1989, p. 85-86, 252-254.

429 On the term *propriétés simultanées* see Pataault 1989, p. 15. Pataault 1983, p. 217 *et seq.*

430 Or *superficies solo cedit,* see Art. 552 C.civ.

431 This includes the application of Art. 815 C.civ to these cases. Pataault 1983, p. 224-226, Terré & Simler 1998, p. 711.

432 *Civ.* 18 May 1858, S. 58.1.661, Pataault 1983, p. 234.

433 See Terré & Simler 1998, p. 712-714, Sagaert 2006, p. 37, Bertrel 1994, p. 768.

434 Art. 553 C.civ, 'Toutes constructions, plantations et ouvrages sur un terrain ou dans l'intérieur sont présumés faits par le propriétaire à ses frais et lui appartenir, si le contraire n'est prouvé; sans préjudice de la propriété qu'un tiers pourrait avoir acquise ou pourrait acquérir par prescription soit d'un souterrain sous le bâtiment d'autrui, soit de toute autre partie du bâtiment'.

435 Terré & Simler 1998, p. 710.

436 Terré & Simler 1998, p. 710-712, Carbonnier 2000, p. 332.

437 Although reimbursement or compensation must be paid, see Art. 555 C.civ, see Carbonnier 2000, p. 333-335.

this has been debated in the past, be seen as a horizontal *démembrement* of the right of ownership.[438]

More complicated has been the classification of a right of *superficies* created on a piece of land where no construction, plantation or work has yet been placed. In this respect, the already existing right of ownership of the land could not be subject to a *démembrement*.[439] However, a group of authors, in particular Bertrel, see the right of *superficies* as a right to build on the land of another as well as a right of ownership on those constructions.[440] They consider the right to build as part of the right of *superficies*. The majority of authors seems to follow this view.[441]

A right of *superficies* can be created either by agreement or come into existence through prescription.[442] Without any other agreement the right of *superficies* will be perpetual.[443] Because the right awards the right-holder a right of ownership, in principle for an unlimited period, the right cannot cease to exist through the non-use of the right.[444] Furthermore, the right of *superficies* can be subject to the creation of a right of hypothec.[445]

The possibility to create a right of *superficies* by agreement is specifically clear in the context of other agreements of which the right of *superficies* is a result. The best illustration is offered by a contract of lease of an immovable object. When an owner leases his land to a lessee, who subsequently erects a building or construction on that land within his general rights to use the leased land, the lessee will become owner of the building or construction for the duration of the lease agreement.[446] A similar rule applies for a right-holder of a right of *emphyteusis*.[447] In general the owner of the land will become owner of the building or construction upon the end of the agreement which gave rise to the right of *superficies*.[448]

438 See Terré & Simler 1998, p. 698, 712-714, interestingly Carbonnier uses the term vertical *démembrement*, see Carbonnier 2000, p. 332.

439 Jourdain, Marty & Raynaud 1995, p. 237-239, Terré & Simler 1998, p. 712-714, on the doctrinal discussion on the subject see Bertrel 1994, p. 758-761.

440 Bertrel 1994, p. 770 *et seq.*, Carbonnier 2000, p. 339-340, Malaurie & Aynès 2005, p. 281, 283.

441 See Carbonnier 2000, p. 339-340, Larroumet 2004, p. 448-449, different see Bertrel 1994, p. 769 *et seq.*

442 Terré & Simler 1998, p. 714-715.

443 See Terré & Simler 1998, p. 713, Malaurie & Aynès 2005, p. 282, Sagaert 2006, p. 38.

444 *Req.* 5 November 1866, DO 1867, 1, 32 and *Req.* 27 April 1891, DP 1892, 1, p. 219, S. 1891, 1, p. 369. Although the decisions are criticised, see Terré & Simler 1998, p. 713, in particular note 2. On the impossibility to lose a right of ownership through prescription see above; 2.1. Ownership.

445 See Terré & Simler 1998, p. 713, Malaurie & Aynès 2005, p. 282-283.

446 *Cass. Civ.* 1er 1 December 1964, JCP 1965, éd. G., II, 14213, Bull. Civ. I, No. 535, D. 1965, p. 473. See Malaurie & Aynès 2005, p. 281-282, Terré & Simler 1998, p. 714-715, Bertrel 1994, p. 762-763.

447 Terré & Simler 1998, p. 715. On the right of *emphyteusis* see below; 3.4. *Emphyteusis*.

448 See Art. 555 C.civ, Terré & Simler 1998, p. 716-717.

3.4. *Emphyteusis*

The right of *emphyteusis*, like the right of *superficies*, has been connected to fragmented ownership that existed under the *ancien régime*. Under the *ancien régime* the right of *emphyteusis*, a property right allowing a person to use a piece of land for a long duration of time, awarded *dominium utile* to the right-holder.[449] Particularly in relation to the feudal system of landholding, in which a person in his personal capacity would be bound to a piece of land with the use of the legal construction of *emphyteusis*, the right would often be constructed as a perpetual right.[450] With the French Revolution and the abolition of the feudal system, all land charges, including the *emphyteusis* were abolished.[451]

It is for this reason that the Civil Code does not mention the right of *emphyteusis* in its enumeration of property rights in Article 543 C.civ or in any other Article in the Code.[452] Nevertheless, the *Cour de cassation* continued to recognise the right of *emphyteusis* under the name *emphytéose* or *bail emphytéotique*, and characterised it as a property right in respect of the object of another.[453] However, it was not until 25 June 1902 that the legislature formally recognised the existence of the right of *emphyteusis* in French law.[454] Following the case law of the *Cour de cassation* the legislature introduced a definition in Article 451-1 of the *Code rural*:

> The right of *emphyteusis* on immovable objects gives the holder a property right susceptible of a right of hypothec; the right may be transferred or seized according to the rules on the seizure of immovable objects.
> The right can be agreed upon for a minimum of 18 years and may not exceed 99 years; it may not be tacitly renewed.[455]

The right of *emphyteusis* is created by a contract and may last for a maximum of ninety-nine years. In order to avoid confusion with a normal right of lease, the right of *emphyteusis* is explicitly characterised as a property right.[456] The proprietary

449 Because of the long duration, the right of *emphyteusis* is also known as long lease, in French *bail emphytéotique*. On the *ancien régime* see Chapter 2; 2.4. Other Property Rights, Patault 1983, p. 218, Patault 1989, p. 167-168.

450 Patault 1989, p. 169, Terré & Simler 1998, p. 699-700.

451 In particular by Loi du 17 juillet 1793, see Patault 1989, p. 168-169. On the French Revolution see Chapter 2; 5. Natural Law and the French Revolution.

452 Terré & Simler 1998, p. 700.

453 Or *droit réel immobilier portant sur la chose d'autrui*, see Terré & Simler 1998, p. 699-700, Crocq 1995, p. 200, *Cass. Civ.* 24 August 1857, DP 1857, I, p. 326, *Cass. Civ.* 26 January 1864, DP 1864, I, 83.

454 Loi du 25 juin 1902 introduced Art. 937, which later by Décret No. 83-212 du 16 mars 1983 became Art. 451-1 of the *Code rural*. See Terré & Simler 1998, p. 700. In the new version of the *Code rural*, which entered into force on 1 January 2008, the Articles dealing with the right of *emphyteusis* remain the same.

455 Art. 451-1 *Code rural*, 'Le bail emphytéotique de biens immeubles confère au preneur un droit réel susceptible d'hypothèque; ce droit peut être cédé et saisi dans les formes prescrites pour la saisie immobilière. Ce bail doit être consenti pour plus de dix-huit années et ne peut dépasser quatre-vingt-dix-neuf ans; il ne peut se prolonger par tacite reconduction'.

456 Malaurie & Aynès 2005, p. 101-102.

nature of the right has been the subject of debate in the past, but leading opinion as well as case law and legislation have confirmed its status as a property right.[457] Furthermore, the provision stating that it may not be tacitly renewed is intended to force the parties to make an express agreement on the renewal of the right.[458] Once the right is created it awards the right-holder rights and obligations very similar to those of an owner. Like a right of usufruct, the right-holder, or *emphyteuticarius*, is entitled to the use and enjoyment, the *usus* and *fructus*, of the object.[459] However, unlike a holder of a right of usufruct, the holder of a right of *emphyteusis* is entitled to alter the purpose for which the object is used. Furthermore, he is entitled to take the fruits and also has the rights to fish or to hunt.[460]

Since the *Code rural* entitles the right-holder to create a right of hypothec and a right to transfer the right, the creation of other property rights, such as a right of servitude, is also held possible.[461] Furthermore, it is, as the *Code rural* provides, the right-holder who takes advantage of the accession of new buildings or constructions for the duration of the property right.[462] The result of this advantage is that the right-holder becomes owner of the constructions, plantings or works, made on the object of his right for the duration of the property right through the application of the rules on the right of *superficies*.[463] Finally, the right-holder also has a right to change the way in which the object is used.[464]

Unlike a right of usufruct, the right of *emphyteusis* is not connected to a person in their personal capacity. The right therefore does not cease to exist upon death of the right-holder and will continue to exist until the end of the period agreed upon or the destruction or expropriation of the object under *emphyteusis*.[465] Furthermore, the right can also come to an end by rescission of the contract creating the property right.

Apart from a right of usufruct, the right of *emphyteusis* resembles a contract of lease. Although a normal lease, also of rural areas, only confers personal rights and obligations to the right-holder, a right of *emphyteusis* resembles a lease because it is created by contract and confers similar rights and obligations on the right-holder. However, beyond those rights and obligations, the holder of a right of *emphyteusis* also holds a right that takes effect against the whole world.

Like a normal lease agreement, the right of *emphyteusis* is usually agreed upon in exchange for a payment of money, known as *canon*. Violation of this obligation can entitle the owner to rescind the agreement. Furthermore, the holder of a right of

457 See Aubry, Rau & Bartin 1935, Paras. 224bis stating it is a contract, see Beudant 1938, p. 57 stating it is a property right. For modern references see Carbonnier 2000, p. 296-297, Atias 2005, 309-311.

458 Terré & Simler 1998, p. 701.

459 Terré & Simler 1998, p. 699, Malaurie & Aynès 2005, p. 101, Atias 2005, p. 309.

460 Art. 451-11 *Code rural*, Terré & Simler 1998, p. 701.

461 Art. 451-9 *Code rural*, Terré & Simler 1998, p. 701.

462 Art. 451-10 *Code rural*, see also Malaurie & Aynès 2005, p. 101, Carbonnier 2000, p. 296-297.

463 *Cass. Req.* 22 June 1885, DP 1886, I, p. 268, *Cass. Civ.* 23 November 1954, Bull. Civ. I, No. 331. On the applicability of the right of *superficies* see above; 3.3. *Superficies*.

464 Carbonnier 2000, p. 296.

465 Terré & Simler 1998, p. 702.

emphyteusis is also under the obligation to make repairs to the object. The holder of the right will be bound to those obligations by nature of the property right but also through the existence of the contract agreed. When the owner manages to rescind the contract, the contract and with it the right of *emphyteusis*, will come to an end.[466]

Finally, because the right of *emphyteusis* is a property right in respect of an immovable object, it must be registered in order to have affect against third parties. Like a right of servitude, the right will come into existence between the parties at the moment of agreement, but for third-party effect registration is required. Consequently, registration is also used in case the right is transferred or made subject of the creation of another property right.[467]

A special type of *emphyteusis* is in the *bail à construction* or construction lease.[468] In 1964 the legislature introduced this special right which was later implemented in the *Code de la construction et de l'habitation*.[469] The construction lease is a property right imposing a duty on the right-holder to build.[470] Like the right of *emphyteusis* the construction lease is created by contract for a minimum duration of eighteen years and a maximum duration of ninety-nine years, with the possibility to renew the contract.[471] The contract will deal with the ownership of the existing buildings as well as the buildings that are to be constructed. Without any agreement the right-holder of the construction lease will become owner of the building he constructed until the end of the construction lease agreement.[472] The rules on the construction lease further resemble those on the right of *emphyteusis*. This includes the possibility to create a right of hypothec or other property rights such as servitudes on the right of *emphyteusis*. The right can be transferred as well as seized, and the object that is built may be leased to another party.[473]

Differently from any other property right, the construction lease, by its nature, imposes a positive duty on the right-holder. When the right-holder does not perform his contractual duties, including the positive duty to erect a building, but also the payment for the construction lease, the owner is entitled to rescind the contract and the construction lease will come to an end.[474] In general the end of the contract will result in the acquisition of ownership of the buildings erected during the

466 Terré & Simler 1998, p. 702.

467 Art. 451-13 *Code rural*, Terré & Simler 1998, p. 701.

468 See Terré & Simler 1998, p. 703-705, Carbonnier 2000, p. 296-297, Atias 2005, p. 179-180.

469 Loi No. 64-1247 du 16 décembre 1964, now in Arts. L251-1 – L251-9 *Code de la construction et de l'habitation*.

470 Art. L251-3 *Code de la construction et de l'habitation*. This article states 'Le bail à construction confère au preneur un droit réel immobilier. Ce droit peut être hypothéqué, de même que les constructions édifiées sur le terrain loué; il peut être saisi dans les formes prescrites pour la saisie immobilière. Le preneur peut céder tout ou partie de ses droits ou les apporter en société. Les cessionnaires ou la société sont tenus des mêmes obligations que le cédant qui en reste garant jusqu'à l'achèvement de l'ensemble des constructions que le preneur s'est engagé à édifier en application de l'article L. 251-1. Le preneur peut consentir les servitudes passives indispensables à la réalisation des constructions prévues au bail'.

471 Art. L251-1 *Code de la construction et de l'habitation*, Terré & Simler 1998, p. 703.

472 Art. L251-2 *Code de la construction et de l'habitation*, Terré & Simler 1998, p. 705.

473 Terré & Simler 1998, p. 704-705. See Art. L251-3 *Code de la construction et de l'habitation*.

474 Terré & Simler 1998, p. 705.

construction lease by the owner of the land. Any property right created on the construction lease will come to an end as well. It is possible that the parties have agreed on a compensation or option to purchase for the right-holder of the construction lease at the end of the property right. However, if no agreement has been made, when the property rights cease to exist, the owner of the land becomes owner of the buildings by operation of the rule of Article 552 C.civ.[475]

Finally, a modification of the construction lease exists in the *bail à réhabilitation* or rehabilitation lease. This specific type of *emphyteusis* was introduced in 1990 to allow particular parties to renovate old buildings that had fallen into disuse.[476] The rules for the rehabilitation lease are almost identical to those for the construction lease, with the restriction that only companies or social housing institutions can use the rehabilitation lease. In general, the rehabilitation lease is a property right that can be transferred, seized and be made subject of the creation of another property right, for example, a right of hypothec.[477] However, restrictions apply on the acquiring party, who must also be involved in social housing or be eligible for social housing.[478]

3.5. *Pledge*

The *Ordonnance* of 23 March 2006 that reformed the law on security rights includes a major reform on the right of pledge.[479] Before the reforms, the right of pledge in the Civil Code had remained unchanged since the introduction of the Civil Code in 1804.[480] The right of pledge, together with the right of hypothec, belonged to the category of accessory property rights or *droits réels accessoires*. The term accessory property right refers to the necessity of a connection, accessority, between these property rights and the obligation the performance of which these rights aim to secure.[481] After the reforms this categorisation of property rights into principal and accessory property rights remains intact, but is no longer fully correct. The right of pledge is dealt with in Article 2333 of the Civil Code:

> A pledge is an agreement under which a pledgor gives a right to a creditor to be paid before his other creditors out of a movable object or a set of movable objects, both present and future.

475 Terré & Simler 1998, p. 705. On the application of Art. 552 C.civ see above; 3.3. *Superficies*.

476 Art. 11 Loi No. 90-449 du 31 mai 1990, now implemented in Art. L252-1 – L252-4 *Code de la construction et de l'habitation*.

477 Art. L252-2 1st paragraph *Code de la Construction et de l'habitation*.

478 Art. L252-2 2nd paragraph *Code de la Construction et de l'habitation*.

479 Ordonnance No. 2006-346 du 23 Mars 2006 relative aux sûretés, JORF 24 March 2006. On the ordonnance in general see above; 1. Introduction.

480 Legeais 2006b, p. 12, Legeais 2006a, p. 349.

481 Aynès & Crocq 2003, p. 5.

> The claim secured may be present and future; in the last case the claim must be determinable.[482]

The right of pledge and the way in which it was dealt with in French law has always been subject to many divisions. When a right of pledge is created on a corporeal movable object it is known as a *gage*. A right of pledge on an incorporeal object, such as a claim, can also be created, but is named *nantissement*.[483] Finally, a pledge can also be held on immovable objects, which always requires a transfer of possession. This last right is known as *antichrèse*.[484] After the 2006 reform, the *antichrèse* is dealt with under the right of hypothec.[485] Furthermore, although the provisions on the right of pledge in the Civil Code did not change, over time several specific types of pledge were introduced by special legislation. These special rights of pledge include a pledge on cars, a life-rent pledge and a commercial pledge.[486]

The provisions of the Civil Code after the reforms continue to recognise the classic right of pledge that existed before the reforms, but now also include special types. The classic right of pledge is a right that requires a transfer of possession of objects from the pledgor to the pledgee. This method of creation is the standard method to create a right of pledge. The Civil Code first and foremost provides general rules for the classic right of pledge. These general rules also apply, as far as possible, to new types of pledge that do not require a transfer of possession. These new types were either placed in the Civil Code from special legislation or newly created by the 2006 reform.[487]

The 2006 reform created a new definition of the classic right of pledge that no longer refers to the transfer of possession.[488] Before the reform, it was especially the reference to the possession of the objects that made the right of pledge into a *droit réel*. Now, with the lack of a reference in this respect, it is held that the new right of pledge has lost its *caractère réel*.[489] The result of this loss of proprietary characteristic is not that the right of pledge is no longer a security right, but that, in exchange for flexibility, the right has lost some of its proprietary characteristics. In the new provisions on the right of pledge, flexibility is offered through the possibility to hold a right of pledge on a single object, but also on a group of objects, both present and future. As long as the objects can be identified, a right of pledge can be created.

482 Art. 2333 C.civ, 'Le gage est une convention par laquelle le constituant accorde à un créancier le droit de se faire payer par préférence à ses autres créanciers sur un bien mobilier ou un ensemble de biens mobiliers corporels, présents ou futurs. Les créances garanties peuvent être présentes ou futures; dans ce dernier cas, elles doivent être déterminables'.

483 Before the reforms, this terminology was different. A *nantissement* was a general term used for a situation where by contract a debtor gave an asset to his creditor for security purposes. See Legeais 2006a, p. 354.

484 Art. 2387 C.civ, see Dupichot 2006, p. 26-28, Legeais 2006a, p. 445-447.

485 See below; 3.6. Hypothec.

486 Loi 29 décembre 1934, (pledge on cars), Art. 2354 C.civ (life rent pledge) and Art. L521-1 *Code de Commerce* (commercial pledge). See Legeais 2006a, p. 359-361.

487 Therefore the title in the Civil Code above Art. 2333 C.civ is now Section 1 *Droit commun du gage* (common rules on pledge).

488 Simler 2006, p. 597 *et seq.*

489 Legeais 2006b, p. 12-13, Legeais 2006a, p. 349, 351.

This includes the possibility to create a right of pledge on a generic set of objects, including the possibility that through an act of the pledgee similar objects replace the original objects included in the pledge.[490]

To create a classic right of pledge, which will have effect against third parties, the agreement underlying it must be in writing and contain a description of the obligation it secures and a description of the objects that are given in pledge.[491] The pledgor must, in principle, be the owner of the objects and possession of the objects needs to be transferred to the pledgee.[492] When the classic right of pledge is created, the pledgee, who will now be in possession of the objects, will be under a duty of care over the objects, including a duty to preserve them.[493] However, in contrast with the duty of care in case of principal property rights, acts of management and administration are not required.[494] Violation of the duty of care will entitle the pledgor to claim restitution of the objects.[495] When a pledge is created on generic objects the duty of care applies as well, unless the parties exempt it in their agreement. In such a situation the pledgee will become owner of the objects, but will be under an obligation to make restitution of similar objects with the same value when the obligation secured by the pledge is performed.[496]

In exchange for his care of the objects, the pledgee is entitled to the fruits that the objects produce.[497] This entitlement, which can be excluded by agreement, will only apply in case the pledgee is the creditor of the secured obligation. This will normally be the situation, but it is possible that the possession of the objects is in the hands of another party than the creditor of the obligation.[498] When the pledgor is unable to perform his obligation, the pledgee will be entitled to realise his right and sell the objects.[499] This right to sell the objects is the core power of the pledgee. In order to sell the objects, the pledgee will have to obtain a court order, but since 2006 may also sell the objects without judicial intervention. The pledgee will be entitled to the proceeds of the sale in order to satisfy his claim on the pledgor.[500] Once the pledge is realised, the conditions under which the sale takes place will be the general rules on enforcement of security rights that cannot be deviated from.[501] Alternatively, the pledgee may approach the court and claim that the objects themselves are attributed to him in ownership.[502] An expert may be appointed who

490 Legeais 2006a, p. 352.
491 Art. 2336 C.civ.
492 Art. 2335 C.civ, Legeais 2006a, p. 353.
493 Art. 2343 C.civ. However, the requirement of a transfer of possession has been abandoned by the 2006 reform; a right of pledge can now also be created without a transfer of possession, but with registration of the right instead.
494 *Cass. Com.*, 12 July 2005, RD *bancaire et fin.* 2005, 174. Legeais 2006a, p. 354.
495 Art. 2344 C.civ.
496 Art. 2344 (1) C.civ, Legeais 2006a, p. 354.
497 Art. 2345 C.civ.
498 Known as a third-party pledge. Legeais 2006a, p. 355.
499 Art. 2346 C.civ.
500 Legeais 2006a, p. 355-356.
501 Art. 2346(2) C.civ.
502 Art. 2347 C.civ.

will establish the value of the objects. When the value of the objects exceeds the value of the outstanding claim on the pledgor, the pledgee is obliged to pay the surplus value to the pledgor.[503] When the court awards the objects to the pledgee, the pledgee becomes owner of the objects and the claim will cease to exist to the extent that it is covered by the value of the object of the pledge.[504] However, in case of insolvency of the pledgor, the claim of a pledgee for the objects is usually temporarily suspended.[505]

The 2006 reform introduced further possibilities for a pledgee to take the objects in case of non-performance of the secured obligation. Before the reform the *pacte commissoire* or *lex commissoria,* as it had been known in Roman law, an agreement between the parties that entitles the pledgee to keep the objects for himself in case of non-performance by the pledgor had been strictly prohibited.[506] One of the main reasons for its prohibition had been the protection of the pledgor.[507] However, with the 2006 reform the inclusion of a *pacte commissoire* became expressly allowed. Article 2348 C.civ states in this respect:

> Parties may agree, when the right of pledge is created or at a later moment, that in case of non-performance of the obligation by the pledgor, the pledgee will become the owner of the objects under pledge.
> The value of the objects shall be determined on the day of the transfer by an expert designated by agreement or by a court, in the absence of an official quotation of the object on a regulated market in the meaning of the monetary and financial code. Any clause to the contrary is deemed not to have been written.
> When that value exceeds the value of the secured claim, the difference shall be paid to the pledgor or, in case there are more secured creditors, shall be deposited.[508]

The requirement of an expert to determine the value of the object is held to protect the pledgor sufficiently and replaces the former outright prohibition of these clauses.[509] This provision allowing the *pacte commissoire* is part of the general rules on pledge and can therefore also be applied to the special types of pledge, unless provided otherwise.[510] The general introduction of the *pacte commissoire* into the

503 Art. 2347 C.civ, Legeais 2006a, p. 357.

504 *Cass. Com.* 24 January 2006, JCP E 2006, 1753.

505 Legeais 2006a, p. 357-358.

506 Legeais 2006a, p. 258. See Chapter 2; 2.4. Other Property Rights.

507 Other reasons include the protection of other creditors from objects of a higher value than the outstanding claim leaving the patrimony of the debtor when the secured creditor claims these for himself.

508 Art. 2348 C.civ, 'Il peut être convenu, lors de la constitution du gage ou postérieurement, qu'à défaut d'exécution de l'obligation garantie le créancier deviendra propriétaire du bien gagé. La valeur du bien est déterminer au jour du transfert par un expert désigné à l'amiable ou judiciairement, à défaut de cotation officielle du bien dur un marché organisé au sens du code monétaire et financier. Toute clause contraire est réputée non écrite. Lorsque cette valeur excède le montant de la dette garantie, la somme égale à la différance est versée au débiteur ou, s'il existe d'autres créanciers gagistes, est consignée'.

509 Legeais 2006a, p. 358.

510 Art. 2354 C.civ.

provisions on pledge introduces a remarkable flexibility in the French law of pledge, that has, until now, not been seen in other civil law systems.[511]

Apart from the classic right of pledge that requires a transfer of possession, French law recognises a non-possessory right of pledge on movable objects. This right of pledge is subject to the same rules as the classic right of pledge, but with the exception of the requirement for the transfer of possession.[512] Because of the lack of a transfer of possession, the creation of a non-possessory pledge is invisible to third parties. Therefore, in order to have effect against third parties, the right of non-possessory pledge must be registered.[513]

Other differences exist between these and the classic right of pledge. Because the possession of the objects remains with the pledgor, the pledgor, and not the pledgee, will be under the duty to take care of the objects. Furthermore, if the agreement allows it, the pledgor may be entitled to sell and transfer generic objects under pledge. When this is allowed, the pledgor is under the obligation to replace the generic objects.[514] When the right of pledge is realised, other differences are apparent. A non-possessory pledge is a less strong security right compared with a classic, possessory, right of pledge. In case of a classic pledge the pledgee will have a right of retention on the objects by nature of his possession.[515] This right allows the pledgee to hold on to the objects, even in respect of other creditors, until his claim is satisfied. In case of a non-possessory pledge, the pledgee does not have possession and therefore also does not have a right of retention.

French law after the 2006 reform recognises several special types of non-possessory pledge. These special types include a commercial pledge, a right of pledge on objects in storage, and a right of pledge on cars.[516] The provisions on these special types of pledge are mostly similar to the common rules on pledge in the Civil Code and are specified depending on the type. For example, in case of a pledge on objects in storage, the *pacte commissoire* cannot be agreed upon.[517]

Finally, a third type of pledge is recognised. This right of pledge, known as a *nantissement*, is a right of pledge on incorporeal objects, usually claims.[518] This category of objects had hardly been dealt with before the reform and this should be seen as one of the principal reasons why a reform of French law in respect of pledges was absolutely necessary.[519] In Article 2355 the Code Civil states:

511 In the other civil law systems of German and Dutch law the *lex commissoria* remains prohibited. See Chapter 4; 3.6. Pledge and Chapter 5; 3.6. Pledge.

512 Legeais 2006b, p. 16, Legeais 2006a, p. 362.

513 See Art. 2337 C.civ, Legeais 2006a, p. 364.

514 Art. 2342 C.civ.

515 Art. 2286 C.civ, Legeais 2006b, p. 15, Legeais 2006a, p. 359. On the right of retention in French law see below; 4.1. Right of Retention.

516 Legeais 2006a, p. 265-366.

517 Art. L527-2 *Code de commerce*. Legeais 2006a, p. 369.

518 See in general Stoufflet 2006, p. 19-22.

519 Legeais 2006a, p. 375. Synvet 2005, p. 64 *et seq.*

> The pledge of an incorporeal object is the allocation, in order to secure the performance of an obligation, of an incorporeal object or a set of incorporeal objects, present or future.[520]

This type of pledge mainly applies to claims, but can be created on other rights as well.[521] Claims, in particular future claims, are a great source of value which, when subject of security rights, may provide for increased financing opportunities for companies. Before the reform, the pledge on claims had been subject to the general rules on classic pledge, making it possible to hold a pledge only over present claims.[522]

Under the new provisions, the right of pledge is created by an agreement which must describe the claims on which it is created.[523] When the claim is future, the agreement must specify the claim in such a way that it can be anticipated. Anticipation can be achieved by stating the name of the debtor, the amount due and the moment when the claim must be paid. When a claim cannot be identified in this manner, it cannot be the subject of a right of pledge.[524] The result of this method of creation is that although the right of pledge will exist, the future claim will not. Therefore, from the moment the claim is created, the right of pledge will burden it.[525] The right of pledge is created on the day on which the agreement is signed and will have effect against third parties on the same date.[526] However, in order to have effect against the debtor, especially to force the debtor to pay the claim to the pledgee in case of non-performance by the pledgor, notification of the pledge must be given to the debtor.[527]

Because of the nature of the objects concerned, the realisation of the pledge on claims is organised differently. In case of a pledge on claims the pledgee may demand payment of the claim to himself by giving notification to the debtors of the claims, but may also, by making use of the *pacte commissoire*, demand assignment of the pledged claims to him.[528] As with all other rights of pledge, any surplus value must be returned to the pledgor.[529] Finally, as with the other types of pledge, special types of pledge are recognised. These include a pledge of a bank account and a pledge of a *fonds de commerce*.[530]

520 Art. 2355(1) C.civ, 'Le nantissement est l'affectation, en garantie d'une obligation, d'un bien meuble incorporel ou d'un ensemble de biens meubles incorporels, présents ou futurs'.

521 Legeais 2006a, p. 375-376.

522 Legeais 2006a, p. 377. In the law of banking and finance, however, a pledge on future claims had already been allowed before the 2006 reform.

523 Art. 2356 C.civ.

524 Art. 2356 C.civ, Legeais 2006a, p. 378.

525 Art. 2357 C.civ.

526 Art. 2361 C.civ, Legeais 2006a, p. 379.

527 Arts. 2362 and 2363 C.civ.

528 Art. 2364 C.civ, Legeais 2006a, p. 380.

529 Art. 2366 C.civ.

530 Art. 2360 C.civ (pledge on bank account), Art. L142-1 *Code de commerce* (pledge on *fonds de commerce*).

3.6. *Hypothec*

The right of hypothec is a property security right in respect of an immovable object.[531] In many respects it resembles a right of pledge, in particular a non-possessory right of pledge, but because of the specific nature of immovable objects, a specific property right is recognised. Like the right of pledge, the right of hypothec was thoroughly restructured by the 2006 reform on security rights. The right of hypothec can be created by agreement, by court decision, or through operation of law.[532] The right of hypothec in French law is defined in Article 2393 C.civ:

> The right of hypothec is a property right created on immovable objects for the performance of an obligation.
> The right is, by its nature, indivisible and exists on all of the objects under hypothec, on each one and on each part of those objects.
> The right of hypothec follows the objects in whatever hands they may pass.[533]

The regular type of hypothec, known as conventional hypothec, can be created by an owner of an immovable object, usually a piece of land, but can also be created on a property right by its holder, such as a bare owner, a holder of a right of usufruct, *superficies, emphyteusis,* and even the holder of a construction lease.[534] When the right of hypothec is created, the immovable object on which it is created must already exist. A hypothec on a future object is in principle not allowed.[535] However, three exceptions exist to this rule. When a debtor does not have any or sufficient objects to secure the claim he may agree to submit all immovable objects that he will acquire in the future to the hypothec. A debtor whose object was damaged and deteriorated in value may do the same. And finally, a debtor who has a right to build for his own benefit on another's land may subject his right to the building to the right of hypothec.[536] The agreement creating the right of hypothec must give a description of the objects or, in case of the exceptions just mentioned, the future objects.[537] The right of hypothec is an *acte solennel,* which requires an agreement to take the form of a notarial deed in order to be validly created.[538] Furthermore, differently from other property rights in French law, the right must be registered in order to come into existence.[539]

531 See Laurent 1878, p. 95, Legeais 2006a, p. 398.
532 Art. 2395 C.civ.
533 Art. 2393 C.civ, 'L'hypothèque est un droit réel sur les immeubles affectés à l'acquittement d'une obligation. Elle est, de sa nature, indivisible, et subsiste en entier sur tous les immeubles affectés, sur chacun et sur chaque portion de ces immeubles. Elle les suit dans quelques mains qu'il passent'.
534 Art. 2397 C.civ, *Cass. Civ.* 12 April 1836, S. 1836, I, 366, Delebecque 2006, p. 29, Legeais 2006a, p. 402.
535 Art. 2419 C.civ.
536 Art. 2420 C.civ, Legeais 2006a, p. 403.
537 Art. 2418 C.civ.
538 Art. 2416 C.civ.
539 Legeais 2006a, p. 454.

The right of hypothec is an accessory right, by which is meant that it cannot exist without the obligation it secures. Apart from the object on which the right is created, the claim that the right of hypothec seeks to secure must also be identifiable, but does not necessarily have to be in existence.[540] Before the reform in 2006, French law adhered strictly to the principle of specificity. Therefore, a right of hypothec could only exist when it secured a single claim that already existed when the right was created. The statutory amendments on hypothec make it possible to create a right of hypothec to secure the performance of a future claim or even of future claims, as long as these can be identified.[541]

By introducing less strict requirements on the specificity of claims, the French legislator has opened up the possibility of creating several new types of hypothec. First, Article 2422 C.civ provides a further provision on the possibility of securing a claim with a right of hypothec:

> A right of hypothec may be used to secure other claims than those mentioned in the contract that created the right, provided that this agreement states so explicitly.
> The right-holder may then offer the right as security, up to the value provided for in the contract that created the right and specified in article 2423, not only to the original creditor, but also to a new creditor, even when the first has not yet been paid.[542]

This new type of hypothec, although technically a conventional hypothec, is known as a *hypothèque rechargeable* or rechargeable hypothec.[543] It enables a debtor to provide a right of hypothec to a creditor in order to obtain finance, but it also enables the debtor to recharge the right when there is more value in the object under hypothec. Moreover, the right of hypothec can also be recharged when the debtor has already paid off some of this loan and the claim the right of hypothec secures has decreased in value.[544] When recharging the right of hypothec, the debtor can not only approach the original creditor, but may also offer the same right of hypothec to another creditor.[545] In order for this special right to be created a specific notarial deed is needed, which must be registered.[546]

The rechargeable hypothec cannot be used by everyone and cannot be held on all objects. The creation of the right may only be agreed by regular, i.e. non-legal, persons on an immovable object that is used as housing, usually a piece of land with a house on it.[547] Furthermore, the notarial deed creating the right must contain information on the duration of the right of hypothec by mentioning the duration of

540 Art. 2421 C.civ.

541 Art. 2421 C.civ, Legeais 2006a, p. 404-405.

542 Art. 2422 C.civ, 'L'hypothèque peut être ultérieurement affectée à la garantie de créances autres que celles mentionnées par l'acte constitutif pourvu que celui-ci le prévoie expressément. Le constituant peut alors l'offrir en garantie, dans la limite de la somme prévue dans l'acte constitutif et mentionnée à l'article 2423, non seulement au créancier originaire, mais aussi à un nouveau créancier encore que le premier n'ait pas été payé …'.

543 See, in general, Grimaldi 2006b, p. 33-36.

544 Legeais 2006a, p. 406.

545 Legeais 2006a, p. 405-406.

546 Art. 2422 C.civ.

547 Art. L313-14 *Code de la consommation*.

registration, a description of the object under hypothec, and, most importantly, the maximum value for which the rechargeable right of hypothec is created.[548] When the right of hypothec is created for an unlimited duration, the debtor may at any time terminate the agreement by giving the creditor three-months' notice. However, the right of hypothec will remain in existence for outstanding claims.[549]

A second new type of hypothec also falls into the general category of conventional hypothecs and is known as the *prêt viager hypothécaire* or life-rent hypothec. This new type is defined by Article L.314-1 *Code de la consommation*:

> The life rent hypothec is a contract by which a credit or financial institution provides a private person, the debtor, with a loan in the form of a sum of money or periodic instalments of money, secured by a right of hypothec on an immovable object used for residential purposes of the debtor and the repayment of the loan - the loan and the interest - are not claimed until the debtor dies or when the object is conveyed or a limited property right is created on the object is made before the debtor dies ...[550]

The new provisions on the specificity of the claims that the right of hypothec must secure create the possibility that the right of hypothec is created to secure a future claim. This type of hypothec cleverly makes use of these new flexible rules and enables the creation of what is also known as a reversed hypothec. Instead of creating a claim fully at once, which is also possible, the claim is build up in instalments, increasing in value each time an instalment is paid. When the debtor receives all the money at once, usually to buy a life-rent scheme from another financial institution, the full claim comes into existence at once. Unlike a standard right hypothec, the agreement between the debtor and the bank is that the claim will not be repaid until the death of the debtor.[551] As in the case of a rechargeable hypothec the agreement will have to take the form of a notarial deed and must be registered. The deed must contain information on the parties, the object concerned, and the maximum value for which the right of hypothec is created.[552]

These rights of hypothec must be created by notarial deed and require registration in order to be enforced against third parties. However, even without registration the right of hypothec is validly created.[553] When the right is validly created it will create a property right in respect of the right of ownership of the debtor. Because the debtor remains the owner of the immovable object under hypothec, the debtor continues to enjoy his right of ownership, but is no longer unrestricted. In

548 Art. L313-13-1 *Code de la consommation*.

549 Art. 2423 C.civ.

550 Art. L314-1 *Code de la consommation*, 'Le prêt viager hypothécaire est un contrat par lequel un établissement de crédit ou un établissement financier consent à une personne physique un prêt sous forme d'un capital ou de versements périodiques, garanti par une hypothèque constituée sur un bien immobilier de l'emprunteur à usage exclusif d'habitation et dont le remboursement - principal et intérêts - ne peut être exigé qu'au décès de l'emprunteur ou lors de l'aliénation ou du démembrement de la propriété de l'immeuble hypothéqué s'ils surviennent avant le décès ...'.

551 See Legeais 2006a, p. 406-407. Grimaldi 2006b, p. 36-37.

552 Arts. L314-5 and L314-7 *Code de la consommation*.

553 Arts. 2426 *et seq*. C.civ, Legeais 2006a, p. 414.

any situation the debtor will be under a duty to preserve the value of the object.[554] For example, the debtor may not create a lease on his object for a long period of time to another person, as this would seriously decrease the value of the immovable object.[555]

When the debtor defaults on his loan the creditor, the holder of the right of hypothec, will have the choice to sell the object under hypothec or to claim the object for himself through a court order, or through an agreement with the debtor.[556] In order to start the procedure of executing the right of hypothec, the creditor must demand payment from the debtor.[557] Although the holder of a right of hypothec has a choice between these actions, most of the time the holder will choose to sell the object. The holder may then satisfy his claim with the proceeds of the sale.[558]

When the object under hypothec is not the principal place of residence of the debtor, the right-holder may approach a court to claim the object for himself.[559] This possibility, which did not exist before the 2006 reform, brings the right of hypothec in line with the reforms on the right of pledge.[560] As in the case of a right of pledge, the court order will transfer the ownership from the debtor to the creditor. The value of the object will be determined by agreement or, if necessary by an expert. Any surplus value must be paid to the debtor or, in case there are more secured creditors, must be deposited.[561]

Finally, the 2006 reform has also introduced the *pacte commissoire* for rights of hypothec.[562] By such an agreement the debtor and creditor may agree that on non-performance by the debtor, the creditor shall become owner of the immovable object under hypothec without a court order.[563] As in the case of acquisition by court order, the *pacte commissoire* will be invalid if the immovable object is the principal place of residence of the debtor.[564] Also, in the case of acquisition by agreement, the value of the object will be determined by the parties themselves, or by an expert.[565] Any surplus value shall be paid to the debtor, or deposited in cases where there are more secured creditors.[566]

In addition to conventional rights of hypothec, a right of hypothec can also come into existence by operation of law or by decision of a court. The first of these types of hypothec is known as *hypothèque légale* or legal hypothec and may arise by application of the Civil Code or other specific legislation.[567] These specific rights

554 Legeais 2006a, p. 421-422.
555 Legeais 2006a, p. 422-423.
556 See Delebecque 2006, p. 29-31.
557 *Cass. Civ.* 3ème 23 January 1973, D. 1973, 427, Malaurie & Aynès 2005, p. 257.
558 Art. 2458 C.civ, Legeais 2006a, p. 424.
559 Art. 2458 C.civ.
560 Legeais 2006a, p. 427.
561 Art. 2460 C.civ.
562 Art. 2459 C.civ. Delebecque 2006, p. 31-32.
563 See Legeais 2006a, p. 428-429.
564 Legeais 2006a, p. 428.
565 Delebecque 2006, p. 32.
566 Art. 2460 C.civ.
567 Legeais 2006a, p. 440.

arise in case of marriage, where one spouse will have a right of hypothec on the objects of the other, and in case of guardianship, where the person subjected to the guardianship has a right of hypothec on the objects of the guardian.[568] Other types exist as well and include rights of legal hypothec held by the State. For example, the tax authority will have a general legal hypothec on the immovable objects of a debtor.[569] The second of these types of hypothec is known as *hypothèque judiciaire* or judiciary hypothec.[570] These rights are of high practical relevance and enable a creditor who has obtained judgement against a debtor for payment to claim recognition of a right of hypothec on the immovable objects of the debtor through the decision of a court. If the court awards the right of hypothec, the creditor may register his right in order for it to have effect against third parties. Therefore, the judiciary hypothec is used to strengthen a personal claim that has been awarded by court decision.[571]

Finally, under the 2006 reform, the already mentioned *antichrèse* or pledge on immovable objects has come under the heading of security rights in respect of immovable objects in the Civil Code.[572] The pledge on immovable objects is not often used as it requires a transfer of possession of the immovable object to the creditor.[573] The right therefore bears characteristics of a right of pledge as well as a right of hypothec.[574] This special property right, once created, must be registered in order to have effect against third parties, and will award its holder with a strong security right in respect of an immovable object. As far as possible the general provisions on hypothec apply, including the execution of the right.[575]

3.7. *Priority Rights*

Article 2324 of the Civil Code states:

> A priority right is a right that a creditor of a claim has by the nature of his claim to have priority over other creditors, even holders of a right of hypothec.[576]

French law has a long tradition of recognising priority rights. Before a reform in 1955 there were many priority rights, most of which were not registered.[577] This reform in 1955 reduced the number of priority rights and changed the publicity requirements of some of these. In particular those priority rights that can be held over an immovable object, were made subject to more publicity requirements.

568 Arts. 2400(1) and (2) C.civ.
569 Art. 2400(3) C.civ, Legeais 2006a, p. 441.
570 Art. 2412 C.civ, Legeais 2006a, p. 442.
571 Legeais 2006a, p. 442-444.
572 Art. 2387 C.civ. See also above; 3.5. Pledge.
573 Legeais 2006a, p. 445-446.
574 Legeais characterises it as a *sûreté mixte*, Legeais 2006a, p. 445.
575 Art. 2388 C.civ.
576 Art. 2324 C.civ, 'Le privilège est un droit que la qualité de la créance donne à un créancier d'être préféré aux autres créanciers, même hypothécaires'.
577 Loi du 4 janvier 1955. Legeais 2006a, p. 453.

Privilèges or priority rights are special property rights that come into existence by operation of law accessory to an existing claim.[578] Because of their special nature, the acceptance of priority rights in French law is debated, even though the 2006 reform chose to reintroduce and therefore re-establish these rights.[579] When a priority right is recognised it will give preference to its holder in violation of the rule of *paritas creditorum*. Contrary to other security rights that deviate from this rule that makes all creditors equal, priority rights are not created by agreement and sometimes not even registered.

Two types of priority rights exist. First, there are general priority rights that are held on a set of objects.[580] Second, there are special priority rights that are held on a single object.[581] Furthermore, most priority rights are divided between immovable and movable objects. The term priority right is therefore a name for a collection of rights that may be different in content but each of which gives priority over other creditors to its holder.

The first category of priority rights comprises general priority rights that are held on all objects of a debtor. These include a right in respect of claims arising from court costs and salaries of the past and present year, but also claims from contributions made during insolvency proceedings in order to stimulate a fresh start for insolvent companies, and claims arising from business with a company under observation, which refers to a company that is almost insolvent.[582]

All other priority rights are held either on immovable or on movable objects. General priority rights in respect of immovable objects are no longer recognised and since 2006 have been replaced with rights of legal hypothec.[583] General priority rights over movables are rare, but include the claim of the tax authorities and social security authorities.[584] The remaining priority rights are not only dealt with by the Civil Code but also by specific legislation. These arise when a seller of an object has a claim for payment of the purchase price, the claim of a manager of an apartment building for the contributions, or the claim of a lessor of an object for rent.[585]

With the 2006 reform most priority rights in respect of immovable objects became capable of registration. Priority rights in respect of movable objects, however, remain undisclosed to third parties.[586] Finally, priority rights may come into conflict with each other. However, since all priority rights follow directly from the Civil Code or other legislation, an order of ranking amongst them may also be

578 Legeais 2006a, p. 451.

579 See Legeais 2006a, p. 452.

580 Known as *privilèges généraux*. Legeais 2006a, p. 453.

581 Known as *privilèges généraux*. Aynès & Crocq 2003, p. 7, Legeais 2006a, p. 453.

582 Arts. 2331-1 and 2375-1 C.civ (Court costs), Arts. 2331-4 and 2375-2 C.civ (Salaries), Art. L611-11 *Code de commerce* (fresh start contributions) and Arts. L622-17 and L641-13 *Code de commerce* (claims on company under observation).

583 On these rights of legal hypothec see above; 3.6. Hypothec.

584 Art. 2331 C.civ, Legeais 2006a, p. 465-468.

585 See Arts. 2332, 2374 and 2375 C.civ.

586 Legeais 2006a, p. 453-454.

provided for by legislation. Therefore, to solve these conflicts Article 2332 C.civ provides an order of ranking.[587]

Priority rights are atypical property rights because they are not created by agreement and only provide priority to a holder of a claim. Unlike other property security rights, priority rights do not entitle the right-holder to sell the object or keep it for himself in case of non-performance by the debtor. A priority right only entitles its holder to a right of preference or *droit de préférence*. The right of preference entitles its holder to claim the sum or performance due to the debtor before other creditors. Depending on the rank of the security rights, the holder entitled to a right of preference will even be entitled to claim before other holders of security rights that entitle them to a right of preference. The entitlement to preference of a priority right is even stronger because its holder may claim payment even before the holders of other property security rights. A final difference from other security rights is that priority rights are so closely connected to the claim they secure that they arise but also cease to exist with that claim. This is in contrast with other property security rights, which only come into existence upon agreement between the parties and, in case of hypothec, after registration.[588]

4. Borderline Cases in French Property Law

Section 3 of this Chapter deals with those property rights that are explicitly recognised as property rights by legislation. However, there are other legal relations in French law that closely resemble property rights. Some of these relations are commonly dealt with in property law handbooks, but traditionally are not recognised as property rights. The reason for their treatment in property law is that these relations have many but not all of the characteristics of a property right. In other words, these rights are on the borderline between contract law and property law, but are traditionally not dealt with by contract law.

4.1. *Right of Retention*

When one party is under an obligation to do something in order to benefit another party, that benefiting party may be entitled to retain possession of an object of the first party until the obligation is performed. Such a situation can occur in many instances, but is best illustrated by a simple situation of sale. Where, under a contract of sale, the purchase price has not been paid and there is reason to believe that payment will not be made soon, the seller may refrain from delivering the object to the buyer.[589] *Vice versa*, the buyer might also withhold the payment of the purchase price when he suspects the seller will not perform.[590] Another example is offered in the area of security rights. When a right of pledge has been created, the

587 See Legeais 2006a, p. 473-474.
588 Legeais 2006a, p. 451.
589 See Piedelièvre 2004, p. 171 *et seq.*, Legeais 1996, p. 318 *et seq.*, Aynès & Crocq 2003, p. 165.
590 Piedelièvre 2004, p. 172.

holder of the right of pledge may retain possession of the object under pledge until he has been paid.[591]

This right, known as the right of retention, can be exercised on movable as well as on immovable objects, and even on incorporeal objects, rights and claims, insofar as they can be retained.[592] There is a debate on whether there must be a relation between the object and the claim for which the right of retention is exercised.[593] Refusing the requirement of such a connection would entitle the retentor, the person using the right of retention, to retain possession of any object of the debtor. However, the leading opinion in France seems to require a connection between the object under retention and the claim the right intends to secure.[594]

The Civil Code does not explicitly deal with the right of retention, but recognises its existence.[595] This recognition can be seen in several instances where the Civil Code specifically excludes the possibility of exercising a right of retention.[596] *A contrario*, the drafters of the Civil Code did accept the possibility that parties would exercise a right of retention. The existence of the right of retention is therefore not debated.[597] However, the legal nature of the right, in particular the question whether the right of retention is a property security right, has been subject to a long debate.

To start with, French legal scholarship is generally divided over the question whether the right of retention is a security right. Although the right of retention secures the performance of an obligation, usually the payment of a debt, the right lacks the basic characteristic of a security right - the entitlement to the value of the object.[598] Although the majority of authors recognise the right of retention as security in the broad sense of the word, as *sûreté*, the question whether it is also a security right is much more complicated.[599] In general the exercise of the right of retention is connected to contract law.[600] It is a method to strengthen the position of a creditor in a situation where a debtor does not perform or threatens not to perform. Therefore, the primary effect of the right of retention is against the non-performing debtor and not against the world. It is because of this aspect of the right of retention that Catala-Franjou has argued that the right of retention is nothing more than a personal right.[601] However, retaining factual control of an object does not only have effect against the non-performing debtor, but also has effect against

591 See Piedelièvre 2004, p. 173. Legeais 1996, p. 320.

592 Piedelièvre 2004, p. 174-177, Simler & Delebecque 2004, p. 482-483, on incorporeal rights see Legeais 1996, p. 320-321.

593 See Piedelièvre 2004, p. 177.

594 Legeais 1996, p. 322-323, Piedelièvre 2004, p. 177-180, Simler & Delebecque 2004, p. 477.

595 Piedelièvre 2004, p. 172, Simler & Delebecque 2004, p. 478-481, Aynès & Crocq 2003, p. 167.

596 See, e.g., Art. 1885 C.civ, Piedelièvre 2004, p. 173-174.

597 Legeais 1996, p. 319-320.

598 Piedelièvre 2004, p. 185-186, Legeais 1996, p. 318-319, Simler & Delebecque 2004, p. 476-477, see Crocq 1995, p. 238-241 who does not consider the right of retention as full security.

599 On the classification as security see Piedelièvre 2004, p. 185-186, Legeais 1996, p. 318-319, Simler & Delebecque 2004, p. 476-477, Crocq 1995, p. 238-241, *contra* see *Cass. Com.* 20 May 1997, D. 1998, p. 479, Aynès & Crocq 2003, p. 178-179.

600 Simler & Delebecque 2004, p. 476.

601 Catala-Franjou 1967, p. 9 *et seq.*, see also Legeais 1996, p. 318.

other parties. It is because of this effect that another group of authors argues that the right of retention is a property security right.[602] But the effect of the right against third parties is not the same as a normal property right. The right of retention lacks the essential characteristics of *droit de suite* and *droit de préférence*. Due to the absence of these characteristics some authors call the right of retention an incomplete property right.[603]

Furthermore, unlike any other property security right, the right of retention allows the holder to withhold the object from the debtor, but does not allow the creditor to sell the object and take the proceeds of the sale to satisfy his claim.[604]

In 1992 the *Cour de cassation* ruled on the subject and decided that the right of retention is a property right with effect against everyone, including third parties not related to the claim.[605] This includes a situation in which the right of retention is not registered and is therefore unknown to these third parties.[606] With this remarkable decision, the *Cour de cassation* enlarged the number of property rights with an additional security right. However, the leading opinion continues to refrain from classifying the right as either a personal or a property right.[607]

The classification problem was even further complicated by the *Cour de cassation* in 1997 when it held that the right of retention was not a *sûreté*.[608] Finally, with the 2006 reforms of the Civil Code, the right of retention has come to be dealt with under the heading of general provisions on security. This new classification therefore somewhat settles the debate.[609] Article 2286 of the Civil Code now provides general rules on when to invoke the right of retention. The Article states:

> The exercise of a right of retention on an object is possible by:
> 1. The person to whom the object was handed over until the payment of his debt;
> 2. The person whose outstanding debt results from the contract that binds him to deliver the object.

[602] Legeais 1996, p. 318, Piedelièvre 2004, p. 185.

[603] Picod 1999, No. 129, Catala-Franjou 1967, p. 40. See also Simler and Delebecque who seem to suggest that the right of retention should be a security right, Simler & Delebecque 2004, p. 476-477.

[604] See Simler & Delebecque 2004, p. 474-475.

[605] *Cass.* Civ. 1er 7 January 1992, RTD civ. 1992.586, JCP 1992.I.3583, Piedelièvre 2004, p. 185, Aynès & Crocq 2003, p. 165 *et seq.* In support also see Recueil complet des travaux préparatoires du code civil 14, p. 507, 516-517.

[606] See *Cass. Civ.* 3ème 16 December 1998, Bull. Civ. III No. 253, DP 1874, p. 457. Aynès & Crocq 2003, p. 175.

[607] See Piedelièvre 2004, p. 185-186, Legeais 1996, p. 318-319, in particular Aynès & Crocq 2003, 178-179. This refusal of French doctrine to recognise the right of retention as a property right is why this right is dealt with in this section and not in the section dealing with property rights.

[608] The *Cour de cassation* states 'Mais attendu que le droit de rétention n'est pas une sûreté et n'est pas assimilable au gage…', *Cass. Com.* 20 May 1997, D. 1998, p. 479, see also *Cass. Com.* 9 June 1998, Bull. 1998 IV No. 181, p. 150.

[609] The Grimaldi-report published to prepare the 2006 reform does not mention the nature of the right of retention either. See Grimaldi et al. 2003.

3. The person whose outstanding debt was created at the moment he started holding the object.

A right of retention is lost through the voluntary release of the power over the object.[610]

The 2006 reform upholds the decision of the *Cour de cassation* on the classification of the right of retention as a property right. Nevertheless, at the same time, legal scholarship seems to remain divided on the issue and refrains from taking a position.[611] Because of this it seems justifiable to deal with the right of retention as an exceptional right amongst the other property rights. Even with the classification of the *Cour de cassation*, the right of retention continues to lack the essential characteristics of *droit de suite* and *droit de préférence* and hence possibly the characteristics of a property right at all.

4.2. *Real Obligations*

Like in any civil law system, the separation between the law of obligations and the law of property in French law creates some classification problems.[612] Certain agreements between parties cannot be characterised as a property right, but are not, strictly speaking, a personal right either. An example of such an agreement is offered by the positive duties connected to a principal negative duty in case of a right of servitude.[613] These secondary obligations are not part of the right of servitude as such, but transfer with the right of servitude to a third party. In other words, the debtor of the obligation is bound to the obligation in his capacity as owner of the servient land. Because of this effect these obligations are known as real obligations or obligations *propter rem*. A real obligation or obligation *propter rem* is an obligation closely related to an object.[614] Because of this relation the obligation bears the characteristics not only of a personal right but also of a property right, including the effect against a third party when the right is transferred.[615] The nature of the real obligation is subject to considerable debate.[616] This debate not only focuses on the recognition of real obligations, but also concerns questions such as the distinction between the law of obligations and the law of property, the recog-

610 Art. 2286 C.civ, 'Peut se prévaloir d'un droit de rétention sur la chose: 1. Celui à qui la chose a été remise jusqu'au paiement de sa créance; 2. Celui dont la créance impayée résulte du contrat qui l'oblige à la livrer; 3. Celui dont la créance impayée est née à l'occasion de la détention de la chose. Le droit de rétention se perd par le dessaisissement volontaire'.

611 See Piedelièvre 2004, p. 185-186, Legeais 1996, p. 318-319, Aynès & Crocq 2003, p. 178-179, Libchaber 2004, p. 399 *et seq*.

612 On German and Dutch law see Chapter 4; 4. Borderline Cases in German Property Law, and Chapter 5; 4. Borderline Cases in Dutch Property Law.

613 See above; 3.1. Real Servitudes.

614 Sometimes also the term *charge réelle* is used. Aberkane 1957, p. 2, Atias 2005, p. 56, De Juglart 1937, p. 33, Terré & Simler 1998, p. 589-590, 655, Jourdain, Marty & Raynaud 1995, p. 8-10.

615 See Sagaert 2004b, p. 59-60, Sagaert 2006, p. 43-45, Terré & Simler 1998, p. 655, Malaurie & Aynès 2005, p. 103, Carbonnier 2000, p. 72-73.

616 See Aberkane 1957, De Juglart 1937, Larroumet 2004, p. 31 *et seq*., Sagaert 2004a, No. 16, Sagaert 2004b, p. 47 *et seq*.

nition of a *numerus clausus* of property rights, and the doctrine of privity of contract in French law.[617]

The theory of real obligations is primarily connected to the existence of property rights. Certain obligations can come into existence that are not part of a property right itself and which should be seen as a separate agreement. However, this agreement does not create a mere personal obligation, but an obligation that transfers with the property right to which it is connected. Therefore the real obligation, like the property right to which it is connected, has effect against third parties. In legal theory, these agreements are considered to be accessory to the property right.[618] In his study on this subject, Aberkane recognises three situations in which the Civil Code, by force of law, recognises the existence of these real obligations.[619] The existence of real obligations by force of the Civil Code resembles the legal property rights which have been dealt with above.[620] First, in case of a right of servitude, the obligation that arises through the application of Article 699 C.civ for the maintenance of the object under servitude can be seen as a real obligation. The maintenance obligation is not part of the right of servitude itself, but is seen as a separate obligation arising from Article 699 when the parties agreed on the maintenance of the object under servitude.[621] Furthermore, Article 701 C.civ also offers an example of a real obligation. Any maintenance or other works under the normal exercise of a right of servitude cannot be a part of the right of servitude itself as they are positive duties.[622] Legal scholarship and case law therefore recognise these positive duties as a real obligation.[623]

Article 655 C.civ offers another example. This Article deals with a situation of co-ownership of a wall and stipulates a duty to repair the wall at the costs of each co-owner. Aberkane holds that also this obligation is a real obligation.[624] Finally, he also mentions the old Article 2168 C.civ, now Article 2463 C.civ, which describes the obligation of a third person holding an object on which a right of hypothec is created or on which a priority right is held to pay interest and capital, or repayment of the debt or claim the performance of which these rights secure, over the object.[625]

Furthermore, a theory of real obligations connected to the right of ownership has become recognised through the works of Ginossar.[626] Although his studies do

617 See Sagaert 2005b, p. 1004-1016, Sagaert 2004b, p. 60-61, Larroumet 2004, p. 31-35. It is De Juglart who focuses the attention on the influence of German doctrine in the development of French doctrine on the real obligation, see De Juglart 1937, p. 50-52.

618 See Aberkane 1957, p. 1-16, Sagaert 2004b, p. 56 *et seq.*

619 Aberkane 1957, p. 1 *et seq.*

620 E.g. the legal pledge and legal hypothec, see above; 3.5. Pledge and 3.6. Hypothec.

621 Aberkane 1957, p. 2-3, see also De Juglart 1937, p. 16-17, 34-36, Terré & Simler 1998, p. 655.

622 This is why Belgian law generally is very restricted to recognise positive real obligations. See Sagaert 2004b, p. 60-61, Sagaert 2004b, p. 1006-1007.

623 *Cass. Civ.* 3ème 26 November 1960, Bull. Civ. III, No. 646, Aberkane 1957, p. 6-9, 117 *et seq.*, Sagaert 2004b, p. 56-57. A similarly real obligation could be recognised in case of the maintenance duty of a usufructuary. See Sagaert 2004b, p. 64-65.

624 Aberkane 1957, p. 2.

625 Aberkane 1957, p. 2.

626 Ginossar 1960, p. 18 *et seq.* On Ginossar see, *inter alia*, Larroumet 2004, p. 31, Snijders & Rank-Berenschot 2001, p. 49-50, Hervieu 1981, p. 176 *et seq.*

not reflect the leading opinion in French law, Ginossar's ideas are worth considering.[627] Ginossar looks at the right of ownership as a set of obligations which should not be defined in terms of personal rights or property rights.[628] Any power exercised over an object constitutes obligations towards the owner of the object, limited property rights are considered obligations towards the owner and *vice versa*.[629] The result of this is that the owner is bound to respect the rights of a holder of a limited property right. When the right of ownership or the limited property right is transferred, the obligation to respect the rights of the other party is transferred with that property right. This effect in case of a transfer is why Ginossar does not see these obligations as personal rights, but recognises the property characteristics of these obligations, naming them real obligations.[630]

Real obligations are therefore considered to be obligations, but with some characteristics of property rights.[631] These characteristics are specifically to be found in the transfer of the real obligation to another party when the property right to which the right is connected is transferred. In terms of a property right, the real obligation achieves a *droit de suite* effect.[632] However, the leading opinion in French law resists the recognition of real obligations as property rights. The primary reason for the refusal is the acceptance of the rule of *numerus clausus* in French law.[633] The recognition of a real obligation would lead to an additional property right, governed by contract law and without restrictions as to its contents.[634] Furthermore, the doctrine of privity of contract, which determines that, in principle, personal rights only have effect against the persons that created them, also resists the recognition of a real obligation with effect against the whole world.[635] In other words, from both property law and contract law there are objections to the recognition of the effect of real obligations.

Finally, next to these real obligations that are created as part of the creation of a property right, there are also authors who argue for the recognition of real obligations that come into existence independently of the creation of a property right.[636] Aberkane has suggested using Article 686 C.civ, which provides the general definition for servitudes created by agreement, as a guideline for the acceptance of these

627 Ginossar's ideas have been taken over by some French authors. See Zenati 1981, p. 18, Larroumet 2004, p. 31, Chabas 1996, No. 166.

628 Ginossar 1960, p. 181 *et seq.*, see Sagaert 2005b, p. 996-997, Larroumet 2004, p. 31, Rank-Berenschot 1992, p. 60-65.

629 Larroumet 2004, p. 32, Sagaert 2005b, p. 996-997.

630 Ginossar 1960, p. 181-185, Sagaert 2005b, p. 996-997. See also Zenati 1981, p. 18-21, 695 *et seq.*

631 See also Carbonnier 2000, p. 72-73, Malaurie & Aynès 2005, 103, on Belgian law see Sagaert 2005a, p. 983 *et seq.*

632 See Sagaert 2005b, p. 1006-1007. However, Aberkane favours only a partial transfer of the real obligation, where the transferee remains bound by the duty, see Aberkane 1957, p. 147-148.

633 On the existence of the *numerus clausus* in French law see below; 5. A *Numerus Clausus* in French Property Law?

634 Sagaert 2004b, p. 60-61, Sagaert 2005b, p. 1013-1014, Larroumet 2004, p. 31-35, implicitly Malaurie & Aynès 2005, p. 103.

635 Sagaert 2004b, p. 61, Sagaert 2004b, p. 1012-1013.

636 Aberkane 1957, p. 117, De Juglart 1937, p. 332.

autonomous real obligations.[637] Also De Juglart in an earlier thesis used the provisions on the right of servitude, in particular Articles 698 and 699 C.civ, to argue for a general category of real obligations created by agreement.[638] Others have also advocated the recognition of non-transferability clauses as real obligations. Non-transferability clauses are part of contracts of sale and usually limit temporarily the powers of the owner to dispose of an object. These clauses are under strict scrutiny from the *Cour de cassation*.[639]

Although the ideas of autonomous real obligations are interesting and persuasive, the majority of French scholarship has not adopted these suggestions, and neither the legislature nor the *Cour de cassation* has adopted them either. Therefore, real obligations, even when they are just recognised as accessory obligations to an existing property right, remain controversial. The doctrine of separation between the law of property and the law of obligations, in particular the law of contract, does not allow for an intermediate category. Maintaining this distinction forces French scholarship into a difficult position. In general the French handbooks deal with real obligations after they explain what a property right is as opposed to a personal right.[640] However, an answer to the exact nature of these rights is usually not provided.

4.3. *Concession Immobilière*

In 1967 a law reform introduced a special type of contract called *concession immobilière*.[641] Article 48 of this 1967 reform Act states:

> The *concession immobilière* is a contract in which an owner of an immovable object or part of an immovable object, built upon or not, gives the use and enjoyment to a person known as *concessionnaire*, for a duration of a minimum of 20 years and for the payment of an annual sum of money ...[642]

The contract cannot just be agreed upon, but must take the form of an authentic act and be registered.[643] When registered, the contract will have effect against third parties, in particular against acquirers of the object.[644] This includes a situation

637 In particular because Art. 686 C.civ does not prohibit positive obligations explicitly, Aberkane considers this Article a good basis for his theory. Aberkane 1957,p . 115-117.

638 De Juglart 1937, p. 332.

639 See Crocq 1995, p. 170-171, Jourdain, Marty & Raynaud 1995, p. 75-77, Chabas 1996, No. 217, p. 314. See above; 2.3. Security Ownership.

640 See Terré & Simler 1998, p. 42-43, Malaurie & Aynès 2005, p. 102-103, Carbonnier 2000, p. 72-73, Larroumet 2004, p. 11-22, Chabas 1994, p. 3, Atias 2005, p. 45-61, Jourdain, Marty & Raynaud 1995, p. 1.

641 Loi No. 67-1253 du 30 décembre 1967 d'orientation foncière.

642 Art. 48 Loi du 30 décembre 1967, 'La concession immobilière est le contrat par lequel le propriétaire d'un immeuble ou partie d'immeuble, bâti ou non bâti, en confère la jouissance à une personne dénommée concessionnaire, pour une durée de vingt années au minimum et moyennant le paiement d'une redevance annuelle'.

643 Art. 48 Para. 2 Loi du 30 décembre 1967, Terré & Simler 1998, p. 706.

644 Terré & Simler 1998, p. 706, Larroumet 2004, p. 471.

where the object under contract is sold and transferred to another person.[645] Furthermore, the right arising from the contract can be subject to a right of pledge.[646]

During the existence of the contract, the *concessionnaire* may change the purpose for which the object is used, make alterations or construct buildings or constructions necessary for the exercise of the contract.[647] Furthermore, the *concessionnaire* is allowed to transfer his right or part of his right to another person.[648] In exchange for his right, the holder must pay a price to the owner of the object. Furthermore, if the object decreases in value, compensation must be paid.[649] The contract will come to an end when the period for which it was agreed comes to an end or when the contract is terminated under the provisions of contract law.[650] Any right created on the basis of the contract will also come to an end.[651]

With the *concession immobilière* the legislature intended to create an instrument that would suit practical needs.[652] Therefore, the contract may be used for any purpose, including habitation.[653] In that case legislation on leases will not be applicable and the 1967 reform law provides its own rules. However, even with these possibilities to avoid undesired application of lessee protection rules, the *concession immobilière* is not much made use of.[654]

The effects of the *concession immobilière* are such that it has been argued that the contract constitutes a property right, particularly because of the registration requirements.[655] Furthermore, the contract resembles a contract creating a right of *superficies*. Terré and Simler, but also Jourdain, argue that the contract of *concession immobilière* constitutes a right of *superficies*.[656] They argue that, as in the case of a contract of lease, a building constructed by the right-holder will be owned by that holder until the end of the contract.

However, although the arguments seem convincing and in line with the case law and legal scholarship in respect to other, similar, contracts, the arguments do not provide that contract of *concession immobilière* is a property right itself. There are authors who argue that the contract is a full property right as well, but these seem to be in the minority.[657] Nevertheless, the contract, introduced by special legislation,

645 Art. 53 Loi du 30 décembre 1967.
646 This is complicated because, would the right be characterised as a property right it would, because of its creation on an immovable object be treated as an immovable right and hence would have to be subject to a right of hypothec and not a right of pledge. See Art. 51 Para. 3 Loi du 30 décembre 1967, Terré & Simler 1998, p. 707.
647 Art. 50 Loi du 30 décembre 1967, Terré & Simler 1998, p. 708, Larroumet 2004, p. 472-473.
648 Art. 51 Loi du 30 décembre 1967.
649 Art. 52 Loi du 30 décembre 1967.
650 Art. 53 Loi du 30 décembre 1967.
651 Art. 55 Loi du 30 décembre 1967, Terré & Simler 1998, p. 710.
652 See Terré & Simler 1998, p. 706.
653 Terré & Simler 1998, p. 708.
654 See Terré & Simler 1998, p. 706, Larroumet 2004, 473-474.
655 See Terré & Simler 1998, p. 706-707, Larroumet 2004, p. 471-472, Jourdain, Marty & Raynaud 1995, p. 235-237.
656 Terré & Simler 1998, p. 707, Jourdain, Marty & Raynaud 1995, p. 236. On the application of the right of *superficies* see above; 3.3. *Superficies*.
657 See Boulanger 1968, p. 99.

functions on the borderline between the law of property and the law of obligations and offers problems for legal scholarship upholding this separation.

4.4. *Real Suretyship*

A suretyship or *cautionnement* is a contract by which one party, the surety, agrees to pay the debt of another person.[658] For the payment of this debt the surety is liable with his full set of objects. Suretyships are a type of contract and are a personal security right. However, French law also recognises a *cautionnement réel* or real suretyship. In a real suretyship, a third party, known as the surety, creates a right of pledge or hypothec on an object that serves as security for the payment of the debt of another person.[659] In a real suretyship the liability of the surety is therefore limited by the value of the object over which he provided security.

The Civil Code does not deal with real suretyship, but recognises some situations in which real suretyship applies.[660] The recognition and development has therefore been a matter for legal scholarship and case law. Partly because of this method of development the nature of the right has been the subject of debate. The debate centred on the question of whether the real suretyship constituted a personal right, as a normal suretyship does, or whether, because of its real nature it can be considered a property right.[661] The characterisation of the right as personal or proprietary is especially relevant for the question of liability of the surety. If the real suretyship constitutes a property right, the surety will only be liable for the object serving as security itself. The creditor to the agreement would therefore only be able to seize that particular object.[662] If the real suretyship constitutes a personal right, the surety is liable for the value of the object for which he provided security. Although scholars following this school of thought do not challenge the nature of the security right established by the surety, they consider the suretyship itself a personal right.[663] The creditor to the agreement would therefore be able to seize any object of the surety, providing the value of the object is not higher than the value of the object for which security was given.[664]

In 1999 the *Cour de cassation* decided that the real suretyship constituted a property security right.[665] In this case the court did not take a position in the dispute between the two schools of thought, but seemed to hint at the former. In a series of

658 On French law see Aynès & Crocq 2003, p. 15 et seq., Simler & Delebecque 2004, p. 59, Piedelièvre 2004, p. 17 *et seq*.

659 Aynès & Crocq 2003, p. 43.

660 Cf. Arts. 1020 and ex. 2077 C.civ, see Simler & Delebecque 2004, p. 59, Houtcieff 2006, p. 458 *et seq*.

661 See Simler & Delebecque 2004, p. 60 *et seq*., Aynès & Crocq 2003, p. 43 *et seq*.

662 Grimaldi 2003, 170, Aynès & Crocq 2003, p. 44.

663 The term mixed approach would therefore be more accurate. See Grimaldi 2003, p. 170 *et seq*., Aynès & Crocq 2003, p. 43-44, Piedelièvre 2004, p. 30, Crocq 2002, p. 546-548.

664 Grimaldi 2003, p. 170, Grimaldi 2006a, p. 454.

665 *Cass. Civ.* 1er 4 May 1999, Bull. Civ. I, No. 144, p. 96, Simler & Delebecque 2004, p. 318.

case law decisions in 2002, however, the court opted for the personal theory.[666] These cases dealt with the question of whether Article 1415 C.civ applied to real suretyships. Article 1415 C.civ concerns marital property law and prevents one spouse from entering into agreements that affect the common marital property. When a contract of suretyship is signed, the liability of the surety includes the matrimonial objects. Article 1415 C.civ prevents one of the spouses, without permission of the other spouse, from entering into such agreements.

Whether an agreement such as a real suretyship falls under Article 1415 C.civ was in question until the 2002 judgments.[667] In particular, the question arose when the object provided as security was an object in the communal property of a married couple. The *Cour de cassation* held that the suretyship was a personal agreement limited to the value of the object given as security. The creditor to the agreement was therefore prohibited to seize a common object, and had to seize another object or series of objects not exceeding the value of the original object.[668]

The decision of the court seemed to have settled the debate on the nature of real suretyship. However, in 2005 the *Cour de cassation* in a joint session revised its opinion and held that real suretyship agreements constitute actual security rights to secure a debt of a third party.[669] Even more remarkable, the court held that a real suretyship created no personal obligations at all and that therefore the real suretyship was not to be considered as a suretyship.[670] Article 1415 C.civ was therefore not applicable in case of real suretyship.[671] In other words, the court returned to its earlier case law, expressly stating that the provisions on normal suretyship would not apply and that the creditor could only seize the particular object over which security was provided.

The case has been received with much criticism, but has been followed in other decisions by the *Cour de cassation*.[672] It is remarkable that the court has recognised the real suretyship as a security right, thus effectively creating a new property right. It is also this definition of a property right that was adopted by the Grimaldi report preparatory to the 2006 reforms of French security law.[673] The proposed Article 2295 C.civ stated:

666 *Cass. Civ.* 1er 20 May 2002, Bull. Civ. I, Nos. 127, 128 and 129, for a critical analysis see Crocq 2002, p. 546 *et seq.* See also *Cass. Com.* 13 November 2002, Bull. Civ. IV, No. 161, Crocq 2003, p. 128-129.

667 I.e., the characterisation of a real suretyship as a real security right could include that the real suretyship was not be considered as a suretyship in the meaning of Art. 1415 C.civ. See Aynès & Crocq 2003, p. 43-44, Simler & Delebecque 2004, p. 60-61.

668 Grimaldi 2003, p. 170 *et seq.*, Grimaldi 2006a, p. 454 *et seq.*, Houtcieff 2006, p. 458 *et seq.*

669 *Cass. Ch.* mixte 2 December 2005, D. 2006, 722, JCP G 2005.II.10183, JCP N 2006, p. 61. On the case see Simler 2005, p. 2425 *et seq.*

670 Hence the title of the contributions of Grimaldi and Houtcie *et seq.* Translated in English these would be 'real suretyship is no suretyship', see Grimaldi 2006a, p. 454, Houtcieff 2006, p. 458.

671 For a critical evaluation of the applicability of Art. 1415 C.civ see Grimaldi 2006a, p. 454 *et seq.*

672 See *Cass. Com.* 21 February 2006, *Cass.* Civ. 1er 7 February 2006. On the criticism see Grimaldi 2006a, p. 454 *et seq.*, Simler 2005, p. 2428.

673 However, the law authorising the Ordonnance did not provide competence to reform the law on suretyship. See Simler 2006, p. 598.

> A real suretyship is a property security right created to guarantee the debt of another. The creditor cannot seize any other object than that provided as security.[674]

This definition followed the most recent case law of the *Cour de cassation*, but was eventually not implemented.[675] Instead, the right of pledge was extended to cover a property security right in respect of the object of another.[676] Nonetheless, the decision of the *Cour de cassation* to accept real suretyship as a property right remains and enlarges the category of available property rights.[677] The classification of the right as such, however, remains controversial.

4.5. *Fiducie*

On 19 February 2007 a law was adopted that introduced the *fiducie*, a trust-like device.[678] This instrument, which is a contract that creates a transfer of ownership of objects, rights or securities, both present and future, to a fiduciary who will hold these objects for a specific purpose on behalf of a beneficiary, has already been dealt with above, under the heading of security ownership.[679] However, the *fiducie* can be used for more purposes than to provide security. By analogy with its Roman law foundations, not only the *fiducia cum creditore*, but also the *fiducia cum amico* is recognised.[680] The latter is a transfer of ownership for management purposes known in French law as a *fiducie à fin de gestion*.[681]

The contract creating the *fiducie* may provide for a specific management purpose and state the rights and duties of the fiduciary in this respect.[682] This enables the parties to make detailed agreements about matters such as the investment powers of the fiduciary. Furthermore, the provision on the requirements for the *fiducie* contract leaves room for unknown beneficiaries at the moment the contract is created. Instead of requiring the beneficiaries to be mentioned, requirements to identify them may be given.[683] Therefore, a *fiducie* might also give the fiduciary discretionary powers to appoint beneficiaries, enabling the institution to be used for scholarships and charitable purposes.

The fiduciary will be under the obligation to take care of the objects in accordance with the *fiducie* contract. For any mistakes the fiduciary makes, he will

674 The proposed Art. 2295 stated 'Le cautionnement réel est une sûreté réelle constituée pour garantir la dette d'autrui. Le créancier n'a d'action que sur le bien qui en forme l'objet'. See, *inter alia*, Grimaldi 2006a, p. 454 *et seq*.

675 This because of political reasons, see above; 3.5. Pledge. Grimaldi 2006a, p. 455, Legeais 2006a, p. 60.

676 Art. 2334 C.civ, Legeais 2006a, p. 60, 353. See above; 3.5. Pledge.

677 See Legeais 2006a, p. 57-61.

678 Loi No. 2007-211 du 19 février 2007, JORF 21 February 2007.

679 Art. 2011 C.civ, see above; 2.3. Security Ownership.

680 See Chapter 2; 2.4. Other Property Rights.

681 See De Roux 2007, p. 12, Kuhn 2007, p. 32.

682 Art. 2018 C.civ.

683 Art. 2018(5) C.civ, De Roux 2007, p. 43-44.

be personally liable with his own set of objects and debts.[684] The liability of the fiduciary is not only against the transferee and beneficiary, who are the parties to the contract, but also against any third parties that suffer damage.[685] Furthermore, when the transferee or the beneficiary is unsatisfied with the performance of the fiduciary, or even when a third party is unsatisfied with the fiduciary, they may approach a court to ask for a replacement.[686]

The *fiducie* creates a right of ownership that is limited by the contract of transfer. These limitations are limitations in time (the right of ownership for management purposes of the fiduciary may last for a maximum of thirty-three years) but are also limitations on the rights and duties of the owner.[687] Although the fiduciary becomes owner, his right of ownership can hardly be qualified as a standard right of ownership, even though doctrinally there is only one right of ownership. The *fiducie* creates a purpose-bound ownership that can, depending on the purpose of the transfer, be called either security ownership or management ownership

In any case the right will be temporary, awarding the transferee a right of 'remainder': at the end of the *fiducie* he will become full owner again. In this sense the *fiducie* approaches the concept of the English trust.[688] However, compared with the English trust, the beneficiary only has a right against the trustee and not a right that he may be able to invoke against third parties.[689] A *fiducie* is, contrary to an English trust, a mere contract creating personal rights. However, at the same time, some proprietary effects, in particular on the right of ownership of the fiduciary, cannot be denied. It remains therefore unclear what is the status of the newly introduced *fiducie* in French law.[690]

4.6. *Lease*

An owner may give a right to use and enjoy his object under ownership not only by creating a limited property right in respect of or on behalf of another person, but he may also create a personal right in respect of or on behalf of another person. Such a personal right can be a right of lease.[691] The agreement creating the lease is therefore not a *démembrement* of the right of ownership and does not constitute a limited property right, but limits the owner in his powers.[692] This limitation on the powers of the owner can be justified by the lease agreement, to which the owner agrees,

684 I.e., with his own patrimony. Art. 2026 C.civ.
685 De Roux 2007, p. 52-53.
686 Art. 2027 C.civ, De Roux 2007, p. 53-54.
687 Art. 2018 C.civ, see above; 2.3. Security Ownership.
688 See Chapter 6; 1.5. Trust Law.
689 The effect of the right of the beneficiary in English law is also not unlimited. But when a property right is the subject of a trust, the beneficiary may have a right to act against third parties. See Chapter 6; 1.5. Trust Law.
690 See critically Crocq 2007, p. 12 *et seq.*
691 See Malaurie & Aynès 2005, p. 100, Carbonnier 2000, p. 295, Hervieu 1981, p. 61.
692 See Carbonnier 2000, p. 296, Patault 1989, p. 168-172.

and, in a normal situation, by the compensation the owner receives from the lessee.[693] In this respect Article 1709 of the Civil Code states:

> A lease of objects is a contract by which one of the parties binds himself to let another enjoy the object for a certain duration of time, and at a certain price which the latter party binds himself to pay.[694]

The definition of a lease comes very close to the definition of a right of *emphyteusis* or the definition of a building or construction lease.[695] These rights give the right-holder a property right, whereas the holder of a lease is entitled to a personal right only. However, legislation on leases has been introduced, mainly to protect the lessee in case of a sale and transfer of the ownership of the lessor, with the effect of making a lease not just a mere personal right either.[696]

The owner of the object under lease is bound by the lease agreement. The result of this is that he is obliged to make the object under lease available to the lessee and perform any maintenance or repair work that are necessary.[697] Especially when the ownership of the leased object is transferred to another person, by operation of law, the new owner becomes bound by the lease agreement, including these duties of repair and maintenance.[698] Article 1743 of the Civil Code states:

> If the lessor sells the object under lease, the acquirer of the object may not evict the lessee, tenant of a part of the object or tenant who has an authentic lease or one of which the date can be ascertained.
> He may however evict a non-rural lessee or tenant when he has reserved a right to do so in the lease agreement.[699]

Article 1743 of the Civil Code expresses the maxim that a sale does not break a lease. In other words, the lease is given a *droit de suite* effect on the part of the owner. It is because of this that some scholars have argued that a lease constitutes a property right.[700] However, already in 1861 the *Cour de cassation* held that a lease did not constitute a *démembrement* and is a personal right.[701] The right of lease is a personal right awarding the lessee nothing more than personal rights, with the exception of the case of a sale and transfer by the owner, in which case the full lease agreement

693 See Carbonnier 2000, p. 295-296.

694 A lease of objects is contrasted by a lease of labour which is also possible under the similar rules in the French Civil Code, see Art. 1708 C.civ. Art. 1709, 'Le louage des choses est un contrat par lequel l'une des parties s'oblige à faire jouir l'autre d'une chose pendant un certain temps, et moyennant un certain prix que celle-ci s'oblige de lui payer'.

695 On these rights see above; 3.4. *Emphyteusis*.

696 See Malaurie & Aynès 2005, p. 100-101.

697 Arts. 1719 and 1720 C.civ.

698 Art. 1743 C.civ.

699 Art. 1743 C.civ, 'Si le bailleur vend la chose louée, l'acquéreur ne peut expulser le fermier, le colon partiaire ou le locataire qui a un bail authentique ou dont la date est certaine. Il peut, toutefois, expulser le locataire de biens non ruraux s'il s'est réservé ce droit par le contrat de bail'.

700 See e.g. Troplong 1845, Nos. 5 *et seq.*, Nos. 473 *et seq.* On this see Sagaert 2005b, p. 1010.

701 *Req.* 6 March 1861, DP, 1861, I, 713, Hervieu 1981, p. 62.

transfers to the new owner or lessor and the personal rights of the lessee can be exercised against that new owner.[702]

In 1975 a legislative reform introduced an extension of the applicability of possessory actions.[703] Before the reform these actions had only been available to possessors, but after the reform the actions were extended to detentors as well. In French law a lessee does not become possessor of the object of lease, but detentor. In other words, the holder of a personal right over an object, a detentor, becomes entitled to claim return of his detention when the object is removed from his factual power.

In order to limit the possibilities of the lessee instituting this action against the lessor, the Civil Code prevents the lessee from taking such action.[704] However, against persons interfering with his detention the lessee may use a possessory action to claim back factual control over the object.

With this extension the lessee has been awarded rights and powers over the object that he can exercise against third parties, albeit a limited class of third parties.[705] Remarkably, these new powers to claim back factual control by the lessee have not led to a renewed debate on the legal nature of the lease.[706]

5. A *Numerus Clausus* in French Property Law?

French law adheres to the separation between the law of obligations and the law of property and therefore also to the separation between personal rights and property rights. This is not just to be deduced from the structure of the Civil Code, but is also the starting point for case law and legal scholarship.[707] Although the separation is not as strictly advocated in the structure of the Civil Code, in which property law seems to take the leading role, the effects of personal rights are considered to be different from those rights created in the area of property law.[708]

The separation between the law of obligations and the law of property can also be seen in the area of security rights. Not only in the Civil Code of 1804, but also in

702 Malaurie & Aynès 2005, p. 101, Carbonnier 2000, p. 301.
703 Loi No. 75-596 du 9 juillet 1975, JORF du 10 juillet 1975.
704 Art. 2282 C.civ, Malaurie & Aynès 2005, p. 101, 153, Carbonnier 2000, p. 301.
705 Carbonnier 2000, p. 319.
706 See Malaurie & Aynès 2005, p. 101, Carbonnier 2000, p. 301. The absence of a debate is remarkable seen the debate on the availability of the possessory action for detentors has created in Germany. On German law see Chapter 4; 4.3. Entitlement to Possession Through the Law of Obligations.
707 With respect to case law see *Cass. Civ.* 3ème 16 November 1988, D. 1989, p. 157. See also Zenati 1989, p. 577, Hervieu 1981, p. 195.
708 Such a structure is different in German or Dutch law where the law of contract is known as the law of contract and not as different ways to acquire property. The leading role of property law in the French Civil Code is deceptive. At least its drafting was not as controversial as other subjects. The collected works of the commission and the debates on the drafts of the Civil Code, collected by Fenet show a 340 page volume dealing with the second book of the Civil Code dealing with property law, whereas 3 books deal with the law of contract, of which e.g. the book on sale comprises 614 pages. See Recueil complet des travaux préparatoires du code civil 11 and Recueil complet des travaux préparatoires du code civil 14.

the 2006 reform on security law, a distinction is made between personal security rights and property security rights. Personal security rights are personal rights and therefore only have effect between parties, property security rights are property rights and therefore have effect against the whole world. However, the strict separation creates classification problems with certain rights.[709] This is partly because of the consensual transfer system. In principle, the conclusion of a contract transfers ownership of an object from one person to another. This same principle also applies to the creation of limited property rights. The conclusion of a contract creates a limited property right and determines the content of that right.

Through this system of transfer and creation the law of contract has a substantial influence on the law of property. The right of servitude offers one of the best examples of this influence. In French law, the right of servitude is not only created by contract, but is also governed by it. Whether the right of servitude concerns a right of way or a right of water or of support depends on the content of the contract creating the right. Not only does the law of contract in this way interfere in the law of property and achieve effect against third parties, it also allows parties to attempt to give any content to a right of servitude that is possible.[710] Nevertheless, property law does not allow parties the same amount of party autonomy as does the law of contract. Therefore, a tension is present between the contract the parties conclude and the effect property law may give to such a contract.[711]

This tension can be illustrated with a case that came before the *Cour de cassation*. In 1984 the court dealt with the question whether a right given to a third party to put a poster on a wall was a right of usufruct.[712] The court of Aix-en-Provence had classified the right to put a poster on a common wall as a right of usufruct, but the *Cour de cassation* held that, from the definition of a usufruct in Article 578 of the Civil Code, the right could not be a right of usufruct.[713] In other words, as a result of the refusal to classify the right to put up a poster as a right of usufruct, the parties had not succeeded in creating a property right in this case.[714] Zenati in his observations on the case considers the possibility that the right to put up a poster might be a real servitude, but rejects the option because of the lack of a dominant piece of land.[715]

Therefore it could be stated that the Civil Code of 1804 does provide guidelines for the restrictions the courts impose on practice in respect to the content parties attempt to give to their legal relations. The definitions provided by the Civil Code and common interpretations of these definitions are used by the courts as a

709 See above; 4. Borderline Cases in French Property Law.

710 On this tension see Hervieu 1981, p. 8 *et seq.*

711 In the same sense see Hervieu 1981, p. 32.

712 *Cass. Civ.* 3ème 18 January 1984, D. 1985, p. 504. In French known as a *droit d'affichage*. See also Crocq 1995, p. 80.

713 On the case see Zenati 1985, p. 504 *et seq.*

714 This case could be seen as an application of the *Typenfixierung*. On this concept see Chapter 4; 5. A *Numerus Clausus* in German Property Law.

715 Zenati 1985, p. 505.

restriction on party autonomy.[716] However, at the same time the definitions provided and the interpretations of these should not be taken as making it impossible to recognise new rights.

As early as 1834 the *Cour de cassation* was asked to decide on a particular situation of co-ownership.[717] This case concerned a situation in which one party, named Caquelard, owned a riverbank and the grass and plants growing on it. Another party, named Lemoine, was the owner of the trees that grew on the riverbank. A lower court in Rouen had decided that both parties were owners, or at least co-owners, of the riverbank, but that Caquelard had to respect the rights of Lemoine over the trees.[718] Lemoine's rights, the court of Rouen held, were recognised as a right of servitude.[719] Caquelard appealed in cassation and argued that the court of Rouen had violated the Civil Code's principles of ownership. The *Cour de cassation* rejected the appeal and ruled that the two parties could very well be co-owners, even with an unfamiliar division of rights as in this case. The court stated that Articles 544, 546 and 552 of the Civil Code are representing the general law on ownership, but that they are not prohibitive.[720]

Somewhat contradictory to the decision of the *Cour de cassation* is Article 543 of the Civil Code which names three possible property rights a person can have in an object; a right of ownership, a right of usufruct or a right of servitude. The contradiction between the judgment of the *Cour de cassation* in *Caquelard v Lemoine* and Article 543 C.civ has been the subject of much debate that is not completely settled today. The debate specifically centres on the interpretation of Article 543 C.civ.

When looking at the Civil Code of 1804 a clear picture is provided. On the structure of the second book of the Civil Code dealing with these property rights, one of its draftsmen, Treilhard, stated:

> See here, in effect, the only modifications to which the owners can be susceptible in our political and social organisation. There can be no other rights in respect of any object than a right of ownership, full and complete, including the right to use and enjoy and to dispose; or a simple right of use and enjoyment, without the right to dispose of a piece of land; or, finally, a right of servitude on the object of another.[721]

716 The interpretation of the definition of property rights is of particular importance with respect to the prohibition to impose positive duties in case of a right of real servitude. Although Article 686 C.civ provides a definition, the restriction to negative duties is interpreted and not explicitly mentioned. See above; 3.1. Real Servitudes.

717 *Req.* 13 February 1834, D.P. 1834.I.218, S.1834.I.205.

718 *Cour royale de Rouen* 14 March 1832, Hervieu 1981, p 57.

719 *A servitude discontinue, non établie par titre*, S. 1834.I.205. See also Patault 1983, p. 222-223.

720 The Court states 'Attendue, en droit, que les articles 544, 546 et 552 du Code civil, sont déclaratifs du droit commun relativement à la nature et aux effets de la propriété, mais ne sont pas prohibitifs'.

721 'Voilà, en effet, les seules modification dont les propriétés soient susceptibles dans notre organisation politique et sociale; il ne peut exister sur les biens aucune autre espèce de droits: ou l'on a une propriété pleine et entière, que renferme également et le droit de jouir et le droit de disposer; ou l'on n'a qu'un simple droit de jouissance, sans pouvoir disposer un fonds; ou enfin on n'a que des services fonciers à prétendre sur la propriété d'un tiers ...', Recueil →

Although this statement seems very clear and unambiguous, on several occasions the *Cour de cassation* has ruled in outright contradiction. Patault has shown that in order to understand the case law of the *Cour de cassation*, the Civil Code should be seen in the light of the abolition of the feudal system.[722] First and foremost, the unitary nature of the right of ownership had to be protected. Only later, at the end of the nineteenth century, did the exclusivity of the right of ownership come to receive greater emphasis.[723] According to Patault, this first method of looking at the right of ownership as a non-feudal right enabled what she calls *propriétés simultanées* or simultaneous ownership.[724] Although the recognition of a unitary concept of ownership in the Civil Code of 1804 brought an end to the multiplicity of property rights in the *ancien régime*, the use of the right of ownership remained controversial.[725]

Patault refers to a case in 1832 in which the court in Nancy was asked to decide on a situation in which both a municipality as well as the State had a right of ownership on the hills surrounding a village.[726] In this case the court stated that it saw no problem in the division between the two rights of ownership. In a decision three months after the decision in *Caquelard v Lemoine*, the *Cour de cassation* upheld this judgment.[727] Patault shows also that on other occasions the courts have had no problem in recognising several persons sharing a right of ownership.[728]

Only in the second half of the nineteenth century does Patault detect a change in the case law of the *Cour de cassation*.[729] She notes that when the Court was asked to decide on a case where one person claimed to own a building and another claimed to own the land on which the building was constructed, the court would recognise a situation of co-ownership entitling the owner of the house to co-ownership of the land.[730] From 1858 onwards the court started to recognise a separate right of ownership from the ownership of the land for the owner of the house.[731] Only in 1873 did the *Cour de cassation* recognise the ownership of the house as a separate and distinct property right in the form of the right of *superficies*.[732] Furthermore, on several other occasions the *Cour de cassation* has recognised other property rights. These include the right of *emphyteusis*, but also most recently the rights of retention and real suretyship.[733]

complet des travaux préparatoires du code civil 11, p. 33. In the same sense see Recueil complet des travaux préparatoires du code civil 11, p. 41. See also Hervieu 1981, p. 109.

722 Patault 1983, p. 217-221, Patault 1989, p. 182 *et seq.*

723 Patault 1983, p. 228 *et seq.* See also Bürge 1991, p. 42 *et seq.*

724 On the term see Patault 1989, p. 15.

725 Libchaber 2004, p. 352.

726 *Cour royale de Nancy* 16 August 1832, S. 34, I, 720, see Patault 1983, p. 221.

727 Patault 1983, p. 222.

728 Patault 1983, p. 224-228. See, *inter alia*, *Req.* 14 January 1840, D. 1840, I, 20.

729 Patault 1983, p. 228 *et seq.*

730 Patault 1983, p. 232.

731 *Cass. Civ.* 18 May 1858, S. 1858, 1, 661, see also above; 3.3. *Superficies*.

732 *Cass. Civ.* 16 December 1873, S. 1874, I, 457, Patault 1983, p. 235.

733 *Cass. Civ.* 24 August 1857, DP 1857, I, p. 326 (right of *emphyteusis*), *Cass. Civ.* 1er, 7 January 1992, RTD civ. 1992.586, JPC 1992.I.3583 (right of retention), *Cass. Ch.* mixte 2 December 2005, D. 2006, 722, JCP G 2005.II.10183, JCP N 2006 (real suretyship).

The recognition of these new property rights seems connected to the approach taken towards the creation of property rights in general. The theory of *démembrement* connects the creation of property rights to the right of ownership itself. In a time when the right of ownership could be simultaneous, there was little need for the creation of new property rights. Bürge has attempted to show that the development of the theories in France on the exclusivity of the right of ownership was influenced by German legal scholarship, in particular Von Savigny and the Historical School.[734] Bürge argues that it was only after Von Savigny and his school of thought became influential in France that French legal scholarship, and with it legal scholarship and also case law, started to adhere to an exclusive *and* unitary concept of ownership.[735] Hervieu in his dissertation on the subject of limitation of property rights underlines this conclusion.[736]

The combination of the two theories could explain why it was only in the second half of the nineteenth century that French courts started to adhere to a more exclusive right of ownership. The exclusive concept of ownership led to a change in approach, the development of the abuse of rights doctrine to limit the powers of the exclusive owner offers a clear example.[737] In any case, only upon the recognition of an exclusive concept of ownership did the need for a clear definition of property rights other than ownership arise.

A property right in French law is either a right of ownership or a limited property right. The limited property rights are further divided into principal property rights; the rights of servitude, usufruct, *emphyteusis* and *superficies*, and accessory property rights; the rights of pledge and hypothec. The second category of rights is known as accessory because these rights are traditionally seen as connected to the claim the performance of which these rights seek to secure.[738]
The traditional system of French property law uses the theory of *démembrement* in order to determine what is a property right. In other words, a property right is seen as a right consisting of certain powers of the owner, who, for the time the limited property right exists, cannot exercise these rights. This narrow definition of a property right created some difficulties in French legal scholarship. Those property rights that can be brought under the narrow definition are the principal property rights.[739] These principal property rights comprise the traditionally recognised powers of the owner; *usus, fructus* and *abusus*.[740]

Accessory property rights do not fit easily in this model. In general the modern handbooks do not deal with the question of *démembrement* of accessory

734 Bürge 1991, p. 42-63, 89-93, Heirbaut 2004, p. 322-323. On Von Savigny see Chapter 4; 1. Introduction.
735 Bürge 1991, p. 521-523.
736 Hervieu 1981, p. 117 *et seq*.
737 Also see above; 2. The Right of Ownership.
738 On the distinction see above; 3. Other Property Rights.
739 Their status as property rights is usually not challenged. See Malaurie & Aynès 2005, p. 99-100, Terré & Simler 1998, p. 40-42.
740 On the recognition of these elements of the right of ownership see above; 2.1. Ownership.

property rights.[741] Whether accessory property rights actually are a *démembrement* of the right of ownership is questionable. Becqué has suggested that the accessory property rights also deprive the owner of some of his powers.[742] Crocq even implies that limiting the powers of the owner in case of non-payment by the debtor constitutes a *démembrement* of the right of ownership when an accessory property right is created.[743] According to Crocq these powers include the powers of the owner to sell and transfer the object.[744]

At the same time, others argue that accessory property rights do not constitute a *démembrement* of the right of ownership as they are focused on the value of the object and not on the use of an object.[745] Partly because of their nature as distinct property rights, the development of security rights in France has been different from the development of the rights to use that certainly comprise a *démembrement* of the right of ownership. Taking into account the origin of security rights, which is usually a contract, their recognition as property rights has been controversial.[746] The recognition of new rights to use, the right of *superficies* and the right of *emphyteusis*, has also been problematic to some extent, but the recognition of new security rights has led to a much fiercer debate.[747] Crocq in his doctoral thesis has argued for the possibility of using contract law to extend the possible security rights in the French system.[748] He argues that a contractual limitation on the right of ownership, for instance a non-transferability clause, would provide the right of ownership with an accessory and therefore also security character.[749]

When combining the above, the complicated situation in French law becomes clear. Only since the second half of the nineteenth century have case law and legal scholarship been forced to clarify the catalogue of property rights. With the recognition of a unitary and exclusive right of ownership, the need to protect that right of ownership also arose. Although this development forced the *Cour de cassation* to recognise several new property rights, a new series of recognitions such as occurred in the first half of the nineteenth century seems unthinkable.[750] Nevertheless, the *Cour de cassation* has continued to hold itself competent to recognise new property rights. This competence is best illustrated by the recognition of the rights of reten-

741 See Terré & Simler 1998, p. 41-42, Malaurie & Aynès 2005, p. 100, Atias 2005, p. 55-56, Libchaber 2004, p. 356 *et seq.*

742 Planiol, Ripert & Becqué 1953, p. 375-376, see also Crocq 1995, p. 78-87.

743 Crocq 1995, p. 81, where Crocq states 'Ceci étant admis, il apparaît que le démembrement du droit de propriété dans le but d'en faire un droit accessoire n'est pas incompatible avec l'essence du droit de propriété. En effet, le créancier a une vocation à recouvrer la plénitude de ses prérogatives en cas de défaut de paiement par le débiteur'. See also Libchaber 2004, p. 364.

744 See Crocq 1995, p. 78-81.

745 Cabrillac & Mouly 2004, No. 504, Aubry, Rau & Eismein 1961, p. 94.

746 See, in general, Chapter 2.

747 On the recognition of the right of *superficies* and *emphyteusis* see above; 3.3. *Superficies* and 3.4. *Emphyteusis*.

748 Crocq 1995, p. 81.

749 Crocq 1995, p. 83-87.

750 See Patault 1983, p. 217 *et seq.*, Libchaber 2004, p. 351-352.

tion and real suretyship as property rights.[751] It can therefore be stated that although Article 543 of the Civil Code enumerates the three most important principal property rights, the list is not as limited as this Article seems to suggest.

Whether the system of property rights in French law is a closed system remains controversial. Von Bar and Drobnig in their study on property law and non-contractual liability law and how these areas of law relate to contract law signal a continuing debate in French law.[752] The debate does not so much centre on the interpretation of Article 543 of the Civil Code, but concerns the tension between party autonomy in contract law and the possible party autonomy in property law as well.[753] Surprisingly, the term *numerus clausus* is also familiar to French authors.[754]

Some of the most influential classic authors in French law, Demolombe, and Aubry and Rau, have recognised a *numerus clausus* in French law.[755] Also modern authors like Chabas, Crocq, Cabrillac and Mouly, Carbonnier, Larroumet and Zenati recognise the existence of the principle.[756] These authors consider the property rights mentioned in the Civil Code, added to those naturally recognised by the *Cour de cassation*, as a closed system and deny parties the freedom to create new property rights. They therefore seem to adhere to a rule of *numerus clausus*.[757]

At the same time, several other influential authors, including the classic authors Eismein, Chauveau, Laurent and Picard, but certainly also modern authors, like Atias and Terré, and Simler. recognise a freedom for parties to create new property rights.[758] This second group of authors examines the classification problems French law faces and conclude that parties must be given the freedom to create new property rights, especially in respect to real obligations.[759]

Currently the first group is considered the leading opinion.[760] Particularly Crocq seems successful in showing that parties should not have the freedom to

751 See above; 4.1. Right of Retention and 4.4. Real Suretyship.

752 Von Bar & Drobnig 2002, p. 312-313.

753 Or the autonomie de la volonté.

754 Although also terms as limitation of property rights and closed system are used. The use of the term in French law is surprising because the term *numerus clausus* seems to have come from German scholarship at the beginning of the nineteenth century. Only through comparative research the term seems to have become known in other legal systems as well. See e.g. Van Erp 2003b, Swadling 2000a. On the origin of the term *numerus clausus* see Struycken 2007, p. 122-123. See also Chapter 7; 1.3. Considering *Numerus Clausus*.

755 Demolombe 1870, p. 436-437, Aubry, Rau & Bartin 1935, p. 69-74.

756 Chabas 1994, p. 4-5, Crocq 1995, p. 191-192, Cabrillac & Mouly 2004, No. 505, Carbonnier 2000, p. 76-77, Larroumet 2004, p. 33-35, Zenati & Revet 1997, No. 196, p. 216. See also Witz 1981, p. 76.

757 There seems only one doctoral thesis on the subject in France itself. Hervieu, the author of this thesis, comes to the conclusion that the system of French property rights is closed. Hervieu 1981, p. 117 *et seq*. In a Swiss thesis Foëx comes, in respect to Swiss law, to this same conclusion. See Foëx 1987, p. 113.

758 Aubry, Rau & Eismein 1961, p. 91-93, Chauveau 1931, p. 562-563, Laurent 1878, p. 107 115, Picard 1952, No. 48, p. 54, Atias 2005, p. 47-50, Terré & Simler 1998, p. 42-43. See very carefully Malaurie & Aynès 2005, p. 91-93.

759 On this see also Sagaert 2004b, p. 47 *et seq*., Sagaert 2005b, p. 983 *et seq*.

760 Crocq 1995, p. 189-191, Malaurie & Aynès 2005, p. 91, Zwalve 2003, p. 154.

recognise new property rights.[761] He argues that the recognition of new property rights would violate Articles 2284, 2285 and 2323 of the Civil Code.[762] These Articles establish that a debtor will be liable with his full set of objects and that all creditors, save those holding a property right giving them a right of preference, are equal. Crocq reasons that the free creation of new property rights would either create a separate patrimony or at least enable the right-holder of such a property right to take an object from the set of objects of the debtor before any creditor could reach it. Such a new property right would infringe on the principle of equality of creditors, or would entitle the creditor to a right of preference not recognised by the Civil Code.[763] Furthermore, Crocq also brings the rule of *numerus clausus* in connection with the impossibility to fragment the right of ownership.[764] Similarly, in a case where the right of ownership is fragmented when a party succeeds in creating a separate patrimony, the three Articles from the Civil Code would be equally violated.

In conclusion, although French law does not award parties the freedom to create new property rights, both the legislature and the *Cour de cassation* have shown they are capable as well as competent to create or recognise new property rights. The interpretation of difficult cases of classification such as real obligations remains strict so that the system does not shift into an open system of property rights. A rule of *numerus clausus* is therefore present in French law, although not as clearly and strictly as in other civil law systems.

761 Crocq 1995, p. 189 *et seq.*

762 Ex Arts. 2092, 2093 and 2094 C.civ.

763 Crocq 1995, p. 189-191, see also Larroumet 2004, p. 33-35. For a very similar approach with respect to Dutch law see Snijders 1997, p. 87 *et seq.*, Snijders 2005a, p. 79 *et seq.*

764 Crocq 1995, p. 191 *et seq.*

Chapter 4

GERMAN LAW

1. Introduction

The development of property law in the territories that now constitute the Federal Republic of Germany has been different from that in France.[1] One of the principal reasons that explains this difference is that, before the unification of private law into a Civil Code, the Germanic countries did not form a unity, nor did they have a central administration, a central court system or a central organisation of lawyers.[2] There was a unifying factor, however, in that the Holy Roman Empire, of which the Germanic countries were the largest part, was focused strongly on restoring the territory and unity of the old Roman Empire.

In 1495 a central court was established, the *Reichskammergericht* (Imperial Court), which was ordered to deliver judgment on the basis of the common law of the Germanic countries. Depending on the substance of the conflict before it, the Court would first look at local customary law. If the Court did not know of this law or could not decide the case on this basis, it would use Roman law to solve the issue.[3] The judges had been educated in Roman law and were far better equipped to decide matters using Roman law than they were using customary law.[4] Furthermore, commentaries based on the jurisprudence of the Imperial Court were written, on the basis of which jurists, who were educated in Roman law, were trained. These jurists were not only Court officers, but also clerks, municipal officers, or legal advisors.[5] In this way, the rediscovered Roman law, the law that had been commented

1 Most literature referred to in this chapter will be German literature. However, if an English source was available I have tried to mention it where I considered it appropriate. Zweigert and Kötz, in their famous introduction to comparative law distinguish the civil law into the romanistic and German legal family. See Zweigert & Kötz 1998, p. 132 *et seq.*

2 Zweigert & Kötz 1998, p. 134-135, Lokin & Zwalve 2001, p. 220 *et seq.*, Zwalve 2003, p. 42 *et seq.*

3 Zwalve 2003, p. 44.

4 Zwalve points out that this leads to a Bartolistic interpretation of the law in order allow for the maximum impact of received Roman Law. See Zwalve 2003, p. 44-45.

5 Zwalve 2003, p. 45, Zweigert & Kötz 1998, p. 135.

on by the Glossators, was received in the Germanic countries as well as applied and altered. Received Roman law was not merely applied, it became a living system of law subject to alterations to fit the circumstances of the Germanic countries.[6] Especially when practice demanded a different or unknown solution, German jurists would seek an answer to the problem in Roman law, or make a new interpretation of Roman law. This method, comparable to the method used by the Glossators, became known as the *usus modernus Pandectarum*.[7]

In the eighteenth century, the Enlightenment movement introduced a new view of the world based on reason.[8] In the legal domain this led to a rediscovery of natural law.[9] Private law in particular became an area of study, which resulted in a systematic overview of principles by, amongst others, Pufendorf and Wolff.[10] With this development, German legal scholarship became a rational and abstract method that was out of touch with actual legal practice.[11] The *usus modernus Pandectarum*, with its enormous theoretical framework, became the principal subject of study and development. It was this Enlightened work that inspired several leaders and administrators to reform and humanise the practice of law. Unlike in France, where the Enlightenment eventually resulted in the French Revolution and the overthrow of the *ancien régime*, the authorities in the Germanic countries wanted to replace the Roman law basis with a modern system based on reason.

One of the most prominent Germanic countries was Prussia. This country, also known as the Prussian States, once part of the Holy Roman Empire, had developed into a powerful organisation. Prussian territories were spread throughout the major parts of the Germanic countries and were only bound by their shared King and the subsidiary application of Roman law.[12] The Prussian King was strongly influenced by natural law and ordered a code of law based on the principles of reason.[13] The code was intended to replace Roman law as the subsidiary system, with customary law continuing to apply as the primary source of law. The drafter of the code, Suerez, created a system based on the ideas developed by Pufendorf and Wolff. Moreover, the code was intended to be a comprehensible document in which the influence of natural law was clearly visible.[14]

The code entered into force on 1 June 1794 as the General Land Law for the Prussian States, *Allgemeines Landrecht für die preußischen Staaten* (ALR).[15] The ALR was in force throughout Prussia until Napoléon defeated some of the Prussian States in 1806, and Napoléon introduced his *Code civil* in the conquered parts. In the unconquered Prussian States the ALR remained in force and, after Napoléon's defeat in 1813, the ALR was restored in the whole of Prussia. However, in the

6 Zweigert & Kötz 1998, p. 135, Zwalve 2003, p. 45.
7 Zwalve 2003, p. 45-46.
8 Zweigert & Kötz 1998, p. 135.
9 On the natural law school see Chapter 2; 5. Natural Law and the French Revolution.
10 Zweigert & Kötz 1998, p. 136.
11 Zweigert & Kötz 1998, p. 136.
12 Lokin & Zwalve 2001, p. 225-227, Zweigert & Kötz 1998, p. 137.
13 Lokin & Zwalve 2001, p. 226, Zweigert & Kötz 1998, p. 137.
14 Lokin & Zwalve 2001, p. 230, Hattenhauer 1989, p. 88.
15 Zweigert & Kötz 1998, p. 137.

conquered territories, the French had abolished the customary law. This customary law was not restored after 1813, and as a result, the ALR, contrary to its original application, had exclusive force of law.[16]

Nevertheless, the Germanic countries in general remained without a general code of law that unified German private law. It is no surprise that at the beginning of the nineteenth century several influential scholars started to call for a German Civil Code. In 1814 Thibaut published his *Über die Nothwendigkeit eines allgemeinen bürgerlichen Rechts für Deutschland*, in which he argued for a general German Civil Code.[17] As the ALR had been intended to provide an overall system of private law and to be a comprehensible document at the same time, it was increasingly considered to be a failed attempt to clarify eighteenth-century law that could not be used to codify German private law. New ideas on the development of law arose that were based on research into the historical evolution of the law. These ideas culminated in the German Historical School of which Von Savigny became the most famous advocate. Von Savigny published a reaction to Thibaut's article in which he agreed that the Germanic countries needed a codification of private law, but that the time to draft such a civil code had not yet come.[18] Instead, Von Savigny argued that both Germanic law and Roman law should first be studied from a historical perspective. It was on the study of Roman law that Von Savigny focused. However, instead of studying Roman law in the form received by the Glossators, which had been the focus of study in the method of the *usus modernus Pandectarum*, he studied the *Corpus Iuris Civilis* itself. Civil Codes such as the ALR and the French *Code civil* could not win his approval.[19] Von Savigny and his followers studied and interpreted what they perceived to be true Roman law, and categorised it under a new system of private law. From this study the *Pandectists*, as they became known, created a doctrinal system of 'current' private law with legal concepts that were similar for all of the Germanic countries.

In 1871, when Bismarck's efforts had resulted in a unified Germany, the draft of a private law code became a subject for consideration. By that time, German legal scholarship was prepared for this task in the way Von Savigny had intended it to be. The study of what the Pandectists called the 'current Roman law' would form the basis of the new Civil Code. Windscheid, one of the most influential members of the Historical School, served in the First Commission that would draft the new code.[20] This commission, which started work in 1874, published its first draft for a German civil code in 1887. This draft was heavily criticised because of its academic nature and the influence of the Historical School, which some critics regarded as detrimental to Germanic principles of law. On this last aspect, especially the criti-

16 Zweigert & Kötz 1998, p. 138, Lokin & Zwalve 2001, p. 232.

17 The title translates as 'On the need for a general private law for Germany', Thibaut 1814, p. 37 *et seq.*

18 Von Savigny 1814, p. 61 *et seq.*

19 Zwalve 2003, p. 46.

20 Zwalve 2003, p. 47, Lokin & Zwalve 2001, p. 253-254, Zweigert & Kötz 1998, p. 142, see Johow 1982.

cism of Von Gierke was very influential.[21] In 1895 a Second Commission submitted an improved draft, but the criticism of the first draft had only resulted in the inclusion of some laymen in the commission and a number of textual revisions.[22] The proposal was adopted by parliament, and it entered info force on 1 January 1900 as the German *Bürgerliches Gesetzbuch*.[23]

The German *Bürgerliches Gesetzbuch* (BGB) is a civil code based on the work of the Historical School. One of its main characteristics, a general part on principles common to the specific parts of private law, had been strongly urged by Von Savigny.[24] The general part of the BGB is followed by specific parts on the law of obligations, the law of property, family law and the law of succession. This system differed from other civil codes where these distinctions, especially between contract law and property law, were not as clear, such as, according to the Historical School, the French *Code civil* and the Prussian ALR.[25]

The ALR did not adhere to a strict separation between the law of contract and the law of property and it enabled parties to create a relation with third-party effect by contract.[26] German legal scholarship strongly opposed this idea. Thibaut had published an article on the distinction between personal rights and property rights in Roman law. In his view, mixing the two was not a Roman-law-based distinction.[27] The Historical School became the most ardent advocate of a strict separation.[28] Already in his *System des Heutigen Römischen Rechts* or System of Current Roman Law, Von Savigny wrote:[29]

> Roman law keeps both [the law of property and the law of obligations. BA] strictly separated, and deals with each part as fully independent of the other'.[30]

Von Savigny provides examples of less strict separation and concludes that mixing the two types of rights could result in a system of obligations in which property rights would naturally follow from these obligations. Alternatively he saw a mixing of property law and the law of obligations leading to a system where property rights would be the only 'proper' rights and obligations, that is to say, 'improper'

21 See Von Gierke 1889, Zweigert & Kötz 1998, p. 142, Pfenning 1997, Füller 2006, p. 14-16.

22 Zweigert & Kötz 1998, p. 142.

23 Zweigert & Kötz 1998, p. 142.

24 Lokin & Zwalve 2001, p. 254. Füller 2006, p. 11.

25 See, explicitly, Motive III 1888, p. 3. Also the Austrian ABGB was included in the criticism. On the French Civil Code see Chapter 3; 1. Introduction. Zwalve 2003, p. 46.

26 Liebs 1975, p. 13, Motive III 1888, p. 2-3.

27 Thibaut 1817a.

28 See Füller 2006, p. 8-10.

29 On Von Savigny and his influence on the system of property law in German law, see Wiegand 1990, p. 112 *et seq.*

30 'Das Römische Recht hält beide [The law of property and the law of obligations. BA] streng aus einander, und behandelt jeden Theil für sich als ganz unabhängig innerhalb seiner Gränzen', Von Savigny 1981, p. 374.

rights, would only serve as a means to create these property rights.[31] Von Savigny considered such approaches incomplete and one-sided.[32]

Von Savigny's observations were closely followed in the draft of the BGB.[33] In fact, under the *Trennungsprinzip* or principle of separation, the separation between the law of property and the law of obligations is at the foundation of the German system of property law.[34] According to the *Motive*, the explanatory memoranda to the Civil Code:

> In the system of the draft of the BGB property law takes an independent position. On the one hand it is independent from the law of obligations and family law and on the other hand from the law of succession. Its independence is founded in the distinction between property and personal rights.[35]

Wiegand has emphasised the connection between the drafter of the property law part in the First Commission, Johow, and Von Savigny's theory on the strict separation between the law of obligations and the law of property.[36] Von Savigny's doctrine sees property rights as instruments to organise nature, not in its entirety but in a limited area. Such a limited area is a corporeal object (*Sache*) to which a property right can exist.[37] Of these property rights the right of ownership is the most extensive right.[38] The law of property provides rules on how nature can be organised. Rights against another person concern either objects or powers over objects (law of property) or rights that follow from a person's acts (law of obligations). The *Motive* further explain the independence of property law:

> Property Law, to safeguard its independence, must deal with the creation of property rights itself.
> ... A person can therefore not be free to create any right in relation to an object with a property effect. Party autonomy as it is used in the law of obligations is therefore not applicable in property law. Here the opposite is the case: persons can only create those

31 For which Von Savigny quotes Domat and the French Code Civil. Von Savigny 1981, p. 374, see also Wiegand 1990, p. 115.

32 Von Savigny 1981, p. 375.

33 Füller 2006, p. 8-9.

34 On this principle see extensively Füller 2006, p. 177 *et seq.* In respect to *numerus clausus* see p. 373 *et seq.*

35 'Das Sachenrecht nimmt in dem System des Entwurfs eine selbständige Stellung ein. Es schließt sich ab einerseits gegen das Recht der Schuldverhältnisse und das Familienrecht, anderseits gegen das Erbrecht. Seine Selbständigkeit beruht wesentlich in dem Gegensatz zwischen dinglichem und persönlichem Rechte', Motive III 1888, p. 1, see also Wiegand 1990, p. 113.

36 Wiegand 1990, p. 113-114, Johow 1982, p. 125-128.

37 In Von Savigny's view, nature comprises tangible objects only. Intangible or incorporeal objects in this reasoning are outside the definition of *Sache*. See below; 2. The Right of Ownership.

38 'Die unfrye Natur kann von uns beherrscht werden nicht als Ganzes, sondern nur in bestimmter räumlicher Begränzung; ein so begränztes Stück derselben nennen wir Sache, und auf diese bezieht sich daher die erste Art möglicher Rechte: das Recht an einer Sache, welches in seiner reinsten und vollständigsten Gestalt Eigenthum heist', Von Savigny 1981, p. 338. On objects see Para 90 BGB. See also Füller 2006, p. 43-47.

> rights that are recognised by the law. The number of property rights is consequently limited.[39]

The inclusion of these, admittedly very short, explanations for the separation between the law of property and the law of obligations should be seen in the light of the development of the right of ownership. Under the influence of the Glossators, for many centuries property law had recognised a fragmented type of ownership. Heavily influenced by the feudal system of landholding, a distinction had been made between *dominium directum*, the right of ownership of a feudal lord, and *dominium utile*, the right to use the land of the feudal vassal.[40] In the eighteenth and nineteenth centuries too, natural law still recognised the distinction between these two types of ownership.[41] Based on the state of legal scholarship at the time the Prussian ALR, and also the Austrian Civil Code, the ABGB, was drafted, such a *duplex dominium* was recognised in these civil codes.[42] It was about this fragmentation of ownership that Thibaut published an article in 1817.[43] Thibaut considered such a fragmentation un-Roman. Instead, he focused on the holder of the *dominium utile*.[44] Many authors agreed with him and in the nineteenth century a unitary concept of ownership came to be considered the only possible type of ownership.[45] Where the ALR permitted separating powers from the owner into another type of ownership, the new approach considered ownership to be the complete and indivisible power over an object. As Von Savigny observed twice in his book on 'current' Roman law: [46]

> ... right of ownership, or the complete and exclusive power of a person over an object.[47]
> Another power, outside ownership, over the unfree nature cannot be imagined.[48]

39 'Das Sachenrecht muss, um seine Selbständigkeit zu wahren, die Erwerbung der dinglichen Rechte nach Gesichtspunkten ordnen, die auf seinem Gebiete liegen. ... Den Betheiligten kann es daher nicht freistehen, jedem beliebigen Rechte, welches sich auf eine Sache bezieht, den Karakter des dinglichen zu verleihen. Der Grundsatz der Vertragsfreiheit, welcher das Obligationenrecht beherrscht, hat für das Sachenrecht keine Geltung. Hier gilt der umgekehrte Grundsatz: die Betheiligten können nur solche Rechte begründen, deren Begründung das Gesetz zulässt. Die Zahl der dinglichen Rechte ist daher nothwendig eine geschlossene', Motive III 1888, p. 3. The limitation of property rights will be dealt with below in 5. A *Numerus Clausus* in German Property Law?

40 See Chapter 2; 4.3. Ownership.

41 Wiegand 1976, p. 130-131.

42 E.g. § 16 of Title 8 of Part I ALR provided: The ownership of an object is divided, when the different rights contained in the ownership belong to several people. 'Das Eigenthum einer Sache ist getheilt, wenn die darunter begriffenen verschiedenen Rechte verschiedenen Personen zukommen' as quoted by Wiegand 1976, p. 131, 139.

43 Thibaut 1817b, on this article see Wiegand 1976, p. 136-138.

44 See also Chapter 2; 6.1. General Summary.

45 See, *inter alia*, Puchta 1873, p. 324-326, Wiegand 1976, p. 139 *et seq.*

46 See Füller 2006, p. 38, 48-50.

47 'Eigenthums, oder der unbeschränkten und ausschließenden Herrschaft einer Person über eine Sache', Von Savigny 1981, p. 367.

Property law should therefore be governed by its own rules in respect to objects, and it should not be subject to alterations made by the law of obligations. The strict separation between the law of obligations and the law of property, emphasised by the *Motive*, forms the basis of the German system of private law.[49] This independent system of property law deals with those legal relations that can be used to control objects. Of these relations, ownership is the most extensive right, but other rights exist as well. However, only those relations that are recognised by law can be property rights. The German property law system is thus characterised by a *numerus clausus* of property rights.

However, although the system of German property law is built on the strict separation between the law of property and the law of obligations (the *Trennungsprinzip*), and the principle of *numerus clausus*, certain developments have resulted in deviations from both principles. This chapter will deal with the recognised list of property rights first, after which these developments and other quasi-property relations are examined. Because of the influence of Germanic law, the list of property rights in German law is longer than the French or the Dutch.[50] Furthermore, because of German legal doctrine, which places distinction upon distinction, some additional explanation is necessary. The right of ownership especially is subject to many of these distinctions. The main distinctions of the right of ownership will be dealt with in separate sections, even though all concern the regular right of ownership. The chapter will conclude with an examination of the system of property law in German law and specify how German law recognises a *numerus clausus*.

2. The Right of Ownership

In German law the right of ownership is the most comprehensive right a person can have to an object. Since the BGB follows the general doctrinal structure of Von Savigny's system, an object or *Sache* susceptible of ownership can only be a corporeal thing.[51] Since this doctrine considers a property right to be a power over nature, and nature consists of corporeal objects and the acts of other persons, a property right can only concern such a corporeal object.[52] What an object is, is clearly described in Paragraph 90 BGB:

> The term object as it is used in this law can only be a corporeal object.[53]

48 'Eine noch außer dem Eigenthum liegende Herrschaft des einzelnen Menschen über die unfreye Natur ist nicht denkbar' Von Savigny 1981, p. 369.

49 More will be stated on this below in 3. Other Property Rights. See Füller 2006, p. 8-11, Baur, Baur & Stürner 1999, p. 6 *et seq*.

50 See Chapter 3; 3. Other Property Rights, and Chapter 5; 3. Other Property Rights.

51 See, *inter alia*, Johow 1982, p. 15 *et seq*.

52 The latter is dealt with in the law of obligations. See above; 1. Introduction, but also Rank-Berenschot 1992, p. 242.

53 Para. 90 BGB, 'Sachen im Sinne des Gesetzes sind nur körperliche Gegenstände'.

Of all property law entitlements, the right of ownership grants the paramount power. Consequently, a power over such an object is considered an absolute power, it can, subject to limitations, be exercised against the whole world.[54] Property rights over objects other than corporeal objects cannot in principle exist.[55] Nevertheless, the power does not grant owners the unrestricted right to do as they wish. When there are several owners or when the right of ownership is used for a specific purpose, such as ownership of an apartment, or ownership for security purposes, the right loses some of its unlimited nature. Because of the distinction between the normal, full, type of ownership and several other types, this section will be divided into subsections, each dealing with a different variant of the right of ownership, yet it should always be kept in mind that, paradoxically, German doctrine regards all these variants as manifestations of one right of ownership.[56]

2.1. *Normal Ownership*

The right of ownership is thoroughly dealt with by German law. Ownership does not only serve a purpose in private law, it is also considered to be a relation between the State and an individual person.[57] To this end, Article 14 of the *Grundgesetz*, the German Constitution, provides:

> (1) The right of ownership and the right of succession is guaranteed. Their content and limit shall be defined by law.
> (2) The right of ownership entails duties. Its use shall also serve the public good.
> (3) Expropriation shall only be permissible for the public good. ...[58]

Although Article 14 of the Constitution concerns a public law relationship, it is considered to guarantee the right of ownership and provide room for the free development of the individual as well as for the protection of individual ownership against the State.[59] Nevertheless, there are differences from the private-law type of ownership. For instance, the definitive interpretation of Article 14 is given by the *Bundesverfassungsgericht* (the Constitutional Court) and not by the private-law courts. Furthermore, the concept of ownership as guaranteed by Article 14 is interpreted much more widely than the private-law concept of ownership. The Constitu-

54 Along the same reasoning, Motive III 1888, p. 2, Johow 1982, p. 619.
55 Baur, Baur & Stürner 1999, p. 269.
56 See, *inter alia*, Baur, Baur & Stürner 1999, p. 27, Schwab & Prütting 2003, p. 8, Wolf 2005, p. 26 *et seq.*
57 At the foundation of this development was an influential article by Wolff, see Wolff 1923. Wolf 2005, p. 19, Baur, Baur & Stürner 1999, p. 134 *et seq.*, 270, Mayer-Maly 1984, p. 145 *et seq.*
58 Article 14 Grundgesetz, '(1) Das Eigentum und das Erbrecht werden gewährleistet. Inhalt und Schranken werden durch die Gesetze bestimmt. (2) Eigentum verpflichtet. Sein Gebrauch soll zugleich dem Wohle der Allgemeinheit dienen. (3) Eine Enteignung ist nur zum Wohle der Allgemeinheit zulässig. ...'.
59 Wolf 2005, p. 20.

tional Court has extended the term ownership to cover not only rights to corporeal objects, but also rights to other, incorporeal, rights and assets.[60]

In German doctrine, the relationship between the owner and the State is considered highly relevant in private law, but at the same time different from the relation governed by the regular right of ownership. It is the BGB that deals with the right of ownership as a relation between private persons. The private-law right of ownership is considered as a relation of the owner against the rest of the world, and is dealt with in Paragraph 903 BGB:

> The owner of an object can, when this does not interfere with the law or other rights of third parties, do with the object what he wishes and exclude others from interfering. The owner of an animal must, in the exercise of his powers, uphold the special conditions for the protection of animals.[61]

At the basis of this definition is the concept of ownership advocated by Von Savigny, the right of ownership is considered the most absolute and total power over a corporeal object.[62] At the same time, the old definition of Bartolus of the right of ownership as a *ius in re corporali perfecte disponendi nisi lege prohibeatur* can also still be distinguished.[63] Any object other than a specific corporeal object is excluded from the right of ownership.[64]

Because the right of ownership is seen as the paramount entitlement to a corporeal object, ownership is regarded as an indivisible power over an object.[65] The right of ownership cannot therefore be separated into several types of ownership, as this would deprive the right of ownership of its primary characteristic. In order to work around this indivisibility, German doctrine follows the reasoning that the creation of a property right will not deprive the right of ownership of its characteristics, the transfer of certain powers of the owner will not make the other party an owner. Instead, the other person will hold a property right as a *ius in re aliena*.[66] Ownership will remain the right of ownership, even if another property right is created.

The right of ownership is an absolute right, it has effect against the world. Any disturbance of the right of ownership itself or of the object encumbered with this

60 See, *inter alia*, BVerfG 17 July 1981, BVerfGE 58, 300, 336, Baur, Baur & Stürner 1999, p. 271.

61 Para. 903 BGB, 'Der Eigentümer einer Sache kann, soweit nicht das Gesetz oder Rechte Dritter entgegenstehen, mit der Sache nach Belieben verfahren und andere von jeder Einwirkung ausschließen. Der Eigentümer eines Tieres hat bei der Ausübung seiner Befugnisse die besonderen Vorschriften zum Schutz der Tiere zu beachten'.

62 Wiegand 1990, p. 117.

63 Wiegand 1976, p. 121 see Chapter 2; 4.3. Ownership.

64 Baur, Baur & Stürner 1999, p. 269. In principle, this also excludes ownership of a general set of assets as e.g. a company (*Unternehmen*). This includes the obligation to transfer each asset of a company through the normal rules of transfer. However, practice has lead to some exceptions enabling the term *Unternehmen* to be seen as an object capable of transfer. For more details see Hattenhauer 1989, p. 101 and Baur, Baur & Stürner 1999, p. 323 *et seq*.

65 Wiegand 1990, p. 117, Rank-Berenschot 1992, p. 243.

66 The relation between the right of ownership and other property rights will be dealt with below in 3. Other Property Rights.

property right can be remedied through a set of special claims available to the owner. First, a removal of the object from the powers of the owner entitles its owner to a claim based on Paragraph 985 BGB:

> The owner can claim the return of the object from the possessor.[67]

This claim is available exclusively to the owner who has lost possession (factual power) over the object.[68] It entitles the owner to reclaim the lost object. Although the provision uses the concept of possession, dealing with factual power over the object, only the owner can initiate the claim, as German doctrine considers that possession follows from the right of ownership.[69] The formulation of Paragraph 985 BGB is therefore slightly misleading. The claim can only be initiated by the owner against a holder of the object. If the object is transferred, or brought into the hands of someone else, the claim will consequently no longer be directed at the old possessor but at the new possessor.[70] The claim of Paragraph 985 BGB thus offers the owner the possibility to retrieve factual power.

Secondly, Paragraph 903 BGB emphasises the power of the owner. German doctrine distinguishes a positive side and a negative side of the powers of the owner.[71] The positive side is that owners may do with their objects as they see fit. However, the powers of the owner are not unlimited. The drafters of the BGB recognised this and wanted to make clear that the powers of the owner can be limited.[72] These limits may concern provisions from public law, general private law, the law of neighbours or property rights.[73]

The negative side of the powers of the owner is visible in the power to exclude others from the use or enjoyment of the object.[74] The owner can claim exclusion through Paragraph 1004 BGB:[75]

> (1) If the right of ownership is influenced in another way as by removal or non-return of the possession, the owner may claim the discontinuation of the influence. If further influences can be expected, the owner may claim the ceasing of the activity.

67 § 985 BGB 'Der Eigentümer kann von dem Besitzer die Herausgabe der Sache verlangen'. Cf. the Roman *rei vindicatio*, see Chapter 2; 2.3. Ownership.

68 The term possession in German law is used in two ways. First, as the Roman *possessio*, but, secondly, also in the sense of the Roman *detentio*. See Chapter 1; 4. Terminology. Wolf 2005, p. 97-98.

69 Wolf 2005, p. 97. In case a possessor exercised factual control over an object, but was not the owner, e.g. in case of a *detentor*, there is another specific claim available. On this see below; 4.3. Entitlement to possession through the law of obligations.

70 See Wolf 2005, p. 100.

71 See Windscheid 1906, p. 856-857, Wolf 2005, p. 24-25, Schwab & Prütting 2003, p. 138-139, Müller 1997, p. 97-99.

72 *Protokolle* § 848, 849 (G. 903-905), Mugdan 1979, p. 577.

73 Motive III 1888, 260. See Aicher 1975, p. 71 *et seq*. The other property rights will be subject below in 3. Other Property Rights. Limitations on the right of ownership by law are not subject of this study. On this see, *inter alia*, Baur, Baur & Stürner 1999, p. 273 *et seq*.

74 Wolf 2005, p. 25.

75 On § 1004 BGB in general see Müller 1997, p. 249 *et seq*.

(2) The claim cannot be initiated if the owner is obliged to endure the influence.[76]

Any disturbance of the owner's use or enjoyment of the object can lead to a claim based on Paragraph 1004 BGB.[77] The threat of a disturbance can be a reason to initiate the claim. The criterion for a threat of disturbance is whether, from the perspective of an independent third party, an act would normally lead to a disturbance of the powers of the owner.[78] Consequently, the claim can only succeed insofar as the owner is not obliged, by law or by agreement, to tolerate such a disturbance.[79] This duty to tolerate includes both the law of neighbours and other property rights.

Finally, there are several other claims protecting the right of ownership, both in property law and in the law of obligations.[80] These claims all serve the purpose of guaranteeing the power of the owner over the object as defined by Paragraph 903 BGB.

The system of claims strengthens the right of ownership as the most comprehensive right. Furthermore, the right of ownership is a unitary right. Influenced by the reasoning of the Historical School, the right of ownership in German law confers an indivisible power on the owner.[81] Primarily a reaction to the *duplex dominium* of former ages, the right of ownership cannot be fragmented into other rights.[82] In doctrinal reasoning the right of ownership is always unitary and complete.

However, there are several applications of the right of ownership which show that its unitary nature is not as clear as it seems. For example, a conditional transfer of ownership presents the legal system with some difficulties. There are two possible conditional transfers of ownership; the transfer under a resolutive condition, under which a transfer is made but the ownership of the object returns to the transferor upon the occurrence of an event described in the condition, and the transfer under a suspensive condition, under which a transfer of ownership is postponed until the event described in the condition occurs.

The transfer under a resolutive condition (*unter auflösende Bedingung*) poses a problem. The acquirer receives a right of ownership, which has to be absolute and unitary, but he will lose it upon fulfilment of the condition. Nevertheless, such a transfer will grant the transferee a full right of ownership. After all, in German doctrine ownership cannot be fragmented.

76 § 1004 BGB '(1) Wird das Eigentum in anderer Weise als durch Entziehung oder Vorenthaltung des Besitzes beeinträchtigt, so kann der Eigentümer von dem Störer die Beseitigung der Beeinträchtigung verlangen. Sind weitere Beeinträchtigungen zu besorgen, so kann der Eigentümer auf Unterlassung klagen. (2) Der Anspruch ist ausgeschlossen, wenn der Eigentümer zur Duldung verpflichtet ist'. Compare in this respect the Roman *actio negatoria*, see Chapter 2; 2.3. Ownership.

77 Müller 1997, p. 250.

78 Müller 1997, p. 270.

79 Müller 1997, p. 267-269.

80 §§ 986 *et seq.* BGB, but also § 823 BGB (tort), see Wolf 2005, p. 97 *et seq.*

81 Von Savigny 1981, p. 367, Puchta 1873, p. 324, Windscheid 1906, p. 856.

82 On the effect of the right of ownership in case of the creation of a limited property right see below; 3. Other Property Rights.

The transfer under a suspensive condition (*unter aufschiebende Bedingung*) creates the opposite situation. Here, the acquirer does not obtain ownership until the condition is fulfilled. The right of ownership therefore remains with the transferor, but the transferee will expect to obtain the right of ownership. In most situations, this transfer takes the form of a reservation of ownership or *Eigentumsvorbehalt*.[83] Unlike the transfer of ownership under a resolutive condition, where the right of ownership and the expectation of ownership are mirrored, the transferor of a right of ownership under a suspensive condition will retain full ownership. The transferee has nothing but an expectation. In principle, therefore, the law of property does not limit the transferor's right to use, enjoy or dispose of his ownership.[84]

The German approach to conditional transfers of ownership emphasises the unitary nature of the right of ownership. The doctrinal attitude of the system creates an unfair situation in which the person who does not have the right of ownership but merely expects to obtain it, is in a very vulnerable legal position. At the outset of the system, the person expecting ownership only has a personal right. When the owner becomes insolvent, the personal right will almost certainly not be sufficient to claim the right of ownership. German legal practice has found a solution in the recognition of a new property right: the *Anwartschaftsrecht* or acquisition right.[85] With the recognition of this new right, the person expecting ownership is granted, through the law of property, a better position than a personal right provides, without affecting the fullness of the right of ownership.

2.2. *Co-Ownership*

There are two types of co-ownership in German law. First, German law recognises a right of co-ownership in equal indivisible shares. These shares entitle their holders to act separately from each other. Secondly, there is a pure co-ownership in which there are indivisible and equal shares held by two or more persons, but these can only act jointly with regard to an object.

The community of indivisible shares, known as *Miteigentum nach Bruchteilen*, is dealt with in Paragraphs 741 and further and 1008 and further of the BGB. The ownership of the object in question will, unless otherwise provided, be separated into equal indivisible shares.[86] Each share will entitle each holder to a part of the ownership but also to a part of the right to use, as well as to a part in the proceeds of the object owned.[87] Although each co-owner will hold a share in the community, only the holders together can manage the object they co-own. Usually, a majority

83 See Baur, Baur & Stürner 1999, p. 741 *et seq.*

84 Such limitations can be imposed by contract, which is normally done in case of a reservation of ownership. See Baur, Baur & Stürner 1999, p. 743.

85 The *Anwartschaftsrecht* will be dealt with below in 3.4. Expectation Rights: Pre-Emptive Right and Acquisition Right.

86 § 742 BGB, Wolf 2005, p. 26-27.

87 Schwab & Prütting 2003, p. 190.

will provide a decision and will also bind any votes against.[88] Doctrinally however, these co-ownership shares are treated as if they constituted normal ownership. The result of this is that they can be transferred and burdened in almost the same way as a normal right of ownership.[89] The community in indivisible shares enables the owner of a share to act independently of the owners of the other shares. Consequently, the claims available to the owner to protect his right of ownership are also available to the owner of a share in a community. At the same time the holders of the shares are also bound to each other. The claim for the return of the object can only be made by the co-owners together.[90] Finally, a co-ownership share itself cannot, subject to certain exceptions, be subject to another co-ownership by a community of indivisible shares.[91]

The second type of co-ownership is known as *Gesamthandseigentum*. This type of co-ownership is characterised by an indivisible community over which the owners can only exercise their powers together. The holders of shares in this community cannot exercise their powers over these shares without the holders of the other shares.[92] This is different from the other type of co-ownership in which each holder of a share can act independently of the other holders in respect of his own share. This second type of co-ownership can only exist where the law provides for it, for instance, partnerships in company law, marriage or the receipt of an inheritance.[93]

Co-ownership in an indivisible community especially can hardly be characterised as an indivisible power over an object. German doctrine offers a solution to the question of whether this type of co-ownership still concerns a right of ownership. In this line of reasoning, the indivisible share itself represents the full and indivisible right of ownership. Consequently, even though several people share the power granted by the right of ownership, that power is not divided among them. In this way, the right of ownership remains unitary and the most comprehensive right a person can have to a corporeal object.

2.3. *Ownership of an Apartment*

The ownership of an apartment, or *Wohnungseigentum*, is a specific type of ownership that gives the owner entitlement to a specified part of a building. The introduction of this special type of ownership required the inclusion of some exceptions to the general provisions of the BGB, such as Paragraph 93 BGB, which prohibits the

88 § 745 BGB, but § 1010 provides an extra requirement of registration in case of an immovable object. See Schwab & Prütting 2003, p. 290-291.

89 Baur, Baur & Stürner 1999, p. 19, Schwab & Prütting 2003, p. 290-291.

90 § 1011 BGB which states 'Jeder Miteigentümer kann die Ansprüche aus dem Eigentum Dritten gegenüber in Ansehung der ganzen Sache geltend machen, den Anspruch auf Herausgabe jedoch nur in Gemäßheit des § 432'.

91 The exception is the specific ownership of an apartment (*Wohnungseigentum*), which is dealt with in the next Section. See Wolf 2005, p. 27, Schwab & Prütting 2003, p. 290.

92 Baur, Baur & Stürner 1999, p. 19, Wolf 2005, p. 27.

93 § 718, 105 *et seq.*, 161 *et seq.*, § 1405 *et seq.* and § 2032 *et seq.* BGB, as mentioned by Baur, Baur & Stürner 1999, p. 18-19. See also Wolf 2005, p. 26-27.

separation of an object into several parts capable of being the subject of property rights, and Paragraph 94 BGB, which considers the land and any building constructed on it a single entity.[94] The *Wohnungseigentum* was introduced in German law through special legislation.[95] The act introducing the ownership of an apartment also introduced the *Dauerwohnrecht*, the right to live in a building for a longer duration of time.[96]

The ownership of an apartment is constructed around a co-ownership in a community with indivisible shares.[97] The *Wohnungseigentum* enables several people to each 'own' a separate area of a building they co-own.[98] The *Wohnungseigentum* thus comprises a share in the community as well as a specific, exclusive ownership of a defined part of the building. Together these two entitlements form the *Wohnungseigentum* that German doctrine considers a normal type of ownership.[99] As such this type of ownership of an apartment can be transferred and be burdened with other property rights in the same way as a normal right of ownership.[100] Furthermore, the claims available to normal owners through Paragraphs 985 and 1004 BGB are available to the holders of this special right of ownership.[101] In addition these special co-owners can use Paragraph 1004 BGB to exclude others, including other co-owners, from the exclusive ownership of their part of the building.[102]

The share in the community and the exclusive part of the ownership of an apartment are inseparable. The owner can only dispose of the indivisible ownership.[103] Because German doctrine considers the ownership of an apartment a normal right of ownership, it is mostly treated as such. However, there are differences between these types of ownership. For instance, the law introducing the ownership

94 § 93 BGB states 'Bestandteile einer Sache, die voneinander nicht getrennt werden können, ohne dass der eine oder der andere zerstört oder in seinem Wesen verändert wird (wesentliche Bestandteile), können nicht Gegenstand besonderer Rechte sein'. § 94 BGB states '(1) Zu den wesentlichen Bestandteilen eines Grundstücks gehören die mit dem Grund und Boden fest verbundenen Sachen, insbesondere Gebäude, sowie die Erzeugnisse des Grundstücks, solange sie mit dem Boden zusammenhängen. Samen wird mit dem Aussäen, eine Pflanze wird mit dem Einpflanzen wesentlicher Bestandteil des Grundstücks'. The latter is a codification of the rule *superficies solo cedit.* See Schwab & Prütting 2003, p. 292-293, Baur, Baur & Stürner 1999, p. 330.

95 Gesetz über das Wohnungseigentum und Dauerwohnrecht (WEG) of 15 March 1951 (BGBl. I 175). See Baur, Baur & Stürner 1999, p. 332.

96 § 31 WEG. The *Dauerwohnrecht* is not to be confused with the *Wohnungsrecht* in the BGB, which is a special type of limited personal servitude. When the *Dauerwohnrecht* is created on a building not fit to live in, the right is known as a *Dauernutzungsrecht.* On this distinction see Baur, Baur & Stürner 1999, p. 342.

97 § 1 WEG (*Wohnungseigentumsgesetz*) see above; 2.2. Co-ownership.

98 § 10 WEG.

99 See BGH 17 January 1968, NJW 1968, 499 = BGHZ 49, 250.

100 Baur, Baur & Stürner 1999, p. 333.

101 Also § 823 will be available to the owner, Baur, Baur & Stürner 1999, p. 333.

102 § 13 WEG, Wolf 2005, p. 68.

103 § 6 WEG, Wolf 2005, p. 67, Baur, Baur & Stürner 1999, p. 337.

of an apartment permits certain limitations that cannot be imposed on normal ownership.[104] Paragraph 12 of the *Wohnungseigentumsgesetz* (WEG) states:

> A provision that the owner of an apartment cannot transfer his right without permission from the other owners or from a third party can be made the content of the special exclusive ownership.[105]

Such a provision limits the powers of the owner and constitutes a contractual interference in the law of property. Under the general theory on the right of ownership, property law provides its own rules, and contractual interferences, especially limitations on property rights, are not allowed, and they therefore do not have third-party effect.[106] As a general rule of German property law, Paragraph 137 BGB states:

> The power to dispose over a transferable right cannot be excluded or limited by juridical act. ...[107]

Certain deviations from the normal right of ownership are also permissible through legislation. The WEG deals with the relation between co-owners and contains a number of provisions that deviate from the provisions on the normal type of ownership. Furthermore, co-owners themselves are allowed to deal with their affairs by contract within the limits of the law.[108] However, such provisions will only have effect against third parties if they are registered as part of the exclusive ownership.[109]

A community of co-owners is created by force of law. The result is a community of shares that cannot be dissolved easily, neither on the request of one of the co-owners nor upon insolvency.[110] Although each of the co-owners has an exclusive right of ownership as part of the ownership of an apartment, which each co-owner can transfer and burden, the community also binds each co-owner. In respect of costs and division of these costs, the co-owners are entitled to deal with their affairs on their own, usually through an association of co-owners.[111]

104 *Bundesgesetz vom 15.3.1951 über das Wohnungseigentum und das Dauerwohnrecht* (WEG or *Wohungseigentumsgesetz*).

105 § 12 WEG, 'Als Inhalt des Sondereigentums kann vereinbart werden, daß ein Wohnungseigentümer zur Veräußerung seines Wohnungseigentums der Zustimmung anderer Wohnungseigentümer oder eines Dritten bedarf'.

106 The agreement is, however, binding on the parties as a contract, but has no effect on the property relation *per se*.

107 § 137 BGB, 'Die Befugnis zur Verfügung über ein veräußerliches Recht kann nicht durch Rechtsgeschäft ausgeschlossen oder beschränkt werden. ...'.

108 § 10 WEG, this could include costs but also a rule that a majority decision concerning the common parts of the building will bind all the owners. A majority decision having impact on the exclusive ownership of a part of the building will not have effect. BGH 20 September 2000, *BGHZ* 145, 158 = NJW 2000, 3500, Schwab & Prütting 2003, p. 295.

109 § 10 (2) WEG.

110 § 11 WEG.

111 § 20 *et seq.* WEG.

Finally, the right of ownership of an apartment can also be used to enable ownership of a separate part of an immovable object other than an apartment. In those cases the right is not known as ownership of an apartment but as *Teileigentum*, which translates as right of ownership of a certain part.[112]

The right of ownership of an apartment is a special type of ownership. Although German doctrine treats this right as a normal type of ownership, contractual or community-imposed restrictions create a more limited type of ownership. Unlike the normal type of ownership, the *Wohnungseigentum* does not confer on its holder the absolute and indivisible power over an object.

2.4. *Treuhand Ownership*

The *Treuhand* is best characterised as a contractual relation with far-reaching property effects.[113] In German doctrine, *Treuhand* does not so much concern the most comprehensive nature of the right of ownership as it concerns the substance and scope of the owner's powers. A *Treuhand* enables parties to limit the powers of the owner by contract.[114] In this respect, the *Treuhand* deviates from a basic principle of the BGB that the law of obligations and the law of property are strictly separated.[115] This separation is especially reflected in Paragraph 137 BGB, which prohibits contractual limitations on the power of the owner.[116]

A *Treuhand* is created by a transfer of ownership whereby the transferee, the *Treuhänder*, is obliged to manage the transferred object for the benefit of the transferor, or *Treugeber*. The *Treuhänder* may appear to be the normal owner, but in relation to the *Treugeber*, the *Treuhänder* is obliged to manage the object as was agreed in the contract of transfer.[117] This special transfer effectively fragments the right of ownership into economic ownership of the *Treugeber* and legal ownership of the *Treuhänder*.[118] This distinction had been recognised in 1899, shortly before the introduction of the BGB. The *Reichsgericht*, or Imperial Court, but a different court than the Imperial Court (*Reichkammergericht*) mentioned above, stated:

> An object or claim, which is transferred to a debtor who is insolvent, however with the agreement that the object or claim is not treated as his ownership ... is legally and formally owned by him, but not economically and practically.[119]

112 Baur, Baur & Stürner 1999, p. 330.

113 Ganter 2004, p. 260. Another classification would be a trust-like device. The comparison to trusts has been made before, see, *inter alia*, Kötz 1963, Marwede 1972, Helmholz & Zimmermann 1998, p. 27 *et seq.*

114 Wolf 2005, p. 27-28, Füller 2006, p. 387-392.

115 See above; 1. Introduction.

116 Although § 137 BGB did and does function as a limitation to what can be agreed upon by the parties. On the development of *Treuhand* in relation to § 137 BGB see Liebs 1975, p. 32-33.

117 Baur, Baur & Stürner 1999, p. 22.

118 See Wolf 2005, p. 29.

119 As cited by Wiegand 1990, p. 126, note 56. 'Ein Gegenstand, der dem Gemeinschuldner zwar zum Eigentum übergeben ist, jedoch mit der Abmachung, daß derselbe gleichwohl von ihm →

Wiegand has emphasised that the decision of the *Reichsgericht*, which was followed by the *Bundesgerichtshof* (BGH) or Federal Court, forms the basis of treating *Treuhand* ownership differently from the normal right of ownership.[120] Nevertheless, German doctrine continues to recognise the unitary right of ownership as the only type of ownership. Judicial recognition of two rights of ownership, economic and legal ownership, does not doctrinally interfere with the notion of absolute and unitary ownership. The recognition of economic ownership does not imply a lesser form of legal ownership. A doctrinal solution is found in the distinction between the internal and external effects of the *Treuhand*.[121] In relation to third parties there is only one type of ownership - the right of ownership of the *Treuhänder*. From a property-law point of view, the *Treuhänder* can freely dispose of the object under *Treuhand*. However, in the internal relation between *Treugeber* and *Treuhänder*, the *Treuhänder* is bound by the terms of the contact. This contract can limit the *Treuhänder*'s power to dispose, but may also stipulate duties to manage and take care of certain objects. In case of non-performance, the *Treugeber* has a set of contractual remedies against the *Treuhänder* at his disposal.[122] However, the legal ownership of the *Treuhänder* is not affected by his personal duties.

The explanation of the *Treuhand* relationship is one thing, but German legal doctrine has developed certain deviations from this doctrinal solution that give rise to interesting problems. First, the personal relation between *Treugeber* and *Treuhänder* is extended in such a way that a third party who knows of the *Treuhand* relation and still decides to act can be affected by the contract.[123] Secondly, in case of insolvency of either the *Treugeber* or the *Treuhänder*, the legal ownership of the *Treuhänder* is not decisive. The *Treuhänder*'s creditors cannot simply seize the object under *Treuhand*, although the *Treuhänder* is the legal owner.[124] Instead, the *Treugeber* is awarded a counter-claim to stop a creditors' seizure of the object through Paragraph 771 of the Civil Procedure Regulation, *Zivilprozeßordnung* (ZPO).[125] Moreover, Paragraph 47 of the Bankruptcy Regulation, *Insolvenzordnung* (InsO), entitles the *Treugeber* to claim the object from the set of assets and debts of the *Treuhänder*.[126] The justification for this exception is the emphasis on the *Treugeber*'s economic ownership.[127] Furthermore, as a result of the recognition of the economic ownership of the

nicht wie sein Eigentum behandelt werden dürfte ... gehört dem Gemeinschuldner zwar formell und juristisch, aber nicht materiell und wirtschaftlich' RGZ 45, 80 *et seq.*, p. 85.

120 Wiegand 1990, p. 126 *et seq.*, for a comparative study of Swiss and German law see Wiegand 1982, p. 565 *et seq.*

121 Wolff & Raiser 1957, p. 354-355, Wiegand 1982, p. 574, Wiegand 1990, p. 127.

122 See Wolf 2005, p. 27-28.

123 A claim for damages through § 823 is awarded. BGH NJW-RR 1993, 367. Wolf 2005, p. 28.

124 Wolf 2005, p. 29.

125 This is the *Drittwiderspruchklage*, Henckel 1982, p. 137, Wolf 2005, p. 29, 362 363.

126 This is the *Aussonderungsrecht*. Before 1994 the *Aussonderungsrecht* was awarded by § 43 of the *Konkursordnung* (KO) which is mentioned in older literature. Baur, Baur & Stürner 1999, p. 726-727.

127 Henckel 1982, p. 137.

Treugeber, creditors of the *Treugeber* can seize the object, even though the *Treuhänder* has legal ownership.[128]

These rules on *Treuhand* apply when a *Treugeber* transfers an object for his personal benefit to a *Treuhänder* through a contract stating the purpose of the transfer as well as the limitations of the *Treuhänder*'s powers. Such a transfer creates two types of *Übertragungstreuhand.*[129] The first of these is the *Verwaltungstreuhand* or *Uneigennützige Treuhand*, whereby the *Treuhänder* becomes the legal owner for the purpose of managing the object that was transferred. Such a *Treuhand* can also be created through a contract giving the *Treugeber* legal ownership but providing the *Treuhänder* with certain powers of management.[130] The second type is the *Sicherungstreuhand* or *Eigennützige Treuhand*, transferring an object with the purpose of providing security.[131]

The *Treuhand* ownership has led to an approach to the right of ownership in which the *Treugeber* is awarded a property-like right to the detriment of the *Treuhänder*'s ownership. With the specified limitations in force, the legal ownership of the *Treuhänder*, although doctrinally pure, can hardly be classified as a right of ownership under Paragraph 903 BGB, but is not a personal right either.[132]

2.5. *Security Ownership*

The right of ownership is not only used for the enjoyment of an object, but can also be used as security for the performance of a certain obligation. Among the security property rights recognised by German law, security ownership takes an important position.[133] The use of ownership as a security right developed through case law as a method next to the security rights dealt with mainly in the BGB.[134] When the trade in movable objects increased, the security rights to these movable objects also rose in importance. Immovable objects, in particular land, were no longer the primary object of value, movable objects such as machines and company inventory were also offered as security in exchange for capital.[135]

128 Henckel 1982, p. 137.

129 Schmidt also distinguishes forms of *Erbwerbstreuhand* and *Vereinbarungstreuhand*. These will be dealt with below in 4.5. *Treuhand* Bank Account. See Schmidt 2005, p. 937, Ganter 2004, p. 251-252.

130 Wolf 2005, p. 28, Marwede 1972, p. 45 *et seq.* A *Treuhand* in which the right of ownership is not transferred to the *Treuhänder* will consequently not require the deviation from the insolvency procedure, as is the case when the *Treuhänder* is legal owner.

131 This type of security-*Treuhand* will be dealt with below in 2.5. Security Ownership.

132 See Wiegand 1990, p. 127, Wiegand 1999a, p. 118-119.

133 On these other rights see below; 3.5. Real Burden (*Reallast*), 3.6. Pledge, 3.7. Hypothec and 3.8. *Grundschuld*.

134 See Schwab & Prütting 2003, p. 199-200, Baur, Baur & Stürner 1999, p. 706.

135 The concept of security ownership is not applicable to immovable objects; it can exist in respect to immovable objects only. In case of rights there is a possibility to assign these for security purposes. However the terms 'transfer' and 'ownership' in German law are restricted to corporeal objects.

However, the existing security rights were not suited for this purpose. The main reason for this was the requirement to transfer possession (factual power) of the object serving as security. Especially, since security over movable objects was sought, the right of pledge demanded such a transfer of possession. By transferring ownership of a movable object, the factual power over the object and the legal entitlement to it can be separated. In other words, transfer of ownership does not necessarily include actual transfer of the object itself.

The German system of property law allows such a transfer.[136] The owner, the transferor, transfers his right of ownership of a movable object to another person, the transferee. The object serves as security for the payment of a claim the transferee has against the transferor. The transferee is intended to retain the right of ownership until the transferee's claim is satisfied, but only for security purposes. Because of this purpose, the right of ownership acquired by the transferee is not normal ownership but security ownership.

Doctrinally, the difference between security ownership and normal ownership is very small. The right of ownership is an indivisible power over an object, regardless of what it is used for. The right of ownership transferred for security purposes is therefore a full right of ownership. However, at the same time, the powers of the security owner are not the same as those of a normal owner. The security owner retains the object serving as security for security purposes and not for personal enjoyment, and will eventually have to return the object to the original owner in the same state as received. In other words, there are specific limitations to the powers of a security owner, and security ownership can therefore be considered a different type of ownership from the normal right of ownership.

In order to create this special type of ownership the parties conclude a contract known as a *Sicherungsvertrag* or security contract. This contract not only serves as the basis for the transfer of the right of ownership, but also limits the powers of the security owner.[137] Moreover, the parties also stipulate what will happen when the claim of the security owner, the transferee, is satisfied. There are two possibilities; the parties can agree that upon satisfaction of the claim the security owner will retransfer the ownership of the object to the original owner, or that the transferor transfers the right of ownership to the transferee under the resolutive condition that when the claim is satisfied, the right of ownership will revert to the original owner.[138] Mutual agreement is required because security ownership is not an accessory right.

An accessory right is a right that is connected to the existence of a claim. Accessority will lead to termination of a security right when the secured debt ceases to exit upon satisfaction. When no accessority between a right and a debt exists, a specific act by the parties is needed to retransfer the right to the transferor or to extinguish the right. As regards security ownership, where no accessority exists, the right of ownership will not automatically revert to the original owner.[139]

136 § 930 BGB, see Van Vliet 2000, p. 52-60.

137 See Wolf 2005, p. 356-359.

138 Wolf 2005, p. 356-357, Baur, Baur & Stürner 1999, p. 710.

139 Baur, Baur & Stürner 1999, p. 710, for an overview in French see Crocq 1995, p. 151 *et seq.*

The security contract will also contain duties for the transferor, including the duty to hand over the factual power over the object when the security owner is contractually entitled to it.[140] However, the most important function of the security contract is to protect the transferor by imposing limitations on the powers of the security owner. The contract will usually ensure that the security owner can only use the object for security purposes and may only exercise his ownership rights if the transferor fails to perform. Until then the transferor remains in control of the object.[141]

The use of ownership for security purposes is not without risk. Parties are relatively free to arrange the division of powers, but only within certain limits. These limits are imposed by analogous application of provisions on other security rights, but they are also determined specifically by case law. The limitations set by case law, especially the case law of the BGH, play a particularly important role in the protection of the rights of the transferor.

The *Sicherungsvertrag* is subject to several requirements, including those of public morals as provided in Paragraph 138 BGB.[142] The application of the principle of public morals severely limits the powers of the security owner. Because the security owner does not own the object to enjoy it, but merely for the purpose of securing the transferor's debt, the security owner cannot simply dispose of the object. In fact, the security owner can only use his powers over the object in case the transferor fails to perform his duty. The security contract will have to describe the security owner's powers in detail. Furthermore, unless otherwise provided and if not to the detriment of the transferor, by analogous application of the provisions on the right of pledge, the security owner must sell the object serving as security in the event that the debtor, usually the transferor, does not perform.[143] In that case the provisions on pledge also apply in such a way that the security ownership is recognised not as a right of ownership but as a type of pledge. The object serving as security is therefore considered part of the set of assets and debts of the transferor to which the security owner has a preferential claim.[144]

Another limitation imposed by Paragraph 138 BGB is known as *Knebelung*. In a situation of *Knebelung* the transferor is so disproportionately dependent on the security owner that the transferor can no longer properly enjoy the object serving as security.[145] Paragraph 138 BGB renders such a security contract void, in which case, assuming ownership has been transferred, the security owner loses his legal basis for retaining the right of ownership. The ownership of the object in case of *Knebe-*

140 This will usually include the situation where the transferor can no longer pay and the security owner 'executes' the contract. See Wolf 2005, p. 357.

141 Wolf 2005, p. 357-358.

142 Or in German, *gute Sitten*. The German translation of the German Ministry of Justice states 'Public Policy' as a translation. See <http://www.gesetze-im-internet.de>.

143 BGH 27 June 1995, NJW 1995, 2221. The Paragraph's on pledge concern §§ 1233 *et seq.*, see Wolf 2005, p. 357-358.

144 Baur, Baur & Stürner 1999, p. 722.

145 Wolf 2005, p. 360-361, Baur, Baur & Stürner 1999, p. 714-715.

lung will not automatically return to the transferor, but the transferor will have a claim in unjust enrichment against the security owner.[146]

A third and more difficult situation occurs when an object is used to secure a debt of much less value than the object. Such a situation, known as over-securitisation or *Übersicherung*, can arise at the moment of creation, but also during the existence of the security right.[147] An *Übersicherung*-situation is not always clear. Following decisions of the German Federal Court, the *Bundesgerichtshof* (BGH), parties commonly included a clause in their *Sicherungsvertrag* specifying a maximum amount of money that the objects serving as security secured. This clause would normally also oblige the transferee to make those objects exceeding the maximum amount available to the debtor.[148] However, parties were not under a strict legal obligation to include such a clause. In a landmark decision, the Grand Senate of the *Bundesgerichtshof* specifically considered a situation where no such clause had been inserted.[149] In this situation, but also when such a clause had been used, the Senate of the BGH used Paragraph 138 BGB to limit the powers of the security owner. The BGH was not only concerned with the imbalance of power between the transferor and the security owner, but also with the relation between the security owner and the other creditors of the transferor. A transfer of ownership would, in principle, bring the object serving as security outside the set of assets and debts of the transferor and into the set of assets and debts of the security owner. In the absence of a clause in the contract stating otherwise, the transferor's creditors could not claim the value of the object. Especially when the value of the object was higher than the debt, the excess value would be available to the other creditors of the transferor. In order to address this problem the Grand Senate of the BGH ruled that in case of *Übersicherung* the *Sicherungsvertrag* is void.[150] Furthermore, the BGH now assumed by implication the existence of clauses limiting the agreement to a certain amount of outstanding debt, and the obligation for the security owner to disclose the excess value of the object.[151]

Most importantly, the Senate of the BGH answered the question of when *Übersicherung* occurs. According to the Court, the lower limit of *Übersicherung* is when the value of the claim for which security is given exceeds 110% of the actual value of the object serving as security, but is not higher than 150% of the estimated

146 This is due to the abstract system of transfer. See Van Vliet 2000, p. 31 *et seq.*

147 These are the *anfängliche* and *nachträgliche* cases of over-securitisation. See Baur, Baur & Stürner 1999, p. 721, Wolf 2005, p. 361.

148 BGH 8 October 1986, BGHZ 98, 303 and 13 January 1994, BGHZ 124, 371. Baur, Baur & Stürner 1999, p. 715-716.

149 BGH GS NJW 1998, 671, 675. For a detailed analysis of this complicated decision and the facts that lead to it see Baur, Baur & Stürner 1999, p. 717-721.

150 Although a distinction should be made between initial *Übersicherung*, in which the contract and the transfer is void, and *nachträgliche Übersicherung* that follows another approach. In such cases the debtor under a *Freigabeanspruch* can reclaim part of the objects. Baur, Baur & Stürner 1999, p. 719, Wolf 2005, p. 361.

151 Wolf 2005, p. 361.

value of the object.[152] The latter requirement connects to the general provision in Paragraph 237 BGB, which limits the value of the object in relation to the debt it secures to 150%.[153] Finally, a contract creating a transfer of ownership for security purposes with an initial surplus value of the object will be void by application of Paragraph 138 BGB as well. According to the BGH, a situation of *Übersicherung* exists when the value of the object is twice the limit of 150% of the secured claim.[154]

Although the transfer of ownership for security purposes does transfer a type of ownership - security ownership -, in insolvency cases, security owners are not treated in the same way as normal owners. In German insolvency law, security ownership is treated as a pledge-like right.[155] The result of this approach is that the object serving as security is not considered to have left the assets of the transferor completely. To the outside world the security owner is the owner, but not to the extent a normal owner is. The principal objective of the transfer for security purposes is to enable the security owner to institute actions in order to protect his position in case the transferor becomes insolvent. Contrary to the claim of a normal owner, the security owner cannot claim the object from the transferor, but has a right to separate the object from the set of assets through Paragraph 51(1) InsO.[156] This claim for separation is awarded for practical reasons. Like a pledgee, the security owner will be entitled to the proceeds of the sale of the complete set of assets of the transferor. This will, at least theoretically, increase the proceeds of the sale.[157] However, to protect the security owner who joins the other creditors in the sale of the total set of assets of the debtor, a counter-claim is awarded to block claims of the creditors of the transferor.[158] These, in their turn, may claim nullity of the *Sicherungsvertrag* based on Paragraph 138 BGB. This would make both the contract and the transfer void, and fully return the object serving as security to the transferor's set of assets and debts.[159] The creditors can claim financial compensation if the security owner mistreats the transferor or gravely disadvantages the other creditors of the transferor.[160] The transferee, who is then no longer the security owner, will no longer be able to use a counter-claim to block the claims of the creditor or claim a separation of the security object.[161]

152 The actual value or *realisierbaren Wert*, is the value which is received upon sale of the object. The estimated value or *Schätzwert* is the estimated worth in money of the object serving as security.

153 Wolf 2005, p. 361, Baur, Baur & Stürner 1999, p. 720.

154 BGH 12 March 1998, NJW 1998, 2047, Wolf 2005, p. 361.

155 Baur, Baur & Stürner 1999, p. 722.

156 And not a claim for revindication of the object, § 51(1) *Insolvenzordnung* or Bankruptcy Code awards a *Absonderungsrecht* or separation claim, Wolf 2005, p. 360, Baur, Baur & Stürner 1999, p. 722.

157 Baur, Baur & Stürner 1999, p. 722-723.

158 § 771 ZPO (*Zivilprozeßordnung* or Civil Procedure Code) awards a *Drittwiderspruchsklage* or third party counter-claim, Wolf 2005, p. 359-360.

159 Baur, Baur & Stürner 1999, p. 721.

160 § 826 BGB, Baur, Baur & Stürner 1999, p. 722, 725.

161 Wolf 2005, p. 360.

Considering the effects of the *Sicherungsvertrag*, security ownership can hardly be described as a right of ownership that grants the owner powers comparable to those of a normal owner. Although doctrinally security ownership is just another form of the regular type of ownership of Paragraph 903 BGB, security contracts severely limit the powers of owners.[162] In fact, security ownership is one of the primary recognised forms of *Treuhand*.[163] The result of this is that the contract establishing the security ownership greatly restricts the property relation between the transferor and the security owner. Security ownership is thus also a special type of ownership at the same time.

3. Other Property Rights

In German law, the right of ownership is considered the supreme property right. The right is absolute, it has effect against the whole world, and it is unitary, it cannot be fragmented. The doctrine of ownership as an indivisible power over an object, as primarily advocated by Von Savigny, firmly establishes and emphasises this position. Nevertheless, German law also recognises property rights other than the right of ownership. Like the right of ownership, these are primarily restricted to corporeal objects and they are known as *Dingliche Rechte*.[164] The absolute and unitary nature of the paramount property right, the right of ownership, also characterises the other property rights, albeit that these other rights are derived from the right of ownership itself. These other property rights are *Beschränkte Dingliche Rechte* or limited property rights.[165]

The relation between the right of ownership and the other property rights is complicated in German law. Doctrinally the right of ownership is the ultimate and indivisible power over an object. In reaction to the situation before the introduction of the BGB, the First Commission stated:

> The specific powers of the owner could be derived ... from the provisions on the protection of the right of ownership and from the planned transfers of the owner; it is not possible to describe a sum of powers, *since ownership cannot be characterised as a sum of powers*. Therefore, ownership also cannot be fragmented in a way in which two parties receive powers contained in the rights of ownership while their rights are still characterised as ownership.[166]

162 See above; 2.1. Normal Ownership. For a similar discussion in French law see Crocq 1995, p. 59 *et seq.*

163 See above; 2.4. *Treuhand* Ownership, Baur, Baur & Stürner 1999, p. 726.

164 However, also property rights in respect to rights are recognised. The term *Dingliche Rechte* best translates as rights in respect to an object. Nevertheless, these property rights in respect to rights are property rights. Therefore property right will be the term with which these rights are dealt with in this chapter.

165 Wolf 2005, p. 3-4, Füller 2006, p. 35.

166 Emphasis by the author, 'Die einzelnen Befugnisse des Eigenthümers würden, ..., aus den Vorschriften über den Eigenthumsschuz und über die von dem Eigenthümer vorzunehmenden Veräußerungsgeschäfte entnommen werden können; sie lassen sich nicht vollständig aufzählen; das Bedürfnis einer solchen Aufzählung liegt auch nicht vor, *da das Eigenthum*
→

The last sentence should be understood as a general rejection of the fragmentation of ownership into *dominium directum* and *dominium utile*.[167] The statement that ownership cannot be characterised as a sum of powers should be understood as the expression of Von Savigny's theory of ownership as an indivised and indivisible power over a corporeal object. However, at the same time limited property rights are recognised that limit the powers of the owner. In modern doctrine, the creation of a limited property right is explained as a transfer of certain powers from the right of ownership to another property right.[168] However, even such a transfer will not deprive the right of ownership of its characteristics, or as Wiegand states: 'Ownership remains ownership, even when powers of the owner are transferred to someone else'.[169] The First Commission itself concluded:

> The primary function of the law of property is to deal with property rights. Of these rights the right of ownership is the most complete and important, its treatment separate from the other rights is commonly accepted. The order in which the other property rights connect to the right of ownership is more or less random, and for the creation and use of the law more or less the same. A specific point follows from this, that the limited property rights receive their content from the power to use and the power to transfer of the owner.[170]

The approach of German property law to limited property rights is twofold. First, the right of ownership is considered absolute and indivisible, the right of ownership remains whole even when a property right is created. Secondly, the limited property rights are considered to receive their content from the right of ownership. In, for example, the French system, such an approach to limited property rights would result in the termination of the property right once it has reverted to the owner. This approach to the creation and termination of property rights is commonly described as elasticity of ownership.[171] The system of creation of property rights in French law is known as *démembrement*.

nicht eine Summe einzelner Befugnisse ist. Deshalb lässt sich das Eigenthum auch nicht so theilen, dass dem Einen und dem Anderen eine Reihe bestimmter im Eigenthume liegender Befugnisse zugewiesen werden und dem beiderseitigen Rechte der Karakter des Eigenthumes beigemessen wird', Motive III 1888, p. 262, see also Hattenhauer 1989, p. 90-91.

167 See also Füller 2006, p. 367-381.

168 Wolf 2005, p. 4 (*Teilinhalte aus dem Eigentum*), Wiegand 1990, p. 117 (*einzelne Befugnisse jemandem anderen übertragen werden*), Baur, Baur & Stürner 1999, p. 17 (*er hat die Möglichkeit, aus seinem Vollrecht beschränkte Befugnisse zugunsten anderer 'abzuspalten'*), see also Müller 1997, p. 100 (*die sich aus dem Eigentum ergebende Herrschaftsbefugnis beschränken*).

169 Wiegand 1990, p. 117, *Eigentum bleibt auch dann Eigentum, wenn einzelne Befugnisse jemandem anderen übertragen werden.*

170 'Die Hauptaufgabe des Sachenrechts ist die Regelung der dinglichen Rechte. Unter diesen Rechten ist das Eigenthum das vollkommenste und wichtigste, seine Behandlung von dem übrigen daher allgemein gebräuchlich. Die Reihenfolge, in welcher die letzteren sich ihm anschließen, ist mehr oder weniger willkürlich, für die Gestaltung und Anwendung des Gesetzes auch ziemlich gleichgültig. Ein gewisser Anhalt ergiebt sich daraus, dass die begrenzten Rechte ihren Inhalt entweder aus dem Nutzungsrechte oder aus dem Veräuserungsrechte des Eigenthümers schöpfen', Motive III 1888, p. 22-23.

171 Wolf 2005, p. 4-5.

The termination of a property right once it has reverted to the owner is known in German law as *Konsolidation*, which does not have a directly equivalent term in English.[172] However, it does not apply to all limited property rights.[173] As regards property rights to immovable objects, German law seems to follow an approach different from the *Konsolidation* approach generally taken under the *démembrement* method, as it is used in French law.[174] This remarkable deviation from the traditional system was included under economic pressure, especially in the area of the right of hypothec.[175]

The law in Prussia before the introduction of the BGB provided for the establishment of a limited property right that would continue to exist after it had returned to the owner, enabling the owner to use the same right again for another transaction.[176] Applying the French approach of *démembrement* would result in the destruction of the limited property right when the powers of the owner and the powers of the holder of the right of hypothec, the hypothecee, were merged. After all, the powers of the hypothecee were originally the owner's and would reunify with the right of ownership once they had returned to the owner.[177]

Furthermore, the drafters of the BGB also considered it undesirable that a third party should be entitled to a right to the limited property right, and this right would be destroyed when the limited property right ceased because of mixing with the right of ownership.[178] For that reason, the German BGB includes Paragraph 889:

> A right to another piece of land does not expire when the owner acquires the piece of land or the holder of the right receives the ownership of the same land.[179]

The effect of this Paragraph is that it is possible for one person simultaneously to have a limited property right to a piece of land and the right of ownership of that same piece of land. Combined with a right of ownership that cannot be characterised as a sum of powers, but from which it is still possible to transfer powers into

172 Füller 2006, p. 468-470. A translation of *Konsolidation* into English is difficult to provide. Possibly terms as coincidence or concurrence could describe the same effect. A concurrence of ownership and property rights would in this sense be a *Konsolidation* in the German doctrinal sense.

173 Wolff & Raiser 1957, p. 128, Schwab & Prütting 2003,p. 10, See Chapter 3; 3. Other Property Rights.

174 § 889 BGB. The *démembrement* method considers a limited property right as a part of the larger right, usually the right of ownership, from which it was derived. See Chapter 3; 3. Other Property Rights and Chapter 7; 2.2. Of Ways to Create a Lesser Property Right.

175 On the previous system see Wolff & Raiser 1957, p. 128-129.

176 Specifically under the ALR., see Motive III 1888, p. 203-204, Wolff & Raiser 1957, p. 128-129, 592-593.

177 Elasticity of ownership, see above; 2. The Right of Ownership.

178 Motive III 1888, p. 201-205. Remarkably, the Dutch civil code has opted for the opposite solution, whereby the property right ceases to exist except for the holder of a property right in respect of that property right. See Chapter 5; 4.5. After-Effects of Property Rights.

179 § 889 BGB, 'Ein Recht an einem fremden Grundstück erlischt nicht dadurch, dass der Eigentümer des Grundstücks das Recht oder der Berechtigte das Eigentum an dem Grundstück erwirbt'.

another property right, German law adheres to a complicated theory describing the relation between ownership and other property rights in respect to immovable objects.[180] Although the First Commission recognised this problem, it observed:

> How the right recognised in § 836 [now § 889 BGB, BA] to a person's own object can be legally constructed, is not dealt with by the law. The construction is a task for legal science. Only this can be stated, that the often heard objection against the owner-hypothec, that the owner cannot have a specific property right in respect of the same object as his ownership, because the ownership already contains the advantages the specific property right provides, is not correct. Until now, the discussion results in the situation that the owner, when the piece of land is transferred, can exercise his specific property right in respect of the same piece of land and, when he continues to have ownership, dispose of it for the benefit of a third party, - both advantages, of which the actual value should not be argued.[181]

In the documents preceding the *Motive*, Johow, the drafter of the Property Law part of the BGB, also addressed the issue. On the relation between ownership and limited property rights, he states:

> The powers of the owner find their natural limitation in the concept of ownership. This concept is provided by objective law and cannot be given content by practice. The owner can do with the object what he wants, he could transfer it out of his assets or give up the right of ownership. However, he cannot continue to hold the object in his assets and at the same time, by randomly trimming several powers, which contain the same as his right of ownership, reduce his right of ownership. If he could do so, then he would have the power to transform his right of ownership on a specific object into another right, which the legal system no longer recognises as a right of ownership. With that the right of ownership would have disappeared ...
> It is now commonly recognised that the opinion advocated by certain writers as, e.g., Puchta, Pand. §145, that a limited right contains powers taken from the right of ownership, cannot be upheld. Ownership is an undividable right, which may consist of a list of powers, but which cannot be characterised as such. The owner is not in the position to take certain of his powers and transfer these to others. The limited right, which he creates, does not comprise of a limitation of the right of ownership; it is simply a right of a non-owner to the object, which limits the power of the owner over the same object. With the ceasing of this right the limitations on the powers of the

180 See Wolff & Raiser 1957, p. 175.

181 'Wie das in dem § 835 [now § 889, BA] anerkannte recht an der eigenen Sache juristisch zu konstruiren ist, entzieht sich der Bestimmung durch das Gesetz. Die Konstruktion ist Aufgabe der Wissenschaft. Nur das mag hier hervorgehoben werden, daß der oft gehörte Einwurf gegen die Eigenthümerhypothek, der Eigenthümer könne ein besonderes Recht an der Sache nicht haben, weil das Eigenthum bereits alle mit der begrenzten Rechten verbundenen Vortheile gewähre, nicht zutreffend ist. Die bisherigen Erörterungen ergeben, daß der Eigenthümer, wenn das Grundstück veräußert wird, das an demselben ihm zustehende Recht vollinhaltlich ausüben und, wenn er das Eigenthum behält, zu Gunsten eines Dritten verfügen kann, - beides Vortheile, deren reeller Werth sich nicht bestreiten läßt', Motive III 1888, p. 205.

> owner cease as well. The right of ownership consolidates itself, without the necessity to re-transfer powers which belong to the holder of the limited right.[182]

Windscheid responds in similar fashion.[183] In discussing servitudes, he states:

> I must explain my position against this opinion [that servitudes consist of parts of the right of ownership. BA]. As little as servitudes are dealt with as parts of ownership, so little they comprise parts of ownership.[184]

Both Johow and Windscheid conclude that the pre-BGB situation, where a property right was considered to comprise a part of the owner's powers, was no longer represented in the system of the BGB.[185] Taking these considerations into account, it could be argued that the doctrinal system of the BGB should be understood as differing from the French system of *démembrement.*

Despite these remarks on the complicated nature of the relation between ownership and limited rights in the BGB, modern handbooks on German property law do not consider the problem as very fundamental.[186] Yet in respect to this

182 'Das Verfügungsrecht des Eigenthümers findet seine natürliche Begrenzung durch den Begriff des Eigenthums. Dieser Begriff ist durch das objektive Recht gegeben und der Bestimmung durch Privatwillkür entrückt. Der Eigenthümer kann allerdings an sich mit die Sache machen, was er will, er kann dieselbe namentlich auch aus seinem Vermögen ausscheiden und also das Eigenthum aufgeben. Aber er kann nicht die Sache in seinem Vermögen behalten und gleichzeitig sein Eigenthum durch willkürliche Abtrennung einzelner Befugnisse, welche dasselbe verleiht, abschwächen. Dürfte er dies, so läge es in seiner Hand, das Eigenthum an einer bestimmten Sache in ein Recht umzuformen, welches die Rechtsordnung nicht mehr als Eigenthum gelten lassen könnte. Damit aber wäre der Eigenthumsbegriff selbst verflüchtigt ... Als unhaltbar ist wohl jetzt allgemein erkannt die von einigen Schriftstellern, z.B. Puchta, Pand. §. 145, aufgestellte Ansicht, dass die dinglichen Rechte aus dem Eigenthum herausgenommene Befugnisse seien. Das Eigenthum ist ein untheilbares Recht, welches zwar eine Reihe von Befugnissen gewährt, aber nicht aus solchen sich zusammenfesst. Der Eigenthümer ist mithin gar nicht in der Lage, ein solche Befugniss aus seinem Rechte herauszunehmen und auf einen Anderen zu übertragen. Das dingliche Recht, welches er bestellt, besteht auch nicht in einer Beschränkung des Eighenthums; es ist einfach ein Recht des Nichteigenthümers an der Sache, welches die Herrschaft des Eigenthümers über deselbe beschränkt. Mit dem Erlöschen dieses Rechts erlischt zugleich die Beschränkung. Das Eigenthum konsolidiert sich wieder, ohne dass es einer Rückerwerbung der dem Berechtigten zugestandenen Befugnis seitens des Eigenthümers bedürfte'. Johow 1982, *Begründung*, p. 126, 127.

183 Windscheid 1875, p. 633, note 3, specifically pages 634-635. See also Vangerow, who is of the same opinion Vangerow II 1876, p. 686-687.

184 'Ich muss mich auch gegen diese Auffassung erklären. So wenig wie die Dienstbarkeiten nach ihrer Begründung Eigenthumsbestandtheile sind, so wenig sind sie aus Eigenthumsbestandtheilen gebildet', Windscheid 1875, p. 634.

185 On the situation before the BGB see also Staudinger & Gursky 2002, § 889, p. 311.

186 See, *inter alia*, Wolff & Raiser 1957, p. 128, Müller 1997, p. 439, Schwab & Prütting 2003, p. 75, Wolf 2005, p. 444, more elaborate Wilhelm 2002, p. 52, 232 and Baur, Baur & Stürner 1999, p. 25.

research, a clear explanation of the relation between the right of ownership and other property rights is highly relevant.[187]

Two modern handbooks, Baur, Baur and Stürner and Wolf, deal with the issue, but not along the same lines as Johow and Windscheid.[188] These modern handbooks describe the powers of the owner as a comprehensive and indivisible unit, but recognise the possibility of transforming some specific powers into a property right other than ownership. This explains the use of the term *abspalten*, which is best translated as separate, in relation to powers of the owner.[189] Wolf even refers to *Teilinhalte aus dem Eigentum*, or parts of the right of ownership, to describe limited rights.[190] However, in this approach it is difficult to explain how a property right, which contains a power that was originally part of the right of ownership, and the right of ownership from which that power is missing, can be held by the same person. In German doctrine, this would be a situation of *Konsolidation*. The doctrinal question seems to be why this power does not revert into the right of ownership.

It is interesting to see that these authors find the answer in Paragraph 889 BGB. Under the BGB, a property right to an immovable object will not cease to exist when the owner acquires the property right; this will only occur if the owner so desires.[191] However, in other situations, the limited right will cease to exist.[192] Baur, Baur and Stürner explain this situation by referring to the ranking of property rights.[193] It is possible for several limited property rights to be created on the same object. Especially in cases of insolvency sale the order and existence of these rights become relevant. Subject to conditions, the right of ownership can also be part of the ranking of the aforementioned limited property rights.[194] If the property right ceased to exist the holders of other property rights would move up in rank.[195] Furthermore, an explanation can be given in respect to third parties holding a property right to the limited right that would cease to exist in a *Konsolidation*. Such a situation can occur specifically when an owner acquires land to which a right of servitude is created and subsequently transfers it to another party. It is held that the necessity to create a new servitude with the same contents as the extinct right would bring unnecessary costs.[196]

Following the reasoning of Baur, Baur and Stürner, if in such a situation the owner has acquired a property right to his own immovable object, the owner will

187 On the relevance of two different models of creating property rights see Chapter 7; 2.2. Of Ways to Create a Lesser Property Right.

188 Baur, Baur & Stürner 1999 and Wolf 2005.

189 Baur, Baur & Stürner 1999, p. 17, Wolf 2005, p. 4.

190 Wolf 2005, p. 4.

191 This power would include a limitation on the owner to decide so, if there are third parties with a right in respect of the property right in question.

192 Wolf 2005, p. 5.

193 Baur, Baur & Stürner 1999, p. 25.

194 Baur, Baur & Stürner 1999, p. 25. See also Kipp 1911, p. 211 *et seq.*

195 See also Staudinger & Gursky 2002, p. 311.

196 Staudinger & Gursky 2002, p. 311.

participate in insolvency proceedings ranking both as the owner and as holder of a property right.[197]

This approach does not, however, consider the statements made by Johow and Windscheid, which are at the foundation of the BGB.[198] The approach does concern the practical application of Paragraph 889 BGB, but does not answer the doctrinal question on the relation between the right of ownership and the other property rights. Such a solution seems to agree with the views of Johow and Windscheid. In German law, a limited property right is modelled on the powers of the owner, but does not comprise them. The right of ownership remains complete, but the powers of the owner are limited for the duration of the existence of the property right. The limited property right that comes into existence will not burden the right of ownership itself but rather the exercise of the powers of ownership. This approach makes it possible for a limited property right and the right of ownership to co-exist and, possibly, to continue to exist when the property right reverts to the owner.

Perhaps the system of the BGB should be understood as follows. When a limited property right is created in respect to an immovable object and the right returns to the owner, Paragraph 889 BGB renders a *Konsolidation* impossible. In this approach, there can be no *démembrement* in German property law. *Konsolidation* would not then be so much a mixing of the powers of the owner with the powers contained in the limited property right, but the situation in which the powers of the owner are still restricted, but in which that restriction is temporarily relative since the owner is also entitled to the limited right restricting his powers as an owner. The transfer of the limited right to another person will not change the right of ownership in any way, nor will it change the limitations on the powers of the owner.

When ownership and property right fall into the same hands, the limited property right will remain to exist. In that situation, the owner is able to exercise his powers in his capacity as owner as well as his powers in his capacity as right-holder of a limited right.[199] Property rights in German law therefore do not limit the ownership as such, but only burden the powers of the owner, with third-party effect. This would be in line with the statement in the *Motive* dealing with restrictions to the right of ownership other than limited property rights:

> 8. The limitations on the ownership by force of law dealt with in this title are not absolute in nature. The owner can establish property rights – real servitudes or limited personal servitudes – on his own land, which decrease or annul the powers of the owner that follow from the current chapter.[200]

197 See also Staudinger & Gursky 2002, p. 314.

198 Also the Staudinger Commentary does not consider the statement by Johow, but only refers to the *Motive* stating the solution is for legal science to decide on. See Staudinger & Gursky 2002, p. 314.

199 Staudinger & Gursky 2002, p. 314.

200 '8. Die in diesen Titel bestimmten gesetzlichen Eigenthumsbeschränkungen sind nicht absoluter Natur. Der Eigenthümer kann an seinem Grundstücke dingliche Rechte – Grunddienstbarkeiten oder beschränkte persönliche Dienstbarkeiten – bestellen, welche die aus →

In terms of doctrine, this would answer the need for the ownership to remain unitary. The owner has not lost the power that characterises him as an owner, and the property right, which co-exists besides the ownership, only burdens these powers.[201] Finally, in case of property rights in respect of movable objects or rights, specifically usufruct and pledge, the situation is different. By force of the BGB these rights cease to exist when they are acquired by the owner.[202]

The conception of limited rights as separate rights co-existing with the right of ownership also enables the owner to create a limited right in respect of his own object, and according to his own terms and conditions. The advantages of this are twofold. First, the limited right will take rank from the moment of its creation. Any property right created at a later moment will be lower in rank than the limited right created by the owner. Secondly, it allows the owner to transfer his ownership while continuing to hold the property right that was created under his own terms and conditions with the ranking he wanted.[203] This can be done with all the rights in respect of land and for some rights other objects.[204]

The relation between ownership and other property rights is therefore highly relevant, but it should be emphasised that this relation, as well as the concept of *Konsolidation*, are not given the attention they deserve.

This Section will deal with the limited property rights recognised by German law. In order to organise the discussion of these property rights, German doctrine makes a distinction between movable and immovable objects on which various limited property rights can be created. Moreover, the system of German property can be divided into rights to use and rights for security.[205] As in other legal systems, property rights created in a movable object and the same property rights created in an immovable object can be different in content.[206] Furthermore, German law also recognises a third category of property rights: acquisition rights.[207] This Section will first deal with the main property rights to use, followed by the acquisition rights.

dem gegenwärtigen Abschnitte sich ergebenden Rechte des Eigenthümers mindern oder aufheben', Motive III 1888, p. 260.

201 This approach seems to be followed by Müller who states 'Rechte Dritter, die im Rahmen des § 903 BGB die sich aus dem Eigentum ergebende Herrschaftsbefugnis beschränken, sind die beschränkte dinglichen Rechte. ... Insofern ist das Eigentum als zunächst allumfassendes Herrschaftsrecht gegenüber den beschränkt dinglichen Rechten subsidiär: Das sich aus dem Eigentum ergebende Herrschaftsrecht wird durch ein beschränktes dingliches Recht im Umfang seines Inhalts verdrängt. Deshalb ist es zutreffend, beschränkte dingliche Rechte auch als Belastung des Eigentums zu definieren', Müller 1997, p. 100. Also affirmative of this view is Schön 1992, p. 12-13.

202 § 1063 and § 1256 BGB, Staudinger & Gursky 2002, p. 313.

203 Hess 1998, p. 501.

204 On the difficulty with usufruct, see Schwab & Prütting 2003, p. 422. On servitudes, see Staudinger et al. 2002, p. 238.

205 These are the *Nutzungsrechte* and the *Sicherungsrechte*. Baur, Baur & Stürner 1999, p. 22-27. On *Nutzungsrechte* in general see Ahrens 2004.

206 The best example would be a usufruct, which the owner can create on his own immovable object, but not on his own movable object. On the right of usufruct, see below; 3.2. Personal Servitudes.

207 These are the *Erwerbsrechte*, Baur, Baur & Stürner 1999, p. 24-27.

The Section will finish with the security property rights.[208] The differences in content of these rights when created in movable objects, immovable objects or claims will be dealt with under the heading of the specific rights respectively.

3.1. *Real Servitudes*

German law does not adhere to a single concept of servitude, but recognises several types of servitudes. Real servitudes or *Grunddienstbarkeiten* are the primary type of servitudes and are dealt with in the BGB.[209] The primary Paragraph on real servitudes is 1018 BGB:

> A piece of land can, for the benefit of an owner of another piece of land, be burdened in such a way that the owner may use this piece of land for specific purposes or certain action cannot be taken on the piece of land or a certain right which follows from the burdened piece of land against the other piece of land cannot be exercised.[210]

The *Grunddienstbarkeiten* are servitudes in the same sense as the Roman law category of real servitudes.[211] The result of this is that the main criteria from Roman law are recognised and applied in German law. A right of servitude binds the holders of the property right in their capacity as owners of two pieces of land, which are known as the dominant and servient land.[212] It is also possible, under conditions, for holders of property rights other than ownership to create a real servitude.[213] The pieces of land must be in the vicinity of each other in order to fulfil the requirement set by Paragraph 1019 BGB. This Paragraph requires the dominant land to benefit from the existence of the right of servitude.[214] In other words, in order for the dominant land, and not the right-holder personally, to benefit from the servitude, the land should be in the neighbourhood of the servient tenement.[215] Furthermore, German law, albeit implicitly, also adheres to the *perpetua causa* rule, according to

208 This chapter will provide an overview of the principal property rights as they are recognised in German law. However, certain variations on certain property rights exist in the respective *Länder*, which, seen the scope of this research, will not be dealt with.

209 Baur, Baur & Stürner 1999, p. 366.

210 § 1018 BGB, 'Ein Grundstück kann zugunsten des jeweiligen Eigentümers eines anderen Grundstücks in der Weise belastet werden, dass dieser das Grundstück in einzelnen Beziehungen benutzen darf oder dass auf dem Grundstück gewisse Handlungen nicht vorgenommen werden dürfen oder dass die Ausübung eines Rechts ausgeschlossen ist, das sich aus dem Eigentum an dem belasteten Grundstück dem anderen Grundstück gegenüber ergibt'.

211 Wolff & Raiser 1957, p. 430, Staudinger et al. 2002, p. 205. See Chapter 2; 2.4. Other Property Rights.

212 Or in German the *herrschendes* and *dienendes Grundstück*, see Staudinger et al. 2002, p. 236.

213 For dominant tenements see Staudinger et al. 2002, p. 237-238, for servient tenements p. 241-242.

214 Such benefit does not have to be a value for Money, but can also be e.g. an aesthetic benefit, see Baur, Baur & Stürner 1999, p. 369.

215 This could include a servitude of view or silence, see Baur, Baur & Stürner 1999, p. 369.

which a servitude is intended to last forever.[216] The creation of a real servitude limited in time is therefore difficult.[217]

Furthermore, German law also recognises the Roman maxim of *servitus in faciendo consistere nequit,* a right of servitude can only impose a negative duty.[218] Any positive duty, even if formulated negatively, is prohibited.[219] However, in this respect German law distinguishes between primary duties and secondary duties. The first category cannot comprise a positive duty, whereas the latter can. A secondary duty can only be positive in cases where such a duty serves the negative primary duty. Examples of such a positive secondary duty include the duty to take care or maintain a construction or a road needed for the exercise of the servitude.[220] However, the exact status of these secondary duties has been highly debated.

Hess has divided the duties of the parties to a right of servitude in two.[221] First of all, there is a property relation that accords property effect to rights and claims. Secondly, there is also an internal relation between the respective owners. This distinction is relevant because this last relation allows for more influence by the parties, since it does not concern a relation that has effect against third parties.[222] After a long debate and initial reluctance of the BGH this internal relation is now recognised as a legal subsidiary relation, known in German as a *gesetzliches Schuldverhältnis,* for which the owner is liable with his personal assets.[223] In other words, for those duties arising from the real servitude during the period of time when the owner is owner of the servient piece of land, he shall be personally liable when these duties are not fulfilled. Contrary to the primary relation, which concerns the servitude itself, the internal relation is a type of obligation.[224] The recognition of this obligation by force of law in the relation between the owner of the dominant and the owner of the servient land is of high practical relevance. Not only does the subsidiary relation comprise the legal duties to maintain and take care of the object, it can also contain positive duties that do not follow specifically from the law.[225] Parties are relatively free to add content to this relationship as well. The internal relation is subject to the law of contract, which results in the availability of contractual remedies upon non-performance. However, the content of the internal relation will, by operation of law, transfer with the servitude to any who subsequently

216 Staudinger et al. 2002, p. 248, 264.

217 Staudinger et al. 2002, p. 221.

218 Staudinger et al. 2002, p. 251. See Chapter 2; 2.4. Other Property Rights.

219 E.g., a prohibition to use the products of the competition implicitly is a duty to take on products of the right-holder of the servitude, BGH 30 January 1959, BGHZ 29, 244. Staudinger et al. 2002, p. 253, Schwab & Prütting 2003, p. 416, see also BayObLG, MDR 1977, 139 and NJW-RR 1990, 600.

220 § 1020 and § 1021 BGB, Staudinger et al. 2002, p. 252, Füller 2006, p. 405-421.

221 Hess 1998, p. 502 *et seq.*, Staudinger et al. 2002, p. 276.

222 Amann 1989, p. 539-540.

223 BGH 28 June 1985, BGHZ 95, 144, 146 = NJW 1985, 2944, Staudinger et al. 2002, p. 276.

224 This type of obligation comes into existence by operation of law and not by agreement between parties. Although such agreement is present, i.e., it is required to establish the right of real servitude, it is not the *causa* for the creation of the subsidiary obligation.

225 Such as a building duty, see Staudinger et al. 2002, p. 277.

acquire the land on which it runs.[226] The possibility for parties to give content to their relation should therefore not be underestimated.[227] In any case, whatever duty a servitude comprises, the duty must be formulated in such a way that it can be objectively identified by an independent party.[228]

The definition of Paragraph 1018 BGB provides three categories of servitudes; the servitude that entitles the holder to do something on the land of another, the servitude that forces an owner not to do something on his land, and the servitude that forces the owner of a piece of land not to exercise certain powers against the owner of the dominant land . First, there is a servitude that will give the owner of one piece of land a specific right to do something on another owner's land.[229] Such a right of servitude is limited to the exercise of a specific right or power that the right-holder of the servitude holds, exclusively or co-operatively.[230] The duty must concern a factual duty, a limitation in the power to dispose of the owner is not allowed.[231] Secondly, a right of servitude may include a duty for the owner of the servient land to refrain from undertaking a specific act on his land.[232] Like the first category of real servitudes, the second type of servitude is restricted to factual acts.[233] However, the duty to refrain can, contrary to the right to do something on another's land, refer to a single act. A reference to a general category of acts is also possible.[234] In practice, it is possible to limit the purpose for which a piece of land is used through this type of servitude, for example, a duty not to build on the land, but also a prohibition to have a petrol station or a cinema on the land.[235] Such a restriction of use can only be imposed insofar as it directly concerns the use of the land on which the right of servitude is created.[236] The justification for such a right of servitude is made by reference to the power of the owner through Paragraph 903 BGB to do with the object as he wishes. This power of the owner is considered to include the power to decide on the purpose for which the land is used, which can consequently be limited by a right of servitude.[237] This can either be done by a

226 The case deciding the issue concerned a servitude of road over which the owner drove with heavy equipment which caused damage to the road surface. The recognition of the subsidiary relation, with the duty to maintain the road following from § 1020 BGB, allowed the holder of the servitude to claim for compensation. A claim for compensation for a violation of the duty in § 1020 BGB had previously not been possible. See Amann 1989, p. 532, 535-536, Staudinger et al. 2002, p. 277.

227 Amann 1989, p. 544-545. More on this at the end of this Section.

228 Staudinger et al. 2002, p. 255, RGZ 117, 326.

229 The is the *Benutzungsdienstbarkeit*. Baur, Baur & Stürner 1999, p. 366.

230 Although a single act cannot be subject of this servitude. Staudinger et al. 2002, p. 257 *et seq.*

231 Staudinger et al. 2002, p. 250.

232 This is the *Unterlassungsdienstbarkeit*. Baur, Baur & Stürner 1999, p. 366.

233 Staudinger et al. 2002, p. 262.

234 This can be the duty not to build a specific building over a certain height, but also a general prohibition to build or have constructions over a certain height. See Staudinger et al. 2002, p. 263.

235 Staudinger et al. 2002, p. 264.

236 § 1019 BGB. For instance, the duty to only use petrol, gas and oil from a certain firm in the tank-station cannot be imposed by real servitude, see Staudinger et al. 2002, p. 265-266.

237 BGH 30 January 1959, BGHZ 29, 244, 249 = NJW 1959, 670, Staudinger et al. 2002, p. 264.

general prohibition on a certain use of the land or the possibility to only permit one type of use.[238]

In German legal practice these general prohibitions are used in order to secure a certain act of the owner of the servient tenement. This can be done through a general prohibition on using the land for a certain purpose, for example, not to have a petrol station, except with permission, through contract, of the right-holder. When the right-holder of the servitude retracts his permission, the right of servitude will prohibit the owner of the land from, to follow the example, having a petrol station.[239]

German legal practice also uses a combination of a real servitude and a contract to create what is known as a security-servitude.[240] The deed creating the right of servitude will contain a general prohibition on the owner of the servient piece of land, for example, where there is a petrol station, on behalf of the owner of the dominant piece of land, for example, a petrol company, to use the land for a certain purpose. The parties then enter into a contract whereby the owner of the servient land agrees to the terms of the contract, for example, to buy and use the petrol of a petrol company or beer from a particular brewery, and the right-holder, the owner of the dominant land, restricts his exercise of the servitude to those situations where the contract is not performed.[241] This contract should not be confused with the abovementioned internal relation that comes into existence by operation of law and that contains secondary duties. The security contract and the right of servitude are connected in the sense that the fulfilment of one of these will lead to the fulfilment of the other. In this way double duties, for example, for payment, arising from two different sources are prevented.[242] However, the contract does not come into existence by operation of law. In other words, the contract will not be accessory to the property right and will give the parties the possibility to keep the terms of the contract secret, since the contract does not need to be registered with the servitude.[243] Upon termination of the contract the servitude will continue to exist.

The security-servitude is modelled after the security-*Grundschuld*, a type of property security right that will be dealt with below.[244] If a situation concerning a security-servitude is not clear, the courts will refer to the security-*Grundschuld*.[245] The contract finds its limits both in Paragraph 138 BGB and in national and

238 The first of these would be an example of a non-competition clause, see BGH 30 January 1959, BGHZ 29, 244, 249 = NJW 1959, 670 on the prohibition to have a petrol station. The latter would be a combination of the first and second type of servitudes, see BGH 22 September 1961, BGHZ 35, 378, 381 = NJW 1961, 2157.

239 See Staudinger et al. 2002, p. 267.

240 Or *Sicherungsdienstbarkeit*, see Walter & Maier 1988, p. 377, Baur, Baur & Stürner 1999, p. 370-371, Staudinger et al. 2002, p. 267, Füller 2006, p. 505-506. See also De Waal 1995, p. 197-205.

241 BGH 18 May 1979, BGHZ 74, 293, 296 = NJW 1979, 2150, BGH 22 September 1961, NJW 1961, 2157.

242 Staudinger et al. 2002, p. 267.

243 Staudinger et al. 2002, p. 267-268.

244 On *Grundschuld* and security-*Grundschuld* see below; 3.8. *Grundschuld*.

245 Walter & Maier 1988, p. 387.

international competition law.[246] However, the invalidity of the contract will not automatically bring the invalidity of the servitude with it.[247] The right of servitude itself will be limited by the general rules on servitudes; a negatively formulated positive duty will still be prohibited. However, it is clear that with a negative real servitude but a positive duty imposed by contract in relation to such a right of servitude, the security-servitude balances on the border of what is allowed.[248]

Thirdly, a servitude can impose a duty on the owner of the servient tenement not to exercise some powers which he has as an owner against the owner of the dominant land under, *inter alia*, Paragraphs 903 and 1004 BGB. This duty can include the agreement not to take action over a right to a path or way by operation of law or a building that leans over on the servient land.[249] Finally, although these three different types of servitudes are distinguished in German doctrine, parties are free to combine several of these types into one right.[250]

The previous examples show that parties are relatively free to give content to their relationship. The *Motive* indeed state that the content of servitudes mainly comprises the act creating the property right. The content of the right is therefore set by the content of the agreement creating the right.[251] Rights of servitude are intended to give freedom to the parties to provide content to their relationship. Nevertheless, there is a tension between the rules of Paragraph 1018 BGB and party autonomy.[252] The recognition of the subsidiary obligations by the BGH has given rise to a renewed discussion on the content of servitudes.[253]

The debate stretches from those authors who claim that the limit of party autonomy follows from the provisions of Paragraphs 1020 and 1021 BGB, which deal with the agreements that can be made between the owner of the servient land and the holder of the right of servitude, to those authors who claim that any party agreement which fits in the system of the law should be recognised.[254] Each of the participants to the debate attempts to answer the question of to what extent the agreement between parties can be considered part of the right of servitude itself in the sense that it will transfer with the right of servitude to any acquirer. Any agreement outside the criteria, whatever these may be, will still be an agreement, but will not automatically transfer with the right of servitude.

246 The former will limit the contract to a 15-20 year period. Baur, Baur & Stürner 1999, p. 370, Füller 2006, p. 509-512. The latter, specifically Art. 81 EC concerns EC competition law and exceeds the scope of this research. Staudinger et al. 2002, p. 271, Stürner 1994, p. 284 *et seq.*

247 This is mainly a result of the abstract system in German law, see BGH 28 January 1988, V ZR 310/86, NJW 1988, 2364, Van Vliet 2000, p. 31-34, Baur, Baur & Stürner 1999, p. 371, Stürner 1994, p. 287.

248 OLG München 4 September 2003, NJW-RR 2004, 164, Staudinger et al. 2002, p. 268, critically see Schwab & Prütting 2003, p. 416-417 and Joost in Quack 1997, p. 1476 *et seq.*

249 See Baur, Baur & Stürner 1999, p. 369, Staudinger et al. 2002, p. 272 *et seq.*

250 Staudinger et al. 2002, p. 275.

251 Motive III 1888, p. 476.

252 Staudinger et al. 2002, p. 249.

253 For a good overview of the discussion see Staudinger et al. 2002, p. 281-286. The discussion concerns articles by Amann, Stürner and Hess, Amann 1989, Stürner 1994 and Hess 1998.

254 Staudinger et al. 2002, p. 281, Füller 2006, p. 410-412, Falckenberg in Quack 1997, p. 1319 *et seq.* (conservative), Hess 1998, p. 510 *et seq.* (progressive).

Amann argues for a wide possibility for parties to include duties to maintain as part of the subsidiary obligations.[255] He recognises agreements between parties that only work between parties but which have a property effect in the sense that they transfer to acquirers of the servitude.[256] In order for an agreement to reach such a proprietary status, he suggests that the agreement is in direct and immediate connection to the content of the right of servitude, that the agreement concerns the land on which the right of servitude is created, the agreement does not constitute a mere personal duty, and that the content of the agreement is not such that it can no longer be considered to be a secondary duty.[257]

Stürner searches for the deciding criteria in the BGB itself. He considers the system of property rights in the BGB and emphasises that the BGB adheres to a model that exclusively prescribes the available property rights.[258] He sees the available property rights as building blocks that form the construction to which party agreement can give content. This party freedom is, for reasons of legal clarity and legal certainty, limited to the property rights the BGB has available.[259] In this approach parties can only give content to the property rights as they are available in the BGB.[260]

Hess has argued against this by showing that the property rights to use in German property law are so abstractly formulated that parties need to give content to their right by agreement.[261] Practically, these agreements on the content will, in order for the law to function, also have to work against those who acquire the right of servitude. Hess argues for criteria following from the general direction of the law.[262] He clearly distinguishes the servitude on the one hand and the internal relation between owner of the servient land and holder of the right of servitude on the other hand. By using examples from other areas of property law where a subsidiary obligation by force of law is recognised, for example, usufruct and *emphyteusis*, he concludes that parties should also have a limited freedom to give content to the servitude relation. The absolute boundary of this limited party autonomy follows from the law, a positive burden is not allowed.[263] When the party agreement remains within the limit of the system of the law, it should be allowed. In his view property rights are not just building blocks, but form the guideline for the decision of what is allowed and what is not.[264]

255 Amann 1989, p. 536 *et seq.*

256 Amann 1989, p. 560-561.

257 Amann 1989, p. 561.

258 This concept, which is part of the *numerus clausus* of property rights, is known as *Typizität*, Stürner 1994, p. 275. For a detailed discussion on the *numerus clausus* of property rights in German law see below in 5. A *Numerus Clausus* in German Property Law?

259 This theory is known in German doctrine as the formal theory, Stürner 1994, p. 275 *et seq.*, Staudinger et al. 2002, p. 282.

260 Stürner 1994, p. 281-282.

261 Hess 1998, p. 509 *et seq.*

262 Or the *gesamtgesetzlichen Leitbild*, Hess 1998, p. 513-515.

263 Hess 1998, p. 504 *et seq.*

264 Hess 1998, p. 513-515.

Each of the criteria suggested raises objections. The law is unclear on the status of party agreements in case of servitudes.[265] Furthermore, the recognition of a subsidiary agreement by force of law to which parties can also give limited content leads to new questions. In any case, Paragraphs 138, 134 and 305 *et seq.* BGB will govern a right of servitude.[266]

3.2. *Personal Servitudes: Usufruct and Limited Personal Servitudes*

The category of personal servitudes in German law includes two different property rights; the right of usufruct and the limited personal servitude.[267] The last is known in German as *beschränkte persönliche Dienstbarkeit.* Both these rights are servitudes that are connected to a person, and not to a piece of land. Such a person can be either a natural or a legal person. Specifically the creation of a personal servitude on behalf of a legal person enables a more flexible application of these property rights. This section will first deal with the right of usufruct, after which the limited personal servitude is dealt with.

The right of usufruct is considered the right that most closely resembles the right of ownership. This right, which limits the powers of the owner, entitles the right-holder to use the object under usufruct. The right-holder is entitled to the usufruct not in his capacity as the owner of a piece of land or other object, but in his personal capacity.[268] An object of a usufruct can be not only a immovable or a movable, but also a claim.[269] The full right of use, which includes the right to take the fruits the object produces, and the personal nature of the right are its defining characteristics. Without any further agreement, the usufructuary will receive a full power to use the object under usufruct. The power to use can be limited, but not to one specific incidence of use. Instead the right must entitle its holder to a particular type of use.[270] The right of usufruct is dealt with in Paragraph 1030 BGB, which states:

> (1) An object can be burdened in such a way, that the person, for whose benefit this burdening occurs, is entitled to the use of the object and to take the fruits. (Usufruct)
> (2) The usufruct can be limited by the exclusion of certain powers to use.[271]

265 Staudinger et al. 2002, p. 284-285.

266 These Paragraphs concern good faith, agreements against the law, and general terms and conditions. Staudinger et al. 2002, p. 286.

267 On the distinction between real and personal servitudes, see Füller 2006, p. 455-460.

268 Schön 1992, p. 29-30.

269 Schwab & Prütting 2003, p. 421, Baur, Baur & Stürner 1999, p. 360.

270 Baur, Baur & Stürner 1999, p. 362-363.

271 § 1030 BGB, '(1) Eine Sache kann in der Weise belastet werden, das derjenige, zu dessen Gunsten die Belastung erfolgt, berechtigt ist, die Nutzungen der Sache zu Ziehen (Nießbrauch). (2) Der Nießbrauch kann durch den Ausschluss einzelner Nutzungen beschränkt werden'.

The right of usufruct creates a property relation between the owner of an object and the usufructuary, whereby the usufructuary receives possession.[272] The usufructuary, i.e., the holder of a right of usufruct, has a property right that has effect against third parties and that enables him to use the same claims the owner has for the protection of the object.[273] This includes both the claim for vindication as well as the *actio negatoria* to stop or prevent interference with the object under usufruct.[274] Because the right of usufruct is connected to a person, the usufruct will end with the death of the usufructuary and in principle cannot be transferred. It is possible, however, to establish a right of usufruct on behalf of a legal person, which creates some transfer possibilities.[275]

German doctrine recognises, as with rights of real servitude, an internal relation between the owner and the usufructuary. This internal relation is recognised as a subsidiary obligation existing by force of law, to which parties can make alterations by agreement.[276] The rights and duties contained in this subsidiary obligation will transfer with the ownership of the object under usufruct.[277] The subsidiary obligation will in any case contain the legal duties of the usufructuary. This includes the duty of the usufructuary to preserve the object and deal with it according to the principles of property management.[278] Other legal duties include the duty to pay certain fees, to insure the object and to replace certain parts of the object under usufruct.[279] Moreover, parties can provide content to their relation through agreement. They can do so without the obligation losing its effect against later acquirers of the property right. As in the case of real servitudes, the content of the agreement will transfer to the new subsidiary obligation between the new holders of the property right.

In order to have effect against subsequent acquirers, the agreements parties make will have to fulfil certain criteria. In the case of usufructs the main criteria for property effect follow from the system of property rights.[280] The general rules on the nature of the usufruct cannot be deviated from.[281] Parties cannot just give any content to their relation, they can only do so if the relevant provisions in the BGB give them permission to do so.[282] If the duty in question concerns third parties the BGB provides almost no freedom at all. Only in respect to the inner relation between owner and usufructuary do the parties have some freedom, but no agreement

272 § 1036 (1) BGB, this is the *mittelbarer Besitz*, § 868 BGB. Schwab & Prütting 2003, p. 422.

273 § 1065 BGB, Baur, Baur & Stürner 1999, p. 363-364, Schwab & Prütting 2003, p. 425.

274 §§ 985 and 1004 BGB. On the claims connected to the right of ownership, see above; 2.1. Normal Ownership.

275 § 1059 BGB, § 1061 BGB and § 1059a, BGB.

276 BGH 21 June 1985, BGHZ 95, 99, 100, Amann 1989, p. 540-541, Baur, Baur & Stürner 1999, p. 364, Staudinger et al. 2002, p. 367-379, Schön 1992, p. 260 *et seq.*, Füller 2006, p. 421-422.

277 A transfer on the side of the usufructuary is possible, but only in case the usufruct is created for the benefit of a legal person, see Baur, Baur & Stürner 1999, p. 364, Schön 1992, p. 30.

278 § 1036 (2) BGB.

279 §§ 1047, 1045 and 1048 (2) BGB, Staudinger et al. 2002, p. 376.

280 Füller 2006, p. 423-431.

281 Staudinger et al. 2002, p. 367, Hess 1998, p. 504, Schön 1992, p. 262.

282 § 1030 (2) BGB is a clear example.

should interfere with the relation between owner and usufructuary as is provided for in the system.[283]

When the right of usufruct ends, the usufructuary is under the duty to return the object to the owner.[284] The owner will have a claim for vindication against the usufructuary from the moment the right of usufruct ends.[285] The object must be returned in the state in which it was received. A decrease in value, other than through normal use, will have to be compensated. Any increase of value of the object will be for the owner.[286]

In legal practice, the usufruct is mainly used for two purposes. First, in the law of succession it is a common arrangement that a usufruct is created for the surviving spouse while appointing the children as heirs.[287] Secondly, the right of usufruct is used for security purposes. When made subject to a right of pledge, the right of usufruct can be used to give advantages to the pledgor to which he normally would not be entitled.[288] The combination of the right of usufruct with the right of pledge effectively creates a situation in which the pledgor becomes entitled to use the object, or at least to take the fruits the object produces, which power was not included in the system of pledge in the BGB.[289]

Furthermore, the right of usufruct can be used to secure a contractual relation of lease. In this flexible application of the right, the function of the usufruct is to effect and secure the lease.[290] However, a property right cannot be created on a right of lease itself. Parties must therefore be careful not to connect the property right to the lease by attempting to make the usufruct accessory, i.e. dependent, on the lease contract, or by referring explicitly to the lease relation in the deed of creation.[291] The *Bundesgerichtshof* has recognised the validity of a usufruct to strengthen a lease.[292] It is possible for two persons to be entitled to the use of an object following from a contract and from a property right at the same time.[293]

Any object mentioned in Paragraph 90 BGB can be the subject of a usufruct.[294] This includes immovable as well as movable objects. The general rules on the right of usufruct are applicable on rights of usufruct on all types of objects. However, because of the different nature of immovable and movable objects, some differences exist. For example, it is possible to limit the exercise of a right of usufruct to a specif-

283 Staudinger et al. 2002, p. 377.
284 Or, in case of death of the usufructuary, the heirs will have to return the object. § 1055 BGB, Schwab & Prütting 2003, p. 424, Staudinger et al. 2002, p. 506.
285 § 985 BGB, Staudinger et al. 2002, p. 506.
286 Staudinger et al. 2002, p. 507-508.
287 Baur, Baur & Stürner 1999, p. 361.
288 E.g., payments of rent, Baur, Baur & Stürner 1999, p. 361.
289 Schön 1992, p. 370. On the concept of fruits in German law see § 99 BGB. On the right of pledge see below; 3.6. Pledge.
290 Schön 1992, p. 371 *et seq.*, Staudinger et al. 2002, p. 380, Füller 2006, p. 512-517.
291 Schön 1992, p. 371.
292 BGH 22 April 1966, WM 1966, 1089, Schön 1992, p. 372.
293 This is the *Dopperlwirkung*, see Schön 1992, p. 373, but also in general Staudinger et al. 2000, p. 41-47, Kipp 1911, p. 220-233.
294 Staudinger et al. 2002, p. 374.

ic part of the land on which the right runs, and the owner can establish a right of usufruct on his own land. A right of usufruct on movable objects cannot be limited to the exercise of a specific piece of such a movable object, nor can an owner create a right of usufruct on his own movable objects.[295] Rights that resemble the right of ownership on immovable objects, such as the right of ownership of an apartment, but also the right of *superficies*, can be subject of a right of usufruct.

Because the usufructuary is under a duty to return the object at the end of the usufruct, movable objects that are either perishable or that can be used up, cannot be subject of a right of usufruct. In order to solve this problem, and to enable the creation of a property right also on these types of objects, German law recognises a right of quasi-usufruct.[296] The right of quasi-usufruct is actually a transfer of the right of ownership combined with the personal duty for the 'holder of the right of quasi-usufruct' to replace the value of the objects he received.[297] Because the right of quasi-usufruct is not really created on an object or set of objects, but is better defined as a transfer with the personal duty to return the object or set of objects, it is not really a property right. This characterisation offers advantages, most importantly in more freedom for parties to decide on the content of their relation.[298]

Furthermore, the BGB provides additional rules for rights of usufruct on rights. Paragraph 1068 BGB states:

> (1) A right may also be the subject of a usufruct.
> (2) The provisions on usufruct on objects apply to the usufruct on rights, insofar as §§ 1069 until 1084 do not provide otherwise.[299]

The usufruct on rights can only exist on a right that is transferable and which can be used in such a way that fruits can be taken from it.[300] The usufruct on a right is mainly used to create a usufruct on a set of assets or on a company.[301] The usufruct on a set of assets will usually concern claims. A usufruct on a claim creates a three-party relationship between the debtor, creditor and usufructuary. The property right will entitle its holder to the proceeds of the claim.[302] A usufruct on a general set of assets is not specifically recognised in the BGB, but is possible under the same conditions as any other right in respect of a set of assets, e.g. those of a company.[303]

295 Staudinger et al. 2002, p. 427, Schwab & Prütting 2003, p. 422.
296 § 1067 BGB, Staudinger et al. 2002, p. 559 *et seq.*, Schwab & Prütting 2003, p. 426. On quasi-usufruct, see Chapter 2; 2.4. Other Property Rights.
297 Schwab & Prütting 2003, p. 426.
298 Staudinger et al. 2002, p. 561.
299 § 1068 BGB, '(1) Gegenstand des Nießbrauchs kann auch ein Recht sein. (2) Auf den Nießbrauch an Rechten finden die Vorschriften über den Nießbrauch an Sachen entsprechende Anwendung, soweit sich nicht aus den §§ 1069 bis 1084 ein anderes ergibt', translation partially taken over from Goren 1994.
300 § 99 BGB and § 1069 (2) BGB, Schwab & Prütting 2003, p. 426-427, Baur, Baur & Stürner 1999, p. 776.
301 Baur, Baur & Stürner 1999, p. 775.
302 Schwab & Prütting 2003, p. 427-428.
303 Schwab & Prütting 2003, p. 428.

In reality, the usufruct on a set of assets will be a sum of rights of usufruct on the individual objects in the set assets.[304]

In respect of a right of usufruct on a set of assets, the relation between the holder of the claim and the holder of the right of usufruct, as well as the relation between the debtor and the creditor, also right-holder, should be separated. The last relation concerns the external relation of the usufruct. The creditor can execute the claim in insolvency of the debtor. The holder of the right of usufruct will have to respect the execution, although he is entitled to its use.[305] The internal relationship between the holder of the claim and the holder of the right of usufruct concerns the question of whether the holder of the usufruct can, following from his right to use and take the fruits of the claim, execute the claim himself. Under conditions, the holder of a usufruct will have this power.[306]

The second personal servitude in German law is the limited personal servitude. Like the right of usufruct, a person holds this right not in his capacity as holder of a property right in respect of an object, but as a person. However, in respect to the rest of its contents, the *beschränkte persönliche Dienstbarkeit* is based on a right of real servitude.[307] Like a right of real servitude, the limited personal servitude does not concern a general power to use, as is the case with a right of usufruct, but a specifically described power for the use of another's land.[308] Although the limited personal servitude is strictly personal, i.e., it will end with the death of the holder of the right, as in case of a usufruct, it can be transferred when created on behalf of a legal person.[309] Furthermore the *beschränkte persönliche Dienstbarkeit* cannot be transferred unless it is created on the immovable object of another for the construction of, *inter alia*, electricity cables, gas, water or a sewer system.[310]

On the limited personal servitude, Paragraph 1090 BGB states:

> A piece of land can be burdened in such a way that a person for whose benefit the right is created is entitled to a specific use of the land or that it awards him a power that can be subject to a real servitude.[311]

Given that the limited personal servitude is modelled on the right of real servitude, the way in which it is applied is also very similar. A limited personal servitude can comprise duties to use land in a specific way, to refrain from doing something on the land, and to refrain from using a power connected to the entitlement to land.[312]

304 Staudinger et al. 2002, p. 375, see also RG 30 October 1936, RGZ 153, 29, in particular, p. 31.
305 Schwab & Prütting 2003, p. 431.
306 See Schwab & Prütting 2003, p. 431.
307 Or a *subjective-persönliches recht,* Staudinger et al. 2002, p. 682.
308 Staudinger et al. 2002, p. 682.
309 §§ 1090 (2) and 1061 BGB, § 1092 (2) BGB.
310 § 1092 (3) BGB.
311 § 1090 BGB, 'Ein Grundstück kann in der Weise belastet werden, dass derjenige, zu dessen Gunsten die Belastung erfolgt, berechtet ist, das Grundstuck in einzelnen Beziehungen zu benutzen, oder dass ihm eine sonstige Befugnis zusteht, die den Inhalt einer Grunddienstbarkeit bilden kann'.
312 Staudinger et al. 2002, p. 692.

Like the right of real servitude, the law imposes limitations on what conditions the parties may agree. A limited personal servitude cannot contain a positive duty or a single factual act.[313] However, secondary duties are recognised. These can be positive, as in the case of rights of real servitude.[314] Just as with the other servitudes, the limited personal servitude also gives rise to a subsidiary obligation by force of law, to which parties are relatively free to give content. The limited personal servitude is therefore of particular interest as a security-servitude.[315] The construction is the same as with a right of real servitude, but the holder of the right will be limited in his personal capacity and not in his capacity as owner or holder of another property right to a piece of land.[316] Moreover, because of the possibility to bind a person, the right is also used to secure lease payments, as can also be done with a usufruct.[317]

Finally, Paragraph 1093 BGB deals with a specific type of limited personal servitude:

> A limited personal servitude (*beschränkte persönliche Dienstbarkeit*) can also include a right to use, to the exclusion of the owner, a building or part of a building as housing accommodation ...[318]

With respect to this right, known as an apartment right or *Wohnungsrecht*, parties are not as free to give content to their relationship as in case of other servitudes.[319] Contrary to the right of ownership of an apartment, this apartment right is strongly connected to the right-holder as a person, i.e., not in his capacity as holder of a property right in respect of land with a building on it, and cannot be transferred.[320] The apartment right only entitles one to the use of an apartment and not to a general right to use as in case of a right of usufruct. The right to live in an apartment will be the main element of the servitude. Paragraph 1093 BGB declares various provisions on the right of usufruct applicable, which include the duty to take care of the building.[321]

The apartment right can be combined with a contract of lease that will function as a security contract. The technique used for this is the same as with security-servitudes and security-*Grundschuld*.[322] In respect of a security apartment right, the

313 See BGH 25 February 1959, V ZR 176/57, DNotZ 1959, 240.

314 Staudinger et al. 2002, p. 693.

315 See BGH 3 May 1985, V ZR 55/84, NJW 1985, 2474, BGH 29 January 1988, V ZR 310/86, NJW 1988, 2364.

316 Staudinger et al. 2002, p. 695. On security servitudes see above; 3.1. Real Servitude.

317 See Staudinger et al. 2002, p. 682.

318 § 1093, 'Als beschränkte persönliche Dienstbarkeit kann auch das Recht bestellt werden, ein Gebäude oder einen Teil eines Gebäudes unter Ausschluss des Eigentümers als Wohnung zu benutzen ...' This specific usage of the *beschränkte persönliche Dienstbarkeit* resembles the Roman personal servitude of *habitatio*, D. 7.8.1 *et seq.*, Kaser 1971, p. 454.

319 Staudinger et al. 2002, p. 728.

320 Staudinger et al. 2002, p. 683.

321 The duties are very similar to those of the usufructuary, excluding the duty to insure the object. Staudinger et al. 2002,p. 744.

322 On security servitudes see above; 3.1. Real Servitude. On security-*Grundschuld*, see below; 3.8. *Grundschuld*.

apartment right will comprise a duty not to use an apartment. At the same time the lease and security contract deviates from the servitude by granting permission to use the apartment in the same way as in case of other security-servitudes. Only in the event that the lessee cannot pay or the contract expires will the servitude be invoked.

3.3. *Superficies*

The *Erbbaurecht* or right of *superficies* was part of German law before the BGB. Although the right of *superficies* came from the received Roman law, Germanic law knew an equivalent as a right that was part of the feudal system of landholding.[323] Over time, the two different concepts became one.[324] The relation between owner and right-holder was often characterised as *dominium directum* and *dominium utile,* which came to be rejected in the BGB.[325] Nevertheless, because of its origin, the right was considered with great suspicion. The drafters of the BGB included the right of *superficies,* mentioned its limited use in practice, and considered the right as relatively unimportant.[326] They therefore only provided minimum regulations in Paragraphs 1012 to 1017 BGB.[327] Nevertheless, a right to hold a building on or under someone else's land that could be transferred and inherited was included.

Practice changed after the introduction of the BGB. More people needed housing and the right of *superficies* could enable them to acquire their 'own home'.[328] However, the provisions in the BGB were so limited that they were not of much use for legal practice. These limited provisions in the BGB created a lot of legal uncertainty, especially in relation to the creation of other property rights in respect of the right of *superficies* in order to finance its acquisition.[329] Under pressure from legal practice a legislative reform was introduced on 15 January 1919 in the *Verordnung über das Erbbaurecht* (ErbbauVO) or Regulation on the right of *Superficies.* This new Regulation was primarily intended to make the right of *superficies* available for practice and to enable the use of the right as an object of security.[330] The Regulation states in Paragraph 1 ErbbauVO:

323 This was the *Bodenleihe,* Staudinger et al. 2002, p. 3-4.
324 Staudinger et al. 2002, p. 4.
325 See above; 2. The Right of Ownership.
326 Von Oefele & Winkler 2003, p. 13, Motive III 1888, p. 466-467.
327 In modern times these Paragraph's are still mentioned in the BGB, but are empty. Hattenhauer 1989, p. 95-96, Von Oefele & Winkler 2003, p. 13.
328 Von Oefele & Winkler 2003, p. 14.
329 Von Oefele & Winkler 2003, p. 14, Staudinger et al. 2002, p. 4.
330 Staudinger et al. 2002, p. 7. For more on the development of the right of *superficies* see Von Oefele & Winkler 2003, p. 13 *et seq.*

> A piece of land can be burdened in such a way that the person for whose benefit the right is created has the transferable and inheritable right to have a building upon or under the surface of that land. (right of *superficies*) ...[331]

The right of *superficies* is a property right to use connected to a person.[332] Although the right is created on behalf of a person, natural or legal, it can be transferred and inherited. The right of *superficies* entitles the holder to have a building on another's land. These elements constitute the nature of the right of *superficies*.[333]

The right to have a building is open for interpretation. First of all, the term 'building' should be interpreted very broadly. It includes constructions that are not buildings but for which work on the land is necessary, for example, a golf course.[334] In order to decide on the content of the right the factual situation and common speech are taken into account.[335]

Secondly, it was already the intention of the First Commission to create a right that would be treated as if it was a piece of land. German law adheres to the Roman maxim of *superficies solo cedit*.[336] The right of *superficies* entitles the right holder to ownership of the building which is already on the land, or which is to be constructed, in which case the right-holder will receive ownership from the moment construction starts.[337] The right of *superficies* is therefore an exception to the rule that buildings on land follow the ownership of the land. Furthermore, because the holder of the right of *superficies* becomes the owner of the building on the land of another, he may use the same actions as an owner to protect his ownership.[338]

The right of *superficies* is treated in the same way as a right of ownership of land. Upon registration the right receives its own page in the register, just like the right of ownership.[339] Consequently, the right of *superficies* can be burdened with other property rights almost as if it was a right of ownership of land. For legal practice this is especially relevant in combination with ownership of an apartment. The combination of a right of *superficies* with *Wohnungseigentum* enables the creation of apartments without the acquisition of the land.[340]

Nevertheless, the right remains a property right and ownership remains ownership. When the holder of a right of *superficies* creates another right of *superficies* the holder of the second right will become owner. No two owners at the same

331 § 1 ErbbauVO, 'Ein Grundstück kann in der Weise belastet werden, dass demjenigen, zu dessen Gunsten die Belastung erfolgt, das veräusserliche und vererbliche Recht zusteht, auf oder unter der Oberfläche des Grundstücks ein Bauwerk zu haben (Erbbaurecht) ...'.

332 A *subjectiv persönliches Recht*. Staudinger et al. 2002, p. 21.

333 RGZ 61, 2; BayObLGZ 14, 254, Staudinger et al. 2002, p. 17.

334 BGH 10 January 1992, BGHZ 117, 19, Staudinger et al. 2002, p. 23.

335 RGZ, 56, 42, Staudinger et al. 2002, p. 22.

336 §§ 93 and 94 BGB, Staudinger et al. 2002, p. 20.

337 Staudinger et al. 2002, p. 20. Especially the ownership of a building that is still to be constructed is debated in French law. On French law see Chapter 3; 3.3. *Superficies*.

338 § 11 ErbbauVO, Staudinger et al. 2002, p. 21, 115 *et seq.*

339 A *Grundbuchblatt*, § 14 ErbbauVO.

340 The right of *superficies* itself resists vertical separation. § 1(3) ErbbauVO. § 30 WEG enables the application of the WEG on the right of *superficies*, on this see Von Oefele & Winkler 2003, p. 84-85, 112 *et seq.*

time can be recognised.[341] It is also impossible to create a right of *superficies* on part of a piece of land. Legal practice solves this in a form of co-ownership whereby one of the co-owners holds the general right of *superficies*.[342] The ErbbauVO specifically intends to allow the possibility to create another property right in respect of the right of *superficies*. The possibility to create another property right enables the creation of a right of hypothec or *Grundschuld*, which allows the holder to obtain finance, and therefore enables people to acquire ownership of a privately owned home without buying the land on which the building is created.

When dealing with the right of *superficies*, parties are more limited in their party autonomy than they are in respect of other property rights to use. Since the right of *superficies* imposes a very large burden on the right of ownership, the ErbbauVO provides specific rules. However, parties still have influence on the exact contents of their relation.[343] A legal subsidiary obligation as is recognised in the case of other property rights to use does not exist.[344] Parties must, therefore, if they want their agreements to have property effects, deal with their relation in the contract creating the property right.

However, not every agreement the parties make will have property effect. Paragraphs 2 to 8 of the ErbbauVO stipulate the content of the right, to which parties can, under conditions, add agreements.[345] Such an agreement remains a contract, even when the law awards it property effect.[346] Paragraph 2 ErbbauVO stipulates cases in which the party agreement will have property effect. These categories of agreements are agreements on the purpose and maintenance of the building, the insurance of the building and re-building in the event of its destruction, the responsibility for private and public law burdens, the duty, under specific conditions, to transfer the right to the owner, a duty to pay contract penalties, the privileged right of the holder of the right to renew the right of *superficies*, and the duty of the owner to sell the land to the right holder.[347] Other agreements with property effect include the duty for the right holder to ask permission from the owner when he wishes to change the building or burden his right.[348] Because of the third-party effect of these provisions they will be interpreted objectively and narrowly.[349] Any other agreement which, either through interpretation or content, falls outside the scope of these Paragraphs will be a contract only having effect between the parties.

Finally, it is possible for the parties to agree on a periodic payment for the right of *superficies*. The provisions on *Reallast* or real burdens will be applicable to

341 Staudinger et al. 2002, p. 20-21.
342 Staudinger et al. 2002, p. 25. For more information see Von Oefele & Winkler 2003, p. 84 *et seq.*
343 See BGH 22 April 1994, NJW 1994, 2024.
344 Motive III 1888, p. 469, Staudinger et al. 2002, p. 42.
345 In this respect the nature of the right of *superficies* is relevant. On the nature of the right of *superficies* see the top of this Section. See Füller 2006, p. 448-451.
346 Staudinger et al. 2002, p. 42.
347 Staudinger et al. 2002, p. 47-60.
348 § 5 ErbbauVO.
349 Von Oefele & Winkler 2003, p. 129.

such payments.[350] The result of this is that the creation of a right of *superficies* for periodic payment of money will also create a real burden. The burden will serve as security for the payments by the holder of the right. However, Paragraph 9 ErbbauVO specifically states that the holder can only be forced to return the right of *superficies* to the owner when there has been no payment for at least two years.[351] In respect to the real burden that came into existence, the general provisions on real burdens apply, including the legal subsidiary obligation between parties, to which parties may also give content.[352]

A return of the right of *superficies* to the owner, because of Paragraph 889 BGB, will not result in the destruction of the right. Furthermore, an owner can also establish a right of *superficies* on his own ownership on his own terms and conditions and subsequently transfer his ownership or his right of *superficies* to a third party.[353]

3.4. *Expectation Rights: Pre-Emptive Right and Acquisition Right*

German law recognises two property expectation rights.[354] The pre-emptive right, or *Vorkaufsrecht*, is dealt with in the BGB. The acquisition right, or *Anwartschaftsrecht*, is fully developed by case law.[355] The introduction of this last right has given rise to a fundamental debate, both on the nature of the right itself as well as on the system of property rights in German law.[356]

The *dingliche Vorkaufrecht*, or property pre-emptive right, has its origins in Germanic property law.[357] The right was widely applied and could have far reaching consequences. These included, for example, the reversal of an already made transfer of ownership. Under the old feudal system the lord would have such a property right in respect of an object that a vassal could sell.[358] The *Vorkaufrecht* is an expectation right, a right that, as such, was unknown to Roman law. The system of the BGB recognises various expectation rights or gives rise to the recognition of expectation rights, of which not all are recognised as property rights. These include the *Vormerkung*, a form of pre-emptive registration, which gives a property effect to a sales agreement, and the already mentioned *Anwartschaftsrecht* or acquisition right which are based on the system of the BGB, but not dealt with by it.[359] Each of these

350 With the limitation that the specific provisions in the different *Länder* do not apply. § 9 ErbbauVO. On real burdens see below; 3.5. Real Burden (*Reallast*).

351 § 9(4) ErbbauVO.

352 Staudinger et al. 2002, p. 85.

353 BGH 142, 231 = JW 1934, 282, Staudinger et al. 2002, p. 18.

354 Or *Erwerbsrechte* Baur, Baur & Stürner 1999, p. 24.

355 On the early development of *Anwartschaftsrechte* see Von Tuhr 1957, p. 180 *et seq.*, Sponer 1965, p. 20.

356 The debate on the nature of the right is dealt with in this Section, the debate on the system of property rights is dealt with below in 5. *A Numerus Clausus* in German Property Law?

357 Wolff & Raiser 1957, p. 498-499, Staudinger et al. 2002, p. 759, Schwab & Prütting 2003, p. 437-438.

358 Wolff & Raiser 1957, p. 499.

359 These rights will be dealt with below in 4. Borderline Cases in German Property Law, see, in particular, 4.2. Pre-emptive registration (*Vormerkung*).

rights operates on the border between contract and property. Not surprisingly therefore, it is debatable in German doctrine whether these last two rights are property rights.

The pre-emptive right is a property right and is dealt with in Paragraph 1094 BGB:

> A piece of land can be burdened in such a way that the person for whose benefit the right is created is entitled to the pre-emptive sale in respect to the owner.[360]

This complicated sentence results in a right that entitles the holder to force the owner to permit the sale and transfer of ownership to him. The right can be created either on behalf of a person in his capacity as holder of a property right or on behalf of a holder personally.[361] Although the right concerns the contract of sale, the right is commonly recognised as a property right since it burdens the land, burdens the owner in his capacity as an owner, has effect against third parties, and remains in existence in insolvency.[362]

The effect of the property right is that when an owner and another person agree on the sale and transfer of an immovable object, they create a property pre-emptive right that is designed to protect the right holder against the owner selling and transferring the object to a third party before the formalities are dealt with.[363] The property right entitles the right holder to preclude the conclusion of a contract of sale concluded between the owner and a third party and, under conditions, to demand a transfer of ownership.[364]

The property right entitles the right-holder to declare his right.[365] Making this declaration will entitle the holder of the right to a claim for the transfer of the ownership. In principle, this claim will only be effective against the owner, and not against third parties. Paragraph 1098 BGB stipulates, however, that the claim can be invoked against third parties by way of *Vormerkung*.[366] When the pre-emptive right is pre-emptively registered, i.e., through *Vormerkung*, the existence of the right will be in a public register. The *Vormerkung* functions as a vehicle to enable the successful claim of the right holder. *Vormerkung* makes a possible transfer of ownership between the owner and a third party invalid in respect to the holder of the pre-emptively registered property right, who by rank of his property right, remains

360 § 1094 BGB, 'Ein Gründstuck kann in der Weise belastet werden, dass derjenige, zu dessen Gunsten die Belastung erfolgt, dem Eigentümer gegenüber zum Vorkauf berechtet ist'.

361 The *subjectiv-persönliches Recht* and the *subjectiv-dingliches Recht*, Staudinger et al. 2002, p. 775.

362 See Staudinger et al. 2002, p. 760-762.

363 § 1094 BGB, also a share in a community of co-owners can be subject of the right, § 1095 BGB. Also other land-like rights, e.g. the right of *superficies* (§ 11 ErbbauVO) can be subject, see Staudinger et al. 2002, p. 765, 772-773.

364 § 1098 BGB. The right itself does not interfere with the party autonomy of the owner and the third party to decide on the contents of their agreement, see Staudinger et al. 2002, p. 796.

365 Staudinger et al. 2002, p. 780.

366 § 1098 (2) BGB, Staudinger et al. 2002, p. 797, Baur, Baur & Stürner 1999, p. 244-245.

entitled to claim the transfer of ownership.[367] A transfer between the owner and a third party will be valid against the rest of the world.[368]

However, the right holder is not just entitled to the transfer of ownership. He can not only ask for the transfer of ownership under the conditions, but he is also allowed to claim, instead of the transfer, the purchase price that the owner and the third party agreed on. As to the price, the holder of the right will be dependent on the agreement of the owner and the third party; a price already contained in the pre-emptive right will be invalid.[369] If the right-holder decides not to invoke his property right, the right will cease to exist.[370]

Parties do not have a great deal of freedom to decide on the exact content of the property right. By force of law a subsidiary obligation will come into existence, but this obligation, like their whole relation, will be covered by Paragraphs 465 until 473 BGB.[371] The application of these provisions from contract law emphasise the contractual nature of the right, which by force of the BGB achieves the status of a property right.

Finally, against the claim of the holder of this right, a third party who enters into a contract of sale with the owner is entitled to invoke Paragraph 1100 BGB. When the third party has already acquired the right of ownership of the immovable object, the position of the holder of the right depends on whether the purchase price has already been paid. If the price has not yet been paid, the holder invokes his right against both the owner and the third party, i.e., because of the *Vormerkung* the transfer of ownership between the owner and the third party takes no effect in respect to him.[372] When the purchase price has been paid, the 'new owner', i.e., the third party, can refuse to transfer the ownership to the holder of the right and vacate the immovable object until the purchase price has been paid to the holder.[373] The contract of sale between the owner and the third party will remain valid, which also entitles the third party to claim for damages.[374]

A special feature of German property law is the recognition of the special nature of the position of a person acquiring a property right as a distinct legal relation with limited third-party effect. These relations are known as acquisition rights or *Anwartschaftsrechte*. Although the term *Anwartschaft* was mentioned during the making of the draft, the acquisition right as such is unknown to the BGB.[375] Predecessors of the currently recognised right were already known in Germanic law, partly based on Roman law as well.[376] However, the current *Anwartschaftsrecht*

367 Staudinger et al. 2002, p. 797, Schwab & Prütting 2003, p. 437.
368 This effect concerns the concept of *Vormerkung*, see below; 4.2. Pre-emptive registration (*Vormerkung*).
369 Staudinger et al. 2002, p. 780.
370 Baur, Baur & Stürner 1999, p. 245.
371 § 1098(1) BGB, Staudinger et al. 2002, p. 795.
372 Staudinger et al. 2002, p. 802-803.
373 § 1100 BGB, Staudinger et al. 2002, p. 803, Schwab & Prütting 2003, p. 437.
374 § 435 *et seq.* BGB, Schwab & Prütting 2003, p. 437.
375 Achilles, Spahn & Gebhard 1897, p. 181, Raiser 1961, p. 2, Konzen 2000, p. 882, Füller 2006, p. 517-519.
376 Sponer 1965, p. 20 *et seq.*

was introduced by the German courts, in particular the BGH, and was also further developed through case law. Whether a new property right was recognised with the recognition of the acquisition right has been highly debated.[377] The leading opinion in German doctrine seems to be to accept the acquisition right as a limited property right or a quasi-property right.[378] However, these proponents of the acquisition right as a property right are also forced to recognise that the acquisition right also lacks certain characteristics.[379]

The acquisition right is connected to the acquisition of a property right and therefore with the system of transfer. The German transfer system is a *traditio* transfer system, meaning that the contract underlying the transfer and the transfer of ownership of the object itself are two different and distinct legal acts. They are related in such a way that the contract functions as justification for the transfer.[380] When a contract of sale is concluded between a seller and a buyer, the buyer acquires a personal right against the seller for the transfer of the object. It is this personal right that is strengthened by the recognition of the acquisition right.

In certain situations the rights of the buyer are stronger than just a personal right against the seller.[381] This is especially so when the seller reserves his right of ownership until payment by the buyer. A reservation of ownership is a transfer of ownership under a condition of suspension.[382] In case of a reservation of ownership the BGB provides that the owner can no longer use his power to dispose to prevent the acquisition of ownership over the object by the buyer.[383] Almost all acts by the owner in this respect will be invalid.[384] Furthermore, the buyer has a claim for compensation when the object is damaged in the care of the owner. When the owner resists the act that would fulfil the condition, the buyer can acquire ownership by force of law.[385] The position of the buyer in case of a reservation of ownership is therefore more than just a personal right against the seller. It is this 'secured' position that has given rise in German doctrine and legal practice to the recognition of the right of the buyer in reservation of ownership cases as a special right. This right of the buyer is considered not just a personal right for the transfer of the object, but a pre-emptive right in respect of the right of ownership itself. In a landmark decision the BGH, dealing with a reservation of ownership case, introduced the concept of acquisition rights.[386] This decision introduced a concept which was as such unknown to the drafters of the BGB.[387]

377 Schwab & Prütting 2003, p. 187, Wolf 2005, p. 315-316, Wiegand 1990, p. 128-129, Baur, Baur & Stürner 1999, p. 755-756, Raiser 1961, p. 45 *et seq.*, Mülbert 2002, p. 912 *et seq.*

378 Soergel et al. 2002, p. 15.

379 For a short overview see Wolf 2005, p. 316.

380 Although, technically, a contract is not required to transfer the right of ownership. For that a real agreement suffices. Van Vliet 2000, p. 31 *et seq.*

381 Baur, Baur & Stürner 1999, p. 755.

382 See above; 2.1. Normal Ownership.

383 Wolf 2005, p. 314-315.

384 § 161 (1) BGB, but see § 161 (3) BGB.

385 §§ 160 and 162 BGB, Wolf 2005, p. 315.

386 BGH 24 June 1958, BGHZ 28, 16, 21, BGH 25 February 1966, BGHZ 45, 186 (192).

387 Konzen 2000, p. 882.

The BGH introduced the acquisition right as a right that so closely resembles a full property right, that the rights and actions available to the holder of such a full right should be a model for the rights and actions of the holder of the acquisition right. The BGH held the acquisition right to be a '*wesensgleiches minus*', i.e., essentially the same as, but a little less than, of ownership.[388] After its introduction into German property law the acquisition right was further developed through case law.

The main result of this development is that the holder of an acquisition right is entitled to possession of the object. Leading opinion considers the right to possession of the right-holder as a right with third-party effect.[389] The result is that the right-holder can claim the return or transfer of possession against an unlawful possessor.[390] Furthermore, because the acquisition rights so closely resemble the full property right the right-holder is about to acquire, leading opinion awards the actions available to the holder of such a full property right to the holder of the acquisition right. This includes the claims for return of the object and the *actio negatoria*.[391] Finally, since the acquisition right is recognised as a property right, also a claim for damages in tort is available when the right is interfered with.[392]

Parallel to the recognition of the acquisition right in case of reservation of ownership, there are other situations where the BGB awards a secured position to the acquirer of a property right. Such a situation also occurs during the acquisition of immovable objects. The transfer of immovable objects requires more formalities than the transfer of movable objects. One of these formalities is that parties must formally agree on the transfer and that such agreement must be registered.[393] This requirement is further specified in Paragraph 925 BGB, which requires the parties to declare their intention and agree to transfer together in front of an official, usually a notary.[394] Such agreement is known as *Auflassung* and should be distinguished from a contract of sale, which is a separate individual agreement.[395] After the *Auflassung* has been made, the agreement can be registered, which, because of the registration system, can take some time. The need for protection of the acquirer of a property right in respect to immovables is different from the acquirer of a movable object under reservation of ownership. Paragraph 925 BGB prohibits a conditional transfer

388 BGH 24 June 1959, BGHZ 28 , 16 = NJW 1958, 1133. Schwab & Prütting 2003, p. 187, Wolf 2005, p. 316.

389 Baur, Baur & Stürner 1999, p. 762, Wolf 2005, p. 318.

390 BGH 21 May 1953, BGHZ 10, 69 = NJW 1953, 1099, §§ 858 *et seq*. and 1007 BGB, Baur, Baur & Stürner 1999, p. 762.

391 §§ 985 and 1004 BGB, Wolf 2005, p. 318, Schwab & Prütting 2003, p. 190. For an overview of the debate on the application of these claims see Baur, Baur & Stürner 1999, p. 762-763.

392 § 823 BGB uses the terms 'Eigentum oder ein sonstiges Recht' or ownership and ownership-like rights. Leading opinion places the acquisition right in the latter category. Schwab & Prütting 2003, p. 190, Wolf 2005, p. 318-319, Baur, Baur & Stürner 1999, p. 762-763.

393 § 873 BGB, Schwab & Prütting 2003, p. 165.

394 § 925 BGB, although the law does not require the parties to appear personally, see Schwab & Prütting 2003, p. 165-166, Wolf 2005, p. 206 *et seq*.

395 § 925a BGB, Schwab & Prütting 2003, p. 166-167.

of immovable objects; a reservation of ownership of an immovable object is therefore not possible.[396]

When the buyer of an immovable object requests registration or when the *Auflassung* was made by official deed in front of a notary, the BGB strengthens the position of the buyer. Naturally, the agreement will bind parties as to its contents, but as such it will only create a personal right for the buyer. However, upon request for registration or passing of a deed the seller can no longer oppose the registration of the *Auflassung*, and, even more, can therefore no longer oppose the acquisition of ownership by the buyer.[397] The right of the buyer can also be protected through a pre-emptive registration or *Vormerkung*.[398] In such a strengthened position, the buyer is awarded an acquisition right.[399] There has been much debate on the exact moment of creation of the right. Leading opinion recognises the acquisition right after *Auflassung* and request for registration.[400] Some authors also recognise an acquisition-like right when the *Auflassung* has been made but no request for registration or *Vormerkung* has yet been made.[401]

Thirdly, a more secured position of the acquirer of a property right also exists in case of the creation of a right of hypothec for a future claim.[402] When the claim to which the right of hypothec will be accessory is not yet in existence, an owner-*Grundschuld* comes into existence, which will automatically change in a right of hypothec for the creditor when the claim comes into existence.[403] If the right of hypothec is constructed as a *Briefschuld*, and not a *Buchschuld*, the same reasoning applies where the document proving the existence of the *Briefschuld* is not yet transferred.[404] The owner-*Grundschuld* is made under resolutive condition of the existence of the claim or the transfer of the brief. Such a situation will give the creditor an acquisition right for the right of hypothec.[405]

Apart from these three primary examples, other types of acquisition rights exist in German law, but are more debated.[406] In any case, all of these rights share the characteristic that they are expectation rights. In other words, these rights are a phase prior to the acquisition of a property right. The examples show that this can relate both to ownership and to other property rights. The character of the acquisition right will be determined by the right the holder intends to acquire. The claims

396 § 925 (2) BGB, Schwab & Prütting 2003, p. 167.

397 § 873 (2) BGB, further protected by §§ 130 (2), 979 BGB and §§ 17 and 45 *Grundbuchordnung* (GBO), Wolf 2005, p. 216-217.

398 BGH 30 April 1982, BGHZ 83, 395, 399, Wolf 2005, p. 216, Konzen 2000, p. 877-878.

399 The *Auflassungsanwartschaft*, Wolf 2005, p. 216, Schwab & Prütting 2003, p. 168, Baur, Baur & Stürner 1999, p. 205, Konzen 2000, p. 875.

400 BGH 18 December 1967, BGHZ 49, 197 = NJW 1968, 493, Schwab & Prütting 2003, p. 168, Konzen 2000, p. 875. Critically see Mülbert 2002, p. 913 *et seq.*

401 Wolf 2005, p. 217, *contra* see Schwab & Prütting 2003, p. 168 and Konzen 2000, p. 884-885.

402 Baur, Baur & Stürner 1999, p. 542 *et seq.*

403 §§ 1113 (2), 1163 (1) BGB, Baur, Baur & Stürner 1999, p. 543. On the owner-*Grundschuld* see below; 3.8. *Grundschuld.*

404 § 1163 (2) BGB, Baur, Baur & Stürner 1999, p. 543. On *Buchschuld* and *Briefschuld* see below; 3.7. Hypothec.

405 Baur, Baur & Stürner 1999, p. 543, Sponer 1965, p. 114 *et seq.*

406 For an overview see Sponer 1965, p. 73 *et seq.*

available will be modelled on the full property right, and will include both personal claims and property claims.

The acquisition right is almost a full property right, but connected, through accessority, to the acquisition of the full right it is modelled after. This accessority has important effects. When the holder of the acquisition right is no longer entitled to acquire the property right, the acquisition right will cease to exist. In case of reservation of ownership this also occurs when the reservation of ownership ends.[407]

Because the acquisition right itself represents a value it can be subject to other property rights.[408] Moreover, the acquisition right can also be transferred to another party.[409] The new holder will acquire the acquisition right under the same conditions as the old holder was holding the right. However, the agreement to which the acquisition right is connected will not transfer automatically to the new right-holder.[410]

It is with the transfer of the acquisition right that doctrinal problems appear. The leading opinion in doctrine is to accept a transfer of the acquisition right. The requirements for transfer are the same as the requirements for transfer the acquisition right is modelled after.[411] This system of transfer fits the nature of the acquisition right. However, it creates serious doctrinal problems. A transfer of an *Auflassung* acquisition right will have to be modelled after Paragraphs 873 and 925 BGB. Mülbert has shown that this means that parties have to agree on the transfer of the acquisition right in a second *Auflassung*, but that the third party acquiring the acquisition right cannot request a registration of the transfer.[412] One of the requirements for the transfer is therefore lacking. The lack of registration will lead to the impossibility of the second acquirer of the acquisition having the right to act against the transfer of ownership of the object to another party. This problem can only be solved by interference of the first holder of the acquisition right, who is entitled to alter his request for registration.[413]

Secondly, Mülbert emphasises that the transfer of an acquisition right that was strengthened through *Vormerkung* is especially problematic.[414] A right that is registered through a *Vormerkung* is accessory to the agreement on which basis it is registered.[415] However, the acquisition right is by its nature not an accessory right. Mülbert argues that the acquisition right through *Vormerkung* changes this nature and creates an accessory right. Doctrinally, accessory rights are transferred with the principal claim underlying the accessory relationship.[416] However, the acquisition

407 Schwab & Prütting 2003, p. 188.

408 Wolf 2005, p. 321, Mülbert 2002, p. 920.

409 According to the leading opinion this also includes the admissibility of an acquisition right as the subject for a legal pledge, i.e. a pledge by force of law, Schwab & Prütting 2003, p. 189. Wolf 2005, p. 321.

410 Therefore, the acquisition right is not an accessory right.

411 Mülbert 2002, p. 920.

412 Mülbert 2002, p. 924.

413 Mülbert 2002, p. 925-926.

414 Mülbert 2002, p. 920 *et seq.*, 933.

415 Mülbert 2002, p. 921, Mülbert 1997, p. 336 *et seq.*

416 § 401 BGB, Mülbert 2002, p. 921.

right must be transferred according to the right after which it is modelled. In many situations, these two transfer requirements will conflict with each other.

The problems with the transfer of the acquisition right illustrate the doctrinal and systematic issues the right creates. Although the proprietary nature of the right is commonly recognised, its characterisation in the system creates problems. On the one hand, the right is recognised as a right to use, i.e., a *wesensgleiches minus* of another property right.[417] On the other hand, which seems to be leading opinion, the right is considered to be a distinct category, i.e. as an expectation right.[418] Although the acquisition right secures the acquisition of a property right it bears characteristics of a right to use as well. In other words, the right secures the right to use, but also the right to acquire.[419]

3.5. *Real Burden (Reallast)*

Unknown as such by Roman law, the *Reallast* in the BGB comes from the influence of Germanic law, and is a perfect example of the influence of Germanic law on the modern German property law system.[420] The *Reallast* is a real burden that finds its origin in the feudal system. A tenant could be under a burden, which was connected to him holding the land for a lord, to provide a lord with, for example, money or proceeds of the land.[421] Because of this system of land holding, these real burdens were an important part of everyday life. Each of the different Germanic countries dealt with real burdens in its own specific way.[422] Especially after the French Revolution and the new ideas on freedom and individuality, certain of them limited the application of real burdens on their territory.[423] Nevertheless, real burdens, especially because they continued to be used, were of great economic importance. The First Commission drafting the BGB recognised this legal diversity as well as the economic importance of real burdens and explicitly decided to include real burdens in the new Civil Code, but to leave the content, except the general provisions on real burdens, to the different states of the German federation.[424] It is therefore for each state to provide exact rules on real burdens.[425]

A real burden as it is dealt with by the BGB is a burden in private law and is described by Paragraph 1105 BGB, which states:[426]

> A piece of land can be burdened in a way, that a person, to whose benefit the right is created, is entitled to returning benefits from the land. (Real Burden). The returning

417 Raiser 1961, p. 65 *et seq.*
418 Baur, Baur & Stürner 1999, p. 25-26.
419 Mülbert 2002, p. 918-919.
420 Staudinger et al. 2002, p. 813, Füller 2006, p. 460-465.
421 Motive III 1888, p. 572 *et seq.*, Wolff & Raiser 1957, p. 510-511, Schwab & Prütting 2003, p. 440.
422 For an overview see Motive III 1888, p. 573-578 and for modern times see Staudinger et al. 2002, p. 814-817.
423 Motive III 1888, p. 578.
424 Motive III 1888, p. 579.
425 Staudinger et al. 2002, p. 813.
426 Staudinger et al. 2002, p. 823.

> benefits can be adapted, without any further action taken, when the expected development of the burden of the land can be decided on the basis of the nature and scope of the burden in the agreement ...[427]

The real burden is different from a right of servitude because it entitles the right-holder to take a benefit from the land of another. The duty in a real burden is therefore a positive duty, whereas a right of servitude cannot consist of a positive duty.[428] Furthermore, a real burden cannot contain a burden to refrain from doing something.[429] The burden can be created between a party and the owner of a certain immovable object but also between a party and another person, not in his capacity as holder of a property right in a certain immovable object.[430] In both types of this right it is not possible to change the real burden to the other type.

The most important difference to other property rights is that a real burden is not a right to use. Leading opinion characterises the real burden as a *Verwertungsrecht*, in other words a right that entitles the holder, under conditions, to claim the value of the object.[431] Nevertheless, the difference between the right to the value and the right to use is very small.[432] A right of servitude allows the holder to take, whereas a real burden allows the right-holder to receive.[433] This difference is best seen in case of non-performance. A non-performance by the owner of the burdened land, i.e., non-delivery of the benefit the real burden entails, will not lead to a claim to the continuation of the duty, but for a claim for the value of the object under burden.[434]

The benefits to which the real burden entitles its holder cannot be one single benefit. The benefit must be repeated or return, even if it is not periodically.[435] A single benefit can only be part of a real burden besides a returning benefit.[436] A returning benefit is usually a duty to perform services or to pay money.[437] Moreover, the content of the burden does not have to be particularly specified. The

427 § 1105 BGB, 'Ein Grundstück kann in der Weise belastet werden, dass an denjenigen, zu dessen Gunsten die Belastung erfolgt, wiederkehrende Leistungen aus dem Grundstück zu entrichten sind. (Reallast). Als Inhalt der Reallast kann auch vereinbart werden, dass die zu entrichtenden Leistungen sich ohne weiteres an veränderte Verhältnisse anpassen, wenn anhand der in der Vereinbarung festgelegten Voraussetzungen Art und Umfang der Belastung des Grundstücks bestimmt werden können'.

428 On the requirement for rights of servitude see above; 3.1. Real Servitude.

429 Staudinger et al. 2002, p. 836.

430 *Subjectiv-dingliche Reallast* § 1110 BGB and *Subjectiv-persönliche Reallast* § 1111 BGB, Wolf 2005, p. 396-397.

431 Baur, Baur & Stürner 1999, p. 23-24, Staudinger et al. 2002, p. 820.

432 Also depending on the content the parties whish to provide the property right with. See Baur, Baur & Stürner 1999, p. 380.

433 See Staudinger et al. 2002, p. 823-824.

434 For an overview of the real burden in insolvency see Amann 1993, p. 222 *et seq.*

435 Staudinger et al. 2002, p. 837-838.

436 Staudinger et al. 2002, p. 838.

437 Or *wiederkehrende Leistungen*, § 1105 BGB, Wolf 2005, p. 396.

second sentence of Paragraph 1105 BGB allows for a connection to index figures in order to increase the value of the burden equally without additional agreement.[438]

The real burden is therefore a property right that entitles to a periodic benefit under pressure of execution against the object under burden. Doctrine distinguishes two parts of the real burden. On the one hand there is the real burden as a general property right which contains all the specific burdens. This part is known as the *Stammrecht* or stem-right.[439] It is this part of the property right that directly burdens the land on which it is created.[440] However the possibilities to execute the right in respect of the land itself are very limited.[441] On the other hand, doctrine recognises the right to the specific benefits, which follow from the stem-right.[442]

The relation between these two parts of the right can be considered by analogy to the right of hypothec. The stem-right is the right of hypothec itself, which entitles the holder of the right to a proprietary claim upon non-payment of the owner. The payments of the owner, to which the right-holder of the hypothec is entitled, are specific benefits the holder of the right receives. In order to protect this second type of benefits, the BGB offers protection for the holder of the right of hypothec.[443] Paragraph 1107 BGB declares the provisions on the protection of the holder of a right of hypothec in respect to the payment for the right of hypothec applicable to the holder of a real burden.[444] Furthermore, in order to enhance the position of the holder of the real burden, through Paragraph 1108 BGB the owner is liable with his personal assets for those benefits that have to be paid during his ownership. As in the case of servitudes, this personal liability is constructed through a subsidiary obligation arising by force of law.[445]

Other resemblances with servitudes exist as well. Besides the legal subsidiary obligation arising between the owner and the holder of the right, an independent agreement can be made which can be connected to the property right. Such a construction enables a security-real burden or *Sicherungsreallast*.[446] As in the case of servitudes, the security-real burden is modelled on the *Sicherungsgrundschuld*.[447] As a result, the security contract is not accessory, but merely connected to the property right, and specific arrangements have to be made to protect the owner. Finally, it is also possible for an owner to create a real burden on his own property. Creating a real burden on the owner's land by the owner enables the owner to establish a real

438 This is not possible in case of a pledge, which adds to the attractiveness of the real burden for practice. See BayOlG 9 December 1992, NJW-RR 1993, 530, Staudinger et al. 2002, p 830.

439 Baur, Baur & Stürner 1999, p. 382, Staudinger et al. 2002, p. 818.

440 Schwab & Prütting 2003, p. 440, Staudinger et al. 2002, p. 818-820.

441 This will especially be the situation in which the owner invokes a right, if available, to pay a sum of money in exchange for a ceasing of the right. Baur, Baur & Stürner 1999, p. 382.

442 § 1107 BGB, Baur, Baur & Stürner 1999, p. 382-383, Staudinger et al. 2002, p. 847.

443 These are the provisions of §§ 1113 *et seq.* BGB, for an overview see Staudinger et al. 2002, p. 848-851.

444 With the limitation of those provisions which particularly concern the objects in the hypothec or the accessory character. See Staudinger et al. 2002, p. 848.

445 § 1108 BGB, Staudinger et al. 2002, p. 821, 853-854.

446 See Amann 1993, p. 222 *et seq.*

447 On this type of *Grundschuld* see below; 3.8. *Grundschuld*.

burden on his own terms after which he can transfer either the burden, or his ownership, and continue to hold the other for himself.[448]

In legal practice the *Reallast* is mostly used in very specific circumstances.[449] Since the real burden originates from before the introduction of the BGB, it is still possible to come across an old pre-BGB type of the right.[450] Its most important present application is in support of a burden following from other rights, such as payments of lease of hypothec.[451] Furthermore, the right is used for the providing of heat, water and electricity on construction sites.[452]

3.6. *Pledge*

The right of pledge was intended to provide German legal practice with a security property right in respect of movable objects and rights. The inclusion of a security right in respect of movable objects and rights was considered very important. The First Commission therefore, following the general opinion at the end of the nineteenth century, introduced a classic right of pledge.[453] This right of pledge, based on the Roman *pignus,* is a security right whereby the pledgor brings the object under pledge into the power of the pledgee. In German law this includes a transfer of possession.[454] The possessory-pledge was already criticised before the BGB entered into force and remains the subject of discussion.[455]

However, the right of pledge, mainly because of the requirement to transfer possession, is overshadowed by the use of ownership for security purposes with which similar results can be achieved without the transfer of possession of the object serving as security.[456] In practice the right of pledge serves a limited function, especially in respect to lease and pledge of claims.[457] This section will first deal with the right of pledge on movable objects, after which the pledge on rights is considered.

The BGB recognises three types of pledge; the contract pledge, the legal pledge and the insolvency pledge.[458] This section will primarily deal with the right of pledge created by contract, *Pfandrecht.* At the end of this section some remarks on the rights of pledge by force of law will be made. The normal pledge, i.e., the pledge

448 Staudinger et al. 2002, p. 834.
449 See in particular Wolf 2006, p. 17-20.
450 Schwab & Prütting 2003, p. 440.
451 Staudinger et al. 2002, p. 830.
452 Wolf 2005, p. 397, Heyman 2003, p. 25.
453 Schwab & Prütting 2003, p. 374, Staudinger, Nöll & Wiegand 2002, p. 4-5.
454 § 1205 BGB. A fictional possession, i.e. a transfer through a *constitutum possessorium,* see Schwab & Prütting 2003, p. 377, Van Vliet 2000, p. 53 *et seq.*, 127 *et seq.*
455 See Staudinger, Nöll & Wiegand 2002, p. 4.
456 This includes both the transfer of ownership for security purposes and the reservation of ownership. See above; 2.5. Security Ownership. Staudinger, Nöll & Wiegand 2002, p. 4, Füller 2006, p. 490.
457 Schwab & Prütting 2003, p. 375-376.
458 Or *Vertragspfand, Gesetzliche Pfandrecht and Pfändungspfandrecht,* Baur, Baur & Stürner 1999, p. 671-672, Schwab & Prütting 2003, p. 374, Staudinger, Nöll & Wiegand 2002, p. 14.

created by agreement between the parties, is dealt with in Paragraph 1104 BGB, which states:

> A movable object can, for purposes of securing a claim, be burdened in such a way that the creditor is entitled to be satisfied from the object's value.[459]

The normal type of pledge can be created on any movable object.[460] For a right of pledge to be created a relation between the pledgor and pledgee is necessary whereby the pledgee has a claim on the pledgor.[461] The standard circumstance is a loan of money whereby the pledge is used as security for the repayment of the loan. In German law, the right of pledge is accessory to the claim.[462]Although the right of pledge is accessory, the claim does not need to be in existence at the moment the right of pledge is created.[463] Also a future claim can be used to create a right of pledge, as long as at the moment of the creation the claim itself can be anticipated.[464] The right of pledge will come into existence at the moment of creation and take its rank from that moment.[465] If it becomes clear that the claim will not come into existence, the right of pledge will cease to exist.[466]

In content the right of pledge is an agreement between parties that focuses on the conditions under which the pledgee is entitled to execute the right of pledge and to sell the object. Because of this primary personal relation the nature of the right of pledge can be questioned.[467] Nevertheless, leading opinion in Germany considers the right of pledge a property right, especially as the right entitles the pledgee to the same actions as the owner, and will also give the pledgee a right to separate the object that was pledged from the other assets of the pledgor in case of insolvency of the pledgor.[468] This protection of the pledgee is different from the Roman law origins where an *actio Serviana* was available. Instead, the BGB awards the pledgee the same actions as an owner. These include the revindication of Paragraph 985 BGB and the *actio negatoria* of Paragraph 1004 BGB.[469]

Furthermore, German law recognises the possibility, in Paragraph 1213 BGB, to create a pledge whereby the pledgee is entitled to use the object under pledge. This *antichresis* clause will, with exceptions, only be effective if the parties specifi-

459 § 1204 BGB, 'Eine bewegliche Sache kann zur Sicherung einer Forderung in der Weise belastet werden, dass der Gläubiger berechtet ist, Befriedigung aus der Sache zu suchen (Pfandrecht)'.

460 Baur, Baur & Stürner 1999, p. 676, Staudinger, Nöll & Wiegand 2002, p. 28.

461 In other words, whereby the pledgee is creditor of the pledgor, the debtor.

462 Baur, Baur & Stürner 1999, p. 672-673.

463 § 1204 (2) BGB.

464 Baur, Baur & Stürner 1999, p. 678, Staudinger, Nöll & Wiegand 2002, p. 26.

465 BGH 26 January 1983, BGHZ 86, 340=NJW 1983, 1619, Baur, Baur & Stürner 1999, p. 678, Staudinger, Nöll & Wiegand 2002, p. 26-27.

466 RGZ 145, 336.

467 See Wiegand 1981, p. 1 *et seq.*

468 § 1227 BGB and § 50 InsO, Staudinger, Nöll & Wiegand 2002, p. 6-7, 9, Baur, Baur & Stürner 1999, p. 671.

469 Staudinger, Nöll & Wiegand 2002, p. 137, 139.

cally agree on it.[470] The *antichresis* will entitle the pledgee to the general benefits of use, but also to the fruits the object produces. When the object under pledge delivers fruits and its possession is transferred solely to the pledgee, in case of doubt, the right to use can be accepted, without proof of an agreement.[471] A general exception is money, for which an irregular right of pledge is used, resulting in the right of the pledgee to use the money, but the duty to replace it.[472]

Between the pledgor and the pledgee a subsidiary legal obligation comes into existence by force of law.[473] The BGB provides regulations on the essential content of the parties' relation, to which the parties themselves can change or add content. The legal provisions include: the duty for the pledgee to refrain, save the already mentioned exception, from using the object serving as security, or from establishing a right of pledge on the right of pledge; the duty of the pledgor to compensate costs the pledgee has incurred while possessing the object; the possibility for the pledgor to claim replacement or repair of the object in the care of the pledgee; the possibility for the pledgor to claim the object back for replacement when it decreases in value; and the claim, *vice versa*, of the pledgee to replace the object, as well as the possibility for the pledgor to claim the object back after the right of pledge ceases.[474]

When the pledgor is not able to fulfil his duties under the security agreement that created the right of pledge, the pledgee is entitled to execute his right. When this occurs, German doctrine considers the claim *Pfandreif* or ripe for execution.[475] The execution in case of a right of pledge on movable objects is effected through a sale of the object. Upon the sale, the pledgee can use the proceeds of the sale to satisfy the claim that remains against the pledgor.[476] Most importantly, the pledgee is under no condition entitled to keep the object for himself; the sale is compulsory.[477] Although the pledgee is not the owner of the object, the acquirer in such a transfer will acquire ownership through Paragraph 1242 BGB.[478]

A right of pledge can also be created on rights. The provisions on the right of pledge on movable objects are also generally applicable to the right of pledge on rights, but the BGB also provides additional regulations.[479] Only those rights that represent a value which can be acquired by a possible pledgee in case of non-performance of the duties of the pledgor can be accepted as the subject of a right of

470 This will create the *Nutzungspfandrecht,* Staudinger, Nöll & Wiegand 2002, p. 88.

471 § 1213 (2) BGB, Staudinger, Nöll & Wiegand 2002, p. 89.

472 Although a normal right of pledge in respect to money is also possible. On both possibilities see Staudinger, Nöll & Wiegand 2002, p. 37-38.

473 Schwab & Prütting 2003, p. 380, Staudinger, Nöll & Wiegand 2002, p. 13, 92.

474 §§ 1215, 1216, 1217, 1218 and 1223 BGB, Schwab & Prütting 2003, p. 380-381, Staudinger, Nöll & Wiegand 2002, p. 98 *et seq.*

475 On the term *Pfandreif* see Baur, Baur & Stürner 1999, p. 470, 682-683, Staudinger, Nöll & Wiegand 2002, p. 141-142.

476 § 1228 BGB, Staudinger, Nöll & Wiegand 2002, p. 140.

477 In other words, the *lex commissoria* in German law is strictly prohibited. § 1229 BGB, Staudinger, Nöll & Wiegand 2002, p. 144.

478 § 1242 BGB, Staudinger, Nöll & Wiegand 2002, p. 167-169.

479 § 1273 BGB.

pledge.[480] Also rights that are treated as immovable objects in the system of German property law cannot be the subject of a right of pledge. This category includes the rights of *superficies* and ownership of an apartment.[481] Also the right of ownership itself cannot be subject to a right of pledge. Since a right of pledge concerns the object and not the right of ownership itself, the nature of the right of ownership resists it being subject to other property rights.[482]

Also future rights, especially claims, can be the subject of a right of pledge. The criteria for the admissibility of future rights are parallel to the transfer of future rights. The result is that as long as the right can be ascertained at the moment of creation of the right of pledge, the right of pledge will be valid. The deciding factor in German law is that if an independent third party would be able to identify the claim, it can be allowed.[483] When the criteria are fulfilled, the right of pledge will come into existence.

The right of pledge is created with the transfer of right or, in case of a claim, the notice to the debtor of the claim that the claim has been pledged.[484] When the transfer of a right requires the transfer of an object, for example, a document proving the existence of the right, the possession of the document must be transferred in order to acquire the right.[485] In case of execution of the pledge on rights, the pledgee will execute by seizure instead of sale.[486]

When claims are subject to the right of pledge a three-party relationship comes into existence between the pledgor, the pledgee and the debtor of the claim. The right of pledge on claims is the most important application of the right of pledge on rights.[487] Before the right of pledge can be executed, both the pledgor and the pledgee are entitled to receive the fulfilment of the claim.[488] The pledgor will become owner or will become entitled to the object or claim that is received from the debtor. Furthermore, the pledgee will receive a right of pledge on the object or claim by the force of law. This will especially be so in case the right to the transfer of an object is pledged.

However, when the right of pledge can be executed the position of the pledgee becomes stronger.[489] The pledgee becomes entitled to demand the fulfilment of the claim. The pledgor can only demand the proceeds of the fulfilment from the pledgee and no longer from the debtor.[490] When the pledgee receives an object for

480 Staudinger, Nöll & Wiegand 2002, p. 251.

481 Or the *Erbbaurecht* and *Wohnungseigentum*, Staudinger, Nöll & Wiegand 2002, p. 252.

482 Staudinger, Nöll & Wiegand 2002, p. 252.

483 Staudinger, Nöll & Wiegand 2002, p. 253-254.

484 BGH 30 November 1977, BGHZ 70, 75, 78 = NJW 1978, 642, Schwab & Prütting 2003, p. 390-391,Baur, Baur & Stürner 1999, p. 785.

485 Schwab & Prütting 2003, p. 390.

486 § 1277 BGB, Schwab & Prütting 2003, p. 391, Baur, Baur & Stürner 1999, p. 783.

487 Schwab & Prütting 2003, p. 391-392.

488 § 1281 BGB, before the pledge is 'ripe' (*Pfandreif*), Baur, Baur & Stürner 1999, p. 785, Staudinger, Nöll & Wiegand 2002, p. 291-292.

489 § 1282 BGB, the pledge is then 'ripe' (*Pfandreif*), Baur, Baur & Stürner 1999, p. 786, Staudinger, Nöll & Wiegand 2002, p. 293.

490 Schwab & Prütting 2003, p. 393, Staudinger, Nöll & Wiegand 2002, p. 297.

the fulfilment of the claim, he will receive a right of pledge on that object by the force of law and the pledgor will become owner.[491] When the pledgee receives money, he can satisfy his claim and will only have to transfer the surplus after compensation to the pledgor.[492]

Finally, the right of pledge can also come into existence by operation of law or in insolvency procedures. On the former, Paragraph 1257 BGB declares the provisions on pledge that are applicable. It should be emphasised that these rights come into existence by operation of law and are rights of pledge in the same sense as the contract-pledge rights. The result is that they take rank against the other property rights and therefore should not be considered lightly. An example of such a right is the right of a lessor of an immovable object on the objects the lessee brings into the immovable object to secure the payment of the rent through Paragraph 562 BGB.[493] The second type of pledge, the insolvency pledge, is not dealt with in the BGB, but in the insolvency regulations, InsO. The insolvency pledge is imposed on the movable assets in the insolvency procedure and will take rank amongst the other security rights.[494]

3.7. *Hypothec*

German law recognises two main property security rights in respect of land. In doctrine, these rights are confusingly known as rights of pledge on land, *Grundpfandrechte*.[495] This is confusing because the terminology of the BGB restricts the right of pledge to movable objects and rights.[496] The *Grundpfandrechte* consist of the right of hypothec and the right of *Grundschuld*, which are similar rights, but with doctrinal differences. Because of the similarities between these rights, the BGB uses a similar approach to deal with each of these. This is particularly so in respect to the way in which they can be created.

Grundpfandrechte can either be a *Briefrecht*, a 'document-right', or a *Buchrecht*, in a 'register-right'.[497] The difference between the two is that in the case of the document-right, the security right is registered and this registration can be proven by a document that also serves as the object of transfer in the event of a transfer of that security right, whereas the registration-right is a security right that is formally registered and whose existence follows only from the registration. The *Buchrecht* is therefore less suited to transfer. Both the right of hypothec and the right of *Grundschuld* can be either a document-right or a registration-right. The main reason that both these property security rights were included is that both of these rights were applied in practice, the right of hypothec in the north and the right of *Grundschuld* in

491 Baur, Baur & Stürner 1999, p. 786, Schwab & Prütting 2003, p. 394.
492 Schwab & Prütting 2003, p. 394, Staudinger, Nöll & Wiegand 2002, p. 296.
493 Baur, Baur & Stürner 1999, p. 690.
494 Baur, Baur & Stürner 1999, p. 693.
495 Baur, Baur & Stürner 1999, p. 384, Staudinger & Wolfsteiner 2002, p. 10.
496 See above; 3.6. Pledge.
497 Baur, Baur & Stürner 1999, p. 406.

the south.[498] This section deals with the right of hypothec and the next section will deal with the right of *Grundschuld*.[499]

The right of hypothec was specifically designed by the drafters of the BGB to be useful for practice. However, from the second half of the twentieth century, the *Grundschuld* has taken over in practice. Because of this, the right of hypothec has lost most of its practical relevance.[500] Nevertheless, the main rules on hypothec find analogous application to the right of *Grundschuld* and therefore remain of importance.[501] Furthermore, the right of hypothec, although not used much anymore, is still a property right in the system of the BGB that is worthy of consideration. The right of hypothec is defined in Paragraph 1113 BGB:

> A piece of land can be burdened in such a way that the person for whose benefit the right is created is entitled to a specific sum of money from the piece of land for the fulfilment of a claim (right of hypothec).[502]

The right of hypothec connects a claim between an owner and a creditor to a property right for security on an immovable object on behalf of that creditor.[503] The right must be created on land or on land-like rights.[504] Also movable objects on the land that are considered part of the land can be subject to the right of hypothec.[505] The right of hypothec is an accessory right, it cannot exist without the claim the performance of which it seeks to secure. Because of this connection the right of hypothec combines a personal relation, i.e., the claim, with a property relation, i.e., the right of hypothec.[506]

The accessory nature of the right of hypothec exists from the moment of creation, and means that there can be no right of hypothec without a claim.[507] When a right of hypothec is created without an existing claim, the creditor cannot become right-holder of the hypothec. Yet, it is possible to hold a right of hypothec without an existing claim. In such a situation, the right will rest with the owner as a *Eigentümerhypothek*, in English 'owner hypothec'.[508] When a right of hypothec is trans-

498 Motive III 1888, p. 604-612, Wolff & Raiser 1957, p. 521-522, Baur, Baur & Stürner 1999, p. 506, Staudinger & Wolfsteiner 2002, p. 12-14.

499 See below; 3.8. *Grundschuld*.

500 Baur, Baur & Stürner 1999, p. 398, Staudinger & Wolfsteiner 2002, p. 74-75.

501 § 1192 BGB.

502 § 1113 BGB, 'Ein Grundstück kann in der Weise belastet werden, dass an denjenigen, zu dessen Gunsten die Belastung erfolgt, eine bestimmte Geldsumme zur Befriedigung wegen einer ihm zustehenden Forderung aus dem Grundstück zu zahlen ist (Hypothek)'.

503 The creditor of the claim and the holder of the property right must be the same person, § 1153 BGB. Baur, Baur & Stürner 1999, p. 420, Schwab & Prütting 2003, p. 322.

504 This includes *inter alia* the *Wohungseigentum* and the *Erbbaurecht*, Staudinger & Wolfsteiner 2002, p. 27-28.

505 § 1120 BGB. The deciding factor is whether these rights are included in the ownership of the land, Schwab & Prütting 2003, p. 317.

506 See Schwab & Prütting 2003, p. 325-328.

507 Schwab & Prütting 2003, p. 305.

508 §§ 1163 and 1177 BGB, Schwab & Prütting 2003, p. 305.

ferred, the transfer cannot take effect without a transfer of the claim and *vice versa*.[509] And, finally, when the claim ceases to exist, the right of hypothec will not cease, but will return to the owner as an owner-*Grundschuld*.[510]

Apart from the right of hypothec itself, the section on hypothec in the BGB also provides regulations concerning the claim. First, the claim must be for money, in whatever currency.[511] Secondly, the claim must be identifiable.[512] A future claim can also be used to establish a hypothec. The right of hypothec will be created if the claim can be sufficiently identified in anticipation of its existence. However, contrary to the right of pledge, the creditor will only become right-holder of the hypothec when the claim comes into existence. Prior to that time a right of owner-hypothec will rest with the owner, but the creditor will have an *Anwartschaftsrecht*.[513]

The BGB recognises two models of hypothec; the *Verkehrshypothek* or transferable-hypothec, and the *Sicherungshypothek* or security-hypothec. The BGB presents the *Verkehrshypothek* as the standard model. The drafters of the BGB specifically started with this type of hypothec, which is intended to allow for a transfer of the right. This type of hypothec can be created in two ways; as a *Briefhypothek* or as a *Buchhypothek*. Especially the former enables parties to transfer the right of hypothec to another party by transferring a document (*Brief*). The document-hypothec is therefore not intended for long-term relations, it is more used for a situation in which it is desirable to change creditors.[514] As a standard in the BGB, a right of hypothec will be of this type unless parties explicitly agree otherwise.[515] In case of doubt the hypothec will be considered to be a document-hypothec.[516]

The registry issues the document, the *Brief*, after the right of hypothec has been registered and gives it, unless specifically provided otherwise, to the owner. However, parties can decide otherwise either by creating a transfer of the document through *constitutum possessorium*, or agreeing that the document will directly be transferred to the creditor.[517] The result of this regulation is that the owner will have an owner-hypothec until he transfers the document to the creditor. A registration after transfer is not necessary.[518]

The document itself will contain the registration data, including the identification of the land on which the right is created, but also the sum of money the right secures.[519] Furthermore, parties can add information to the document as well, e.g.,

509 § 1153 BGB, Schwab & Prütting 2003, p. 305-306.

510 § 1163 (1) 2nd sentence BGB, Schwab & Prütting 2003, p. 306. The right of hypothec can, because of its accessory nature, never be held by the owner on his own object. See Füller 2006, p. 471-472.

511 § 1113 BGB, Schwab & Prütting 2003, p. 308, Staudinger & Wolfsteiner 2002, p. 19.

512 Baur, Baur & Stürner 1999, p. 421-422.

513 Schwab & Prütting 2003, p. 310, Baur, Baur & Stürner 1999, p. 543. On *Anwartschaftsrechte* see above; 3.4. Expectation Rights: Pre-Emptive Right and Acquisition Right.

514 Schwab & Prütting 2003, p. 307.

515 § 1116 BGB, Schwab & Prütting 2003, p. 307.

516 Schwab & Prütting 2003, p. 314, Baur, Baur & Stürner 1999, p. 406.

517 § 1117 BGB, Schwab & Prütting 2003, p. 313.

518 § 1154 BGB.

519 Schwab & Prütting 2003, p. 314.

information on the payment.[520] Finally, the document proves the existence of the right of hypothec, but the registry will remain to give the overriding correct information, unless explicitly proven otherwise.[521]

The second type of hypothec, the *Buchhypothek,* is created when parties agree on the claim and the establishment of the right of hypothec, which is then registered under specific exclusion of a document.[522] Upon registration the right of hypothec comes into existence and the creditor immediately becomes right-holder of the hypothec. This type of hypothec is specifically used for long-term relations where there is no change in creditor to be expected.

The second model of hypothec, the *Sicherungshypothek,* is presented as the exception to the main type of hypothec.[523] However, in fact, the security-hypothec is the purest form of hypothec.[524] The security-hypothec is completely dependent on the existence of the claim. Different from the *Verkehrshypothek,* the security-hypothec must be connected to the owner of the land.[525] Furthermore, the security hypothec will come into existence with the claim and will cease to exist with the claim as well. The security-hypothec is always a *Buchhypothek.*[526]

The right of hypothec, on whichever model, enables the holder of the right to put pressure on the owner to fulfil his duties under the claim. The nature of the right brings with it specific claims the holder of a right of hypothec can initiate, both before and after the owner does not fulfil his duties. In order to safeguard the value of the object the holder of the hypothec is entitled to prevent damage to the object under hypothec.[527] If the object under hypothec is damaged or its condition has become worse in such a way that the security of the holder is in danger, he can require the owner to repair or maintain the object. If the owner does not do so, the right holder will be able to execute his right of hypothec.[528] Furthermore the right holder has a similar possibility to stop others from interfering with the object when the object is damaged or its condition has deteriorated in such a way that the value is affected.[529]

When the owner does not fulfil his duties under the claim the holder of the right of hypothec becomes entitled to execute his right. The execution of the right of hypothec is typically effected through a sale of the object under the rules of execution.[530] In order to do so the holder of the right must present the document proving

520 Schwab & Prütting 2003, p. 315-316.
521 § 1140 BGB, Schwab & Prütting 2003, p. 316.
522 § 1116 (2) BGB, Schwab & Prütting 2003, p. 313.
523 § 1184 *et seq.* BGB.
524 Staudinger & Wolfsteiner 2002, p. 76-77.
525 In case of a *Verkehrshypothek,* it is possible that the owner and the debtor are two different persons, as long as the creditor and the holder of the right are the same person. Schwab & Prütting 2003, p. 358.
526 § 1185 BGB.
527 These actions are also available for damage to any part of the object, which is not the land itself. § 1135 BGB, Baur, Baur & Stürner 1999, p. 472-473.
528 § 1133 BGB.
529 § 1134 BGB.
530 A private sale is prohibited. § 1147 BGB, Baur, Baur & Stürner 1999, p. 467.

his right or refer to the official register in the case of a *Buchhypothek*.[531] In order to prevent the acquisition of the right by a third party during or just after the execution, the owner may claim the document.[532] When the owner repays the holder and therefore fulfils the duty under the claim, the execution will stop. However, when the owner does not pay, the right-holder can execute his right of hypothec through seizure of the immovable object.[533] The holder cannot claim the object for him, he will only be entitled to the proceeds of the object after execution.[534] Furthermore, also in case of insolvency of the owner, the holder of the right of hypothec will have a preferential position in relation to other creditors.[535]

Although the right of hypothec is not used much in practice anymore, two special types should be mentioned that do have relevance for legal practice. The first of these types is the *Höchstbetraghypothek* or maximum-amount-hypothec.[536] This type of hypothec is a security-hypothec, but is valid as long as the maximum amount of the claim connected to the right of hypothec is created. The result of this type of hypothec is that not only the claim underlying the right can change, but also that different claims can be used under the same right.[537] However, in respect of the rest of the right, it is similar to the security hypothec.[538] The second type, the *Gesamthypothek* or combined-hypothec, enables several pieces of land to be used to secure one claim.[539] This special type of hypothec enables several owners to combine forces and secure one claim. However, the danger is that the creditor of the claim can execute his right in respect of any or part of any of the land securing his claim.[540]

3.8. *Grundschuld*

The second type of *Grundpfandrecht* is the right of *Grundschuld*. The right of *Grundschuld* is of Germanic origin and was in force in various countries including Prussia prior to the introduction of the BGB.[541] Different from the right of hypothec, the right of *Grundschuld* is a property security right in respect of an immovable object that is not connected to a claim.[542] The right is therefore a non-accessory right. In practice this non-accessory nature allows parties much more freedom than they

531 § 1160 BGB.
532 § 1144 BGB, Schwab & Prütting 2003, p. 340.
533 § 1147 BGB, Staudinger & Wolfsteiner 2002, p. 47.
534 Also in respect to the right of hypothec German law strictly prohibits the *lex commissoria*. Baur, Baur & Stürner 1999, p. 476.
535 Baur, Baur & Stürner 1999, p. 484-485.
536 § 1190 BGB.
537 Staudinger & Wolfsteiner 2002, p. 78.
538 This type of hypothec is similar to the Dutch trust-*hypotheek*, see Staudinger & Wolfsteiner 2002, p. 13, see Chapter 5; 3.7. Hypothec.
539 § 1132 BGB, Baur, Baur & Stürner 1999, p. 497 *et seq.*, Schwab & Prütting 2003, p. 355.
540 Baur, Baur & Stürner 1999, p. 498.
541 Motive III 1888, p. 605.
542 Baur, Baur & Stürner 1999, p. 505. On the danger of non-accessority in modern finance practice see Clemente 2007, p. 737 *et seq.*

would have in respect to the right of hypothec. Especially the *Sicherungsgrundschuld* or security-*Grundschuld* is widely applied.[543]

The definition of the right in Paragraph 1191 BGB is identical to the definition of the right of hypothec, but without the reference to the claim.[544] Upon registration the parties only need to mention the holder of the right of *Grundschuld*, the amount of money the right represents and, if agreed, the sum of payment.[545] In most other situations the right of *Grundschuld* is similar to the right of hypothec. The provisions on hypothec are, therefore, declared applicable, with the exception of the provisions dealing with the accessority of the right to the claim.[546]

The non-accessory nature of the right has major consequences in practice. The independence from the claim is the main characteristic of the right of *Grundschuld*. The right will not only come into existence without any claim, but will also remain with the creditor if any claim, to which parties attempted to connect the right, ceases.[547] In the past several authors have attempted to include a claim into the right itself, but leading opinion has continued to resist such a development.[548]

Like the right of hypothec, the right of *Grundschuld* can be created as a document-right, *Briefschuld*, or as a register-right, *Buchschuld*. The main advantage of the document-right in the specific situation of a *Grundschuld* is that, since there is no registered claim identifying the creditor, the creditor can remain secret to his competitors. This is achieved by the owner creating a right of *Grundschuld*, then receiving the document and transferring it, without the need for further registration, to the creditor.[549] Also similar to the right of hypothec, the right will be an owner-*Grundschuld* until the owner transfers the document to the creditor, who will become holder of the right from that moment.[550] However, the property right itself will take rank from the moment of its creation.

Two different types of *Grundschuld* are distinguished; the isolated *Grundschuld* and the security-*Grundschuld*. The isolated type, which is not used much, exists in a situation where the right is created without the existence of any claim. This would occur in a situation where the owner wishes to entitle another person to the value of part of his land and not his general set of assets, for example, by way of gift from a parent to a child.[551] This type of *Grundschuld* is completely independent of a claim and will not need a claim in its further existence.[552] The second type is actually the primary type of *Grundschuld*.[553] The use of the right for security purposes is widely applied in practice. It is this right which was the model for the acceptance of the

543 Schwab & Prütting 2003, p. 367.
544 § 1191 BGB.
545 § 1115 BGB.
546 § 1192 BGB, Staudinger & Wolfsteiner 2002, p. 671, Baur, Baur & Stürner 1999, p. 507.
547 § 1163 BGB, Schwab & Prütting 2003, p. 364.
548 Staudinger & Wolfsteiner 2002, p. 675.
549 Baur, Baur & Stürner 1999, p. 507.
550 Baur, Baur & Stürner 1999, p. 507.
551 Baur, Baur & Stürner 1999, p. 507.
552 § 1196 BGB.
553 See Füller 2006, p. 499-500.

different rights to use for security purposes.[554] The security-*Grundschuld* combines the property right with an independent security contract. This independent agreement can be a completely separate agreement, but also part of a larger contract.[555] In effect, the security-*Grundschuld* creates a property right securing a claim. The contract creating or identifying the claim remains independent of the security property right.[556]

Nevertheless, the security contract is not completely independent. The transfer of the right of *Grundschuld* for security purposes in the fulfilment of a security contract with a creditor creates a *Treuhand* relation in the same way as this occurs in case of a transfer of ownership for security purposes.[557] The right-holder is therefore bound as *Treuhänder* in his exercise of the right of *Grundschuld*. Furthermore, the security contract is also under control in case of securing overvalue, i.e., *Übersicherung*, or agreements which are so seriously disadvantageous for the debtor that he can no longer exercise his property right, i.e., *Knebelung*.[558]

The security-*Grundschuld* connects the property right to any claim. This can be a claim against the owner, but also against a third party. Furthermore, the right can be used to secure both current and future claims. In the latter situation there is a strict control over the possibilities. Any future claims of the holder of the right against the owner can be secured, but those against a third party are subject to some more criteria.[559]

In any of these situations the security-contract remains a contract. It will contain the duty to create a right of *Grundschuld* and the duty to transfer the right to the creditor, an agreement on the maximum value the right represents, an agreement on the execution powers of the holder of the right, and an agreement on re-transfer of the right when the claim has been fulfilled.[560] Because the right of *Grundschuld* will not automatically return to the owner upon fulfilment of the claim, an agreement on re-transfer is needed. The owner will have contractual remedies to claim the return of the right of *Grundschuld*.[561] When the owner receives the right of *Grundschuld* he is free to use it again under another security contract. Should the contract fall away, i.e. when it is void or avoided, the owner will have a claim in unjust enrichment against the creditor.[562] Finally, the right of *Grundschuld* is, like the right of hypothec, executed by way of an executionary sale. The *lex commissoria* is also prohibited in respect to the right of *Grundschuld*.[563]

554 The *Sicherungsdienstbarkeiten* and *Sicherungsreallast*, see above; 3.1. Real Servitude, 3.2. Personal Servitudes: usufruct and limited personal servitudes, and 3.5. Real Burden (*Reallast*).

555 Staudinger & Wolfsteiner 2002, p. 677-678.

556 Baur, Baur & Stürner 1999, p. 513.

557 Baur, Baur & Stürner 1999, p. 515, Füller 2006, p. 500-501, BGH NJW 1080, 1732, 1733, see above; 2.4. *Treuhand* Ownership.

558 On these concepts see above; 2.5. Security Ownership, § 1136 BGB. Staudinger & Wolfsteiner 2002, p. 689-691.

559 Baur, Baur & Stürner 1999, p. 516, Staudinger & Wolfsteiner 2002, p. 687.

560 Schwab & Prütting 2003, p. 368, Staudinger & Wolfsteiner 2002, p. 676-677.

561 Baur, Baur & Stürner 1999, p. 519-520.

562 Baur, Baur & Stürner 1999, p. 519.

563 § 1147 BGB, Baur, Baur & Stürner 1999, p. 509.

The security-*Grundschuld* provides legal practice with a very flexible security right. It is not surprising that the right is used far more than the right of hypothec, which is more restricted in the ways it can be used. The security-*Grundschuld* can be used for any type of claim in money, both for current and for future claims. This flexibility allows the right to be used for credit facilities, but also in complicated multi-party financing constructions.[564] The construction of a security-*Grundschuld* enables parties to use a property right for security purposes under terms and conditions on which they are very much free to decide. The conditions that they set will be governed by contract law and therefore also party autonomy exists. It effectively enables parties to leave the strict and limited area of property law and give content to a property relation beyond the scope of property law by entering the law of contract.

4. Borderline Cases in German Property Law

In Section 3 of this chapter the standard set of property rights in German law is dealt with. In the discussion on these various property rights certain other relations have been mentioned that are not a property right, but nevertheless bear many of the same characteristics.[565] Mainly for historical reasons, but also because of current developments in German law, there are some other additional relations that should be examined. Some of these are actual property rights, whereas others are relations that bear so many property characteristics that, although not recognised as such, they might be treated as a property right.[566]

4.1. *Old Property Rights*

The entry into force of the BGB on 1 January 1900 ended most of the fragmentation of law throughout Germany. However, property rights that existed prior to the introduction of the BGB partly remained in force. Article 184 of the *Einführungsgesetz zum Bürgerlichen Gesetzbuche* (EGBGB), or Law Introducing the BGB, provides in one general provision for the continuation of property rights from before the BGB, known as old property rights.[567] The starting point under this Article is the continuation of old property rights, although under certain conditions. Any old right, also those rights that are no longer included in the system of property rights in the BGB, remains in existence and is to be dealt with according to the law under which it was created. For instance, a property right of lease, as was recognised in Prussian law, falls under the Prussian ALR by force of Article 184 EGBGB.[568]

564 See Baur, Baur & Stürner 1999, p. 514.
565 For a general discussion of current developments in German property law see Staudinger et al. 2000, p. 38 *et seq.* and Soergel et al. 2002, p. 56 *et seq.*
566 See Baur, Baur & Stürner 1999, p. 28.
567 Staudinger et al. 1998, p. 774.
568 On lease as a property right in Prussian law see below; 4.4. Lease of Immovable Objects.

The application of the old law specifically also applies to the interpretation of the content of the right.[569] This also includes the relation of the old property right to the right of ownership and the way in which the right burdens the right of ownership. Moreover, also the rank of the right will have remained in existence.[570] Exempted from the continuation under the old law are the rights of hypothec, *Grundschuld*, *superficies* and real servitudes, in other words, those rights for which the BGB provides rules itself. In general, the rules in the BGB are declared applicable to those rights in as far as is possible.[571]

The law on ownership of an apartment in a building or *Stockwerkseigentum* also remained, but the relation between the owners of the building falls under the new law.[572] Furthermore, a normal right of ownership continues under different conditions. From 1 January 1900 the new rules of the BGB apply to as many cases as possible.[573]

Because of the recognition of old property rights, i.e., pre-BGB property rights, in theory, it is possible that a property right from before the introduction of the BGB is still in existence and should be considered as an exceptional right outside the system of the BGB.

4.2. *Pre-Emptive Registration (Vormerkung)*

Vormerkung was mentioned above under the heading of the *Vorkaufrecht* or pre-emptive property right where the *Vormerkung* functions as the vehicle to achieve the effect of the claim of the holder of the pre-emptive right against the third party who enters into a contract of sale with the owner.[574] However, the technique of *Vormerkung* is much wider than its application in case of pre-emptive rights.

The *Vormerkung* is a form of pre-emptive registration of a personal right, usually a claim, against an owner or holder of a property right. The technique of *Vormerkung* was known in the Prussian system before the introduction of the BGB and, although it applied in a wider range of cases, it formed the basis for provisions in the BGB.[575] The BGB deals with the *Vormerkung* in Paragraph 883 BGB:

> (1) In order to secure the claim for the creation or ceasing of a right to a piece of land or of a right burdening a piece of land, or for the alteration of the contents or the rank of such a right, a pre-emptive registration can be made in the registry…
> (2) An act of disposition, which is conducted after the pre-emptive registration, does not have effect insofar as it interferes with the claim. …[576]

569 Staudinger et al. 1998, p. 777.
570 Staudinger et al. 1998, p. 778.
571 For a detailed overview see Staudinger et al. 1998, p. 780 *et seq.*
572 Art. 182 EGBGB, Staudinger et al. 1998, p. 767 *et seq.*
573 Art. 181 EGBGB.
574 See above; 3.4. Expectation Rights: Pre-Emptive Right and Acquisition Right.
575 Staudinger & Gursky 2002, p. 14-15.
576 § 883 BGB, '(1) Zur Sicherung des Anspruchs auf Einräumung oder Aufhebung eines Rechts an einem Grundstück order an einem das Grundstück belastenden Recht oder auf Änderung →

A pre-emptive registration enables the registration of a claim in respect of an immovable object or a property right in respect of an immovable object. Pre-emptive registration for movable objects or rights in respect of movable objects is not possible.[577] The claim that is registered is a personal claim, but can be both a current claim as well as a future claim.[578] The use of pre-emptive registration in German law is very wide. In order for a claim to be suitable for registration it must be made to bring about a change in the legal situation of a property right in respect of an immovable object. Moreover, the claim must concern a change that is suitable for registration, and the claim must be made in respect of a private law situation.[579]

When such a claim is registered through *Vormerkung* Paragraph 883 BGB awards certain effects. After registration the holder of the claim has a stronger position against the owner or holder of a property rights than his personal claim would normally allow. Any act of the owner or holder that interferes with the registered claim will not have effect against the holder of the registered claim.[580] Against the rest of the world any act of the owner or holder of a property right will be valid. A third-party acquirer will therefore acquire ownership in respect to the rest of the world if the owner transfers his ownership contrary to the agreement and to the pre-emptively registered claim of the buyer. However, for the buyer who pre-emptively registered his claim, the old owner is still owner and not the third party. The first buyer can demand from the old owner an *Auflassung*.[581] However, when both the old and new owner, i.e., a third party, have registered their *Auflassung*, the new owner will have been registered as the holder of the right.[582] In that situation, the buyer will not have a right based on his agreement with the old owner against the new owner. In such a situation the buyer can use a claim based on Paragraph 888 BGB that entitles him to claim, after the formalities with the old owner are fulfilled, his registration as the rightful owner. In other words, through *Vormerkung* the claim that is registered is strengthened so that the registered right is granted limited third-party effect.[583]

Furthermore, the claim and the registration are closely connected. If the claim ceases to exist, so will the rights arising from the registration.[584] The connection is so

des Inhalts oder des Ranges eines Solchen Rechts kann eine Vormerkung in das Grundbuch eingetragen werden. … (2) Eine Verfügung, die nach der Eintragung der Vormerkung über das Grundstück oder das Recht getroffen wird, ist insoweit unwirksam, als sie den Anspruch vereiteln oder beeinträchtigen würde …'.

577 Wolf 2005, p. 222.

578 § 883 (1)(2) BGB, Staudinger & Gursky 2002, p. 33.

579 Staudinger & Gursky 2002, p. 25 *et seq.*, Wolf 2005, p. 225.

580 § 883 BGB, Wolf 2005, p. 226.

581 On the concept of *Auflassung* see above in 3.4. Expectation Rights: Pre-Emptive Right and Acquisition Right.

582 This premature registration is known as *Voreintragung* in the registry, not to be confused with the *Vormerkung*. Wolf 2005, p. 227-228.

583 Wolf 2005, p. 226-227.

584 Staudinger & Gursky 2002, p. 22-23.

strong that the term accessory is used.[585] However, the registration will not change the character of the claim. The right is personal and will remain personal. The effect of *Vormerkung* is that the claim can be invoked in such a way that a property act of the owner or right holder is ineffective.

Apart from the function to strengthen a claim as described above, the *Vormerkung* can also be used to secure the rank of a future right. Paragraph 883(3) BGB enables parties to register a future claim with a certain rank that is later replaced by a property right that takes over the rank of the pre-emptively registered claim.[586] Furthermore, in case of insolvency or in case of seizure of the object the pre-emptively registered claim will be treated as if the right for which the claim is registered is already in existence.[587]

In legal practice *Vormerkung* is used to secure many claims, which especially includes registration of the claim to the transfer of the object that follows from a sales agreement.[588] Furthermore, it can also concern the claim for the creation of property rights or the termination of property rights. In case of hypothecs the agreement on the termination of property rights is specifically dealt with in Paragraph 1179 BGB.[589] A holder of a property right can agree with the owner that, when the owner acquires another property right which is equal or higher in rank, the owner will make sure such a property right ceases to exist.[590] In order to secure that claim, a special *Vormerkung* is allowed. Such an agreement is favourable to the holders of other property rights in respect to the same debtor, because with the ceasing of another property right that is equal or higher in rank, their rank is strengthened or even increases.[591]

The nature of the *Vormerkung* has been highly debated.[592] The leading doctrine agrees that a claim itself does not achieve a property status through *Vormerkung*.[593] However, the effects the *Vormerkung* produces closely resemble a property right. The procedure creates a claim that takes effect not just against the other contracting party but also against a third-party acquirer. It therefore entitles the holder of the claim, who is also holder of the registration, to the transfer or alteration of a property right. The concept of *Vormerkung* therefore balances on the line between the law of obligations, specifically contract law, and property law.[594] It is clear that

585 Baur, Baur & Stürner 1999, p. 219, Mülbert 2002, p. 921, Schwab & Prütting 2003, p. 94, Staudinger & Gursky 2002, p. 176, Wolf 2005, p. 223. Very extensive see Mülbert 1997, p. 335 *et seq.*

586 § 883 (3) BGB, Wolf 2005, p. 229, Baur, Baur & Stürner 1999, p. 229-230.

587 § 106 InsO, § 48 ZVG, Wolf 2005, p. 229, Baur, Baur & Stürner 1999, p. 229.

588 Cf. the Dutch '*Vormerkung*' in Article 7:2 BW, see Chapter 5; 4.4. Registration of a Consumer Contract of a Sale of a House.

589 Schwab & Prütting 2003, p. 349, Baur, Baur & Stürner 1999, p. 218, 546 *et seq.*

590 § 1179 BGB, Baur, Baur & Stürner 1999, p. 547.

591 Staudinger & Gursky 2002, p. 17.

592 Baur, Baur & Stürner 1999, p. 232-234, Staudinger & Gursky 2002, p. 172-176, Wilhelm 2002, p. 25.

593 Schwab & Prütting 2003, p. 93, Baur, Baur & Stürner 1999, p. 232, Staudinger & Gursky 2002, p. 23.

594 See Staudinger & Gursky 2002, p. 172.

the drafters of the BGB, although the inclusion of the *Vormerkung* was somewhat complicated, did not intend the *Vormerkung* to be a property right.[595] The *Vormerkung* is a separate method to secure a personal claim with third-party effects.[596]

4.3. *Entitlement to Possession through the Law of Obligations*

The BGB uses a concept of possession that includes both the Roman *possessio* as well as the *detentio*.[597] In other words, German law distinguishes possession between a person who is entitled to the possession, i.e., has power over an object, and he who holds the object through usufruct, pledge or lease and for the duration of that right is entitled to factual power.

In respect to these types of possession, i.e., by way of a limited property right or lease, the owner of the object will have *mittelbarer Besitz*, the holders of property rights will have *unmittelbarer Besitz*.[598] When there is no right to possession in existence, there will only be *unmittelbarer Besitz*. German law also distinguishes *Eigenbesitz* and *Fremdbesitz*.[599] He who holds the object is entitled to possession in the sense of *Eigenbesitz*. However, when such a possessor has to recognise another with a better right to possession, the possession will be a *Fremdbesitz*. The latter is the situation in case of lease where the lessee, *unmittelbarer Fremdbesitzer*, is forced to recognise the possession of the lessor, *mittelbarer Eigenbesitzer*.

The concept of possession in German law, especially the recognition of the *Fremdbesitz*, makes it possible to hold possession through a contract. Although a lease only awards personal rights, the right still entitles the lessee to possession of the object.[600] In respect to movable objects, a personal right that entitles a party to possession achieves certain property characteristics. These property characteristics are awarded on the basis of Paragraph 1007 BGB. This Paragraph awards a claim for the return of possession against the person who took possession away.[601] The claim does not so much flow from the possession, but more from a property right granting possession. Nevertheless, the claim is also available to possessors who are not entitled on the basis of a property right but on the basis of a contract or other personal relation.[602] With this inclusion, German law partly follows the Prussian law

595 This can be seen from the placement in the General part of the Book 3 on property. Mugdan 1979, p. 567, Staudinger & Gursky 2002, p. 173.

596 Wolf 2005, p. 231 writes: '... als Sicherungsmittel eigener Art zur Verwirklichung von Ansprüchen ausgestaltet worden miet einzelnen dingliche Wirkungen'.

597 See Otte 1978, p. 463. On different forms of possession see Chapter 1; 4. Terminology.

598 § 868 BGB, the term *unmittelbarer Besitz* is not used by the BGB, but follows from the definition of *mittelbarer Besitz*, Wieling 2001, p. 43.

599 § 872 BGB, the term *Fremdbesitz* is not used by the BGB, but follows from the definition of *Eigenbesitz*. Wieling 2001, p. 43.

600 This applies for lease of movable as well as immovable objects. On the latter see 1.1. Lease of Immovable Objects.

601 In that respect the claim resembles the *actio Publiciana*. Wieling 2001, p. 205.

602 The Protocols state 'Der Anspruch solle auch dem Miehter, dem Finder usw. zustehen', Mugdan 1979, p. 699. Wieling 2001, p. 206.

from before the introduction of the BGB in which a personal right to possession entitled the holder to a property right.[603]

Paragraph 1007 BGB entitles the possessor who has lost possession to claim the return of the object, unless the current possessor of the object holds in good faith.[604] Furthermore, when the current possessor of the object holds a right of possession himself, e.g., the lessee sublet the object to the current possessor, the claim cannot succeed.[605] Between the current possessor and he who lost his possession a subsidiary legal obligation will come into existence.[606] The obligation will entitle the holder of the personal right who is entitled to possession to claim damages.[607] Finally, Paragraph 1007 BGB will entitle the holder of a claim to separate the object in insolvency of the current possessor and a counter-claim to resist a seizure of a creditor.[608]

A right to possession of a movable object flowing from a personal right therefore entitles the right-holder to claim his possession also against a third party. However, it should be emphasised that the claim based on Paragraph 1007 BGB will succeed if the right-holder has a better right than the person against whom he exercises the claim, but another third party might hold an even better right, for example, the owner.[609] Therefore, there is third-party effect, but not in the sense of a property right.

4.4. *Lease of Immovable Objects*

German law recognises the lease of immovable property as a special right. Although the right, like a lease of movable objects, is a personal right, it bears many characteristics of a property right. The principal characteristic is dealt with in Paragraph 566 BGB, which states:[610]

> If the leased living space, after the lessee has taken up the lease, is transferred to a third party, the acquirer will take the place of the lessor by force of law under the obligations following from the lease for the duration of his ownership.[611]

The Paragraph codifies the maxim that sale does not break a lease.[612] When an agreement is made for the lease of an immovable object, which includes room to

603 Wieling 2001, p. 206.
604 § 1007 BGB.
605 §§ 1007 (3)(2), 986 BGB, Wieling 2001, p. 207, Staudinger & Gursky 1999, p. 601.
606 § 1007 (3)(2) BGB, Wieling 2001, p. 207.
607 Staudinger & Gursky 1999, p. 605.
608 § 771 ZPO, Staudinger & Gursky 1999, p. 595, Wieling 2001, p. 208.
609 Staudinger & Gursky 1999, p. 594-595.
610 Since 1 January 2001 this Paragraph contains the 'sale does not break lease' maxim. Before 2001 this subject was dealt with in Para. 571 BGB.
611 § 566 BGB, 'Wird der vermietete Wohnraum nach der Überlassung an den Mieter von dem Vermieter an einen Dritten veräußert, so tritt der Erwerber anstelle des Vermieters in die sich während der Dauer seiner Eigentums aus dem Mietverhältnis ergebenden Rechte und Pflichten ein'.
612 In German *Kauf bricht nicht Miete*, see Schön 2001, p. 119-120.

live in, but also land, parts of land or parts of buildings, a personal relation arises between lessee and lessor.[613] However, by force of Paragraph 566 BGB, the personal relation will transfer to a new owner in case the old owner transfers his right of ownership on the object to someone else. In other words, in specific situations the right of the lessee has effect against a third party.

The maxim that sale does not break a lease is not entirely accurate, since in German law it is not a sale which 'breaks' a lease, but a transfer. The rule of Paragraph 566 BGB will also apply when a transfer occurs for another cause other than sale, for example, a gift.[614] Furthermore, the right of lease will also be effective in the insolvency of the owner or the seizure of the object by a creditor. Any person dealing with the object or acquiring the object will also have to respect the lease.[615]

The recognition of the third-party effect of a lease agreement has given rise to a debate on the nature of the right. The debate already started before the introduction of the BGB. The maxim that a sale does not break a lease came from Germanic law.[616] In the Prussian ALR a general rule stated:

> When he who has a personal right to an object is entitled by that right to possession, a property right in respect of the object comes into existence.[617]

In Prussian law, as well as in current German law, lease of an immovable object entitles the lessee to possession. In Prussian law this made the right of lease a property right that would also have effect against the acquirer of the ownership of the object under lease.[618] However, the right of lease did not need to be registered.[619] The First Commission mainly based its draft of the BGB on Roman law. In Roman law, lease was a personal right and a transfer of ownership therefore did not force the new owner to deal with the lessee and allowed the new owner to evict him.[620] In other words, in the first draft of the BGB a lease was as a purely personal right.[621] However, lease as a property right was reality in Prussia, and under severe criticism from legal practice the Second Commission included a compromise in the provision of Paragraph 566 BGB.[622] However, the lease itself remained a personal right, not suitable for registration.

613 Staudinger, Emmerich & Rolfs 2003, p. 61-62, Baur, Baur & Stürner 1999, p. 349, Wilhelm 2002, p. 26.
614 Schön 2001, p. 119.
615 §§ 108, 110 and 111 InsO, Baur, Baur & Stürner 1999, p. 350.
616 See Otte 1978, p. 463 *et seq.*
617 § 135 ALR I. 2. 'wenn demjenigen, der ein persönliches Recht zu einer Sache hat, der Besitz derselben auf den Grund dieses Rechtes eingeräumt wird, so entsteht dadurch ein dingliches Recht auf die Sache'. Wieling 2001, p. 205, Wieling 2003, p. 201.
618 Wieling 2003, p. 202, Staudinger, Emmerich & Rolfs 2003, p. 59, Otte 1978, p. 464.
619 Wieling 2003, p. 203, Otte 1978, p. 471-472.
620 Wieling 2003, p. 205-206.
621 Wieling 2003, p. 207, Staudinger, Emmerich & Rolfs 2003, p. 59.
622 Wieling 2003, p. 209, Staudinger, Emmerich & Rolfs 2003, p. 60.

Since the introduction of the BGB several authors have tried to argue for the re-introduction of the lease as a property right and for its wider application.[623] The courts have, until now, followed a strict line restricting the application of Paragraph 566 BGB to leases.[624] The courts continue to characterise the lease as a personal right with an extraordinary protection provided by Paragraph 566 BGB.[625]

The lessee is under even more protection than just Paragraph 566 BGB. The lease awards the lessee possession, the importance of which should not be underestimated. First, if the lessee is interrupted in his possession or his use of the object, this can lead to a claim in tort following from Paragraph 823 BGB.[626] Doctrinally it is not the lease, but the possession which entitles the lessee to the claim.[627] Secondly, although the lessee only has a personal right, he is entitled to a counter-claim to stop the seizure of the object by a creditor of the lessor.[628] Thirdly, and even more important, the possession of the lessee entitles him to the possessory claims in order to protect his possession. When another takes the possession from the lessee, the lessee will, through Paragraph 861 BGB, have a claim for a return of the possession.[629] However, this claim will not entitle the lessee to claim use of the object or compensation. Furthermore, the lessee may also use a claim as laid down in Paragraph 862 BGB. When the lessee does not lose his possession, but his possession is interfered with, in whatever way, the lessee can use this claim against the person interfering with his possession to stop the interference.[630] Even more, the BGH also admitted a claim based on Paragraph 1007 BGB, albeit by analogy, since Paragraph 1007 BGB is restricted to movable objects.[631]

The recognition of the possession of the lessee or any other possession of an object through a personal right therefore awards the personal right property characteristics.[632] The right of lease breaks with the system of property law, especially since third party effect is awarded although the right of lease is not registered. A registered right concluded later than a lease will therefore come after the lease.[633] Primarily based on these arguments, Wieling has argued for the recognition of lease

623 For an overview see Schön 2001, p. 120 *et seq.*

624 This includes lease of a building or of land, in German classified as *Miete* and *Pacht*, RG LZ 1921, S. 414, Schön 2001, p. 120.

625 Wilhelm 2002, p. 27.

626 RGZ 54, 233 *et seq.*, Baur, Baur & Stürner 1999, p. 346, Wieling 2003, p. 214-215, Wilhelm 2002, p. 26, Otte 1978, p. 467 *et seq.*

627 Baur, Baur & Stürner 1999, p. 346.

628 § 771 ZPO, Wilhelm 2002, p. 26.

629 § 861 BGB, Wieling 2001, p. 65-66.

630 § 862 BGB, Baur, Baur & Stürner 1999, p. 345-346, Wieling 2001, p. 66-68, Otte 1978, p. 465.

631 BGH 25 September 1952, BGHZ 7, 208 *et seq.*, Otte 1978, p. 466, Wilhelm 2002, p. 26.

632 Such rights are known as *verdinglichte Rechte*, see Dulckeit 1951, Canaris 1978, Weitnauer 1983, Wieling 2003. A similar discussion is held in English law in respect to bailment of chattels. Also a bailment might entitle to possession, but this does not make bailment itself a property right. See Chapter 6; 3.2. Leases / Bailment?

633 Schön 2001, p. 127.

as a property right.[634] However, in the system of German property rights, the lease remains a personal right.

4.5. *Treuhand Bank Account*

German law recognises three types of *Treuhand;* the transfer-*Treuhand* or *Übertragungstreuhand,* the acquisition-*Treuhand* or *Erwerbstreuhand,* and the agreement-*Treuhand* or *Vereinbarungstreuhand.*[635] These three types differ in the way in which the *Treuhand* originates. The transfer-*Treuhand* was the first type that was recognised. The transfer-*Treuhand* is created through a transfer of an object under agreement that the transferee will hold the object for the transferor. Its basic characteristics and main application in practice, i.e., *Sicherungstreuhand,* have already been dealt with under the heading of *Treuhand*-ownership.[636] The second type of *Treuhand* is created when a person receives an object from a third party which he agrees to hold for another. These two types are not as problematic as the third type, in which the *Treuhänder* agrees to hold assets that he already holds for the benefit of a *Treugeber.* In other words, the creation of the last type of *Treuhand* does not require a transfer.

The *Treuhand* is a concept widely applied in German law. The transfer-*Treuhand* is mostly used in respect to corporeal objects, but the other two types of *Treuhand* are mainly used in respect to claims and money. The *Treuhand* for claims and money is usually a receive-*Treuhand* and creates what is known as a *Treuhandkonto* or *Treuhand* bank account. The *Treuhänder* agrees to receive money on a separate account for the fulfilment of claims of the *Treugeber.* The claims are paid by third parties.[637] The *Treuhandkonto* is part of the development of the *Treuhand* as a general device for the management of objects. The inclusion of incorporeal objects, i.e., claims and money, enables a wide variety of applications. The inclusion of such objects under a *Treuhand* is possible because a *Treuhand* is a contract with some specific third-party effect.[638] In practice, the *Treuhandkonto* is widely used to protect money by making a separate account, for example, for the payment of a lease or a client's fund for advocates.

A *Treuhand* is mainly a contract, which results in the applicability of contract law. However, if an object is transferred and the parties agree in the contract in what way the *Treuhänder* will deal with those objects, the *Treugeber* will not only have a personal right against the *Treuhänder,* but also a claim for the objects in case of insolvency of the *Treuhänder.*[639] The *Treuhand* therefore consists of two elements; a contract, and what is called a quasi-property right. The contract will set out the content of the relation between the parties, whereas the latter will entitle the enforce-

634 Wieling 2003, p. 212, see also Otte, Otte 1978, p. 474-475, Hattenhauer 1989, p. 100-101, different see Hess 1998, p. 504-505.

635 Schmidt 2005, p. 936-937.

636 See above; 2.4. *Treuhand* Ownership.

637 Ganter 2004, p. 253.

638 Ganter 2004, p. 260.

639 BGH NJW 2002, 3414, § 47 InsO, Ganter 2004, 253.

ment of that relation against third parties.[640] As long as the *Treuhänder* keeps the *Treuhand* objects separated from his private assets, the *Treugeber* will have a claim for the objects in case of insolvency. However, when the objects are mixed the claim can no longer succeed.[641]

A *Treuhandkonto* can also be created under the third type of *Treuhand*, the agreement-*Treuhand* or *Vereinbarungstreuhand*. However, in such a case no objects have been transferred, but the parties attempt to create a *Treuhand* relation by mere agreement.[642] Such an attempt is recognised as a *Treuhand* but will not entitle the *Treugeber* to a claim to separate the assets in case of insolvency of the *Treuhänder*.[643] The transfer of assets is considered a principal criterion for the quasi-property right side of the *Treuhand* and is therefore not awarded to a *Treuhand* created without a transfer.[644]

5. A *Numerus Clausus* in German Property Law?

As a result of the influence of the Historical School the BGB is *Pandektenrecht* at its best. The influence of Roman law is visible in every area, but especially in property law. The solutions that were implemented are not always pure Roman law; the Historical School also developed Roman law and adapted it to modern conditions.[645] Under the heavy influence of Von Savigny's system, the BGB was founded on a separation between the law of property and the law of obligations. In this system each of these areas fulfils an independent function.[646] The system of the BGB was intended to break with the tradition of civil codes under influence of natural law theory, in which ownership could rest on everything, objects and rights, and in which the separation between the law of property and the law of obligations did not exist. The BGB deviated strongly from those systems, especially from the Prussian ALR.[647]

The First Commission on the BGB restricted property rights to corporeal objects, with the exception of the rights of usufruct and pledge, which can also be created on rights, and in no more than three pages, justified the separate and independent position of property law.[648] In German law the right of ownership is absolute and unitary. The right of ownership is the paramount right a person can have in a corporeal object. In order to protect this right of ownership and to guarantee its absolute nature, the German property law system restricts other property

640 Ganter 2004, p. 262-263.
641 BGH 12 December 2003, NJW 2004, 954, Schmidt 2005, p. 960-961.
642 In terms of English law this would be a declaration of trust. See Swadling 2000a, p. 280.
643 Ganter 2004, p. 259-260.
644 Critically to this lack of protection for the *Treugeber*, see Schmidt 2005, p. 954-958.
645 Cf. Von Savigny's System of *Current* Roman Law, Von Savigny 1981.
646 Von Savigny 1981, p. 374 *et seq.*, Staudinger et al. 2000, p. 7, Wiegand 1987, p. 630, Wiegand 1990, p. 133, Wiegand 1999a, p. 115 *et seq.*, Füller 2006, p. 8-13. Not as in French law where the law of obligations is dealt with in order to support property law. See Chapter 3; 1. Introduction.
647 Motive III 1888, p. 2-3.
648 Motive III 1888, p. 1-3, Wiegand 1999a, p. 107 *et seq.*, Füller 2006, p. 10-11.

rights. Such other property rights are possible, but these function, in contrast with the Prussian ALR, in a closed system. Furthermore, the First Commission made it very clear that a property right other than ownership can never be a right of ownership.[649]

The property rights other than the right of ownership function in a closed system or *numerus clausus* of property rights.[650] Doctrine expresses *numerus clausus* in two ways, which, although not generally recognised as such in the *Motive*, form the foundation for the doctrine of *numerus clausus* in German law.[651] Contrary to the law of contract where party autonomy is the starting point, the law of property is characterised by a severe limitation on party autonomy. Parties are not free to give content to their relation in the way they desire. First of all, parties must choose one of the available property rights if they wish to give a property effect, i.e., third-party effect, to their relation. German doctrine uses the term *Typenzwang* for this part of the *numerus clausus*.[652] Secondly, when the parties choose a property right, they are bound by the content the law prescribes for that property right. In other words, parties are also not free to decide on the content of their chosen relation. A property right to which parties attempt to give a content it cannot have, will not be a property right. German doctrine uses the term *Typenfixierung* for this latter concept.[653]

Especially in respect to *Typenfixierung*, party autonomy is limited but not absent.[654] The *Typenfixierung* should be understood in the sense that parties can give content to their relation within the boundaries set by law. For example, a right of real servitude cannot comprise a positive duty as a primary duty. Although parties can agree on the content of their relation, for example, a right to walk over a specific area of another's land in exchange for the payment of a price, they cannot agree on a positive duty. The effect of the *Typenfixierung* is that such a right containing a positive duty will be a contract and will therefore lack third-party effect. However, within the limits of the property right, parties are free to decide.[655] What these limits are will depend on the nature of the property right.[656]

The *numerus clausus* should be seen in relation to the absolute and unitary right of ownership.[657] The specific refusal of the system to recognise fragmented ownership is strengthened by the recognition of a limited set of property rights other than ownership which burden the powers of the owner.[658] The connection

649 Motive III 1888, p. 3, Wiegand 1990, p. 117, Füller 2006, p. 367-378.

650 See Füller 2006, p. 370.

651 Staudinger et al. 2000, p. 24.

652 Baur, Baur & Stürner 1999, p. 3, Schwab & Prütting 2003, p. 9, Wilhelm 2002, p. 5, Staudinger et al. 2000, p. 24, Füller 2006, p. 371.

653 Baur, Baur & Stürner 1999, p. 3, Schwab & Prütting 2003, p. 9-10, Wilhelm 2002, p. 5-6, Füller 2006, p. 371-372, critically on the recognition of a separate *Typenfixierung* from the *Typenzwang* see Staudinger et al. 2000, p. 24.

654 Seiler emphasises that the *Motive* should not be read to strictly regarding the lack of party autonomy in property law, see Staudinger et al. 2000, p. 25, Motive III 1888, p. 3.

655 Staudinger et al. 2000, p. 25, Schwab & Prütting 2003, p. 9-10.

656 See, *inter alia*, Hess 1998, p. 508 *et seq.*

657 See also Füller 2006, p. 367-381.

658 Johow 1982, p. 126, Wiegand 1987, p. 635, 638.

between the two is very clear. Recognising a fragmentation of ownership would make a restriction of the other property rights less useful, recognising a fully open system of property right other than ownership would make a unitary right of ownership less useful. Also the recognition of a property right, not as a part of the right of ownership, but as a separate right limiting the powers of the owner, should be understood as a method to safeguard the absolute and unitary concept of ownership.[659]

Furthermore, recognising a limited category of property rights enables objects to remain relatively free and transferable. The intention of the German legislator to limit the possibilities for restriction of the transferability of objects should not be underestimated. Wiegand has emphasised that the German system of private law in the nineteenth century was primarily intended to stimulate the economy through an efficient and clear transfer system.[660] The *numerus clausus* of property rights in German law should certainly also be understood as a method to restrict the number of possible burdens that could be imposed on an object in order to make it as freely transferable as possible.[661] Moreover, the limited number of property rights also restricts the possibilities for an owner to keep his objects from his creditors. In the law of insolvency, the starting point is the possibility for the creditors to execute their claims on the full set of assets of the owner. Only the holder of a property right might have a right to separate the object, in order to take it outside the set of assets of the owner, or such holder may have a preferential position in relation to the other creditors. Neither in the *Motive*, nor in the BGB itself, are these reasons explicitly mentioned.[662] Nevertheless, Wiegand, as well as Füller, has shown that Paragraph 137 BGB, which was originally intended for the third book on Property law, fulfils these functions as the main protector of the *numerus clausus*.[663] This Paragraph prohibits parties from limiting the powers of the owner with property effect, other than those limitations, i.e., property rights, recognised by law.

Prussian law recognised the possibility to restrict the powers of the owner by contract but with effect against third parties.[664] Wiegand emphasises that Paragraph 137 BGB should be read as a reaction against the Prussian ALR, and a protection of the unitary nature of the right of ownership, as well as securing the independent position and closed nature of the law of property.[665] Secondly, Paragraph 137 BGB also limits the powers of the owner to take his objects outside the reach of his

659 On the relation between ownership and property rights other than ownership see above; 3. Other Property Rights.

660 The system as such was known as *Verkehrsrecht,* Wiegand 1990, p. 118-119, Wiegand 1999a, p. 113. See also Füller 2006, p. 558-559.

661 Füller 2006, p. 394-397.

662 Staudinger et al. 2000, p. 24.

663 Liebs 1975, p. 15, Wiegand 1987, p. 637 *et seq.*, Wiegand 1990, p. 118, Hattenhauer 1989, p. 91, Füller 2006, p. 384-386.

664 Liebs 1975, p. 13.

665 Wiegand 1990, p. 118. See also Füller 2006, p. 559.

creditors.[666] In this last sense, Paragraph 137 BGB ensures the transferability of the object and the good functioning of the law of insolvency.[667]

The choice made by the drafters of the BGB for the *numerus clausus* of property rights as well as the distinction between the law of obligations and the law of property has come under heavy criticism.[668] The Germanic law, especially Prussian law, had not known such a closed system, or such a sharp distinction between contract and property. The choice of the First Commission was therefore criticised as a choice that would result in a discontinuation of the development of property law as well as of the development of the law in general.[669]

However, recognising a closed system of property rights does not necessarily result in an absolutely closed list of property rights. Unlike other civil law property systems, German doctrine does not consider the list closed in an absolute sense at all.[670] To the contrary, the system of the BGB, as it was intended to facilitate the economy by referring to the maximum unburdened transferability of objects, does not restrict the development and recognition of new property relations.[671] German doctrine focuses on the *numerus clausus* as a limitation of party autonomy - it is not for parties themselves to create new property relations. However, legislation and case law are not restricted to adapt the system of property law to modern developments.[672]

Several new property rights have been recognised since the entry into force of the BGB in 1900. These developments concern both the right of ownership and property rights other than ownership. First of all, the *Wohnungseigentumsgesetz* (WEG) introduced a new type of ownership that could be limited in content by contract as well as by the community of owners, deviating from the protection of Paragraph 137 BGB.[673] Secondly, case law also limited the rights of the owner in a *Treuhand* situation. The primary example of such limitation was developed in the case of a transfer of ownership for security purposes, which creates *Sicherungseigentum*.[674] In the case of a transfer of ownership creating a *Treuhand*, the right of ownership is limited by contract, in the case of security ownership in such a way that it is difficult to characterise the right that results as ownership under Paragraph 903 BGB.[675] Furthermore, the development of the *Treuhand* by case law should also be

666 Wiegand 1990, p. 118.

667 Or the well functioning of the *Verkehrsrecht*, see Wiegand 1990, p. 119. This application of § 137 BGB should be compared to the function of Art. 3:84(3) BW in Dutch law. See Chapter 5; 5. A *Numerus Clausus* in Dutch Property Law?

668 Wiegand 1999a, p. 114-115.

669 Especially Von Gierke had fierce comments on the draft of the BGB, see, *inter alia*, Von Gierke 1889, p. 281 *et seq.*, see also Fuchs 1889, p. 71-75. Wiegand 1999a, p. 114, note 18, Pfenning 1997, p. 156 *et seq.*

670 Cf. The Netherlands, where the *numerus clausus* is considered an absolutely closed list.

671 Canaris 1978, p. 376, Liebs 1975, p. 26, Wiegand 1987, p. 640, Staudinger et al. 2000, p. 24.

672 Canaris 1978, p. 376, Wiegand 1987, p. 640-641, Wiegand 1999a, p. 115, Schwab, 2003, p. 10, 187.

673 See above; 2.3. Ownership of an Apartment, Staudinger et al. 2000, p. 27.

674 See above; 2.5. Security Ownership.

675 Staudinger et al. 2000, p. 27.

seen in the recognition of a property relation other than ownership. The *Treuhand* of claims and money, especially in case of a *Treuhandkonto*, also creates a protected position for the *Treugeber* which closely resembles a property right.[676] The possession of movable property through a contractual relation and the lease of immovable property should be mentioned as property-like rights.[677]

Finally, perhaps the best example of the enlargement of the available property rights is offered through the recognition of the *Anwartschaftsrechte*.[678] The *Anwartschaftsrechte* awards a property-like position to the person who expects to acquire a right and who is awarded extra protection by the BGB already. These acquisition rights were recognised by case law and developed into a new property right, although the subject remains controversial.[679]

Besides the recognition of new property relations, the development of German law since the entry into force of the BGB should also be seen in the relation between the law of obligations and the law of property.[680] Already the criticism of the draft BGB concerned the sharp distinction between the law of obligations and the law of property. Traditionally, neither Germanic law nor the Prussian ALR had adhered to such a strict separation.[681] Already the BGB of 1900 itself was forced to accept a certain influence of contract law as a means to transfer and create property rights.[682] The sharp separation between the two was difficult to maintain. The development of German private law after the introduction of the BGB shows a development towards a less strict separation in contract law as well as in property law.

In the area of property law there is an increasing influence of contract law, described by doctrine as an *Obligatoriserung der dinglichen Rechte*.[683] The influence of contract law in property law is twofold. First, contracts are used to explain the relation between the current holder of a property right and the current owner of the object the property right burdens. By way of a subsidiary legal obligation German law justifies the applicability of certain contractual or delictual remedies. The recognition of these legal obligations in case of real servitudes and real burdens should not be underestimated. The existence of the obligation enables the current holder of the right to claim performance of the duties and compensation for non-performance of the current owner.[684]

Secondly, and perhaps most interesting, contract law is also used to achieve what cannot be achieved by property law, i.e., it enables parties to work around the *Typenfixierung*. The development and recognition of the *Sicherungsgrundschuld* is the best example. A security-contract is used to create a right of *Grundschuld* on a claim,

676 See above; 4.5. *Treuhand* Bank Account.

677 See above; 4.3. Entitlement to Possession through the Law of Obligations and 4.4. Lease of Immovable Objects.

678 See above; 3.4. Expectation Rights: Pre-Emptive Right and Acquisition Right.

679 Staudinger et al. 2000, p. 27-28.

680 See Füller 2006, p 526 *et seq.*

681 Wiegand 1999a, p. 115.

682 Fuchs 1889, p. 79 *et seq.*, Staudinger et al. 2000, p. 43-44.

683 Hattenhauer 1989, p. 100, Wiegand 1990, p. 133, Wiegand 1999a, p. 118-119, Füller 2006, p. 560.

684 Staudinger et al. 2000, p. 44-45.

but, because of its effect in property law, it will still enable the right-holder to enjoy the benefits of a *Grundschuld* over a hypothec. It is this security-*Grundschuld* that has been the model for security-servitudes and security-usufructs. Especially in case of security-servitudes, the combination of contract and property creates a positive burden, which is contrary to the property law requirements concerning servitudes, with quasi-property effect.[685]

Also in the area of contract law as such, there is a development towards property law. Parties attempt to create a contractual relation with property effect. This process is described by doctrine as *Verdinglichung obligatorischer Rechte*.[686] To a certain extent German property law also facilitates property effect of contractual relations through *Vormerkung*. Although *Vormerkung* itself does not create a property right, it enables the holder of a personal right to invoke his right against a third party as if such a person was holding a property right.[687] Secondly, the increasing influence of the law of property on the law of contract should also be seen in relation to the *Treuhand*. A *Treuhand* enables a *Treugeber* to limit the powers of the *Treuhänder* by contract with effect against third parties, especially in case of insolvency of the *Treuhänder*.[688] However, doctrinally the *Treuhand* remains a contract.[689] Thirdly, a personal right that entitles the holder to possession of an object is also awarded a property-like status. The clearest example of such a situation is a lease. If the lease concerns movable objects, the lessee, i.e., the holder of the right of lease, is awarded a right to possession that he can, in case the possession is lost or interfered with, enforce against third parties. When the lease concerns an immovable object, the lessee is awarded extra protection through Paragraph 566 BGB, which entitles the lessee to assert his right against a new owner in case the old owner transfers his ownership. Nevertheless, a lease remains a contract, but a holder of a lease can claim his right against more than just the lessor.

Wiegand, based on the *Motive* and texts of Johow, who drafted the parts on property law, argues that it was the intention of the legislator to create a system of law that would facilitate the economy.[690] He argues that the criticism of the abstract and autonomous property law has partly proven itself to be correct.[691] Wiegand sees the development of property law after the entry into force of the BGB as a materialisation, i.e., as opposed to abstracting from reality, and a mixing of property and contract.[692]

As early as 1930, Heck emphasised that the choice of the legislator for a closed system might not have been the best choice.[693] He emphasises the richness of property rights in Germanic law and states that if a property right is seen as a tree

685 Staudinger et al. 2000, p. 27, see above; 3.8. *Grundschuld*.
686 Dulckeit 1951, 7 *et seq.*, Canaris 1978, p. 371 *et seq.*, Weitnauer 1983, p. 705 *et seq.*
687 Schwab & Prütting 2003, p. 93, Baur, Baur & Stürner 1999, p. 232, Staudinger & Gursky 2002, p. 23.
688 See above; 4.5. *Treuhand* Bank Account.
689 Ganter 2004, p. 260.
690 Wiegand 1987, p. 640, Wiegand 1990, p. 133-134, Wiegand 1999a, p. 115,
691 Wiegand 1990, p. 133-134. See also Füller 2006, p. 526 *et seq.*
692 Wiegand 1990, p. 134.
693 Heck 1930, p. 84-87.

resting on the land that is ownership, Germany was a rich and dense forest before the introduction of the BGB.[694] The restriction of the number of property rights to the Roman categories, complemented with the Germanic pre-emptive right, real burden and *Grundschuld*, has severely cut the forest away and left only a few trees standing.[695] Even more, the pre-emptive right was adapted to fit in the Roman system of property rights and the right of *Grundschuld* was considered a less useful right than the Roman right of *hypothec*.

It is not surprising that the developments in the law of property have come from its Germanic origins. First, the Prussian ALR, which adhered to an open system of property rights, has proven itself to be very influential, even after it was replaced by the BGB.[696] Although the Prussian system of property rights conflicts with the strict Roman system of property rights, the developments in German property law described in this chapter all share a Germanic and often also a Prussian origin. Therefore, modern developments often create doctrinal problems. Already in the *Motive* of the BGB itself, the influence of the Prussian ALR is immanent. The discussion on the possibility of the combination of a holder of a property right and an owner of the same object, especially in the case of a right of hypothec, directly follows from Prussian law.[697] The *Motive* explain the economic relevance of such a possibility and leave legal science to deal with the doctrinal justification.[698] Secondly, the acceptance of the right of *Grundschuld* should be seen as a compromise between the north of Germany, where the right of hypothec was used, and the south, i.e., Prussia, which used the right of *Grundschuld*.[699] However, a non-accessory security right clearly breaks with the Roman system of pledge and hypothec. Thirdly, the *Vormerkung*, which enables a limited third-party effect of a personal right, was also known to the Prussian ALR.[700] The *Vormerkung* in the ALR gave the holder of a registered personal right a stronger position since it resulted in a claim against a third party as well.[701] The current BGB saw the *Vormerkung* as a mixture between the law of obligations and the law of property and took away the claim, which returned in the form of Paragraph 899 BGB, and therefore outside the scope of pre-emptive registration, in order to deprive the *Vormerkung* of its main proprietary characteristics.[702]

694 Although Heck also states that the forest was a *Mischwald* comprising many different types of rights, Heck 1930, p. 85.

695 Although the Motive consider the right of *Superficies* a Germanic right, Roman law knew a very similar right and the *Erbbaurecht* should not be considered to be purely Germanic, nor as purely Roman. Motive III 1888, p. 2-3.

696 § 135 ALR, Wieling 2001, p. 205, note 2, Heck 1930, p. 86, Wiegand 1990, p. 114.

697 §§ 52, 63-66 ALR, Motive III 1888, p. 201, Baur, Baur & Stürner 1999, p. 408 *et seq.*, Staudinger & Wolfsteiner 2002, p. 61 *et seq.*

698 Motive III 1888, p. 205, more on this subject above in 3. Other Property Rights.

699 Motive III 1888, p. 604-612, Wolff & Raiser 1957, p. 521-522, Staudinger & Wolfsteiner 2002, p. 12-14.

700 However, it should be emphasised that also other Germanic legal systems used the *Vormerkung*, Staudinger & Gursky 2002, p. 14-15.

701 Staudinger & Gursky 2002, p. 14.

702 Motive III 1888, p. 239 *et seq.*, Staudinger & Gursky 2002, p. 14-15.

Furthermore, the developments after the entry into force of the BGB should also be seen in the light of the influence of Germanic law and the Prussian ALR. This includes the position of a lessee in relation to the lessor. The maxim that sale does not break a lease is commonly interpreted as a deviation from the classical Roman system in favour of the Prussian system.[703]

The influence of Germanic, non-Prussian, law itself should not be underestimated. It is this law that formed the basis for the recognition of the acquisition rights. Although Roman law knew situations in which a person expecting to acquire a property right had some extra protection, the distinction in ownership and a property right to the expectation of ownership is Germanic.[704] The acquisition right was as such not unknown to the Prussian system, but should be seen as a general Germanic concept.[705]

Furthermore, the *Treuhand* also originates party in Germanic law. Although the *Treuhand* in the sense of a transfer of ownership for security purposes also resembles the Roman *fiducia cum creditore*, and also the influence of the Roman *fiducia cum amico* is recognised, the Germanic roots that enable the restriction of the powers of a right-holder with third-party effect are part of the current *Treuhand*.[706] The development in which a personal right is awarded limited third-party effect as such also fits the Prussian ALR.

The development of property law is especially characterised by an increasing influence of contract law in the law of property. Wiegand emphasises that this should be seen as a result of a less strict approach towards the independence and autonomy of the law of property.[707] In fact, he proposes to use the law of contract, specifically party autonomy, to develop the law of property insofar as the rights of third parties and the general interest does not object to such a development.[708]

Wiegand argues for the recognition of property-like rights as property rights. He mentions *Treuhand*-ownership as a specific example. A right of ownership of which the powers are limited in such a way that the right can no longer be defined as absolute and complete ownership under Paragraph 903 BGB should be recognised as a separate right of ownership.[709] Along the same lines Hess argues in favour of allowing any party agreement that falls within the nature of a property right and the legal system as a whole, or the *gesamtgesetzlichen Leitbild*, as an agreement with third-party effect.[710] Such a development could put a stop to the doctrinal difficulties with property-like rights in which doctrine recognises limited property effects only in case of certain contracts.

703 Schön 2001, p. 119-120, Wieling 2003, p. 202, Staudinger, Emmerich & Rolfs 2003, p. 59, Otte 1978, p. 464.

704 Sponer 1965, p. 20 *et seq.*

705 Sponer 1965, p. 28, Heck 1930, p. 449.

706 Enneccerus & Nipperdey 1960, p. 921 *et seq.*, Schulze 1967, p. 1 *et seq.*

707 Wiegand 1990, p. 134. See also Füller 2006, p. 558-560.

708 Wiegand states: 'Der Parteiwille und die Gestaltungsfreiheit haben Vorrang vor der Autonomie des Sachenrechts, sofern und soweit nicht schützwerte Dritt - oder höherwertige Allgemeininteressen entgegenstehen', Wiegand 1990, p. 134-135.

709 Wiegand 1990, p. 136-137.

710 Hess 1998, p. 513-515.

Finally, perhaps the function the law of obligations fulfils at the moment should be maintained. The way in which obligations and contracts are used to create what cannot be created under property law, as it is seen in doctrinal legal thinking, resembles the development of praetorian law in Roman law and the development of equity in English law. Specifically the acquisition rights show a development in this direction. The *Anwartschaftsrecht* entitling the acquisition of ownership is modelled on the right of ownership. In fact, it is so much like a right of ownership that the claims the owner can use are also available to the right-holder. Strauch has argued that the situation very closely resembles a situation of *duplex dominium*.[711] The same could be said for *Treuhand*-ownership of the *Treuhänder* in relation to the rights of the *Treugeber*. Strauch's argument is interesting because it attempts to justify deviations from the Roman system of private law, specifically property law, within the system itself. After all, in Roman law also he who could not have ownership under Quiritian law, could still have bonitary ownership through the Praetor's jurisdiction.[712]

German law should therefore be studied closely as one of the leading civil law systems. Its complicated and compromising nature deserves to be understood. The consequences of the many compromises German law has made between Roman law and Germanic law create many doctrinal problems. The possibility to have a property right and ownership at the same time in the same object is perhaps the best example. When German law is subsequently used as a model that could be applied in other civil law systems, for instance, in a European legislative project, this may cause unexpected and serious consequences, especially if that civil law system or legislative project does not share with German law its compromising nature leading to a mixture of Germanic and Roman principles.[713]

711 Strauch 1984, p. 288, Hattenhauer 1989, p. 83 *et seq.*

712 On bonitary or Praetorian ownership see Kaser & Wubbe 1971, p. 135, Chapter 2; 2.3. Ownership. Also in respect to pre-emptive property rights, a close resemblance to the option to purchase in English law can be made. On this see Chapter 7; 2.6. Lesser Rights Used to Acquire a Certain Legal Position (Anticipatory Rights).

713 In case of the property right in respect of the own object this would include a serious deviation from the system of property rights in e.g. France and the Netherlands. See Chapter 3; 3. Other Property Rights, and Chapter 5; 3. Other Property Rights. On the European initiatives see Chapter 8; 2.1.3. European Commission Initiatives for Future Legislation.

Chapter 5

DUTCH LAW

1. Introduction

The law of the Netherlands holds a special and separate place amongst the civil law systems in Europe.[1] With the introduction of a major part of the new code in 1992, the Dutch legal system combines elements from both the French and the German legal systems. Dutch law has not always been in this special position. The specific nature of Dutch law in relation to French and German law, but also English law, is a result of its historical development. Therefore, before this chapter proceeds to deal with modern Dutch law, some remarks about its history and development have to be made.

Before the French Revolution, which reached the Netherlands in 1795, the Netherlands was internally divided into several states with a large diversity of law.[2] The primary source of law was customary law, supplemented by Roman law when necessary.[3] Specifically the law of the province of Holland, the *Rooms Hollands recht*, confusingly translated as 'Roman-Dutch law', was very influential.[4] Moreover, there was a strong influence from the natural law school because of the influence of Grotius.[5] In 1806, after France had gained more and more influence in the Netherlands, the Republic of the Netherlands concluded a treaty with Napoléon which included the imposition of a king. In 1807, the new king, Louis Bonaparte, brother of Napoléon, was ordered to introduce the French Civil Code, known as the *code Napoléon*, in the Netherlands.[6] However, Louis Bonaparte did not obey his

1 Most literature referred to in this chapter will be Dutch literature. However, if an English source was available I have tried to mention it where I considered it appropriate.

2 Lokin & Zwalve 2001, p. 293.

3 It was only externally that the Republic acted as one, with the estates general as the representative organ. Lokin & Zwalve 2001, p. 284-290.

4 Confusingly because it was only the law of the province of Holland and not of the Netherlands entirely. Roman Dutch law is the law that was brought to South Africa where it still, although modified, applies today. See, *inter alia*, De Waal 2004, p. 83.

5 Zwalve 2003, p. 48-50, Lokin & Zwalve 2001, p. 289. On the natural law school see Chapter 2; 5. Natural Law and the French Revolution.

6 Lokin & Zwalve 2001, p. 296-298.

brother's orders and ordered the redrafting of the *code Napoléon* adapted to the situation in the Netherlands. With this procedure more influences from local Dutch law could be introduced in the Dutch Civil Code. The work on this adapted version resulted in the introduction of the *code Napoléon* as adapted for the kingdom of the Netherlands.[7] However, in 1810 Napoléon forced the introduction of the *code Napoléon* on the Netherlands when he included the country in his empire.[8] In this way the Netherlands were forced to use and apply French law. When the Netherlands became independent again in 1813, work was started on a properly Dutch code of private law.[9]

The Civil Code that resulted from this work, now known as the old Civil Code, *Oud Burgerlijk Wetboek* (or old BW), entered into force in the major part of the Netherlands in 1838. Because of the circumstances it was primarily based on French law, but also showed some Roman-Dutch influences.[10] This influence of French law was visible in particular in the traditional structure the code followed. Because of the circumstances under which the code had been drafted, there had been pressure to introduce a code quickly while French law continued to apply. The code was therefore never perceived as a purely Dutch product.[11] During the next century several proposals were made to create a new Dutch Civil Code, but none of these were successful. The existing Dutch law was reformed in some areas.[12]

After the Second World War, Professor E.M. Meijers was commissioned to develop a new Civil Code.[13] Meijers introduced a new approach, partly based on comparisons with German law, French law and other legal systems. Whereas the old Civil Code had been primarily based on French law, Meijers especially introduced concepts from German law.[14]

One of the results of this new approach is that the Dutch Civil Code breaks with traditional distinctions, both in structure and in contents. The Dutch Civil Code has a layered structure, in which general rules are dealt with before specific rules. In the area of property law, the consequence of this approach is that there is no longer one single book of property law in the Code, but several books in which rules of property law are provided.

In content the Dutch Civil Code does not follow a traditional approach either. As in most civil law systems, the code is founded on the distinction between personal rights and property rights and the related separation between the law of

7 The *Wetboek Napoleon, ingerigt voor het Koningkrijk Holland*, see Lokin & Zwalve 2001, p. 297.
8 However, the Southern part of the Netherlands has already been part of France since 1795, on the status of the different provinces see Ketelaar 1978, p. 46-47, Lokin & Zwalve 2001, p. 299.
9 Ketelaar 1978, p. 56.
10 Only in the province of Limburg the old BW entered into force in 1842, see Ketelaar 1978, p. 1.
11 Lokin & Zwalve 2001, p. 306.
12 Levenbach 1838, p. 129 *et seq.*
13 Unfortunately, Professor Meijers died before the first version was completed.
14 German law belongs to another legal family or legal tradition, i.e. has a different origin, and is therefore based on different concepts than French law. On legal families see Zweigert & Kötz 1998, p. 63 *et seq.*, on legal traditions see Glenn 2006, p. 421 *et seq.*

obligations and the law of property.[15] The separation between the law of obligations and the law of property had been recognised before, but had not been taken into the structure of the Civil Code. In 1905, the *Hoge Raad*, the Supreme Court of the Netherlands, delivered a landmark decision in which the distinction between personal rights and property rights was first strongly affirmed.[16] With this decision the separation became a fundamental principle of Dutch law. The new Civil Code, the *Burgerlijk Wetboek* (BW), although adhering to this separation, expresses it less strongly in the structure of the code than do other civil law systems. Moreover, there are several concepts in Dutch law that deviate from this principal separation, specifically in the area of contract law. However, at the outset, the system continues to adhere to the strict separation between personal and property rights.[17]

The separation between personal rights and property rights has been the subject of only a few studies in the Netherlands.[18] Both in case law and literature the separation has been perceived as a basic principle of Dutch law.[19] However, the exact distinction between personal rights and property rights in the Netherlands has not been the subject of much research. In 1932 Kisch defended a doctoral thesis on this subject in which he argued that the essential characteristic of a property right should be found in its consequences.[20] He understood the absolute nature of a property right as an effect against the world. In 1992 Rank-Berenschot defended her thesis in which she criticised Kisch's viewpoints and developed her own theory.[21] Furthermore, in 2007 Struycken was the first to deal with the closed system of property rights in the Netherlands, also dealing with the separation between per-

15 Like the German Civil Code, the Dutch Civil Code takes the distinction between personal rights and property rights as its starting point. Only from the distinction between these two rights, the separation between the law of obligations and the law of property follows. On the German approach see Füller 2006, p. 8-13.

16 HR 3 March 1905, W 8191 (*Blaauboer/Berlips*). In this case the *Hoge Raad* (Supreme Court) stated: Considering that when every owner would be under an obligation and that the performance of this obligation would have a property effect, although created by a contract, without a specific legal basis, especially in these circumstances, cannot be accepted, because with that the existing sharp distinction in our Civil legislation between property law and the law of obligations would be erased. 'O. verder, dat, waar de verbintenis zoude rusten op elken eigenaar als zoodanig het recht op de vervulling dier verbintenis een zakelijk karakter bekomt, hoewel voortspruitende uit een overeenkomst, iets, dat zonder eene wetsbepaling, dit bepaaldelijk voor een geval als het besprokene veroorlovende, niet kan worden aangenomen, omdat daarmede de in onze burgerlijke wetgeving bestaande scherpe onderscheiding tusschen zakenrecht en verbintenissenrecht, wordt uitgewischt', *Hoge Raad* (Supreme Court) 3 March 1905, W 8191 (*Blaauboer/Berlips*). On this decision see, *inter alia*, Pitlo 1968, Rijtma 1969 and Heyman 2003.

17 Meijers 1948, p. 266, Parlementaire Geschiedenis NBW - Boek 5 1981, p. 3, Asser, Mijnsen, De Haan & Van Dam 2006, No. 20, p. 19-20.

18 See Rank-Berenschot 1992 and Struycken 2007.

19 Rank-Berenschot 1992, p. 309-310.

20 Kisch 1932, p. 206 *et seq.*

21 Rank-Berenschot 1992, p. 53-54. On Rank-Berenschot's views see below; 5. A *Numerus Clausus* in Dutch Property Law?

sonal and property rights as well as the separation between the law of obligations and the law of property.[22]

In 1948 Meijers published his work on the general concepts of Dutch private law, in which he developed the theory that would become the foundation of the modern Dutch system of property law and the law of obligations.[23] In this book on general concepts of Dutch private law, or the *Algemene Begrippen*, Meijers developed a theory on 'subjective' rights. This type of right is further divided into absolute and relative rights that correspond with property rights and personal rights.[24] Meijers states that it is not possible to identify and list criteria that would apply to all property rights.[25] Instead he developed a theory of normal types. A normal type would be characterised by a set of criteria. Once a certain relation fulfils the majority of the criteria set for a type of right, the right would be characterised under that type. According to Meijers the normal-type absolute right is characterised by; an exclusive power of the holder of the right, a duty on third parties to refrain from interfering with the right, a possibility to claim the object over which the right is created in insolvency as if there was no insolvency, where registration of the right is required this concerns an object and not a person, where two rights cannot exist at the same time the older right prevails over the newer, and the powers of the holder of the right are considered to come from the right itself.[26]

It is on this basis that the Dutch system of property law is built. The Civil Code uses the distinction between personal rights and property rights and consequently provides separate rules dealing with property law. For reasons of legal certainty only those property rights that are dealt with by law are recognised.[27] The property rights in Dutch law therefore form a closed list or closed system of rights. However, as in other legal systems there are other legal relations recognised in Dutch law that closely resemble property rights, either in content or in their effect against third parties. This chapter will examine the list of property rights first, after which these other relations with some property effects are examined. The chapter will conclude with an examination whether the system of property law in Dutch law recognises a *numerus clausus*.

2. The Right of Ownership

In Dutch law the concept of 'subjective' right, which refers to a right that can be brought in relation to a specific person, forms the basis for the private law system.[28]

22 Struycken 2007, p. 11-240.
23 Meijers 1948.
24 Meijers 1948, p. 266 *et seq*.
25 Asser, Mijnsen, De Haan & Van Dam 2006, No. 22, p. 20-21.
26 Meijers 1948, p. 269-270.
27 Art. 3:81 BW, Parlementaire Geschiedenis NBW - Boek 5 1981, p. 3. This can include rights dealt with outside the BW, such as the right to a grave dealt with in Art. 28(1) *Wet op de Lijkbezorging*.
28 Also in German law this concept of 'subjective' right is the starting point. See Füller 2006, p. 27 *et seq*.

Subjective rights are divided into rights to a person and *vermogensrechten*. Personal subjective rights are, for example, fundamental rights, *vermogensrechten* are those rights dealing with 'patrimony', or *vermogen*, best described as the full set of assets and debts a person can have.[29] It is with this second group that property law is concerned. Dutch law deals with *vermogensrechten* in Article 3:6 BW:[30]

> Rights that, either separately or together with another right, are transferable, or give the right-holder material benefit, or are acquired in exchange for material benefit, are patrimonial rights.[31]

Vermogensrechten are divided into relative rights and absolute rights. In Dutch law relative rights include personal rights, whereas absolute rights include property rights.[32] As was mentioned in the introduction, the distinction between relative and absolute rights is at the foundation of Dutch private law.[33] The Dutch BW deals with rules on *vermogensrechten* in book 3, property rights are subsequently dealt with in book 5, and personal rights in book 6.[34] This division is different from the traditional division between property law and the law of obligations which is followed in other Civil Codes.[35] In respect to property rights, the Dutch legal system makes a distinction between *goederen* and *zaken*. Both can be objects of property rights but differ in content. *Zaken* are, according to Article 3:2 BW, corporeal objects susceptible of human control.[36] *Goederen* are, according to Article 3:1 BW, all *zaken*, which are corporeal objects, and *vermogensrechten*, or, in other words, *goederen* are all corporeal and incorporeal objects. The relevance of the distinction comes with the definition of the right of ownership in Article 5:1 BW that states:

29 Asser, Mijnsen, De Haan & Van Dam 2006, No. 1, p. 1-2.

30 Art. 3:6 BW refers to Art. 6 of book 3 of the Dutch *Burgerlijk Wetboek* (Civil Code).

31 Art. 3:6 BW, 'Rechten die, hetzij afzonderlijk hetzij tezamen met een ander recht, overdraagbaar zijn, of er toe strekken de rechthebbende stoffelijk voordeel te verschaffen, ofwel verkregen zijn in ruil voor verstrekt of in het vooruitzicht gesteld stoffelijk voordeel, zijn vermogensrechten'.

32 The category of absolute rights is wider than the list of property rights, it also includes, *inter alia*, intellectual property rights. Meijers 1948, p. 266, Asser, Mijnsen, De Haan & Van Dam 2006, Nos. 1, 21, p. 1-2, 20, Van der Steur 2003, p. 11.

33 For an overview of the discussion on the difference between personal rights and property rights see Rank-Berenschot 1992, p. 35 *et seq.*

34 However, only those property rights in respect to corporeal objects are dealt with in book 5. Those property rights that can also be held on incorporeal objects, e.g. claims, are dealt with in book 3. Asser, Mijnsen, De Haan & Van Dam 2006, Nos. 21 *et seq.*, p. 20 *et seq.*

35 As, for instance, the German BGB that uses the second book for the law of obligations (*Recht der Schuldverhäldnisse*) and the third book for property law (*Sachenrecht*). Also the French Civil Code deals with property law in the second book (*Des biens et des différentes modifications de la propriété*) and in the third book with the law of obligations as a way to acquire ownership (*Des différentes manières dont on acquiert la propriété*), see, *inter alia*, Westra 1992, p. 287.

36 Art. 3:2 BW states 'voor menselijke beheersing vatbare stoffelijke objecten'. Translation by Haanappel & Mackaay 1990.

1. The right of ownership is the most extensive right a person can have on a corporeal object.[37]

In other words, the concept of ownership is restricted to corporeal objects which means that incorporeal objects in the Netherlands cannot be owned. However, it is possible to have a position very much comparable to ownership of a corporeal object. The Dutch Civil Code uses the term *rechthebbende*, right-holder, for the person entitled to incorporeal objects. In other words, Dutch law recognises entitlement to rights, either the right of ownership on *zaken* or other property rights in respect of *goederen*.[38] However, the division in rights in respect of corporeal and rights in respect of incorporeal objects is not as logical as it seems. *Zaken* are corporeal objects capable of ownership while *vermogensrechten* are not, but ownership of *zaken* is included in the concept of *vermogensrechten*. The Dutch legislature has explained this illogical choice by stating that in normal terminology it is not the ownership of an object that is sold, but the object itself. Although it is actually the right of ownership that transfers to the acquirer, the law uses the term *zaak* to indicate the object. It is the right of ownership itself that is regarded as a patrimonial right, a *vermogensrecht*.[39] Nevertheless, the system of property law is structured around the categorisation of corporeal and incorporeal objects.

2.1. *Normal Ownership*

Article 5:1 BW states that the right of ownership is the most extensive right a person can have in a corporeal object. This definition of ownership is the result of a development of opinions on the right of ownership throughout the ages. In the old BW of 1838, the right of ownership was defined in Article 625 Old BW as:

> Ownership is the right to the free enjoyment of an object and to dispose of it in the most absolute manner, subject to limitations imposed by law or public regulation, imposed by the authority provided by the constitution, subject to the rights of others; all under the condition of expropriation for the public benefit for a reasonable compensation as provided by the Constitution.[40]

37 Art. 5:1 BW '-1 Eigendom is het meest omvattende recht dat een persoon op een zaak kan hebben'. Another translation reads ownership is the most comprehensive right which a person can have in a thing, Haanappel & Mackaay 1990.

38 Van der Steur 2003, p. 14.

39 Parlementaire Geschiedenis NBW - Boek 3 1981, p. 63-64, Van der Steur 2003, p. 15, Asser, Mijnsen, De Haan & Van Dam 2006, No. 68, p. 61-62.

40 Art. 625 old BW: 'eigendom is het regt om van eene zaak het vrij genot the hebben en daarover op de volstrekste wijze te beschikken, mits men er geen gebruik van make, strijdende tegen de wetten of de openbare verordeningen, daargesteld door zoodanige magt, die daartoe volgens de Grondwet, de bevoegdheid heeft, en mits men aan de regten van anderen geen hinder toebrenge; alles behoudens de onteigening ten algemeenen nutte tegen behoorlijke schadeloosstelling, ingevolge de Grondwet'.

The definition in the old BW was strongly based on the French equivalent in Article 544 C.civ.[41] It is immediately clear from the definition that the right of ownership is a special right. The right gives the holder free enjoyment of an object and a seemingly unlimited power to dispose of that object in the most absolute manner.

The development of the concept of the right of ownership is visible in this definition. It has long been held that the enjoyment of objects and the power to dispose of these are based on the Roman concept of *dominium*. However, Van der Bergh has shown that the definition of Article 625 old BW was not so much based on Roman law, but the result of a development of opinion about the right of ownership from Bartolus through to nineteenth-century scholars.[42] Under the influence of natural law scholars, specifically Grotius, the power to dispose of the object under ownership was firmly established in Dutch law.[43] In this respect, the definition in Article 625 old BW is an echo of Bartolus' definition of ownership as *ius in re corporali perfecte disponendi nisi lege prohibeatur*.[44] The definition in the new BW turns away from the emphasis on the powers of the owner and focuses more on the nature of the right of ownership itself. Nevertheless, in content, the powers of the owner remain of importance and are further qualified in section 2 of Article 5:1 BW, which states:

> 2. To the exclusion of everybody else, the owner is free to use the thing provided that this use not be in violation of the rights of others and that it respects the limitations based upon statutory rules and rules of unwritten law.[45]

The right of ownership in Dutch law is absolute and unitary. The absoluteness of the right of ownership lies in the fact that everybody must respect the right and the holder of the right.[46] The right of ownership is not the only absolute right, nor are all other property rights. Intellectual property rights, in Dutch law not part of the regular law of property, are also absolute rights.[47]

Traditionally there are two characteristics of absolute rights. First, an absolute right will follow the object on which it is created. This effect is known as *droit de suite*. Second, in case of bankruptcy, the holder of an absolute right receives preference over holders of other rights, specifically holders of relative rights. This effect is known as *droit de préférence*.[48]As well as being absolute the right of ownership is also

41 Art. 544 CC states: 'La propriété est le droit de jouir et disposer des choses de la manière la plus absolue, pourvu qu'on n'en fasse pas un usage prohibé par les lois ou par les règlements', Feenstra 1976, p. 250 *et seq.*, Feenstra 1990, p. 40. See Chapter 3; 2.1. Ownership.

42 Van den Bergh 1988, p. 39-50.

43 Van den Bergh 1988, p. 56, Feenstra 1990, p. 40, Smits 1996, p. 56.

44 Wiegand 1976, p. 121, see Chapter 2; 4.3. Ownership.

45 Translation by Haanappel & Mackaay 1990, Art. 5:1 (2) '-2 Het staat de eigenaar met uitsluiting van een ieder vrij van de zaak gebruik te maken, mits dit gebruikt niet strijdt met rechten van anderen en op wettelijke voorschriften en regels van ongeschreven recht gegronde beperkingen daarbij in acht worden genomen'.

46 Pitlo et al. 2006, No. 22, p. 13.

47 See Pitlo et al. 2006, Nos. 22 *et seq.*, p. 13 *et seq.*

48 Pitlo et al. 2006, Nos. 23, 24, p. 14.

unitary. The unitary nature of the right of ownership forms the basis of the system of property law in the Netherlands. It is impossible to have several types of ownership on the same object. It is possible for several persons to have ownership at the same time as co-owners, but in situations of co-ownership, co-owners will always share the right, instead of each of them having a separate right of ownership.[49] In other words a fragmentation of ownership is deemed impossible.[50] This strict approach towards the right of ownership is expressed in other provisions in the Civil Code as well. Specifically in relation to the various forms of transfer of ownership the Dutch legislature has included Article 3:84 section 3 BW:

> A transfer of ownership for security purposes, or a transfer that does not intend to transfer the object to the patrimony of the acquirer, cannot be a valid title for transfer.[51]

Dutch law only allows the transfer of ownership if there is a valid cause, which is confusingly named a title, a power to dispose of the current owner and an act of delivery.[52] The cause needed for the transfer is usually a contract, but can have other forms as well, for instance, a legacy.[53] The provision in Article 3:84 section 3 BW is a specific protection of the unitary concept of ownership. A transfer of ownership for security purposes, in Roman law known as a *fiducia cum creditore*, would deviate from the unitary nature of the right.[54] A debtor who transfers his ownership to a creditor with the knowledge that, once he repays the loan that the transfer secures, the right of ownership will return to him, will continue to hold a certain right to the object. The question of the nature of the right of the debtor to the return of the object has been much debated. This debate is part of a larger debate on another problem with transfer of ownership that must be dealt with first. This problem concerns the conditional transfer of ownership. In Dutch law the right of ownership can be transferred under condition in two ways. First, the right of ownership can be transferred from A to B under a resolutive condition. Under such a transfer, B acquires ownership, but not full ownership, because, on occurrence of the situation described in the condition, the right of ownership will return to A. Secondly, the right of ownership can be transferred from A to B under condition of suspension. Under such a transfer, A will remain the owner, but not full owner, because, on occurrence of the situation described in the condition, the ownership will transfer to B. In the first situation of transfer, it is held that B has ownership under resolutive condition, ownership

49 The co-owners will hold property in community or *gemeenschap*. See Arts. 3:166 *et seq.* BW, Asser, Mijnsen, De Haan & Van Dam 2006, Nos. 445 *et seq.*, p. 496 *et seq.*, Asser, Van Dam & Mijnsen 2002, No. 55, p. 66-67.

50 Smits 1996, p. 57.

51 Art. 3:84 sub 3 BW, 'Een rechtshandeling die ten doel heft een goed over te dragen tot zekerheid of die de strekking mist het goed na de overdracht in het vermogen van de verkrijger te doen vallen, is geen geldige titel voor overdracht'. On this article see Heyman 1994, p. 1-14, Kleijn 1994, p. 15-17, Kortmann 1994, p. 18-23.

52 Art. 3:84 sub 1 BW. On the Dutch system of transfer of ownership see Van Vliet 2000, p. 133 *et seq.*

53 Pitlo et al. 2006, No. 113, p. 83-84.

54 See Chapter 2; 2.4. Other Property Rights.

onder ontbindende voorwaarde. In the second situation of transfer A has ownership under condition of suspension, ownership *onder opschortende voorwaarde.*[55] The condition that is subject to these special transfers can be practically anything except a period of time, which is specifically prohibited by Article 3:85 BW.[56] In Dutch law there is only one concept of ownership and, because the right of ownership is unitary, it can only belong to one party. The result of this fundamental starting point is that either B will have ownership in case of a resolutive transfer, or that A will have ownership in case of a transfer under condition of suspension. The other party, A or B respectively, can have a right in respect of the object under condition, but this right logically cannot be ownership.[57]

The debate centres on the nature of the remaining right. Granting a property right to the person expecting ownership would allow a better position than a personal right, especially in case of insolvency. However, in the system of Dutch property law recognising such a property right is a difficult matter. The limited number of property rights recognised by the Civil Code does not include a lesser form of ownership or a property right similar to the position of the remaining party. Kortmann has argued that this other right is nothing more than an expectation of ownership or an *eigendomsverwachting* and that this is not a form of ownership, nor is it any other property right.[58] In Dutch law, the expectation of ownership is just a personal right to acquire the right of ownership in case the condition for transfer is fulfilled.

With this explanation the unitary nature of the right of ownership is upheld and no property rights are created outside the exhaustive list of property rights. It will depend on the situation which party is owner and which party will have an expectation of ownership. As a standard situation Kortmann mentions that the transferor will have ownership and the transferee an expectation of ownership. Only in case there has already been an actual delivery based on a resolutive condition, will the right of ownership transfer and the transferor will have an expectation of ownership.[59]

55 Kortmann 1992, p. 199, Bartels 1997, p. 82, Van Vliet 2000, p. 36.

56 A title for transfer of ownership under a condition of a certain period is changed, by operation of law to a title for the creation of a right of usufruct. A suspensive transfer of ownership for a certain period is changed to a full transfer of ownership and the creation of a right of usufruct for the benefit of the transferor. Art. 3:85 BW states: '-1 een verbintenis strekkende tot overdracht van een goed voor een bepaalde tijd, wordt aangemerkt als een verbintenis tot vestiging van een vruchtgebruik op het goed voor de gestelde tijd. -2 Een verbintenis strekkende tot overdracht van een goed onder opschortende tijdsbepaling, wordt aangemerkt als een verbintenis tot onmiddellijke overdracht van het goed met gelijktijdige vestiging van een vruchtgebruik van de vervreemder op het goed voor de gestelde tijd'.

57 Kortmann 1992, p. 201, Aertsen 2004, p. 63-64.

58 Kortmann 1992, p. 211. Compare in this respect the remainder in English law that is treated as a property right, but also the German *Anwartschaftsrecht*. See Chapter 4; 3.4. Expectation Rights, and Chapter 6; 1.1. Terminology.

59 A transfer of ownership for security purposes, which is also a transfer under resolutive condition, is not allowed in Dutch law. See Art. 3:84(3) BW and below; 2.3. Security Ownership.

2.2. *Co-Ownership*

As mentioned in the last section, in Dutch law it is also possible for more than one person to share the right of ownership of an object. Like the German Civil Code, Dutch law makes use of the concept of community of objects, in Dutch *gemeenschap*, and the concept of shares in that community for the co-owners.[60] The shares in the community of objects enable two or more persons to share the entitlement to an object between them.[61] Instead of a right of ownership for each of them, the co-owners will hold the ownership of the object between them. Because the concept of community is wider than just co-ownership, it can also include co-entitlement to other rights, the concept of community is dealt with in the third book of the Dutch Civil Code. Article 3:166(1) BW provides that a community of objects exists, when two or more persons are entitled to the same object.[62]

The shares in a community are indivisible shares, reflecting the unitary nature of the right of ownership that is the object of the community. The share itself is a patrimonial right in the meaning of Article 3:6 BW and can be transferred to a third party, who will then hold the share in the community.[63] Furthermore, a share can be burdened with a property right itself.[64] The relation between the co-owners can be complicated depending on the number of co-owners and the nature of the right they are sharing. When nothing is specified each holder will hold an equal share in the community.[65] The relation between the co-owners will be governed by the principles of fair and equal dealing, in Dutch, *redelijkheid* and *billijkheid*.[66] Consequently, parties may reach agreements on the division of the shares and the ways in which the objects of the community are managed.[67]

The nature of the right granted through the share in the community will therefore depend on the nature of the right that is object of the community. In case of a right of ownership, the co-owners, who are holders of the shares in the community of ownership, will be entitled to the benefits of the right of ownership proportional to their share.[68] Also in the event that the community is dissolved and the objects must be divided or sold, each holder will be entitled to his share in the objects or in the proceeds proportional to his share.

60 Pitlo et al. 2006, p. 349 *et seq.*, Asser & Perrick 2007, No. 3, p. 5.
61 Asser, Mijnsen, De Haan & Van Dam 2006, No. 445, p. 496.
62 Art. 3:166 BW, 'Gemeenschap is aanwezig, wanneer een of meer goederen toebehoren aan twee of meer deelgenoten gezamelijk'.
63 Pitlo et al. 2006, p. 352.
64 Pitlo et al. 2006, p. 352-353, 364-366.
65 Art. 3:166(2) BW, Pitlo et al. 2006, p. 352.
66 Art. 3:166(3) BW. Asser & Perrick 2007, No. 7, p. 11.
67 See Pitlo et al. 2006, p. 253, Struycken 2007, p. 636-637.
68 Asser & Perrick 2007, Nos. 10 *et seq.*, p. 15 *et seq.*

2.3. *Security Ownership*

The best example of a resolutive transfer of ownership is the transfer of ownership for security purposes, although this is no longer allowed under the new Civil Code. An example of a transfer under the condition of suspension is the reservation of ownership, known in Dutch as *eigendomsvoorbehoud*, provided by Article 3:92 BW.[69] The latter type of security can be created in three situations that are specifically listed by the Civil Code itself.[70] Each of these situations concerns two parties involved in a transaction that includes a transfer of ownership. The first is when the transferee must still perform his obligation under a contract to deliver objects or future objects. The claim on the performance of the obligation, for which a reservation of ownership can be made, creates a wide variety of possibilities to use the reservation instrument.[71] Although usually the obligation will be the payment of money, the reservation of ownership is not restricted to this. The second is when the transferee must still perform an obligation under a contract to carry out some work or deliver an object. The third is when a claim arises on the transferee for non-performance of the obligation to carry out work or to deliver an object.

The reservation of ownership results in a right of ownership for the seller and a personal right to the expectation of ownership for the buyer. Only when the buyer performs his obligation under the contract entered into with the seller, will he acquire the right of ownership.

The theory of expectation of ownership, which was dealt with above, applies both to transfer of ownership for security purposes and to the conditional transfer of ownership, but the difference in Dutch law is that the transfer for security purposes is prohibited by Article 3:84 sub 3 BW, while the reservation of ownership is not.[72]

Under the old BW there was the possibility for a transfer of ownership for security purposes.[73] The old BW provided very strict rules for the rights of pledge and hypothec. Specifically in respect of the right of pledge, Article 1198 sub 2 old BW provided that a right of pledge could not be created when the object would remain with the pledgee or when the object would immediately return to the pledgee after the creation of the property right.[74] The *Hoge Raad* interpreted this article in a

69 See also Pitlo et al. 2006, p. 101-104, 730 *et seq.*

70 Art. 3:92(2) BW.

71 See Pitlo et al. 2006, p. 734.

72 Art. 3:84 section 4 BW restricts a transfer under suspensive condition but does not prohibit it, Art. 3:92 BW specifically authorises the transfer under suspensive condition for movable objects. On the Dutch approach to the expectation of ownership as a purely personal right see above; 2.1. Normal Ownership. See also Struycken 2007, p. 60 *et seq.*

73 HR 25 January 1929, *NJ* 1929, 616, Feenstra 1990, p. 98-99, Kliebisch 1997, p. 75-78, Asser, Beekhuis, De Haan 1985, No. 296, p. 184-185, Struycken 2007, p. 60-61.

74 Art. 1198 section 2 reads 'het [the right of pledge, BA] is niet bestaanbaar op zaken, die in de magt van den schuldenaar of den pandgever worden gelaten of met den wil van den schuldeischer terugkeren'. It [the right of pledge, BA] can not exist on objects that are left within the possession of the debtor or pledgee or which, with consent of the creditor, return to him. Asser, Mijnsen & Van Velten 1986, No. 172, p. 137-138.

strict sense and held that it only applied to rights of pledge. With this decision the *Hoge Raad* created the possibility of transferring ownership for security purposes, or in Roman terms, a *fiducia cum creditore*.[75] In the event of such a transfer the possession, factual control, would remain with the transferor.[76]

In other words, allowing a transfer of ownership for security purposes solved the lack of a non-possessory pledge in Dutch law. This specific transfer of ownership was carried out by the creation of a title of transfer, a contract and a special form of delivery, whereby the parties agree that the transferor would hold the property for the transferee, known as a delivery *constitutum possessorium*.[77]

As a result of this transfer of ownership, the creditor would now have more rights than he needed and the debtor would have to trust the creditor to treat the object properly until it was returned. Not surprisingly, in later cases the *Hoge Raad* corrected some of this inequality in powers. When, in 1929, the *Hoge Raad* accepted the obligation of the debtor to give his objects as security as a valid contract leading to a transfer of the ownership of those objects, it accepted the contract as a valid cause for transfer. At a later stage the *Hoge Raad* accepted that a contract to transfer ownership of an object for security purposes is not the same as a regular contract for the transfer of ownership. Moreover, the *Hoge Raad* accepted that there are situations in which the transfer of ownership for security purposes should be neglected.[78]

Neglecting the transfer for security purposes could be necessary in respect to the recognition of rights of third parties with regard to the objects serving as security. These third parties could be creditors of the debtor that, under specific provisions of the law, had a priority right. Examples of such priority rights include the right of an unpaid seller, because he delivered the object serving as security to the debtor, and the debtor would not have had the object if the seller had not delivered. Other examples are the right of a transport company that provided Customs services by paying levies for the debtor, and the right of a seller who transferred the object that was transferred for security purposes, but who had not yet received payment.[79]

As a result of the case law of the *Hoge Raad*, the right of ownership acquired for security purposes is different from the right of ownership acquired in another situation. Moreover, because there are certain situations in which the transfer of ownership for security purposes can be neglected in respect to certain persons, security ownership is not as absolute as regular ownership. In those situations where the creditors have priority rights, the transfer is considered not to have occurred and the debtor will be treated as owner instead. Consequently, the debtor

75 On Roman law see Chapter 2; 2.4. Other Property Rights.

76 HR 25 January 1929, *NJ* 1929, 616 (*Beer brewery*) and HR 21 June 1929, *NJ* 1929, 1096 (*Luxury car-lease*), on delivery *constitutum possessorium* see Van Vliet 2000, p. 51 note 96.

77 The power to dispose of the debtor is highly relevant since if the debtor is not owner himself there can be no transfer of ownership Asser, Mijnsen & Van Velten 1986, No. 175, p. 141, Van Vliet 2000, p. 53, 127.

78 HR 6 March 1970, *NJ* 1970, 433, HR 7 March 1975, *NJ* 1976, 91, Asser, Mijnsen & Van Velten 1986, No. 178, p. 144, Brahn 1988, p. 90 *et seq.*

79 HR 6 March 1970, *NJ* 1970, 433, HR 7 March 1975, *NJ* 1976, 91, Brahn 1988, p. 92-93.

will have a certain right of ownership that can only be used in these specific cases. In respect to the rest of the world, the creditor will be owner.

Apart from this relative concept of ownership there is also fragmentation of ownership in another sense, because both parties continue to have rights of ownership. In other words, both debtor and creditor continue to hold a fragment of the right of ownership during the existence of the bargain. In this respect, the characterisation of the right of ownership for security purposes in a situation where the secured claim has ceased to exist is problematic. The majority of authors have concluded that the right of security ownership was of an accessory nature, dependent on the claim whose performance it secured. Therefore ownership was considered to revert to the debtor the moment the claim ceased to exist, with no further action needed.[80] In this theory the right of the debtor to the return of the right of ownership was considered a fragment of the right of ownership.[81]

The *Hoge Raad* never decided on this matter, but did decide that a transfer for security purposes was a resolutive transfer of ownership and that, with the payment of the debt, the condition would be fulfilled and the right of ownership would fully transfer back to the debtor.[82] This accessory nature of the ownership for security purposes has led some authors to conclude that this transfer creates nothing more than a right of pledge, although a non-possessory type of pledge.[83]

The *Hoge Raad* even decided that the rules in the old BW on the right of pledge should also be applied to the right of ownership for security purposes.[84] As a result the right of ownership of the creditor could hardly be qualified as normal ownership any longer.[85] However, in theory, the rights of the debtor in respect to the object serving as security remained personal, an expectation of ownership, unless there was a specific situation where a creditor held a priority right and the transfer could be neglected. Moreover, in theory, the right of the creditor continued to be ownership.

However, in effect the absolute and unitary concept of ownership under the old BW was deviated from and Meijers, the drafter of the new BW, refused to accept a transfer for security purposes in this new civil code.[86] The result of this refusal eventually became known as the *fiducia*-ban of Article 3:84 section 3 BW. The second part of section 3 of this Article prohibits a transfer of ownership whereby the transferred object does not end up in the transferee's set of assets and debts, and refers to the Roman *fiducia cum amico*.[87] Even though, in a strict sense, this type of transfer is not a transfer of ownership for security purposes, the approach Dutch law takes in respect to both forms of *fiducia, cum creditore* and *cum amico*, is almost

80 Asser, Mijnsen & Van Velten 1986, No. 181, p. 146-147.
81 See also Struycken 2007, p. 62.
82 HR 3 October 1980, *NJ* 1981, 60, Asser, Mijnsen & Van Velten 1986, No. 182, p. 147-148.
83 Asser, Mijnsen & Van Velten 1986, No.181, p. 147.
84 HR 3 January 1941, *NJ* 1941, 470 (*Boerenleenbank Hazerswoude/Los*), see Van Mierlo 1988, p. 15.
85 Struycken 2007, p. 62.
86 Meijers 1948, p. 89 *et seq.*, Kortmann 1995, p. 455 *et seq.*
87 Heyman 1994, p. 5.

the same.[88] During the drafting of the *fiducia*-ban Article this second type of transfer, the transfer for management purposes, was also discussed thoroughly. The reason for this discussion was the possible introduction of a common law trust in Dutch law.[89]

A transfer that does not result in the object becoming part of the set of assets and debts of the acquirer is, at least in the interpretation of the Dutch legislature, a trust.[90] A trust is a special device that can, under certain circumstances, entitle the acquirer to a property right in respect of the acquired object, but without the object becoming part of the set of assets and debts of the acquirer. Instead, the object falls into the set of assets and debts of the person managing them who will, under circumstances, also have a property right.[91]

The Dutch legislature specifically refused to recognise such a construction where both the acquirer and the transferee of an object would have a property right. It especially rejected the possibility that these property rights are considered as ownership, a situation in which both the manager as well as the transferee would hold a right of ownership, the unitary concept of ownership in Dutch law does not allow for such a fragmentation.[92]

In a landmark decision the *Hoge Raad* dealt with the application of Article 3:84 sub 3 BW. This case dealt with a sale-and-lease-back of certain machinery, financed by a financial company called Sogelease.[93] Although most of the decision focuses on the security aspects of the sale-and-lease-back, the *Hoge Raad* also dealt with the prohibition of the *fiducia cum amico*.[94] The case concerned a transaction whereby a firm, De Zaaiers BV, bought and took delivery of certain printing presses from a supplier, and contracted with Sogelease for the transfer of ownership of the presses and for the payment of the original purchase price by Sogelease to the supplier. At the same time a leasing agreement was entered into that obliged De Zaaiers BV to pay a yearly sum to Sogelease for seven years, after which the printing presses could be bought back for a token sum of money.

The whole bargain was executed before the BW came into force and the question before the *Hoge Raad* was whether this was a transfer of ownership for security purposes as was now prohibited under Article 3:84 sub 3 BW. In dealing with this question, the *Hoge Raad* distinguished between transfers for security purposes, in which there is at least some fragmentation of the right of ownership, and actual transfers, in Dutch *werkelijke overdrachten*, in which there is a full transfer of owner-

88 Also in French law, both forms of *fiducia* are usually considered together. See Chapter 3; 4.5. *Fiducie*.

89 See below; 4.9. EC and International Influences.

90 On the law of trust see Chapter 6; 1.5. Trust Law.

91 In any case, the subject of the trust must be a property right. A trust of a personal right will not give the manager, i.e. the trustee, or the beneficiary a property rights. Trusts are simply a way of holding rights. On this see Swadling 2000a, p. 275-276.

92 Parlementaire Geschiedenis NBW – Boek 5 1981, p. 17-18. More will be stated about this debate below in 5. A *Numerus Clausus* in Dutch Property Law? Against this conception of a trust as a fragmentation of ownership see Chapter 6; 1.5. Trust Law.

93 HR 19 May 1995, *NJ* 1996/119 (*Sogelease*).

94 See also Struycken 2007, p. 63.

ship and the seller is left with only personal obligations, not a fragment of the right of ownership.[95] The first type, a transfer for security purposes, is prohibited by Article 3:84 sub 3 BW, but the second type, the actual transfer, can escape the ambit of the Article. In this case escaping the ambit of the Article required an actual transfer of ownership to Sogelease, leaving De Zaaiers BV with a mere contractual duty of payment, and a personal right to purchase the printing presses after the lease had expired for a set amount of money. Finally, the *Hoge Raad* specifically stated that the doctrine of actual transfers would also apply in case of a *fiducia cum amico*.[96] In other words, in Dutch law it is only possible to transfer ownership of an object for management purposes if the full right of ownership is transferred to the manager and the beneficiary is left with only personal rights.

About ten years later, the *Hoge Raad* delivered another judgment on the concept of an actual transfer.[97] In this case, the *Hoge Raad* refined its judgment in the *Sogelease* case and held that, in order to decide whether a transfer is an actual transfer, the contract underlying the transfer must be interpreted.[98] The case concerned a transfer of agricultural machines in a sale-and-lease-back transaction. The value of the machines was about twice the value of the sum of money that was received in return.[99] The *Hoge Raad* held that for the purposes of the transfer, the over value of the machines had no effect, but that over value could be an indication for the court interpreting the contract underlying the transfer to decide that the transfer would fall under the *fiducia*-ban of Article 3:84(3) BW.[100] When an actual transfer has been made, the acquirer will still become full owner and will be entitled to vindicate the objects in case of insolvency of the other party.

These examples of cases show the rigidity of Dutch law in respect of the unitary and absolute nature of the right of ownership. The judgment in the *Sogelease* case shows that the absolute and unitary nature of the right of ownership are connected; a limitation to the absoluteness will usually imply a deviation from the unitary nature of the right of ownership. Awarding a lesser form of ownership to a creditor, leaving the debtor with the remaining ownership, would mean a deviation in content of the right as well as creating multiple forms of ownership, since the debtor will continue to have a limited form of ownership as well.[101]

However, many elements restrict the absoluteness of the right of ownership in Dutch law. Both public law and private law regulations ensure that the absoluteness of the right, as far as the form the right takes and the content of the right is concerned, is less absolute than it was considered in the eighteenth and nineteenth

95 HR 19 May 1995, *NJ* 1996/119 (*Sogelease*), Para. 3.4.3. For a similar discussion in French law see Crocq 1995, p. 59 *et seq.*

96 HR 19 May 1995, *NJ* 1996/119 (*Sogelease*), Para. 3.6.

97 HR 18 November 2005, *NJ* 2006/151 (*BTL Lease*).

98 HR 18 November 2005, *NJ* 2006/151 (*BTL Lease*), Para. 3.5.2.

99 On the case see also Struycken 2007, p. 504-505.

100 HR 18 November 2005, *NJ* 2006/151 (*BTL Lease*), Para. 3.5.2.

101 On the same conclusion see Struycken 2007, p. 64.

centuries.[102] Nevertheless, in Dutch legal doctrine the right of ownership remains absolute and unitary.[103] Two examples will illustrate this. First, in respect to third-party protection, the fair and equal results that Dutch law seeks to achieve create a relative element in the right of ownership.[104] If owner A lends a certain object to B, who subsequently sells the object to C, and C has no reason to suspect B is not the owner and pays a good price, there is no transfer of ownership.[105] B is not an owner but a detentor of the object and therefore cannot transfer more right than he has. In terms of Article 3:84 sub 1 BW, B lacks the power to dispose over the object.[106] However, through application of Article 3:86 sub 1 BW, if he acted in good faith and for a reasonable price, C still acquires ownership over the object.[107] A has not committed himself to a transfer of ownership, nor has he fulfilled any of the relevant requirements in Article 3:84 sub 1 BW himself. Nevertheless, the result of the application of Article 3:86 sub 1 BW is that A has to respect that his right of ownership transfers to C. Because in Dutch doctrine ownership is unitary, only one of them can have the right of ownership.[108]

Secondly, in the last few decades there has been a discussion on the possible recognition of economic ownership in Dutch law. Proponents of this theory argue for a distinction between legal ownership and economic ownership.[109] During the debate on the concept of ownership, the drafters of the new BW specifically refused a division between legal and economic ownership by explicit statement that they wanted to preserve the unitary nature of the right of ownership. Furthermore, as mentioned above, Dutch law refuses to recognise a trust device, which in the eyes of the majority of Dutch doctrine, leads to a fragmentation of ownership.[110]

Nevertheless, economic ownership is recognised in Dutch law, but because of the clear doctrine on the unitary nature of the right of ownership, economic owner-

102 In public law this is mainly due to developments in society and new ideas on the function of the government. Van den Bergh 1988, p. 56 *et seq.* See also Chapter 3; 2.1. Ownership, and Chapter 4; 2.1. Normal Ownership.

103 Kortmann & Van Hees 1995, p. 994.

104 In Dutch *redelijkheid en billijkheid,* see Art. 6:248 BW.

105 Art. 3:84 sub 1 BW. Dutch law requires a valid cause, i.e. underlying agreement, a power to dispose, and an act of delivery for a valid transfer.

106 This is an application of the *nemo potest plus iuris ad alium transferre quam ipse habet* or *nemo plus* principle. Asser, Mijnsen, De Haan & Van Dam 2006, Nos. 331 *et seq.*, p. 357 *et seq.*

107 Art. 3:86 sub 1 BW states: Despite the lack of power to dispose on the side of the transferor, a transfer according to Arts. 90, 91 or 93 of a movable non-registrable object, is valid if the transfer is for due value and the transferee is in good faith. 'Ondanks onbevoegdheid van de vervreemder is een overdracht overeenkomstig artikel 90, 91 of 93 van een roerende zaak, niet-registergoed, of een recht aan toonder of order geldig, indien de overdracht anders dan om niet geschiedt en de verkrijger te goeder trouw is'.

108 HR 5 May 1950, *NJ* 1951, 1 (*Damhof/State*), Asser, Mijnsen, De Haan & Van Dam 2006, No. 325, p. 351, Pitlo et al. 2006, p. 132-133.

109 See, *inter alia*, Slagter 1992, p. 357 *et seq.*, Huijgen 1995. The Netherlands is not the only country to consider recognition of economic ownership. See e.g. for French law Crocq 1995, p. 149 *et seq.*

110 Parlementaire Geschiedenis NBW – Boek 5 1981, p. 17-18.

ship can be nothing more than a set of personal rights and obligations.[111] Economic ownership was originally introduced into Dutch law through case law of the *Hoge Raad* on taxation.[112] Until legislative interference, it frequently happened that an immovable object was sold, with the payment of the purchase price, and the agreement that the benefits and risks would be for the purchaser, and that no transfer of the legal ownership would take place. Instead economic ownership would be transferred and no transfer taxes or levies were due.[113]

As a further development in the area of private law, the concept of economic ownership has become recognised. Examples include certificate holders in case of certification of shares in company law, and rights of holders of property rights of rights of *emphyteusis* or usufruct on certain parts of the object, for example, buildings or improvements to buildings made by them.[114] The certification of shares deserves some extra attention. In Dutch law a certificate is a set of personal rights and obligations in respect to a certain object or set of objects, which itself can be subject of property rights.[115] With the use of the possibility of certification it is possible to transfer the right of ownership of these objects to someone else under agreement that this person will manage the object for the benefit of the transferee. In Dutch law this construction is known as the transfer for management purposes, or *eigendomsoverdracht ten titel van beheer*, and is used for family estate planning.[116] This solution allows parents to transfer certain objects, say shares and other equities, to a legal person, such as a foundation, which will issue certificates in return to the parents, combined with the agreement that the legal person will manage the objects for the benefit of the certificate holder. The certificates entitle the certificate holder to the value of the objects. The parents then donate the certificates to their children.[117] The construction enables parents to provide wealth to their children without concerns about whether the children could manage such property.[118] Furthermore, the power of the manager to dispose of the objects is limited, by the agreement for transfer for management purposes and, if applicable, the rules applying to the foundation.[119] This situation is an appearance of the *fiducia cum amico* as well and is held possible because the full ownership of the objects is transferred, constituting an actual transfer, and the creditors remain with personal rights. Certification therefore allows parties to work around the *fiducia*-ban of Article 3:84 sub 3 BW.

111 Asser, Mijnsen, De Haan & Van Dam 2006, No. 483, p. 547.

112 Asser, Mijnsen, De Haan & Van Dam 2006, No. 483, p. 547 *et seq.*, Huijgen 1995, p. 12 *et seq.*

113 All requirements, but the act of delivery from Art. 3:84 BW are fulfilled, Huijgen 1995, p. 12.

114 Under the rule of *superficies solo cedit*, the ownership of buildings is with the owner of the land, unless a right of *superficies* has been created. On the right of *superficies* and the rule of *superficies solo cedit* see below; 3.3. *Superficies*. Asser & Maeijer 2000, Nos. 403 *et seq.*, p. 571 *et seq.*, Asser, Mijnsen, De Haan & Van Dam 2006, No. 483, p. 547, Bos 2005, p. 164 *et seq.*

115 Aertsen 2004, p. 118-119, Asser & Maeijer 2000, Nos. 403 *et seq.*, p. 570 *et seq.*

116 Vegter 2004, p. 108.

117 Example taken from Vegter 2004, p. 108, see also Aertsen 2004, p. 114 *et seq.*

118 Furthermore, there are many fiscal advantages to a transfer of ownership for management purposes, which fall outside the scope of this study. See, *inter alia*, Vegter 2004, p. 105 *et seq.*

119 Aertsen 2004, p. 114.

3. Other Property Rights

The new definition of the right of ownership in Article 5:1 BW defines the right as the most extensive right a person can have. The words 'most extensive' emphasise the absolute and unitary nature of the right of ownership, but suggest that there may also be other, less extensive, property rights. In Dutch law, property rights other than ownership are known as *beperkte rechten*, or limited rights. Like the right of ownership, these limited property rights are absolute and unitary rights. These rights have effect against the world and cannot be fragmented so that two persons each hold a fragment of the same limited right. However, like the right of ownership, two or more persons can share a limited right as a whole by making use of a community, *gemeenschap*.[120]

In Dutch property law, a limited property right is considered as a part of the right of ownership that is in the hands of another person. Based on the French approach of *démembrement* of property rights, the creation of property rights in the Netherlands is perceived as a transfer of parts of the powers contained in the right of ownership to another person in the form of a property right.[121] In this respect Article 3:8 BW states:

> A limited right is a right that is derived from a more comprehensive right.[122]

From this description of limited rights in Dutch law, the creation of a property right in respect of a property right is also possible, and is also considered to be a transfer of parts of the powers of the more comprehensive property right to the more limited right.[123] Article 3:8 BW, in other words, specifically enables parties to build limited property rights on top of each other, a method also known as stacking of rights.

The method of creation of property rights in Dutch law is not debated. Struycken has shown that, alternatively from the *démembrement* method, which he terms the subtraction method, there is also the limitation method, which he terms the mirror method, which was considered during the draft of the new BW.[124] Struycken further shows that in Dutch doctrine there is no consensus, but also no debate, on the method that is followed by Dutch law.[125]

Under the currently applied *démembrement* method, property rights comprise parts of the mother right from which they are derived. Therefore, these rights are known as limited rights or *beperkte rechten*. Furthermore, property rights created on corporeal objects, *zaken*, are known as *zakelijke rechten*. Because of their method of creation these rights are, in principle, also limited rights.[126]

120 On this type of co-entitlement see above; 2.2. Co-Ownership.
121 Art. 3:8 BW, Asser, Mijnsen, De Haan & Van Dam 2006, No. 10, p. 11.
122 Art. 3:8 BW, 'Een beperkt recht is afgeleid uit een meer omvattend recht'.
123 In support of this statement the Dutch Civil Code declares the provisions on transfer of property rights applicable to the creation of property rights as well. Art. 3:98 BW.
124 Struycken 2007, p. 361-363.
125 Struycken 2007, p. 363-366.
126 The exception is the right of apartment that is dealt with in below in 3.5. Right of Apartment.

Rights created on incorporeal objects cannot be *zakelijke rechten* and therefore are only limited rights. For the purposes of consistent terminology, and to serve comparative conclusions, this chapter uses the expression 'property rights' to denote limited rights as well as limited *zakelijke rechten*, unless stated otherwise.

Through the *démembrement* method there is a specific relation between the right of ownership and limited rights. All are considered property rights, but ownership will always be the principal right from which limited rights are derived.[127] It is possible that limited rights function as a source for other limited rights. However, the right of ownership, as the most extensive right, can only function as the principal right. Moreover, like in French law, a property right that comes back to the owner of the same object, in principle, ceases to exist.[128] When the powers that were transferred from the right of ownership to another person in the form of a property right other than ownership return to the owner, through mixing the right of ownership becomes full and complete again.[129] However, there is an exception to this rule, although not to the extent that it is accepted in German law.[130] Also in Dutch law the legislature was confronted with the rights of third parties in a property right that ceases to exist through mixing with the powers of the owner when the property right and the right of ownership from which that property right was derived fall into the same hands. Therefore, some property rights will not cease to exist in relation to those who already had a property right in respect of the property right that falls into the hand of the owner. Furthermore, mixing of powers and, with that, the destruction of a property right, also does not have effect in respect to those who held another property right in respect of the same object and were forced to recognise the existence of the destroyed property right.[131] For example, a holder of a right of pledge on a right of usufruct will not automatically acquire a right of pledge on the ownership of an object once the right of usufruct and the right of ownership fall into the same hands. In other words, in respect to the *démembrement* model in Dutch law, the destruction of property rights through mixing with the rights and powers of the right of ownership – when ownership and limited property right fall into the same hands – is given relative effect in respect to third parties with a right in respect of that same right or on the same object.

Dutch law is traditionally held to adhere to a closed list of property rights.[132] In Dutch law only those property rights that are recognised by law can be property rights. Especially after the interference of the *Hoge Raad* in respect to security owner-

127 Dutch law uses the terms mother and daughter rights, Asser, Van Dam & Mijnsen 2002, Nos. 7, 10, p. 7, 11, Pitlo et al. 2006, p. 15.

128 Art. 3:81(3) BW, Asser, Van Dam & Mijnsen 2002, No. 13, p. 15-16.

129 Asser, Mijnsen, De Haan & Van Dam 2006, No. 10, p. 11.

130 On the German exception through Para. 889 BGB, see 4 German Law; 3. Other Property Rights.

131 See below; 4.5. After-Effects of Property Rights.

132 Although not everybody agrees on this, the parliamentary history states that at the outset the system is closed. Whether this is the case will be subject of examination below in 5. A *Numerus Clausus* in Dutch Property Law? See Parlementaire Geschiedenis NBW – Boek 5 1981, p. 3, Struycken 2007, p. 211-216.

ship under the old BW, the recognition of new property rights under the new civil code is, in principle, for the legislature.[133]

3.1. *Real Servitudes*

In Dutch law the right of real servitude is known as the right of *erfdienstbaarheid*. The Dutch term reveals that a right of servitude exists in relation to a specific piece of land, in Dutch *erf*, and that these are not personal servitudes such as exist in French and German law.[134] Dutch law deals with rights of servitude in the civil code. Article 5:70 BW provides a definition of the right:

> 1. A right of servitude is a burden, with which an immovable object, the servient land, is burdened for the benefit of another immovable object, the dominant land.[135]

The requirement of two pieces of land is essential for the right of servitude to exist. The old BW of 1838 stated in Article 721 that the servitude had to be for the benefit, in Dutch *ten nutte*, of the dominant land.[136] Under the old BW, the terminology *ten nutte* gave rise to a debate on the interpretation of the right of real servitude. Van Oven argued for a broad interpretation and a central place of the intention of the parties.[137] In legal practice, the requirement of benefit was further connected to the requirement that the two pieces of land should be in close vicinity of each other, and that the right of servitude itself must be created perpetually.[138] The new definition provided by Article 5:70 BW uses a different wording, which is to be interpreted as no longer including the requirement of vicinity. Therefore, under the new Civil Code it is possible to create a right of servitude between pieces of land that are far apart.[139] Article 5:71 BW provides further requirements for the content of the servitude:

> 1. The burden that a right of servitude imposes on the servient land consists of a duty to allow or refrain from something on, above or under one of the pieces of land. In addition, the deed of creation can contain an agreement that the burden includes a duty to construct buildings, works or plantings that are required for the exercise of

133 See above; 2.3. Security Ownership.

134 In Roman law terms, the right of real servitude in Dutch law includes both rural and urban praedial servitudes. Asser, Van Dam & Mijnsen 2002, No. 169, p. 195, Pitlo et al. 2006, p. 472. See Chapter 2; 2.4. Other Property Rights. On French and German Law see Chapter 3; 3.1. Real Servitudes, and Chapter 4; 3.1. Real Servitudes.

135 Art. 5:70 '-1 Een erfdienstbaarheid is een last, waarmede een onroerende zaak - het dienende erf - ten behoeve van een andere onroerende zaak - het heersende erf - is bezwaard'.

136 Art 721 stated 'Erfdienstbaarheid is een last waarmede een erf bezwaard is, tot gebruik en ten nutte van een erf, hetwelk aan eenen anderen eigenaar toebehoort', Asser, Van Dam & Mijnsen 2002, No. 172, p. 198, Chapter 2; 2.4. Other Property Rights.

137 See Maeijer 1966, p. 8.

138 Asser, Beekhuis & Davids 1990, Nos. 210, 211, p. 203-204, Smalbraak 1966, p. 90, Davids 1988, p. 138.

139 The interpretation centres on the terms *ten nutte van* and *ten behoeve van*. Asser, Van Dam & Mijnsen 2002, No. 172, p. 198-199.

> the right of servitude, under the condition that these buildings, works or plantings are entirely or partly on the servient land.[140]

The Dutch legislature deliberately left the definition of servitudes as open as possible.[141] There are as few restrictions as possible and parties are left as free as possible to decide on the contents of their right themselves.[142] Furthermore it is clear that the legislature, although using the word *erf*, indicating a piece of land, included the possibility to create a right of servitude on all immovable objects.[143] The result of this is that a right of servitude can also be created in relation to objects on the land, for instance, a certain building or plants or trees.

Article 5:71 sub 1 BW defines the outer limits of party autonomy. It connects the burden to servient land. This first sentence of the Article is intended to emphasise that a right of servitude is a property right that is attached to an *erf*. A right of servitude will therefore transfer with the ownership of either piece of land.[144] A right of servitude must impose a negative burden. However, it is possible to include certain positive duties in a right of servitude. These positive duties, which should be seen as an exception to the rule that servitudes can only impose a negative burden, are mentioned in the Article. However, the positive duties mentioned by Article 5:70 BW cannot be the main burden of the right of servitude.[145] Another possibility to include positive duties is mentioned by the second paragraph of Article 5:70 BW:

> 2. The burden that a right of servitude imposes on the servient land can also consist of a duty to maintain the servient land or buildings, works or plantings that are, or will be, entirely or partly on the servient land.[146]

Paragraph 2 of Article 5:70 BW allows a right of servitude to comprise a positive burden in specific situations. The reason for this is that the legislature specifically intended to allow municipalities to impose burdens of maintenance on residents facing a public road.[147] Such a burden could contain a duty to put up fences to separate pieces of land and to maintain gardens on behalf of the right of servitude in respect to this public road. However, the burden a right of servitude imposes cannot comprise a duty to conduct a legal act, in Dutch a *rechtshandeling*. The

140 Art. 5:71 '-1 De last die een erfdienstbaarheid op het dienende erf legt, bestaat in een verplichting om op, boven of onder een der beide erven iets te dulden of niet te doen. In de akte van vestiging kan worden bepaald dat de last bovendien een verplichting inhoudt tot het aanbrengen van gebouwen, werken of beplantingen die voor de uitoefening van die erfdienstbaarheid nodig zijn, mits deze gebouwen, werken of beplantingen zich geheel of gedeeltelijk op het dienende erf zullen bevinden'.

141 Parlementaire Geschiedenis NBW – Boek 5 1981, p. 254-255.

142 Art. 5:73 BW.

143 Asser, Van Dam & Mijnsen 2002, No. 170, p. 196.

144 Art. 3:7 BW.

145 Pitlo et al. 2006, No. 614, p. 474.

146 Art. 5:71 BW, '-2 De last die een erfdienstbaarheid op het dienende erf legt, kan ook bestaan in een verplichting tot onderhoud van het dienende erf of van gebouwen, werken of beplantingen die zich geheel of gedeeltelijk op het dienende erg bevingen of zullen bevinden'.

147 Pitlo et al. 2006, p. 615-616.

burden must impose a duty to refrain from a factual act, not a legal act. As a result of this restriction there are limitations on the use of servitudes in certain situations. For example, a duty to prohibit the sale of the object on which a right of servitude is created cannot be a valid right of servitude.[148]

Even though there are restrictions on the content of servitudes, the Dutch legislature has left the category of servitudes itself wide open. Contrary to the old Dutch Civil Code, the old BW, there is just one type of servitude and there is no distinction in treatment. The old Civil Code made distinctions between visible, invisible, continuing, and non-continuing rights of servitudes.[149] This distinction was particularly relevant in respect to acquisitive prescription, which is the acquisition of a right of servitude through lapse of time.[150] Furthermore, the old civil code recognised specific servitudes that were subject to different criteria.[151]

In the new Civil Code there is only one type of servitude which, as long as parties remain within the criteria stipulated by the provisions on the right of servitude in the code, is a property right, and will transfer with the ownership of the respective pieces of land. Moreover, it is also possible to create a right of servitude between holders of property rights in respect of two pieces of land; the holders of the right of servitude need not be owners.[152] These holders will create the servitude in their capacity as holder of a property right in respect of the land and the right of servitude will therefore be connected to the property right and not directly to the ownership of the land. If the property right of the right-holder ceases to exist, so will the servitude.[153] A right of servitude will also cease to exist when the two pieces of land fall in the ownership of the same person and there are no holders of property rights in respect of either of the pieces of land.[154] In these situations, the right of servitude will mix with the right of ownership of both pieces of land and can therefore no longer exist. Even if at a later stage the tenements are separated in ownership once more, the servitude will have to be re-created.[155]

148 Asser, Van Dam & Mijnsen 2002, No. 174, p. 201.

149 Arts. 724 and 725 OBW, Asser, Van Dam & Mijnsen 2002, No. 170, p. 195-196.

150 Van Vliet 2004, p. 223.

151 Arts. 727-734 OBW, these rights include *inter alia* rights of view (*uitzicht*), light (*licht*) and watercourse (*waterloop*).

152 Art. 5:84 BW. These property rights are usufruct, *emphyteusis* or *superficies*, Asser, Van Dam & Mijnsen 2002, Nos. 173, 207, p. 199, 223.

153 Asser, Van Dam & Mijnsen 2002, No. 207, p. 224.

154 It is possible to have a right of servitude when both the dominant and servient tenement are owned by the same person but the servitude is created between the owner and the right-holder of a property right in respect of either of the tenements. See Asser, Van Dam & Mijnsen 2002, No. 173, p. 199.

155 Asser, Van Dam & Mijnsen 2002, No. 204, p. 222. A right of servitude for the *pater familias* as is recognised in French law is therefore unknown to Dutch law. On this French type of servitude, see Chapter 3; 3.1. Real Servitudes.

3.2. *Usufruct*

In Roman law the right of usufruct fell under the general category of servitudes. Specifically a right of usufruct on land was widely used. However, the personal nature of the right, which refers to the connection of the property right to a person, and the fear of associating the right with personal burdens that existed under the *ancien régime*, have led to the recognition of a distinct property right in Dutch law.[156] A right of usufruct is a property right that entitles the holder to the user and the fruits of a certain object. This object can be corporeal, immovable or movable, and incorporeal. However, the right of usufruct remains connected to the usufructuary as a person. The property right will exist as long as the usufructuary lives or for a period of time agreed in the agreement that created the right. If the right of usufruct is created on behalf of a legal person, the maximum duration of the right is thirty years.[157]

Contrary to the requirements in Roman law, that have been adopted in both French and German law, the Dutch civil code does not require the usufructuary to return the object in the state he received it when the usufruct comes to an end. With the introduction of the new Civil Code, the Dutch legislature has chosen to extend the scope of usufructs, opening the possibilities for a wide variety of applications of the right.[158]

Book 3 of the new BW provides a general set of rules applicable to usufructs, but different parts of the Civil Code are also applicable to specific situations.[159] These specific parts include the law of succession, where specific rules for specific types of usufructs are provided.[160] Insofar as no specific legislation applies, the general rules on usufruct from book 3 of the BW will apply. In this general part, the right of usufruct is dealt with in Article 3:201 BW, which states:

> Usufruct provides the right to use and take the fruits of objects that belong to someone else.[161]

The legislature left the definition of the right of usufruct open, with the intention that the content of the right of usufruct can be further defined by the parties themselves. Article 3:207 BW states in this respect:

> 1. A usufructuary can use and use up the objects under usufruct in accordance with the agreement made upon creation, or when such agreement is missing, in accord-

156 Lévy & Castaldo 2002, p. 639, Asser, Beekhuis & Davids 1990, No. 350, p. 300 *et seq.*

157 Art. 3:203 BW.

158 Art. 3:215 BW, Parlementaire Geschiedenis NBW - Boek 3 1981, p. 639 *et seq.*, Van Gaalen 2001, p. 23 *et seq.*, 76-77, Bos 2005, p. 5.

159 Arts. 3:201 *et seq.* BW.

160 See, *inter alia*, Arts. 4:30 *et seq.* BW, Van Gaalen 2001, p. 4 *et seq.*, but also Asser, Van Dam & Mijnsen 2002, No. 278, p. 307 *et seq.*

161 Art. 3:201 BW: 'Vruchtgebruik geeft het recht om goederen die aan een ander toebehoren, te gebruiken en daarvan de vruchten te genieten'.

> ance with the nature of the objects in respect to the local practice of use and using up.[162]

Furthermore Article 3:215 BW provides:

> 1. When upon creation of a right of usufruct, or after that, the power to partially or completely alienate or use up the objects under usufruct is given to the usufructuary, the principal right-holder may demand the retro-transfer of the objects under usufruct or the objects substituted for these, unless the usufructuary or acquirers of his right prove that the objects were used up or vanished by coincidence.[163]

These definitions show that it is possible that the usufructuary can be allowed to use up or consume the objects under usufruct. The inclusion of the power to use up, in Dutch *verteringsbevoegdheid*, breaks with the Roman tradition where the usufructuary is under the obligation to maintain the objects under usufruct.[164] With the inclusion of the power to use up or consume, the scope of the right of usufruct is extended. Where in the Roman tradition a usufruct on objects which by nature decay or vanish was, because of the obligation to maintain, not possible, the Dutch right of usufruct can easily be created.[165] The recognition of a quasi-usufruct, as in French and German law, is therefore not necessary.[166]

When a right of usufruct is validly created, the usufructuary is under a duty to manage the objects under usufruct.[167] The consequence of his management powers can very well include the necessity to conclude a contract in respect to or to transfer the objects under usufruct. In this respect a distinction between acts within the law of obligations and acts within the law of property should be made.

A contract that is made in respect to the objects under usufruct will be valid, unless one of the contracting parties was not aware of the existence of the right of usufruct, and successfully invokes a rule of third-party protection.[168] Acts made by the usufructuary within the law of property, such as a transfer of ownership of the objects under usufruct, are more complicated. In order to decide on the validity of

162 Art. 3:207 BW: '-1. Een vruchtgebruiker mag de aan het vruchtgebruik onderworpen goederen gebruiken of verbruiken overeenkomstig de bij de vestiging van het vruchtgebruik gestelde regels of, bij gebreke van zodanige regels, met inachtneming van de aard van de goederen en de ten aanzien van het gebruik of verbruik bestaande plaatselijke gewoonten'.

163 Art. 3:215 BW: '-1. Is bij de vestiging van een vruchtgebruik of daarna aan de vruchtgebruiker de bevoegdheid gegeven tot gehele of gedeeltelijke vervreemding en vertering van aan het vruchtgebruik onderworpen goederen, dan kan de hoofdgerechtigde bij het einde van het vruchtgebruik afgifte vorderen van de in vruchtgebruik gegeven goederen of hetgeen daarvoor in de plaats getreden is, voor zover de vruchtgebruiker of zijn rechtverkrijgenden niet bewijzen dat die goederen verteerd of door toeval tenietgegaan zijn'.

164 Asser, Van Dam & Mijnsen 2002, No. 261, p. 289, No. 288, p. 323-324, Rank-Berenschot 1985, p. 178, Van Gaalen 2001, p. 23, 118-122.

165 Asser, Van Dam & Mijnsen 2002, No. 261, p. 289, Parlementaire Geschiedenis NBW - Boek 3 1981, p. 639. See Chapter 2; 2.4. Other Property Rights.

166 See Chapter 3; 3.2. Personal Servitudes, and Chapter 4; 3.2. Personal Servitudes: usufruct and limited personal servitudes.

167 Art. 3:207(2) BW, Van Gaalen 2001, p. 215-216, Rank-Berenschot 1985, p. 173 *et seq.*

168 Art. 3:36 BW Van Gaalen 2001, p. 218.

these property law acts, Dutch law follows a functional approach. The usufructuary only has a power to dispose over the objects under usufruct insofar as is useful for the exercise of the right of usufruct. If an act of the usufructuary does not classify as an act within the exercise of the right of usufruct, it will be invalid. Consequently, the objects will not have left the usufruct.[169] Only in the event that a third party successfully invokes a provision of third-party protection, the lack of power to dispose of the usufructuary will be remedied and the object will have left the usufruct.[170]

However, what exactly constitutes an act within the exercise of the right of usufruct is not at all clear. It certainly includes the right to insure, to collect claims, to transfer those objects under usufruct that are supposed to be transferred, for instance, shares, to invest money, to transfer or consume if such powers or rights exist, and the right to repair.[171] Van Gaalen refers to the general management power in case of a community of objects in Article 3:170 BW, which states:[172]

> 1. Acts for the normal maintenance or to maintain a common object, and, in general, acts which cannot be delayed, can be, if necessary, performed by one of the holders of a share in the community. Each of the holders of a share is entitled to act in order to stop prescription.[173]

When shares in a company are the objects under usufruct, the management duty of the usufructuary will usually include an obligation to invest these objects. However, high-risk investments are usually considered a violation of the management duties of the usufructuary and are not allowed.[174] The circumstances of the case will determine whether a usufructuary has acted within his powers. The position of the third party is decisive: an act that seems valid for a third party and is made within the powers of exercise of the usufruct can be relied upon.[175] In all other circumstances only the usufructuary and the owner together can dispose of the object.

The act of the usufructuary can constitute a breach of his management powers in respect of the owner, or principal right-holder, of the objects under usufruct.[176]

169 Van Gaalen remarks that the exact consequence of an act made by the usufructuary outside his powers is not clear, Van Gaalen 2001, p. 218, see also Bos 2005, p. 24 on the extension of the powers of the usufructuary.

170 Art. 3:86 BW, Van Gaalen 2001, p. 218.

171 Respectively Arts. 3:209, 3:210, 3:212, 3:214, 3:215, 3:217, and 3:220 BW, Asser, Van Dam & Mijnsen 2002, No. 283a, p. 316.

172 On co-ownership, which is one of the forms of a community, in Dutch *gemeenschap*, see above; 2.2. Co-Ownership.

173 Art. 3:170 BW '-1 Handelingen dienende tot gewoon onderhoud of tot behoud van een gemeenschappelijk goed, en in het algemeen handelingen die geen uitstel kunnen lijden, kunnen door ieder der deelgenoten zo nodig zelfstandig worden verricht. Ieder van hen is bevoegd ten behoeve van de gemeenschap verjaring te stuiten'.

174 Specifically not in a situation where the owner of these shares is a minor. See HR 9 January 1998, *NJ* 1999, 285, Mellema-Kranenburg 1999, p. 30-31.

175 Parlementaire Geschiedenis NBW – Boek 3 1981, p. 650-651, Asser, Van Dam & Mijnsen 2002, No. 283a, p. 315.

176 In Dutch *hoofdgerechtigde*.

This internal relation between usufructuary and owner is dealt with in Article 3:207(3) BW:

> 3. In relation to the owner the usufructuary is under the obligation to act as a diligent usufructuary in respect to the objects under usufruct and the management thereof.[177]

The distinction between the external effects and internal effects of the right of usufruct allow for the possibility that an act would be valid against a third party, but would lead to a claim of damages by the owner against the usufructuary for a violation of this requirement of diligence.[178] The result of such an act would be that the object leaves the usufruct, therefore decreasing the value of the property right.

In order to maintain the value of the usufruct Article 3:213 BW introduces the possibility of substitution.[179] Substitution is a technique under which those objects that the usufructuary receives in exchange for the object leaving the usufruct will fall under the usufruct instead.[180] However, substitution is only possible in respect to certain objects. Immovable objects and claims cannot be easily substituted. Both need to be registered in the name of the owner or right-holder, before they fall under the usufruct.[181]

A right of usufruct in Dutch law not only allows its holder the use of objects, but also allows the holder of the right to take the fruits the object produces. In respect to fruits Dutch law makes a distinction between natural fruits and civil fruits. Natural fruits are part of the object before they separate and can be used by the usufructuary. Examples are apples from a tree, the calf of a cow and the wool of a sheep. Civil fruits are proceeds such as dividend of shares, interests from sums of money, and income from rent, that the object produces.[182] Generally, the usufructuary is also entitled to receive these civil fruits. However, fruits can only be used when they can be identified. The principal rule is that at the moment the fruits are separated from the object, the usufructuary receives ownership of them and can therefore use the fruits.[183] Consequently, the owner of the object will lose ownership of the fruits upon separation, but the object itself will, if not used up, eventually return to the owner.

177 Art. 3:207(3) '-3. Jegens de hoofdgerechtigde is de vruchtgebruiker verplicht ten aanzien van de aan het vruchtgebruik onderworpen goederen en het beheer daarover de zorg van een goed vruchtgebruiker in acht te nemen'. The old BW used the criterion of *pater familias* (goede huisvader) in Art. 831 Old BW, Mellema-Kranenburg 1999, p. 30-31.

178 Parlementaire Geschiedenis NBW - Boek 3 1981, p. 651, Van Gaalen 2001, p. 216, Asser, Van Dam & Mijnsen 2002, No. 283, p. 314.

179 See Bos 2005, p. 29 *et seq.*

180 Van Gaalen 2001, p. 94.

181 HR 23 September 1994, *NJ* 1996, 461 (*Kas-associatie case*), Bos 2005, p. 31.

182 Pitlo et al. 2006, No. 686, p. 521-522, Mellema-Kranenburg 1999, p. 25.

183 Art. 5:17 BW.

In practice the right of usufruct is used as a management device.[184] The right of usufruct is used in cases of succession as well as *inter vivos*.[185] For example, if the surviving spouse is not the only heir of the deceased, in Dutch law the other heirs are under the obligation to co-operate with the spouse in order to create a right of usufruct on the matrimonial home and its contents, usually household furniture.[186] Another good example is offered by usufructs on shares in a company. Articles 2:88 and 2:197 BW specifically allow the creation of a usufruct on shares.[187] The usufruct will give the usufructuary the right to manage the shares, but will not give him the voting right connected to these shares.[188] The voting right will, unless the parties agree otherwise, remain with the owner. Furthermore the owner and the usufructuary can agree to distribute more powers to the usufructuary. In fact, the possibility to distribute powers to the usufructuary makes the usufruct a very flexible device. Specifically in case of a usufruct on shares, the possibility to award the usufructuary more powers of investment is very interesting. The diligence requirement of Article 3:207(3) BW does not require the usufructuary to successfully invest the shares in order to increase the fund under usufruct. To the contrary, any loss made while investing shares are to be paid by the usufructuary, while, as a standard situation the profits made by shares are not considered fruits and therefore are for the owner.[189] The possibility of agreement will usually allow for a workable distribution of powers.

Based on the right of usufruct, Dutch law recognises two usufruct-like rights in the right to use and the right to live in a building.[190] Dutch doctrine considers these rights as special forms of the right of usufruct.[191] Article 3:226 BW declares the provisions on the right of usufruct applicable to the right of use or the right to live in a building, also known as the right of habitation. However, because of the different nature of these two rights, some provisions on usufruct will not apply. A right of use will give the right to use an object of another, but not the right to take the fruits that object produces. Only those fruits the holder needs for his family can be taken.[192] A right of habitation grants a right to use a building, but only to live in, not to use it in another way.[193] These rights can be created on a right of ownership, but also on other property rights. This includes, for example, a right of apartment, a

184 Especially in Dutch law where the transfer of ownership for management purposes, i.e. the *fiducia cum amico*, is prohibited by Art. 3:84(3) BW there is a need for other management devices.

185 See Bos 2005, p. 41 *et seq.*

186 Art. 4:29 BW.

187 Art. 2:88 BW for shares in public limited companies (*NV*) and Art. 3:197 for shares in private limited companies (*BV*) Mellema-Kranenburg 1999, p. 25.

188 Art. 3:88(2) or Art. 3:197(2) BW.

189 HR 9 January 1998, *NJ* 1999, 285, Bos 2005, p. 113.

190 Based on the Roman law rights of *usus* and *habitatio*. See Chapter 2; 2.4. Other Property Rights.

191 Asser, Van Dam & Mijnsen 2002, No. 328, p. 351. Under the old Dutch Civil Code these two rights were treated separately by Arts. 865-874 old BW.

192 Art. 3:226(2) BW.

193 Art. 3:226(3) BW.

special property right which is dealt with below, which may be burdened with a right of habitation.[194]

Finally, the rights of use and habitation are strictly personal rights. These rights are held, like a right of usufruct, by a person not in his capacity as holder of a property right to an object, but are connected to that person specifically. When, as with a right of usufruct, the holder of the right dies, the right of use or habitation will end. However, in contrast with a right of usufruct in Dutch law, the rights of use and habitation cannot be transferred, nor can they be made subject of another property right.[195]

3.3. *Emphyteusis*

The right of *emphyteusis*, in Dutch *erfpacht*, is a property right that entitles one to hold and use an immovable object that is owned by someone else.[196] Of all the property rights available in Dutch law, the right of *emphyteusis* most closely resembles the right of ownership.[197] The scope of the right is established by book 5 of the Civil Code, but also through agreement between parties contained in the deed of creation.[198] Such agreements are known as conditions, in Dutch *voorwaarden*, and are part of the property right itself.[199] The Articles in book 5 of the Civil Code can, in certain circumstances, be deviated from through these conditions. Furthermore, the conditions can also contain additional agreements governing the relationship between the owner and the holder of the right of *emphyteusis*.

Although these conditions are an agreement between parties, they are treated as part of the property right insofar as they have a *sufficient connection* to the right of *emphyteusis* and are not contrary to the *nature* of the right.[200] These open criteria make it difficult to establish which agreements are included in the property right and which are not.[201] Leading opinion in Dutch law seems to be that these agreements can be both negative and positive.[202] Van Velten, however, has argued that the conditions cannot contain a positive duty unless there is a specific legal basis.[203] Struycken has held that there are limits to the freedom of parties to make these

194 See 3.5. Right of Apartment.

195 Art. 3:226(4) BW, Asser, Van Dam & Mijnsen 2002, No. 328, p. 351-352.

196 Art. 5:85 BW, Asser, Van Dam & Mijnsen 2002, No. 215, p. 236.

197 In German doctrinal terms it could be held that the right of *emphyteusis* is an *Eigentumsähnliches* right. However, German law itself does not recognises a right of *emphyteusis* in its catalogue of property rights. See Chapter 4; 3. Other Property Rights.

198 De Jong 1995b, p. 1, Asser, Van Dam & Mijnsen 2002, Nos. 215 *et seq.*, p. 236 *et seq.*

199 See Vonck 2007, p. 598.

200 HR 16 March 1977, *NJ* 1977, 399, Plantenga & Treurniet 1957, p. 177, Van Velten 1995, p. 47, De Jong 1995b, p. 17, Rank-Berenschot 1992, p. 110-111, Struycken 2007, p. 391-392. Although this case dates from before the introduction of the new Civil Code, it can be assumed its reasoning applies to the new right of *emphyteusis* as well. See the opinion of Advocate General De Vries Lentsch-Kostense at 10, HR 27 April 2007, *RvdW* 2007/469.

201 See also Struycken 2007, p. 394.

202 Asser, Van Dam & Mijnsen 2002, No. 217, p. 241, De Jong 1995b, p. 17-19, Vonck 2007, p. 603.

203 Van Velten 1995, p. 49, see also Snijders 1995, p. 155.

agreements, explicitly referring to the method in which property rights are created. Through the *démembrement* model, which he terms the subtraction model, Struycken explains that in respect to positive duties a problem arises.[204] Under this model, property rights are composed of powers that follow from the mother right from which the property right is derived. Positive duties are not part of the mother right, so neither can they be part of a property right derived from that right.[205]

The powers of the holder of the right can be so extensive that the owner is left with nothing but a completely empty right of ownership. Such an empty right of ownership will only provide the owner with the expectation that, eventually, when the right of *emphyteusis* comes to an end, his ownership will be full and complete again. In other words, the extensive influence of the conditions on the right of *emphyteusis* makes this the property right most closely resembling the right of ownership.

Dutch doctrine distinguishes between urban and rural types of *emphyteusis*. Rights of rural *emphyteusis*, for instance, a right to use a piece of agricultural land for a long duration of time, are mainly used for agricultural purposes and include combinations with, for example, milk quotas.[206] The urban *emphyteusis* is the result of developments originating in Amsterdam from 1896.[207] The city of Amsterdam decided that henceforth it would no longer transfer rights of ownership, but instead rights of *emphyteusis* would be created. In the conditions to these rights, the city of Amsterdam would provide additional rules and regulations that supplemented the powers of the city for regulating public law.[208] The Amsterdam approach was soon followed by other cities as well and has become standard in the Netherlands. Because of this development, the urban *emphyteusis* became the most common form of *emphyteusis*, but the rural type also continues to be used.[209]

Dutch cities establish general terms and conditions that apply to all rights of *emphyteusis* created on behalf of the city. These terms and conditions provide regulations on the powers of the municipality as owner and on the holder of the right. Furthermore, remuneration is paid in exchange for the right. The terms and conditions will also deal with the establishment and powers of alteration of this remuneration, also known as the *canon*. The general terms and conditions make the right of urban *emphyteusis* a very suitable method for regulation.

The right of *emphyteusis* can be created for a limited or unlimited duration, either with full payment of the *canon* in advance or through a system of payments over time. A right of *emphyteusis* created for an unlimited period of time with a full payment of the *canon* in advance will very much resemble ownership. Article 5:89 BW states:

204 Struycken 2007, p. 412-415.

205 Struycken 2007, p. 415-422. The nature of additional conditions to property rights will be dealt with extensively in the next section. See below; 4.7. Obligations as Part of Property Rights.

206 See Snijders 1995, p. 89 *et seq.*

207 De Jong 1995b, p. 3, Van Velten 1995, p. 17-18.

208 De Jong 1995b, p. 4-6, Van Velten 1995, p. 18-28.

209 See, *inter alia*, Snijders 1995, p. 89 *et seq.*

1. Unless provided otherwise in the deed of establishment, the *emphyteuticarius* will have the same power to enjoy the object as the owner.[210]

The consequence of the comparison to the powers of the owner is that the holder of a right of *emphyteusis* is allowed to use and enjoy the object exclusively.[211] The power to use the object includes the power to erect buildings or other constructions for which the owner will have to provide compensation once the right of *emphyteusis* ends.[212] The holder of the right will not become the owner of the buildings or other constructions he erects.[213] Like in other civil law systems, the rule of *superficies solo cedit* applies in Dutch law. The result of the application of this rule is that the owner of the land will become owner of the buildings on it.[214] This consequence leads to the unfair situation that for as long as the right of *emphyteusis* exists, the holder of the right remains liable for both the land and the buildings or constructions erected on it, but is not automatically entitled to compensation of the value after termination of the right of *emphyteusis*.[215] Van Velten has proposed to solve this problem by awarding ownership of the buildings to the holder of the right of *emphyteusis*.[216]

The contents of a right of *emphyteusis* resemble the contents of a right of usufruct. Both rights entitle the holder to the use and the enjoyment of an object, as well as the right to take and enjoy the fruits the object produces.[217] However, the right of *emphyteusis* is not connected to the holder personally, as is the case with a right of usufruct. Therefore, a right of *emphyteusis* is capable of existing well beyond the life of the original right-holder.[218]

Municipalities usually combine the creation of a right of *emphyteusis* on a parcel of land with the duty to erect a building.[219] Any subsequent holder of the right of *emphyteusis* will take over the rights and duties concerning this building. Therefore, according to leading opinion, the holder of the right of *emphyteusis* is awarded economic ownership of the building.[220] However, in practice, the powers of enjoyment will usually be limited by the terms and conditions. These limitations can include, for example, a prohibition on altering the purpose for which the building is used, the duty to park cars on one's own land, and a prohibition against polluting the environment.[221]

210 Art. 5:89 BW '-1. Voor zover niet in de akte van vestiging anders is bepaald, heeft de erfpachter hetzelfde genot van de zaak als een eigenaar'.

211 Asser, Van Dam & Mijnsen 2002, No. 221, p. 247.

212 Art. 3:99 BW, Asser, Van Dam & Mijnsen 2002, No. 221, p. 248.

213 This is different in French law, where the contract creating the right of *emphyteusis* breaks with the *superficies solo cedit* rule. See Chapter 3; 3.4. *Emphyteusis*.

214 This is the rule of *superficies solo cedit*. See below; 3.4. *Superficies*.

215 Art. 6:174 BW, Asser, Van Dam & Mijnsen 2002, No. 221, p. 248, Van Velten 1995, p. 78.

216 Van Velten 1995, p. 78-79, see also Asser, Van Dam & Mijnsen 2002, No. 221, p. 248.

217 De Jong 1995b, p. 46, Asser, Van Dam & Mijnsen 2002, No. 223, p. 249.

218 De Jong 1995b, p. 21-22.

219 HR 8 March 1991, *NJ* 1991, 379, Asser, Van Dam & Mijnsen 2002, No. 217, p. 241, De Jong 1995b, p. 46.

220 Asser, Mijnsen, De Haan & Van Dam 2006, No. 483, p. 547.

221 De Jong 1995b, p. 43-45.

Furthermore, the right-holder's power to dispose can be limited.[222] Without these limitations it is possible to create other rights, both personal and property rights, on the object under *emphyteusis*. It is also possible to transfer the right itself.[223] The limitations can only exist in the form of a requirement to ask permission from the owner before a transfer or creation of another right. If such permission is refused without reasonable grounds, the holder of the right can approach the court for an order to replace the required permission of the owner with permission from the court.[224] The possibility to create rights in respect of the right of *emphyteusis* includes the creation of rights of hypothec, rights of apartment and possibly, but controversially, also rights of *superficies*.[225]

Finally, the right of *emphyteusis* can impose a substantial burden on the right of ownership. In particular when the right has been created for an unlimited duration of time. In order to remedy property burdens still existing when they are no longer needed, Article 5:97 BW offers the possibility to approach the court to change the right or to bring it to an end.[226] Both the holder of the right and the owner of the object may approach the court. The idea behind this Article is, in case a perpetual property right may be created, to allow parties, when circumstances have changed and twenty-five years have passed since the creation of the right, to change the content of their legal relation or to bring the legal relation to an end.[227] In this way the unwanted effects of perpetual property rights, which sometimes recall the feudal rights that burdened generations of tenants, can be remedied, but only if the parties to the property right are in agreement.

3.4. *Superficies*

The right of *superficies* or *opstalrecht* is defined in Article 5:101 BW, which states:

> 1. The right of *superficies* is a property right to have or acquire a right of ownership in, on or on top of buildings, constructions or plantings on an immovable object, that belongs to someone else.[228]

The right of *superficies* breaks with the general rule in Dutch property law that what can be considered part of the main object is part of that object.[229] In case of immovable objects, ownership of land brings with it ownership of everything that is attached to the land.[230] This rule of *superficies solo cedit* was known in Roman law and

222 See Vonck 2007, p. 603.

223 Art. 5:91 BW, Asser, Van Dam & Mijnsen 2002, Nos. 224 *et seq.*, p. 250 *et seq.*

224 Art. 5:91(4) BW, Asser, Van Dam & Mijnsen 2002, No. 224, p. 251.

225 Asser, Beekhuis & Davids 1990, No. 224, p. 250, Heyman 1999, p. 52 *et seq.*

226 Vonck 2007, p. 600, Asser, Van Dam & Mijnsen 2002, No. 237, p. 263-264.

227 Asser, Van Dam & Mijnsen 2002, No. 238, p. 265.

228 Art. 5:101 BW, '-1. Het recht van opstal is een zakelijk recht om in, op of boven een onroerende zaak van een ander gebouwen, werken of beplantingen in eigendom te hebben of te verkrijgen'.

229 Art. 3:4 BW, Ploeger 1997, p. 2, Staudinger et al. 2002, p. 20.

230 Art. 5:20 BW.

remains to be applied in Dutch law today. However, contrary to Roman law, Dutch law allows exceptions to this principle.[231]

In fact, the main exception to the rule is provided by Article 5:101 BW which allows ownership of objects in, on or on top of an immovable object, which is in the ownership of someone else. The right of *superficies*, in other words, creates a split in the object of the right of ownership and results in two rights of ownership; one on the immovable object, one on the object that is split from that object.

Unlike the other property rights, the right of *superficies* not only provides the holder with powers derived from the right of ownership, but also provides a right of ownership itself. This ownership is a right of ownership in the meaning of Article 5:1 BW - absolute and unitary. The result of the creation of a right of *superficies* is therefore that the owner of the land remains the owner, and that the accession rule of *superficies solo cedit* does not apply. The ownership of a building on land is therefore in the hands of someone other than the owner of that land.

The right of *superficies* resembles the right of *emphyteusis*. Both property rights are rights to use and enjoy immovable objects and can be created for an unlimited duration.[232] Furthermore, rights of *superficies* and *emphyteusis* can be created in combination with one another. In legal literature these two rights have often been dealt with together.[233] The Dutch civil code only provides a very short set of articles on the right of *superficies* and declares that several articles on the right of *emphyteusis* are applicable.[234] Amongst those common rules is the possibility for parties to decide on additional agreements that become part of the right itself.[235]

Nevertheless, there are also important differences.[236] The possibility to break with the *superficies solo cedit* rule of Article 5:20 BW seems the principal example.[237] The right of ownership of the buildings, constructions or plantings will give the holder of the right of *superficies* the full powers of an owner.[238] The right of *emphyteusis* will only give a right to use and enjoy the land on which the building, construction or planting is placed.[239]

In practice the right of *superficies* is used as an independent right, but also as a right dependent on another right of enjoyment.[240] When the right is used dependent on another right, the right of *superficies* will fall under the general category of accessory, or dependent, rights of Article 3:7 BW. In practice this will specifically be so in combinations with the right of lease and the right of *emphyteusis*. In regard to lease, the relationship between the parties will be personal, but the property right of

231 See Chapter 2; 2.4. Other Property Rights. Ploeger 1997, p. 3.

232 De Vries & Pleysier 1995, p. 110, Ploeger 1997, p. 169. This is different in French law where the maximum duration for a right of *superficies* is 99 years. See Chapter 3; 3.3. *Superficies*.

233 See, *inter alia*, Asser, Van Dam & Mijnsen 2002, No. 243, p. 250, De Vries & Pleysier 1995, De Jong 1995b, Ploeger 1997, p. 169 *et seq*.

234 Art. 5:104 BW.

235 Asser, Van Dam & Mijnsen 2002, Nos. 251, 253, p. 279, 281.

236 See also Asser, Van Dam & Mijnsen 2002, No. 254, p. 281 *et seq*., Ploeger 1997, p. 177.

237 Asser, Van Dam & Mijnsen 2002, No. 247, p. 274.

238 Ploeger 1997, p. 176.

239 Art. 5:103 BW, Asser, Van Dam & Mijnsen 2002, No. 253, p. 280.

240 Art. 5:101(2) BW, Asser, Van Dam & Mijnsen 2002, No. 250, p. 278, Ploeger 1997, p. 169, 203.

superficies can function as a method to ensure compensation for any building remaining at the end of the lease.[241] Because the right of *superficies* is dependent on the lease, the end of the agreement will bring with it the end of the right of *superficies*. Furthermore, the right of *emphyteusis* could be combined with a right of *superficies* to arrange for the ownership of any buildings or constructions on the land. A right of *emphyteusis* only gives a right to use and enjoyment comparable to those of the owner, whereas the right of *superficies* enables the holder of the right to actually have ownership.[242]

However, not just any right of *superficies* created in relation to another right or relation will necessarily be accessory, in the meaning of Article 3:7 BW. The right will be accessory if it cannot exist without the relation to which it is connected.[243] Furthermore, the deed of creation can provide clarity.

The holder of a right of *superficies* has the power to create other property rights in respect of his right of *superficies*. In theory, these other property rights will have to be created on the right of *superficies* itself. Therefore, these newly created rights will become accessory rights within the meaning of Article 3:7 BW. The end of the right of *superficies* will then bring an end to the property right. A different doctrinal possibility would be the creation of a property right in respect of the ownership of, for instance, a building in the hands of the holder of the right of *superficies*. However, when the right of *superficies* came to an end and the ownership of the building, construction or planting returned to the owner of the land, the owner of the land would be bound by the property right which he had nothing to do with.

This case should be distinguished from that of an acquirer of the object who, in his decision to acquire the object, can check the register and see which property rights are created. An accessory property right in respect of the right of *superficies* and not the ownership of the holder of the *superficies* solves this problem. It will result in a termination of the property right in relation to the termination of the right of *superficies*.[244]

Another solution is provided in case of the creation of servitudes. Article 5:84 BW provides that a right of servitude can be created on an immovable object, both as servient and as dominant land. If the right of servitude has been created from the right of *superficies* as the dominant land it will only cease to exist if the parties agreed to this possibility in the deed of creation.[245] A right of servitude on the object under the right of *superficies*, where the object is the servient land, will terminate with the right of *superficies* itself.[246]

241 Asser, Van Dam & Mijnsen 2002, No. 250, p. 278, see also De Vries & Pleysier 1995, p. 114.

242 Although De Jong remarks that it is not very likely that this combination is used much. See De Jong 1995b, p. 77, Asser, Van Dam & Mijnsen 2002, No. 243, p. 270, Heyman 2005, p. 19 *et seq*.

243 Asser, Van Dam & Mijnsen 2002, No. 250, p. 278-279, see also HR 7 March 1979, *NJ* 1980, 116.

244 In the same line see De Vries & Pleysier 1995, p. 116-117, Asser, Van Dam & Mijnsen 2002, No. 255, p. 283.

245 Art. 5:84 (2) BW, Asser, Van Dam & Mijnsen 2002, No. 255, p. 283.

246 Art. 5:84 (3) BW.

Other property rights that could be created include apartment rights, but also a right of hypothec.[247] Also those rights will be accessory to the right of *superficies* and therefore terminate with the termination of the right of *superficies*. In order to avoid over-complicated situations, in Dutch law a right of *superficies* that is already an accessory right in relation to another right or relation cannot in itself be burdened with another property right.[248] Only if the mother right to which the right of *superficies* is accessory is burdened as well, will this be possible.[249] The termination of the mother right will then bring with it the termination of the right of *superficies* as well as the newly created accessory right. However, this power of the holder of the right of *superficies* can be limited in the deed of creation.[250]

3.5. *Right of Apartment*

Appartementsrecht, the right of apartment, is dealt with by Article 5:106 BW. It is difficult to define the right of apartment in Dutch law since it includes a share in the ownership of a building as well as of the land on which the building is built, an exclusive right to use a certain part of that building and a right to use certain parts of the building together with the others who hold a right of apartment in the same property.[251] Moreover, the term apartment is, both in Dutch and in English ambiguous. In the first place, it refers to flats, used for residential purposes. However, the right of apartment in Dutch law can also include rights to commercial and industrial spaces, both in and outside of buildings.

The foundation of the right of apartment can be found in the general rules on co-ownership. The apartment right in Dutch law is constructed around the ownership of the land and the building that is constructed on it. The holders of the various rights of apartment together have the right of ownership of the land and of the complete building.[252] This form of co-ownership is characterised as a community.[253] Each holder of a right of apartment holds a share in the community. Consequently, the holders of the shares together have the full right of ownership amongst them.

The share that each of the holders of a right of apartment has in the community is an indivisible share that represents a specifically defined fraction.[254] As a result,

247 It follows from Arts. 3:227 and 3:228 BW that a right of hypothec can be established on registered incorporeal objects (*registergoederen*), Asser, Van Dam & Mijnsen 2002, No. 255, p. 283.

248 Ploeger 1997, p. 208, De Vries & Pleysier 1995, p. 117, Asser, Van Dam & Mijnsen 2002, No. 255, p. 283.

249 De Jong 1995b, p. 76.

250 Arts. 5:104 and 5:91 BW.

251 Art. 5:106(3) BW, Asser, Van Dam & Mijnsen 2002, No. 343, p. 366.

252 Asser, Van Dam & Mijnsen 2002, No. 343, p. 367.

253 Or *gemeenschap*, see Art. 3:166 BW. The term community is preferred over co-ownership since in Dutch law ownership is restricted to corporeal objects. See Art. 5:1 BW. A right of apartment can also be established on other property rights as e.g. a right of *emphyteusis*. Mertens 1989, p. 3-4, Asser, Mijnsen, De Haan & Van Dam 2006, Nos. 445 *et seq.*, p. 496, Asser, Van Dam & Mijnsen 2002, No. 343, p. 367. See above; 2.2. Co-Ownership.

254 Art. 5:113(1) BW, Mertens 1999, p. 25.

the holder of a share is not entitled to specific objects in the community, but only to a share of the whole. A division at the end of the community will therefore require a division of the object amongst the holders of shares, usually a division of the economic value of the community.[255]

The share in the community is combined with an exclusive right to use a specifically defined part of the building. This right to use is not a property right itself, not a type of ownership, but an accessory right to the share in the community.[256] The right to use cannot be transferred separately but can be given to someone else to use.[257] The deed of separation in which the various shares are created contains a drawing in which is specified which parts of the building are for the right-holder's exclusive use. Any other parts of the building will be for common use for all the holders of the shares. These common parts are also shown on the drawing.[258] Also the right to use the common parts of the buildings can be given to someone else to use.[259]

Furthermore, besides the share in the community and the exclusive and common rights to use, the holder of a share becomes a member of the association of owners, in Dutch *vereniging van eigenaars*. The membership of this association is 'qualitative' in the sense that the holder of a share automatically becomes a member of the association. When the share is transferred to another person, so is the membership of the association.[260] In the last few decades there has been much debate on the applicability of the rules on association of book 2 of the Civil Code. This second book provides rules on legal persons, including associations. However, the rules on the property law aspects, specifically on the community in which all holders of all shares together have a complete right of ownership, conflict with the majority voting system in book 2 on legal persons.[261] Recently these problems have been solved by new legislation that introduces a more workable solution inspired by the law of associations.[262]

Within the community, and therefore also within the association of owners, the holders of the shares are linked to each other. Even though on some issues the association may make majority decisions, the relation between the members is governed by the principles of good faith and fair dealing.[263] In other words, the majority will have to take the minority into account as well.

Apart from the right of ownership, the right of apartment can also be created on other property rights. These other property rights, most often the rights of *emphyteusis* and *superficies*, can therefore be subject to a separation into rights of

255 Pitlo et al. 2006, p. 366 *et seq.*, the general rules on community in book 3 of the BW are not applicable to apartment rights, although the concept is the same, Art. 3:189 BW. Title 9 of book 5 of the BW provides specific rules for apartment-rights, Art. 5:143 BW.

256 Art. 5:106(3) BW, Asser, Van Dam & Mijnsen 2002, No. 344, p. 368, Mertens 1999, p. 3.

257 Art. 5:120 BW, Asser, Van Dam & Mijnsen 2002, No. 344, p. 368.

258 Asser, Van Dam & Mijnsen 2002, No. 407, p, 424-425, Mertens 1999, p. 12.

259 Asser, Van Dam & Mijnsen 2002, No. 344, p. 369.

260 Art. 5:125 (2) BW.

261 Van Velten 2004, 554 *et seq.*

262 Art. 5:139 BW, Van Velten 2004, p. 555.

263 In Dutch the *redelijkheid en billijkheid*. HR 30 October 1998, *NJ* 1993, 83.

apartment.[264] In those situations the holders of the rights of apartment together will share the full right of *emphyteusis* or right of *superficies* among them.[265] However, in order to separate the property right, the permission of the owner from whom that property right is derived is required.[266] The creation of a right of apartment on another property right creates additional problems. The problems most likely to arise is when the property right that is separated into rights of apartment ceases to exist. For example, when the *canon* for a right of *emphyteusis* is no longer paid, the owner might bring the right to an end. As a general rule, the rights of apartment will cease to exist when the property right from which they are derived ceases to exist as well.[267]

In the case of payment of a *canon* for a right of *emphyteusis*, the duty for payment is divided among the different shareholders in the community. If all holders should stop their payment, the owner would have a right to terminate the right of *emphyteusis*. In the event that there is just one holder that does not pay, the owner can demand the transfer of the right of apartment of the non-payer instead.[268] Furthermore, the rights of apartment will not cease to exist when the underlying property right is extended or renewed.[269]

The right of apartment is dealt with in book 5 of the Civil Code, which deals with property rights in respect of corporeal objects.[270] Furthermore, the right is dealt with after the rights of *emphyteusis* and *superficies*. Systematically this would give rise to the assumption that the right of apartment is a limited property right in the same sense as the other rights dealt with in that part of the Civil Code. Nevertheless, there is a difference. As explained in the beginning of this section, property rights in Dutch law are considered to be limited property rights in the sense that they are derived from the paramount right of ownership.[271] The right of apartment, which was originally known as just 'apartment', is a complex of rights and competences. Dutch doctrine therefore treats it as a separate and distinct property right.[272] After all, upon creation of the right of apartment the original right of ownership will disappear and will be replaced by several shares in a community. In case of a limited right, the right of ownership continues to exist and is burdened by the limited property right. Moreover, the right of apartment is placed in book 5 of the Civil Code, which deals with property rights in respect of corporeal objects, whereas the

264 However, also other property rights could be subject to separation into rights of apartment, see Asser, Van Dam & Mijnsen 2002, No. 376, p. 400.
265 Asser, Van Dam & Mijnsen 2002, No. 374, p. 397-399, Mertens 1999, p. 4.
266 Art. 5:106 (6) BW, Asser, Van Dam & Mijnsen 2002, No. 374, p. 397-399.
267 Asser, Van Dam & Mijnsen 2002, No. 382, p. 406.
268 Art. 5:116 (4)(5) BW, Asser, Van Dam & Mijnsen 2002, No. 381, p. 405.
269 Although this is a doctrinally difficult construction, see Asser, Van Dam & Mijnsen 2002, No. 383, p. 406.
270 This is not an entirely correct placement, since also a right of *emphyteusis* and a right of *superficies* can be separated into rights of apartment. Following this reasoning, the right of apartment should have been included in book 3 that deals with property rights in respect to both corporeal objects and rights. On this see Mertens 1999, p. 4.
271 See above; 3. Other Property Rights.
272 Van Velten 1989, Asser, Van Dam & Mijnsen 2002, Nos. 347, 348, p. 371-372.

right of apartment can also be created on property rights. Its place in the Civil Code is therefore not immediately evident.

The different shares that arise after a separation into rights of apartment have a different character from the other limited property rights. For example, they can be in the hands of the same person without mixing and coming to an end.[273]

3.6. *Pledge*

Apart from rights to use someone else's object, Dutch law also recognises property rights that are used to secure the performance of an obligation. Security rights are intended to provide the holder with a preferential position compared with other creditors, and to allow the holder to sell the object serving as security and use the proceeds of sale to satisfy the debt, usually a sum of money, for which security was given.[274] In Dutch law these security rights are the right of pledge and hypothec. Like their Roman predecessors, the rights of pledge and hypothec share many characteristics.[275] In this section the right of pledge will be dealt with, and the next section will deal with the right of hypothec.[276]

The right of pledge is a property right in respect of a movable object or claim that gives security to the holder. The main element of this security is the power of the holder to sell the object under pledge and use the proceeds of the sale to satisfy a debt.[277] The right of pledge is created to provide security for the payment of a certain debt. In the event that the debtor cannot pay his debt, the holder of the right of pledge can use his power to sell the object.

Traditionally, the right of pledge in Dutch law has been a classic, possessory, security right. In a classic right of pledge, the pledgor brings the object under pledge into the power of the pledgee in order to provide security.[278] Because of the obligation to bring the object in the power, the possession, of the pledgee, the type of objects that could be used was limited. Only those objects that the pledgor could miss would be brought into the power of the pledgee. The result of this was that objects used for normal business purposes, such as inventory or company cars, could not be used to provide security. It was for this reason that in 1929 the *Hoge Raad* acknowledged the transfer of ownership for security purposes.[279] Such a transfer enabled the passing of the ownership without the loss of control over the object. When possession remained with the transferor, he could continue to use these objects and trade in order to pay his debt.

Meijers, the founding father of the Dutch Civil Code, was a fierce opponent of this transfer of ownership for security purposes. He claimed that such a transfer

273 See above; 3. Other Property Rights.
274 Art. 3:227 BW.
275 See Chapter 2; 2.4. Other Property Rights.
276 See below; 3.7. Hypothec.
277 The pledgee is not entitled to keep the object under pledge for himself; a sale is compulsory. Art. 3:235 BW, Asser, Mierlo, Mijnsen & Van Velten 2003, No. 26, p. 25.
278 Art. 1198(1) Old BW, Asser, Mierlo, Mijnsen & Van Velten 2003, No. 13, p. 9.
279 See above; 2.3. Security Ownership.

effectively created a right of pledge without the object being brought into the power of the pledgee.[280] Following this reasoning, the scope of powers received by the owner for security purposes was, compared with the powers he needed, far too broad. A right of pledge only awards those powers to the pledgee that are necessary for the exercise of the pledge.

In the new Civil Code the classic right of pledge remains, but is supplemented by a so-called silent or non-possessory pledge. The silent pledge creates a right of pledge on a certain object without the pledgor having to bring the object into the power of the pledgee. Combined with the introduction of this right of silent pledge, the legislature introduced Article 3:84(3) BW which prohibits transfers of ownership for security purposes.[281]

A right of pledge, both classic and silent, can be created on all objects, or *goederen*, that are capable of pledge, except registered objects.[282] This includes corporeal objects and also incorporeal objects such as claims. The corporeal object as well as the claim must be transferable. Non-transferability would make it impossible for the pledgee to execute his right of pledge and sell and transfer the object or claim to a third party.[283] A right of pledge created on an incorporeal object is considered a so-called patrimonial right.[284] Because a right of pledge can also be created on an incorporeal object, the right is dealt with in book 3 of the Civil Code which deals with patrimonial law in general, and not in book 5, which deals with property rights in respect of corporeal objects only.

The right of pledge entitles the pledgee to preferential treatment over other creditors and awards the exclusive power to sell the object under pledge and use its proceeds to satisfy a debt. Also in the event of insolvency of the pledgor, the pledgee is entitled to sell the object and satisfy the debt as if there were no insolvency.[285] The pledgee will be entitled to make such a sale as an executor of the pledge and not as a representative of the owner.[286] When a non-possessory or silent pledge is created, the pledgee has the power to claim possession or actual power over the object before he realises his right.[287] However, the pledgee must sell and is not allowed to take the object under pledge and keep it for himself. Any agreement that attempts to give this power to the pledgee is therefore void.[288] Nevertheless,

280 Meijers even used security ownership as an example of evasion of the law, see Meijers 1937, p. 65, Meijers 1948, p. 89 *et seq.*, see also Van Mierlo 1988, p. 176, Molenaar 1991, p. 7.

281 But not so-called actual transfers, see above; 2.3. Security Ownership. See further Molenaar 1991, p. 6 *et seq.*

282 The right of hypothec deals with registered objects. Any other object, corporeal and incorporeal, can be subject to a right of pledge, Art. 3:227(1) BW.

283 Art. 3:228 BW, Asser, Mierlo, Mijnsen & Van Velten 2003, Nos. 16a, 28, p. 14, 31.

284 In Dutch, *vermogensrecht*, Art. 3:6 BW.

285 Art. 57 Bankruptcy Act (Fw).

286 Molenaar 1999, p. 50.

287 See Asser, Mierlo, Mijnsen & Van Velten 2003, No. 66, p. 76.

288 Arts. 3:235, 3:250 and 3:253 BW, this prohibition is a remainder of the prohibition of the *lex commissioria* in Roman Law, see Chapter 2; 2.4. Other Property Rights, and 3.4. Other Property Rights. The discussion on the prohibition was raised again with in the Netherlands on the occasion of the implementation of Directive 2002/47/EC of 6 June 2002 on Financial Collateral arrangements. This Directive introduces a specific type of pledge where the pledgee is →

parties can agree that, when the pledgee is entitled to execute, the court may be approached for an order stating the price at which the pledgee may keep the object for himself.[289]

The right of pledge is an accessory right. Therefore, the right of pledge must be dependent upon a claim or other relation in order to exist. Its accessory nature is visible when the claim or object for which the pledge was created is transferred to another person. In that situation, the right of pledge will transfer with that claim or relation and will remain in existence.[290] When the claim for which the right of pledge was created ceases to exist, the right of pledge will cease as well.[291]

Moreover, a right of pledge is also dependent on the existence of the object on which it is created. The ceasing of the claim that is the object of the right of pledge will also lead to the ceasing of the right of pledge itself. However, in some cases, a new right of pledge will arise in substitution. This new right of pledge will cover those claims that replace the original object or claim through substitution.[292] This right of pledge on those new claims arises by operation of law and strengthens the position of the pledgor since this substitution is intended to preserve the value of the object or claim serving as security. However, this substitution will not work in all situations; a purchase price received for the sale of a corporeal object will not fall under the right of pledge.[293] The *Hoge Raad* has stated that a specific legal basis is required for substitution.[294] Such a legal basis is offered by Article 3:229 BW:

> 1. The right of pledge or the right of hypothec includes a right of pledge by operation of law on all *claims for compensation* that substitute the object under pledge or hypothec, including claims for the devaluation of the object.[295]

A paid purchase price is not considered as a 'claim for compensation' in the meaning of Article 3:229 BW. The intention of the legislature was to only include insurance claims or claims for unlawful destruction or damage.[296]

The pledgee who holds the object will be under a duty of care in respect of it. The standard used is the standard of a good pledgee.[297] The duty of care is linked to the obligation the pledgee has against the pledgor. A breach of the obligation

entitled to keep the objects under pledge for himself in case of non-payment of the debt. See Keijser 2004, p. 768, Van Vliet 2005, p. 195.

289 Art. 3:251 BW, Asser, Mierlo, Mijnsen & Van Velten 2003, No. 26, p. 25.

290 This is the *droit de suite* effect. Arts. 3:7 and 6:142 BW, see also Molenaar 1999, p. 43-44.

291 Art. 3:81(2) BW. On the destruction of property rights see also above; 2.3. Other Property Rights.

292 Art. 3:229 BW, Asser, Mierlo, Mijnsen & Van Velten 2003, No. 25, p. 22 *et seq.*

293 HR 23 April 1999, *NJ* 2000, 158, Asser, Mierlo, Mijnsen & Van Velten 2003, No. 25, p. 23.

294 HR 17 February 1995, *NJ* 1996, 471 (*Mulder q.q./CLBN*), 3.3.3, see also Van Mierlo 2000, p. 59.

295 Emphasis by author, Art. 3:229 BW '1- Het recht van pand of hypotheek brengt van rechtswege mee een recht van pand op *alle vorderingen tot vergoeding* die in de plaats van het verbonden goed treden, waaronder begrepen vorderingen ter zake van de waardevermindering van het goed'.

296 Van Mierlo 2000, p. 59, Parlementaire Geschiedenis NBW – Boek 3 1981, p. 734-735.

297 Art. 3:243(1) BW uses the term *goed pandhouder*.

against the pledgor is also considered a breach of the duty of care.[298] Dutch law distinguishes two types of breaches. First, if the object is devalued or is damaged in the care of the pledgee, the pledgor can demand that the object is taken into the possession of a third party.[299] Consequently, the third party will also be under a duty of care.[300] Secondly, only in case of 'grave' breaches can the pledgor approach the court for an order to return the object or place it into special care with a third party.[301] This special care of a third party is the so-called *gerechtelijke bewaring*.[302] The same remedy will be available for a pledgee against the pledgor in case of a silent pledge.

A right of pledge can be created for debts not only that are already in existence, but also for debts that will come into existence in the future.[303] A future claim can be pledged, but only if such claim can be ascertained sufficiently.[304] Although at the moment of creation of the pledge the debt does not yet exist, the subject of the pledge should be ascertainable.

A classic right of pledge can only be created on objects and claims that exist at the time of creation. Other objects and claims cannot be brought into the power of the pledgee. However, a right of silent pledge may be created on future objects, since bringing these objects in the power of the pledgee is not necessary for the valid creation of the right. However, Article 3:239 BW limits this possibility by stating:

> 1. A right of pledge on a claim against one or more persons that is not payable to bearer or to order, or on the right of usufruct of such a claim, can also be created by authentic deed or registered informal deed, without notification to those persons, if at the moment of creation of the right of pledge this claim exists or directly results from an existing legal relationship.[305]

298 Arts. 3:243(1) and 6:74 BW, Asser, Mierlo, Mijnsen & Van Velten 2003, No. 45, p. 55, Molenaar 1999, p. 45.

299 Arts. 3:243 and 3:237(3) BW, Asser, Mierlo, Mijnsen & Van Velten 2003, No. 45, p. 55.

300 Arts. 3:236(1) and 2:243 BW, Asser, Mierlo, Mijnsen & Van Velten 2003, No. 45, p. 54.

301 Art. 3:257 BW, mentions *ernstige mate van tekortschieten* (grave breach), Asser, Mierlo, Mijnsen & Van Velten 2003, No. 45, p. 54, Molenaar 1991, p. 68.

302 Special care is dealt with in Arts. 853 *et seq.* Civil Procedure Code (Rv).

303 Art. 3:231 BW states: '1- A right of pledge or a right of hypothec can be established both for existing and for future claims ...', '-1 Een recht van pand of hypotheek kan zowel voor een bestaande als voor een toekomstige vordering worden gevestigd ...'. For examples see Wibier 2007, p. 9 *et seq.*

304 Art. 3:231(2) BW, Asser, Mierlo, Mijnsen & Van Velten 2003, No. 32, p. 34.

305 Art. 3:239 BW, '-1 Pandrecht op een tegen een of meer bepaalde personen uit te oefenen recht dat niet aan toonder of order luidt, of op het vruchtgebruik van een zodanig recht kan ook worden gevestigd bij authentieke of geregistreerde onderhandse akte, zonder mededeling daarvan aan die personen, mits dit recht op het tijdstip van vestiging van het pandrecht reeds bestaat of rechtstreeks zal worden verkregen uit een dan reeds bestaande rechtsverhouding'. This article brings a difficulty with a right of pledge on claims. A company will establish a right of pledge on its current claims, but these will be paid in the course of business causing the right of pledge to disappear. Practice solves this difficulty by using lists that are signed and periodically registered. This practice was allowed by the *Hoge Raad* in its case HR →

Although many rules are applicable both to classic pledge and silent pledge, the right of silent pledge is a somewhat weaker right than its classic equivalent. Specifically with regard to a right of pledge on claims, the debtor of the claim that is subject of the right of pledge, not the debt the payment of which the right of pledge secures, will not know the claim has been pledged. The debtor of that claim will pay his debt to the pledgor after which the right of pledge will cease to exist. The pledgee will only become entitled to the payment of the claim once he notifies the debtor of the existence of his right of pledge. With his notification the silent pledge becomes public and the pledge will henceforth be a classic right of pledge.[306] The debtor of the claim will then have to pay his debt to the pledgee and can no longer pay to the pledgor. The received money will substitute the claim on which the right of pledge was created. The pledge will then continue to exist on the received money.[307]

Before notification the pledgee is in a difficult position. The new Civil Code banned ownership for security purposes because the security owner was considered to have too many powers.[308] Given the prohibition of Article 3:84(3) BW, Dutch legal practice is left with the right of pledge to fulfil its need for security.[309] The silent pledge, the only real alternative for the ownership for security purposes, awards just enough rights to the pledgee. Especially in a case where a silent pledge has been created and no notification has been given, the pledgee, usually a bank, can lose its security right and, with that, its preferential position over the other creditors if the claims under pledge are paid to the pledgor. To address this problem, the *Hoge Raad*, in its landmark decision of *Mulder q.q. v CLBN*, ruled that although a right of pledge will cease to exist once the debt has been paid to the pledgor, the preferential position of the former pledgee remains to exist in insolvency.[310] Therefore, the right of pledge is granted effects after it ceases to exist, a development that solves practical problems, but creates some doctrinal difficulties.[311]

3.7. *Hypothec*

The right of hypothec is the property security right that can be created on registered objects. These objects are land and buildings upon land, but can also be registered ships and registered aircraft.[312] Furthermore, the category of registered objects also

14-10-1994, *NJ* 1995, 447 (*Stichting Spaarbank Rivierland/Gispen q.q.*) and was further developed. On this see Asser, Mierlo, Mijnsen & Van Velten 2003, Nos. 126 *et seq.*, p. 143 *et seq.*

306 Brahn 1988, p. 176, Van Mierlo 1988, p. 182, Asser, Mierlo, Mijnsen & Van Velten 2003, No. 116, p. 130.

307 Art. 3:246(5) BW, Asser, Mierlo, Mijnsen & Van Velten 2003, No. 115, p. 129, more detailed see Rank-Berenschot 1997, p. 237 *et seq.*

308 On Ownership for security purposes see above; 2. The Right of Ownership, but also Van Mierlo 1988.

309 Asser, Mierlo, Mijnsen & Van Velten 2003, No. 65, p. 75, Van Mierlo 1988, p. 175.

310 HR 17 February 1995, *NJ* 1996, 471 (*Mulder q.q./CLBN*).

311 More will be stated about this below in 4.5. After-Effects of Property Rights.

312 Arts. 3:227(1) and 3:10 BW, see Asser, Mierlo, Mijnsen & Van Velten 2003, No. 169, p. 198. A hypothec on a building without the land as such is not possible. A right of *superficies* can be →

includes those property rights that are created on these objects.[313] The right of hypothec is a property right for security that grants the person holding the right of hypothec, the 'hypothecee', the right to sell the registered object serving as security. Similar to the right of pledge, the right of hypothec entitles the holder to a preferential treatment over other creditors in case of insolvency of the debtor. The right of hypothec is an accessory right, connected with the obligation creating the debt the payment of which the property right seeks to secure.[314] However, there are special types of hypothec where this accessority of the right of hypothec does not apply, or at least in a different way than with a regular right of hypothec.[315]

Because the right of hypothec is mainly used for immovable objects, compared with the right of pledge, additional requirements exist for the creation of the right. The right of hypothec can only be created by a notarial deed, which is subject to several requirements.[316] These include the identity of the parties, the identity of the notary, a description of the object serving as security, the explicit use of the word 'hypothec', but also specifically mentioning the obligation creating the debt for which security is given, as well as the amount of the debt.[317] In case the sum of the debt is not yet certain, the potential maximum amount of the debt will have to be mentioned.[318]

One of the principal characteristics of the right of hypothec is that the hypothecee will only have a right of hypothec and will not have physical control over the object under hypothec itself. The owner will only have to give up his power over the object from the moment the hypothecee executes his right of hypothec. This is the reason why the right of hypothec is so often used in practice.[319] However, the fact that the hypothecee cannot exercise any power of the right creates a more risky position than if the hypothecee had such power, for example, if the object decreases in value once the hypothecee decides to execute. In order to avoid this, the owner is usually obliged to take care of the object under hypothec. In principle, an owner who causes a devaluation of the object will be liable for the devaluation.[320] This liability is not part of the right of hypothec and is usually created by general terms and conditions applying to the right of hypothec. These terms and conditions can also impose limitations on the owner, such as the duty to ask permission before the

used to separate the ownership of the land from the ownership of the building. The right of *superficies* will then be subject of a right of hypothec, not the ownership of the building itself. See Asser, Mierlo, Mijnsen & Van Velten 2003, Nos. 171, 174, p. 201, 203.

313 These are the main categories of registered objects. For more examples see, *inter alia*, Heuff & Huijgen 2000, p. 10.

314 Arts. 3:7 and 3:227 BW, Asser, Mierlo, Mijnsen & Van Velten 2003, No. 201, p. 232, Heuff & Huijgen 2000, p. 13.

315 These will be dealt with in this section.

316 Art. 3:260 BW.

317 Art. 40 Law for the office of notaries (Wn), Art. 24(2)(b) Law for the Cadaster (Kw), Arts. 3:260(1), 24(2)(a) Kw, and 24(2)(a)(2) Kw.

318 Asser, Mierlo, Mijnsen & Van Velten 2003, No. 202, p. 233, Heuff & Huijgen 2000, p. 18.

319 See, *inter alia*, Heuff & Huijgen 2000, p. 3.

320 Although the law does not explicitly state this, it does mention a liability for devaluation resting on a third party in Art. 3:233 BW. The basic duty of care for the owner is read into this article, see Asser, Mierlo, Mijnsen & Van Velten 2003, No. 256, p. 288.

purpose for which the object is used can be changed, or they may contain additional agreements on the conditions of execution of the hypothecee.[321] The duty of care of the owner includes the duty to insure the object.[322] In order to strengthen the position of the hypothecee, Article 3:229 BW, as in a right of pledge, creates a right of pledge by operation of law on any claim for compensation, which substitutes the object, including claims for devaluation of the object.[323] This right of pledge will rank over any other right of pledge created on such a claim.[324]

When the owner defaults on his payments, the hypothecee can execute his right of hypothec.[325] The execution of the right of hypothec is effected through a sale of the object serving as security. The sale is compulsory, a clause that entitles the hypothecee to keep the object for himself is void.[326] Similar to the powers of execution of a pledgee, the hypothecee may sell the object once the owner defaults on the payments. Furthermore, in case of insolvency of the owner, the hypothecee may act as if there were no insolvency.[327] The right of hypothec gives the hypothecee the power to sell and transfer the object and to keep sufficient of the proceeds of the sale to satisfy the debt.[328] The sale of the object will have to be concluded in the presence of a notary who will fulfil the formalities and receive the purchase price.[329] The costs of the execution will be deducted from the price and the notary will pay the hypothecee and, when there is any money left after the hypothecee has received his part of the proceeds, the owner.[330]

The rules on the right of hypothec leave freedom for the parties to decide on the content of their relation. Apart from general terms and conditions, book 3 of the Civil Code offers rules on certain clauses that the parties may include in the deed of creation and which aim at protection of the hypothecee.[331] One of these clauses, the lease-clause, deserves some attention.[332] A contract of lease of an immovable object in Dutch law can be invoked against a new owner.[333] This would normally include the situation in which the object under hypothec is sold by way of execution. The new owner would then be forced to recognise the lease agreement. This would

321 See Stein 2004, p. 89-90.
322 Heuff & Huijgen 2000, p. 33.
323 Heuff & Huijgen 2000, p. 34.
324 Asser, Mierlo, Mijnsen & Van Velten 2003, Nos. 25, 179, p. 22, 209.
325 Art. 3:268 BW. The terms and conditions will usually describe when the owner will be in default, see Asser, Mierlo, Mijnsen & Van Velten 2003, No. 302, p. 337.
326 Art. 3:235 BW, Asser, Mierlo, Mijnsen & Van Velten 2003, No. 291, p. 328. This article provides another example of the prohibition on the *lex commissoria* in Dutch law.
327 Art. 57 Fw, although Art. 58 Fw entitles the curator in insolvency the power to set a reasonable time limit for the execution. Asser, Mierlo, Mijnsen & Van Velten 2003, No. 342, p. 369.
328 Asser, Mierlo, Mijnsen & Van Velten 2003, Nos. 298, 322, p. 333, 354, Heuff & Huijgen 2000, p. 48-49, 55.
329 Arts. 3:268 and 3:270(1) BW.
330 Asser, Mierlo, Mijnsen & Van Velten 2003, No. 344, p. 372, Heuff & Huijgen 2000, p. 55.
331 Stein 2004, p. 105 *et seq.*
332 For a detailed overview of these clauses see, *inter alia*, Stein 2004, p. 105 *et seq.*, Asser, Mierlo, Mijnsen & Van Velten 2003, Nos. 262 *et seq.*, p. 295 *et seq.*
333 Art. 7:226 BW, Stein 2004, p. 105, more will be stated on this rule of sale does not break lease below in 4.3. Lease of Immovable Objects.

result in a considerable devaluation of the object. The lease-clause contains a prohibition to lease the object under hypothec without permission of the hypothecee.[334] An agreement of lease concluded after the lease-clause was created will be valid in general but not against the hypothecee. Upon execution the hypothecee can, because of the lease-clause, terminate the lease agreement. The termination will have to be respected by the lessee. Without the lease agreement in force the hypothecee can then sell and transfer the object under hypothec without burdens.[335]

Like a right of pledge, a right of hypothec can be created for a current claim, usually a debt, but also for a future, not yet existing, claim.[336] However, unlike a right of pledge, the right of hypothec cannot be created on a future registered object.[337] As a result of this complication, objects that are in existence are used as a security object for a debt that has to arise in the future. This is specifically so with a so-called credit-hypothec.[338] This special type of hypothec is used to secure a credit facility, usually provided by a bank. This credit facility comprises an account with the bank from which the client can take money until a certain maximum sum. Once the client withdraws money from the credit account, a debt will come into existence and the bank will have a claim for repayment. However, the client might not withdraw the maximum amount immediately; the claim of the bank will therefore depend on the withdrawal of the client. The debt the credit facility creates can therefore be a future debt, which can still be secured by creating a right of hypothec.[339] The right of hypothec will come into existence at the moment the deed that creates the right is registered, regardless of whether the client has withdrawn money and the debt has arisen.[340]

The complication of this type of hypothec comes with the freedom of the client to do as he wishes within the limits set by the bank. This includes the possibility that the client fully repays his debt to the bank before he withdraws money again. This type of hypothec therefore creates a doctrinal difficulty with regard to the principle of accessority. If the debt and the right of hypothec are dependent on each other, the repayment of the debt will cause the right of hypothec to terminate. The purpose of this type of hypothec is to use a property right to secure the debt the client will have and the termination of the right of hypothec is therefore the opposite of what the parties want. Because of the practical relevance of credit-hypothecs this doctrinal difficulty is put aside. Van Velten concludes that, in fact, there are two different types of hypothecs.[341] He distinguishes rights of hypothec that are dependent on the debt for which it is created, and those rights of hypothec that are inde-

334 See Art. 3:264 BW.

335 Stein 2004, p. 106, Asser, Mierlo, Mijnsen & Van Velten 2003, No. 264, p. 298-299.

336 Art. 3:231 BW, Timmerman 2002, p. 412.

337 Arts. 3:97(1) and 3:98 BW, Asser, Mierlo, Mijnsen & Van Velten 2003, No. 186, p. 214-215, Polak & Van Mierlo 1998, p. 106.

338 See Stein 2004, p. 91-92.

339 See Asser, Mierlo, Mijnsen & Van Velten 2003, Nos. 205 *et seq.*, p. 237 *et seq.*, Polak & Van Mierlo 1998, p. 11 *et seq.*

340 HR 25 February 1955, *NJ* 1955, 711 and HR 16 June 2000, *NJ* 2000, 733. Pitlo et al. 2006, p. 572-573, Stein 2004, p. 90, different see Asser, Mierlo, Mijnsen & Van Velten 2003, No. 205, p. 237.

341 Asser, Mierlo, Mijnsen & Van Velten 2003, No. 209, p. 243.

pendent from the debt and will exist as long as the relation between the owner and the hypothecee exists.[342] The credit-hypothec is an example of the second type of hypothec.[343] The principle of accessority seems to apply in a different way to these rights of hypothec than to a normal right of hypothec. If accessority exists at all in these cases, the right is more connected to the relation between hypothecee and owner in general than to the content of this relationship, the debt.[344]

Finally, in legal practice the right of hypothec is also used for major transactions where more than one bank is involved. In these situations the banks will have to share the right of hypothec. This sharing is done through the general principles of *gemeenschap* or community in which each of the creditors holds an indivisible share.[345] Through an agreement, the holders of the shares in the community can decide on the management of the security right. For instance, they can appoint one of them to act as a representative of the creditors. A right of hypothec granted to a community of creditors is also known as a trust-hypothec.[346]

Using the concept of community is not always the best solution. In practice, the so-called security-trustee construction is also used, in which a special-purpose vehicle (SPV), commonly a foundation, is used to act as holder of the security right. This includes situations in which an SPV is founded, banks give credit to the SPV, which, in its turn, gives credit to a client who will grant the SPV a right of hypothec. Moreover, it includes a situation in which a SPV is used to function as a guarantor in a surety agreement. In this last situation the debtor grants a personal security right to the SPV to secure the amount of money that creditors need to receive.[347] Another solution is offered through the use of a *bewind*, a construction where entitlement and management powers over an object are separated. The SPV can act as an administrator or manager, in Dutch *bewindvoerder*, of the security right on behalf of the creditors.[348] These solutions open the possibility of creating a security right for as yet unknown creditors. The trust-hypothec is used, for instance, in case of a bond loan.[349]

The development of the use of the right of hypothec illustrates the search for practical solutions. In the case of credit-hypothecs this is visible in the flexible use of

342 See also Heuff & Huijgen 2000, p. 56-57, Pitlo et al. 2006, p. 572-573.

343 See also Timmerman 2002, p. 410.

344 Asser, Mierlo, Mijnsen & Van Velten 2003, No. 209, p. 243, but also see Timmerman 2002, p. 423-424.

345 Art. 3:166 BW. The community is the same concept as used with rights of apartment, see above; 3.5. Right of Apartment. See also Van Weverwijk 1995, p. 257, Timmerman 2002, p. 416 *et seq.*, Asser, Mierlo, Mijnsen & Van Velten 2003, No. 218, p. 252, Asser & Perrick 2007, No. 78, p. 105-107. See above; 2.2. Co-Ownership.

346 The term confusingly invokes connotations with the English trust. Nevertheless, the Dutch trust-hypothec is a different legal instrument. The term is used because a third party is used to represent the common interest of the creditors. On this see Polak & Van Mierlo 1998, p. 22 *et seq.*

347 On this complicated structure see Polak & Van Mierlo 1998, p. 21 *et seq.*, Van Weverwijk 1995, p. 259-260. A combination of a community and a SPV is also very possible. On this see Polak & Van Mierlo 1998, p. 27.

348 Stein 2004, p. 92-93, Asser, Mierlo, Mijnsen & Van Velten 2003, Nos. 220 *et seq.*, p. 254 *et seq.*

349 Stein 2004, p. 93.

the principle of accessority. Furthermore, trust-hypothecs open the possibilities for syndicate security solutions. The trust-hypothec searches for the boundaries of what is possible with the Dutch system of property law and creatively uses different concepts such as community and *bewind* to allow a security system with multiple creditors.

4. Borderline Cases in Dutch Property Law

The third section of this chapter dealt with the standard set of recognised property rights in Dutch law. However, because of both historical and current developments there are some other relations that should be examined. Some of these are actual property rights, whereas others are relations that bear so many property characteristics that, although not recognised as such, they might be treated as a property right.

4.1. *Priority Rights*

Like French law, Dutch law recognises a set of rights that arise by operation of law and that provide the holder of such a right with a preferential position over other creditors. These rights are known as priority rights, or in Dutch *voorrechten*.[350] Article 3:278 BW specifically mentions priority rights as one of the grounds for preferential treatment over other creditors.[351]

Priority rights in Dutch law are divided into two categories. First, general priority rights are held on a full set of assets and debts of a person or company. These rights include rights in respect of the reimbursement of costs of insolvency proceedings, the costs of burials, pension claims of employees and former employees, and claims of employees for salary.[352] Second, specific priority rights are held on a specific object. These rights are more common in Dutch law. They include claims for costs that were incurred in order to prevent the physical destruction of an object, both immovable and movable, claims for costs incurred as a result of work on a certain object based on a contract of work, and claims from the association of co-owners or all the holders of a share in a community of apartment rights together on the payment of the costs by one of them.[353]

In Dutch law priority rights are not property rights, even though they provide the holder with a preferential position over other creditors. At the same time, because of the same effect, priority rights are not purely personal rights either.[354] Most priority rights end when the object on which they rest is transferred to someone else.[355] However, under certain conditions some of the priority rights can also have a right to follow, a *droit de suite*. For example, Article 3:287 BW which provides for a

350 In the old Dutch Civil Code these rights were still known as *privileges*, resembling the French term *privilège*. Fesevur 1992, p. 9. See Chapter 3; 3.7. Priority Rights.

351 Art. 3:278 BW. The other grounds are through the right of pledge or the right of hypothec.

352 Art. 3:288 BW. See Fesevur 1992, p. 20 *et seq.*

353 Arts. 3:281(1) BW, 3:285(1), 3:286(2), and 3:286(1) BW. Fesevur 1992, p. 17-18.

354 Fesevur 1992, p. 25-26.

355 HR 22 May 1931, *NJ* 1931, 1429, Parlementaire Geschiedenis NBW – Boek 3 1981, p. 843.

priority right in respect of a claim for damages, which is intended to provide priority over the claim of the debtor on his insurance, still rests on that claim after assignment. When the claim is assigned the priority right will transfer with it.[356]

Priority rights are therefore best characterised as situated between personal and property rights. They have characteristics of both. In any case, they are not included in the closed list of property rights, and therefore, at least in Dutch doctrine, they should not be considered as a property right.[357]

4.2. *Old Property Rights*

Besides the menu of property rights recognised by the Dutch Civil Code, there are also property rights that were created before the entry into force of the property law part of the new Civil Code in 1992, sometimes even before the entry into force of the old Civil Code in 1838.[358] When the new Civil Code was introduced, the transitional legislation dealt specifically with these old property rights.

These rights include; *pootrecht*, the right to plant trees on another's land, *weiderechten*, rights to let cattle graze on another's land, *recht van eendenkooi*, the right to catch ducks with a special device on another's land, *recht van windvang*, the right of an owner of a windmill to stop anyone from building or planting constructions or plants that would interfere with the flow of wind, *cijnzen*, the right of an owner to a periodic performance, in money or *in natura*, *recht van de 13e penning*, the right to receive 1/13 share (7.69%) of the purchase price of another's land, *visrecht*, the exclusive right to catch fish in another's water, *veerrecht*, the exclusive right to transport people and objects over the water, *recht van aanwas*, the right to the part of a river- or seabed that becomes visible when the tide is low, *stuwrecht*, the right to a certain level of water and the right to use this water, *recht op kerkgestoelte*, the right to have a set seat in a church, and *recht van beklemming*, the right to use another's land for a long duration of time and have buildings on that land.[359]

Whereas, at first, these rights had been abolished as a result of developments after the French Revolution, after the occupation of the Netherlands by the French at the beginning of the nineteenth century, the sovereign ruler reinstated them by sovereign decree.[360] This sovereign, William I, was petitioned to reinstate them by many holders of former seigniorial rights, which included these old property rights, but also by others who believed the reinstatement of these property relations would help structure the rural areas.[361]

356 Fesevur 1992, p. 26.

357 Different in French law, see Chapter 3; 3.7. Priority Rights.

358 Ketelaar 1978, p. 1, this book provides a detailed overview of old property rights in Dutch law, their development, recognition and abandonment. See also Meijers 1907, p. 272, Struycken 2007, p. 50-52.

359 Descriptions taken from Ketelaar 1978, p. 154, 163, 174, 192, 198, 206, 219, 234, 250-251, 262 and 267. The last mentioned right, the right of *beklemming*, is best seen as a combination of a right of *emphyteusis* and a right of *superficies*. It was also mentioned in Art. 1654 of the Old Dutch Civil Code, but not further dealt with.

360 SB 26 March 1814, Ketelaar 1978, p. 57-58.

361 Ketelaar 1978, p. 57.

However, recognition of old property relations did not include the automatic application of the old law. The new legislation, after 1838 the old Dutch Civil Code, would recognise them, but would not allow the creation of these rights.[362] The *Hoge Raad* supported this decision with several judgements stating that these old property rights had returned as *vermogensrechten*, but also allowed old law to apply in certain situations.[363]

The new Civil Code also allows for the continuation of old property rights.[364] In order to deal with old property rights, Article 150 of the Transition Act, in Dutch *Overgangswet*, stipulates specific rules and requirements. A right that existed under the old Civil Code or which was recognised under the old Civil Code as an old property right, remains in existence and takes effect as a registered object as described in Article 3:10 BW.[365] Although no new 'old' property rights can be created, old rights still exist and function within the legal system. The courts do not have the authority to abolish them, this is a sole competence of the legislature.[366] Article 3:24 BW allows the old property rights to be registered, but even without registration these property rights have an affect against the world.[367]

4.3. *Lease of Immovable Objects*

As in other civil law systems, in Dutch law lease is a personal right.[368] A lease is created by contract and only creates personal rights and claims. The relation between lessor and lessee is strictly personal. By application of the general rules on contract law, in case another person substitutes either the lessor or lessee, the contract of lease ceases and a new contract should be concluded. This situation is the result of the fact that personal rights do not work against third parties. However, in case of lease, as in other civil law systems, these effects are sometimes considered undesirable, especially in case of a sale of the leased object by the owner. By application of the rules on contract law, the new owner would not be bound to the lease and could evict the lessee. Therefore, the position of the lessee has become protected by legislation.[369] To this effect Article 7:226 BW states:

> 1. The transfer of an object to which a lease agreement applies and the creation or transfer of an independent right of usufruct, *emphyteusis* or *superficies* on the object

362 Art. 1 *Overgangswet* 1829, Ketelaar 1978, p. 3, 133, Struycken 2007, p. 50-51.

363 Ketelaar 1978, p. 133-134, HR 28 March 1890, W 5858 and HR 13 November 1914, W 9810 and HR 20 February 1931, W 12314. See also HR 17 March 1981, *NJ* 1981, 338.

364 Art. 69 *Overgangswet*, under (a). Struycken 2007, p. 50. See also, for example, HR 27 April 2007, *RvdW* 2007/469 concerns a right of *emphyteusis* created in 1741.

365 Art. 150(1) *Overgangswet*. With this Article, property rights become incorporeal objects.

366 Asser, Van Dam & Mijnsen 2002, No. 208, p. 225.

367 Asser, Van Dam & Mijnsen 2002, No. 208, p. 225, Art. 150 *Overgangswet* (Transition Act)

368 Art. 7:201 BW. On the origins of lease in Dutch law and the origins of the protection central in this section, see Schrage 1984.

369 Art. 7:226 BW. For an overview of the development protecting the lessee under the *adagium* sale does not break lease, in Dutch *koop breekt geen huur*, see Westrik 2001, p. 189 *et seq.*

> to which the lease agreement applies by the lessor transfers the right and claims of the lessor ... to the acquirer.[370]

Because this provision protects lessees, it cannot be deviated from by the lease contract.[371] The Article codifies the maxim that a sale does not break a lease.[372] Different from other civil law systems, the description of the object that is leased in Article 7:226 BW is so broad that it not only includes immovable objects, specifically land and buildings on land, but may also apply to movable objects.[373]

The provision of Article 7:226 BW also deals with the effects of a lease agreement in respect to the creation of a property right. This part of the Article refers to the creation of a right of usufruct, which will transfer the lease contract to the usufructuary. When a right of usufruct is created the owner will therefore be free of his obligations against the lessee. The result of the rule of Article 7:226 BW is that a contract of lease will have effect against the holder of a newly created property right. In the system of property law this is a normal effect, as older rights go before new rights.[374] However, to award such effect to a contract, or, better, to a personal right, does not fit in the system in which the law of property and the law of obligations are separated.[375] Mainly because of this systematic problem it has been suggested to transform lease into a property right.[376]

Furthermore, with the introduction of the protection of lessees, the Dutch legislature awards effects to a contract that, although it is a special contract, it cannot have. Hartkamp has described this effect as a transfer of the contract prescribed by law.[377] However, the effect could also be described in property law terms as a *droit de suite* effect.[378] In property law terminology, the possibility that the contract of lease becomes enforceable against a third party is in effect a *droit de suite* effect.

370 Art. 7:226 BW '1- Overdracht van de zaak waarop de huurovereenkomst betrekking heeft en vestiging of overdracht van een zelfstandig recht van vruchtgebruik, erfpacht of opstal op de zaak waarop de huurovereenkomst betrekking heeft, door de verhuurder doen de rechten en verplichtingen van de verhuurder uit de huurovereenkomst ... overgaan op de verkrijger'.

371 Art. 7:226 (4) BW.

372 Like in German law, because of the tradition transfer system in which the contract underlying the transfer and the transfer of ownership itself are separated, the better way to describe the maxim is a transfer does not break a lease.

373 See also HR 15 June 2007, *NJ* 2007/445. On the protection of the lessee in French and German law see Chapter 3; 4.6. Lease, and Chapter 4; 4.4. Lease of Immovable Objects.

374 *Prior tempore potior iure*, see Parlementaire Geschiedenis NBW - Boek 5 1981, p. 3, Van Erp 2006b, p. 16.

375 See below; 5. A *Numerus Clausus* in Dutch Property Law?

376 Asbreuk-van Os 2000a, p. 32 *et seq.*, in reaction Van Erp 2000b, p. 465 *et seq.*, with a contra-reaction by Asbreuk-van Os 2000b, p. 458 *et seq.* and on the fiscal implications of such a development see Thomas & Ziepzeerder 2000, p. 859 *et seq.*

377 Or *wettelijke contractsovername*, HR 25 January 1991, *NJ* 1992, 172, Asbreuk-van Os 2000a, p. 32.

378 Westrik 2001, 27-28.

Nevertheless, systematically, the contract of lease, although a special contract, remains a contract and not a property right.[379]

4.4. *Registration of a Consumer Contract of a Sale of a House*

In the Dutch system of transfer of ownership the agreement between the parties to transfer and the actual transfer itself are separated. In this so-called *traditio* system, property law provides its own rules on the transfer of the right of ownership.[380] Therefore, when a contract of sale is concluded, but a deed has not yet been made and registered, the seller cannot be stopped in property law from a sale and transfer, including, registration to another person.[381]

In respect to consumers, the strict rules of property law do not always have a fair effect. In 2003, after a lengthy legislative procedure, Article 7:2 BW was added to the Dutch Civil Code to help consumers in the acquisition of an immovable object that is used for habitation.[382] Article 7:2 BW states:

> 1. The sale of an immovable object or a part of that object that will be used to live in, when the buyer is a natural person not acting in the exercise of a business or profession, is made in writing.
> 2. The deed made between the parties, or a true copy thereof, must be delivered, on demand, to the buyer, in return for, on demand, a dated receipt. Within three days of this having been delivered to him, the buyer has a right to terminate the sale. Where, after the buyer has made use of this right, a new sale is made in respect to the same object or part of that right, the right does not arise anew ...[383]

This Article introduces aspects of consumer protection through requiring the contract of sale to be in writing and by providing the buyer a period of three days to think about the sale.[384] This aspect of the reform therefore interfered with the consensus principle of contract law. There was also an aspect of the reform that interfered with basic property law rules. Now that the contract of sale of a consumer

379 HR 15 June 2007, *NJ* 2007/445. Book 7 BW deals with special contracts, lease is dealt with in Title 4 (Arts. 7:201 *et seq*. BW).

380 Art. 3:89 BW requires a notarial deed and registration of that deed in the public register. Pitlo et al. 2006, p. 166-169. On the Dutch transfer system see Van Vliet 2000, p. 133 *et seq*.

381 Van Velten 2005, p. 29.

382 On the legislative procedure see Van Velten 2005, p. 29-31.

383 Art. 7:2 BW, '1.- De koop van een tot bewoning bestemde onroerende zaak of bestanddeel daarvan wordt, indien de koper een natuurlijk persoon is die niet handelt in de uitoefening van een beroep of bedrijf, schriftelijk aangegaan. 2.- De tussen partijen opgemaakte akte of een afschrift daarvan moet aan de koper ter hand worden gesteld, desverlangd tegen afgifte aan de verkoper van een gedateerd ontvangstbewijs. Gedurende drie dagen na deze terhandstelling heeft de koper het recht de koop te ontbinden. Komt, nadat de koper van dit recht gebruik gemaakt heeft, binnen zes maanden tussen dezelfde partijen met betrekking tot dezelfde zaak of hetzelfde bestanddeel daarvan opnieuw een koop tot stand, dan ontstaat het recht niet opnieuw. ...'.

384 Especially the requirement for the contract of sale to be in writing was not evident in Dutch law. See Van Velten 2005, p. 29-30, Pitlo et al. 2006, p. 166.

transaction of a house had to be made in writing, registration of that agreement became possible. Article 7:3 BW provides to this effect:

> 1. The sale of a registered object can be entered into the public register, as mentioned in Section 2 of Title 1 of Book 3, unless, at the time when such registration is made, no delivery of the object by the seller would have been possible yet due to the exclusion made in Article 97 of Book 3 on the anticipated delivery of future registered objects. On a sale of an immovable object or a part thereof which is destined to be used to live in, there may be no derogation from the provision in the preceding sentence to the detriment of the buyer who is a natural person and does not act in the conduct of a profession of business....[385]

Article 7:3 BW is reminiscent of the technique of the German *Vormerkung*, which also enables the registration of a personal right.[386] The Article allows the consumer, after the reflection period of Article 7:2 BW, to register the contract of sale in anticipation of the transfer of the right of ownership to him.[387]

Unlike the effects of a German *Vormerkung*, the effects of the registration of Article 7:3 BW are mentioned by the Article itself. Registration makes it possible for the buyer to invoke the sale in case of a transfer of the same object or the creation of a property right in respect of that same object; against the administrator when the object is placed under administration, in Dutch *bewind*, after the registration, against a contract of lease concluded after the registration, against a qualitative duty created after the registration, and, most importantly against the insolvency administrator in an insolvency procedure.[388]

Registration, in other words, provides the contract of sale with a limited third-party effect by creating the possibility, directly based on the Civil Code, of invoking the contract against persons who were not party to it. Especially in case of insolvency of the seller, the buyer can invoke the agreement against the administrator and claim performance of the agreement through a transfer of the right of ownership.[389] Because of these effects, the registration will only be valid for a period of six months.[390] When these six months have passed, the registration will end with retroactive effect. Nevertheless, within this six-month period, the registered consumer contract for the sale of a house is awarded effects that the personal right that follows from the contract would normally not have. Like its German equivalent, the technique of registration awards the personal rights some property effects.

385 Art. 7:3 BW, '1.- De koop van een registergoed kan worden ingeschreven in de openbare registers, bedoeld in afdeling 2 van titel 1 van Boek 3, tenzij op het tijdstip van de inschrijving levering van dat goed door de verkoper nog niet mogelijk zou zijn geweest wegens de in artikel 97 van Boek 3 vervatte uitsluiting van levering bij voorbaat van toekomstige registergoederen. Bij de koop van een tot woning bestemde onroerende zaak kan, indien de koper een natuurlijk persoon is die niet handelt in de uitoefening van een beroep of bedrijf, van het in de vorige zin bepaalde niet ten nadele van de koper worden afgeweken. ...'.

386 Pitlo et al. 2006, p. 165. See Chapter 4; 4.2. Pre-emptive Registration (*Vormerkung*).

387 Art. 7:3(2) BW, Van Velten 2005, p. 42.

388 The grounds are mentioned in Art. 7:3(3) BW. See also Pitlo et al. 2006, p. 173-178.

389 Van Velten 2005, p. 46, Pitlo et al. 2006, p. 174-175.

390 Art. 7:3(4) BW.

4.5. *After-Effects of Property Rights*

Dutch property law adheres to the theory of *démembrement* to describe the relation between the right of ownership and other property rights.[391] In this method of creation of property rights, these rights are considered as a part of the mother rights from which they were derived.[392] Consequently, once a property right and the mother right fall into the same hands, the powers resulting from the property right and of the mother right mix, the right of ownership becomes complete again, and the property right ceases to exist.

This method of creation of rights forms the foundation of the Dutch system of property law and has several important consequences. For one, as a property right is seen as a part of the right from which it was derived, it is impossible to have a property right in respect of one's own object or right.[393] Connected to this is the accessoriness of property security rights. When the claim a property security right secures ceases to exist, the property right returns to the owner. When this happens, the property right and the right of ownership fall into the same hands and the property right will cease to exist when the powers of that right mix with the powers of the right of ownership.[394] However, to this general rule, Dutch law makes one general exception. Article 3:81 BW, which deals with ways in which a property right can end, states:

> 3. Renunciation and mixing of property rights do not have effect against those who have a property right in respect of the property right that ceases to exist. Mixing of property rights also does not have effect against those who had a property right in respect of the same object as the property right that ceases to exist and they should respect that property right.[395]

The result of the general rule, following from the method of *démembrement*, is that a right of *emphyteusis* ceases to exist when the holder of the right becomes the owner, or the holder of a right of usufruct inherits the bare ownership.[396] However, if an-

391 On this concept in Dutch law see above; 3. Other Property Rights.

392 Art 3:8 BW.

393 This is different in German where one could have a property right in respect of his own object or right such as a *Grundschuld*. See Chapter 4; 3. Other Property Rights.

394 Another theory would be to state that property security rights in Dutch law, because of their accessory nature, simply cease to exist from the moment the claim they secured ceased to exist, as one cannot exist without the other once the property rights is created.

395 Art. 81(3) '-1 Afstand en vermenging werken niet ten nadele van hen die op het tenietgaande beperkte recht op hun beurt een beperkt recht hebben. Vermenging werkt evenmin ten voordele van hen die op het bezwaarde goed een beperkt recht hebben en het tenietgaande recht moesten eerbiedigen'.

396 Another effect of the article is that the property right that was created on the property right that ceases to exist should not just also cease to exist. If the destruction of the property right is to the disadvantage of the holder of the property right in respect of the property right, the right can, in certain circumstances, continue to exist on the object itself and no longer on the property right, which has, after all, cease to exist. See Asser, Mijnsen, De Haan & Van Dam 2006, No. 15, p. 14-15. Examples taken from Pitlo et al. 2006, p. 468-469.

other property right had been created on the property right that ceased to exist, the effect of Article 3:81(3) BW is a re-activation of the property right. If, for instance, a right of hypothec was created on a parcel of land that was burdened with a right of servitude and the dominant and servient land fall into the same hands, the right of servitude will cease to exist. However, the right of hypothec will continue to rest on one of the parcels of land. If the holder of the right of hypothec executes his right the right of servitude will revive for the benefit of the new owner.[397] Another example would arise where more than one right of hypothec is created on the same object. When the holder of the first right of hypothec becomes owner of the object, the right of hypothec mixes with the right of ownership and ceases to exist. However, this mixing will not work to the advantage of the second hypothecee, who will remain to hold a right of second hypothec in respect to the holder of the first right of hypothec.[398]

The effect of a termination of a property right through mixing with the powers of the owner is therefore a relative effect. It is no surprise that in Dutch property law this effect causes some doctrinal difficulties. These difficulties especially concern the relative nature of the effect. The leading opinion is that the property right ceases to exist but that this has no effect against the holder of a property right in respect of such a property right.[399] Effectively this means that a property right can have a 'second life', even after it has ceased to exist.[400]

The right of pledge offers another example of an after-effect of property rights. The end of the discussion on the right of pledge made notice of the landmark decision of the *Hoge Raad* in *Mulder q.q. v CLBN*.[401] This case dealt with a right of silent pledge created on several claims for the benefit of a bank. The pledgor became insolvent, and the bank wanted to execute the right of pledge. Since the pledge had not been notified to the debtors, it was a silent pledge, the debtors could pay their debts to the pledgor.[402] Because the right of pledge is an accessory right, the payment of the claims caused the right of pledge to cease to exist. The bank therefore lost its security right in respect of the pledgor regarding the paid claims.

Following the strict rules laid down in case law of the *Hoge Raad*, the result of this was that the bank became a normal creditor in the insolvency procedure and could not use its preferential position anymore than the right of pledge would have

397 Example from Asser, Van Dam & Mijnsen 2002, No. 13, p. 15-16 and Asser, Mijnsen, De Haan & Van Dam 2006, No. 19, p. 18-19, see also Parlementaire Geschiedenis NBW - Boek 3 1981, p. 311, Rank-Berenschot 1992, p. 235 *et seq.*

398 In other words, the mixing of the right of first hypothec with the right of ownership must not have an effect to the advantage of the holder of a second right of hypothec. However, this situation only arises when the claim for which the right of first hypothec was created remains in existence. Parlementaire Geschiedenis NBW - Boek 3 1981, p. 840-841, Asser, Mierlo, Mijnsen & Van Velten 2003, No. 353, p. 378, Asser, Mijnsen, De Haan & Van Dam 2006, No. 19, p. 18-19.

399 Asser, Mijnsen, De Haan & Van Dam 2006, No. 18, p. 17-18.

400 See also Rank-Berenschot 1992, p. 238.

401 See above; 3.6. Pledge.

402 Art. 3:246 BW.

granted it.[403] However, the *Hoge Raad* intervened against this effect and decided that, although the right of pledge had ceased to exist because the claims had been paid, the bank continued to hold the preferential position it had when the right of pledge had still been in existence.

With this very interesting decision the *Hoge Raad* has provided for an after-life of the right of pledge, in which, although doctrinally the right of pledge ceases to exist when a debtor pays the claims the right secures, the preferential position of the bank remains. In the system of security rights such a preferential position can only be achieved by establishing a property security right or by having a priority right prescribed by law.[404] The judgment in the case *Mulder q.q. v CLBN* has added a third possibility.

4.6. *Privative Mandate*

The systematic nature of Dutch property law creates some undesirable rigidity in respect to the power of disposal over another's assets. The inclusion of Article 3:84(3) BW, the *fiducia*-ban Article, and the limitations of its application by the *Hoge Raad*, still prohibit a legal construction whereby one person brings his objects in the power of another who deals with the administration of these objects.[405] Such a legal relation is considered a transfer for management purposes where the actual acquirer does not become the owner of the assets.[406] The other person is only administrator. Such relations invoke a regime that resembles an Anglo-American trust concept, which the system of Dutch property law fiercely resists.[407]

Consequently, solutions to provide for management of the object of another are found in contract law, specifically in the law on representation. In these situations a certain person, *mandatory*, acts on behalf of another person, *mandator*. In respect to representation the new Dutch Civil Code introduced a new concept that best translates as privative mandate. Article 7:423 BW states:

> When it is agreed between the mandator and mandatory that the mandatory will exercise a right of the mandator in his own name and with the exclusion of the mandator, the mandator will lack the power to act on his own for the duration of the agreement also against third parties. The exclusion cannot be invoked against third parties who did not know, nor ought to have known about it.[408]

403 HR 10 January 1975, *NJ* 1976, 249 (*Giro-case*), HR 7 October 1988, *NJ* 1989, 449 (*AMRO-Curators THB*), see also HR 17 February 1995, *NJ* 1996, 471 (*Mulder q.q./CLBN*), Para. 3.4.3.

404 Art. 3:278 BW.

405 See above; 2. The Right of Ownership.

406 Or a so-called *fiducia cum amico*. See above; 2.3. Security Ownership.

407 Van Erp 2000b, p. 456, Parlementaire Geschiedenis NBW - Boek 5 1981, p. 17-18, see below; 4.9. EC and International Influences.

408 Art. 7:423 BW '-1 Indien is bedongen dat de lasthebber een aan de lastgever toekomend recht in eigen naam en met uitsluiting van de lastgever zal uitoefenen, mist deze de bevoegdheid tot deze uitoefening voor de duur van de overeenkomst ook jegens derden. De uitsluiting kan niet worden tegengeworpen aan derden die haar kenden noch behoorden te kennen'.

This mandate is created when the stipulator, or mandator, agrees that he will not exercise his power over a certain object for the duration of the agreement.[409] This power can be twofold. Either it concerns acts that create obligations, such as the lease of immovable objects, or acts that have property law consequences, such as the transfer of the right of ownership of immovable objects.[410]

Depending on the act from which the stipulator agrees to refrain, he will lose his power to act, or his power to dispose.[411] The power to dispose is a concept in property law and therefore only applies in case of acts in the area of property law.[412] Consequently the agreement to refrain from taking acts concerning obligations will result in a prohibition to act for the stipulator.[413] The effect of the agreement, in particular the third-party effect, has been debated. Under the old Civil Code the *Hoge Raad* held that there was no third-party effect.[414] The Court stated that, because of the contractual nature of the agreement, no so-called 'privative effect', the exclusive power of the mandatory to act that could also be invoked against third parties, could be awarded.[415] Nevertheless, the legislature chose a different way in the new Civil Code. Article 7:423 BW awards this 'privative effect' when the parties agree that the mandatory will act in his own name and the stipulator will refrain from taking acts concerning the object. Such agreement will have effect against all who knew or ought to have known about its existence.[416] A third party who did not have such knowledge can rely on the third-party protection rules of Articles 3:86 and 3:88 BW. In Struycken's view the distinction between acts resulting in obligations and also having property effect remains relevant, because in the system of Dutch law no privative effect can be awarded to property law acts outside those dealt with by property law itself.[417]

Van der Grinten has named the introduction of the provision introducing the privative mandate in the new Civil Code 'opportunity legislation'.[418] He states that under pressure from private organisations, the Minister of Justice has opted for a concept that is situated between contractual and property solutions. Especially the fact that a privative mandate can now be registered means that it is almost impossible to prove lack of knowledge of its existence, and make successful use of the third-party protection provisions mentioned earlier.[419] In effect, therefore, the privative

409 Aertsen points out that this concept has been specifically mentioned as an alternative for trusts in Dutch law, see *Kamerstukken II* 1992-1993, 23 027, No. 3, p. 5, Aertsen 2004, p. 128. See also Struycken 2007, p. 586.

410 Worst 2002, p. 195.

411 Worst 2002, p. 197.

412 Worst 2002, p. 197.

413 Although in effect there is almost no difference, the system of property law forces the distinction to be made.

414 HR 29 September 1989, *NJ* 1990, 397.

415 Van der Grinten 1993, p. 12.

416 Van der Grinten 1993, p. 12, Worst 2002, p. 197, Rank 1997, p. 469.

417 Struycken 2007, p. 591-592.

418 Van der Grinten 1993, p. 13, see also Rank 1997, p. 474, Snijders 1993, p. 236-238, Struycken 2007, p. 612.

419 Rank 1997, p. 470, Worst 2002, p. 198.

mandate creates a relation that has effect against third parties. Third parties that deal with the stipulator of such an agreement should realise that the mandator lacks the power to act or even the power to dispose. In other words, with the inclusion of this provision in the Civil Code, like the lease of immovable objects, the privative mandate offers another example of property-like effects granted by the Dutch Civil Code to what is, in essence, a contractual relation.[420]

Finally, the usefulness of the privative mandate to legal practice is shown by its application in fund investments. Investors transfer their money to a third party who is known as a 'keeper', who will hold the money in a separate set of assets from his own. The 'keeper' creates a contract creating a privative mandate with a 'manager' who will invest the money by using the power over the money of the 'keeper'. The 'manager' agrees to act in his own name so that the privative mandate will have effect against third parties.[421] The terms of the contract will limit the powers of both the 'keeper' and of the 'manager', safeguarding the interest of the investors.[422]

4.7. *Obligations as Part of Property Rights*

The discussion of the Dutch system of property law in this chapter shows that, although at the outset the system of property rights is closed, within the closed system parties have, depending on the right in question, some freedom to decide on the content of those rights.[423] This freedom is visible in case of rights of servitude and rights of *emphyteusis*, but certainly also in case of rights of usufruct or rights of apartment.[424] Parties are left to make agreements that deal with the exact contents of their relationship. These agreements, as far as they are included in the deed of creation, can become part of the property right.[425]

The criteria for when these agreements are an inherent part of the property right was developed in relation to the right of *emphyteusis*. The *Hoge Raad* held that agreements between parties would be part of the property right itself if they have a *sufficient connection* to the *emphyteusis* and are not contrary to the *nature* of the right.[426] The criterion of sufficient connection was introduced by the legislature in the discussion on the introduction of the new Dutch Civil Code.[427] Struycken has

420 See also Rank 1997, p. 469.

421 Example taken from Worst 2002, p. 196.

422 See Worst 2002, p. 200.

423 For a perspective on this same problem from Belgian law see Verbeke & Snaet 2007, p. 365 *et seq*.

424 In case of servitudes the legislator explicitly stated that it kept the definition of Art. 5:71 BW as open as possible. See Parlementaire Geschiedenis NBW - Boek 5 1981, p. 253.

425 The interesting suggestion that a burden could both comprise a personal obligation as well as a property obligation was put forward by Eggens, see Eggens 1960, p. 4 *et seq*. However, this suggestion is generally rejected, see Van Opstall 1966, p. 398, Asser, Van Dam & Mijnsen 2002, No. 176, p. 202. In respect to French law see Chapter 3; 4.2. Real Obligations.

426 HR 16 March 1977, *NJ* 1977, 399, Plantenga & Treurniet 1957, p. 177, Van Velten 1995, p. 47, De Jong 1995b, p. 17, Rank-Berenschot 1992, p. 110-111.

427 Parlementaire Geschiedenis NBW - Boek 5 1981, p. 3.

examined this criterion and shown that the Dutch legislature intended to leave parties freedom to give shape and content to their own property relations.[428] In his view the criterion of a sufficient connection is vague and most likely the legislature intended to set boundaries that parties must stay within. If such a requirement were to be fulfilled Struycken considers the agreement is awarded the same effect as the rights and duties that follow from the description of the property right in the Civil Code.[429] However, it is also possible to argue that, once an agreement has a sufficient connection to the property right to which it relates, the agreement becomes an inherent part of the property right itself.

These open criteria of sufficient connection and the nature of the right make it difficult to establish which agreements are included in the property right and which are not. Struycken has held that the addition made by the *Hoge Raad* of the requirement for an agreement not to be contrary to the nature of the right offers a more objective view and allows the court to take the property relation and the intention of the legislature as a starting point.[430]

It has been argued that agreements that are part of a property right can be both negative and positive.[431] The possibility for parties to impose positive burdens is not open with respect to every property right. The system of Dutch property law also imposes restrictions on the content of certain rights. Especially rights of servitude are subject to this restriction. Article 5:71 BW stipulates that a duty imposed by a right of servitude can, in principle, only be negative.[432] The right of *emphyteusis* offers more extended possibilities for parties to impose positive duties. A right of *emphyteusis* can include a duty to erect a building as a principal duty, whereas in case of a right of servitude such a duty can only be imposed insofar as the erection of a building is necessary for the performance of the principal duty.[433] However, because of the broad criteria to establish which agreements are inherent parts of a property right, the inclusion of any of these duties remains the subject of debate.

An agreement that falls within the criteria of the *Hoge Raad* will be an inherent part of the property right. In other words, the scope of the property right can be extended, be it within the limits set by the law, through party agreements. Dutch law, contrary to German law, follows the principle of *démembrement* to explain the relation between ownership and property rights.[434] In strict application this approach considers property rights as temporarily separated parts of the right of ownership. Suijling and Van Opstall defended the principle, known in Dutch law as the principle of deduction, or *aftrekprincipe*.[435] These authors argued that because a property right consists of parts of the right of ownership, it can never comprise

428 Struycken 2007, p. 386-387.

429 Struycken 2007, p. 387.

430 This requirement was additional besides the requirement of sufficient connection provided by explanation of the Civil Code, Struycken 2007, p. 394.

431 Asser, Van Dam & Mijnsen 2002, No. 217, p. 241, De Jong 1995b, p. 17-19. Of a different opinion see Van Velten 1995, p. 49, Struycken 2007, p. 112-115.

432 See above; 3.1. Real Servitudes for a more detailed explanation.

433 Asser, Van Dam & Mijnsen 2002, No. 217, p. 241, See above; 3.3. *Emphyteusis*.

434 This is, *inter alia*, expressed by Art. 3:8 BW.

435 See Van Opstall 1966, p. 383 *et seq.*, Suijling 1940, No. 345, p. 363.

more than the right of ownership itself. The owner cannot be under a duty to erect a building; ownership cannot easily be burdened with a positive duty, so the holder of a right of *emphyteusis* cannot either.

The new Dutch BW does not follow this strict approach. In modern Dutch law a property right can consist of more than just parts of the powers of the owner.[436] However, the principle of *démembrement* does still exist; once a property right and ownership come into the same hands, the property right ceases to exist.[437] Nevertheless, the arguments of Suijling and Van Opstall can still be found. Van Velten has argued that a positive duty imposed by conditions in an *emphyteusis* can only exist if there is a specific legal basis.[438] Van Velten also extends this argumentation to agreements included in deeds of creation of property rights in general.[439] In this approach any agreement made by the parties, which cannot be classified as a part of the right of ownership, and which does not have an explicit legal basis, is a separate contract. Any rights and claims created by these contracts are personal.

Struycken also has argued that the possibility for parties to create an agreement that becomes part of a property right should be interpreted restrictively.[440] He focuses upon the method in which property rights are created, in Dutch law the *démembrement* method, and concludes that following this method most agreements cannot be part of the property right itself.[441] Perhaps some party agreements can have third-party effect as 'qualitative' or real obligations, but never as a part of the property right itself. When the mother right from which the limited property right was derived did not contain the powers now contained in the agreement, the limited property right cannot contain these either.[442] As a primary example, Struycken mentions that positive burdens can therefore certainly not be created as a part of a property right.[443]

Vonck has argued for a much more broader view of possible party agreements as a part of property rights.[444] In his view, which centres on the right of *emphyteusis*, the criterion of the *Hoge Raad* should be relaxed, and all agreements that are used to support the agreements that can be made directly based on the Civil Code itself, should be allowed as part of a property right.[445] As an example Vonck provides the agreement that parties can make, directly based on the Civil Code, on the right of

436 Art. 3:8 BW, Parlementaire Geschiedenis NBW - Boek 5 1981, p. 3, 257, Asser, Mijnsen, De Haan & Van Dam 2006, Nos. 44-45, p. 38-41.

437 However, a property right will not always cease to exist in relation to those who already had a property right in respect of the property right that falls into the hand of the owner. Art. 3:81(3) BW, see above; 3. Other Property Rights.

438 Van Velten 1995, p. 49, see also Snijders 1995, p. 155, *contra* see De Jong 1995a, p. 525, Asser, Van Dam & Mijnsen 2002, No. 217, p. 241.

439 This would include rights of servitude, *superficies*, usufruct and apartment, Van Velten 1995, p. 49.

440 Struycken 2007, p. 412-413.

441 Struycken 2007, p. 404-405.

442 Struycken calls this the subtraction model. Struycken 2007, p. 401 *et seq*.

443 Struycken 2007, p. 414-415.

444 Vonck 2007, p. 598 *et seq*.

445 Vonck 2007, p. 599-600.

the holder of the right of *emphyteusis* to take the fruits the object produces. He sees no reason why parties should not be allowed to agree that those fruits may be enjoyed by the owner, instead of the holder of the right of *emphyteusis*, and why that agreement should not be part of the property right.[446] Such inclusion would allow parties considerable freedom to include party agreements in property rights.

In order to restrict parties and to uphold the closed system of property rights in Dutch law, Vonck suggests that, when his criterion would be adopted, only those agreements that are in direct relations to the object as to which the right of *emphyteusis* is created, can be allowed as part of the right itself.[447]

The categorisation of party agreements as a part of a property right is relevant for its enforcement. The first approach, the property approach, will treat agreements that fulfil the criteria as parts of the property right. In my opinion such an agreement will lose its status as a contract and will be considered a property right. The agreement will have effect against the world, will transfer together with all the other rights and claims the property right entails, and property law remedies will be available. That means that interference will lead to a claim for damages based on Article 6:162 BW, and a claim based on unlawful action, but not a claim based on Article 6:74 BW and further, which deal with breach of contract. The possibility to include agreements in property rights offers an example where, not based on legislation, but based on case law, a contract can achieve a property effect. Its development shows the possibilities to use the current legal framework to its maximum extent. Practice will constantly search for the border between property and contract and a vague criterion of sufficient connection and non-contrariness to the nature of the right will indeed be very helpful.

Consequently, a theory like Struycken's in which these party agreements are not considered as parts of the property right will not allow the parties access to proprietary remedies. This second approach is more of a contractual approach. Here, the parties will be left with the law of obligations to enforce their legal relation.[448] In some circumstances these agreements will still have third-party effect. However, this will only be so when they can be characterised as a qualitative right or a qualitative duty, which will be dealt with below. Only then will third-party effect in the law of obligations be ensured.[449]

4.8. *'Qualitative Duties' and Chain Clauses*

With the introduction of the new Civil Code, the Dutch legislature has introduced a concept situated between the area of contract and property, the qualitative duty of Article 6:252 BW. The qualitative duty allows the creation of a negative burden on a registered object that is transferred to successive acquirers. The duty will not only

446 Vonck 2007, p. 600.
447 Vonck 2007, p. 603.
448 Arts. 6:74 *et seq.* BW, Struycken 2007, p. 422-425.
449 A qualitative right is dealt with by Art. 6:251 BW, which grants third party effect to a right that is connected to an object held by a creditor and is only of use as long as the creditor holds that object. Struycken 2007, p. 423-424.

bind the parties that agreed to its creation, but will also bind acquirers of the land on which the qualitative duty is created, not by contract but by operation of law. In other words, qualitative duties have a *droit de suite* effect. It was exactly with this argument that many authors opposed the introduction of the qualitative duty into Dutch law.[450] Nevertheless, the qualitative duty was included in the Civil Code and forms an intermediate category between the law of obligations and the law of property.[451] Article 6:252 BW states:

1. It can be agreed by contract that the duty of one of the parties to tolerate or not to do something in respect to a registered object that belongs to him will transfer to those who acquire the object under special title, and that also those who will have a right to use that object will be bound.
2. In order for the contract mentioned under sub 1 to have this effect, the agreement must take the form of a notarial deed and be registered in the public registry...
4. When, in exchange for the duty, the performance of another duty for compensation has been agreed upon, this duty for compensation will transfer with the duty when this duty for compensation relates to the period after transfer and was also registered.
5. This Article does not apply to duties that restrict the holder in his power to transfer or create limited property rights.[452]

A qualitative duty is an agreement between two parties, one of whom is the owner or holder of a property right in respect of a registered object, an immovable, ship or aircraft, who will be bound by its terms in his capacity, 'quality', as owner.[453] The other party to the agreement will be bound by its terms not in his capacity as owner or holder of a property right, but in his personal capacity. The qualitative duty will transfer with the property right in respect of the registered object over which the

450 See, *inter alia*, Van Opstall 1966, p. 471, Pitlo 1968, Maeijer 1966, p. 80, Rijtma 1969, p. 229, Stein 1976, p. 650, in favour see Smalbraak 1966, p. 110, Asser & Hartkamp 2001, No. 411, p. 430.

451 See Sagaert 2005a, p. 343, Asser & Hartkamp 2001, No. 411, p. 430, Van Oostrom-Streep 2005, p. 786.

452 Art. 6:252 BW, '1.-Bij een overeenkomst kan worden bedongen dat de verplichting van een der partijen om iets te dulden of niet te doen ten aanzien van een haar toebehorend registergoed, zal overgaan op degenen die het goed onder bijzondere titel zullen verkrijgen, en dat mede gebonden zullen zijn degenen die van de rechthebbende een recht tot gebruik van het goed zullen verkrijgen. 2.-Voor de werking van het in lid 1 bedoelde beding is vereist dat van de overeenkomst tussen partijen een notariële akte wordt opgemaakt, gevolgd door inschrijving daarvan in de openbare registers. ... 4.-Is voor de verplichting een tegenprestatie overeengekomen, dan gaat bij de overgang van de verplichting het recht op de tegenprestatie mee over, voor zover deze betrekking heeft op de periode na de overgang en ook het beding omtrent deze tegenprestatie in de registers ingeschreven is. 5.-Dit artikel is niet van toepassing op verplichtingen die een rechthebbende beperken in zijn bevoegdheid het goed te vervreemden of te bezwaren'.

453 Art. 3:10 BW, Cahen 2004, p. 34-35.

duty is established. Subsequent acquirers of the object will then be bound by the terms of the agreement.[454]

The qualitative duty is dealt with in the Dutch Civil Code in the law of obligations. However, because of the effects of the qualitative duty, it could possibly also be a property relation. In respect to the legal nature of the duty, Van Oostrom-Streep recognises two different obligations; one between the parties with regard to the content of the duty, and one between the parties with regard to the duty to register the agreement in order to make it qualitative, to give it third-party effect.[455] Making this distinction permits the explanation of which provisions of contract law apply to which agreement and in which way. In other words, the main agreement, the agreement in respect to the duty, is governed by the ordinary rules on contract law. The agreement in which parties express their intention to provide their relation with third-party effect is subject to more formalities.[456]

Because of this third-party effect there are several requirements for the duty to exist. First, the contents of the duty are limited to a negative burden.[457] Contrary to the requirements for a right of servitude, parties may include a prohibition to take legal acts as well. In Dutch law a right of servitude can only comprise factual acts, for example, a duty to tolerate that the holder of the right walks over the owner's land.[458] A qualitative duty can also contain a prohibition to lease the object.[459] Different from a right of servitude, the Dutch Civil Code does not explicitly provide for specific situations where a positive duty can be imposed.[460] Hartkamp considers that the broader scope of qualitative duties, which can be used for more purposes than just rights of servitude because of the possibility of creating the right on behalf of a person not holding a property right, is compensated for by the restriction on parties to impose positive duties.[461] Secondary positive duties, as these can exist in relation to a right of servitude, can, in principle, not be made with respect to a qualitative duty.[462] The only exception is that of a penalty clause to strengthen the qualitative duty, which was specifically mentioned by the legislature during the drafting of the Article.[463] Van Oostrom-Streep has examined this prohibition and shows that the legislature intended to be careful not to reintroduce feudal relations.[464] She argues that the introduction of the Civil Code was a missed chance for the legislature actually to allow the creation of positive duties, and that there can be

454 This *droit de suite* effect is not applicable in case of transfer under so-called general title (*algemene titel*). This would include the acquisition through an inheritance. See Pitlo et al. 2006, No. 382, p. 335.

455 Van Oostrom-Streep 2005, p. 786, Van Oostrom-Streep 2006, p. 218.

456 Van Oostrom-Streep 2006, p. 220-221.

457 Art. 6:252(1) BW.

458 Cahen 2004, p. 34, Asser & Hartkamp 2001, No. 407, p. 427. See above; 3.1. Real Servitudes.

459 Cahen 2004, p. 33-34.

460 Art. 5:71 BW.

461 Asser & Hartkamp 2001, No. 407.

462 Van Oostrom-Streep 2006, p. 55-57. See also, but less specific, Asser & Hartkamp 2001, No. 407, Du Perron 1999, p. 246 *et seq.*

463 Van Oostrom-Streep 2006, p. 59-61, Parlementaire Geschiedenis NBW – Boek 6 1981, p. 944.

464 Van Oostrom-Streep 2006, p. 54-59, Parlementaire Geschiedenis NBW – Boek 6 1981, p. 944.

situations where a positive secondary duty can be useful.[465] One example of a useful positive duty would be an obligation for an owner against the holder of the qualitative duty to inform this holder of the identity of person to whom he granted a right to use the immovable object, so that the holder of the qualitative duty does not have to find out for himself.[466]

Secondly, the agreement will only have effect against third parties when it is made by notarial deed and registered in the public registry.[467] This requirement shows another difference in comparison with a right of servitude. A right of servitude will only come into existence upon registration of the notarial deed of creation, whereas a qualitative duty will exist between the contracting parties from the moment of agreement. Also here the explanation by Van Oostrom-Streep of the qualitative duty as two agreements is insightful. The main agreement can already have come into being, even if the agreement, in which the parties agree to provide for third-party effect, will not. Until the moment of registration of the notarial deed the qualitative duty will therefore only have effect between parties.[468] There is no other possibility to see the legal nature of the qualitative duty as contractual.[469] A failure to comply with the duty will result in a breach of contract and contractual remedies should be used.[470]

Nevertheless, the qualitative duty fulfils the main criteria for a property right; it has effect against third parties upon registration and it will transfer to subsequent acquirers of the object on which it is created.[471] Also in situations of insolvency the qualitative duty remains in force. If it has been registered before the holder of the object became insolvent, the Insolvency Act stipulates that the duty will remain in existence. The object will then have to be sold burdened with the duty.[472]

In effect the Dutch legislature has created a relation that takes effect against third parties and remains in existence in case of insolvency. Although it fulfils the main criteria for a property right, the relation is contractual in nature. The duty itself is personal and only takes effect against third parties upon registration. Furthermore, the question of the nature of this qualitative duty remains a point of academic debate, since the legislature has decided that the answer lies in the law of obligations.[473] Because of its place in the Civil Code an interference with the qualitative duty will result in a claim for damages based on Article 6:74 BW and further.

Besides the qualitative duty, contract law offers another possibility for parties to provide for third-party effect of their relation. In fact, this last method allows parties also to impose positive duties. In return, the enforcement of the agreement in respect to third parties is more difficult.

465 Van Oostrom-Streep 2006, p. 218-219.
466 Van Oostrom-Streep 2006, p. 113-115.
467 Art. 6:252(2) BW, Van Oostrom-Streep 2005, p. 786.
468 Asser & Hartkamp 2001, No. 411, p. 430, Cahen 2004, p. 39.
469 Asser & Hartkamp 2001, No. 412, p. 431.
470 Art. 6:74 BW, Cahen 2004, p. 35.
471 See also Van Oostrom-Streep 2006, p. 234.
472 Art. 35a FW.
473 Parlementaire Geschiedenis NBW – Boek 6 1981, p. 942 *et seq.*, Du Perron 1999, p. 250, Van Oostrom-Streep 2006, p. 217-219.

The principle of party autonomy in contract law allows the parties, as long as they stay within the limits of the law, to create any relation they desire.[474] In return, the doctrine of privity of contract prevents general third-party effect of such an agreement. However, parties can agree to impose the same rights and duties on subsequent parties upon occurrence of a set event. For example, the owner of a shopping centre may agree with the owner of a restaurant that the latter will be the only restaurant in the shopping centre, and subsequently include a contractual clause in all agreements with other businesses trading in the shopping centre which prescribes a duty not to establish a restaurant, plus an obligation to impose the same duty on subsequent acquirers of these businesses. Such an agreement is concluded under a penalty clause to pay damages to the original restaurant owner per day of violation.[475] These agreements are accepted in Dutch law and are known as chain clauses.

The result of the use of a chain clause is the creation of a third-party effect. The effect is relative because the original agreement will only take effect against those third parties that agree to the chain clause. In other words the duty transfers *ex contractu* and not by operation of law, as in case of property rights and the qualitative duty.[476] The penalty clause allows the original party to take action in case of violation. However, only contractual remedies will be available, so the original party can only sue for performance and damages.[477] In very limited circumstances only, the original party may claim for a reinstatement of the clause by way of specific remedy as a part of a claim in tort.[478] The *Hoge Raad* has exercised extreme caution not to allow reinstatement of the clause through the law of tort, as that would effectively grant the chain clause the status of a property right.[479]

Chain clauses offer the possibility to provide for a specific third-party effect of an agreement, but only through another act, which is the agreement of a third party to the terms of the agreement. Because it is necessary to act in order to transfer the chain clause, and, once the agreement is violated, only limited possibilities exist to claim for specific performance of the clause, this solution is usually considered undesirable and unnecessarily complicated in Dutch legal practice.[480]

4.9. *EC and International Influences*

The last part of this Section deals with the influences of European and international law on the Dutch system. Under pressure from both European law and international law, the Netherlands is forced to recognise and implement alterations to existing concepts as well as concepts completely foreign to the system. Although these influ-

474 Art. 3:40 BW.
475 HR 10 May 1996, *NJ* 1996/537 (*Coscun/Van Sommeren*).
476 See Art. 6:155 BW, Wijting 2001, p. 937 *et seq.*
477 Arts. 6:74 *et seq.* BW.
478 HR 17 May 1985, *NJ* 1986/760 (*Curaçao/Boyé*), Asser & Hartkamp 2001, No. 413, p. 432, Rank-Berenschot 1992, p. 83-84.
479 HR 17 May 1985, *NJ* 1986/760 (*Curaçao/Boyé*), Van Oostrom-Streep 2006, p. 219.
480 See, *inter alia*, Van Opstall 1966, p. 471, Heyman 2003, p. 10, Wijting 2001, p. 938 *et seq.*

ences also exist in French and German law, in Dutch law, because of the rigidity of the legal system, serious problems arise. Two of these influences are of great importance; the implementation of the EC Financial Collateral Arrangements Directive and the international Hague Convention on Trusts.[481]

The Financial Collateral Arrangements Directive creates two additional property relations; a collateral transfer and a collateral pledge.[482] The Directive is intended to provide rules for the market in equities and money.[483] It applies to security rights created by companies or organisations that have a connection to the financial market. These include governments, banks and other financial institutions.[484] In this respect there is a difference between these and normal property rights which can generally be used by anyone and applied to all objects, or to a general set of objects as immovable or registered objects. The security rights that the Financial Collateral Directive introduces are, in principle, only available for financial institutions and large companies, but they still have a significant impact on the Dutch system of property law.[485] From a systematic point of view, the most remarkable development is the introduction of the collateral transfer. This security instrument enables one party to transfer his equities or money to another party for security purposes in return for finance. However, the transfer for security purposes, which was formerly recognised under the old Dutch Civil Code, is now clearly prohibited in Article 3:84(3) BW.[486]

Regardless of Article 3:84(3), several property law authors, among whom are Keijser, Westrik and Van Erp, have argued that the Directive re-introduces the possibility of a transfer for security purposes.[487] At the end of the legislative process, the Minister of Justice felt the need to respond specifically to the last two of these authors. The Minister argues that the prohibition of Article 3:84(3) BW was introduced to stop the old fiduciary transfer of ownership that resulted in a fragmentation of ownership.[488] The Minister recalls that is was the specific intention of the legislature to supplement the ownership for security purposes with a right of silent pledge.[489] The prohibition in Article 3:84(3) BW should therefore be read as prohibiting this relative and fragmented type of security ownership. As was dealt with

481 Directive 2004/47/EC of 6 June 2002 on Financial Collateral Arrangements and the Hague Convention on the Law Applicable to Trusts and on Their Recognition.

482 On this Directive see Chapter 8; 2.1.2. Legal Framework: Secondary Community Law.

483 Article 1 Directive 2004/47/EC. Keijser 2004, p. 761, Van Vliet 2005, p. 190.

484 Van Erp 2004c, p. 540.

485 The original proposal of the Minister of Justice was to extend the application of the Directive to small and medium sized enterprises (SMEs). The legislative proposal made it through most of the legislative process but was put to a halt by the First Chamber of Parliament (Senate) who voted against the proposal. See *First Chamber of Parliament* proceedings of 8 March 2005, *Handelingen I* 2004-2005, No. 18, p. 781-782, Van Vliet 2005, p. 190.

486 See above; 2.3. Security Ownership.

487 Keijser 2004, p. 765-767, Van Erp 2004c, p., 541-543, furthermore in reaction to *inter alia* Keijser see Van Erp 2004d, on which see Meulman 2005, and Van Erp in a final reaction in Van Erp 2005.

488 *Nadere Memorie van Antwoord* 5 January 2005, p. 7-8 and 22-23. More detailed see above; 2. The Right of Ownership.

489 See above; 3.6. Pledge.

above, following the *Hoge Raad* in its *Sogelease* judgment, an actual transfer of ownership for security purposes is possible in Dutch law.[490] In such a transfer the full right and not a fragment of the right of ownership is transferred to the acquirer. The Minister emphasises that there should be no mistake about this and that the collateral transfer is such an actual transfer.[491]

However, the acceptance that a collateral transfer is an actual transfer leads to complications for the transferor. The security ownership of the old Civil Code only comprised those powers of the right of ownership that were necessary for the transferee to exercise his security right. Over time, the provisions on the right of pledge became applied by analogy.[492] The result was that the security owner could only sell the object serving as security and satisfy his claim with the proceeds of the sale.

An actual security transfer as introduced by the Collateral Directive transfers the full powers of the transferor to the transferee. Consequently the transferee will have full right of ownership and will be under no obligation to sell the object serving as security.[493] Even more so, Van Vliet has emphasised that the Dutch implementation act does not contain a rule stipulating that any excess value of the object is for the transferor and that the transferee will be under no obligation to return this excess value.[494] A mere personal obligation to remedy this will not be enough. Van Vliet uses a comparative example from Germany to show that in German law also a property law solution or a *Verdinglichung* of personal rights is used to strengthen the position of the transferor.[495]

Secondly, the collateral pledge also creates complications with regard to the general rules of property law.[496] The implementation act provides special provisions on a right of collateral pledge. Only when these special rules do not apply will the general rules on pledge be applicable.[497] These general rules include the provisions in book 3 of the Civil Code, but also the Dutch Insolvency Act. Under these provisions, the pledgee may act as if there was no insolvency and execute his right of (collateral) pledge. The result is that at the outset the legislature has chosen to implement the collateral pledge as a species of the normal right of pledge.[498] One of the most specific characteristics of the collateral pledge is that the pledgee will have the power to dispose and the right to use the object serving as security.[499] A transfer of the objects under collateral pledge will lead to substitution. Therefore, a right of collateral pledge will come into existence by operation of law on the substituted

490 See above; 2.3. Security Ownership.

491 Art. 7:55 BW and *Nadere MvA I, Kamerstukken I* 2004/05, 28 874, E, p. 9-10.

492 HR 3 January 1941, *NJ* 1941, 470 (*Boerenleenbank Hazerswoude/Los*), Van Mierlo 1988, p. 15, Van Vliet 2005, p. 198.

493 Van Vliet 2005, p. 198.

494 Van Vliet 2005, p. 198-199.

495 Van Vliet 2005, p. 200.

496 See Van Vliet 2005, p 196.

497 Lieverse & Wiggers-Rust 2005, p. 60, Keijser 2004, p. 761.

498 See Van Vliet 2005, p. 191, 196, but also Lieverse & Wiggers-Rust 2005, p. 60.

499 Art. 5 Directive 2004/47/EC, Keijser 2004, p. 767, Van Vliet 2005, p. 193-194.

object.[500] At the end of the relationship between pledgor and pledgee, the pledgee is under the obligation to return the objects or objects comparable to the originals.[501]

Furthermore, the Directive provides specific rules on the execution of the collateral pledge. The general rules on execution of a right of pledge force the pledgee to sell the object and to satisfy his claim with the proceeds of sale.[502] However, the Collateral Directive allows the pledgee to keep the object for himself and does not require such a sale.[503] In order to protect the position of the pledgor in such a situation the pledgee will be under a duty to transfer any excess value to the pledgor.[504]

The implementation of the Financial Collateral Directive shows the influence of EC legislation on the Dutch legal system.[505] Although the collateral pledge shares many characteristics with the normal types of pledge, in effect a new type of pledge is added to the catalogue of property rights. The right created is a limited security property right to which special rules apply.[506] The implementation shows the effect EC legislation can have on the Dutch property law system and raises the question of whether Dutch law is ready for these developments.[507]

Another strong influence on the Dutch property law system comes from international law. The Hague Convention on the Law Applicable to Trusts and on Their Recognition introduces the Anglo-American concept of a trust into the Dutch system of private law.[508] A trust is a legal instrument whereby one person, the settlor, transfers objects to another person, the trustee, who will be under the obligation to manage these assets, separately from his own, for the benefit of a third person, a beneficiary. Although Dutch law itself does not recognise a trust, the Hague Convention allows persons to set up a trust under a foreign law that does recognise a trust, and thereby forces the contracting states to recognise the foreign trust.[509]

Although the Convention especially deals with rules of private international law, the Convention itself is not intended to supply a legal basis for the creation of a trust. It merely opens the possibility of choosing an applicable law that does provide such a basis, which consequently has to be recognised.[510] Article 2 of the Convention states:

500 Art. 7:52(4) BW, Keijser 2004, p. 767, Van Vliet 2005, p. 194.
501 Art. 7:53(2) BW, Van Vliet 2005, p. 194.
502 Art. 3:250 BW, see above; 3.6. Pledge.
503 Art. 7:54 BW, Keijser 2004, p. 768, Van Vliet 2005, p. 195.
504 Art. 7:54 BW, *Nadere MvA I, Kamerstukken I* 2004/05, 28 874, E, p. 16-17, Van Vliet 2005, p. 196.
505 See Van Erp 2004c.
506 Van Vliet 2005, p. 196.
507 Van Erp 2004c and in reaction the Minister of Justice in *MvA I, Kamerstukken I* 2004/05, 28 874, E, p 22-23. This issue is returned to below in 5. A *Numerus Clausus* in Dutch Property Law?
508 The Convention was signed by the Netherlands on 1 July 1985 and was ratified on 28 November 1995. The Convention entered into force in the Netherlands on 1 February 1996. The Netherlands is one of the only countries that is Contracting Party to the Convention. Other Contracting Parties include England and Italy, but not Germany and France.
509 Art. 11 Hague Convention. The Hague Convention entered into force in the Netherlands on 1 January 1996, Aertsen 2004, p. 103.
510 See also Graziadei 2002b, p. 336-340.

> For the purposes of this Convention, the term 'trust' refers to the legal relationship created – *inter vivos* or on death – by a person, the settlor, when assets have been placed under the control of a trustee for the benefit of a beneficiary or for a specified purpose.
> A trust has the following characteristics:
> (a) the assets constitute a separate fund and are not part of the trustee's own estate;
> (b) title to the trust assets stands in the name of the trustee or in the name of another person on behalf of the trustee;
> (c) the trustee has the power and the duty, in respect of which he is accountable, to manage, employ or dispose of the assets in accordance with the terms of the trust and the special duties imposed upon him by law.

The reservation by the settlor of certain rights and powers, and the fact that the trustee may himself have rights as a beneficiary, are not necessarily inconsistent with the existence of a trust.[511]

Article 2 states the material scope of the Convention. Legal relations that fall under this definition of a trust are covered by it. These basic criteria create a difficulty for the Dutch legislature. Specifically the recognition of a trust under Dutch law, but also the obligation to make sure that the trust objects constitute a separate set of assets from the assets of the trustee, causes problems.

The creation of a trust requires a transfer of objects from the settlor to the trustee, who will not acquire a right of ownership of the objects for himself but actually for the beneficiary. The purpose of a trust is not to have the beneficiary, but the trustee, receive ownership of the objects, although the beneficiary still has an entitlement to the trust objects. In Dutch law, such a transfer is considered as a transfer whereby the object does not fall in the set of assets of the acquirer, which is strongly opposed to by the second part of Article 3:84(3) BW.[512] Furthermore, the trust objects being treated as a set of assets separate from the assets of the trustee interferes with the provision of Article 3:276 BW, which allows creditors to seize all assets of the debtor if they are not paid. A separate set of trust assets would disable the creditors from having access to these assets.[513]

In order to solve these problems, new legislation on the private international law aspects of trusts, the *Wet Conflictenrecht Trusts* (WCT), was introduced. Article 4 WCT states:

> Provisions of Dutch law concerning the transfer of ownership, security rights or protection of creditors in case of insolvency do not affect the legal effects of a recognition provided by Article 11 of the Convention.[514]

511 Art. 2 Hague Convention.

512 Koppenol-Laforce 1997b, p. 547, also see above; 2.3. Security Ownership.

513 Art. 3:275 BW and Art. 20 Fw.

514 Art. 4 WCT 'Bepalingen van Nederlands recht inzake eigendomsoverdracht, zekerheidsrecht of de bescherming van schuldeisers in geval van insolventie laten de in artikel 11 van het Verdrag omschreven rechtsgevolgen van de erkenning van een trust onverlet'. On the effects of Art. 4 WCT see Koppenol-Laforce 1997b, p. 545.

The effect of the Hague Convention is not to make it possible for everyone to create a trust. The Hague Convention explicitly states that a trust under the Convention only has to be recognised if significant elements, specifically the habitual residence of the trustee, are closely connected to a legal system that does recognise a trust.[515] Therefore, the creation of a trust by a Dutch national using trust assets located in the Netherlands is not a trust under the Hague Convention.[516]

Once a trust is recognised by Dutch law, the result of the Hague Convention and the WCT is that several essential elements of Dutch property law no longer apply. Dutch law will be forced to recognise a legal relation where both the trustee and the beneficiary have a claim with regard to the trust objects. General Dutch property law does not know what to do with it.

5. A *Numerus Clausus* in Dutch Property Law?

The parliamentary history of the fifth book of the Dutch Civil Code states that the system of property rights in Dutch law is closed.[517] The parliamentary history presents this as a clearly established fact. It states:

> In continental legal systems the system of property law is, different than in the area of contract law ..., a closed system.[518]

Under the old Civil Code this was not as certain as the parliamentary history suggests. A very clear example was provided in 1914, when the Brotherhood of Notaries had an official meeting to discuss the question of whether property rights could be created outside the list of recognised property rights.[519] During the debate, the answer seemed not at all clear. At the centre of this debate was Article 584 old BW. This Article, which is based on Article 543 of the French Civil Code, mentioned several property rights:

> One can have, on an object, a right of possession, or a right of ownership, or a right of hereditary title, or a right to enjoy fruits, or a right of servitude or a right of pledge or hypothec.[520]

Meijers, in an influential article in 1907, emphasised that this Article was a result of an historical development and invoked Hahn's Pentarchy to explain its origin.[521] On

515 Art. 13 Hague Convention. Aertsen 2004, p. 104-105.

516 This is different in Italian law, where an internal trust is recognised. See Graziadei 2002b, p. 336-340, Lupoi 2005, p. 10 *et seq.*, Braun 2006, p. 795 *et seq.*

517 Parlementaire Geschiedenis NBW - Boek 5 1981, p. 3.

518 Parlementaire Geschiedenis NBW - Boek 5 1981, p. 3 states '3. In de continentale rechtstelsels vormt het Zakenrecht, anders dan het contractenrecht ..., een gesloten stelsel'.

519 Broederschap der Notarissen in Nederland 1914. See also Struycken 2007, p. 161-166.

520 Art. 584 Old BW stated 'Men kan op zaken hebben, hetzij een recht van bezit, hetzij een recht van eigendom, hetzij een recht van erfgenaamschap, hetzij een vruchtgenot, hetzij een recht van erfdienstbaarheid, hetzij een regt van pand en hypotheek'.Further underlined by the Council of State (*Raad van State*) and the affirmation of this by the Minister of Justice, see Parlementaire Geschiedenis NBW - Boek 5 1981, p. 6 and 9.

the question whether this list provided a limitation to the number of property rights recognised under the old Civil Code, he stated that, although the *Hoge Raad* had not dealt with any new property rights outside the recognised list in the Civil Code, in lower instances this question had been decided.[522] Meijers concluded that property rights can only exist when there is a specific legal basis for their existence, and that this was possible outside the scope of Article 584 old BW.[523] At the end of the meeting of the notaries, the questions of whether any new property rights, other than those recognised by law, could be created, and whether it is desirable that there should be a power to create new rights in Dutch law, were answered negatively.[524]

Struycken has examined this period of Dutch history closely and has shown that, possibly under the influence of German legal thinking, around 1900 the system of Dutch property rights was considered closed.[525] Struycken invokes several proposals for a Dutch Civil Code that were drafted in the second half of the nineteenth century to show that, at least in the eyes of the Dutch legislators, the system of property rights in Dutch law was not open.[526] However, these proposals never made it into a Civil Code and Dutch practice remained divided over the question. The 1914 meeting of the Brotherhood of Dutch Notaries only confirms this.[527]

The starting point in Dutch law is the landmark decision of the *Hoge Raad* in *Blaauboer v Berlips*, in which the Court firmly established the separation between the law of property and the law of obligations.[528] Moreover, the *Hoge Raad* refused to classify the agreement made in the case – the duty to construct a road – as a right of servitude, because the agreement lacked some of the characteristics of a servitude prescribed by the Civil Code. Struycken explains this final part of the reasoning of the *Hoge Raad* as an expression of *Typenfixierung*.[529]

Since 1905 the Dutch legal system has been based on a strict separation between the law of property and the law of obligations, in particular the law of contract.[530] Before that, it had been possible to create contracts with a property effect.[531] The decision of the *Hoge Raad* reinstated the strict separation and prohibited these effects.[532] In legal literature, the separation between the law of contract and the law of property became linked to the different rules applying to these two areas. The law of contract was considered an area in which parties were as free as possible. The

521 Meijers 1907, p. 271 *et seq*. See Chapter 2; 4.4. Other Property Rights. On this theory in Dutch law see, *inter alia*, Nève 1996, p. 231, Feenstra 1982, Ketelaar 1978, p. 140.

522 Meijers 1907, p. 10.

523 Meijers 1907, p. 10, 24. He mentions the rights of *genot van weide and recht van ettinge*.

524 Broederschap der Notarissen in Nederland 1914, p. 345.

525 Struycken 2007, p. 170 *et seq*. On the influence of German legal scholarship in the 19th century in France see Bürge 1991. Possibly the influence of German legal thinking in Dutch law has had similar effects. See, in this respect, Struycken 2007, p. 169, 205.

526 These include the proposals of 1816 and 1820, see Struycken 2007, p. 129-131.

527 See also Struycken 2007, p. 161-166.

528 HR 3 March 1905, W 8191, see above; 1. Introduction.

529 Struycken 2007, p. 41-42.

530 HR 3 March 1905, W 8191 (*Blaauboer/Berlips*), see above; 1. Introduction.

531 See Struycken 2007, p. 42-50.

532 On this development see Struycken 2007, p. 40-50.

law of property, in contrast, was characterised by its strictness and the closed system of property rights.[533]

The system of property rights and the separation between the law of property and the law of contract are connected. A less strong separation between contract law and property law could result in the possibility for parties to create contracts with property effects. It is exactly against this development that the *Hoge Raad* delivered its 1905 decision in *Blaauboer v Berlips*.[534]

The opinion in the Netherlands in the twentieth century was that there could be no new property rights created outside those prescribed by law. Nevertheless, in 1929 the *Hoge Raad*, under pressure to help Dutch legal practice to solve growing problems caused by the strict provisions on the right of pledge, recognised a transfer for security purposes resulting in a new type of ownership known as security ownership. From that moment until the entry into force of the new Dutch Civil Code, besides the already recognised types of ownership, a right of security ownership existed.[535] The result of these decisions was that the list of property rights was extended with the right of security ownership which found no exact legal basis, either in the Civil Code, or in another legislative provision.

The decisions of 1929 and the subsequently developed ownership for security purposes were heavily condemned. Meijers especially heavily criticised the developments and argued that security ownership was nothing more than an attempt to create a right of pledge without the obligation to transfer the object under pledge to the pledgee.[536] When Meijers was asked to develop a new Civil Code he made certain that the system would not know any property rights other than those recognised by law. Therefore, Article 3:81(1) BW states:

> 1. He who is entitled to an independent and transferable right can, within the limits of that right, create the limited rights that are recognised by law.[537]

If the Article was not clear enough, the parliamentary history adds to this Article that the Civil Code only recognises those property rights that are dealt with by law and that this applies both to the limited rights, in Dutch *beperkte rechten*, as well as to the property rights in respect of corporeal objects, in Dutch the *zakelijke rechten*.[538] This limitation by the legislature applies not only to the number of rights, but also to their content. Only those rights that fulfil the criteria of one of the recognised and described property rights can be a property right in the sense of Article 3:81(1) BW. With that the Dutch legislature has firmly set a rule of *numerus clausus* in Dutch law.

533 See Kisch 1932, p. 5-11, Suijling 1940, p. 1-2, Asser & Scholten 1913, p. 31-35.

534 See also Pitlo 1968 and Heyman 2003.

535 HR 25 January 1929, *NJ* 1929, 616 (*Beer brewery*) and HR 21 June 1929, *NJ* 1929, 1096 (*Luxury car-lease*), on delivery *constitutum possessorium* see Van Vliet 2000, p. 51, Van Mierlo 1988, p. 7-9.

536 Meijers 1937, p. 65, Meijers 1948, p. 89 *et seq.*

537 Art. 3:81(1) BW '-1 Hij aan wie een zelfstandig en overdraagbaar recht toekomt, kan binnen de grenzen van dat recht de in de wet genoemde beperkte rechten vestigen'.

538 On limited rights and *zakelijke rechten* see above in 3. Other Property Rights. Parlementaire Geschiedenis NBW - Boek 5 1981, p. 3. See also Snijders 1997, p. 88 and Snijders 2002, p. 28.

However, within the limits of this definition, parties are free to decide on the content of the property right.[539]

At the outset of the system the creative activity to find new solutions will therefore have to take place within these boundaries. The system of the Civil Code does not explicitly prohibit the creation of one property right in respect of another property right.[540] This so-called stacking of rights creates interesting possibilities for parties that want to create certain specific legal relations. Many provisions in the Civil Code explicitly create this possibility.[541] These include the possibility that can be found in Article 5:84 BW to create a right of servitude on a right of *emphyteusis*, *superficies* or usufruct, or the possibility of Article 5:93 BW to create a right of *emphyteusis* on a right of *emphyteusis*.[542] Moreover, stacking of property rights is also possible with security property rights.[543] These property rights in respect of property rights will, except for the situation described in Article 3:81(3) BW, be dependent on the existence of the mother right. When the mother right therefore ceases to exist, so, generally, will these property rights.[544]

Another possibility is to create several property rights in respect of the same object. Specifically in the case of security rights this can create certain doctrinal difficulties. Parties can agree that the pledgee will have a right to create a second right of pledge for the benefit of himself on the object under pledge. This so-called re-pledging, in Dutch *herverpanding*, is a special power for which a specific clause in the deed of creation is needed.[545] Theoretically, this power would include the creation of a new property right, but the pledgee will never have the power to transfer more rights than he already has. However, the new right of pledge will take rank above his own right and will therefore be a stronger right than the original right of pledge.[546] The most sensible doctrinal justification for this is that holders of security rights in respect of the same object have the right to renounce their rank for the benefit of another holder of a security right.[547] In this respect it could be held that by inserting the clause that authorises the pledgee to re-pledge, the pledgee agrees to give up his rank on behalf of the newly created property right. However, the new right of pledge comprises more than the holder of the original right of pledge could theoretically transfer.

539 The agreement will be part of the property right if it fulfils set criteria. See Parlementaire Geschiedenis NBW - Boek 5 1981, p. 3, but also above; 4.7. Obligations as Part of Property Rights.

540 See in particular Struycken 2007, p. 368-378.

541 Although at the outset the rights dealt with in book 5 of the BW were intended to be excluded from this possibility, see Heyman 1999, p. 53.

542 The application of Art. 5:104 BW allows the same possibility for the right of *superficies*. See Heyman 1999, p. 53.

543 See e.g. Arts. 3:212 and 3:223 BW on the establishment of a right of hypothec on a right of usufruct. On this see also Asser, Mierlo, Mijnsen & Van Velten 2003, No. 174, p. 203.

544 See above; 3. Other Property Rights.

545 Art. 3:242 BW, see Breken 2002, p. 365, Snijders 2002, p. 30-32.

546 Breken 2002, p. 372-373.

547 Breken 2002, p. 386-387.

Moreover, Article 3:84(3) BW restricts the freedom that parties have within the set of recognised property rights. The prohibition, known as *fiducia*-ban, which has been dealt with on several occasions in this Chapter, is intended to prevent a separation of powers included in a property right that does not fit within the system of property law.[548] The inclusion of the Article recalls the strong words of Meijers who used to condemn the ownership for security purposes.[549] The transfer of ownership for security purposes did not constitute a transfer of the full powers of the owner, but merely those powers required for the protection of the transferee. The interpretation of the *Hoge Raad* in its *Sogelease* judgement requiring an actual transfer of ownership, a transfer of the full set of powers of the owner, to pass the test of Article 3:84(3) BW was a reiteration of Meijers' views.

One of the principal instances in which not all powers of an owner are transferred is the creation of a trust. A trust requires a separation of powers between a trustee, who holds the trust objects separate from his own objects and who manages them, and a beneficiary, who is entitled to the benefits and proceeds of the trust objects. In the past few decades the discussion about whether a trust should be implemented in Dutch law has been the subject of a lively debate.[550] However, it has been the specific intention of the legislature to exclude a trust, which, at least in the eyes of the Dutch legislature, would result in a separation of powers that, according to the system of Dutch property law, should be in one hand.[551] The prohibition of any attempt to create a situation where not all the powers of the right of ownership are transferred is strengthened by Article 3:276 BW.[552] This article states that a debtor will be liable with his full set of assets unless the law provides otherwise.[553] The creation of a trust whereby the objects included in the trust are separated from the private objects of the trustee is therefore generally not possible.[554] The *Hoge Raad* indeed held in 1937 that such a separate set of assets can only exist insofar as there is a specific legal basis.[555] According to the *Hoge Raad*, allowing this would introduce the possibility for parties to create a position in which they have a preferential position, to the disadvantage of other creditors. Effectively a creditor to a separate set of objects of person X would not have to deal with a possible insolvency of the private objects of person X.

548 Snijders 1997, p. 91, in the same sense Asser, Van Dam & Mijnsen 2002, p. 22.

549 See above; 2.3. Security Ownership.

550 See, *inter alia*, Raaijmakers 1994, Koppenol-Laforce 1997b, Koppenol-Laforce 1997a, Snijders 1997, Snijders 1999b, Hayton, Kortman & Verhagen 1999, Vriesendorp 2003 and Aertsen 2004.

551 Final report on Art. 5.1.1 (now Art. 5:1 BW). See Parlementaire Geschiedenis NBW – Boek 5 1981, p. 18.

552 The creation of property rights is a general exception to this rule. However, property rights can only be created when specifically authorised by the Civil Code, Art. 3:81 BW.

553 The exceptions are dealt with by Art. 3:278 BW that mentions the right of pledge, hypothec and priority rights. On the (non) applicability of Art. 3:276 BW outside the scope of property law, in particular in respect to a contractual security on bank accounts see Wibier 2007, p. 99-104.

554 Although such results can be achieved in Dutch law by, e.g. creating a legal person that will manage the assets.

555 HR 4 January 1937, *NJ* 1937, 586, Snijders 1997, p. 95. The reasoning of the court became, once more, established in HR 13 June 2003, *NJ* 2004/196 (*Pro-Call*).

The result of these three provisions, Articles 3:81, 3:84 and 3:276 BW, is that, at the outset, the system of Dutch property law is built on a closed list of property rights. This is widely accepted, and most basic handbooks on property law state that the system of property rights is closed.[556] Based on the general theory on 'normal types' of Meijers, the system of Dutch private law makes a distinction between relative rights and absolute rights. Among the absolute rights are the property rights that are dealt with in a system separate from the law of contract.

The reason for such a closed system in Dutch law is also clear - allowing parties to create their rights would burden the right of ownership and create legal uncertainty in respect to which rights apply to which objects.[557] With a clear reference to the reasons stated by the *Hoge Raad* in the *Blaauboer v Berlips* decision on the separation between property law and contract law, the parliamentary history brings the discussion on the nature of the system of property rights in Dutch law to an end.[558]

Nevertheless, this Chapter has dealt with several situations in which the Dutch system of property law is under pressure. Legal relations such as leases, privative mandates and qualitative duties bear many characteristics of property rights, except that they are dealt with in other areas of the Civil Code than in the parts dealing with property law.[559] Moreover, even within the parts on property law, security rights can, after their existence has ended, still have after-effects against third parties.[560] Also, new types of property relations under the influence of European law and international law create doctrinal difficulties. The Collateral Directive introduces both a right of pledge as well as a security ownership, but it is still implemented in book 7 and therefore considered a contract in Dutch law.[561]

It appears to be the system of Dutch property law itself that withholds these personal legal relations from becoming what they essentially and effectively already are - property rights. A trust recognised under the Hague Convention creates so many problems with the system that Article 4 WCT declares Article 3:81(1) and Article 3:84(3) BW, the basis of the system of Dutch property law, not applicable. At the same time, a similar relation that cannot be brought under the definition of the Hague Convention will fall under these same provisions and will be prohibited. It can be questioned why an international obligation would be a sufficient reason to deviate from the foundations of Dutch property law, where the same type of arrangement under Dutch law as such is rejected on grounds of legal certainty.

556 See Snijders & Rank-Berenschot 2001, p. 56-57 (using the 'term more or less closed'), Pitlo et al. 2006, p. 459-460 and Asser, Mijnsen, De Haan & Van Dam 2006, No. 39, p. 34-35 (using the definition no other property rights than those recognised by law).

557 With a reference to the old law prior to the Old BW, where such a creation of rights was possible, see Parlementaire Geschiedenis NBW - Boek 5 1981, p. 13.

558 Parlementaire Geschiedenis NBW - Boek 5 1981, p. 13.

559 See above; 4.3. Lease of Immovable Objects, 4.6. Privative Mandate and 4.7. Obligations as Part of Property Rights, respectively.

560 See above; 4.5. After-Effects of Property Rights.

561 See above; 4.9. EC and International Influences.

The strongest arguments against such a development are put forward by Snijders.[562] As one of the founders of the system of the new BW, Snijders, in a series of articles, puts forward that the system of Dutch private law was designed to cope with new developments and that there is no need to change it.[563] He argues that the drafters of the Civil Code made a legal-political choice to prohibit a separation of powers that does not fit within the system of property law.[564] Consequently, a separation of powers that can be brought within the system can be allowed. Snijders' reasoning is primarily based on an analogy with the theory of sources of obligations dealt with in Article 6:1 BW. This Article states that obligations can only arise if this follows from the law. In 1959 the *Hoge Raad* rendered a landmark decision in *Quint v Te Poel* in which the Court held that an obligation can also arise in circumstances other than as prescribed by law, if that obligation fits into the system and is in line with cases that are already dealt with.[565] Consequently, Snijders argues that a fiduciary relation that has no basis in the law could be recognised if it fits in the system and is in accordance with the property rights already dealt with.[566] As an example he mentions forms of *bewind*, a type of administration or management, that are not dealt with specifically by the Civil Code but which he considers should be recognised if demanded by practice.

Furthermore, Snijders searches for developments in other areas than the right of ownership and other property rights. In his articles, Snijders looks specifically at Article 3:6 BW on patrimonial rights, in Dutch *vermogensrechten*. This concept is, as a consequence of Meijers' normal-types theory, an open concept under which Snijders argues new rights can be brought. In his view, these new patrimonial rights include, for instance, domain-names and licences.[567] Snijders argues that the BW should be read in a free and not overly legalistic way. When practice and societal developments require the recognition of new legal relations he considers that they should be recognised.[568]

In a strict approach to the system of Dutch private law, these new legal relations should be either personal or property rights, in traditional terms, relative or absolute rights. Snijders does not agree with this strict approach and points out that Meijers, the founder of the Dutch Civil Code, also intended to leave room for intermediate forms.[569] Snijders proposes to characterise new legal relations, which could be patrimonial rights under Article 3:6 BW, in terms of exclusivity and not in terms

562 Snijders was commissioner responsible for the introduction of books 3, 5 and 6 of the New Civil Code, vice president of the *Hoge Raad* and is Professor of Private Law at the University of Amsterdam. See, *inter alia*, Storme, De Theije & Delbecke 2004.

563 Snijders 1991, Snijders 1993, Snijders 1997, Snijders 2002, Snijders 2005a and Snijders 2005b.

564 Snijders 1997, p. 91.

565 HR 30 January 1959, *NJ* 1959, 548 (*Quint/Te Poel*).

566 Snijders 1997, p. 91-92.

567 Snijders 2005a, p. 81, 84, Snijders 2005b, p. 96. As such, these patrimonial rights can be an object of a property right. The interesting part of this development is that because of these new objects of property law, the existing property rights might no longer offer sufficient possibilities for parties to deal with their affairs.

568 Snijders 2005b, p. 101, see also Van Erp 2006a, p. 1057.

569 Snijders names these *sui generis*. Snijders 2005a , p. 81.

of relative or absolute rights. Also here, Snijders proposes to search for connections to the cases that are already dealt with by the Civil Code under the *Quint v Te Poel* doctrine mentioned above.[570] In this approach a domain-name is an exclusive right, not dealt with by law, but which, according to Snijders, fits in the system of the Dutch Civil Code. A right to a domain-name is transferable, but does not answer to the characterisation between relative and absolute rights well. It should therefore, in Snijders' words, be an exclusive right under Article 3:6 BW.[571]

In her dissertation, Rank-Berenschot emphasises that the distinction between personal rights and property rights should not be taken as the essential characteristic of the system of private law.[572] Partly based on the works of Ginossar, she explains private law as a system of relations between persons, where a property right is a personal right with qualitative or property effects.[573] Rank-Berenschot states that partly because the distinction between personal rights and property rights is less strong than is often suggested, the new Dutch Civil Code introduced several elements, mainly personal rights with third-party effect, that blur the distinction.[574] However, at the outset the system remains based on the distinction between property law and contract law, whereby the former provides rules on a limited set of relations in a closed system of rights that are derived from the right of ownership.

In a system, as suggested by Rank-Berenschot, where the basis is a personal right, the distinguishing element is third-party effect. She proposes a scale where on the one side there is a pure personal right and on the other side a pure property right. In order to place a certain relation on the scale several questions have to be answered.[575] Starting with the closed system of property rights, parties must use one of the provided property rights if possible, ending with the doctrine of privity of contract. When the first question is answered positively there is a property right and therefore also third-party effect. A negative answer to the first question, in the theory of Rank-Berenschot, will bring the matter of third-party effect into the realm of personal rights.[576] In the latter situation the starting point will be no third-party effect unless provided otherwise. In this system the law of property becomes the primary system and contract the leftover category.[577]

The dissertation of Struycken primarily deals with the closed system of property rights.[578] Struycken's analysis of the *numerus clausus* brings him to the conclusion that in Dutch law *numerus clausus* is a question of who is entitled to develop the law of property. In his view this is either the legislature or the judiciary.[579]

570 HR 30 January 1959, *NJ* 1959, 548 (*Quint/Te Poel*), Snijders 2005a, p. 81-82.
571 Snijders 2005a, p. 84-85.
572 Rank-Berenschot 1992, p. 309-310, see also Snijders 2002, p. 28-29.
573 Ginossar 1960, p. 121 *et seq.*, Rank-Berenschot 1992, p. 313, Sagaert 2005b, p. 996-997. On Ginossar see also Chapter 3; 4.2. Real Obligations.
574 Rank-Berenschot 1992, p. 318, see also Snijders 2002, p. 29.
575 Rank-Berenschot 1992, p. 320-321.
576 Rank-Berenschot 1992, p. 321.
577 Rank-Berenschot 1992, p. 335.
578 Struycken 2007, p. 1-2.
579 Struycken 2007, p. 753-761.

Struycken makes a firm choice for the legislature.[580] At the same time he recognises that, bringing the responsibility for the development of the law of property fully back to the legislature, an active legislature is required.[581] In this approach the case-law based approach of Snijders is rejected, but replaced by an active legislature that should adapt the law of property to changes in society.[582]

Struycken's approach has consequences for the system of Dutch property law. Especially in respect to the influence of party autonomy in the law of property, his theory makes a firm decision. When the primacy, which refers to the rule-making power, of the *numerus clausus* is with the legislature, a rule of *numerus clausus* exists in Dutch law. Under this rule the legislature is the only actor that decides on the freedom of the judiciary, but also of parties, in the law of property. Struycken is unequivocally against the development of the law of property through case law.[583] Consequently, he sees little role for party autonomy in the development of the law of property.[584]

Parties are allowed, within the boundaries set by the legislature in the exercise of its primacy to shape the law of property, to provide content to their legal relations. The boundaries set by the legislature are part of the rule of *numerus clausus* in Dutch law, either explicitly in Articles of the Dutch Civil Code dealing with the various property rights, or through the principle of sufficient connection and what Struycken calls the subtraction principle, the model in which a property right is derived from a more extensive right, both of which were also created by the legislature.[585] Struycken therefore affirms the choices made by the legislature with the introduction of the property and contract parts of the new Dutch Civil Code in 1992.[586]

It is interesting that the new Dutch Civil Code allows for the creation of several situations where the law provides legal relations, other than property relations, with some proprietary effect. These quasi-property relations include the lease, the privative mandate and the qualitative obligation. Regardless of the theory on the nature of the Dutch law of property, these legal relations exist and must be dealt with.

The explanation of the system as proposed by Rank-Berenschot opens possibilities for the argument of Snijders that new relations can be recognised if they fit within the system of the law. The system of property rights remains closed, in other words there is a pure rule of *numerus clausus*, but the number of other relations with third-party effect can be extended if there are good reasons to do so. Whether these new relations are characterised as other absolute rights, as proposed by Snijders, or

580 Struycken 2007, p. 762-764.
581 Struycken 2007, p. 770-771.
582 Struycken 2007, p. 778-779.
583 Struycken 2007, p. 762.
584 Struycken 2007, p. 779-780.
585 Struycken 2007, p. 779. On Struycken's subtraction principle see above; 3. Other Property Rights and 4.7. Obligations as Part of Property Rights.
586 On Struycken's opinion on *numerus clausus* see Chapter 7; 3.4. Struycken: Why we Need a *Numerus Clausus*.

as other relations with third-party effect in the area of contract law, does not matter. The legislature or the judiciary could equally effect the inclusion of such a legal relation in the system of Dutch private law.[587] In my view, a choice such as that suggested by Struycken does not necessarily have to be made. When the inclusion of a new right is made by case law, the line of reasoning of the *Hoge Raad* as created in its case law on chain clauses should be followed, and restraint should be exercised when recognising third-party effect of personal rights.[588]

The system of Dutch private law remains founded on the distinction between personal and property rights, but this distinction is not sacrosanct. The deciding factor on whether a relation is a property right or a personal right is primarily offered by the rule of *numerus clausus* to which the property system of Dutch law seems to adhere. After the introduction of the new Dutch Civil Code, it is common opinion that only the legislature has the authority to recognise new types of property rights. However, at the same time there are already many quasi-property relations that operate in the grey area between property law and contract law. The doctrinal problems these quasi-property relations create, in combination with a strict separation between property and contract, has led several authors to search for better distinguishing criteria. Snijders proposes using exclusive rights, Rank-Berenschot third-party effect.[589]

In any event, the question remains whether any other rights besides those recognised by the rule of *numerus clausus* should be awarded third-party effect. Within the Dutch rule of *numerus clausus*, parties have an extensive freedom to decide on the content of their relations which, if the appropriate criteria are fulfilled, will have property-right and therefore third-party effect.

587 This suggestion is also in line with Snijders' theory, see Snijders 2005b, p. 101.
588 HR 17 May 1985, *NJ* 1986/760 (*Curaçao/Boyé*). Also see Rank 1997, p. 471.
589 Snijders 2005a, p. 81, Rank-Berenschot 1992, p. 320.

Chapter 6

ENGLISH LAW

1. Introduction

The law of England is traditionally seen as a system distinct from the other legal systems in Europe. The difference between the common law system of England and the civil law systems of France, Germany and the Netherlands is most visible in the Civil Codes that the civil law countries have adopted. In these Civil Codes, each of the civil law systems has, after the development of a system of feudal landholding from the time of the fall of the Roman Empire, returned to a Roman-law basis of property law. This does not only apply to land, but to the property law systems in general. However, English law, after the famous battle of Hastings in 1066, continued to develop the common law through decisions of the judiciary whilst maintaining a system of feudal landholding.[1]

The property law system of English law is therefore different from civil law and is often used in support of the argument that no common ground between the legal systems in Europe can be found. However, the two traditions of civil law and common law are not completely separate, there have been many influences from continental systems on English law and *vice versa*.[2]

Because of the origin of English law and the absence of a clear break with the legal system of the past, no separate account of the development of property rights in English law will be given. To the contrary, the development of property rights in English law is English law in force at this moment. Therefore the historical development is part of the discussion of English modern property law in this chapter.

In English law, property law is not a subject that is usually considered as a whole. Based on the historical development of property relations, a distinction between personal property law and land law is made. The concepts that are used in these two different systems of property law are different depending on which division of property law applies. This chapter will therefore start with a description of the common law, its specific terminology, and some important doctrines and

1 Holdsworth 1927, p. 10 *et seq.*
2 Many of these cross influences in the area of property law will be dealt with in this study.

concepts necessary to explain the content of the currently recognised property rights.

1.1. *Terminology*

English law uses different words from the civil law systems to describe the objects on which property rights can be created. First and foremost, there is a general distinction between land and chattels.[3] As a very general definition, 'chattels' are those things that are not land. Because of the development of the system of property law in England, property law comprises two areas of law in line with the distinction between land and chattels. These areas are land law and personal property law.

The common law has developed since 1066, and the common law terminology has evolved over time. In old terminology, land is also known as realty and land law as real property law. This specific terminology refers to the real action, or *actio in rem*, that, under old procedural law, could be used to protect a legal interest in land.[4] Chattels are also known as personalty, which refers to the personal action or, *actio in personam*, that could be used to protect a legal interest in a chattel. The difference in the availability of these actions has determined some of the most fundamental differences between land law and personal property law today. Briefly stated, only real actions could result in a specific remedy, personal actions could only lead to damages.[5]

Another word used for chattel is the French word *chose*. With this term, English law, with the law of Normandy in force from 1066, and French law share a common basis. Of chattels types, there are two; choses in possession, which are all chattels that can be held in possession, and choses in action, which are chattels that cannot be held in possession.[6] In other words, choses in possession are tangible objects on which factual control can be exercised. Consequently, choses in action are those objects on which no factual control or power can be exercised, usually intangible or incorporeal objects.[7] Choses in action comprise basically any object that is not real or a chose in possession. The main examples are shares in a company, bills of exchange, intellectual property and debts.[8] A separate category, mainly used in commercial transactions, is an intangible, which are rights one person can exercise against another for a certain performance.[9] A last term for chattel is a 'good', when it comes to a sale of objects that fall under the Sale of Goods Act 1979. Because of the

3 Tyler & Palmer 1973, p. 3, Bridge 2002, p. 1-2. English law therefore does not follow a general distinction between immovable and movable objects, see *Freke v Lord Carbery* (1873), L.R. 16 Eq. 461 and *Re Hoyles* [1911] 1 Ch. 179.
4 Tyler & Palmer 1973, p. 6-7, Simpson 1986, p. 25 *et seq.*, Holdsworth 1927, p. 11 *et seq.*
5 Tyler & Palmer 1973, p. 6-7, Holdsworth 1927, 3-4, 10, Pollock & Maitland 1898b, p. 150-151.
6 Tyler & Palmer 1973, p. 11, Bridge 2002, p. 3.
7 Tyler & Palmer 1973, p. 11-14, Bridge 2002, p. 4-12.
8 Bridge 2002, p. 4-5.
9 See Goode 2004, p. 29.

important position tangible things and in particular sale of these objects take in commercial settings, in commercial law, the word 'good' is normal terminology.[10]

Other distinctions exist, but are for the purposes of this study less relevant. These include hereditaments, which is another word for all types of real property, but also the term chattels real.[11] A chattel real is an old category that mainly comprised leasehold interests.[12] Originally, the feudal system of landholding did not recognise leases as a proprietary interest and therefore leases were treated as chattels, but with a special status as chattels real.[13]

When the object of property law has been defined and the relevant property law regime can be determined, the question remains as to what right or interest a person can exercise on these objects. In general, the terms interest and right are both used, interest as a slightly more general term.[14] Depending on the area of property law, land law or personal property law, the terminology differs.

In the area of land law, the terminology is very specific. It is in particular in land law that the remains of the feudal system can be seen from the use of terms such as estate, landlord and tenant. An estate is a feudal grant that can be made by the Crown or another estate holder, which entitles its holder to immediate possession, known as 'seisin'.[15] Based on this possession the holder can protect his land, and grant a further estate to another person, for example, to a tenant.[16] Even today, although numerous reforms have been made, the relation between landlord and tenant remains feudal in character.[17] The landlord holds an estate that is known as a 'fee simple', which is the only remaining freehold estate at common law. The term freehold refers to the fact that the holder of this type of estate holds freely, without any condition or collateral limitation. In the old feudal system, tenants were those people who held an estate from the crown.[18] In other words, anyone but the king was a tenant. In modern terminology the term tenant is used, as mentioned above, for the relation between a landlord and a tenant, but is also used to deal with situations of co-ownership, where both parties to a community are also known as tenants, whatever right they hold.[19]

The term ownership should be used with care in English law, in particular land law. English law does not know a concept of ownership as is used in civil law systems, but uses the term ownership in a very broad sense to describe the most

10 Lawson and Rudden 2002, p. 26-27, See Goode 2004, p. 29.
11 Swadling 2007, p. 227.
12 Tyler & Palmer 1973, p. 8-9, Bridge 2002, p. 3.
13 Pollock & Maitland 1898b, p. 115-116, Holdsworth 1927, p. 19-21. For a more detailed discussion on the origin of leasehold interests see below; 2.2. Lease of Land.
14 See, *inter alia*, Honoré 1961, p. 108.
15 See Pierre 1997, p. 242-244. On possession see Harris 1961, p. 69 *et seq.*
16 See Burn & Cartwright 2006, p. 31-33. For a more detailed discussion on land law see below; 2. Property Rights in Respect of Land.
17 Burn & Cartwright 2006, p. 27.
18 Those who held directly from the Crown were known as tenants in chief. People who held from them were known as tenants.
19 See below; 2.1. Fee Simple.

extensive entitlement.[20] When it comes to land, this right is usually the fee simple, which was mentioned above. When the holder, in English law terminology, rather than the owner, of a fee simple grants part of his estate to another person for what is known as a 'term of years absolute', he grants a leasehold estate to that person.[21] Leaseholds are entitlements to land for a limited period of time. At the end of this period the right that was granted will revert back to the holder of the fee simple. This right to the return of the grant is known as 'reversion' and can, as a right, be granted to other parties. When the holder of a fee simple grants his reversion to another person the right granted is called remainder.[22] To provide an example, A is holder of a fee simple and has granted a term of years absolute for ten years to B with remainder to C. As a result, B will be in possession of the land for ten years, after which C will be entitled to take possession of the land. First B and later C will have seisin.

Personal property law terminology is even more complicated. Personal property law is, compared to land law, an underdeveloped area of law.[23] In particular conceptually there are still many uncertainties. In general, the term ownership in the civil law sense of the word does not exist in personal property law either.[24] Instead, personal property law talks of entitlement to a chattel, in short 'title'.[25] The concept of title therefore usually describes the person with the best right, which is the right to hold possession forever. However, in certain settings, in particular commercial law, the term ownership is freely used, but should be understood to mean title.[26]

When it comes to a term of years, the concept is, because of its connection to the feudal system and to land, unknown in personal property law. Instead, the general term 'bailment' is used, which describes the situation when possession of an object is transferred from one party to another for a limited duration of time. Whether bailment creates a property right is debatable and is discussed below.[27] Again, in certain settings, in particular commercial law, the term lease is also used. However, this should not be automatically understood as giving bailment the status of a property right.

1.2. *Common Law and Equity*

English law as a common law system is considered to have started to develop after the Norman Conquest in 1066.[28] William the Conqueror became King of England

20 See below; 2. Property Rights in Respect of Land.

21 See below; 2.2. Lease of Land.

22 See Holdsworth 1927, p. 65 *et seq.*, Burn & Cartwright 2006, p. 510 *et seq.*

23 See Birks who states that 'With the exception of a few specialisms, our law of personal property is in a bad state'. Birks 2000, p. 1.

24 See below; 3.1. Title / Ownership.

25 Swadling 2006a, p. 280.

26 Swadling 2006a, p. 280-282.

27 See below; 3.2. Leases / Bailment?

28 Also before 1066 there was a legal system in existence, but 1066 is usually chosen as a starting date. See, *inter alia*, Pollock & Maitland 1895, p. 57, Simpson 1986, p. 2-3, Pollock & Mailand →

and succeeded to all the rights of the previous Anglo-Saxon kings, and became the supreme landholder in England.[29] From this time onwards, the common law was developed through decisions of the centralised jurisdiction of the king's court and, occasionally, legislation issued by the king.[30] In the area of property law this mainly concerned land law, which was of a feudal nature. However, English land law was strict and sometimes led to unjust or unwanted results.

Under the feudal system the king granted estates to his major supporters in certain types of *tenure* from him for which he received various *incidents*.[31] In their turn, these supporters of the King would grant estates to others. This process is known as *subinfeudation* and was, because of its fragmenting effect on English land, banned by the statute *Quia Emptores* in 1290.[32]

The common law rules on landholding prohibited women and children from holding land in tenure. When the holder of such tenure was absent, for example, a knight who went on crusade with the king, he would have to leave his land with his wife and children.[33] However, under the strict rules of the common law, women and children were not allowed standing in court, and were therefore unable to protect the land against interference by other parties.[34] To remedy this and to protect his wife and children, the knight was forced to convey his land to another man, one of his friends who stayed behind, for instance. The friend would promise the knight to protect the land against interference and take care of the land on behalf of the wife and children of the knight.

Problems arose at common law when, for instance, the friend had burdened the land with another estate, or had conveyed it to another person. At common law, the knight's wife and children would be helpless because the knight had conveyed the land and all his rights in the land to his friend, be it for the benefit of the knight's wife and children, but this was not recognised by the common law. In these instances, the wife and children would petition to the king claiming that it was unfair that they could not protect themselves. The king would refer such a petition to the Chancellor, the King's closest advisor and head of the secretarial division.[35] The Chancellor would then decide on the case. At first this power was delegated but from 1473 onwards the Chancellor passed judgment alone.[36] As the number of cases and the importance of his work increased, the Chancellor came to sit in what became known as the Court of Chancery or Chancellor's Division, which began to systematically develop its own rules.[37] These rules developed into a separate system

1898a, 79 *et seq.*, Digby focuses on the influence of pre-1066 legislation on the beginning of the common law, Digby & Harrison 1897, p. 26 *et seq.*

29 Digby & Harrison 1897, p. 27.

30 See Pollock & Maitland 1895, p. 57 *et seq.*

31 Hayton 1998, p. 9.

32 Hayton 1998, p. 9. The Law abandoning this is called *Quia Emptores* 1290, a statute that remains in force today.

33 See Biancalana 1998, p. 114-115, Burn & Cartwright 2006, p. 18-21, Swadling 2007, p. 234-235.

34 Biancalana 1998, p. 113.

35 One could say that the Chancellor was a kind of royal secretary of state.

36 Biancalana 1998, p 142.

37 Hayton 1998, p 10.

of law known as equity which came to exist alongside the common law.[38] Until 1875 common law and equity were administered in different courts, but were eventually joined.[39] Now, common law and equity are both dealt with before the same courts.

It is the system of equity that has been very important for the development of property law in England. The common law has generally been reluctant to recognise new property relations. One of the basic starting points in equity, known as a maxim, is that 'equity follows the law' and therefore property rights that exist at common law also exist in equity. However, the special nature of equity allows it to go beyond the common law. Equity, under the development of maxims like 'equity looks upon that as done which ought to be done', has awarded proprietary rights to certain parties that have a 'mere' personal right at common law.[40] It has in particular done so where equity, contrary to common law, awards specific performance of a certain agreement. Specific performance is an exceptional remedy in English contract law, which usually awards damages in case of non-performance. Equity can, while anticipating the coming into existence of a property right at common law, award a property right in advance of the common law right.[41] Furthermore, equity is the source of the law of trusts, enabling parties to hold several property rights in the same object at the same time.[42]

Finally, through the operation of law of trusts, equity can remedy a wrong done to a holder of a right. For instance in *Macmillan Inc v Bishopgate Investment Trust* a gratuitous transfer of Macmillan's shares had been made by a Mr Maxwell.[43] Macmillan tried to argue that the shares were held on trust for him, giving him a right in equity to the shares as a beneficiary. According to the Court of Appeal, under the rules of equity, the circumstances of the case gave rise to the coming into being of a specific type of trust, a resulting trust. The transferee of the shares had therefore become resulting trustee. Birks has emphasised that this creates a *de facto vindicatio* of the assets, a remedy that is not possible at common law.[44] He argues, this remedy is a *vindicatio*, because under the rules of *Saunders v Vautier* the beneficiary can ask the trustee for a transfer of the object and thus assert his property right in respect of the assets directly.[45]

However, there is a disadvantage to the interference of equity in property law. The rights that equity creates are not as strong as the property rights at common law. In general, property rights in equity are to be respected by anyone, with one major exception. A *bona fide* purchaser for value without notice of the right will not

38 For a short and concise overview see Lawson and Rudden 2002, p. 15-16.

39 The Judicature Acts 1873-1875 comprised two acts: the Supreme Court of Judicature Act 1873, 36 & 37 Vict. c. 66, and the Supreme Court of Judicature Act 1875, 38 & 39 Vict. c. 77.

40 See below; 2.7 Estate Contracts, 2.8. Options to Purchase and for a discussion see below; 4. A *Numerus Clausus* in English Property Law?

41 See Swadling 2007, p. 231-233.

42 Civil lawyers tend to characterise this as fragmentation of entitlement to an object. See Lawson and Rudden 2002, p. 90-91, 97-100, Parlementaire Geschiedenis NBW - Boek 5 1981, p. 17, *contra* see Swadling 2008, p. 99-100.

43 *Macmillan Inc. v Bishopgate Investment Trust* [1996] BCC 453, CA.

44 Birks 2000, p. 4-5, see also Swadling 2000a, p. 218-219.

45 *Saunders v Vautier* (1841) 4 Beav 115, Birks 2000, p. 5.

be bound by equitable property rights.[46] This is usually not the case with common law property rights, which are therefore stronger.

1.3. *Personal Property Law and Land Law*

Another distinction made in English law is the distinction between the law of property with respect to land, usually named land law or real property law, and the law of property with respect to movable objects or chattels, usually referred to as personal property law. In English doctrine these areas are distinct and, apart from distributing property rights to private parties, have little to do with each other.[47]

The explanation for this difference with civil law systems can be found in the historical development of the legal system. When the common law began in 1066, the customary law of Normandy, which was feudal law, started to apply to all land in England.[48] William the Conqueror, as the King of England, owned all land, and all others held from him. The area of law that developed around this system of property law only applied to land.[49] Chattels were considered to be of such a different nature that they were not subject to feudal law.[50]

The difference between land and chattels therefore caused the creation of two separate property law systems; land law and personal property law. In respect to land law, the common law developed by awarding a real action to the holder of a right in a piece of land allowing him to regain seisin of the land.[51] A holder of a right in a chattel was only awarded a personal action allowing him to claim damages, but not the specific return of seisin, as this was only possible for freehold land.[52] Therefore, in contrast with civil law systems, personal property law uses actions in tort, in other words the law of obligations, to protect property interests.[53]

It was only from the nineteenth century onwards that personal property law became more important. The objects that are subject to personal property law grew in value and now, usually within the setting of commercial law, form a great source of value, usually exceeding the value of land.[54] Amongst these objects are claims that companies have on their debtors.

It is the distinction between the availability of real and personal actions that still forms the difference between land law and personal property law today. This chapter will deal with this distinction as the available property rights in land law and personal property law differ greatly.

46 Swadling 2007, p. 275.
47 See Pretto-Sakmann 2005, p. 3-4, Tyler & Palmer 1973, p. 3, Lawson and Rudden 2002, p. 13-14.
48 Tyler & Palmer 1973, p. 4.
49 Holdsworth 1927, p. 3-9.
50 See Pollock & Maitland 1898b, p. 149 *et seq.*
51 Tyler & Palmer 1973, p. 6, Pollock & Maitland 1898b, p. 570.
52 Tyler & Palmer 1973, p. 6-7, Burn & Cartwright 2006, p. 36.
53 On the protection of personal property rights see Bridge 2002, p. 47 *et seq.*
54 See below; 1.4. Commercial Law.

1.4. *Commercial Law*

A third area of law, besides land law and personal property law, deserves to be dealt with separately. Generally stated, commercial law is the law dealing with trade.[55] In civil law classification, commercial law deals with contract, tort and property law. In English law, commercial law is a distinct area of law that , at the same time, overlaps with personal property law and land law to a large extent. Goode states that commercial law deals with rights and duties that arise from the supply of goods and services in the way of trade.[56]

It is in the area of commercial law that mainly aspects of personal property law are dealt with in a different way than in the traditional personal property law.[57] In this separate area of law, different terminology applies. In fact, terminology is used that is much more closely connected to everyday language than the old, sometimes archaic, terms of personal property law. In commercial law, no one speaks of chattels, but instead of goods.[58] Where in personal property law, many are hesitant to speak of ownership, in commercial law the term is more easily employed.[59] And where personal property law retains the term choses in action, commercial law rather uses the generic term intangibles.[60] Furthermore, the term lease, which is a property right in land law, is used instead of bailment.[61]

In the last century commercial law has developed as one of the most important areas of property law.[62] In many cases the value of goods and intangibles now exceeds the value of land and commercial law is used in particular for security to obtain finance.[63] Moreover, objects of property law that were difficult to deal with by personal property law, for example, claims, have also found their place in commercial law. It is, in other words, the area of commercial law that deals with these developments. Therefore, when in this chapter rules of commercial law are used, connection will be sought to the terminology used in commercial law. Where commercial law is absent, the terminology of personal property law will be used.

1.5. *Trust Law*

Trust law is a final area of English law that should be dealt with in this introduction.[64] In order to understand the law of trust, the history of equity has to be taken into account. Referring back to the earlier example of a knight going on a crusade

55 See Goode 2004, p. 3 *et seq.*
56 Goode 2004, p. 8.
57 See Birks 2000, p. 1-2.
58 Goode 2004, p. 24.
59 See Goode 2004, p. 31 *et seq.*
60 See Goode 2004, p. 29.
61 See below; 3.2. Leases / Bailment?
62 See Holdsworth 1927, p. 6.
63 Birks 2000, p. 2.
64 For an account of English trust law in Dutch see Aertsen 2004, p. 11 *et seq.* For a short account of the elemental principles of trust law in English see *Westdeutsche Landesbank Girozentrale v Islington LBC* [1996] AC 669, HL, *per* Lord Browne-Wilkinson.

with the king, leaving his land entrusted to a friend until he returned, the king, through the Lord Chancellor, awarded a remedy to the wife and children against the entrusted friend.[65] The remedy the Lord Chancellor, or better, Chancery, gave in equity eventually formed an interest in equity.[66] In equity, the standing in court of the wife and children became recognised and Chancery made the agreement specifically enforceable.[67]

Through this development, tenants could use this legal instrument to leave their wives and children behind safely. The instrument became known as a 'use', and came to be employed in a wide variety of situations to avoid the strict rules of the common law.[68] In the fourteenth, fifteenth and sixteenth centuries, most persons were in the feudal hierarchy, holding land in tenure. In case of death of the right-holder of the land, inheritance taxes had to be paid to the feudal lord.[69] An heir who was an adult, before he could claim his inheritance, would have to pay a fixed sum to the feudal lord. An heir who was an infant was in an even worse position. In that case the lord would be entitled to use the land for his own benefit until the heir reached the age of majority.[70] Furthermore the infant had to either submit to the feudal lord's choice of a spouse or, if he could not live with the choice of the feudal lord, pay the lord for the value of the marriage.[71]

All of these cases, but also problems with the common law on, for example, wardships, could be avoided if the person in tenure conveyed the land, during his life, to third parties for the use of himself during the remainder of his life and thereafter for the use of his heir.[72] In other words, he would declare the land on use for himself.[73] The holder of the land would then enjoy all the benefits from the land, without the feudal restrictions, and upon his death the third parties would transfer the land to the heir, or when the heir reached the age of majority. The heir would receive the land as if he himself held the land in *tenure*, but did not technically inherit it, so the feudal lord could not claim taxes.

This avoidance of common law rules was prohibited by the Statute of Uses of 1536.[74] The king, who felt he was losing his control of the land, had passed the Statute to prevent this. Nevertheless, after the Statute of Uses 1536, legal practitioners continued to search for possibilities to work around the strict rules of the common law. Therefore, situations kept arising in which one person entrusted assets to

65 Biancalana 1998, p. 111, Yale 1961, p. 93-94.
66 Biancalana 1998, p. 141.
67 Biancalana 1998, p. 149-151.
68 See Pollock & Maitland 1898b, p. 230-239.
69 At first to all Lords, but after the Statute of Marlborough 1267, c. 16, only to one feudal lord. Oakley 1998, p. 3-4, Swadling 2007, p. 271-272.
70 See Oakley 1998, p. 4, note 20: '21 for males, 14 for women (unless death occurred when the woman was already over 14 and unmarried, in which case she came of age at 16 or upon earlier marriage)'.
71 Oakley 1998, p. 4.
72 Most of the time land was conveyed to multiple parties to avoid the risk of death of the third party. Biancalana 1998, p. 131-137.
73 Swadling 2008, p. 79.
74 Maitland 1936, p. 34-42, Holdsworth 1927, p. 151-161.

another person on behalf of a third party, which did not fall under the prohibition of the Statute of Uses.[75] These creations became known as trusts. It is especially these trusts that the Lord Chancellor and his Court of Chancery protected in equity. In modern times, trusts are much desired for management, security and succession purposes, in all cases attempting to keep taxes as low as possible.[76]

The relevance of trust law from the point of view of property law is that trusts are a way of holding a property right. In a normal situation a property right is, as Swadling puts it, held outright.[77] This term is used to explain that the holder of the right holds a property right for his own benefit whilst managing it at the same time. Another possibility is, by making use of equity, to hold a property right on trust.[78] When a property right is held on trust, the right holder at common law is under the obligation to hold the property right for the benefit of another person in equity. Holding a property right in this way gives rise to a new property right in equity. This method of holding the property right is therefore different from holding outright. The holder on trust, also known as trustee, must respect and take into account the right in equity of the person on whose behalf he is holding the property right, also known as the beneficiary. Through the workings of equity, the trustee is therefore limited in his powers over the property right. The trustee is manager and the beneficiary benefits.[79]

Through a trust objects can be held for the benefit of another. These objects can, in principle, be anything. Examples are shares in a company, other equities and land. One of the most interesting aspects of a trust is the right in equity that is awarded to the beneficiary. Once a trustee receives trust objects he is under the obligation to keep these objects separate from his own.[80] Furthermore, the trustee is under the obligation to manage the trust assets as a 'prudent man of business'. In other words, the trustee must take the interest of the beneficiary seriously.[81] The protection for the beneficiary, who does not have management powers over the trust object, is that he is entitled to claim damages from a trustee who acts in breach of trust. Additionally, under certain criteria, when objects are sold from the trust in what is known as breach of trust by the trustee, the beneficiary has the right to follow any trust objects which end up in other hands.[82] This right to follow is known as tracing and provides the beneficiary with some rights against third parties that were not part of the bargain. In this approach, a trust is an intermediate form between the law of obligations, which covers the relation between the beneficiary and the trustee, in particular the duties of the trustee, and the law of property, which enables the beneficiary to claim from the trust assets which are held separate from

75 Swadling 2007, p. 271-272.
76 Swadling 2007, p. 276.
77 Swadling 2007, p. 270-271.
78 Swadling 2007, p. 271-272.
79 Swadling 2007, p. 272 *et seq.*
80 Another possibility is that the trustee declares himself trustee for the benefit of another. The effects in English law are the same. *Westdeutsche Landesbank Girozentrale v Islington LBC* [1996] AC 669, HL, Swadling 2007, p. 279, Hayton 1998, p. 132.
81 *Speight v Gaunt* (1882) 22 Ch D 727, 739.
82 Lawson and Rudden 2002, p. 88-89.

the assets of the trustee, even in case of insolvency of the trustee, and to follow the trust objects to third parties.[83]

In order to create a trust three requirements must be fulfilled. First, it must be clear for whose benefit the trust is made.[84] This requirement is known as certainty of object. As a minimum standard, a trustee should be able to identify the beneficiaries in order to know which beneficiary takes which share in the trust objects.[85] When a trustee is given more discretionary powers to appoint beneficiaries, at least a certain class of beneficiaries must be identified from which the trustee may choose.[86] Secondly, the objects that are in the trust must be identifiable. This requirement is known as certainty of subject matter.[87] When the objects cannot be identified, a trust cannot come into existence. The trustee will hold the property rights outright, and not on trust.[88] But like the certainty of object, a class of objects, for instance 5% of a share capital, has been held sufficiently precise for a trust to come into existence.[89] Thirdly, there must also be certainty of intention.[90] When a trust is created, the initiator, known as the settlor, must declare his intent to be bound by the trust or to bind the trustee.[91] In normal situations, certainty of intention is established by looking first and foremost at the words used, but the words should be interpreted in the context of the whole and external circumstances should be taken into account.[92]

A trust relation can easily come into existence, but it remains subject to requirements of specificity. This also justifies the proprietary elements connected to the trust. A specific person benefits from specific objects that are held on trust for him or her. Therefore, this beneficiary can claim his or her share in these specific objects from the trustee and, if necessary from a third party who knew or should have known about the trust as well.[93]

Finally, trusts can come into existence not only by agreement or declaration, but also by operation of law. These trusts are known as constructive trusts. In particular the way in which they are used, which is also outside the sphere of private law, forms an important element of English law.[94] One famous example of a constructive trust was when a high official in Hong Kong accepted bribes from criminals. The Privy Council held that the official breached his fiduciary duty towards the government of Hong Kong and decided that the official held the bribes on

83 *Westdeutsche Landesbank Girozentrale v Islington LBC* [1996] AC 669, HL, Swadling 2007, p. 296, 322-327.

84 Swadling 2007, p. 280.

85 Swadling 2007, p. 281-284.

86 *Re Gulbenkian's Settlement Trust (No. 1)* [1970] AC 508, HL and even wider for so-called discretionary trusts, *McPhail v Doulton* [1971] AC 424, HL.

87 Swadling 2007, p. 285.

88 See *Palmer v Simmonds* (1854) 2 Drewry 221, 61 ER 704.

89 *Hunter v Moss* [1994] 1 WLR 452, CA.

90 Swadling 2007, p. 286.

91 *Richards v Delbridge* (1874) LR 18 Eq 11.

92 *Milroy v Lord* (1862) 4 De G.F. & J. 264, 45 ER 1185, Swadling 2000a, p. 291-293.

93 This exception is for the *bona fide* purchaser for value without notice, see Swadling 2007, p. 264.

94 Birks 1996, p. 92-96, Swadling 2007, p. 321 *et seq.*

constructive trust for the government.[95] This trust had to be constructive because no one declared the trust or agreed on it. Instead, its existence was presumed.

Another type of trust is known as a resulting trust, which comes into existence through a presumption of law. In particular when objects are transferred gratuitously between persons, under particular circumstances, this can give rise to a presumption that the transferee will hold the rights conveyed on trust for the transferor.[96] This presumption can be rebutted by a clear and expressed intention to the contrary.[97]

According to a widely-held view, a resulting trust can also arise when objects are transferred on trust and for some reason the creation of the trust is void.[98] This could happen in the event that the trust lacks objects.[99] Also in such a case a resulting trust could arise whereby the transferee holds the objects on trust for the transferor. Swadling has shown that this type of resulting trust, which he names a 'failed trust resulting trust', creates very interesting problems in respect of its creation.[100]

The other type of resulting trust arises because of a presumption that when certain facts are proven, the transferor is considered to have declared a trust in his own favour.[101] However, the failing trust resulting trust, Swadling argues with reference to the House of Lords, operates without a presumption.[102] In this case, *Vandervell v Inland Revenue Commission*, Lord Upjohn and Lord Wilberforce considered the question of where the right in equity of the transferor comes from in case of a failed trust resulting trust.[103] In their view, the right in equity was with the transferor all along, besides his right at law, and the resulting trust arises because the transferor fails to give the right in equity away. Swadling is very critical of this decision and refers to a later statement made by Lord Browne-Wilkinson in another case, *Westdeutsche Landesbank Girozentrale v Islington LBC*, to prove this 'retention theory' is false.[104] In this case Lord Browne-Wilkinson stated:

> 'A person solely entitled to the full beneficial ownership of money or property, both at law and in equity, does not enjoy an equitable interest in that property. The legal title carries with it all rights. Unless and until there is a separation of the legal and equitable estates, there is no separate equitable title. Therefore to talk about the [transferor]

95 *A-G for Hong Kong v Reid* [1994] 1 AC 324, PC. However see *Halifax Building Society v Thomas* [1996] Ch 217, CA, Pretto 2002, p. 76-77.

96 Swadling 2008, p. 72-73.

97 *Re Vandervells Trust (No 2)* [1974] Ch 269, CA, at 294 *per* Megarry J. On other types see Swadling 2007, p. 329-330, Swadling 2008, p. 98-99.

98 Swadling 2008, p. 73.

99 *Morice v Bishop of Durham* (1804) 9 Ves 399. Swadling 2008, p. 94.

100 Swadling 2008, p. 94-96.

101 Swadling 2008, p. 101-102.

102 *Vandervell v Inland Revenue Commission* [1967] 2 AC 291, HL, at 329 *per* Lord Wilberforce. Swadling 2008, p. 96-99.

103 *Vandervell v Inland Revenue Commission* [1967] 2 AC 291, HL at 313 *per* Lord Upjohn, and at 329 *per* Lord Wilberforce. See Swadling 2007, p. 329-330, Swadling 2008, p. 99-100.

104 *Westdeutsche Landesbank Girozentrale v Islington LBC* [1996] AC 669, HL, *per* Lord Browne-Wilkinson. Swadling 2008, p. 100. See also Swadling 2007, p. 272-273.

> 'retaining' its equitable interest is meaningless. The only question is whether the circumstances under which the money was paid were such as, in equity, to impose a trust on the [transferee]. If so, an equitable interest arose for the first time under that trust'.[105]

Apart from attempting to settle an important point for resulting trusts, this statement by Lord Browne-Wilkinson explains the approach of English law to trusts in general. It is not the case that the right in equity of the beneficiary is formed out of the legal right of the settlor of the trust. In other words, a trust does not create a fragmentation of a title or estate that previously existed at common law.[106] Swadling emphasises that in this respect the use of the word 'separation' is unfortunate and it seems to conflict with the other part of the statement.[107] Under the rule formulated by Lord Browne-Wilkinson an equitable right comes into existence from nothing and is added onto the right at common law, which will now be in the hands of the trustee.[108]

2. Property Rights in Respect of Land

English land law is an area that is closely connected with its history. As on the continent of Europe, England was also governed by the feudal system of landholding. However, contrary to the development in other European legal systems, the impact of the French Revolution, the abolition of the feudal system and a resulting return to the Roman law concepts in property law, did not occur in England.

From the beginning of the common law, English land law has been governed by feudal law.[109] When all land was feudal land, the Crown was entitled to all land and, consequently, all others must have a lesser right than the Crown.[110] Furthermore, English law did not concern itself with the attempt to explain feudal law in terms of Roman law concepts such as *dominium directum* or *dominium utile*.[111] It is because of these reasons that English land law does not have a concept of ownership in the civil law sense of the word.[112] The lack of a 'revolution' in English land law does not imply that no reforms have been made to land law since the eleventh century. To the contrary, English land law has continued to develop and has modernised the sometimes unjust application of the law to bring the law into conformity with modern needs.

105 *Westdeutsche Landesbank Girozentrale v Islington LBC* [1996] AC 669, HL, at 706 *per* Lord Browne-Wilkinson, Swadling 2008, p. 99-100.

106 See Swadling 2007, p. 271-273.

107 Swadling 2008, p. 100, note 144.

108 This approach to the creation of an equitable right that burdens the trustee is similar to the original German conception of property rights. On this German approach see Chapter 4; 3. Other Property Rights.

109 Burn & Cartwright 2006, p. 11 *et seq*., Holdsworth 1927,p. 3-4, Swadling 2007, p. 233-235.

110 See Lawson and Rudden 2002, p. 101, who describes the title of the Crown in land as 'demesne'. Holdsworth 1927, p. 4-5.

111 See Chapter 2; 4. The *Ius Commune*.

112 However, see Honoré 1961, p. 107 *et seq*., Burn & Cartwright 2006, p, 27.

Originally, the relation between the landlord and tenant was strictly personal, resulting in a return of the feudal grant to the lord when the tenant died. However, already in the early common law the lord would accept the heir of the tenant, allowing the grant to continue.[113] When the grant could pass to the heir of the tenant, it lost some of its strictly personal status. Over time this grant became known as an estate.[114] In a normal situation, the tenant would be allowed to use and enjoy the land freely. This type of estate therefore became known as fee simple estate.[115]

When the concept of estate developed, the possibility of leaving the estate to heirs, or to even conveying it to another person, became tested. Only through the Statute of Wills 1540 could estates be left by will.[116] Before that, this restriction was avoided through a 'use' as dealt with above.[117] Furthermore, tenants tried to grant estates to other persons, usually family members, in an attempt to keep the estate within the family.[118] At first, courts interpreted these attempts as a conditional gift, requiring the existence of heirs, but allowing the holder of the estate to freely convey it to other persons as well. This undesired result was remedied by the statute *De Donis Conditionalibus* of 1285, under which it became possible to grant a different type of estate, the estate tail, which would pass on to the heirs of the tenant.[119]

Another of the first land reforms was mentioned above, the statute *Quia Emptores* of 1290 which restricted the possibilities of feudal lords to give further feudal grants to others.[120] This practice, known as subinfeudation, was disadvantageous to landlords who owned large pieces of land, because subinfeudation fragmented the entitlements to the land. As a result of the statute, only the full estate that was granted could be conveyed to another party.[121] Combined with the statute *De Donis Conditionalibus* it remained possible to grant a lesser estate in land, sometimes made for the life of a tenant. These estates became known as life estates.[122] When conveyed, these estates remained dependent upon the life of the grantee, and meant that the tenant granted an estate *pur autre vie*.[123]

English land law developed into a complicated system in which these three estates; the normal fee simple estate, the estate in tail, and the estate for life, were the standard types. However, adapting this system to developments in society

113 Swadling 2000a, p. 224-225. Simpson emphasises the fact that already in early feudal law freehold tenurial disputes became exclusively considered in Royal courts, rather than in local seignorial courts, and that this transfer of jurisdiction changed the nature in which freeholds were protected from personal to real actions. See Simpson 1986, p. 36-37.

114 Holdsworth 1927, p. 50 *et seq.*, Swadling 2007, p. 234-235.

115 See Pierre 1997, p. 244-246.

116 Swadling 2000a, p. 224.

117 See Para. 1.5. Trust Law.

118 Swadling 2000a, p. 224-225.

119 13 Edward I, st. 1, C. 1, Holdsworth 1927, p. 55-60, Swadling 2000a, p. 225-226, Simpson 1986, p. 66-68.

120 18 Edward I, c. 1, Holdsworth 1927, p. 104-109. See above; 1.2. Common Law and Equity.

121 Holdsworth 1927, p. 106-107.

122 Holdsworth 1927, p. 60-65.

123 Holdsworth 1927, p. 62, Swadling 2000a, p. 226.

consequently meant mixing some of these categories, depending on the wording the parties had given to the grant. As a result a large variety of estates existed.[124]

Until the beginning of the twentieth century, land law continued to use these feudal concepts of estates. However, when society developed from being mainly agricultural and land-based to a society based on cities and industries, reforms in the land law were necessary.[125] From the beginning of the nineteenth century, law reforms were made, eventually resulting in a major property law reform in 1925 with the Law of Property Acts.[126] The Law of Property Acts include the Settled Land Act 1925, the Trustee Act 1925, the Land Registration Act 1925, the Land Charges Act 1925, the Administration of Estates Act 1925, the Universities and College Estates Act 1925 and, the most important for the subject of this study, the Law of Property Act 1925. The Law of Property Act 1925 limited the types of estate that could be held, and registered, at common law. Section 1 of the Law of Property Act 1925 provides:

> '1. Legal estates and equitable interests
> The only estates in land which are capable of subsisting or of being conveyed or created at law are –
> a) An estate in fee simple absolute in possession;
> b) A term of years absolute.
> (2) The only interests or charges in or over land which are capable of subsisting or of being conveyed or created at law are—
> (a) An easement, right, or privilege in or over land for an interest equivalent to an estate in fee simple absolute in possession or a term of years absolute;
> (b) A rentcharge in possession issuing out of or charged on land being either perpetual or for a term of years absolute;
> (c) A charge by way of legal mortgage;
> (d) . . . and any other similar charge on land which is not created by an instrument;
> (e) Rights of entry exercisable over or in respect of a legal term of years absolute, or annexed, for any purpose, to a legal rentcharge.
> (3) All other estates, interests, and charges in or over land take effect as equitable interests'.

Consequently, there could only be two estates at common law, and other estates, which included the estate in tail and the life estate, could only be created in equity.[127] The result of this provision is that, since equity must be used to create these estates, the law of trusts must be used to create these last two types of estates. Moreover, in 1996, the Trusts of Land and Appointment of Trustees Act 1996 ended the possibility to create an estate in tail.[128]

124 Burn & Cartwright 2006, p. 7 *et seq.*

125 Holdsworth 1927, p. 302 *et seq.*, Burn & Cartwright 2006, p. 7-8.

126 Examples of reform include the Reform Act 1832, the Partition Act, the Vendor and Purchasor Act, the Conveyancing Acts and the Settled Land Acts (1882), see Holdsworth 1927, p. 316.

127 Swadling 2007, p. 234-235.

128 Trusts of Land and Appointment of Trustees Act 1996, s. 5, sch 1. See Swadling 2000a, p. 226-227, Burn & Cartwright 2006, p. 9-10.

The most important recent English land law reform is the Land Registration Act 2002, which repealed the Land Registration Act 1925.[129] The Land Registration Act 2002 creates a mandatory registration system for all entitlements in respect to land in England, which had not existed before.[130] Behind the Act is the idea that the entitlements to any geographically described piece of land are registered, so that a prospective purchaser can investigate the rights registered on a certain piece of land.[131] As a result the conveyance of an unregistered right to land will now lead to registration.[132]

It could be held that the law therefore limited the possible estates that can be held at common law. Furthermore, the Law of Property Act 1925 also limited other property rights which can exist at common law. As Section 1 (3) shows, all other rights and estates can only exist in equity.

At common law, therefore, the Law of Property Act 1925 creates a closed system of property rights, to which parties cannot add a new property right. Swadling has argued that therefore at common law a *numerus clausus* of property rights exists.[133] Whether such a closed system also exists in equity is a matter of debate. This section will discuss the various property rights that can exist at common law and in equity. Although equity follows the law, some property rights can only exist in equity. The subject of *numerus clausus* will be returned to at the end of this chapter.[134]

2.1. *Fee Simple*

The estate in fee simple absolute in possession, after 1925 also known as freehold estate, is the most extensive entitlement a person can have on land in English law.[135] This most extensive entitlement is meant both in time and in space. A holder of a fee simple is allowed to exercise his right to possession forever and, in principle, exclusively. The term 'fee' refers to the feudal grant, which is the origin of this estate.[136] The term 'simple' refers to the fact that the estate will pass to the heirs of the holder, not of any particular category, as was the case with a fee tail or estate in tail.[137] The right is 'absolute' in the sense that the estate is not subject to any condition.[138] 'In possession', finally, refers to the requirement that the holder of the

129 Burn & Cartwright 2006, p. 10.

130 Compulsory registration of entitlements to land had existed before the LRA 2002 already, but with the new Act, all conveyances, including gratuitous transfers, must be registered. See Swadling 2007, p. 390-391.

131 Gray & Gray 2005, p. 160-161.

132 There are a few exceptions to this rule, but most entitlements will be subject to a compulsory registration. See Gray & Gray 2005 , p. 164-166.

133 Swadling 2007, 223-224.

134 See below; 4. A *Numerus Clausus* in English Property Law?

135 Before 1925 more types of freehold were available. See Burn & Cartwright 2006, p. 167, Holdsworth 1927, p. 52.

136 Burn & Cartwright 2006, p. 167.

137 Burn & Cartwright 2006, p. 167.

138 Burn & Cartwright 2006, p. 168-170.

estate must have control over the land. This control is there, even if the factual control is with someone else for the time being. In that respect the term 'in possession' refers to the control over the fee simple that allows the holder to receive payments of rent or profits.[139]

The most extensive entitlement also refers to the fact that, under the rules of the common law, the holder of the estate is entitled to everything in, on or above the land according to the maxim *cujus est solum, ejus est usque ad coelum et ad inferos.*[140] Any objects that are on the land as so-called fixtures belong to the holder of the fee simple. Moreover, any mines or minerals under his land are also his, except for silver and gold, coal and petroleum.[141]

As a general starting point, a holder of a fee simple may take action against any interference with his right. However, that does not imply that the holder of a piece of land can sue those who fly over his land but do not interfere with his use of the land in trespass.[142] The right can therefore not be held to actually extend from the heavens to the centre of the earth.[143] However, when such an invasion of airspace does interfere with the use of the land, the holder of the fee simple may claim an injunction to stop such interference.[144] Generally, holder of a property right in the land may use an action in trespass to protect his right is another characteristic feature of English land law. Trespass is a tort and should be placed in the law of obligations and not property, it will therefore lead to a claim of damages. However, because the right-holder holds an entitlement to land, he may also ask for a specific order for possession. This specific claim is available to right-holders of land only. A successful order will return the possession of the land or allow the holder to continue his possession.[145]

This specific recovery is a central characteristic of land law, making it distinct from personal property law where specific recovery is, in principle, impossible.[146] The specific recovery of possession as opposed to the recovery of the abstract legal title in the land is another feature of English law, which distinguishes it from the civil law tradition where a specific recovery in the form of vindication returns the object of ownership to the owner and not possession to the possessor.[147]

139 Burn & Cartwright 2006, p. 170.

140 'To whomsoever the land belongs, to him also belongs [the space] up to heaven and down to the deepest depths'. Translation taken from Swadling 2007, p. 235. See also Burn & Cartwright 2006, p. 173. Or 'everything under the sky down to the centre of the earth' *Poutney v Clayton* (1883) 11 QBD 820 at 838 *per* Bowen LJ.

141 Swadling 2007, p. 235. Silver and Gold and petroleum belong to the Crown. Coal to the Coal Authority.

142 *Lord Bernstein v Skyviews & General Ltd* [1978] QB 479.

143 See also the Privy Council in *Commissioners for Railways v Valuer-General* [1974] AC 328, 351.

144 *Anchor Brewhouse Developments Ltd v Berkley House (Docklands Development) Ltd* [1987] 2 EGLR 173.

145 Swadling 2007, p. 228.

146 Bridge 2002, p. 47.

147 Only when possessor and owner are the same person, the results of the action will coincide. See Simpson 1986, p. 37-38, Swadling 2006a, p. 283. On revendication in civil law see Chapter 2. The Development of Property Rights; Para. 2.3 Ownership. However, see e.g. Art. 5:2 in the →

In a model situation the fee simple will be held by only one person. However, in reality there are numerous situations where people share entitlement to objects, for instance, marriage or partnership. Rather confusingly, in English law this co-entitlement is known as co-ownership, although English law does not recognise ownership in the civil law sense of the word.[148] In English law there are two types of co-ownership; joint tenancy and tenancy in common.[149]

Joint tenancy is a situation in which two tenants hold rights together. In case of a co-ownership of a fee simple the result is that the two tenants together hold the fee simple.[150] A joint tenancy is created when the fee simple is conveyed to more than one person.[151] The connection between the co-owners is such that none of the tenants can be held to hold a share. Instead, they can only dispose of the fee simple by acting together. However, for a situation of joint tenancy to arise, more is needed than just two persons entitled to a right in the same piece of land. As described above, through the working of common law and equity, it is possible for multiple parties to have different rights in the same piece of land at the same time.[152] In order for a joint tenancy to arise the so-called four unities must be present:[153]

First, there must be unity of possession. This means that each tenant must be entitled to the full possession of the land concerned. In other words, one tenant must not be able to exclude the other tenant by bringing an action in trespass against him.[154] Without this requirement, the tenants can never be held to share the whole of the fee simple among them.

Secondly, there must be unity of interest. Because the tenants hold one right or interest between them, the content of that interest must be the same. This requirement excludes simultaneous interests with different content, such as a fee simple held on trust, from the rules on tenancy in common.[155]

Thirdly, there must be unity of title, which usually refers to the document under which the tenants acquired the fee simple.[156] This requirement ensures that the tenants became entitled to the fee simple under the same conditions.

Fourthly, there must be unity of time. English law allows the possibility to divide an interest or right in time. For example, A can grant a lease to B and, after B's death to the heirs of C. Under English law, the right of C is also a property right known as the remainder.[157] These interests that are created are called concurrent, as

Dutch Civil Code that allows the owner to vindicate his right of ownership by claiming possession.

148 See above; 1.1. Terminology.

149 Swadling 2007, p. 342, Lawson & Rudden 2002, p. 92-93.

150 See *Hammersmith & Fulham LBC v Monk* [1992] 1 AC 478, 492, HL *per* Lord Browne-Wilkinson.

151 Burn & Cartwright 2006, p. 453.

152 See above; 1.5. Trust Law.

153 Burn & Cartwright 2006, p. 454-455, Swadling 2007, p. 343-344.

154 *Martyn v Knowllys* (1799) 8 Term Rep 145, 101 ER 1313, *Wilkinson v Haygarth* (1847) 12 QB 837, 116 ER 1090. See Burn & Cartwright 2006, p. 454, Swadling 2006a, p. 284-285.

155 Swadling 2007, p. 343-344.

156 Swadling 2007, p. 344.

157 Swadling 2007, p. 344.

they do not give a right to possession at the same time. A joint tenancy can only exist if the interest that is shared is held at the same time.

The interest of a single tenant cannot be identified as the tenants hold the whole of the property right together. Therefore, when one of the tenants dies, the interest cannot pass on to his heirs and therefore ceases to exist. The interest of the remaining tenants will remain until there is only one left. The last surviving tenant will hold the property right, in this case the fee simple, outright once more.[158] This last rule is known as the right of survivorship or *ius accrescendi*.[159]

Whether a joint tenancy comes into existence depends on the wording with which it was created. If a fee simple is conveyed to A and B, a joint tenancy will result.[160] However, when words of qualification, such as restriction, exclusion, or another explanatory statement, are added, the result might also be a tenancy in common.

Tenancy in common is the second type of co-ownership in English law. In a tenancy in common, each of the tenants holds a share that can be identified. The share itself is indivisible, but it can be conveyed or left by will to other persons.[161] Because of this possibility to pass the interest on by will, there is no survivorship rule here. Also, the requirements of unity apply in a different way. First, there must be unity of possession, as without that no common interest can exist. Secondly, the interest of the tenants must also coincide in time in order to exclude a situation where a remainder has been assigned.[162]

Traditionally, common law has favoured joint tenancy, because this would eventually lead to a property right held outright in relation to the feudal incidents that had to be paid.[163] A tenancy in common could, theoretically last as long as the property right in respect of which it was created and was therefore considered less desirable. Equity, however, has shown a preference for tenancy in common because of the sometimes undesirable results of the rule of survivorship.[164] It is therefore possible that in equity a different situation of co-ownership arises than is the case at common law.

In cases where land is acquired and the purchase money is provided in unequal shares common law would, unless otherwise provided, assume a joint tenancy. However, in equity a tenancy in common is the result, unless parties particularly provide otherwise, as was the case in *Goodman v Gallant*.[165] In this case the parties explicitly provided that a conveyance had been made as 'joint tenants at law and equity'.[166] Another situation where equity has deviated from common law is where two or more persons holding shares, irrespective of whether these shares are equal,

158 Swadling 2007, p. 343.
159 Swadling 2007, p. 343, Burn & Cartwright 2006, p. 455.
160 Burn & Cartwright 2006, p. 453, Swadling 2007, p. 345.
161 Swadling 2007, p. 344.
162 Swadling 2007, p. 344.
163 Burn & Cartwright 2006, p. 41-42, 455.
164 *R v Williams* (1735) Bunb 342, 145 ER 694, see Swadling 2007, p. 345-346.
165 *Goodman v Gallant* [1986] Fam 106, CA.
166 See Swadling 2007, p. 346, Burn & Cartwright 2006, p. 456.

advance money on mortgage. These creditors will, at law, hold the interest they receive as joint tenants, but in equity as tenants in common. Finally, also in case of partnerships, equity prevents the rule of survivorship from operating so that the surviving partner does not receive the part that belonged to the deceased partner and, instead, this share can pass on to the heirs of the deceased.[167]

Finally, apart from holding a fee simple outright, on trust or as a co-owner, the Commonhold and Leasehold Reform Act 2002, which entered into force on 27 September 2004, created a fourth way: commonhold.[168] The commonhold allows private parties to have a freehold estate in a separate space that could, without that, not be held in fee simple alone. This in particular applies to a part of a building that, under the rules of common law, could only be held in fee simple in full. Holding a fee simple on commonhold provides a means of apartment ownership, although it can be used for other purposes than apartments as well.[169]

Before the introduction of commonhold, tenure of apartments was managed through the use of leases. However, although in English law a lease in land is a property right, its existence is limited in time.[170] Many leases granted for 99 years in the 1930s are now approaching their end, making it increasingly difficult to obtain finance on the purchase of such a lease.[171] A commonhold therefore allows a freehold estate in a certain piece of land under certain conditions. In this respect Section 1 of the Commonhold and Leasehold Reform Act 2002 states:

> '(1) Land is commonhold land if–
> (a) the freehold estate in the land is registered as a freehold estate in commonhold land,
> (b) the land is specified in the memorandum of association of a commonhold association as the land in relation to which the association is to exercise functions, and
> (c) a commonhold community statement makes provision for rights and duties of the commonhold association and unit-holders (whether or not the statement has come into force).
> (2) In this Part a reference to a commonhold is a reference to land in relation to which a commonhold association exercises functions.
> ...
> (4) Sections 7 and 9 make provision for the vesting in the commonhold association of the fee simple in possession in the common parts of a commonhold'.

For the creation of commonhold land three requirements must be fulfilled. First and foremost, the land must be registered as a freehold estate held in commonhold. After the registration, the common parts of a building are held by an association, and the parts of a building that are to be used privately are held by so-called unit-

167 *Hamond v Jethro* (1611) 2 Brownl & Golds, 97, 99, 123 ER 836, 839. See Burn & Cartwright 2006, p. 457, Swadling 2007, p. 346.
168 Burn & Cartwright 2006, p. 183, Swadling 2007, p. 244.
169 Burn & Cartwright 2006, p 183-184.
170 On lease of land see below; 2.2. Lease of Land.
171 Burn & Cartwright 2006, p. 184.

holders, who hold a fee simple on their exclusive part.[172] Consequently, the unit-holders are also registered as holders of a fee simple in their respective unit.[173]

The second requirement is the mandatory creation of a commonhold association. This association is a private limited company under English law, capable of holding the freehold estate in commonhold.[174] The unit-holders are members of the association for the duration of their entitlement to the fee simple in their unit. When the fee simple is conveyed to another person, this other person replaces the old unit-holder as a member.[175] The purpose of the commonhold association is to manage the commonhold scheme, including maintenance and repairs of the common parts. Furthermore, the association will also function as holder of the fee simple in the total land when the commonhold comes to an end.[176] When the commonhold ends, the unit-holders no longer have a fee simple in their unit. Instead, they will have a share in equity, they are equitable tenants in common, proportional to their contribution or according to a previously arranged division. The fee simple in the land will be held on trust for the former unit-holders.[177]

Thirdly, a commonhold community statement must make provisions for the distribution of rights and duties between the commonhold association and the unit-holders. These rights and duties include payment of fees, maintenance duties, but also duties to refrain from causing nuisance or to refrain from any specified behaviour.[178] Provisions contained in this community statement, also covenants, will bind the unit-holders and their successors.[179]

The unit-holders therefore have a fee simple that approaches a normal fee simple in land as much as possible. Their interest can be leased, transferred and even charged in order to obtain finance.[180] However, the existence of the fee simple will remain, and this is different from a normal fee simple in land, connected to the existence of the commonhold.

2.2. *Lease of Land*

Leases of land or leasehold interests or term of years absolute began life as personal rights.[181] Unlike the holder of a freehold estate, a lessee of land was awarded possession, but not seisin, which refers to actual control of the land.[182] It is most likely because of this that an evicted or dispossessed lessee was not given access to the

172 S. 9 Commonhold and Leasehold Reform Act 2002 (CLRA 2002).
173 S. 7 CLRA 2002 states that registration of the fee simple of the unit-holders can also occur at a later moment. See also Burn & Cartwright 2006, p. 186.
174 S. 34, Sch 3, CLRA 2002.
175 Sch 174 3, CLRA 2002.
176 S. 49 (3) CLRA 2002.
177 Burn & Cartwright 2006, p. 184.
178 Scc S. 31 CLRA 2002.
179 Such obligations can be enforced in court. See S. 37 CLRA 2002.
180 Burn & Cartwright 2006, p. 187-188.
181 Simpson 1986, p. 71-74, Burn & Cartwright 2006, p. 36.
182 On the concept of seisin see above; 1.1. Terminology.

real action protecting freeholders.[183] In practice, leases developed and were used to circumvent the medieval rules against usury. These rules prohibited a creditor from lending money with interest.[184] Instead a person who needed money would grant a lease to a creditor who would enjoy the profits the land produced as interest for a loan.[185]

A lease of land was therefore used to circumvent some of the strict real property law rules. However, in doing so, parties could only create a strictly personal relationship. The lessee, in early law also known as termor, would be in a weak position. Around the twelfth century a writ was introduced that allowed the termor a remedy against the holder of the fee simple by which land could be recovered.[186] However, when a third party interfered the termor remained dependent on the holder of the fee simple to use his real action.[187] Around 1235 a new writ, *quare ejecit infra terminum*, gave the termor a remedy against third parties who ejected him from the land after a sale made by the lessor.[188] However, soon a writ, *ejectione firmae*, which created a form of tort of trespass, allowed the termor a remedy against any ejector.[189] However, this remedy was only in damages, not in specific performance. It was not until the fifteenth century that this changed and the lessee could recover possession of the land in *ejectione firmae*.[190] The availability of this remedy changed the legal nature of the lease from a personal to a property right. However, these developments were too late to fit the lease into the feudal system and for it to be recognised as a legal estate.[191] Already before the fifteenth century, the legal nature of the lease of land had been considered. Leases were commonly made to a person and his heirs to ensure that the lease would not come to an end upon the death of the lessee. Instead the heirs, when this wording was used to create the lease, continued to enjoy it until the term of years ended.

Furthermore, a lease, as it did not fit in the feudal system, was subject to different rules than those regulating the feudal estates. In particular the right of the lessee to leave his interest by will to a third party, which was at that time not allowed at common law at all, became recognised by the ecclesiastical courts. However, the lease never became a feudal estate. Instead it was considered as something connected to the feudal system, but not part of it. Pollock and Maitland look at the way leases were used, in particular to avoid the common law rules on usury, and

183 Burn & Cartwright 2006, p. 36, Swadling 2000a, p. 232-233, Pollock & Maitland 1898b, p. 110-111. Simpson offers another possibility: the writ giving access to relevant real action required the affected person to have had seisin of a free tenement. Simpson considers the possibility that a leasehold was not considered a free tenement. See Simpson 1986, p. 71-74. On this see Pollock & Maitland 1898b, p. 113.

184 Swadling 2000a, p. 233, Burn & Cartwright 2006, p. 37.

185 Burn & Cartwright 2006, p. 37.

186 Although the remedy was contractual, it did, rather exceptionally, allow specific performance of the contract.

187 Simpson 1986, p. 74.

188 Simpson 1986, p. 73-75, Holdsworth 1927, p. 71-73.

189 Simpson 1986, p. 73-74, Pollock & Maitland 1898b, p. 108-109.

190 Simpson 1986, p. 74-75.

191 Swadling 2000a, p. 233.

consider that the lease was actually a financial investment in land, and they therefore consider it situated between land law and personal property law and give a lease its classification as a chattel real.[192]

A lease is considered personal property with land law characteristics and it was this qualification with which the lease ended up in the Law of Property Act 1925. In that Act it became recognised as one of the possible estates at common law.[193] However, technically a lease remains a chattel real.[194] Moreover, the lease also remains partly contractual in nature. It is an agreement between a lessor and a lessee that gives rise to its creation, and that continues to set the terms for the relation between these parties.[195] Depending on whether the lease is created at common law or is created in equity, which remains a possibility because equity follows the law, these contractual elements will be stronger or less strong.[196]

A lease or leasehold interest is a property right entitling a person to exclusive possession of land for a limited period of time that can be determined.[197] However, not every agreement to grant a person possession of a piece of land will constitute a lease. It is possible to give a person a personal right, a licence, to have access to the land of the holder of the fee simple. The distinctions between leases and licences are in particular relevant for the application of the so-called Rent Acts, in particular the Rent Act 1977, which only apply to leases.[198]

Finding the distinction between leases and licences centres around the question of whether there is exclusive possession or not. In the nineteenth century, the courts used a rigid test that when an agreement gave a person exclusive possession, that person would be tenant. If it did not, the agreement would be a licence.[199] In the course of the twentieth century this test shifted to a flexible and subjective interpretation of the intention of the parties.[200] However, in *Street v Mountford* the House of Lords rejected this flexible test and held that the subjective intentions of the parties as such are irrelevant and that the distinction between a lease and a licence centres on the intention to grant exclusive possession.[201]

Whether such exclusive possession is granted remains a subject of interpretation. In *Street v Mountford*, a Mrs Mountford was given exclusive possession of furnished rooms in exchange for the payment of a sum of £ 37 a week. She had

192 Pollock & Maitland 1898b, p. 116-117. See also above; 1.1. Terminology.

193 Burn & Cartwright 2006, p. 193-194, Swadling 2006a, p. 233.

194 Burn & Cartwright 2006, p. 192-193, Tyler & Palmer 1973, p. 8-9, Bridge 2002, p. 3.

195 *Linden Gardens Trust Ltd v Lenesta Sludge Development Ltd* [1994] 1 AC 85 at 108 *per* Lord Browne-Wilkinson, *Prudential Assurance Co Ltd v London Residuary Body and Others* [1992] 2 AC 386, see also *Bruton v London & Quadrant Housing Trust* [2000] 1 AC 406 at 415 *per* Lord Hoffmann.

196 When the lease is created in equity, it will not hold against the *bona fide* purchaser for value without notice.

197 *Street v Mountford* [1985] AC 809, HL at 818 *per* Lord Templeman.

198 See Burn & Cartwright 2006, p. 197.

199 *Lynes v Snaith* [1899] 1 QB 486, *Glenwood Limber Co Ltd v Phillips* [1904] AC 405. See Burn & Cartwright 2006, p. 198, Swadling 2007, p. 236-239.

200 *Somma v Hazelhurst* [1978] 1 WLR 1014, CA, *Abbeyfield (Harpenden) Society Ltd v Woods* [1968] 1 WLR 374, CA, *Marchant v Charters* [1977] 1 WLR 1181, CA.

201 *Street v Mountford* [1985] AC 809, HL at 827 *per* Lord Templeman.

accepted and signed a statement that the agreement did not and was 'not intended to give me a tenancy protected under the Rent Acts'. Subsequently, Mrs. Mountford attempted to invoke application of the Rent Acts in order to have a fair rent registered. The Court of Appeal, following the flexible test, concluded this agreement could not constitute a lease.[202] The House of Lords overturned this judgment and discussed the relevant requirements for a lease.

On the subject of exclusive possession Lord Templeman stated that if an agreement grants exclusive possession to a person, that person is allowed to exclude others, including the landlord. When a landlord enters the premises upon specific terms made in the agreement, for instance, for maintenance or repair works, this only emphasises the fact that exclusive possession has been granted.[203] In fact, in this case, the fact that Mrs Mountford had exclusive possession was not further debated.

However, in other cases, landlords have attempted to avoid granting exclusive possession in order to avoid the application of the Rent Acts by granting a licence to occupy, and not a lease. Not granting exclusive possession can be achieved by granting permission to use rooms in a house, but not of a certain room or rooms.[204] The case of *Westminster City Council v Clarke* concerned a special house for single men, including those with personality disorders and physical disabilities.[205] The defendant lived in the house, paid a weekly accommodation charge and had agreed that he could be moved to another room from time to time, or could be required to share a room with others. The House of Lords, again by way of a judgment of Lord Templeman, agreed with the claimant that in this particular case a licence had been granted.[206] However, when no special circumstances arise, it is very difficult not to grant exclusive possession of a space granted to someone to live in.[207]

Another difficulty with the requirement of exclusivity arises in case of multiple or joint occupations. When a couple lives in a certain space, it is difficult to prove that each of them has been granted exclusive possession, unless exclusive possession is considered to have been granted to both of them together at the same time. In other words, a lease in such a situation can only be accepted if it is co-owned.[208] The House of Lords, in two cases heard simultaneously, discussed these issues.[209]

In *AG Securities v Vaughan and others,* a four-bedroom flat was occupied by four persons at a time, each entering into a separate agreement of licence with the landlord, a company holding an interest in the building in which the flat was situated. The agreements were almost identical, giving exclusive use of a bedroom and common use of common facilities such as a kitchen and bathroom. The defen-

202 *Street v Mountford* (1984) 271 EG 1261.

203 *Street v Mountford* [1985] AC 809, HL at 818 *per* Lord Templeman.

204 *Westminster City Council v Clarke* [1992] 2 AC 288, HL. See Swadling 2007, p. 238-239.

205 See Swadling 2007, p. 238-239.

206 *Westminster City Council v Clarke* [1992] 2 AC 288, HL.

207 Swadling 2007, p. 239, Burn & Cartwright 2006, p. 199-200.

208 See Swadling 2007, p. 239-240.

209 *AG Securities v Vaughan and Others* and *Antoniades v Villiers and Another* [1990] 1 AC 417, HL.

dants tried to argue they were joined tenants and therefore fell under the ruling of *Street v Mountford.* The House of Lords, under careful consideration of whether this arrangement was not just intended to avoid application of the Rent Acts, disagreed.[210]

However, in *Antoniades v Villiers and another,* a couple entered into two separate agreements of licence with the holder of the fee simple of a house. The couple expressed preference for a double bed, which was provided by Mr Antoniades, the licensor. The agreement further provided that the licensor did not intend to grant exclusive possession of any of the rooms. However, the House of Lords, Lord Templeman in particular, argued that in this case the licence agreements were interdependent and that therefore the couple could be considered as joint occupiers.[211] Under the judgment of *Street v Mountford,* the couple was held to be joint tenants of the lease.[212]

The second requirement for a lease concerns the certainty of term. The requirement of a term of years absolute has no limit in how long it might be, as long as there is a definite end.[213] The requirement to define the end of the lease with certainty has given rise to a series of cases. For example, in *Lace v Chantler,* a lease for the 'duration of the war' was held void by the Court of Appeal, and in *Prudential Assurance Co Ltd v London Residuary Body,* a lease of a strip of land until that land was required by the council 'for the purposes of widening the road' was held void by the House of Lords.[214] This reasoning also applies for periodic tenancies, which are renewed each week or each year. The certainty in those cases is offered by the possibility for each of the parties to determine the lease at the end of the year.[215]

The reasoning of the courts in these cases has been that the time at which the specified event would take place was uncertain and therefore could not, under a rule more than 500 years old, constitute a lease. However, the result of the strict application of this rule is not always as fair. Swadling points out that had the lease been made 'to X for the duration of the war or until the land is needed for road-widening purposes' it would have been allowed.[216] Lord Browne-Wilkinson in his judgment in *Prudential Assurance Co Ltd v London Residuary Body* therefore appeals to the Law Commission for England and Wales to review this rule and consider its abolition.[217] The Law Commission has, however, not responded.[218]

210 *AG Securities v Vaughan and Others* [1990] 1 AC 417, HL. See Swadling 2007, p. 240-241, Burn & Cartwright 2006, p. 203-204.

211 *Antoniades v Villiers and Another* [1990] 1 AC 417, HL, *per* Lord Templeman.

212 For a critical view on the application of joint tenancy, but not tenancy in common because the parties did not argue this, see Swadling 2007, p. 239-240.

213 See Bright 1993, p. 38 *et seq.*, Burn & Cartwright 2006, p. 207-208, Swadling 2007, p. 241.

214 *Lace v Chantler* [1944] KB 368 CA, 1 All ER 305, *Prudential Assurance Co Ltd v London Residuary Body* [1992] 2 AC 386, HL, 3 All ER 504. See Bright 1993, p. 39.

215 *Prudential Assurance Co Ltd v London Residuary Body* [1992] 2 AC 386, HL, at 394 *per* Lord Templeman. See also Burn & Cartwright 2006, p. 214-217.

216 Swadling 2007, p. 242.

217 *Prudential Assurance Co Ltd v London Residuary Body* [1992] 2 AC 386, HL, at 394 *per* Lord Browne-Wilkinson. See Bright 1993, p. 48 *et seq.*

218 See <http://www.lawcom.gov.uk/>.

A possible third requirement for a lease to arise is a matter for debate. In *Street v Mountford*, Lord Templeman held that a tenancy requires a premium or periodical payment.[219] However, in *Ashburn Anstalt v Arnold*, although overruled by the House of Lords in *Street v Mountford* on the ground of uncertainty of term, the Court of Appeal held that there was no rule requiring rent to be paid for a lease.[220] Leading opinion seems to maintain this rule and usually considers the agreement to pay rent as a covenant to the lease.[221]

When a lease is created, the holder of the fee simple, who will usually be the lessor, will not be entitled to use and enjoy the land because he has granted exclusive possession to someone else.[222] However, the certainty of term allows the lessor to re-enter the land and reclaim exclusive possession at the end of the lease. Such a right to a return of possession of the land can also arise when a certain condition, under which the lease was made, has been fulfilled.[223] This right, under English law, has been given a property qualification called reversion. The holder of the fee simple can even grant this reversion itself to another person. In that situation that other person receives a future interest known as a remainder.[224] For example, A, holder of a fee simple, grants a lease to B for 30 years, remainder to C.

Finally, the content of a lease determines the rights and duties of the lessor and lessee.[225] When no arrangements have been made between the parties, a standard set of implied rights and obligations apply. These include the obligation of the landlord to ensure that the lessee can enjoy the premises, that these premises are fit for habitation, and that a reasonable rent is paid.[226]

However, in most situations landlord and tenant will have made explicit agreements on the enjoyment of the lease.[227] Such agreements are known as covenants and can be both positive and negative in nature. Generally speaking, these covenants concern the payment of the rent, of rates, and of insurance premiums, as well as agreements on the enjoyment of the premises, and the division of costs and duties for maintenance and repair works.[228] As already mentioned, in certain circumstances, legislation has interfered with the common law to introduce rules for lessee protection. These interferences comprise the Rent Acts, which interfere in the amount of rent to be paid, but also the Landlord and Tenant Act 1988, which forces

219 *Street v Mountford* [1985] AC 809, HL at 818 *per* Lord Templeman.

220 *Ashburn Anstalt v Arnold* [1989] Ch 1, CA. See Burn & Cartwright 2006, p. 196-197, Swadling 2007, p. 242-243.

221 Burn & Cartwright 2006, p. 241 *et seq.*, 265 *et seq.*

222 However see *Bruton v London and Quadrant Housing Trust* [2000] 1 AC 406, where the lessor was a trust, which had no estate out of which it could grant a tenancy.

223 See Burn & Cartwright 2006, p. 169-170.

224 See Burn & Cartwright 2006, p. 510 *et seq.*

225 Burn & Cartwright 2006, p. 230.

226 See Burn & Cartwright 2006, p. 230-240.

227 Burn & Cartwright 2006, p. 241.

228 The payment of rent is known as rent service, not to be confused with a rent charge on land that is closely connected to it. See Burn & Cartwright 2006, p. 241-265. On rent charges see below; 2.6. Rentcharges over Land.

duties on landlords in respect to applications for consent to an assignment and subleasing of the lease.[229]

These covenants, because they are agreements, apply between the landlord and the tenant. On the application of the doctrine of privity of contract, the doctrine that only the parties to the contract can be bound by the terms of the contract, they cannot be enforced against third parties. When, for example, a lessor conveys his right to another person, the agreement between lessor and lessee does not automatically transfer. The same applies for the situation when the lessee assigns his right to another person. That conclusion therefore raises the question of whether a lease is really a property right. In this respect Lord Browne-Wilkinson stated in *Linden Gardens Trust Ltd v Lenesta Sludge Disposals Ltd*:

> 'A lease is a hybrid, part contract, part property'.[230]

Already in the early common law, covenants made through a lease agreement were not considered purely contractual.[231] Instead, there was an understanding that the agreements made through a lease were part of the estate. It is especially because of this last argument, that leases in English law, in contrast with leases in civil law, are considered property rights.

Before the Landlord and Tenant (Covenants) Act 1995, which resulted in major reforms in this area of English land law, a covenant could transfer to a new party to the lease when it touched and concerned the land or, under the terminology as reformed by the Law of Property Act 1925, had reference to the subject-matter of the lease.[232] In short, the covenant had to concern the lease itself, the use of land, and not the lessor or lessee personally.

When a covenant was part of a lease agreement and the agreement was followed by a grant of a term of years, not only privity of contract applied between the parties to the lease agreement, but there was also privity of estate between the holders of those legal estates created by the lease.[233] It is the concept of estate, as was dealt with above, which made it possible to assign the right to another person. The landlord could therefore transfer his estate, in this case the reversion, to another person, who, under the doctrine of privity of estate, became bound by the lease. The same would apply for the lessee who assigned his term of years to another person. A covenant which touched and concerned the land would transfer with the estate to the assignee. However, liability could and would usually remain with the original landlord and tenant.[234]

229 Burn & Cartwright 2006, p. 258.

230 *Linden Gardens Trust Ltd v Lenesta Sludge Development Ltd* [1994] 1 AC 85 at 108 *per* Lord Browne-Wilkinson. See Burn & Cartwright 2006, p. 194-196.

231 Burn & Cartwright 2006, p. 294, Swadling 2007, p. 243.

232 Burn & Cartwright 2006, p. 294-295, Swadling 2007, p. 245-246.

233 *Bickford v Parson* (1848) 5 CB 920, 136 ER 1141, *City of London v Fell* [1994] 1 AC 458 HL, Burn & Cartwright 2006, p. 302.

234 Swadling 2007, p. 244.

Those negative effects were remedied by the Landlord and Tenant (Covenants) Act 1995, which came into force on 1 January 1996.[235] The objective of the Act was to avoid a landlord or tenant from enjoying rights or being under any obligation arising from the lease after it has been assigned to another party.[236] The departure from the old regime is that all covenants, except those which are personal, are binding upon the successors in title of both the landlord and the tenant and no contractual liability remains for the original parties.[237] A covenant is personal when it is not intended to bind successors in title.[238]

The effects of the new Act are such that a new set of terminology is introduced to enable differentiation between leases under the old regime and so-called new tenancies, which fall under the Landlord and Tenant (Covenants) Act 1995.[239] Furthermore, covenants are now divided into landlord covenants and tenant covenants.[240]

With the introduction of the new Act, the requirement of touching and concerning has been removed. The Act ensures that all covenants, save personal covenants, automatically transfer with the assignment of a lease. Therefore the new lessor and lessee will, in principle, become bound by the terms of the lease agreement. However, when the lease is not transferred itself, but a sub-lease is created, the Act does not apply. In such a situation the assignor continues to hold a legal estate and the Act does not operate. In other words, there is no privity of estate effect in the case of a sub-lease.

The interference in contract law by the Landlord and Tenant Act 1995 is severe. Unless parties decide on and formulate their covenants in such a way that they are strictly personal and do not bind their successors in title, the covenants will transfer with the lease when it is assigned in full to another party. In order to ensure the application of the Act, Section 25 prohibits parties from contractually deviating from these rules.

With the Landlord and Tenant Act 1995, leasehold estates have therefore become strengthened in their status as property rights. The new rules now provide for third-party effect, not only of the lease itself, but also of the majority of the contractual provisions agreed to by landlord and tenant.

Leases mostly exist at common law, but equitable leases are also recognised. A lease can arise in equity when parties agree to create a lease but not all the formalities have been fulfilled. In such a case, as will happen in the case of estate contracts, where a right in equity comes into existence in anticipation of a right at common

235 See Swadling 2007, p. 248.

236 Burn & Cartwright 2006, p. 310.

237 S. 3, 5 and 6 Landlord and Tenant (Covenants) Act 1995. See Burn & Cartwright 2006, p. 310-316, Swadling 2007, p. 248-249.

238 *London Diocesan Fund v Phitwa* [2005] 1 WLR 3956.

239 S. 1(1) Landlord and Tenant (Covenants) Act 1995. Swadling 2007, p. 248-249.

240 S. 2(1), 2(2) Landlord and Tenant (Covenants) Act 1995.

law, as will be discussed below, the lease will already come into existence, equity anticipating the common law.[241]

2.3. *Easement*

Apart from estates or interests that grant the holder possession, English law also recognises other property rights that grant rights to the holder on the land of another. Burn and Cartwright name these rights *in alieno solo.*[242] In the Roman tradition these rights would be known as *iura in re aliena.*[243] Of this category of rights, the right of easement is the most important. Easements exist both at common law and in equity.[244]

An easement is a right attached to one particular piece of land that allows the holder of the right in that piece of land to use the land of another or, to a certain extent, restrict its use by that other.[245] An easement therefore, can be both positive and negative. In contrast with the civil law systems, the law on easements is looked at from the side of the party benefiting from the right instead of the party that is under the burden of the right.[246] Although, in particular in this respect, the term servitude is sometimes used, English law prefers the term easement.[247] In order for an easement to arise several requirements must be met:[248]

First, there must be two pieces of land. The land on which the easement runs is known as the servient tenement and the land that benefits from the existence of the easement is known as dominant tenement.[249] This requirement ensures that there are no easements in gross, which is an easement without a benefiting tenement.[250]

Second, the easement must accommodate the dominant tenement. This requirement adds to the previous requirement that not only a dominant tenement must exist, but that there must also be a benefit to this tenement.[251] The reasoning behind this requirement is that the use of the land benefits from the existence of the tenement, and it is not the holder of the land himself who benefits.[252] When such benefit for the land does not exist, no easement can come into existence.[253] The fulfilment of the criterion that the land benefits from the existence of an easement will differ from case to case.

241 See Swadling 2000a, p. 228-229, 259. On estate contracts see below; 2.7. Estate Contracts.
242 Burn & Cartwright 2006, p. 583-584.
243 See Chapter 2; 2.4. Other Property Rights.
244 Burn & Cartwright 2006, p. 599-600.
245 See Swadling 2006b, p. 123,
246 Burn & Cartwright 2006, p. 586-587, Swadling 2006b, p. 123.
247 Burn & Cartwright 2006, p. 586, note 2.
248 *Re Ellenborough Park. Re Davies (deceased). Powell and Others v Maddison and Another* [1956] Ch 131, CA, *per* Lord Evershed MR.
249 *King v David Allen & Sons, Billposting, Ltd* [1916] 2 AC 54, HL, *Re Ellenborough Park. Re Davies (deceased). Powell and Others v Maddison and Another* [1956] Ch 131, CA.
250 Swadling 2007, p. 250-251, Burn & Cartwright 2006, p. 587-588.
251 *Ackroyd v Smith* (1850) 10 CB 164, Burn & Cartwright 2006, p. 588.
252 Swadling 2007, p. 251-253.
253 *Hill v Tupper* (1863) 2 H & C 121, 159 ER 51.

In *Re Ellenborough Park*, Lord Evershed MR considered whether a right to stroll around a common park, built to serve a group of houses that had no gardens themselves but instead were to use the common park, could constitute an easement.[254] Normally, a right to stroll around a garden would not automatically constitute a benefit to the dominant tenements, but as in this case the houses on the dominant tenements had no gardens, and the park was specifically constructed to allow the holders of the dominant tenements enjoyment of the park, in this specific case a benefit and therefore also an easement could be recognised.[255] The line between benefiting the dominant tenement and benefiting the holder of the dominant tenement is sometimes difficult to establish. In *Moody v Steggles* a right to have a sign to indicate that a business was held on the dominant tenement was held to constitute an easement.[256] However, in *Hill v Tupper* an exclusive right to put pleasure boats on a canal was held to benefit a business and not the dominant land.[257] The difference between these cases is explained through the relevance of the easement for the business. In *Moody v Steggles* the easement supported the business, whereas the easement in *Hill v Tupper* was the subject matter of the business. Furthermore, the right of easement in *Hill v Tupper* merely prevented others from doing something, whereas the right of easement in *Moody v Steggles* allowed the business to do something.[258]

Third, there must be both a holder of the dominant tenement and a holder of the servient tenement. This requirement prevents an easement from coming into existence when both dominant and servient land are held by the same person. When two pieces of land are held by the same person and the holder makes use of one piece of land to reach the other, he is merely using his own land, not exercising an easement.[259]

Fourth, the easement must be capable of forming the subject matter of a grant.[260] This requirement introduces some certainties for the creation of easements. A right of easement must be granted by a capable grantor to a capable grantee and must contain a clear description of the grant.[261] In particular the last requirement, the certainty of description, limits the possible easements. A right of easement to allow light on the dominant tenement will usually not be allowed, whereas an easement to allow light through a certain window usually will.[262] A right to stroll in the park, known as a *jus spatiandi*, would normally not constitute an easement. How-

254 *Re Ellenborough Park. Re Davies (deceased). Powell and Others v Maddison and Another* [1956] Ch 131, CA, at 175 *per* Lord Evershed MR.

255 See Swadling 2007, p. 252, Burn & Cartwright 2006, p. 588.

256 *Moody v Steggles* (1879) 12 Ch D 261, see Swadling 2007, p. 252-253.

257 *Hill v Tupper* (1863) 2 H & C 121, 159 ER 51.

258 Swadling 2007, p. 252-253, 255, *Re Ellenborough Park. Re Davies (deceased). Powell and Others v Maddison and Another* [1956] Ch 131, CA, at 175 *per* Lord Evershed MR.

259 *Bolton v Bolton* (1879) 11 Ch D 968.

260 Burn & Cartwright 2006, p. 599, Swadling 2007, p. 254-255.

261 Burn & Cartwright 2006, p. 591-592.

262 *Harris v De Pinna* (1886) 33 Ch D 238, *Hunter v Chanary Wharf Ltd* [1997] AC 655, HL, at 709 *per* Lord Hoffmann, Burn & Cartwright 2006, p. 591.

ever, when the *jus spatiandi* was granted specially to accommodate a certain group of houses it can be allowed.[263]

When a right fulfils these four requirements it can be an easement. The list of easements is therefore not limited to existing easements.[264] New easements can be recognised, but depending on their nature with more or less scrutiny. When an easement forces the holder of the servient tenement to spend money or allow the holder of the dominant tenement full or joint use of the land it will most likely not be recognised.[265] Furthermore, what are known in English law as negative easements will not easily be recognised. Negative easements, known in civil law systems as positive easements, are easements that give the holder of the dominant tenement the right to prevent the holder of the servient land from doing something on his own land. Examples include easements of light or of support.

A right of easement that has validly been created will run with the dominant land and continue to bind the servient land.[266] When the holder of the dominant tenement conveys his estate to another person, the benefit of the easement will transfer with the land.[267] When the holder of the servient land conveys his estate, the burden of the easement will also transfer to the new holder of the estate.[268]

However, when an easement exists in equity, the burden will not transfer to the new holder of the servient land. In some cases an equitable easement can be registered under the Land Charges Act 1972, which will make it capable of binding successive holders of the servient land.[269] When no such registration has or could be made, the equitable easement will not bind a purchaser without notice of its existence.[270]

2.4. *Profit à Prendre*

A profit à prendre is very similar to a right of easement, but allows the holder to take something from the burdened land.[271] The holder of a profit à prendre may therefore enter the burdened land and take something that the land produces from

263 *Re Ellenborough Park. Re Davies (deceased). Powell and Others v Maddison and Another* [1956] Ch 131, CA.

264 *Dyce v Lady Hay* (1852) (1 Macq 305), *per* Lord St. Leonards LC, who states 'the category of servitudes and easements must alter and expand with the changes that take place in the circumstances of mankind'. See also Burn & Cartwright 2006, p. 595.

265 Burn & Cartwright 2006, p. 595-596.

266 See Burn & Cartwright 2006, p. 631 *et seq.*

267 S. 62 Law of Property Act 1925, S. 11(2) and 12(3) Land Registration Act 2002.

268 However, in case of registered land the Land Registration Act 2002 imposes some restrictions. These include situations in which the land was registered but the easement not and the holder of the servient land could not have known about the existence of the easement, see Burn & Cartwright 2006, p. 633-634.

269 Burn & Cartwright 2006, p. 634-635.

270 S. 199 (1)(ii) Law of Property Act 1925.

271 Swadling 2007, p. 255-256, Burn & Cartwright 2006, 640 *et seq.*

that land.[272] Like rights of easement, profits can exist both at common law and in equity.[273] Four types of profits are recognised:

(1) The profit appurtenant is a right that exists for the benefit of an estate in land. It therefore very closely resembles a right of easement, but differs in nature because it allows the holder to do something on the burdened land.[274]
(2) A profit appendant is a right that was created when a feudal lord granted a freehold estate to a tenant.[275] When such a grant was given, the common law automatically assumed a right to pasture on the land, including the right to have cattle on the land, as was necessary to plough and work the land.[276] Different from the profit appurtenant, which requires a grant, the profit appendant came into existence upon the grant of the feudal estate. By the statute *Quia Emptores*, these profits have been abandoned, but they can still exist today if they were granted before 1290.[277]
(3) A profit in gross is a profit that allows a certain person, or a group of persons, to have a profit in land without holding a tenement themselves. Different from a right of easement, a profit can therefore exist without a dominant tenement.[278]
(4) Finally, a profit *pur cause de vicinage* is a profit that allows cattle from one piece of land to stray and graze upon another piece of land without being treated as trespassers.[279]

Profits can be held in two ways. They can give the holder a right to the exclusion of everybody else, or they can give the holder a right to enjoy the right in common with the holder of the servient tenement.[280] In particular the second category, known as rights of common or *commons*, is relevant today. Examples are rights of pasture, allowing the holder of the profit to have his cattle graze on the land of another, rights of piscary, allowing the holder of the profit to catch fish in inland waters, or rights to take resources such as turf or wood from the land of another.[281]

As in the case of rights of easement, when the profit exists at common law it is capable of binding acquirers of the servient land. When the right exists in equity, unless a registration under the Land Charges Act 1972 is possible, it will not bind a purchaser without notice.[282] The benefit of a profit appurtenant to land will transfer to a new holder of an estate in the land in the same way as a right of easement

272 *Duke of Sutherland v Heathcote* [1892] 1 Ch 475, 484.
273 Burn & Cartwright 2006, p. 648-649.
274 Burn & Cartwright 2006, p. 641.
275 Burn & Cartwright 2006, p. 641.
276 Holdsworth 1942, p. 147 *et seq.*, Burn & Cartwright 2006, p. 641.
277 Burn & Cartwright 2006, p. 641.
278 *Wickam v Hawker* (1840) 7 M & W 63, Burn & Cartwright 2006, p. 641.
279 *Tyrringhamm's Case* (1584) 4 Co Rep 36b, [1558-1774] All ER Rep. 646. *Newman v Bennett* [1981] QB 726. See Burn & Cartwright 2006, p. 641-642.
280 Burn & Cartwright 2006, p. 642-643.
281 Burn & Cartwright 2006, p. 643-645.
282 Burn & Cartwright 2006, p. 651.

does.[283] Profits that are not connected to a piece of land, profits in gross, can be assigned or left by will to other parties.[284]

2.5. *Restrictive Covenant*

In 1808, Tulk sold and conveyed a piece of land, now known as Leicester Square in London, to Elms. The parties agreed in a covenant to 'maintain the land as a garden and pleasure ground in an open state uncovered with any buildings and to allow residents, on payment of a reasonable rent, to use the gardens'.[285] Elms conveyed his land on to several parties until the right in the land ended up with the defendant, Moxhay, who, whilst knowing about the covenant, made plans to build on the land. Tulk, who still held several pieces of land, sought an injunction, which is an equitable remedy, against Moxhay to prevent him from building.[286]

Moxhay tried to rely on an earlier judgment, *Keppel v Bailey*, in which the court had held that an agreement that limestone for an ironworks would be bought exclusively from a particular quarry, not only by the previous holder of the ironworks, but also by his successors in title, could not constitute a property right.[287] Lord Brougham LC had emphasised that this was not a property right and that parties themselves could not create new property rights as they liked.[288]

However, in *Tulk v Moxhay* Lord Cottenham LC held that it could not be justified that the defendant acted in breach of the agreement. If Moxhay paid a purchase price for the land with an equity, in this case the covenant, on it, and would be able to sell it the next day without, he would make a considerable profit and this could not be allowed. Lord Cottenham LC held that this was therefore not a question of whether the covenant ran with the land, as would be the case with a right of easement and a profit à prendre, or covenants in case of a lease, but a question of whether a purchaser should be allowed to use the land in a manner inconsistent with the contract entered into by his seller, while knowing about that contract.[289]

In doing so, the Lord Chancellor's Court created a new property right, which can only exist in equity, termed a restrictive covenant. An agreement made between parties that restricts the holder of an estate in land will acquire third-party effect and becomes a property right in equity. However, under the broadly formulated rules of *Tulk v Moxhay*, almost all personal agreements with the holder of a right in land would have become property rights.[290]

283 Burn & Cartwright 2006, p. 651. On rights of easement see above; 2.3. Easement.

284 *Goodman v Saltash Corpn* (1882) 7 App Cas 633, Burn & Cartwright 2006, p. 641.

285 *Tulk v Moxhay* (1848) 2 Ph 774.

286 See Swadling 2007, p. 256-257.

287 *Keppel v Bailey* (1834) 2 My & K 517, 39 ER 1042. On this case see below; 4. A *Numerus Clausus* in English Property Law?

288 *Keppel v Bailey* (1834) 2 My & K 517, 39 ER 1042, at 535-536 or 1049 *per* Lord Brougham LC.

289 *Tulk v Moxhay* (1848) 2 Ph 774, at 778 *per* Lord Cottenham LC, Burn & Cartwright 2006, p. 666-668, Swadling 2007, p. 256-257.

290 Burn & Cartwright 2006, p. 668-670, Swadling 2007, p. 257.

In *Haywood v Brunswick Permanent Building Society*, the Court of Appeal considered the scope of the ruling in *Tulk v Moxhay*.[291] In that case, one Charles Jackson conveyed a fee simple to an Edward Jackson with a promise that the latter would keep the buildings on the land in repair. Brett LJ considered the positive nature of the duty this covenant imposed and held that the covenant to repair is not restrictive and therefore could not be enforced against the land.[292] This reasoning by analogy to rights of easement therefore restricted the content of restrictive covenants to negative covenants.[293]

The Court of Appeal introduced another restriction to the ruling of *Tulk v Moxhay* in 1914 in *London County Council v Allen*.[294] In this case, a holder of a certain estate applied to London County Council for permission to build a new street on the land. London County Council granted permission on the condition that this holder entered into a covenant agreeing that that piece of land would not be built on, by the holder or by his successors in title. The holder of the land conveyed his right to the defendant in this case, who knew about the covenant, but proceeded to build on the land. The London County Council argued that under the rules of *Tulk v Moxhay* the defendant was bound by the covenant. Buckley LJ held that London County Council had no land that could benefit from the existence of the covenant and that therefore a restrictive covenant could not exist.[295] Through this judgment another analogy with rights of easement had been made. Not only does a restrictive covenant require a dominant tenement to exist, there must also be some benefit to this dominant tenement in order for the property right to exist.[296] In order for the benefit to bind third parties, it must therefore touch and concern the land.[297] Finally, it must be the intention of the parties that the burden of the covenant runs with the servient tenement.[298] With the introduction of the Law of Property Act 1925, this intention is supplied by statute.[299]

The rules on the binding effect of restrictive covenants in respect to later acquirers, although limited by case law, were further dealt with in the 1925 property law reforms. Restrictive covenants created before 1926 bind all persons who acquire the land on which the covenant runs, except *bona fide* purchasers for value of the legal estate without notice.[300] Covenants entered into after 1925 are void against a purchaser for value of the legal estate in the land on which the covenant runs.[301] In

291 *Haywood v Brunswick Permanent Benefit Building Society* (1881) 8 QBD 403, Burn & Cartwright 2006, p. 668-669.

292 *Haywood v Brunswick Permanent Benefit Building Society* (1881) 8 QBD 403, *per* Brett LJ.

293 See also *Austerberry v Oldham Corporation* (1885) 29 Ch D 750 and *Rhone v Stephens* [1994] 2 AC 310, HL. On easements see above; 2.3. Easement. Positive covenants can still be made, but only as part of leases. On leases see above; 2.2. Lease of Land.

294 *London County Council v Allen* [1914] 3 KB 642.

295 *London County Council v Allen* [1914] 3 KB 642, at 654 *per* Buckley LJ.

296 See Burn & Cartwright 2006, p. 669-670, Swadling 2007, p. 258.

297 Burn & Cartwright 2006, p. 670.

298 Burn & Cartwright 2006, p. 670, Swadling 2007, p. 258-259.

299 S. 79 Law of Property Act 1925, *Rhone v Stephens* [1994] 2 AC 310, HL.

300 Burn & Cartwright 2006, p. 673.

301 Except covenants in a lease, *Dartstone Ltd v Cleveland Petroleum Co Ltd* [1969] 1 WLR 1807.

order for a restrictive covenant to bind the holder of a legal estate it must be registered as a land charge.[302] When the land is registered, notice of the restrictive covenant can be registered with the servient tenement.[303]

2.6. *Rentcharges over Land*

A rentcharge is a right to receive a payment of money that is secured against an estate in land.[304] When the money is not paid, the creditor has a right of distress, he can enter the debtor's land and seize and sell chattels found there.[305] Rentcharges originated in cases where there was no tenure between the creditor and debtor, for example when A conveyed his fee simple to B and accepted a periodic payment instead of the purchase price all at once.[306] In such a case no tenure would exist between A and B and therefore A, as a creditor to B, could not use the common law remedy of distress. Instead, the parties would enter into a separate covenant that would entitle A to a similar remedy he would have had in case of tenure.[307]

Rentcharges are connected to the legal estates that could exist before 1926. After the Law of Property Act 1925 only those rentcharges on land that are held on a legal interest, confer a legal right. Rentcharges on other interests in land confer an equitable right.[308] However, the right on which the rentcharge rests must be a right that confers exclusive possession on land. A right of easement cannot be the subject of a rentcharge, as an easement cannot entitle the holder to come and seize, for instance, a right of way.[309]

Rentcharges have been used in cases where, as already mentioned, there is not a purchase price in full, but rather an annual payment is made. This could be done to secure family annuities and to strengthen the effects of a restrictive covenant.[310] However, with the Rentcharges Act 1977 most rentcharges were abolished. New rentcharges made to strengthen the annual payment of a purchase price were prohibited and, if existing before 1977, will run until 2037.[311] The other two types, those for family annuities and restrictive covenants, survived.[312]

302 SS. 2(5), 4(6) and 17(1) Land Charges Act 1972.
303 S. 32 Land Registration Act 2002. Burn & Cartwright 2006, p. 673-674.
304 Swadling 2007, p. 256.
305 Burn & Cartwright 2006, p. 706.
306 Burn & Cartwright 2006, p. 266.
307 Burn & Cartwright 2006, p. 705-706.
308 Burn & Cartwright 2006, p. 706.
309 However, see S. 122 Law of Property Act 1925 which enables a creditor of a rentcharge on a rentcharge to appoint a receiver on the rent after non-payment of twenty one days. See Burn & Cartwright 2006, p. 707.
310 Burn & Cartwright 2006, p. 707-708.
311 S. 2(1) and S. 3 Rentcharges Act 1977.
312 S. 2(4) Rentcharges Act 1977. See also S. 2(3) Rentcharges Act 1977.

2.7. *Estate Contracts*

The limited recognition of property rights at common law does not necessarily result in equity refraining from recognising additional rights. As was seen in the case of restrictive covenants, although equity is said to follow the law, protection was granted in equity that was not available at common law.[313] The rules of equity are different from the rules of common law. In view of its origin and function, granting remedies where the common law would not, equity often takes a different view from the common law.

One of the prime examples in which equity takes such a different view is in the case of estate contracts.[314] When one party agrees to sell an interest in land to another party, the common law takes the view that this only creates personal rights for the buyer. Common law requires a deed to be passed in order for the interest to pass.[315] Therefore, under the general rule that there is no specific performance of contracts, the buyer can only claim damages in case of non-performance of the contract.[316] Nevertheless, equity recognises exceptional situations in which specific performance of a contract can be allowed. A contract that seeks to transfer land is said to have such a specific subject matter, land, that it can be specifically enforced in equity.[317] The fact that equity holds this contract to be specifically enforceable changes the nature of the rights the contract awards to the buyer. At common law these rights are only personal, but in equity this is different. Equity takes the view of something 'as done which ought to be done', meaning that when parties agree to do something that requires a formality, in this case passing a deed, and the objective of the contract, the conveying of an interest in land, has not yet taken place at common law, equity, fictitiously, will see the conveyance as already having taken place.[318]

The buyer will acquire an interest in the land in equity and the seller will still have the legal interest in the land at law.[319] In order to explain this situation where two persons hold an interest in the same piece of land, English law uses the law of trusts. When an estate contract is concluded, a constructive trust arises under which the seller will hold the land on trust for the buyer.[320] This trust is constructive because the parties have not specifically agreed to the trust coming into existence.[321] Instead, the trust arises by operation of law and is known as constructive.[322] The interest in equity will remain in existence until the legal interest is also transferred to the buyer. Before that, the buyer will hold a property right in equity which he can enforce against third parties and assign if he wants to.

313 See above; 2.5. Restrictive Covenant.

314 See Burn & Cartwright 2006, p. 65-66, Swadling 2007, p. 259.

315 Swadling 2007, p. 259.

316 Goode 2004, p. 113-123.

317 Burn & Cartwright 2006, p. 66, Swadling 2007, p. 259-260.

318 *Lysaght v Edwards* (1876) 2 Ch D 499, *Walsh v Lonsdale* (1882) 21 Ch D 9.

319 Furthermore, the seller will have an equitable lien on the land. See e.g. *Re Stucley Stucley v Kekewich* [1904-1907] All ER 281, CA. See Para. 3.6. Liens.

320 *Lysaght v Edwards* (1876) 2 Ch D 499, *per* George Jessel MR.

321 Which is known as an express trust. See above; 1.5. Trust Law.

322 See Swadling 2007, p. 259-260.

2.8. *Options to Purchase*

Another situation in which equity recognises a property right and the common law does not is in the case of options to purchase land. An option to purchase exists in a phase before the contract to purchase is concluded. As in the case of estate contracts, an option to purchase has land as its subject matter, and is therefore specifically enforceable in equity.[323]

In *London and South Western Railway v Gomm*, the Court of Appeal affirmed that options to purchase are also equitable property rights.[324] The case concerned a conveyance that had been made under covenant that the claimant, who conveyed the interest in land, could repurchase the land by giving notice and paying the purchase price. The buyer of the land conveyed his interest in the land to the defendant, who, when the claimant tried to invoke his option to purchase, refused to accept that he was bound by the covenant. Jessel MR held that the contract created a property right in equity and that therefore the defendant was bound by it, even though the contract was made between the claimant and the original buyer and the claimant was not a party to that contract. Such a property right would run with the land and transfer to a new acquirer of the land such as the defendant.[325]

An option to purchase therefore also awards its holder with a property right which he can enforce against the owner of the land on which the purchase may be exercised, regardless of whether the owner at the moment the purchase is invoked was a party to the contract. The equitable property right will not bind an owner who had no knowledge of the existence of the purchase and who acquired his interest in the land for value.[326]

2.9. *Mortgage of Land and Equity of Redemption*

As in other legal systems, entitlements to land in English law can be used not only for the use and enjoyment of land, but also as security for the performance of an obligation. In many cases this obligation will be for the repayment of money.[327] The primary property security right in English law is known as a right of mortgage. Originally the mortgage was a form of pledge of which two types existed.[328] A lender of money could be entitled to enter the land and be allowed to take the rents and profits the land produced as payments of a loan as well as its interest.[329] This type of agreement was called a living pledge or *vivum vadium*.[330] Another type was by an agreement that allowed the lender to take the rents and profits of the land in

323 *London and South Western Railway v Gomm* (1882) 20 Ch D 562 *per* Lindley LJ, Swadling 2007, p. 260.

324 *London and South Western Railway v Gomm* (1882) 20 Ch D 562.

325 *London and South Western Railway v Gomm* (1882) 20 Ch D 562, *per* George Jessel LJ.

326 The *bona fide* purchaser for value without notice, see above; 1.2. Common Law and Equity.

327 Swadling 2007, p. 261, Smith 2000, p. 385.

328 Pledge is used here in the widest sense of the word, denoting a security right in general.

329 Burn & Cartwright 2006, p. 720-721.

330 See Burn & Cartwright 2006, p. 721.

order to pay the interest only, which was called a dead pledge or *mortuum vadium*, as it did not result in a complete payment of the debt.[331]

In the early common law the mortgage developed and became a conveyance of a fee simple or other interest in land, legal or equitable, by the mortgagor to the mortgagee.[332] Therefore, from the beginning there were legal and equitable mortgages.[333] This conveyance was made under the condition that when the mortgagor, the debtor in a loan agreement, repaid the loan to the mortgagee, the creditor in the agreement, the conveyance would be reversed.[334] If repayment was not made before a certain precise date, the mortgagee would hold the land absolute and the title of the mortgagor would be lost.[335] However, this would not relieve the debt of the mortgagor, but would just deprive him of his property interest.[336]

The common law provided strict rules on the repayment of the loan that the mortgage secured. For instance, it required the mortgagor to pay the mortgage debt on a specific date. The application of this rule would often result in the impossibility of the mortgagor redeeming his title to the land, and this led the Court of Chancery to intervene with remedies in equity. The term redeem or redemption here describes the right to pay off the debt and re-acquire the title in the land because of the fulfilment of the condition.

In equity the rule developed that time is not the most essential matter of the transaction. In equity, the mortgagor must be allowed to redeem his property right despite his failure to make a payment on the exact date.[337] Therefore, where at common law the right to redeem would be lost after a specific date when no payment was made, in equity the right to redeem remained.[338] When the mortgagor repaid his loan, equity would allow specific performance in order to retrieve the fee simple or other estate in land, which had been conveyed on mortgage. It is important to recognise that this transaction does not give rise to the creation of a trust, and that therefore the mortgagee does not become trustee for the mortgagor.[339] Instead, equity recognised the position of the mortgagor through a specific property right.

This recognition in equity awarded the mortgagor what became known as an equity of redemption. However, until payment, the mortgagee remained entitled to the fee simple or other estate in both common law and equity.[340] Equity could award the mortgagor an equitable right through the equity of redemption, but could not award the mortgagor the legal right to the land. Therefore, as a result of the existence of the equity of redemption, which would entitle its holder to retrieve

331 Hence the term mortgage, which refers to the French term *mort gage*, literally meaning dead pledge.

332 Burn & Cartwright 2006, p. 717-718, 723, Smith 2000, p. 385-386.

333 Smith 2000, p. 386-388.

334 Burn & Cartwright 2006, p. 721.

335 Burn & Cartwright 2006, p. 721.

336 *Kreglinger v New Patagonia Meat and Cold Storage Co Ltd* [1914] AC 25 at 35 *per* Lord Haldane.

337 Burn & Cartwright 2006, 721-722, Smith 2000, p. 386-387.

338 Burn & Cartwright 2006, p. 722.

339 See e.g. *Cuckmere Brick Company Ltd v Mutual Finance Ltd* [1971] Ch 949, CA, at 965 *per* Salmon LJ.

340 *Kreglinger v New Patagonia Meat and Cold Storage Co Ltd* [1914] AC 25 at 48 *per* Lord Parker.

the full equitable title, the entitlements in common law and equity were divided between mortgagee and mortgagor.

With the property law reforms of 1925 the provisions on mortgages changed. The 1925 legislation revived another old type of mortgage that had fallen out of use since the sixteenth century.[341] In this type of mortgage, a mortgagor would grant the land to the mortgagee for a short term of years. When the debt was not repaid at the end of the lease, the term of years of the mortgagee would automatically enlarge to a fee simple that vested in the mortgagee.[342] If the subject of this type of mortgage had been a lease itself, a sub-lease would create the same result. The mortgage by demise for a term of years absolute, the formal term used by the Law of Property Act 1925, fitted in the objectives of the law reform project to change the law so that the fee simple was vested in the person truly entitled to it.[343] This was not the case with the other mortgages, as there, through the recognition of the equity of redemption, actually the mortgagor and not the mortgagee would have the entitlement. The use of a right of lease enabled the legal fee simple to remain with the mortgagor.

In order to solve the unfair situation in respect to the other type of mortgage, the mortgage created by a conveyance of the fee simple or other interest in land, this type was abolished and replaced by a charge by deed expressed to be by way of legal mortgage. After 1925 a mortgage, besides by demise for a term of years absolute, could also be created through a charge, which was a special and new type of property right.[344] This charge was called a 'charge by deed expressed to be by way of legal mortgage'.[345] A charge does not give the mortgagee an estate in the land, but instead gives a legal interest equivalent to a position if he had taken a term of years.[346]

In practice, this last type of mortgage, the charge by way of legal mortgage, became the method used to create mortgages. In 2002 the mortgage by way of granting a lease was abolished and several reforms were made.[347] These reforms include the provision that when land is registered, a charge by way of legal mortgage can only be made as a legal charge over registered land.[348] Since 2002, the law on mortgages has become less complicated. However, in order to understand the rights and duties of the holder of a charge by way of legal mortgage, the origins of the mortgage as a lease given for security should be understood.[349]

Although, after the reforms in 1925, the mortgagee did not become holder of the legal estate in the land anymore, the equity of redemption of the mortgagor

341 S. 85 Land of Property Act 1925, Smith 2000, p. 387.

342 Burn & Cartwright 2006, p. 722.

343 Burn & Cartwright 2006, p. 723.

344 Charges over registered land had been first introduced in 1875 through the Land Transfer Act 1875, Burn & Cartwright 2006, p. 724.

345 S. 85(1) Law of Property Act 1925.

346 S. 1(2)(c) and S. 87 Law of Property Act 1925, Burn & Cartwright 2006, p. 724, Smith 2000, p. 387.

347 S. 23(1) Land Registration Act 2002.

348 See below; 2.10. Charges of Land, Gray & Gray 2005, p. 726.

349 S. 87(1) Law of Property Act 1925, see Burn & Cartwright 2006, p. 725.

remained recognised.[350] The recognition of the equity of redemption has several consequences for the relationship between the mortgagor and mortgagee.[351] Although, now the mortgagor no longer conveys his legal estate in the land, the equity of redemption limits the holder of the legal estate so that the holder can only keep the estate as security, and not use it for himself, and ensures that the interest of the mortgagee is only effective as a security right.[352] The equity of redemption is therefore necessary for the mortgage to work as a security device. Parties are not allowed to deviate by excluding or altering or postponing it. As a result of such an attempt the transaction will be void.[353] The right to redeem may be temporary at law; it is indefinite in duration in equity.[354]

Furthermore, when parties attempt to go beyond the creation of a mortgage in their agreement, beyond the recovery of the debt with interest, a court might invalidate the mortgage.[355] The equity of redemption, in other words, must be taken seriously.[356] Parties may not agree on the exclusion of the equity of redemption, or on postponing the equity of redemption.[357] The interference with the freedom of contract is extensive. Therefore, when parties have entered into agreements that are made through a separate contract and are not directly part of the contract creating the mortgage, the House of Lords has refused to accept the invalidity of that contract.[358]

When the mortgagor is a company, there is a possibility to alter the way in which the equity of redemption works. Under the Companies Act 1983 a company may create so-called 'debentures', which can be made irredeemable, or redeemable only after a certain period of time.[359]

When the mortgage contract is created, the mortgagee may take possession of the land.[360] However, the mortgagee may only do so *bona fide* as a part of the mortgage agreement and not for another purpose, such as to avoid legislation on leases.[361] In practice the right to take possession is mostly used for purposes of enforcement. Before using his ultimate power of selling the land to another party, the mortgagee will usually take possession of the land. This enables the mortgagee

350 Burn & Cartwright 2006, p. 735-736, Smith 2000, p. 388.

351 See *Biggs v Hoddinott* [1898] 2 Ch 307.

352 Smith 2000, p. 388.

353 *Samuel v Jarrah Timber and Wood Paving Corpn Ltd* [1904] AC 323, *Jones v Morgan* [2002] 1 EGLR 125, *Knightsbridge Estates Trust Ltd v Byrne* [1939] Ch 441, CA, Burn & Cartwright 2006, p. 736-738, Smith 2000, p. 393-395.

354 Smith 2000, p. 394.

355 Smith 2000, p. 396-397.

356 See *England v Codrington* (1758) 1 Eden 169, 28 ER 649, *Barnhart v Greenshields* (1853) 9 Moo PC 18, 14 ER 204.

357 *Vernon v Bethell* (1762) 2 Eden 110, 28 ER 838, *Fairclough v Swan Brewery Co Ltd* [1912] AC 565.

358 *Kreglinger v New Patagonia Meat and Cold Storage Co Ltd* [1914] AC 23, HL, Smith 2000, p. 397, Burn & Cartwright 2006, p. 741-745.

359 S. 193 Companies Act 1985, Smith 2000, p. 396. *Knightsbridge Estates Trust Ltd v Byrne* [1940] AC 613, HL.

360 *Four-Maids Ltd v Dudley Marshall (Properties) Ltd* [1957] CH 317.

361 *Quennell v Maltby* [1979] 1 WLR 318, CA, *Albany Home Loans Ltd v Massey* [1997] 2 All ER 609, CA.

to lease the land and enjoy the income from the lease, before the sale is concluded.[362] In order to protect the mortgagor against the use of this power of the mortgagee, the parties may contractually exclude it, or the mortgagor may use his statutory right under the Administration of Justice Act 1970 to ask the court to postpone the possession in case he can pay off his debt within a reasonable period.[363]

When the mortgagor defaults on his payments under the agreement, usually after six months, the mortgagee will have a right to sell.[364] However, in order to use his right to sell, the mortgagor must have received three-month's notice in writing summoning him to pay, the mortgagor must have defaulted on at least two periodical payments of interest, and there must be a breach by the mortgagor of the mortgage agreement or the Law of Property Act 1925.[365] The purchaser of the land will take the land free of the rights of the mortgagor, who will no longer have his right of redemption.[366] Finally, if the mortgagee wishes, he may appoint a receiver to take control of the land and receive income thereof. Depending on the nature of the mortgage, whether the charge is fixed or floating, this appointment can have severe consequences.[367]

A mortgage is an important security right that can exist both at law and in equity. Equitable mortgages arise when a right in equity is the subject of the mortgage or when, as in case of leases of land and estate contracts, an agreement to create a mortgage has been reached, but the formalities have not yet been fulfilled. In that case an equitable mortgage will arise anticipating the coming into existence of a legal mortgage.[368]

2.10. *Charges of Land*

The most important charge on land is the charge by way of legal mortgage discussed above.[369] The term charge, however, is used in a very wide sense and may include all cases where land is liable for the payment of a debt.[370] The charge in case of a mortgage is special because the types of action the mortgagee, as chargee, may take, are equivalent to those of a mortgage before 1925. However, 'normal' charges, in other words non-mortgage charges, do award protection to the chargee, but not to the same degree.[371]

English law recognises many charges, both on land and on chattels, legal and equitable. When charges of land are concerned, the common law only recognises the

362 Smith 2000, p. 401.
363 S. 36 Administration of Justice Act 1970, Smith 2000, p. 401-402, Burn & Cartwright 2006, p. 760-762.
364 S. 101 Law of Property Act 1925, Burn & Cartwright 2006, p. 769-771, Smith 2000, p. 403.
365 S. 103 Law of Property Act 1925.
366 S. 104 Law of Property Act 1925, Smith 2000, p. 404.
367 On fixed and floating charges see below; 2.10. Charges of Land. Smith 2000, p. 407.
368 Smith 2000, p. 389.
369 See above; 2.9. Mortgage of Land and Equity of Redemption.
370 Gray & Gray 2005, p. 724, Smith 2000, p. 423.
371 The terms mortgage and charge are often used interchangeably. See *Swiss Bank Corp v Lloyds Bank Ltd* [1980] 2 All ER 419, at 425 *per* Buckley LJ.

registered charge. Under the Land Registration Act 2002, anyone registered as entitled to a registered estate in land may charge this estate at law with the payment of money.[372] A mortgage of registered land can consequently only be made by registered charge.[373] When a mortgage is made over unregistered land, the mortgage itself still must be registered, unless the title deeds are deposited.[374] Consequently, any other charge created cannot exist at common law and must be equitable.

When a mortgage is equitable, when an equitable interest is the subject matter of the mortgage, or the mortgage agreement was made, but the formalities to create a legal mortgage have not been fulfilled, the charge will be equitable and can be registered as such in order to give protection to the mortgagee.[375] Another type of charge arises by operation of law and will always be equitable. These types of charges arise without the consent of the holder of the charged object, and are often referred to as equitable liens.[376] Liens are, in civil law terminology, rights of retention exercised by someone in possession, in order to ensure payment of a certain debt. Situations of equitable liens also arise in order to secure a judgment debt or a confiscation order.[377]

The most extensive class of charges arise by consent and are also equitable. These charges can be either fixed or floating. A charge is fixed when, upon creation, it immediately attaches.[378] This is the standard way in which charges operate. A charge is floating when the moment of attachment is postponed until a certain event, usually insolvency.[379] Floating charges are mainly created by companies and are especially relevant in commercial law. These charges mainly concern chattels, but may exist on land as well.[380] More will be said on fixed and floating charges in the section on charges on chattels.[381]

Charges are tailor-made security rights, referring to the fact that their exact content will depend on the agreement that gives rise to its creation. However, once a charge is created, the chargee has access to a certain number of remedies which closely resemble, but are not the same, as those of a mortgagee. The chargee may apply for a possession order or appoint a receiver to take possession of the land on

372 S. 24 Land Registration Act 2002, Gray & Gray 2005, p. 726-727.
373 Gray & Gray 2005, p. 728.
374 *Ministry of Housing & Local Government v Sharp* [1970] 2 WB 223 *per* Cross LJ, Sparkes 2003, p. 426.
375 S. 2(4) Land Charges Act 1972, Sparkes 2003, p. 426-427.
376 On liens see below; 3.6. Liens, Smith 2000, p. 424.
377 These liens arise, *inter alia*, under the Charging Orders Act 1979 and the Criminal Justice Act 1988, see Smith 2000, p. 424.
378 Goode 2004, p. 587.
379 Goode 2004, p. 587.
380 S. 396(1)(d) Companies Act 1985.
381 See below; 3.4. Charges, Fixed and Floating.

his behalf.[382] Furthermore, the chargee may use his ultimate power, the right to sell the land.[383]

3. Property Rights in Respect of Personalty

Apart from real property law or land law, English law uses a different system to deal with movable objects, known as chattels or goods.[384] As a generic term, movable objects are known as personalty.[385] Contrary to land law, this other area of property law, known as personal property law, has not been subject to development from the beginning of the common law. As a result it has never been subject to the feudal system and therefore lacks a central system binding the various elements together.[386]

For that reason it is also more difficult to provide a list of property rights in personalty, and if a list is drawn, it is, as in the other legal systems discussed above, considerably shorter. For instance, no property rights can attach to the object in order to run with the object to another holder, excluding easements, profits and restrictive covenants.[387] Personal property law is an area of law under development and different from any other system discussed so far. The property law nature of some of these property rights is debated.[388] Nevertheless, English lawyers consider these rights in the area of property law. Therefore, contrary to the content of previous chapters, these borderline cases between property and contract law, will be dealt with in this section and not in a separate section dealing with borderline cases.

3.1. *Title / Ownership*

There is no doctrine of estates in personal property law.[389] Therefore, the entitlement to chattels or goods is not expressed in feudal terminology. However, ownership in the sense in which it is used in civil law jurisdictions is not used either.[390] Instead, and this seems comparable to the approach taken in land law, possession plays a decisive role. Ownership, if the word is used at all, is taken to describe entitlement to possession of a chattel forever. As a short word, the word title is

382 Goode 2004, p. 638.

383 The chargee does not have the right of foreclosure, which causes the equity of redemption to cease to exist as a 'normal' chargee is not mortgagee and therefore there is no equity of redemption. See Bridge 2002, p. 186-187.

384 Due to the Sale of Goods Act 1979 that governs the sale of movable assets, the most common form to transfer title.

385 On the distinction between land law and personal property law, see above; 1.3. Personal Property Law and Land Law.

386 Swadling 2007, p. 267.

387 See Tyler & Palmer 1973, p. 16-17, *Taddy v Steropis* [1904] 2 Ch 306.

388 See above; 3.2. Leases / Bailment?

389 However see *Re Swan, Witham v Swan* [1915] 1 Ch 829, in which an estate for life was recognised on personal property, no longer possible under the present law. See Swadling 2000a, p. 264.

390 See Swadling 2000a, p. 264-265, Tyler & Palmer 1973, p. 39-55, Bridge 2002, p. 28-29.

used. This does not seem to be different in essence from the civil law concept of ownership, but English lawyers insist on describing what they call relativity of title.[391]

Relativity of title means that, in a certain procedure, two parties face each other and the party with the best possessory right will win. However, this adjudication of the better right of possession does not establish that the party who won this particular case also has the best right of possession.[392] Ownership, as the most extensive right a person can have, is by nature unitary or absolute as opposed to relative.[393] Therefore, ownership as a unitary and absolute right is in tension with the relative concept of title in English law.[394]

However, English personal property lawyers do use the term ownership. Especially under the influence of commercial law, which is better connected to everyday speech than personal property law, the term ownership is used. In this respect ownership should be understood in the light of the concept of relativity of title. An owner, Bridge explains, should be seen as the person with the best possessory interest in a chattel.[395]

A second reason English lawyers resist the recognition of a civil law concept of ownership is that in English law the holder of a title in personal property does not enjoy the same protection as the owner in civil law systems.[396] Closely connected to the civil law concept of ownership is the possibility for an owner to vindicate his object in case someone else takes it.[397] In English law, personal property interests are protected through the law of torts, the tort of conversion being the most important.[398] The tort of conversion protects possession and is seen as connected to possession of the title holder, and not to the title itself.[399] However, and that is considered different from the right of ownership, as a result of the action, the holder of a title will recover damages and not possession of the chattel or good he lost.

The use of the term ownership in English law remains debatable. Already in 1961, Honoré described the concept of ownership for English lawyers and argued that, even though it is traditionally argued that English law does not adhere to a concept of ownership, the term could very well be used.[400] Honoré argues that in English law there are also entitlements that fulfil the criteria for ownership.[401]

391 See Pollock & Maitland 1898b, p. 149 *et seq.*, Bridge 2002, p. 28 *et seq.*

392 Bridge 2002, p. 28-29.

393 See Chapter 2; 2.3. Ownership, and 3.3. Ownership.

394 See, in this respect, the discussion by legal historians on the relative concept of ownership in Roman law, an idea advocated by Kaser. Kaser 1964, p. 5 *et seq.* and Kaser & Wubbe 1971, p. 108-110. See Chapter 2; 2.3. Ownership.

395 Bridge 2002, p. 29.

396 See Bridge 2002, p. 47 *et seq.*, Tyler & Palmer 1973, p. 19 *et seq.*

397 See Chapter 2; 2.3. Ownership.

398 Tyler & Palmer 1973, p. 19-21, Bridge 2002, p. 52-56, Swadling 2006a, p. 285-286, Swadling 2007, p. 228.

399 Harris 1961, p. 70-71, Bridge 2002, p. 52 *et seq.*

400 Honoré 1961, p. 107 *et seq.* On Honoré's views Clarke & Kohler 2005, p. 192 *et seq.*

401 Honoré 1961, p. 124, 136-141.

A question that remains is what the concept of title comprises. Bridge describes the content of title in the following way.[402] Title, or ownership, comprises the right to possession forever, the right to enjoy the thing and the right to take the fruits and profits generated by it forever and the right to alienate, bequeath or destroy it. Honoré in his 1961 article ascribes a similar content to the right of ownership.[403] Although he distinguishes more 'incidents of ownership' than does Bridge, the general distinction in the right to use, enjoy and dispose can also be seen in Honoré's division.[404] After this qualification of ownership he describes the power of the owner to grant others parts of his rights and considers that generally these granted powers constitute a new property right, less in content than ownership. It is in particular here that Honoré explains what he sees as the true nature of the right of ownership. In his view ownership is the right that remains at the end and that entitles its holder to receive the powers back.[405] Therefore, it is the 'greatest possible interest in a thing which a mature system of law recognizes'.[406]

This description of title in English law brings to mind the traditional division of the right of ownership into *usus, fructus* and *abusus* used by civil lawyers.[407] The creation of property rights by granting parts of the title to another party also resembles the French approach of property rights as a *démembrement* of the right of ownership.[408] These property rights may concern a right to use or enjoy, but certainly also a right to transfer in case of property security rights.[409]

Like its civil law equivalent, title can also be used for security purposes in two ways. First, a transfer can be made under condition that it will only take place when a certain payment has been made, or another obligation is performed. This type of security is created through a contract with a so-called retention of title clause.[410] When a sale of goods is concerned, the parties are free to decide themselves when the title in these goods is transferred between them.[411] When, in a standard situation, the parties do not specifically decide on this matter, the Sale of Goods Act 1979 provides presumptions to determine when title passes.[412]

However, parties may specifically deviate from these presumptions and create an effective security device.[413] Deviation from the standard presumptions may be

402 Bridge 2002, p. 30.
403 Honoré 1961, p. 112-124.
404 Honoré distinguishes the right to possess, the right to use, the right to manage, the right to the income, the right to the capital, the right to security, the incidents of transmissibility and absence of term and the prohibition of harmful use and liability to execution. Honoré 1961, p. 112-124.
405 The residuary character of ownership. Honoré 1961, p. 126-128.
406 Honoré 1961, p. 108.
407 See, e.g., Chapter 3; 2.1. Ownership.
408 See Chapter 3; 3. Other Property Rights.
409 See Chapter 7; 2.2. Of Ways to Create a Lesser Property Right.
410 *Aluminium Industrie Vaassen BV v Romalpa Aluminium Ltd* [1976] 1 WLR 676. See Goode 2004, p. 585-586, Smith 2000, p. 420.
411 S. 17 Sale of Goods Act 1979. See *McDougal v Aeromarine of Emsworth* [1958] 1 WLR 1126, 3 All ER 431.
412 Bridge 2002, p. 82, Smith 2000, p. 420.
413 S. 19 Sale of Goods Act 1979. See Bridge 2002, p. 170, 184.

necessary in case of the manufacture of goods. When a supplier delivers supplies to the manufacturer but has not yet received payment, he may retain his title until payment. However, when the manufacturer transforms the supplies into new products, the title to the supplies is destroyed and a new title vests in the producer.[414] The retention of title clause cannot be extended to these new products.[415] Therefore parties, in order to include the new products in the security device, have to create a separate and new proprietary security right, usually a charge.[416]

Parties may also attempt to create a situation in which a company is authorised to sell the products that are under retention of title. In such cases, the agreement may stipulate that the supplier of the chattels, exercising his retention of title, shall lose his title to the product but become entitled to the proceeds of sale. The courts have qualified this right as an equitable charge, a property right that enables the supplier to extend his security to the proceeds of sale.[417]

Secondly, another possibility is that, in case a party needs finance, he transfers his title to a certain chattel or group of chattels to a financer. Such a transfer creates a mortgage in the same way as the conveyance of an estate in land.[418] Similarly, the creation of a mortgage on chattels gives rise to an equity of redemption, which will be dealt with separately later in this section.[419]

3.2. *Leases / Bailment?*

The possibility in English law for the holder of a title to grant parts of his right to another person in the form of a property right for a limited duration of time is debated. A term of years absolute, affirmed by the Law of Property Act 1925 as one of the two possible legal estates, cannot be used, as it only applies to land.[420] However, the granting of possession of a chattel for a limited duration is possible under English law. A general concept of bailment is used to describe these situations. As Bridge puts it:

> 'Bailment is a possessory relationship by which a bailor transfers possession of a chattel to a bailee. The bailment may be at will, in which case the bailor has the right to call for the return of the goods at any time, or it may be for a fixed or terminable

414 Due to what is known as specification. See *Borden (UK) Ltd v Scottish Timber Products Ltd and Another* [1981] Ch 25.

415 *Modelboard Ltd v Outer Box Ltd (in liquidation)* [1992] BCC 945.

416 *Modelboard Ltd v Outer Box Ltd (in liquidation)* [1992] BCC 945, On charges on chattels See below; 3.4. Charges, Fixed and Floating.

417 *E Pfeiffer Weinkellerei-Weineinkauf GmbH & Co v Arbuthnot Factors Ltd* [1988] 1 WLR 150, *Tatung (UK) Ltd v Falex Telesure Ltd* [1989] BCC 325, *Compaq Computer Ltd v Abercorn Group Ltd* [1993] BCLC 602. On charges on chattels See Para. 3.4. Charges, Fixed and Floating.

418 See above; 2.9. Mortgage of Land and Equity of Redemption. Bridge 2002, p. 179, Bridge 2002, p. 268.

419 Swadling 2007, p. 261. See below; 3.3. Mortgage of Chattels and Equity of Redemption.

420 S. 1 Law of Property Act 1925, Swadling 2000a, p. 261.

> period, in which case the bailee has the right to resist a demand for the early return of the chattel ...'.[421]

The relation of bailment is therefore covered by contract in which the bailor and bailee agree on the terms.[422] A very common example of bailment is the case of hire, which is a bailment for value. Furthermore, in a commercial context the term lease is even used.[423] In any case a bailment creates a relationship between bailor and bailee in which both can be liable in case of misconduct or when in violation of the terms and conditions agreed upon.[424] However, whether bailment or lease of chattels creates a property right, remains unanswered.

Swadling has attempted to classify bailment.[425] Referring to the case law on leases of land and licences to occupy, the latter used by landlords in an attempt to avoid the application of the Rent Acts, Swadling emphasises that not every covenant awarding possession constitutes a property right.[426] Even though the possession the bailee receives gives him remedies against third parties who interfere with his possession, an action in the tort of conversion, Swadling states that this does not make bailment into a property right.[427] Also holders of a licence have remedies granted through their possession, but do not hold a property right.[428]

Furthermore, there is an argument that once a bailor has granted possession to the bailee, he no longer is entitled to possession himself and that therefore under the *nemo dat quod non habet* rule, that no one may give more away than he already has, a property right must exist. The reasoning behind this is that once the right to possession has been given away, it can no longer reside with the grantor. Also in respect to this argument Swadling argues that it cannot be maintained, as the *nemo dat* rule only applies to property rights, and in case the right in question is not found to be a property right, the title holder will still be allowed to possession himself.[429]

Therefore, the fact that a bailment awards possession as such does not make it into a property right.[430] However, that does not exclude the possibility that a bailment constitutes a property right. When possession of a chattel is transferred to another person to serve as security, a pledge is created. The right of pledge is a recognised property right, but at the same time is also a type of bailment.[431]

The question whether there are other types of bailment that are also proprietary, is very difficult to answer. Because of the granting of possession, a bailee will

421 Bridge 2002, p. 33. For a similar description see Tyler & Palmer 1973, p. 70.
422 Bridge 2002, 37-38.
423 Goode 2004, p. 721 *et seq.*, Swadling 2007, p. 268.
424 *Coggs v Bernard* (1703) 2 Ld Raym 909, 92 ER 107, *per* Holt CJ, Bridge 2002, p. 36-38, Tyler & Palmer 1973, p. 86-99.
425 For a general discussion on bailment see Palmer 1991.
426 On leases of land and licences to occupy see above; 2.2. Lease of Land. Swadling 2007, p. 262.
427 Different see Holdsworth 1933, p. 580.
428 Swadling 2007, p. 263-267.
429 Cf., *King v David Allen & Sons, Billposting, Ltd* [1916] 2 AC 54, HL.
430 See, in this respect, the discussion in German law on the question of the proprietary nature of personal rights that grant possession. See Chapter 4; 4.3. Entitlement to Possession through the Law of Obligations.
431 On the right of pledge in English law see below; 3.5. Pledge. Swadling 2007, p. 269.

have access to a claim in the tort of conversion. However, this right to claim follows from his possession and not from his status as bailee, and can only be exercised against a party with a weaker right of possession than that of the bailee.[432] Therefore, a bailment does not generally create a property right at common law.

There are also difficulties in equity. From its general maxim that regards that as done which ought to be done, equity has awarded specific performance and, with that, the status of a property right, in cases of estate contracts and options to purchase.[433] Also here Swadling is very careful in explaining that equity only recognises a property right when eventually a property right would have resulted anyway.[434] Therefore, Swadling argues, licences to occupy, which are also specifically enforceable, do not constitute property rights.[435]

In this respect there is a controversial judgement by Sir Nicholas Browne-Wilkinson V-C in *Bristol Airport plc v Powdrill*.[436] In this case an airline was insolvent but was placed in administration in order to allow the business to continue and repay the creditors. The Insolvency Act 1986 specifically allowed this under the condition that no steps were taken to enforce any security over the company's objects, except with permission of the administrator or through a leave of the court.[437] The airline owed landing fees to the company running the airport. This company had a statutory power of detention in case of non-payment of the landing fees.[438] Following this right, the company running the airport blocked one of the aircraft of the airline without consent from the administrator or leave from the court. The company claimed it did not need such consent as the aircraft was leased and therefore did not constitute 'property', in the meaning of objects, under the Insolvency Act 1986. On the question of what a lease of an aircraft is, Sir Nicholas Browne-Wilkinson V-C states:

> '... But modern commercial methods have introduced chattel-leasing ... Although a chattel lease is a contract, is does not follow that no property interest is created in the chattel. The basic equitable principle is that if, under a contract A has certain rights over property as against the legal owner, which rights are specifically enforceable in equity, A has an equitable interest in such property. I have no doubt that a court would order specific performance of a contract to lease an aircraft, since each aircraft has unique features peculiar to itself. Accordingly in my judgment the 'lessee' has at least an equitable right of some kind in that aircraft which falls within the statutory definition ...'.[439]

Swadling has argued against this judgment that Sir Browne-Wilkinson misunderstood the law of equity.[440] Equity, Swadling argues, can only anticipate the existence

432 *Gordon v Harper* (1796) 7 Term Rep 9, 101 ER 828, Swadling 2000a, p. 270-271.
433 See above; 2.7. Estate Contracts and 2.8. Options to Purchase.
434 Swadling 2000a, 271-272.
435 Swadling 2000a, p. 272, Swadling 2007, p. 263-264.
436 *Bristol Airport plc v Powdrill* [1990] Ch 744, CA *per* Sir Nicholas Browne-Wilkinson.
437 S. 11(3) Insolvency Act 1986, see Swadling 2000a, p. 272.
438 S. 88 Civil Aviation Act 1982.
439 *Bristol Airport plc v Powdrill* [1990] Ch 744, CA at 759 *per* Sir Nicholas Browne-Wilkinson.
440 Swadling 2000a, p. 272-273, Swadling 2007, p. 233.

of a property right in case of specific performance under the maxim that equity regards that as done what ought to be done. Chattel leases do not create property rights at law and therefore equity cannot anticipate their existence in equity.[441]

A bailment, therefore, even if it takes the form of hire or lease, does not generally constitute a property right. It does, however, award possession, which entitles its holder to sue in tort when necessary.[442] Bailment as such is a contract, but in effect not just a contract either. Tyler and Palmer explain that bailment is *sui generis,* and 'that most modern writers adopt this view mostly without question'.[443]

3.3. *Mortgage of Chattels and Equity of Redemption*

A conveyance of chattels for security of payment of a debt creates a mortgage, as it did with land until 1925. In 1925, the mortgage by conveyance of an estate or interest in land to a creditor was replaced by a mortgage by demise, now also abolished, and by a charge by deed expressed by way of legal mortgage.[444] However, these changes of the Law of Property Act 1925 only apply to land, so that a transfer of chattels as security remains possible.[445]

A mortgage of a chattel offers an advantage over a right of pledge because it does not require a transfer of possession to the mortgagee. However, not transferring possession of a chattel creates a false impression of which party has title in the chattel. When a mortgagor remains in possession, it is unclear that in fact the mortgagee holds title.[446] Therefore, courts have resisted a mortgage on chattels without a transfer of possession by making such transaction void on the grounds that it misleads other creditors.[447] It was not until a registration system for mortgages was created, that, once more, mortgages without a transfer of possession could be created.[448]

As in the case of mortgages of land, a mortgage of chattels also gives rise to an equity of redemption for the mortgagor, enabling him to redeem the mortgage when he fully repays his debt.[449] Also in this respect, the existence of the equity of redemption strengthens the position of the mortgagor and ensures that the mortgagee only uses his right as security.[450]

A mortgage of chattels is created by agreement and the transfer of title in the chattels. The Bills of Sale Acts 1878 and 1882, which introduced the registration system mentioned above, require the document containing the agreement to be in a certain form. When the document does not comply with the Bills of Sale Acts, it will

441 Swadling 2000a, p. 273, Swadling 2007, p. 232-233.
442 Swadling 2000a, p. 273, Tyler & Palmer 1973, p. 76-77.
443 Tyler & Palmer 1973, p. 77.
444 See above; 2.9. Mortgage of Land and Equity of Redemption.
445 Smith 2000, p. 415-416, Bridge 2002, p. 179.
446 Smith 2000, p. 416.
447 Smith 2000, p. 416.
448 Bills of Sale Act 1854, Bills of Sale Act 1878 amended by Bills of Sale Act (1978) Amendment Act 1882.
449 See above; 2.9. Mortgage of Land and Equity of Redemption, Smith 2000, p. 416.
450 Smith 2000, p. 415-416.

be void. However, as in the case of land, a mere agreement to create a mortgage will give rise to an equitable mortgage, equity anticipating the common law.[451]

The requirements for the mortgage document depend on whether the mortgage is of tangible or intangible objects. Tangibles require a specific description of existing objects.[452] Future objects cannot be specified, and therefore cannot be included in a legal mortgage. However, an agreement to transfer future tangible objects to the mortgagee will give rise to a mortgage in equity when the agreement constitutes a binding contract.[453] A mortgage of intangibles can be created almost without formality.[454] When the mortgagee is a company, less restrictive provisions apply. A company may create a mortgage of chattels without complying with these requirements for a document, but under the Companies Act 1985 will usually have to register the mortgage.[455]

Finally, the mortgagee of chattels will enjoy almost the same actions as a mortgagee of land. When the mortgagor is in default of payment the mortgagee may lift the mortgagor's equity of redemption and acquire full and unrestricted title. He may take possession of the chattel, but when the mortgage falls under the Bills of Sale Acts 1878 and 1882 this power is restricted, and, if necessary, the mortgagee may appoint a receiver.[456] Whether the mortgagee also has a power to sell the chattels is debatable. In case of intangibles, the power of sale is recognised.[457] However, in case of tangible objects, the law may grant the mortgagee a power to sell.[458] The power to sell is usually considered to be implied in the Bills of Sale Acts. These hold that chattels can only be sold after they have been held for five days, or after a seven-day notice, which must be issued, has not resulted in the default in the payment being made good.[459]

3.4. *Charges, Fixed and Floating*

Charges can exist both on land as well as on chattels.[460] As in respect to land, the most common charge is usually used interchangeably with mortgage. However, other charges than mortgages may exist. These charges are created by operation of law or by agreement and can only exist in equity.[461] Charges arising by operation of law, sometimes also referred to as equitable liens, arise in case of an unpaid vendor,

451 See above; 2.9. Mortgage of Land and Equity of Redemption, Bridge 2002, p. 180.
452 S. 4 Bills of Sale Act (1878) Amendment Act 1882.
453 I.e., when consideration has been given. *Re Clarke* (1887) 36 Ch D 348, Bridge 2002, p. 180-181, Smith 2000, p. 419.
454 S. 4 Bills of Sale Act (1878) Amendment Act 1882, Smith 2000, p. 417.
455 S. 395 Companies Act 1985.
456 See above; 2.9. Mortgage of Land and Equity of Redemption. S. 101 and S. 205(1) Law of Property Act 1925, S. 7 Bills of Sale Acts (1878) Amendment Act 1882. See Smith 2000, p. 419.
457 *Stubbs v Slater* [1910] 1 Ch 632, CA.
458 Smith 2000, p. 419, Bridge 2002, p. 187.
459 Goode 2004, p. 639.
460 See above; 2.10. Charges of Land.
461 Goode 2004, p. 587.

or when trust property is disposed of without authority.[462] These charges by operation of law do not need to be registered.

Nevertheless, most charges will be consensual. Because a charge does not involve a transfer of title, the agreement creating the charge is the charge itself. These charges may be either fixed or floating. A fixed charge, also known as specific charge, attaches immediately to the chattels.[463] As a result, the chargor is no longer authorised to dispose of any of the charged objects without consent of the chargee.[464] A floating charge does not attach immediately, and will only do so upon the occurrence of a certain event, usually insolvency of the chargor. Consequently, the chargor will be authorised to dispose of any charged chattels as he desires until the charge attaches and becomes fixed.

Floating charges were introduced through case law when fixed charges no longer fulfilled all the needs commercial practice demanded. As a normal method of security, a lender would acquire security by creating a charge on objects of a company.[465] However, when a company could only offer equipment as security and this equipment was charged, the charge was only effective until the equipment needed replacing. The common law did not allow the creation of a charge by agreement over future chattels. Already in 1862 the courts intervened and allowed a charge in equity on the new equipment as soon as it was acquired.[466] However, this only provided for security over additional objects of the debtor. Under the rules on charges, the debtor was not allowed to dispose of charged objects, unless the chargee explicitly agreed. Therefore, stocks could not be used as security.[467]

In practice a solution was attempted through the creation of a floating charge, which was allowed by the Court of Appeal in Chancery in *Re Panama, New Zealand and Australian Royal Mail Company*.[468] In later cases, more content has been given to the floating charge. As a guideline Romer LJ offers three elements to help decide whether a charge is floating.[469] A floating charge would cover a class of objects present and future; the content of that class would change over time; and the chargor would be at liberty to conduct his business until the charge attaches. It is in particular the third requirement that is of high relevance for legal practice.[470]

The difference between a floating charge and a fixed charge is relevant when it comes to the ranking of the security rights. A fixed charge will go before a floating

462 Smith 2000, p. 424.

463 Although the term specific is somewhat ambiguous, see *National Westminster Bank plc v Spectrum Plus Ltd (In Creditors Voluntary Liquidation)* [2005] 2 AC 680, HL, at 711 *per* Lord Scott of Foscote. Goode 2004, p. 587.

464 *Agnew v Commissioner of Inland Revenue* [2001] 2 BCLC 188, PC, Smith 2000, p. 424.

465 See Goode 2004, p. 676.

466 *Holroyd v Marshall* (1862) 10 HL Cas 191.

467 See also *National Westminster Bank plc v Spectrum Plus Ltd (In Creditors Voluntary Liquidation)* [2005] 2 AC 680, HL at 716 per Lord Scott of Foscote.

468 *Re Panama, New Zealand and Australian Royal Mail Company* (1870) 5 Ch App 318. See Goode 2004, p. 676-677.

469 *Re Yorkshire Woolcombers Association Ltd* [1903] 2 Ch D 284, at 295 *per* Romer LJ.

470 *Agnew v Commissioner of Inland Revenue* [2001] 2 BCLC 188, PC.

charge, even when it was created later, without notice of the floating charge.[471] Also other creditors, such as employees, who have a preference ranking for arrears of wages are given priority over an existing floating charge.[472] Usually the charge must be registered in order to have effect against later creditors.[473]

To avoid the company creating a fixed charge during the existence of the floating charge, parties may agree on a so-called negative pledge clause.[474] Although a floating charge allows the company to trade in the ordinary course of business, the negative pledge clause prohibits the company from creating a security right in respect of the charged objects, which would take priority over the floating charge.[475] It is subject to debate whether such a clause has third-party effect, judicial authority holding against it.[476] Goode holds that the question of third-party effect depends on notice of the third party of the charge.[477]

The distinction between a floating charge and a fixed charge is not always a clear one.[478] In the past, there has been some confusion over the question of whether a fixed charge could be created on so-called book debts. These book debts are outstanding claims a company has, which follow from the company's administration, and which are by their nature liable to change from time to time. In *Siebe Gordman & Co Ltd v Barclays Bank Ltd*, the Court of Appeal held that a fixed charge could be created over a fluctuating body of objects, so long as the chargor was not free to deal with the proceeds.[479] This case raised many uncertainties, in particular because it blurred the distinction between fixed and floating charges, with serious results in respect to the ranking of the chargee.

In *National Westminster Bank plc v Spectrum Plus Ltd*, the House of Lords was of a different opinion.[480] This case concerned a charge given by Spectrum over all its book debts to the bank. When the charge that was created was a floating charge, under the rules of priority in insolvency, Spectrum's preferential creditors would be entitled to have their debts paid out of the proceeds of the book debts. If the charge were a fixed charge, the preferential creditors would have no priority and the bank would be entitled to the whole of the proceeds.[481] On considering the facts of this case, the House of Lords held that this charge by its nature must be a floating charge because it was created on a fluctuating set of claims, and overruled the decision in

471 *Re Cosslett (Contractors) Ltd* [1998] Ch 495 *per* Millett LJ.
472 S. 386, Sch 6 Insolvency Act 1986.
473 S. 344 Insolvency Act 1986, but especially S. 396(1) Companies Act 1985.
474 Smith 2000, p. 427.
475 *Wheatley v Sikstone and Haigh Moor Coal Co* (1885) 29 Ch D 715.
476 *Griffiths v Yorkshire Bank Ltd* [1994] 1 WLR 1427, Smith 2000, p. 427.
477 Goode 2004, p. 686-687.
478 See Worthington 1996, p. 73-78.
479 *Siebe Gordman & Co Ltd v Barclays Bank Ltd* [1979] Lloyd's Rep 142, CA. See Smith 2000, p. 425-426.
480 *National Westminster Bank plc v Spectrum Plus Ltd (In Creditors Voluntary Liquidation)* [2005] 2 AC 680, HL.
481 *National Westminster Bank plc v Spectrum Plus Ltd (In Creditors Voluntary Liquidation)* [2005] 2 AC 680, HL at 710-711 *per* Lord Scott of Foscote.

Siebe Gordman.[482] This last case illustrates the importance of distinguishing between fixed and floating charges, especially when it comes to enforcement of the security right. A fixed charge will grant the chargee actions equivalent to a mortgagee, including a power to take possession, sell the object and appoint a receiver. Furthermore, a fixed charge will give its holder a strong position in the insolvency of the debtor.

When a floating charge is enforced it crystallises. Crystallisation means the charge attaches to the objects that are in a company at that specific moment. The floating charge will then become a fixed charge and the chargor will no longer be allowed to manage the charged objects.[483] Crystallisation occurs when a company ceases to trade, voluntarily or involuntarily.[484] Furthermore, parties may also agree that crystallisation takes place at the occurrence of another event, for example, the default of a loan, or the exceeding of a certain credit facility.[485] This last type of crystallisation is known as automatic crystallisation, as it occurs without third parties being able to take notice of it.[486] Involuntary crystallisation can take place in the event of a winding-up petition or the appointment of a receiver by the chargee of the floating charge.[487]

The chargee will then have become authorised to intervene in the management of the company, but must exercise that right in order for the enforcement of the charge to become effective.[488] Usually, the chargee will appoint a receiver who will take over the administration of the company. The chargee will then also be entitled to the other actions a charge awards him; the power to take possession and the power to sell the charged assets.

Fixed charges are property rights and take effect against third parties from the moment they are validly created. However, the legal nature of floating charges has been debated. In this debate there are two problems. First, a floating charge does not attach to any objects when it is created, and because of that it could be argued no property right can exist. Secondly, the floating charge allows the company to trade in the ordinary course of business, which could also imply that a property right does not yet exist. Some have held there is no property right at all, until the charge crystallises.[489] Goode and Worthington have held that a property right already exists before crystallisation.[490] Goode emphasises that a floating charge is held on a fund of objects rather than on specific objects, and that, by the analogy of a trust

482 *National Westminster Bank plc v Spectrum Plus Ltd (In Creditors Voluntary Liquidation)* [2005] 2 AC 680, HL, at 705-707 *per* Lord Hope of Craighead.

483 Smith 2000, p. 426, Goode 2004, p. 681.

484 *National Westminster Bank plc v Jones* [2002] 1 BCLC 55, Goode 2004, p. 682.

485 Goode 2004, p. 684, Smith 2000, p. 426-427.

486 *Re Horne & Hellard* (1885) 29 Ch D 736, *Davey & Co v Williamson* [1898] 2 QB 194, *Illingworth v Houldsworth* [1904] AC 355, HL.

487 *Re Colonial Trusts Corporation* (1879) 15 Ch D 454, *Re Panama, New Zealand and Australian Royal Mail Company* (1870) 5 Ch App 318, *Evans v Rival Granite Quarries Ltd* [1910] 2 KB 979, CA.

488 *Governments Stock and Other Securities Investment Co Ltd v Manila Railway Co Ltd* [1897] AC 81, HL. Goode 2004, p. 685.

489 Goode 2004, p. 681-682. On this theory see Worthington 1996, p. 79-80.

490 See Goode 2004, p. 678-679, 684, Worthington 1996, p. 98-100.

fund, objects may go in and out until the moment of attachment.[491] Also the Court of Appeal has held that a floating charge creates a security right from the moment it is created.[492]

In answer to the second element, Goode holds that it is only by contract that the chargor is entitled to manage the fund under the charge.[493] Worthington has argued that a fixed and a floating charge create the same property right. Only through a licence is the chargor of a floating charge entitled to deal with the objects.[494] This view is also endorsed by Smith, and it offers several advantages.[495] First and foremost, the use of a contractual licence will enable the parties to set the terms of the licence and a failure to stay within those terms will immediately result in liability for the company.[496] Secondly, Worthington argues, this analysis can also be used on other security rights, such as liens.[497]

Whatever the status of the powers of the chargor to deal with the charged objects, it seems convincing to argue that a floating charge creates a property right from the moment it is created. Therefore, as a general security right, the floating charge is one of the most important property security rights in English law.[498]

3.5. *Pledge*

A right of pledge is created with a transfer of possession from a pledgor to a pledgee to hold as security.[499] Because of the requirement of possession, a right of pledge can only exist on tangible objects. The pledgee will have possession of the chattel and receive a property right.[500] As discussed above, a pledge is a special type of bailment. It is a special type because, unlike other situations of bailment, it confers a property right on the bailee.[501]

A right of pledge is created by the transfer of possession without other formalities being needed.[502] In order to protect third parties, possession fulfils a publicity function. This also applies in case a right of pledge was created and possession is in the hands of a third party.[503] However, the requirement to transfer possession makes the pledge an unattractive security right in most cases. The pledgor will often need possession of the chattels under pledge in order to make money and repay the loan that the pledge secures.

491 Goode 2004, p. 678.
492 *Evans v Rival Granite Quarries Ltd* [1910] 2 KB 979, CA at 999 *per* Buckley LJ. See Goode 2004, p. 678-679.
493 Goode 2004, p. 684.
494 This is the so-called 'defeasible charge' theory. See Worthington 1996, p. 82-83.
495 Smith 2000, p. 426.
496 Worthington 1996, p. 88-91, 96-98.
497 Worthington 1996, p. 92-93.
498 See Goode 2004, p. 689.
499 Goode 2004, p. 617-618.
500 *The Odessa* [1916] 1 AC 145, PC.
501 On bailment see above; 3.2. Leases / Bailment?
502 Smith 2000, p. 412.
503 *Meyerstein v Barber* (1870) LR 4 HL 317, Smith 2000, p. 413.

Therefore, English legal practice has attempted to allow the pledgor to remain in possession or for a retransfer of possession back to him. For instance, in *Dublin City Distillery Co Ltd v Doherty*, the House of Lords suggested that a pledgor could be allowed by attornment to transfer chattels to the pledgee, making him the pledgor's bailee.[504] In any case, once a pledge has been validly created, possession can be returned to the pledgor, as long as it is for a limited purpose.[505] Such a limited purpose can arise in the event that the pledgor needs the chattels in order to conduct his business. This is done through a 'trust receipt' which makes the pledgor trustee for the benefit of the pledgee.[506]

With its proprietary status, the right of pledge remains one of the most powerful security rights in English law.[507] When the pledgor can no longer pay his debt, the pledgee becomes entitled to enforce his security right. Enforcement in case of a right of pledge will usually only take effect as a right to sell the objects under pledge.[508] The taking of possession is not necessary as a pledgee usually will already have possession. Should possession have been transferred to another party, upon enforcement the pledgee may re-claim it.[509]

3.6. *Liens*

There are certain situations where, as a method of security, a party retains possession of a chattel until a debt is paid.[510] The right to do so usually arises by operation of law, either common law or statute, but may also arise by agreement.[511] The party entitled to retain possession of the chattel is known as the lienee, the party against whom the right is exercised the lienor.[512] Moreover, a lien is different from a right of pledge, which is also a type of possessory security, in that there is no transfer of possession, and the retaining of possession is usually for another purpose than the purpose for which the possession of the chattels was acquired by the lienee.[513] A lien is therefore more a right used as a remedy than as a right *per se*.[514]

At common law a lien will come into existence when there is a possessory relationship between the lienee and the chattel.[515] For example, the mechanic who operates a garage may exercise a lien against his client who has not yet paid for repairs to a vehicle, an innkeeper has a lien on the chattels of guests to secure pay-

504 *Dublin City Distillery Ltd and Another v Doherty* [1914] AC 823, HL.
505 *Mercantile Bank of India Ltd v Central Bank of India Ltd* [1938] AC 287, PC. Smith 2000, p. 413.
506 *North Western Bank Ltd v John Ponter, Son & Macdonalds* [1895] AC 56, HL. Smith 2000, p. 413-414.
507 See Goode 2004, p. 584-585.
508 This is a common law implied right of sale, *Deverges v Sandeman, Clark & Co* [1902] 1 Ch 579, CA, Goode 2004, p. 639-640.
509 Goode 2004, p. 637-638.
510 Smith 2000, p. 414.
511 Civil law systems refer to this type of right as a right of retention.
512 Bridge 2002, p. 170.
513 *Re Cosslett (Contractors) Ltd* [1998] Ch 495, CA, Smith 2000, p. 414.
514 *Tappenden v Artus* [1964] 2 QB 185 *per* Diplock LJ, Bridge 2002, p. 170-171.
515 Bridge 2002, p. 171.

ment for their food and lodging, and common law confers a lien on anyone in possession of a chattel to employ his work or skill on it.[516]

In other situations a lien may arise through statute. On example was mentioned above in respect to the decision of the Court of Appeal in *Bristol Airport plc v Powdrill*.[517] In that case, a company managing an airport was granted a statutory lien to detain the aircraft of airlines that had not paid their landing fees.[518] As a final example, a lien will also arise when a seller of goods has not yet been paid.[519]

These examples show that a lien can also be exercised when the lienee himself does not have possession of the chattels as such, but becomes entitled to prevent the party in possession from enjoying the rights he normally has. Therefore, a lien is an effective method to ensure payment of a debt.

In English law, liens may be special or general, depending on their origin. A special, or particular, lien is a right exercised on chattels specifically related to the claim the lien concerns. This includes the lien on the luggage of guests in an inn for payment of a stay in that inn, or the lien on a car that has been brought in for repair. A lien is general when there is no such connection to a specific payment. These types of liens are rarer, but can be exercised by those who render professional services such as lawyers, bankers, factors, stockbrokers and insurance brokers.[520]

Liens are special rights and, because of the way in which they originate, they are connected to the party exercising the right. This connection does not exist in respect of the claim it secures, but neither does it exist in respect of possession. The right can therefore not be assigned and when possession is lost the lien ceases to exist.[521] However, through agreement, parties may alter the conditions under which a lien arises. This includes the possibility to make a special lien into a general lien.[522]

Finally, liens may also arise in equity. Unlike common law liens, equitable liens can only arise through operation of equity. In contrast with common law liens they do not depend on the possession of the creditor. Therefore the difference with an equitable charge is difficult to find. Equitable liens are therefore usually referred to as charges, as most equitable security rights are charges.[523] Examples of an equitable lien are difficult to find. The equitable lien mostly arises in cases of unjust enrichment. One example is the equitable lien of an insurer in relation to an action to recover money or money actually recovered by the insured himself from a third party.[524]

516 S. 1 Innkeepers Act 1878, S. 2 Hotel Proprietors Act 1956, *Tappenden v Artus* [1964] 2 QB 185, Bridge 2002, p. 171.

517 *Bristol Airport plc v Powdrill* [1990] Ch 744, CA. See above; 3.5. Pledge.

518 S. 88 Civil Aviation Act 1982, Bridge 2002, p. 171, Smith 2000, p. 415.

519 S. 41 *et seq.* Sale of Goods Act 1979.

520 *Woodworth v Conroy* [1976] QB 884, *per* Lawton LJ, *Eide UK Ltd v Lowndes Lambert Group Ltd* [1998] 1 All ER 945, CA.

521 *Albemarle Supply Co v Hind* [1928] 1 KB 307, Bridge 2002, p. 172.

522 *Service Motor Policies at Lloyds v City Recovery Ltd* [1997] CLY 3167, CA.

523 One difference between equitable liens and charges is that the first are non consensual. Smith 2000, p. 422.

524 See *Lord Napier and Ettrick and Another v Hunter and Others* [1993] AC 713, HL.

4. A *Numerus Clausus* in English Property Law?

This discussion of the property rights in English law shows how English property law is characterised by historical development and its ability to adapt to changes in society. This includes the desire to create both new property rights and new property security rights. However, that is not to say that parties enjoy an unlimited freedom to create new property rights themselves. As in other legal systems, in English law parties need authority by judgment or statute for the creation new property rights. However, there is one important difference between civil law systems and English law. English law does not have a civil code and therefore it lacks a general statutory framework in which the law of property is set out. Instead, English law, in particular property law, has developed over time and was almost fully formed by case law until the legislature intervened and brought limitations in respect to the number of estates.[525] However, the legislation did not, in principle, create new property rights, but merely re-organised the English property law system.[526]

In this respect English law is not different from civil law systems, where legislation also re-organised the property law systems, as these existed before the Civil Codes, almost without introducing new property rights. A common exception is for apartment rights, which were introduced by legislation in all the legal systems under study. However, whereas civil law systems with their Civil Codes froze the law as it stood at that moment, enabling the possibility to enumerate the available property rights in a law code, English courts continue to develop property law until they are stopped by legislation.[527]

Like the civil law systems, English law adheres to a separation between the law of property, which creates property rights that have third-party effect, and the law of obligations, in particular contract law, which is governed by the doctrine of privity of contract.[528] Also in English law, parties are free to provide content to their contractual relations, but enjoy a more limited freedom when these relations take effect against third parties as property rights. English law therefore must also use criteria to determine which rights are property rights and which are not. This section will deal with the question of how English law recognises and uses these types of criteria and in what way it adheres to a *numerus clausus* of property rights.

525 Think of, *inter alia*, the Law of Property Act 1925 and the Land Registration Act 2002.

526 For instance, under S. 1 Law of Property Act 1925 a term of years absolute, before that a chattel real, became one now two legal estates. However, this is not a substantive change. See above; 2.2. Lease of Land.

527 E.g. the running of positive covenants in case of leases, where the Landlord and Tenant (Covenants) Act 1995 brought substantive changes that must now be uphold by the courts. See above; 2.2. Lease of Land. Another example is offered by the 1925 property law reform legislation in respect to the binding effect of restrictive covenants. On this, see above; 2.5. Restrictive Covenant. It should be noted, however, that was not the objective of these legislative reforms to stop courts from developing property law. The argument made here is that this is, nonetheless, an effect.

528 *Hill v Tupper* (1863) 2 H & C 121, 159 ER 51, *National Provincial Bank ltd v Ainsworth* [1965] AC 1175, HL, at 1247 *per* Lord Wilberforce, Swadling 2007, p. 223-225.

The question of whether English law adheres to a *numerus clausus* of property rights should be answered by taking into account the major distinctions English law makes between law and equity and between land law and personal property law. However, as eventually law and equity form one legal system, English law, the recognition of a property right in one will ultimately also have an effect on the other.[529]

In 1795 a firm operating an ironworks constructed a railway to enable limestone to be transported from a quarry to the ironworks more efficiently and at less expense than before. Upon construction of the railway, the operator of the ironworks and the operator of the limestone quarry entered into a covenant that the former would, for themselves and their 'heirs, executors, administrators, and assigns', procure all the limestone they might want from that particular quarry. In 1833, part of the ironworks business came, after a few changes in title-holders, into the hands of Joseph and Crawshay Bailey, who had full notice of the covenant. The Bailey's started construction on a railway to other quarries in the area. Upon this, the shareholders of the limestone quarry brought an action to prevent the Bailey's from constructing the railway and to force them to use the already constructed railway.[530]

In 1834, the case came before Lord Brougham LC who considered the question of whether Messrs Bailey were bound by the agreement. On discussing whether the covenant might have created a property right, which would result in third-party effect, and therefore that the Bailey's were bound by the agreement, even though they had no connection to the agreement except that they now held the ironworks, he stated:

> 'There are certain known incidents to property and its enjoyment; among others, certain burthens wherewith it may be affected, or rights which may be created and enjoyed over it by parties other than the owner; all which incidents are recognized by the law. In respect of possession the property may be in one, while the reversion is in another ; in respect of interest, the life estate in one, the remainder in tail in a second, and the fee in reversion in a third. So in respect of enjoyment, one may have the possession and the fee simple, and another may have a rent issuing out of it, or the tithes of its produce, or an easement, as a right of way upon it, or of common over it ... All these kinds of property, however, all these holdings, are well known to the law and familiarly dealt with by its principles. But it must not therefore be supposed that incidents of a novel kind can be devised and attached to property, at the fancy or caprice of any owner. It is clearly inconvenient both to the science of law and to the public weal, that such a latitude should be given. There can be no harm in allowing the fullest latitude to men in binding themselves and their representatives, that is, their assets, real and personal, to answer in damages for breach of their obligations. This tends to no mischief, and is reasonable liberty to bestow; but great detriment would arise and much confusion of rights, if parties were allowed to invent new modes of holding and enjoying real property, and to impress upon their lands and tenements a peculiar character, which should follow them into all hands, however remote. Every

529 In respect to the relations between law and equity as debate is sometimes held on the so-called 'fusion' of law and equity. See, *inter alia,* Lobban 2004a, p. 389 *et seq.*, Lobban 2004b, p. 589 *et seq.*

530 *Keppel v Bailey* (1834) 2 My & K 517, 520-526.

> close, every message, might thus be held in a several fashion; and it would hardly be possible to know what rights the acquisition of any parcel conferred, or what obligations it imposed'.[531]

Lord Brougham LC is very clear on the subject and not only established that the covenant in question cannot be a new property right, he also explains why English law cannot allow parties to create new property rights at their 'fancy or caprice'.[532] In short, legal certainly in English law would not be served with a freedom for parties to make new property rights at will.

In the case of *Hill v Tupper*, in 1860 a holder of a fee simple in a piece of land with a canal on it granted a lease to a boat proprietor stating, *inter alia*, that it was the 'sole and exclusive right or liberty [of the boat proprietor] to put or use boats on the said canal. And let the same for hire for the purpose of pleasure only'. However, an inn-keeper who ran a business on the side of the canal also started letting boats out for hire. The lessee brought an action against the inn-keeper claiming that this inn-keeper violated the property right of the lessee.[533] The Court of Exchequer considered his claim. Pollock CB held:

> 'This grant merely operates as a licence or covenant on the part of the grantors, and is binding on them as between themselves and the grantee, but gives him no right of action in his own name for any infringement of the supposed exclusive right. It is argued that, as the owner of an estate may grant a right to cut turves, or to fish or hunt, there is no reason why he may not grant such a right as that now claimed by the plaintiff. The answer is, that the law will not allow it. So the law will not permit an owner of estate to grant it alternatively to his heirs male and heirs female. A new species of incorporeal hereditament cannot be created at the will and pleasure of the owner of property; but he must be content to accept the estate and the right to dispose of it subject of the law as settled by decisions or controlled by act of parliament. A grantor may bind himself by covenant to allow any right he pleases over his property, but he cannot annex to it a new incident, so as to enable the grantee to sue in his own name for an infringement of such a limited rights as that now claimed'.

The other judges agreed and the covenant was not allowed to exist as a property right, the decision being reached along the same line of reasoning as used by Lord Brougham LC in *Keppel v Bailey*. However, that does not imply the agreement of exclusivity was not allowed. Martin B added to the judgment that the covenant was not invalid, but just took effect between the parties.[534]

Further, in 1916 the House of Lords dealt with the question of whether an agreement granting a right to put up posters at the side of a cinema building was a property right. The question arose because the cinema building was leased to another party who knew about the agreement, but the lease did not mention the agreement at all. This other party, the lessee, did not want to grant permission to affix posters. The holder of the right to put up posters sued the title-holder of the

531 *Keppel v Bailey* (1834) 2 My & K 517, 520-526, at 535-536 *per* Lord Brougham LC.
532 *Keppel v Bailey* (1834) 2 My & K 517, 520-526, at 546-548 *per* Lord Brougham LC.
533 *Hill v Tupper* (1863) 2 H & C 121, at 123-124. See Swadling 2007, p. 223.
534 *Hill v Tupper* (1863) 2 H & C 121, at 128 *per* Martin B.

cinema building for breach of contract.[535] The title-holder argued that the lessee of the building was bound by the agreement because of its proprietary nature. Lord Buckmaster LC held:

> 'The matter then is left in this way. There is a contract between the appellant and the respondents which creates nothing but a personal obligation. It is a licence given for good and valuable consideration and to endure for a certain time. But I fail to see - although I have done my best to follow the many authorities which the learned Solicitor-General has thought it right to place before our consideration - that there is any authority for saying that any such document creates rights other than those I have described'.[536]

These cases show that the English courts have been very careful in dealing with parties that attempt to give effect to their legal relations beyond the privity of contract. While considering the nature of the legal relation the parties have created, the courts go over the list of available property rights and, even though sometimes they express a dislike of the law in this respect, hold that since the relation in question does not fall under any of the recognised property rights, it must be personal.[537]

In the area of land law this line of reasoning became confirmed through the limiting effect of the Law of Property Act 1925. In this statute, the available estates capable of existence at common law as well as other interests capable of existence at law were mentioned in one section.[538] Although the aim of the 1925 legislation was by no means to change the substantive rules of land law, there are some effects that should be considered. Before the Law of Property Act 1925 the courts themselves had held authority to classify new and existing types of property rights. The introduction of the Law of Property Act 1925 changed this authority in respect to rights that could exist at common law, but not in equity. After the Act, the legislature had limited the possible estates in land that can exist at common law.

Although it is not a conclusion an English lawyer may draw, the effects of the Law of Property Law Act 1925 very much resemble a standardising effect.[539] After the entry into force of the Law of Property Act 1925, the two possible estates in land at common law were specifically mentioned. When, after the introduction of the 1925 Act, courts are confronted with an unknown type of property right, they are not only restricted by their own case law, but now also by an Act of Parliament. It remains to be doubted, whether a common law court could recognise a third, yet unknown, type of property right that is not mentioned in the Law of Property Act 1925. It seems, therefore, that the exclusive authority to recognise new property

535 *King v David Allen and Sons, Billposting, Ltd* [1916] 2 AC 54, HL.

536 *King v David Allen and Sons, Billposting, Ltd* [1916] 2 AC 54, HL, at 61 *per* Lord Buckmaster LC. See Swadling 2007, p. 224.

537 E.g., 'My Lords, it is impossible to approach the consideration of this case without feeling and expressing great regret for the unfortunate position in which the appellant, Mr. King, has found himself'. *King v David Allen and Sons, Billposting, Ltd* [1916] 2 AC 54, HL, at 57-58 *per* Lord Buckmaster LC.

538 S. 1 Law of Property Act 1925. See above; 2. Property Rights in Respect of Land.

539 It is therefore that no authority in this respect can be mentioned.

rights at common law, but not in equity, has shifted with the Law of Property Act 1925 from the courts to the English legislature.

Finally, a natural consequence of this line of reasoning could that the Law of Property Act 1925 effectively established a rule of *numerus clausus* of property rights in land at common law.[540] In other words, from 1926 on, the courts of law are limited by statute in their ability to create new property rights at law. In terms of a *numerus clausus* of property rights, the courts now apply a *Typenzwang*, meaning that a legal relation must fit within one of the recognised types of property rights in land at common law in order to be allowed as such.[541]

However, this conclusion is relevant in theory only, as in equity courts remain to hold authority to recognise new types of property rights. In this respect, the courts are only bound by their own case law and not by a statute equivalent to the Law of Property Act 1925.[542]

In personal property law the courts have also been reluctant to recognise new property rights at law. This is best illustrated when returning to bailment.[543] Bailment is a relation that is created when possession of a chattel is transferred to another party. The fact that possession is transferred gives rise to actions to protect this possession when it is interfered with, but does not create a property right as such.[544] A personal right granting possession does not make it into a property right just because of that.[545] As discussed above, bailment does not create a property right and, although courts, at certain moments, have been tempted to make it into a property right, in general, the relationship between bailor and bailee remains personal.[546]

Nevertheless, in some cases that have been discussed above, the courts have given rise to the recognition of new property rights. They have done so not at common law but in equity. Although common law and equity are connected, and property rights at common law exist in equity as well, there are some differences.[547] In some cases the courts have used a different approach to the limited list of available property rights. *Tulk v Moxhay* concerned a covenant on the use of a garden.[548] The parties to the covenant had agreed that a garden would be used as a pleasure garden only. When Moxhay acquired the land, he attempted to build on the garden and Tulk, one of the other residents, brought proceedings against him. Lord Cottenham LC recognised a new property right, known as a restrictive covenant, which could only exist in equity.[549]

540 Swadling 2007, p. 233-234, more in general see Gray & Gray 2005, p. 1, Swadling 2006b, p. 121-122.
541 On *Typenzwang* see Chapter 1. Introduction; 1.2.2. *Numerus Clausus* of Property Rights.
542 It is in this way that S. 1 (3) LPA 1925 should be understood in this line of reasoning.
543 See above; 3.2. Leases / Bailment?
544 Swadling 2000a, p. 269.
545 Swadling 2000a, p. 269, Swadling 2007, p. 231-233.
546 E.g., *Bristol Airport plc v Powdrill* [1990] Ch 744, CA *per* Sir Nicholas Browne-Wilkinson.
547 Swadling 2007, p. 229-231.
548 *Tulk v Moxhay* (1848) 2 Ph 774, see above; 2.5. Restrictive Covenant.
549 *Tulk v Moxhay* (1848) 2 Ph 774, at 778 *per* Lord Cottenham LC, Burn & Cartwright 2006, p. 666-668, Swadling 2007, p. 256-259.

Equity has also made other contributions to the recognition of property rights in English law. Due to the operation of the maxims of equity, in particular that equity considers 'that as done, which ought to be done', it can anticipate the coming into existence of a property right.[550] The first category of these rights comes into existence when an agreement is made to create a recognised property right at common law, but certain formalities are not fulfilled. For example, an agreement in writing is made that is not a deed. In such cases equity recognises the existence of a property right before it comes into existence at common law. As discussed above, the application of this maxim of equity concerns most property rights, except liens, which by their nature are more of a remedy than a property right.[551]

A second category of equitable property rights should be distinguished. Equity has also given rise to new property rights when certain agreements are made. This applies in case of estate contracts and options to purchase, which anticipate a conveyance of an estate in land.[552] The recognition of these property rights became paired with the fact that such agreements would be specifically enforceable in equity.[553] The result is a constructive trust that enables both seller and buyer to have a property right in the same land.[554]

The above could indicate that although at law the list of property rights is closed, parties are free in equity to create new property rights.[555] Especially when the law of trusts is taken into account, this conclusion may be reached. Any right that can be held outright can also be held on trust.[556] The creation of a trust gives rise to an additional right in equity for the beneficiary. When the subject-matter of the trust is a property right, this equitable right of the beneficiary is also a property right, which, in its turn, can be assigned, leased, charged to third parties, and, if necessary, can be enforced. Apart from the requirements avoiding fraud, the content of a trust and therefore also the content of the right in equity of the beneficiary can be formed according to the parties' wishes.

However, the cases on estate contracts and options to purchase show that, due to the exceptional specific enforceability of these contracts, a constructive trust and thus an equitable right might arise. Swadling adds to this that these rights remain anticipatory in nature. When the agreement, such as an estate contract or option to purchase, ultimately does not give rise to the creation or the conveyance of a property right it cannot be a property right in equity either.[557] In other words, when at common law no property right or transfer of a property right results, equity cannot just make a property right out of nowhere. Also, when at common law a personal

550 Swadling 2007, p. 231-233.
551 On liens, see above; 3.6. Liens.
552 See above; 2.7. Estate Contracts and 2.8. Options to Purchase.
553 Swadling 2007, p. 259-260, Burn & Cartwright 2006, p. 66.
554 *Lysaght v Edwards* (1876) 2 Ch D 499, *Walsh v Lonsdale* (1882) 21 Ch D 9, *London and South Western Railway v Gomm* (1882) 20 Ch D 562.
555 Against this, see Swadling 2007, p. 231.
556 See above; 1.5. Trust Law.
557 *Booker v Palmer* [1942] 2 All ER 674, 677, CA, Swadling 2007, p. 262-263.

right would result, equity cannot make the entitlement to a personal right into a property right.

In this respect it has been argued that through proprietary estoppel, especially after the introduction of the Land Registration Act 2002, a licence of land that comes into existence through the workings of estoppel can lead to the creation of an equitable property right.[558] However, here also equity does not have the power to transform what would be a personal right at common law, a licence of land, into a property right in equity.[559] In other cases, anticipating the law through the recognition of another property right in equity will most likely not occur. When parties create an express trust on a property relation, they do create a property right in equity, but this does not exist without the legal right existing as well. Therefore, an express trust could be considered creating equitable rights in the first category, rather than the second.

These cases show that it might be possible for English courts to recognise new property rights. In one case in particular, this possibility was considered. In *National Provincial Bank v Ainsworth*, the House of Lords considered the nature of a right to live in the matrimonial home by a wife who had been deserted by her husband.[560] The husband had used the matrimonial home as security for debts and defaulted on his payments. The question before the House of Lords was whether the wife had a property right to live in the house that would bind the creditor bank as a chargee.

Lord Hodson, delivering the first judgment, looked into the available property rights in respect of land, and came to the conclusion that the right of the wife was not one of them. Therefore, he held, the other law lords agreed with him, the right of the wife was personal between the wife and the husband and did not bind the bank as chargee.[561] Moreover, Lord Wilberforce added additional reasoning to explain why this right of the wife could not be a property right. He held:

On any division, then, which is to be made between property rights on the one hand, and personal rights on the other hand, however broad or penumbral the separating band between these two kinds of rights may be, there can be little doubt where the wife's rights fall. Before a right or an interest can be admitted into the category of property, or of a right affecting property, it must be definable, identifiable by third parties, capable in its nature of assumption by third parties, and have some degree of permanence or stability. The wife's right has none of these qualities, it is characterised by the reverse of them.[562]

With this judgment, Lord Wilberforce implies that the category of property rights in equity is open and that, once the criteria he mentions are fulfilled, a new property right may come into existence. However, a right not falling under these criteria, such as the wife's right in this case cannot be a property right in any case.[563]

558 S. 116 Land Registration Act 2002, McFarlane 2003, p. 695-696.
559 See Swadling 2007, p. 226-227.
560 *National Provincial Bank Ltd v Ainsworth* [1965] AC 1175, HL.
561 *National Provincial Bank Ltd v Ainsworth* [1965] AC 1175, HL at 1220-1225 *per* Lord Hodson.
562 *National Provincial Bank Ltd v Ainsworth* [1965] AC 1175, HL at 1247-1248 *per* Lord Wilberforce.
563 See Swadling 2007, p. 225.

Lord Wilberforce's criteria have not since been followed, not even in cases where the court considered the possible existence of a new property right.[564]

When it comes to *numerus clausus* and *Typenzwang*, after *Tulk v Moxhay* the courts have not created any new independent property rights, even though there have been cases attempting to achieve this. In equity, the courts have allowed anticipatory property rights to come into existence, but these rights are always connected to an eventual creation or conveyance of an already recognised type of property right.

A second element of *numerus clausus* is *Typenfixierung*.[565] The term *Typenfixierung* covers the idea that once a property right from the list has been selected, the law prescribes which criteria must be fulfilled. Failure to comply will lead to the non-existence of the right in property law. The application of *Typenfixierung* to English property law is, like the application of *Typenzwang*, not something an English property law would undertake. However, in the light of a comparative study, some reflections in *Typenfixierung* by the English courts might offer insights that can be used further.[566]

In *Clore v Theatrical Properties*, a lease included an agreement that granted 'front of house rights' to a theatre.[567] In this respect the agreement stated that 'the lessor doth hereby demise and grant unto the lessee the free and exclusive use of all the refreshment rooms of the theatre for the purpose only of the supply to and the accommodation of the visitors to the theatre and for no other purpose whatsoever'. The lessor then assigned his interest, and the new holder tried to prevent the lessee from exercising his rights under the lease.

Lord Wright MR, although sympathetic with the 'lessee' in this case, held that this agreement did not result in exclusive possession because the refreshment rooms of the theatre were shared with the title-holder and his licensees.[568] Because a lease requires the grant of exclusive possession, the right granted in this case could not be a property right, and consequently, as a personal right, could not bind the new lessor, as he was not a party to the agreement.

Also in other cases dealing with leases, the courts have considered what criteria need to be fulfilled in order to distinguish them from licences to occupy, which are 'mere' personal rights. These include the decision by Lord Templeman on the three criteria required for a lease; exclusive possession, for a term and at a rent, in *Street v Mountford*, and the removal by Fox LJ in *Ashburn Anstalt v Arnold* on the requirement of a rent.[569]

564 *Ashburn Anstalt v Arnold and Another* [1989] Ch 1, CA. See Swadling 2007, p. 225, 242-243.

565 On *Typenfixierung* see Chapter 1; 1.2.2. *Numerus Clausus* of Property Rights.

566 See Chapter 7; 2. The Content of Property Law Systems in Europe.

567 *Clore v Theatrical Properties Ltd and Westby & Co Ltd* [1936] 3 All ER 483, CA.

568 *Clore v Theatrical Properties Ltd and Westby & Co Ltd* [1936] 3 All ER 483, CA *per* Lord Wright MR.

569 *Street v Mountford* [1985] AC 809, HL at 818 *per* Lord Templeman, *Ashburn Anstalt v Arnold* [1989] Ch 1, CA at 9 *per* Fox LJ. See also *Booker v Palmer* [1942] 2 All ER 674 *per* Lord Greene MR on the certainty of term.

Also in respect to other property rights, case law has set criteria that must be fulfilled for a property right to come into existence. These include *Re Ellenborough Park* setting the requirements for easements, and *Rhone v Stevens* prohibiting positive burdens in case of restrictive covenants.[570] These criteria are subsequently applied when parties attempt to bring their legal relation under the definitions of property rights.

One clear example of this is offered by the abovementioned case of *King v David Allen Billposting Ltd*, in which the right to put up posters could also not be an easement as it did not fulfil one of the criteria set by *Re Ellenborough Park*, namely that there was no dominant tenement.[571] Another example is offered by the facts of the *Hill v Tupper* case that could also not amount to an easement, as the right to let out pleasure boats benefited one of the parties themselves rather than the land, and therefore failed another criterion for easements set by *Re Ellenborough Park*.[572]

As in other legal systems, the degree of party autonomy depends on the property right in question. This applies to easements and restrictive covenants, but also to agreements made in case of a term of years absolute.[573] However, one feature that is exceptional in comparison with other legal systems are equitable charges.[574] Equitable charges are tailor-made security rights that can have any content, burdening the object on which they are created with a property right. In this respect there is a constant tension with the property law element of *Typenfixierung* of the *numerus clausus* and the party autonomy the parties enjoy under contract law.[575] However, as long as parties stay within the boundaries of these property rights, the rights come into existence.

The sources of English law - common law, equity and statute - mean that the answer to the question of whether English law recognises a *numerus clausus* of property rights should be approached differently than in civil law systems with their Civil Codes. In English law, the primary source of property law is case law and it is through case law that the system of property law, both real and personal, developed. Statutes fulfil a subsidiary role, usually standardising the common law, and only occasionally, in particular the Land Registration Act 2002, altering the system.

Legislation has not created any new property rights, and from an English point of view this task should not be for the legislature, but rather for the courts, preferably in equity. The courts of equity have shown their willingness to remedy novel situations with the recognition of a new property right. However, the result of this is not that the system of property law is open.

570 *Re Ellenborough Park. Re Davies (deceased). Powell and Others v Maddison and Another* [1956] Ch 131, CA, *per* Lord Evershed MR, *Rhone v Stephens* [1994] 2 AC 310, HL *per* Lord Templeman.

571 *King v David Allen and Sons, Billposting, Ltd* [1916] 2 AC 54, HL, see Swadling 2007, p. 224.

572 *Hill v Tupper* (1863) 2 H & C 121.

573 See above; 2.2. Lease of Land, 2.3. Easement, and 2.5. Restrictive Covenant.

574 See above; 2.10 Charges of Land, and 3.4. Charges, Fixed and Floating.

575 Smith 2000, p. 425-426.

To the contrary, unless authorised through one of the sources of law, parties cannot create new property rights.[576] The courts give good reasons for that and keep using the same line of arguments to prevent parties from creating new property rights or 'fancies'.

Rudden has attempted to analyse English property law and explain why a *numerus clausus* must exist.[577] As one of the main reasons why it must exist, he contends that a purchaser of an object would have many problems finding out which property rights are created on it.[578] Registration, he argues, is not the solution here, as notice of the existence of a property right is not enough for it to bind third parties. In Rudden's view the allowance to register any right would make even personal rights enforceable against third parties, even without their consent.[579]

Another reason Rudden uses is that freedom for parties to create property rights would create a pyramid of rights, in which each successive right-holder would want to create property rights himself.[580] Allowing this, in Rudden's view, would lead to a decrease in the value of the land.

The result of an examination of English property law is that, from the perspective of private parties, the system of property law in England is closed. Parties are not free themselves to create new, as yet unknown, property rights. Only when they are authorised to do so by statute, or by a court decision, whether at law or in equity, can new property rights that were not recognised before, come into existence. In those cases it will not be the parties themselves that create the right, although the parties do create the legal relation, but the legislature or judiciary granting third-party effect, and therefore making it into a property relation. In this respect a *numerus clausus* may be held to exist in English law.[581]

576 Or 'fancies', see Rudden 1987, p. 240.

577 Rudden 1987, p. 245 *et seq.*

578 Rudden 1987, p. 246.

579 Rudden 1987, p. 247.

580 Rudden 1987, p. 248.

581 Rudden 1987, p. 260-261, Swadling 2000b, p. 354 *et seq.*, Swadling 2006b, p. 121-122, Gray & Gray 2005, p. 152-154, Sparkes 2003, p. 88-97, Swadling 2007, p. 223.

Chapter 7

COMPARATIVE OVERVIEW

1. Introduction

The property law systems of France, Germany, the Netherlands and England represent a large part of the legal traditions in Europe.[1] In the past, the comparative study of the law of France, Germany and England, in particular, consisted of the search for similarities and dissimilarities between these legal systems.[2] These three legal systems have also been used to draw initial conclusions for a European Private law.[3] Not only have comparative studies led to a better understanding of foreign legal systems, they have also led to initiatives providing common rules on the basis of comparative analysis.[4]

These developments have mainly taken place in an area of private law where there is a common basis in Roman law[5] - the law of obligations, in particular the law of contract. It is also in contract law that the well-known Principles of European Contract Law, the UNIDROIT principles on international commercial contracts, and, most recently, the Principles of European Law, have been drafted.[6] Partly based on these comparative law efforts, it is also in this area that the European Union has issued a series of Directives, mainly for the purpose of consumer protection.[7] Furthermore, the European Commission continues to work on a 'more coher-

1 Zweigert & Kötz 1998, p. 63 *et seq.* For a critical view on using European legal traditions as a standard in comparative law, see Glenn 2006, p. 434-436.

2 See, *inter alia*, Koschaker 1995, Zimmermann 2006, p. 546-547, 549-550.

3 See, e.g., Zimmermann 1996a, Gordley 1993, p. 498 *et seq.*, Van Vliet 2000, Sagaert 2003.

4 See Zimmermann 2006, p. 557-560.

5 See, e.g., Zimmermann 1996a, Gordley 1991, Van Dam 2006.

6 See Goode 2004, p. xix, Zimmermann 2006, p. 560-564. On the Principles of European Law (PEL) see Chapter 8; 2.1.3. European Commission Initiatives for Future Legislation.

7 See, e.g., Council Directive 93/13/EEC of 5 April 1993 on unfair terms in consumer contracts, Directive 97/7/EC of the European Parliament and of the Council of 20 May 1997 on the protection of consumers in respect of distance contracts, and Council Directive 85/577/EEC of 20 December 1985 to protect the consumer in respect of contracts negotiated away from business premises. On these Directives see Zimmermann 2006, p. 543-545.

ent' European contract law with the development of a Common Frame of Reference (CFR) as the latest issue.[8]

In comparison with the law of contract, the law of property has often been held to be underdeveloped. The study of comparative law has been considered less interesting in this area in Europe because of the major differences between the laws of the EU Member States.[9] Traditionally, it is held that these differences are due to the national character of property law, in particular with respect to land, and the role property law plays in taxation issues.[10] Property law systems are traditionally perceived as very different from each other, and common principles covering the whole area of law, such as the Principles of European Contract Law, the UNIDROIT principles, or the Principles of European Law, have not been drafted. However, in specific areas that touch upon property law aspects, such as trust law and insolvency law, attempts to draft common principles have been made.[11]

One of the most important reasons for the lack of comparative initiatives is that in the area of property law the differences between the civil law and the common law tradition have been considered to be unbridgeable.[12] Once more, compared with contract law, relatively few studies have been devoted to the comparison of these legal systems to determine whether this is actually the case.[13] The results of studies in comparative property law show two things. First, differences between common law and civil law certainly exist. Second, there are also differences amongst civil law systems and these are sometimes just as big as the differences between common law and civil law. However, these studies also show that differences in and between both areas, common law and civil law, can be bridged.[14]

1.1. *Property Law in Development*

The developments in the study of comparative and European property law go hand in hand with the changing field of property law. In the last few decades, property law has moved itself away from the very static system it has been since the period of Roman law. With the exception of the *ancien régime*, where, under the feudal

8 See Communication from the Commission to the European Parliament and the Council on European Contract Law, COM(2001) 398, Communication from the Commission to the European Parliament and the Council. A more Coherent European Contract Law. An Action Plan. COM(2003) 68, Communication from the Commission to the European Parliament and the Council. European Contract Law and the revision of the *acquis*: the way forward. COM(2004) 651, and Green Paper on the Review of the Consumer *Acquis* COM(2006) 744. On the Common Frame of Reference (CFR) see, *inter alia*, Rutgers 2006, p. 217 *et seq.*, Van Erp 2006b, p. 10-11, Smits 2006, Smits 2007, p. 281 *et seq.*

9 See Van Erp 2006a, p. 1044, Sagaert 2007, p. 301.

10 See also Gray & Gray 2005, p. 1-2.

11 See Hayton, Kortman & Verhagen 1999, McBryde, Flessner & Kortmann 2005.

12 See Van Erp 2006a, p. 1044-1046.

13 See, e.g., Van Vliet 2000, Zwalve 2003, Sagaert 2003. For a similar observation see Zimmermann 2006, p. 570-571.

14 See, e.g., Van Vliet 2000, p. 201 *et seq.*

system, new property rights were created, the list of property rights in most legal systems remained static and Roman-law inspired.

On the occasion of the 200th anniversary of the French Civil Code, Libchaber took the opportunity to plead for a re-codification of French property law.[15] A re-codification is needed, he argues, because property law has developed in recent decades in such a way that the current regulations can no longer be sufficiently applied.[16] In his view, property law has been subject to three developments; changes in concepts, changes in objects and the development of new techniques.[17] Although Libchaber's ideas are based on French law and the French Civil Code, his remarks are of a general European importance. In fact, it is partly because of the influence of ideas from other legal systems, and the increasing Europeanisation as well as internationalisation of property law, that Libchaber comes to his ideas. Of course, these European and international influences are also present in other legal systems.

The first challenge for property law that Libchaber recognises is the change in concepts. This change is visible, in particular, in the changed applications of the right of ownership.[18] When the French Civil Code was drafted, its drafters had a certain idea of society and the function of the law of property, in particular of the right of ownership. As a reaction against the fragmentation of ownership in the *ancien régime,* the new definition of the right of ownership created a unitary right.[19] The right of ownership of the makers of the Civil Code was a concept of ownership of an immovable object.[20] However, in modern property law, the concept of ownership is more and more seen as the paramount set of legal relations in respect of an object.[21] This includes questions of whether the right of ownership also includes intellectual property rights, and whether the right of ownership can also be held on other rights.[22]

Furthermore, the unitary concept of ownership as a rejection of fragmentation is increasingly confronted with types of co-ownership in which either legislation or party agreement modifies the relations between the co-owners in such a way that the right of ownership in its natural form is no longer recognisable.[23] This in particular includes the law in respect of apartments.

Secondly, Libchaber signals that property law is faced with an increase in the types of objects that do not fulfil the criteria of the original objects the drafters of the Civil Code had in mind, which were immovable objects, and, possibly, movable

15 Libchaber 2004, p. 297 *et seq.*
16 Libchaber 2004, p. 297-302.
17 Libchaber 2004, p. 302-303.
18 Libchaber 2004, p. 304.
19 Art. 544 C.civ. see Chapter 3; 2.1. Ownership.
20 Libchaber 2004, p. 315.
21 Libchaber 2004, p. 311-314, Zenati 1981, p. 84-104, Zenati 1993, p. 305.
22 Although this study deliberately excludes intellectual property rights from the spheres of property law, in many, mainly Anglo-American systems, intellectual property law is considered a part of property law.
23 See Libchaber 2004, p. 315-323.

objects.[24] More and more incorporeal objects, for example, ideas and other intellectual property rights, as well as claims, are becoming subjects of property law in a system that is not specifically intended to deal with them.[25] For example, general rules on acquisition and transfer might be difficult or sometimes even impossible to apply.[26]

The third and final challenge Libchaber recognises is the development of new techniques of property law. This challenge combines the two former challenges and brings the focus on to *numerus clausus*.[27] New techniques of holding property rights include modifying existing property rights, as well as possibly creating new types. In respect to new techniques, this includes the development of rules on substitution or real subrogation, which allow the object of a property right to be replaced by substituting other objects, for instance, money instead of corporeal objects.[28] Changing property rights themselves include the law on apartment ownership just mentioned, but also the development of real or qualitative obligations, and the development of the right of lease.[29] Especially in respect of real obligations, usually as a part of a recognised type of property right, and rights of lease, there are strong arguments for these rights to be recognised as property rights because of the third-party effect these legal relations have been granted.[30]

1.2. *The Increasing Role of Contract Law*

Since the introduction of the Civil Codes in the civil law systems, these legal systems have undergone important developments. In the French Civil Code, the law of contract was subjected to the law of property, contract law was presented as providing ways to acquire ownership. In the German Civil Code, contract law achieved an equal status with property law.[31] In the decades that followed the introduction of the Civil Codes, contract law played an increasingly important role, eventually, in particular in commercial law, for some purposes thus becoming more important than property law.[32]

In the area of property law itself, which is traditionally an area of law where private parties do not enjoy much freedom, private parties now opt for contractual solutions whenever possible. In fact, certain property law systems have allowed property law to develop by awarding some contractual relations the status of property law. Examples of these include the German *Anwartschaftsrechte*, in English 'acquisition rights', and the restrictive covenants in English law. Furthermore,

24 See, e.g., Art. 516 C.civ that states that all objects are movable or immovable. See Libchaber 2004, p. 329. See also Reich 1964, p. 733 *et seq.*, Rudden 1994, p. 83 *et seq.*

25 Libchaber 2004, p. 341-350.

26 Libchaber 2004, p. 329-341.

27 Libchaber 2004, p. 353.

28 Libchaber 2004, p. 303, 368-369.

29 Libchaber 2004, p. 359-364. See also Smits 1996, p. 41 *et seq.*, Sagaert 2004a, p. 353.

30 Libchaber 2004, p. 364-371, Van Erp 2006a, p. 1052-1053.

31 See Motive III 1888, p. 1-3.

32 See Goode 2004, p. 11-20.

German and French law give certain property effects to contractual relations characterised as *Treuhand* or *fiducie*.[33] Other legal systems, Dutch law in particular, have not followed these developments, not even when an opportunity arose with the introduction of a new Civil Code in 1992.

Within the existing structures of property law, the law of contract plays an increasingly important role.[34] In those areas where property law allows for party autonomy, parties make use of it to the maximum. Examples of these developments are in the field of servitudes, *emphyteusis*, *superficies* and apartment rights. These rights are now used to fulfil functions, for instance, in project development schemes, that did not exist in the nineteenth century. This includes possibilities for parties to separate ownership of a building from ownership of land, divide the building into apartments and grant access to the building and parking spaces. In this sense, contract law is used to combine or 'stack' property rights to create modern-day solutions.

German law presents an optimal system to make use of contract law in property law. In these developments, property law has become the servant of contract law - in order to strengthen the performance of an obligation, the *Sicherungsdienstbarkeit*, or security-servitude, is recognised. Here, property law plays a passive role until the non-performance of the obligation. Only upon non-performance of the obligation are the property right and its strong remedies invoked.[35]

Finally, the increasing importance of claims and other rights as objects of property rights, as dealt with in the previous section, have influence on the content of property rights as well.[36] A claim is, in essence, a personal right shaped through party agreement. When parties shape their personal right in a certain way and this right subsequently becomes the object of a property right, it could be argued that these agreements become part of the property right in it as well. Lebon provides an example of a non-transferability clause of a claim that makes a property right in respect of a claim also non-transferable.[37] The impact of this last development is such that the underlying object influences the content of the property right. In other words, the content of the claim influences the content of the property relation created on that claim. In terms of civil law doctrine, with this development the distinction between the object of a property right and the property right itself becomes less clear, and possibly it can no longer be maintained.[38]

German doctrine has appropriately named these developments *Verdinglichung obligatorischer Rechte*, which translates as 'property-isation of personal rights', and *Obligatoriserung dinglicher Rechte*, 'obligation-isation of property rights'.[39] These

33 See Libchaber 2004, p. 369-371.

34 See, e.g., Kieninger 2004, p. 656-667.

35 On German security-servitudes see Chapter 4; 3.1. Real Servitude, and 3.2. Personal Servitudes.

36 See above; 1.1. Property Law in Development.

37 See, e.g., HR 17 January 2003, *NJ* 2004, 281 (*Oryx*), Lebon 2007. See also Wibier 2007, p. 49-51.

38 Struycken points out the danger of this development for civil law doctrinal thinking, see Struycken 2007, p. 117-119.

39 Dulckeit 1951, p. 7 *et seq*., Canaris 1978, p. 371 *et seq*., Weitnauer 1983, p. 705 *et seq*. Wiegand 1984, p. 107 *et seq*. Another example is provided by Wibier, who argues that property security →

developments have consequences for the property law systems and also for the content of the recognised property rights. In other words, there is also an effect on the *numerus clausus* of property rights. Therefore, in the course of this Chapter, many influences of contract law will be dealt with.

First, this Chapter will recall the essentials of *numerus clausus* (Section 1.3), then consider the property law systems of France, Germany, the Netherlands and England (Section 2) and see to which developments these systems are subject. Only after that will the Chapter return to *numerus clausus* and will deal with if and how it functions (Sections 3 and 4).

1.3. *Considering Numerus Clausus*

1.3.1. Requirements of *Numerus Clausus*

It is useful to recall the function of the *numerus clausus* of property rights before embarking on a comparative discussion of the various property rights. When it comes to general principles of property law, the *numerus clausus* is the principle that decides which legal relations create a property right and which do not achieve this status.[40] This filtering role the *numerus clausus* plays is present in each system that distinguishes property law from the law of obligations.[41] In fact, for most, it is the essential function of the principle.[42] Following the basic German doctrinal distinctions, the filter of the *numerus clausus* comprises of two different elements. First, a legal relation must fall under one of the recognised property rights (*Typenzwang*) and, secondly, the rules on that recognised property right will determine how and whether the right may exist (*Typenfixierung*).[43]

After considering the origin of *numerus clausus* it will be easier to place it in a comparative overview. In each of the legal systems discussed in earlier chapters, a *numerus clausus* has been found to exist in some form. This Chapter will not therefore repeat the search. Instead, it will, through comparison of the legal systems dealt with, analyse the property law systems of France, Germany, the Netherlands and England, in search of similarities in the existence and content of the *numerus clausus*.[44]

rights on bank accounts can be replaced with a contractual solution. See Wibier 2007, p. 49 *et seq*.

40 This role *numerus clausus* plays has also been named its organisational function (*organisatorische dimensie*), see Struycken 2007, p. 350-356, 759.

41 See Van Erp 2006b, p. 14, Sagaert 2005b, p. 1030-1031.

42 Struycken 2007, p. 350-356, Rank-Berenschot 1992, p. 335, Van Erp 2006b, p. 14, Wiegand 1999a, p. 111.

43 See Chapter 1; 1.2.2. *Numerus Clausus* of Property Rights.

44 See below; 2. The Content of Property Law Systems in Europe.

1.3.2. *Numerus Clausus* as a Principle or as a Rule?

Apart from the basic features of *numerus clausus*, this Chapter also addresses how legal systems deal with *numerus clausus*. As a general principle, *numerus clausus* ensures that private parties are limited in their freedom to create property rights. However, depending on the nature of a legal system, whether it is a civil law or a common law system, and within that distinction, a strict or a flexible system, the degree of freedom will differ.

In all legal systems under discussion, the principle of *numerus clausus*, the idea that there are limitations on the number and the content of property rights available for private parties, is present. In a system adhering to such a general idea, parties are not necessarily prohibited from creating new property rights, but the addition of new rights might be subject to serious restrictions. However, in other legal systems, such as the strict civil law systems of Germany and the Netherlands, parties may be prohibited by law from creating new property rights altogether. In these systems the principle of *numerus clausus* finds expression in such a way that it might be called a *rule* of *numerus clausus*.

This distinction between systems using a principle of *numerus clausus* and those using a rule of *numerus clausus* has consequences for the discussion on whether a *numerus clausus* is recognised in a legal system. Although the concept might be best developed and most discussed in the systems adhering to the rule of *numerus clausus*, these systems do not necessarily set the norm for a *numerus clausus* from a comparative perspective. Making the rule of *numerus clausus* into the standard for other legal systems should not be the way in which this concept is considered comparatively. First of all, it provides an inaccurate view of the reality of legal systems. As can be seen from the discussion on German law, even though doctrinally there is a strictly closed system of property rights, new elements, such as the transfer of ownership for security purposes, and even new property rights, such as the acquisition rights, have been added through case law.

Secondly, *numerus clausus* as a basic principle of property law should be looked at from a comparative point of view. When the system with the highest standard is taken as the example for the other legal systems, comparison will not lead to results that can be used to develop further thought. Using the minimum standard of the *principle* of *numerus clausus* enables comparison between the legal systems, taking into account the differences and degrees to which the principle is adhered. As a result a much more nuanced overview can be gained.

1.3.3. Historical Origins of *Numerus Clausus*

In order to provide a complete overview of *numerus clausus*, a look at its historical origin is necessary. Following the development of property rights in civil law dealt with in Chapter 2, one might expect to find the origin of *numerus clausus* in the development of property rights in Roman law. However, in considering Roman law as a basis of our current legal system, caution should be exercised. As was discussed in Chapter 2, ancient Roman law used a system of actions, not of rights. Therefore Roman law took a procedural rather than a substantive approach to private law.[45]

As was also discussed in Chapter 2, the system of actions in Roman law formed a closed system, both for property law and contract law. In an approach to *numerus clausus* that takes a system of property *rights* as opposed to *actions* as a starting point, the fact that the system of property actions in Roman law was closed tells us nothing about whether a *numerus clausus* of property rights was also in place. Struycken warns us about this approach and quotes Lokin, who states:

> Concerning absolute rights, in which respect Roman law knew a closed system, modern law coincidentally also recognises a closed system, but on the basis of completely different arguments than those of the Romans. Roman law knew, due to its limited number of formulas, nothing but closed systems; in our system, absolute rights are limited in number, because with each absolute right, interests of third parties are at stake. It could paralyse trade when absolute rights that can be enforced against third parties can be created without limitations.[46]

Although the argument that the system of actions can be opposed to the system of rights should be awarded its place in the reasoning on whether a *numerus clausus* existed in Roman law, it is not the sole factor that should be looked at. First of all, modern legal systems also prescribe the actions a holder of a property right may take in the case of interference or a threat of interference with his right. The best examples of this follow from German law, which, for instance, in the Civil Code, provides the actions to protect possession in case of dispossession and interference of possession, in case of re-vindication of ownership or in case of interference with the right of ownership.[47] However, there is not necessarily a closed system at its base. In modern law, Lokin seems right in that respect, the decision to recognise another property right is not the decision to recognise a new real action.

Secondly, the fact that Romans thought in concepts of actions and not in concepts of rights should not end the discussion on the closed nature of the property law system. Just like in modern law, the recognition of a property right is dependent on its authorisation by the legal system. Depending on the sources of law and the hierarchy between them in a legal system, recognition of a new property right is achieved through legislation or case law.[48] In (pre-) classical Roman law, the sources were edicts of Praetors and legal writers, and only in Emperor Justinian's time was

45 See Chapter 2; 2.5. A *Numerus Clausus* in (Pre-) Classical Roman Law? and 3.5. A *Numerus Clausus* in the *Corpus Iuris Civilis*?

46 Lokin 2003, p. 273, 'Ten aanzien van de absolute rechten, waar het Romeinse recht natuurlijk ook een gesloten stelsel heeft, kent het huidige recht toevallig ook een gesloten stelsel, maar op grond van geheel andere overwegingen dan die voor de Romeinen bepalend waren. Het Romeinse recht kende door zijn beperkte aantal formula's niet anders dan gesloten stelsels; bij ons zijn de absolute rechten beperkt in aantal, omdat bij ieder absoluut recht de belangen van derden op het spel staan. Het zou op het rechtsverkeer verlammend kunnen werken wanneer de absolute rechten die tegen derden gehandhaafd kunnen worden in onbeperkte aantallen zouden kunnen worden gevestigd'. See Struycken 2007, p. 124-125.

47 See, §§ 861, 862, 985 and 1004 BGB respectively.

48 More on this reasoning see below in 3. *Numerus Clausus* in Comparative Analysis.

there legislation that took the form of the *Corpus Iuris Civilis*. The question of awarding an action of course took place in the legal environment of procedural law, but awarding a new action to a new situation was not unthinkable. In fact, at the time of the development of property rights, new actions were created or old ones were modified so as to adapt to the newly recognised situations.[49]

Behind this line of argumentation is the question of when a new property right is recognised. If the development of property rights is taken into consideration, new property rights come with changes in society, and, most of the time, they demand adaptation of the already existing rights. When Roman society developed from a purely agricultural into a more urban economy, the category of rural servitudes was complemented by the development of urban servitudes.[50] Whereas a transaction for security purposes could function in a small society where everyone knew each other, and could survive because of the requirement to have witnesses with a *mancipatio*, the new Roman society, with its larger communities and many *peregrini*, strangers, required a transfer of possession for a new security right, *pignus*. This was originally a contract, but only later became a property right through the development of the *actio Serviana*.[51]

Moreover, the real actions awarded in Roman law led to a parallel recognition of property *rights* when Roman law was received, from the twelfth century onwards, by the efforts of the jurists Bartolus and Baldus.[52] Following this method, the *rei vindicatio* led to the right of ownership, the *actio confessoria* led to rights of servitude, and the *actio Serviana* to a right of pledge.[53] In this period, the recognition of the list of rights became accepted and led to a more or less closed system.[54] When legal doctrine developed, and concepts became clearer, for instance, the distinction between the right of ownership and other property rights in Donellus' work, new property rights were added in a logical system at a time when legal writers could do so.

Finally, in the period of the drafting of the Civil Codes, when the concept of a closed system of property rights was dealt with, this led to a change in hierarchy of sources of law.[55] In the Civil Codes of both France and Germany, it is provided, albeit implicitly in the German Civil Code, that only those property rights mentioned by the Civil Code could be property rights.[56] It is only in this period that a rule of *numerus clausus* surfaced.

Therefore, the real origin of *numerus clausus* could very well be found in the drafting of the Civil Codes. However, whether the origin of the rule of *numerus clausus* should be found in French or German law remains a subject of debate.

49 See Chapter 2; 2.4. Other Property Rights, and 3.4. Other Property Rights.
50 See Chapter 2; 2.4. Other Property Rights.
51 See Chapter 2; 2.4. Other Property Rights, and 3.4. Other Property Rights.
52 See Chapter 2; 4.4. Other Property Rights.
53 Furthermore Baldus recognised the right to succession, the *ius heriditatis*. See Feenstra 1979, p. 14, Feenstra 1989, p. 113.
54 Of course, in the period of the *Ius Commune*, there was always local customary law that could also be the source of property rights. See Chapter 2; 4. The *Ius Commune*.
55 In the same sense, see Struycken 2007, p. 169.
56 Art. 543 CC, Motive III 1888, p. 3.

Treilhard, a member of the commission drafting the French Civil Code, made his intentions about Article 543 C.civ very clear when he stated that, in his view, the Article contained the only 'modifications to which the owners can be susceptible in our political and social organisation'.[57] Although, at a later stage, rights have been added, and a decision of the *Cour de cassation* from 1834 has led to a lively debate on whether Article 543 C.civ constitutes an exhaustive list, the intention of the legislators with this Article seems clear.

However, in German law, express limitations on party autonomy are made by the legislature which, in the *Motive,* explicitly stated that 'the number of property rights is … limited'.[58] However, the term *numerus clausus* is not used by either of the explanatory memoranda. Struycken mentions he has found the earliest mention of the term *numerus clausus* in a textbook by Heck from 1930.[59] I have not been able to find an earlier reference to the term *numerus clausus* before that. In French literature the term *numerus clausus* is not much used either. French writers have written more about limiting property rights, or in terms of the private autonomy of the owner.[60]

Considering *numerus clausus* as a principle and not as a rule, the general idea of limiting property rights could be as old as law, or at least as old as systematisation of law. Any right with an effect against third parties deserves special treatment and should be approached differently from those rights that do not have this effect. Granting a certain legal relation, which we now call a right, an action that enables one of the parties to act against any third party, is, although technically perhaps different, at least functionally similar to stating that a property right has effect against third parties. In order to give effect to these rights an action is also needed that enables the holder of the right to react appropriately.

Reasoning that Roman law can be excluded when looking at the historical origin of *numerus clausus* may very well hold true for the *rule* of *numerus clausus* and the use of the term *numerus clausus,* which indeed seems to be a German 'invention' dating from after the French Revolution, but it does not provide us with a full overview of the development of property rights and the system in which they function. For that, an understanding of property relations from Roman law and their development into those property rights that eventually received their place in the legal systems is required as well.

57 '… les seules modification dont les propriétés soient susceptibles dans notre organisation politique et sociale …', Recueil complet des travaux préparatoires du code civil 11, p. 33. See Chapter 3; 5. A *Numerus Clausus* in French Property Law?

58 '… Die Zahl der dinglichen Rechte ist daher ... eine geschlossene', Motive III 1888, p. 3. See Chapter 4; 1. Introduction.

59 Heck 1930, Paras. 22 and 23, Struycken 2007, p. 122-123.

60 *Limitation des droits réels or l'autonomie de la volonté.* See, *inter alia,* Hervieu 1981.

1.3.4. *Numerus Clausus* as a Principle of 'Constitutional' Property Law, or as a Framework Principle

It is Struycken's contention that *numerus clausus* should also be looked at as a principle of what I call 'constitutional' property law.[61] This term does not refer to the human rights dimension of property law, but to the organisational function in the separation of powers doctrine.[62] Another term would therefore be to describe *numerus clausus* as a framework principle of property law. Struycken has shown that *numerus clausus* is also a question of which party or institution has authority to create new property rights. He comes to this conclusion after careful analysis of the development of Dutch property law in respect to the *numerus clausus*, and decides that *numerus clausus* shows the primacy of the legislature in this area.[63] This primacy should not only be seen in respect of private parties, in the sense of limiting party autonomy, but also in respect of the judiciary, which, in Struycken's view, in Dutch law has not been given the authority from the legislature to create new property rights.[64] Struycken finds reasons for this in the legislative process, in which, in his view, the interests of all potentially interested parties can be weighed and a decision can be made. Furthermore, when a law is promulgated, its existence is made known to all, and this is done before the rule enters into effect. Furthermore, it will never have retroactive effect.[65] Thus, in such a system legal certainty would be optimal.

Although, in this study, *numerus clausus* has mainly been considered from the point of view of party autonomy, its relation with the legislature or the judiciary has also been dealt with. In respect of the hierarchy of sources of law in civil law countries, the legislature holds the prime position when it comes to law making. In common law jurisdictions, in England in particular, in most areas of property law dealt with, the judiciary holds this prime position. The internal struggle between legislature and judiciary in a certain system has not been considered explicitly. However, examples of judicial activism have been dealt with in the light of co-ownership, security-ownership and expectation rights.[66] In each of these cases, in each of the civil law countries, the judiciary gave recognition to a new property right, without permission to do so by the legislature. Possibly because in the Netherlands a new Civil Code was drafted relatively recently, the question on the constitutional division of powers in the area of property law was dealt with more specifically than it was in other legal systems. However, the results of the debate and the conclusion Struycken draws could be equally applied to other legal systems.

61 However, also see Merrill & Smith 2000, p. 58 *et seq.*, Van Erp 2003b, p. 11.

62 On constitutional property law in the sense of human rights law see Van der Walt 2005, p. 1 *et seq.*

63 Or, *primaat van de wetgever*, Struycken 2007, p. 91, 350, 753 and 762.

64 Struycken 2007, p. 764-765.

65 Struycken 2007, p. 765.

66 See *Req.* 13 February 1834, D.P. 1834.I.218, S.1834.I.205 (*Caquelard*), HR 25 January 1929, *NJ* 1929, 616 (*Beer brewery*) BGH 24 June 1959, BGHZ 28, 16 = NJW 1958, 1133 (*Anwartschafts-recht*).

On the other hand, still in respect of Dutch law, some have argued that, as a result of a development in legal practice, courts are the appropriate actors to authorise new property rights, even if there is no explicit legal basis.[67] Snijders, who is one of the proponents of this approach, bases his arguments on a decision of the Dutch *Hoge Raad* in the area of unjust enrichment. This case, known by Dutch lawyers after the parties, *Quint v Te Poel*, concerned a claim in unjust enrichment that was not based on a specific provision in the old Dutch Civil Code.[68] Instead of rejecting the claim, the Court held that a solution could be found that fitted the system of the law, and that was connected with the cases already dealt with in the Civil Code.[69]

The Dutch *Hoge Raad* further developed this line of reasoning in other cases that were also outside the law of unjust enrichment, including the law of property.[70] Based on this case and its general application beyond unjust enrichment, Snijders argues new objects of property law, and possibly also new property rights, can be recognised through court decisions.[71] Struycken, who sees a clear primacy for the legislature in respect to the *numerus clausus*, remarks that this argument does not hold true, as parties only have a (limited) freedom where the legislature specifically allows them to have this. Therefore, there can never be so much freedom as to allow parties, with permission *ex post* or *ex ante* of the judiciary, to recognise new property rights.[72]

Although this debate seems to concern Dutch law specifically, proposals like those of Snijders have been made in other legal systems too. As discussed in Chapter 4, on German law, Hess has made proposals to treat any party agreement that falls within the nature of a property right and the legal system as a whole, or the *gesamtgesetzliches Leitbild*, as an agreement with third-party effect.[73] The arguments of Struycken can also be used against this statement.

These discussions show the 'constitutional' dimension of *numerus clausus* that should be taken into account when discussing the existence of the concept in the various legal systems. Not only should the relation between private parties, judiciary and legislature be considered, but also the hierarchy of sources of law that each of these three produce.

2. The Content of Property Law Systems in Europe

The recognition of a *numerus clausus* is closely related to the separation between the law of obligations and the law of property. The separation between the law of

67 Snijders 2005a, p 82, on Snijders' argument see, in English, Van Erp 2006a, p. 1056-1057.

68 HR 30 January 1959, *NJ* 1959, 548 (*Quint/Te Poel*), see Struycken 2007, p. 774.

69 '... de oplossing moet worden aanvaard, die in het stelsel van de wet past en aansluit bij de wèl in de wet geregelde gevallen'.

70 HR 13 June 2003, *NJ* 2004, 196 (*ProCall*). On this case and the application of the *Quint/Te Poel* case, see Struycken 2007, p. 774-775.

71 Snijders 2002, p. 57-58, Snijders 2005a, p. 82.

72 Struycken 2007, p. 775, 777-778 and 782.

73 Hess 1998, p. 513-515.

obligations and the law of property is a fundamental starting point of each legal system under discussion, although differences exist between them in terms of application. It might be useful to recall once more that *numerus clausus* is the filter that determines which right is a property right and which right is not. Only in a system where there is a distinction between property rights and personal rights and, connected to that, between the law of property and the law of obligations, does using such a filter makes sense.[74]

The discussion on the division between personal rights and property rights is conducted along the same theoretical lines in each legal system. In each system there are classical theorists, who see a property right as a relation between a person and an object. In other words, they require an object, or a *res*, to exist on which the property right is exercised.[75] For classical theorists, a personal right is a right, not against a *res*, but against another person. From the entitlement to the object, the classical theorists hold that the holder of the property right has a right to follow the object, the *droit de suite* and the right of preference, the *droit de préférence*, to take the object back before other creditors.[76] However, this theory comes into difficulties when the object of ownership is incorporeal, especially when it is a right. A relation between a person and a right is more difficult to conceive than a relation between a person and a corporeal object.[77] Furthermore, personal rights can also have a *res* as their object, for example, in case of a right of lease.[78]

On the other side are relationalists, who see a property right as a relation between two persons in respect of an object.[79] They also require a *res*, but in this theory the *res* has a less prominent place. The way in which property rights differ from personal rights, in this view, is that a property right creates an obligation for everyone, the whole world, whereas the personal right creates an obligation in respect of a particular person.[80]

Whether a property right can be held on an object that is corporeal, or whether an object can also be incorporeal, is a complicating factor with which each legal system deals in a specific way. French law takes the broadest view and considers all objects, corporeal and incorporeal, as *biens* and therefore capable of being the subject of property rights, in particular, the right of ownership. English law also recognises incorporeal rights as objects capable of being subject to personal property law.[81] On the other hand, German law and Dutch law recognise incorporeal rights, in particular, claims, and these can be the subject of property rights, but the most important property right, ownership, is restricted to corporeal objects.[82]

74 See, along the same line of reasoning, Van Erp 2006b, p. 14.

75 See Sagaert 2005b, p. 990-991, Smits 1996, p. 54.

76 See, *inter alia*, Sagaert 2005b, p. 992.

77 See Gretton 2007, p. 831.

78 See Sagaert 2005b, p. 992-993, Reid 1997b, p. 225-226.

79 In Dutch literature also known as the respect theory, see Smits 1996, p. 54-55, Rank-Berenschot 1992, p. 42-48, Struycken 2007, p. 707.

80 In French literature also known as the personalist theory. Sagaert 2005b, p. 993-994, Ginossar 1960, p. 4-11.

81 Tyler & Palmer 1973, p. 8-14, Goode 2004, p. 47-50.

82 See § 90 BGB, Art. 3:2 BW.

Moreover, when parties agree on the creation of a new legal relation and wish to give third-party effect to that legal relation by making it a property right, they create a limited property right, not a right of ownership. In legal systems that recognise a right of ownership, the civil law systems, the right of ownership is unitary and cannot be fragmented in such a way that two different types or forms of ownership come into existence. This rule is a direct result of the rejection of the feudal system in which the fragmentation of ownership into *dominium directum* and *dominium utile* existed.

Connected to this unitary concept of ownership, but not the same issue, are the property rights derived from the right of ownership, the limited property rights. These limited property rights are dealt with by the *numerus clausus*. In this respect the right of ownership falls outside the scope of the *numerus clausus*, as it is the right from which the limited property rights are usually derived.[83] However, without a unitary concept of ownership, there is little use for a *numerus clausus* of property rights. When parties can simply fragment the right of ownership in such a way that any desired division of rights and duties between them is created, with third-party effect, there is no longer any need to use limited property rights from a closed list.[84] With a unitary concept of ownership, however, the limited property rights are needed to allow parties to create some of those legal relations they would otherwise create through fragmentation of the right of ownership. The choices the legal systems have made, in particular, in respect to the number and types of property rights they recognise, have an effect on the way in which the *numerus clausus* operates. It is therefore necessary first to analyse the property law systems and see how they operate before returning to the subject of *numerus clausus*.

2.1. *Of Primary Property Rights and Lesser Property Rights*

In order to analyse the property law systems of France, Germany, the Netherlands and England, to compare them, and to come to comparative conclusions, a set of terminology is needed in which the property law of these systems can be expressed.[85] Traditionally, most property law terminology is considered to be restricted to the legal system that uses it. Without some 'neutral' terminology, comparison will be burdened by the use of different terms which nevertheless have similar meanings; such as ownership and fee simple, or servitude and easement.[86]

83 In some legal systems a limited property right can also be derived from another limited property right. See, e.g., Gretton 2007, p. 832, 840-841.

84 It is in this respect that the decision of the *Cour de cassation* in *Caquelard* has given rise to a discussion on the existence of a *numerus clausus* in French law. See Chapter 3; 3. Other Property Rights, and 5. A *Numerus Clausus* in French Property Law?

85 In the same sense, see Jansen 2006, p. 314-318.

86 Of course, choosing different terminology does not make the analysis objective or the terminology neutral. However, using a set of terminology that is not used by the four legal system at hand enables comparison on a different, possibly higher abstract lever, thus enabling to see similarities that have until now been hidden under the level of system-specific terminology.

On the other hand, we have seen that the civil law systems share a common Roman-law basis. As a result of this common basis, civil law systems share similar terminology. A good example is the use of the term ownership, which the civil law systems all use.[87] However, the apparent differences between civil law and common law, and the need to find a language in which both of these traditions can be expressed might justify the use of a novel terminology.

In civil law systems, the most extensive right a person may have in an object is the right of ownership. The right of ownership entitles the owner to exclude everyone from his object, to use it, enjoy it and, when he wants to, to transfer the right to someone else.[88] Moreover, from the right of ownership, limited property rights can be derived, which, in civil law systems, share common names, like usufruct, servitude, pledge and hypothec.

In common law systems, the terminology used is different. Although the term ownership is also used in English law, an immediate caveat is required. 'Ownership' in English law is that right which grants the best right of possession, whether exclusive possession forever, in the case of fee simple in land, or possession forever, in the case of title to a chattel. Especially when it comes to personal property law, the relativity of title, which refers to the possibility that certain rights of possession are stronger than other rights of possession, means that the use of the word ownership can be, and usually is, confusing.

In English law the term 'ownership' is used as a general word denoting entitlement as well. Although the verb 'to own' a property right is avoided by making use of the verb 'to hold', the phrase 'owning a fee simple' is not uncommon.[89] Ownership in this sense is used as a generic word for entitlement, to whatever extent. Therefore, in trust relations, legal ownership and equitable ownership are synonyms for legal interest and equitable interest, or for a right at law and a right in equity. However, in content these rights at law and in equity are very different from the right of ownership in civil law systems.[90]

The differences between civil law and common law in respect of terminology create difficulties for the comparison between these legal systems.[91] However, the existence of different terminology should not mislead us into emphasising the differences between the civil law and common law systems. The fact that ownership of land and fee simple tenure of land have different names does not immediately result in a different content between these two rights. The same could be said, for instance, of servitudes and easements.

In order to avoid the impression that property rights in civil law systems and common law systems are different, and in order to avoid the traditional assumption that difference in terminology is a clear sign of different content, a set of system-neutral terminology should be used. Describing the legal systems in such neutral

87 In the same sense see Reid 1997b, p. 228.

88 This is the classical division into *usus, fructus* and *abusus*.

89 Burn & Cartwright 2006, p. 27-28, 34, Gray & Gray 2005, p. 590 (fee simple ownership). The technically correct statement would be holding a fee simple.

90 On trust law, see Chapter 6; 1.5. Trust Law.

91 Trying to overcome such difficulties see, e.g., Gordley 2006, p. 46-65.

terminology will focus the discussion on the content of property rights and the system in which they function, as opposed to differences between these rights and systems just because they bear different names.

In his article on ownership and things capable of ownership, Gretton provides valuable neutral terminology with which to analyse property law systems.[92] He defines property rights in terms of primary rights and limited real rights.[93] Primary rights are those rights that give persons the most extensive entitlement to an object a legal system can provide.[94] As a criterion, therefore, primary rights are the rights that last for the longest duration of time a legal system can provide.[95] When a primary right is temporarily limited by the existence of another property right, the right remains a primary right, in particular because the limitation will be temporary and the primary right will eventually become full and unburdened once more. In this sense, Honoré's residuary character of ownership may be added to Gretton's characteristics of primary rights, although Gretton himself observes that the residuary character is not exclusive to ownership, but belongs to any right from which a limited real right is created.[96]

The term limited real right, however, is a typical civil law term to denote those property rights that are formed from the primary right.[97] A more neutral term could be used in this respect also. Limited real rights are less extensive in content than primary rights and may be termed 'lesser rights'.[98] Lesser rights are those rights that are derived from the primary right. The relation between primary and lesser rights is such that the primary right functions as a mother right on which the lesser right, as a 'daughter right', is modelled.[99] Traditionally, the characteristics of primary rights are defined in terms of prerogatives of the holder of that right. These include the rights to use and enjoy and to dispose of objects.

Corresponding to this division, the lesser rights may be divided into two major groups. The first group contains the rights that are modelled after the right to use and enjoy objects that is enjoyed by holders of primary rights. The second group contains rights that focus on the right of disposal over objects that is enjoyed by the holders of primary rights. The right to dispose of objects can be transferred to another party who, under certain conditions, will be allowed to exercise this right, which will usually in the end also deprive the holder of the primary right of his

92 Gretton 2007, p. 802.

93 Gretton 2007, p. 831-832, 834-835.

94 However, the term primary right has also been used in a different context, which is not meant here. See Pretto 2002, p. 65 *et seq.*

95 Struycken uses the term complete (*volledig*) right to denote primary rights in this respect. See Struycken 2007, p. 237-240.

96 Honoré 1961, p. 126-128, Gretton 2007, p. 835. In this respect there is an interesting distinction in Spanish property law, where the term 'limits' is reserved for limits contained in the right of ownership, and the term 'limitations' for those limits placed upon, or imposed on, property rights. See Sáez 2006, p. 281-283.

97 On this concept of limited real right in a common law jurisdiction, see Hohfeld 1917, p. 710 *et seq.*

98 In the same sense, see Honoré 1961, p. 124.

99 Gretton 2007, p. 834-835.

right to use and enjoy the object. This second group comprises security property rights.

A third group of rights, that does not correspond to the division of primary rights into use, enjoyment and disposal, should also be recognised. This group of rights comprises rights that are temporary in nature, existing in anticipation of the lesser right of the first two groups to come into existence, or anticipating the conveyance of a primary right. This third group of rights is modelled on a right to use or enjoy, but contrary to the other lesser rights, not to the right to use and enjoy of the primary right that already exists, but the right to use and enjoy of the lesser right or the primary right they are anticipating.[100]

2.2. *Of Ways to Create a Lesser Property Right*

In Gretton's division, primary rights function as a mother right of what should be named lesser property rights.[101] He arrives at this conclusion by reference to German doctrine on the general concepts of private law, but emphasises that he thinks this theory is of European importance.[102] The analysis in this Chapter will illustrate that all of these legal systems follow this model of 'mother' and 'daughter' rights. Before exploring the content of primary and lesser rights it might be useful to see in which ways a primary right can be a mother right.

Comparative analysis of the civil law systems of France, Germany and the Netherlands shows two methods.[103] First, the most visible method is used in French law, where lesser rights are considered a *démembrement* of the primary right, which is the right of ownership. *Démembrement* is a term that does not translate well into English but could be described as subtraction or taking away part of something whole and complete.[104] In this method, a lesser right is created by taking parts of the right of ownership, the primary right, and by transferring these parts to another party. In the hands of the other party these parts of the right of ownership form a new property right, a lesser property right, which will burden the right of ownership from which it is derived.[105] For the duration of the existence of the lesser right, the primary right will not be full and complete; in French law the right of owner-

100 In case of a normal lesser right, the content of that right is modelled after the rights and powers of the primary right from which it is derived. In case of these 'anticipatory rights' or lesser rights used to acquire a certain legal position, the content of the right is modelled on the right the holder of the anticipatory right is about the acquire. See below; 2.6. Lesser Rights used to Acquire a Certain Legal Position (Anticipatory Rights).

101 See Gretton 2007, p. 838-839.

102 Gretton 2007, p. 803-804, 838, 851. On the German doctrine, see Larentz 1989, p. 38-40.

103 Struycken also comes to a division in two methods that he calls *aftrekking*, or subtraction, and *afspiegeling*, or mirroring. See Struycken 2007, p. 361-363.

104 The general English term dismemberment, although a literal translation, should be avoided as it generally calls into recollection the losing of body parts and not an abstract concept as taking parts from another abstract entity, such as a primary right. South African law also follows this method under the name subtraction from the *dominium*, see below; 3.8. A Legal System without a *Numerus Clausus*: South African Law. See also Struycken 2007, p. 361-363.

105 See Chapter 3; 3. Other Property Rights.

ship is known as nude or bare ownership.[106] The method of *démembrement* is accompanied by a division of the primary right, the right of ownership, into three different parts, which in their turn can each form the content of a lesser property right. These three parts are the right to use, the right to enjoy and the right of disposal.[107] Consequently, a lesser property right may exist out of any of these rights of the owner or a combination of them.[108]

This method of creating lesser property rights is not only applied in French law, but is followed by Dutch law, and also English law. In Dutch law, the Civil Code explicitly states that a lesser property right, a limited property right in Dutch legal terminology, is derived from a more comprehensive right.[109] Furthermore, the general distinction of the elements of the primary right, the right of ownership, into rights to use and enjoy, and of disposal, is also followed. Dutch law also uses the term nude or bare ownership to denote the primary right when a lesser property right is created.

English law follows this same method when it comes to creating lesser property rights at common law. When a holder of an estate in fee simple grants a term of years absolute to another party, he conveys part of his rights to the tenant. The tenant will now enjoy some of the rights that previously belonged to the holder in fee simple.[110] The holder in fee simple will still hold the fee simple but its content will be less. English law uses a specific term for the right granted to the holder in fee simple remaining after the lease, the reversion. The reversion itself is a right that the holder of an estate in fee simple may grant as a remainder to a third party.[111]

The method of *démembrement* creates certain difficulties with the existence of lesser rights. To start with, legal systems have difficulties explaining how the holder of a lesser right may enjoy a right that the holder of the primary right is still entitled to enjoy as well. For example, when a right of servitude is created, the holder of this lesser right may walk over the owner's land, but the existence of the right does not necessarily deprive the owner, the holder of the primary right, of his right to walk over his own land as well. In order to solve this, the legal systems answer that the transfer of rights to use and enjoy that form the right of servitude is not necessarily a transfer of all the rights to use and enjoy of the owner.[112]

106 See Grotius who considered these rights *gebreckelicke eigendom*, De Groot 1926, II.3.11, p. 34.

107 Or the classic terms *usus, fructus* and *abusus*.

108 The use of the method of *démembrement* by a legal system does not necessarily result in a *numerus clausus* of property rights. However, French, Dutch law and English law, which follow this method, do recognise a *numerus clausus* and have therefore made a choice for private parties in what way they may combine these elements. In other words, the menu for private parties has been set; it is build out of these three different ingredients.

109 Art. 3:8 BW. See Chapter 5; 3. Other Property Rights. However, also in Dutch law, most likely under influence from German Pandectist writers of the nineteenth century, another model has been defended in which property rights do not comprise parts of the primary right from which they are derived. See Diephuis 1880, p. 474, Land 1901, p. 7, Rank-Berenschot 1992, p. 105-107.

110 See Chapter 6; 2.2. Lease of Land.

111 See Chapter 6; 1.1. Terminology.

112 Asser, Mijnsen, De Haan & Van Dam 2006, p. 10-11.

Furthermore, as a consequence of the way in which lesser rights are created, when the lesser right and the primary right fall into the same hands, the two rights will merge and the lesser right will no longer exist. The reason for this is that the lesser right can only exist because certain rights of the holder of the primary right are temporarily in the hands of another person. When the rights return to the holder of the primary right, these rights merge with the rights that remained, and it can no longer be established which rights belonged to the primary right, and which to the lesser right. The same will also apply when the holder of the lesser right acquires the primary right.

The way in which lesser property rights cease to exist is recognised in the civil law systems of France and the Netherlands.[113] Although the method of *démembrement* is primarily a civil law method it can be applied to English common law as well. Evidence for this may be taken from the surrender of a lease. When a lease is surrendered and the landlord agrees, the lease will merge with the landlord's reversion and cease to exist.[114] The same will happen when the lease and the reversion fall into the same hands.[115]

Whether this method is also followed in German law is not entirely clear. In German law, a primary right and a lesser right can exist at the same time in the hands of the same person.[116] In other words, the holder of a primary right may create a lesser property right on his own behalf on his own object. Under the method of *démembrement* the creation of a lesser property right without a transfer of rights to another person is theoretically not possible. In this respect it seems that German law cannot adhere to this method.

The drafters of the German Civil Code in fact offered another solution in the method of limitation.[117] Limitation as opposed to *démembrement* does not require a transfer of rights from the primary to the lesser right, but involves the creation of additional rights, which are modelled after the content of the primary right. Under this method, the primary right remains full and complete. Its exercise will be limited by the existence of a lesser right, but not because certain rights have been taken out of the primary right.[118]

This method of limitation seems also to be followed by English law when it comes to the creation of lesser rights in equity. When, in English law, a right is created in equity, that right is additional to the right that already exists at common law. This is best observed in the case of trusts, on which Lord Browne-Wilkinson stated in *Westdeutsche Landesbank Girozentrale v Islington LBC* that when a property right grants the full right of use and enjoyment to a person at common law, no equitable

113 In the Netherlands there is even a special provision in the Civil Code that deals with this method of destruction of property rights: Art. 3:81(2)(e) BW.

114 Swadling 2007, p. 393.

115 Swadling 2007, p. 393.

116 See § 889 BGB.

117 See Chapter 4; 3. Other Property Rights.

118 See, in this respect, Thibaut who also does not consider lesser rights as parts of the primary right. See Thibaut 1817a, p. 62, Thibaut 1817b, p. 86-87, 91, 92-93. I owe gratitude to André van der Walt for drawing my attention to this and the contrast with Grotius' *gebreckelicke eigendom*.

right exists.[119] Instead, when a trust is created, a new additional right in equity comes into existence on behalf of the beneficiary that burdens the right of the trustee at common law. This reasoning holds for trusts, but there is no reason why it could not be applied to other property rights in equity.

However, where in English law the limitations method continues to apply for rights in equity, modern German property law literature writes in terms of *démembrement* as opposed to the traditional method of limitation.[120] It seems, therefore, that German doctrine might be moving away from its limitations theory in favour of the *démembrement* approach. However, it is difficult to explain how a lesser property right and the primary property right, from which the lesser right was formed, can exist at the same time with the same right holder.[121]

In German law especially the possibility for a right-holder of a primary right to create a lesser property right in respect of his own immovable object is recognised and has drawn the attention of the European legislators.[122] In fact, this method of creation, the creation of an *Eigentümergrundschuld*, is a model for developments on a European level towards a Euro-mortgage, a European right of hypothec.[123]

The method by which a lesser property right is created is of relevance to the *numerus clausus* as it determines the boundaries of the content of lesser property rights. However, it does not automatically result in a *numerus clausus* of property rights.[124] In a *démembrement* system, the lesser property right can never have a different content than the primary right from which it is derived.[125] In a limitation system, which traditionally requires the property right to be modelled after the primary right, but does not take away rights of the right-holder of a primary right, this is in principle the same.

Modelling an additional right as opposed to using an already existing part of a primary right creates possibilities to deviate from the rights of the holder of the primary right. These possibilities are twofold. It could be argued that, because a primary right does not contain a positive duty, no positive duty can be part of a lesser right that is derived from that primary right.[126] A system that models additional

119 *Westdeutsche Landesbank Girozentrale v Islington LBC* [1996] AC 669, HL, at 706 *per* Lord Browne-Wilkinson. Swadling 2007, p. 271-272. See Chapter 6; 1.5. Trust Law.

120 For examples see Chapter 4; 3. Other Property Rights.

121 One explanation is offered through the *Doppelwirkung* under which a person can hold property rights in two capacities; once as holder of the primary right, and once as holder of a lesser rights. See Kipp 1911, p. 211 *et seq.* On other explanations, see Chapter 4; 3. Other Property Rights.

122 § 889 BGB.

123 Green Paper Mortgage Credit in the EU COM(2005) 327. See also White Paper on Mortgage Credit Markets COM(2007) 807 final, where the right of Euro-mortgage has disappeared from the proposals of the European Commission. More about these developments in Chapter 8; 2.1.3. European Commission Initiatives for Future Legislation.

124 South African law with its subtraction from *dominium* test is held not to recognise a *numerus clausus*, but still follows the method of *démembrement* (subtraction) to decide which rights are property rights. See, *inter alia*, De Waal 2004, P. 83 *et seq.*

125 Struycken calls this the subtraction principle that limits the content of lesser rights to negative duties. See Struycken 2007, p. 404-405.

126 Struycken 2007, p. 404-405.

rights on the content of primary rights, however, is not entirely restricted to limiting the content of lesser rights to negative duties. Of course, systems adhering to a limitation method are very cautious about recognising these positive burdens. Secondly, legal systems following the limitations method have taken a more lenient approach to the recognition of additional property rights, best seen in the case of anticipatory rights. In these systems, German and English, anticipatory property rights are more developed than in French and Dutch law, which follow a *démembrement* method of creation. Systems adhering to a limitations model award proprietary status to an expectation right, because the recognition of property rights does not require these systems to express the content of a property right in terms of powers of the primary right. Under a liberal interpretation of the requirement to model the lesser right on the content of a primary right, expectation rights have been given a place as a third category of lesser rights. For now, legal systems adhering to the *démembrement* method have not taken this step.[127]

2.3. *Primary Property Rights*

The analysis of property law as a system of primary rights and lesser rights can be applied to the Roman system of property law. Although Roman law did not work with property rights as such, the primary entitlement to an object, *dominium*, was that right protected with the *rei vindicatio*, enabling an owner to get his object back if it had been taken or interfered with.[128] Lesser rights, such as servitudes, were modelled on the powers of the *dominus* and were protected with the respective action.

This analysis also holds true for the modern legal systems, the civil law systems, with their Roman law basis, as well as the English common law. In civil law systems, like in Roman law, there is only one primary right - the right of ownership. Ownership, with its paramount entitlement to an object, forms the foundation for the law of property in French, German and Dutch law. The right of ownership entitles its holder to do with an object what he wants, as long as this is not contrary to law or public order. When a lesser right is created, the right of ownership, sometimes referred to as bare or nude ownership, remains into existence and will return to its full and unburdened scale when the lesser right ceases to exist.

In English law this analysis is more difficult to apply. Traditionally English law does not recognise a right of ownership in the civil law sense, either in land law or in personal property law. Instead, as a starting point English law uses the right to possession. In English property law, the person with the stronger right to possession will succeed against the person challenging his right.[129] This concept is known

127 See below; 2.6. Lesser Rights used to Acquire a Certain Legal Position (Anticipatory Rights).

128 See Chapter 2; 2.3. Ownership.

129 Interesting in this respect are the land law reforms in Ireland, that, like English law, knows a feudal system of land holding. See Land and Conveyancing Reform Bill 2006. See also the preparing report of the Irish Law Reform Commission No. LRC 70-2003 to be found at <http://www.lawreform.ie>.

as relativity of title, and in this sense English property law takes its viewpoint from procedural law.[130]

However, the exercise of searching for the best right of possession results in two property rights, one for land law and one for personal property law. In land law the person with the best right is the holder of an estate in fee simple. The holder in fee simple is entitled to exclusive possession of land forever.[131] Other rights in respect of land also give a right to possession, but never one as strong a right as fee simple. One exception to this might be the *demesne* title of the Crown, which owns all land.[132] Allodial land, which is land that is not subjected to the feudal system of landholding, is therefore subject to its own primary title. However, for the system of land law and the search for primary rights that can be used by private parties, this is of less relevance. In personal property law, a right to possession forever is also recognised. Title to a chattel grants its holder possession forever. Also here, other rights exist which give right to possession, but these are never as strong as a title to a chattel.

The division of English law into land law and personal property law therefore has consequences for the recognition of a primary right. In fact, technically there must be two primary rights, one corresponding to each area of property law.[133] However, the difference between the two primary rights, fee simple to land and title to chattels, the last including claims, should not be overstated. Both rights entitle the holder to exclusive possession for an unlimited period and are, like the right of ownership in civil law systems, the paramount entitlement a person can have in an object.

Granting the paramount entitlement to the holder, primary rights are mostly intended to provide use and enjoyment. The holder of a primary right is therefore entitled to use and enjoy an object to the exclusion of everyone else. By its nature, as this analysis shows, there can only be one primary right in a legal system. In that sense there is no competition between holders of primary rights and usually, if at all, the holder of a primary right will compete with a holder of a lesser property right.

A primary right can also be used for different purposes than for use and enjoyment. As the right is the most important property right, it is interesting for banks and other financers to use it for security purposes. In French, German, Dutch and English law, primary rights can be used for security purposes in two ways.

First, a conveyance of a primary right can be postponed until a certain obligation has been fulfilled, usually the payment of a purchase price. This postponement

130 See Chapter 6; 1.1. Terminology.

131 Theoretically, the Crown holds all land and therefore the *demesne*-title of the Crown should be mentioned. However, as this right can only be held by the Crown and not by a private person it is functionally outside the area of property law. See Lawson and Rudden 2002, p. 78. Sparkes states on this matter: 'It is much easier to bring together the English and civilian systems than would have been the case with the pre-1925 common law (that is to say Irish and American Systems). … whereas the 1925 scheme for the undivided freehold estate is quite close to the civilian conception of absolute *propriété* or *Eigentum*'.

132 Burn & Cartwright 2006, p. 955-956, Lawson and Rudden 2002, p. 78.

133 This is, for sake of clarity, excluding the *demesne*-title of the Crown.

can be achieved by making a condition of suspension in the contract that underlies the conveyance of the primary right, or by making the conveyance itself under condition of suspension. As a result a strong security right is created. Civil law systems speak of reservation of ownership, and common law systems of retention of title.[134]

The reservation or retention of a primary right provides the holder reserving or retaining the right with the most powerful security right. Although the buyer of the object will usually already have the right to use and enjoy the object, he has not yet received the primary right and will usually only have a personal right against the holder of primary right.[135] When the buyer does not perform his obligation, the seller remains the holder of the primary right.

A second method is using the primary right as security by conveying it under resolutive condition to another pending the performance of a certain obligation. In contrast to the transfer under suspensive condition, this conveyance takes immediate effect, but only until the obligation is performed. Such a conveyance, modelled on the Roman rule *fiducia cum creditore*, is also used in all legal systems.[136] In civil law systems it is known as a transfer of ownership for security purposes. It includes a transfer of ownership with an additional contract, called a security agreement, in which the rights of the transferee are limited. These limitations are not only contractual but have some property effects, through the working of the law on trust-like devices, *Treuhand* and *fiducie*. In many situations a third party dealing with the transferee with knowledge of the additional contract, the security agreement, will be bound by the terms of the agreement on acquiring the object which was transferred for security purposes.[137] In Dutch law, a transfer of ownership for security purposes is also recognised, but only if the full right of ownership is transferred, leaving the transferor relatively unprotected with only personal rights.[138] There are also no trust-like devices, as in the common law, to strengthen the position of the transferor. The primary right for security purposes is therefore not used as much as in other civil law systems.

English law also recognises a conveyance of a primary right for security purposes in the form of a mortgage. However, the Law of Property Act 1925 abolished this method in land law. In personal property law the creation of a mortgage remains possible through a transfer of the primary right. Although for civil lawyers the use of the term mortgage invokes the lesser right for security, in particular hypothec, a mortgage was created when a property right, including a primary right, was conveyed to secure the performance of a certain obligation.[139] In civil law sys-

134 See Chapter 3; 2.3. Security Ownership; Chapter 4; 2.5. Security Ownership, Chapter 6; 2.3. Security Ownership, and Chapter 6; 3.1. Title / Ownership.

135 German law provides the exception where the buyer under reservation of ownership is awarded an *Anwartschaftsrecht*. See Chapter 4; 3.4. Expectation Rights.

136 However, Dutch law prohibits the most common form of transfer of ownership for security purposes in Art. 3:84(3) BW. See Chapter 5; 2.3. Security Ownership.

137 Art. 2023 CC, Dupichot 2007, p. 5-8.

138 Struycken 2007, p. 504-508. See Chapter 5; 2.3. Security Ownership.

139 See Chapter 6; 2.9. Mortgage of Land and Equity of Redemption.

tems, a right of hypothec is deliberately used to allow a private person to keep his house, while the bank will have a right to sell the house in case of non-payment of the loan the right of hypothec secures. Also in English law the creation of a mortgage gave rise to the recognition of a property right for the former holder of the house, the equity of redemption. Since 1926, the mortgage in English law is, like in civil law systems, created through a lesser right, namely a charge by deed by way of legal mortgage.[140]

A third way, next to usage and security, in which primary rights are used, is through co-entitlement. By sharing the primary right between several parties under special provisions, the legal systems enable parties to have exclusive rights to use and enjoy as well as to dispose of specific parts of a piece of land, usually of a building in the form of an apartment. The effect, however, of such 'apartment ownership' is that the normal rules on the primary right hardly apply anymore and are qualified through the existence of other rights. In that sense effectively a lesser right is created that will be dealt with later. However, a few remarks in respect to the primary right should be made here.[141]

A remarkable resemblance between the systems exists. Although some legal systems provide a specific right, whether a primary or a lesser right, and some solve apartment rights through a deviation of the rules on the primary right, each solution consists of three elements; a right to exclusive use and enjoyment of a certain space, a right to common use and enjoyment of certain joint space, and compulsory membership of an association of 'co-owners'. Even when a lesser right is created, it still contains these three elements, making the lesser right an atypical property right.[142]

2.4. *Lesser Rights to Use*

Most of the property rights that grant a right to use in French, German, Dutch and English law are derived from the Roman category of servitudes, but exceptions do exist. The lesser rights to use are based on the right to use and enjoy the object of the holder of the primary right, whether exclusively or not.[143] The lesser right is categorised depending on its content. In civil law systems there is a strong division between rights to use for a limited period of time, usually a person's life, and rights granted forever. The property rights to use from English law can also fit into this division.

140 See Chapter 6; 2.9. Mortgage of Land and Equity of Redemption.

141 The rest of apartment ownership is dealt with below in 2.4. Lesser Rights to Use.

142 In Dutch law this is also recognised by the statement in the Asser handbook that an apartment right is a property right but not a limited property right (*zakelijk recht, geen beperkt recht*). See Asser, Van Dam & Mijnsen 2002, Nos. 347, 348, p. 371-372. In comparative law, the work of Van der Merwe offers invaluable information on the law on apartments. See Van der Merwe 1994.

143 Of course, also depending on the method of creation, on the actual parts of the primary right or on rights modelled after the content of the primary right. See above; 2.2. Of Ways to Create a Lesser Property Right.

2.4.1. Lesser Rights to Use for a Limited Period of Time

The first right to use for a limited period of time is a right of usufruct, recognised in all civil law systems but, as such, unknown to modern English law. Before the introduction of the Law of Property Act 1925 a holder of a fee simple could grant a life estate to another person. After 1925, and until 1996, a holder of a fee simple could do the same, but only in equity.[144] If, before 1925, the holder of the fee simple did this, he would carve out parts of his rights and grant those rights as an estate at common law to another person. This method of creation makes the life estate a lesser right. The life estate was a fully-fledged property right that could even be assigned to another person. When the holder of the life estate assigned his estate to another person, the estate remained in existence, but would be known as an estate *pur autre vie*, always remaining connected to the life of the person to whom the right was granted. The life estate, whether *pur autre vie* or not, gave exclusive possession to its holder, thus depriving the holder of the estate in fee simple completely of his right to use, but always for a limited period of time.

In the other estate at common law, the term of years absolute, the exclusive possession of land is also given to another person for a limited duration of time.[145] The holder of the fee simple cannot use his land for the duration of the lease. However, the limited duration of a lease should be looked at with care, as a lease for a million years is also a valid lease.[146] When a lease is created, the lesser right of lease, which remains a lesser right as it is derived from the primary fee simple right, achieves almost the status of a primary right. The holder of such a long lease will have exclusive possession as well as the possibility to assign the lease to another person or make it subject to another lesser right. The reversion of the lease, which is the right that eventually entitles the holder of the fee simple to enjoy the object once more, will be practically worthless.

In civil law also the creation of a right of usufruct may be combined with the possibility to assign the usufruct.[147] When the right of usufruct was created for the duration of its holder's life, and the holder assigns the property right to another person, the legal effects are usually the same as in English law; the existence of the right of usufruct remains connected to the life of the person on whose behalf the right was created.[148]

The right of usufruct in civil law systems is influenced by the increasing importance of contract law. The owner and the holder of the right of usufruct may shape their relation in any way they wish through an agreement, staying within the

144 Swadling 2007, p. 234. See Chapter 6; 2. Property Rights in Land.

145 Swadling 2007, p. 236, 238.

146 See Swadling 2007, p. 241-242.

147 In German law the starting point is that a right of usufruct cannot be assigned. When it is created for the benefit of a legal person, this rule can be lifted. See § 1059 BGB, § 1061 BGB and § 1059a, BGB, Art. 595 CC, Terré & Simler 1998, p. 616-617, Art. 3:223 BW, Asser, Van Dam & Mijnsen 2002, p. 329-330.

148 In French law there is specific case law on this point, see *Cass.* 3e civ. 26 January 1972, D. 1975, p. 22, JCP 1972, éd. G, II, 17104.

boundaries of the provisions on usufruct.[149] This contractual freedom allows parties to shift some additional rights of the owner to the holder of the usufruct, making the usufruct into an effective management device. An example of this is the usufruct on shares in a company. In a normal situation, the owner will profit from an increase in value of the shares, but the holder of the right of usufruct will have the voting rights and will be entitled to the dividend the shares produce. In this way the owner of the shares does not need to bother with administration and merely profits from the arrangement. By agreement the parties may give content to the standard of a good usufructuary by imposing a duty to invest and re-invest the shares on the right holder. Shares leaving the usufruct will be freed from the property right, but will be substituted with the new shares or money received in exchange for them.[150] It is this way of using rights of usufruct that shifts the similarities of the right of usufruct away from a right of lease, and in the direction of the law of trusts.[151]

Other civil law property rights also resemble leases in English law. These are the rights of *emphyteusis* and *superficies*. These two property rights, already known in Roman law, were not part of the law of property as introduced by the Civil Codes in each legal system. In French law, these rights were not mentioned by the Civil Code at all, but survived and were developed through case law before the legislature intervened.[152] Consequently, the old Dutch Civil Code, which was heavily based on the French Civil Code, did not mention these rights either. In the Netherlands a special law applied.[153] In German law, the right of *emphyteusis* is not recognised at all because of its connotation of the feudal system, and the right of *superficies* was introduced by special legislation.[154]

The right of *emphyteusis* grants exclusive use of a piece of land for a long time, in Dutch law even potentially forever.[155] However, traditionally, as can be seen in French law, the duration of the right of *emphyteusis* is limited to ninety-nine years. The right of *superficies* grants a right of ownership of a building to its holder, while the right of ownership of the land remains with the original owner. This property right is atypical because it awards the holder of the right a right of ownership by breaking with the rule of *superficies solo cedit*, that what is on the land follows the land.[156] Depending on the agreement between the parties that gives rise to the creation of the right of *superficies*, the right may be perpetual in nature. However, like the right of *emphyteusis*, traditionally the right of *superficies* is limited to ninety-nine years.[157]

Although these rights are usually considered together, they differ in content. A right of *emphyteusis* grants an exclusive right to use land, but does not grant a right

149 As a result of the *Typenzwang* of the *numerus clausus* of property rights.
150 Bos 2005, p. 31-39.
151 See Bos 2005, p. 176 *et seq*.
152 See Chapter 3; 3.3. *Superficies*, and 3.4. *Emphyteusis*.
153 See Chapter 5; 3.3. *Emphyteusis*, and 3.4. *Superficies*.
154 See Chapter 4; 3.4. *Superficies*.
155 The right of *Emphyteusis* is not recognised in German law.
156 See Chapter 2; 2.4. Other Property Rights.
157 See Chapter 3; 3.3. *Superficies*.

of ownership of buildings on that land. In order for the holder of a property right to acquire ownership of buildings on a piece of land, a right of *superficies* is needed. It is therefore not uncommon for both rights to be created together. In French law, with its consensual system of transfer, and therefore also of creation, an agreement is sufficient to give rise to the creation of a property right, even on land.[158] Under that system of creation, a right of *superficies* may, for instance, come into existence as part of an agreement creating a lease, a personal right in French law, or a right of *emphyteusis*.

With these special characteristics, the rights of *emphyteusis* and *superficies* are situated between rights granted for a limited period of time and those granted forever. Nevertheless, they are recognised as typical lesser property rights in civil law, although a right of *emphyteusis* very much resembles an English term of years absolute. Both give the holder the right to use land for a limited period of time. The right of *superficies* does not really have an equivalent in English law. With the introduction of the commonhold, it becomes possible to separate entitlement to land from the entitlement to part of a building.[159] However, commonhold schemes more resemble apartment rights than they resemble the right of *superficies*.[160]

2.4.2. Lesser Rights to Use for an Unlimited Period of Time

The second type of lesser rights that entitle the holder to the use of an object are rights that are usually granted for an unlimited period of time. In turn for their longer duration, these rights are less extensive in content. Civil law systems call them servitudes, English law easements.[161] The criteria used to create these rights are derived from Roman law and comprise, in all cases, the requirement of two pieces of land, with two different persons holding a right in those pieces of land, the description of a burden on one of the pieces of land known as the servient tenement and, thus, constituting a right in respect of the other piece of land known as the dominant tenement, and, last, the requirement that the burden that is imposed on the servient land must not result in a positive duty for the holder of the servient tenement. Furthermore, the burden that is imposed should benefit the land and not the owner himself, except in Dutch law, where this requirement was abolished in 1992 when the relevant part of the new Civil Code entered into force. These requirements are Roman in nature and apply in all civil law systems, but they have also been adopted in English law by the Court of Appeal in *Re Ellenborough Park*. Therefore, they also apply to rights of easement.[162]

What exactly comprises the burden imposed by the servitude or easement depends on the agreement that the parties made. Especially in German doctrine, a

158 Van Vliet 2000, p. 73-74.

159 Commonhold and Leasehold Reform Act 2002. See Chapter 6; 2.1. Fee Simple.

160 On entitlement to apartments see below; 2.4.3. Lesser Rights to Use of an Apartment.

161 Although also in civil law, especially in comparative law the term easements are also used for servitudes. See, e.g., Sagaert 2004b, p. 51.

162 *Re Ellenborough Park. Re Davies (deceased). Powell and Others v Maddison and Another* [1956] Ch 131, CA.

threefold distinction has been developed that provides a useful analysis of the law on servitudes.[163] First, there are servitudes or easements that entitle the holder of the dominant tenement to do something on the land of the holder of the servient tenement.[164] Secondly, there are servitudes or easements that impose a burden on the holder of the servient land to refrain from doing something on his land.[165] Thirdly, there are servitudes or easements that impose a burden on the holder of the servient land not to exercise some of the rights he has, as holder of a primary right, against the holder of the dominant land.[166] Usually, this third type of servitude or easement concerns the actions or remedies the holder of the primary right in respect of the servient tenement has to protect his right. For example, the servitude or easement may concern the right to claim removal of a fence that has been placed on the servient land. When there is indeed a fence on the servient land, the servitude or easement may contain the duty for the holder of the primary right in respect of that land, the servient tenement, to refrain from initiating an action for removal against the holder of the primary right of the dominant tenement.

Rights of servitudes or easement are special lesser property rights in the sense that the parties creating the right are free to give content to their relation as long as they stay within the general criteria of servitudes or easements mentioned above.[167] The right that is created is held by two parties, one whose land benefits and one whose land is burdened. Therefore, there are two parties to this property right, one who holds the right, one who holds the duty. These parties are not necessarily both holders of a primary right in respect of the land on which the right of servitude or easement was created. Other lesser property rights are created between a holder of a primary right and a holder of a lesser right. They can also affect parties other than the holder of a primary right, but this is because these rights must be respected.

The freedom that the parties enjoy to provide content to their right of servitude means that servitudes or easements are rights that are very suitable to be adapted to modern conditions. English law has recognised this in particular. In the words of Lord St Leonards LC:

> 'The category of servitudes and easements must alter and expand with the changes that take place in the circumstances of mankind'.[168]

When it comes to developments in servitude or easement law, it is especially the second type of servitude or easement, the right imposing the duty to refrain from doing something, which has developed. In French and German law, a right of servitude may be used to restrict the holder of the servient tenement from conducting a

163 See, e.g., De Waal 1995, p. 193 *et seq.*

164 German doctrine names these types *Benutzungsdienstbarkeiten*, Baur, Baur & Stürner 1999, p. 366, Staudinger et al. 2002, p. 257 *et seq.*

165 German doctrine names these types *Unterlassungsdienstbarkeiten*, Baur, Baur & Stürner 1999, p. 366, Staudinger et al. 2002, p. 262.

166 See Baur, Baur & Stürner 1999, p. 369, Staudinger et al. 2002, p. 272 *et seq.*

167 Again, this is due to the *Typenzwang* of the *numerus clausus* of property rights.

168 *Dyce v Lady Hay* (1852) (1 Macq 305), per Lord St. Leonards LC, Burn & Cartwright 2006, p. 595.

certain business activity on his premises. However, these non-competition servitudes are used in a different way in both systems. Dutch law and English law do not allow these servitudes or easements.

In French law the non-competition servitude is used to restrict the use of a piece of land when the neighbouring piece of land is used in the same way. For example, if a certain business, such as a supermarket, is established on the dominant tenement, the holder of the servient tenement may be under a restriction not to open a similar business on his land.[169]

In German law, the non-competition servitude is used to 'secure' the performance of an obligation arising from a contract.[170] There, the non-competition clause will stipulate that a certain business activity cannot be employed on the land, when in reality there already is such a business activity, or there will be in the near future. For example, a clause will state that no petrol station can operate on the land, when in reality a petrol station is there already. Through contract law the parties will enter into a contract in which the holder of the dominant tenement promises not to invoke the servitude as long as the holder of the servient tenement fulfils the terms of the contract. To follow the example, as long as the holder of the servient tenement buys the petrol for his petrol station from the holder of the dominant tenement, a petrol company, the petrol company will not invoke the servitude.

This specific use of the non-competition servitude creates a new type of servitude, in German known as *Sicherungsdienstbarkeit*, which translates into English as security-servitude.[171] Technically, the security-servitude falls within the second category of servitudes mentioned above, but by making maximum use of the party autonomy the law on servitude allows, parties can almost achieve the creation of a new property right that, contrary to the requirement for servitudes and easements, imposes a positive duty, the performance of the contract, on the right holder of the servient tenement. In any case, by making optimal use of contract law, the parties avoid the provisions on servitudes that restrict these rights to negative duties.[172]

Although this development has not taken place in other legal systems, it is not inconceivable that in these systems also parties may attempt to achieve similar results. The use of contract law, not only to give form and content to property rights, but also the use of contract law in addition to property law, is a concept which is much more developed in German law in comparison with other legal systems. More will be said on this below.[173]

Furthermore, several legal systems recognise other types of servitudes that do not fully fit in this main division. First, German law recognises a right of servitude

169 See Chapter 3; 3.1. Real Servitude.

170 See Chapter 4; 3.1. Real Servitude, and 3.2. Personal Servitudes.

171 See also De Waal 1995, p. 201-207.

172 And therefore work around the *Typenzwang* of the *numerus clausus* of property rights. Note that in English law generally the term negative easement is used for a right of easement that, in civil law terms, imposes a positive duty. The reason for this difference is the different perspective that a legal system takes on rights of servitude or easement. Civil law systems look at the servient land, whereas English law looks at the dominant land. On this difference see Chapter 6; 2.3. Easement.

173 See below; 3. *Numerus Clausus* in Property Law Systems in Europe?

without a dominant tenement. With this right, a person can benefit from the existence of the servitude. This type, known as *beschränkte persönliche Dienstbarkeit*, or limited personal servitude, should be placed between a right of usufruct and a right of servitude. The right authorises the specific use of a piece of land like a right of servitude, but the right benefits not a piece of land, but a person, as does a right of usufruct. In that sense, the limited personal servitude has been named as a real burden. In the other legal systems, such burdens may exist as well, but they are not part of the law of property.[174]

The limited personal servitude is in particular useful as a security-servitude. Because this type of servitude does not require the existence of a dominant tenement, a company burdening a piece of land that is remote from its own location can still use the right. The effects of the limited personal servitude are the same as a real servitude and therefore enable the holder to enforce the burden the servitude imposes on the servient land.

Secondly, English law recognises restrictive covenants, which impose a restriction on the use of the land of another. These covenants are different from easements as they benefit a person and not a dominant tenement. These property rights were first recognised and developed by case law. A restrictive covenant is a contract and therefore awards the maximum freedom to the parties. However, although originally allowed, a restrictive covenant may not impose a positive burden.[175]

The parties may prevent the holder of a piece of land from conducting a certain business on his land. However, 'security' restrictive covenants, like the German security-servitudes, are unknown in English law, and it is not very likely the courts will recognise them. The reason for that is that restrictive covenants are created by contract in equity, and, when a separate contract is made, it is very likely that the courts under the law of equity will consider these two contracts as a whole and hold that a positive covenant has been created. Even though they technically do not grant a right to use, but only restrict it, restrictive covenants fit into the category of lesser rights to use in the same way as servitudes of the second type do. They have effect on the right to use and are not intended *per se* to serve as security for the performance of an obligation.

Thirdly, German law recognises another type of real burden. This type, known in German as *Reallast*, imposes a positive burden on the holder of the servient tenement. The burden the *Reallast* imposes must consist of returning benefits of the land. The *Reallast* creates a duty on an owner to give these benefits to the holder of the real burden. However, because of its positive nature, when the duty is not performed, the holder of the real burden cannot specifically enforce it. Instead, he will be entitled to the value of the objects.[176] This is different from a right of servitude that can be specifically enforced under German law.

It is this difference that gives rise to the German classification as a right for the value, a *Verwertungsrecht*, and not a right to use. This difference, however, is a very

174 E.g., Dutch qualitative duties of Art. 6:252 BW. On these duties see Chapter 5; 4.8. 'Qualitative Duties' and Chain Clauses.

175 *Haywood v Brunswick Permanent Benefit Building Society* (1881) 8 QBD 403, *per* Brett LJ.

176 See Amann 1993, p. 222 *et seq.*

fine and technical distinction. Although French and Dutch law do not recognise an equivalent right, English law does, under the name *profit à prendre,* and characterises it as a right to use. A profit under English law creates the same burden as the German *Reallast,* but is formulated from the perspective of the other party.

Profits, which form the fourth type of servitude- or easement-like rights, are rights to take something from another's land. In order to take something from the land of another, the profit includes a right of access to the land of another. These rights can be held by a holder of a dominant tenement, like an easement, but also by a person for his own benefit. In the last case the profit is said to be held in gross.

The right to take something from another's land in civil law systems is covered by a right of usufruct, but in German law, although formulated from the point of view of the other party, it can be formed as a *Reallast* as well. A piece of land that produces fruits, which are by their nature returning benefits, such as turves or fishes, can be made subject to a right of usufruct and *Reallast,* entitling its right holder to enter the land and take these fruits.

2.4.3. Lesser Rights to Use of an Apartment

A third type of rights to use was mentioned above as a special species of primary rights, but it should also be dealt with separately. These rights concern the entitlement a person can have in respect of an apartment. Apartments create specific problems for legal systems. Apartment buildings become part of the ownership of the land they are constructed on, not only through application of the *superficies solo cedit* rule, vertical accession, but also through the general rules on horizontal accession, apartments themselves cannot be considered as objects separate and individual from the building in which they situated, and are therefore they are incapable of being the subject of a primary right.

In order to solve this problem, legal systems have come up with a solution that, although different in technicalities, comprises of three elements. First, the possibility is created for a party to be entitled to the exclusive use of a certain space in an apartment building. Secondly, all the parties entitled to exclusive use are co-entitled to use the common parts of a building. Thirdly, an association is formed in which all these parties are members, usually called an association of co-owners, which makes decisions, preferably by majority decision.

In French law apartment rights are created by making use of a special type of co-ownership. Through the application of special provisions, an apartment in a building can be co-owned but with rights of exclusive use.[177] Dutch law follows a different approach and has recognised a separate and distinct property right, known as 'apartment right'.[178] German and English law, on the other hand, make use of the general primary right and have created specific provisions to enable the primary right to be capable of granting exclusive use of an apartment and joint use

177 See Chapter 3; 2.2. Co-Ownership including Apartments.
178 See Chapter 5; 3.5. Apartment Right.

of the common parts of a building.[179] However, should the apartment rights cease to exist, the primary right that existed before the creation would return to its full state. In that sense, apartment rights could be categorised as lesser rights, although in many systems they are not considered as limited property rights.[180]

2.4.4. Evaluation

In the past few decades, under the influence of contract law, the use of each of these three different types of lesser rights to use has been further developed. Servitudes are no longer employed just to provide use of a certain part of another's land, but they are also used to secure performance of an obligation. Usufructs are more and more used as management devices. A usufruct on shares enables an owner to profit from an increase in value of the shares, substitution included, but without the investment duties, which are on the holder of the usufruct.[181] Also apartment rights, an invention of the last two centuries, make use of contractual freedom. The legal provisions dealing with apartments set the boundaries, but parties are free to design the content of their relation. This includes agreement on which parts of a building are exclusive, which are common, and how these parts should be dealt with, as well as the rules on the association of co-owners, how votes are cast, how decisions are made, and how costs are divided. Those agreements are not just contractual agreements, but because they are part of the apartment right structure as a whole they will also bind new holders who acquire apartment rights.

With the increasing influence of contract law, the lesser rights to use, apart from their traditional use, have received a new dimension that suits the development of property law in general. Before this new property law is dealt with, the other lesser property rights should be examined.

2.5. *Lesser Rights as Security*

Apart from lesser rights to use, each of the legal systems also recognises lesser rights for security purposes, sometimes however under different names. French law divides lesser rights into principal and accessory lesser rights. In this division the principal rights entitle the holder to the use of object, which corresponds to the first category of lesser rights, and the accessory rights are security rights, which correspond to the second category. German, Dutch and English law, although they make divisions into rights to use and for security, are less strict in their categorisation. Partly this is so because not all property rights for security purposes in these systems are accessory rights. In other words, the existence of the property rights is not necessarily dependent on the existence of an obligation.

179 See Chapter 4; 2.3. Ownership of an Apartment, and Chapter 6; 2.1. Fee Simple.

180 E.g., in French and German law, apartment rights are seen as types of ownership and not limited property rights. In Dutch law, the apartment right is a property rights, but is seen as an exception to the rule and is not characterised as a *limited* property right.

181 See Bos 2005, p. 28.

When it comes to security rights, the division into movable and immovable objects is much more relevant than in the case of rights to use, where in civil law systems certain rights to use can be held both in movable and immovable objects.[182] However, security rights are divided along the lines of movable and immovable objects or, in case of English law, land and chattels.

2.5.1. Security Rights in Respect of Movables and Chattels

When it comes to security rights in respect of movable objects and chattels, all of the legal systems recognise the same lesser property right. In order to secure the performance of an obligation, possession of a movable object or of a chattel can be transferred to another party. That other party, known as the pledgee, will hold possession of the object until the party, known as pledgor, performs the obligation. If the obligation, usually the repayment of a loan, is not performed, the pledgee has the right to take the object and sell it. It is this last power that makes this right, known as pledge, a property right. The right is usually held to comprise or to be modelled after the right of disposal, the *abusus*, of the holder of the primary right. In each of the legal systems this right, once validly created, has third-party effect.

The use of the right of pledge requires a transfer of possession, which makes it less usable as a security right in practice because most of the time the pledgor will need to retain possession of the pledged objects in order to carry on trading and so be able to repay his loan. Therefore, all of the legal systems have found solutions to provide security on movable objects or chattels that do not require the transfer of possession.

German law uses the primary right in respect of movable objects, which is a transfer for security purposes in a *fiducia cum creditore* as dealt with above.[183] This transfer of the primary property right also provided an alternative in the Netherlands before the introduction of a new Civil Code.[184] In a transfer of the primary right for security purposes, the factual control over the object remains with the transferor so that he can trade and perform his duty under the obligation the transfer secures.[185] Once the duty the transfer secures is performed, a retro-transfer will return the primary right over the objects to the original transferor, the debtor in the agreement.

After the introduction of the main part of the new Civil Code in the Netherlands in 1992, a new lesser right, a right of pledge without the transfer of possession, was introduced. This lesser property right functions in the same way as an ordinary right of pledge, in Dutch law referred to as a classic right of pledge, but does not require the transfer of possession. Consequently, in case of non-performance by the pledgor, the pledgee will have an additional right to take possession of the objects before selling them.[186]

182 E.g., a right of usufruct.

183 See above; 2.3. Primary Property Rights. See Chapter 4; 2.5. Security Ownership.

184 See Chapter 5; 2.3. Security Ownership.

185 In German law the transferor retains possession, in Dutch law this is a type of detention.

186 See Chapter 5; 3.6. Pledge.

English law also makes use of another lesser right that exists in equity. Through a charge that is either fixed or floating, the parties can create a property right that enables the chargee to take possession of the objects and sell them, or appoint a receiver over them in case of non-performance of the obligation by the chargor.[187] The charge is a lesser property right in equity, so not as strong as a property right at law, but is still made use of in most situations.

Finally, French law did not have a general alternative for movable objects until 2006, when a new non-possessory right of pledge, similar to the Dutch lesser property right mentioned above, was introduced as part of a series of reforms.[188] In French law also a right of pledge can be created without the transfer of possession. Upon non-performance by the pledgor, the pledgee may take possession and sell the objects.[189]

Furthermore, in 2007, the French legislature introduced a *fiducie*, which may be used by companies, banks and financial institutions to transfer the primary right over objects for security purposes. This transfer, as in German law, creates a *fiducia cum creditore* in which the holder of the primary right is limited in his power over the object and must re-transfer it when the obligation the transfer secures has been performed.

These developments towards non-possessory security rights also enable the application of these lesser property rights to claims instead of corporeal objects. The possession of a claim needed for the creation of a traditional security right would require notice of the transaction to be given to the debtor of the claim. However, preferably, the debtors of claims subject to lesser security rights are left alone until the lesser security right is executed. As a development of non-possessory security rights, security rights and assignment of incorporeal objects, usually claims, without notice to the debtor, have become possible.

In German law, both an assignment for security purposes and a right of pledge of claims can be created.[190] In Dutch and French law, the non-possessory right of pledge can also be used with regard to claims. Additionally, in French law a transfer of claims for security purposes, known as a *cession Dailly*, now a type of *fiducie*, is recognised.[191] In English law a claim, as a chose in action, can be the subject of an equitable charge.

2.5.2. Security Rights in Respect of Immovables and Land

Security rights in respect of immovable objects or land in French, German, Dutch and English law are very similar. Each of these legal systems recognises a lesser property right connected to the performance of an obligation.

[187] See Chapter 6; 3.4. Charges, Fixed and Floating.

[188] French law did know a pledge on cars and a life rent pledge through special legislation. See Loi 29 décembre 1934, (pledge on cars), Art. 2354 C.civ (life rent pledge) and Art. L521-1 *Code de Commerce* (commercial pledge). See Legeais 2006a, p. 359-361.

[189] See Chapter 3; 3.5. Pledge.

[190] See Chapter 4; 3.6. Pledge.

[191] See Chapter 3; 2.3. Security Ownership.

In French law this right is the right of hypothec, which is a property right in respect of an immovable object that enables the holder to sell the object when the obligation is not performed. However, until that moment the owner is entitled to use, enjoy and dispose of his immovable object. When the obligation is performed, the lesser property right will cease to exist and the ownership will be full and complete again. In other words, the right of hypothec in French law is a strictly accessory right. It cannot exist without the obligation it secures.

The 2006 reforms of securities law in France introduced new types of hypothec that deviate from the ordinary, traditional, type of hypothec, in particular, from the accessory nature of the traditional right. First, a rechargeable hypothec is created that enables parties to reuse an already created right. In order to achieve this, the right of hypothec is not accessory to the obligation it secures in the traditional meaning. The obligation remains necessary to create the right, but once the obligation is performed, usually a loan has been repaid, and the parties have specifically so agreed, the right of hypothec will remain in existence. When the owner of an immovable object wants to re-use his right of hypothec to secure another obligation, the right of hypothec is re-charged. Until that moment, the right of hypothec exists without a corresponding obligation. Secondly, a reversed hypothec, or life-rent hypothec, is recognised, which enables an owner to build up a loan in instalments.[192] At the moment this right of hypothec is created no obligation to secure exists. In other words, the claim the right secures is a future claim.

In German law, a traditional type of hypothec also exists. It is a similar property right to the French ordinary hypothec and cannot exist without an obligation. However, German law recognises another, non-accessory, lesser property right, the *Grundschuld*. This property right grants the same rights to its holder as a right of hypothec, a right to sell the object in case of non-performance, but is not dependent on the existence of an obligation. Therefore, and differently from French law, a right of *Grundschuld* can also be created by an owner on his own immovable object, and then transferred to another party in exchange for finance.[193]

The terms under which the right of *Grundschuld* may be exercised are mostly for the parties to determine. In fact, because the property right itself will usually already be in existence, a separate contract will deal with the transfer of the lesser property right and the terms and conditions. These terms and conditions are not subject to the law of property and therefore parties enjoy maximum contractual freedom. If a right of *Grundschuld* is transferred by this method, under the conclusion of a security contract, it becomes a security-*Grundschuld*.[194] The legal technique used for this is the same as a transfer of ownership for security purposes and the creation of a security-servitude, making use of the law on *Treuhand*, the law on fiduciary relationships.

Dutch law recognises only one lesser property security right, in the form of the right of hypothec. As in French law and German law, the Dutch right of hypothec is

192 See Chapter 3; 3.6. Hypothec.

193 See Chapter 4; 3.8. *Grundschuld*.

194 It is this type of *Grundschuld* that has been model for the security servitudes to develop.

an accessory security right, incapable of existing without the obligation it secures. However, in legal practice an important deviation from this principle has developed. Although the Dutch Civil Code does not expressly deal with it, a right of hypothec can be created for a future obligation, usually a future claim. This is the case when a bank gives credit to a company and the company does not make immediate use of that credit. Until the company does make use of that credit, but also when it repays the credit during the agreement, no claim will exist, and therefore the obligation the right of hypothec secures will not exist either, or will have been performed. This special type of hypothec, known as credit-hypothec, will continue to exist until the end of the agreement between the bank and the company.[195]

English law also recognises a lesser security right in respect of land, the charge. Contrary to its equivalent on chattels, this charge is capable of existence at common law. When the conveyance of a fee simple for security purposes was prohibited in 1925, it was replaced by a charge by deed by way of legal mortgage. In this transaction, the land is charged with a lesser property right granting its holder the same rights as if the holder of a fee simple had granted a lease for security purposes, a different type of mortgage that existed until 2002.[196] The holder of the charge is therefore entitled, in case of non-performance of the obligation, to take possession, sell the land or appoint a receiver over it. The English solution very much resembles the civil law use of hypothecs as security rights over land.[197]

2.5.3. Evaluation

Property security rights have also been under the influence of the increasing role of contract law. As in the case of other property rights, contract law has always been used to provide content to property security rights. The increasing influence is best seen in Germany where the *Grundschuld* is used as the subject of a security contract setting the terms and conditions under which the property right is transferred, almost without interference from property law. Also the French new rechargeable hypothec will make it possible to use the rights in a similar way.

In these cases property law is used to strengthen what would otherwise be a personal right. It is in this respect that a final category of rights that are used as security should be mentioned. These rights are created by law and arise in a factual situation where a creditor holds possession of an object of a debtor as a method to strengthen his claim for performance. Here, the legal systems use different solutions. French and Dutch law recognise a right of retention, which in French law alone is recognised as a property right.[198] German law also uses a property solution

195 See Chapter 5; 3.7. Hypothec.

196 See Chapter 6; 2.9. Mortgage of Land and Equity of Redemption.

197 Furthermore, civil law systems recognise the right of *antichresis* in respect of land. A property security right to the movables on the land for payment of a sum of money. In civil law systems this right is considered less relevant. On the origin of the right see Chapter 2; 2.4. Other Property Rights.

198 See Chapter 3; 4.1. Right of Retention.

through the recognition of a right of pledge by force of law in certain cases.[199] Finally, English law also recognises a category of special property rights that come into existence by force of law, the liens.[200]

In connection with this, civil law systems also recognise priority rights. English law recognises similar rights in case of statutory liens. The legal nature of priority rights is debated and only in French law are they explicitly recognised as security property rights.[201]

2.6. *Lesser Rights Used to Acquire a Certain Legal Position (Anticipatory Rights)*

Contract law and property law must work together in order to transfer property rights, but also in order to create lesser property rights. Depending on the legal system, the effects of concluding a contract will differ. In French law, with its consensual system of transfer, the conclusion of a contract will normally result in an immediate transfer. In the case of land, registration is required for third-party effect, but between the parties the transfer takes effect upon agreement.[202] The same system generally applies for the creation of property rights. A lesser property right is created by agreement. In the case of immovable objects, in order to achieve third-party effect, registration is required.[203]

German and Dutch law have a *traditio* system of transfer that starts from the general idea that contract law and property law are separate. Besides a contract, which functions as the cause for the transfer, a real agreement is needed to result in a transfer of a property right. In the case of immovable objects, registration is a constitutive requirement.[204] The same rules apply for the creation of property rights.

When it comes to the transfer of property rights or the creation of lesser property rights in English law, the division in consensual and *traditio* systems does not seem to be a subject of debate.[205] As in the other systems, the transfer and creation of property rights is initiated by contract. At common law these transfers or acts to create lesser rights may be subject to certain formalities. Equity generally resists formalities and will give proprietary effect at an earlier stage than the common law.[206] It is in particular in the different requirements between law and equity that a separate category of property rights arises.

For the creation of property rights in respect of land at common law, such as leases and rights of easement, the common law requires certain formalities to be

[199] See Chapter 4; 3.6. Pledge.
[200] See Chapter 6; 3.6. Liens.
[201] See Chapter 3; 3.7. Priority Rights, Chapter 4; 3.6. Pledge, Chapter 5; 4.1. Priority Rights, and Chapter 6; 3.6. Liens.
[202] See Van Vliet 2000, p. 73 *et seq.*
[203] The exception is the right of hypothec that without registration cannot come into being. See Chapter 3; 3.6. Hypothec.
[204] See Art. 3:89 BW, Van Vliet 2000, p. 30, Baur, Baur & Stürner 1999, p. 202 *et seq.*
[205] Briefly, see Swadling 2006a, p. 287-290.
[206] Swadling 2007, p. 233.

fulfilled. Mostly these concern the requirement to make a deed. However, when an agreement is made to create a lease or a right of easement, equity will give effect to these rights, anticipating their existence at common law. Because the property rights are already recognised in equity as equitable leases or equitable easements, parties do not necessarily have to conclude a deed. They will usually do so, however, because rights in equity are less strong than rights at common law.[207]

Moreover, another category of equitable rights may come into existence, which does not mirror the property rights at common law. Instead, these equitable property rights exist separately from the common law rights and, by their nature, only until the common law rights have come into existence. It is this category of equitable rights that can be considered as a distinct group of lesser property rights.

In order to transfer an estate in land, a deed and, after 2002, registration is required.[208] However, when parties conclude an agreement to sell, make a deed, and send this deed for registration, the process may take some time. The courts of equity, by reference to the fact that the contract to convey an estate in land can be specifically enforced in equity, and that equity looks at 'that as done which ought to be done', have recognised a property right in equity for the transferee. Until registration of the deed is completed, the transferor will remain entitled to the estate at common law.[209] As a result, another person will have a right in equity on the land through the workings of the law of trusts. From the moment the agreement to convey an estate, known as an estate contract, is concluded, the holder of the property right at common law will hold it on trust for the transferee. With reference to the same arguments the courts of equity have also recognised the property effect of an option to purchase.[210]

Similarly, in German law, the courts have intervened in the property law system in cases where the Civil Code awards additional protection to a person waiting for a property right to be transferred to him. This occurs in the case of reservation of ownership clauses where the transferee will only become owner upon full payment of the purchase price. Until that moment, the Civil Code offers additional protective measures for the transferee against the transferor, but not in the form of a property right. With reference to this special protection, the German federal court introduced an additional property right known as an *Anwartschaftsrecht* or acquisition right.[211]

The acquisition right is also recognised in other situations, the most important being when an agreement to sell and transfer a primary right in land has been made and a deed is passed that is sent for registration. In that case, the German Civil Code

207 See Chapter 6; 1.2. Common Law and Equity.

208 Swadling 2000a, p. 256.

209 See Chapter 6; 2.7. Estate Contracts.

210 *London and South Western Railway v Gomm* (1882) 20 Ch D 562 *per* Lindley LJ, Swadling 2007, p. 260-261, 334.

211 BGH 24 June 1958, BGHZ 28, 16, 21, BGH 25 February 1966, BGHZ 45, 186 (192). See Chapter 4; 3.4. Expectation Rights.

also offers additional protection to the transferee, and the courts, with reference to that protection, have recognised an acquisition right.[212]

Furthermore, German law recognises the *dingliche Vorkaufrecht*, which literally translates as a pre-emptive property right to a sale. The right is created through an agreement between an owner and another person containing a right for the latter to claim the sale and transfer of the ownership under certain conditions. In comparison with other systems, therefore, the pre-emptive right to sale is effectively an option to purchase with property law effects, as in English law. The effect of the German option to purchase is that it enables the holder to invoke the right against a third party who made an agreement of sale with the owner, contrary to the option to purchase and, in certain circumstances, to demand the transfer of ownership to himself.[213] However, once the sale and transfer is concluded with that third party, the option ceases to exist and a personal claim for damages remains.

Finally, German law recognises the possibility to provide certain rights with third-party effect through *Vormerkung* or pre-emptive registration. Any claim that involves a change in the legal situation of a property right in respect of an immovable object can be registered.[214] The registration changes the effect of the pre-registered claim, and makes it possible for its holder to invoke it against third parties. Doctrinally, the registration does not transform a personal right into a property right, but the effects are the same.[215]

Moreover, certain property rights that are less strong in nature, such as the German option to purchase, can be pre-emptively registered. Upon the pre-emptive registration, the holder of the right will not only be able to invoke his right against the owner, but also, albeit under conditions, against a third party who entered into a sale and transfer with the owner.[216]

In Dutch law pre-emptive registration also exists, but it can only be used to register a contract of consumer sale of a house.[217] When such a contract of sale is registered and the owner enters into another contract of sale, transfers ownership of the house to a third party, or becomes insolvent, the holder of that pre-emptively registered personal right may invoke his right against the third party or against the insolvent estate.[218]

Both German and Dutch doctrine insist that pre-emptive registration does not transform personal rights into property rights. Nevertheless, registration does give these personal rights property law effects. If a right is created in respect of an object and it can be invoked and specifically enforced against a third party who did not

212 § 873 (2) BGB, further protected by §§ 130 (2), 979 BGB and §§ 17 and 45 *Grundbuch Ordnung* (GBO), Wolf 2005, p. 216-217. See Chapter 4; 3.4. Expectation Rights.

213 § 1098 BGB, Staudinger et al. 2002, p. 796.

214 Furthermore, the claim must concern a private law relation. See Chapter 4; 4.2. Pre-Emptive Registration (*Vormerkung*).

215 A similar discussion is held in South African law where personal rights can sometimes be registered under Art. 63 of the Deeds Registries Act 47 of 1937. See, *inter alia*, Sonnekus 1991, p. 173 *et seq.*, Van der Walt 1992, p. 171 *et seq.*

216 See Chapter 4; 4.2. Pre-Emptive Registration (*Vormerkung*).

217 See Chapter 5; 4.3. Lease of Immovable Objects.

218 Arts. 7:2 and 7:3 BW.

agree to it, it fulfils the main criteria for a property right and it is difficult to maintain that it is a special type of personal right.[219]

From a comparative point of view, this category of rights contains rights that are temporary in nature. They anticipate events, usually the creation or transfer of primary and lesser rights, and will cease to exist once the event takes place. In that sense, it could be held that these rights form a general category of anticipatory rights. Anticipatory rights are subject to different requirements compared with lesser property rights.

In order to create these rights a contract is usually sufficient, but sometimes registration is required. However, the effect of these rights is that they can be invoked against third parties, which makes them different from personal rights. Anticipatory rights are therefore situated between the law of obligations and the law of property.

However, as all of these legal systems operate on a distinction between these systems of law, a choice should be made. By stating that anticipatory rights are rights *sui generis* or invoking the old category of *iura ad rem*, no real solutions are achieved and the dynamic side of property law is neglected. Anticipatory rights should be part of property law and enable property law systems to develop. The fact that contract law is used to develop the law of property, and provide new uses for it, should not hinder, but stimulate its development.[220]

3. *Numerus Clausus* in Property Law Systems in Europe?

Now that a categorisation of property rights in the various legal systems has been made, and a model is developed that makes use of terminology in which the characteristics of each of the legal systems can be expressed, the concept of *numerus clausus* can be revisited. First, we will take another look at why legal systems operate a *numerus clausus*. From within the legal systems, legal arguments are used to justify the existence as well as the maintenance of the closed system of property rights.[221] Moreover, *numerus clausus* has also received attention from Law and Economics scholars, who provide explanations for why a *numerus clausus* exists.[222]

When the arguments that justify and clarify the existence of a *numerus clausus* are taken into consideration, the question can be asked whether a legal system needs *numerus clausus* to function.[223] There are legal systems in the world that do not adhere to a closed system of property rights, in other words, where parties enjoy freedom to create new property rights themselves. One of these legal systems, South African law, will be examined to see if a legal system can function without a closed system.[224]

219 See Chapter 1; 1.1. Personal Rights and Property Rights.

220 This topic will return in below in 3. *Numerus Clausus* in Property Law Systems in Europe?

221 See below; 3.1. Justifications for a *Numerus Clausus* from within the Legal System.

222 See below; 3.2. Law and Economics on *Numerus Clausus*.

223 See below; 3.3. *Numerus Clausus* in Comparative Analysis.

224 See below; 3.8. A Legal System without a *Numerus Clausus*: South African Law.

Finally, when the reasons for and against a closed system have been discussed, we can return to the *numerus clausus* in the property law systems in Europe. *Numerus clausus* as a principle of property law is adhered to by all of the legal systems under consideration, albeit to different degrees. The final section of this Chapter will therefore be devoted to the place of the *numerus clausus* of property rights in the European legal systems.[225]

3.1. *Justifications for a Numerus Clausus from within the Legal System*

There can be several reasons for the fact that even in an open system of property rights, in a system where no *numerus clausus* exists, there is not unlimited freedom to create new property rights. First, the primary reason for a *numerus clausus* to be recognised is to ensure legal certainty. A system that does not recognise a *numerus clausus* does not, however, desire a system of legal uncertainty. Therefore, even in such a system, criteria exist with which property rights must comply. Examples of these criteria are the 'subtraction from *dominium* test' of South African law, and also the requirements for new property rights of Lord Wilberforce from *National Provincial Bank Ltd v Ainsworth* in English law.[226] A *numerus clausus* offers optimal legal certainty in the sense that it ensures no other property rights can exist than those recognised by the legal system and, therefore, when parties are confronted with a property right they can establish what property right they are dealing with. However, even in a system without a *numerus clausus*, parties should not be confronted with a group of unknown property rights.

Only a few authors have searched for the reasons behind the *numerus clausus*. Rudden has offered several legal reasons why a *numerus clausus* might exist.[227] First of all, he offers an argument that the current list of property rights might offer all the property rights that are needed. Under the heading of absence of demand, Rudden almost immediately rejects this argument, mentioning some attempts to create new property rights such as in *Clore v Theatrical Productions*, which was dealt with in Chapter 6 on English law.[228] Other examples, such as the German acquisition right, or the new French lesser security rights introduced by the 2006 reforms, also show that there can be much demand for new property rights.

A second reason Rudden mentions is the absence of notice.[229] By this Rudden means the argument often used, that third parties dealing with the right will not know about its existence. However, although this is a valid argument, Rudden focuses attention on the fact that notice by itself will not suffice as a reason to create

225 See below; 4. Conclusion: *Numerus Clausus* in Property Law Systems in Europe.
226 *National Provincial Bank Ltd v Ainsworth* [1965] AC 1175, HL at 1247-1248 *per* Lord Wilberforce. See Chapter 6; 4. A *Numerus Clausus* in English Property Law? On South African law see below; 3.8. A Legal System without a *Numerus Clausus*: South African Law.
227 Legal reasons, a term used by Rudden himself, because there might be other, additional, reasons for a *numerus clausus* such as in Law and Economics. See below; 3.2. Law and Economics on *Numerus Clausus*. Rudden 1987, p. 245-249.
228 *Clore v Theatrical Properties Ltd and Westby & Co Ltd* [1936] 3 All ER 483, CA.
229 Rudden 1987, p. 246.

new property rights. In other words, just the fact that other parties know about the existence of a right does not automatically make that right into a property right.[230] Knowledge about a property right is therefore not as such a requirement for the validity of a property right.

A third reason is offered in the form of absence of consent. Property rights bind parties beyond privity of contract. Therefore when it comes to property rights imposing positive duties on the right-holder, these rights should not be allowed. Parties, when they acquire a property right, should not be compelled to do something they did not agree to. A new property right would result in another right to which parties can be bound without their consent.

A final reason is what Rudden calls *pyramiding*. By this Rudden refers to the idea that if one owner is allowed to create new property rights in respect of his land, his successors in title will expect to be able to do the same. As a result a pyramid of obligations will rest on the land, which is generally considered an undesirable effect.[231] Rules prohibiting this type of pyramiding include, for instance, the statute *Quia Emptores* which prohibited sub-infeudation.[232] In mentioning these reasons, Rudden does not explain *numerus clausus* as such, but provides arguments he has come across in legal writings.[233]

In a thesis on Swiss law, Foëx examined the *numerus clausus* of property rights in respect of movables, and also provided legal arguments for why a *numerus clausus* might exist.[234] First, Foëx examines the publicity function of the *numerus clausus*. Property rights are rights against the world and therefore the world should know about their existence in order to justify this effect. Therefore, the law prescribes the number of these rights that have an effect against third parties, as well as the rules of publicity they are subject to.[235] Second, *numerus clausus* ensures that the available property rights and their content are clear. Under the heading of simplicity and predictability, Foëx holds that parties must know which legal relations they might have to confront, and what the content of these relations is.[236] Third, the limited number of property rights is there to protect the freedom of ownership, the idea that the right of ownership is such an important right that it deserves special protection.[237] This is a typically French-inspired argument, which holds that after the unitary concept of ownership was introduced, as an effect of the French Revolution, fragmentation of this right was only allowed by law in the form of a *démembrement* of the right of ownership. If parties were free to fragment the right of ownership, either into different types of co-ownership, or in the form of new, as yet unrecognised, lesser property rights, the reason the right of ownership was made a unitary right would be taken away. The legal system would then return to the feudal

230 Rudden 1987, p. 246.
231 Rudden 1987, p. 248.
232 See Chapter 6; 1.2. Common Law and Equity.
233 Rudden 1987, p. 245.
234 Foëx 1987. For a discussion of Foëx's ideas in Dutch, see Struycken 2007, p. 290 *et seq*.
235 In Foëx's words, *fonction de publicité*, Foëx 1987, p. 29-30.
236 Or *fonction de clarification*, Foëx 1987, p. 30-31.
237 Or *fonction de protection de liberté de la propriété*, Foëx 1987, p. 31-34.

system of fragmentation of ownership.[238] Fourthly, in Foëx's view, *numerus clausus* also serves an ethical purpose.[239] In Foëx's view, *numerus clausus* refers to the idea that only the legislature may add property rights.[240] Therefore, the legislature has made choices on which property rights to recognise and which not. In that respect, the choice and all its elements, the ethical dimension Foëx seems to refer to, is part of *numerus clausus* as well.[241] Finally, Foëx mentions that *numerus clausus* also serves a function of support to other principles and rules of property law.[242] In this respect Foëx seems to adhere to a strict interpretation of *numerus clausus* as a rule that limits the number and content of the lesser property rights. In my view, he refers to the filtering-function of *numerus clausus* as dealt with above.[243] In this respect, when under the rule of *numerus clausus* the legislature decides that a certain legal relation is a property right, the law of property and the specific rules of the law of property, and even more specific rules on a certain property right, apply.

Struycken has analysed Foëx's arguments and concludes that the first function is more about the principle of publicity than the *numerus clausus*, and that also the second function, that of simplicity and predictability, can be brought under the heading of publicity.[244] Furthermore, according to Struycken, the ethical objective is not a part of *numerus clausus* as such, but a general principle of good legislation in which the legislature takes into account as many relevant dimensions as possible. In that respect, these arguments show that in a system adhering to the rule of *numerus clausus*, the legislature takes prime position and *numerus clausus* serves to organise the law of property and decide which rules apply.[245]

In my view, these arguments seem to justify the existence of *numerus clausus* more than to explain why it must be there. Possibly, legal arguments alone do not clarify or even justify the existence of a *numerus clausus*. What appears certain is that the law of property needs legal certainty and that therefore publicity and *numerus clausus* go together to a large extent.[246] The legal certainty argument could be seen as a leading consideration behind the existence of a *numerus clausus*. Possibly, looking more to the effects of the property law system and of *numerus clausus* in particular will offer more clarity. It is in particular in this respect that Law and Economics can offer assistance.

238 Foëx 1987, p. 34.

239 Or *fonction d'ordre éthique*, Foëx 1987, p. 34-35.

240 Foëx 1987, p. 113.

241 As an example, he mentions the choice to prohibit the *lex commissoria*, Foëx 1987, p. 34-35.

242 Or *fonction d'appoint d'autres principes de nos droits réels*, Foëx 1987, p. 35-36.

243 See above; 1.3.1. Requirements of *Numerus Clausus*.

244 Struycken 2007, p. 305-306.

245 In particular in Foëx's view, who recognises the supremacy of the legislator in this area and does not favour the influence of the judiciary in this respect. See Foëx 1987, p. 113.

246 However, publicity and *numerus clausus* are not the same, see Chapter 1; 1.2.1. Principles of Property Law, and 1.2.2. *Numerus Clausus* of Property Rights.

3.2. *Law and Economics on Numerus Clausus*

The study of Law and Economics is concerned with an economic analysis of the law, not so much on what ought to happen and what ought to be done, but more an analysis to explain the functioning of the law.[247] In this respect, Law and Economics offers explanations of the workings of the law that lawyers who only consider law might overlook, or simply ignore. In the law of property, and in respect to property rights in particular, Law and Economics is concerned with scarcity of resources and individual choice.[248] Property law concerns objects that are resources for which there is more demand than supply. Because of that, the law offers rules on the allocation of these resources. Individuals, natural persons, subsequently have a choice as to which resources they want. The study of Law and Economics recognises the costs to individuals of choices they may make.[249] The way in which individuals make decisions can be expressed in terms of weighing the benefits and costs of a certain decision. In property law, this decision concerns the choice to acquire or not to acquire a certain scarce resource.[250]

In order to analyse property law there are three basic concepts of relevance; externalities, transaction costs and efficiency. First, externalities are the effects a decision has on parties other than the decision maker. When looking at a decision to use a certain resource, where the effects against third parties are not taken into account, the effects are external to the decision.[251] In an optimal situation a decision maker would take all externalities of his decision into account. However, the world is far from optimal and therefore externalities may be neglected and a resource may be inefficient, because costs and benefits were not taken fully into account. Second, transaction costs are costs incurred with making a decision to act and the costs that come with the act.[252] An important part of transaction costs are information costs, which are the costs incurred in gathering information that would normally lead to a decision. Depending on the decision to be made, these information costs will be higher or lower. Other transaction costs may include the costs of acquiring an object or of failing to reach an optimal bargain with the seller. Third and finally, the concept of efficiency in relation to property law means that for economists the value of a resource is maximised. It is this concept that law should strive for, although it might, in reality, never achieve this.[253] Analysis towards an efficient use of a resource, so that its value is maximised, leads to interesting insights in the workings of the law. In respect to *numerus clausus*, Law and Economics theorists have offered several explanations that will be dealt with in this section.

Before entering into three different theories, there are some general concepts that need clarification. When it comes to property rights, Law and Economics is also

247 Clarke & Kohler 2005, p. 42.
248 Posner 1973, p. 10, Clarke & Kohler 2005, p. 42.
249 See Anderson & McChesney 2003, p. 2.
250 Posner 1973, p. 10 *et seq.*, Anderson & McChesney 2003, p. 4.
251 Mattei 2000, p. 60-61, Clarke & Kohler 2005, p. 45-46.
252 Clarke & Kohler 2005, p. 47-48.
253 Mattei 2000, p. 51-53, Clarke & Kohler 2005, p. 48-49.

concerned with the efficient allocation of these property rights, particularly to ensure that entitlements to objects are not fragmented. When the entitlement to an object becomes so fragmented that decision making over that object, or protection of that object, becomes so difficult that the costs are larger than the benefits the fragmented entitlements to the object earn its holders, the object is no longer held efficiently.[254]

When it comes to *numerus clausus*, Law and Economics can tell us something about the reasons for its existence. Rudden has offered several economic explanations for the existence of a closed system. His approach is to look at why a legal system does not want to recognise a new, as yet unknown, property right, which he names, after Lord Brougham VC in *Keppel v Bailey*, a 'fancy'.[255] In doing so, Rudden discovered legal reasons that have been dealt with above.[256] Apart from these legal reasons, Rudden also offers a scheme of economic explanations, without going into detail. By way of introduction to the subject, Rudden's economic reasons will be dealt with here, before three specific economic theories on *numerus clausus* are dealt with.

First of all, Rudden argues that the existence of too many property rights would decrease the marketability of land. Land could no longer be freely transferred, which would have an effect on its value.[257] Secondly, Rudden signals that economists point out that a market would benefit from a standardisation of property rights.[258] Trading in a non-standard commodity, in this case a property right, would increase the costs of other market participants. Standardising the market would reduce these externalities. Thirdly, Rudden mentions the market economy.[259] In order to ensure trade, objects of property law should be as unrestricted as possible. Imposing too many burdens would restrict the 'free circulation of things'.[260] Fourthly, Rudden mentions information costs.[261] In Rudden's view these costs occur in two ways; when parties are at the 'screening stage', looking at what entitlements are available on the market, and when parties have made a selection and are faced with the application of their entitlement to specific circumstances. In particular these information costs are of high importance for *numerus clausus* and have been further elaborated on by other Law and Economics scholars.[262] Fifthly, Rudden mentions there are transaction costs that are incurred by parties if they have to negotiate the terms of their legal relation.[263] When, at the initial stage, parties have screened the rights available, which in an optimal situation would have been

254 Mattei 2000, p. 58-60, Shavell 2002, p. 20-21, Heller 1998, p. 621 *et seq.*
255 Rudden 1987, p. 239-240. *Keppel v Bailey* (1834) 2 My & K 517, 520-526, at 535-536 *per* Lord Brougham LC. See Chapter 6; 4. A *Numerus Clausus* in English Property Law? For a discussion of Rudden's views in Dutch see Struycken 2007, p. 311-322.
256 See above; 3.1. Justifications for a *Numerus Clausus* from within the Legal System.
257 Rudden 1987, p. 252-253.
258 Rudden 1987, p. 253.
259 Rudden 1987, p. 254.
260 Rudden 1987, p. 254.
261 Rudden 1987, p. 254-255.
262 See above; 3.2.2. *Numerus Clausus* as Optimal Standardisation of Property Rights.
263 Rudden 1987, p. 256.

standardised by the market, they are unlikely to be confronted with surprises when they do acquire the entitlement they have been looking at. Transaction costs thus will be at a minimum level. Sixthly, Rudden suggests land utilisation is ensured by the idea that entitlements to land are limited to ensure efficient development.[264] Too many 'fancies' on the land will hinder this development and lead to, in economic terms, non-efficient use of the resource. Seventhly, and finally, Rudden emphasises that property relations are static, in the sense that they are durable, intended to last for a long time.[265] In the law of obligations, to the contrary, relations are dynamic in the sense that they are intended to last only for a limited period. Therefore, *numerus clausus* also ensures that there are not too many rights that last for a very long time, possibly forever, and that, *a contrario*, dynamic relations must be renegotiated.[266]

These basic concepts can be summarised under two different headings; first, fragmentation issues and, secondly, costs incurred from property transactions. Both of these provide an economic answer for why *numerus clausus* might be useful, and they are dealt with in the next sections.

3.2.1. Fragmentation: Not too Many Rights; on Commons and Anti-Commons

In his influential article, 'The Tragedy of the Commons' (1968), the biologist Garrett Hardin drew attention to what he called problems for which there is no technical solution.[267] In relation to the debate on the threat of nuclear war, and the conclusion of many that there is no technical solution to this, Professor Hardin focused on a concept called 'commons'. A commons is a situation in which the privilege to use an object is shared between several persons in the absence of any rules or agreements in respect of the right of exclusion.[268] Hardin offered the example of a pasture on which several herdsmen attempt to have as many cattle as possible. There are no specific rules or agreements on the use of the pasture. The herdsmen cannot exclude each other and the pasture is therefore a commons. The problem Hardin identified is that each herdsman will gain for himself by adding cattle to the pasture, but all the herdsmen will share the cost of adding an animal to the pasture together. On this he states:

> 'Therein is the tragedy. Each man is locked into a system that compels him to increase his herd without limit – in a world that is limited. Ruin is the destination towards which all men rush, each pursuing his own best interest in a society that believes in the freedom of the commons. Freedom in a commons brings ruin to all'.[269]

The example shows what has become known as the tragedy of the commons, a situation in which a destructive situation is created through over-use.[270] In later

264 Rudden 1987, p. 256-257.
265 Rudden 1987, p. 259-260.
266 Rudden 1987, p. 259, Struycken 2007, p. 319-320.
267 Hardin 1968, p. 1243 *et seq.*
268 See also Heller 1998, p. 623-624, Sagaert 2005b, p. 1047-1049.
269 Hardin 1968, p. 1244.
270 See also Parisi, Schulz & Depoorter 2005, p. 578-579.

writings, the commons problem described by Hardin has been divided into two types of commons.[271] First there are public commons, such as national parks, forests and other public areas. These areas generally allow access to the public and are subject to problems of over-use. Such over-use can occur through physical use of land, but also by pollution, for instance.[272] Other commons are known as private commons, and have been mostly described as common-pool problems, describing the effects of a group of tenants or landowners sharing a swimming pool together.[273] In those situations, too, in the absence of rules or agreements, the pool is subject to dangers of over-use.

However, a tragedy does not occur automatically, and even if it does, the result is not necessarily disadvantageous.[274] In the case of public parks, Central Park in New York City is a prime example, where a 'tragedy of the commons' may prevent the land from being used as a building development site.[275] There, the landowners neighbouring the park have a clear incentive not to allow the park to be developed as their interest clearly benefits from the presence of the park. Although they do not have a right to exclude others, including a developer coming in to build commercial buildings in the park, these neighbouring owners have a clear incentive to prevent development from taking place by ensuring everyone exercises their privilege to use the park.[276]

Nevertheless, the analysis offered by Hardin shows that when too many people enjoy a privilege to use, without the necessary right to exclude others, the drive for maximisation of personal gain will lead to a situation of over-use of a scarce resource. It is there that Hardin sees the tragedy occurring. Therefore, theorists have offered private ownership as a solution to prevent the tragedy from happening.[277] In a private ownership regime, specific parties will receive rights to exclude others and to make decisions in respect of the object that is no longer strictly a commons.

Creating rights of ownership in such a situation will prevent a tragedy of the commons from occurring, but will not necessarily solve the problem. At the other end of the spectrum, too many 'ownership rights' with a power to make decisions over an object will lead to another phenomenon in Law and Economics - an anti-commons.[278] 'The tragedy of the anti-commons' was formulated in 1998 by a legal scholar, Michael Heller.[279] Anti-commons is a situation in which the power to make decisions over an object is divided between so many actors that no decision can be

271 Munzer 2006, p. 150-151.
272 Heller 1998, p. 624, Hardin 1968, p. 1245.
273 Munzer 2006, p. 150-151.
274 Heller 1998, p. 676-677, Hansmann & Kraakman 2002, p. 160-161.
275 Parchomovsky & Bell 2006, p. 138-141.
276 Parchomovsky and Bell name these rights anti-property interests. Parchomovsky & Bell 2006, p. 142-146.
277 Heller 1998, p. 678, Munzer 2006, p. 151-152.
278 Of course, in terms of property law the term should not be ownership rights, i.e., in plural, but rather property right as the right of ownership, as a primary right, is a unitary right.
279 Heller 1998, p. 622. See also Parisi, Schulz & Depoorter 2005, p. 579, Fusaro 2001, p. 3-4.

made. As an example, Heller mentions the shops in post-Soviet Russia.[280] As part of the transition from a socialist property regime to a system of private ownership, ownership in Russia remained partly fragmented among several actors. Fragmentation of ownership therefore remained in the sense that the power to make decisions over an object was divided between several actors. As an example Heller shows how for a right to sell an object, six actors are involved.[281]

A tragedy of the anti-commons occurs because the actors cannot come to a decision. As a result the object is not over-used, as is the case with a tragedy of the commons, but under-used.[282] In the case of the Moscow shops, these remained empty, and meanwhile small kiosks selling goods erupted in the streets in front of the shops. Law and Economic analysis shows that fragmentation of decision-making power leads to under-use and this can only be solved through '[unification] of fragmented property rights into a usable bundle'.[283] As a final remark Heller states:

> 'Property theory and transition practice have given insufficient weight to the role that the bundling of rights plays in avoiding anti-commons tragedy. Both theorists and practitioners assume that the key to creating private property is to define rights clearly, enforce contracts predictably, and let the market sort out entitlements. The experience of anticommunist property in transition suggests that the content of property bundles, and not just the clarity of property rights, matters more than we have realized. We pay a high price when we inadvertently create anticommunist property'.[284]

The examples of the commons and anti-commons illustrate a danger each property law system faces. When through either not enough or too many rules an object becomes over-used or under-used, the system fails and inefficiency results.

In respect of *numerus clausus* it has been argued that this reasoning applies directly.[285] Through the existence of too broadly formulated, or too many, property rights, a tragedy of the commons or anti-commons may occur.[286] When, in other words, the list of property rights is examined, the system of property law must ensure there are not too many rights granting a privilege to use without a right to exclude others from using on the one hand, but, on the other hand, these rights should not divide the decision-making powers over the object amongst too many right-holders. The danger of fragmentation of property rights lies in a tragedy occurring.[287]

280 Heller 1998, p. 633-642.

281 The local administration, property committee, Committee for Architecture and Historical Preservation, State enterprise or institute (as balance-sheet holder), budget organisation and the relevant council. Heller 1998, p. 638.

282 See Fusaro 2001, p. 5-6.

283 Heller 1998, p. 640, 678.

284 Merrill & Smith 2000, p. 688.

285 Heller 1999, p. 1167, Shavell 2002, p. 21, Baffi 2007, p. 6 *et seq.*, however see Munzer 2006, p. 153-154.

286 See Parisi, Schulz & Depoorter 2005, p. 583-585.

287 See Parisi, Schulz & Depoorter 2005, p. 590-591.

The effect of this theory on *numerus clausus* is debated. Merrill and Smith challenge the fundamental nature of the fragmentation argument.[288] Although they do not challenge the relevance of the analysis of the danger of fragmentation of property rights for many areas of property law, they challenge the assumption that dangers of fragmentation can explain the existence of a *numerus clausus*.[289] In the view of Merrill and Smith, fragmentation is fragmentation in respect of the number of right-holders, not in respect of the *types* of property rights. Therefore, the danger of fragmentation is part of the discussion of *numerus clausus*, but does not explain its existence.

3.2.2. *Numerus Clausus* as Optimal Standardisation of Property Rights

If fragmentation does not provide the answer for the existence of the *numerus clausus*, additional analysis could offer help. Merrill and Smith argue that the answer lies in the view of *numerus clausus* as a standardisation of property rights. In creating this view they discuss the costs and benefits of standardisation and to what extent government should be involved in standardisation.[290]

They come to this view through an analysis of the judgment by the Lord Chancellor, Lord Brougham, in *Keppel v Bailey*, dealt with in Chapter 6 on English law.[291] In that judgment Lord Brougham LC stated that no new property rights should be recognised because third parties would hardly be able to know what rights and duties would be included when they acquired a piece of land. According to Merrill and Smith, recognising new property rights 'would create unacceptable information costs to third parties'.[292] They argue that costs incurred by third parties, which refers to parties other than those creating the right, are the deciding factor. These costs, which they call information costs, can be divided into two types; measurement costs and frustration costs.

Measurement costs are those costs that individuals face when they encounter property rights. As these are not costs faced by the parties creating a property right, but by third parties confronted with the right, they are an 'externality involving measurement costs'.[293] Merrill and Smith therefore distinguish between the originating parties, who were participants in the transaction creating the property right, potential successors in interest of the object in which the property right is created, and other market participants.[294] Each of these three groups is affected by the creation of a new property right. The parties creating the property right mainly enjoy benefits and will usually not take the measurement costs they impose on third

288 Merrill & Smith 2000, p. 6, 51 *et seq*. See also Hansmann & Kraakman 2002, p. 418, Munzer 2006, p. 156-157, Parisi, Schulz & Depoorter 2005, p. 587.

289 Merrill & Smith 2000, p. 52. On the similarities between fragmentation and *numerus clausus*, see also Struycken 2007, p. 791.

290 Merrill & Smith 2000, p. 8.

291 See Chapter 6; 4. A *Numerus Clausus* in English Property Law?

292 Merrill & Smith 2000, p. 26. On this theory see Baffi 2007, p. 16-19.

293 Merrill & Smith 2000, p. 26.

294 Merrill & Smith 2000, p. 27-28.

parties into account. Potential successors in interest are confronted with the specific property right that was created by the originating parties. This 'internal' effect of *numerus clausus*, which does not include the costs imposed on other market participants, is also covered in other explanations of *numerus clausus*, such as fragmentation as dealt with above.[295]

In Merrill and Smith's view, their explanation of measurement costs also affects market participants other than just the parties dealing with the property right. As an example they describe a situation in which one hundred people own watches and one of them, A, sells and transfers his watch to B. He does not transfer it fully, but only the right to use the watch on Monday.[296] Not only are A and B and their respective successors in interest affected by this transfer, but also all other market participants will now be confronted with a situation where not only a 'normal' property right in watches exists, the right to use the watch, but also a 'time-share' of watches. Now that another property right exists, anyone acquiring a watch will have to investigate whether such a watch does not include a 'time-share' or 'Monday-right'.

With these costs of *numerus clausus*, which they term 'external costs' and which I would call the 'external' effect, taking other market participants who are not directly confronted with the existence of the property right into account, Merrill and Smith claim their explanation of *numerus clausus* is different from others. This difference can best be seen in solutions proposed to solve the problems created by the example of 'Monday-rights' in watches. Theories that focus on the 'internal' effects of *numerus clausus*, which are those theories that do not take the other market participants into account, seek solutions to this problem in concepts such as notice and other forms of specific publicity. When it comes to the other market participants, notice cannot provide a solution, because other market participants are not party to the transaction creating the property right, nor do they intend to acquire the property right in question.

Translated into costs, Merrill and Smith show that when the price of 'Monday-right' is 10, but the existence of this right raises the processing costs for all other of the hundred watch owners by 1, A's net benefit will be 9, however, the social cost will be 90. In other words, the benefit for A to create a 'Monday-right' is much more than the increase in costs for him. There is no incentive to prevent A and any other watch-owner creating 'Tuesday-rights', 'Wednesday-rights' and so on. A tragedy of the commons, a private common in this case, may result.[297] As a solution Merrill and Smith offer the following:

> 'One way to control the external costs of measurement to third parties is through compulsory standardization of property rights. Standardization reduces the costs of measuring the attributes of such rights. Limiting the number of basic property forms allows a market participant or a potential violator to limit his or her inquiry to whether

295 Merrill & Smith 2000, p. 28, 30.

296 Merrill & Smith 2000, p. 27.

297 See above; 3.2.1. Fragmentation: Not too Many Rights; on Commons and Anti-Commons. Merrill & Smith 2000, p. 32.

> the interest does or does not have the features of the forms on the menu. Fancies not on the closed list need not be considered because they will not be enforced. When it comes to the basic legal dimensions of property, limiting the number of forms thus makes the determination of their nature less costly. The 'good' in question here might be considered to be the prevention of error in ascertaining the attributes of property rights. Standardization means less measurement is required to achieve a given amount of error prevention. Alternatively, one can say that standardization increases the productivity of any given level of measurement efforts'.[298]

However, the proposed standardisation solution of Merrill and Smith comes at the price of an increase of other costs. The authors realise this and deal extensively with the additional costs a regime of standardisation creates.[299] These costs, which they term 'frustration costs', occur because parties can no longer create any property right they wish to create, but they must make use of the 'building blocks' the property law system offers. In this respect, a standardised regime creates an unequal position for market participants. Parties with money and knowledge can afford to spend both time and money on the optimal 'stacking' of building blocks so that the most optimal combination of property rights for their specific situation results.[300] Although the increase in frustration costs limits the party autonomy that exists in a completely open system, the standardisation into building blocks also makes these complex combinations of property rights easier to process for third parties, thus lowering measurement costs.[301] Nevertheless, the situation remains one of balancing costs. Therefore Merrill and Smith do not strive for maximum, but rather for optimal, standardisation. Their attention is therefore to the middle range of the spectrum between no standardisation and complete standardisation. [302]

When this *equilibrium* between the number of types of property rights and the measurement costs for third parties, both successors in interest and other market participants, is reached depends on the degree of publication of property rights.[303] The more third parties can acquire knowledge about possible property rights, the more property rights can exist in a system of optimal standardisation. In other words, a lesser degree of standardisation is required with more publicity of property rights. However, just creating a property right with a publicity requirement, such as notice, does not necessarily allow it onto the market. As the example of the 'Monday-right' in a watch shows, even with notice, the costs might be higher than the benefits, and a tragedy of the commons, with all the costs related to that, is likely to occur.[304]

298 Merrill & Smith 2000, p. 33-34, footnotes omitted.

299 Merrill & Smith 2000, p. 35 *et seq.*

300 This in the words of Merrill and Smith is a form of price discrimination or, by analogy, a sort of 'pollution tax', Merrill & Smith 2000, p. 35.

301 Merrill & Smith 2000, p. 37.

302 Merrill & Smith 2000, p. 38.

303 In their article, Merrill and Smith provide two figures that show that when the degree of publication is higher, the number of property rights in a situation of optimal standardisation may be larger than in an system with a lesser degree of publicity. See Merrill & Smith 2000, p. 39, 41.

304 Merrill & Smith 2000, p. 44.

Finally, in Merrill and Smith's view, standardisation is not something the market achieves on its own, but something for which intervention from rule makers is necessary. Because they see the role of courts more in maintaining the *status quo* of the current system of property rights, they argue the legislature should ensure a system of property rights at the optimal rate of standardisation.[305] Furthermore, new property rights created by the legislature produce much more information to third parties at less cost than a property right created by the judiciary. Such a system would reduce information costs, in particular measurement costs, for new property rights.[306]

The views of Merrill and Smith have been criticised, in particular by other Law and Economy scholars.[307] Their focus on costs for third parties and therefore *numerus clausus* as a standardisation of property rights especially has raised questions. If costs for third parties are relevant, why should the system of property law offer standardisation and not just ensure that information costs for third parties are reduced through notice or other forms of publication?

3.2.3. *Numerus Clausus* as Verification of Property Rights

One criticism of the views on *numerus clausus* as the optimal standardisation of property rights has been offered by Hansmann and Kraakman.[308] These authors agree with Merrill and Smith that third-party information costs are relevant, but they propose a different view on how these affect the system of property law.

In the view of Hansmann and Kraakman, the law does not take the form of standardisation of property rights to reduce information costs for third parties, but it offers a set of rules enabling parties to verify property rights.[309] In this respect this theory differs from the standardisation theory that focuses on the communication between the parties about the existence of (new) property rights. Hansmann and Kraakman emphasise that verification rules are closely connected with the existence of property rights and that some property rights require different verification rules than others. It is in this relation, they argue, that the explanation for *numerus clausus* can be found.[310]

In the view of Hansmann and Kraakman, a property right is a right that 'runs with the object'. The question they focus on is therefore why the law limits the possibility for parties to create a property right that runs with an object.[311] When two parties are dealing with a potential property right they need, in their view, a method to verify the other party's understanding of the parties' respective rights.[312]

305 Merrill & Smith 2000, p. 58.
306 Merrill & Smith 2000, p. 61, Van Erp 2003b, p. 9.
307 See Munzer 2006, p. 156-157, Hansmann & Kraakman 2002, p. 373 *et seq.*, Parisi, Schulz & Depoorter 2005, p. 588-590.
308 Hansmann & Kraakman 2002, p. 373.
309 Hansmann & Kraakman 2002, p. 374. On this theory see Baffi 2007, p. 19-21.
310 Hansmann & Kraakman 2002, p. 375.
311 Hansmann & Kraakman 2002, p. 379.
312 Hansmann & Kraakman 2002, p. 383.

In the case of a contract, verification lies in the mutual consent the parties give to the conclusion of the contract. However, when a property right is at stake, the parties in question might not be bound through privity of contract.[313] An example is a situation in which A sells most of his rights in an object to B, while retaining some rights in respect of the object for himself. In the contract of sale A and B deal with this division, and stipulate that B may assign his own rights in the object to another party, but not A's right in the object. When B subsequently contracts with C, there is no means by which A can verify that C shares the understanding of A and B on the division of the right to which they agreed.[314]

It is, in particular, in situations such as these that Hansmann and Kraakman search for the existence of *numerus clausus*. On this they state:

> 'A central problem of property is to provide mechanisms for solving these verification problems - or, as it is more commonly put, to assure effective notice. To solve these problems, property law employs a variety of *verification rules*. A verification rule sets out the conditions under which a given right in a given asset will run with the asset. There is a strong relationship between verification rules and the types of property rights - or, rather, the forms of ownership - that the law is prepared to recognise. Indeed, the two are inextricably intertwined in any legal regime for property rights'.[315]

These authors argue that a prime example of this theory can be found in the concept of possession. A strict rule of possession in a theoretical system could indicate that he who has physical possession of an object holds the complete property right in that object and that a transfer of possession will transfer that property right to another party.[316] In a more realistic and complicated world, different verification rules apply, imposed by legislation as either an opt-in or an opt-out rule, parties can have the choice whether to add a form of publicity to their legal relation or not. An example is an artist who may choose to add some form of information on his work of art to assert his intellectual property right in respect of the piece of work, or legislation might impose such an intellectual property right through a mandatory system.[317]

In Hansmann and Kraakman's view, property law systems rarely offer a set of well-defined property rights, but rather a set of property categories for which additional verification rules may apply.[318] In this respect they differ in opinion from Merrill and Smith, who focus their theory on types of property rights and not categories. A property law system is therefore not closed because no new rights can be created, but because, especially in common law systems, for the creation of new property rights, such difficult and costly verification rules apply that parties do not make use of this possibility.[319]

313 Hansmann & Kraakman 2002, p. 383-384.
314 Hansmann & Kraakman 2002, p. 384.
315 Hansmann & Kraakman 2002, p. 384. Footnotes omitted.
316 Hansmann & Kraakman 2002, p. 384-385.
317 Hansmann & Kraakman 2002, p. 385-395.
318 Hansmann & Kraakman 2002, p. 398-399.
319 Hansmann & Kraakman 2002, p. 399.

As in the case of the optimal standardisation theory, there seems to be a link between the number of rights and the costs for third parties. On this Hansmann and Kraakman state:

> '... there is a great discontinuity between permitting a single form of property rights and permitting more than one. Verification is simple and cheap when a single form of property rights is mandated for a given type of claim in a given type of asset. As soon as choice is permitted - even if that choice is only between two well-defined alternatives - much more costly verification rules are generally required. On the other hand, a verification rule that is adequate for a choice between even a small number of different property rights will commonly be adequate for a choice among an indefinitely number of alternatives'.[320]

A new property right therefore should only be created if the benefits to users of the right exceed the costs a new property right creates for non-users of the right. These costs for non-users will comprise a new or extended verification rule. The law therefore does not limit the kinds of property rights that can be created, but only affirms certain property rights.[321] *Numerus clausus,* in the view of Hansmann and Kraakman, can therefore be explained as the balance between these costs and benefits.[322]

3.2.4. Critical Analysis of the Approach to *Numerus Clausus* in Law and Economics

The reasons behind a *numerus clausus* of property rights have not been discussed in legal writings in great detail. It can therefore be no surprise that Law and Economics has only recently given attention to the subject.[323] In the writings of Law and Economics scholars three approaches can be distinguished. First, the fragmentation argument focuses attention on the limitation of the law of property in respect of the number of property rights, showing that too many property rights with the wrong content, too many or too few rights to exclude others, can lead to economically inefficient results in a tragedy of the commons or anti-commons.[324] Secondly, when not looking at the property rights themselves, but at third parties, the problem of information costs created by a new property right leads to a legal system standardising the available property rights or, thirdly, leads to the legal system only affirming certain property rights with verification rules.[325] On these approaches, a number of observations can be made.

In general, each of these three approaches brings highly relevant arguments to the discussion on the reasons for a *numerus clausus,* but none of them provides a

320 Hansmann & Kraakman 2002, p. 399.
321 Hansmann & Kraakman 2002, p. 419.
322 Hansmann & Kraakman 2002, p. 419-420.
323 Furthermore, as Anderson and McChesney signal, economists have only become recently interested in the law of property. See Anderson & McChesney 2003, p. 1-5.
324 See above; 3.2.1. Fragmentation: Not too Many Rights; on Commons and Anti-Commons.
325 See above; 3.2.2. *Numerus Clausus* as Optimal Standardisation of Property Rights and 3.2.3. *Numerus Clausus* as Verification of Property Rights.

conclusive answer.[326] The explanation for this can partly be found in the fact that all of the authors behind these approaches are American lawyers, and they primarily attempt to clarify *numerus clausus* doctrine in US law. Since US law differs from European legal systems, even English common law, the arguments these authors use are not automatically applicable to civil law or English common law.

A second explanation is closely connected to this last statement. Heller, Merrill and Smith, and Hansmann and Kraakman, renowned Law and Economics scholars, are all American lawyers and not civil law property lawyers.[327] As discussed at the beginning of this chapter, the debate on *numerus clausus*, although in principle applicable to all legal systems, finds its origin in civil law systems.[328] Therefore, possibly, the understanding of these authors of what exactly *numerus clausus* is might be different from the civil law approach.

When looking at this Law and Economics analysis of *numerus clausus* from a property law point of view, several remarks can be made. First of all, the discussion on the fragmentation of property rights is highly relevant in respect of the method in which property rights are created.[329] A lesser right or limited property right is a property right derived, either through subtraction, *démembrement* or limitation, from a primary right. Consequently, a property right will have characteristics similar to the primary right after which it was modelled. In systems that use the *démembrement* or subtraction method, creating a limited property right is regarded as a fragmentation of the primary right.[330] In some cases, for example, when a lesser right to use, such as a right of servitude of way, is created, both the holder of the primary right and the holder of the lesser right have a right to walk over a certain piece of land. Theoretically, the holder of the primary right may create as many lesser rights to use as he wants.[331]

The criticism of the fragmentation theory, that it would look only at the number of right-holders and not at the types of property rights, in this respect, does not seem completely accurate. When parties want to create a new, as yet unknown, property right, such as a right to take minerals from a piece of land, as occurred in South Africa, the question can be raised whether not too many privileges to use, without the right to exclude others, are created, and the threat of a tragedy of the commons is more imminent with the new property right.

Even when it comes to the fragmentation of a single property right among multiple holders in a co-entitlement or co-ownership regime, the danger of under-use and over-use occurs. Theoretically, when several co-holders of a primary right want to transfer the object on which they have a right, they must all agree to the transfer. When one party refuses his consent, in the absence of any rules, a tragedy

326 See Van Erp 2003b, p. 10-12.

327 E.g., Van Erp who states that for him the analysis of Merrill and Smith comes (very) 'close to how a civil property lawyer looks at the content, historical background and justification of the *numerus clausus* doctrine'. Van Erp 2003b, p 10.

328 See above; 1.3. Considering *Numerus Clausus*.

329 See above; 2.2. Of Ways to Create a Lesser Property Right.

330 See above; 2.2. Of Ways to Create a Lesser Property Right.

331 However, see Fusaro 2001, p. 7.

of the anti-commons occurs. Even more, when, as was the case in France until very recently, permission is needed from the other co-holders to assign a co-entitlement share to another party, the danger of a tragedy of the anti-commons arises.[332]

The Law and Economics scholars do not make the distinction between *Typenzwang* and *Typenfixierung*. They therefore ignore the principle that both of these elements are part of *numerus clausus*.[333] The first example, the recognition of new lesser rights to use without sufficient regulations, is a question of recognising new rights or *Typenzwang*. The second, the question of whether a specific property right, whether primary or lesser, can be shared in a co-entitlement regime, is also a question of *Typenfixierung*, an element that these American authors seem to miss. Although generally all legal systems allow parties to create such a co-entitlement regime, in respect of some lesser rights that are closely connected to a specific person, a right of usufruct, for example, a co-entitlement regime might be denied.

Secondly, in the Law and Economics analysis of *numerus clausus*, the discussion about costs for third parties when new property rights are created is entangled with a discussion on the publicity principle. As was set out in Chapter 1, the subject of *numerus clausus* should be distinguished from that of the publicity of property rights.[334] Although these two elements are very closely connected, a system of property rights is not closed because there are certain rules on publicity. The order of reasoning is the other way around. Because there are property rights that have effect against third parties, in some cases the legal system demands publicity in order to justify the effect of these property rights against third parties.[335]

What these two elements share with each other is their desire for legal certainty. In particular, civil law systems start from the presumption that the list of available property rights is closed because it concerns rights that have effect against third parties. Therefore, in order to ensure legal certainty, the number and content of property rights should be as standardised as possible. In case of publicity, the reasoning is connected, but not the same. Some property rights have effect against third parties even if these parties do not know about the existence of these property rights. In order to justify this effect against third parties, the legal system demands publicity. The principle of publicity therefore justifies the effect of property rights against third parties, but not the closed nature of the system of property rights.

The counter-arguments of Hansmann and Kraakman on the analysis of Merrill and Smith should be reviewed in the light of the distinction between *numerus clausus* and publicity. Verification rules, or rules that enable a party to investigate if a property right exists are, at least in my view, rules of publicity and not of *numerus clausus*.[336] Explaining the existence of *numerus clausus* through a system of publicity, which, in my view, results from the nature of property rights more than from the fact that the list of property rights is closed, does not answer the question posed by

332 On French law see Chapter 3; 2.2. Co-Ownership including Apartments.

333 See Chapter 1; 1.2.2. *Numerus Clausus* of Property Rights.

334 See Chapter 1; 1.2.1. Principles of Property Law.

335 Of a different opinion see Epstein 1982, p. 1360.

336 See also Struycken, who makes a distinction between *numerus clausus* and publicity. Struycken 2007, p. 305 and p. 797-798. See also Sagaert 2005b, p. 1052-1053.

Hansmann and Kraakman. Instead, it offers insight in how the property law system functions and how *numerus clausus* and publicity are connected.[337]

Finally, the explanation of Merrill and Smith seems to be the one that most closely connects to the way in which continental lawyers perceive the closed system of property rights.[338] This could possibly be explained because Merrill and Smith connect their theory to the traditional distinction between property rights and personal rights, and the different effects these rights have in respect to third parties. Their presumption therefore seems to be that, because of the third-party effect, property rights should be limited.[339]

What Merrill and Smith have done is qualify the effect against third parties that deserves limitation in terms of measurement costs, externalities and frustration costs.[340] Their explanation of a system of property rights as the search for the optimal balance between these two types of costs and therefore a search for the optimal standardisation of property rights might explain the tension civil lawyers feel between legal certainty and party autonomy.

The analysis of Merrill and Smith certainly connects to the marketability argument put forward by Rudden.[341] An optimal standardisation of property right will ensure that not too many property rights are recognised in a legal system. Too many property rights make it difficult to execute transfers in particular primary rights, as it is more difficult and more costly to find out what lesser property rights burden the primary right. In this respect the marketability argument might be further specified into a 'finance-ability' argument. When, in order to offer finance for the acquisition of a primary right, the party offering the finance has to undertake a disproportionate effort to find out with what property rights the primary right is burdened, in order to estimate the risk of the transaction, the primary right loses not only value, but also transferability because finance is more difficult to obtain.

3.3. *Numerus Clausus in Comparative Analysis*

The analysis above shows that it is possible to analyse the property law systems in France, Germany, the Netherlands and England in terms of primary rights and three categories of lesser rights.[342] However, a common analysis does not result in four similar legal systems. To the contrary, many technical differences between the legal systems exist, in particular when it comes to the requirements for the creation of property rights.

However, technical difficulties, although highly relevant, should not be the main concern when considering the topic of *numerus clausus* from a comparative

337 In the same sense see Van Erp, who, in his Van Gerven lecture, distinguishes between *numerus clausus* and transparency (publicity) as basic, but distinct, principles of property law. See Van Erp 2006b, p. 14-15.

338 Van Erp 2003b, p. 10.

339 See Motive III 1888, p. 3. See also above; 1.3. Considering *Numerus Clausus*.

340 See above; 3.2.2. *Numerus Clausus* as Optimal Standardisation of Property Rights.

341 See above; 3.2. Law and Economics on *Numerus Clausus*.

342 See above; 2.1. Of Primary Property Rights and Lesser Property Rights.

point of view. The *numerus clausus* of property rights is a principle of property law.[343] It is this principle that is a filter through which legal relations pass on their way to becoming property rights. The *numerus clausus* decides which relations can have property effect and which cannot.

Numerus clausus operates in a twofold manner. First, the legal relation is analysed and characterised as one of the property rights a legal system recognises. This function is known as *Typenfixierung*. Secondly, when the type of property right has been created, the provisions on that type of property right will be applied to the legal relation. This function is known as *Typenzwang*. The method by which *numerus clausus* operates is to require both elements to be fulfilled. When this occurs, the legal relation passes the 'test' and property law will be applicable.[344] It is only after this 'test' that other principles, and also ground rules such as the *nemo dat* principle, apply.[345]

In each of the discussions on the different national legal systems in the chapters above, the conclusion has been reached that each legal system adheres to a *numerus clausus*. However, in each legal system developments can be seen which put the traditional *numerus clausus* under pressure. When the Civil Codes were adopted in the civil law systems, the legislators claimed these codes to be the primary source of law. In these legal systems, legislation comes before case law and doctrine.[346] In common law systems the hierarchical order between the sources of law is different – case law takes the primary place unless the legislature has intervened by statute.

Property law is a very important area of law, which in each of these systems is dealt with primarily by the most important, primary, source of law. As a result the way in which the property law system operates is different between civil law and common law countries. In civil law, the Civil Code, by its nature as a code of law, stipulates which rights are property rights and what provisions apply to these. In common law, with its case-law nature, rules have been made through court decisions, on a case-by-case basis, to decide which property rights exist and what provisions apply to these rights.

This difference does not necessarily result in a legal system different from the civil law. In English law too, over time, a standardisation of rights at common law was achieved, which eventually became affirmed by the Law of Property Act 1925. By statutory intervention, but in fact already before that, the number of estates that could exist at common law had been reduced to three types. Through legislation in this area of law, the hierarchical order between the sources of law shifted and Section 1 of the Law of Property Act 1925 became an expression of the *numerus clausus* of property rights in land at common law in the same way as the Civil Codes became such an expression in the civil law systems. Equity, in English law, remains different. In equity, analysis of the case law on equitable property rights is needed to come to a list of property rights. No case or statute provides a list of all equitable property rights. Theoretically, a new case could arise tomorrow and, with case law

343 Van Erp 2006b, p. 14.
344 See, in this respect, Chapter 8; 3. The Making of European Property Law.
345 Van Erp 2006b, p. 16-17. Van Erp 2008, forthcoming.
346 Zweigert & Kötz 1998, p. 74-75, 143-144.

being the primary source of law in this area, the courts could recognise a new property right. However, here the House of Lords has restricted itself to criteria that must be fulfilled for a new equitable property right to be created, if at all.[347]

In all these legal systems, therefore, private parties are prevented from creating new property rights themselves.[348] In other words, in order for private parties to create a new property right, they require either legislative or judicial permission in the form of a statute or a decision. The *numerus clausus* of property rights provides that only the legislature or the judiciary has the power to authorise new property rights. Since the nineteenth century, this is exactly what has happened. Originally outside the Civil Codes, all legal systems have in some form recognised a right to an apartment. Furthermore, in all of the legal systems, the judiciary has also intervened by recognising new property rights. These include the French retention of title and real suretyship[349], the German security ownership and acquisition right[350], the Dutch security ownership, although later abolished in the new Civil Code[351], and the English restrictive covenants, estate contracts and options to purchase.[352]

In particular, under the increasing influence of contract law, parties have attempted to create new property rights and have found authorisation from courts in three areas. First, in respect of the anticipatory lesser property rights, mentioned above as the third category of lesser property rights, the influence of contract law has led to a series of new property rights. Second, contract law has also enabled parties to combine property rights, either with each other or with general contract law. Although these developments do not technically and doctrinally create new property rights, they provide new uses for existing property rights that were, thus far, unknown. These include the stacking of rights, the combination of property rights to achieve a specific situation. Examples include a right of apartment on a right of *superficies,* combined with a right of *emphyteusis,* on a right of ownership of land. Although doctrinally three lesser property rights are created, it is the combination of rights that are enjoyed by the holder of an apartment that provides a unique situation that could not be achieved without the stacking of these rights.

Property rights are also combined with contract law to create new situations in which these property rights can be applied. As mentioned above, in particular, German law is highly developed when it comes to security-*Grundschuld* and security-servitudes. This use of these lesser property rights does not doctrinally create a new property right, but in fact achieves a result that could not have been created with these lesser property rights alone. For example, in respect to a security-*Grundschuld,* the addition of contract law is the re-introduction of accessority to the

347 *National Provincial Bank Ltd v Ainsworth* [1965] AC 1175, HL at 1247-1248 *per* Lord Wilberforce. See Chapter 6; 4. A *Numerus Clausus* in English Property Law?

348 It is this function of the *numerus clausus* that is emphasised by Reid and Van der Merwe, see Reid & Van der Merwe 2004, p. 654.

349 See Chapter 3; 2.3. Security Ownership, and 4.1. Right of Retention.

350 See Chapter 4; 2.5. Security Ownership, and 3.4. Expectation Rights.

351 See Chapter 5; 2.3. Security Ownership.

352 See Chapter 6; 2.5. Restrictive Covenants, 2.7. Estate Contracts, and 2.8. Options to Purchase.

property right. The German legislature explicitly removed accessority in respect of the right of *Grundschuld*, but through conclusion of the security contract, accessority to a claim that the right of *Grundschuld* secures is created. In property law, the right of *Grundschuld* remains non-accessory, but in effect an accessory property right is created.[353] Moreover, in case of a security-servitude this is the creation of a *de facto* positive burden on the holder of the servient tenement.[354]

Third, in contract law itself, several rights can be created that have more effect than just between the parties themselves. These rights include contractual relations already mentioned such as *Treuhand* and *fiducie*, but also rights of lease in civil law systems that, through special protection measures for the lessee, create a personal right that can be invoked against a new owner of the leased object. These rights have been dealt with under the heading of borderline cases because they are situated between the law of obligations and the law of property.[355]

This analysis shows that, compared with the nineteenth century, when the Civil Codes were first introduced, property law is now a more open system. Even in Germany, where property law and contract law are strictly separated, the influence of contract law has opened up the system of property law considerably. The fear of the creation of disproportionate and unnecessary burdens on the primary right, and so also the fear of the recreation of feudal relations, has not fully stopped the development of property law. Several lesser property rights can be enjoyed by a person without the requirement of that person being a holder of a property right of the object on which it is created, for instance, limited personal servitudes and real burdens in German law.[356] Moreover, several property rights can be enjoyed almost perpetually.

Property law in the twenty-first century faces completely different challenges than the property law of the nineteenth century. Nevertheless, the catalogue of property rights that all these legal systems use is almost the same as in Roman law 2000 years ago. Of course, the law of property has been adapted to suit modern-day business, but this has led to an increase in party autonomy in the existing catalogue of property rights. No new property rights have been created and private parties are still not authorised to create new property rights themselves. This line of argumentation can be used against property law as well. Because private parties do not get sufficient freedom in property law to create the legal relations they want, they resort to the law of contract and attempt to achieve similar results. They do this either by making creative use of property law or by abandoning property law altogether.

When Civil Codes were introduced in the civil law systems, the legal systems were recovering from the effects of the French Revolution. The feudal system of landholding, which had resulted in a fragmentation of ownership into *dominium directum* and *dominium utile*, was abolished and replaced by a unitary, Roman-law

353 See Chapter 4; 3.8. *Grundschuld*.
354 See Chapter 4; 3.1. Real Servitudes.
355 See Chapter 3; 4. Borderline Cases in French Property Law, Chapter 4; 4. Borderline Cases in German Property Law, Chapter 5; 4. Borderline Cases in Dutch Property Law, and Chapter 6; 4. A *Numerus Clausus* in English Property Law?
356 See Chapter 4; 3.2. Personal Servitudes, and 3.5. Real Burden.

based, concept of ownership. Furthermore, in the feudal system, property rights that were held by lords had forced tenants or vassals to provide labour and give up large parts of their income, just because they held a feudal interest in the land of the lord. Therefore, the abolition of the feudal system not only resulted in a return to a unitary concept of ownership, but also in the abolition of feudal burdens that had forced positive duties on landholders. In France, Germany and the Netherlands, although different Civil Codes applied, these two elements were included. In the name of legal certainty, a unitary concept of ownership was established that would be protected by the legal system. Unlike the feudal burdens, which could be many, only a selected group of property rights could burden the ownership of a landholder. The selection of which property rights could exist was made by the legislators under the inspiration of Roman law, and was taken into the Civil Code. In this way, the freedom of ownership became protected. Moreover, third parties dealing with an owner and possibly acquiring the right of ownership were also protected, because only a limited number of property rights affecting the use and the value of the land could exist. Once a third party found out which of the selected property rights existed on the land, that party would know the contents of that right because the Civil Code offered explicit provisions on it.

The *numerus clausus* therefore fulfilled a *contra*-feudal function and enhanced legal certainty. It is possibly therefore that the French *Cour de cassation* in 1834, when considering an old feudal relation, was more concerned with the characterisation of the right of ownership than when considering the possibility that the right the parties wanted to create could have been a lesser property right.[357] In modern property law, the feudal system, although not forgotten, is less of relevance. Land is no longer the sole source of wealth and more and more movable and incorporeal objects are gaining importance. English law, although technically still adhering to a feudal system of landholding, long ago abolished its negative effects and, as was discussed above, also developed a restricted set of property rights.

In order to adapt property law to modern developments, the focus today is more on party autonomy than on fear of feudal relations, and more on lesser property rights than on the right of ownership. The role *numerus clausus* therefore plays in modern-day property law is different from the role it played in the nineteenth century. It still seeks to provide legal certainty and protect the law of property, no longer against feudal law, but in order to maintain the separation from the law of contract.

With the development of movable and incorporeal objects, especially claims, into separate subject matters of property law, the catalogue of property rights or the content of the *numerus clausus*, which is mainly focused on land, has not always proven to be sufficient. Therefore, in the most recent law reforms, the traditional requirements for some property rights have been relaxed by allowing for more party autonomy. This is the case with security rights, in particular, which in the Netherlands and France can also be non-possessory rights or, in case of a security

357 *Req.* 13 February 1834, D.P. 1834.I.218, S.1834.I.205. See Chapter 3; 5. A *Numerus Clausus* in French Property Law?

right in respect of a claim, can be created without notice to the debtor of the claim. This relaxation enables the creation of these rights in respect of future claims. Furthermore, these rights can be created not only to secure the performance of an already existing obligation, but also, under conditions of specificity, to secure a future obligation.[358] Therefore, by contract, parties may specify the obligations or set of obligations the property right secures, and also the claim or set of claims on which it is created, both present and future.

The combination of these developments, the increasing role of contract law and the increasing importance of new objects of property law, can lead to two questions. First, in the light of these developments, is the *numerus clausus* of property rights the modern legal systems recognise still sufficient? Second, especially with regard to the role contract law plays in modern legal practice, and its increasing importance, also in the law of property, as well as the fading of fears about a return to the feudal system, do we still need a *numerus clausus* of property rights?

3.4. *Struycken: Why we Need a Numerus Clausus*

The first question is less difficult to answer than the second. The above analysis shows that, at this moment, the *numerus clausus* is under more pressure than ever, but that at the same time it seems to function adequately. Struycken, in his thesis on this subject, argues for the continuation and maintenance of the *numerus clausus*. Although he is critical of the content of the *numerus clausus*, he explicitly states that the rule itself should remain.[359]

In terms of this Chapter, the concept of *numerus clausus* Struycken uses is a rule of *numerus clausus*.[360] In that respect, his analysis is that of a Dutch civil lawyer of Dutch law, albeit taking into account several foreign jurisdictions. In Struycken's view, *numerus clausus* should be seen in a broad sense, taking not only the number and content of lesser rights into account, but *numerus clausus* is the system of rules in the system of property law that governs the creation, transfer and destruction of property rights.[361] In this view, *numerus clausus*, even as a rule, should be placed in the general doctrinal context of the legal system. The doctrinal context in this respect is that of the Pandectist system as developed by Von Savigny and others, as dealt with in Chapter 4 on German law.[362] In this system, the law of obligations and the law of property are strictly separated, and the law of property provides its own rules for the creation, transfer and destruction of property rights.[363] These rules should be seen as part of the rejection of the system that prevailed before the Civil Codes, in which there was not a strict separation between these areas of law, and in

358 The difference between the future claim, i.e., the object of the property right, and the future obligation is that the lesser security right seeks to secure the performance of the obligation by existing on the claim.
359 Struycken 2007, p. 796.
360 See above; 1.3.2. *Numerus Clausus* as a Principle or as a Rule?
361 Struycken 2007, p. 9-10, 799-801.
362 See Chapter 4; 1. Introduction.
363 On this see also Füller 2006, p. 8 *et seq.*

which the right of ownership could be fragmented in such a way as to impose positive duties on persons in their feudal relations to their feudal lords.[364]

As a rejection of this system of property law, a unitary concept of ownership was introduced in which ownership could no longer be fragmented in such a way as to create several forms of ownership. Instead, the right of ownership could only be fragmented in those ways that are prescribed by law, and these take the form of lesser property rights. In order to continue protecting the right of ownership, consequently the number, but certainly also the content, of property rights was limited.[365]

Placing *numerus clausus* in this partly historical perspective - the Pandectist system was developed after the beginning of the nineteenth century - provides strong arguments for maintaining the closed system of property rights. First of all, *numerus clausus* is part of a system in which the legislator has taken the principal position in authorising the recognition and regulation of property rights.[366] Changing this in favour of private parties is not only 'opening up' the *numerus clausus* with the creation of new property rights created by parties themselves, but also changing the primacy in respect to the authority to recognise property rights from the legislator to private parties themselves. Such a change would bring a movement away from a system in which the legislature imposes and enforces the strict separation between the law of obligations and the law of property.

Secondly, *numerus clausus* fulfils a function to determine the applicability of the law of property.[367] When a legal relation passes through the filter of the *numerus clausus*, the law of property will apply and thus legal certainty is ensured. When, as Struycken emphasises, no *numerus clausus* exists, there should be clear criteria to decide which legal relations are property rights.[368] The existence of a rule of *numerus clausus* compensates for a less clear definition of what constitutes a property right. With reference to Meijers, who drafted a large part of the current Dutch Civil Code, Struycken concludes that all sorts of problems concerning registrability, destruction, and execution, including seizure, would arise.[369] In this respect, *numerus clausus* creates legal certainty in respect of information to third parties about the property rights and the provisions applicable to that property right.[370]

Moreover, when looking further into the content of the legal system, arguments in favour of *numerus clausus* can be found. As stated above, although Struycken's analysis is based on Dutch law, his arguments are valid for, and can be applied to, any other legal system as well. When it comes to the *numerus clausus* as a

364 See Chapter 2; 4. The *Ius Commune*.

365 It is these two elements of the Pandectist system that Struycken seems to focus on. See Struycken 2007, p. 695-724.

366 Struycken 2007, p. 762-765, in the same sense see Foëx 1987, p. 113. See above; 1.3.4. *Numerus Clausus* as a Principle of 'Constitutional' Property Law.

367 Struycken 2007, p. 350-356, 759-760, see above; 1.3.1. Requirements of *Numerus Clausus*.

368 Struycken 2007, p. 759.

369 In Dutch law the concept of property right is based on the 'normal-type' (*normal type*), which is a set of criteria to which a certain legal relation can confirm. As long as the majority of these criteria are fulfilled, the legal relation can be a property right. See Struycken 2007, p. 759, Meijers 1948, p. 269-270, Meijers 1907, p. 24. See also Chapter 5; 1. Introduction.

370 In the words of Struycken *oriënteringszekerheid*, Struycken 2007, p. 759-760.

closed system of property rights, it is the limitation on party autonomy that is its consequence.

Party autonomy is that concept, usually identified in the area of contract law, and hence also known as the principle of freedom of contract, that allows parties to agree on anything they wish (albeit between themselves) within the scope of the law, public order or public morality. In contrast with contract law, in property law this principle of party autonomy is limited, and in some cases even absent. In legal systems adhering to the rule of *numerus clausus*, the *numerus clausus* is enforced through legislation, usually a Civil Code. In those systems, party autonomy in the law of property is only allowed under specific authorisation of the legislature. However, in modern property law systems, in particular in Dutch law, the legislature has created several areas in which parties are allowed to shape their legal property relation through agreement. This is the case in the area of real servitudes, *emphyteusis* and *superficies*.[371]

In Dutch law, there are two elements that are connected to the recognition of party autonomy. One is offered through a criterion formulated by the Supreme Court in the context of the right of *emphyteusis*, stating that an agreement between parties that has a *sufficient connection* to the *emphyteusis*, and that is not contrary to the *nature* of the right, is treated as part of the property right.[372] Struycken deals with this decision and the criteria following from it in respect to party autonomy, and shows that as a part of the *Typenfixierung*, the limitations on the content of property rights, parties have to stay within the limitations the property right offers.[373] In this respect, *Typenfixierung* also ensures that parties do not modify a property right in such a way that it fulfils the function of another property right. As an example, Struycken mentions the right of usufruct formed in such a way that a right of *superficies* is created.[374] In his view, this is an unauthorised use of party autonomy that is prevented by the closed system. The closed system thus ensures legal certainty in the sense that parties remain within the boundaries set by the legislature.

Struycken finds a second element in what he calls the subtraction principle. Inspired by the South African test of subtraction from the *dominium*, Struycken's principle of subtraction refers to the starting point that a lesser right can only comprise part of the rights or powers of the primary right, or mother right, from which it is derived.[375] Following a method of *démembrement*, as is done in Dutch law, in which lesser rights are conceived as rights or powers from a primary right that are transferred to another person and take the form of a lesser right, there are several

[371] See Arts. 5:73 (servitudes), 5:85 and 5:86 (*emphyteusis*) and 5:101 and 5:102 (*superficies*) BW. See, e.g., also the discussion in Epstein 1982, p. 1353 *et seq.*

[372] HR 16 March 1977, *NJ* 1977, 399. See Struycken 2007, p. 386 *et seq.* See Chapter 5; 3.3. *Emphyteusis*.

[373] Struycken 2007, p. 400-401.

[374] Struycken 2007, p. 625-627. He also mentions the right of *emphyteusis*, apartment rights and the footprint, p. 627-632.

[375] Struycken 2007, p. 401. On South African law see also below; 3.6. A Legal System without a *Numerus Clausus*: South African Law.

consequences for the content of these lesser rights.[376] A prime result of Struycken's subtraction principle is that a lesser right cannot contain a positive duty, usually seen as one of the best expressions of the existence of a rule of *numerus clausus*, because the primary right from which it is derived does not contain a positive duty either.[377] Again, this theory is part of the *Typenfixierung* as a part of *numerus clausus*. The content of lesser rights that is outside the specific provisions of the law, which is that content the parties give to the right themselves, cannot exceed the content of the mother right from which it is derived or subtracted.[378] Struycken emphasises that the subtraction principle is a theoretical model, connected to the criterion of sufficient connection dealt with above, that does not necessarily apply for all lesser rights, but certainly applies to clarify why in principle no positive duties, or duties *in faciendo*, can be imposed.[379]

The two elements of party autonomy again illustrate the link of the *numerus clausus* to the separation between the law of obligations, where parties can make agreements containing a positive duty for one of them or both of them, and the law of property, which provides its own rules and regulations, and in which party autonomy has a very limited place. As a general guideline, parties must remain within the boundaries set by the legislature, even when they have been granted a certain amount of party autonomy.[380]

Struycken adds another strong argument for why a rule of *numerus clausus* should be recognised by illustrating how parties can make use of the space within the limits set by law, or, in other words, within the *Typenfixierung*. Under the heading of forming property rights in three dimensions, he discusses content, object, and time or, in other words, fragmentation, space and time.[381]

As to the first dimension, fragmentation, a *numerus clausus* is strongly related to the prohibition on fragmenting a property right beyond the possibilities to do this authorised by law. Creating a lesser right, at least in Dutch law, but also in French law, and partly in English law, brings with it a fragmentation of the primary right or the right from which it is derived.[382] These forms of fragmentation, in Struycken's view, can only exist if there is a specific legal basis for it, as the rule of *numerus clausus* would lose its meaning because the other property rights would be neglected.[383] Forms of fragmentation, which have been dealt with in terms of content above, as well as earlier in the discussion on the several legal systems, are the transfer of a primary right, in this case ownership, for security purposes, which is not considered as a full transfer because the transferee continues to have some property right in the object he transferred. Therefore such a fragmentation is limited in Dutch

376 See above; 2.2. Of Ways to Create a Lesser Property Right.
377 Struycken 2007, p. 402-403.
378 Struycken 2007, p. 404-405.
379 Struycken 2007, p. 407-415.
380 Struycken 2007, p. 427-431. See also Rank-Berenschot 1992, p. 335. On Rank-Berenschot see Struycken 2007, p. 445-446.
381 Struycken 2007, p. 447, 448 (content), 453 (space), 463 (time).
382 Struycken 2007, p. 467.
383 Struycken 2007, p. 467-470.

law and is usually seen as enforcing the rule of *numerus clausus*, because only those fragmentations that are authorised by law can be made.[384] Another form of fragmentation is a transfer of a primary right, again in this case ownership, for management purposes.[385] In a Dutch perspective, a transfer for management purposes brings the English trust to mind.[386] In the way in which English trust law is traditionally conceived in Dutch law, a fragmentation of the primary right is required so that both trustee and beneficiary hold a part of the primary right.

Finally, there is another danger resulting from fragmentation of the right of ownership, in the creation of a separate set of objects to which normal creditors do not have access.[387] The rule in any civil law system that all creditors are equal and that a person is liable to these creditors with all his assets can be violated with a fragmentation of ownership in two ways. First, the fragmentation of ownership might violate the equality rule, known as *paritas creditorum*, in the form of lesser rights for security such as pledge and hypothec. However, these special rights only exist when explicitly dealt with by law. Second, fragmenting the right of ownership will divide the right of ownership over two sets of assets. Where formerly creditors of the full right of ownership could acquire the object's full value, now only a part of the value remains, as only one fragment of ownership remains with the original owner and the other fragment of ownership is with someone else.[388]

As to the second dimension, there are the requirements of space to which the parties must conform.[389] Through the use of their party autonomy when creating property rights, parties may attempt to fragment ownership in such a way that a horizontal or vertical separation occurs. In this way, parties can split a building from the ownership of the land on which the building is constructed, or parties can separate the ownership of floors in a building from each other. Such separations are known as horizontal separations. In order to achieve this, parties usually make use of a right of *superficies*.[390] A second way is that parties can vertically divide the land, such as splitting a piece of land in two or splitting a building into two different entities, each capable of being subject to a property right.[391] Here also, Struycken emphasises, parties should remain within the limits of the law, although many solutions can be found there.[392]

Thirdly, a final form of separation is that in time. As an example of a separation in time, a property right can be fragmented through a conditional transfer.[393] Such a transfer either takes place under suspension, with the result that the transfer will only take effect upon the occurrence of a certain condition, or under resolution, with the result that the transfer will take place until the occurrence of a certain

384 Struycken 2007, p. 510-512.
385 Struycken 2007, p. 512.
386 Struycken 2007, p. 513. See also Sagaert 2005b, p. 1018-1021.
387 Or a separate patrimony (*afgescheiden vermogen*), see Struycken 2007, p. 539.
388 Struycken 2007, p. 539-548. See also Sagaert 2005b, p. 1029-1030.
389 Struycken 2007, p. 453.
390 Struycken 2007, p. 455-460.
391 Struycken 2007, p. 453-455.
392 See, e.g., on the Footprint-construction Struycken 2007, p. 461-462.
393 Struycken 2007, p. 549.

condition. The property right that is transferred, or not yet transferred, under condition is best described as a temporal property right that will only regain its full form when the condition under which is was created has taken effect.[394]

The effects of a transfer under condition of a property right are debated in many systems, and these systems offer different solutions. In French law, both parties to a transfer receive a property right, one under condition of suspension, and the other under resolutive condition.[395] In German law, a separate lesser right, the expectation right, is recognised.[396] In English law, the entitlement to a property right that is transferred under condition is solved through the law of trust.[397] In Dutch law, unlike any of the other legal systems, the other party that is not the owner only has a personal right.[398] Creating a type of ownership limited in time is in direct conflict with the unitary concept of ownership as the primary right, and therefore also in direct conflict with the closed list of lesser rights.[399] It is also in this context that Struycken concludes that, without a specific legal basis, fragmentation of property rights in time should not be allowed.[400]

It is, in particular, the argument that property law is a coherent system of law, built on the foundations of Pandectist legal thinking, as civil law jurisdictions are, that justifies the existence of and need for a rule of *numerus clausus* of property rights that is enforced by the legislator.[401] In Struycken's view, it is undesirable to leave complete freedom for parties to shape their own legal relations with third-party effect.[402] Arguments used in favour of more freedom for parties to create new property rights have an enormous and unpredictable impact on the system of property law, and are therefore not convincing enough to accept.[403]

However, that does not imply that property law should not be subject to change. Through the analysis of the content of property law, such as the transfer system, specificity and publicity requirements, deduced into principles of property law, which form a part of *numerus clausus* as Struycken sees it, we can move away from the Pandectist legal thinking and move forward.[404] In the 'constitutional' dimension of the *numerus clausus*, renewing the law of property and moving towards a more dynamic property law is a task for the legislator, with whom the authority to recognise and regulate new property rights is entrusted in the system of property law as it is adhered to by civil law systems.[405]

394 Struycken 2007, p. 551-553.
395 See Chapter 3; 2.1. Ownership.
396 See Chapter 4; 2.1. Ownership.
397 See Chapter 6; 2.9. Mortgage of Land and Equity of Redemption.
398 Struycken 2007, p. 557-558. See Chapter 5; 2.1. Ownership.
399 See above; 2. The Content of Property Law Systems in Europe.
400 Struycken 2007, p. 567.
401 Struycken 2007, p. 753-762. See also Smits 1996, p. 53-54.
402 Struycken 2007, p. 796.
403 Struycken 2007, p. 796-797.
404 Struycken 2007, p. 784.
405 Struycken 2007, p. 809-810. On the 'constitutional' dimension see above; 1.3.4. *Numerus Clausus* as a Principle of 'Constitutional' Property Law.

3.5. *Füller: Restructuring Property Law but Maintaining a Closed System*

In a German thesis Füller discusses the state of modern German property law.[406] His study concerns German law only, especially the influence of the Pandectist legal thinking on the law of property, but it is of general European importance.[407] Many European legal systems have taken over influences from German law. These influences include the separation between the law of obligations and the law of property, the primary subject of Füller's work.

Füller analyses the influence of contract law on the German law of property. He emphasises that even though the German legislature created an autonomous, independent, property law, contract law was not left out completely.[408] To the contrary, the German legislature placed the law of property into a separate book to show the independence of property law from contract law, but this did not prevent it from including contract law in the book on property law at all. Füller shows that in many places the property law part of the German Civil Code recognises obligations between holders of property rights, for example, the subsidiary legal obligations between holders of a primary right and the holder of a lesser right, but also the relation between possessor and owner, between finder and owner, and between co-owners.[409]

In other words, even though, as a fundamental principle of German private law, the law of property is separate from the law of contract, there are explicit and deliberate links between the two. However, at the same time there are also influences of contract law on German property that were not foreseen by the legislature.[410] Füller mentions *Treuhand* as an example of these unwanted influences.[411] Füller's central issue is therefore whether the strict separation between the law of contract and the law of property in German law should be maintained.[412] Apart from influences of contract law on aspects of property law, such as the system of transfer and creation of property rights, Füller sees a direct influence on the rule of *numerus clausus* of property rights in German law.[413]

He argues that through the influence of contract law, rights such as the right of *superficies*, the ownership of an apartment, and security ownership, can hardly be categorised as a normal right of ownership anymore.[414] Furthermore, the acquisition right and ownership for management purposes also cause problems in respect of the normal right of ownership.[415] Also in respect of lesser rights, the demarcations

406 Füller 2006, p. 2-7. For a discussion of Füller's opinion on German substantive property law see Chapter 4; 4. Borderline Cases in German Property Law.

407 Füller 2006, p. 571.

408 Füller 2006, p. 528.

409 See Füller 2006, p. 529-542. See also Chapter 4; 3. Other Property Rights.

410 Füller 2006, p. 528-529.

411 Füller 2006, p. 527.

412 Füller 2006, p. 543.

413 Füller 2006, p. 558-560.

414 In German the *Erbbaurecht, Wohnungseigentum* and *Treuhandeigentum*. On the same conclusion see Chapter 4; 4. Borderline Cases in German Property Law. Füller 2006, p. 559.

415 Füller 2006, p. 559.

between various rights, because of the freedom parties enjoy to shape these rights through contract law, have become blurred and unclear. As an example, Füller mentions the distinction between a right of usufruct and a right of real servitude.[416] Moreover, the case law on the possibility of both ownership and a lesser right in respect of the same object being held by the same person, and the case law on the co-entitlement of lesser property rights, especially security rights, enlarge the category of types of lesser property rights.[417]

The reason for the limitations that are imposed on parties in the creation of property rights, according to Füller, is the third-party effect of property rights.[418] However, with these developments in respect of the right of ownership and the blurring of the distinctions between the lesser property rights, he asks the question whether the limitations, the *Typenzwang*, can still be justified. In Füller's view, the *Typenzwang* is an over-reaction to the problem of the third-party effect of property rights, the fact that parties can be bound by a right to which they did not consent.[419]

Moreover, Füller emphasises that a system that adheres to a rule of *numerus clausus*, and therefore a strict *Typenzwang*, hinders the development of property law. On this he states:

> He who wants to maintain the *Typenzwang* as fundamental principle of property law, must consequently deny the case law concerning the rights in respect of the own object and the co-entitlement to lesser rights, reject the ownership for management purposes and declare the acquisition right as incompatible with the *Typenzwang*.[420]

Instead of such an approach, but without leaving the *Typenzwang* as an essential element of the rule of *numerus clausus*, Füller proposes to reform the law of property. His proposal is to bring the law of property, together with the law of obligations, into a general system of patrimonial law, the law dealing with the set of assets and debts of a person.[421] In other words, Füller proposes abandoning the strict separation between the law of property and the law of obligations. However, the consequence of a re-organisation of property law is not to abolish the separation between property rights and personal rights. Füller proposes to maintain this distinction, but to reform the right of ownership and lesser property rights so that they better fit the demands of modern property law.

First, Füller concentrates on the lesser rights to use. He recalls the blurring of the demarcations between the various lesser rights and proposes to replace the various rights to use, which are distinguished from one another for mainly historical

416 Füller 2006, p. 560-561.

417 Füller 2006, p. 468-489, 560.

418 Füller calls this the *verkehrsschützende Funktion*, see Füller 2006, p. 559.

419 Füller 2006, p. 559.

420 'Wer den Typenzwang als Strukturprägendes Prinzip aufrechterhalten möchte, muss folgerichtig die Rechtsprechung zu den eigenen Rechten und dem Gesamtrechten ablehnen, das Treuhandeigentum als unzulässig ansehen und das Anwartschaftsrecht für unvereinbar mit dem Typenzwang erklären'. Füller 2006, p. 560.

421 Füller 2006, p. 567.

reasons, with one lesser right to use.[422] Moreover, he compares the current lesser rights to use with the right of lease, in German law a personal right, and comes to the conclusion that the lesser right created for a limited period of time, in particular, now the right of usufruct, is almost similar to a lease.[423] Also the housing-right, a special type of limited personal servitude, very much resembles a lease of land.[424] A single lesser right to use could embody all of these, including the right of lease.

Secondly, Füller deals with three lesser rights that do not fit in the traditional distinction between lesser rights to use and lesser rights for security purposes. The real burden, for example, is a relic of the feudal system and cannot be entirely fitted in the separation between the law of property and the law of obligations.[425] Füller mentions how the German courts treat real burdens and personal rights to the performance of an owner, *Rentenschulden*, alike.[426] Therefore, Füller proposes to abolish the real burden and let the function it fulfils be taken over by these personal rights.[427]

As another example, Füller deals with pre-emptive registration and the German option to purchase.[428] He considers the possibility of removing the option to purchase in exchange for a full possibility to pre-emptively register personal rights in respect to land. When these personal rights can be registered through *Vormerkung*, pre-emptive registration, the option to purchase will, in his view, no longer be needed.[429]

In Füller's view, the autonomy of the law of property is under great pressure and a restructuring of property law is needed to free it from its isolation.[430] He therefore proposes to enlarge the general part of the German Civil Code so that it also deals with the right of ownership and the law between neighbours.[431] Matters like pre-emptive registration and actions to revindicate the right of ownership should be moved to the law dealing with registration, the *Grundbuchordnung*.[432]

The part of the German Civil Code dealing with contract law should, according to Füller, be enlarged with rules on third-party protection. Leases should be removed from contract law and take over the function of the lesser rights to use as property rights. The end of this part on contract law in the German Civil Code could deal with co-entitlement, as the nature of the rights of the co-owners and the relations between them is almost fully defined by contract law.[433] Lesser rights for security are deliberately left out of his proposals. Füller recognises that there is so much to say about property security rights that a separate reform is needed to deal

422 Füller 2006, p. 560-561.
423 Füller 2006, p. 561-563.
424 Füller 2006, p. 563-564.
425 Füller 2006, p. 564.
426 BGH WM 1970, 92, 93, Füller 2006, p; 564.
427 Füller 2006, p. 564.
428 Füller 2006, p. 565.
429 Füller 2006, p. 565.
430 Füller 2006, p. 567.
431 Füller 2006, p. 567-568.
432 Füller 2006, p. 567.
433 Füller 2006, p. 567-568.

with these. He does mention aspects that need reform, amongst which publicity is the most important. Füller considers property security rights without registration a danger for the appearance of a persons' set of assets and debts. When a property security right is created, the holder of that right is entitled to separate objects from the set of assets and debts of the debtor, or to claim from that set of assets and debts, before other creditors. A secret lesser security right will not inform the other creditors about the existence of such preferential rights and should therefore be considered with great caution by the legal system.[434] Especially in respect of lesser security rights in respect of concerning movables and claims, Füller considers publicity should be reintroduced.[435]

In Füller's view it is remarkable that the strict separation between the law of property and the law of obligations is so strongly defended by German lawyers, but broken by practice when needed. In his view, there is nothing against removing this strict separation in favour of a more workable system in which the law of obligations and the law of property would work together.[436] Such a re-organisation would restructure the law of property, but would not give up the rule of *numerus clausus*. Instead, the content of the closed system would be reorganised such that it fulfils the demands of modern practice again.[437]

3.6. *Van Erp: a Less Rigid Numerus Clausus*

Adhering to a rule of *numerus clausus* limits the development of property law in such a way that parties themselves cannot create any new property rights.[438] When we follow Struycken in arguing that it is only for the legislator to add rights to the list of recognised property rights, this might not lead to the desired developments, as the politics of the legislative process would come into play.[439] Others have therefore chosen a more flexible approach. Among these is Van Erp who has offered an analysis of *numerus clausus* in the context of developing ideas, on a comparative basis, about the future of European property law.[440]

After recalling the impact of the French revolution, Van Erp focuses attention on the role *numerus clausus* plays in a legal system.[441] The *numerus clausus* of what he calls 'absolute rights' is the limitation imposed by a Civil Code on private parties to

434 Füller 2006, p. 568-569.
435 Füller 2006, p. 569.
436 Füller 2006, p. 571-572.
437 Füller himself refers to the developments in European Union law in respect to property law, in particular the development of a Euro-hypothec or Euro-mortgage, which will require the national property law systems to be rethought in any case. Füller 2006, p. 572. On these European developments see Chapter 8; 2.1.3. European Commission Initiatives for Future Legislation.
438 See Füller 2006, p. 558-560.
439 In the same sense see Van Velten 2007, p. 376.
440 Hence the title of Van Erp's contribution a *numerus quasi-clausus* of property rights as a constitutive element of a future European property law?
441 Van Erp 2003b, p. 5 *et seq.*

create new property rights, introduced after the French Revolution.[442] In this respect, civil law is different from common law, although Van Erp also sees a standardisation of property rights in the common law system.[443] However, like Füller, Van Erp considers the developments of property law, and recognises that a *numerus clausus* that is too rigid will prevent innovation.[444]

Van Erp mentions the trust and time-share arrangements as examples of innovations that property law is facing.[445] These two forms of holding property rights are especially difficult for a civil lawyer coming from a 'unitary' system, which is a system that applies to both movables and immovables as much as possible.[446] A trust creates a situation in which two parties hold property rights in the same object, without, for a civil lawyer, it being clear what these rights are. There is no lesser property right in the *numerus clausus* of any civil law system that covers the rights of the beneficiary or the rights of a trustee in a trust. In the case of time-share arrangements, there is also a separation, but different from a trust, a separation in time, so that several holders can be entitled to 'own' an object for a limited, but recurring, period of time.

Van Erp is correct in focussing on trusts and time-shares now that civil law systems are increasingly confronted with these two common law methods of holding rights.[447] However, civil law systems have dealt with them differently. In the case of trusts, several civil law systems, in particular France and Germany, have offered their own civil law solution to create a similar device in the form of *fiducie* or *Treuhand*.[448] The Netherlands continues to reject trusts, but has created several forms of trust-like devices for particular purposes, for example, the certification of shares in a public company. As the Netherlands is also a party to the Hague Convention on the Law Applicable to Trusts and their Recognition, Dutch law is obliged to recognise foreign trusts.[449]

Another example is the transfer of ownership for security purposes which effectively creates a type of security ownership, although according to strict Dutch doctrine it does not.[450] In Dutch law, the transfer of ownership for security purposes was introduced through case law under the old Civil Code and was later prohibited by the legislature when the new Dutch Civil Code entered into force in 1992.[451] In

442 Absolute rights in civil law systems are rights that are good against the whole world, but include a larger number of rights than just property rights. Also intellectual property rights such as copyrights or patents are absolute rights. Therefore it is better to speak of a *numerus clausus* of property rights instead. See Struycken 2007, p. 109-114, Snijders 2002, p. 36.

443 Van Erp 2003b, p. 8-10.

444 On Füller's view see above; 3.5. Füller: Restructuring Property Law but Maintaining a Closed System.

445 Van Erp 2003b, p. 11.

446 Van Erp 2003b, p. 4.

447 See also Reid 1997b, p. 229-230.

448 See Chapter 3; 4.5. *Fiducie*, and Chapter 4; 2.5. Security Ownership, 4.5. *Treuhand* Bank Account.

449 See Chapter 5; 4.9. EC and International Influences.

450 Van Erp 2003b, p. 11.

451 HR 25 January 1929, *NJ* 1929, 616, see Chapter 5; 2.3. Security Ownership.

German law, however, the transfer of ownership for security purposes was also created by case law, but has not been prohibited at all.[452]

Van Erp concludes that the *numerus clausus* in civil law systems also serves an economic purpose and that this purpose should always be borne in mind.[453] Therefore a too strict approach to *numerus clausus* could be economically harmful. In Van Erp's view, *numerus clausus* should develop in the direction of a *numerus quasi-clausus*, a more flexible system in which new property rights, such as those enabling trusts and time-shares, as well as security ownership, can be recognised.[454] In Van Erp's view, the legislature should preferably recognise new property rights, but if the legislature fails to act, he would allow the courts to act, but with extreme care.[455]

3.7. *Smits and Sagaert: Property Law as a System of Obligations*

Apart from Van Erp's suggestion, Sagaert, but also, before him, Smits, have gone much further in their attempts to bring more dynamics into the law of property.[456] Smits, in his analysis of property law, tries to translate the Pandectist concept of *numerus clausus*, in particular that of Von Savigny, into what he calls modern concepts of third-party effect of obligations. In this view, *numerus clausus* refers to the concept that the law only authorises specific situations in which parties are allowed to create a legal relation that will have third-party effect.[457] The requirement for this approach in Smits' view is that a property right is conceived as a relation between two persons in respect of a thing.[458]

In this approach, the law of obligations and the law of property are brought under one single concept - an obligation, with or without third-party effect. This single concept is needed, Smits argues, because the legal system is increasingly confronted with hybrid figures situated between the law of obligation and the law of property.[459] In the current system, Smits continues, a top-down approach is followed, by which he refers to the approach in which the law decides that a certain legal relation is a property right and that therefore third-party effect results.[460] Instead, a bottom-up approach is needed; if there is third-party effect, a property right is created. Smits seems to be correct when he states that it is this approach that is

452 See Chapter 4; 2.5. Security Ownership.

453 Van Erp comes to this conclusion, *inter alia*, through reference to several American Law and Economics Scholars who dealt with *numerus clausus*. These are dealt with later in this chapter. Van Erp 2003b, p. 11. See above; 3.2.2. *Numerus Clausus* as Optimal Standardisation of Property Rights and 3.2.3. *Numerus Clausus* as Verification of Property Rights.

454 Van Erp 2003b, p. 11-12.

455 Van Erp 2003b, p. 11.

456 Smits 1996, p. 41 *et seq*. Sagaert 2005b, p. 986 *et seq*.

457 Smits 1996, p. 54.

458 I.e., relationalist theory as mentioned above. See above; 2. The Content of Property Law Systems in Europe.

459 These include Dutch qualitative duties, lease and right of retention (lien). See Smits 1996, p. 41, 63.

460 Smits 1996, p. 55.

followed in English law, where, in small steps, personal rights, a right of lease, for instance, have gradually developed into property rights.[461]

With reference to South African law, which will be dealt with in the next section, Smits comes to the conclusion that it is the Pandectist system that enforces the separation between the law of obligations and the law of property, and the separation between personal rights and property rights connected to that.[462] *Numerus clausus* is the decision-making device with which it becomes clear *ex ante* whether a legal relation is personal or proprietary. If we want to break free from the Pandectist tradition, and Smits thinks we should, we should abandon the separation between the law of obligations and the law of property.[463]

A property right in this perspective is no longer dependent on a mother-right, but on the basis of other criteria for an obligation with third-party effect. Smits offers the intention of the parties and the publicity of the right so that third parties know about its existence as criteria to decide which relations have third-party effect and which do not.[464] However, what exactly is the relation between these criteria, and if there are any additional criteria, remains unanswered.

Along the same lines of reasoning, Sagaert has developed ideas on property law as an open system of obligations.[465] Following the ideas of Ginossar, Sagaert describes what he calls the *neo-personalist* approach to property rights.[466] This approach takes the relationalist theory, dealt with at the beginning of this Section, one step further. It can therefore be seen as a neo-relationalist theory, which sees all property rights as obligations against third parties.[467] The content of the obligation corresponding to a property right is that a third party must refrain from interfering.[468] However, the obligation is not a normal obligation but is connected to the holder of the right in respect of the object and runs with the object to a new holder. In that regard, the obligation is a qualitative obligation. Ginossar analyses the system of the law of obligations and the law of property together in a system of ownership, qualitative obligations and normal obligations.[469]

In Ginossar's view, in other words, there is no longer a place for the separation between the law of obligations and the law of property. Instead one system of 'patrimonial law' should take its place.[470] It is with this idea that Sagaert offers four

461 Smits 1996, p. 55. The best example is a lease, see Chapter 6; 2.2. Leases of Land. Swadling 2000a, p. 232-233, Swadling 2007, p. 234-236.

462 Smits 1996, p. 56-61. With the same line of reasoning see Füller 2006, p. 525 *et seq*. On South African law see below; 3.6. A Legal System without a *Numerus Clausus*: South African Law.

463 Smits 1996, p. 61-62.

464 Smits 1996, p. 63.

465 Sagaert 2005b, p. 983.

466 Sagaert 2005b, p. 996-998, Ginossar 1960, p. 181 *et seq*.

467 On the classic theory and relationalist theory see above; 2. The Content of Property Law Systems in Europe.

468 Sagaert 2005b, p. 996-997.

469 Qualitative obligations because they are connected to a person in his quality as the holder of a property right (in Sagaert's words *qualita qua*). See Sagaert 2005b, p. 997, Ginossar 1960, p. 181 *et seq*.

470 For the same solution, but a different approach, see Füller above in 3.5. Füller: Restructuring Property Law but Maintaining a Closed System.

new categories of rights, which are no longer based on the distinction between personal right and property right, but on the effects a right can have against third parties.[471] The need for these new categories comes, in this respect Sagaert and Smits agree, from the difficulties presented to the current legal systems by hybrid figures such as qualitative duties as parts of property rights, as well as trusts or trust-like devices.[472]

Sagaert's new distinction is based on the analysis of a right. He assumes that both property rights and personal rights have an active and a passive side. The active side is the party that is entitled to the right, the passive side the party that is bound by the right.[473] Depending on the content of the right, the right is in respect of performance by another party or it is related – in Sagaert's words, accessory – to an object with which it may transfer to another party. In other words, those rights are qualitative rights in respect of the active side or rights that follow, the *droit de suite*, on the passive side. The first new category comprises rights that are not accessory to an object, neither on the passive, nor on the active side.[474] These rights comprise the current category of personal rights, now dealt with by the law of obligations. The second new category comprises rights that are accessory to an object, both on the passive and on the active side.[475] These rights are property rights in the traditional sense of the word, with third-party effect on both sides. Sagaert classifies servitudes, pledge, hypothec and special priority rights under this heading. The third new category comprises rights that are accessory to an object on the passive side, but not on the active side.[476] These are property rights that only exist in respect of an owner, for example, a right of usufruct, *superficies* or *emphyteusis* and co-ownership. They are different from the rights in the second category where, apart from the right of ownership, the property right is defined in terms of two parties, in case of servitudes in the holder of the dominant and the holder of the servient land for instance, or in case of pledge, the pledgor and the pledgee. In case of a right of usufruct there is ownership and the holder of the right of usufruct.

The fourth and final new category comprises rights that are accessory to an object on the active side, but not on the passive side.[477] It is this category, Sagaert argues, that has been mostly neglected.[478] Rights included would be personal servitudes, unknown to French law, but known in German, Dutch and English law.[479]

471 Sagaert 2005b, p. 1022.
472 Sagaert 2005b, p. 1022-1023.
473 Sagaert 2005b, p. 1023.
474 Sagaert 2005b, p. 1023.
475 Sagaert 2005b, p. 1024.
476 Sagaert 2005b, p. 1026.
477 Sagaert 2005b, p. 1027.
478 Sagaert 2005b, p. 1027-1028.
479 These are limited personal servitudes, qualitative duties and restrictive covenants. See Chapter 4; 2.2. Personal Servitudes, Chapter 5; 4.8. 'Qualitative Duties' and Chain Clauses, and Chapter 6; 2.5. Restrictive Covenants.

In respect to *numerus clausus*, Sagaert shows that, depending on the category of rights, the legislature and judiciary have used different approaches.[480] In respect of the first category, which contains purely personal rights, there is the starting point of freedom of contract, but there are more and more limitations in, for instance, the areas of consumer protection, environmental protection, and through good faith.[481] Nevertheless, the starting point remains an open system in which parties have maximum freedom to shape their legal relations. In respect of the second category, in particular as a reaction against the feudal system of landholding, a *numerus clausus* has been enforced. In respect to servitudes, this can best be seen from the prohibition against imposing a positive burden on another party.[482] However, insofar as the parties stay within the boundaries set by law, within the *Typenfixierung*, there is some limited freedom to shape legal relations. In this respect, most legal systems recognise the possibility to impose positive duties as secondary obligations to a primary negative duty.[483] In respect of the third category, Sagaert asserts the *numerus clausus* is less important, and that in French and Belgian doctrine it is sometimes held that the rules of, in particular, *Typenfixierung* do not apply.[484] As examples he mentions possibilities to shape the right of ownership in a co-ownership regime and the decision of the Dutch Supreme Court quoted above, in which a party agreement becomes part of a property right if there is a sufficient connection to the property right and the parties stay within the nature of the right.[485] Finally, in respect of the fourth category, Sagaert explains that this category of rights has been traditionally neglected in French and Belgian law, because the rights in this category might resemble old feudal duties, as property rights bind persons.[486] Therefore, *numerus clausus* has traditionally not been applied to this category.

The current system of property law uses an *ex ante* method to decide which rights have effect against third parties and which have not. With Sagaert's new division, it might be possible to choose a more modern approach, in which an *ex post* method allows for more freedom to create new property rights.[487] Creating new rights, however, is subject to conditions:

> ... on the condition that they do not cause damage from an economic point of view. When, after creation, it becomes apparent that it does cause damage, this method should have sufficient gravity to re-integrate the separated right back into the right of ownership. The gravity can be created for instance through extinction of a property

480 Sagaert 2005b, p. 1062 *et seq.*
481 Sagaert 2005b, p. 1063.
482 Sagaert 2005b, p. 1064-1065.
483 Sagaert 2005b, p. 1067-1068.
484 Sagaert 2005b, p. 1073.
485 HR 16 March 1977, *NJ* 1977, 399, see above; 3.4. Struycken: Why we Need a *Numerus Clausus*.
486 Sagaert 2005b, p. 1076.
487 Sagaert 2005b, p. 1079.

> right when its purpose is gone, it has not been used for a long duration of time ..., when it can no longer be used, when using the right would be unreasonable, etc.[488]

Sagaert therefore seems to want to retain a principle of *numerus clausus* through an *ex post* model that does not limit party autonomy before parties create their relation, but controls the effect of the relation they choose with criteria of economic relevance. In such a way the separation of the law of obligations and the law of property is no longer needed and a gradual system in which more, or less, third-party effect, on the active or on the passive side of a right, can be awarded.[489]

3.8. *A Legal System without a Numerus Clausus: South African Law*

The above analysis shows how civil law systems, in particular, all adhere to a *numerus clausus* of property rights, albeit to different degrees, and also how legal scholarship in these systems continues to value *numerus clausus* as a fundamental principle of property law. Although the *numerus clausus* fulfils an important filtering function to restrict the application of property law to those legal relations that are not property rights, other solutions that achieve the same result can be imagined.

Until now, the *numerus clausus* has always been defended with the argument of legal certainty. As stated above, this argument is twofold. It seeks to protect the unitary nature of the right of ownership, as well as seeking to protect third parties from a large amount of unknown property rights. In the name of legal certainty, therefore, party autonomy is seriously restricted.[490] However, without such restrictions to party autonomy, an unworkable system will not necessarily result. There are legal systems in the world in which no *numerus clausus* is recognised. One of these legal systems, that of South Africa, deserves special attention.[491] South African law is interesting in particular because it combines the civil law and common law

488 Sagaert 2005b, p. 1079-1080, '... op voorwaarde dat zij vanuit economisch oogpunt niet schadelijk zijn. Indien naderhand blijkt dat zij wel schadelijk zijn, moet dit model voldoende gravitatiekracht bieden om de afgesplitste beperkt zakelijke rechten terug te integreren in het eigendomsrecht. Die gravitatiekracht kan bv geboden worden door de uitdoving van het zakelijk recht indien het kennelijk onnuttig is geworden, indien het lange tijd niet meer uitgeoefend..., indien het niet meer kan worden uitgeoefend, indien een beroep op het beperkt zakelijk rechte kennelijk onredelijk zou worden ..., enz.'.

489 Sagaert 2005b, p. 998-999. By analysing property rights in their content as a set of obligations perhaps Sagaert also approaches the approach of the American Hohfeld who developed a theory of property rights as a bundle of rights. See Hohfeld 1917, p. 710 *et seq.*

490 On the disproportionality of this see Füller 2006, p. 558-559.

491 Apart from South African law, also in Spanish law no *numerus clausus* of property rights is recognised although most authors argue in practice a *numerus clausus* exists, as no new property rights have been recognised. See Goni Rodriguez de Almeida 2006, O'Callaghan 2002, Fulgencia Angosto Sáez 2006, p. 281 *et seq.* Also in Scotland no *numerus clausus* is recognised, but it is argued that, since the last new property right, the real burden, was recognised in 1840 a virtual *numerus clausus* exists. See *Tailors of Aberdeen v Coutts* (1840) 1 Rob 296, Reid & Van der Merwe 2004, p. 654.

tradition in one legal system.[492] Therefore, South African law is also confronted with doctrine from civil law and common law. Over and above that, South African law has also developed its own doctrine to deal with property rights and the limitations on party autonomy in the creation of property rights. The system of South African law is therefore particularly interesting.[493]

In South African law it is traditionally held that no *numerus clausus* exists.[494] South Africa is a mixed legal system, where English law and Roman-Dutch law are combined into one legal system.[495] South Africa does not have a Civil Code, and applies the South African common law in the same way as the English legal system applies the English common law. However, in content, South African common law is different from English common law.[496]

As a result of its Roman-Dutch origins, the foundation of the South African property law system is the general catalogue of property rights derived from Roman law. First and foremost, the primary right is a unitary concept of ownership. This right of ownership is a right of ownership in the civil law sense, including a *vindicatio* for the owner to protect his right. Secondly, there are lesser rights to use and for security purposes. These lesser rights, following the Roman law categories, are; rights of servitude, both real and personal, pledge and hypothec.[497] However, unlike the civil law systems, apart from these traditional property rights, South African law has seen the development of new types of property rights. Some of these rights result from the influence of English common law, for example, a lease of land, but others are very specific to the South African environment, for example, mineral rights. Furthermore, with the entry into force of the Constitution there is a discussion on the recognition of human rights, and other rights that are protected under the Constitution as property rights.[498] These highly complicated constitutional influences will be left aside.

Without a Civil Code or a judgment stating that the Roman law property rights mentioned by the Roman-Dutch writers are an exhaustive list of property rights, both the courts as well as the legislature have given recognition to new property rights. When the courts recognise new property rights, they characterise a legal relation created by two private parties as constituting a property right. Remarkably, these new property rights in South African law have all been property

492 See, *inter alia*, Zimmermann 1983, Zimmermann 1992, p. 9 *et seq.*, Sonnekus 1996, p. 285, Zimmermann 2004, p. 1 *et seq.*

493 Also other studies on *numerus clausus* have recognised the importance of South African law. See, e.g., Reid 1997b, p. 228-229, De Waal 1999a, De Waal 2000, p. 439 *et seq.*, Struycken 2007, p. 257-265.

494 See, *inter alia*, Van Warmelo 1959, p. 84, De Waal 2004, p. 83, 85, Van der Merwe 2004, p. 99, Badenhorst & Coetser 1991, p. 357, Badenhorst 2000, p. 509, Badenhorst et al. 2003, p. 56, Van der Walt 1987, p. 343, Van der Walt 1992, p. 171, Van der Merwe, De Waal & Carey-Miller 2002, p. 84-85. However see Reinsma 1970, p. 141 ('toch kan men, dacht ik, niet zeggen dat zij uitgaat van een open zakenrechtelijk systeem').

495 Zimmermann 2004, p. 4-8.

496 De Waal 2004, p. 83.

497 Van Warmelo 1959, p. 87-89, De Waal 1999a, De Waal 2004, p. 83-84.

498 See Van der Walt 2005, p. 58 *et seq.*, Badenhorst et al. 2003, p. 69-70.

rights in respect of land. The reason for this is that recognition of new property rights in South African law is dealt with as a question of registration. It is through registration, in particular the law dealing with registration of property rights, that parties can be allowed to register rights that are, as yet, unknown as property rights. The effect of this approach is that the decision whether a right is a property right or a personal right is dealt with as a question of registration.[499] In particular, the combination of property rights and other rights that are capable of registration has caused some confusion when personal rights have been offered for registration.[500]

In *Ex Parte Geldenhuys* the Orange Free State Provincial Division was asked to rule on the registrability of a clause in a testament stating that the children of the testator would be entitled to a piece of land.[501] The relevant portions of the clause stated:

> 'As soon as our first child reaches his or her majority, the survivor of the testators shall be bound to subdivide the said land in equal portions and distribute it among the children, such distributions to be made by the survivor and such major child by drawing lots ... and we declare and direct that the child who by such lot obtains the portion comprising the homestead of the farm Jakhalskop shall pay the sum of £200 to our other children within a specified time'.[502]

The Registrar of Deeds had refused to register the deed with the argument that the rights created by the clause were only personal rights, and that, following previous case law, personal rights could not be registered.[503] In dealing with the question of registrability De Villiers JP held:

> 'The reference is to rights, which are merely binding on the present owner of the land, and which thus do not bind the land, and do not constitute *jura in re aliena* over the land, and do not bind the successors in title of the present owner. These are the 'personal rights' which are not registrable, according to the above cited case of *Hollins v Registrar of Deeds* 1904 TS 603... One has to look not so much to the right, but to the correlative obligation. If that obligation is a burden upon the land, a subtraction from the *dominium*, the corresponding right is real and registrable; if it is not such an obligation, but merely an obligation binding on some person or other, the corresponding right is a personal right, or right *in personam*, and it cannot as a rule be registered'.[504]

In this case the court developed a test to determine which rights are property rights and therefore can be registered and which rights are personal rights and can therefore not be registered. This test, by which the court looks at the corresponding obligation of a right and sees if this obligation is a burden upon the land, in other words a subtraction from the *dominium*, would become known as the subtraction from

499 This question is becoming increasingly relevant in the human rights aspects of property law, the constitutional property law, as it is known by in South Africa. On this aspect see Van der Walt 2005, p. 101 *et seq.*

500 Van Warmelo 1959, p. 85, Boraine 1987, p. 77, Badenhorst 2000, p. 509.

501 *Ex Parte Geldenhuys* 1926 OPD 155.

502 *Ex Parte Geldenhuys* 1926 OPD 155, at 155.

503 *Hollins v Registrar of Deeds* 1904 TS 603, *Ex Parte Geldenhuys* 1926 OPD 155, at 157.

504 *Ex Parte Geldenhuys* 1926 OPD 155, at 164 *per* De Villiers JP.

dominium test.[505] Applied to the facts of this case, in *Ex Parte Geldenhuys* the court held that the rights of the children to the subdivision, at the moment of registration of the indivisible shares in the land, directly affected the ownership of land and therefore constituted a real burden on the current ownership that was capable of registration. The obligation to pay the sum of money was held to be personal and not registrable *per se*.[506]

This judgment was delivered under the Deeds Registries Act of 1918, which dealt with the registrability of rights.[507] In 1937, a new Act was adopted that restated the requirements a legal relation had to fulfil in order to be registered as a property right.[508] Furthermore, the introduction of the 1937 Act was used to restate the available property rights, without closing the possibility for parties to create new rights.[509] These rights include leases of land and of mineral rights, mortgage bonds, notarial bonds, personal and real servitudes and notarial prospecting contracts.[510]

The South African system of registration of rights is complicated and has caused several uncertainties, mostly because the Deeds Registries Act 1937 is not concerned with property rights, but with registrable rights.[511] Usually, only property rights are rights capable of registration, but as a result of the focus on registrability of rights, personal rights can also be included. Furthermore, Section 102 of the Deeds Registries Act 1937 defines property rights as any right that becomes a property right on registration, which could imply that personal rights that are registered become property rights.[512] In order to provide some guidelines to the Registrar of Deeds, Section 63(1) of the Deed Registries Act 1937 states:

> 'No deed, or condition in a deed, purporting to create or embodying any personal right, and no condition which does not restrict the exercise of any right of ownership in respect of immovable property, shall be capable of registration: Provided that a deed containing such a condition as aforesaid may be registered if, in the opinion of the registrar, such condition is complementary or otherwise ancillary to a registrable condition or right contained or conferred in such deed'.[513]

It is in particular the end of the first sentence, the requirement for a deed to restrict any right of ownership in respect of immovable property, of which it is argued that it embodies the subtraction from *dominium* test.[514] Therefore, the introduction of the Deeds Registries Act 1937 has not put a hold on the courts applying the subtraction

505 Best formulated in *Erlax Properties (Pty) Ltd v Registrar of Deeds* 1992 (1) SA 879 (A). De Waal 2004, p. 87-88, Van der Walt 1992, p. 171, Badenhorst et al. 2003, p. 58, Van der Merwe, De Waal & Carey-Miller 2002, p. 84-87.

506 *Ex Parte Geldenhuys* 1926 OPD 155, at 164-166, *per* De Villiers JP.

507 Sec. 3(1) Deeds Registries Act 13 of 1918.

508 Deeds Registries Act 47 of 1937.

509 Sec. 3(1)(r) Deeds Registries Act 1937, see Badenhorst 2000, p. 509.

510 Sec 3(1) Deeds Registries Act 1937, see Badenhorst & Coetser 1991, p. 376.

511 See Boraine 1987, p. 53-83, Reid 1997b, p. 228-229.

512 Badenhorst et al. 2003, p. 58, Van der Walt 1992, p. 179.

513 Sec 63(1) Deeds Registries Act 1937.

514 Van Warmelo 1959, p. 91, De Waal 2004, p. 86, Badenhorst & Coetser 1991, p. 377, Badenhorst 2000, p. 509, Van der Walt 1992, p. 171.

from *dominium* test. In fact the test was refined in later case law and achieved a standardised form. The test now comprises the following two elements; in order for a right to be registrable, it must be the intention of the parties to bind not only themselves but also their successors in title, and the nature of the right or condition must be such that registration of it results in a subtraction from the *dominium* of the land against which it is registered.[515] However, the application of the test does not always answer the question about the division between personal rights and property rights. In particular, the criterion that an arrangement must restrict the exercise of the right of ownership, in other words, be a subtraction from the *dominium*, is not always helpful, as personal rights can also limit the exercise of a right of ownership.[516] Therefore in some cases the courts have struggled with the correct application of the test.

In *Ex parte Pierce and Others*, the court held that a clause in a testament stating that the profits from any minerals or precious stones, metals or oils that were found on the land should be divided between the heirs, did constitute a property right as it resulted in a 'diminution of the ownership' and therefore should be seen 'as creating real rights'.[517]

An even better illustration was offered three years later in *Oldensaalsrus Gold, General Investments and Extensions Ltd v Registrar of Deeds*.[518] In this case the Oldensaalsrus Gold company owned several farms for the purpose of township development. The land had been proclaimed a public digging site for precious metals.[519] When certain parts of the land were developed, the company attempted to sell and transfer this land under the condition that a share of any income received from the land, in licence money, rent profits, or profits otherwise, would be reserved for the company.[520] The deed containing this provision was refused registration with the argument that it constituted a personal right and that registration under Section 63(1) Deeds Registries Act 1937 was not allowed. The court, however, argued that the company had acquired a property right, which, looking at the corresponding obligation, entitled it to claim that the transferee should refrain from claiming a share in the money received from the land.[521] In the opinion of the court, such a clause constituted a subtraction from the *dominium*, and would therefore have to be capable of registration.[522]

515 See *Erlax Properties (Pty) Ltd v Registrar of Deeds* 1992 (1) SA 879 (A).

516 See *Registrar of Deeds (Transvaal) v The Ferreira Deep Ltd* 1930 AD 169 at 176 *per* De Villiers CJ, *Low Water Properties (Pty) Ltd v Wahloo Sand CC* 1999 1 SA 655 (SE), Van der Walt 1987, p. 346, Van der Walt 1992, p. 171, Sonnekus 1991, p. 179-180, Lewis 1987, p. 601.

517 *Ex parte Pierce and Others* 1950 (3) SA 628 (O), at 635D. Lewis 1987, p. 605-606.

518 *Oldensaalsrus Gold, General Investments and extensions Ltd v Registrar of Deeds* 1953 (1) SA 600 (O).

519 Badenhorst et al. 2003, p. 60-61.

520 *Oldensaalsrus Gold, General Investments and extensions Ltd v Registrar of Deeds* 1953 (1) SA 600 (O), at 607B-C.

521 *Oldensaalsrus Gold, General Investments and extensions Ltd v Registrar of Deeds* 1953 (1) SA 600 (O), at 606A-D, *per* Horwitz AJP, at 611G *per* Smit J.

522 *Oldensaalsrus Gold, General Investments and extensions Ltd v Registrar of Deeds* 1953 (1) SA 600 (O), at 606D, *per* Horwitz AJP.

These cases have been criticised on the grounds that a monetary obligation cannot constitute a subtraction from the *dominium*. Behind this reasoning is the idea that an owner does not have an obligation to pay money, so this part of the right of ownership cannot be made part of a property right either.[523] In *Lorenz v Melle and Others*, the Transvaal Provincial Division considered another case with a profits clause.[524] In this case, two parties had acquired a farm in co-ownership and had agreed on a division of a certain part of the farm. As a part of the notarial deed creating the division, the parties granted each other rights to receive half of the income of minerals, grazing or hunting rights, but also for profits of a township that would possibly be developed. The parties explicitly stated that these clauses were not only applicable to them, but also to their 'heirs, executors and assigns'.[525] One of the heirs of one of the parties creating the deed became owner of the land and wanted to transfer part of the land to a company for the development of a township, but wanted to ensure that she would not have to give half of the profits to the heirs of the other party who had created the deed. Therefore, she sought and obtained, at first instance, a declaratory order that the profit clause only created personal rights. On appeal, the nature of the rights created by the clause was reviewed. The court considered, because of the arguments brought forward by the appellant, the question of whether the clause in the deed constituted a real servitude. The court came to the conclusion that it could not be a real servitude, as the right did not bind the land to pay but merely the owner of that land to do so.[526] However, if the requirement of subtraction from *dominium* have been applied alone, the court admitted it would have come to the conclusion that a property right was created.[527] Therefore, an additional argument was used to come to the conclusion that a right is a property right – the right must relate to the enjoyment of the land in the physical sense.[528]

The additional requirement might have brought some clarification as to which rights would classify under the subtraction from *dominium* test, but in *Pearly Beach Trust v Registrar of Deeds*, in which the Cape Provincial Division dealt with the registrability of a clause in a deed of sale, this additional requirement was not followed.[529] In *Pearly Beach Trust v Registrar of Deeds*, the nature of a clause granting a third party the right to receive certain benefits in the event of a grant of prospecting rights, contained in a deed of sale of land, was considered. The clause provided that a third party was entitled to:

523 See Badenhorst et al. 2003, p. 61, De Waal 2004, p. 88.

524 *Lorenz v Melle and Others* 1978 (3) SA 1044 (T).

525 *Lorenz v Melle and Others* 1978 (3) SA 1044 (T), at 1045F *per* Nedstadt J.

526 *Lorenz v Melle and Others* 1978 (3) SA 1044 (T), at 1052E *per* Nedstadt J.

527 *Lorenz v Melle and Others* 1978 (3) SA 1044 (T), at 1052A *per* Nedstadt J. De Waal 2004, p. 90, Badenhorst & Coetser 1991, p. 377, Badenhorst et al. 2003, p. 61-62, Lewis 1987, p. 606-607, Van der Merwe, De Waal & Carey-Miller 2002, p. 87-88.

528 *Lorenz v Melle and Others* 1978 (3) SA 1044 (T), at 1052E *per* Nedstadt J. Badenhorst et al. 2003, p. 62, De Waal 2004, p. 90.

529 *Pearly Beach Trust v Registrar of Deeds* 1990 (4) SA 614 (C).

> '... receive from the transferee and/or its successors in title -:
> (a) one third of the net consideration received from the grantee of any option or rights to prospect for minerals etc. on the property;
> (b) one third of the net compensation received in consequence of the expropriation of the property;
> (c) one third of the net consideration received upon the disposal of the property to any authority who is vested by law with the power of expropriation'.[530]

The Registrar, probably relying on the interpretation of Section 63(1) in *Lorenz v Melle and Others*, refused registration because the clause did not restrict any right of ownership in the land.[531] However, the court, in dealing with the issue of registration, returned to the classic definition of the subtraction test from *Ex parte Geldenhuys* and *Ex parte Pierce*, and neglected the additional requirement from *Lorenz v Melle*.[532] On the applicability of the subtraction test in *Lorenz v Melle and Others*, King J. stated:

> 'Lorentz' case recognises (at 1052A - B) that a clause requiring an owner to give up of his profits amounted to a subtraction from the 'dominium, however this fact did not make the clause a real servitude; what was required (1052E) was a curtailment of the right of the owner to the enjoyment of the land in the physical sense'.
> In my view one of the rights of ownership is the jus disponendi or right of alienation and if this right is limited in the sense that the owner is precluded from obtaining the full fruits of the disposition it can be said that one of his rights of ownership is restricted'.[533]

With this case the court therefore also returned to the acceptability of profit clauses as property rights. The decision of the court has therefore been received with criticism and was not followed, when the opportunity arose in a different context in respect to a profit clause.[534] The case of *Kain v Kahn* concerned not a profit clause, but a clause in a contract of sale reserving the right to occupy one of the rooms in a house for a monthly rent of R10.[535] After some years of occupation, the applicant making use of this right sought registration of the clause. The Registrar refused on the ground that the clause only granted a right to occupy a part of a building and therefore did not result in a restriction on the right of ownership of the whole.[536] When considering the registrability of the clause, the court came to the conclusion that the right granted was a subtraction from the *dominium* in the form of a lease and was therefore capable of registration.[537]

530 *Pearly Beach Trust v Registrar of Deeds* 1990 (4) SA 614 (C), at 615B-C *per* King J.

531 *Pearly Beach Trust v Registrar of Deeds* 1990 (4) SA 614 (C), at 615E *per* King J. See also Badenhorst & Coetser 1991, p. 383. Sonnekus 1991, p. 173, Van der Merwe, De Waal & Carey-Miller 2002, p. 89-90.

532 *Pearly Beach Trust v Registrar of Deeds* 1990 (4) SA 614 (C), at 615G *per* King J.

533 *Pearly Beach Trust v Registrar of Deeds* 1990 (4) SA 614 (C), at 617G-I *per* King J.

534 *Denel (Pty) v Cape Explosive Works Ltd* 1999 (2) SA 419 (T). See Sonnekus 1991, 173 *et seq.*, Van der Walt 1992, p. 202-203, De Waal 2004, p. 92.

535 *Kain v Kahn* 1986 (4) SA 251 (C).

536 *Kain v Kahn* 1986 (4) SA 251 (C), at 253B-C.

537 *Kain v Kahn* 1986 (4) SA 251 (C), at 253G-H. On this conclusion, see Lewis 1987, p. 600.

Finally, in *Denel (Pty) Ltd v Cape Explosive Works Ltd*, the Transvaal Provincial Division was confronted with two clauses contained in a contract of sale of a piece of land.[538] The clauses had been made before the transaction under review by the court, and had in fact been part of several transactions before that.[539] One of these clauses stipulated that the land could only be used for the manufacture of armaments by the government for any defence or military purpose. The other clause granted the seller the first right to repurchase the land.[540] However, deciding not to follow *Pearly Beach,* the court considered that it was bound by *Lorenz v Melle,* and applied a more conservative test. Hartzenberg J, on behalf of the court, developed a two-stage test approach.[541] First, the court determined whether a clause in a contract was capable of being a property right. In order to determine this, the court applied the *Ex parte Geldenhuys* version of the subtraction from *dominium* test.[542] As a result, the court looked at the correlative obligation to see whether the burden rested on the land itself, or rather on the owner. In deciding this, the court recalled earlier case law and held that the owner's rights must be curtailed in relation to the enjoyment of the land in the physical sense, as was held in *Lorenz v Melle*.[543] Furthermore, the court held that other arguments that could answer the question whether a right is a personal or a property right could be admitted. When, for example, the right has as its object a performance of the owner, the right could be a personal right. When the right is made in respect of an object, the right could be a property right.[544] Secondly, only if the result of the first stage is that a property right is created, must the court establish whether or not the creator of the right intended it to be a property right.[545] On this aspect, Hartzenberg J held that if the parties agree that the right is a personal right, then registration is not possible. If the parties agree that the right is a property right, then it may be registered.[546]

Badenhorst has emphasised that originally the courts would look at the intention of the parties first and only after that would consider whether a right could be a subtraction from the *dominium*. She emphasises that by changing the order of these

538 *Denel (Pty) Ltd v Cape Explosive Works Ltd and Another* 1999 (2) SA 419 (T).

539 *Denel (Pty) Ltd v Cape Explosive Works Ltd and Another* 1999 (2) SA 419 (T), at 423D-H *per* Hartzenberg J.

540 *Denel (Pty) Ltd v Cape Explosive Works Ltd and Another* 1999 (2) SA 419 (T), at 422-423 *per* Hartzenberg J.

541 See Badenhorst 2000, p. 512-513.

542 *Denel (Pty) Ltd v Cape Explosive Works Ltd and Another* 1999 (2) SA 419 (T), at 435E-H per Hartzenberg J.

543 Or, following another earlier case of *Fine Wool Products of South Africa Ltd v Director of Valuations* 1950 4 SA 490, in which it was held that the obligation must affect the land or run with the land, *Denel (Pty) Ltd v Cape Explosive Works Ltd and Another* 1999 (2) SA 419 (T), at 435H-I *per* Hartzenberg J.

544 *Denel (Pty) Ltd v Cape Explosive Works Ltd and Another* 1999 (2) SA 419 (T), at 435I-J *per* Hartzenberg J.

545 *Denel (Pty) Ltd v Cape Explosive Works Ltd and Another* 1999 (2) SA 43619 (T), at 436C-D *per* Hartzenberg J.

546 *Denel (Pty) Ltd v Cape Explosive Works Ltd and Another* 1999 (2) SA 419 (T), at 436C-E *per* Hartzenberg J.

requirements around, the results can be much more predictable.[547] The result of the case of *Denel v Cape Explosive Works*, before it was considered on appeal, was therefore that the first clause, containing a restriction on the use of the land, could be registered, but that the second clause, the repurchase agreement, could not be registered, as this clause did not affect the land itself, but required a performance by an owner.[548] Unfortunately, on appeal, the Supreme Court of Appeal confirmed the two-stage approach, but came partly to the opposite conclusion on the interpretation of the facts of the case.[549] The Court of Appeal held that the two clauses in the contract should be read together, because the right to repurchase the land contained in the second clause would only apply if the land was no longer used for the purpose set by the first clause. Streicher JA therefore held that as a whole a subtraction from the *dominium* of the land resulted.[550] De Waal states that this case on appeal illustrates the inherent unpredictability of the subtraction from *dominium* test.[551] Other authors have also been critical of the predictability of the outcome of the test.[552] This criticism should not be taken as an argument in favour of a *numerus clausus*, but more as a plea for a stricter and more coherent application of the criteria to determine which right is a property right and which right is not.

A short analysis of South African law in terms of this Chapter may reveal some of the problems with the subtraction from *dominium* test. In terms of the property law system, South African law recognises a primary property right in the right of ownership. As this is a right of ownership in the civil law sense of the word, the paramount entitlement a person can have to an object, there is only one primary right in South African law. From this primary right, lesser rights may be derived in the form of property rights with effect against third parties. The South African method of creation of property rights is through a subtraction from *dominium* test. South African law finds its inspiration here in the Roman-Dutch author Grotius who wrote about lesser rights as *gebreckelicke eigendom* or limited ownership.[553] This method is essentially the same as the French method of *démembrement*, in which parts of the rights of ownership are taken, subtracted, and transferred to another person for a limited duration in the form of a lesser property right.[554]

Like other legal systems, South African law recognises property rights to use and property rights for security purposes. The third category, anticipatory rights, is unknown as such to South African law, although, as can be seen from *Denel (Pty) Ltd v Cape Explosive Works Ltd*, an option to purchase can be part of a lesser right re-

547 Badenhorst 2000, p. 512.

548 *Denel (Pty) Ltd v Cape Explosive Works Ltd and Another* 1999 (2) SA 419 (T), at 437-439 *per* Hartzenberg J. See Badenhorst 2000, p. 512-513, De Waal 2004, p. 94-95.

549 *Cape Explosive Works Ltd; AECI Ltd v Denel (Pty) Ltd; Armaments Corporation of SA Ltd and the Registrar of Deeds* (3) SA 569 (SCA).

550 *Cape Explosive Works Ltd; AECI Ltd v Denel (Pty) Ltd; Armaments Corporation of SA Ltd and the Registrar of Deeds* (3) SA 569 (SCA), at 578F-I, *per* Streiger JA.

551 De Waal 2004, p. 95.

552 See Badenhorst 2001, p. 195, Badenhorst et al. 2003, p. 66-67, Van der Walt 1992, p. 200-201, Lewis 1987, p. 615, Reid 1997b, p. 228-229.

553 De Groot 1926, II, 3, 11, p. 54, See Van der Walt 1992, p. 175.

554 See above; 2.2. Of Ways to Create a Lesser Property Right.

stricting the use of a piece of land. In fact, it is in particular with this third category of lesser rights that South African law has had problems. In South African law, these rights are pre-emptive rights, rights against the alienation of land and options to land.[555] Taking into account that lesser rights in South Africa are a subtraction from the primary right, it can be seen how the legal system would experience problems with rights that cannot be defined in terms of rights of the holder of the primary right.[556] Therefore, in particular, lesser rights of the third category (anticipatory rights) have been generally characterised as personal rights in South African law.[557] The method of creating lesser rights does not determine, although it has an influence on, the open or closed nature of the catalogue of property rights. As South African law illustrates, following a method of subtraction or *démembrement* to create lesser property rights can still lead to an open system in which private parties are free to offer new property rights for registration. Nevertheless, the open system of property rights in South African law has not led to a large increase in the recognition of new property rights.

4. Conclusion: *Numerus Clausus* in Property Law Systems in Europe

Numerus clausus as a principle of property law can be found, albeit in a different form and with a different content, in French, German, Dutch and English law. Even in legal systems that are traditionally considered not to recognise a *numerus clausus*, such as South African and American law, limitations on the number and content of property rights can be found. In the terminology of this Chapter, South African law might not adhere to a rule of *numerus clausus*, but, at least to some extent, it does apply a principle of *numerus clausus* by imposing a test and therefore limitations on the creation of new property rights.

Besides the adherence to a principle of *numerus clausus* in French, German, Dutch and English law, there is also a clear similarity in the catalogue of property rights that they recognise. Each of these systems uses a primary right, from which lesser rights are derived, either through subtraction or *démembrement*, or through the method of limitation.[558] Inside the catalogue of lesser rights, each legal system recognises rights to use and rights for security, and struggles with the recognition of lesser rights used to acquire a certain legal position.[559]

When considering the method of creation of property rights, it is not surprising that the legal systems adhering to a method of limitation on the creation of lesser property rights have fewer difficulties with the recognition of lesser rights

555 *Crous v Utilitas Belville* 1994 (3) SA 720 (C), *Lazerus and Jackson v Wessels, Olivier, and the Coronation Freehold Estates, Town and Mines Ltd* 1903 TS 499, *Vansa Vanadium SA Ltd v Registrar of Deeds* 1997 (2) SA 784 (T).

556 On this same analysis in respect to other systems adhering to the *démembrement* method of creating property rights, see above; 2.6. Lesser Rights used to Acquire a Certain Legal Position (Anticipatory Rights).

557 See Badenhorst et al. 2003, p. 67.

558 See above; 2.2. Of Ways to Create a Lesser Property Right.

559 On this distinction see above; 2.1. Of Primary Property Rights and Lesser Property Rights.

used to acquire a certain legal position. At the same time, legal systems that follow the other method, the method of *démembrement*, are increasingly confronted with the demand to recognise anticipatory property rights. In particular, when an object is transferred and additional legal certainty for one of the parties is required, the strict separation between the law of obligations and the law of property is under pressure. Such a situation can occur when the primary right is transferred or the primary right is retained for security purposes. Legal systems adhering to a *démembrement* model generally refuse to recognise a special position for the party not holding the primary right. Legal systems adhering to the limitation model seem to recognise these rights more easily. However, with the *démembrement* method in mind, those systems that award a lesser property right for the acquisition of a property right are accused of being doctrinally impure. Those systems that do not award a lesser property right in these cases are criticised for their inflexibility and are sometimes avoided by legal practice.

Another distinction that is shared by French, German, Dutch and English law is the separation between the law of obligations and the law of property. This separation is strongly connected to the *numerus clausus*, regardless of whether *numerus clausus* appears as a rule or as a principle. Those systems adhering to a separation between these two areas of law must have criteria to decide which relations belong to either of these areas. In other words, as a result of this distinction, which is generally modelled on the distinction already used in Roman law, a legal relation cannot belong to both.[560]

The way in which *numerus clausus* is implemented in a legal system seems to depend on the hierarchy of sources of law. In those systems where the legislature has taken prime position amongst the sources of law, necessarily legislation also has exclusive authority to recognise and regulate property rights. In other words, the legislature has the authority to make the decision which legal relations have third-party effect. In doing so, legislators, in particular in civil law systems, have recognised property rights in a very traditional way, mainly by falling back on the Roman categories.[561] Moreover, as a reaction to the fragmented feudal concept of ownership, one unitary primary right and only a very limited category of lesser rights is recognised. Legislators mostly reject new solutions, even if these are needed in legal practice.

In German law the *Eigentümergrundschuld*, or owner-*Grundschuld*, offers an exception. Under pressure from legal practice, the Commission drafting the German Civil Code decided to keep this type of property right, even though it did not exactly fit in the Roman categories of property rights.[562] In some other countries legislators have also responded to the demands in practice. The French property reforms illustrate this. However, mostly, legislators leave property law to remain a static area of law. In this respect it is, in particular, the Dutch legislature that failed to take the opportunity on the occasion of the new Civil Code of 1992 to make changes to

560 In particular the strict separation as it was devised in German law under the influence of, *inter alia*, Von Savigny.

561 Gordley 1994, p. 459 *et seq.*

562 On the German owner's-*Grundschuld* see Chapter 4; 3.8. *Grundschuld*.

the menu of property rights. In fact, with its rejection of the use of the primary right for security and management purposes, the Dutch legislature seems to have placed Dutch law outside the current European developments.

Even in English law, traditionally held to be a very different system from civil law, the legislature interfered with Section 1 of the Law of Property Act 1925. It could be that with this interference the legislature granted itself exclusive authority to deal with the recognition of property rights at common law. In equity, primacy of the judiciary remains, and, not surprisingly, the courts have acted and recognised new property relations such as restrictive covenants, estate contracts, and options to purchase.

The above analysis focuses on *numerus clausus* as an expression of the actor with the primary authority to make law. It shows three elements of comparison. First, there are many similarities in the approach legal systems take towards the recognition of property rights. In each legal system the legislature has interfered in one area or another, and after reforms in that area, the system has become dependent on further legislative reform. Examples of this include apartment ownership, security rights, and the use of registration systems.

Secondly, all of these legal systems adhere to a separation between the law of obligations and the law of property. For reasons of legal certainty, usually expressed as justification for the third-party effect of property relations, the number and content of available property rights is restricted. Although the term legal certainty is vague and has been avoided as much as possible, the term does cover all objections made against an open system of property rights. In this respect, the objections against an open system can be brought under the heading of internal arguments, which focus on the relation between the holder of a lesser property right and the holder of a primary right, or the holder of another right from which the lesser right was derived, and external reasons, which focus on the relation of a holder of a lesser right against the rest of the world. Internal arguments include the argument that the system of property law as devised by Von Savigny and built by the Pandectists does not allow for a fragmentation of ownership in any way other than that prescribed by law, in other words, in another way than specifically authorised by the legislature. Ownership in this system is a unitary right and this unitary nature needs to be protected above all. Arguments derived from this line of reasoning are protection of the freedom of ownership, protection against over-fragmentation of the right leading to its inefficient use, pyramiding of rights, and standardisation of rights to create the optimal use of property rights. External arguments are also based on the doctrinal concepts made by the Pandectists and include problems of orientation on the market of property rights, information costs, transaction costs, externalities, justification of third-party effect through publicity, and standardisation to ensure the minimum costs for third parties.

Thirdly, the analysis of *numerus clausus* as an expression of the exclusive authority to regulate property rights shows the underlying justification for a (rule of) *numerus clausus*. Although, in my view it does not explain the existence of *numerus clausus*, the taking of a leading role by the legislator shows how, when through the source of legislation the menu of property rights is set, the rest of the system consequently also must be dealt with by legislation. By this I intend to state that *numerus clausus* as the criterion to decide on the applicability of the law of property would make little sense if the law of property as such was a set of unclear principles. Instead, in this way of systematic thinking, *numerus clausus* is the beginning of the path a legal relation follows, and from which it gains direction on the way to other general principles of property law, such as the principle of publicity and specificity.[563] Moreover, behind these two other principles there are further specific rules that must be followed.[564]

However, what all these arguments do not show or explain is how a system without a rule of *numerus clausus* can be fully functional. English equity or South African law might impose restrictions on party autonomy, but a rule of *numerus clausus* could not be discovered. Nevertheless, these legal systems seem to function well, but sometimes invoke harsh criticism, from both inside and outside that legal system, because of the flexibility and hence possible unpredictability of the law. It could be that, in exchange for flexibility, these systems have given in to some legal uncertainty. It could also be the case that this lower standard of legal certainty comes from the fact that not the legislator, but the courts are in charge here. The system of equity is intended to correct the strict rules of the common law, making the outcome of a certain case more just for the parties which are involved. As a result, new or different property rights may be recognised. Also in legal systems where no system of equity exists, frequently the courts have taken the authority to alter the menu of property rights. In this respect balancing interests and reaching the optimal result is of the utmost importance.

These open systems or open aspects of a system of property rights invoke more criticism, in my view, due to their lower standard of legal certainty, in this respect possibly translated as lesser degree of predictability, but they also allow the law of property to develop. It is precisely because of this that authors such as Füller, Smits, Sagaert and Van Erp present arguments for the development of a more flexible property law, in which there is more room for the increasing role of contract law in the law of property, the increasing role of property law in the law of contract, and for the development of new objects of property law, including claims and other intangible objects.[565]

However, for the time being, especially in civil law systems, the development of property law remains stuck in the Roman law-inspired separation between the law of obligations and the law of property and the Roman law-inspired categories of property rights. Other legal systems are less rigid when it comes to the effects of these distinctions. In a system such as South African law, contractual relations, such as the lease, have been allowed to grow into a property relation, whereas rigid civil law systems remain behind, struggling with these hybrid legal relations. As this Chapter shows, the civil law systems of France, Germany and the Netherlands continue to uphold a closed system of property rights based on their own national doctrinal arguments. However, when these national doctrinal arguments are com-

563 See specifically Chapter 8; 3.4.2. A Limited Open System of Property Rights.

564 These include ground rules of property law, such as the *prior tempore* and *nemo plus* or *nemo dat* rule. On this distinction see Van Erp 2006b, p. 16-17.

565 These include, e.g., emission rights, see Van Erp 2006a, p. 1065-1066.

pared, it seems that they are not strictly national at all. In fact, all of these arguments seem based on the post-Revolutionary ideas of a unitary concept of ownership, sharply distinguished from lesser property rights that, in their turn, fall into different categories. Moreover, these categories are all based on Roman law. Even in English law, where it is usually held that the French Revolution never had a direct effect, the systematic way of thinking in terms of the relation between primary and lesser rights is very much the same as civil law doctrine. The way in which most property rights are approached in English law is not very different from the civil lawyer's approach. Numerous examples can be found; rights to use fall into a general category of user rights, they either run with the land or they are held in gross. Other property rights are security rights, and these are used to secure the performance of a certain obligation. Also in English law, the obligation is contractual and therefore creates personal rights, but the right that secures the performance of that obligation is a property right.[566]

What is remarkable is that, even though these similarities in approach can be seen, the list of property rights in one legal system is different from the list in another system. The comparison between the legal systems shows that German law has a larger catalogue of property rights than French and Dutch law. Moreover, the list of property rights also differs between French and Dutch law. Finally, the list of property rights in English law is altogether different because of the separation between law and equity and personal property law and land law.

A likely explanation for these differences can be found in history. As a rejection of the feudal system, civil law systems introduced the use of one single primary right, clearly distinguished from several categories of lesser rights. In English law, the system of land law and the system of personal property law each recognise one primary right. Because Roman law was never received in English law as it was in civil law systems, the feudal concepts were not explained in terms of Roman law and no *duplex dominium* resulted. Civil law systems, in their turn, struggle with the relics of the feudal system. For example, neither the French nor the German Civil Code included the right of *emphyteusis* at the moment these entered into force. Later, under pressure from practice, this right came to be reintroduced by special legislation.[567] German law offers another example; in order to make a compromise between the north and the south of Germany, the legislator included both the right of hypothec and the right of *Grundschuld*. In other legal systems only the right of hypothec is recognised.[568]

In other words, in order to understand the differences between the lists of property rights in the various legal systems, the historical development of each of these systems must be taken into account. Even though the historical development of property rights, especially between the civil law systems, is partly a shared history, the peculiarities of each legal system influence the list of property rights that it recognises.

566 Other examples could include the use of a primary right and the carefulness the property law system uses to approach lesser property rights in relation to this primary right.

567 See Chapter 3; 3.4. *Emphyteusis*.

568 See Chapter 4; 3.7. Hypothec, and 3.8. *Grundschuld*.

Although these differences between legal systems, both civil law and common law, should be taken seriously, in the twenty-first century it is no longer possible to consider the systems of property law in Europe from a purely national point of view. European legal systems are increasingly confronted with legal relations, and therefore also doctrinal choices, from other jurisdictions. When in one legal system the courts have recognised a legal relation as a property right, and the object on which that property right is created is transported to another legal system, the other legal system, the receiving system, will be confronted with a decision it did not choose to make itself. In respect of *numerus clausus*, the principle of property law that French, German, Dutch and English law share, these increasing contacts between the doctrines of property law and the systems of property rights from these various countries mean that the principle of *numerus clausus* can no longer be considered from a purely national point of view.[569]

569 Therefore the final Chapter of this study will pay attention to the principle of *numerus clausus* as a principle of European property law. See Chapter 8.

Chapter 8

NUMERUS CLAUSUS IN A EUROPEAN PROPERTY LAW?

1. Introduction

1.1. *European Property Law*

In the previous Chapters, *numerus clausus* has been looked at from the perspective of the national legal systems of France (Chapter 3), Germany (Chapter 4), the Netherlands (Chapter 5) and England (Chapter 6). In Chapter 7 the divergences and similarities between these legal systems, as well as *numerus clausus* theory in general, have been examined. One of the findings of the comparative analysis of the legal systems discussed in these Chapters is that the national closed systems of property rights are under increasing pressure.[1] This pressure comes, first of all, from within the system of property law, for example, the increasing use of combinations of property rights, the stacking of rights, and the increased use of property rights for a different purpose than that for which they were originally intended. Furthermore, influences from outside the system of property law, but also from within the legal system itself, in particular, from contract law, were discussed.

In this final Chapter, the pressure on the national systems of property law from outside the legal system will be central. Although it is not the objective to provide a complete overview of international property law, some influences of international law, in particular, its subspecies European law, have such an influence on national property law systems that a discussion of the property law systems in France, Germany, the Netherlands and England, and in particular in respect of *numerus clausus* in these systems, brings a different view to the nation-based analysis. Moreover, aspects of French, German, Dutch and English law in respect of private international law, especially the recognition of property rights created in another country, also have an influence on *numerus clausus*.

It could be stated that international property law draws attention to aspects of *numerus clausus* that sometimes cannot be clearly seen when the principle is looked at from a purely national perspective. This is not only because at a national level

1 See Chapter 7; 4. Conclusion: *Numerus Clausus* in Property Law Systems in Europe.

property law is a doctrinally coherent system, with which many lawyers argue any new situation can be solved, but also because, without influences from other legal systems, in particular, when different doctrinal arguments are used, some problems just do not come up at a national level.

In a national legal system, *numerus clausus* filters legal relations and only allows a certain set of rights to be recognised as property rights. All other rights are consequently personal rights and belong to the law of obligations. When it comes to the recognition of foreign property rights, *numerus clausus* fulfils another filtering function; determining whether a legal relation entered into in another country that constituted a property right in the originating country can be recognised as a property right in the national, host jurisdiction. The result of the application of *numerus clausus* in this respect is different from the result at a purely national level. At a national level, a legal relation that is not recognised as belonging to the law of property can still be enforced as a personal right. Perhaps it will not be enforceable against a third party, but at least the legal relation will still have some effect. In contrast, a foreign legal relation that is not recognised by reference to the national closed list of property rights cannot be enforced in that jurisdiction.

Through the increasing development of European rules, national private law, including the law of property, is subject to the development of the Internal Market in the European Union. As a result of this development, national legal systems are no longer strictly national. They also face influences from other national legal systems, as well as influences from the international legal order, the European Union in particular.

The influence of these external factors creates a separate pressure on *numerus clausus* in the national systems, but it also raises the question of whether the approach to property law whereby we look purely at national systems of property law is, especially in the light of the increasing influence of the law of the European Union, still sufficient to provide a complete overview.[2] Instead, the question will be raised whether we should not speak of a European property law, as opposed to systems of national property law, in which *numerus clausus*, to use the formulation by Van Erp, is a 'constitutive element'.[3]

1.2. *Private International Law*

The external pressure on national property law systems is twofold. First, due to an increase in international trade, legal systems are increasingly confronted with property rights created in another country. When such a situation occurs, national law will decide whether a foreign property right should be recognised and what its place is within the national property law system. However, recognition of foreign property rights is not easy, especially when the nature and the content of the right that must be recognised is different from the rights within the closed list that the national legal system recognises. In such a case it will be uncertain whether a prop-

2 See below; 3.2. The Status of European Property Law.
3 Van Erp 2003b.

erty right can be recognised at all. This decision depends on a special area of national law, known as private international law.[4] This is not necessarily always an effective system, and parties may lose their property security right through operation of a legal system other than the legal system under which the right was created.[5]

As a general rule of private international law, many countries recognise the doctrine of vested rights or *droits acquis*.[6] Under this doctrine, a country commits itself to grant effect to a right created in another country as far as possible. However, such a foreign right must fit within the national legal system. When the receiving jurisdiction cannot fit the right into its system, it reserves the right to refuse recognition.

When it comes to property law and property rights, there are situations in which it is necessary to determine which law applies to the creation, existence, exercise or destruction of a property right. In terms of property law, the standard rule of private international law to determine the applicable law is the *situs* rule, or *lex rei sitae*. According to this rule it is the law of the place where an object is located that applies.[7] In respect of immovable objects, the *lex rei sitae* offers a clear decision on the applicable law.[8] In terms of movable objects, which can be moved from the territory of one country to that of another, the *lex rei sitae* rule is used here also to determine the applicable law. When a property right in respect of an object is validly created under the law of one country and the object is moved onto the territory of another country, and when the property right in respect of that object must be exercised, a rule of private international law is needed to determine which of the two countries' laws applies. Such a situation is known in private international terms as a *conflit mobile*.[9]

In order to provide a solution, private international law must determine, as well as the place where an object is located, also at what time a certain object was in a certain place. The element of time allows the national courts to decide with reasonable precision on the applicable law.[10] For example, to determine the applicable property regime in the case of a sale of goods, the time of the conclusion of the contract usually determines the applicable law.[11] However, when an object moves to another jurisdiction, so do the property rights in respect of that object. In order to

4 The term conflict of laws is also used to describe the national provisions that decide on the applicable law. In that sense, the rules of private international law or conflict of law rules do not decide on the substantive matter of a specific case, but only result in a substantive solution because a certain law applies.

5 Drobnig mentions Italian cases in which the Italian courts have refused to recognise a right of ownership under retention of title or reservation of ownership because the date of the creation of the retention or reservation had not been certified according to the Italian standards. (the *data certa*-requirement). See Drobnig 2006, p. 110. See also Kieninger 1996b, p. 46-47.

6 See, e.g., Grodecki 1976, p. 4, Rutgers 1999, p. 93-94, Van der Weide 2006, p. 36, 93-94, Michaels 2006b, p. 18 *et seq.*

7 Van der Weide 2006, p. 15-19, Rutgers 1999, p. 69-73, Kieninger 1996a, p. 165-167.

8 See, in particular, Sparkes 2007, p. 439-441.

9 See Grodecki 1976, p. 33-42, Rutgers 1999, p. 93-94, Kieninger 1996b, p. 47-48, Kieninger 1996a, p. 30-34.

10 Van der Weide 2006, p. 46-52.

11 Van der Weide 2006, p. 51.

determine the applicable law on that object, French, German, Dutch and English law use the doctrine of transposition. This doctrine uses the *lex rei sitae* in the strict sense of its meaning, according to which, when an object crosses the border of a jurisdiction, the law of the receiving jurisdiction governs the rights in respect of that object. Depending on the content of the national law, the recognition of a foreign property right will be more or less difficult.

In national systems of property law that adhere to a closed system of property rights, a foreign property right cannot be recognised as such. In order for the foreign property right to be recognised it must be 'transformed' into a property right from the national catalogue of property rights.[12] In many cases, recognition by way of transformation will not lead to problems. After all, as was shown in the previous Chapter, most legal systems use the same set of property rights as a basis.[13] However, according to some, automatic transformation when there is no imminent need to do so is unnecessary. They argue that only when the property right in respect of the object in question is exercised does the need arise to decide on the applicable law and, if necessary, for the recognition of a foreign property right.[14]

In any case, a situation may arise where the *lex rei sitae* rule determines that in a specific situation the law of the receiving country is applicable, and that, when the substantive national property law of that country is applied, in particular when that system adheres to a closed system of property rights, a foreign property right will be transformed into one of the recognised national types of property rights. The result of this transformation will not always be favourable to the holder of the right. Even if countries apply a very flexible and pragmatic approach to the recognition of foreign rights, the rights granted under the law of the receiving jurisdiction will not always be comparable to rights granted under the law of the original jurisdiction. There are many examples of holders of, for instance, security rights, who lose their rights or part of their rights when their property right is transformed into a property right known in the receiving country.[15] One example can be offered by looking at the Dutch case of *Sisal v TNBC*.[16] In that case, the Dutch courts were confronted with the exercise of a floating charge, later a fixed charge, created under Tanzanian law. Although the courts were willing to recognise the effects of the floating charge by transforming it into a right of non-possessory pledge under Dutch law, the right that the holder of a floating charge had under Tanzanian law to appoint a receiver could not be granted.[17]

Other examples could result from the differences in property law between countries. When it comes to reservation of ownership or retention of title clauses, some jurisdictions, Germany, for instance, allow parties to agree that the reservation

12 Van der Weide 2006, p. 35-39, Kieninger 1996b, p. 48-49.

13 On the same conclusion, see Reid 1997b, p. 228.

14 In case of a 'crystallisation' of rights, in German known as *Hinnahmetheorie* see Grodecki 1976, p. 37-38, Van der Weide 2006, p. 3941.

15 For other examples, see Kieninger 1996b, p. 47-48, Kieninger 1996a, p. 188-206, Drobnig, Snijders & Zippro 2006, p. 3 *et seq.*

16 HR 14 December 2001, *NJ* 2002, 241 (*Sisal/TNBC*).

17 See Van der Weide 2006, p. 68-69.

of ownership will extend to a newly formed object, formed with the object on which a reservation of ownership clause was held.[18] When, subsequently, such an object is transported to another country that does not recognise such an extension of the reservation of ownership clause, such as the Netherlands, the security owner will lose his right in the transformation process.[19]

To facilitate an effective trade between countries and to prevent certain property rights not being recognised, several international initiatives have been taken. In the area of security rights, in respect of highly valuable objects, for example, trains, ships and aeroplanes, international agreements have been reached under which a 'security interest' can be created and registered that will subsequently be recognised in all legal systems of the Contracting Parties.[20] Another, very interesting, example is the Hague Convention on the Law Relating to Trusts and their Recognition. Under this convention, which has already been dealt with briefly in Chapter 5 on Dutch law, trusts created under a foreign jurisdiction are recognised by all Contracting Parties.[21] In Dutch law, the ratification and entry into force of the convention has not led to remarkable results. In Italy, however, the recognition of trusts under this convention has led to the creation of a trust known as domestic trust, not only open to foreigners under the convention, but also to Italian nationals.[22]

This Italian example, although outside the scope of this study, illustrates how private international law can, under certain circumstances, lead to a change in substantive national law, including property law. The pressure from foreign jurisdictions on national law, in particular, as a result of the recognition of foreign property rights under the rules of private international law, is therefore to be taken seriously.

Besides the applicable law, international agreement has also been reached in matters concerning jurisdiction. On a European Union level, the Brussels – I Regulation has resolved questions of jurisdiction.[23] Article 22 of the Regulation states that regardless of domicile of the parties to a dispute, the courts of the legal system in which 'rights in rem in immovable property' or 'tenancies in immovable property' are situated have jurisdiction. Under these rules, therefore, jurisdiction also follows the *lex rei sitae* rule.[24]

18 On German law and reservation of ownership, see Chapter 4; 2.5. Security Ownership.
19 See Kieninger 1996a, p. 207-208, Van der Weide 2006, p. 90-93.
20 Cape Town Convention on International Interests in Mobile Equipment, see, *inter alia*, Goode 2002, p. 3 *et seq.*, Van Erp 2004a, p. 91 *et seq.*, Van der Weide 2006, p. 72-81.
21 See Chapter 5; 4.9. EC and International Influences.
22 See Graziadei 2002b, p. 317 *et seq.*, Lupoi 2005, p. 10 *et seq.*, Braun 2006, p 795 *et seq.*
23 Council Regulation (EC) No. 44/2001 of 22 December 2000 on jurisdiction and the recognition and enforcement of judgments in civil and commercial matters (Brussels – I).
24 Art. 22 of the Brussels – I Regulation was preceded Art. 16 of the Brussels Convention on jurisdiction and the enforcement of judgments in civil and commercial matter, a treaty between the original six Member States of the European Economic Community (EEC), to which new Member States acceded. Therefore, at the moment of creation of the Convention, no English term for property relation in respect to an immovable object was needed. Only when the United Kingdom became party to the EEC in 1973 (1 January 1973) and to the Convention in 1978 (9 October 1978), an English translation was needed. Eventually, the term 'rights in rem in immovable property' was settled on. The term 'in rem' can sometimes lead →

1.3. *European Union Law*

A second influence comes from the legal order created by the European Union, to establish and maintain an internal market in which there is free movement of goods, persons, services and capital.[25] Under the policy of the accomplishment of the internal market, the European Union's institutions, in particular the European Commission, have taken various legislative measures, harmonising areas of former national law, so as to ensure a better movement of goods, persons, services and capital.[26]

In the spheres of private law, which in this respect are rules that can have an effect on the functioning of the Internal Market, in particular, the attempts of the Commission to harmonise contract law have already been mentioned in the introduction of Chapter 7 above.[27] The harmonisation of private law has been part of the European Union's general agenda for some time. In the *Tampere* programme of the European Council, the convergence of private law systems in the area of the European Union was mentioned as one of the three main areas in which the EU would stay active.[28] However, at the same time, in the area of property law the European Union has been much more restrictive, sometimes excluding property aspects as much as possible, as in case of the Directive on time-share agreements, where this property law concept is reduced to rules on information duties on a contractual level.[29]

Nevertheless, from the very beginning, the European Commission has included some property concepts in its attempts to harmonise contract law. In particular in the area of property security rights, 'credit securities' in the words of the official Commission communications, the Commission seems always to have been willing to consider including these in its programme for harmonisation.[30] Recently, a study

to difficulties. See e.g. Case C-294/92 *Webb v Webb* [1994] ECR I-467 in which the European Court of Justice held Art. 16 of the Brussels Convention did not apply to an action declaring an immovable object was held on trust.

25 See Arts. 28, 39, 43 and 56 EC.

26 Barnard 2007, p. 3.

27 See Chapter 7; 1. Introduction. See also Rutgers 2006, p. 217 *et seq.* and Weatherhill 2005, p. 405 *et seq.*

28 Tampere European Council, 15 and 16 October 1999, Presidency Conclusions, <http://www.europa.eu.int/council/off/conclu/oct99/oct99_en.htm>. See Israël & Saarloos 2007, p. 669-670.

29 In this respect Chalmers, Hadjiemmanuil, Monti and Tomkins are mistaken when they state that the European Union has created its own system of property rights in the course of the creation of the Internal Market. Chalmers et al. 2006, p. 470. See Directive 94/47/EC of the European Parliament and the Council of 26 October 1994 on the protection of purchasers in respect of certain aspects of contracts relating to the purchase of the right to use immovable properties on a timeshare basis. See also the newly proposed Directive on the protection of consumers in respect of certain aspects of timeshare, long-term holiday products, resale and exchange of the European Commission of 7 June 2007, 2007/0113 (COD). See also Kieninger 2007, p. 187-188.

30 See Communication from the Commission to the Council and the European Parliament on European Contract Law, Com(2001) 398 final, No. 13. See Rutgers 2006, p. 218.

has been published by Von Bar and Drobnig, at the invitation of the Commission, on the effects of harmonisation of contract law on the areas of property law and unjust enrichment, rules on transfer of movables, on property security rights in respect of movables, and on rules on trust. The results of this study show that these areas of property law would be seriously affected in the event that contract law were to be harmonised.[31] In the project of the Commission to create a Common Frame of Reference (CFR), a toolbox of rules on the harmonisation of European contract law, these areas of property law are now included.[32]

Apart from these 'positive' harmonisation efforts, the European Court of Justice (ECJ) has made use of the EC Treaty provisions, which are all formulated in the form of a prohibition, to declare provisions of national law inapplicable when they form an obstacle to one or more of the 'four freedoms'.[33] This 'negative' harmonisation of national law was originally most visible in the area of free movement of goods, but was also used analogously with regard to the other freedoms; the free movement of persons, services, and capital.[34] From the line of jurisprudence of the ECJ, some cases have become well known, such as *Dassonville* and *Cassis de Dijon* and, for instance, in the sphere of free movement of persons, *Bosman*.[35]

In the initial phase of European integration, many national provisions discriminated on the grounds of country of origin or on the grounds of nationality. It was, at first, against these provisions that the ECJ took action by prohibiting what are known as distinctly applicable rules. Examples of these are a rule that would only apply to foreign products, or a rule that required imported products to fulfil higher standards than domestic products.[36] However, soon after the start of this line of jurisprudence, the Court extended its case law to national provisions applying indistinctly, regardless of the country of origin or nationality, but which still have an effect on the trade within the internal market. It is especially the case law on these indistinctly applicable rules that is of relevance to European private law today.[37] In short, under the case law of the ECJ, Member States can be forced to recognise a product that was lawfully produced in another Member State under the principle that has become known as 'mutual recognition'. In particular, in situations where an object, to stay within the definitions of the free movement of goods, has been subject

31 Von Bar & Drobnig 2002. On this study see, *inter alia*, Drobnig, Snijders & Zippro 2006, p 3 *et seq.*, Rutgers 2006, p. 221.

32 See <http://www.sgecc.com>. On the applicability of such proposals to property law, see Sparkes 2007, p. 523-524.

33 On these forms of harmonisation, see Craig & De Búrca 2007, p. 604-606. On the effects of the freedoms on private law, see Israël 2005, p. 106 *et seq.*

34 Barnard 2007, p. 10-11. On negative harmonisation or negative integration see Case 15/81 *Gaston Schul Douane Expediteur BV v Inspecteur der Invoerrechten en Accijnzen, Roosendaal* [1982] ECR 1409, Para. 33.

35 Case 8/74 *Procureur du Roi v Dassonville* [1974] ECR 837, Case 120/78 *Rewe-Zentrale AG v Bundesmonopolverwaltung für Branntwein* [1979] ECR 649, Case C-415/93, *Union Royale Belge des Sociétés de Football Association ASBL v Jean-Marc Bosman*, [1995] ECR I-4921, [1996] 1 CMLR 645.

36 E.g., Case 251/87 *Firma Denkavit Futtermiteel GmbH v Minister für Ernährung* [1979] ECR 3369, Case C-320/93 *Lucien Ortscheid GmbH v Eurim-Pharm Arzneimittel GmbH* [1994] ECR I-5243.

37 Israël & Saarloos 2007, p. 649-650, Joerges 1997, p. 381.

to rules and requirements in one Member State, another Member State under this principle of mutual recognition is not allowed to impose another set of rules with the same aim or purpose, known as a double burden.[38]

In other words, besides the national rules on the recognition of objects - known as goods in European law terminology - that originate in other countries, and rights in respect of these objects, European Law, in particular Internal Market law, applies when there is a European Community dimension to the case. National rules of private international law on recognition are therefore also subject to the scrutiny of the Court.[39] In this respect, the rules of private international law are also subject to what might be called EC-private international law, which is sometimes based on principles other than the private international law system of some of the Member States.[40]

National property law, especially *numerus clausus*, is therefore under increasing pressure to facilitate the development of the Internal Market in the European Union. National rules of a Member State stating that national law applies when an object is situated in that territory, known as the *lex rei sitae* rule, are closely watched by the European Court of Justice.[41] It might very well be that the application of the *lex rei sitae* rule in some instances will be contrary to EC law, making national property law, and thus the national *numerus clausus*, inapplicable.[42] It is with this European pressure that this Chapter is concerned. The next section will therefore deal with EC Internal Market law and its influence on private law in more detail.[43] After that, some conclusions for property law will be drawn and *numerus clausus* is visited once more to see if it could play a role in the development of a European property law, and if so, what that role might be.[44]

2. The European Union and the Need for a European Property Law

Of all the external influences on the national property law systems, and on *numerus clausus* specifically, the European influence is the broadest, but at the same time most challenging, influence. The focus on the law of the European Union, in particular the law of the European Community (EC Law) is relevant because of the active roles that both the European Commission as a legislator, in the case of positive harmonisation, and the European Court of Justice, in the case of negative harmonisation, have played in the achievement of the Internal Market by breaking down barriers to trade.

The active involvement of the European Community (EC), as was already mentioned in the introduction to this Chapter, has not only included public law, but

38 See Kieninger 1996a, p. 181-183.

39 See Israël & Saarloos 2007, p. 629-631, 649.

40 Israël & Saarloos 2007, p. 656-658, Michaels 2006b, p. 18 *et seq.*, Basedow 2007, p. 172 *et seq.*

41 See Israël & Saarloos 2007, p. 649-652.

42 Kieninger 2006, p. 166, Basedow 1995, p. 44, Kieninger 1996a, p. 122 *et seq.*, Rutgers 1999, p. 167 *et seq.*, Roth 1999, p. 40 *et seq.*

43 See below; 2. The European Union and the Need for a European Property Law.

44 See below; 3. The Making of European Property Law.

also private law, lately in particular in the area of company law dealing with the freedom of establishment.[45] Although the 'core areas' of private law, especially contract law, tort law and property law as a whole, have been left alone for the most part, at least the legal environment in which private law functions has changed with the rise and development of the Internal Market.[46] Undoubtedly, this 'Europeanisation' has an effect on the way in which national private law functions, including scrutiny by the EU's Institutions of the national performance in respect to the functioning of the Internal Market.

In order to understand and fully appreciate the European efforts and their effect on private law, some basics on the law of the European Communities are needed. This section will therefore deal first with general EC law in respect to private law, from contract law to company law, after which some more specifics of European law, in particular the case law of the ECJ, can be discussed. Finally, but most importantly for this study, these aspects of EC law will be applied to the law of property.

2.1. *EC Private Law*

Within the legal order of the European Union, there are various sources of law that affect private law. Moreover, there are also initiatives towards law making by the European Union's Institutions, in particular the European Commission, that deserve to be mentioned as they are likely to end up as a form of either primary or secondary Community law. Following the general hierarchy of sources, first the EC Treaty as the primary source of Community private law, in particular property law, is briefly dealt with. After that some secondary legislation in the area of private law will be mentioned. As will be seen, there is an unavoidable connection between the primary and secondary legal framework. This is primarily because some secondary Community law requires a legal basis in a primary legal instrument. In describing these sources of law, the focus will be on legislative efforts in the area of property law as much as possible.

2.1.1. Legal Framework: Primary Community Law

The Treaty establishing the European Community, the EC Treaty, set as the objective of the Community the creation of an Internal Market in which there is free movement of goods, persons, services and capital.[47] These four areas in which free movement is ensured in the Treaty are known as the four freedoms.[48]

45 Joerges 1997, p. 382.

46 See Joerges 1997, p. 382 *et seq.*, Van Erp 2006b, p. 5-7.

47 Arts. 2 and 3(1)(C) EC. Art. 2 EC uses the term single market, whereas Art. 3 EC uses the term Internal Market. It seems however, that there is no real difference between these two terms. On this terminological issue see Barnard 2007, p. 10-12, Craig & De Búrca 2007, p. 6-7. In the new Treaty Art. 2 and 3(1) EC Treaty have been repealed and replaced, although slightly amended, in Art. 3 TFEU.

48 Craig & De Búrca 2007, p. 605-606, Barnard 2007, p. 3.

When it comes to primary Community law, and its effect on private law especially, the EC Treaty is of relevance.[49] In the system of European law, the European Union needs a legal basis in the Treaty to be able to legislate. In many subject areas there are specific provisions that have been included over the years to give the European Union more competences. Examples of these include Article 174 EC Treaty on environmental protection and Article 153 EC Treaty on consumer protection. At this moment, the EC Treaty is subject to reform. Although this reform is primarily focused on reforming the structure of the EU and its Institutions, the reformed Treaty, known as the Lisbon Treaty, also reforms the substantive articles in the EC Treaty, affecting the legal basis for Community legislation.[50] The new articles in the EC Treaty will also be dealt with.

No specific provisions have been included to harmonise private law. However, the EC Treaty provides some general provisions that can and have been used as a legal basis for private law harmonising measures. In this respect three articles in the EC Treaty should be considered.

First, Article 94 EC Treaty provides a general basis for legislative measures harmonising law when the Internal Market is concerned:

> 'The Council shall, acting unanimously on a proposal from the Commission and after consulting the European Parliament and the Economic and Social Committee, issue directives for the approximation of such laws, regulations or administrative provisions of the Member States as directly affect the establishment or functioning of the common market'.[51]

Although Article 94 offers a general basis for the harmonisation of private law when it comes to the functioning of the Internal Market, the requirement of unanimity in the Council provides a major obstacle. Moreover, Article 94 only offers the possibility to draft a Directive, which can sometimes be problematic.[52]

Article 95 EC Treaty also allows the EU to legislate in order to promote the establishment or functioning of the Internal Market, but does not require unanimity.[53] This Article states:

> '1. By way of derogation from Article 94 and save where otherwise provided in this Treaty, the following provisions shall apply for the achievement of the objectives set out in Article 14. The Council shall, acting in accordance with the procedure referred to

49 There is another Treaty in respect to the European Union, i.e. the Treaty on European Union or EU Treaty.

50 Treaty of Lisbon amending the Treaty on European Union and the Treaty establishing the European Community. On the process towards the making of this Treaty see Craig & De Búrca 2007, p. 31-36.

51 Again, this Article uses a different term to describe the Internal Market. Like the term single market that was shortly dealt with above in respect to Art. 2 EC, the term common market probably also synonym for the Internal Market. See Barnard 2007, p. 10-12.

52 E.g., in case of an optional instrument of European Contract law, a Directive cannot offer the desired 28th regime. See Hesselink, Rutgers & de Booys 2007, p. 58-59.

53 See Rutgers 2005, p. 145 *et seq.*, Smits 2007, p. 282-285, Hesselink, Rutgers & de Booys 2007, p. 44 *et seq.*

> in Article 251 and after consulting the Economic and Social Committee, adopt the measures for the approximation of the provisions laid down by law, regulation or administrative action in Member States which have as their object the establishment and functioning of the internal market'.

This Article especially has been used to issue Directives in the area of private law, contract law in particular.[54] The reference to Article 14 EC Treaty, which refers to the progressive establishment of the Internal Market, allows room to include private law. For many years Article 95 was used with a statement in the preamble of Regulations and Directives that differences in private law between the Member States led to an obstacle to the functioning of the Internal Market.[55] However, as Weatherhill states, there have been two principal objections to this assumption. First, the connection between the diversity of law and market fragmentation, more specifically the functioning of the Internal Market, has not always been shown.[56] Second, even when the need for harmonisation based on the first assumption has been shown, the question remains whether that is enough to justify the adoption of the measure.[57]

The European Court of Justice, in the *Tobacco Advertising* case, has addressed the first point.[58] When confronted with Directive 98/43, based on Article 100a, now Article 95 EC Treaty, on the advertising of tobacco products, the Court was asked to rule on the use of Article 95 as a legal basis. It stated in this respect:

> 'Those provisions, read together, make it clear that the measures referred to in Article 100a(1) of the Treaty are intended to improve the conditions for the establishment and functioning of the internal market. To construe that article as meaning that it vests in the Community legislature a general power to regulate the internal market would not only be contrary to the express wording of the provisions cited above but would also be incompatible with the principle embodied in Article 3b of the EC Treaty (now Article 5 EC) that the powers of the Community are limited to those specifically conferred on it'.[59]

As Weatherhill explains, the Court made very clear that the Treaty does not provide the European legislature with a competence to harmonise *per se*, but forces the legislature to show that an act of European law will make a contribution to the establish-

54 See Weatherhill 2005, p. 411, Craig & De Búrca 2007, p. 615-620. Moreover, this is also the Article that the Commission intents to use to create the horizontal instrument or horizontal directive in the area of EC Consumer Law. See Communication from the Commission to the European Parliament, the Council, the European Economic and Social Committee and the Committee of the Regions - Commission Legislative and Work Programme 2008, COM(2007) 640, p. 28.

55 Weatherhill 2006, p. 136. See also Case 15/81 *Gaston Schul Douane Expediteur BV v Inspecteur der Invoerrechten en Accijnzen, Roosendaal* [1982] ECR 1409.

56 Weatherhill 2006, p. 137, Van Erp 2006b, p. 12.

57 Weatherhill 2006, p. 137.

58 Case C-276/98 *Germany v Parliament and Council* [2000] ECR I-8419. Weatherhill 2005, p. 412-413.

59 Case C-276/98 *Germany v Parliament and Council* [2000] ECR I-8419, Para. 83.

ment and functioning of the internal market.[60] In order to harmonise private law, therefore, the Community legislature must not only show divergences between the various national legal systems, but must also show that these divergences lead to an obstacle to the functioning of the Internal Market.[61]

A third Article on which the European legislature could legislate in the area of private law is Article 308 EC Treaty. This Article states:

> 'If action by the Community should prove necessary to attain, in the course of the operation of the common market, one of the objectives of the Community, and this Treaty has not provided the necessary powers, the Council shall, acting unanimously on a proposal from the Commission and after consulting the European Parliament, take the appropriate measures'.

Article 308 EC is one of the final Articles in the EC Treaty, offering last resort for the European legislature seeking a legal basis for a measure of European law. As in the case of Article 94 EC Treaty, unanimity in the Council is required.[62] The legislative procedure of a measure adopted under Article 308 is different from the co-decision procedure that is followed under Article 95, however. Article 308 only calls for consultation of the European Parliament, thus lowering the democratic legitimacy of a measure adopted.[63]

2.1.2. Legal Framework: Secondary Community Law

When it comes to secondary Community private law, which mainly comprises Regulations and Directives, the EU has been mainly active in the field of contract law.[64] Examples of legislation issued in European contract law are the Directive on unfair terms in consumer contracts, the Directive on distance selling and the Directive on time-share agreements.[65] All of these, although sometimes the name suggests otherwise, as in the case of time-shares, deal specifically with issues of contract law.

In the field of property law, the Commission has been much more restrictive, but has, since 1993, carefully touched upon some property law aspects. Usually, these property law aspects are dealt with in the context of a very specific issue. However, as property law and, in particular, the system of property rights is based

60 Weatherhill 2006, p. 138-139, see also Rutgers 2005, p. 157-158, Van Erp 2006b, p. 12.

61 In this sense the requirement on the legislator can be compared to the requirement of an individual claiming infringement of a national measure under Article 28 EC. On this see below; 2.2.1. Free Movement of Goods. See also Hesselink, Rutgers & de Booys 2007, p. 52 *et seq.*

62 Weatherhill 2005, p. 415, 417-418.

63 See on this last point of democratic legitimacy Hesselink, Rutgers & de Booys 2007, p. 59-65. In the new Treaty the requirement will not be consultation with the European Parliament, but consent of the European Parliament.

64 On Regulations and Directives see Art. 249 EC.

65 Directives 93/13 (Unfair Terms), 97/7 (Distance Selling), 94/47 (Timeshare). See also below; 2.1.3. European Commission Initiatives for Future Legislation. The vast majority of these Directives are based on Art. 95 EC as a legal basis.

on coherence and systematic application of property rights to all possible cases, the introduction of a specific European type of property right will usually, because of the coherent nature of the national property law systems implementing European legislation, lead to a change of the current national property law as a whole.

The best example of this is provided by the Directive on late payments.[66] In this Directive, the European Parliament and the Council specifically wanted to deal with late payments and non-payments in commercial transactions. Because of that, the Directive focuses on resolving diverging contractual payment periods in the Member States.[67] As a part of combatting the problem of late payments, the Parliament and the Council emphasise that creditors should have the possibility to strengthen their position by making use of a retention of title or reservation of ownership clause.[68] The legislature leaves open what exactly the effects of a retention of title clause would be when it defines such a clause in Article 1 of the Directive as 'the contractual agreement according to which the seller retains his title to the goods in question until the price has been paid in full'.[69] Article 4 of the Directive obliges the Member States to ensure that a retention of title clause is recognised in their national law, and that a retention of title clause made in conformity with national law of one of the Member States shall be given effect.[70] Moreover, the Insolvency Regulation also deals with retention of title.[71] In Article 7, the Regulation deals with 'reservation of title', a different term than the term used in the Directive on late payments. Article 7 of the Regulation attempts to ensure that the commencement of insolvency proceedings against a buyer who has made a reservation of title agreement does not affect the validity of the reservation of title. Furthermore, the commencement of insolvency proceedings against the seller who has made a reservation of title agreement does not constitute a ground for rescinding that agreement.[72] Although the Directive on late payments and the Insolvency Regulation do not create a European right of retention of title, they do attempt to ensure effective use of retention of title clauses throughout the Internal Market.[73] The inclusion of property law in a Directive on contract law shows the willingness of the EU to deal with matters of property law when they have an effect on the functioning of the Internal Market.

Another area of property law in which the European legislature has been active is the protection of cultural objects.[74] In a Directive of 1993, the Council pro-

66 Directive 2000/35 of the European Parliament and of the Council of 29 June 2000 on combating late payment in commercial transactions.

67 Directive 2000/35, Preamble Paras. 8-10.

68 Directive 2000/35, Preamble Para. 21.

69 Art. 1(3) Directive 2000/35/EC. On the tension between the contractual aspects and the proprietary aspects of a retention of title clause see Rutgers 1999, p. 167.

70 Art. 4 Directive 2000/35.

71 Council Regulation 1346/2000 of 29 May on insolvency proceedings.

72 Art. 7 Council Regulation 1346/2000. See e.g. Remien 2005, p. 2, Van Erp 2006b, p. 8.

73 See also Sagaert 2007, p. 316-321.

74 See Biondi 1997, p. 1173 *et seq.*

vided rules on prescription periods and rules of third-party protection.[75] Although the topic of this Directive is very specific, the results of its application have a serious impact on national property law systems. Rules of third-party protection and prescription, which are key concepts of property law, can be set aside in order to ensure the return of a stolen or lost cultural object.[76]

In environmental law, the Parliament and the Council have issued a Directive on emission rights, the tradable right to produce a certain amount of carbon dioxide (CO_2) in the air.[77] As a result, new objects of property law are created to which a new regime, ensured by the Directive, applies.[78] The specific nature of emission rights in the Directive forced some national property law systems, such as the Netherlands, to adopt an abstract transfer system, which is a system in which invalidity of the underlying agreement does not automatically lead to invalidity of the transfer.[79] In other words, as a result of the Directive, systems adhering to a different model of transfer were forced to adapt their law, at least in respect of emission trading.[80]

Recently Sparkes has focused attention on rules of secondary EC Law that have an effect on immovable objects.[81] These include environmental concerns, such as the energy performance of buildings, but also rules on competition law and state aid, that have an effect on how a market in immovable objects is organised.[82] Especially in respect to immovables there is a growing body of European Community legislation that does not explicitly deal with these objects, but which nevertheless has an effect on them.[83] Possibly the clearest example of this is offered through the development of a European family law.[84] For example, in respect of marriage and the law applicable to marriage and divorce, property law questions in respect to immovables, especially matrimonial homes, are very important.[85] Moreover, also in

75 Directive 93/7/EEC of the Council on of 15 March 1993 on the return of cultural objects unlawfully removed from the territory of a Member State. On this Directive see Salomons 2002, Van der Weide 2006, p. 9.

76 See e.g. Arts. 2, 4 and 12 Directive 93/7/EEC.

77 Directive 2003/87/EC of the European Parliament and the Council of 13 October 2003 establishing a scheme for greenhouse gas emission allowance trading within the Community and amending Council Directive 96/61/EC.

78 On this Directive see, *inter alia*, Van Erp 2004c, p. 539-540, Van Erp 2006a, p. 1065-1066.

79 See Van Erp 2006a, p. 1066.

80 Van Erp 2006a, p. 1065-1066.

81 Sparkes 2007, p. 130-137.

82 See, *inter alia*, Proposal for a Directive of the European Parliament and of the Council establishing a framework for the protection of soil and amending Directive 2004/35/EC COM (2006) 232 final, Directive 2002/91/EC of the European Parliament and of the Council on Energy Performance of Buildings, Council Regulation 1184/2006/EC applying certain rules of competition to the production of, and trade in, agricultural products. Sparkes 2007, p. 130-137.

83 Sparkes 2007, p. 153. This, according to Sparkes, also includes EC Consumer protection rules. See Sparkes 2007, p. 191 *et seq.*

84 Sparkes 2007, p. 475 *et seq.*

85 See Green Paper on the Conflict of Law Matters concerning matrimonial property regimes, including the question of jurisdiction and mutual recognition, Brussels 17 July 2006, Memo/06/288, Regulation 861/2007 of the European Parliament and of the Council establishing →

respect to succession law, similar questions arise. In this respect also the European legislature is becoming active.[86]

Finally, and most importantly, in 2002 the European Parliament and the Council adopted a directive on financial collateral arrangements.[87] In this Directive, a security right in respect of cash or financial instruments, and the possibility to transfer title in such cash or financial instruments for security purposes, is created throughout the Internal Market.[88] Regardless of the rules on national property law, the Directive on financial collateral establishes a new regime, to which different rules apply. These new rules include the possibility of a *lex commissoria* and the possibility of a transfer of ownership for security purposes with, from a civil law point of view, all its problems of fragmentation of ownership.[89] As a result, Member States that did not recognise a transfer of ownership for security purposes, either in the form of a repurchase agreement or as a transfer under condition, will now be forced to recognise such a transfer in respect of the applicability of the Directive.[90] Member States that hitherto did not allow a *lex commissoria* will be forced to recognise this possibility, at least for those transactions falling under the Directive.[91]

The Directive on financial collateral arrangements has forced Member States either to reform their currently existing property rights, or to adopt new, additional, property rights. The entry into force of the Directive therefore directly affects the closed system of property rights in the national property laws of the Member States. Those systems that have created a new type of security right by implementation of the Directive, for instance, a special right of pledge, have added one more property right to the menu of national property rights. Those systems that have chosen to change the existing provisions have, under the influence of European law, changed the contents of the already existing menu of national property rights. In any of these cases, the effect of European law, and the problems its effect may create for national property law systems, has become clearly visible.

2.1.3. European Commission Initiatives for Future Legislation

Apart from the currently existing legislation, both primary and secondary, that has an effect on property law, there are several European Commission initiatives on legislation or investigation into possibilities to prepare legislation that will have an

a European Small Claims Procedure, Art. 2(2)(b), Green Paper on Applicable Law and Jurisdiction in Divorce Matters (Rome III), COM(2005), 82 final.

86 Green Paper on Succession and Wills COM(2005) 65 final. See Sparkes 2007, p. 493-499.

87 Directive 2002/47/EC of the European Parliament and the Council of 6 June 2002 on financial collateral arrangements. See Sagaert 2007, p. 321-327, Kieninger 2007, p. 195-197.

88 Art. 1(4)(a), 5, and 6 Directive 2002/47/EC. See Van Vliet 2005, p. 190 *et seq.*

89 On the problems of implementation of the Financial Collateral Arrangements Directive see, *inter alia*, Van Erp 2004c, Keijser 2004,Van Erp 2004d, Van Erp 2005, Van Vliet 2005.

90 In terms of the Member States included in this study this in particular applies to the Netherlands.

91 In 2006 the French reforms introduced the general possibility of a *lex commissoria*. Other Member States have not and are forced to deal with it in terms of transactions falling under the Directive.

effect on property law. These initiatives are relevant not only because they are likely to change the substance of property law, also property law at a national level, but also because their adoption would result in the European Union becoming active in the field of property law. When this happens, not only the specific legislation but also the full body of European law methodology and legal thinking will become applicable to aspects of, property law. This European methodology includes the jurisdiction of the European Court of Justice and its exclusive competence to interpret EU law through answering preliminary questions submitted by national courts.[92] The European legal thinking includes the impressive line of case law of the European Court of Justice in respect of the four freedoms, in particular, the free movement of goods which might apply to property law as well. In this line of reasoning, traditional distinctions between public law and private law play a less important role, as the European legal thinking does not follow the traditional national distinctions between private and public law. Instead, the effects of national law on the functioning of the internal market are central.[93]

Before going into these aspects of the case law of the European Court of Justice, some Commission initiatives should be examined. Because these initiatives do not yet have the force of legislation, and some of them do not directly, but only indirectly, affect property law, they will only be dealt with briefly.

With the publication of the European Commission's action plan in 2001 on a more coherent European Contract law, the work on a Common Frame of Reference was begun.[94] Led by the Directorate General (DG) on Consumer Affairs, the Commission is undertaking a revision of the currently existing consumer contract law, also known as the consumer *acquis*.[95] In terms used by the Commission, and therefore in the terms of European law that does not concern itself specifically with the traditional distinction between private law and public law, the consumer *acquis* is part of EC consumer law.[96] EC consumer law, however, is, in content, restricted largely to contract law.

That is not to say that the Commission is not aware of the traditional distinctions used in the Member States and does not investigate whether other areas of private law should also be included. In 2002 the Commission published a study on the effects of harmonisation of contract law on other areas of private law, in particular tort and property law.[97] The results of this study include the conclusion that some areas of property law are affected so much by contract law, that they should at least be included in the academic research that is at the foundation of this EU

92 See Art. 234 EC.

93 See e.g. Case 8/74 *Procureur du Roi v Dassonville* [1974] ECR 837.

94 Action plan 2001, COM(2001) 98.

95 The term *acquis* is derived from the term *acquis communautaire*, the term that is used in European law to describe those legislative instruments that have been created and have entered into force thus far.

96 The use of the term EC Consumer Law has led to some problems of understanding with national contract lawyers. For a discussion of the terms and their relation see, *inter alia*, Schuze 2005, p. 17 *et seq.*

97 Von Bar & Drobnig 2002.

legislative project.[98] These areas of property law include the transfer of movables, security rights in movables, and trusts.[99]

The exact political, and therefore also future legal, status of the Common Frame of Reference is unknown at the time of writing. Two major research projects are being conducted at the same time to prepare its contents. Under the presidency of Professor Von Bar, the Study Group on a European Civil Code is working on a set of principles based on the Principles of European Contract Law (PECL) but with added new insights and, of importance to this study, the abovementioned aspects of property law.[100] At the same time, under the co-ordination of Professor Schulte-Nölke, another group of legal scholars, called the *Acquis* Group, is working on a review of the existing consumer law *acquis*.[101] This consumer *acquis*, for the purposes of the research conducted by this group, comprises eight Directives.[102] The result of the study provides an overview on how these eight Directives have been implemented in the different Member States, and concludes that there is an increasing need for more legislative measures.[103] In line with its consumer policy and expecting the results of the study of the *Acquis* Group, the Commission proposes to adopt a horizontal instrument in the form of a Directive.[104] With a horizontal instrument the EU intends to harmonise aspects of EC consumer law with a single legal instrument, replacing the currently existing fragmentary legislation.[105]

Because the nature of the work of the *Acquis* Group is restricted to the existing *acquis*, the group is not directly confronted with property law.[106] Nevertheless, the group does make proposals affecting general contract law, which, according to the results of the Commission study mentioned above, could have an impact on property law as well.[107]

98 Von Bar & Drobnig 2002, Nos. 730-736, p. 442-444.

99 In particular in the area of security rights there have been voices for many years to come to more European legislation. See, *inter alia*, Kreuzer 1999, Kieninger 1996b, p. 41 *et seq.*, Drobnig, Snijders & Zippro 2006, p. 3 *et seq.*

100 See <http://www.sgecc.com and www.copecl.org>.

101 The group is headed by Prof. Gianmaria Ajani. On the work of the *Acquis* Group see Schulze 2007, p. 130 *et seq.* The first results of this group were published in 2007. See *Acquis* Group 2007, p. IX *et seq.*

102 Directives 85/577 (Doorstep-selling), 90/314 (Package Travel), 93/13 (Unfair Terms), 94/47 (Timeshare), 97/7 (Distance Selling), 98/6 (Price Indication), 98/27 (Injunctions) and 99/44 (Consumer Sales). See also <http://www.eu-consumer-law.org>.

103 In particular a horizontal instrument. Schulte-Nölke, Twigg-Flesner & Elbers 2007, p. 746. See also Briefing Note: Review of the Consumer *Acquis*, (IP/A/IMCO/FWC/2006-168/C4/SC1), PE 385.641 EN, available at <http://www.europarl.europa.eu/comparl/imco/studies/0705_consumeracquis_en.pdf>.

104 Green Paper on the Review of the Consumer *Acquis*, 8 February 2007, COM(2006) 744 final, p. 8.

105 Smits 2007, p. 285-289.

106 Although the *Acquis* Group has taken a somewhat wider view on what exactly should be in the *acquis*. See Jansen & Zimmermann 2007, p. 1113 *et seq.*, *Acquis* Group 2007, p. XXIII *et seq.*

107 Von Bar & Drobnig 2002. For a critical view on the initial results of the *Acquis* Group see Jansen & Zimmermann 2007, p. 1113-1115.

The work of the Study Group on a European Civil Code and the *Acquis* Group resulted in the publication of a first draft of the Common Frame of Reference (DCFR), known as the 'academic CFR', at the end of 2007. Another version of the DCFR is expected to be published in 2008. The academic CFR was presented to the Commission, and from this the Commission will have to make a selection in order to compose a horizontal instrument in the field of EC consumer contract law.[108]

A second field in which the Commission is active is in the field of financial services.[109] When it comes to property law, the mortgage market in particular is of relevance. In this area, the European Commission has made several initiatives in the past, but has most recently published a Green Paper and a White Paper, which will now be discussed in turn.[110] In the Green Paper, the European Commission, as part of the improvement of the Internal Market, in particular of the Lisbon criteria to enhance the competitiveness of the EU, considers that intervention in the mortgage market by creating a European right of mortgage or right of hypothec would contribute to the economic growth in Europe, and solve many problems of cross-border financing.[111] In order to investigate the possibilities and possible threats of a potential Commission intervention in the national legal systems, the Commission commissioned an out-sourced study. This study showed a real need for European legislation in this field.[112] Already the Commission's early proposals and the results of this study show that there are two aspects to the European mortgage market.[113]

Firstly, there is the perspective of the consumer, the primary mortgage market. Market research results show that in 2004 only 1% of all transactions in immovables in the European Union concerned a cross-border sale of immovable objects.[114] In this respect, in particular, to increase cross-border mortgage lending, the Commission is investigating possibilities for a more flexible, consumer-friendly type of mortgage,

108 At the end of 2007 it was unclear what exactly the Commission considers a horizontal instrument and what will be its legal status. In the Commission Working Programme 2008, there is mention of a Consumer Contract Law Directive as a legal instrument. See Communication from the Commission to the European Parliament, the Council, the European Economic and Social Committee and the Committee of the Regions. Commission Legislative and Work Programme 2008 COM(2007) 640 final, p. 28.

109 See Green Paper on Financial Services Policy (2005-2010) COM(2005) 177, p. 12. Communication from the Commission to the European Parliament, the Council, the European Economic and Social Committee and the Committee of the Regions A Single Market for 21st Century Europe COM(2007) 724 final. Remien 2005, p. 12-14.

110 Green Paper Mortgage Credit in the EU COM(2005) 237 final. White Paper on Mortgage Credit Markets COM(2007) 807 final.

111 The terminology of European law in this respect is restricted to the term mortgage, although of course also rights of hypothec, and even *Grundschuld*, are considered to be included. As a result of possible legislation in this field, the term Mortgage will become a concept of EU law, i.e., a term to which European law gives its own meaning and to which the European Court of Justice has exclusive authority of interpretation. See Art. 234 EC. Green Paper Mortgage Credit in the EU COM(2005) 237 final, p. 3-4. See Sparkes 2007, p. 379-380, 396-397.

112 London Economics 2005, p. 105-107, see also Mortgage Credit Funding Group 2004, p. 47.

113 On the development see also Sparkes 2007, p. 397-398.

114 European Opinion Research Group 2004, p. 58. Green Paper Mortgage Credit in the EU COM(2005) 237 final, p. 5.

known as a right of Euro-mortgage. This includes abstract mortgages, which are property security rights not strictly connected to or dependent on a loan agreement, so that the property right can be used again.[115] French law has recently adopted the *hypothèque rechargeable* and the *prêt viager hypothécaire*, or reverse mortgage, which create possibilities to release the value of the immovable object in different ways than with a traditional type of hypothec.[116] Furthermore, the right of Euro-mortgage would be accompanied with a document proving its existence, as is the case with the German *Grundschuld*. The right could then also be transferred and executed by making use of the document issued by the Registrar.[117]

Secondly, there is also the perspective of the banks and large financial investors. In this respect, there is a secondary mortgage market in which mortgage credit that is granted to consumers is funded.[118] Such financing is achieved by complicated financial structures known as mortgage-backed security and covered bonds.[119] Integration of the mortgage market in this field is considered to have an immediate positive effect on the primary mortgage market.[120]

Although there is no exact proposal for a Euro-mortgage yet, academics have been working on proposals for several decades.[121] One of the older proposals for a pan-European right of mortgage came from the *Segré* report, in which a group of experts proposed to create a flexible European property right in line with the German *Briefgrundschuld* and the Swiss *Schuldbrief*.[122] Although later studies changed many details, the core of this original proposal, a flexible, non-accessory European property security right in respect of immovable objects, remains today.[123]

At the end of 2007 the European Commission published a White Paper on Mortgage Credit.[124] In contrast with the perspectives raised in the Green Paper, the Commission postpones the question of legislation in this area, including the question of introducing a right of Euro-mortgage to a later stage.[125] It does recognise

115 On the danger of the use of abstract, i.e., non-accessory, security rights, especially in case of security-*Grundschuld*, see Clemente 2007, p. 737.

116 Green Paper Mortgage Credit in the EU COM(2005) 237 final, p. 5-6. On the French forms of hypothec see Chapter 3; 3.6. Hypothec. Sparkes 2007, p. 398-401.

117 On the workings of the German *Briefgrundschuld* see Chapter 4; 3.8. *Grundschuld*.

118 See Sparkes 2007, p. 409-412.

119 See Forum Group 2005, Nasarre-Aznar 2004, p. 5 *et seq*.

120 Green Paper Mortgage Credit in the EU COM(2005) 237 final, p. 13-14.

121 See, *inter alia*, the Segré-report 1966 on the integration of the financial market, to be found at: <http://europa.eu.int/comm/economy_finance/emu_history/documentation/chapter1/19661130en382develeurocapitm_a.pdf>.

122 *Segré*-report 1966, p. 23. On the right of *Grundschuld* in particular *Briefgrundschuld* see Chapter 4; 3.8. *Grundschuld*. Swiss law is, as such, outside the scope of this study.

123 See, *inter alia*, Wehrens & Gresser 1992, Stöcker 1992, and Mortgage Credit Funding Group 2004.

124 White Paper on Mortgage Credit Markets COM(2007) 807 final.

125 White Paper on Mortgage Credit Markets COM(2007) 807 final, p. 5. On 18 December 2007 Commissioner for the Internal Market McCreevy stated in the European Parliament Committee on Economic and Monetary Affairs (ECON), *de auditu*, that it was not his intention, nor had it ever been his intention, to propose a Directive in this area. Such a statement is remarkable because several studies, including those contained in he Impact Assessment →

the diversity in legal systems in the mortgage credit market and recognises these as an obstacle to trade, but it does not seek a legislative solution.[126] Instead, the Commission seeks to stimulate the development of a wide spectrum of mortgage products, by which it refers to applications of the rights of hypothec in the Member States themselves, and seeks to remove barriers to distribution and sale of these products. For now, therefore, it seems that the Commission has shifted its focus to information duties and the development of national types of property security rights in respect of immovable objects. These information duties, however, include the further promotion of access to information from other Member States, for instance through EULIS, the European Land Information System.[127] National property rights are to remain for the time being, although naturally some convergence will occur. The White Paper clearly states that, at this moment, the Commission sees no reason to deviate from the *lex rei sitae* rule in respect of the applicable law.[128]

Even more than with the Common Frame of Reference, and a horizontal instrument redefining the EU Consumer *acquis*, the proposals of the Commission in the mortgage credit market, will have considerable effects on the national property law systems, and on *numerus clausus* in particular. More types of property security rights in respect of immovable objects, or a different application of currently existing property rights, possibly with new or altered provisions governing creation, existence, execution and destruction, will have to be recognised throughout the European Union.

Creating a right of Euro-mortgage would take this development one step further.[129] In many systems the legal nature of this new European property right will be contrary to the existing national provisions on property security rights in respect of immovable objects. The introduction of such a European property right could cause problems, including the non-accessory nature of the new European right of mortgage in legal systems that require all property security rights to be accessory. Moreover, it could cause problems in legal systems that do not have a positive registration system.[130] A positive registration system is a system in which the content of the register is guaranteed. Opposed to positive systems are negative registration systems, in which only the documents relating to immovable objects are registered, but the content is not checked. As a result the negative registration systems cannot

accompanying the White Paper make mention of legislation as a solution for the integration of the EU Mortgage Market. More information available on <http://europa.eu.int/comm/internal_market/finservices-retail/index_en.htm>.

126 White Paper on Mortgage Credit Markets COM(2007) 807 final, p. 3-5.

127 White Paper on Mortgage Credit Markets COM(2007) 807 final, p. 8.

128 White Paper on Mortgage Credit Markets COM(2007) 807 final. p. 7.

129 The White Paper makes no mention at all of a European right of mortgage, which could lead to the conclusion the Commission has left its legislative intentions in this area. However, it could also be argued that, not that the legislative option has been postponed, this topic, as it is the most far-reaching legislative solution, has been postponed with it.

130 The White Paper promises a Recommendation for 2008 in which the Commission will address the issue of land registration systems. White Paper on Mortgage Credit Markets COM(2007) 807 final, p. 8.

guarantee the content of the registration system in the same way as positive registration systems can. A document proving the existence of a property right can only be issued in systems adhering to a positive registration system. England and Germany adhere to a positive system of registration, France and the Netherlands to a negative system.[131]

A large part of this reasoning can also be applied to the current Commission initiative as advocated by the White Paper.[132] Through convergence of the legal systems of the Member States, new applications of current lesser rights of hypothec or mortgage will arise, possibly requiring substantial adaptation of the national system of property law. Even without a pan-European property right, the results of this line of policy can be expected to be severe.[133]

These Community initiatives show that, as a result of European legislation, national property law systems are under pressure, and that not all national property law systems are likely to be able to cope with European property rights, at least not in a way of creating truly European property rights. The legislative initiatives especially show that when property law is looked at from a purely national point of view, these European developments are overlooked. Instead, property law should be looked at from a more European perspective. Changing this perspective, which does not exclude national property law, will enable the appreciation of developments on a European level and the problems these are likely to cause at a national level.

2.2. *The ECJ as a Motor for the Development of European Private Law*

By allowing both the Commission and private parties to challenge national rules that hinder intra-Community trade and, if necessary, declaring these rules inapplicable, the European Court of Justice (ECJ) has played an immensely important role in shaping the Internal Market.[134] The provisions on the Internal Market, with its freedom of goods, services, persons and capital, were originally mostly applied to those rules of public national law that formed a direct burden or threat to intra-

131 On registration systems, see Cámara-Lapuente 2005, p. 797 *et seq.*, Zevenbergen 2002. More on the impacts of EC legislation on national property law below in 2.4. The Effects of European Law on the Law of Property.

132 On convergence of national legal systems below; 2.3. Voluntary Harmonisation.

133 Possibly, but this is contrary to the statements made by the Commission in its White Paper, the 2007 crisis on the US Sub-Prime Market, in which loans were granted to clients that could not afford to pay these loans, plays part in a careful legislative approach of the Commission. As a result of the financial turmoil the Commission seeks to create and enhance transparency in financial services, in particular in structure finance products, for which rights of mortgage and hypothec are often used. On the US Sub-Prime Mortgage crisis and the relation to the White Paper see White Paper on Mortgage Credit Markets COM(2007) 807 final, p. 2, 4, but see p. 7.

134 In particular the procedures under Arts. 226 and 234 EC.

Community trade, such as levies on products, requirements of nationality or requirements of language.[135]

At a later stage, other areas of law also became included, as the ECJ extended its case law to measures which hindered intra-Community trade, but which were not necessarily aimed at foreign products only. Examples of these cases include cases on the marketing of products.[136] It is in this respect that private law, contract and property law in particular, became subject to European supervision. In particular the free movement of goods, the freedom of establishment, the free movement of persons, and the free movement of capital have been used to challenge rules of private law.[137] This Section will deal with the free movement of goods, an area in which the ECJ has developed a particular method of case law in respect of the Internal Market. Furthermore, it will deal with the application of this case law to private law, company law in particular, before returning to the subject of property law.

The case law of the ECJ in this field is an impressive list of cases, each contributing to the development of the approach towards the Internal Market. However, in this Section only that case law that is of relevance to property law, *numerus clausus* in particular, will be dealt with.

2.2.1. Free Movement of Goods

2.2.1.1. Obstacles to Trade

At the heart of the case law of the ECJ on free movement is the EC Treaty provision on the free movement of goods. In terms of European law, the definition of goods is not altogether clear. In the ECJ's definition, goods are products 'which can be valued in money and which are capable, as such, of forming the subject of commercial transactions'.[138] However, electricity has also been considered a good in terms of the free movement of goods.[139] The provision in the EC Treaty dealing with free movement of goods is Article 28 EC Treaty:

[135] Famous older cases on free movement include Case 26/62 *Van Gend & Loos (NV Algemene Transport- en Expeditie Onderneming) v Nederlandse Administratie der Belastingen* [1963] ECR 1, Case 2/73 *Geddo v Ente Nationale Risi* [1973] ECR 865 and, although slightly later Case C-213/89) *R v Secretary of State for Transport, ex parte Factortame Ltd (Factortame I)* [1990] ECR I-2433.

[136] See, e.g., Case 120/78 *Rewe Zentrale v Bundesmonomolverwaltung für Branntwein (Cassis de Dijon)* [1979] ECR 649, Joined Cases C-267 & 268/91 *Keck and Mithouard* [1993] ECR I-6097 and Joined Cases C-34-36/95 *Konsumentombudsmannen (KO) v De Agostini (Svenska) Förlag AB and TV-Shop I Sverige AB* [1997] ECR I-3843.

[137] On the applicability of the freedom of capital to property law, see also Von Wilmowsky 1996, p. 82-86, Kieninger 2007, p. 188-189, Sparkes 2007, p. 521-522.

[138] Case 7/68 *Commission* v *Italy (Art treasure)* [1968] ECR 423, 428-9, Barnard 2007, p. 27.

[139] Case C-393/92 *Gemeente Almelo and Others v Energiebedrijf IJsselmij* [1994] ECR I-1477, Para. 28.

> 'Quantitative restrictions on imports and all measures having equivalent effect shall be prohibited between Member States'.[140]

This provision prohibits two types of national measures; quantitative restrictions (QR) and measures having the equivalent effect of a quantitative restriction (MEQR).[141] Of course the ECJ has done much work in the prevention of QR, but, for purposes of private law especially, the second category, that of MEQRs, is of relevance.[142] It has been under the heading of MEQRs that the ECJ has managed to declare many measures of national law inapplicable due to hindrance of the functioning of the Internal Market. The ECJ has used a very wide interpretation of what may constitute a measure. In general it can be any measure of national law, as long as there is an effect on the Internal Market.[143] It is the effect of national measures that is central in the case law of the ECJ. This is evident in its landmark ruling, *Dassonville*, in which the ECJ held in respect to MEQRs:

> 'All trading rules enacted by Members States which are capable of hindering, directly or indirectly, actually or potentially, intra-Community trade are to be considered as measures having an effect equivalent to quantitative restrictions'.[144]

The definition formulated by the ECJ in *Dassonville* shows that this aspect of European law is concerned with the trade between Member States and not with the production process. Although a national measure can demand products to be composed in a specific way and therefore also concern the production phase, the emphasis is on the trade between Member States.[145]

In respect of MEQRs, the Court makes a distinction between measures that make a distinction based on the country of origin of the good and national measures that apply irrespective of the country of origin of a good, but nevertheless have an impact on intra-Community trade. The former are discriminatory measures or, as they have been termed in the literature, distinctly applicable measures, and the latter are non-discriminatory, also known as indistinctly applicable measures.[146]

Measures applying specifically to imported products, distinctly applicable measures, are fewer in number than indistinctly applicable measures. Distinctly

140 Art. 28 EC is to return in its present form, most likely in Art. 35 of the Treaty on the Functioning of the European Union (TFEU). Also when a new treaty would take a different form, it is not likely that these 'technical' provisions would change.

141 See Barnard 2007, p. 64, Craig & De Búrca 2007, p. 668-669.

142 Quantitative Restrictions (QR) are essentially quotas or product bans. On QRs see Barnard 2007, p. 64-65, Craig & De Búrca 2007, p. 669.

143 Case 2/73 *Geddo v Ente* [1973] ECR 865.

144 Case 8/74 *Procureur du Roi v Dassonville* [1974] ECR 837, Para. 5.

145 Barnard 2007, p. 92.

146 On distinctly applicable measures see Case C-320/93 *Lucien Ortscheid GmbH v Eurim-Pharm Arzneimittel GmbH* [1994] ECR I-5243. On indistinctly applicable measures see Joined Cases C-267 & 268/91 *Criminal Proceedings against Keck and Mithouard* [1993] ECR I-6097. Barnard 2007, p. 98, 105, Craig & De Búrca 2007, p. 669, 677.

applicable measures include rules favouring domestic products and price fixing.[147] It could be implied that, at least from a private-law perspective, rules of private international law could possibly fall in this category also, as they are specifically aimed at dealing with a non-domestic situation, and its relation to national law.[148] This is however highly controversial.[149]

Indistinctly applicable measures are the broadest category, as they can include almost any measure of national law. The Court's definition of a MEQR in *Dassonville*, in particular its emphasis on the effects a measure has on intra-Community trade, is therefore of specific relevance to this category of national measures. In a series of decisions starting in 1979, the ECJ has shaped a European legal method to deal with national measures that do not make a distinction based on the origin of the good, and that have an effect on intra-Community trade. In 1979 the ECJ rendered its *Cassis de Dijon* judgment, in which it explained its position towards indistinctly applicable rules. The case concerned a measure of German law prescribing the minimum alcohol strength for a beverage classified as a liqueur on the German market. Based on this measure, the German authorities refused to allow the French product *cassis de Dijon*, a blackcurrant liqueur, to be sold on the German market. The claimant, the French producer, argued the rule was an MEQR, as it formed an obstacle to trade because the French producer could not directly export its products from France to Germany. The ECJ agreed with the claimant and held that, as a rule of Community law, a product lawfully produced in one Member State should also be recognised as such in other Member States, unless some good reason can be demonstrated in justification.[150]

The judgment of the ECJ introduced a new concept and, with that, a new approach in European law, the principle of mutual recognition. As a result, the Court removed the need for extensive harmonisation and allowed the Commission to focus its attention elsewhere.[151] Furthermore, from an international trade point of view, the Court emphasised that it does not approve of double burdens being imposed. When a product has been lawfully produced, it has been subject to a set of national requirements and if the product is exported to another Member State it cannot, in principle, be made subject to similar rules again.

147 One of the most famous cases is the 'Buy Irish' case, in which the Irish government tried to promote domestic products, according to the ECJ, to the detriment of imported products. Case 249/81 *Commission v Ireland* (*Buy Irish*) [1982] ECR 4005.

148 See Israël & Saarloos 2007, p. 649-653. Along the same line of reasoning, see Von Wilmowsky 1996, p. 51-52.

149 Although there are good arguments to deal with rules of private international law in this perspective, the topic of measure of private international as subject of EC law is outside the scope of this study. However, as far as the *lex rei sitae* rule is concerned, I feel it could be argued this is a distinctly applicable measure.

150 Case 120/78 *Rewe Zentrale v Bundesmonomolverwaltung für Branntwein* (*Cassis de Dijon*) [1979] ECR 649, Para. 8.

151 EC Commission, Communication from the Commission regarding the *Cassis de Dijon* judgment [1980] OJ C256/2. Barnard 2007, p. 114-115, Craig & De Búrca 2007, p. 677-679.

2.2.1.2. *Grounds for Justification*

If a Member State can provide a good reason why it should impose national measures on products from another Member State, it can still be allowed to do so. The EC Treaty provides a list of reasons a Member State may invoke to justify restrictions in respect of QRs or distinctly applicable MEQRs. Article 30 EC Treaty states:

> 'The provisions of Articles 28 and 29 shall not preclude prohibitions or restrictions on imports, exports or goods in transit justified on grounds of public morality, public policy or public security; the protection of health and life of humans, animals or plants; the protection of national treasures possessing artistic, historical or archaeological value; or the protection of industrial and commercial property'.[152]

In its *Cassis de Dijon* judgment, the ECJ added to this that when an indistinctly applicable measure is concerned, the grounds of justification of Article 30 EC Treaty are complemented with a set of 'mandatory requirements'.[153] Mandatory requirements, also known as imperative requirements, are additional reasons a Member State may use to justify restrictions it imposes to trade.[154] These requirements often follow from policy areas defined in the Treaty and include consumer protection, environmental protection and the protection of fundamental human rights.[155] Mandatory requirements should, because of the functioning of the Treaty, not be of a purely economic nature.[156] In any case the current list of mandatory requirements is not exhaustive and new types may be added.[157]

2.2.1.3. *Proportionality*

The ECJ does not accept justifications invoked by Member States readily. The role of the Court is the protection of the Internal Market and the promotion of intra-Com-

152 Art. 30 is most likely to return, in its present form, in Art. 36 TFEU.

153 See also Case 788/79 *Criminal Proceedings against Gilli and Andres* [1980] ECR 2071, Joined Cases C-1 & 176/90 *Aragonesa* [1991] ECR I-4151.

154 Barnard 2007, p. 115-117.

155 Barnard mentions the mandatory requirements that the ECJ has thus far recognised. These include the effectiveness of fiscal supervision, the protection of public health, the fairness of commercial transactions, the defence of the consumer, the protection of the environment, the protection of working conditions, the protection of cinema as a form of cultural expression, the protection of national or regional socio-cultural characteristics, the maintenance of press diversity, preventing the risk of seriously undermining the financial balance of the social security system, the protection of fundamental rights, and preserving the maintenance of order in society. Barnard 2007, p. 116.

156 Case C-254/98 *Schutzverband gegen unlauteren Wettbewerb v TK-Heimdienst Sass GmbH* [2000] ECR I-151. Barnard 2007, p. 117.

157 Barnard 2007, p. 116.

munity trade. The Court will therefore examine a national measure closely before it allows derogation from the Treaty.[158] In its decision in *Rau* the ECJ added that:

> 'It is also necessary for such rules to be proportionate to the aim in view. If a Member State has a choice between various measures to attain the same objective it should choose the means which least restricts the free movement of goods'.[159]

In the case law of the ECJ, the proportionality test comprises two elements; a test of suitability, if the measure used is suitable for the aim pursued, and a test of necessity, whether there are adverse consequences of the national measure worthy of legal protection.[160] The proportionality test allows the Court a far-reaching ground for legislative review and allows it to demand extensive proof from Member States that a national measure is really necessary.[161]

This basic methodology allows the ECJ to ensure the continuous building of the Internal Market, ensuring that all Member States comply with these basic rules on the free movement of goods.[162] Because the measures the Court initially accepted to take under review were indistinctly applicable national measures, most national law was included. It is not surprising, therefore, that in later case law the court restricted the scope of application of Article 28 EC Treaty to some extent.

2.2.1.4. *Moving Towards a Market Access Test?*

In *Keck and Mithouard*, the ECJ was confronted with a French legislative act prohibiting the selling of products below their cost price.[163] Keck and Mithouard argued that they needed to sell products under the cost price in order to be able to gain access to the French market. The Court, having faced criticism on the wide scope of its definition of national measures falling under Article 28 EC Treaty, restated its case law by making a distinction between measures concerning a product characteristic, which are those measures directly affecting the content of a certain product, and 'certain selling arrangements', which are those rules not directly affecting a product, but concerning more the way in which the product is placed on a national

158 Craig 2006, p. 687-689, Barnard 2007, p. 66.

159 Case 261/81 *Rau* [1982] EXCR 3961, Para. 12.

160 Case 72/83 *Campus Oil Ltd and others v Minister for Industry and Energy and others* [1984] ECR 2727, Para. 37, Case C-368/95 *Vereinigte Familiapress Zeitungsverlags- und vertriebs GmbH (Familiapress) v Heinrich Bauer Verlag* [1997] ECR I-3689, Barnard 2007, p. 81, 119-120. Craig discusses whether a third element to this test, 'whether the measure was disproportionate to the restrictions thereby involved', is also part of the proportionality test. It seems EC law is unclear about this. Craig 2006, p. 656.

161 Case C-17/93 *Openbaar Ministerie v Van der Veldt* [1994] ECR I-3537, [1995] CMLR 621. See Craig 2006, p. 655, 690, Barnard 2007, p. 119-124.

162 See, e.g., Case C-292/92 *Ruth Hünnermund and others v Landersapothekerkammer Baden-Württemberg* [1993] ECR-6787, Para. 1.

163 Joined Cases C-267 & 268/91 *Criminal Proceedings against Keck and Mithouard* [1993] ECR I-6097.

market.[164] In respect to product characteristics, the Court reaffirmed its *Cassis de Dijon* judgment and held that any product rules forming an obstacle to intra-Community trade would have to be justified under Article 30 EC Treaty, or the mandatory requirements. If the measure could not be justified, Article 28 EC Treaty would prohibit it.[165] However, in respect to certain selling arrangements, the Court stated:

> 'Contrary to what has previously been decided, the application to products from other Member States of national provisions restricting or prohibiting certain selling arrangements is not such as to hinder directly or indirectly, actually or potentially, trade between Member States within the meaning of the *Dassonville* judgment... provided those provisions apply to all affected traders operating within the national territory and provided that they affect in the same manner, in law and in fact, the marketing of domestic products and those from other Member States ...
> Where those conditions are fulfilled, the application of such rules to the sale of products from other Member States meeting the requirements laid down by that State is not by nature such as to prevent their [foreign goods'] access to the market or to impede access any more than it impedes the access of domestic products'.[166]

In other words, those selling arrangements that apply to all traders without distinction, both in their application and in their effect, are excluded from the scope of Article 28 EC Treaty. However, it is in respect of the requirement of non-distinction, in particular the way in which a national measure affects traders, that Article 28 continues to play an important role. In its judgments in *De Agostini* and *Heimdienst* the ECJ returned to this element of the effect of certain selling arrangements, and held that those selling arrangements that do not affect all traders in the same way, especially not in fact, would either prevent or at least hinder market access for foreign traders. These measures would therefore fall under the scope of Article 28 EC Treaty.[167]

With these two judgments, the Court has put an emphasis on market access, including for selling arrangements.[168] When a national product characteristic rule falls under Article 28, the *Cassis de Dijon* line of case law assumes that the measure

164 These selling arrangements have also been named market circumstances rules, see Barnard 2007, p. 137-138, Craig & De Búrca 2007, p. 684-686.

165 Joined Cases C-267 & 268/91 *Criminal Proceedings against Keck and Mithouard* [1993] ECR I-6097, Para. 15.

166 Joined Cases C-267 & 268/91 *Criminal Proceedings against Keck and Mithouard* [1993] ECR I-6097, Paras. 16 and 17.

167 Joined Cases C-34-36/95 *Konsumentombudsmannen (KO) v De Agostini (Svenska) Förlag AB and TV-Shop I Sverige AB* [1997] ECR I-3843, Case C-254/98 *Schutzverband gegen unlauteren Wettbewerk v TK-Heimdienst Sass GmbH* [2000] ECR I-151. See, before these cases were held the opinion of AG Jacobs in Case C-412/93 *Société d'Importation Edouard Leclerc-Siplec v TFI Publicité SA* [1995] ECR I-179. Craig & De Búrca 2007, p. 688-690.

168 See also Case C-322/01 *Deutscher Apothekerverband eV v 0800 DocMorris NV, Jacques Waterval* [2003] ECR I-14887, Case C-145/88 *Torfaen Borough Council v B & Q Plc* [1989] ECR I-3851. Craig & De Búrca 2007, p. 692-693.

impedes market access.[169] The burden of proof is then on the Member State to show either that the measure falls outside the scope of Article 28, or that it can be justified on one of the grounds mentioned in Article 30, or on one of the mandatory requirements, the open-ended but exclusive list of justifications that can be used to justify indistinctly applicable measures.[170] When a selling arrangement is concerned, there is no automatic assumption of a hindrance to market access. In those cases the burden of proof is on the trader, and not on the Member State. Moreover, the proof the trader must provide is more than just a potential hindrance. A trader will have to show a substantial disadvantage that is actual, rather than potential.[171]

The emphasis on market access also enables the Court to consider the final set of selling arrangements that could potentially fall under Article 28 EC treaty - those selling arrangements that are indistinctly applicable, which is non-discriminatory, but that nevertheless prevent or hinder market access. It is in this field that many uncertainties remain. An example of a rule preventing market access is a total product ban, applying both to domestic as well as foreign products. In a pre-*Keck and Mithouard* decision, the Court held that a product ban would constitute a Quantitative Restriction (QR) as none is also a quota.[172] However, Barnard adds that it is not completely certain this case can still be upheld.[173] On the analogy of similar cases from the free movement of services and the free movement of persons, it could be argued that where a national measure prevents market access or provides a substantial hindrance to market access, such a measure would fall under Article 28.[174]

2.2.1.5. *Conclusion*

This method of the ECJ in its approach to the free movement of goods, in particular the focus on national measures preventing market access, provides Internal Market lawyers with a systematic way of thinking to deal with rules that hinder intra-Community trade. The wording of Article 28 EC Treaty shows that the Article is addressed to Member States. Unlike some of the other freedoms, it has not been

169 Case C-463/01 *Commission v Germany (deposit and return)* [2004] ECR I-11705. See Barnard 2007, p. 155-156.

170 Barnard 2007, p. 156. On the mandatory requirements, see the discussion on the *Cassis de Dijon* judgment in this same section.

171 Joined Cases C-34-36/95 *Konsumentombudsmannen (KO) v De Agostini (Svenska) Förlag AB and TV-Shop I Sverige AB* [1997] ECR I-3843, Case C-405/98 *Konsumentombudsmannen v Gourmet International Products (GIP)* [2001] ECR I-1795. In this respect there is a deviation from the ECJ's formula in Dassonville.

172 Case 34/79 *R. v Henn and Darby* [1972] ECR 3795.

173 Barnard 2007, p. 159-160.

174 Case C-275/92 *Her Majesty's Customs and Excise v Schindler* [1994] ECR I-1039 (Free movement of services) and Case C-384/93 *Alpine Investments v Minister van Financiën* [1995] ECR I-1141 (Free movement of persons). Barnard 2007, p. 159-165, Craig & De Búrca 2007, p. 690-695.

awarded horizontal direct effect. In other words, the Article applies vertically between a trader and a Member States and not between private parties.[175]

However, when private parties do violate the principles contained in Article 28, in particular mutual recognition and market access, a Member State doing nothing to prevent this could violate European law nonetheless. Member States are under an obligation to be loyal to the European Union, including the duty to take action when one of the Community's objectives is at stake.[176] Furthermore, not taking action when one of the fundamental freedoms is systematically breached may also lead to a violation of a duty of a Member State under Community law.[177]

In this respect, all measures of national law, including those of private international law and substantive law, are subject to the rules on free movement of goods in the Internal Market insofar as they have an effect on its functioning.[178] Furthermore, they are subject to the other fundamental freedoms as well. A further example, that of free movement of persons, especially the freedom of establishment, will be provided before moving to the effects of Internal Market law on property law.

2.2.2. Freedom of Establishment and its Effect on Substantive Private Law

Within the Internal Market, persons also enjoy freedom of movement.[179] When it comes to the self-employed and companies, there is a freedom of movement in the form of a freedom of establishment.[180] In respect to companies, Article 43 EC Treaty ensures the freedom to set up a company, as well as to set up subsidiaries, agencies or branches of a company in another Member State. However, in order for EU law to apply, a Community dimension is needed. A company from within the EU must therefore first be established, or attempting to establish itself, in another Member State.[181]

When such establishment takes place, and a national measure hinders the company's access to the market, a very similar approach to that used in respect of

175 Case C-159/00 *Sapod-Audic v Eco-Emballages SA* [2002] ECR I-5031, see Barnard 2007, p. 94-95. The exception to the strict vertical effect of Art. 28 EC is found in the area of European intellectual property law where the Court has assumed horizontal direct effect. See e.g. Case 15/74 *Centrafarm BV and others v Sterling Drug* [1974] ECR 1147, Van den Bogaert 2002, p. 129-134, Barnard 2007, p. 173 *et seq.*

176 Art. 10 EC, the objectives of the Community include those mentioned in Art. 2 EC. In the new Treaty Art. 4 (3) EU (i.e. not the TFEU) will deal with the same subject matter. See e.g. Case 235/87 *Matteucci v Communauté française de Belgique* [1988] ECR 5589, Case C-251/89 *Nikolaos Athanasopoulos and others v Bundesanstalt für Arbeit* [1991] ECR I-2797. See Van den Bogaert 2002, p. 150-151, Craig 2006, p. 703, Israël & Saarloos 2007, p. 645-657.

177 See Case C-265/95 *Commission v France (Spanish Strawberries)* [1997] ECR I-6959. Barnard 2007, p. 95-96, Craig & De Búrca 2007, p. 675-676.

178 Case C-339/89 *Alsthom Atlantique v Compagnie de construction mécanique Sulzer SA* [1991] ECR I-107, Case C-93/92 *CMC Motorradcenter GmbH v Pelin Baskiciogullari* [1993] ECR I-5009. See Rutgers 1999, p. 174-175, 183-184, Kieninger 1996a, p. 124-125, Basedow 1995, p. 5, 15.

179 Art. 39 EC.

180 Art. 43 EC, Case C-268/99 *Aldona Malgorzata Jany and others v Staatsecretaris van Justitie* [2001] ECR I-8615, Barnard 2007, p. 308.

181 Case C-196/04 *Cadbury's Schweppes v Commissioners of the Inland Revenue* [2006] ECR I-000.

the free movement of goods applies. Article 43 EC Treaty provides for equal, non-discriminatory, treatment in cases of both direct and indirect discrimination. This distinction, between direct and indirect discrimination, is the same as the distinctly and indistinctly applicable measures in respect of the free movement of goods.[182] A national measure preventing a national or a company of one Member State from becoming established, based on the fact that the person or company has a foreign nationality or originates in another Member State, will breach the EC Treaty unless it can be justified.[183] As in the case of the free movement of goods, indirectly discriminatory measures also fall under the scope of the Treaty, and are prohibited unless they can be justified.[184] Furthermore, once a person or company has established itself in another Member State, it must be treated and continue to be treated in the same way as a national person or company.[185] With respect to companies, Article 48 EC Treaty provides that companies are treated in the same way as natural persons.[186] However, primary and secondary establishment of companies, which refers to setting up the primary office or establishment of an agency, branch or subsidiary, are slightly different in content than the free movement of persons.

Since the 1980s, the ECJ has especially been active in the area of secondary establishment.[187] The right of secondary establishment enables a company to establish itself in the Member State with the least strict regulations and then make use of the right of secondary establishment to create subsidiaries throughout the EU.[188] Initially, the ECJ was very reluctant to accept this method of working around Member States with stricter regulations, but in a series of judgments the Court has also applied the Internal Market method of thinking to secondary establishment.[189]

The first of these cases, known as *Centros*, concerned a private limited company established in England by two Danish citizens.[190] The Danish citizens had no intention of trading in England, but simply registered their company there, as England had no rules on minimum capital requirements. Had they established their company in Denmark, they would have had to comply with Danish law, which set a minimum capital of 200,000 DKr. Once the company was validly created in England, the Danish citizens applied to the Danish registry to have a subsidiary of the English company registered in Denmark. The Danish Registrar refused to register the subsidiary on the grounds that the Danish citizens did not trade in England, and that they simply used English law to avoid the undesirable consequences of

182 On the free movement of goods see above; 2.2.1. Free Movement of Goods.

183 E.g., Case 2/74 *Jean Reyners v Belgian State* [1974] ECR 631. Barnard 2007, p. 312.

184 E.g., Case 340/89 *Vlassopoulou v Ministerium für Justiz, Bundes- und Europaangelegenheiten Baden-Wüttemberg* [1991] ECR I-2357.

185 See Barnard 2007, p. 345-346.

186 Barnard 2007, p. 330-331, Dohrn 2004, p. 31-32.

187 On primary establishment, see, *inter alia*, Case 81/87 *Ex parte Daily Mail* [1988] ECR 5483.

188 Barnard 2007, p. 341. See also Charny 1991, p. 423 *et seq.*

189 See e.g. Case 33/74 *Van Binsbergen v Bedrijfsvereniging Metaalnijverheid* [1974] ECR 1299, Case C-373/97 *Diamantis v Elliniko Dimosio and Organismos Ikonomikis Anasygkrotisis Epicheiriseon AE (OAE)* [2000] ECR I-1705.

190 Case C-212/97 *Centros v Erhverves- og Selskabsstyrelsen* [1999] ECR I-1459. See, *inter alia*, Dohrn 2004, p. 35-38.

Danish law. The ECJ rejected the argument that this was a fraud case, and held that the refusal to register constituted an obstacle to the freedom of establishment.[191] The Danish government sought to justify the refusal by stating that the capital requirements were there to ensure the financial soundness of companies as well as to protect creditors against a company without any financial means.

As in the case of the free movement of goods, the justifications used by the Member States, in this case the Danish government, are also subject to a test of proportionality. In this case the ECJ held the first justification inadequate as well as disproportional and, although it accepted the validity of creditor protection, the Court held that outright refusal to register was not a proportionate measure.[192]

The ECJ returned to the question of creditor protection in the *Inspire Art* case.[193] In this case a Dutch national had set up a private limited company in the UK and established and registered a subsidiary of that UK company in the Netherlands. The Netherlands had adopted a law allowing recognition of a 'foreign company'. Under this law, a 'foreign company' is a company registered in and governed by the law of another country but with which the company has no real link. Connected to the characterisation as a foreign company, Dutch law imposed all sorts of obligations, including a capital requirement equal to that of Dutch private limited companies.[194]

The Dutch registration authority, in this case the chamber of commerce, applied to a Dutch court to change the registration of the UK company to a 'foreign company' under this new Dutch law. The UK company argued such a rule infringed the freedom of establishment under Articles 43 and 48 EC Treaty. The ECJ held that the rules of Dutch law had the effect of treating a company like Inspire Art as a Dutch company, including the provisions on capital requirements and liability.[195] However, the company had already fulfilled the requirements of establishment under English law, and therefore the creation of a subsidiary of that company elsewhere in the EU would have to fall under the Treaty provisions on the freedom of establishment. The rules on capital requirements and liability therefore could not be imposed again on the company, also not on a subsidiary. They were therefore contrary to the provisions on the freedom of establishment.[196] Nevertheless, the Court acknowledged that taking measures to stop foreign companies on the grounds of fraud prevention could be justified, but only on a case-by-case basis.[197]

The decision of the ECJ in *Centros* and the further elaboration on this issue in *Inspire Art* have led to the question whether Member States remain allowed to restrict the recognition of foreign companies. In some Member States, Germany in

191 Case C-212/97 *Centros v Erhverves- og Selskabsstyrelsen* [1999] ECR I-1459, Paras. 29 and 30.

192 Case C-212/97 *Centros v Erhverves- og Selskabsstyrelsen* [1999] ECR I-1459, Para. 38.

193 Case C-167/01 *Kamer van Koophandel en Fabrieken voor Amsterdam v Inspire Art Ltd* [2003] ECR I-10155. See De Kluiver 2004, p. 122-123, Kersting & Schindler 2003, p. 1277 *et seq.*

194 Art. 4(1) Wet op de Formeel Buitenlandse Vennootschappen (WFBV).

195 Case C-167/01 *Kamer van Koophandel en Fabrieken voor Amsterdam v Inspire Art Ltd* [2003] ECR I-10155, Para. 100.

196 Case C-167/01 *Kamer van Koophandel en Fabrieken voor Amsterdam v Inspire Art Ltd* [2003] ECR I-10155, Paras. 104 and 105. See also Barnard 2007, p. 342-343.

197 On this aspect see De Kluiver 2004, p. 128, Kersting & Schindler 2003, p. 1288-1289.

particular, a foreign company form is not immediately recognised. Under the doctrine used, known as the real-seat theory or *siège réel*, the court looks at the actual situation at hand. When a company is actually conducting its business in another Member State than that in which it was created, the law of the Member State in which the company has its real, in the sense of actual, seat will be applied. As a result, a foreign limited company conducting its actual business in Germany will not be treated in Germany as a limited company, because the company has not fulfilled the German rules on the creation of private or public limited companies.[198] The decision of the Court in *Centros* raised questions on the conformity of the real-seat theory with Community law.[199] The Danish nationals in that case exercised their business in Denmark, but UK law nevertheless allowed this. In a country applying the real-seat theory this could not have been the case.[200]

The ECJ was confronted with the question of the conformity of the real-seat theory in the case of *Überseering*.[201] The case concerned a Dutch company that sued a German company for defective work carried out on its behalf in Germany. Prior to the case, two German nationals had acquired all the shares in the Dutch company.[202] The German court, applying the real-seat theory, argued that since *Überseering* had transferred its activities to Germany, German law applied, and, because it was a Dutch company, this company did not have legal capacity in Germany. The German court therefore did not allow the Dutch company standing in court, even though *Überseering* continued to enjoy legal capacity in the Netherlands.[203]

The ECJ held that since the Dutch company was validly created under the law of the Netherlands, the rule requiring it to incorporate in Germany was contrary to the freedom of establishment of Articles 43 and 48 EC Treaty.[204] This 'outright negation of the freedom of establishment' could not be justified because a general refusal would not pass the test of proportionality.[205] The German court subsequently had to recognise the Dutch company.

The approach taken by the ECJ in cases of freedom of establishment resembles the approach taken in cases of free movement of goods. However, the nature of the cases is sometimes so different that different tests are used to investigate whether Community law has been breached. In the case of free movement of goods, the Court seems to be moving towards a market access test, seen best in the *De Agostini* decision discussed above.[206] In cases concerning the freedom of establishment, only

198 See Barnard 2007, p. 343, Dohrn 2004, p. 31-33.

199 See Dohrn 2004, p. 37-38, Kieninger 2005, p. 742.

200 Barnard 2007, p. 343.

201 Case C-208 *Überseering BV v Nordic Construction Company Baumanagement GmbH (NCC)* [2002] ECR I-9919.

202 Dohrn 2004, p. 39.

203 Barnard 2007, p. 343-344.

204 Case C-208 *Überseering BV v Nordic Construction Company Baumanagement GmbH (NCC)* [2002] ECR I-9919, Paras. 80 and 81.

205 Case C-208 *Überseering BV v Nordic Construction Company Baumanagement GmbH (NCC)* [2002] ECR I-9919, Paras. 81, 92-93. For a critical view on this judgment, see Dohrn 2004, p. 44-46.

206 See Joined Cases C-34-36/95 *Konsumentombudsmannen (KO) v De Agostini (Svenska) Förlag AB and TV-Shop I Sverige AB* [1997] ECR I-3843. See also Case C-322/01 *Deutscher Apothekerver-* →

the *Centros* case deals with a refusal of access. Other company law cases have been decided following the more traditional test of discrimination on the grounds of nationality. In the case of companies, this concerns discrimination based on the country where the seat of the company is established.[207] However, in other cases based on Article 43 EC Treaty, the general article on the freedom of establishment, the European Court of Justice seems to have held in favour of the market access test, focussing on removing obstacles and hindrances to access.[208]

The tendency towards market access brings the case law of the European Court of Justice outside the spheres of traditional distinctions between discriminatory and non-discriminatory measures, favouring a more functional approach. It is under this approach that Member States themselves might be more stimulated to act in order to remove obstacles to the Internal Market. In some cases, in company law and contract law, Member States have acted, and this will be dealt with in Section 2.3 below.[209]

2.3. *Voluntary Harmonisation*

In the history of European integration, the European Institutions especially have created legislation resulting in harmonisation of the law in the Internal Market. Although Member States are represented in the Council, the Commission and the Parliament also take many initiatives themselves. As a result, many Member States tend to conceive of European law as law forced upon their national legal systems.[210]

Nevertheless, as a result of the development of European law, Member States also take action themselves. Possibly the best example can be seen when looking at the development of European contract law. Germany used the project of reforming contract law to integrate European legislation in this area into German private law.[211] The new law, which entered into force in 2002, brings the German Civil Code into line with the applicable European contract legislation. In this respect the communications of the Commission concerning the work on a more coherent contract law have resulted in the adaptation of national contract law.[212] It is certainly also the intention of the Commission to investigate the possibilities of convergence of national laws without Community intervention.[213]

band eV v 0800 *DocMorris NV, Jacques Waterval* [2003] ECR I-14887. See above; 2.2.1. Free Movement of Goods.

207 On this distinction, see Barnard 2007, p. 345.

208 Case C-55/94 *Reinhard Gebhard v Consiglio dell'Ordine degli Avvocati e Procuratori di Milano* [1995] ECR I-4165, Case C-415/93 *Union Royale Belge de Société de Football Association v Bosman* [1995] ECR I-4921. See Barnard 2007, p. 312-315.

209 This has included adaptation of national law to bring national law in line with the case law of the ECJ. See below; 2.3. Voluntary Harmonisation.

210 See, e.g., Van Erp who discusses this problem under the term antagonism, Van Erp 2006b.

211 See, *inter alia*, Zimmermann 2002b, p. 265, 276, 280-282, Zimmermann 2005.

212 See Weatherhill 2005, p. 407-408.

213 See Commission Action Plan on a More Coherent Contract Law, COM(2001), 98.

Another example of voluntary harmonisation can be seen in the aftermath of the decisions of the ECJ in *Überseering* and *Inspire Art*, discussed above.[214] As a result of these decisions, some Member States have feared a race towards the Member State with the most attractive company legislation. Instead of allowing such an open competition between legal systems, some Member States, such as France, have introduced an alternative company form in their national company law, for which creation no capital requirements exist.[215] In France this is the One Euro SARL.[216] As a result of this introduction, when parties choose to establish a One Euro SARL company, French law will remain applicable.[217] This development also shows how Member States bring their national legislation into line with legislation from other Member States, in particular that of a Member State whose law is often applied, as is the case with English law in the field of company law. In doing so, these Member States ensure that mutual recognition of company forms is less problematic and, as in case of the French developments, national law remains applicable.[218]

In the area of property law also, some convergence can be seen. Especially in the area of security rights, it has been argued by Drobnig that 'natural harmonisation' is a serious option.[219] Because of intra-Community trade, Member States bring their national law into line with that of their trading partners, even though there is no European legislation yet. The French reforms of 2006 can certainly also be seen from this perspective, especially the introduction of non-possessory security rights and the abandonment of the prohibition on the *lex commissoria* in the light of the Financial Collateral Directive discussed above.[220]

2.4. *The Effects of European Law on the Law of Property*

The foregoing has focused on issues of European law and when possible on issues of European private law. As was stated in the introduction to this Chapter, private law is most definitely affected by European law.[221] Section 2.2.1. above, on the case law of the ECJ on the free movement of goods, shows that the emphasis the ECJ puts on the effect of a national measure on intra-Community trade enables the Court to include private law.[222] The ECJ has dealt with issues of private law, company law and contract law in particular, although not often. In only very few cases, the European Court of Justice has examined aspects of property law. This Section will deal with aspects of property law in the European Union in general, but

214 See Kieninger 2005, p. 768.

215 In fact the requirement is a minimum capital of 1 Euro. Kieninger 2005, p. 768.

216 See Kersting & Schindler 2003, p. 1291.

217 See De Kluiver 2004, p. 132.

218 Kersting & Schindler 2003, p. 1291, Kieninger 2005, p. 768-770. On the effects of the *Inspire Art* decision in Dutch law, see De Kluiver 2004, p. 131-132, Bouwes 2006, p. 105 *et seq.*

219 See Cox 2006, p. 239. See also Kieninger 2004, p. 647-655.

220 See above; 2.1.2. Legal Framework: Secondary Community Law. On the French 2006 reforms see Chapter 3; 1. Introduction.

221 See above; 1. Introduction.

222 On the focus of the ECJ on the effect of national measures see also Craig & De Búrca 2007, p. 669.

especially those which have already been dealt with by the ECJ. Moreover, this Section will examine the applicability of the case law of the ECJ in the area of the free movement of goods to the law of property and the consequences thereof for the national property law systems.[223]

The application of Internal Market law to property law is not new, but has remained an area that has been relatively undiscovered by property lawyers and European lawyers alike.[224] Exceptions are those authors who look at property law from an international point of view. In international property law, aspects of private international law, in particular the *lex rei sitae* rule, have always forced scholars to look at the relation of one system of property law to another. The influence of European law on private international law, especially since the decision of the ECJ in *Cassis de Dijon*, in which the Court introduced the concept of mutual recognition, has led scholars to raise questions about the validity of traditional rules of private international law.[225] In the field of property law these especially include the work by Von Wilmowsky, Kieninger and Rutgers on retention of title or reservation of ownership clauses.[226]

2.4.1. Article 295 EC Treaty and European Property Law

Before applying the ECJ's case law to property law, and to property rights in particular, some aspects of primary European law with respect to property law should be mentioned. From the very beginning of European integration, the Treaty has contained an article in which the relation between the Community and Member States with respect to the system of ownership was dealt with. This is Article 295 EC Treaty (formerly Article 222), which states:

> 'This Treaty shall in no way prejudice the rules in Member States governing the system of property ownership'.[227]

Although the Commission and the Parliament have occasionally claimed that the EU has no competence to regulate property law based on Article 295 EC Treaty, the ECJ, as the primary interpreter of Treaty provisions, has taken a different view.[228] In a series of cases, the Court has held that although Member States are entitled to

223 See below; 2.4. The Effects of Internal Market Law on Property Law.

224 See, e.g., Basedow 1995, p. 41-48, Kieninger 1996b, p. 41 *et seq.*

225 See, e.g., Basedow 1995, Von Wilmowsky 1996, Kieninger 1996b, Rutgers 1999, Roth 1999, Israël & Saarloos 2007.

226 Von Wilmowsky 1996, Kieninger 1996a, Rutgers 1999.

227 Art. 295 EC will return in its current form, most likely, in Art. 345 TFEU.

228 See, e.g., Green Paper on Wills and Succession (COM(2005) 65 final) and on this Report of the JURI-committee of the European Parliament No. 6/2006-6L of 3 May 2006, Answer to Written Question asked by Bert Doorn MEP (PPE-EP) to the Commission. Restitution of property to Jewish citizens and Jewish communities in the applicant countries. OJ 12/12/2002, C 309E, p. 15. A clear summary of the ECJ's position is provided in Case C-503/04 *Commission v Germany* [2007] ECR I-6153, Para. 37. See also Bartels 1995, p. 244 *et seq.*, Sagaert 2007, p. 302-307, Kieninger 2007, p. 190-191.

provide rules on their national property law, they are bound by the principles governing the Internal Market.[229] In one of its 'Golden Share' cases, the ECJ held that Article 295:

> '... merely signifies that each Member State may organise as it thinks fit the system of ownership of undertakings whilst at the same time respecting the fundamental freedoms enshrined in the Treaty'.[230]

The ECJ seems to emphasise that the provision in Article 295 EC does not prevent internal market law from having an influence on the right of ownership.[231] Although Member States are free to create their own system of ownership, in the absence of harmonisation, they are required to exercise their competences in the field of property law in conformity with EC law.[232] When this is not the case, the Court is not afraid to interfere. In fact, in the area of intellectual property law, the Court has interfered and established a line of case law dealing with the mutual recognition of patents, trademarks and copyrights.[233] Especially in the area of trademarks, where there is Community legislation, the Court has ruled on the relation between EC intellectual property law and Article 295 EC Treaty:

> 'With regard, first of all, to Article 295 EC, it must be borne in mind that according to that provision the Treaty shall in no way prejudice the rules in Member States governing the system of property ownership. That provision merely recognises the power of Member States to define the rules governing the system of property ownership and does not exclude any influence whatever of Community law on the exercise of national property rights'.[234]

As a result of this interpretation, the Treaty does not prevent the creation of secondary Community law in the area of property law in respect to the right of ownership. Moreover, the Court's interpretation of Article 295 also has an effect on its case law in the area of free movement. The fact that rules of national property law can be subject to European law restricts the possibilities of Member States to

229 See Case 182/83 *Robert Fearon and Company Ltd v The Irish Land Commission* [1984] ECR 3677, and Case C-367/98 *Commission v Portugal* [2002] ECR I-4731, Case C-483/99 *Commission v France* [2002] ECR I-4781, Case C-503/99 *Commission v Belgium* [2002] ECR I-4809 ('Golden Share Cases').

230 C-367/98 *Commission v Portugal* [2002] ECR I-4731, Para. 28. See also Van Erp 2006b, p. 12-13.

231 Basedow 1995, p. 44-45, Bartels 1995, p. 248-251, Kieninger 1996a, p. 127-128, Rutgers 1999, p. 174-175, Remien 2005, Weatherhill 2006, p. 144-147, Van Erp 2006b, p. 12-13, Barnard 2007, p. 174-176, Sagaert 2007, p. 306-307, Sparkes 2007, p. 112-114, Hesselink, Rutgers & de Booys 2007, p. 57-58.

232 Weatherhill 2006, p. 146.

233 See Case 78/70 *Deutsche Grammophon v Metro* [1971] ECR 487, Case 15/74 *Centrafarm v Sterling Drug* [1974] ECR 1147, Case 35/87 *Thetford Corporation v Fiamma SpA* [1988] ECR 3585, Case C-16/03 *Peak Holding v Exolin-Elinor AB* [2004] ECR I-11313. For an overview of the Courts case law in the field of Intellectual Property Law see Van den Bogaert 2002, p. 131-134, Barnard 2007, p. 173-210.

234 Case C-491/01 *R v Secretary of State ex parte BAT & Imperial Tobacco* [2002] ECR I-11543, Para. 147. See Weatherhill 2006, p. 145-146, Craig & De Búrca 2007, p. 616-617.

invoke peculiarities of their national system of property law in respect of ownership as a possible ground for justification for an infringement on one of the four freedoms.[235]

In respect of other areas of property law, not regarding the system of ownership, Article 295 remains silent and therefore does not form an obstacle to the creation of secondary legislation in the field of European property law. In fact, the Community has issued legislation in areas other than the right of ownership.[236]

2.4.2. The Effects of Internal Market Law on Property Law

There have not been many cases in which the ECJ has been confronted with aspects of national property law. There has never been a case in which the ECJ was actually concerned with the content of a property right and the system of property rights itself.[237] Nevertheless, the Court has touched upon various aspects of property law in the 'Golden Share' cases mentioned in Section 2.4.1. above. Moreover, while dealing with the free movement of capital, the Court has included property law aspects in its decisions.[238] Although these cases deal with the freedom of capital and the freedom of establishment, the Court has declared that the reasoning applies to all fundamental freedoms.[239] It is therefore worth investigating to what extent aspects of property law are subject to the rules on the Internal Market as developed by the ECJ. Of particular interest to this Chapter is the recognition of property rights created in another Member State under these rules.[240] In respect to property security rights and the right of security ownership in cases of retention of title or reservation of ownership, these questions are becoming increasingly relevant.

2.4.2.1. Obstacles to Trade

In her study, Kieninger has applied the case law of the ECJ up to the decision of that same Court in *Keck and Mithouard* to the law of property, the law on international retention of title clauses in particular.[241] Kieninger shows that in a combined application, the rules of private international law and the rules on substantive property

235 Case C-503/04 *Commission v Germany* [2007] ECR I-6153, Para. 37. See also Para. 2.4. The Effects of Internal Market Law on Property Law.

236 See Para. 2.1.2. Legal Framework: Secondary Community Law. I owe gratitude to Jona Israël for the focus on Art. 295 EC and ownership.

237 The only case that comes close to a property law case deals with insolvency law and the effects of a seizure made by the Dutch tax authorities. In this case the ECJ had to deal with property law questions because of the effect this seizure of objects had on a German reservation of ownership. See Case C-69/88 *H. Krantz GmbH & Co v Ontvanger der Directe Belastingen en de Staat der Nederlanden* [1990] ECR I-583.

238 See e.g. Case C-222/97 *Manfred Trummer v Peter Mayer* [1999] ECR I-1661. On this subject see, specifically, Sparkes 2007, p. 25-35.

239 See, e.g., Case C-350/92 *Spain v Council* [1995] ECR I-1985, Case C-503/04 *Commission v Germany* [2007] ECR I-6153, Para. 37. On this general applicability, see also Rutgers 1999, p. 175.

240 See also Sparkes 2007, p. 112.

241 Kieninger 1996a, p. 122 *et seq*. See also Kieninger 1996b, p. 41 *et seq*.

law can lead to results that hinder the free movement of goods. It is the combination of these rules that, in her view, constitutes a measure that, under the *Dassonville* formula, might hinder intra-Community trade.[242]

In order to be able to apply Article 28 EC Treaty to rules of property law, first the rule must be characterised as a measure having the effect equivalent to a quantitative restriction (MEQR). The system of property law does have a direct effect on the quantity of goods entering the market of a Member State, however, its rules are not the same as directly setting a quota for the importation of goods. Rules on property law are therefore not likely to constitute a QR. Instead, the question Kieninger addresses is whether a measure of national property law can be a MEQR.[243] Providing an affirmative answer to this question, according to the distinction made in the *Keck and Mithouard* decision, results in a question whether a measure can be qualified as relating to a product characteristic or as relating to a certain selling arrangement.[244] Although she provides arguments why a measure of national property law could be related to a product characteristic, in particular the effect a security right's quality can have on the price of a product, Kieninger concludes that these measures most likely relate to a certain selling arrangement.[245] In other words, when a choice must be made, the measures of national and international property law are in her view rules dealing with market circumstances.[246]

In order to understand this line of reasoning, the effect of a measure of national property law in an international property law setting must be looked at. When, because of the application of *lex rei sitae*, a national system of property law applies, and a property right created according to the law of one Member State is not recognised by another Member State, this will affect the way in which trade between these Member States is conducted. In Kieninger's terms of marketing rules, a sales promotion used in one Member State cannot be used in another Member State or is made more difficult and more expensive than the marketing of domestic products.[247] In terms of selling arrangements in general, but in particular when the concept of selling arrangements is applied to property law, it becomes clear that it is very difficult to draw a line between what rules relate to product characteristics, or the whether nature of the property security right influences the product itself directly, and what rules relate to selling arrangements, or whether the rules on property law are best compared with sales promotions.[248]

242 Case 8/74 *Procureur du Roi v Dassonville* [1974] ECR 837, Kieninger 1996a, p. 129.

243 Kieninger 1996a, p. 152 *et seq*. See also the recent case C-297/05 *Commission v The Netherlands* [2007] ECR I-7467, in which the ECJ held that Dutch law that imposed a compulsory roadworthiness test prior to registration of vehicles coming from another Member State, was in violation of Art. 28 (and Art. 30) EC. See, in particular, Paras. 73 and 74.

244 Joined Cases C-267 & 268/91 *Keck and Mithouard* [1993] ECR I-6097, Kieninger 1996a, p. 152-153. On difficulties establishing whether measures are selling arrangements see Craig & De Búrca 2007, p. 694-695.

245 Kieninger 1996a, p. 152-153.

246 On the term market circumstances, see Barnard 2007, p. 137-138.

247 Kieninger 1996b, p. 58-59.

248 Kieninger 1996b, p. 59.

Kieninger bases her arguments on a post-*Keck and Mithouard* decision of the ECJ. In this case, *Clinique*, the Court held that a prohibition in German law on marketing a product under the name 'Clinique', as that term could only be used for products with medicinal properties, was not in conformity with EC law. Moreover the ECJ held that this imposed additional costs for the alteration of labelling, packaging and advertising and was therefore covered by Article 28 EC Treaty. Kieninger argues that the formula the ECJ applied in that case, known as the *Oosthoek* formula, continues to apply.[249] In *Oosthoek*, a pre-*Keck and Mithouard* decision, the ECJ stated:

> '15. Legislation which restricts or prohibits certain forms of advertising and certain means of sales promotion may, although it does not directly affect imports, be such as to restrict their volume because it affects marketing opportunities for the imported products. The possibility cannot be ruled out that to compel a producer either to adopt advertising or sales promotion schemes which differ from one Member State to another or to discontinue a scheme which he considers to be particularly effective may constitute an obstacle to imports'.[250]

Kieninger argues that the granting of credit is probably the most basic form of promoting the sale of goods and that, in particular, when an international transaction is concerned, the seller will want a security right strengthening his claim as he cannot check, or would find it very difficult to check, a buyer's creditworthiness.[251] She therefore argues that the granting of credit together with the creation of a property security right, in her terms a retention of title, can be seen as a method for a seller to market its products.[252]

A national measure of property law in combination with rules on private international law restricting a seller to use the same security right in the same way as he would in a purely domestic situation, might therefore, as a MEQR, be contrary to Article 28 EC Treaty.[253] This reasoning remains in line with the *Keck and Mithouard* decision because the certain selling arrangement affects the traders in the same way in law, but not in fact. Rules of property law are therefore not excluded from the scope of Article 28.[254]

Rutgers agrees with Kieninger's conclusion, but does not base her conclusion on the *Oosthoek* formula.[255] Instead, she bases her conclusion directly on the application of *Keck and Mithouard* to rules of property law.[256] In Rutgers' view, these rules relate to certain selling arrangements that are capable of discriminating against

249 Case C-315/92 *Verband socialer Wettbewerb e.V. v Clinique Laboratories S.N.C. and others* [1994] ECR I-317. Kieninger 1996b, p. 59-60, Kieninger 1996a, p. 153-155.

250 Case 286/81 *Criminal proceedings against Oosthoek's Uitgeversmaatschappij BV* [1982] ECR 4575, Para. 15. On the same conclusion see Basedow 1995, p. 43.

251 Kieninger 1996b, p. 60, Rutgers 1999, p. 199.

252 Kieninger 1996b, p. 61.

253 Kieninger 1996b, p. 62, see also Kieninger 2006, p. 166. See also Von Wilmowsky 1996, p. 111-112, Israël 2005, p. 110-111.

254 This would only be so when the burden would apply in the same way in law and in fact. Kieninger 1996a, p. 159-162.

255 Rutgers 1999, p. 199.

256 See Rutgers 1999, p. 176 *et seq.*

foreign nationals using property security rights.[257] When a property right created in one Member State is not recognised in another Member State, in other words it cannot be effectively transformed into a property right that is recognised in the receiving Member State, the measure affects traders in a different way. In fact it hinders intra-Community trade, and therefore constitutes a MEQR under Article 28 EC Treaty.[258]

Von Wilmowsky also considers the applicability of Article 28 EC Treaty to property law, especially in the light of limitations on party autonomy in respect of the creation of property security rights through the operation of private international law.[259] He comes to the conclusion that, in an international setting, party agreements made in relation to security rights, for example, reservation of ownership clauses, will always be treated differently than agreements in a purely national setting. After all, the question on the applicable law of a security right will only be at stake in an international setting. Therefore, the requirement of equal burden in *Keck and Mithouard* will never be met in these cases.[260]

Moreover, the analysis of Kieninger, Rutgers and Von Wilmowsky is of renewed relevance because of the movement of the ECJ towards a market access test in the area on the free movement of goods.[261] The emphasis on market access as opposed to requiring a strict distinction between rules relating to product characteristics and to certain selling arrangements, in particular, when the selling arrangements do have an effect of discriminating against foreign goods, allows for a consistent approach with the other freedoms, where this type of distinction has not been recognised. In respect to private law and the applicability of European law, a market access test allows the focus to remain on the effect of a measure without the need to unnecessarily characterise the rules in terms of marketing concepts first.

In order for private law to be subject to the rules of the Internal Market under the market access test, an effect on intra-Community trade will have to be proven. Under the market access test, a return to the *Dassonville* criteria might be possible and a potential indirect effect might be sufficient. The distinction between product characteristics and selling arrangements would lose some significance.[262] However, for as long as it remains unclear whether the market access test is sufficient, the rules under *Keck and Mithouard* and the case law after that require the trader himself

257 Rutgers 1999, p. 195, 200.

258 Rutgers 1999, p. 196-198.

259 Von Wilmowsky comes to the question of selling arrangements after a discussion of the *Krantz* judgment of the ECJ. On this case see below in this same Section. Von Wilmowsky 1996, p. 51-52.

260 Von Wilmowsky 1996, p. 52.

261 See, in this respect, Weatherhill 2006, p. 132-133, Barnard 2007, p. 150-151, Craig & De Búrca 2007, p. 690-695. See, recently, Case C-297/05 *Commission v The Netherlands* [2007] ECR I-7467, on Dutch law imposing a roadworthiness test prior to registration of foreign vehicles. Limitations on roadworthiness because of environmental reasons and limitations on publicity because of creditor protection can possibly be compared. In this case the ECJ simply applies the *Dassonville*-formula without going into the question of product characteristics or certain selling arrangements.

262 On this development in case law see above; 2.2.1. Free Movement of Goods.

to show the actual and substantial effect on intra-Community trade of a national measure of property law.[263]

2.4.2.2. *Grounds for Justification*

When the conclusion is drawn that a measure is contrary to Article 28 EC Treaty, whether as a product characteristic or as a selling arrangement, the method followed by the ECJ requires consideration of whether the receiving Member State might offer a justification for the effect its measure has on intra-Community trade. Because all these cases concern MEQRs the Court's decision in *Cassis de Dijon* applies. As a result, the national measure can be justified based on the grounds mentioned in Article 30 EC Treaty as well as the mandatory requirements.[264]

Of the grounds for justification mentioned in Article 30, public policy might be used to justify the application of the *lex rei sitae* in combination with substantive property law, with the effect being the non-recognition or partial loss of a foreign property security right in a certain Member State. The closed system of property rights, which is the reason why a foreign property security right must be transformed, could be held to be of public policy. Moreover, in respect of the mandatory requirements it could be argued that the coherence of the system of property rights can be invoked as a ground for justification. The list of mandatory requirements is not exhaustive, new types can be added.

Basedow expresses the most conservative view.[265] In considering whether the application of the combination of *lex rei sitae* and national property law, and its negative effects on intra-Community trade, might be justified, he states:

> Furthermore the system of property law, that is to say the clear descriptions of property rights in respect of objects subject to trade, is a concept of economic constitutional importance for the organisation of markets; in so far the system of property rights is part of public policy, in which interests a Member State under Art. 36 EC [now 30 EC] may justify discriminatory restrictions to trade.[266]

Kieninger examines the underlying principles of the *lex rei sitae* rule. She states that the predominant principle behind the *lex rei sitae* is 'the protection of third parties who trust that property being within the territory of a certain jurisdiction can only

263 See above; 2.2.1. Free Movement of Goods. Joined Cases C-34-36/95 *Konsumentombudsmannen (KO) v De Agostini (Svenska) Förlag AB and TV-Shop I Sverige AB* [1997] ECR I-3843, Case C-405/98 *Konsumentombudsmannen v Gourmet International Products (GIP)* [2001] ECR I-1795.

264 See Case 120/78 *Rewe Zentrale v Bundesmonomolverwaltung für Branntwein (Cassis de Dijon)* [1979] ECR 649. See above; 2.2.1. Free Movement of Goods.

265 Basedow 1995, p. 41 *et seq.*

266 'Um übrigen besitzt aber die Güterordnung, d.h. die eindeutige Umschreibung der dinglichen Rechte an Handelsgütern, eine geradezu wirtschaftsverfassungsrechtliche Bedeutung für die Organisation von Märkten; insofern ist die Güterordnung Teil der öffentliche Ordnung, in deren Interesse der einzelne Mitgliedstaat gemäß Art. 36 EGV diskriminierende Handelsbeschränkungen verhängen kann'. Basedow 1995, p. 45. On this quote Rutgers 1999, p. 202. For a similar conclusion in respect of Dutch law, see Van der Weide 2006, p. 226-229.

be charged according to the laws of that jurisdiction'.[267] She also examines the closed system of property rights as well as the rules on publicity. Also in respect to these elements, Kieninger, in agreement with Basedow, argues that they exist to protect third parties against unknown property rights, either, in case of publicity, in respect to ranking and existence of other security rights, or, in case of the system of property rights, against unknown property rights in general.[268] She therefore agrees with Basedow that the system of property rights, but in her case in combination with the protection of third parties, in particular other creditors, could be a sufficient reason to justify a restrictive measure falling under Article 28 EC.[269]

Von Wilmowsky also deals with the question of grounds for justification. He focuses, like Kieninger, on the justifications for the *lex rei sitae* rule. In his view, each Member State has the exclusive authority to deal with the organisation of property security rights in its own legal system. Member States do this to protect third parties who do not have a property security right against secured creditors that allows these creditors to take the full set of assets of an insolvent debtor.[270] Therefore, Von Wilmowsky argues, Member States should be allowed to invoke this authority as a justification for imposing measures that might fall under Article 28 EC Treaty.[271]

2.4.2.3. *Proportionality*

The next step in the process of evaluating grounds for justification is to see whether the measure imposed by a Member State is proportional to the aim pursued.[272] When it comes to the question of proportionality, Kieninger raises the question of whether outright refusal of recognition of a foreign property right within the Community is the most moderate method possible.[273] In this respect, the type of justification that is used must be closely examined. When public policy is of importance, the rule in question must be applied consistently in the Member State in order for the Member State to be able to invoke it. When the rule is not applied consistently it can no longer be part of public policy and hence it cannot be used as a possible justification for a measure falling under Article 28 EC Treaty.[274]

Taking into consideration the current state of property law, as well as the increased pressure on the system of property law from contract law, Kieninger questions whether the ECJ would accept that public policy as a ground for justification would pass the proportionality test.[275] Rutgers agrees with this conclusion and

267 Kieninger 1996b, p. 63, see also Kieninger 1996a, p. 165-167.
268 Kieninger 1996a, p. 168-173.
269 Kieninger 1996a, p. 173-174. See also Kieninger 1996b, p. 63-64.
270 Von Wilmowsky 1996, p. 123.
271 Von Wilmowsky 1996, p. 122-124.
272 On the proportionality test and private law see, *inter alia*, Israël 2005, p. 119-120.
273 Kieninger 1996a, p. 210. See also *Centros*, in which the court also held an outright refusal of legal capacity of a company could be disproportional. See above; 2.2.2. Freedom of Establishment and its Effect on Substantive Private Law.
274 Kieninger 1996b, p. 64-65.
275 Kieninger 1996b, p. 65. See e.g. Case 178/84 *Commission v Germany* [1987] ECR 1227. On this case see, *inter alia*, Barnard 2007, p. 122-123.

affirms that, if there is no consistency in national property law, the ECJ will not easily accept the argument of a Member State that, because of the consistency of a national system, foreign influences may be rejected.[276]

A possible example of a less disproportionate solution can be taken from Swiss private international law, which does not automatically recognise a reservation of ownership created in another jurisdiction. However, instead of refusing recognition immediately, a period of three months is given to the security owner to register his right in Switzerland, and so to bring his right in conformity with Swiss law.[277] When the three-month period is not complied with, Swiss law refuses recognition.[278]

Von Wilmowsky also deals extensively with the question of proportionality.[279] The justification of Member States that they have the exclusive authority to deal with the organisation of property security rights to protect creditors, especially unsecured creditors, is, in his view, not likely to pass the proportionality test. Many Member States use a restricted number of property security rights in respect of movable objects. These restrictions are usually explained with a statement that a restricted number of rights protect creditors. However, at the same time these Member States might recognise additional preferential positions in insolvency through, for example, priority rights.[280]

Proportionality is not an easy subject. The outcome of the proportionality test very much depends on the reasoning of the Court. What is clear is that in cases where the European legislature has not been active, the Court will allow Member States more freedom to choose a certain degree of regulation.[281]

The first part of the proportionality test of the ECJ comprises the question of suitability. When other solutions can be employed that have a less extensive effect on intra-Community trade, this is a sign that the measure is not suitable for the aim pursued.[282] Von Wilmowsky states that the justification of Member States to be allowed to organise their own national systems of property security rights is aimed at protecting unsecured creditors from an empty set of assets after the secured creditors have claimed their share. By only allowing a limited set of property security rights, it is likely that the unsecured creditors will be left with something in the insolvency to claim from. Von Wilmowsky argues that enacting a rule that a percentage of all objects in insolvency is open specifically for unsecured creditors is another way of protecting unsecured creditors.[283]

The second part of the proportionality test is the question of necessity. It is in this part of the test that the Court looks at the effect of the measure and critically reviews it in the light of the aim that is pursued.[284] The creditor protection rule is

276 Rutgers 1999, p. 205-206.
277 Art. 102(2) IPRG, see Van der Weide 2006, p. 38-39.
278 Bundesgericht 6 July 1967, JDI 1976, 469-470, Art. 715(1) ZGB. Van der Weide 2006, p. 39.
279 Von Wilmowsky 1996, p. 133-149.
280 Von Wilmowsky 1996, p. 134-135.
281 See Case 178/84 *Commission v Germany* [1987] ECR 1227. Craig & De Búrca 2007, p. 706-709.
282 On the proportionality test see above; 2.2.1. Free Movement of Goods. Von Wilmowsky 1996, p. 135-136.
283 Von Wilmowsky 1996, p. 136.
284 See Case 178/84 *Commission v Germany* [1987] ECR 1227.

founded on the principle of *paritas creditorum*, which is the equality of creditors. In respect of this principle, Von Wilmowsky holds that Member States themselves choose to make exceptions by granting holders of a property security right a preferential position compared with unsecured creditors.[285] This, in his view, is also necessary, because the functioning of the economy is dependent on the existence of secured creditors.[286] The protection of unsecured creditors is therefore in his view less important than the protection of the functioning of the Internal Market through the recognition of secured creditors. As a general group, therefore, unsecured creditors should not be protected.[287] However, there are unsecured creditors that deserve protection, for example, employees and consumers, but Von Wilmowsky argues these should be protected in a different way than by refusal to recognise foreign property security rights.[288] In Von Wilmowsky's view, therefore, the measure of a Member State and the statement that this measure is taken because the Member State has the exclusive authority to organise the system of property security rights in order to protect unsecured creditors is not likely to be proportional to the aim pursued. A measure restricting intra-Community trade that falls under Article 28 EC Treaty would therefore be in violation of EC law.

The same reasoning can be used in respect of the justifications advocated by Basedow and Kieninger. When the closed system of property rights is presented as a measure to protect third parties against unknown property rights, the same questions of suitability and necessity must be asked. Possibly, in this respect, because of the complete absence of Community law, the ECJ will take into account the exclusive powers of the Member States in this field.[289] In the absence of Community legislation, Member States are free to choose the measures they deem appropriate to fulfil the aim they seek to pursue. However, although the ECJ will accept this, Member States must choose those measures that have the least restrictive effect on the Internal Market.[290] The Court will investigate whether there are other, less restrictive measures in respect to trade which could fulfil the same aim. In respect to property rights, publicity could possibly offer a less restrictive measure.[291] Therefore, the general refusal of a Member State to recognise the full validity and effect of property rights created in another Member State, even though Member States are entitled to give form and content to their own system of property relations, is not likely to pass the test of proportionality.

2.4.2.4. *Example: Krantz*

In one of the relatively few cases touching upon aspects of property law, the ECJ exactly focused on this aspect. In its decision in *Krantz*, the Court was confronted

285 Von Wilmowsky 1996, p. 140-143.
286 Von Wilmowsky 1996, p. 147.
287 Von Wilmowsky 1996, p. 148.
288 Von Wilmowsky 1996, p. 148-149.
289 Case 178/84 *Commission v Germany* [1987] ECR 1227.
290 Case 178/84 *Commission v Germany* [1987] ECR 1227, Para. 28.
291 Craig & De Búrca 2007, p. 708-709.

with a reservation of ownership clause in a contract of sale of a machine concluded between a German company, Krantz GmbH, and a Dutch company, J. Krantz & Zoon NV.[292] The Dutch company placed the machine in the possession of another Dutch company, Vaalser Textielbedrijf BV. When both of the Dutch companies became insolvent, the Dutch collector of taxes seized all movable objects available on the premises of the insolvent companies to recover unpaid tax. The machine had not been paid for, and the German company invoked its reservation of ownership, claiming it was still the owner of the machine and could revindicate it. The Dutch collector of taxes, based on a provision of Dutch law, did not allow this until the German company paid the outstanding taxes.[293] After payment, the Germany company went to court claiming the seizure made by the tax collector was contrary to Article 28 EC Treaty, because the application of Dutch law restricted trade between Germany and the Netherlands.[294] The ECJ was not convinced and held that:

> 'It must, however, be observed that the national provision referred to by the national court applies without distinction to both domestic and imported goods, and does not seek to control trade with other Member States.
> ... Furthermore, the possibility that nationals of other Member States would hesitate to sell goods on instalment terms to purchasers in the Member State concerned because such goods would be liable to seizure by the collector of taxes if the purchasers failed to discharge their Netherlands tax debts is too uncertain and indirect to warrant the conclusion that a national provision authorizing such seizure is liable to hinder trade between Member States'.[295]

In this slightly disappointing judgment the ECJ did not accept that there was substantial hindrance to intra-Community trade. It is not entirely clear why the Court did not investigate the effects of the restrictions to property security further. When closely examined, it could very well be that the trade between Member States is affected because parties will demand a different, more demanding and more expensive, but safer, security right.

In respect of these more expensive security rights, the reasoning of Advocate General Darmon could be of relevance. The Advocate General argued that because of the specific nature of the right of seizure of the Dutch tax authorities, which is restricted to movables available on the premises, but not stocks of the company, the restriction to trade was minimal.[296] In other words, if the case would have had a more general application, the result could have been that foreign traders would

292 Case C-69/88 *H. Krantz GmbH & Co v Ontvanger der Directe Belastingen en de Staat der Nederlanden* [1990] ECR I-583.

293 Specifically, Art. 16 Invorderingswet.

294 On this case see, *inter alia*, Kieninger 1996a, p. 156-157, Rutgers 1999, p. 197, Barnard 2007, p. 139-140.

295 Case C-69/88 *H. Krantz GmbH & Co v Ontvanger der Directe Belastingen en de Staat der Nederlanden* [1990] ECR I-583, Paras. 10 and 11.

296 Case C-69/88 *H. Krantz GmbH & Co v Ontvanger der Directe Belastingen en de Staat der Nederlanden* [1990] ECR I-583, Opinion AG Darmon, Paras. 12 and 16. Although it is generally held that Art. 28 EC is not subject to a *de minimis* rule. On this subject, see Barnard 2007, p. 162-165.

demand more expensive security rights for an international transaction. Domestic traders in a purely domestic situation can rely on the national system and will not require the creation of such more demanding or more expensive security rights. Therefore the application of the *lex rei sitae* rule in combination with domestic law could result in an actual and substantial hindrance to intra-Community trade under Article 28 EC. Whether such a rule can be justified under Article 30 or one of the mandatory requirements will depend on the ground for justification and the circumstances of the case.

2.4.2.5. *Evaluation*

It is very likely that a Member State will try to invoke the public policy exception and state that its domestic law is intended to safeguard the system of property law, as well as third-party protection, both for creditors as well as for other third parties. Whether such justifications will be allowed will depend on the Member State in question. It is clear, as this study shows, as well as those conducted by Kieninger and Rutgers, that the closed system of property rights is not always applied consistently at a national level. It will be difficult under the standing case law for the ECJ to accept that a foreign property right is not recognised, whereas in domestic law several new property rights have been recognised.[297]

In deciding whether a measure can be justified under Article 30 EC Treaty or the mandatory requirements, the ECJ will look at the aim that the measure seeks to protect. When, however, such an aim has already been fulfilled under the law of the Member State in which the good originates, it is not likely to accept the double burden imposed on it by the receiving Member State.[298]

In other words, the case law of the ECJ requires a Member State to accept the actions taken by one Member State in the pursuit of a certain aim, in this case third-party protection and creditor protection, and does not allow the receiving Member State to impose measures pursuing the same aim. When a Member State does impose such a double burden, this burden must not only fall within the categories mentioned in Article 30 EC or one of the mandatory requirements, but must also be proportionate, or, in other words, suitable and necessary.

It seems unlikely that the outright refusal to recognise a foreign property right from within the EU will pass the test the ECJ imposes.[299] Even in case of transformation or assimilation of a property right, the application of national law would fall under Article 28 EC Treaty, with the result being the loss of certain rights the right

297 See Barnard 2007, p. 122-123.

298 See Case 220/81 *Criminal proceedings against Timothy Frederick Robertson and others* [1982] ECR 2349, Para. 12, Case 27/80, *Criminal proceedings against Anton Adriaan Fietje* [1980] ECR 3839, Para. 12. Basedow 1995, p. 22, Kieninger 1996a, p. 181-183, 191.

299 In this respect, a direct comparison to *Cassis de Dijon* can be made. In that case the Court held that an outright refusal of blackcurrant liqueur on the German market as 'liqueur' was disproportionate and labelling requirements could solve the same objections than those underlying the refusal. In respect to property law the same question could be asked. What measures, i.e. labelling requirements, can be taken by the producer at the time of bringing the product on the market to fulfil the same objections as the outright refusal does?

holder had under the law of the original Member State. These measures could hardly be justified. Moreover, should a ground for justification be accepted, the proportionality test of the ECJ is likely to capture the ground for justification, making the measure in violation of EC law.

When a Member State uses third-party and creditor protection as a possible ground for justification, the case law of the ECJ in respect of the freedom of establishment is recalled. Especially in *Inspire Art*, the Dutch government argued that, in Dutch law, a private limited company requires a certain capital in order to protect creditors against an 'empty' company.[300] The ECJ held that creditors have some responsibility of their own and must rely on the national law of the original Member State that protects their interests, or insist on additional security form the company when dealing with it.[301] In this respect the Court stated:

> '... with regard to protection of creditors, and there being no need for the Court to consider whether the rules on minimum share capital constitute in themselves an appropriate protection measure, it is clear that Inspire Art holds itself out as a company governed by the law of England and Wales and not as a Netherlands company. Its potential creditors are put on sufficient notice that it is covered by legislation other than that regulating the formation in the Netherlands of limited liability companies and, in particular, laying down rules in respect of minimum capital and directors' liability ...'[302]

As a result of this reasoning, there is at least a possibility, if not an obligation, for Member States to deal effectively with property rights created in other Member States. However, the burden of proof will be on the trader to show that there is an actual and substantive impediment to intra-Community trade. When the trader succeeds, the burden of proof is placed on the Member State, which will to attempt to use the system of property law, creditor and third-party protection as possible grounds for justification. When these grounds for justification of a national measure that actually and substantially hinders intra-Community trade have been put forward, the Court will examine the proportionality of such measure, and might conclude that the measure refusing to recognise or only partly recognise a property right is contrary to European law.[303]

From a property law perspective, we see *numerus clausus* playing a different role in the field of European private international law. The reasons used to justify a closed system of property rights are the same in private international law as they are in national law. In particular, when the public policy exception is invoked, and

300 See Case C-167/01 *Kamer van Koophandel en Fabrieken voor Amsterdam v Inspire Art Ltd* [2003] ECR I-10155, Paras. 82 and 142. See also Case 212/97 *Centros Ltd v Erhvervs- of Selsabsstryrelsen* [1999] ECR I-1459.

301 Case C-167/01 *Kamer van Koophandel en Fabrieken voor Amsterdam v Inspire Art Ltd* [2003] ECR I-10155, Para. 125.

302 Case C-167/01 *Kamer van Koophandel en Fabrieken voor Amsterdam v Inspire Art Ltd* [2003] ECR I-10155, Para. 135. Although it should be added that in respect of the information for creditors there is some Community law guaranteeing information that does not exist in the area of property law.

303 See Kieninger 2005, p. 166.

the effect of the application of the *numerus clausus* is a direct limitation on party autonomy, an alteration of party autonomy when a foreign property right is transformed into the national property law system in the same way as a domestic party agreement would be altered by the *numerus clausus*, the effect of the application of the *numerus clausus* is a protection of the domestic market to the detriment of a foreign market that imposes its own regulations of public policy on the existence of property rights already.

Another function, therefore, of *numerus clausus* is the protection of the national system of property law. However, when it comes to European law and, especially, the creation of an Internal Market, there is a tension between this protective function of *numerus clausus* and the principle of mutual recognition, most visible in the area of free movement of goods.

2.4.2.6. *Other Freedoms*

When it comes to a relation between two private parties, whereby one of the parties is in violation of EU law, possibly one of the other freedoms can be invoked.[304] An example can be found in the area of free movement of services, in particular the freedom to provide services. Invoking other freedoms, in particular the freedom of services of Article 49 EC Treaty, could result in a case against a Member State for the contra-European effect of a provision of private international law in combination with a provision of substantive property law, but could also enable a private party to invoke European law directly against another private party.

In respect to the freedom to provide services, a bank losing the security right that it received in exchange for the granting of credit, a commercial service that banks provide, could possibly invoke Article 49 EC Treaty. In order for a measure which has the effect of depriving the bank of its security right to be justified it would have to fulfil four conditions. The measure must be applied in a non-discriminatory manner, it must be justified by a imperative requirement in the public interest, which is the equivalent of mandatory requirements in the area of free movement of goods, the measure must be suitable for the aim it pursues, and, finally, it must not go beyond what is necessary to achieve that aim.[305]

The requirements for the justification of measures in the area of free movement of goods are very similar to those required in the case of freedom to provide services. The fact that a measure must not discriminate in its application either, creates special difficulties for the justification used by a Member State. In the case of freedom to move goods, it is exactly the discriminatory effect of the *lex rei sitae* rule in combination with a provision of substantive property law depriving a national of another Member State from his property right, that might bring the combination of

304 It should be noted that Art. 28 EC has not been awarded horizontal direct effect, but that this effect has been recognised in respect to the other freedoms. See Van den Bogaert 2002, p. 144-145.

305 See, in case of freedom of establishment, Case C-167/01 *Kamer van Koophandel en Fabrieken voor Amsterdam v Inspire Art Ltd* [2003] ECR I-10155, Para. 133.

national measures under Article 28 EC. There is no reason to assume that, in case of the freedom to provide services, this conclusion would be different.

The freedom to provide services might be highly relevant when it comes to immovable objects. Traditionally, property law in respect of immovable objects has been seen as a purely domestic aspect of property law, not subject to European law. However, as the developments towards a right of Euro-mortgage show, there is an increasing need for banks to create a European property security right in respect of immovables.[306]

In terms of the freedom to provide services, the question can be posed why a bank in one Member State can provide a service, mortgage lending, to nationals in the same Member State by using one property right, but is required to create another, more expensive, property right in another Member State in respect of that same national? Possibly a bank could also invoke the freedom of services if it is able to show that the requirement of creating a foreign security right constitutes a hindrance to intra-Community trade.[307] With respect to Article 49 EC Treaty, the Member State would face the same problems with the justification of a national measure; both in selecting a possible justification and in showing that the measure is proportional. With regard to public policy and creditor and third-party protection, Kieninger's and Rutgers' conclusions on the lack of consistency and proportionality remain valid.[308]

As a final possibility, horizontal direct effect might be helpful in a case where a private party provided a service, such as a bank, in the granting of credit, and the bank refuses to recognise a property security right created in another Member State. In such a situation the bank's client that offered the security right might argue that the refusal of the bank is contrary to the free movement of services.

2.4.2.7. *Conclusion*

The effect of Internal Market law on substantive property law is substantial. The national property laws of the Member States are designed as coherent systems, especially as systems of property rights, no deviations are accepted. Internally, these systems are under pressure, in particular from influences coming from contract law. This analysis shows that there is also serious pressure externally, from outside the national system of property law.

In terms of *numerus clausus* it could very well be that a national legal system is forced by European law to recognise an unknown, foreign, type of property right. When this happens, the *numerus clausus* in that Member State will be extended with an additional property right and the legal system will face difficulties. To what extent the legal system of a Member State will experience difficulties depends on

306 See, for the most recent developments in this area, White Paper on Mortgage Credit Markets COM(2007) 807 final.

307 On the shift in focus to services in respect to immovable objects, see Sparkes 2007, p. 521-522. Moreover, a bank could invoke the free movement of capital. See Case C-222/97 *Manfred Trummer v Peter Mayer* [1999] ECR I-1661.

308 Kieninger 1996b, p. 65, Rutgers 1999, p. 205-206.

the analysis of the effect of the applicability of European law. Some might argue that a newly recognised property right can only be used in case of an intra-Community trade situation, whereas others may argue that this new property right should also be available to nationals of the receiving Member State. Preventing nationals access to a property right that is available to competitors, in the case of intra-Community trade, seems unequal treatment and might be covered by European law as well.[309]

In any case, European law adds a dimension to the discussion on the remaining validity of a closed system of property rights by adding an imminent external pressure. It is therefore not surprising that authors such as Basedow and Kieninger expect Member States to use the public policy exception to save their national systems of property law.[310] However, should a Member State not succeed in justifying restrictive measures, it would be confronted with the pragmatism of European law.

If the national property law systems of the Member States of the European Union are connected through the application of Internal Market law, it can be questioned whether these national property law systems are still really purely national. If all these systems are linked and property rights created in one Member State might have effect in another Member State if needed, this signals the rise of a new system of property law, a European property law. However, what the status of the system of property rights in European property law is depends on how a European property law is constructed.

3. The Making of European Property Law

The above analysis has shown that there is a substantial influence of European law on national property law.[311] This influence comes not only from European rules on national contract law, but also from European rules on property law itself. Moreover, there is a potential influence of European law on the rules of private international law, in particular on the rules of private international law in respect to property law. When this increasing influence is taken into account, and an overview is provided of the consequences and possible consequences on national systems of property law, a fragmented picture arises. The explanation why this is a fragmented picture can be found in the method the European legislature must follow in order to be able to legislate.

Without proof of a hindrance to the functioning of the Internal Market under one of the provisions in the EC Treaty, legislation cannot be adopted. Therefore,

309 See Art. 12 EC. It has been argued, although the courts have not explicitly dealt with this, that because of the Constitutional concept of equality in the Italian Constitution, a trust relation recognised under the Hague Convention should also be open to Italian nationals. The Italian courts have recognised this through the recognition of an internal trust, but not specifically on the basis of equality. See Braun 2006, p. 797 *et seq.*

310 Basedow 1995, p. 45, Kieninger 1996a, p. 210, Kieninger 1996b, p. 65. See also Roth 1999, p. 57-58, Von Wilmowsky 1996, p. 122.

311 The title of this section is inspired by the title used by Smits. See Smits 2002.

European legislation is issued in specific areas that require harmonisation. In European private law, legislation therefore virtually does not deal with general aspects of private law. Decisions of the European Court of Justice are also taken in specific areas that require the Court's attention. In these cases, a specific barrier to the functioning of the Internal Market has arisen.

In other words, the European method of legislating and guarding the functioning of the Internal Market might allow the development of general underlying principles in respect to the functioning of the Internal Market, but this method does not necessarily allow room for underlying principles of the substantive private law they are dealing with.[312]

Private law, and property law in particular, is an area of law in which underlying concepts and principles are highly relevant. When, under the influence of the functioning of the Internal Market, a European property law is formed, the need to answer some fundamental questions of European private law, in particular European property law, arises. These questions have been answered, be it to different degrees, in the private law systems of the Member States. Consequently, now that the European legislature is involved in law-making in this area, there is no reason why this European legislature should be exempted from answering these questions. As a minimum, therefore, the European legislature should deal with fundamental principles of private law.

In dealing with European property law, the principle of *numerus clausus* should take centre stage. The principle of *numerus clausus* is the fundamental principle of property law guarding the door that grants access to the other principles and rules of property law.[313] Possibly, the European legislature could take the principle of *numerus clausus* as its starting point and, with it, give form to a more coherent European property law.

This final section will deal with these three aspects of European property law. First, the influence of European law on the national legal systems will be placed in the perspective of the general development of a European property law, and a closer look will be taken at the current state of European property law.[314] Second, when a European property law is created, two fundamental choices should be made, one on the separation between the law of obligations and the law of property and one on the system of property rights.[315] Thirdly and finally, after these fundamental questions have been answered, the principle of *numerus clausus* could fulfil a leading role in the further development of European property law.[316] A model,

312 There is an increasing body of literature that examines the influence of general principles of Community law. For a good overview and also a discussion on the influence of these principles on private law relations, see Devroe 2007, p. 133 *et seq.*

313 Van Erp 2006b, p. 14-17.

314 Below; 3.1. The Influence of European Law on National Property Law Systems, and 3.2. The Status of European Property Law.

315 Below; 3.3. Two Fundamental Questions for a Coherent European Property Law.

316 Below; 3.4. A Possible Model for a European Property Law: *Numerus Clausus* as a Constitutive Element of European Property Law.

based on the comparative research in this study, will be presented as a possible solution to take the development of European property law forward.

3.1. *The Influence of European Law on National Property Law Systems*

The influence of European law on private law is twofold. Through European legislation, issued in the form of Regulations and Directives, the European legislature can harmonise law in the Member States to different degrees.[317] Furthermore, through the case law of the European Court of Justice, certain areas of private law can be strongly affected.[318]

The effect of European legislation on the private law of the Member States is that, either based directly on European law, or based indirectly on European law through the implementation of a Directive into the national law of a Member State, the contents of the laws of the Member States are made similar.[319] In the area of property law, where national legal systems form a doctrinally coherent system, European legislation, based on different, usually pragmatic, considerations, will not automatically fit in. In the case of Directives, the most often used method of European legislation in the area of European private law, the Member States are allowed freedom to implement the European rules in the national doctrinally coherent system. Implementation allows the Member States some freedom to maintain the national coherence of the private law system.

However, on some occasions, choices that were made by national legislatures must be set aside to enable the implementation of European legislation. In the area of property law, the Late-payments Directive forced Member States to create the possibility for private parties to reserve the right of ownership for security purposes by introducing a reservation of ownership or retention of title.[320] Furthermore, the Directive on Financial Collateral Arrangements forced Member States to adopt the possibility for parties to transfer the right of ownership for security purposes, as well as the recognition of a right of pledge that allows the pledgee to keep the object under pledge in case of non-performance by the debtor.[321]

Member States that had made different doctrinal choices were forced to reconsider these choices and possibly to create exceptions. The Netherlands offers two clear examples of solutions that were found to circumvent an undesirable application of international and European rules to the general provisions on proper-

317 Art. 249 EC.

318 E.g., in the area of company law the ECJ's case law on the freedom of establishment has led to a change in substantive company law in some Member States. See above; 2.2.2. Freedom of Establishment and its Effect on Substantive Private Law.

319 For examples of European legislation in the area of private law, see above; 2.1.2. Legal Framework: Secondary Community Law.

320 See Art. 4 Directive 2000/35 of the European Parliament and of the Council of 29 June 2000 on combating late payment in commercial transactions.

321 Directive 2000/35 of the European Parliament and of the Council of 29 June 2000 on combating late payment in commercial transactions. This Directive caused a discussion in the Netherlands whether an actual introduction of a transfer of ownership for security purposes was required. For an overview of the discussion, see Van Vliet 2005, p. 190 *et seq.*

ty law.[322] First, the introduction of the Directive on Financial Collateral Arrangements was implemented in the section of the Civil Code on special contracts. This implementation was effected under explicit statement that the proprietary effects of financial collateral arrangements would not violate the general principles of Dutch property law, in particular the prohibition of a transfer of ownership for security purposes. Secondly, the Dutch legislature had already been creative with this *fiducia*-ban, which is the prohibition of a transfer of ownership for a specific purpose, when the Hague Trust Convention was ratified.[323] Although this Convention is not directly an example of European law, the ratification of the Hague Convention shows the unwillingness of the Dutch legislature to amend the general rules of property law in the light of international developments.

The law that ratified the Convention explicitly states that the *fiducia*-ban does not apply in case of a trust that is recognised under the application of the Convention.[324] There is no reason to assume that in case of the implementation of European legislation, the Dutch legislature would make a different choice. This argument is only strengthened by the implementation of the Financial Collateral Arrangements Directive in the Netherlands.

Next to the influence of European substantive law on the property law systems of the Member States, the European Court of Justice has also contributed to the creation and perfection of the Internal Market. Not only in the area of free movement of goods, services, persons and capital, but also in the area of competition law, the Court has been a motor for European integration.[325] In the area of private law, the four freedoms have been particularly important.[326] Especially in the area of company law, the free movement of persons, in the form of the freedom of establishment, has led to major changes.[327]

In respect to the free movement of goods, beginning with the Court's landmark decision in *Cassis de Dijon*, in which the Court introduced the concept of mutual recognition, the Court has made a substantial contribution to the formation of the Internal Market.[328] The recognition of the principle of mutual recognition, the idea of equivalence of national standards, allowed the European Commission to focus its lawmaking activities on those areas that the ECJ left aside.[329] In other

322 Another example is offered through the implementation of Directive 2003/87/EC of the European Parliament and the Council of 13 October 2003 establishing a scheme for greenhouse gas emission allowance trading within the Community and amending Council Directive 96/61/EC. The implementation of this Directive forced the Dutch legislator to adapt an abstract transfer system for emission rights, but only for emission rights under the directive, leaving the causal transfer system in the general provisions on property law untouched. On this development see Van Erp 2004c, p. 539-540, Van Erp 2006a, p. 1065-1066.

323 The Hague Convention on the Law Applicable to Trusts and on Their Recognition. On this convention and property law, see Sparkes 2007, p. 509-517.

324 Art. 4 Wet Conflictenrecht Trusts (WCT), see Chapter 5; 4.9. EC and International Influences.

325 Barnard 2007, p. 17-23.

326 See above; 2.2. The ECJ as a Motor for the Development of European Private Law.

327 See above; 2.2.2. Freedom of Establishment and its Effect on Substantive Private Law.

328 Barnard 2007, p. 18-19.

329 See Communication from the Commission regarding the *Cassis de Dijon* judgment [1980] OJ C256/2. Barnard 2007, p. 114-115, Craig & De Búrca 2007, p. 714-716.

words, in those areas where the ECJ was active, the Commission could focus its attention elsewhere. The Court, in its turn, would accept the existence of European legislation in its case law on free movement.[330]

The interpretation the Commission attached to the *Cassis de Dijon* judgment has consequences for the law-making authorities in the Member States. National legislators remain free to regulate their own national market, but must accept and recognise the market rules from other Member States as well.[331]

In respect to the law of property, the case law of the ECJ in the area of the free movement of goods is of special interest. When the law of property is, in European law terminology, considered as a measure, or as a set of measures, the rules on the Internal Market can certainly be applied to property law.[332] The analysis of the case law of the ECJ and the work of Kieninger, Rutgers, and Von Wilmowsky in this field shows that it could very well be possible that rules of property law of the Member State, in their application in the Internal Market, constitute a violation of the principles on the free movement of goods.[333] Applying the case law of the ECJ to property law centres on the application of rules of national property law in an Internal Market setting. In the law of property, this Internal Market setting arises when the property law systems of two Member States come into conflict with each other, and, most importantly, the application of one of these legal systems leads to an actual and substantial disturbance of the functioning of the Internal Market.

In terms of traditional private law, the case law of the ECJ in respect of the four freedoms therefore also concerns private international law. The effects of this are substantial. Whereas national legal systems are traditionally free to decide on the application of foreign law and on the recognition of rights created under the law of another jurisdiction, the law of the Internal Market forces Member States to accept rules and rights created under those rules from other Member States under the principle of mutual recognition.

3.2. *The Status of European Property Law*

The influence of the case law of the European Court of Justice on the national systems of private law, both substantive rules of private law and private international law, in combination with legislative measures taken by the European legislature, lead to a constant influence of European law on national law. Central to this approach is that when a national legislature creates a measure of national private law, this national legislature is bound by the rules on the Internal Market. This reasoning does not only apply to contract law but also to the law of property, con-

330 As a result of European legislation, the Court will not accept justifications from Member States when a violation of one of the four freedoms has been found. After all, when there is European legislation in an area, Member States cannot argue that national legislation resists against the application of European law.

331 Barnard calls this competitive federalism, see Barnard 2007, p. 19-21. See also Craig & De Búrca 2007, p. 715-716.

332 See Kieninger 1996b, p. 41 *et seq.*, Rutgers 1999, p. 167 *et seq.*

333 Kieninger 1996a, p. 122 *et seq.*, Rutgers 1999, p. 169 *et seq.*, Von Wilmowsky 1996, p. 111-112.

sidering the possible application of the free movement of goods, and also potentially of services and capital.[334] National property law, therefore, is no longer purely national property law.[335]

Through the adoption of Regulations and Directives, the European Union has already taken the opportunity to regulate some specific areas of property law. Even though some of this legislation takes the form of national property law through the implementation of Directives, the content of these rules as well as the final interpretation is for the European Union.[336] Furthermore, through the potential case law of the ECJ on national property law and the application of the *lex rei sitae* rule, the Member States are not only confronted with European law in the area of property law, but also with the property law systems of the other Member States. When, under the case law of the ECJ, a Member State is forced to recognise a property right created in another Member State, elements of foreign property law enter the law of the receiving Member State.

Theoretically, the result of this case law is that there is no longer a comprehensive national list of property rights, as, potentially, property rights created in other Member States must be recognised. Unlike under normal rules of private international law where jurisdictions themselves decide on the rules concerning recognition, the rules on the Internal Market take away that power from the Member States. Although it will be controversial, if the ECJ should compel Member States to recognise property rights created in another Member State, the rules of private international law in respect to the law of property will be made subject to the scrutiny of Internal Market law, or, potentially, even be replaced by rules of European law.

The influence of national property law systems of the Member States on each other and the possible forced recognition of property rights created in other Member States confront Member States with doctrinal choices made in other Member States. Under the traditional model of national property law, the national legislature has made doctrinal choices on the separation between the law of obligations and the law of property, as well as on the available menu of rights that are dealt with by property law.[337]

When in a national legal system a choice has been made not to recognise a certain property relation, for example security-ownership or anticipation rights, but the legal system is forced to recognise such a legal relation under the rules of the Internal Market, the receiving jurisdiction is likely to have problems with the recognition.[338] Under ordinary rules of private international law it is not likely that legal relations which were decided against by the receiving legal systems will be accepted. But without the possibility to create rules of private international law that

334 On the application of these three freedoms to the law of property, see above; 2.4. The Effects of European Law on the Law of Property.

335 See Joerges 2005, p. 16-19.

336 On Directives and Regulations that have effect on property law, see above; 2.1.2. Legal Framework: Secondary Community Law.

337 See also Joerges 1997, p. 385.

338 On these types of rights, see Chapter 7; 2. The Content of Property Law Systems in Europe.

are not subject to Internal Market law, Member States are left with only a limited possibility to justify non-recognition under the rules of the Internal Market.[339]

As a ground for justification, Member States could try to invoke the internal coherence of the legal system. However, is not likely that the ECJ will accept this argument easily. Especially when comparative research shows that the internal coherence is also deviated from by the Member States themselves, either by legislation or by case law, the ECJ will not be inclined to accept a national coherent system, in other words, a rule of *numerus clausus*, as a valid ground for justification.[340] The consequence of acceptance of the principle of mutual recognition implies therefore also mutual recognition of property law doctrines from other Member States.[341] The conflicts that arise in national legal systems, therefore, not only concern the specific recognition of a certain foreign property right, but also the doctrinal choices that support the creation of that certain foreign property right in that other Member State. The receiving Member State will have to accommodate these doctrinal choices that will often be contrary to its own choices.

The current fragmented approach, in which there is some European legislation and a constant threat of a decision of the ECJ on the law of property, creates uncertainty in respect to the relation between European and national property law. In theory, all rules of national property law are subject to the rules of the Internal Market if they, in combination with the *lex rei sitae* rule, lead to an actual and substantial hindrance of intra-Community trade.[342] In terms of the modern law on free movement of goods, when the application of national property law actually and substantially prevents access to the market from another Member State, the national measure might be contrary to the rules of the Internal Market, unless it is justified and proportional.

European property law is an area of law in which the pragmatic approach of European law reigns. Fundamental aspects, which have been dealt with at the level of national property law, are neglected by the European legislature. When property law systems were formed or created, national legislatures as well as national courts formed the law of property based on assumptions of a separation between the law of obligations and the law of property, on the policy question of what can be property rights, and on the decision as to which criteria these property rights should be subject.[343]

National property law systems form a coherent system of law in which concepts and rules are connected to each other to form a system that provides legal certainty. At the same time, under the influence of, especially, contract law, there is

339 See above; 2.2. The ECJ as a Motor for the Development of European Private Law.

340 See also Rutgers 1999, p. 202. See further above; 2.4. The Effects of Internal Market Law on Property Law.

341 See Joerges 1997, p. 385.

342 As formulated under the *Dassonville*-formula. See above; 2.2.1. Free Movement of Goods.

343 Although this formulation sounds very civil law oriented, also in English law these same questions have been dealt with. One of the best examples is offered by *National Provincial Bank Ltd v Ainsworth* [1965] AC 1175, HL at 1247-1248 *per* Lord Wilberforce. On this case see Chapter 6; 4. A *Numerus Clausus* in English Property Law?

a tendency to create more flexibility in the law of property and to move to a more dynamic system of property law.[344] These influences of contract law are received carefully and placed in the coherent national system in order to prevent uncertainty in respect to the legal status of legal relations. Property law concerns legal relations that have effect against third parties. In order to safeguard this third-party effect, and having learned lessons from history in which too many property rights led to an unbalanced system, for instance under the *ancien régime*, each property law system must strike a balance between legal certainty and flexibility.

Against the possibility that the ECJ might rule on a question of property law, it could be argued that in fact the European Union, as well as the ECJ, has not dealt with principal questions of property law yet. Furthermore, in a case where the ECJ did go into property law, the Court was very careful in accepting a violation of provisions of property law.[345] The critical argument would be that, because there is no or almost no European activity in this area, the Court would refrain from making a fundamental decision.

Against this argument the ECJ's judgment in *Centros* can be recalled. In that case the Court held that the fact that company law was not completely harmonised did not prevent the Court from giving a decision in which European company law was further developed.[346] In respect to property law, now that some EU legislation is passed on aspects of property law, the same argument could possibly be used.[347] In fact, in a very recent case the ECJ did not refrain from holding a transfer of ownership of land invalid, based on European law.[348] This decision adds more weight to the threat of another ECJ decision ruling against the non-recognition of a property right created in another Member State.[349]

At this moment, under the current pragmatic decision-making procedure of the European Union, if a decision of the ECJ on national property law should arise, the confrontation between the balanced systems of national property law and the pragmatic system of European property law could lead to undesirable results. The coherence of national property law suffers under the pragmatic approach of European Internal Market regulation. Not surprisingly, therefore, an increasing number of authors argue that in those fields where it is very likely that the European Union

344 On these aspects see Chapter 7; 1.1. Property Law in Development and 4. *Numerus Clausus* in Property Law Systems in Europe.

345 See, e.g., Case C-69/88 *H. Krantz GmbH & Co v Ontvanger der Directe Belastingen en de Staat der Nederlanden* [1990] ECR I-583.

346 Case C-212/97 *Centros v Erhverves- og Selskabsstyrelsen* [1999] ECR I-1459, Para. 28.

347 On EC property law, see above; 2.1.2. Legal Framework: Secondary Community Law.

348 Case C-117/06 *Gerda Mölendorf v Christiana Mölendorf-Niehuus* [2007] ECR I-8361. This case concerns the transfer of ownership of land in violation of Regulation 467/2001 prohibiting the export of certain goods and services to Afghanistan strengthening the flight ban and extending the freeze of funds and other financial resources in respect of the Taliban of Afghanistan, as amended by Council Regulation 561/2003 of 27 March 2003.

349 On this threat see, in particular, Kieninger 2006, p. 166.

will interfere or, to put it positively, where the Internal Market would benefit, harmonisation of aspects of property law is needed.[350]

Alternatively, European law could regulate the interaction between the national legal systems. European property law as a federation of national legal systems, or better as a federation of national property law doctrines, a system in which European law would only regulate the interaction between these systems, offers a solution but does not fulfil doctrinal objections on the balance of legal certainty and flexibility. When arguments of legal certainty are used, and, under pressure from European law, foreign, as yet unknown, property rights are recognised in a legal system, legal certainty is not well served.

In respect of property law as a coherent system with many highly developed doctrinal foundations justifying its existence, the method of positive harmonisation through enactment of EU law is well worth considering. Such an approach has an advantage over negative harmonisation in that legal certainty is safeguarded through a clear formulation of rules instead of a judgment of a court on the status of substantive law. Furthermore, positive harmonisation allows the European legislature to make choices on the doctrinal foundations of European property law itself.

Legal certainty would be served through European legislation because in matters of Community legislation the ECJ has the right to interpret these provisions.[351] By granting one court the right to interpret rules of European law, a more consistent interpretation can be guaranteed. Especially in cases of property law, consistent interpretation of provisions that provide rules in respect to third parties, whether these provisions deal with third party effect or with third party protection, will lead to increased legal certainty.

In short, European property law is not just a vague prospect for the future, but is a system already in development. At present European property law is fragmented. It is actually a combination of a federation of national property law systems with specific European legislation in some areas.[352] This leads to legal uncertainty in respect of a possible ECJ decision on the validity of a measure of national property law in a setting of intra-Community trade. Furthermore, without a European doctrine on fundamental aspects of property law, future European legislation is likely to upset the national property law systems when they are confronted with this legislation.

These objections could be solved by looking at the possibilities of creating a basic framework of European property law from an Internal Market perspective. This would contribute to the further creation of a European property law.

350 See, *inter alia*, Snijders 2006, p. 153 *et seq.*, and on this proposal, Kieninger 2006, p. 165 *et seq.*, Rank 2006, Rutgers 2006, Kieninger 1996a, p. 215 *et seq.*, Roth 1999, p. 225 *et seq.*, Kieninger 2004, p. 664-672, Von Bar & Drobnig 2002, p. 321-322, Nasarre-Aznar 2004, Kieninger 2007, p. 198-202.

351 Art. 234 EC.

352 On a similar conclusion see Van Erp 2006b, p. 7-11.

3.3. *Two Fundamental Questions for a Coherent European Property Law*

If we look at European property law as more than a federation of national legal systems of the Member States, and accept that there is already some European legislation in the area of property law, the need to deal with two fundamental aspects of European private law, property law in particular, arises.

At this moment, European property law is a pragmatic system of law, increasing in volume through the adoption of legislation or through decisions of the ECJ. These types of legislation and court decisions are issued without fundamental principles of European private law. In order to ensure the continuous development and to provide more legal certainty, European property law therefore is in need of more coherence and, although perhaps not to the same extent or in the same form as in the Member States, a doctrinal basis. Only with these can a balance be found between flexibility and legal certainty.

Based on the model adhered to by French, German, Dutch and English law, that was discussed in Chapter 7, two fundamental questions can be formulated.[353] First, should a European property law make a distinction between the law of obligations and the law of property? Part of this question is whether a European property law should recognise the difference between personal rights and property rights. Second, should a European property law adhere to the principle of *numerus clausus,* and if so, in what form? These two fundamental questions will be discussed in the next two sections.[354]

3.3.1. Separation between the Law of Obligations and the Law of Property?

The separation between the law of obligations and the law of property has, like the principle of *numerus clausus,* taken different forms in different Member States. As was discussed in Chapter 7, there is a strong connection between the separation of the law of obligations and the law of property, and the way in which a legal system adheres to a *numerus clausus.*[355] French, German, Dutch and English law all adhere to the principle of separation between the law of obligations and the law of property, as well as to the principle of *numerus clausus.* Both are fundamental principles of property law.[356] As a result, each of these legal systems has rules on the basis of which it is possible to decide which legal relation is granted access to the realm of property law and which legal relation must remain in the realm of the law of obligations.

The European Commission, in its current activities, also seems to be adhering to some separation between the law of obligations and the law of property, as the work on the Common Frame of Reference as well as of the *Acquis* group is in par-

353 On this model see Chapter 7; 2. The Content of Property Law Systems in Europe.

354 See below; 3.3.1. Separation between the Law of Obligations and the Law of Property?, and 3.3.2. *Numerus Clausus*: the Available Menu of Property Rights?

355 See Chapter 7; 1.2. Considering *Numerus Clausus.*

356 On this theme, see Füller 2006, p. 526 *et seq.*

ticular concerned with contract law.[357] It was only through the study of Von Bar and Drobnig on contract law and how it relates to property law that the law of property became included in the academic work on a Common Frame of Reference.[358] However, at the same time, the Commission has dealt with credit securities, including property security rights, as a part of the sale of goods, and therefore as a part of contract law.[359] It seems therefore that, at this moment, the European legislature is adhering to some degree of separation, but only insofar as it seems practical.

The European Union does not adhere to a clearly formulated set of fundamental principles, except those mentioned in the EC and EU Treaties.[360] Article 6 of the EU Treaty mentions the foundations of the European Union. Among these foundations is respect for fundamental freedoms, which is one of the principles that are common to the Member States.[361] When the separation between the law of obligations and the law of property is seen as a fundamental principle of private law that is common to the Member States, be it in different degrees, it seems that the European legal order will also have to adhere to some degree of separation. Subsequently, the European legal order will also have to adhere to the distinction between legal relations without third-party effect, personal rights, and legal relations with third-party effect, property rights.

Only when the law of obligations and the law of property are also separated at a European level to the degree that it remains possible to distinguish between legal relations with and without third-party effect, in other words between the law of property and the law of obligations, will the legal systems of the Member States be able to cope with the influence of European law in this area. European law and national law will then be able to co-operate in the development of a system of property law for the European Union.

3.3.2. *Numerus Clausus*: the Available Menu of Property Rights?

A second question concerns the adherence to the principle of *numerus clausus*. Adhering to *numerus clausus* brings systematic reasoning to the law of property, even when an open system of property rights is used, as in a legal system such as South Africa. When the system of European property law adheres to a separation between the law of obligations and the law of property, the question of how property law must deal with those legal relations that fall under it, relations with third-party effect, becomes important to answer.

357 See above; 2.1.3. European Commission Initiatives for Future Legislation.

358 See Von Bar & Drobnig 2002, p. 309 *et seq.*

359 See above; 2.1.2. Legal Framework: Secondary Community Law.

360 After the Lisbon Treaty these will be the EU Treaty and the TFEU.

361 Art. 6 EU mentions liberty, democracy and respect for human rights as other principles, which are common to the Member States. See also Case 155/79 *AM & S v Commission* [1982] ECR 1575, see also Devroe 2007, p. 134-135, 138-139. On the effect of general principles of Community law on private relations see Case C-144/04 *Werner Mangold v Rüdinger Helm* [2005] ECR I-9981.

The discussion of the legal systems of France, Germany, the Netherlands and England shows that there are different degrees of adherence to the principle of *numerus clausus*. It could be held that Germany and England are on opposite sides in the way in which they adhere to the principle.[362] However, in none of these systems are parties completely free to create new property relations themselves.

In a system that is traditionally held not to adhere to a *numerus clausus* but to a *numerus apertus*, like South African law, parties do have freedom to create new property relations, but this freedom is severely limited. I have argued therefore that, although South Africa does not have a closed system of property relations, it does adhere to the principle of *numerus clausus* to some degree.[363]

When, under pressure from decisions of the ECJ, Member States are forced to recognise property relations created in another Member State, a federation of legal systems will be formed in which the national closed systems are no longer closed. When a property relation from another Member State is imported under the rules of the Internal Market, the receiving Member State will have to accommodate that relation. Member States will therefore be confronted with legal relations and doctrinal choices of another Member State.[364]

This could result in recognising German *Anwartschaftsrechte* or English estate contracts and options to purchase in legal systems that have explicitly chosen not to recognise these. Furthermore, most visible in case of property security rights, questions of publicity and third-party protection may show undesirable results when, in a purely national situation, a national property security right must be registered, but a foreign property security right that is recognised does not have to fulfil this requirement or must fulfil this requirement to a different degree.[365]

In any case, the principle of mutual recognition could lead to competition between Member States for the best law. However, what the best law is depends on the perspective that is taken. As in the case of company law, a Delaware effect may occur. A Delaware effect arises when companies choose the most favourable legal system and then, under the freedom of establishment, create branches in other Member States that must be recognised.[366] For the law of property this could include a rush on German law or English law to create, for example, options to purchase or other anticipation rights.

In respect of property law, such competition between Member States could result in enlarging the number of recognised property rights in the national legal systems. However, these results will not be so dramatic as they seem at first sight. As long as the national legal systems in Europe do not use an open system of property rights, a *numerus apertus*, the national legal systems will also remain closed. Private parties will not be granted the possibility to create new property rights to their own liking.

362 See Chapter 7; 4. Conclusion: *Numerus Clausus* in Property Law Systems in Europe.
363 See Chapter 7; 3.8. A Legal System Without a *Numerus Clausus*: South African Law.
364 See Joerges 1997, p. 385, Rank 2006, p. 206-207.
365 Although most of the time a property relation that is recognised will also be subject to the rules of registration in the receiving legal system.
366 See Charny 1991, p. 428 *et seq.*, Barnard 2007, p. 342, 20-21.

However, when an open system of property rights does exist in one Member State, theoretically this would, in combination with a decision by the ECJ that property rights from other Member States must be recognised, open the other national property law systems to some degree.[367] Concerning France, Germany, the Netherlands and England, in the previous chapters the conclusion was reached that the menu of property relations in these systems is not absolutely closed, but parties do not enjoy the freedom to create new, as yet unrecognised types of property rights themselves in those systems. However, in respect of other legal systems in the European Union that have not been included in this research, open systems of property rights do exist. Spain is the best example of such a system, where Spanish authors hold the system, at least in respect to property rights in respect of immovables, to be open.[368] Nevertheless, no new property rights have been recognised in Spanish law.

What would be the result of an open competition can only be predicted. Based on the studies in Law and Economics, standardisation of property rights through either voluntary harmonisation or changes made by the European legislature might occur to enhance legal certainty and to create the optimal standardisation.[369]

Numerus clausus theory therefore also applies to European property law, and, not surprisingly, much in the same way as it applies at a national level. Given that European contract law already exists, it makes sense to reinvestigate whether there should be a European property law that is separated, at least to some degree, from European contract law.[370] The national legal traditions, in particular of France, Germany, the Netherlands and England, all adhere to the distinction between personal rights and property rights. There is, and there seems, no need to change this.

3.4. A Possible Model for a European Property Law: Numerus Clausus as a Constitutive Element of European Property Law.[371]

The term European property law offers at least two interpretations. First, the term can be interpreted as the current European legislation that deals with property law or has an effect, or could have an effect, on property law of the Member States. It is this type of European property law that has been central in this Chapter so far. A second interpretation of European property law, with a perspective of the future in mind, could be that of a true property law system on a European level, possibly replacing or partly replacing the national systems of property law in the Member

367 I.e., in as far as they are forced under Community law to recognise an unknown property right in cross-border situations originating in a Member State adhering to an open system of property right.

368 On Spanish law, see Goni Rodriguez de Almeida 2006, O'Callaghan 2002, Fulgencia Angosto Sáez 2006, p. 281 *et seq.*

369 See Boeckaert 2006, p. 182-184, 187 (solution), Merrill & Smith 2000. On *numerus clausus* and Law and Economics, see Chapter 7; 3.2. Law and Economics on *Numerus Clausus*.

370 See, in respect to the separation between the law of obligations and the law of property, the remarks by Füller, who holds that a completely autonomous property law can no longer be maintained. Füller 2006, p. 525 *et seq.*

371 See Van Erp 2003b.

States. This interpretation of the term European property law should be handled with great care.

As this Chapter seeks to illustrate, at this moment there is no European legislation replacing national property law provisions.[372] Moreover, this Chapter also emphasises that with the current system of European legislation, primary law does not offer a basis for general harmonisation of property law. Not only can Articles 95 and 308 EC Treaty themselves not be interpreted as providing the European Union with a general competence to harmonise private law, including property law, but also the decision of the ECJ in the *Tobacco Advertising* case makes very clear that an obstacle to the functioning of the Internal Market must be shown in order to authorise legislation.[373] Furthermore, the renewed version of the European Treaties will not offer a more general competence of harmonisation. The judgment of the ECJ in the *Tobacco Advertising* case should also be read in combination with the principle of subsidiarity as contained in Article 5 EC Treaty. This Article, which was inserted in the EC Treaty by the Treaty of Maastricht, forces the European Community to remain within the powers conferred to it by the Treaty.[374] Subsidiarity is in particular relevant in cases where the European Community does not have exclusive competence. Article 5 EC Treaty states that the Community can only act if 'the objectives of the proposed action cannot be sufficiently achieved by the Member States and can, therefore, by reason of the scale or effects of the proposed action, be better achieved by the Community'.[375]

Describing European property law as a system of property law on a European level, replacing or partly replacing the national property law of the Members States, is not a realistic issue for the moment. However, as this Chapter also seeks to illustrate, problems with the current system of European property law are increasing. A lack of legislative competences for the European Community and a possible ECJ decision on the recognition of foreign property rights, might increase the need for the development of a European property law in the second, truly European, meaning.

The harmonisation of property law in the European Union is a controversial issue, which has raised and will continue to raise many legal and political objections. Nevertheless, it could be interesting, without further taking the current legal and political objections to harmonisation of property law in Europe into consideration, to investigate a possible future for a truly European property law. The results of such an investigation are not a proposal for legislation, but could possibly offer food for thought in the debate on the making of European property law. This Section therefore offers a possible model for the development of European property law, not with a simple argument for the full harmonisation of property law in the European Union, but with a more nuanced system of interaction between European competences and national substantive property law.

372 See above; 2.1. EC Private Law.

373 Case C-276/98 *Germany v Parliament and Council* [2000] ECR I-8419, Para. 83. See above; 2.1.1. Legal Framework: Primary Community Law.

374 Craig & De Búrca 2007, p. 100.

375 Art. 5 EC. See further Craig & De Búrca 2007, p. 101-105.

The model that was developed as a result of a comparative analysis of French, German, Dutch and English law in Chapter 7 could serve as a basis for the development of a model for European property law. Such a model would not be based on an analysis of all the Member States, but would be formed on a combination of civil law and common law traditions.

All of these legal systems adhere to a system of property law, or systems of property law in case of English law, in which there is one primary right from which several lesser property rights are derived, either through subtraction or through limitation of the primary right.[376] However, as a result of varying doctrinal choices, differences between Member States exist that do have an actual effect on the functioning of the Internal Market. This is especially so when, through the application of a *lex rei sitae* rule together with a more restrictive national property law in the receiving Member State, a property relation, or part of a property relation, can be lost.

Coherence between the national systems of property law is needed in order for the system of European property law to function. Only when national property law systems efficiently deal with property rights from other jurisdictions without a negative effect on the functioning of the Internal Market, can national doctrinal arguments of legal certainty and third-party protection be maintained. However, when not only European law, but also other national legal systems are involved, unavoidably some national doctrinal arguments must be set aside. In particular when it comes to a confrontation between static and dynamic systems of property law, compromises will have to be made. The pragmatic, as opposed to doctrinal, approach of the European Union, especially with regard to the functioning of the Internal Market, could result in doctrinal reasons giving way in favour of market access. However, as a ground for justification for refusing to accept a certain solution, national doctrinal arguments may remain valid.

3.4.1. Towards a European Property Law as a Flexible System of Property Rights

In view of the pragmatic approach the European Court of Justice, but also European law in general, takes in respect to systems of private law, a pragmatic and dynamic solution for a European property law seems to fit better than a discussion on which national model of static property law should prevail. In other words, national doctrinal arguments and arguments of doctrinal coherence of property law systems should only be taken into account in so far as they have an actual effect on the functioning of the Internal Market.

A dynamic property law is altogether more suitable in respect of what is happening in the national property law systems of France, Germany, the Netherlands and England. As discussed in the previous Chapter, national property law systems are under increasing pressure from contract law, both from within the system of property law, and from outside the system, in particular from contract law itself, to

[376] See Chapter 7; 2.1. Of Primary Property Rights and Lesser Property Rights.

develop into a more open and flexible, pragmatic, system.[377] Although no one questions the need for limitations on private parties when it comes to the creation of those legal relations that have effect on third parties, and a full limitation through an outright rejection of party autonomy is also not realistic, the balance between these two extremes remains to shift to the side of rejecting party autonomy. At the same time, systems that do not reject the influence of party autonomy, but nevertheless limit the creation of property relations, also adhere to the principle of *numerus clausus*.[378] In legal systems like South Africa, the economy has not collapsed and legal certainty and third-party protection remain assured through the requirement of registration. The publicity principle is thus awarded a more important role in South African law than it is in systems adhering to a rule of *numerus clausus*, which are those systems with a strictly closed list of property rights.[379]

Taking into account these two developments; the increased internal, national, problems the *numerus clausus* system faces from contract law, and the external, international and European, pressure from private international law and European Internal Market law, it is worth considering further development of European property law so that it better fulfils the needs of modern legal practice.[380]

3.4.2. A Limited Open System of Property Relations

A European property law could adhere to a limited open system of property relations. In such a system the fundamental distinction between property rights and personal rights, the law of property and the law of contract, continues to be upheld, but at the same time more responsibility is granted to private parties to opt for a combination of the two areas of law to create new legal relations with third-party effect.[381] At the same time, under a limited open system, parties should not be completely free to give any legal relation third-party effect. As a principle of this system, parties should have an interest in granting third-party effect, not just because it is convenient or to avoid certain other aspects of law, for example the law of succession, from applying. A limited open system of property relations therefore also adheres to the principle of *numerus clausus*. It imposes restrictions on the freedom for private parties to create new property rights.

With such a new approach to property law, the focus of the legal system shifts from a closed system, what parties may not do, to an open system, what parties may do. Nevertheless, at the same time, the system of European property law should strike a balance between flexibility, which implies a pure dynamic system of

377 See Chapter 7; 4. Conclusion: *Numerus Clausus* in Property Law Systems in Europe.

378 See Chapter 7; 1.3.2. *Numerus Clausus* as a Principle or as a Rule?

379 On South African law see Chapter 7; 3.8. A Legal System Without a *Numerus Clausus*: South African law. An example of registration in legal systems adhering to a rule of *numerus clausus* can be seen in Dutch law in case of a silent right of pledge on (future) claims that is only registered to be able to determine when the right of pledge was created in case the right must be executed, not to inform third parties. On this, see Van der Weide 2006, p. 67-68.

380 For similar conclusions see, *inter alia*, Van Erp 2003b, Sagaert 2005b, Smits 1996.

381 On this distinction, see Reid 1997b, p. 444.

property law, and legal certainty, which implies a pure static system of property law.[382]

When the focus of a system of property rights is more directed towards the possibilities parties have to create new rights, inspiration can be drawn from those systems that already adhere to this model. South African law provides an opportunity to see the effects of a limited open system of property rights.[383] The system of property law in South Africa starts with the traditional set of property rights following from Roman-Dutch law. These include a primary right, in the case of South African law, the right of ownership, lesser rights to use of servitude and usufruct, and lesser rights for security of pledge and hypothec. Under the famous 'subtraction from the *dominium* test', which was discussed in the previous Chapter, new lesser property rights in respect of immovable objects have been created when it was the intention of the parties to bind not only themselves but also their successors in title and when the right that results constituted a subtraction from the right of ownership. When this two-stage test is fulfilled, the new lesser right in respect to an immovable object can be registered under Section 63(1) of the Deed Registries Act 1937.

In many aspects, South African law fulfils the requirements for a limited open system of property rights needed in Europe. It limits the possibilities for private parties to create new property rights in two ways. First, it must be the expressed intention of the parties to bind successors in title, third parties, and second, the right the parties seek to create must be able to be expressed in terms of a subtraction from the primary right of ownership. In South African law, therefore, a lesser right can never comprise more than the primary right from which it is derived. As was dealt with in Chapter 7, the requirement of subtraction itself represents a limitation on party autonomy.[384] However, the effects of the subtraction test have led to situations of unpredictability, demonstrating its failure in respect of legal certainty so badly needed in the field of property law.[385] Many have, therefore, both from within and from outside South Africa, criticised the subtraction test for leading to unpredictable results.[386]

Criticism does not mean the test should be abandoned altogether. South African law continues to adhere to its principles. Systems adhering to a closed system of property rights are also under criticism. As a rule it could be held that the more strict a system is, the more criticism it invokes from those seeking more flexibility. Consequently, the less strictly the system is applied, the more criticism it invokes from those seeking more legal certainty.

382 In the words of Reid, 'certainty and rigidity are familiar companions', Reid 1997b, p. 445.

383 On South African law see Chapter 7; 3.8. A Legal System Without a *Numerus Clausus*: South African law.

384 See Chapter 7; 2.2. Of Ways to Create a Lesser Property Right.

385 E.g., *Pearly Beach Trust v Registrar of Deeds* 1990 (4) SA 614 (C), at 615B-C *per* King J.

386 See, e.g., De Waal 2000, De Waal 2004, Van der Walt 1992, Sonnekus 1991, Badenhorst 2000, Badenhorst 2001, but also Reid 1997b, p. 228-229.

3.4.3. Formulating the Access Test

Possibly, a fine-tuning of the subtraction from *dominium* test by adapting it to the European circumstances, specifically based on comparative analysis made in Chapter 7, could provide inspiration for a *numerus clausus* in European property law. Such a solution will not answer all questions in respect of European property law, but could provide a solid basis for discussion. In any case, it will bring the discussion on principles of property law to a European level and will offer one possible solution in which the principle of *numerus clausus* as a principle of European property law can be expressed.

When the South African subtraction test and the experiences with that test are used as an example for Europe, some changes are necessary to increase the predictability of its outcome. As was seen in the discussion on South African law in the previous Chapter, changing the order in which the test is applied by bringing the focus onto the objective element, the subtraction from the primary right, could offer a better, and especially more predictable, solution.[387] Such a test would allow the courts to look at the content of the lesser right first, before deciding if any third-party effect should be awarded through registration. When a lesser right cannot be formulated in terms of powers contained in the primary right from which it is supposed to be derived, the intention of the parties is no longer needed. When, however, such a lesser right can be brought under the powers contained in the primary right, it is up to the parties if they wish to provide third-party effect. In other words, if the parties have expressed and shown a sufficient interest in creating third-party effect, it can be granted. The focus of the European test should therefore be on the objective part, which suits property law best as it offers a strong element of predictability. However, the content of the objective test could also be made the subject of fine-tuning in order to achieve even more predictable results.

When the subtraction test is taken as a basis, the European system is immediately confronted with a choice between the *démembrement*, or subtraction, model and the limitation models as set out in Chapter 7.[388] Although a choice does not necessarily have to be made, subtraction could be interpreted in a broad sense as including both methods of creating lesser property rights, making an explicit choice will enhance the predictability of the outcome of the test. When looking at the current developments in European property law, in particular, the Commission's proposals for a Euro-mortgage, a non-accessory type of lesser security right in respect of immovables based on lesser property rights originating in a system adhering to the limitations method, it seems that the Commission has already, although implicitly, made a choice.[389] When indeed a lesser property right is introduced which limits the primary right and which can be held by the same person holding the primary right, such as the German owner-*Grundschuld* or *Eigentümergrundschuld*, the

387 See Badenhorst 2000, p. 512. See Chapter 7; 3.8. A Legal System Without a *Numerus Clausus*: South African law.

388 See Chapter 7; 2.2. Of Ways to Create a Lesser Property Right.

389 See above; 2.1.3. European Commission Initiatives for Future Legislation.

limitation model must be followed.[390] Furthermore, it seems, when looking at the contents of the list of property rights in systems adhering to a limitations method - German law and English law in respect of equity - that especially these systems have succeeded to some extent in developing new property rights under pressure from contract law. A more dynamic property law therefore seems better served by the limitations method.

Therefore, reformulating the very first requirement of the subtraction test to the requirement that the legal relation created must be able to be expressed in terms of rights or powers of the holder of the primary right, would offer flexibility to follow the limitation model. However, the concept of subtraction would no longer cover the test. Instead, looking at the test from a functional point of view, as the test that grants legal relations access to the law of property, could result in naming it the access test. The link to the primary property right remains of relevance as many criteria contained in the test follow from the requirements of a primary right. When, for example, a primary right cannot be held on a certain object, for example, the human body, no lesser right can be created on that human body either. In order to avoid confusion, a second part of the access test could therefore be that the legal relation must be made with regard to an object capable of being subject to property law. This nuance will give more power to the courts applying the access test in deciding on the matter of whether a property right should be recognised or whether there are serious objections to its recognition. By withholding the effect of a primary right in respect of a certain object, no lesser property rights in respect of such an object can be created either.

To summarise, the first step of the access test would consist of two parts. The first part would require examining whether a legal relation entered into by the parties can be expressed in terms of rights of the holder of a primary right. The second part would require examining whether a legal relation can be held in respect to the object in question.

As a second step, the intention of the parties should be examined. In this second phase of the European access test, the courts could examine whether the parties have a sufficient interest to create a legal relation with third-party effect. A sufficient interest exists when the party agreement is not made for fraudulent purposes, and the court can understand why parties would desire a third-party effect. For example, in the case of a simple contract of sale of an object there is no need to provide for eternal third-party effect and the court should not allow this. This second part, which acknowledges the role of contract law, is therefore more of a subjective nature.

When the court is satisfied that the parties have indeed validly expressed their interest in granting third-party effect, a third additional element to the access test could be the attempt of the court to characterise the property right in terms of the already existing categories of property relations.[391] When, for example, two parties draft a document including terms in which one party has the right to walk over the

390 See Chapter 4; 3.7. Hypothec, and 3.8. *Grundschuld*.

391 In the same sense, see Reid 1997b, p. 445.

other party's land, in exchange for a yearly sum of money, and the parties have expressed that this right as well as the duty to pay money should remain connected to the land with which the right runs, the court must acknowledge the document as validly creating a property relation and try to categorise it in terms of a lesser right of use, in particular, of servitude.

The categories of lesser rights should be examined in the third phase of the test and should allow more legal certainty in respect of the exact nature of the property relation. As a starting point, a European property law could work with the existing categories of lesser rights to use, for security and in anticipation of the acquisition of another property right, be it a primary or another lesser right.[392]

Under the access test, which is the expression of a limited open system of property relations, adding a new category of property relations would be possible. Creating the requirement for a court to deal explicitly with the category of property relations in the third phase of the test will require that court to deal explicitly with a new category of lesser property rights. Accepting a new property relation will require a weighing of the balance between more flexibility and maintaining legal certainty. Allowing a new category of property rights would, as suggested by Van der Walt, become a matter of public policy.[393]

As a result of the test, the filtering function of the *numerus clausus* decides that property law applies. The result of the test, however, is not necessarily application of European property law legislation. Depending on the legal relation in question, the characterisation and categorisation of the legal relation will usually lead to the applicability of national law. Only in cases where the European legislature has acted, which implies it has had the competence to act, will European property law legislation be applicable. In this respect, the test is of a somewhat procedural character. It is the European principle of *numerus clausus* that decides whether the applicable property law is EU law or national law, but the test does not decide on the content of that law. The *numerus clausus* test only decides that a legal relation has third-party effect and shall be governed by property law. When the European legislature has chosen to harmonise a certain area of property law, the applicable law will be Community law and, under the principle of precedence of Community law, it will apply throughout the EU.[394]

The access test is also functional in its categorisation of rights as primary and lesser rights. As the comparative analysis in Chapter 7 shows, it is possible to express the property law systems of France, Germany, the Netherlands and England in terms of these rights. Using functional categorisations offers some advantages. For instance, by requiring a lesser right to be expressed in terms of a primary right, the system of European property law for now does not have to choose between ownership and title, either to land or to personalty. When a property relation from England is brought under the test, the courts can look at that right in terms of

392 On these categories, see also Reid 1997b,p. 228. On this distinction, see Chapter 7; 2. The Content of Property Law Systems in Europe.

393 Van der Walt 1992, p. 197-200, 202-203.

394 Case 6/64 *Faminio Costa v ENEL* [1964] 585.

English law. Consequently, the primary right will not be ownership but one of the English primary rights, depending on the content of the lesser right.

The courts could do this and at the same time maintain the access test, because comparative analysis shows that, although there are differences between ownership and title as primary rights, these rights, in terms of their function as primary rights, are similar.[395] Expressing an easement in terms of a fee simple, or expressing a right of servitude in terms of ownership will not lead to changes in categorisation of easements and servitudes as lesser rights.

Finally, although not as such part of the test, but together with its implementation, parties should be given the possibility of approaching a court to terminate their legal relation when such a relation becomes too much of a burden, or when, in terms of Sagaert's suggestions, the right no longer fulfils its purpose, is no longer used, can no longer be used, or its use would be unreasonable.[396] Allowing the possibility to terminate a property relation allows for more flexibility in deciding on the third-party effect by way of a test. As a result, the doctrinal argument that a property right lasts forever and that therefore we should be very careful in deciding which legal relations have this effect, is removed in some, undesirable, aspects.

Schematically, *numerus clausus* in a system of European property law could be formulated as an access test, which, in case of problems or uncertainties, a court applies to see whether a certain legal relation constitutes a property relation:

1. Phase I - Objective Part
   (a) Can a legal relation in respect of an object be expressed in terms of competences contained in the primary right?
   (b) Is the object with respect to which the legal relation is created capable of being subject to a property relation?
2. Phase II - Subjective Part
   (a) Do the parties have a sufficient interest to provide third-party effect to their legal relation?
   (b) Have the parties sufficiently expressed their intention to provide third-party effect?
3. Phase III - Characterisation
   Can the legal relation be fitted into one of the categories of property rights?
   If not, what new category does the right belong to? (public policy)
   Result: (European) property law applies.

3.4.4. Advantages of an Access Test and a Limited Open System of Property Rights

Using the access test combines elements of national property law doctrine into what could possibly be a workable system. While *numerus clausus* is about filtering legal relations to decide whether property law applies, this test offers guidance on how to do so. While *numerus clausus* is about deciding which property relation is involved and which rules apply, the test also provides an answer. In that respect, the German

[395] See Chapter 7; 2.3. Primary Property Rights.

[396] Sagaert 2005b, p. 1079-1080. See also Heyman 2003, p. 23. On Sagaert's ideas, see Chapter 7; 3.7. Smits and Sagaert: Property Law as a System of Obligations.

concepts of *Typenzwang* and *Typenfixierung* can be recalled.[397] As a part of the principle of *numerus clausus*, the legal system decides on how the legal relation is characterised and which requirements this legal relation must fulfil. The European access test decides on the question of whether property law applies, and through categorising of the legal relation provides guidance as to which property law rules apply. When, for example, a right of way is concerned, the property law on servitudes can apply. When a property security right is concerned, provisions on security rights can apply.

The advantage of this system is that it will transfer the competence to decide if property law applies to a European level. Although this transfer of competence takes away powers from the Member States, it may help avoid a conflict between national doctrinal systems under the principle of mutual recognition and the case law of the European Court of Justice. It can therefore no longer be that in one Member State a legal relation does not have third-party effect, while it does in another Member State. A European principle of *numerus clausus* would enable European property law to decide on what legal relation is a property right and which property law provisions apply. As stated above, these provisions of property law are not necessarily of European law. Insofar as there is no need to provide European rules, national property law may apply as a result of the test. The principle of subsidiarity as contained in Article 5 EC Treaty, and the judgment of the European Court of Justice in the *Tobacco Advertising* case, therefore would remain strongly upheld in this system of reasoning.[398] The balance between taking away competences from the Member States and providing legal certainty on the status of legal relations as property rights or personal rights, should shift to the European Union while taking into account the further competences to frame property law by the Member States as much as possible.

As an advantage, because the fundamental question of what is property relation has become an issue of Community law under this test, the ECJ becomes the highest interpretative authority. However, this would not place the national legal systems on the side at all. National courts are also courts of European law and must apply Community law, but when a difficult case on the interpretation of Community law, in this case most likely the adding of a new category of property rights comes along, the ECJ will have the final say.[399] In matters of substantive national property law the national supreme courts would remain the highest authority. However, already under the current situation, national property law is subject to

397 On these concepts of *Typenfixierung* and *Typenzwang*, see Chapter 1; 1.2.2. *Numerus Clausus* of Property Rights.

398 In the new Treaty the principle of subsidiarity will return as Art. 5 EU. On the *Tobacco* case see above; 2.1.1. Legal Framework: Primary Community Law. On subsidiarity in respect to property law, especially land law, see Sparkes 2007, p. 118-120.

399 Case 26/62 *Van Gend & Loos (NV Algemene Transport- en Expeditie Onderneming) v Nederlandse Administratie der Belastingen* [1963] ECR 1, Case 6/64 *Costa v ENEL* [1964] ECR 585, Claes 2004, p. 51 *et seq*. Moreover, in respect to the completion of the Common Frame of Reference (CFR) there is now also a coherent body of principles and rules that will enable the ECJ to interpret national law in conformity with this new standard. On this idea specifically, see Basedow 2007, p. 184-185.

the rules on the Internal Market and therefore even national courts must accept the binding judgments of the ECJ on the interpretation of national law in the light of European law.[400]

In terms of substantive property law, what exactly is the primary right from which a lesser right under this access test is derived, can be, at least for the moment, left to the legal systems of the Member States. Under Article 295 EC Treaty, Member States remain free to create their own rules on property law. However, as a principle of property law following from the approach taken by *numerus clausus* as an access test, it follows that a legal system should recognise only one primary right per set of property law rules.[401]

The system of *numerus clausus* as a test in European property law offers an *ex post* decision model as opposed to the currently recognised *ex ante* decision models. In other words, only after the legal relation has been created will the system of property law decide on the property effect. Traditionally, *ex ante* models mean that only when certain criteria are fulfilled can a property relation come into existence. The great advantage of an *ex post* system is that it offers more flexibility and that only in cases where something goes wrong with the characterisation of the right, does the test need to be invoked. Moving towards an *ex post* model would require some alterations to the national systems of property law, but not too many alterations. The creation of property rights has, under the test, become partly a matter of Community law, especially the decision whether a legal relation is a property right or not. However, the remaining rules on its existence and the rules on its exercise and, partly, its destruction, continue to belong to national property law, at least until Community legislation in that field is passed.

A further advantage offered through the use of a test is that it could be a way to avoid the stacking of property rights. In particular in civil law systems property rights are sometimes created on top of each other to reach a desired solution. For example, ownership of a building is split from the ownership of the land through a lesser right of *superficies* and the right of *superficies* is subsequently divided into apartment rights. Instead, parties could attempt to create an apartment right in a building, but not in the land, directly. Although the result of the test might be more variations of property rights, it would be more clear which primary right is burdened in which way by which lesser rights. Solutions of up to three to five property rights stacked on top of each other could belong to the past.

A final advantage is that the access test offers a model on which the system of European property law could be built. By allowing the courts, or legislators, to recognise new property rights as a matter of public policy, the development of the dynamic system of property law is ensured. At the same time, however, the development of property law can also be carefully guarded as only the legislature and the ECJ, as the highest court in this matter, will have the power to authorise new categories of property rights. A new category of rights, such as anticipatory rights,

400 See, in this respect, *inter alia*, the critical remarks by Baroness Hale of Richmont in *Kola (FC) and another (FC) (Appellants) v Secretary of State for Work and Pensions (Respondent)* [2007] UKHL 54, at 149 *per* Baroness Hale of Richmont.

401 On Art. 295 EC, see above; 2.4.1. Article 295 EC Treaty and European Property Law.

will therefore be closely examined before it will be recognised as allowing legal relations with third-party effect.

3.4.5. Possible Objections to an Access Test and to a Limited Open System of Property Rights

Of course there can be objections towards a limited open system as well as a *numerus clausus* by way of an access test. Especially in the light of arguments used at a national doctrinal level, some objections can be answered immediately with counter-arguments.

A first possible objection could be that a test that requires a legal relation just to be expressed in terms of a primary right, but which does not require the lesser right to comprise parts of the primary right, may not prevent the creation of a positive burden. According to many national doctrinal arguments, positive burdens are considered undesirable, as in particular the experiences under the *ancien régime* before the French Revolution.[402] Furthermore, in the systems adhering to a *démembrement* method for the creation of lesser rights, the argument is used that because a lesser rights comprises part of the more extensive primary right, and such a right does not contain positive duties, a lesser right cannot contain a positive duty.

Such an argument against the test would not hold automatically as even legal systems that do recognise the method of limitation, such as German law, do not recognise positive burdens. However, it is correct that in a system adhering to the limitations model, positive burdens can be accepted more easily than in a system adhering to the *démembrement* or subtraction model.[403] Accepting positive burdens is a matter of public policy, which also under the test, for now, is a matter for the Member States.

Moreover, even when positive burdens are recognised, there are other ways of preventing the unnecessary consequences of long-lasting positive burdens. The suggestion that a party could approach a court and ask for a relief from the burden could provide a sufficient solution.[404] Furthermore, a requirement to re-evaluate the burden every few years and allowing a decision on its continuation to be made by the parties, could also provide a less disproportionate solution than an outright prohibition.

The acceptance of a positive burden will depend on the circumstances of the case, which is exactly why an approach using a test can provide much more protection than a simple prohibition. In respect of the outright prohibition of a positive duty in the field of servitudes, German law has shown that an effective use of contract law creates a *de facto* positive burden with the recognition of security-servitudes.[405] Even worse, these positive burdens in the case of security-servitudes are usually secret in respect of third parties. In a test approach, more circumstances can

402 On the idea of allowing a positive burden in the law of property, see Reid 1997b, p. 445.

403 Also here possibly German law could offer illustration with the recognition of the Real Burden or *Reallast*.

404 In the same sense, see Heyman 2003, p. 23.

405 See Chapter 4; 3.1. Real Servitudes.

be taken into account and it is not automatically said that security-servitudes will be denied access to property law. In particular because the content of the contracts underlying these security-servitudes will also be subject to rules on competition law, either national or EU competition law, which provide protection to the original as well as third parties. When the courts look at the intention of the parties these questions can be taken into account.

A further objection of civil lawyers might be that there is no longer a statute that contains the list of available property rights and that the available menu will depend on court decisions. However, reliance on court decisions, especially of the ECJ, is necessary in many areas of law. The case law on the free movement of goods offers a good example. In English law, too, although Section 1 of the Law of Property Act 1925 mentions most property relations, English lawyers continue to rely on court decisions in respect of relations not mentioned by the Law of Property Act 1925, as well as in respect of the content of property relations.[406]

Another objection could be that this test does not provide for registration of lesser property rights, in particular not when immovable objects are concerned. However, this possible objection does not take into account the function of the principle of *numerus clausus*. When through the application of *numerus clausus* the decision is made that the law of property applies to a certain legal relation, the other principles of property law, including the principle of publicity, will start to apply.[407] When, as a result of the test, the law of property does not apply, no registration is necessary, as the legal relation will not have third-party effect. Registration is not a question of *numerus clausus*, but of publicity. Registration of lesser rights in respect of immovable objects is a matter of national property law, or, in case of harmonisation of registration systems in Europe, of substantive Community law.[408]

A final objection might be that an open system would create an impenetrable forest, or a web of property relations, in which no one could recognise the content of rights anymore, or to whom they belong.[409] Two arguments can be put forward against this. First, in those legal systems that openly do not recognise a rule of *numerus clausus*, such as South African law, such an outbreak of rights has not occurred. Only in exceptional circumstances, even with a test of which the outcome could not always be predicted, have new property rights been created.[410]

Second, Law and Economics, especially the theory on the optimal standardisation of property rights, but also the theories on the tragedy of the commons and of the anti-commons, explain why this effect does not happen. When too many property rights exist, the information costs of finding out about the existence of all available property law will outweigh the benefits of the creation of an as yet unknown

406 On the English approach, see Chapter 6; 1. Introduction.

407 See Van Erp 2006b, p. 14-17.

408 See Cámara-Lapuente 2005, p. 797 *et seq*. On the European Land Information Service (EULIS) - project, which links land registration systems in Europe see <http://www.eulis.org>.

409 Cf., the rich forest of property rights that according to Heck existed before the introduction of the German BGB. See Heck 1930, p. 85.

410 The same applies for other jurisdiction with a rule of *numerus apertus*, e.g., Spain. See Fulgencia Angosto Sáez 2006, p. 281 *et seq*.

property right.[411] As a result there will be a standardisation of property rights, leading to the opposite of an impenetrable forest of property rights.

4. Conclusions

The making of European property law by which, at a Community level, the principle of *numerus clausus* is expressed through a test, or, stated differently, as an access test to property law, could provide a way forward. When the criteria of test have been fulfilled at a Community level, a legal relation created by two private parties will be a property relation and subsequently it will be governed by property law. Depending on the situation and on the state of harmonisation of property law in the European Union, the applicable property law will be national law, especially when there is no Community dimension or when no Community law has been drafted, or has not yet been drafted. Alternatively, the applicable law will be EU law, in which case an actual and substantial hindrance to the functioning of the Internal Market, under the ECJ's case law and following the principle of subsidiarity, has been proven.

Such a test, however, should not just be arbitrarily applied, but should be carefully drafted. After all, the principle of *numerus clausus* safeguards the law of property. As Reid suggests:

> 'Modern life, and more especially modern commercial life, may make demands which the traditional categories find difficult to meet. For example, there may be a need for positive obligations which bind successive owners of land, or for preferential rights for purchasers who have paid for property without having received ownership. If the traditional categories are to survive, they may require to be adapted.
> ..., any adoption or innovation must work as far as possible within the traditional categories. The alternative is structural incoherence, conceptual drift and, if pressed too far, the collapse of the law of property into the law of obligations'.[412]

The European property law access test suggests changing the focus from static property law to dynamic property law where there is more room for party autonomy. In the light of the developments in national property law, as well as in international and European property law, such a change in focus seems justified.

What the test does is maintain the distinction between the law of property and the law of obligations, the law of contract in particular. Furthermore, it upholds the difference between personal and property relations. In other words, it brings fundamental questions of property law to a European level. When carefully applied by the courts of the European Union, and this also includes all national courts, the test could allow property law to move into the twenty-first century as a modern, dynamic, system of property law with respect for the traditions from whence it came in the form of the traditional categories of property rights.

411 See Chapter 7; 3.2.2. *Numerus Clausus* as Optimal Standardisation of Property Rights.
412 Reid 1997b, p. 245.

Numerus clausus is thus a principle of property law that may find expression, as it has done in many civil law systems, in a rule. However, *numerus clausus* can also be adhered to in other ways. As a principle of property law, *numerus clausus* is nothing more than the idea that a system of private law imposes limitations on private parties in their attempts to create new property relations. The principle of *numerus clausus* determines that there is a set of existing property relations and that, once it has been decided that the law of property applies, and not the law of contract, the content of the property relation is governed by that law of property. The principle of *numerus clausus* can therefore not exist without the distinction between the law of property and the law of obligations. When such distinction does not exist, there is no need to determine whether a legal relation is a property right to which property law applies.

Until now, the principle of *numerus clausus* has found expression in a rule created by a legislature, or as a principle of law advocated by a court, depending on the hierarchy of sources in a legal system. When it comes to the further making of European property law, property law in the European Union, applying in all the Member States, the principle of *numerus clausus* might possibly find expression as an access test, using an *ex post* approach to the creation of property relations. Not only the pragmatic nature of European law, but also the increased danger of potential conflicts between the doctrinally internal coherent systems of the Member States, demands an approach different from any approach that has been taken so far.

Using an access test to determine to which law of property, national or European, a legal relation is granted access, could provide a solution to avoid Europeanisation of national property law where this is not, or not yet, necessary. With that development the principle of *numerus clausus* would become the first true principle of European property law.

SUMMARY

Numerus clausus is a fundamental principle of property law. It is the principle that is strongly connected to the distinction between the law of obligations, in particular, contract law, and the law of property. Moreover, it is connected to the distinction between personal relations and property relations. A personal relation is a relation between two or more persons that only binds the parties to that legal relation. The law of obligations governs this type of relation. A property relation is a relation between two or more persons in respect to an object with third-party effect. The law of property governs this type of relation. *Numerus clausus* as a fundamental principle of property law decides on which legal relation belongs to the law of property, and is therefore awarded third-party effect. *Numerus clausus* is, in other words, the access test to the law of property. Only after the *numerus clausus* test is passed, other principles of property law, such as specificity and publicity, begin to apply.

The *numerus clausus* as an access test comprises of two parts. First, the principle of *numerus clausus* sets the available menu of property rights. Only a limited number of property rights are recognised. In French, German, Dutch and English law, the catalogue of property rights starts with a primary right. Moreover, there are a limited number of property rights other than the primary right, which can be named lesser rights. In respect to the creation of these rights, the principle of *numerus clausus* limits private parties in the creation of these lesser rights. There is, in other words, a *Typenzwang* of property rights.

The second part of the access test concerns the content of property rights. Once parties have selected a property relation from the available menu, the system of property law also determines the content of this property relation. Private parties are not free to give content to their property relation outside the freedom to do this that is allowed by the system of property law. In other words, there is also a *Typenfixierung* of property rights.

Numerus clausus as a principle of property law finds expression in French, German, Dutch and English law, but to different degrees. Depending on the hierarchy of sources of law and the doctrinal choices legislatures in a legal system have made, there is a *rule* of *numerus clausus*. A rule of *numerus clausus* exists if there is an absolutely limited list of property rights. Private parties have no freedom to create new types of property rights at all in these systems, and are only granted limited freedom under the rule of *numerus clausus* to provide content to existing types of property relations.

Other systems adhere to a *principle* of *numerus clausus*. The principle of *numerus clausus* refers to the idea that there is a more or less clear set of property rights established by one or more sources of law, but parties are nevertheless limited in the free creation of new, thus far unrecognised, types of property rights. These systems also impose limitations on parties in respect to the content of property rights. When parties create an already recognised property relation, they must stick to the boundaries set for this relation by the legal system.

When the rule of *numerus clausus* and the principle of *numerus clausus* are seen as two ends of the same spectrum, French, German, Dutch and English law all find there place in this system of classification. German law, with its pandectist origin, is at the most rigid side (that of the rule of *numerus clausus*). Dutch law, having been strongly influenced by German law also finds itself on the more rigid side of the spectrum. French law takes a much more pragmatic approach to the creation of property rights. It is therefore in between adhering to a rule and a principle of *numerus clausus*. English law, finally, adheres to a principle of *numerus clausus* that is, contrary to the civil law systems, clearly formulated by case law.

With the start of the twenty-first century, property law is subject to various new developments. These developments form a pressure on the currently existing systems of property law. This includes pressure to recognise new objects of property law, a stronger influence of contract law in the law of property, and pressure to recognise new, yet unknown, types of property rights.

All four legal systems adhere to a similar classification of property rights. In each system of property law, there is a primary right. In civil law systems, this is the right of ownership. In English law, which recognises two systems of property law, there are two primary rights. In land law this is the fee simple, in personal property law it is title to chattels. Connected to the recognition of a single primary right, in each of the legal systems there is a limited list of property rights other than the primary right. These rights are lesser rights, as they are lesser in content than the primary right. They are created either through a *démembrement*, or subtraction, of powers contained in the primary right in the form of a lesser property right, or through a limitation of the primary right by the creation of a lesser right that is modelled to the content of the primary right. There is a subtle difference in the two methods of creation.

In the civil law systems, the number and content of lesser property rights can mostly be directly derived from Roman law. Although property law systems have developed since (pre-) classical Roman law, the main property rights have remained the same. Only in the last century, some legal systems have added new types of property right to the Roman law inspired catalogue. English property law, although it should be considered not to share a basis in Roman law, recognises a similar list of property rights. However, because of this different historical development, the list of property rights in English law is slightly longer than in most civil law systems.

In French, German, Dutch and English law, lesser rights are organised in two main categories: lesser rights to use and lesser rights for security. Lesser rights to use exist either for a long duration of time, which usually results in a more limited content of the right, or they exist for a short period of time, which usually results in a more extensive content of the right. In civil law systems these lesser rights to use for a longer period are rights of servitude. Lesser rights to use for a shorter period of time are rights of usufruct. In English law there are easements and profits à prendre that fulfil the same requirements. Moreover, an estate for life, a right for a shorter period of time, does no longer exist as a distinct property right, but can be created by making use of trust law.

Lesser rights for security are usually divided depending on the type of object they can be created on. Lesser rights on movables include rights of pledge in civil law systems and rights of pledge and charges in English law. Lesser rights for security on immovables are rights of hypothec in the civil law and mortgage in English law. Although there are variations in the content of these rights, they grant the holder of the lesser right for security a right to sell the object under security, the right to satisfy their claim from the proceeds of that sale, and the right of preference in case of insolvency of the debtor.

The characterisation in primary rights and lesser rights to use and for security is a division that was mainly developed historically since the period of Roman law, which adhered to a similar division in real actions. Also in English law, the distinction between rights to use and rights for security is a historical one. Apart from this general characterisation, also due to historical development and due to different doctrinal choices that legal systems have made, there are additional property rights that not fit this general characterisation.

Examples of additional property rights that do not fit these classical distinctions are German acquisition rights, French real suretyships and English estate contacts. Moreover, also options to purchase, recognised by both German and English law create problems. The right of lease, which, in civil law systems remains a personal right, but in English law has developed into a property relation, offers a final example. The recognition of these additional types of property rights seems linked to the method of creation of property rights that is followed in a legal systems. Systems adhering to a limitation method have recognised more additional property rights than systems adhering to the subtraction method.

In addition, the law of property is subject to influences, both from within the own legal system as well as from the increasing development of the Internal Market in the European Union. These developments lead to a different use of already existing property rights as well as the recognition of new types of property rights, either through positive harmonisation, or, through the recognition of property rights validly created in another Member State under the case law of the European Court of Justice.

Influences from within the own legal system include developments from within the system of property law, but also the increased influence of the law of contract in the law of property. Mainly due to changes in society and the increasing demand for a more flexible property law, parties attempt to create property rights on top of other property rights, the so-called stacking of rights, to achieve a situation that a single property right cannot achieve. Examples of such stacking include a right of apartment on a right of *superficies* to separate the right of ownership from a building from the right of ownership of land, in order to be able to divide the ownership of the building into apartment rights.

Other influences include the increased influence of contract law in the law of property. Especially regarding security rights, the law of contract has become more and more important. Through the recognition of trust-like relations such as *Treuhand* and *fiducie*, the use of a primary right for security purposes has become much more attractive. Also in English law, the possibility to give shape and content to a charge by agreement between the parties creates many possibilities for parties in legal practice.

Traditionally, the law of property is a system of mandatory rules that cannot be deviated from by the law of contract. Contract law is considered an area of law from which the law of property is separated. Traditional property law is therefore a static area of law in which there is relatively little, or at least limited, party autonomy. Due to the influence of contract law property law becomes much more dynamic.

Examples of this are the recognition of subsidiary legal obligations that arise in German law between the holder of a primary right and the holder of a limited property right by operation of law. Through developments in case law it has become accepted that parties may provide new and additional content to these legal relations. Another example includes the German security-servitudes, in which a contract is made to create a *de facto* positive burden next to a negatively formulated right of servitude.

The second group of influences comes from outside the own legal system. The European Union is increasingly also becoming active in the field of property law. This does not only include already existing European legislation in the area of retention of title, insolvency, emission rights, the protection of cultural objects, and financial collateral arrangements, but also developments in the work on a Common Frame of Reference that will possibly include rules on personal property security rights, systems of transfer, and trusts.

Moreover, the property law systems of the Member States are increasingly confronted with property rights originating in another Member State. Through the operation of the rules on private international law in the national law of the Member States, in particular the *lex rei sitae* rule, the national menu of property relations becomes applicable to the recognition of foreign property rights. As a result, a property right created in another Member State may not fit in the national list, because of a different historical development or a different doctrinal choice made by the original Member State. In this respect, *numerus clausus* shows a different face: it protects the national legal system.

When the law of property is seen as a set of rules that have an effect on trade in the Internal Market of the European Union, in particular rules that have an effect on the free movement of goods, it could very well be that through a court decision by the European Court of Justice Member States become forced to recognise a property right validly created in another Member State. Member States may try to justify their refusal to recognise or limited recognition by offering grounds for justification and by showing their measure is proportional to the aim that is pursued. As a justification against recognition of foreign property rights, Member

States may try to invoke their national sovereignty to deal with property rights in order to protect third parties, especially creditors. Moreover, they may argue for the national coherence of the legal system. Whether these grounds for justification will be accepted remains questionable. Moreover, even when these justifications are accepted, whether the measures the Member State has taken will pass the proportionality test remains to be seen.

When, through a decision of the ECJ, property rights from other Member States must be recognised, a federation of property law systems arises. The national systems of property law will then no longer be closed, but will, at least, be open to property rights from the lists of other Member States. Such a development might lead to more legal uncertainty that it seeks to solve.

Property law, in other words, is becoming an increasingly dynamic area of law. However, the current European systems of property law are all formed and designed as static areas of property law. Therefore, the need to rethink the traditional elements of property law, including especially the way in which the principle of *numerus clausus* is adhered to, arises.

It could be necessary to rethink *numerus clausus* in the light of the development of, or the making of, a European property law. In a system of European property law two fundamental questions would have to be answered. When a European property law would be formed, should the system adhere to a separation between the law of obligations and the law of property, as well as to a corresponding division in personal and property relations? When this question is answered positively, and that is the second fundamental issue, European law would have to develop rules that make it possible to decide which relations are personal and which a property relations.

The making of a European property law offers possibilities to rethink the structure of the law of property and to allow property law to develop into a more dynamic system of law, in which there is more place for party autonomy. The principle of *numerus clausus* does not oppose party autonomy at all, it merely limits party autonomy in such a way that a balance between legal certainty, which in this case results in rigidity, and flexibility can be found. Even in legal systems that adhere to an open system of property rights, there are limitations on party autonomy in the creation of new property rights. South African law, with its subtraction from *dominium* test, offers an example of one of these systems.

Moreover, law and economic scholars have explained why, even in a system where parties would be completely free to create new types of property rights, no unlimited number of property rights would arise. Either through the prevention of fragmentation, when a tragedy of the commons or of the anti-commons would arise, or through the increase in information costs, either by third parties dealing with property rights or by third parties in general, an optimal standardisation of property rights may result.

A European property law might, possibly, provide expression to the principle of *numerus clausus* by forming an access test. When a legal relation would pass the European access test, that legal relation would become a property relation and will be governed by property law, either national law or, in case there is European legislation, by Community law.

The access test could be formulated in three phases. First, when parties attempt to create a relation, that relation must be expressed in terms of powers contained in the primary right, and the relation must be made in respect to an object that is capable of being subject to that primary right. Secondly, the parties must have expressed their intent to bind not only themselves, but also their successors in title. Parties must have a sufficient interest to do so. Thirdly and finally, as a matter of policy, the relation that is created must be classified in terms of one of the existing categories of property relations: lesser rights to use, lesser rights for security, or anticipatory rights. When the legal relation cannot be expressed in terms of one of these categories, express attention, and this is the policy part, must be paid to the creation of a new, additional category.

The access test of European property law is an *ex post* model that is applied by the courts. Because it would be a test of EU law, all courts in the European Union would have to apply it. Moreover, because the ECJ will have the final interpretation over it, the question of recognition of a new category of property rights would be a subject for the ECJ to decide on through a preliminary ruling.

With this creation of a substantive *ex post* test at a European level, the principle of *numerus clausus* would find new, yet unknown, expression. As a result there will be more legal certainty on the status of property relations throughout the EU. In other words, the principle of *numerus clausus* could become the first true principle of European property law.

SAMENVATTING

Numerus clausus is een fundamenteel beginsel in het goederenrecht. Dit beginsel is sterk verbonden met het onderscheid tussen het verbintenissenrecht, in het bijzonder het contractenrecht, en het goederenrecht. Daarnaast is het beginsel ook sterk verbonden met het onderscheid tussen persoonlijke en goederenrechtelijke rechtsbetrekkingen. Een persoonlijke rechtsbetrekking is een rechtsrelatie die enkel partijen bindt. Deze rechtsbetrekkingen worden beheerst door het verbintenissenrecht. Een goederenrechtelijke rechtsbetrekking is een rechtsrelatie tussen twee of meer personen ten opzichte van een object. Deze relaties hebben derdenwerking. Deze rechtsrelaties worden door het goederenrecht beheerst. Het fundamenteel beginsel van de *numerus clausus* bepaalt welke rechtsbetrekking tot het goederenrecht hoort en daarom derdenwerking heeft. *Numerus clausus* is, met andere woorden, de toegangstest tot het goederenrecht. Pas als de toets van de *numerus clausus* is doorstaan, zijn andere beginselen van goederenrecht, zoals specificiteit en publiciteit van toepassing.

De *numerus clausus* als toegangstest omvat twee delen. Ten eerste stelt het *numerus clausus* beginsel het beschikbare menu van goederenrechtelijke rechten vast. In elk rechtstelsel worden slechts een beperkt aantal goederenrechtelijke rechten erkend. In het Franse, Duitse, Nederlandse en Engelse recht vangt het menu van goederenrechtelijke rechten aan met een 'primair recht'. Naast het primaire recht zijn er een beperkt aantal rechten, welke 'mindere rechten' genoemd kunnen worden. Het is in de vestiging van deze laatste groep rechten dat partijen beperkt worden door het *numerus clausus* beginsel. Er is, met andere woorden een *Typenzwang* van goederenrechtelijke rechten.

Het tweede deel van de toegangstest heeft betrekking op de inhoud van goederenrechtelijke rechten. Wanneer partijen een recht van het menu van beschikbare rechten hebben gekozen, bepaalt het stelsel van goederenrecht ook de inhoud van deze rechtsbetrekking. Het staat partijen niet vrij om inhoud aan hun rechtsbetrekking te geven die buiten de grenzen van het door het goederenrecht aangegeven gebied gaat. Met andere woorden, er is ook een *Typenfixierung* van goederenrechtelijke rechten.

Numerus clausus als beginsel van goederenrecht vindt uitdrukking in het Franse, Duitse, Nederlandse en Engelse recht, zij het in andere mate. Afhankelijk van de hiërarchie van rechtsbronnen en de dogmatische keuzes die wetgevers in de verschillende rechtsstelsels gemaakt hebben, is er een *regel* van *numerus clausus*. Een *numerus clausus* regel bestaat als er een absoluut gesloten stelsel van goederenrechtelijke rechten aanwezig is. In deze stelsels hebben partijen geen vrijheid om nieuwe typen goederenrechtelijke rechten te vestigen en genieten slechts een beperkte, door de *numerus clausus* regel vastgestelde, vrijheid om inhoud aan hun goederenrechtelijke rechtsbetrekkingen te geven.

Andere rechtssystemen erkennen een *beginsel* van *numerus clausus*. Het *numerus clausus* beginsel verwijst naar het idee dat een min of meer duidelijke set van goederenrechtelijke rechten is vastgesteld door middel van één of meer rechtsbronnen, en dat partijen enigszins beperkt zijn om nieuwe, tot op heden onbekende, typen van goederenrechtelijke rechten te vestigen. Deze stelsels leggen ook beperkingen op aan partijen met betrekking tot de inhoud van goederenrechtelijke rechten. Als partijen een reeds erkende goederenrechtelijke rechtsbetrekking kiezen, dienen zij zich te houden aan de grenzen die voor deze rechtsverhouding gelden.

Als de *numerus clausus* regel en het *numerus clausus* beginsel als twee uiteinde van hetzelfde spectrum worden gezien, vinden het Franse, Duitse, Nederlandse en Engelse recht allen een plaatst in dit kwalificatiestelsel. Duits recht, dat zijn oorsprong vindt in het pandektistische systeem, staat aan de meest statische kant (dat van de *numerus clausus* regel). Het Nederlandse recht is sterk beïnvloed door het Duitse recht en kan ook aan de meer statische kant van het spectrum geplaatst worden. Het Franse recht kent een meer pragmatische benadering met betrekking tot het vestigingen van goederenrechtelijke rechten. Het dient daarom geplaatst te worden tussen een stelsel dat de *numerus clausus* regel en het *numerus clausus* beginsel volgt. Het Engelse recht, ten slotte, volgt het *numerus clausus* beginsel dat, anders dan in de *civil law* stelsels, duidelijk door jurisprudentie geformuleerd is.

Met het begin van de 21e eeuw is het goederenrecht onderhevig geworden aan nieuwe ontwikkelingen. Deze ontwikkelingen vragen om nieuwe objecten van goederenrecht te erkennen, om meer invloed van het contractenrecht in het goederenrecht te erkennen, en om nieuwe, tot op heden onbekende, typen van goederenrechtelijke rechten te erkennen.

Zowel het Franse, Duitse, Nederlandse als Engelse recht volgen een vergelijkbare benadering van kwalificatie van goederenrechtelijke rechtsbetrekkingen. In elk stelsel is er een primair recht. In *civil law* systemen is dit het recht van eigendom. In het Engelse recht, dat twee stelsels van goederenrecht kent, zijn er twee primaire rechten. In het onroerende zaken recht (*land law*) is dit de *fee simple*, in het recht met betrekking tot roerende zaken en vorderingen (*personal property law*) is dit de *title to chattels*.

Verbonden aan het erkennen van een enkel primair recht is een lijst van goederenrechtelijke rechten anders dan het primaire recht. Dit zijn de mindere rechten. Deze zijn minder omdat zij minder tot inhoud hebben dan het primaire recht. Deze rechten worden gevestigd door een, met een Franse term uitgedrukt, *démembrement*, of, in het Nederlands, subtractie van bevoegdheden van het primaire recht, of door beperking van het primaire recht met bevoegdheden die gemodelleerd worden naar het primaire recht. Er bestaat een subtiel verschil tussen deze twee vormen van vestiging.

In de *civil law* stelsels is het aantal en de inhoud van de goederenrechtelijke rechten vrijwel geheel geïnspireerd op het Romeinse recht. Hoewel het goederenrecht in ontwikkeling is geweest sinds het (pre-) klassieke Romeinse recht, zijn de belangrijkste goederenrechtelijke rechten hetzelfde gebleven. Pas in de laatste eeuw hebben verschillende rechtsstelsels nieuwe typen van goederenrechtelijke rechten aan de door het Romeinse recht geïnspireerde catalogus toegevoegd. Het Engelse recht, dat niet direct op het Romeinse recht gebaseerd is, erkent een vergelijkbare catalogus van goederenrechtelijke rechten. Echter, door andere historische ontwikkelingen is de lijst met goederenrechtelijke verhoudingen in het Engelse recht langer dan de lijst in de meeste *civil law* stelsels.

In het Franse, Duitse, Nederlandse en Engelse recht worden mindere rechten ingedeeld in twee categorieën: mindere gebruiksrechten en mindere zekerheidsrechten. Mindere gebruiksrechten bestaan voor een lange tijdsperiode en hebben meestal een minder verstrekkende inhoud, of voor een korte tijdsperiode en hebben doorgaans een meer omvattende inhoud. Deze gebruiksrechten voor een langere periode zijn erfdienstbaarheden in de *civil law* stelsels. Gebruiksrechten voor een kortere periode zijn rechten van vruchtgebruik. In het Engelse recht zijn er rechten van *easement* en *profits à prendre* die aan dezelfde kenmerken voldoen. Daarnaast kan, hoewel deze niet meer als zelfstandig recht kan bestaan, een *life estate* via een trustconstructie gerealiseerd worden.

Mindere zekerheidsrechten worden verder verdeeld naar gelang het type van object waarop ze gevestigd kunnen worden. Zekerheidsrechten op roerende zaken zijn rechten van pand in *civil law* stelsels en rechten van *pledge* en *charges* in het Engelse recht. Zekerheidsrechten op onroerende zaken in *civil law* systemen zijn het recht van hypotheek. In het Engelse recht wordt hier het recht van *mortgage* gebruikt. Hoewel er variaties zijn in de inhoud van deze rechten, schenken alle rechten de rechthebbende de bevoegdheid het object dat tot zekerheid is gegeven te verkopen en met de opbrengst van deze verkoop hun vordering te voldoen. Daarnaast geven deze rechten ook een voorrangsrecht in geval van faillissement van de debiteur.

De indeling in primaire en mindere gebruiks- en zekerheidsrechten is een indeling die vanaf de periode van het Romeinse recht, dat ook een vergelijkbare indeling in zakelijke acties aanhing, ontwikkeld is. Ook in het Engelse recht wordt er onderscheid gemaakt tussen gebruiksrechten en zekerheidsrechten. Echter, door de historische ontwikkeling van de verschillende rechtsstelsels en met name ook door de verschillende dogmatische keuzes die de verschillende wetgevers gemaakt hebben, worden ook additionele goederenrechtelijke rechten erkend die niet (goed) in deze indeling passen.

Voorbeelden van deze additionele mindere rechten die niet in het systeem van goederenrechtelijke rechten passen zijn de Duitse verkrijgingrechten, de Franse zakelijke borgtocht en de Engelse *estate contracts*. Daarnaast vallen ook koopopties, erkend als goederenrechtelijke verhouding in zowel Duitsland als Engeland, onder deze voorbeelden die problemen veroorzaken met het goederenrechtelijke stelsel. Tot slot kan het recht van huur, dat in *civil law* stelsels een persoonlijk recht is, maar in het Engelse recht zich tot een goederenrechtelijk recht ontwikkeld heeft, genoemd worden. De erkenning van deze additionele mindere rechten lijkt verband te houden met de methode van vestiging die wordt gevolgd. Stelsels die een methode van beperking aanhouden hebben meer additionele rechten erkend dan stelsels die de subtractie methode volgen.

Het goederenrecht recht is onderhevig aan invloeden van binnen het eigen rechtssysteem, maar ook van daarbuiten. Het gaat dan met name om de invloed die komt door de ontwikkeling van de interne markt in de Europese Unie. Deze ontwikkeling leidt tot een andere toepassing van de reeds bestaande goederenrechtelijke rechtsbetrekkingen, maar ook tot de erkenning van nieuwe typen goederenrechtelijke rechten door positieve harmonisatie, en ook door, onder druk van de rechtspraak van het Europese Hof van Justitie, erkenning van goederenrechtelijke verhoudingen die geldig in een andere lidstaat van de Europese Unie zijn gevestigd.

Binnen het eigen rechtssysteem ondergaat het goederenrecht druk van binnen het stelsel van goederenrecht, maar ook door de toenemende invloed van het contractenrecht in het goederenrecht. Met name door maatschappelijke veranderingen en de stijgende vraag naar meer flexibele goederenrechtelijke verhoudingen, proberen partijen in toenemende mate goederenrechtelijke rechten te combineren, met andere woorden, te stapelen, om zo resultaten te bereiken die voorheen onmogelijk waren met het gebruik van een enkel goederenrechtelijk recht. Een voorbeeld van een dergelijke stapeling is het recht van appartement op een opstalrecht om het eigendomsrecht van een gebouw van het eigendomsrecht van de grond te scheiden, om zo alleen het gebouw in appartementsrechten te kunnen splitsen.

Andere invloeden betreffen de toenemende invloed van het contractenrecht. Met name in verband met zekerheidsrechten is het contractenrecht belangrijker geworden. Door de erkenning van trustachtige verhoudingen als de *Treuhand* en de *Fiducie*, wordt het gebruik van primaire rechten tot zekerheid interessanter. Ook in het Engelse recht biedt de mogelijkheid een *charge* met een partij afspraak vrijwel geheel vorm te geven voor de praktijk interessante mogelijkheden.

Het goederenrecht is van oorsprong een systeem van dwingende regels waarvan niet kan worden afgeweken door het gebruik van het contractenrecht. Het contractenrecht is oorspronkelijk een rechtsgebied waarvan het goederenrecht is afgescheiden. Klassiek goederenrecht is daarom een statisch rechtsgebied waar geen, of althans weinig, partij autonomie wordt getolereerd. Door de toenemende invloed van het contractenrecht wordt het goederenrecht meer dynamisch.

Voorbeelden hiervan zijn de erkenning van de wettelijke verbintenissen tussen de houder van een primair recht en de houder van een minder recht in het Duitse recht. Via de ontwikkeling van deze verbintenissen in de Duitse jurisprudentie is het mogelijk geworden dat partijen zelf additionele inhoud aan deze verhouding geven door het maken van verdere partijafspraken. Een ander voorbeeld wordt geboden door de Duitse dienstbaarheden tot zekerheid, waarbij een contract gemaakt word om een *de facto* positieve plicht te creëren naast een negatief geformuleerde dienstbaarheid.

De tweede groep van invloeden komt van buiten het eigen rechtssysteem. De Europese Unie wordt in toenemende mate actief in het goederenrecht. Het gaat hierbij dan niet alleen om bestaande Europese wetgeving over eigendomsvoorbehoud, insolventie, emissierechten, de bescherming van cultuurgoederen, en finan ciëlezekerheidsovereenkomsten, maar ook om het werk aan het zogenaamde Europese Gemeenschappelijk Referentiekader dat waarschijnlijk regels over zekerheden op roerende zaken, stelsels van overdracht en trustverhoudingen zal bevatten.

Nationale stelsels van goederenrecht in toenemende mate geconfronteerd met goederenrechtelijke rechten die gevestigd zijn in een andere lidstaat. Door de werking van de regels van het internationale privaatrecht in het nationale recht van de lidstaten, met name de *situs*-regel, wordt het nationale menu van goederenrechtelijke rechten van toepassing op de erkenning van buitenlandse goederenrechtelijke rechten. Het resultaat hiervan is dat een goederenrechtelijke verhouding die gecreëerd is in een andere lidstaat niet altijd past in de lijst van de ontvangende lidstaat. De lijst van de ontvangende lidstaat is bepaald door een andere historische ontwikkeling en andere dogmatische keuzes. De *numerus clausus* laat zich zo van een andere kant zien: de bescherming van het nationale recht.

Wanneer het goederenrecht wordt gezien als een set van regels die een effect hebben op de handel tussen lidstaten in de interne markt van de Europese Unie, met name als regels die gevolgen hebben voor het vrij verkeer van goederen, zou het kunnen zijn dat door een beslissing van het Europese Hof van Justitie lidstaten gedwongen worden om buitenlandse goederenrechtelijke rechten te erkenning in hun eigen stelsel. Lidstaten mogen gronden aanvoeren om hun weigering tot erkenning of beperkte erkenning te rechtvaardigen. Daarnaast dienen zij aan te tonen dat de door hen getroffen maatregel proportioneel is ten opzichte van het doel dat de maatregel nastreeft. Lidstaten zouden kunnen proberen om tegen deze erkenning hun nationale bevoegdheden op het gebied van het goederenrecht als rechtvaardiging aan te voeren. Met name als het gaat om derdenbescherming, of bescherming van andere crediteuren, zou dit argument gebruikt kunnen worden. Daarnaast zou een lidstaat kunnen proberen de interne coherentie van het systeem van goederenrecht aan te voeren. Of deze rechtvaardigingsgronden geaccepteerd zullen worden is maar zeer de vraag. Zelfs als deze geaccepteerd worden is het niet zeker dat deze argumentatie de proportionaliteitstest van het Europese Hof van Justitie zal doorstaan.

Als lidstaten, door een beslissing van het Europese Hof van Justitie, gedwongen worden om buitenlandse goederenrechtelijke rechtsverhoudingen te erkennen, ontstaat een federatie van goederenrechtelijke stelsels in Europa. De nationale stelsels van goederenrecht zullen dan niet langer gesloten zijn, maar zullen, ten minste, open zijn voor goederenrechtelijke rechten die voorkomen op de lijst van goederenrechtelijke rechten in andere lidstaten. Een dergelijke ontwikkeling zou wel eens tot meer rechtsonzekerheid kunnen leiden dan het op moet lossen.

Goederenrecht, met andere worden, wordt in toenemende mate een dynamisch rechtsgebied. Echter, de huidige stelsels van goederenrecht in de lidstaten zijn ontwikkeld als een statisch goederenrechtelijk stelsel. Het is daarom nodig om de traditionele uitgangspunten van het goederenrecht te heroverwegen, met name de manier waarop het *numerus clausus* beginsel wordt aangehangen.

Het zou nodig kunnen zijn om de *numerus clausus* te heroverwegen in het licht van de ontwikkeling van een Europees goederenrecht. In een stelsel van Europees goederenrecht zouden twee fundamentele aspecten behandeld moeten worden. Als een Europees goederenrecht gevormd zou worden, zou dit stelsel moeten vast houden aan de scheiding tussen het verbintenissenrecht en het goederenrecht en het daarbij behorende onderscheid tussen persoonlijke en goederenrechtelijke rechten? Als deze vraag positief wordt beantwoord, en dat is het tweede aspect, dan zou het Europese goederenrecht regels moeten hebben om te beslissen welke rechtsverhoudingen goederenrechtelijk zijn en welke niet.

De ontwikkeling van een Europees goederenrechten biedt de mogelijkheid de structuur van het goederenrecht te heroverwegen en het goederenrecht tot een meer dynamisch rechtsgebied te maken, waarin er meer plaats zal zijn voor partij autonomie. Het *numerus clausus* beginsel verzet zich zeker niet tegen partij autonomie, de *numerus clausus* regel doet dit wel. Het beginsel beperkt partij autonomie voor zover het nodig is om een juiste balans tussen rechtszekerheid, wat in dit geval tot starheid leidt, en flexibiliteit. Zelfs in rechtsstelsels die een open stelsel van goederenrechtelijke rechten aanhangen zijn er beperkingen voor partijen in de vestiging van nieuwe goederenrechtelijke rechten. Het Zuid-Afrikaanse recht, met de bekende *subtraction from dominium* test, biedt een voorbeeld van een dergelijk stelsel.

Rechtseconomen hebben verklaard waarom, in een stelsel waarin partijen volkomen vrij zijn om nieuwe goederenrechtelijke verhoudingen te creëren, geen oneindig aantal goederenrechtelijke verhoudingen zal ontstaan. Door het voorkomen van te vergaande fragmentatie die een *tragedy of the commons of anti-commons* zou kunnen veroorzaken, of door de toename van informatiekosten voor derden die of met het beperkte recht in aanraking komen, of derden in het algemeen, zou een optimale standaardisatie van goederenrechtelijke rechten het gevolg zijn.

Een Europees goederenrecht zou, wellicht, uiting kunnen geven aan het beginsel van *numerus clausus* via een toegangstest. Wanneer een rechtsverhouding deze voor deze test zou slagen, wordt deze verhouding een goederenrechtelijke verhouding die beheerst wordt door het, nationale goederenrecht of, indien er Europese wetgeving bestaat, het Europese goederenrecht.

Deze toegangstest zou uit drie onderdelen kunnen bestaan. Ten eerste, wanneer partijen proberen een rechtsverhouding te creëren moet deze rechtsverhouding uitgedrukt worden in bevoegdheden die besloten zijn in een primair goederenrechtelijke recht. Daarnaast moet het object waarop ze deze verhouding willen vestigen onderwerp van dat primaire recht kunnen zijn. Ten tweede moeten partijen hun intentie kenbaar maken om niet slechts elkaar, maar ook hun rechtsopvolgers aan deze rechtsverhouding te willen binden. De partijen moeten hier een voldoende belang bij hebben. Ten derde, als een beleidspunt, de verhouding die resulteert moet worden gecategoriseerd als een van de bestaande typen van goederenrechtelijke rechten: mindere rechten tot gebruik, mindere rechten tot zekerheid of verkrijgingrechten. Als de verhouding niet in een van deze categorieën past, en dat is het beleidspunt, dient uitdrukkelijke aandacht besteed te worden aan het maken van een nieuwe, additionele, categorie.

Een dergelijke toegangstest van het Europese goederenrecht zou een *ex post* model kunnen zijn dat door de gerechtshoven en rechtbanken zal moeten worden toegepast. Omdat het een EU rechtelijke test betreft, zal deze door alle gerechtelijke instanties in de Europese Unie toegepast moeten worden. Het Europese Hof van Justitie zal de uiteindelijke interpretatie in handen hebben. De vraag naar de erkenning van een nieuwe categorie van goederenrechtelijke rechten zou dan ook aan het Europese Hof van Justitie moeten worden voorgelegd via een prejustitiële procedure.

Met het maken van deze inhoudelijke *ex post* toegangstest op een Europees niveau zou een nieuwe, tot op heden onbekende, invulling van het *numerus clausus* beginsel gegeven worden. Het resultaat zou meer rechtszekerheid over de status van rechtsbetrekkingen in de Europese Unie moeten zijn. Met andere woorden, met deze ontwikkeling zou het *numerus clausus* beginsel het eerste werkelijke beginsel van Europees goederenrecht worden.

BIBLIOGRAPHY

Aberkane 1957
Aberkane, H., *Essai d'une théorie générale de l'obligation propter rem en droit positif français (diss.)*, 26 Bibliothèque de la Faculté de droit de l'Université d'Alger; Paris: R. Pichon et R. Durand-Auzias 1957.

Achilles, Spahn & Gebhard 1897
Achilles, Spahn & Gebhard, *Protokolle der Kommission für die zweite Lesung des Entwurfs des Bürgerlichen Gesetzbuchs, Band I. Allgemeiner Theil und Recht der Schuldverhältnisse Abschn. I, Abschn. II Tit. I.*, Berlin: J. Guttentag 1897.

Acquis Group 2007
Research Group of the Existing EC Contract Law, Acquis Group (ed.), *Contract I. Pre-Contractual Obligations, Conclusion of Contract, Unfair Terms Principles of Existing EC Contract Law (Acquis Principles)*, München: Sellier European Law Publishers 2007.

Aertsen 2004
Aertsen, D.W., *De Trust – Beschouwingen over invoering van de trust in het Nederlandse recht* (*diss.*) (Onderneming en Recht, 29), Deventer: Kluwer 2004.

Ahrens 2004
Ahrens, C., *Dingliche Nutzungsrechte*, Berlin: Erich Schmidt Verlag 2004.

Aicher 1975
Aicher, J., *Das Eigentum als subjektives Recht. Zugleich ein Beitrag zur Theorie des subjektiven Rechts*, Berlin: Duncker & Humblot 1975.

Akkermans 2006
Akkermans, B., 'The New Dutch Civil Code: The Borderline between Property and Contract', in: S. van Erp & B. Akkermans (eds.), *Towards a Unified System of Land Burdens?* (Ius Commune Europaeum, 59), Antwerp-Oxford: Intersentia 2006, p. 163-183.

Amann 1989
Amann, H., 'Leistungspflichten und Leistungsansprüche aus Dienstbarkeiten. Ein Beitrag zur Lehre vom Begleitschuldverhältnis', *Deutsche Notar-Zeitschrift,* 1989, p. 531-536.

Amann 1993
Amann, H., 'Durchsetzung der Reallast ohne Verlust der Reallast', *Deutsche Notar-Zeitschrift,* 1993, p. 222-232.

Anderson & McChesney 2003
Anderson, T.L. & McChesney, F.S. (eds.), *Property Rights. Cooperation, Conflict, and Law,* Princeton: Princeton University Press 2003.

Ankum & Pool 1989
Ankum, H. & Pool, E., 'The Development of Roman Double Ownership', in: P. Birks (ed.), *New Perspectives in the Roman Law of Property - Essays for Barry Nicholas,* Oxford: Clarendon Press 1989, p. 5-41.

Ankum 1985
Ankum, J.A., 'Le droit Romain classique a-t-il connu un droit de propriété bonitaire relatif?' in: J.A. Ankum, J.E. Spruit & F.B.J. Wubbe (eds.), *Satura Roberto Feenstra sexagesimum quintum annum aetatis complenti ab alumnis collegis amicis oblata, Fribourg*: University Press *Fribourg* 1985, p. 125-139.

Asbreuk-van Os 2000a
Asbreuk-van Os, M.M., 'De regel 'koop breekt geen huur' in wetsvoorstel 26 089 vertoont (verborgen) gebreken', *Weekblad voor Privaatrecht, Notariaat en Registratie,* (6386) 2000, p. 31-35.

Asbreuk-van Os 2000b
Asbreuk-van Os, M.M., 'Naschrift bij Wordt huur een verhandelbaar goed? door prof. mr. J.H.M. van Erp in *WPNR* (6407), 2000', *Weekblad voor Privaatrecht, Notariaat en Registratie,* (6407) 2000, p. 458-459.

Asser, Beekhuis & Davids 1990
Asser, C., Beekhuis, J.H., Davids, W.J.M., Mijnssen, F.H.J. & Van Velten, A., *Zakenrecht 3 - II Eigendom en* beperke *zakelijke genotsrechten,* 12th edition, Mr. C. Asser's handleiding tot de beoefening van het Nederlands burgerlijk recht; Zwolle: W.E.J. Tjeenk Willink 1990.

Asser, Beekhuis & De Haan 1985
Asser, C., Beekhuis, J.H. & De Haan, P., *Zakenrecht 3 - I Algemeen deel,* 12th edition, Mr. C. Asser's handleiding tot de beoefening van het Nederlands burgerlijk recht; Zwolle: W.E.J. Tjeenk Willink 1985.

Asser, Van Dam & Mijnsen 2002
Asser, C., Van Dam, C.C., Mijnssen, F.H.J. & Van Velten, A., *Goederenrecht 3 - II Zakelijke rechten*, 14th edition, Mr. C. Asser's handleiding tot de beoefening van het Nederlands burgerlijk recht; Deventer: Kluwer 2002.

Asser & Hartkamp 2001
Asser, C. & Hartkamp, A., *Verbintenissenrecht 4 - II algemene leer der overeenkomsten*, 11th edition, Mr. C. Asser's handleiding tot de beoefening van het Nederlands burgerlijk recht; Deventer: W.E.J. Tjeenk Willink 2001.

Asser & Maeijer 2000
Asser, C. & Maeijer, J.M.M., *Vertegenwoordiging en rechtspersoon 2 - III De naamloze en de besloten vennootschap*, 2nd edition, Mr. C. Asser's handleiding tot de beoefening van het Nederlands burgerlijk recht; Deventer: W.E.J. Tjeenk Willink 2000.

Asser, Mierlo, Mijnsen & Van Velten 2003
Asser, C., Van Mierlo, A.I.M., Mijnssen, F.H.J. & Van Velten, A.A., *Goederenrecht 3 - III Zekerheidsrechten*, 13th edition, Mr. C. Asser's handleiding tot de beoefening van het Nederlands burgerlijk recht; Deventer: Kluwer 2003.

Asser, Mijnssen & De Haan 2001
Asser, C., Mijnssen, F.H.J. & De Haan, P., *Goederenrecht 3 - I Algemeen Goederenrecht*, 14th edition, Mr. C. Asser's handleiding tot de beoefening van het Nederlands burgerlijk recht; Deventer: W.E.J. Tjeenk Willink 2001.

Asser, Mijnsen, De Haan & Van Dam 2006
Asser, C., Mijnssen, F.H.J., De Haan, P., Van Dam, C. & Ploeger, H.D., *Goederenrecht 3 - I Algemeen Goederenrecht*, 15th edition, Mr. C. Asser's handleiding tot de beoefening van het Nederlands burgerlijk recht; Deventer: Kluwer 2006.

Asser, Mijnsen & Van Velten 1986
Asser, C., Mijnssen, F.H.J. & Van Velten, A., *Zakenrecht 3 - III Zekerheidsrechten*, 11th edition, Mr. C. *Asser's* handleiding tot de beoefening van het Nederlands burgerlijk recht; Zwolle: W.E.J. Tjeenk Willink 1986.

Asser & Perrick 2007
Asser, C. & Perrick, S., *Goederenrecht 3 - IV Gemeenschap*, Mr. C. Asser's handleiding tot de beoefening van het Nederlands burgerlijk recht; Deventer: Kluwer 2007.

Asser & Scholten 1913
Asser, C. & Scholten, P., *2. Zakenrecht*, Mr. C. Asser's handleiding tot de beoefening van het Nederlandsch burgerlijk recht, Zwolle: Tjeenk Willink 1913.

Atias 2005
Atias, C., *Droit Civil - Les Biens*, 8th edition, Paris: Lexis Nexis S.A. 2005.

Atiyah 1979
Atiyah, P.S., *The rise and fall of freedom of contract*, Oxford: Clarendon Press 1979.

Aubry, Rau & Bartin 1935
Aubry, Rau & Bartin, E., *Cours de droit civil français d'après la méthode de Zachariae*, Tome 2, 5th edition, Paris: Librairie Marchal & Billard 1935.

Aubry, Rau & Eismein 1961
Aubry, Rau & Eismein, P., *Droit civil français,* Tome 2, 7th edition, Paris: Librairies Techniques 1961.

Aubry, Rau, Eismein & Ponsard 1968
Aubry, Rau, Eismein, P. & Ponsard, A., *Droit civil français,* Tome 3, 7th edition, Paris: Librairies Techniques 1968.

Aubry, Rau, Falcimaigne & Gault 1897
Aubry, Rau, Falcimaigne, C. & Gault, M., *Cours de droit civil français d'après la méthode de Zachariae,* Tome 2, Paris: Imprimerie et librairie générale de jurisprudence 1897.

Aynès & Crocq 2003
Aynès, L. & Crocq, P., *Les sûretés; la publicité foncière,* Droit Civil; Paris: Defrénois 2003.

Badenhorst 2000
Badenhorst, P.J., 'Registrability of rights in the deeds office', *Tydskrif vir Hedendaagse Romeins-Hollandse Reg*, 2000, p. 509-519.

Badenhorst 2001
Badenhorst, P.J., 'Erroneous omission of real rights from subsequent title deeds', *Obiter*, 2001, p. 190-203.

Badenhorst & Coetser 1991
Badenhorst, P.J. *& Coetser*, P.P.J., 'Pearly Beach Trust v Registrar of Deeds 1990 4 SA 614 (C) - The subtraction from the dominium test revisited', *De Jure*, 1991, p. 375-389.

Badenhorst et al. 2003
Badenhorst, P.J., Pienaar, J.M., Mostert, H. & Van Rooyen, M., *Silderberg and Schoeman's The Law of Property*, 4th edition, Durban: LexisNexis Butterworths 2003.

Baffi 2007
Baffi, E., *The Anticommons and the Problem of the numerus clausus of Property Rights, Università degli Studi Roma Tre* - Faculty of Law - Working Paper, 2007, <http://ssrn.com/abstract=1023153>.

DCFR Interim Outline 2008
Von Bar, C., Clive, E., Schute-Nölke, H., Beale, H., Herre, J., Huet, J., Schlechtriem, P., Storme, M., Swann, S., Varul, P., Veneziano, A. & Zoll, F. (eds.), *Principles, Definitions and Model Rules of European Private Law. Draft Common Frame of Reference (DCFR)*, Interim Outline Edition, München: Sellier European Law Publishers 2008.

Von Bar & Drobnig 2002
Von Bar, C. & Drobnig, U., *Study on Property Law and Non-contractual Liability Law as they relate to Contract Law*, <http://europa.eu.int/comm/consumers/cons_int/safe_shop/fair_bus_pract/cont_law/study.pdf, 2002>.

Barnard 2007
Barnard, C., *The Substantive Law of the EU. The Four Freedoms*, 2nd edition, Oxford: Oxford University Press 2007.

Bartels 1995
Bartels, S., 'Europees privaatrecht: over de bevoegdheidsverdeling tussen Unie en *Lid-Staat* met betrekking tot het eigendomsrecht', *Ars Aequi* (44/4), 1995, p. 244-251.

Bartels 1997
Bartels, S.E., 'Voorwaardelijke eigendom en relatieve beschikkingsbevoegdheid', in: B.W.M. Nieskens-Ipshording, E.M. Hemmen & T.H.D. Struycken (eds.), *Discussies omtrent beslag, verhaal en beschikkingsbevoegdheid*, Deventer: W.E.J. Tjeenk Willink 1997, p. 79-103.

Bartels 2004
Bartels, S.E., *De titel van overdracht in driepartijenverhoudingen*, Den Haag: Boom Juridische uitgevers, 2004.

Bartels & Milo 2000
Bartels, S.E. & Milo, J.M., 'Open normen in het goederenrecht. Flexibiliteit met behoud van zekerheid?', in: *S.E.* Bartels & J.M. Milo (eds.), *Open Normen in het goederenrecht*, Den Haag: Boom Juridische uitgevers 2000, p. 1-20.

Bartels & Milo 2004
Bartels, S.E. & Milo, J.M., 'Contents of Real Rights: Personal or Proprietary. A Principled History', in: S.E. Bartels & J.M. Milo (eds.), *Contents of Real Rights*, Nijmegen: Wolf Legal Publishers 2004, p. 5-23.

Basedow 1995
Basedow, J., 'Der kollisionsrechtliche Gehalt der Produktfreiheiten im europäischen Binnenmarkt: *favor offerentis*', *Rabels Zeitschrift für ausländisches und internationales Privatrecht*, (59) 1995, p. 1 55.

Basedow 2007
Basedow, J., 'Conflict of Laws and the Harmonization of Substantive Private Law in the European Union', in: M. Andenas, A. Diaz, S.B. Markesinis, H. Micklitz & N. Pasquini (eds.), *Liber Americorum Guido Alpa,* London: British Institute of International and Comparative Law 2007, p. 168-185.

Baudry-Lacantinerie et al. 1930
Baudry-Lacantinerie, G., Bonnecase, J., Barde, Bonnecarrère, Chauveau, M., Chéneaux, Colin, Houques-Fourcade, Courtois, L., Loynes, D., Saignat, Surville, Tissier & Wahl, *Traité théorique et pratique de Droit Civil,* supplément 5, Paris: Recueil Sirey 1930.

Baudry-Lacantinerie & Chauveau 1905
Baudry-Lacantinerie, G. & Chauveau, M., *Traité théorique et pratique de Droit Civil. Des Biens,* Tome 6, 3rd edition, Paris: Librairie de la société recueil J.-B. Sirey et du journal du palais 1905.

Baur 1961
Baur, F., 'Der Beseitigungsanspruch nach § 1004 BGB - Zugleich ein Beitrag zum Problem der Rechtswidrigkeit auf dem Gebiet des Güterschutzes', *Archiv für die civilistische Praxis,* (Band 160), 1961, p. 465-293.

Baur, Baur & Stürner 1999
Baur, F., Baur, J.F. & Stürner, R., *Sachenrecht,* 17th renewed edition, München: C.H. Beck'sche Verlagsbuchhandlung 1999.

Bayard-Jammes 2003
Bayard-Jammes, F., *La nature juridique du droit du copropriétaire immobilier. Analyse critique,* Tome 409, Bibliothèque de droit privé; Paris: LGDJ 2003.

Bean 1968
Bean, J.M.W., *The Decline of English Feudalism 1215-1540,* Manchester: The University Press 1968.

Bell 2002
Bell, J., 'Property and Legal Culture in France', in: P. Birks & A. Pretto (eds.), *Themes in Comparative Law - In Honour of Bernard Rudden,* Oxford: Oxford University Press 2002, p. 83-96.

Van den Bergh 1988
Van den Bergh, G.C.J.J., *Eigendom. Grepen uit de geschiedenis van een omstreden begrip,* 2nd edition, Deventer: Kluwer 1988.

Van den Bergh 1994
Van den Bergh, G.C.J.J., *Geleerd recht: een geschiedenis van de Europese rechtswetenschap in vogelvlucht,* 3rd edition, Deventer: Kluwer 1994.

Bertrel 1994
Bertrel, J.-P., 'L'accession artificielle immobilière. Contribution à la définition de la nature juridique du droit de superficie', *Revue trimestrielle de droit civil,* (88) 1994, p. 737-775.

Beudant 1938
Beudant, R., *Cours de droit civil français,* Tome 4, 2nd edition, Paris: Rousseau & Cie 1938.

Biancalana 1998
Biancalana, J., *'Medieval Uses',* in: R. Helmholz & R. Zimmermann (eds.), *Itinera Fiduciae; Trust and Treuhand in historical perspective,* Berlin: Duncker & Humblot 1998, p. 111-152.

Biondi 1997
Biondi, A., 'The merchant, the thief & the citizen: the circulation of works of art within the European Union', *Common Market Law Review,* (34) 1997, p. 1173-1195.

Birks 1985
Birks, P., 'The Roman Law concept of Dominium and the idea of Absolute Ownership', *Acta Juridica,* 1985, p. 1-27.

Birks 1996
Birks, P., 'Equity in the Modern Law: An Exercise in Taxonomy', *The University of Western Australia Law Review,* (26/1) 1996, p. 1-99.

Birks 2000
Birks, P., 'Personal Property: Proprietary Rights and Remedies', *King's College Law Journal,* 2000, p. 1-18.

Birks & McLeod 1987
Birks, P. & Mcleod, G., *Justinian's Institutes,* London: Duckworth 1987.

Blanchard 2006
Blanchard, C., 'Présentation de la réforme des successions et des libéralités', *Droit et patrimoine,* (153) 2006, p. 24-28.

Blokland, Klinkert-Cino & Schutte 1998
Blokland, T., Klinkert-Cino, J.A.M. & Schutte, N.J., *De praktijk van het vruchtgebruik,* Den Haag: Sdu Uitgevers 1998.

Boeckaert 2006
Boeckaert, B., *'Divergences of the Law on Securities. A Law and Economics Approach', in:* U. Drobnig, H.J. Snijders & E.-J. Zippro (eds.), *Divergences of Property Law, an Obstacle to the Internal Market?,* München: Sellier. European Law Publishers 2006, p. 175-194.

Van den Bogaert 2002
Van den Bogaert, S., 'Horizontality: the Court Attacks?', in: C. Barnard & J. Schott (eds.), *The law of the Single European Market: Unpacking the Premises*, Oxford: Hart Publishing 2002, p. 123-152.

Boraine 1987
Boraine, A., *Probleme rakende die registreerbaarheid van regte* (LL.M. thesis University of Witwatersrand), Johannesburg: 1987, unpublished.

Borkowski 1997
Borkowski, A., *Textbook on Roman Law*, 2nd edition, London: Blackstone Press Ltd. 1997.

Bos 2005
Bos, E.C., *Vruchtgebruik op aandelen. Over de grenzen van goederenrecht, erfrecht en vennootschapsrecht* (diss.) (Serie vanwege het Van der Heijden instituut, 81), Deventer: Kluwer 2005.

Van den Bos 2004
Van den Bos, J.A., 'Niet gespitst, maar toch gescheiden: de zelfstandigheid van grond en opstal', *Bouwrecht*, (7) 2004, p. 584-591.

Boulanger 1968
Boulanger, F., 'Un des nouveaux aspects des "métamorphoses" du droit au bail : la concession immobilière de la loi du 30 décembre 1967', *Recueil Dalloz (Chron.)*, 1968, p. 99.

Bouwes 2006
Bouwes, M., 'De opkomst en ondergang van een anti-misbruikwet', in: P.V.D. Grinten & T. Heukels (eds.), *Crossing Borders. Essays in European and Private International Law, Nationality Law and Islamic Law in Honour of Frans van der Velden*, Deventer: Kluwer 2006, p. 105-111.

Brahn 1988
Brahn, O.K., *Fiduciaire overdracht. stille verpanding en eigendomsvoorbehoud naar huidig en komend recht* (Studiepockets privaatrecht, 13), 6th revised and extended edition, Zwolle: W.E.J. Tjeenk Willink 1988.

Braun 2006
Braun, A., 'Italy', in: J. Glasson & G. Thomas (eds.), *The International Trust*, 2nd revised and updated edition, Bristol: Jordans 2006, p. 795-825.

Breken 2002
Breken, K., 'Herverpanding, geen standaard 'nemo plus' situatie', in: S.C.J.J. Kortmann, C.J H. Jansen, G. van Solinge & N.E.D. Faber (eds.), *Onderneming en 10 jaar nieuw burgerlijk recht*, Deventer: Kluwer 2002, p. 365-387.

Bridge 2002
Bridge, M., *Personal Property Law*, 3rd edition, Oxford: Oxford University Press 2002.

Bright 1993
Bright, S., 'Uncertainty in leases - Is it a vice?', *Legal Studies*, (13) 1993, p. 38-53.

Broederschap der Notarissen in Nederland 1914
Broederschap der Notarissen in Nederland, *'Kort Verslag van de op 29 en 30 Juli 1914 te Groningen gehouden Algemeene Vergadering, onder leiding van den voorzitter der Broederschap, den heer Chs. Miseroy, notaris te Amsterdam', Weekblad voor het Notariaat: gewijd aan privaatrecht, notariaat en fiscaalrecht,* (461) 1914, p. 340-346.

Buckland & McNair 1974
Buckland, W.W. & Mcnair, A.D., *Roman Law and Common Law*, 2nd edition, Cambridge: Cambridge University Press 1974.

Bund 1956
Bund, E., 'Begriff und Einteilung der Servituten im römischen Recht', *Zeitschrift der Savigny-Stiftung für Rechtsgeschichte, Romanistische Abteilung*, (367) 1956, p. 155-219.

Bürge 1991
Bürge, A., *Das französische Privatrecht im 19. Jahrhundert. Zwischen Tradition und Pandektenwissenschaft, Liberalismus und Etatismus* (Ius Commune, Veröffentlichungen des Max-Planck-Instituts für Europäische Rechtsgeschichte, 52), Frankfurt am Main: Vittorio Klostermann 1991.

Burn & Cartwright 2006
Burn, E.H. & Cartwright, J., *Cheshire and Burns's Modern Law of Real Property*, 17th edition, Oxford: Oxford University Press 2006.

Cabrillac & Mouly 2004
Cabrillac, M. & Mouly, C., *Droit des sûretés*, Paris: *Litec* 2004.

Van Caenegem 1988a
Van Caenegem, R.C., *The Birth of the English Common Law*, 2nd edition, Cambridge: Cambridge University Press 1988.

Van Caenegem 1988b
Van Caenegem, R.C., *An Historical Introduction to Private Law* (*Introduction historique au droit privé*), trans. D. Johnston, Cambridge: Cambridge University Press 1988.

Van Caenegem 2002
Van Caenegem, R.C., *European Law in the Past and the Future; Unity and Diversity over Two Millennia*, Cambridge: Cambridge University Press 2002.

Cahen 2004
Cahen, J.L.P., *Overeenkomst en derden* (Monografieën Nieuw BW - B57), 2nd edition, Deventer: Kluwer 2004.

Cámara-Lapuente 2005
Cámara-Lapuente, S., 'Registration of Interests as a Formality of Contracts: Comparative Remarks on Land Registers within the Frame of European Private Law', *European Review of Private Law*, (6) 2005, p. 797-839.

Campana 2001a
Campana, M.-J., 'La clause de réserve de propriété - son évolution dans la législation française', in: M.-J. Campana (ed.), *Étude comparée sur la propriété utilisée comme sûreté*, EUI Working Paper LAW, No. 2001/2, Firenze: 2001, p. 3-12.

Campana 2001b
Campana, M.-J., 'Le mécanisme du bordereau Dailly en droit français', in: M.-J. Campana (ed.), *Étude comparée sur la propriété utilisée comme sûreté*, EUI Working Paper LAW, No. 2001/2, Firenze: 2001, p. 43-53.

Canaris 1978
Canaris, C.-W., 'Die Verdinglichung obligatorischer Rechte', in: K. Ballerstedt, F.A. Mann, H.H. Jakobs, B. Knobbe-Keuk, E. Picker & J. Wilhelm (eds.), *Festschrift für Werner Flume zum 70. Geburtstag 12. September 1978*, Köln: Verlag Dr. Otto Schmidt KG 1978, p. 371-427.

Cantero 1998
Cantero, G.G., 'Les différentes fonctions de la possession en droit privé', *European Review of Private Law*, (6) 1998, p. 363-383.

Carbonnier 2000
Carbonnier, J., *Droit Civil 3 / Les biens: Monnaie, immeubles, meubles*, 19th edition, Thémis; Paris: Presses Universitaires de France 2000.

Carey Miller 1998
Carey Miller, D.L., 'Property', in: E. Metzger (ed.), *A companion to Justinian's Institutes*, Ithaca, New York: Cornell University Press 1998.

Carey Miller & Pope 2000
Carey Miller, D.L. & Pope, A., *Land Title in South Africa, Kenwyn: Juta* & Co, Ltd 2000.

Catala 1991
Catala, P., 'L'évolution contemporaine du droit des biens. Expose de synthèse', *L'évolution contemporaine du droit des biens. Troisièmes Journées Renée Savatier*, Paris: Presse Universitaires de France 1991, p. 181-190.

Catala-Franjou 1967
Catala-Franjou, N., 'De la nature juridique du droit de rétention', *Revue trimestrielle de droit civil*, (65) 1967, p. 9-44.

Cervelli 2001
Cervelli, S., *I Diritti Reali*, Milano: Giuffré Editore 2001.

Chabas 1994
Chabas, F., *Biens: Droit de propriété et ses démembrements*, Tome 2, 8th edition, Leçons de droit civil; Paris: Montchrestien 1994.

Chabas 1996
Chabas, F., *Introduction à l'étude du droit. Leçons de droit civil*, Tome 1, vol. 1, Paris: Montchrestien 1996.

Chalmers et al.
Chalmers, D., Hadjiemmanuil, C., Monti, G. & Tomkins, A., *European Union Law. Text and Materials*, Cambridge: Cambridge University Press 2006.

Charny 1991
Charny, D., 'Competition amongst Jurisdictions in Formulating Corporate Law Rules: An American Perspective on the Race to the Bottom in the European Communities', *Harvard International Law Journal*, (32/2) 1991, p. 423-456.

Chauveau 1931
Chauveau, M., 'Classification nouvelle des droits réels et personnels', *Revue critique de législation et de jurisprudence*, (LXXI) 1931, p. 539-612.

Chirac 2004
Chirac, J. (ed.), *Le code civil, 1804-2004: livre du bicentenaire*, Paris: Dalloz Litec 2004.

Claes 2004
Claes, M.L.H.K., *The national courts' mandate in the European constitution* (diss.), Maastricht: Maastricht University Press 2004.

Clarke & Kohler 2005
Clarke, A. & Kohler, P., *Property Law. Commentary and Materials, Law in Context*, Cambridge: Cambridge University Press 2005.

Clemente 2007
Clemente, C., 'Verwertung der nicht akzessorischen Grundschuld im Rahmen eines Forderungsverkaufs', *Zeitschrift für Immobilienrecht*, (21) 2007, p. 737-746.

Coing 1953
Coing, H., 'Zur Eigentumslehre des Bartolus', *Zeitschrift der Savigny-Stiftung für Rechtsgeschichte, Romanistische Abteilung*, (70) 1953, p. 348-371.

Coing 1962
Coing, H., 'Zur Geschichte des Begriffs "subjektives Recht"', in: H. Coing (ed.), *Zur Geschichte des Privatrechtsystems*, Frankfurt am Main: Vittorio Klostermann 1962, p. 29-55.

Coing 1985
Coing, H., *Europäisches Privatrecht*, Band I, München: C.H. Beck'sche Verlagsbuchhandlung 1985.

Corbino 1995
Corbino, A., 'La struttura della dichiarazione di acquisto nella mancipatio e nella in iure cessio', in: R. Feenstra, A. Hartkamp, J.E. Spruit, P.J. Sijpesteijn & L.C. Winkel (eds.), *Collatio Iuris Romani – études dédiés à Hans Ankum à l'occasion de son 65e anniversaire*, Vol. I., Amsterdam: J.C. Gieben 1995, p. 81-85.

Cox 2006
Cox, K., 'Summary of the Discussion at Leiden University', in: U. Drobnig, H.J. Snijders & E.-J. Zippro (eds.), *Divergences to Property Law, an Obstacle to the Internal Market?*, München: Sellier, European Law Publishers 2006, p. 231-240.

Craig 2006
Craig, P., *EU Administrative Law*, Oxford: Oxford University Press 2006.

Craig & De Búrca 2007
Craig, P. & De Búrca, G., *EU Law. Text, Cases and Materials*, 4th edition, Oxford: Oxford University Press 2007.

Crocq 1995
Crocq, P., *Propriété et garantie* (Bibliothèque de droit privé, Tome 248), Paris: LGDJ 1995.

Crocq 2002
Crocq, P., 'Sûretés et publicité foncière', *Revue trimestrielle de droit civil*, 2002, p. 546-550.

Crocq 2003
Crocq, P., 'Cautionnement réel', *Revue trimestrielle de droit civil*, 2003, p. 128-129.

Crocq 2006
Crocq, P., 'La réserve de propriété (I 6)', *La Semaine Juridique Edition Générale*, (20, 17 May) 2006, p. 23-25.

Crocq 2007
Crocq, P., 'Le cœur du dispositif fiduciaire', *Revue Lamy droit civil*, (40) 2007, p. 1-6.

Van Dam 2006
Van Dam, C., *European Tort Law*, Oxford: Oxford University Press 2006.

Dannemann 2006
Dannemann, G., 'Comparative Law: Study of Similarities or Differences?', in: M. Reimann & R. Zimmermann (eds.), *The Oxford Handbook of Comparative Law*, Oxford: Oxford University Press 2006, p. 383-419.

Darmstaedler 1950
Darmstaedler, F., 'Der Eigentumsbegriff des Bürgerlichen Gesetzbuchs', *Archiv für die civilistische Praxis*, (151) 1950, p. 311-342.

Davids 1988
Davids, W.J.M., *Burenrecht, mandeligheid en erfdienstbaarheden* (Serie Recht en Praktijk, 13), 3rd edition, Deventer: Kluwer 1988.

Davids 1994
Davids, W.J.M., *Mandeligheid en erfdienstbaarheden* (Monografieën Nieuw BW, B27), 2nd edition, Deventer: Kluwer 1994.

Davies 1997
Davies, N., *Europe a history*, London: Pimlico 1997.

Delebecque 2006
Delebecque, P., 'Le régime des hypothèques', *La Semaine Juridique Entreprise et affaires*, Supplément au No. 20, 2006, p. 29-32.

Delmas Saint-Hilaire 2007
Delmas Saint-Hilaire, P., 'Les ajustements techniques de la loi du 23 juin 2006: entre modernisation, correction et interprétation', *Droit et patrimoine*, (157) 2007, p. 40-48.

Demolombe 1870
Demolombe, C., *Traité de la distinction des biens; de la propriété; de l'usufruit de l'usage et de l'habitation*, Tome I, 4th edition, Paris: Auguste Durand/L. Hachette et Cie 1870.

Depoorter & Parisi 2003
Depoorter, B.W.F. & Parisi, F., 'Fragmentation of Property Rights: A Functional Interpretation of the Law of Servitudes', *Global Jurist Frontiers*, (3/1) 2003, Article 2.

Derine 1955
Derine, R., *Grenzen van het eigendomsrecht in de negentiende eeuw. Bijdrage tot de geschiedenis van het moderne privaatrecht* (diss.), Antwerpen: De Sikkel 1955.

Devroe 2007
Devroe, W., 'Impact van door het Europees hof van justitie ontwikkelde algemene beginselen op privaatrechtelijke verhoudingen', in: A.S. Hartkamp, C.H. Sieburgh & L.A.D. Keus (eds.), *De invloed van het Europese recht op het Nederlandse privaatrecht*, Deel I, Deventer: Kluwer 2007, p. 133-189.

Diephuis 1880
Diephuis, *Het Nederlandsch burgerlijk regt*, Deel VI, Groningen: Wolters 1880.

Digby & Harrison 1897
Digby, K.E. & Harrison, W.M., *An introduction to the history of the law of real property*, 5th edition, Oxford: Clarendon Press 1897.

Dockès 1995
Dockès, E., 'Essai sur la notion d'usufruit', *Revue Trimestrielle de Droit Civil*, 1995, p. 479-507.

Dohrn 2004
Dohrn, H., *Die Kompetenzen der Europäischen Gemeinschaft im Internationalen Privatrecht*, 133, Studien zum ausländischen und international Privatrecht; Tübingen: Mohr Siebeck 2004.

Drobnig 1996
Drobnig, U., 'Mobiliarsicherheiten Vielfalt oder Einheit? – Vergleichender Generalbericht', in: K.F. Kreuzer (ed.), *Mobiliarsicherheiten Vielfalt oder Einheit?*, Baden-Baden: Nomos Verlagsgesellschaft 1996.

Drobnig 2006
Drobnig, U., 'Recognition and Adaptation of Foreign Security Rights', in: U. Drobnig, H.J. Snijders & E.-J. Zippro (eds.), *Divergences of Property Law, an Obstacle to the Internal Market?*, München: Sellier, European Law Publishers 2006, p. 105-115.

Drobnig, Snijders & Zippro 2006
Drobnig, U., Snijders, H.J. & Zippro, E.-J., 'Divergences of Property Law, an Obstacle to the Internal Market?' in: U. Drobnig, H.J. Snijders & E.-J. Zippro (eds.), *Divergences of Property Law, an Obstacle tot the Internal Market?*, München: Sellier, European Law Publishers 2006, p. 3-13.

Dulckeit 1951
Dulckeit, G., *Die Verdinglichung obligatorischer Rechte*, Tübingen: Verlag J.C.B. Mohr (Paul Siebeck) 1951.

Dümchen 1909
Dümchen, E., 'Schuld und Haftung', *Jheringer Jahrbücher für die Dogmatik des heutigen römischen und deutschen Privatrechts*, (54) 1909, p. 355-468.

Van Dunné 1991
Van Dunné, J.M., 'Het zakenrecht als open systeem (van verbintenissen)', in: B.W.M. Nieskens-Ipshording, M.J.G.C. Raaijmakers, J. Spier & J.B.M. Vranken (eds.), *In het nu, wat worden zal – Opstellen aangeboden aan prof. mr. H.C.F. Schoordijk ter gelegenheid van zijn afscheid als hoogleraar aan de Katholieke Universiteit Brabant*, Deventer: Kluwer 1991, p. 45-64.

Dupichot 2006
Dupichot, P., 'L'antichrèse', *La Semaine Juridique Entreprise et affaires*, Supplément au No. 20, 2006, p. 26-28.

Dupichot 2007
Dupichot, P., 'Opération fiducie sur le sol français', *La Semaine Juridique Edition Générale*, (11) 2007, p. 5-8.

Eggens 1960
Eggens, J., 'Over de verhouding van eigendom en verbintenis', *Mededelingen der Koninklijke Nederlandse Akademie van Wetenschappen, afd. Letterkunde* (Nieuwe reeks, 23), No. 7, 1960, p. 3-20.

Enneccerus & Nipperdey 1960
Enneccerus, L. & Nipperdey, H.C., *Allgemeiner Teil des Bürgerlichen Rechts. Ein Lehrbuch*, Tübingen: J.C.B. Mohr 1960.

Epstein 1982
Epstein, R., 'Notice and Freedom of Contract in the Law of Servitudes', *Southern California Law Review*, (55) 1982, p. 1353-1368.

Van Erp 2000a
Van Erp, J.H.M., 'Via open normen naar Europees goederenrecht?', in: S.E. Bartels & J.M. Milo (eds.), *Open normen in het goederenrecht*, Den Haag: Boom Juridische uitgevers 2000, p. 61-78.

Van Erp 2000b
Van Erp, J.H.M., 'Wordt huur een verhandelbaar goed? Een reactie op het artikel "De regel 'koop breekt geen huur' in wetsvoorstel 26 089 vertoont (verborgen) gebreken" van mr. *M.M. Asbreuk-van Os* in *WPNR* (6386), 2000)', *Weekblad voor Privaatrecht, Notariaat en Registratie*, (6407) 2000, p. 456-457.

Van Erp 2003a
Van Erp, J.H.M., 'Civil and Common Property Law: Caveat Comparator - The Value of Legal Historical-Comparative Analysis', *European Review of Private Law*, (3) 2003, p. 394-411.

Van Erp 2003b
Van Erp, J.H.M., 'A Numerus Quasi-Clausus of Property Rights as a Constitutive Element of a Future European Property Law', *Electronic Journal of Comparative Law*, (7/2) 2003.

Van Erp 2004a
Van Erp, J.H.M., 'The Cape Town Convention: a Model for a European System of Security Interests Registration?', *European Review of Private Law*, (1) 2004, p. 91-110.

Van Erp 2004b
Van Erp, J.H.M., 'Positive duties in the grey area between contract and property law', in: S.E. Bartels and J.M. Milo (eds.), *Contents of Real Rights*, Nijmegen: Wolf Legal Publishers 2004, p. 149-162.

Van Erp 2004c
Van Erp, J.H.M., 'De osmose van Nederlands en Europees goederenrecht', *Nederlands Tijdschrift voor Burgerlijk Recht*, (10, Special Issue, No. 94), 2004, p. 533-546.

Van Erp 2004d
Van Erp, J.H.M., 'Reactie Financiëlezekerheidsovereenkomsten', *Weekblad voor Privaatrecht, Notariaat en Registratie*, (6601) 2004, p. 967-971.

Van Erp 2005
Van Erp, J.H.M., 'Naschrift. De implementatie van de richtlijn financiëlezekerheids-overeenkomsten vanuit Europeesrechtelijk en rechtsvergelijkend oogpunt', *Weekblad voor Privaatrecht, Notariaat en Registratie*, (6615) 2005, p. 252-256.

Van Erp 2006a
Van Erp, J.H.M., 'Comparative Property Law', in: M. Reimann & R. Zimmermann (eds.), *The Oxford Handbook of Comparative Law*, Oxford: Oxford University Press 2006, p. 1043-1070.

Van Erp 2006b
Van Erp, J.H.M., *European and National Property Law: Osmosis or Growing Antagonism?* (Walter van Gerven Lectures, 6), Groningen: Europa Law Publishing, 2006.

Van Erp 2008
Van Erp, J.H.M., 'From "classical" to modern European property law?', *FS Kerameus*, forthcoming 2008.

Van Erp & Van Vliet 2002
Van Erp, J.H.M. & Vliet, L.P.W., 'Real and Personal Security', *Electronic Journal of Comparative Law*, (6/4) 2002.

European Opinion Research Group 2004
European Opinion Research Group, *Standard Eurobarometer 205 / Wave 60.2 – Public Opinion in Europe: Financial Services – Report B*, Brussels: European Communities 2004.

Farnsworth 2006
Farnsworth, E.A., 'Comparative Contract Law', in: M. Reimann & R. Zimmermann (eds.), *The Oxford Handbook of Comparative Law*, Oxford: Oxford University Press 2006, p. 899-935.

Feenstra 1974
Feenstra, R., 'Les origines du dominium utile chez les glossateurs (avec une appendice concernant l'opinion des Ultramontani)', in: R. *Feenstra* (ed.), *Fata Iuris Romani,* Leyde: Presse Universitaire de Leyde 1974, p. 215-259.

Feenstra 1976
Feenstra, R., 'Historische aspecten van de private eigendom als rechtsinstituut', *Rechtsgeleerd Magazijn THEMIS,* 1976, p. 250-275.

Feenstra 1978
Feenstra, R., 'Der Eigentumsbegriff bei *Hugo Grotius', in: O. Behrends, M. Diesselhorst, H. Lange, D. Liebs, J.G. Wolf & C. Wollschläger* (eds.), *Festschrift für Franz Wieacker zum 70. Geburtstag, Göttingen: Vandenhoeck & Ruprecht* 1978, p. 209-234.

Feenstra 1979
Feenstra, R., *Ius in re. Het begrip zakelijk recht in historisch perspectief* (Thorbecke Colleges, 4), Leiden: Universitaire Pers 1979.

Feenstra 1982
Feenstra, R., 'Real Rights and their classification in the 17th century: the role of Heinrich Hahn and Gerhard Feltmann', *The Juridical Review,* 1982, p. 106-120.

Feenstra 1989
Feenstra, R., 'Dominium and ius in re aliena: The Origins of a Civil Law Distinction', in: P. Birks (ed.), *New Perspectives in the Roman Law of Property; essays for Barry Nicholas,* Oxford: Clarendon Press 1989, p. 111-122.

Feenstra 1990
Feenstra, R., *Romeinsrechtelijke grondslagen van het Nederlands privaatrecht,* 5th edition, Leiden: E.J. Bril/Universitaire Pers Leiden 1990.

Feenstra 1998
Feenstra, R., 'Dominium utile est chimaera: nouvelles réflexions sur le concept de propriété dans le droit savant', *Tijdschrift voor Rechtsgeschiedenis,* (66/3-4) 1998, p. 381-397.

Recueil complet des travaux préparatoires du code civil 11
Fenet, P.A., *Recueil complet des travaux préparatoires du code civil,* 11, Osnabrück: Otto Zeller 1968; repr. of the 1827 edition.

Recueil complet des travaux préparatoires du code civil 14
Fenet, P.A., *Recueil complet des travaux préparatoires du code civil,* 14, Osnabrück: Otto Zeller 1968; repr. of the 1827 edition.

Fesevur 1992
Fesevur, J.E., *Voorrechten en retentierecht* (Monografieën Nieuw BW, B13), 2nd edition, Deventer: Kluwer 1992.

Fikker 1998
Fikkers, H.A.G., 'Over erfdienstbaarheden - HR 27 september 1996, NJ 1997, 496; HR 14 februari 1997, NJ 1997, 542; HR 30 januari 1998, RvdW 1998, 35 C', *Nieuwsbrief BW*, (6) 1998, 70-72.

Flossmann 1996
Flossmann, U., *Österreichische Privatrechtgeschichte*, 3rd improved edition, Vienna-New York: Springer 1996.

Foëx 1987
Foëx, B., *Le numerus clausus des droits réels en matière mobilière* (diss.), Lausanne: Payot 1987.

Forum Group 2005
Forum Group on Mortgage Credit, *Basic Guidelines for a Eurohypothec*, Warsaw: Mortgage Credit Foundation 2005.

Fuchs 1889
Fuchs, E., *Das Wesen der Dinglichkeit. Ein Beitrag zur allgemeinen Rechtslehre und zur Kritik des Entwurfs eines bürgerlichen Gesetzbuches für das Deutsche Reich*, Berlin: Carl Heymanns Verlag 1889.

Fulgencia Angosto Sáez 2006
Fulgencio Angosto Sáez, J., 'Limitations to property', in: J.H.M. van Erp & A. Vaquer (eds.), *Introduction to Spanish patrimonial law*, Grenada: Editorial Comares 2006, p. 281-292.

Füller 2006
Füller, J.T., *Eigenständiges Sachenrecht?* (Jus Privatum. Beitrage zum Privatrecht, 104) Tübingen: Mohr Siebeck 2006.

Fusaro 2001
Fusaro, A., 'The Numerus Clausus of Property Rights', in: E. Cooke (ed.), *Modern Studies in Property Law*, Oxford - Portland, Oregon: Hart Publishing 2001, 1, p. 309-319.

Van Gaalen 2001
Van Gaalen, M.S., *Vruchtgebruik* (Ars Notariatus, XCI), Deventer: Kluwer 2001.

Gambaro & Mattei 2002
Gambaro, A. & Mattei, U., 'Property Law', in: J.S. Lena & U. Mattei (eds.), *Introduction to Italian Law*, The Hague, London, New York: Kluwer Law International 2002, p. 283-316.

Ganter 2004
Ganter, H.G., 'Die Rechtsprechung des Bundesgerichtshofs zu Treuhandkonten in der Insolvenz des Treuhänders', in: Haarmeyer, Hirte, Kichhof & Graf von Westphalen (eds.), *Verschulding, Haftung, Vollstreckung, Insolvenz. Festschrift für Gerhart Kreft zum 65. Geburtstag*, Kevelaer: Bercker 2004, p. 251-266.

Gaunt & Morgan 1997
Gaunt, J. & Morgan, P., *Gale on Easements*, 16th edition, London: Sweet & Maxwell 1997.

Gauthier 1996
Gauthier, A., *Roman Law and its Contribution to the Development of Canon Law*, Ottawa: Ottowa University Press 1996.

Von Gierke 1889
Von Gierke, O., *Der Entwurf eines Bürgerlichen Gesetzbuchs und das Deutsche Recht*, Veraenderte und vermehrte Ausgabe, Leipzig: Verlag von Dunker & Humblot 1889.

Von Gierke 1905
Von Gierke, O., *Deutsches Privatrecht*, Zweiter Band Sachenrecht, Leipzig: Verlag von Duncker & Humblot 1905.

Ginossar 1960
Ginossar, S., *Droit réel, propriété et créance – élaboration d'un système rationnel des droits patrimoniaux*, Paris: LGDJ 1960.

Giuffrè 1992
Giuffrè, V., *L'emersione dei <iura in re aliena> ed il dogma del 'numero chiuso'*, Napoli: Jovene Editore 1992.

Glenn 2006
Glenn, H.P., 'Legal Families and Legal Traditions', in: M. Reimann & R. Zimmermann (eds.), *The Oxford Handbook of Comparative Law*, Oxford: Oxford University Press 2006, p. 421-440.

Goni Rodriguez de Almeida 2006
Goni Rodriguez de Almeida, M., 'Examen de la evolución jurisprudencial y doctrinal hacia la admisión de un numerus apertus en los derechos reales y su estrecha relación con el principio de especialidad', (693) *Revista Crítica de Derecho Inmobiliario*, 2006.

Goo 1997
Goo, S.H., *Sourcebook on Land Law*, London – Sydney: Cavendish Publishing Ltd. 1997.

Goode 1996
Goode, R., 'Landesbericht England', in: K.F. Kreuzer (ed.), *Mobiliarsicherheiten Vielfalt oder Einheit?*, Baden-Baden: Nomos Verlagsgesellschaft 1996, p. 43-74.

Goode 2002
Goode, R., 'The Cape Town Convention on International Interests in Mobile Equipment: a Driving Force for International Asset-Based Financing', *Uniform Law Review*, (1) 2002, p. 3-15.

Goode 2004
Goode, R., *Commercial Law*, 3rd edition, London: Penguin Books 2004.

Gordley 1991
Gordley, J., *The Philosophical Origins of Modern Contract Doctrine*, Oxford: Clarendon Press 1991.

Gordley 1993
Gordley, J., 'Common law und civil law: eine überholte Unterscheidung', *Zeitschrift für europäisches Privatrecht*, (1) 1993, p. 498-518.

Gordley 1994
Gordley, J., 'Myths of the French Civil Code', *The American Journal of Comparative Law*, (42) 1994, p. 459-505.

Gordley 1995
Gordley, J., 'Comparative Legal Research: Its Function in the Development of Harmonized Law', *The American Journal of Comparative Law*, (43) 1995, p. 555-567.

Gordley 1998
Gordley, J., 'Contract, Property and the Will - The Civil Law and Common Law Tradition', in: H.N. Scheiber (ed.), *The state and freedom of contract (Making of Modern Freedom)*, Stanford University Press 1998, p. 66-88.

Gordley 2000
Gordley, J., 'The Common Law in the Twentieth Century: Some Unfinished Business', *California Law Review*, (88) 2000, p. 1-59.

Gordley 2006
Gordley, J., *Foundations of Private Law. Property, Tort, Contract, Unjust Enrichment*, Oxford: Oxford University Press 2006.

Gordley & Von Mehren 2006
Gordley, J. & Von Mehren, A.T., *An introduction to the comparative study of private law. Readings, cases, materials*, Cambridge: Cambridge University Press 2006.

Gordon 1989
Gordon, W.M., 'The Importance of the iusta causa of traditio', in: P. Birks (ed.), *New Perspectives in the Roman Law of Property - Essays for Barry Nicholas*, Oxford: Clarendon Press 1989, p. 123-135.

Gordon & Robinson 1988
Gordon, W.M. & Robinson, O.F., *The Institutes of Gaius, Texts in Roman Law*, London: Duckworth 1988.

Goré 1997
Goré, M., 'Cour de Cassation (1re Ch. civ.) - 17 décembre 1996', *Revue critique de droit international privé*, (86/4) 1997, p. 725-732.

Goren 1994
Goren, S.L., *The German Civil Code*, Littleton, Colerado: Fred. B. Rothman & Co 1994.

Gray 1996
Gray, K., 'Property in Common Law Systems', in: G.E. van Maanen & A.J. van der Walt (eds.), *Property law on the threshold of the 21st century*, Antwerp: MAKLU 1996, p. 235-283.

Gray & Gray 2001
Gray, K. & Gray, S.F., *Land Law*, Butterworths Core Text Series, 2nd edition, London: Butterworths 2001.

Gray & Gray 2005
Gray, K. & Gray, S.F., *Elements of Land Law*, 4th edition, Oxford: Oxford University Press 2005.

Graziadei 2002a
Graziadei, M., 'Tuttifrutti', in: P. Birks & A. Pretto (eds.), *Themes in Comparative Law - In Honour of Bernard Rudden*, Oxford: Oxford University Press 2002, p. 121-133.

Graziadei 2002b
Graziadei, M., 'Trust Law', in: J.S. Lena & U. Mattei (eds.), *Introduction to Italian Law*, The Hague/London/New York: Kluwer Law International 2002, p. 317-340.

Gretton 2004
Gretton, G., 'Ownership and Insolvency: Burnett's Trustee v Grainger', *Edinburgh Law Review*, (8) 2004, p. 389-395.

Gretton 2007
Gretton, G., 'Ownership and its objects', *Rabels Zeitschrift für ausländisches und internationales Privatrecht*, 2007, p. 802-851.

Grimaldi 1991a
Grimaldi, M., 'La fiducie: réflexions sur l'institution et sur l'avant-projet de loi qui la consacre (I)', *Répertoire du notariat Defrénois*, (35085) 1991, p. 897-923.

Grimaldi 1991b
Grimaldi, M., 'La fiducie: réflexions sur l'institution et sur l'avant-projet de loi qui la consacre (II)', *Répertoire du notariat Defrénois*, (35094) 1991, p. 961-997.

Grimaldi 2003
Grimaldi, M., 'La nature juridique du cautionnement réel: de la mixité en droit des sûretés', *Revue des Contrats*, (1) 2003, p. 170.

Grimaldi 2006a
Grimaldi, M., 'Le cautionnement réel n'est plus un cautionnement... et ne relève donc plus de l'article 1415 du Code civil', *Revue des Contrats*, (2) 2006, p. 454.

Grimaldi 2006b
Grimaldi, M., 'L'hypothèque rechargeable et le prêt viager hypothécaire', *La Semaine Juridique Entreprise et affaires*, Supplément au Nos. 20-21, 2006, p. 33-37.

Grimaldi et al. 2003
Grimaldi, M., Aynès, L., Bac, A., Crocq, P., Dos-Reis, D., Frémaux, É., Gourio, A., Provansal, A., Simler, P. & Synvet, H., *Groupe de travail relatif a la reforme du droit des sûretés; rapport a monsieur Dominique Perpen, garde des Sceaux, ministre de la justice*, <http://www.justice.gouv.fr/publicat/rapport/rapportgrimaldi.pdf>, 2003.

Grimaldi et al. 2005
Grimaldi, M., Aynès, L., Bac, A., Crocq, P., Dos-Reis, D., Frémeaux, E., Provansal, A., Simler, P. & Synvet, H., *Rapport relatif à la réforme du droit des sûretés remis au garde des Sceaux par le groupe de travail présidé par M. Michel Grimaldi*, 2005.

Van der Grinten 1993
Van der Grinten, W.C.L., *Lastgeving* (Monografieën Nieuw BW, B81), Deventer: Kluwer 1993.

Grodecki 1976
Grodecki, J.K., 'Private International Law, chapter 8 Intertemporal Conflicts of Laws', in: K. Lipstein (ed.), *International Encyclopedia of Comparative Law*, Volume III, Mouton: J.C.B. Mohr 1976.

De Groot 1926
De Groot, H., *Inleidinge tot de Hollandsche rechts-geleerdheid*, Arnhem: S. Gauda Quint 1926.

De Groot 1995a
De Groot, J.J.A., 'Privatieve last en economische eigendom (I)', *Weekblad voor Privaatrecht, Notariaat en Registratie*, (6180) 1995, p. 314-316.

De Groot 1995b
De Groot, J.J.A., 'Privatieve last en economische eigendom (II)', *Weekblad voor Privaatrecht, Notariaat en Registratie*, (6181) 1995, p. 328-330.

Grosheide 1982
Grosheide, F.W., *Eigendom in de overgang? (1838-1985)*, Assen: Calvinistische Juristen Vereniging 1982.

Grosheide 1995
Grosheide, F.W., 'Enkele opmerkingen over ABC-contracten - in het bijzonder in verband met onroerend goed transacties', *Weekblad voor Privaatrecht, Notariaat en Registratie*, (6172) 1995, p. 181-184.

Guarino 2001
Guarino, A., *Diritto Privato Romano*, 12th edition, Napoli: Jovene 2001.

Gunther 1998
Gunther, W., 'De invloed van de redelijkheid en billijkheid op erfdienstbaarheden', *Ars Aequi*, (116) 1998, p. 170-179.

Haanappel & Mackaay 1990
Haanappel, P.P.C. & Mackaay, E., *New Netherlands Civil Code Patrimonial Law – Nouveau code civil Néerlandais le droit patrimonial*, Deventer, Boston: Kluwer Law and Taxation Publishers 1990.

Hage 2004
Hage, J., 'Vermogensrechten en hun objecten', *Nederlands Tijdschrift voor Burgerlijk Recht*, (8) 2004, p. 355-362.

Halpérin 1992
Halpérin, J.-L., *L'impossible code civil, Histoires*, Paris: Presses Universitaires de France 1992.

Hansmann & Kraakman 2002
Hansmann, H. & Kraakman, R., 'Property, Contract and Verification: The Numerus Clausus Problem and the Divisibility of Rights', *Journal of Legal Studies*, (31/2) 2002, p. 373-420.

Hardin 1968
Hardin, G., 'The Tragedy of the Commons', *Science*, (162) 1968, p. 1243-1248.

Harris 1961
Harris, D.R., 'The Concept of Possession in English Law', in: *A.G. Guest* (ed.), *Oxford Essays in Jurisprudence*, Oxford: Oxford University Press 1961, p. 69-106.

Harris 1996
Harris, J., *Property and Justice*, Oxford: Clarendon Press 1996.

Harris 2002
Harris, J., 'Property - Rights in Rem or Wealth?', in: *P. Birks & A. Pretto* (eds.), *Themes in Comparative Law - In Honour of Bernard Rudden*, Oxford: Oxford University Press 2002, p. 52-63.

Hart 1970
Hart, H.L.A. (ed.), *The Collected Works of Jeremy Bentham - Of Laws in General*, The collected works of Jeremy Bentham; London: The Athlone Press 1970.

Hartkamp et al. 1998
Hartkamp, A., Hesselink, M., Hondius, E., Joustra, C. & Du Perron, E. (eds.), *Towards a European Civil Code*, 2nd revised and expanded edition, Nijmegen: Ars Aequi Libri 1998.

Hartmann 1879
Hartmann, G., 'Recht an eigener Sache', *Jheringer Jahrbücher für die Dogmatik des heutigen römischen und deutschen Privatrechts*, (17) 1879, p. 69-144.

Hattenhauer 1989
Hattenhauer, H., 'Über vereintes und entzweites Eigentum', in: J.F. Baur (ed.), *Das Eigentum. Vorträge gehalten auf der Tagung des Joachim Jungius-Gesellschaft der Wissenschaften Hamburg am 10., 11. und 12 Dezember 1987, Göttingen: Vandenhoeck & Ruprecht* 1989, p. 83-101.

Hayton 1998
Hayton, D.J., *The Law of Trusts*, 3rd edition, London: Sweet & Maxwell 1998.

Hayton, Kortman & Verhagen 1999
Hayton, D.J., Kortmann, S.C.J.J. & Verhagen, H.L.E., *Principles of European trust law*, The Hague/Deventer: Kluwer 1999.

Heck 1930
Heck, P., *Grundriss des Sachenrechts*, 3. Aalen: Scienta Verlag 1994, Tübingen: J.C.B. Mohr 1930.

Heirbaut 2003
Heirbaut, D., 'Feudal Law: the Real Ius Commune of Property in Europe, or: Should We Reintroduce Duplex Dominium', *European Review of Private Law*, (3) 2003, p. 301-320.

Heirbaut 2004
Heirbaut, D., 'Conclusions: codification, a new beginning for the nation? The relationship of the code civil to the old law and to nationalism', in: R. Beauthier & I. Rorive (eds.), *Le Code Napoléon un ancêtre vénéré? Mélanges offerts à Jacques Vanderlinden*, Brussel: Bruylant 2004, p. 319-333.

Heller 1998
Heller, M.A., 'The Tragedy of the Anticommons: Property in the Transition from Marx to Markets', *Harvard Law Review*, (111/3) 1998, p. 621-688.

Heller 1999
Heller, M.A., 'The Boundaries of Private Property', *The Yale Law Journal*, (108) 1999, p. 1164-1223.

Helmholz & Zimmermann 1998
Helmholz, R. & Zimmermann, R., 'Views of Trust and Treuhand: An Introduction', in: R. Helmholz & R. Zimmermann (eds.), *Itinera Fiduciae, Trust and Treuhand in historical perspective*, Berlin: Duncker & Humblot 1998, p. 27-44.

Hemel 1998
Hemel, W.H., *Beschikken over een aandeel in een gemeenschap*, Deventer: Kluwer 1998.

Henckel 1982
Henckel, W., 'Haftungsfragen bei der Verwalungstreuhand', in: N. Horn (ed.), *Europäisches Rechtsdenken in Geschichte und Gegenwart. Festschrift für Helmut Coing zum 70. Geburtstag* (Band II), München: *C.H. Beck'sche* Verlagsbuchhandlung 1982, p. 137-147.

Hervieu 1981
Hervieu, A., *De la limitation des droits réels. Contribution a l'étude de la distinction des droits réels et personnels* (diss.), Caen: 1981.

Hess 1998
Hess, B., 'Dienstbarkeit und Reallast im System dinglicher Nutzungs- und Verwertungsrechte', *Archiv für die civilistische Praxis*, (198) 1998, p. 489-515.

Hesselink, Rutgers & De Booys 2007
Hesselink, M.W., Rutgers, J.W. & De Booys, T., *The legal basis for an optional instrument on European contract law*, Centre for the Study of European Contract Law Working Paper Series/04, 2007, p. 1-83.

Heuff & Huijgen 2000
Heuff, W. & Huijgen, W.G., *Hypotheek* (Monografieën Nieuw BW, B12b), 3rd edition, Deventer: Kluwer 2000.

Heyman 1994
Heyman, H.W., 'De reikwijdte van het fiducia-verbod – In het bijzonder in verband met leasing', *Weekblad voor Privaatrecht, Notariaat en Registratie*, (6119) 1994, p. 1-14.

Heyman 1999
Heyman, H.W., 'Kan een opstalrecht worden gevestigd door een erfpachter of een appartementseigenaar?', *Weekblad voor Privaatrecht, Notariaat en Registratie*, (6342) 1999, p. 52-56.

Heyman 2003
Heyman, H.W., 'Blaauboer/Berlips (HR 3-3-1905)', in: E. Hondius & G.E. van Maanen (eds.), *Civiele klassiekers revisited; Van Blaauboer/Berlips tot Breda/Antonius – Zestien standaardarresten opnieuw geannoteerd*, Deventer: Kluwer 2003, p. 9-34.

Heyman 2004
Heyman, H.W., 'Contents of the Real Right: Dogmatic Rigidity and Pragmatic Flexibility of Dutch Property Law', in: S.E. Bartels & J.M. Milo (eds.), *Contents of Real Rights*, Nijmegen: Wolf Legal Publishers 2004, p. 71-81.

Heyman 2005
Heyman, H.W., 'Het mysterie van het eigendomsrecht van de opstaller', *2000 jaar eigendom en beperkte rechten*, Deventer: Kluwer 2005, p. 19-31.

Hillman 2004
Hillman, R.A., *The Many Dimensions of Private Law; commentary on Stephen Waddams, Dimensions of Private Law*, Cornell Law School Legal Studies Research Paper Series, No. 04-013, 2004.

Hinteregger 2006
Hinteregger, M., 'Servitudes - The Austrian Concept', in: J.H.M. van Erp & B. Akkermans (eds.), *Towards a Unified System of Land Burdens?* (Ius Commune Europaeum, 59), Antwerpen-Oxford: Intersentia 2006, p. 21-30.

Hofer 2001
Hofer, S., *Freiheit ohne Grenze? Privatrechtstheoretische Diskussionen im 19. Jahrhundert* (Jus Privatum. Beiträge zum Privatrecht, 53), Tübingen: Mohr Siebeck 2001.

Hohfeld 1917
Hohfeld, W.N., 'Fundamental Legal Conceptions as Applied in Judicial Reasoning', *Yale Law Journal*, (26) 1917, p. 710-770.

Holdsworth 1927
Holdsworth, W., *An historical introduction to the land law*, Oxford: Oxford University Press, 1927; repr. 2004, The Lawbook Exchange Ltd, Clark, New Jersey.

Holdsworth 1933
Holdsworth, W., 'Review of Ashburner's Principles of Equity. Second edition. By Denis Browne B.A., of Lincoln's Inn, Barrister-at-Law. London: Butterworth & Co., Ltd. 520, xlix, and 31pp. (32s. 6d. net.)', *Law Quarterly Review*, (49) 1933, p. 576-583.

Holdsworth 1942
Holdsworth, W.S., *1066-1485. The mediaeval common Law.* Part 2, III, A history of English law in sixteenth volumes; London: Sweet & Maxwell 1942.

Hondius 1998
Hondius, E., 'Towards a European Civil Code, General Introduction', in: A. Hartkamp, M. Hesselink, E. Hondius, C. Joustra & E. Du Perron (eds.), *Towards a European Civil Code*, 2nd revised and expanded edition, Nijmegen: Ars Aequi Libri 1998.

Honoré 1961
Honoré, A.M., 'Ownership', in: *A.G. Guest* (ed.), *Oxford Essays in Jurisprudence*, Oxford: Oxford University Press 1961, p. 107-147.

Honoré et al. 2003
Honoré, A.M., Cameron, E., De Waal, M.J., Wunsh, B., Solomon, P. & Kahn, E., *Honoré's South African Law of Trusts*, 5th edition, Lansdowne: JUTA Law 2003.

Honsell 1997
Honsell, H., *Römisches Recht*, 4th edition, Berlin; Heidelberg; New York, London, Paris, Tokyo: Springer Verlag 1997.

Houtcieff 2006
Houtcieff, D., 'Le cautionnement réel n'est pas un cautionnement', *Revue des Contrats*, (2) 2006, p. 458.

Huc 1893
Huc, T., *Commentaire théorique & pratique du Code Civil* (4), Paris: Librairie *Cotillon*, 1893.

Huijgen 1995
Huijgen, W.G., *Economische Eigendom* (Studiepocket Privaatrecht, 50), Zwolle: W.E.J. Tjeenk Willink 1995.

Israël 2005
Israël, J., *European Cross-Border Insolvency Regulation*, Antwerpen Oxford: Intersentia 2005.

Israël & Saarloos 2007
Israël, J. & Saarloos, K., 'Europees internationaal privaat- en procesrecht', in: A.S. Hartkamp, C.H. Sieburgh & L.A.D. Keus (eds.), *De invloed van het Europese recht op het Nederlandse privaatrecht*, Deel II, Deventer: Kluwer 2007, p. 629-698.

Jansen 2006
Jansen, N., 'Comparative Law and Comparative Knowledge', in: M. Reimann & R. Zimmermann (eds.), *The Oxford Handbook of Comparative Law*, Oxford: Oxford University Press 2006, p. 305-338.

Jansen & Zimmermann 2007
Jansen, N. & Zimmermann, R., 'Grundregeln des bestehenden Gemeinschaftsprivatrechts?', *Juristen Zeitung*, (23) 2007, p. 1113-1164.

Janssen 1991
Janssen, A.J.G., 'Kwalitatieve verplichtingen en erfdienstbaarheid: lood om oud ijzer?', in: *W.C.L. van der Grinten, S.C.J.J. Kortmann, A.J.M. Nuytinck & H. Wammes* (eds.), *Onderneming en nieuw burgerlijk recht,* Zwolle: W.E.J. Tjeenk Willink 1991, p. 269-278.

Joerges 1997
Joerges, C., 'The Impact of European Integration on Private Law: Reductionist Perceptions, True Conflicts and a New Constitutional Perspective', *European Law Journal,* (3/4) 1997, p. 378-406.

Joerges 2005
Joerges, C., *Rethinking European Law's Supremacy. With comments by Damian Chalmers, Rainer Nickel, Florian Rödel, Robert Wai,* EUI Working Paper LAW/2005/12, 2005.

Johnston 1989
Johnston, D., 'Successive Rights and Successful Remedies: Life Interests in Roman Law', in: P. Birks (ed.), *New Perspectives in the Roman Law of Property – Essays for Barry Nicholas,* Oxford: Clarendon Press 1989, p. 153-167.

Johnston 1999
Johnston, D., *Roman Law in Context,* Cambridge: Cambridge University Press 1999.

Johow 1982
Johow, R. (ed.), *Sachenrecht., Teil 1 Allgemeine Bestummungen, Besitz und Eigentum,* Die Vorlagen der Redaktoren für die erste Kommission zur Ausarbeitung des Entwurfs eines Bürgerlichen Gesetzbuches, Berlin - New York: Walter de Gruyter & Co 1982; Reprint of the original manuscript from 1876-1888 editions.

De Jong 1995a
De Jong, J., 'Erfpacht. Bespreking van het preadvies "Erfpacht" van mr W.G. Huijgen, prof. mr G.M.F. Snijders en prof. mr A.A. van Velten uitgebracht voor de Algemene Ledenvergadering van de Koninklijke Notariële Broederschap op 22 september 1995', *Weekblad voor Privaatrecht, Notariaat en Registratie,* (6190) 1995, p. 523-527.

De Jong 1995b
De Jong, J., *Erfpacht en opstal* (Monografieën Nieuw BW, B28), 2nd edition, Deventer: Kluwer 1995.

Jörs, Kunkel & Wenger 1987
Jörs, P., Kunkel, W. & Wenger, L., *Römisches Recht,* 4th edition, Berlin/*Heidelberg*/ New York/London/Paris/Tokyo: Springer Verlag 1987.

Jourdain, Marty & Raynaud 1995
Jourdain, P., Marty, G. & Raynaud, P., *Les biens,* Paris: Dalloz 1995.

De Juglart 1937
De Juglart, M., *Obligation réelle et servitudes en droit privé français* (diss.), Bordeaux: Imprimerie Fredou & Manville 1937.

Kaden 1951
Kaden, E.H., 'Heinrich Vogt, Das Erbbaurecht des klassischen römischen Rechts - Review', *Zeitschrift der Savigny-Stiftung für Rechtsgeschichte, Romanistische Abteilung,* (68) 1951, p. 607-614.

Kaser 1964
Kaser, M., 'The Concept of Roman Ownership', *Tydskrif vir hedendaagse Romeins-Hollandse reg,* 1964, p. 5-19.

Kaser 1971
Kaser, M., *Das römische Privatrecht; 1. Abschnitt,* 2nd renewed edition, München: C.H. Beck'sche Verlagsbuchhandlung 1971.

Kaser 1975
Kaser, M., *Das römische Privatrecht; 2. Abschnitt,* 2nd renewed edition, München: C.H. Beck'sche Verlagsbuchhandlung 1975.

Kaser & Knütel 2003
Kaser, M. & Knütel, R., *Römisches Privatrecht,* 17th renewed and extended edition, München: C.H. Beck 2003.

Kaser & Wubbe 1971
Kaser, M. & Wubbe, F.B.J., *Romeins Privaatrecht* (*Römisches Privaatrecht*), trans. F.B.J. Wubbe, 2nd revised and updated edition, Zwolle: Tjeenk Willink 1971.

Keijser 2004
Keijser, T.R.M.P., 'De implementatie van de Europese Richtlijn betreffende financiëlezekerheidsovereenkomsten', *Weekblad voor Privaatrecht, Notariaat en Registratie,* (6592) 2004, p. 761-770.

Kerridge 2000
Kerridge, R., 'Succession', in: P. Birks (ed.), *English Private Law,* Volume I, Oxford: Oxford University Press 2000, p. 509-588.

Kersting & Schindler 2003
Kersting, C. & Schindler, C.P., 'The ECJ's Inspire Art Decision of 30 September 2003 and its Effects on Practice', *The German Law Journal,* (4/12) 2003, p. 1277-1291.

Ketelaar 1978
Ketelaar, F.C.J., *Oude zakelijke rechten - vroeger, nu en in de toekomst,* Leiden/Zwolle: Universitaire pers Leiden/W.E.J. Tjeenk Willink 1978.

Kieninger 1996a
Kieninger, E.-M., *Mobiliarsicherheiten im Europäischen Binnenmarkt. Zum Einfluß der Warenverkehrsfreiheit auf das nationale und internationale Sachenrecht der Mitgliedstaaten*, Baden-Baden: Nomos Verlagsgesellschaft 1996.

Kieninger 1996b
Kieninger, E.-M., 'Securities in Movable Property within the Common Market', *European Review of Private Law*, (4) 1996, p. 41-66.

Kieninger 2004
Kieninger, E.-M., 'Evaluation: a common core? convergences, subsisting differences and possible ways for harmonisation', in: E.-M. Kieninger (ed.), *Security Rights in Movable Property in European Private Law*, Cambridge: Cambridge University Press 2004, p. 647-673.

Kieninger 2005
Kieninger, E.-M., 'The Legal Framework of Regulatory Competition Based on Company Mobility: EU and US Compared', *The German Law Journal*, (6/4) 2005, p. 741-770.

Kieninger 2006
Kieninger, E.-M., 'European Regulation of Security Rights', in: U. Drobnig, H.J. Snijders & E.-J. Zippro (eds.), *Divergences of Property Law, an Obstacle to the Internal Market?*, München: Sellier. European Law Publishers 2006, p. 165-171.

Kieninger 2007
Kieninger, E.-M., 'Das Mobiliarsachenrecht als Objekt differenzierter Integrationsschritte', in: P. Jung & C. Baldus (eds.), *Differenzierte Integration im Gemeinschaftsprivatrecht*, München: Sellier. European Law Publishers 2007, p. 187-202.

Kipp 1911
Kipp, T., 'Über Doppelwirkungen im Recht', *Festschrift der Berliner Juristischen Fakultät für Ferdinand von Martitz zum fünfzigjährigen Doktorjubiläum am 24. Juli 1911*, Berlin: Verlag von Otto Liebmann 1911, p. 211-233.

Kisch 1932
Kisch, I., *Beschouwingen over de onderscheiding tusschen zakelijke en persoonlijke rechten* (diss.), Alphen a/d Rijn: N. Samson N.V. 1932.

Kleijn 1991
Kleijn, W.M., 'Het erfpachtsrecht als middel tot ruimtelijke ordening', in: W.C.L. van der Grinten, S.C.J.J. Kortmann, A.J.M. Nuytinck & H. Wammes (eds.), *Onderneming en nieuw burgerlijk recht*, Zwolle: W.E.J. Tjeenk Willink 1991, p. 279-281.

Kleijn 1994
Kleijn, W.M., '"Conversie voor alle zekerheid" De reikwijdte van het fiducia-verbod', *Weekblad voor Privaatrecht, Notariaat en Registratie*, (6119) 1994, p. 15-17.

Kliebisch 1997
Kliebisch, T.A.L., 'Vijf jaar fiducia-verbod', in: S.C.J.J. Kortmann, N.E.D. Faber, A.A. van Rossum & H.L.E. Verhagen (eds.), *Onderneming en 5 jaar nieuw burgerlijk recht* (Serie Onderneming en Recht, 7), Deventer: W.E.J. Tjeenk Willink 1997, p. 75-86.

De Kluiver 2004
De Kluiver, H.-J., 'Inspiring a New European Company Law? - Observations on the ECJ's Decision in Inspire Art from a Dutch Perspective and the Imminent Competition for Corporate Charters between EC Member States', *European Company and Finance Law Review*, 2004, p. 121-134.

Knöchlein 1991
Knöchlein, G., *Das Recht and der eigenen Sache. Die Eigentümerbriefgrundschuld nach deutschem und österreichischem Recht. Die Rechtsüberlagerung in ihren rechtsgeschichtlichen Grundlagen, ihre Gestaltungsbereiche und Grenzen in einem modernen Rechtssystem. Ein Beitrag zur Fortschreibung eines Eigentümergrundpfandes im österreichischen Zivilrecht*, Wien, Köln, Weimar: Böhlau Verlag 1991.

Konzen 2000
Konzen, H., 'Das Anwartschaftsrecht des Auflassungsempfängers in der Judikatur des Bundesgerichtshofs', in: C.-W. Canaris, A. Heldrich, K.J. Hopt, C. Roxin, K. Schmidt & G. Widmaier (eds.), *50 Jahre Bundesgerichtshof. Festgabe aus der Wissenschaft*, Band I. Bürgerliches Recht, München: Verlag C.H. Beck 2000, p. 871-895.

Koppenol-Laforce 1997a
Koppenol-Laforce, M.E., *Het Haagse Trustverdrag* (diss.) (Serie Recht en Praktijk, 101), Deventer: Kluwer 1997.

Koppenol-Laforce 1997b
Koppenol-Laforce, M.E., 'Inbreng van Nederlandse goederen in een trust', *Weekblad voor Privaatrecht, Notariaat en Registratie*, (6281) 1997, p. 545-551.

Kortmann 1992
Kortmann, S.C.J.J., 'Eigendom onder voorwaarde', in: E. Hondius, W.G. Huijgen, J. Hijma, T.J. Mellema-Kranenburg & J.H. Nieuwenhuis (eds.), *Quod Licet; Kleijn-Bundel*, Deventer: Kluwer 1992, p. 199-211.

Kortmann 1994
Kortmann, S.C.J.J., 'Struikelt leasing over de dode letter van art. 3:84 lid 3 BW?' *Weekblad voor Privaatrecht, Notariaat en Registratie*, (6119) 1994, p. 18-23.

Kortmann 1995
Kortmann, S.C.J.J., 'Van fiducia-fobie naar fiducia-filie', *Weekblad voor Privaatrecht, Notariaat en Registratie*, (6187) 1995, p. 455-457.

Kortmann & Van Hees 1995
Kortmann, S.C.J.J. & Van Hees, J.J., 'Reïncarnatie in het recht, ofwel: de nieuwe gedaante van de zekerheidsoverdracht. Het arrest Keereweer q.q./Sogelease BV', *Nederlands Tijdschrift voor Burgerlijk Recht*, (27) 1995, p. 991-996.

Koschaker 1995
Koschaker, P., *Europa en het Romeinse recht* (*Europa und das römische Recht*), trans. T. Veen, Zwolle: W.E.J. Tjeenk Willink 1995.

Kötz 1963
Kötz, H., *Trust und Treuhand. Eine Rechtsvergleichende Darstellung des anglo-amerikanishen trust und funktionsverwandter Institute des deutschen Rechts* (diss.) (Jurisprudenz in Einzeldarstellungen), Göttingen: Vandenhoeck & Ruprecht 1963.

Kreuzer 1999
Kreuzer, K.F. (ed.), *Mobiliarsicherheiten. Vielfalt oder Einheit? Verhandlungen der Fachgruppe für vergleichendes Handels- und Wirtschaftsrecht anläßlich der Tagung der Gesellschaft für Rechtsvergleichung in Jena vom 20. - 22. März 1996*, Baden-Baden: Nomos 1999.

Kriechbaum 1996
Kriechbaum, M., *Actio, ius und dominium in der Rechtslehren des 13. und 14. Jahrhunderts, Abhandlungen zur Rechtswissenschaftlichten Grundlagenforschung* (Münchener Universitätschriften, Juridische Fakultät, 77), Ebelsbach: Aktiv Druck & Verlag GmbH 1996.

Kuhn 2007
Kuhn, C., 'Une fiducie française', *Droit et patrimoine*, (158) 2007, p. 32-44.

Kunkel 1973
Kunkel, W., 'Hypothesen zur Geschichte des römischen Pfandrechts', *Zeitschrift der Savigny-Stiftung für Rechtsgeschichte, Romanistische Abteilung*, (90) 1973, p. 150-170.

Van Laarhoven 2005
Van Laarhoven, M.J., 'Over derdenwerking van overeenkomsten en samenhangende rechtsverhoudingen. Enkele beschouwingen n.a.v. HR 24 september 2004, RvdW 2004. 108 (Vleesmeesters-Alog)', *Nederlands Tijdschrift voor Burgerlijk Recht*, (108) 2005, p. 48-59.

Land 1901
Land, N.K.F., *Verklaring van het Burgerlijk Wetboek – II*, Haarlem: *De Erven F. Bohn 1901.*

Lange 1997
Lange, H., *Römisches Recht im Mittelalter*, Band I Die Glossatoren, München: C.H. Beck'sche Verlagsbuchhandlung 1997.

Larentz 1989
Larentz, K., *Allgemeiner Teil des Deutschen Bürgerlichen Rechts*, 7th renewed edition, München: C.H. Beck'sche Verlagsbuchhandlung 1989.

Larroumet 2004
Larroumet, C., *Les Biens. Droits réels principaux*, Droit Civil, Tome II, 4th edition, Paris: Economica 2004.

Laurent 1878
Laurent, F., *Principes de droit civil français*, Tome 6, 3rd edition, Bruxelles/Paris: Bruylant-Cristophe & Ce - Librairie A. Marescq 1878.

Lawson 1975
Lawson, F.H. (ed.), *Property and trust, chapter 2 Structural variations in property law, VI*, International encyclopedia of comparative law; Mouton: J.C.B. Mohr 1975.

Lawson & Rudden 2002
Lawson, F.H. & Rudden, B., *The Law of Property*, 3rd edition, New York: Oxford University Press 2002.

Lebon 2007
Lebon, C., *Het zakenrechtelijk statuut van schuldvorderingen* (diss.), Leuven: 2007.

Legeais 1996
Legeais, D., *Sûretés et garanties du crédit*, Paris: LGDJ 1996.

Legeais 2006a
Legeais, D., *Sûretés et garanties du crédit*, 5th edition, Paris: LGDJ 2006.

Legeais 2006b
Legeais, D., 'Le gage de meubles corporels', *La Semaine Juridique Entreprise et affaires*, Supplément au No. 20, 2006, p. 12-18.

Legrand 1996a
Legrand, P., 'Sens et non-sens d'un code civil Européen', *Revue Internationale de Droit Comparé*, (4) 1996, p. 779-812.

Legrand 1996b
Legrand, P., 'European Legal Systems are not Converging', *International and Comparative Law Quarterly*, (45/January) 1996, p. 52-81.

Legrand 1997
Legrand, P., 'Against a European Civil Code', *Modern Law Review*, (60/1) 1997, p. 44-63.

Legrand 1999
Legrand, P., 'Sur l'analyse différentielle des jurisultures', *Revue Internationale de Droit Comparé*, (4) 1999, p. 1053-1071.

Lenel 1927
Lenel, O., *Das edictum perpetuum. Ein versuch zu seiner weiderherstellung*, Leipzig: Verlag B. Tauchnitz 1927; repr. 1985, Scientia Verlag Aalen.

Levenbach 1838
Levenbach, M.G., 'Het B.W. en de maatschappelijke verhoudingen van 1838 tot heden', in: P. Scholten & E.M. Meijers (eds.), *Gedenkboek Burgerlijk Wetboek 1838-1938*, Zwolle: Tjeenk Willink 1938, p. 129-168.

Lévy & Castaldo 2002
Lévy, J.-P. & Castaldo, A., *Histoire du droit civil*, Paris: Dalloz 2002.

Levy-Bruhl 1947
Levy-Bruhl, H., *Nouvelles Études sur le Très Ancien Droit Romain*, Paris: Recueil Sirey 1947.

Lewis 1987
Lewis, C., 'Real Rights in Land: a New Look at an Old Subject', *The South African Law Journal*, (104) 1987, p. 599-615.

Libchaber 2004
Libchaber, R., 'La recodification du droit des biens', *Le Code civil 1804-2004* (Livre du Bicentenaire), Paris: Dalloz/Lexis Nexis Litec 2004, p. 297-372.

Liebs 1975
Liebs, R., 'Die unbeschränkbare Verfügungsbefugnis', *Archiv für die civilistische Praxis*, (175/1-2) 1975, p. 1-43.

Lieverse & Wiggers-Rust 2005
Lieverse, C.W.M. & Wiggers-Rust, L.F., 'Verslag van de themamiddag Vereniging voor Burgerlijk Recht 2004: "De financiëlezekerheidsovereenkomst"', *Nederlands Tijdschrift voor Burgerlijk Recht*, (2) 2005, p. 59-63.

Lobban 2004a
Lobban, M., 'Preparing for Fusion: Reforming the Nineteenth-Century Court of Chancery, Part 1', *Law and History Review*, (22/2) 2004, p. 389-428.

Lobban 2004b
Lobban, M., 'Preparing for Fusion: Reforming the Nineteenth-Century Court of Chancery, Part 2', *Law and History Review*, (22/3) 2004, p. 565-600.

Lokin & Zwalve 1992
Lokin, J.H.A. & Zwalve, W.J., *Hoofdstukken uit de Europese codificatie geschiedenis*, 2nd edition, Groningen: Wolters-Noordhoff/Forsten 1992.

Lokin 2003
Lokin, J.H.A., *Prota. Vermogensrechtelijke leerstukken aan de hand van Romeinsrechtelijke teksten uitgelegd*, 6th edition, Groningen: Chimaira 2003.

Lokin & Zwalve 2001
Lokin, J.H.A. & Zwalve, W.J., *Hoofdstukken uit de Europese Codificatiegeschiedenis*, 3rd completely revised edition, Deventer: Kluwer 2001.

London Economics 2005
London Economics, *The Costs and Benefits of Integration of EU Mortgage Markets*, Report for European Commission DG-Internal Market and Services, Brussels: European Communities 2005.

Lupoi 2000
Lupoi, M., *The Origins of the European Legal Order* (*Alle radici del mondo giuridico europeo*), trans. A. Belton, Cambridge: Cambridge University Press 2000.

Lupoi 2005
Lupoi, M., 'A civil law perspective on trusts and the Italian case', *Trusts & Trustees*, (11/2) 2005, p. 10-14.

Van Maanen 1987
Van Maanen, G.E., *Eigendomsschijnbewegingen. Juridische, historische en politiek-filosofische opmerkingen over eigendom in huidig en komend recht*, Nijmegen: Ars Aequi Libri 1987.

Van Maanen 1998
Van Maanen, G.E., 'Ondergronds en bovengronds bouwen. De juridische infrastructuur. Enkele beschouwingen naar aanleiding van H.D. Ploeger, Horizontale splitsing van eigendom, Serie Ars Notariatus, Deventer 1997, diss. Leiden 1997, en D. Samkalden en B. van den Berg, Juridische aspecten van ondergronds bouwen, preadviezen van de Vereniging voor Bouwrecht, Deventer 1997', *Weekblad voor Privaatrecht, Notariaat en Registratie*, (6326) 1998, p. 553-557.

Maeijer 1966
Maeijer, J.M.M., *Erfdienstbaarheden en kwalitatieve verbintenissen (huidig en wordend recht), Preadviezen uitgebracht ... ter behandeling in de algemene vergadering van de Broederschap van Candidaat-Notarissen*, 1966.

Maitland 1936
Maitland, F.W., *Equity. A course of lectures*, Cambridge: Cambridge University Press 1936; repr. 1969 Cambridge, Cambridge University Press.

Malaurie & Aynès 2003
Malaurie, P. & Aynès, L., *Les biens* (Droit civil), Paris: Defrénois 2003.

Malaurie & Aynès 2005
Malaurie, P. & Aynès, L., *Les biens* (Droit civil), 2nd edition,; Paris: Defrénois 2005.

Marcadé 1873
Marcadé, V., *Explication théorique et pratique du Code Civil*, Tome 2, 7th edition, Paris: Delamotte et fils 1873.

Marquet 2004
Marquet, H.P., 'La présentation du droit des biens', in: J. Béguin, C.P.P. Maistre Du Chambon, P. Simler & F. Terré (eds.), *Le discours et le code. Portalis, deux siècles après le Code Napoléon* (Éditions du Juris-Classeur), Paris: Litec 2004, p. 269-278.

Marwede 1972
Marwede, J., *Rechtsnatur und aussenschutz des trust und der Treuhand. Zugleich ein Beitrag zur Dinglichkeit und zum System subjektiver Privatrechte* (diss.), Bonn: Rheinische Friedrich-Wilhelms-Universität 1972.

Mattei 2000
Mattei, U., *Basic Principles of Property Law. A Comparative Legal and Economic Introduction*, Contributions in Legal Studies, Westport, Connecticut: Greenwood Press 2000.

Mattei 2003
Mattei, U., *The European Codification Process: Cut and Paste*, Private Law in European Context Series; The Hague, London, New York: Kluwer Law International 2003.

Mayer-Maly 1984
Mayer-Maly, T., 'Das Eigentumsverständnis der Gegenwart und die Rechtsgeschichte', in: G. Baumgärtel, H.J. Becker, E. Klingmüller & A. Wacke (eds.), *Festschrift für Heinz Hübner zum 70. Geburtstag am 7. November 1984*, Berlin - New York: Walter de Gruyter 1984, p. 145-158.

Mayer-Maly 1985
Mayer-Maly, T., 'Die Verpfändbarkeit von Grunddienstbarkeiten', in: J.A. Ankum, J.E. Spruit & F.B.J. Wubbe (eds.), *Satura Roberto Feenstra sexagesimum quintum annum aetatis complenti ab alumnis collegis amicis oblata*, Fribourg: University Press Fribourg 1985, p. 173-182.

Mayer-Maly 1991
Mayer-Maly, T., *Römisches Privatrecht*, Wien/New York: Springer-Verlag 1991.

Mayer-Maly 1999
Mayer-Maly, T., *Römisches Recht*, 2nd extended edition, Wien: Springer-Verlag 1999.

Mayer-Maly 2003
Mayer-Maly, T., 'Commercium', *Tijdschrift voor Rechtsgeschiedenis,* (1) 2003, p. 1-5.

McBryde, Flessner & Kortmann 2005
McBryde, W.W., Flessner, A. & Kortmann, S.C.J.J. (eds.), *Principles of European Insolvency Law,* Deventer: Kluwer Law International 2005.

McFarlane 2003
McFarlane, B., 'Proprietary estoppel and third parties after the Land Registration Act 2002', *Cambridge Law Journal,* (62/3) 2003, p. 661-696.

Meijer 1991
Meijer, R.S., 'Het eerste van vijf; de exclusiviteit van eigendom', *Liber Amicorum NBW - Opstellen aangeboden aan mr drs B.C. de Die,* Arnhem/Deventer/Zwolle: Gouda Quint/Kluwer/W.E.J. Tjeenk Willink 1991, p. 73-78.

Meijer 1994
Meijer, W.R., 'Is een appartementsrecht een beperkt recht? Reactie naar aanleiding van het artikel van mr. R.J. Holtman "Mandeligheid en beperkte rechten" in WPNR, 1993) 6085, en de reactie van mr. L.C.A. Verstappen en het naschrift van mr. R.J. Holtman over dit onderwerp in WPNR (6089), 1993)', *Weekblad voor Privaatrecht, Notariaat en Registratie,* (6126) 1994, p. 166-168.

Meijers 1907
Meijers, E.M., 'Art. 584 B.W. en de zakelijke rechten', *Verzamelde privaatrechtelijke opstellen van Prof. Mr E.M. Meijers - Deel II,* Leiden: Universitaire Pers Leiden, 1955, p. 8-26, *Rechtsgeleerd Magazijn,* (26) 1907, p. 271-299.

Meijers 1937
Meijers, E.M., 'Misbruik van recht en wetsontduiking', *Verzamelde privaatrechtelijke opstellen van Prof. Mr E.M. Meijers - Deel I,* Leiden: Universitaire Pers 1954, p. 63-81, Lezingen van 9-11 Maart 1937 te Leuven gehouden. Annalen voor rechtsgeleerdheid en staatswetenschappen. Universiteit te Leiden, Brussel, J. Vromans 1937.

Meijers 1948
Meijers, E.M., *Algemene leer van het burgerlijk recht - deel I - De Algemene Begrippen van het Burgerlijk Recht,* Leiden: Universitaire Pers 1948.

Meijers 1955
Meijers, E.M., *Ontwerp voor een Nieuw Burgerlijk Wetboek - Toelichting Boek 5,* Den Haag: Staatsdrukkerij- en uitgeverijbedrijf 1955.

Mellema-Kranenburg 1999
Mellema-Kranenburg, T.J., 'Vruchtgebruik algemeen', in: J.P.M. Stubbé, T.J. Mellema-Kranenburg, C.A. Kraan & I.J.F.A. van Vijfeiken, (eds.), *Vruchtgebruik,* Preadviezen, 's-Gravenhage: Koninklijke Vermande 1999, p. 15-63.

Merrill & Smith 2000
Merrill, T.W. & Smith, H.E., '*Optimal Standardization in the Law of Property: The* Numerus Clausus Principle', (110) *Yale Law Journal*, 2000, p. 1-70.

Mertens 1989
Mertens, R.F.H., *Appartementsrecht en de welstandsbepalingen. Een rechtsvergelijkende studie* (diss.), Deventer: Kluwer 1989.

Mertens 1999
Mertens, R.F.H., *Appartementen* (Monografieën Nieuw BW, B29), Deventer: Kluwer 1999.

Mertens 2004
Mertens, R.F.H., 'Het appartementsrecht vernieuwd!', *Bouwrecht*, (1) 2004, p. 28-34.

Van der Merwe 1994
Van der Merwe, C.G., 'Ch. 5 Apartment Ownership', in: F. Lawson & A.N. Yiannopoulos (eds.), *International Encyclopedia of Comparative Law*, Deventer: Kluwer Law International 1994.

Van der Merwe 2004
Van der Merwe, C.G., 'Numerus Clausus and the Development of new Real Rights in South Africa', in: S.E. Bartels & J.M. Milo (eds.), *Contents of Real Rights*, Nijmegen: Wolf Legal Publishers 2004, p. 99-113.

Van der Merwe & De Waal 1993
Van der Merwe, C.G. & De Waal, M.J., *The law of things and servitudes*, Durban: Butterworths 1993.

Van der Merwe 1989
Van der Merwe, C.G., *Sakereg*, 2nd edition, Durban: Butterworths 1989.

Van der Merwe & Pienaar 1999
Van der Merwe, C.G. & Pienaar, J.M., 'Law of property (including real security) - Case Law - Registrable Rights', *Annual Survey of SA Law*, 1999, p. 284-290.

Van der Merwe, De Waal & Carey-Miller 2002
Van der Merwe, C.G., De Waal, M.J. & Carey Miller, D.L., *Property and Trust Law - South Africa*, International Encyclopaedia of Laws, Suppl. 2 (July 2002), Deventer: Kluwer Law International 2002.

Van der Merwe 1996
Van der Merwe, D., 'Property in Mixed Legal Systems: South Africa', in: G.E. van Maanen & A.J. van der Walt (eds.), *Property Law on the threshold of the 21st century*, MAKLU 1996, p. 355-389.

Mestre, Putman & Billiau 1996
Mestre, J., Putman, E. & Billiau, M., *Droit spécial. Des sûretés réelles* (Traité de droit civil), Paris: LGDJ 1996.

Meulman 2005
Meulman, J., 'Reactie op "Financiëlezekerheidsovereenkomsten" van prof. mr. *J.H.M. van Erp in* WPNR (6601), 2004. Nogmaals de Richtlijn financiëlezekerheids-overeenkomsten - Een Europese barrière voor de Nederlandse implementatie wet? -', *Weekblad voor Privaatrecht, Notariaat en Registratie*, (6615) 2005, p. 248-251.

Michaels 2006a
Michaels, R., 'The Functional Method of Comparative Law', in: M. Reimann & R. Zimmermann (eds.), *The Oxford Handbook of Comparative Law*, Oxford: Oxford University Press 2006, p. 339-382.

Michaels 2006b
Michaels, R., *EU Law as Private International Law? Re-conceptualising the Country-of-Origin Principle as Vested Rights Theory*, ZERP Discussion Paper, 5/2006, Bremen: ZERP 2006.

Michel 1995
Michel, J.-H., 'Les articles historiques du code civil', in: R. Feenstra, A. Hartkamp, J.E. Spruit, P.J. Sijpesteijn & L.C. Winkel (eds.), *Collatio Iuris Romani – études dédiés à Hans Ankum à l'occasion de son 65e anniversaire*, Volume I, Amsterdam: *J.C. Gieben* 1995, p. 349-362.

Van Mierlo 1988
Van Mierlo, A.I.M., *Fiduciaire zekerheid, vuistloos en stil pand. Enige beschouwingen omtrent het rechtskarakter van de fiduciaire zekerheidsoverdracht naar huidig recht en van de haar opvolgende regeling in het Nieuwe Burgerlijk Wetboek* (diss.), Deventer: Kluwer 1988.

Van Mierlo 2000
Van Mierlo, A I M., 'Van Gorp q.q./Rabobank Breda', *Ars Aequi*, (49/1) 2000, p. 55-61.

Mincke 1995
Mincke, G.W., 'Sale en lease back, art. 3:84 lid 3 BW, eigendomsvoorbehoud en de numerus clausus', *Nederlands Tijdschrift voor Burgerlijk Recht*, (8) 1995, p. 175-179.

Molenaar 1991
Molenaar, F., *Pandrecht* (Monografieën Nieuw BW, B12a), Deventer: Kluwer 1991.

Molenaar 1999
Molenaar, F., *Algemene bepalingen zekerheidsrechten op goederen* (Monografieën Nieuw BW, B11), Deventer Kluwer 1999.

Mortgage Credit Funding Group 2004
Mortgage Credit Funding Group, Ducoulombier, E. & Shewaram, H., *The Integration of the EU Mortgage Credit Market*, Report by the Forum Group on Mortgage Credit, Brussels: European Communities 2004.

Motive III 1888
Motive zu dem Entwurfe eines Bürgerlichen Gesetzbuches für das Deutsche Reich – Sachenrecht, III, Berlin: Verlag von J. Guttentag 1888.

Van Mourik 1999
Van Mourik, M.J.A., 'Erfrecht en vruchtgebruik', *Weekblad voor Privaatrecht, Notariaat en Registratie*, (6368) 1999, p. 621-624.

Mugdan 1979
Mugdan, B., *Die gesamtem Materialien zum bürgerlichen Gesetzbuch für das Deutsche Reich – III Sachenrecht*, Neudruck der Ausgabe Berlin 1899, Aalen: Scienta Verlag 1979.

Mülbert 1997
Mülbert, P.O., 'Der redliche Vormerkungserwerb – oder: Die Vormerkung als akzessorisches Recht', *Archiv für die civilistische Praxis*, (197) 1997, p. 335-397.

Mülbert 2002
Mülbert, P.O., 'Das inexistente Anwartschaftsrecht und seine Alternativen', *Archiv für die civilistische Praxis*, (202) 2002, p. 912-950.

Müller 1997
Müller, K., *Sachenrecht*, Academia Iuris. Lehrbücher der Rechtswissenschaft, 4th revised edition, Köln-Berlin-Bonn-München: Carl Heymanns Verlag KG 1997.

Munzer 2006
Munzer, S.R., 'The Commons and the Anticommons in the Law and Theory of Property', in: M.P. Golding & W.A. Edmundson (eds.), *The Blackwell Guide to the Philosophy of Law and Legal Theory*, Malden: Blackwell Publishing 2006, p. 148-162.

Nasarre-Aznar 2004
Nasarre-Aznar, S., *Securitisation & Mortgage Bonds*, Legal aspects and harmonisation in Europe, Saffron Walden: Gostick Hall Publications 2004.

Nève 1995
Nève, P.L., 'Ius Commune oftewel "gemeen recht": traduttore traditore?', in: O.E. Tellegen-Couperus, P.L. Nève & J.W. Tellegen (eds.), *Tertium Datur; Drie opstellen aangeboden aan prof. mr. J.A. Ankum*, Tilburg: Tilburg University Press 1995, p. 3-58.

Nève 1996
Nève, P.L., 'Uit de bonte berm van de juridische begrippenflora: ons 'gesloten stelsel' van beperkte rechten', in: S.C.J.J. Kortmann, J.M.M. Maeijer, A.J.M. Nuytinck & S. Perrick (eds.), *Op Recht - Bundel opstellen aangeboden aan prof. mr. A.V.M. Struycken ter gelegenheid van zijn zilveren ambtsjubileum aan de Katholieke Universiteit Nijmegen*, Zwolle: W.E.J. Tjeenk Willink 1996, p. 223-232.

Nicholas 1962
Nicholas, B., *An Introduction to Roman Law*, Clarendon Law Series, New York: Oxford University Press 1962.

Nieskens-Ipshording 1996
Nieskens-Ipshording, B.W.M., 'Koophuur: een juridische variant van de nieuwe kleren van de keizer', *Nederlands Juristenblad*, (44/6) 1996, p. 1845-1848.

Nieskens-Ipshording 1997
Nieskens-Ipshording, B.W.M., 'Na de 'Vormerkung' nu ook de 'Anwartschaftsrechte'?,' in: B.W.M. Nieskens-Ipshording, E.M. Hemmen & T.H.D. Struycken (eds.), *Discussies omtrent beslag, verhaal en beschikkingsbevoegdheid*, Deventer: W.E.J. Tjeenk Willink 1997, p. 105-118.

Noordraven 1999
Noordraven, G., *Die Fiduzie im römischen Rechts*, trans. K.E. Mitting, Amsterdam: Gieben 1999.

Nörr 1992
Nörr, K.W., 'Zur Frage des subjektiven Rechts in der mittelalterlichen Rechtswissenschaft', in: D. Medicus (ed.), *Festschrift für Hermann Lange zum 70. Geburtstag am 24. Januar 1992*, Stuttgart: Kohlhammer 1992, p. 193-204.

O'Callaghan 2002
O'Callaghan, X., 'Derechos reales reconocidos en la legislatión Espanola', *Compendio de Derecho Civil*, Tomo 3 (Derechos reales e hipotecario), Madrid: EDERSA 2002.

Oakley 1998
Oakley, A.J., *Parker & Mellows: The Modern Law of Trusts*, 7th edition, London: Sweet & Maxwell 1998.

Von Oefele & Winkler 2003
Von Oefele, H.F. & Winkler, K., *Handbuch des Erbbaurechts*, 3rd renewed edition, München: Verlag C.H. Beck 2003.

Van Oostrom-Streep 2005
Van Oostrom-Streep, N.C., 'De kwalitatieve verplichting als twee-eenheid?', *Weekblad voor Privaatrecht, Notariaat en Registratie*, (6638) 2005, p. 786-788.

Van Oostrom-Streep 2006
Van Oostrom-Streep, N.C., *De kwalitatieve verplichting* (diss.), Den Haag: Boom Juridische uitgevers 2006.

Van Opstall 1966
Van Opstall, S.N., 'Zakelijke rechten en kwalitatieve verbintenissen', *Weekblad voor Privaatrecht, Notariaat en Registratie,* (4919-4926) 1966, p. 383-388, 395-399, 407-411, 419-422, 431-434, 443-446, 455-459, 467-473.

Otte 1978
Otte, G., 'Die dingliche Rechtsstellung des Mieters nach ALR und BGB', in: O. Behrends, M. Diesselhorst, H. Lange, D. Liebs, J.G. Wolf & C. Wollsläger (eds.), *Festschrift für Franz Wieacker zum 70. Geburtstag,* Göttingen: Vandenhoeck & Ruprecht 1978, p. 463-475.

Out 2002
Out, J.C., 'Hypotheekrecht op eigen goed?', in: S.C.J.J. Kortmann, C.J.H. Jansen, G. van Solinge & N.E.D. Faber (eds.), *Onderneming en 10 jaar nieuw burgerlijk recht,* Deventer: Kluwer 2002, p. 425-443.

Paisley 2004
Paisley, R.R.M., 'Contents of the Real Right: Practical Problems and Dogmatic Rigidity', in: S.E. Bartels & J.M. Milo (eds.), *Contents of Real Rights,* Nijmegen: Wolf Legal Publishers 2004, p. 115-148.

Palmer 1991
Palmer, N.E., *Bailment,* 2nd edition, London: Sweet & Maxwell 1991.

Palmer 1959
Palmer, R.R., *The Age of Democratic Revolution – a political history of Europe and America, 1760 – 1800 – The Challenge,* Princeton: Princeton University Press 1959.

Palmer 1970
Palmer, R.R., *The Age of Democratic Revolution – a political history of Europe and America, 1760 – 1800 – The Struggle,* 1st paperback edition, Princeton: Princeton University Press 1970.

Parchomovsky & Bell 2006
Parchomovsky, G. & Bell, A., 'Land burdens in the service of conservation', in: J.H.M. van Erp & B. Akkermans (eds.), *Towards a Unified System of Land Burdens?* (Ius Commune Europaeum, 59), Antwerpen - Oxford: Intersentia 2006, p. 137-162.

Parisi 2001
Parisi, F., *Entropy in property,* 2004, George Mason University Faculty of Law Working Paper, No. 01-14, 2001.

Parisi, Schulz & Depoorter 2005
Parisi, F., Schulz, N., Depoorter, B., 'Duality in Property: Commons and Anticommons', *International Review of Law and Economics*, (25) 2005, p. 578-591.

Parlementaire Geschiedenis NBW - Algemeen Deel 1961
Van Zeben, C.J., Belinfante, W.G. & Van Ewijk, O.W., *Algemeen deel – Voorgeschiedenis en algemene inleiding*, Deventer-Antwerpen: Æ.E. Kluwer 1961.

Parlementaire Geschiedenis NBW - Boek 3 1981
Van Zeben, C.J. & Du Pon, J.W., *Vermogensrecht in het algemeen* (Parlementaire Geschiedenis van het Nieuwe Burgerlijk Wetboek, Boek 3), Deventer: Kluwer 1981.

Parlementaire Geschiedenis NBW - Boek 5 1981
Van Zeben, C.J. & Du Pon, J.W., *Zakelijke Rechten* (Parlementaire Geschiedenis van het Nieuwe Burgerlijk Wetboek, Boek 5), Deventer: Kluwer 1981.

Parlementaire Geschiedenis NBW - Boek 6 1981
Van Zeben, C.J. & Du Pon, J.W., *Algemeen gedeelte van het verbintenissenrecht* (Parlementaire Geschiedenis van het Nieuwe Burgerlijk Wetboek, Boek 6), Deventer: Kluwer 1981.

Patault 1983
Patault, A.M., 'La propriété non exclusive au XIXe siècle: histoire de la dissociation juridique de l'immeuble', *Revue historique de droit français et étranger*, 1983, p. 217-237.

Patault 1989
Patault, A.M., *Introduction historique au droit des biens*, Paris: Presses universitaires de France 1989.

Paulick 1953
Paulick, H., 'Zur Dogmatik des Wohnungseigentums nach dem Wohnungseigentumsgesetz vom 15. März 1951', *Archiv für die civilistische Praxis*, (152) 1953, p. 420-232.

Du Perron 1999
Du Perron, C.E., *Overeenkomst en derden; Een analyse van de relativiteit van de contractswerking* (diss.) (Kluwer Rechtswetenschappelijke Publicaties), Deventer: Kluwer 1999.

Peters 1954
Peters, C., 'Die Ansprüche aus dem Eigentum', *Archiv für die civilistische Praxis*, (153) 1954, p. 454-465.

Pfenning 1997
Pfenning, C.M., *Die Kritik Otto von Gierkes am Ersten Entwurf eines Bürgerlichen Gesetzbuches* (diss.), Göttingen: Cuvillier Verlag 1997.

Picard 1952
Picard, M., *Traité pratique de droit civil français. Les biens*, Tome 3, Paris: LGDJ 1952.

Picod 1999
Picod, Y., *Leçons de droit civil. Sûretés - Publicité foncière*, Tome 3, 7th edition, Paris: Montchrestien 1999.

Piedelièvre 2004
Piedelièvre, S., *Les sûretés*, 4th edition, Paris: Dalloz 2004.

Pierre 1997
Pierre, B., 'Classification of Property and Conceptions of Ownership in Civil Law and Common Law', *Revue Générale de Droit*, (28/2) 1997, p. 235-274.

Pitlo 1968
Pitlo, A., 'Na 3 maart 1905', in: P.A.N. Houwing (ed.), *Onroerend goed: opstellen geschreven ter gelegenheid van het 125-jarig bestaan van de Broederschap der Notarissen in Nederland*, Deventer: Kluwer 1968, p. 231-248.

Pitlo et al. 2001
Pitlo, A., Rheehuis, W.H.M., Heisterkamp, A.H.T., Van Maanen, G.E. & De Jong, G.T., *Goederenrecht*, 11th revised and extended edition, Deventer: Gouda Quint 2001.

Pitlo et al. 2006
Pitlo, A., Rheehuis, W.H.M., Heisterkamp, A.H.T., Van Maanen, G.E. & De Jong, G.T., *Goederenrecht* (Het Nederlands burgerlijk recht, 3), 12th revised and expanded edition, Deventer: Kluwer 2006.

Planiol, Ripert & Becqué 1953
Planiol, M., Ripert, G. & Becqué, E., *Suretés réelles. Première partie* (Traité pratique de droit civil français), Tome XII, 2nd edition, Paris: LGDJ 1953.

Plantenga & Treurniet 1957
Plantenga, W.B. & Treurniet, W.C., *Erfpacht en Erfpachtsvoorwaarden, Preadviezen uitgebracht ... ter behandeling in de algemene vergadering van de Broederschap van Candidaat-Notarissen*, 1957.

Pleysier 1996
Pleysier, A.J.H., 'Why is Dutch Law not hampered by a numerus clausus (gesloten systeem, geslote kategorie) of real rights?', *Fundamina*, (2) 1996, p. 298 - 307.

Ploeger 1997
Ploeger, H.D., *Horizontale splitsing van eigendom* (Ars Notariatus, LXXXIII), Deventer: Kluwer 1997.

Polak 2006
Polak, M.V., 'Recognition, Enforcement and Transformation of Foreign Proprietary Rights - a handful of observations and suggestions', in: U. Drobnig, H.J. Snijders & E.-J. Zippro (eds.), *Divergences of Property Law, an Obstacle to the Internal Market?*, München: Sellier, European Law Publishers 2006, p. 117-128.

Polak & Van Mierlo 1998
Polak, M.V. & Van Mierlo, A.I.M., *Verstrekking van zekerheden aan internationale syndicaten* (NIBE-Bankjuridische Reeks, 31), 2nd revised edition, Amsterdam: Nederlands Instituut voor het Bank- en Effectenbedrijf 1998.

Pollock & Maitland 1895
Pollock, F. & Maitland, F.W., *The History of English Law - before the time of Edward I*, Volume I, Cambridge: Cambridge University Press 1895.

Pollock & Mailand 1898a
Pollock, F. & Maitland, F.W., *The History of English Law - before the time of Edward I*, Volume I, 2nd edition (1968 reprinted edition), Cambridge: Cambridge University Press 1898.

Pollock & Maitland 1898b
Pollock, F. & Maitland, F.W., *The History of English Law - before the time of Edward I*, Volume II, 2nd edition (2004, 5th reprinted edition (The Lawbook Exchange)), Cambridge: Cambridge University Press 1898.

Pool 1995
Pool, E.H., *Een kwestie van titels. Causa van bezit, verjaring en eigendom naar klassiek Romeins recht* (diss.), Amsterdam: 1995.

Portalis 1844
Portalis, J.E.M., *Discours rapports et travaux inédits sur le Code Civil*, Paris: Joubert, Libraire de la cour de cassation 1844.

Posner 1973
Posner, R., *Economic Analysis of Law*, Boston: Little Brown 1973.

Pothier 1772
Pothier, R.J., *Traité du droit de domaine de propriété*, Tome I, Paris/Orléans: Debure pere/La veuve Rouzeau-Montaut 1772.

Pretto 2002
Pretto, A., 'Primary Rights and Rights in Rem', in: P. Birks & A. Pretto (eds.), *Themes in Comparative Law - In Honour of Bernard Rudden*, Oxford: Oxford University Press 2002, p. 65-80.

Pretto-Sakmann 2005
Pretto-Sakmann, A., *Boundaries of Personal Property. Shares and Sub-Shares* (diss.), Oxford-Portland, Oregon: Hart Publishing 2005.

Puchta 1873
Puchta, G.F., *Vorlesungen über das heutige römische Recht – I*, 6th extended and improved edition, Leipzig: Verlag von Bernhard Tauchnitz 1873; Aus dessen Nachlass herausgegeben von A.A.F. Rudorff.

Quack 1997
Quack, F., *Münchener Kommentar zum Bürgerlichen Gesetzbuch. Sachenrecht (§§ 854-1296)*, Band 6, 3rd edition, München: C.H. Beck'sche Verlagsbuchhandlung 1997.

Raaijmakers 1994
Raaijmakers, G., 'De externe werking van een trustverhouding tegenover derden naar Engels en Nederlands recht', *Ars Aequi*, (43/5) 1994, p. 331-339.

Radke 2000
Radke, W.W., *Bedingungsrecht und Typenzwang – Eine Untersuchung zu Grundlagen und Granzen privatautonomer Gestaltung* (diss.), Berlin: Dunker & Humblot 2000.

Rainer 1989
Rainer, J.M., 'Superficies und Stockwerkseigentum in klassischen römischen Recht', *Zeitschrift der Savigny-Stiftung für Rechtsgeschichte, Romanistische Abteilung*, (106) 1989, p. 327-357.

Rainer 1995
Rainer, J.M., 'Zum Typenzwang der Servituten: vom Römischen Recht zum BGB', in: R. Feenstra, A. Hartkamp, J.E. Spruit, P.J. Sijpesteijn & L.C. Winkel (eds.), *Collatio Iuris Romani – études dédiés à Hans Ankum à l'occasion de son 65e anniversaire*, II, Amsterdam: J.C. Gieben 1995, p. 415-424.

Rainer 1998
Rainer, J.M., 'Max Kaser und die dinglichen Rechte', *Zeitschrift der Savigny-Stiftung für Rechtsgeschichte, Romanistische Abteilung*, (115) 1998, p. 161-167.

Raiser 1961
Raiser, L., *Dingliche Anwartschaften*, Tübingen: J.C.B. Mohr (Paul Siebeck) 1961.

Rank 2006
Rank, P.W., 'Harmonisation of National Security Rights', in: U. Drobnig, H.J. Snijders & E.-J. Zippro (eds.), *Divergences in Property Law, an Obstacle to the Internal Market?*, München: Sellier, European Law Publishers 2006, p. 201-215.

Rank 1997
Rank, W.A.K., 'Privatieve last tot hypotheekvestiging: een nieuwe zakelijke zekerheid?', in: S.C.J.J. Kortmann, N.E.D. Faber, A.A.V. Rossum & H.L.E. Verhagen (eds.), *Onderneming en 5 jaar nieuw burgerlijk recht*, Deventer: W.E.J. Tjeenk Willink 1997, p. 465-479.

Rank-Berenschot 1985
Rank-Berenschot, E.B., 'Enige aspecten van de plaats van het vruchtgebruik in het vermogensrechtelijk systeem', *Weekblad voor Privaatrecht, Notariaat en Registratie*, (5730) 1985, p. 170-179.

Rank-Berenschot 1992
Rank-Berenschot, E.B., *Over de scheidslijn tussen goederen- en verbintenissenrecht* (diss.), Deventer: Kluwer 1992.

Rank-Berenschot 1997
Rank-Berenschot, E.B., 'Substitutie na inning van een openbaar verpande vordering', in: S.C.J.J. Kortmann, N.E.D. Faber, A.A. van Rossum & H.L.E. Verhagen (eds.), *Onderneming en 5 jaar nieuw burgerlijk recht* (Serie Onderneming en Recht, 7), Deventer: W.E.J. Tjeenk Willink 1997, p. 237-252.

Rank-Berenschot 1998
Rank-Berenschot, E.B., 'Overdracht en toebehoren onder tijdsbepaling. Achtergrond en betekenis van art. 3:85 BW', in: S.I. Grotius (ed.), *Van Beheering – 'goederenrechtelijke beschouwingen'*, Deventer: Gouda Quint 1998, p. 149-162.

Recueil des lois composant le code civil, Livre Deuxième. Des Biens et des différent Modifications de la Propriété, 1804
Recueil des lois composant le code civil, avec les Discours des Orateurs du Gouvernement, les rapports de la commission du Tribunat, et les Opinions émises pendant le cours de la discussion, tant au Tribunat qu'au Corps législatif, et dont on a ordonné l'impression., Livre Deuxième. Des Biens et des différent Modifications de la Propriété, Paris: Rondonneau 1804.

Reedt Dortland 1997
Reedt Dortland, G.J.N., 'Koophuur: economische eigendom van de binnenkant van huurwoningen', *Weekblad voor Privaatrecht, Notariaat en Registratie*, (6258) 1997, p. 127-130.

Reich 1964
Reich, C.A., 'The New Property', *Yale Law Journal*, (73/5) 1964, p. 733-787.

Reid 1997a
Reid, K.G.C., '700 Years at One Blow: The Abolition of Feudal Land Tenure in Scotland', in: P. Jackson & D.C. Wilde (eds.), *The Reform of Property Law*, Aldershot: Darthmouth/Ashgate 1997.

Reid 1997b
Reid, K.G.C., 'Obligations and property: Exploring the Border', *Acta Juridica*, (227) 1997, p. 225-245.

Reid 2003
Reid, K.G.C., 'Vassals No More: Feudalism and Post-feudalism in Scotland', *European Review of Private Law*, (3) 2003, p. 282-300.

Reid 2004
Reid, K.G.C., 'Real Rights and Real Obligations', in: S.E. Bartels & J.M. Milo (eds.), *Contents of Real Rights*, Nijmegen: Wolf Legal Publishers 2004, p. 25-45.

Reid & Van der Merwe 2004
Reid, K.G.C. Van der Merwe, C.G., 'Property Law: Some Themes and Some Variations', in: R. Zimmermann, D. Visser & K.G.C. Reid (eds.), *Mixed Legal Systems in Comparative Perspective. Property and Obligations in Scotland and South Africa*, Oxford: Oxford University Press 2004, p. 637-670.

Reimann 1993
Reimann, M. (ed.), *The reception of continental ideas in the common law world* (Comparative studies in continental and Anglo-American legal history, 13), Berlin: Duncker & Humblot 1993.

Reinsma 1970
Reinsma, M., *Het onderscheid tussen zakelijke en persoonlijke rechten met betrekking tot onroerend goed in het zuidafrikaanse recht* (diss.), Pretoria: Universiteit van Suid-Afrika 1970.

Remien 2005
Remien, O., 'Real Property Law and European Private Law - A Sketch of Unsurveyed Territory -', in: C. Schmid & C. Hertel (eds.), *Real Property and Procedure in the European Union*, Florence/Würzburg: EUI and DNotI 2005, <http://www.iue.it/LAW/ResearchTeaching/EuropeanPrivateLaw/ProjectRealPropertyLaw.shtml>.

Rey 1991
Rey, H., *Die Grundlagen des Sachenrechts und das Eigentum, Grundriss des schweizerischen Sachenrechts*, Band I; Bern: Verlag Stämpfli & Cie AG 1991.

De Richemont 2006
De Richemont, H., Rapport fait au nom de la commission des Lois constitutionnelles, de législation, du suffrage universel, du Règlement et d'administration générale (1) sur la proposition de loi de M. Philippe MARINI instituant la fiducie, version PDF: N. 11, session 2006-2007, annexe au procès-verbal de la séance du 11 octobre 2006, 2006.

Rijtma 1969
Rijtma, H.J., 'Kwalitatieve rechten', Op de grenzen van komend recht, *Opstellen aangeboden aan prof. mr. J.H. Beekhuis*, Deventer/Zwolle: Kluwer/Tjeenk Willink 1969, p. 215-229.

Von Roth 1886
Von Roth, P., *System des Deutschen Privatrechts*, Dritter Theil Sachenrecht, Tübingen: Verlag der H. Laupp'schen Buchhandlung 1886.

Roth 1999
Roth, T., *Vereinheitlichichung des Rechts der Mobiliarsicherheiten. Möglichkeiten und Grenzen im Kollisions-, Europa-, Sach- und Vollstreckungsrecht unter Berücksichtigung des US-amerikanischen Systems der Kreditsicherheiten*, Tübingen: Mohr Siebeck 1999.

Rotherham 2002
Rotherham, C., *Proprietary Remedies in Context. A Study in the Judicial Redistribution of Property Rights*, Oxford/Portland/Oregon: Hart Publishing 2002.

De Roux 2007
De Roux, X., *Rapport fait au nom de la commission des lois constitutionnelles, de la législation et de l'administration générale de la république sur la proposition de loi (n. 3385), adopté par le sénat, instituant la fiducie*, version PDF: N. 3655 Enregistré à la Présidence de l'Assemblée nationale le 1er février 2007, 2007.

Rudden 1987
Rudden, B., 'Economic Theory v. Property Law: The Numerus Clausus Problem', in: J. Eekelaar & J. Bell (eds.), *Oxford Essays on Jurisprudence*, 3rd edition, Oxford: Clarendon Press 1987, p. 239-263.

Rudden 1994
Rudden, B., 'Things as Things and Things as Wealth', *Oxford Journal of Legal Studies*, (14) 1994, p. 83-97.

Rutgers 1999
Rutgers, J.W., *International Reservation of Title Clauses. A study of Dutch, French and German Private International Law in the Light of European Law* (diss.), The Hague: T.M.C. Asser Press 1999.

Rutgers 2005
Rutgers, J.W., 'The Rule of Reason and Private Law or the Limits to Harmonization', in: A. Schrauwen (ed.), *Rule of Reason. Rethinking another Classic of European Legal Doctrine*, Groningen: European Law Publishing 2005, p. 143-159.

Rutgers 2006
Rutgers, J.W., 'Harmonisation of Security Rights and the Communications on Contract Law', in: U. Drobnig, H.J. Snijders & E.-J. Zippro (eds.), *Divergences of Property Law, an Obstacle to the Internal Market?*, München: Sellier, European Law Publishers 2006, p. 217-227.

Sáez 2006
Sáez, J.F.A., 'Limitations to Property', in: J.H.M. van Erp & A. Vaquer (eds.), *Introduction to Spanish Patrimonial Law*, Granada: Editorial Comares 2006, p. 281-292.

Sagaert 2003
Sagaert, V., *Zakelijke Subrogatie* (diss.), Antwerpen - Oxford: Intersentia, 2003.

Sagaert 2004a
Sagaert, V., 'Les interférences entre le droit des biens et le droit des obligations: une analyse de l'évolution depuis le code civil', in: P. Wery (ed.), *Le droit des obligations contractuelles et le Bicentenaire du Code civil*, Brugge: die Keure 2004, p. 353-396.

Sagaert 2004b
Sagaert, V., 'Real rights and real obligations in Belgian and French law', in: S.E. Bartels & J.M. Milo (eds.), *Contents of Real Rights*, Nijmegen: Wolf Legal Publishers 2004, p. 47-70.

Sagaert 2004c
Sagaert, V., 'Preadvies. Het zakenrechtelijk statuur van nutsleidingen in het Belgische recht', *Tijdschrift voor Privaatrecht*, (41/4) 2004, p. 1-50.

Sagaert 2005a
Sagaert, V., 'Kwalitatieve verbintenissen in het Belgische en Nederlandse recht', in: J.M. Smits & S. Stijns (eds.), *Inhoud en werking van de overeenkomst naar Belgisch en Nederlands recht* (Ius Commune Europaeum, 50), Antwerpen - Groningen: Intersentia 2005, p. 341-363.

Sagaert 2005b
Sagaert, V., 'Het goederenrecht als open systeem van verbintenissen? Poging tot een nieuwe kwalificatie van de vermogensrechten', *Tijdschrift voor Privaatrecht*, (42/3) 2005, p. 983-1086.

Sagaert 2006
Sagaert, V., 'The Fragmented System of Land Burdens in French and Belgian Law', in: J.H.M. van Erp & B. Akkermans (eds.), *Towards a Unified System of Land Burdens?* (Ius Commune Europaeum, 59), Antwerpen - Oxford: Intersentia 2006, p. 31-52.

Sagaert 2007
Sagaert, V., 'De verworvenheden van het Europese goederenrecht', in: A.S. Hartkamp, C.H. Sieburgh & L.A.D. Keus (eds.), *De invloed van het Europese recht op het Nederlandse privaatrecht*, Deel I, Deventer: Kluwer 2007, p. 301-333.

Salomons 2002
Salomons, A.F., *De genade en ongenade van de eigenaar*, Deventer: Kluwer 2002.

Sauter & Schepel 2007
Sauter, W. & Schepel, H., *'State' and 'Market' in the Competition and Free Movement Case Law of the EU Courts*, 2007-24, TILEC Discussion Paper; Tilburg: Tilburg University 2007.

Von Savigny 1814
Von Savigny, F.K., 'Vom Beruf unsrer Zeit für Gesetzgebung und Rechtswissenschaft', in: H. Hattenhauer (ed.), *Thibaut und Savigny. Ihre programmatischen Schriften*, München: Verlag Franz Vahlen, 2002, p. 61-130, Heidelberg, Mohr und Zimmer 1814.

Von Savigny 1981
Von Savigny, F.K., *System des heutigen römischen Rechts*, 1, Aalen: Scienta Verlag 1981, repr. of the 1840 edition.

Schim 2004
Schim, B.F.L.M., 'Recensie "Effectengiro-recht in beweging"', *Nederlands Tijdschrift voor Burgerlijk Recht*, (8), 2004, p. 383-392.

Schmidt 2005
Schmidt, K., 'Das Rätsel Treuhandkonto - Gedanken über <Unmittelbarkeit>, <Mittelherkunft> und <Offenkundigkeit> als Kriterien der Verwaltungstreuhand', in: E. Bucher, C.-W. Canaris, H. Honsell & T. Koller (eds.), *Norm und Wirkung. Beiträge zum Privat- und Wirtschaftsrecht aus heutiger und historischer Perspektive. Festschrift für Wolfgang Wiegand zum 65. Geburtstag*, Bern: Stämpfli Verlag AG 2005, p. 933-963.

Schön 1992
Schön, W., *Der Nießbrauch and Sachen. Gesetzliche Struktur und recksgeschäftliche Gestaltung*, Köln: Verlag Dr. Otto Schmidt KG 1992.

Schön 2001
Schön, W., 'Zur Analogiefähigkeit des § 571 BGB', *Juristen Zeitung*, 2001, p. 119-127.

Schoordijk 1991
Schoordijk, H.C.F., 'Economische eigendom, vooral in het licht van Beslag-, Executie- en Bewijsrecht', in: *Verspreid werk van prof. mr. H.C.F. Schoordijk*, Deventer: Kluwer 1991, p. 363-381.

Schoordijk 1992
Schoordijk, H.C.F., 'Recensie; Over de scheidslijn tussen goederen- en verbintenissenrecht', *Nederlands Juristenblad*, (37/22) 1992, p. 1202-1206.

Schrage 1977
Schrage, E.J.H., *Actio en Subjectief Recht; over romeinse en middeleeuwse wortels van een modern begrip*, Amsterdam: VU 1977.

Schrage 1984
Schrage, E.J.H., *Koop breekt geen huur. Enige grepen uit de geschiedenis van het geleerde recht inzake de gevolgen van de vervreemding van een verhuurde zaak* (Rechtshistorische Cahiers), Deventer: Kluwer 1984.

Schrage 1996
Schrage, E.J.H., 'Ius in re corporali perfecte disponendi: Property from Bartolus to the New Dutch Civil Code of 1992', in: G.E. van Maanen & A.J. van der Walt (eds.), *Property Law on the threshold of the 21st century*, MAKLU 1996, p. 35-67.

Schrage 2002
Schrage, E.J.H., 'Why is English law so different?' in: M.J. Schermaier, J.M. Rainer & L.C. Winkel (eds.), *Festschrift für Theo Mayer-Maly zum 70. Geburtstag*, Köln/ Weimar/Wien: Böhlau Verlag 2002, p. 237-273.

Schrage & Dondorp 1987
Schrage, E J.H. & Dondorp, J.H., *Utrumque Ius; een inleiding tot de studie van de bronnen van het middeleeuwse geleerde recht*, Amsterdam: VU Uitgeverij 1987.

Schulte-Nölke, Twigg-Flesner & Elbers 2007
Schulte-Nölke, H., Twigg-Flesner, C. & Elbers, M., *EC Consumer Law Compendium – Comparative Analysis -*, 2007.

Schulz 1956
Schulz, F., *Principles of Roman Law*, trans. M. Wolff, Oxford: Oxford University Press 1956; repr. 2nd, 1936.

Schulz 1992
Schulz, F., *Classical Roman Law*, Aalen: Scientia Verlag 1992; repr. 1992, 1951.

Schulze 1967
Schulze, A., 'Treuhänder im geltenden bürgerlichen Recht', *Jheringer Jahrbücher für die Dogmatik des heutigen römischen und deutschen Privatrechts*, (43) 1967, p. 1-104.

Schulze 2005
Schulze, R., 'Verbraucherrecht und europäisches Vertragsrecht', in: P. van der Grinten & T. Heukels (eds.), *Crossing Borders. Essays in European and Private International Law, Nationality Law and Islamic Law in Honour of Frans van der Velden*, Deventer: Kluwer 2005, p. 17-30.

Schulze 2007
Schulze, R., 'Gemeinsamer Referenzrahmen und acquis communautaire', *Zeitschrift für Europäisches Privatrecht*, (1) 2007, p. 130-144.

Schwab & Prütting 2003
Schwab, K.H. & Prütting, H., *Sachenrecht. Ein Studienbuch* (Juridische Kurz-Lehrbücher), 31st edition, München: Verlag C.H. Beck, 2003.

Shavell 2002
Shavell, S., *Economic Analysis of Property Law*, Harvard John M. Olin Center for Law, Economics and Business, Discussion Paper No. 399/12/2002, 2002.

Simler 2005
Simler, P., 'Sûretés. Une sûreté réelle consentie pour garantir la dette d'un tiers n'impliquant aucun engagement personnel n'est pas un cautionnement', *La Semaine Juridique, Edition Générale*, (52), 2005, p. 2425-2429.

Simler 2006
Simler, P., 'La réforme du droit des sûretés. - Un Livre IV nouveau du Code civil', *La Semaine Juridique, Edition Générale*, (13), 2006, I 124, p. 597-600.

Simler & Delebecque 2004
Simler, P. & Delebecque, P., *Droit civil - Les sûretés. La publicité foncière*, 4th edition, Paris: Dalloz 2004.

Simpson 1986
Simpson, A.W.B., *A History of the Land Law*, 2nd reprinted edition, Oxford: Oxford University Press 1986.

Slagter 1992
Slagter, W.J., 'Eigendom en pseudo-eigendom', in: E. Hondius, W.G. Huijgen, J. Hijma, T.J. Mellema-Kranenburg & J.H. Nieuwenhuis (eds.), *Quod Licet; Kleijn-Bundel*, Deventer: Kluwer 1992, p. 357-374.

Smalbraak 1966
Smalbraak, J.T., *Erfdienstbaarheden en kwalitatieve verbintenissen (huidig en wordend recht), Preadviezen uitgebracht ... ter behandeling in de algemene vergadering van de Broederschap van Candidaat-Notarissen*, 1966.

Smith 2000
Smith, L.D., 'Security', in: P. Birks (ed.), *English Private Law*, Volume I, Oxford: Oxford University Press 2000, p. 385-463.

Smits 1996
Smits, J.M., 'Van partijen en derden; over interpretaties van de numerus clausus van zakelijke rechten', *Groninger Opmerkingen en Mededelingen: magazijn voor leerstellige rechtsvergelijking op historische grondslag*, (XIII) 1996, p. 41-64.

Smits 1999
Smits, J.M., *Europees Privaatrecht in wording*, Antwerpen-Groningen: Intersentia 1999.

Smits 2002
Smits, J.M., *The Making of European Private Law*, Antwerpen - Oxford - New York: Intersentia 2002.

Smits 2003
Smits, J.M., 'Scotland as a mixed jurisdiction and the development of European private law: Is there something to Learn from Evolutionary Theory?' *Electronic Journal of Comparative Law*, (7.5) 2003.

Smits 2004
Smits, J.M., 'Europa en het Nederlandse privaatrecht', *Nederlands Tijdschrift voor Burgerlijk Recht*, (10 (Special Issue)/N. 87) 2004, p. 490-500.

Smits 2006
Smits, J.M., *Common Frame of Reference and Optional Code: How to Find the Best Rules for European Contract Law?* (Vorträge und Berichte; Rheinische Friedrich-Wilhelms-Universität, 151), Bonn: 2006.

Smits 2007
Smits, J.M., 'De toekomst van het Europees privaatrecht: gemeenschappelijk referentiekader, optionele code en implementatie van richtlijnen', in: A.S. Hartkamp, C.H. Sieburgh & L.A.D. Keus (eds.), *De invloed van het Europese Recht op het Nederlandse privaatrecht*, Deel I, Deventer: Kluwer 2007, p. 281-297.

Snijders 1995
Snijders, G.M.F., 'Agrarische erfpacht', *Erfpacht, Preadvies uitgebracht voor de jaarlijkse Algemene Ledenvergadering van de Koninklijke Notariële Broederschap te houden te Nijmegen op 22 september 1995*, Lelystad: Koninklijke Vermande B.V. 1995, p. 89-116.

Snijders 2006
Snijders, H.J., 'Access to Civil Securities and Free Competition in the EU, a plea for One European Security Right in Movables', in: U. Drobnig, H.J. Snijders & E.-J. Zippro (eds.), *Divergences in Property Law, an Obstacle to the Internal Market?*, München: Sellier, European Law Publishers 2006, p. 153-164.

Snijders & Rank-Berenschot 2001
Snijders, H.J. & Rank-Berenschot, E.B., *Goederenrecht*, 3rd edition, Deventer: Kluwer 2001.

Snijders 1991
Snijders, W., 'De toekomst van de eigendom', in: B.W.M. Nieskens-Ipshording, M.J.G.C. Raaijmakers, J. Spier & J.B.M. Vranken (eds.), *In het nu, wat worden zal – Opstellen aangeboden aan prof. mr. H.C.F. Schoordijk ter gelegenheid van zijn afscheid als hoogleraar aan de Katholieke Universiteit Brabant*, Deventer: Kluwer 1991, p. 249-265.

Snijders 1993
Snijders, W., 'Trustverdrag en Nederlands materieel recht', in: *Grensoverschrijdend privaatrecht. Een bundel opstellen over privaatrecht in internationaal verband. Aangeboden aan Mr. J. van Rijn van Alkemade bij gelegenheid van zijn afscheid als raadsadviseur bij het Ministerie van Justitie*, Deventer: Kluwer 1993, p. 231-243.

Snijders 1997
Snijders, W., 'Nog een duit in de zak van de trust', in: S.C.J.J. Kortmann, N.E.D. Faber, A.A. van Rossum & H.L.E. Verhagen (eds.), *Onderneming en 5 jaar nieuw burgerlijk recht*, Deventer: W.E.J. Tjeenk Willink 1997, p. 87-105.

Snijders 1999a
Snijders, W., 'Wilsrechten, in het algemeen en in het nieuwe erfrecht', *Weekblad voor Privaatrecht, Notariaat en Registratie*, (6365, 6366 and 6367) 1999, p. 558-565, 583-589, and 601-608.

Snijders 1999b
Snijders, W., 'Overpeinzingen naar aanleiding van de bundel Inzake kwaliteit, de kwaliteits- of derdenrekening naar Belgisch en Nederlands recht', *Tijdschrift voor Insolventierecht*, (7), 1999, p. 149-154.

Snijders 2002
Snijders, W., 'De openheid van het vermogensrecht; van syndicaatzekerheden, domeinnamen en nieuwe contractsvormen', in: S.C.J.J. Kortmann, C.J.H. Janssen, G. van Solinge & N.E.D. Faber (eds.), *Onderneming en 10 jaar nieuw burgerlijk recht* (Serie Onderneming en Recht, 24), Deventer: Kluwer 2002, p. 27-58.

Snijders 2005a
Snijders, W., 'Ongeregeldheden in het vermogensrecht (I)', *Weekblad voor Privaatrecht, Notariaat en Registratie*, (6607) 2005, p. 79-85.

Snijders 2005b
Snijders, W., 'Ongeregeldheden in het vermogensrecht (II)', *Weekblad voor Privaatrecht, Notariaat en Registratie*, (6608) 2005, p. 94-102.

Soergel et al. 2002
Soergel, T., Stadler, A., Stürner, R., Baur, J.F. & Henssler, M., *Bürgerliches Gesetzbuch mit Einführungsgesetz und Nebengesetzen. Kohlhammer-Kommentaar. Sachenrecht 1 – §§ 854-984*, Band 14, 13th revised edition, Stuttgart: Verlag W. Kohlhammer 2002.

Sohm 1931
Sohm, R., *Institutionen – Geschichte und System des Römischen Privatrechts*, 17th edition, München: Duncker & Humblod 1931.

Sonnekus 1991
Sonnekus, J.C., 'Saaklike regte of vorderingsregte? – Traditionele toetse en 'n petition principii', *Tydskrif vir Suid-Afrikaanse Reg*, 1991, p. 173-180.

Sonnekus 1996
Sonnekus, J.C., 'Property Law in South Africa: Some Aspects Compared with the Position in Some European Civil Law Systems - the Importance of Publicity', in: G.E. van Maanen & A.J. van der Walt (eds.), *Property law on the threshold of the 21st century*, MAKLU 1996, p. 285-331.

Sparkes 2003
Sparkes, P., *A New Land Law*, 2nd edition, Oxford - Portland: Hart Publishing 2003.

Sparkes 2007
Sparkes, P., *European Land Law*, Oxford: Hart Publishing 2007.

Sponer 1965
Sponer, W.D., *Das Anwartschaftsrecht und seine Pfändung* (Schriften zum Deutschen und Europäischen Zivil-, Handels- und Prozessrecht, 31), Bielefeld: Verlag Ernst und Wener Gieseking 1965.

Spruit 2003
Spruit, J.E., *Cunabula Iuris; elementen van het Romeinse privaatrecht*, 2nd edition, Deventer: Kluwer 2003.

Spruit & Feenstra 1987
Spruit, J.E. & Feenstra, R., *Textus Iuris Romani*, 3rd edition, Deventer: Kluwer 1987.

Staudinger et al. 1998
Von Staudinger, J., Albrecht, K.D., Hönle, J., Mayer, J. & Merten, D., *J. von Staudingers Kommentar zum Bürgerlichen Gesetzbuch mit Einfürungsgesetz und Nebengesetzen. Einführungsgesetz zum Bürgerlichen Gesetzbuche - Art. 1, 2, 50-218 EGBGB*, Berlin: Sellier - de Gruyter 1998.

Staudinger et al. 2002
Von Staudinger, J., Amann, H., Frank, J., Mader, P., Mayer, J. & Rapp, M., *J. von Staudingers Kommentar zum Bürgerlichen Gesetzbuch mit Einfürungsgesetz und Nebengesetzen. Buch 3 Sachenrecht - Erbb VO; §§ 1018-1112*, Berlin: Sellier - de Gruyter 2002.

Staudinger, Emmerich & Rolfs 2003
Von Staudinger, J., Emmerich, V. & Rolfs, C., *J. von Staudingers Kommentar zum Bürgerlichen Gesetzbuch mit Einfürungsgesetz und Nebengesetzen. Buch 2. Recht der Schuldverhältnisse - §§ 563-580a (Mietrecht 2)*, Berlin: Sellier - de Gruyter 2003.

Staudinger & Gursky 1999
Von Staudinger, J. & Gursky, K.-H., *J. von Staudingers Kommentar zum Bürgerlichen Gesetzbuch mit Einfürungsgesetz und Nebengesetzen. Buch 3 Sachenrecht - §§ 985-1011*, Berlin: Sellier - de Gruyter 1999.

Staudinger & Gursky 2002
Von Staudinger, J. & Gursky, K.-H., *J. von Staudingers Kommentar zum Bürgerlichen Gesetzbuch mit Einfürungsgesetz und Nebengesetzen. Buch 3 Sachenrecht - §§ 883-902*, Berlin: Sellier - de Gruyter, 2002.

Staudinger, Nöll & Wiegand 2002
Von Staudinger, J., Nöll, H.-H. & Wiegand, W., *J. von Staudingers Kommentar zum Bürgerlichen Gesetzbuch mit Einfürungsgesetz und Nebengesetzen. Buch 3 Sachenrecht - §§ 1204-1296, §§ 1 -84 SchiffsRG*; Berlin: Sellier - de Gruyter 2002.

Staudinger & Wolfsteiner 2002
Von Staudinger, J. & Wolfsteiner, H., *J. von Staudingers Kommentar zum Bürgerlichen Gesetzbuch mit Einfürungsgesetz und Nebengesetzen. Buch 3 Sachenrecht - §§ 1113-1203*; Berlin: Sellier - de Gruyter 2002.

Staudinger et al. 2000
Von Staudinger, J., Bund, E., Gursky, K.-H., Kutter, H.-D. & Seiler, H.H., *J. von Staudingers Kommentar zum Bürgerlichen Gesetzbuch mit Einfürungsgesetz und Nebengesetzen. Drittes Buch - Sachenrecht. Einleitung zum Sachenrecht; §§ 854-882*, Berlin: Sellier - de Gruyter 2000.

Stein 1976
Stein, P.A., 'Van kettingbeding naar kwalitatieve verbintenis', *Weekblad voor Privaatrecht, Notariaat en Registratie*, (5365) 1976, p. 644-650.

Stein 2004
Stein, P.A., *Zekerheidsrechten. Hypotheek*, 4th edition, Deventer: Kluwer 2004.

Stein 1984
Stein, P.G., *Legal Institutions. The Development of Dispute Settlement*, London: Butterworths 1984.

Stein 1989
Stein, P.G., '"Equitable" Remedies for the Protection of Property', in: P. Birks (ed.), *New Perspectives in the Roman Law of Property*, Oxford: Clarendon Press 1989, p. 185-194.

Stein 1992
Stein, P G., 'Roman Law, Common Law, and Civil Law', *Tulane Law Review*, (66) 1992, p. 1591-1603.

Stein 1999
Stein, P.G., *Roman Law in European History*, Cambridge: Cambridge University Press 1999.

Steneker 2005
Steneker, A., *Kwaliteitsrekening en afgescheiden vermogen* (diss.) (Serie Onderneming en Recht, 31), Deventer: Kluwer 2005.

Van der Steur 2003
Van der Steur, J.C., *Grenzen van rechtsobjecten; een onderzoek naar de grenzen van objecten van eigendomsrechten en intellectuele eigendomsrechten*, Deventer: Kluwer 2003.

Stöcker 1992
Stöcker, O.M., *Die Eurohypothek*, Berlin: Duncker & Humblot 1992.

Storme, De Theije & Delbecke 2004
Storme, M., De Theije, M. & Delbecke, B., 'Wouter Snijders: interview met de vader van het nieuwe vermogensrecht', in: T. Veen, C. Coppens, G. Donker & S. Faber (eds.), *Prominenten kijken om. Achttien rechtsgeleerden uit de Lage Landen over leven, werk en recht* (Pro Memorie. Bijdragen tot de rechtsgeschiedenis der Nederlanden 6. 1-2, 2004), Hilversum: Stichting tot uitgaaf der bronnen van het Oud-Vanderlandse Recht. Uitgeverij Verloren, 2004, p. 118-143.

Stoufflet 2006
Stoufflet, J., 'Le nantissement de meubles incorporels', *La Semaine Juridique Entreprise et affaires*, Supplément au No. 20, 2006, p. 19-22.

Strauch 1984
Strauch, D., 'Das geteilte Eigentum in Geschichte und Gegenwart', in: G. Baumgärtel, H.J. Becker, E. Klingmüller & A. Wacke (eds.), *Festschrift für Heinz Hübner zum 70. Geburtstag am 7. November 1984*, Berlin - New York: Walter de Gruyter 1984, p. 273-293.

Struycken 2007
Struycken, T.H.D., *De numerus clausus in het goederenrecht* (diss.) (Serie Onderneming en Recht), Deventer: Kluwer 2007.

Stürner 1994
Stürner, R., 'Dienstbarkeit heute', *Archiv für die civilistische Praxis*, (194) 1994, p. 265-294.

Suijling 1940
Suijling, J.P., *Inleiding tot het burgerlijk recht - 5 - Zakenrecht*, Haarlem: De erven F. Bohn N.V. 1940.

Swadling 2000a
Swadling, W.J., 'Property: General Principles', in: P. Birks (ed.), *English Private Law*, Volume I, Oxford: Oxford University Press 2000, p. 203-384.

Swadling 2000b
Swadling, W.J., 'Opening the Numerus Clausus', *Law Quarterly Review*, (116) 2000, p. 354-360.

Swadling 2006a
Swadling, W.J., 'Unjust Delivery', in: A. Burrows & Lord Rodger of Earlsferry (eds.), *Mapping the Law. Essays in Memory of Peter Birks*, Oxford: Oxford University Press 2006, p. 277-298.

Swadling 2006b
Swadling, W.J., 'Land Burdens - An English Perspective', in: J.H.M. van Erp & B. Akkermans (eds.), *Towards a Unified System of Land Burdens?* (Ius Commune Europaeum, 59) Antwerpen - Oxford: Intersentia 2006, p. 117-135.

Swadling 2007
Swadling, W.J., 'Property: General Principles', in: A. Burrows (ed.), *English Private Law*, Oxford: Oxford University Press 2007, p. 219-401.

Swadling 2008
Swadling, W.J., 'Explaining Resulting Trusts', *Law Quarterly Review*, (124) 2008, p. 72-102.

Synvet 2005
Synvet, H., 'Le nantissement des meubles incorporels', *Droit et patrimoine*, (140) 2005, p. 64-71.

Terrat 1904
Terrat, B., 'Du régime de la Propriété dans le Code civil', in: A. Sorel (ed.), *Le code civil. 1804-1904: livre du centenaire*, Tome Premier, Généralités - Études spéciales, Paris: Arthur Rousseau 1904, p. 329-353.

Terré & Simler 1998
Terré, F. & Simler, P., *Droit civil - Les biens*, 5th edition, Paris: Dalloz 1998.

Tetley 2000
Tetley, W., 'Mixed Jurisdictions: common law vs civil law (codified and uncodified)', *Louisiana Law Review*, (60) 2000, p. 677-738.

Thibaut 1817a
Thibaut, A.F.J., 'Ueber dingliches und persönliches Recht', *Versuche über einzelne Teile der Theorie des Rechts*, 2. verbesserte Ausgabe, (Neudruck Scientia Verlag Aalen 1970): Jena 1817, p. 23-66, 1801 same title.

Thibaut 1817b
Thibaut, A.F.J., 'Ueber dominium directum und utile', *Versuche über einzelne Teile der Theorie des Rechts*, 2. verbesserte Ausgabe, (Neudruck Scientia Verlag Aalen 1970): Jena 1817, p. 67-99.

Thibaut 1814
Thibaut, A.F.J., 'Ueber die Nothwendigkeit eines allgemeinen bürgerlichen Rechts für Deutschland', in: H. Hattenhauer (ed.), *Thibaut und Savigny. Ihre programmatischen Schriften*, 2nd extended edition, München: Verlag Franz Vahlen 2002, p. 37-60, Heidelberg, Mohr und Zimmer, 1814.

Thomas & Ziepzeerder 2000
Thomas, E. & Ziepzeerder, M.J., 'Huur als beperkt zakelijk recht: fiscale consequenties (I). Een reactie op het artikel van prof. mr. J.H.M. van Erp in WPNR (2000) 6407, die daar de vraag poneerde of wetsvoorstel 26089 fiscale consequenties heeft', *Weekblad voor Privaatrecht, Notariaat en Registratie*, (6425) 2000, p. 857-859.

Thomas 1976
Thomas, J.A.C., *Textbook of Roman Law*, Amsterdam: North-Holland Publishing Company 1976.

Timmerman 2002
Timmerman, L., 'Bankhypotheek en afhankelijkheid', in: S.C.J.J. Kortmann, C.J.H. Jansen, G.V. Solinge & N.E.D. Faber (eds.), *Onderneming en 10 jaar nieuw burgerlijk recht*, Deventer: Kluwer 2002, p. 409-424.

Trebilcock 1993
Trebilcock, M.J., *The Limits of Freedom of Contract*, Cambridge, Massachusetts, and London, England: Harvard University Press 1993.

Triola & Rosario Vignale 2000
Triola, R. & Rosario Vignale, M., *Diritti Reali, La Cassazione Civili*, Milano: Giuffré Editore 2000.

Troplong 1845
Troplong, F., *Le droit civil expliqué suivant l'ordre du Code. De l'échange et du louage ou Commentaire des titres VII et VIII du Code civil*, Brussel: Wahlen 1845.

Von Tuhr 1957
Von Tuhr, A., *Der Allgemeine Teil des Deutschen Bürgerlichen Rechts* (Systematisches Handbuch des deutschen Rechtswissenschaft, Ester Band), Berlin: Verlag von Duncker & Humblot 1957.

Tyler & Palmer 1973
Tyler, E.L.G. & Palmer, N.E., *Crossley Vaines on Personal Property*, 5th edition, London: Butterworths, 1973.

Vangerow II 1876
Vangerow, K.A.V., *Lehrbuch der Pandekten - Zweites Buch*, Marburg: Elwert'sche Universitäts-Buchhandlung 1876.

Vareilles-Sommières 1905
Vareilles-Sommières, M.D., 'La définition et la notion juridique de la propriété.' *Revue trimestrielle de droit civil,* (4) 1905, p. 443-495.

Varga 1991
Varga, C., *Codification as a socio-historical phenomenon,* trans. S. Eszenyi, J. Petranyi, C. Varga & J. Payne, Budapest: Akademiai Kiado, 1991.

Vegter 1995a
Vegter, J.B., 'Over de strekking van het fiduciaverbod bij een financiële sale - lease back (I)', *Weekblad voor Privaatrecht, Notariaat en Registratie,* (6190) 1995, p. 534-536.

Vegter 1995b
Vegter, J.B., 'Over de strekking van het fiduciaverbod bij een financiële sale - lease back (II)', *Weekblad voor Privaatrecht, Notariaat en Registratie,* (6191), 1995, p. 555-557.

Vegter 2004
Vegter, J.B., 'Bescherming van familievermogens met behulp van de rechtsfiguur van eigendom ten titel van beheer', *Bewind en aan bewind verwante vormen, Preadviezen voor de jaarlijkse algemene ledenvergadering van de Koninklijke Notariële Beroepsorganisatie te houden te Amsterdam op 8 oktober 2004;* Lelystad: Koninklijke Vermande 2004, p.105-130.

Van Velten 1989
Van Velten, A.A., *Regels zijn regels. Enkele opmerkingen over het hybride karakter van het begrip appartementsrecht in het Nederlandse privaatrecht* (Rede uitgesproken bij de aanvaarding van het ambt van bijzonder hoogleraar op de leerstoel privaatrechtelijke aspecten van onroerend goed bij de faculteit der rechtsgeleerdheid aan de Vrije Universiteit te Amsterdam op donderdag 14 december 1989) (Ars Notariatus, XLIV), Deventer: Kluwer 1989.

Van Velten 1991
Van Velten, A.A., 'Eigendomsvormen van de toekomst', in: B.W.M. Nieskens-Ipshording, M.J.G.C. Raaijmakers, J. Spier & J.B.M. Vranken (eds.), *In het nu, wat worden zal - Opstellen aangeboden aan prof. mr. H.C.F. Schoordijk ter gelegenheid van zijn afscheid als hoogleraar aan de Katholieke Universiteit Brabant,* Deventer: Kluwer 1991, p. 281-294.

Van Velten 1995
Van Velten, A.A., 'Privaatrechtelijke aspecten van stedelijke erfpacht', *Erfpacht, Preadvies uitgebracht voor de jaarlijkse Algemene Ledenvergadering van de Koninklijke Notariële Broederschap te houden te Nijmegen op 22 september 1995,* Lelystad: Koninklijke Vermande B.V. 1995, p. 17-88.

Van Velten 1996
Van Velten, A.A., 'Enkele opmerkingen over een nieuwe maatvoering in het goederenrecht', *Nederlands Juristenblad,* (27) 1996, p. 1040-1045.

Van Velten 2003
Van Velten, A.A., *Privaatrechtelijke aspecten van onroerend goed* (Ars Notariatus, 120), Deventer: Kluwer 2003.

Van Velten 2004
Van Velten, A.A., 'De indiening en voortgang van het wetsvoorstel tot herziening van het appartementsrecht', *Weekblad voor Privaatrecht, Notariaat en Registratie,* (6585) 2004, p. 547-559.

Van Velten 2005
Van Velten, A.A., *Koop van onroerende zaken* (Monografieën Nieuw BW, B65c), Deventer: Kluwer 2005.

Van Velten 2007
Van Velten, A.A., 'Boekbespreking. V. Sagaert, Het goederenrecht als open systeem van Verbintenissen? Poging tot een nieuwe kwalificatie van de vermogensrechten, oratie Leuven 2005, TPR 2005-3, p. 983-1086. T.H.D. Struycken, De numerus clausus in het goederenrecht, diss. Nijmegen 2007, serie Onderneming & Recht deel 37 (Kluwer 2007), XIX en 870p', *Weekblad voor Privaatrecht, Notariaat en Registratie,* (6708) 2007, p. 372-376.

Van de Ven 2001
Van de Ven, K.M.L.L., 'Het vruchtgebruiktestament', *Weekblad voor Privaatrecht, Notariaat en Registratie,* (6433) 2001, p. 124-131.

Verbeke 1999
Verbeke, A., 'Creatief met vruchtgebruik', *Tijdschrift voor notarissen,* 1999, p. 530-579.

Verbeke & Snaet 2007
Verbeke, A. & Snaet, S., 'Meccano-goederenrecht', in: W. Pintens, A. Alen, E. Dirix & P. Senaeve (eds.), *Vigilantibus Ius Scriptum. Feestbundel voor Hugo Vandenberghe,* Brugge: Die Keure 2007, p. 365-393.

Verstappen 1994
Verstappen, L.C.A., 'Reactie naar aanleiding van het artikel van mr. R.J. Holtman "Mandeligheid en beperkte rechten" in WPNR (1993) 6085, en de reactie van mr. L.C.A. Verstappen en het naschrift van mr. R.J. Holtman over dit onderwerp in WPNR (1993) 6089'. *Weekblad voor Privaatrecht, Notariaat en Registratie,* (6126) 1994, p. 166-169.

Verstijlen 2004
Verstijlen, F.M.J., *Vergissingen in het goederenrecht* (Rede in verkorte vorm uitgesproken bij de aanvaarding van het ambt van hoogleraar in het privaatrecht, in het bijzonder het goederenrecht, aan de Rijksuniversiteit Groningen op dinsdag 4 november 2003), Den Haag: Boom Juridische uitgevers 2004.

Verstijlen & Vriesendorp 2004
Verstijlen, F.M.J. & Vriesendorp, R.D., 'Geen "zekerheidseigendom" ter verzekering van vorderingen uit geldlening naar huidig Nederlands recht', *Weekblad voor Privaatrecht, Notariaat en Registratie,* (6145) 1994, p. 518-520.

Van Vliet 2000
Van Vliet, L.P.W., *Transfer of movables in German, French, English and Dutch law,* Nijmegen: Ars Aequi Libri 2000.

Van Vliet 2002a
Van Vliet, L.P.W., 'Accession of Movables to Land: I', *Edinburgh Law Review,* (6/1) 2002, p. 67-84.

Van Vliet 2002b
Van Vliet, L.P.W., 'Accession of Movables to Land: II', *Edinburgh Law Review,* (6/2) 2002, p. 199-216.

Van Vliet 2004
Van Vliet, L.P.W., 'Verjaring en erfdienstbaarheid', *Nederlands Tijdschrift voor Burgerlijk Recht,* 2004, p. 206-225.

Van Vliet 2005
Van Vliet, L.P.W., 'De financiëlezekerheidsovereenkomst, een tussenbalans', *Nederlands Tijdschrift voor Burgerlijk Recht,* 2005, p. 190-204.

Vogt 1950
Vogt, H., *Das Erbbaurecht des klassischen römischen Rechts* (Forschungen zum römischen Recht, 3. Abhandlung), Marburg Lahn: Simons Verlag 1950.

Vonck 2007
Vonck, F.J., 'De zakelijke werking van erfpachtvoorwaarden', *Weekblad voor Privaatrecht, Notariaat en Registratie,* (6717) 2007, p. 598-603.

De Vries 1984
De Vries, A.E., *Het recht van erfpacht volgens BW en NBW* (Studiepockets privaatrecht, 33), Zwolle: W.E.J. Tjeenk Willink 1984.

De Vries & Pleysier 1995
De Vries, A.E. & Pleysier, A.J.H., *Erfpacht en opstal* (Studiepockets privaatrecht, 33), 2nd edition, Zwolle: W.E.J. Tjeenk Willink 1995.

Vriesendorp 2003
Vriesendorp, R.D., 'De Nederlandse trust, het vertrouwen waard!' in: M.J.G.C. Raaijmakers, S.E. Eisma, J.M.M. Maeijer, G.T.M.J. Raaijmakers, H.C.F. Schoordijk, J.A.W. Schreurs, A.F. Verdam, P. Vlas, R.D. Vriesendorp & W.J. Zwalve (eds.), *Trust en onderneming* (Schoordijk Instituut. Center for Company Law), Den Haag: Boom Juridische uitgevers 2003, p. 151-161.

Van der Vyver 1988a
Van der Vyver, J.D., 'Expropriation, Rights, Entitlements and Surface Support of Land', *The South African Law Journal*, (105) 1988, p. 1-16.

Van der Vyver 1988b
Van der Vyver, J.D., 'The doctrine of private-law rights', in: S.A. Strauss (ed.), *Huldigingsbunder vir WA Joubert*, Durban: Butterworths 1988, p. 201-246.

De Waal 1990
De Waal, M.J., *'Die vereistes vir die vestiging van grondsewitute: 'n herformulering'*, *Stellenbosch Law Review*, (2) 1990, p. 171-187.

De Waal 1992
De Waal, M.J., 'Servitudes', in: R. Feenstra & R. Zimmermann (eds.), *Das römisch holländische Recht; Fortschritte des Zivilrechts im 17. und 18. Jahrhundert*, Berlin: Duncker & Humblot 1992, p. 567-595.

De Waal 1995
De Waal, M.J., 'Die moderne aanwending van grondserwitute: eiendomsreg en die beheer oor die ontwikkeling van ander saaklike regte', *Tydskrif vir Suid-Afrikaanse Reg*, (2) 1995, p. 193-220.

De Waal 1999a
De Waal, M.J., 'Numerus Clausus and the development of new real rights in South African Law', *Electronic Journal of Comparative Law*, (3/3) 1999.

De Waal 1999b
De Waal, M.J., 'Die strekwijdte van trustees se bellegingsbevoegdheid', *Tydskrif vir die Suid-Afrikaanse reg*, 1999, p. 370-378.

De Waal 2000
De Waal, M.J., 'The Uniformity of Ownership, Numerus Clausus and the Reception of the Trust into South African Law', *European Review of Private Law*, (3) 2000, p. 439-452.

De Waal 2004
De Waal, M.J., 'Identifying Real Rights in South African Law: the 'Subtraction from the Dominium' Test and its Application', in: S.E. Bartels & J.M. Milo (eds.), *Contents of Real Rights*, Nijmegen: Wolf Legal Publishers 2004, p. 83-98.

Wacke 1998
Wacke, A., 'Max Kasers Lehren zum Ursprung und Wesen des römischen Pfandrechts', *Zeitschrift der Savigny-Stiftung für Rechtsgeschichte, Romanistische Abteilung*, (115) 1998, p. 168-202.

Waddams 2003
Waddams, S., *Dimensions of Private Law; Categories and Concepts in Anglo-American Legal Reasoning*, Cambridge: Cambridge University Press 2003.

Van der Walt 1986
Van der Walt, A.J., 'Bartolus se omkrywing van dominium an die interpretasis daarvan sedert die vyftiende eeu', *Tydskrif vir hedendaagse Romeins-Hollandse reg*, 1986, p. 305-321.

Van der Walt 1987
Van der Walt, A.J., 'Saaklike regte en persoonike serwitute', *Tydskrif vir Hedendaagse Romeins-Hollandse Reg*, (50) 1987, p. 343-352.

Van der Walt 1992
Van der Walt, A.J., 'Personal rights and limited real rights: an historical overview and analysis of contemporary problems related to the registrability of rights', *Tydskrif vir Hedendaagse Romeins-Hollandse Reg*, (55) 1992, p. 171-203.

Van der Walt 2005
Van der Walt, A.J., *Constitutional Property Law*, Wetton: Juta & Co Ltd. 2005.

Van der Walt & Kleyn 1989
Van der Walt, A.J. & Kleyn, D.G., 'Duplex Dominium: The History and Significance of the Concept of Divided Ownership', in: D.P. Visser (ed.), *Essays on the History of Law*, Cape Town: Juta & Co 1989, p. 213-260.

Van der Walt & Pienaar 2002
Van der Walt, A.J. & Pienaar, G.J., *Inleiding tot die sakereg*, 4th edition, Lansdowne: Juta 2002.

Walter & Maier 1988
Walter, G. & Maier, A., 'Die Sicherung von Bezugs- und Abnahmeverpflichtungen durch Dienstbarkeiten', *Neue Juristische Wochenschrift*, (7) 1988, p. 377-388.

Van Warmelo 1959
Van Warmelo, P., 'Real Rights ', *Acta Juridica*, 1959, p. 84-98.

Watson 1968
Watson, A., *The Law of Property in the Later Roman Republic*, Oxford: Oxford University Press 1968.

Watson 1985
Watson, A. (ed.), *Digest of Justinian* (with Latin text edited by T. Mommsen & P. Krüger), Philadelphia: University of Pennsylvania Press 1985.

Weatherhill 2005
Weatherhill, S., 'Reflections on the EC's Competence to Develop a "European Contract Law"', *European Review of Private Law*, (3) 2005, p. 405-418.

Weatherhill 2006
Weatherhill, S., 'Diversity between National Laws in the Internal Market', in: U. Drobnig, H.J. Snijders & E.-J. Zippro (eds.), *Divergences of Property Law, an Obstacle to the Internal Market?*, München: Sellier, European Law Publishers 2006, p. 131-150.

Wehrens & Gresser 1992
Wehrens, H.G. & Gresser, E., *L'Eurohypotheque/Die Eurohypothek*, Amsterdam: Union Internationale du Notariat Latin 1992.

Van der Weide 2006
Van der Weide, J.A., *Mobiliteit van Goederen in het IPR. Tussen situsregel en partij-autonomie* (diss.), Amsterdam: 2006.

Weitnauer 1983
Weitnauer, H., 'Verdinglichte Schuldverhältnisse', in: C.-W. Canaris & U. Diederichsen (eds.), *Festschrift für Karl Larenz zum 80. Geburtstag am 23. April 1983*, München: C.H. Beck'sche Verlagsbuchhandlung 1983.

Westra 1992
Westra, H., 'Nut en noodzaak van het begrip eigendom in het nieuwe BW', *Recht en Kritiek*, (18) 1992, p. 286-299.

Westrik 2000
Westrik, R., 'Koop breekt geen huur in het Ontwerp BW. Reactie op het artikel 'De regel 'koop breekt geen huur' in wetsvoorstel 26089 vertoont (verborgen) gebreken' van mr. M.M. van Asbreuk-van Os in WPNR (2000) 6383', *Weekblad voor Privaatrecht, Notariaat en Registratie*, (6395) 2000, p. 214-217.

Westrik 2001
Westrik, R., *Koop breekt geen huur* (diss.), Den Haag: Vermande 2001.

Van Weverwijk 1995
Van Weverwijk, A., 'De trusthypotheek: vertrouwen in zekerheid', in: S.C.J.J. Kortmann, N.E.D. Faber, A.A. van Rossum & H.L.E. Verhagen (eds.), *Onderneming en 5 jaar nieuw burgerlijk recht* (Serie Onderneming en Recht, 7), Deventer: W.E.J. Tjeenk Willink 1995, p. 253-270.

Wibier 2007
Wibier, R.M., *Alternatieven voor zekerheid op bankrekeningen* (diss.), Tilburg: 2007.

Wieacker 1995
Wieacker, F., *A History of Private Law in Europe; with a particular reference to Germany* (*Privatrechtsgeschichte der Neuzeit*) trans. T. Weir, Oxford: Clarendon Press 1995.

Wiegand 1976
Wiegand, W., 'Zur theoretischen Begründung der Bedenmobilisierung in der Rechtswissenschaft: der abstracte Eigentumsbegriff', in: H. Coing & W. Wilhelm (eds.), *Wissenschaft und Kodification des Privatrechts im 19. Jahrhundert - III Die rechtliche und wirtschaftliche Entwicklung des Grundeigentums und Grundkredits*, Frankfurt am Main: Vittorio Klostermann 1976, p. 118-157.

Wiegand 1981
Wiegand, W., 'Zur Entwicklung der Pfandrechtstheorien im 19. Jahrhundert', *Zeitschrift für Neuere Rechtsgeschichte*, (3) 1981, p. 1-15.

Wiegand 1982
Wiegand, W., 'Treu, schau wem - Bemerkungen zur Entwicklung des Treuhandrechts in der Schweiz und in Deutschland', in: N. Horn (ed.), *Europäisches Rechtsdenken in Geschichte und Gegenwart. Festschrift für Helmut Coing zum 70. Geburtstag*, Band II, München: C.H. Beck'sche Verlagsbuchhandlung 1982, p. 565-591.

Wiegand 1984
Wiegand, W., 'Sachenrecht im Obligationenrecht', in: P. Caroni (ed.), *Berner Ringvorlesung zum Jubiläum des schweizerischen Obligationenrecht*, Bern & Stuttgart: Verlag Paul Haupt, 1984, p. 107-137.

Wiegand 1987
Wiegand, W., 'Numerus clausus der dinglichen Rechte. Zur Entstehung und Bedeutung eines zentralen zivilrechtlichen Dogmas', in: G. Köbler (ed.), *Wege europäischer Rechtsgeschichte - Festschrift Kroeschell*, Frankfurt a.M.: Peter Lang 1987, p. 623-643.

Wiegand 1990
Wiegand, W., 'Die Entwicklung des Sachenrechts', *Archiv für die civilistische Praxis*, (190) 1990, p. 112-138.

Wiegand 1999a
Wiegand, W., 'Funktion und systematische Stellung des Sachenrechts im BGB', in: M. Martinek & P.L. Sellier (eds.), *100 Jahre BGB - 100 Jahre Staudinger. Beiträge zum Symposion vom 18. - 20. Juni 1998 in München* (J. von Staudingers Kommentar zum Bürgerlichen Gesetzbuch mit Einführungsgesetz und Nebengesetzen), Berlin: De Sellier Gruyter 1999, p. 107-127.

Wiegand 1999b
Wiegand, W., 'Achtzehnter Titel: Allgemeine Bestimmungen; - Vorbem. art 641 ff,' in: H. Honsell, N.P. Vogt & T. Geiser (eds.), *Schweizerisches Zivilgesetzbuch*, II, Basel: Helbing & Lichtenhahn 1999, Rn. 61-65.

Wieling 2003
Wieling, H., 'Die Grundstücksmiete als dingliches Recht', in: J. Jickeli, P. Kreuz & D. Reuter (eds.), *Gedächtnisschrift für Jürgen Sonnenschein. 22. Januar 1938 bis 6. Dezember 2000*, Berlin: De Guter Recht, 2003, p. 201-220.

Wieling 2001
Wieling, H.J., *Sachenrecht*, 4th edition, Berlin - Heidelberg - New York: Springer Verlag 2001.

Wijting 2001
Wijting, W., 'Kwalitatieve rechten en verplichtingen in de bouw', *Bouwrecht*, (11) 2001, p. 927-942.

Wilhelm 2002
Wilhelm, J., *Sachenrecht*, 2nd renewed edition, Berlin - New York: Walter de Gruyter 2002.

Williams et al. 1979
Williams, Muir Hunter, Graham, D. & Crystal, M., *The Law and Practise in Bankruptcy*, 19th edition, London: Stevens & Sons 1979.

Von Wilmowsky 1996
Von Wilmowsky, P., *Europäisches Kreditsicherungsrecht. Sachenrecht und Insolvenzrecht unter dem EG-Vertrag*, (Beiträge zum ausländischen und internationalen Privatrecht, 60), Tübingen: J.C.B. Mohr (Paul Siebeck) 1996.

Windscheid 1875
Windscheid, B.J.H., *Lehrbuch des Pandektenrechts*, 1. Band, 4th edition, Düsseldorf: Verlagshandlung von Julius Buddeus 1875.

Windscheid 1906
Windscheid, B.J.H. & Kipp, T., *Lehrbuch des Pandektenrechts - I*, 9th with BGB compared edition, Frankfurt am Main: Literarische Anstalt Rütten & Loenig 1906.

Witz 1981
Witz, C., *La fiducie en droit privé français*, Paris: Economica 1981.

Wolf 1987
Wolf, M., 'Beständigkeit und Wandel im Sachenrecht', *Neue Juristische Wochenschrift*, (42) 1987, p. 2647-2652.

Wolf 1994
Wolf, M., *Sachenrecht* (Grundrisse des Rechts), 12th edition, München: C.H. Beck'sche Verlagsbuchhandlung 1994.

Wolf 1999
Wolf, M., *Sachenrecht*, München: C.H. Beck'sche Verlagsbuchhandlung, 1999.

Wolf 2001
Wolf, M., *Sachenrecht*, 17th revised edition, München: C.H. Beck'sche Verlagsbuchhandlung 2001.

Wolf 2005
Wolf, M., *Sachenrecht* (Grundrisse des Rechts), 21st edition, München: Verlag C.H. Beck 2005.

Wolf 2006
Wolf, M., 'Marketability contra Freedom of Parties in the Law of Land Burdens', in: J.H.M. van Erp & B. Akkermans (eds.), *Towards a Unified System of Land Burdens?* (Ius Commune Europaeum, 59), Antwerpen-Oxford: Intersentia 2006, p. 11-20.

Wolfert 2003
Wolfert, E.C.M., 'Bestanddeel of zaak? Over het onderscheid en de samenhang tussen de artikelen 3:4 en 5:20 BW', *Weekblad voor Privaatrecht, Notariaat en Registratie,* (6523 & 6525), 2003, p. 191-197 & p. 279-285.

Wolff 1923
Wolff, M., 'Reichsverfassung und Eigentum', in: *Festgabe der Berliner Juristischen Fakultät für Wilhelm Kahl zum Doktorjubiläum am 19. April 1923,* Tübingen: Verlag von J.C.B. Mohr 1923, p. 1-30.

Wolff 1929
Wolff, M., *Das Sachenrecht* (Dritter Band, Achte Bearbeitung, Lehrbuch des Bürgerlichen Rechts), Marburg: R.G. Elwert'sche Verlagsbuchhandlung 1929.

Wolff & Raiser 1957
Wolff, M. & Raiser, L., *Sachenrecht. Ein Lehrbuch,* 10th edition, Tübingen: J.C.B. Mohr (Paul Sibeck) 1957.

Worst 2002
Worst, D.A., 'Het gebruik van de privatieve last bij de inrichting van beleggingsfondsen', *Tijdschrift voor Effectenrecht,* (10) 2002, p. 193-200.

Worthington 1996
Worthington, S., *Proprietary Interests in Commercial Transactions,* Oxford: Clarendon Press, 1996.

Wubbe 1976
Wubbe, F.B.J., 'Der Streitwert bei der actio serviana', in: D. Medicus & H.H. Seiler (eds.), *Festschrift für Max Kaser,* München: C.H. Beck'sche Verlagsbuchhandlung 1976, p. 179-200.

Yale 1961
Yale, D.E.C., *Lord Nottingham's Chancery Cases,* Volume II, London: Selden Society 1961.

Zachariae, Massé & Vergé 1855
Zachariae, K.-S., Massé, G. & Vergé, C., *Le Droit Civil Français,* 2, Paris: Auguste Durand 1855.

Zenati 1981
Zenati, F., *Essai sur la nature juridique de la propriété. Contribution à la théorie du droit subjectif* (diss.), Lyon: 1981.

Zenati 1985
Zenati, F., 'Cour de Cassation (3e ch. civ.) 18 janvier 1984', *Recueil Dalloz Sirey*, 1985, p. 504-506.

Zenati 1989
Zenati, F., 'Propriétés et droits réels', *Revue trimestrielle de droit civil*, (88/3) 1989, p. 577-598.

Zenati 1992
Zenati, F., 'Propriété et droits réels', *Revue trimestrielle de droit civil*, (86/1) 1992, p. 791-799.

Zenati 1993
Zenati, F., 'Pour une rénovation de la théorie de la propriété', *Revue trimestrielle de droit civil*, (87) 1993, p. 305-232.

Zenati 1996
Zenati, F., 'Propriété et droits réels', *Revue trimestrielle de droit civil*, (95/1), 1996, p. 420-429.

Zentati 2001
Zenati, F., 'La nature juridique du quasi-usufruit (ou la métempsycose de la valeur)', in: J.C. Carbonnier (ed.), *Le droit privé français à la fin du XXème siècle. Études offertes à Pierre Catala*, Paris: Litec 2001, p. 605-640.

Zenati-Castaing 2006
Zenati-Castaing, F., 'La propriété, mécanisme fondamental du droit', *Revue trimestrielle de droit civil*, 2006, p. 446-466.

Zenati & Revet 1997
Zenati, F. & Revet, T., *Les biens*, 2nd edition, Paris: Presse Universitaires de France 1997.

Zevenbergen 2002
Zevenbergen, J.A., *Systems of Land Registration* (diss.), Delft: Technical University of Delft / NCG 2002.

Zimmermann 1983
Zimmermann, R., *Das römisch-holländische Recht in Südafrika*, Darmstadt: 1983.

Zimmermann 1992
Zimmermann, R., 'Römisch-holländisches Recht - ein Überblick', in: R. Feenstra & R. Zimmermann (eds.), *Das römisch-holländische Recht; Fortschritte des Zivilrechts im 17. und 18. Jahrhundert*, Berlin: Duncker & Humblot 1992, p. 9-58.

Zimermann 1994
Zimmermann, R., 'Rechtsvergelijking, rechtsgeschiedenis en ius commune: Enkele opmerkingen naar aanleiding van een recente polemiek', *Ars Aequi*, (43/5) 1994, p. 276-283.

Zimmermann 1996a
Zimmermann, R., *The Law of Obligations. Roman Foundations of the Civilian Tradition*, Oxford: Oxford University Press 1996.

Zimmermann 1996b
Zimmermann, R., 'Savigny's Legacy; Legal History, Comparative Law, and the Emergence of a European Legal Science', *Law Quarterly Review*, (112) 1996, p. 576-605.

Zimmermann 1998a
Zimmermann, R., 'Max Kaser und das moderne Privatrecht', *Zeitschrift der Savigny-Stiftung für Rechtsgeschichte, Romanistische Abteilung*, (115) 1998, p. 99-114.

Zimmermann 1998b
Zimmermann, R., 'Roman Law and European Legal Unity', in: A. Hartkamp, M. Hesselink, E. Hondius, C. Joustra & E. Du Perron (eds.), *Towards a European Civil Code*, 2nd Revised and Expanded Edition, Nijmegen: Ars Aequi Libri 1998, p. 21-40.

Zimmermann 2001
Zimmermann, R., *Roman Law, Contemporary Law, European Law; The Civilian Tradition Today*, Oxford: Oxford University Press 2001.

Zimmermann 2002a
Zimmermann, R., 'Europa und das römische Recht', *Archiv für die civilistische Praxis*, (202) 2002, p. 243-316.

Zimmermann 2002b
Zimmermann, R., 'Modernising the German Law of Obligations', in: P. Birks & A. Pretto (eds.), *Themes in Comparative Law – In honour of Bernard Rudden*, Oxford: Oxford University Press 2002, p. 265-288.

Zimmermann 2004
Zimmermann, R., '"Double Cross": Comparing Scots and South African Law', in: R. Zimmermann, D. Visser & K. Reid (eds.), *Mixed Legal Systems in Comparative Perspective*, Oxford: Oxford University Press 2004, p. 1-33.

Zimmermann 2005
Zimmermann, R., *The New German Law of Obligations, Historical and Comparative Perspectives*, Oxford: Oxford University Press 2005.

Zimmermann 2006
Zimmermann, R., 'Europeanization of Private Law', in: M. Reimann & R. Zimmermann (eds.), *The Oxford Handbook of Comparative Law*, Oxford: Oxford University Press 2006, p. 539-578.

Zwalve 2003
Zwalve, W.J., *Hoofdstukken uit de Geschiedenis van het Europese Privaatrecht*, 2nd edition, Deventer: Kluwer 2003.

Zwalve & Uniken Venema 2000
Zwalve, W.J. & Uniken Venema, C.A., *Common Law & Civil Law*, Deventer: W.E.J. Tjeenk Willink 2000.

Zweigert & Kötz 1998
Zweigert, K. & Kötz, H., *Introduction to Comparative Law*, trans. T. Weir, 3rd revised edition, Oxford: Clarendon Press 1998.

Zwitser 1993
Zwitser, R., 'De betekenis van 'Anwartschaftsrecht' voor de rangorde van zakelijke rechten', *Weekblad voor Privaatrecht, Notariaat en Registratie*, (6099) 1993, p. 524-530.

INDEX

Access Test 520, 528, 556-558, 560-561, 563-564
Action 22-28, 35-36, 39-42, 47, 49-55, 60-61, 63-64, 66, 179, 206, 218, 225, 239, 332, 405
  Personal Action 38, 40, 78, 332, 337
  Real Action 332, 337, 344, 352, 404, 405
Anticipatory Right (see also expectation right) 413, 417, 436, 481, 560
Anti-Commons 443, 444, 450, 452, 562
Apartment
  Ownership 176, 181-184, 208, 212, 227, 236, 464
  Right 105, 210, 270, 279, 286-288, 298, 387, 401, 420, 423, 427-428, 455, 460, 560

Bailment 242, 334, 338, 373, 376, 379, 384, 391

Cassis de Dijon 495, 510, 512-513, 515-516, 523, 529, 534, 541-542
Centros 518-519, 521, 530, 535, 545
Chain Clause 315, 329
Charge 118, 126, 129, 151, 345, 354, 356, 365, 369, 371-372, 376, 379, 380-384, 386, 420, 430, 432, 485, 492
  Fixed Charge 381-383, 492
  Floating Charge 371- 372, 381-384, 492
Commercial Law 333, 334, 337, 338, 372, 374, 400
Common Law 9-12, 45, 58, 59, 78, 85, 117, 169, 266, 331-337, 339, 340, 343, 344-350, 352-353, 356-359, 362, 365-368, 371, 373, 378, 380-381, 385-386, 390-393, 395, 398, 403, 407, 411-412, 414-415, 417-419, 421, 432-434, 449, 451, 454, 468, 473-474, 484-485, 487, 552
Commons 362, 442, 443, 444, 446, 450, 452
Concession Immobilière 154, 155
Construction Lease 135, 136, 142, 160
Co-Ownership 28-29, 49, 50, 88-89, 91, 99-105, 117, 119, 123, 131, 152, 163-164, 180-182, 213, 260, 262, 277, 286, 333, 348, 349, 399, 407, 427, 438, 451, 471, 472, 478
Corpus Iuris Civilis 21-22, 45-47, 49-53, 55-57, 59, 60, 67, 69, 80, 83-85, 171, 404-405

Démembrement method 95, 98, 114-117, 126, 132, 144, 159-160, 165-166, 192-193, 195, 197, 270-271, 281, 304, 309-310, 375, 413-417, 438, 451, 460, 481-483, 555, 561

Easement (see also servitude)............................345, 359-365, 388, 395, 410, 423-425, 427, 433, 558
EC Treaty 495, 497-500, 510, 513-521, 524, 526-530, 532-534, 536-538, 551, 559
Article 295.. 523-524, 560
Article 95... 498, 499
Emphyteusis 6, 36, 43, 52, 53, 61, 63, 65-66, 71-72, 74-75, 79-80, 132-136, 142, 160, 164-166, 204, 269, 274, 280-284, 286-288, 299-300, 304, 308-311, 323, 401, 422-423, 455, 460, 471, 486
Equity 11-12, 29, 252, 334, 336, 338, 340, 342-346, 348-349, 351, 353, 358-359, 361-363, 366-371, 373, 376, 378-381, 386, 388, 390-396, 411, 415-416, 419-421, 426, 430, 432-434, 438, 454, 463, 484-486, 556
Equity of Redemption 73, 367-371, 373, 376, 379-380, 419-420, 432, 463
Estate Contract 358-359, 366-367, 371, 378, 392, 434, 455, 484, 549
Euro-Mortgage 8, 15-16, 416, 467, 507-508, 537, 555
European Commission 7-8, 15-16, 252, 397, 416, 467, 494, 496-497, 500, 503-504, 506-507, 541, 547-548, 555
European Property Law.............................454, 489-490, 496, 523, 538-539, 542, 547, 550, 552, 560
Expectation Right (see also Anticipatory Rights) 10, 28, 180, 214, 219, 221, 230, 236-237, 248, 261, 407, 417, 419, 434-435, 455, 463
Expectation Rights..28, 214, 216, 230, 248, 400, 549

Fee Simple.........................90, 114, 333-334, 344-353, 355-356, 364-365, 368-369, 388-389, 410-411, 414, 418, 421, 432, 558
Fiducie 88-89, 106, 112-116, 158-159, 266, 401, 419, 430, 456, 468
Finance-Ability.. 453
Fragmentation 28, 49, 88, 98, 100, 116, 174, 192, 235, 246, 260, 265-266, 268, 316, 336, 343, 399, 410, 438, 442, 444-446, 450-451, 456, 461-463, 484, 499, 503
Free Movement of Capital 510, 525, 537
Free Movement of Goods.....494-495, 497, 504, 510, 514, 516-520, 522, 526, 528, 536, 541-544, 562
Free Movement of Services.. 516, 536-537
Freehold (see also fee simple)... 333, 337, 344, 346, 350, 351, 362, 418, 482
French Revolution.......................6, 11-12, 21, 58, 67-70, 72, 74, 76-81, 83, 85, 89, 91, 117, 133, 170, 221, 253, 299, 343, 406, 438, 456, 468, 486, 561

Grundschuld...........................186, 202, 210, 213, 219, 223, 228-230, 232-236, 248-250, 304, 431-432, 455-456, 483, 486, 506-507, 555-556

Hypothec.......................130, 137, 142, 147, 152, 186, 219, 228, 232, 289, 293, 431-433, 486, 507, 556
Life Rent Hypothec 144, 507
Rechargeable Hypothec... 143, 507

Inspire Art..519, 522, 535, 536
Ius Commune 19, 21, 56, 59-60, 66-72, 75, 77, 78-79, 81, 83, 343, 405, 459
Ius Proprium 58

Justinian 19, 21-22, 26, 30-31, 35, 43, 46-56, 60, 83, 404

Keck and Mithouard...510-511, 514-516, 525, 526-528
Krantz.. 525, 528, 532-533, 545

Land Law 9, 11, 16, 331-335, 337-338, 343-347, 353, 357, 373, 388, 390, 417-419, 486, 559
Lease 3-4, 13, 48, 72, 89, 109, 114, 128, 132-136, 145, 155, 159-161, 207, 210, 224, 235, 239-243, 248-249, 251, 264, 266-267, 284, 295, 300-303, 307-308, 313, 322, 325, 328, 333-334, 338, 348, 350-358, 363-364, 369, 371, 377, 378-379, 387, 389, 390, 394-395, 400, 409, 414-415, 421-423, 432, 434-435, 456, 466, 469-470, 474, 479, 485
Leasehold (see also term of years) 333-334, 350-353, 358, 423
Lesser Right 343, 412-417, 419-421, 423-424, 426, 428, 429-430, 433, 436, 451-453, 458, 460-466, 474, 481-484, 486, 509, 554-558, 560-562
Lex Commissoria 42, 54, 110, 112, 139-140, 226, 232, 234, 295, 439, 503, 522
Lex Rei Sitae 491-493, 496, 508, 512, 523, 526, 529-530, 534, 536, 543-544, 552
Lien 366, 385-386, 469
Limitation Method 270, 417

Marketability 441, 453
Mortgage 8, 15-16, 111, 345, 350, 367-372, 376, 379-380, 416, 419-420, 432, 463, 476, 506, 507-509, 537

Natural Law 58, 67, 70, 74, 133, 170, 253
Numerus Clausus 4-9, 11-12, 14,-17, 19-20, 22, 31, 33, 43-45, 55-56, 60, 67, 76-77, 80-81, 89, 91, 112, 117-118, 152-153, 161-162, 167, 173-175, 204, 214, 244-247, 255-256, 266, 271, 301, 318, 320, 328-329, 336, 346, 363, 387-388, 391, 394-396, 400, 402-408, 410, 413-414, 416, 422, 424-425, 436-442, 444, 445-446, 448-461, 463, 467-470, 472-474, 481-485, 487, 489-490, 496, 508, 510, 535-537, 539, 544-545, 547-550, 553-555, 557- 564
  Rule 7, 19-20, 22, 43, 45, 55-56, 77, 89, 153, 167, 168, 323, 328-329, 391, 403, 405-406, 439, 458-461, 463-465, 467, 482, 485, 544, 553, 562

Obligatoriserung 248, 401
Old Property Rights 235, 236, 299-300
Optimal Standardisation 447, 448, 450, 453, 550, 562
Option to Purchase 136, 252, 367, 392, 434, 435, 466, 481
Ownership 1, 6, 10-13, 19, 21-31, 34-35, 37-40, 42, 44-56, 60-66, 68-72, 74, 75-76, 78- 81, 86-89, 91-120, 122, 124-127, 129-133, 135, 138, 144-145, 152, 154, 158-160, 162-166, 168, 173-199, 205-206, 208, 210-220, 223-224, 226-227, 229, 234, 236-237, 240-241, 243-247, 249-252, 256-274, 276-290, 293-294, 297, 301-307, 309-310, 316-317, 319-322, 324-327, 333-334, 338, 342-343, 347-348, 350, 373-375, 399-401, 403-405, 407, 409-414, 417-420, 422-423, 427-431, 434-435, 438, 443, 449, 452, 455-457, 459, 461-466, 468-474, 476-479, 481, 483-484, 486, 491-493, 501, 503, 523-525, 528, 531, 533, 540-541, 543, 545, 554, 557-558, 560, 563
  Dominium 19, 25-27, 29, 35, 38, 44-45, 47-50, 52, 61-66, 70-72, 74, 76-77, 79-80, 133, 174, 179, 192, 211, 252, 259, 343, 410, 413, 416-417, 437, 456, 460, 475-481, 486, 554-555
  Praetorian Ownership 27, 28, 45

Personal Property Law 9, 11, 16, 78, 331-334, 337-338, 347, 353, 373-374, 388, 391, 409, 411, 417-419, 486

Personal Right 2-4, 7, 12-13, 23, 33, 35-36, 65-67, 74, 77-79, 81, 86, 90, 109, 120-121, 134, 149, 151, 153-156, 159-162, 172-173, 180, 186, 217, 219, 236, 239-243, 249-251, 254-257, 261, 263, 266-267, 269-280, 298, 300-301, 303, 317, 327, 329, 336, 351, 353, 366, 377, 391, 393, 394, 396, 401, 409, 419, 423, 432, 435-436, 453, 456, 463, 465-466, 470-472, 475, 476, 477-478, 480, 482, 486, 490, 547-548, 550, 553, 559
Personal Servitudes 29, 31, 33-34, 43, 50-52, 118, 125, 129, 197, 205, 234, 272, 276, 456, 471
Pledge 40-43, 54, 65, 75, 79, 91, 110, 112, 136-142, 145-146, 148, 152, 155-156, 158, 165, 186-188, 190, 198, 207, 220, 223-228, 230, 239, 244, 250, 263-265, 271, 289-296, 298, 305-306, 316-318, 321-325, 367-368, 377, 379, 382, 384-386, 405, 411, 429-430, 433, 462, 471, 474, 492, 503, 540, 553, 554
Pre-Emptive Registration (*Vormerkung*) 214-216, 219-220, 236-238, 249-250, 303, 435, 466
Primary Right 412-421, 424, 427, 429-430, 434, 443, 451, 453, 456, 460-461, 463-464, 474, 481-484, 486, 552, 554-558, 560-561
Priority Right 146-148, 152, 264-265, 298-299, 306, 324, 433, 471, 531
Privative Mandate 306-308, 325, 328
Profit à Prendre 361, 363, 427
Proportionality 513-514, 519-520, 530-532, 535, 537

Qualitative Duty 303, 311-315

Real Burden 186, 213-214, 221-224, 234, 248, 250, 426-427, 456, 466, 473, 476, 561
Real Obligation 122, 151-154, 167-168, 310, 400
Real Suretyship 156-158, 164, 167, 455
Rentcharge 345, 365
Restrictive Covenant 363-366, 373, 387, 392, 395, 400, 426, 455, 471, 484
Right of Retention 140, 149-151, 164, 385, 432, 469, 501

Security Servitude 202, 401, 425
Servitude 29-30, 32-35, 47, 50-52, 65, 72-73, 77, 79, 88, 106, 117-125, 134-135, 151-152, 154, 162-163, 165, 182, 196, 199-206, 209-211, 222, 234, 245, 272-274, 285, 305, 308-310, 313-314, 321, 323, 359, 401, 405, 410-411, 414, 423-427, 431, 451, 456, 465-466, 474, 478-479, 554, 557, 558
South Africa 7, 12, 67, 253, 413, 416, 435-437, 451, 460, 470, 473-476, 480-482, 485, 548-549, 553-555, 562
Standardisation 44-45, 55, 441, 445, 447-448, 450, 453-454, 468-469, 484, 550, 563
Superficies 6, 36-37, 43, 53, 61, 63, 65-66, 75, 79, 130-134, 136, 142, 155, 164-166, 182, 208, 211-215, 227, 236, 250, 269, 274, 282-288, 293, 299, 300, 310, 323, 401, 422-423, 427, 455, 460, 462, 464, 471, 560
Suretyship 156-157, 167

Term of Years (see also leasehold) 334, 345, 351-352, 355, 357, 369, 376, 387, 395, 414, 421, 423
Title 14, 16, 24, 25, 26, 48, 87, 118, 121, 124, 130, 137, 157, 171, 174, 197, 260, 261, 264, 287, 302, 303, 312-313, 319, 321, 334, 342-343, 347-348, 358, 363-364, 368-369, 372-377, 379-381, 388, 390, 394, 411, 418-419, 438, 455, 467, 475, 477-478, 491-492, 501, 503, 523, 525, 527, 538, 540, 554, 557-558
Tobacco Advertising 499, 524, 551, 559

Tragedy of the commons 442-444, 446-447, 450-451, 562
Treuhand 184-186, 191, 234, 243-244, 247-249, 251-252, 401, 419, 431, 456, 464, 468
Treuhand Bank Account 243-244, 248
Trust 12, 38, 89, 112-113, 158-159, 184, 232, 244, 264, 266, 268, 297-298, 306, 318-320, 324, 326, 336, 338, 340-345, 348, 350-351, 353, 356-357, 366, 368, 370, 381, 384-385, 392-393, 398, 411, 416, 419, 434, 462-463, 468, 471, 478-479, 493-495, 529, 538, 541, 554

Überseering 520, 522
Usufruct 33-34, 43, 51-52, 71, 75, 79, 94, 106, 117, 125-130, 134, 142, 162-163, 165, 198, 204-210, 234, 239, 244, 261, 269, 271, 274-280, 282, 292, 300-301, 304, 308, 310, 323, 411, 421, 426-429, 452, 460, 465-466, 471, 554

Verdinglichung 249, 317, 401
Verification Rule 448-450, 452
Voluntary Harmonisation 522, 550

CURRICULUM VITAE

Bram Akkermans was born on 27 October 1979 in Nijmegen, the Netherlands. He studied European and Comparative law at the European Law School in Maastricht (LL.M. 2002). As a part of his studies he spend time at Stellenbosch University, South Africa, where he followed courses in South African Trust law and Comparative Constitutional law.

After his graduation, Bram Akkermans was lecturer in European and International Law and Course Developer at the Institute Marketing Management, Fontys University of Professional Education in Eindhoven, the Netherlands. In February 2002 he started as a junior researcher European and Comparative property law at Maastricht University. As a part of this research he was visiting researcher in Oxford, Bremen, Hamburg and Stellenbosch.

During his work as a junior researcher Bram Akkermans was Ph.D. representative of the Ius Commune Research School Ph.D. researchers for Maastricht, president of the Ius Commune Research School Ph.D. Council, and advisor to the Board of Governors of that same research school.

Since February 2008, Bram Akkermans is a lecturer and post-doctoral fellow in European Private Law, specifically in European and Comparative Property Law at Maastricht University.

IUS COMMUNE EUROPAEUM

A peer-reviewed book series in which the common foundations of the legal systems of the Member States of the European Community are the central focus.

The *Ius Commune Europaeum* series includes horizontal comparative legal studies as well as studies on the effect of treaties within the national legal systems. All the classic fields of law are covered. The books are published in various European languages under the auspices of METRO, the Institute for Transnational Legal Research at the Maastricht University.

Recently published:

Volume 61: *Selected Issues in Equal Treatment law: A Multi-layered Comparison of European, English and Dutch Law*, M. GIJZEN
Volume 62: *Food Safety Regulation in Europe. A Comparative Institutional Analysis*, E. VOS and F. WENDLER (eds.)
Volume 63: *Quality of Judicial Organisation and Checks and Balances*, G.Y. NG
Volume 64: *Suspects in Europe. Procedural Rights at the Investigative Stage of the Criminal Process in the European Union*, E. CAPE, J. HODGSON, T. PRAKKEN and T. SPRONKEN (eds.)
Volume 65: *Constitutions Compared. An Introduction to Comparative Constitutional Law*, A.W. HERINGA AND PH. KIIVER
Volume 66: *Nordic Law – Between Tradition and Dynamism*, J. HUSA, K. NUOTIO and H. PIHLAJAMÄKI (eds.)
Volume 67: *Ondergrondse constructies in het Belgische en Nederlandse recht*, C. ADRIAANSENS en V. SAGAERT (eds.)
Volume 68: *Administrative Law of the European Union, Its Member States and the United States*, 2nd edition, R.J.G.H. SEERDEN (ed.)
Volume 69: *Vennootschappelijke beleidsbepaling in geval van financiële moeilijkheden; de positie van bestuurders en aandeelhouders*, M. OLAERTS
Volume 70: *Judicial Case Management and Efficiency in Civil Litigation*, C.H. VAN RHEE (ed.)
Volume 71: *Specific Performance in Contract Law: National and Other Perspectives*, J.M. SMITS, D. HAAS, G. HESEN (eds.)
Volume 72: *Environmental Liability in a Federal System. A Law and Economics Analysis*, K. DE SMEDT
Volume 73: *De optimale inrichting van de verkeersboete in België en Nederland vanuit een strafrechtelijk en bestuursrechtelijk perspectief. Een juridische en rechtseconomische analyse*, L. DEBEN
Volume 74: *Civil Justice between Efficiency and Quality: From Ius Commune to the CEPEJ*, C.H. VAN RHEE and A. UZELAC (eds.)
Volume 75: *The Principle of Numerus Clausus in European Property Law*, B. AKKERMANS

www.ingramcontent.com/pod-product-compliance
Ingram Content Group UK Ltd.
Pitfield, Milton Keynes, MK11 3LW, UK
UKHW051924100926
8556IPUK00022B/1364

9 789050 958240